DICTIONARY OF ANTIQUES

Also by George Savage

A Concise History of Bronzes
Forgeries, Fakes and Reproductions
The Art and Antique Restorer's Handbook
French Decorative Art

GEORGE SAVAGE

DICTIONARY
OF
ANTIQUES

PRAEGER PUBLISHERS
NEW YORK · WASHINGTON

BOOKS THAT MATTER

Published in the United States of America in 1970
by Praeger Publishers, Inc.
111 Fourth Avenue, New York, N.Y. 10003

© 1970, in London, England, by George Savage

Library of Congress Catalog Card Number: 75–107216

Printed in Great Britain by Butler & Tanner Ltd, Frome and London

FOR CONSTANCE

COLOUR PLATES

PREFACE

This Dictionary has been devised primarily to help both collectors and dealers in antiques of one kind or another to date and attribute those specimens which come their way. To this end considerable emphasis has been laid on styles or fashions in art at various periods because these are of great assistance in dating. A knowledge of forgeries, fakes, and reproductions is also essential to determining whether or not any object is what it purports to be. There are numerous entries relating to these.

Naturally, individual entries are far from exhaustive, and a Bibliography is appended which is intended to be a select reading list for further study. The inclusions range from works likely to appeal to the general reader to detailed and scholarly monographs intended for those whose purpose is more serious. It is to be regretted that so many of the books discussing Continental antiques and works of art are not in English, but wherever possible translations, or suitable works in English, have been included. Certainly in these days of inflation, when antiques are being eagerly bought as an investment, Continental antiques offer the best chance for the collector who would like to use his knowledge for this purpose, since they are not yet well understood in England or America.

The illustrations have, for the most part, been selected to bring out points in the text, and are positioned as nearly as possible to the appropriate article. Some are of more general interest, and are intended to show interiors furnished with antiques of a particular type or period. My thanks are due to those who have provided the photographs, the sources of which are noted under the captions.

Certain subjects have been treated in slightly more detail than others. The criteria here have been popularity among collectors, a special bearing on other aspects of the subject, or scarcity of information in English. The latter reason applies especially to some of the articles on Continental pottery, specimens of which can often be found in England and America. These are increasingly attracting collectors in search of comparatively neglected fields. American readers will find ample coverage of American wares and of the craftsmen who made them, and an attempt has been made to show where American and British or European terminology differs.

Cross-references are to related subjects, and enable the reader to follow a particular course of interest through several articles. The headings to the articles adopted have been those which it was considered would be most likely first to occur to the reader in search of information. The principal articles have been grouped under generic headings—Furniture, Glass, Pottery, Silver, etc.

I am much indebted to several of my friends who have helped me in the completion of this work. My special thanks go to Constance Chiswell, who made valuable suggestions while it was in progress, provided information about subjects which are her special interest, and spent many hours proof-reading. Diana Imber has given considerable assistance with the articles relating to Continental faïence factories. Donald B. MacMillan provided generous help with American material and John Cushion special help with the provision of suitable photographs. Lionel Evans and Leslie Curtis both assisted greatly in many small ways too numerous to detail.

Lodève–Boxford   GEORGE SAVAGE
February 1970

ABAT-JOUR (French)

Candle-shade; sometimes referred to in contemporary records as *garde-vue* (sic). Lazare Duvaux (q.v.) invoiced two silver-plated examples in 1749, and there is an 18th-century specimen in the Musée des arts décoratifs, Paris.

ABTSBESSINGEN (GERMANY) FAÏENCE FACTORY

A factory existed here during the first half of the 18th century under the patronage of Prinz Schwarzburg-Sonderhausen, whose mark it used. Several important pieces include vases with panels painted in blue reserved on a yellow ground, a large blue-and-white garden vase, and a similarly decorated stove.

Otherwise the factory produced tankards, jugs, ink-stands, and so on, in a rather pale low-fired clay, thickly potted, with a creamy glaze. The date when the factory closed is unknown; perhaps some time after 1816.

ACANTHUS (BEAR'S BREECH)

The most widely used of all plant-forms in the decorative arts. It is comparatively common in southern Europe, and there are two principal varieties. They are often cultivated as decoration. The Greeks and Romans both used the leaf in a stylized version for decorative purposes, and it forms part of the capital of the Corinthian and Composite Orders. The Roman version inclines to be more realistic, and the Greek and Byzantine somewhat stiffer and more formal. It was employed in Gothic decoration, and it was especially popular in the 17th and 18th centuries, appearing during the currency of the rococo style with its tip twisted to one side to preserve the prevailing air of asymmetry. It is also used in profile as a scroll.

ACID ENGRAVING ON GLASS

Only one acid will attack glass and such silica products as porcelain glazes, and this acid, hydrofluoric (q.v.), is employed to etch glass. A method of glass etching is said (by Doppelmayr, writing in 1730) to have been devised by Heinrich Schwanhardt (see *Schwanhardt, The Family*), and a specimen which

Acanthus. A George I walnut armchair covered with contemporary needlework, the cabriole legs terminating in ball-and-claw feet carved with acanthus foliage on the knees. *Mallett & Sons.*

may have been done in this way is preserved in the Germanisches Nationalmuseum at Nürnberg. Nevertheless, the date of the discovery of hydrofluoric acid is usually given as late in the 18th century, so some doubt remains.

Generally, the surface of the glass to be decorated with acid is covered with a resistant varnish, through which the design is drawn with a steel point. Subsequent immersion in acid 'bites' the design into the unprotected part, in the same way as nitric acid acts on a copper plate. The same acid is used for polishing glass, which it does extremely well, but the vapour from a loosely stoppered bottle will eat into the surface of any glassware nearby and damage it. The technique of glass etching has been largely confined to the 19th and 20th centuries.

ACIER, MICHEL-VICTOR (1736 to after 1781)

Modeller of porcelain figures at Meissen, and joint *Modellmeister* with Kändler (q.v.) after 1764. Of French origin, Acier was brought to Meissen to introduce the neo-classical style, then beginning in France, with the object of reviving the factory's export trade after the Seven Years' War. Some of the designs for his models were provided by Johann Elias Zeissig, who had worked in Paris, and who was art-adviser to the factory until 1796. Acier modelled in the prevailing sentimental style much at variance with that of Kändler. His earliest figures have bases with slight and degenerate rococo scrollwork, but these soon developed into flat oval bases decorated with such classical motifs as the key-fret. It is probable that Acier introduced the use of lace-work in porcelain. He retired with a pension in 1781. His assistant, Johann Karl Schönheit, worked somewhat in his style, retiring in 1805.

'ACT OF PARLIAMENT' CLOCKS

These wall-clocks have little or nothing to do with the Act of 1797, from which they take their name, which imposed a duty on clocks and watches. It has been said that such clocks, common enough in inns and public places, were installed for the benefit of those unable to pay the tax, but since it was repealed after a year, and similar clocks were not at all uncommon both before and after, the supposition is unlikely. 'Act of Parliament' clocks were made for inns, and it is likely that they were first installed as a convenience for coach passengers. The earliest appear in the 1750s.

In principle they are all the same: a large clear dial with a trunk of variable length below to contain weights and pendulum. This was long at first, but became much shorter in the early years of the 19th century, when spring-driven clocks made their appearance. Japanned cases, with a black face, are among the earliest to be found, although the white painted dial was adopted well before 1800.

They are still to be seen occasionally in old inns, and public clocks on this pattern were made throughout the 19th century. The names on the dial are as often those of the owners as of the makers.

ADAM, ROBERT (1728–1792)

Neo-classical architect; designer of household furniture of all kinds in this style, some of which was made by Chippendale (q.v.). In 1754 Adam journeyed to Italy and thence to Dalmatia (Yugoslavia) where his drawings of Diocletian's palace at Spalatro (Split) influenced his early work as a designer. Adam returned to Britain in 1762 and was appointed architect to George III, who was himself a student of architecture. For over twenty-five years thereafter Robert Adam was in partnership with his brother, James. Among their most notable works was the Adelphi (Strand, London), and they published their *Works in Architecture* in 1773, which was based on a series of engravings of their principal designs.

Acier, Michel-Victor. Family group in a sentimental style associated with 18th-century neo-classicism (q.v.). Note the relatively plain and symmetrical base, and the swag (q.v.) decorating the footstool. Meissen. c. 1755. *British Museum.*

Although the Adam version of the neo-classical style was extremely popular, influencing not only many of their contemporaries in architecture but such manufacturers as Wedgwood and Boulton, it was by no means universally accepted. Sir William Chambers commented adversely on its early phases, and Walpole in 1773 wrote, 'from Kent's mahogany we are dwindled to Adam's filigree', while the King, according to Farington (*Diaries*), eventually came to think that Adam had introduced 'too much of neatness and prettiness'. See *Neo-classical Style; Louis Seize.*

AFFENKAPELLE (German)

The Monkey Band. A series of porcelain figures first modelled at Meissen (q.v.) about 1750 by J. J. Kändler and Peter Reinicke. These have often been said to be a satire on the Dresden Court Orchestra, but they were undoubtedly inspired by the fashion for *Singeries*, or monkeys in costume portrayed taking part in various human activities, of which the most notable example is the mural decoration by Christoph Huet at Chantilly. There are twenty different instrumentalists in the Meissen series, as well as the conductor. The *Affenkapelle* was extensively copied by other Continental porcelain factories, especially Fürstenberg (q.v.) and Vienna (q.v.), as well as in England at Chelsea (where they occur in the sale-catalogue of 1756) and at Derby. There are many 19th-century reproductions, but old specimens are very rare. The complete set includes flautist, violinist, 'cellist, trumpeter, horn player, bagpiper,

Agate. One of a pair of vases of red agate mounted with two infant satyrs holding swags of vine-leaves and grapes, the base with a central shell and Vitruvian scrolls, on *pied de biche* supports. Louis XVI. *Wallace Collection.*

Affenkapelle. Singer, and drummer and piper, from the Monkey Band of Kändler and Reinicke. Meissen. c. 1750. *Victoria and Albert Museum.*

side-drummer, kettle-drummer, bassoonist, cymbalist, oboe player, bugler, harpsichord player, French horn player, recorder player, drummer with drum suspended from a wrist-strap, drummer with twin drums on his back, triangle player, female hurdy-gurdy player, and *chanteuse.* Lazare Duvaux (q.v.) sold a set to Mme de Pompadour in 1753.

AGATA GLASS
Made at Cambridge, Mass., by the New England Glass Company, agata glass resembles peachblow (q.v.) with some added mottling.

AGATE
A translucent quartzose mineral, of which there are several varieties distinguished by the colour and the arrangement of the veining. Onyx is lightly veined; cornelian is cherry-red; sardonyx is orange-red; blue chalcedony is sky-blue; chalcedony is milky-white tinged with blue; chrysoprase is apple-green. The veining of agate is varied, one variety having circular veins, while another has veins which

branch in a way which resembles plants, trees, or moss—moss-agate and *agate arborisée*, both of which were much in favour in the 18th century.

Agate has always been extensively used in the decorative arts either shaped by grinding, as in the making of cups, or in the form of flat plaques made into such things as caskets with the aid of metal mounts. From the beginning of the Renaissance to the end of the 18th century agate plaques were frequently set in either gold or silver mounts, especially in the case of small works. The *Livre-Journal* of Lazare Duvaux refers to: 'Mme de Pompadour—a plaque of *agate arborisée* for the top of a snuff-box.'

AGATE GLASS   See *Slag Glass*

AGATE WARE
Agate or marbled wares made by wedging together clays of several colours were commonly produced both in England and on the Continent. The patterns were largely fortuitous, but an attempt was made to control them in some cases. Since the marbling is in the body itself, this kind of ware is usually termed 'solid agate'.

Agate Ware. Whieldon solid agate sauce-boat based on a well-known contemporary silver pattern. c. 1760. *Hove Museum.*

3

A somewhat similar effect was sought by using coloured slips (q.v.) which were trailed on to the surface of the ware and then 'combed' or 'feathered' into a variety of patterns. Large baking-dishes thus decorated were made in considerable numbers from the 17th to the 19th centuries, and have not uncommonly survived.

A somewhat similar effect was sometimes achieved by blending coloured lead glazes, to be found in the work of Palissy (q.v.) and of Whieldon (q.v.).

AIR–TWISTS
These are to be found running through the stems of English wine-glasses made after 1740. The air-twist began in the same way as the tear (q.v.), but as a number of small tears which were then drawn out and twisted. The earliest such glasses were made in two pieces, and air-twists in glasses of this kind are usually simple and often slightly defective. The development of glasses made in three pieces—bowl, stem, and foot—made more elaborate twists easier. Finally, workmen became so adept at drawing out the air-twists that they were even able to make stems with knops in which the convolutions of the twist were continuous, and these are the most highly valued. Twists are either a single spiral, comparatively simple in appearance, or more elaborate multiple spirals.

See *Opaque Twists.*

ALABASTER
Although less durable than marble, which it somewhat resembles in appearance, alabaster, a white lime sulphate, is much more easily worked, and it has therefore often been popular. It usually shows traces of coloration, and is translucent when sufficiently thin. The medieval alabaster figures of Nottingham (England) are somewhat outside the scope of this volume. As a medium for sculpture it declined during the Renaissance, but returned to popularity during the 18th century for clock-pedestals and similar kinds of ornament in conjunction with gilt-bronze mounts, and its use for table-tops is recorded, although, being softer than marble, these have rarely survived intact. Occasionally it was employed for such large decorative works as chimney-pieces, but examples are rare. The purest colour came from the Near East, but supplies came also from deposits in France, Germany, and Italy. (See *Onyx Marble.*)

ALBARELLO
A term of Arabic derivation used to describe an almost cylindrical jar with an incurving waist to facilitate its removal from a shelf of similar jars. It was used to contain dry drugs and ointments, and those of maiolica were also ornamental. The name of the drug is often lettered on the side, although its nature is now usually difficult to identify. The albarello is to be found in the pottery of the Near East, in the lustre-decorated Hispano-Moresque wares (q.v.), and in European tin-enamelled wares generally.

Albarello. A late 16th-century dry-drug jar of the kind termed an *albarello* from Nîmes, Gard (France). Perhaps made for the medical school at Montpellier. *Victoria and Albert Museum.*

ALCORA FAÏENCE (Spain)
A factory was established in this Spanish town about 1726 by the Duke of Aranda making porcelain and excellent faïence in the style of Moustiers (q.v.). The factory ran a school of design where Spanish potters were taught their craft by French workmen, among whom Joseph Olerys is the best known. After his return to Moustiers in 1732 no more French workmen were employed, but the factory continued to produce high-quality faïence as good as, if not better, than Moustiers.

ALLA PORCELLANA (Italian)
A trailing pattern of blue foliate scrolls in the style of Wan-li porcelain (1573–1619) used to decorate the backs of dishes and plates from some Italian maiolica factories.

See *Chinese Export Porcelain.*

ALLEGORY
A subject which recalls another by reason of its analogous context. For instance, a bunch of grapes, because of the time of year in which it is harvested, is symbolic or allegorical of Autumn. Allegorical subjects were very popular during the 17th and 18th centuries. The gods of classical mythology all had objects sacred to them. The laurel was sacred to Apollo (Helios); the vine to Bacchus (Dionysius); the lightning bolt and the eagle to Jupiter (Zeus); the lion-skin and club to Hercules (Heracles); and the

caduceus to Mercury (Hermes), the names in brackets being the Greek equivalents of the Roman names first given. These attributes, standing by themselves, were symbolic of the gods who bore them. In Christian art both the lamb and the fish symbolized Jesus Christ. Groups of musical instruments represented music, and of arms, war. Groups of this kind were termed trophies (q.v.). Symbolism was carried to great lengths, especially in the 18th century, when sets of porcelain and bronze figures represented the Seasons, Continents, Elements (Earth, Fire, Air, and Water), etc., the meaning of which could be deduced from the symbols they carried. Thus, flowers represented Spring; a sheaf of corn, Summer; grapes, Autumn; and a brazier, Winter. Everyone was expected to be sufficiently well acquainted with this kind of symbolism to be able to identify the meaning.

Allegory. **The River Nile, after Giovanni da Bologna. Meissen porcelain. c. 1750.** *Metropolitan Museum, New York.*

ALMANACKS

In Europe almanacks began to be common at the end of the 15th century, usually providing astronomical and astrological information. A Paris almanack of 1652 was the first to list the great events of the time, and the type became popular. In the 18th century almanacks providing information about the royal family, the Court, the clergy, members of the government, and the ambassadors were popular, as well as those devoted to providing various kinds of scientific information. These, of course, were in volume form, but almanacks meant to be hung on a wall for reference were also made. One of this kind from France is in the Wallace Collection (London).

Allegory. **The River Nile. Clay. By Giovanni da Bologna. c. 1580.** *Victoria & Albert Museum.*

Allegory. **Liberty and Matrimony. Two lovers with a bird in a cage. Bow (England). c. 1753.**

Allegory. **Hearing, from a set of the Five Senses. An** *amorini* **(q.v.) listening to a watch. Ludwigsburg (Germany). c. 1765.** *Mr and Mrs Henry Stern.*

ALTARE (near Genoa)

Glass-making centre rivalling Venice, which flourished especially during the 15th century. The glassmakers of Altare encouraged craftsmen to emigrate and take their skill elsewhere and since their production was presumably very similar to that of Venice, it was often in this way that Venetian styles made their way to the rest of Europe. Actual specimens made at Altare can only be identified conjecturally, but it is probable that some glasses attributed to Venice, or termed *façon de Venise*, were made here. See *Venetian Glass*.

ALTO–RILIEVO (Italian)

Carving in high relief in wood, stone, etc., or castings in plaster or metal in this style. See *Hochschnitt*.

ALUMINIUM

A lightweight silvery metal which can be cast and welded. Since it was only discovered in the 19th century few works of art have been made from it, but an instance is the statue of Eros in Piccadilly Circus, London.

AMALGAM

An alloy of mercury with another metal, usually gold, silver, or tin. If sufficient mercury be added to the metals referred to a liquid alloy is formed which can be applied with a brush. Subsequent heating drives off the mercury as a vapour, leaving the remaining metal evenly deposited. This property of mercury was once extensively employed in the gilding and silvering of such base metals as copper and bronze, and in gilding silver (silver-gilt). Gilding of this kind is sometimes called fire-gilding in England and *dorure d'or moulu* in France. In combination with tin, mercury was used for backing glass in the manufacture of mirrors.

Amalgam. A Paris gilders' workshop about 1750. Workmen on the left are brushing on the amalgam of gold and mercury preparatory to heating. *After Diderot.*

AMARANTH

The French *bois d'amarante*, sometimes termed purple wood in England. The appearance of the wood is characterized by violet or purplish shades, and it was used as a marquetry wood by French *ébénistes*, especially during the reign of Louis XV. Limited use of it was made in England for the same purpose. In appearance it is not unlike violetwood (q.v.), with which it is sometimes confused, but the latter has a figuring which is much more obviously marked.

AMBER

A yellow translucent fossil resin chiefly found on the southern shore of the Baltic Sea. From medieval times until the 17th century amber was used in jewellery, for the decoration of furniture, and for making certain kinds of vases. One of the gifts of Louis XIV to the Siamese ambassadors in 1687 was mirrors with amber frames, as well as 'a large amber vase carved with reliefs and gold ornaments'. A number of amber vases were in the King's collection, one in the form of a ship with three hippocampi (q.v.) of 'white amber'. Amber declined from favour in the 18th century, and was principally used for beads and similar small objects.

AMBERINA GLASS

A lead glass of a lustrous pale amber colour with ruby tinges first made by the New England Glass Company of Cambridge, Mass., and then by its successors, the Libbey Glass Co. A similar glass was also made elsewhere by other American glass companies.

AMBRY

An English Gothic cupboard originally, like the French *armoire*, for the storage of arms, but later used as a pantry or a store-cupboard. The word has largely fallen into disuse, but both this and the French *armoire* (q.v.) appear to have had their origin in the Latin *armarium*, a chest for storing arms.

Ambulantes. A Louis XV parquetry table. c. 1765. *Christie, Manson & Woods Ltd.*

AMBULANTES (French)

Meaning (literally) 'strolling', the term was used to describe certain small furniture of the second half of the 18th century in France which did not, either by custom or etiquette, have a fixed position, but was moved about as convenience required. The category includes numerous toilet-tables, work-tables, bedside-tables, and so forth. Bedside-tables were often provided with hand-holds or handles for ease of removal from the bedroom to the dressing-room during the daytime. The term is more or less equivalent to the English 'occasional' table, of which an excellent example is the Pembroke table (q.v.). Many English occasional tables during the last quarter of the 18th century were based on French designs, and dual-purpose specimens, such as combined toilet- and writing-tables, were sometimes termed 'harlequin' tables.

The earliest use of the term is probably an entry in the *Journal du Garde-Meuble* (q.v.) referring to a small writing-table delivered by Gaudreaux, who died in 1751. This was described as 'une petite table ambulante de bois satiné et amarante'—a small occasional table of satinwood and amaranth. The top measured 23 *pouces* by 15, the *pouce* being approximately an inch.

AMELUNG GLASS WORKS

This glasshouse at New Bremen, Maryland, was also known as the New Bremen Glass Works, the Etna Glass Works, and the American Glass Manufactory. It was founded by John Frederick Amelung, a German immigrant who arrived in 1784. With the aid of German glass-workers who came with him, Amelung produced glass for many purposes— window-glass, mirror-glass, table-glass, decanters, and so forth of excellent quality. Amelung glass is now very rare and difficult to authenticate, but one or two marked pieces exist.

AMMANATI, BARTOLOMMEO (1511–1592)

A Tuscan sculptor and architect, active in Florence, Padua, Venice, and Rome in the time of Cosmo de' Medici. (See *Medici Family.*) Among his small bronzes, the *Venus Amphitrite* of 1573 is in the Palazzo Vecchio in Florence, and his marble Neptune fountain is in the Piazza della Signoria in the same city. He was one of the leading representatives of the Mannerist school (q.v.).

AMORINI (Italian)

Also called *putti* (small boys). *Amorini* are figures of Cupid, or winged Cupids' heads, often used as decoration in carved form, especially during the 16th and 17th centuries. *Amorini* were derived from Roman sources, and a well-known series appears in one of the excavated houses in Pompeii in a wall-painting. They occur commonly in porcelain, bronze and wood-carving.

ANDIRONS

Originally wrought-iron supports for holding logs while burning on the old open-hearth. Andirons later lost some of their original purpose when sea-coal became generally available as fuel instead of wood,

Amelung, J. F. Covered beaker wheel-engraved with the subject of Tobias and the Angel, and an inscription which includes the name of Carolina Lucia Amelung. Dated 1788. New Bremen glass-house of John Frederick Amelung, Maryland. *Corning Museum of Glass, Corning, N.Y.*

Amorini. Cupid as a sculptor modelled by F. E. Meyer (q.v.). Meissen. c. 1755. *Señor José M. Mayorga.*

which necessitated a basket-grate, but they developed into highly decorative objects, sometimes, in the 17th century, of silver. Much fine craftsmanship was lavished on them in France, where they were known as *chenets*, and during the late 17th and 18th centuries some of the most noted silversmiths and bronzesmiths produced *chenets* which were very considerable works of art.

ANGOULÊME FAÏENCE

This factory in the suburb of Houmeau was started by the son of Louis Sazerac (see *Saintes*) about 1748. It was continued by his widow and son after his death in 1771. Some signed pieces from this period are known, and typical are large faïence animals—lions, dogs, cats or sphinxes, with heavy manganese outlines to their features. They may have been intended for garden ornaments. See *La Rochelle.*

ANIMALIERS, LES

A group of French animal sculptors of the early 19th century. The best known is Antoine-Louis Barye (1795–1875), who represented a new departure in bronze sculpture. He interested himself in animals at an early stage in his career, studying in

zoological gardens and improving his anatomical knowledge by dissection. As a sculptor of animals he has rarely been excelled, and he was undoubtedly the founder of the school. His work is especially sought, although sand-cast versions by Émile Martin between 1848 and 1857 are inferior in quality. Barye was skilled in the colouring and patination of bronze.

Barye's intensive study of animals, responsible for the remarkable realism of his work, was perhaps common to the whole school. Christophe Fratin (1800–1864) was the son of a taxidermist, noted for his horses. Jules Moigniez (1835–1894) specialized in birds which are remarkable for acute observation skilfully rendered. One of the most successful of the school was Pierre Jules Mêne (1810–1879), who was much influenced by Landseer, then enjoying a considerable vogue in France. Emmanuel Fremiet (1824–1910) was no less successful and rather more ambitious, modelling an equestrian figure of Napoleon III. Minor members of the school include Auguste Nicolas Cain (1821–1894), who married Mêne's daughter, and Paul Delabrière (1829–1912), but their work is largely derivative.

Bronzes by the *Animaliers* usually bear an incised signature.

ANNEALING

The shaping of metal, especially by processes involving hammering such as raising (q.v.), and spinning (q.v.), sets up stresses which, unless they were relieved, would cause it to crack and tear. For this reason metal is reheated at intervals during the process of shaping and allowed to cool. After this the work can safely continue. Early glass also suffered from this defect, unrelieved stresses set up during the process of manufacture causing it to break easily when hot liquids were poured into it, or even if a sustained musical note of the right pitch was played near it. The defect in English glass was largely overcome after 1770 by improved methods of annealing, in which manufactured glass was first heated and then allowed to cool slowly. Firecracks in pottery and porcelain arise from the same cause, and are due either to the object losing heat too quickly, or to some parts losing heat more quickly than others. Annealing, however, is not possible in this case, and the design has to be amended to obviate the defect.

Animaliers, Les. Bronze dog by Emmanuel Frémiet (1824–1910). Signed. *Mallett of Bourdon House, London, W.1.*

ANSBACH FAÏENCE

The factory was founded about 1710 by Matthias Baur, in collaboration with J. K. Ripp who left two years later to go to Nürnberg (q.v.). The town belonged to the Margraf of Ansbach/Bayreuth. Another painter, Georg Johann Taglieb, worked at Ansbach between 1722 and 1734, and subsequently became manager of the Swedish factory of Rörstrand. Wares were produced in imitation of Rouen in blue-and-white, and no real factory style emerged before 1730. After that date Georg Christoph Popp began to influence the factory's

Ansbach Porcelain. Gallant and Lady. c. 1765.

Ansbach Faïence. Enghalskrüg (narrow-necked jug) enamelled in colours derived from the Chinese *famille verte* (q.v.)—the so-called 'Green Family'. Ansbach. c. 1735. *Germanisches Nationalmuseum, Nürnberg.*

affairs and in 1747 became manager. He was responsible for the *Green Family*, Ansbach's greatest claim to fame. This was an adaptation of the Chinese *famille verte* (q.v.) done in high-temperature pigments with brilliant effect. The Chinese originals are very carefully followed, except on the rims of dishes, where *Laub- und Bandelwerke* was preferred. Sometimes Coats of Arms were done in this colour scheme. There is another group painted in the *Imari* style of high-temperature blue, enamel decoration in iron-red, cold gilding, and lacquer, most of which has rubbed off. A deep blue glaze characterizes these wares. Shapes were the customary ones of South Germany—pear-shaped jugs, tankards, dishes, etc.—but there are also domestic wares painted in high-temperature colours of rather indifferent quality. Figure-subjects are primitively painted on these, and chosen from the usual stock of huntsmen, peasants, etc. After the death of the original G. C. Popp about 1791, the factory began to decline and closed finally in 1804.

ANSBACH PORCELAIN FACTORY

'Ansbach' is the modern version of the earlier name of this town, which was formerly Onolzbach. Here a successful faïence factory (above) was established in 1710, and the Margraf Karl Alexander conceived the idea of starting a porcelain factory as an extension to it in 1757, when Meissen was already experiencing the difficulties caused by the Seven Years' War. Some Meissen workmen came to Ansbach, including Johann Friedrich Kändler, nephew of the Meissen *Modellmeister*. Despite this, the influence was rather of Berlin after the foundation of the royal factory there, and a large collection of 18th century Berlin porcelain is housed in the palace at Ansbach. Frederick ordered a table-service in 1765 for the decoration of the palace at Potsdam. Production was also influenced by the two mistresses of the Margraf, a French actress named Hippolyte Clairon and Lady Craven—Elisabeth, Gräfin Berkeley. By 1762 'groups; big antique figures, medium, and small ones; candelabra; tea and coffee services, white, blue and coloured; butter dishes and baskets; *chacans* [walking-stick handles in the form of figures in Oriental dress], and walking-stick handles [i.e. those otherwise modelled]' were listed. Modelling and painting were excellent in quality.

ANTHEMION

Ornament in the form of stylized honeysuckle flowers and leaves originally derived from classical architecture. It was especially popular during the currency of the Adam style (q.v.).

ANTICO (c. 1460–1525)

Piero Jacopo Alari Bonacolsi, called Antico from the antique (or classical) models which inspired his small bronzes, was an Italian medallist and sculptor active at Padua. He also achieved some fame as a goldsmith. Much of his surviving work is in the Kunsthistorisches Museum, Vienna, but the Victoria and Albert Museum (London) has the recently discovered *Meleager*, which is among the most notable of his bronzes.

9

Antico. Bronze figure of Meleager after the antique by Antico (1460–1525), partially gilt. *Victoria and Albert Museum.*

ANTIMONY
A metal with a silvery lustre occasionally used as an alloy, especially with lead.

ANTIQUE
The meaning of this word has changed very considerably during the last century or so. Originally it meant an object, usually classifiable as a work of art, which had been made in Greek or Roman times. Increasingly 'antique' has been taken to mean almost anything made before a certain date. Until recently the accepted date was 1830, because this was the year laid down by the U.S. Government as the limit for importation free of duty for many categories (furniture, porcelain, and so forth) which did not fall within the Customs' definition of works of art, and would otherwise have suffered the imposition of import duty. This date has now been altered to take in anything made one hundred years before the date of import, thus bringing the U.S. into line with most other countries admitting antiques free of duty.

While anything can be described as an antique the term is usually limited in practice to decorative objects of the kind described in this book, although it is sometimes applied to objects more strictly utilitarian which are valued for one reason or another.

It is not possible to divide antiques and works of art satisfactorily, since the division in many cases is strictly one which has only been made in modern times. For Customs purposes works of art are usually taken to be original works of painting or sculpture. A better definition, and one taking account of the past as well as the present, would be works of good quality which are decorative in intent, made with hand-tools, and this would inevitably include many objects normally classified as antiques.

APPLIED RELIEF
Term employed principally in describing pottery and porcelain manufacture to designate relief ornament separately cast or modelled and applied to the ware before firing, as distinct from relief ornament cast integrally with the piece in one operation.

APPLIQUÉ (French)
The term is most commonly used to denote the decoration of one textile material by sewing on to it patterns cut from another. Velvet on damask is a typical example. In France the word is more widely employed, although the meaning is comparable. Wall-sconces and brackets, for instance, are thus called. See also *Cut-card Work; Stump-work.*

APREY (Haute-Marne, France) FAÏENCE
A factory founded by Jacques Lallemant, Baron d'Aprey, in 1744 and later carried on with his brother, Joseph. Jacques retired about 1769, and Joseph engaged a Nevers potter, François Ollivier, who directed the factory till 1792. After the Revolution Ollivier's son started it again, making copies of early pieces in the original moulds. About 1810 these copies were furnished with the old marks *AP, APR.* Early wares were rococo in shape, and in colours painted on a tin-glaze that had already been fired. The glaze united badly with the body and is inclined to flake. Decoration was usually blue-and-white, of birds, flowers, and Chinese designs. The muffle-kiln technique was introduced about 1760, and painting changed from the broad, somewhat heavy style to the much more delicate manner of Protais Pidoux, a Swiss who worked here from 1760 to 1762. After 1766 the *style fin* supersedes the so-called broad style, attaining its greatest success after 1772. A bird-painter, Jacques Jarry (see

Aprey Faïence. Dish of the second half of the 18th century. Aprey (France). See also *Agate Ware.*

Sceaux), neatly divides the periods, as he painted with a very fine brush in miniature style. The colours now remained stable in the kiln and no longer ran. In 1776 Jarry was joined by Antoine Mege, a painter of birds and miniatures, and landscapes framed in rococo scrolls, or with backgrounds striped like textile patterns. *Chinoiseries* of Chinese figures and flowers were painted in crude, flat, heavily outlined colours. Porcelain was made experimentally at Aprey, but no specimens of certain attribution appear to exist.

ARABESQUE

(In Islamic art.) An intricate decoration of intersecting lines, of curves and angles, accompanied by stylized ornamental motifs, usually of fruit and flowers. To be found in Near Eastern, Moorish, and Hispano-Moresque work. It was not an Islamic invention, but derived by the Arabs from old Roman sources.

(In Renaissance art.) The term is properly employed to describe ornament influenced by imports of Islamic works of art, and especially Hispano-Moresque pottery, but it is often inaccurately applied to copies of Roman ornament derived from Nero's Golden House, discovered shortly after 1500, which are more accurately described as *grotesques* (q.v.). Arabesques (It. *arabeschi*) and grotesques continued to be a popular kind of ornament in one form or another until the early years of the 19th century.

ARCADE

A series of arches. In furniture design the arcade takes the form of arches either panelled between the pillars or open, the latter sometimes forming the backs of 16th- and early 17th-century chairs. Furniture thus designed was based on contemporary architecture.

Arcade. Ornamental arcade in the 18th-century revived Gothic style from Strawberry Hill, Twickenham, London, once the residence of Horace Walpole (q.v.).

ARCANIST

A workman professing to have knowledge of the secret (or arcanum) of porcelain-making, or of the making of some kinds of pottery, notably faïence, during the 18th century. Some were impostors, but many were recognized as competent workmen who helped to start a number of factories.

Archambo, Peter. Silver tea-kettle with lampstand and tray. Period of George II. *Sotheby & Co.*

ARCHAMBO, PETER (d. 1767)

English silversmith of French origin, formerly Archambaud. He is first recorded in 1720, when his mark was entered at the Goldsmiths' Hall. Like other French silversmiths working in London at the time he eventually adopted a restrained version of French rococo, but his early work was in the plain styles of the first decades of the 18th century, and much of his surviving silver is of this nature. By 1733 he had adopted a style hardly distinguishable from French Régence, and nothing is apparently known which comes much nearer to rococo than this. His son, also Peter Archambo, was apprenticed to Paul de Lamerie in 1728, and was in partnership from 1749 with Peter Meure at his father's shop, the Golden Cup, Coventry Street, London. Much of their joint production was devoted to services of plate. Meure died in 1755, and the younger Archambo in 1768. There is no record of him having made anything after the death of his partner.

ARCHITECTURAL FURNITURE

There are two meanings for this term. The first is to describe furniture, especially from early Renaissance times onwards, which is based on contemporary architectural design. Ultimately most old furniture is based on architectural features of one kind or another, and the influence of architecture is equally to be seen in cabinets in the classical style and in the designs of Chippendale and others which utilize the Gothic style. The term is also employed, in discussing English furniture, to refer to furniture-designs by architects, such as William Kent and the Brothers Adam.

Architectural Furniture. A 16th-century chest decorated with architectural *motifs* inlaid and applied. *Victoria and Albert Museum.*

ARDUS (Tarn-et-Garonne, France) FAÏENCE

Collondre and Dupre, workers of Montpellier, assisted a new enterprise founded in the town of Ardus between 1737 and 1739 by François Duval. It was noted for faïence portraits and wall-plaques after 1744. Vessels decorated with *lambrequins*, bunches of grapes, or friezes, are sometimes attributed to this factory. In 1752 the factory changed hands, and its owner David Lestrade, and Arnaud Lapierre, manufactured armorial services and drug-jars. The original founder's son, Duval de Varaire, acquired it in 1770, and enamel decoration was then introduced. It manufactured *faïence-fine* (q.v.) in 1783, and closed in 1786.

ARGYLE (or ARGYLL)

A silver gravy-warmer resembling a coffee-pot, which is first recorded about 1760, although it was probably introduced earlier. It is said, without reliable confirmation, to have been named after the 4th Duke of Argyll. The gravy was kept warm in a variety of ways, of which perhaps the hot-water jacket is the most frequent. Argyles were also made in pottery, first appearing in Wedgwood's creamware catalogue in 1774. They are known in English delft ware. No foreign specimen seems to have been recorded.

Argyle. An argyle of Sheffield plate, with a central compartment for a piece of hot iron. Late 18th century. *Victoria and Albert Museum.*

'ARMADA' CHEST

Iron chests intended as safes or strong-boxes. They were made in the Netherlands and South Germany during the 16th and 17th centuries, and are notable for an elaborate locking system. They have no connection with the Spanish Armada.

Armoire. Late 18th-century walnut *armoire* in the Louis XV style. French Provincial furniture made at Nîmes in the style of Arles. *Musée de Vieux Nîmes.*

ARMOIRE (French)

A large cupboard, usually with two doors, somewhat resembling a wardrobe, with shelves and hanging-space. *Armoires* were used for storage, and were sometimes built in, being little more than a pair of doors of the kind sometimes to be found in the shops of French antique dealers. Doors were sometimes solid, but were often glazed, or trellised with a silk backing.

The *armoire* became popular at the end of the 17th century, when sumptuous examples were made by A.-C. Boulle (q.v.), in his characteristic brass and tortoiseshell marquetry. By far the greater number of surviving specimens, however, are provincial, made by the *menuisier* in a well-marked Louis Quinze style and decorated with carving. The type continued to be fashionable until well into the 19th century and is difficult to date from the style.

The various regions of provincial France made *armoires,* usually in a style which enables their origin to be guessed fairly easily. The type most often met in the south of England came originally from Normandy. The one illustrated is southern, and many well-carved specimens come from Provence, usually from Arles.

Less often seen is the *armoire d'angle,* a tall corner-cupboard not to be confused with the *encoignure* (q.v.). The low *armoire* or *bas d'armoire,* is a large cupboard of a height low enough to lean on —*meuble d'hauteur d'appui.* It was often a book-case and is at its best decorated in the characteristic Paris style, although provincial examples are not uncommon. These, like the *armoire* proper, are often decorated with carving.

Although most provincial specimens are carved fairly elaborately, exceptionally other kinds of decoration may be noticed, such as painting. Uzès, in the south, is the origin of some good examples.

The *armoire* should not be confused with the *buffet à deux corps,* an equally large cupboard, but in two parts.

ARM-RESTS

(French *manchette.*) Padded elbow rests to be found on the wooden arms of *fauteuils,* either French, or in the French taste.

ARRAS

The famous tapestry looms at Arras (Artois, France) were removed elsewhere, to Brussels and Tournai, after the sack of the city by the French in 1477, but the name survived as a generic term for Gothic wall-hangings of this type well into the 16th century. For example, *Hamlet,* Act II, Scene ii, 'Polonius: Be you and I behind an arras then.'

ART NOUVEAU

Despite its name the style known as *art nouveau* in England and America was, in France, far more often termed *le style moderne.* In Germany it was the *Jugendstil* ('youth style'), and in Austria the *Sezession.* In Italy it became the *stile liberte.*

Of *art nouveau* it may be said that after the confusion of styles, and of thinking about the subject, which marked most of Queen Victoria's reign, it represented a style in its own right. By classification it was romantic, and it had its roots in the Gothic style and its revivals, even though the relationship is a fairly distant one, and overlaid in many cases by the elements of styles drawn from other sources, such as Far Eastern art. One of its predecessors was

the Japanese-Gothic of the 1860s. *Art nouveau* was the precursor of many styles in contemporary art, and led more or less directly to them. Among those well known in France who were strongly influenced by it, and in turn helped to develop it, were Toulouse-Lautrec, Emil Gallé, and René Lalique. In architecture it still survives in some of the stations of the Paris Metro, and in its more extreme form, in the work of the Spanish architect Antonio Gaudi at Barcelona.

Art Nouveau. Chair of carved wood by Hector Guimard (1867–1942). Paris. Art nouveau style. 1908. *Cooper-Hewitt Museum of Decorative Art and Design, Smithsonian Institution.*

Like the Gothic style it is essentially curvilinear, although it does not have the preciseness of the compass-work of much Gothic ornament. Straight lines in *art nouveau* are comparatively rare. Ornament is largely based on plant-forms, especially the lily. Like the baroque style it is theatrical, and frequently depends for its effect on an incongruous juxtaposition of ornamental elements. It often borrows the principle of asymmetry from Japanese art, and its debt to the Japanese print and imported Japanese furniture is comparatively easy to recognize. Prints obviously inspired some of the work of Aubrey Beardsley. Some of the earlier designs which can be regarded as belonging to *art nouveau* also show the pronounced influence of William Blake.

The beginnings of the new movement first crystallized round the theories of William Morris in England and, significantly, *art nouveau* was often termed *le style anglais* in France. The characteristic women in *art nouveau* decoration owe more than a little to the pre-Raphaelites, especially Rossetti, and

James McNeill Whistler, the American painter who made his home in England, was deeply interested in Chinese art, and did much to start a vogue for blue-and-white porcelain and Japanese fans and screens. Interest was fostered by the still existing English art-magazine *The Studio*, which was first published in 1893.

The first designer to combine the trends and tendencies current in their day so that they began to assume coherence as a style was Arthur Heygate Mackmurdo who, in 1881, founded the Century Guild in association with Selwyn Image, producing the first recognizably *art nouveau* textile and book designs. Mackmurdo's furniture also broke new ground, the earliest dating from 1880. Harking back to earlier times, before the artificial division of the applied and fine arts, Walter Crane, an English designer, declared that the objective was to turn artists into craftsmen and craftsmen into artists, and on the Continent artists like the Belgian Henri van der Velde turned from painting to the production of decorative objects.

By 1900 the convolutions of plant-forms had become too complex, and the style obviously needed simplification. This task fell to Charles Rennie Mackintosh, a Glasgow architect, helped by his wife, and Herbert and Frances McNair. Greater use was made of the straight line and the cube, and a more austere style was born which was later to influence Walther Gropius and the Bauhaus designers of Weimar, starting in 1919. Commercially, the style was popularised by the English store of Liberty & Co. London, W.1, and it is because of this that the Italians call *art nouveau* the *stile liberte*. A branch establishment was opened in Paris in 1889 which continued until 1931, and some of the textiles in which the company specialized were more or less based on the designs of Mackmurdo. Liberty's also employed many other *art nouveau* artists of the day, mostly English, in the design of fabrics, metalwork, and furniture. Ambrose Heal, founder of the firm which still exists in London, also produced *art nouveau* furniture which was, perhaps, more soundly designed than that of Liberty's. In America, Louis Comfort Tiffany of New York, son of the famous jeweller, who worked mainly in glass, produced his Favrile glass (q.v.), which was extensively exported to Europe in the 1890s.

In architecture perhaps the most widely known exponent of the style, who carried it further than anyone else, was the Spaniard Antonio Gaudi, who favoured poured cement as a material. This gave him much more scope for eccentric form than any other. His furniture designs carry the principle of asymmetry to far greater lengths than had been seen before, and he has had no serious followers in this direction.

Art nouveau as a style spans the period between about 1880 and 1914. Its development was interrupted by the war of 1914–18. It continued to influence the architecture of such men as Frank Lloyd Wright until recent times, and its influence can also be seen in such relatively modern designs as the Barcelona chair of Mies van der Rohe of 1929. The best of its decorative art has now become part of the international scene so far as collectors are concerned, and occasional sales devoted to its products are held by the principal auction-rooms. These may confidently be expected to increase in number in the future.

ART UNION OF LONDON

This society, devoted to the fostering of the arts, was founded in 1836. At first each member was entitled, after payment of an annual subscription, to participate in a lottery, the principal prizes being works of art, the paintings often being those previously shown in Royal Academy Exhibitions. Also as prizes the Union began to commission limited editions of figures in Parian porcelain. Other prizes included lithographs, engravings, medallions, and bronzes, and these bear inscriptions recording the circumstances. Other Art Unions came into existence, notably the Ceramic Art Union and Crystal Palace Art Union of 1858, which were encouraged by the Prince Consort. The latter was intended to improve public taste in ceramics, and commissions are appropriately marked.

ARTISANS-LIBRES See 'Free' Craftsmen

ASH

The European ash (French *frêne*) is a tough, cream-coloured wood with a straight grain, elastic enough to be bent by steaming, although this is a modern development. Generally, it was popular among country craftsmen as a solid wood, and among the fashionable metropolitan furniture-makers as a veneer or inlay. There are two American varieties—white ash and black ash. In the case of the latter the colour approaches a fairly deep brown. The burrs particularly are used for veneers. American or Canadian ash was employed in England during the 19th century for such purposes as drawer-lining. Like walnut, ash is very susceptible to attacks of woodworm.

'ASTBURY' WARES

A number of Staffordshire wares presumably made by John Astbury (1686–1743), and his son, Thomas, as well as by other contemporary potters, are loosely grouped under the heading of 'Astbury' wares. The most important of these are wares of all kinds in which a red clay has been ornamented with applied and stamped reliefs in white clay, the whole being covered with a lead glaze. Teapots and jugs have fairly commonly survived, but figures are extremely rare, much sought, and forgeries exist. These figures include musicians, equestrian subjects, and soldiers in a naive but spirited style. It is very difficult to assign the earliest date for wares of this kind, but none can be much before 1730, and some can be dated by the appearance of Admiral Vernon, the victor of Portobello, as decoration, which places them to 1739. Some specimens are as late as 1745, but this is probably the latest date, and they may have been made by Whieldon (q.v.).

Astbury is credited with the introduction of calcined and ground flint into Staffordshire pottery, which, by giving a whiter, more closely grained body than had been in use in Staffordshire hitherto, helped to lay the foundation for the later drab-white stone-ware, and the creamware of Wedgwood.

The mark, *Astbury*, impressed, occurring on such wares as black basaltes and engine-turned red stone-ware, both introduced after 1760, was presumably employed by a later member of this family.

'ASTBURY-WHIELDON' WARES

Staffordshire wares in the styles presumed to have been introduced by John Astbury (q.v.), but covered with the mottled glazes characteristic of Thomas Whieldon (q.v.), are often referred to as 'Astbury-Whieldon'. They were not necessarily manufactured by either, since both types of ware were made by potters in Staffordshire other than those named.

Attribution. A group of two lovers modelled by J. J. Kändler at Meissen about 1740. *Christie, Manson & Woods Ltd.*

ATTRIBUTION

The consensus of informed opinion on the origin, authorship, and date of an object is termed its attribution. In a few cases a history exists which puts the correct attribution beyond doubt. Obviously a piece of furniture accompanied by an invoice from Thomas Chippendale, which has been in a particular place since it was made, can reliably be attributed to Chippendale's workshop, and even if the invoice were not dated, the object itself could be placed to within a few years by its style. Most antiques, and many things which might better be defined as works of art, have no reliable history, and often they have passed from hand to hand for so long that it is now impossible to trace them to their original source. In such cases an attribution must be made on the available evidence, that is to say, the piece itself. This is a task for the expert accustomed to such judgments, since many factors need to be weighed and

Astbury-Whieldon. An Astbury-Whieldon figure of a mounted dragoon. Staffordshire. c. 1745. *Victoria and Albert Museum.*

ATHÉNIENNE (French)

A small table or stand on three legs, usually made to hold a *jardinière* or a perfume-burner, and based on the old Roman and Etruscan bronze tripods. First to be seen in France during the reign of Louis Seize, most *athéniennes* are decorated with rams'-head *motifs*, and the legs often terminate in hoof feet (*pieds de biche*). Specimens are rare.

ATLANTES

(Latin *Telamones*.) Male figure in the form of a supporting column, usually to be found on furniture of the 16th and 17th centuries. The female equivalent is the caryatid.

Attribution. A group of two lovers imitated from Kändler by A. C. Luplau at Fürstenberg. c. 1770. *Señor José M. Mayorga.*

15

considered. Someone of sufficient experience often finds it easy to make an attribution on the basis of analogy with other known examples, and perhaps most attributions are made in this way. To do this ultimately depends on the existence of key pieces with a reliable history of one kind or another with which the unattributed object may be compared, and for the vast number of antiques this is adequate. Occasionally difficult problems present themselves, and the final verdict is then arrived at by process of elimination. By discarding what it could not possibly be, we eventually arrive at what it could be. The first question to be decided is whether the object is as old as its style suggests or a later copy or a forgery (q.v.). Most such things can usually be dated (when they are genuine) from the style (q.v.), and style will usually suggest country of origin. It then remains to be considered whether sufficient ·evidence exists to venture an attribution to a particular source.

It is always tempting to accept marks at their face value, and the question of their reliability is discussed elsewhere (see *Hall-marks* and *Marks on Pottery and Porcelain*). As an aid to attribution they should only be accepted as confirmatory evidence when everything else is seen to be in agreement. The easiest part of any forgery is usually the addition of a signature or maker's mark.

Many of the books listed in the Bibliography are illustrated, and good photographs and illustrations are of considerable assistance in suggesting possible sources for a piece of which the attribution is in doubt. Mere resemblance, however, is not enough. Porcelain factories copied each other's models, and furniture-makers drew inspiration from published books of designs.

It must also be remembered that research is still going on into many of the categories discussed here, and that this may result in changes of attribution in

Attribution. A Chinese porcelain plate of about 1750, the octagonal form derived from Japanese porcelain of the Kakiemon type (q.v.), the decoration apparently copied from a Bristol delft *chinoiserie* plate of similar form.

the future. A notable instance of this is to be found in the group of porcelain formerly considered to be Chelsea (q.v.) and now known to be from a separate Chelsea factory. This change in attribution has meant, if anything, an increase in value for the secedent group, although this is not always the case.

Attribution in certain instances, therefore, must not be regarded as fixed and immutable, but the most likely statement of the facts in the light of what is known at the time. In the vast majority of cases, however, no change is likely which will significantly alter either value or attribution.

AUBUSSON TAPESTRY

The manufacture of tapestry at Aubusson, and at Felletin not far away, goes back to before the establishment of the *Manufacture royale* (q.v.). In 1665 Colbert gave the looms financial assistance, on condition that each piece should be woven with a blue galloon border and the name 'Aubusson', which was often abbreviated to MRD (*Manufacture royale d'Aubusson*). Not every piece was marked.

With the Revocation of the Edict of Nantes in 1687 the Aubusson looms lost many of their skilled Huguenot (q.v.) workers, and all kinds of makeshifts were resorted to for the purpose of keeping them working. The designs of other looms, such as those of Beauvais, were copied, and at one time even pile-carpets were produced. Manufacture was considerably extended in the 1730s in consequence of assistance given by Louis XV, but designs were still far from original. The work of Oudry and Boucher (including the latter's Chinese scenes) was laid under contribution, and some late rococo *chinoiseries* were taken from the designs of Pillement (q.v.). Pastoral scenes and landscapes were always a favourite subject.

Wall-hangings, coverings for seat-furniture, and carpets were produced in relatively large quantities, but few 18th-century carpets survive. Those of the 19th century are not uncommon, and are of good quality. Generally the tapestries of Aubusson are inferior to those of Gobelins or Beauvais (q.v.).

The looms are still working and can be visited. There is also a local museum.

AUCTION, SALES BY

Sales by auction were common in Imperial Rome. A spear (the *hasta publica*) was struck into the ground in the market-place as a sign that an auction, presided over by the *magister auctionum*, was about to take place. It is evident from Cicero, Suetonius, Pliny the Elder, and others that Roman practice was generally very similar to our own.

Auction sales were commonly held in the 18th century in both France and England, and surviving catalogues are valuable indications of the taste of the time. During the 19th century Christie's especially played an important part in establishing the auction-room as a customary way of disposing of art-property, and sales became a fashionable event.

Aubusson Tapestry. A pair of Chinese Chippendale chairs covered with contemporary Aubusson tapestry. For a fitted room with chair covers *en suite* see *Gobelins, Tapestry.* Mid-18th century. *Parke-Bernet Galleries, New York.*

It has been reserved for today, however, for auction sales to become popular among all classes, and to be organized on an increasingly large scale, to which the resources of modern technology contribute.

In England and the U.S.A. the property to be sold is taken to a suitable auctioneer, who appraises it and includes it in a printed catalogue of goods to be auctioned. It is open to public inspection before the sale, and is then sold competitively to the highest bidder. On the Continent the system is slightly different. The property is usually appraised and catalogued by an *expert*, who is a man of special experience in his particular field and independent of the auctioneer. In France, the sale is conducted by a *commissaire-priseur*, who usually hires premises for the purpose. Elsewhere auction-rooms are privately owned or state owned. An example of the latter is the Dorotheum in Vienna.

The leading auctioneers in England and the U.S.A. maintain a staff of experts whose duty it is to identify provenance and describe the object in the catalogue, as well as helping the owner in suitable cases to fix a minimum price below which an object may not be sold (reserve price). This protects the vendor against combinations of dealers, colloquially known as a 'knock-out', or an absence of interested buyers. The auctioneer's attention should always be drawn, where possible, to any special features, such as illustration in a work of reference, or aspects of an object's previous history, which are likely to enhance the price offered. This will be included in the catalogue description.

Some Continental sale-rooms, especially those of Germany and Austria, provide the prospective buyer with a list of estimated prices below which an object will not normally be sold.

The selection of a suitable auctioneer is sometimes difficult, but if an object is antique, of good quality, and likely to command a worthwhile price, it is safest to offer it to one of the large auctioneers in London, New York, or Paris, and be guided by their advice. Auctioneers act as agents for the vendor and charge a variable rate of commission for their services. To this may be added such expenses as insurance, and the cost of illustrating an object in the catalogue,

Aubusson Tapestry. Tapestry depicting a pastoral scene with trophies (q.v.) above woven at Aubusson. c. 1780. *Parke-Bernet Galleries, New York.*

where this is deemed advisable. In some countries, notably France, a sales-tax is levied on the purchase price.

It is the auctioneer's duty to protect the interests of the vendor, and to get the highest possible price for his property consistent with fair business practice. Conditions of sale can be obtained from them, and are printed in the catalogues. An example of the usual conditions is given at the end of this article.

The large auctioneers supply their catalogues on subscription terms, and some provide a price-list after the sale. Priced catalogues are a valuable addition to the library of the collector, especially when illustrated. Outstanding objects can often be traced through former sales, sometimes for more than a century. It must be remembered, however, that descriptions rarely indicate condition, which sometimes affects price more or less seriously, and prices given can, therefore, only be regarded as an approximate guide at a particular point in time.

Buying at auction requires both skill and experience. Catalogue descriptions are not intended to be a guarantee of authenticity but a statement of the auctioneer's opinion. The old adage, *Caveat emptor*, applies with especial force to buying at auction, and the property offered should be examined with great care before the sale, and the catalogue description should be read with similar care, bearing in mind that it means what it says and no more. The maximum price to be offered ought to be marked against the lot in the catalogue and not subsequently exceeded without very good reason.

There are several malpractices to be found in certain sale-rooms. The most common is raising the price against a single bidder by the auctioneer (sometimes known as 'trotting'), which is made easier by the general custom of signalling bids by nods of the head or in similar ways. Bidding by the vendor of the property, or his agent, is hardly dangerous to the professional buyer, but the uninitiated are sometimes deceived into paying a higher price in the belief that they are genuinely in competition with another buyer. Dealers of the less reputable kind sometimes try to reduce competition by making denigratory remarks about certain lots, suggesting, for instance, that they are forgeries. The soundness of the advice to examine lots carefully beforehand, and to mark the catalogue with the highest price it is proposed to pay, is therefore evident.

CONDITIONS OF SALE

1. The highest bidder shall be the Purchaser; and if any dispute arises between two or more bidders the Lot shall, at the discretion of the Auctioneer, be put up again; the Auctioneer's decision to be final.

2. No person to advance less than 10/-. The Auctioneer has the right to advance the bidding at his absolute discretion.

3. The Purchasers to give in their Names and Addresses and to pay down 5/- in the £ or more in part payment if required, in default of which the Lot

or Lots so purchased will immediately be put up again and resold.

4. All Lots sold by the Auctioneers are to be taken away at Purchaser's risk and expense within TWO DAYS FOLLOWING THE SALE, in default of which the Auctioneers will not accept responsibility if the same are lost, stolen, damaged or destroyed, but the Lots will remain at the sole risk of the Purchaser and subject to a charge for warehousing. If at the expiration of two days after the conclusion of the sale, unless otherwise agreed, the Lots have not been cleared or paid for, the Auctioneers have the right to re-sell them by auction or private treaty, or to have them removed to a Warehouse at the Purchaser's risk and expense, and without notice having been given to the Defaulter.

5. The Owner of any Lot or Lots which have been offered for Sale and not sold or withdrawn before the Sale should give instructions within seven days regarding such Lots. The Auctioneers reserve the right of selling or disposing of any such uncleared Lots at their convenience without regard to any instructions they may have received, written or otherwise, prior to the sale in which the Lots were last offered, nor can the Auctioneers be answerable for any loss, damage or deterioration to the said Lots after the seven days' lapse of time.

6. All Lots to be sold as shown with all faults, imperfections and errors of descriptions. *Purchasers to satisfy themselves as to conditions, quality and description of Lots before bidding.* The Auctioneer not to be responsible for the correct description, genuineness, authenticity or condition of Lots; and to make no warranty whatever.

7. The Auctioneers to act as Agents only and not to be responsible for any default on the part of either Purchaser or Seller, and in particular not to be liable for payment to the Seller for any Lot or Lots until they have themselves received payment from the Purchaser.

8. The Auctioneers have the right to refuse any bid or to withdraw any Lots from the sale without previous notice.

9. No Lots to be transferred and no Lots removed during the time of sale.

10. The Auctioneers not to be held responsible in any matter connected with the commissioning of their staff to buy or bid for any Lots in the sale. *Reserves and Commissions sent by Telephone are accepted only at the Sender's risk and must be confirmed by letter or telegram.*

11. Notwithstanding that the Auctioneers have no legal responsibility in the event of loss or damage by fire, burglary or water, the Auctioneers have in force a special insurance policy to enable them to settle, *at their own discretion*, any claims arising from the above-mentioned causes. Owners of property are of course at liberty to make their own arrangements for insurance if they so desire.

12. All goods sent to these rooms are considered by the Auctioneers as sent for unreserved sale, and unless written instructions intimating reserves are

received prior to the commencement of the sale, such properties will be sold without reserve.

13. The Auctioneers, while taking every reasonable care to protect the respective Lots after they are sold, do not hold themselves responsible for any loss or damage that arises to any such Lots after the fall of the hammer, the Purchaser taking all the risks.

AUDRAN, CLAUDE III (1658–1734)

French designer and painter; *conservateur* at the Luxembourg. He is especially noted for tapestry designs, and his series, *The History of Don Quixote*, for the Gobelins *atelier* (q.v.) is probably the best known of them. Watteau became his pupil in 1709.

AUFENWERTH, JOHANN

Hausmaler (q.v.) of Augsburg. Augsburg was not only renowned for its gold and silver work, but it had a small group of enamellers who were among the earliest to enamel porcelain in colours. Of these, Johann Aufenwerth was the first to decorate the newly invented porcelain of Meissen, and he continued to do so until his death in 1728. He was

Auliczek, Dominicus. Group of hounds attacking their prey. One of the hunting groups which Auliczek made a speciality. Nymphenburg. c. 1770. *The Antique Porcelain Co. Ltd, London and New York.*

success. Later, his services proved to be unsatisfactory, and after years of dispute with the factory director, the Graf von Haimhausen, and his successor, Auliczek was ordered to leave Bavaria in 1797, being replaced as *Modellmeister* by Johann Peter Melchior (q.v.). As a modeller Auliczek was influenced by Meissen, but he is perhaps best known for his realistic groups of animals fighting, and for hunting groups, some derived from engravings by Riedinger.

Aufenwerth, Johann. Cup and saucer painted in iron-red, lilac, and gold enamels, signed 'IAW Augsburg'. c. 1725. *British Museum.*

assisted by his daughter, Sabrina. There has been much dispute, and a great deal of confusion, on the subject of the work actually done by Aufenwerth, but a cup and saucer in the British Museum signed *IAW Augsburg* is of some assistance in identifying it. Much of the work attributed to him by Pazaurek (*Deutsche Fayence und Porzellan Hausmaler*), however, seems much more likely to have been done by Seuter (q.v.). Aufenwerth's palette was more limited than that of Seuter. A signed example of *chinoiserie* in gilt silhouette by Aufenwerth has been recorded.

AULICZEK, DOMINICUS (1734–c. 1800)

Modellmeister and factory inspector at the Nymphenburg Porcelain Factory (q.v.). Auliczek succeeded Bustelli as *Modellmeister*, and became factory inspector in 1773, at first with considerable

AUTOMATA

The term is usually applied to moving figures decorating clocks, although at most periods those which has no set purpose except to amuse or mystify the owner were made. As early as the 3rd century B.C. there is record of a pigeon which flapped its wings, and hydraulic operation was a feature of some Roman automata, none of which have survived, although they are recorded in the surviving fragments of the works of Hero of Alexandria. Automata were very popular at the Byzantine Court, and at the Court of Burgundy, and French goldsmiths introduced them to the Mongol Court in the 13th century.

At the end of the 16th century the clockmakers of Augsburg were skilled in the making of automata, and often used them to decorate clocks. Louis XIV had a well-known clock with moving figures which operated at the hour, and he also had two Chinese

Automata. Gold snuffbox with enamelled mechanical musicians and musical movement, bearing the monogram of Princess Ekaterina Petrovna. By I. D. Piguet, c. 1810. *Christie, Manson & Woods Ltd.*

figures which moved automatically. We find in his inventory 'two Chinese ladies, each one on a peacock, carrying a small silver cup in her hands, silver and enamel, the said peacocks walking on a table by means of a spring according to how they are placed'.

During the 18th century many ingenious devices were made in London, principally by watchmakers, and the best were objects of great luxury, of gold and silver, set with pearls and precious stones. Especially popular in England and France was the *serinette*—a bird which, when actuated by a concealed spring, both moved and sang. These varied from full-size cages, often superb works of craftsmanship containing a canary with real plumage, to cages about the size of a tobacco box. Lazare Duvaux sold a small cage of gold with a bird in enamel to Mme de Pompadour in 1751. J. de Vaucanson (1708–1782), a clockmaker, specialized in automata during the Louis XVI period—pictures which moved, musical clocks, and similar mechanisms. In London Christopher Pinchbeck (q.v.) was making automata in 1721 which played a melody on a miniature organ, and James Cox, also of London and established in 1760, gained his reputation from his mechanical singing birds, although he made many other kinds of automata. Some of these were of superb workmanship and highly valued, and he received commissions from the East India Company for gifts to Oriental rulers, such as China's Emperor Ch'ien Lung, who seems always to have been fascinated by these ingenious toys. The work of Francis Magniac was no less sought at the time.

The popularity of automata did not diminish in the 19th century. Birds in cages, and birds which moved from branch to branch of a tree, were great favourites, the latter usually accompanied by a clock. These were a speciality of Charles Bontemps of Paris. Pictures, parts of which moved, had been made in Paris in the late 18th century, but they were even more popular during the early Victorian period, and they have not uncommonly survived. They were often combined with a small clock set in a church tower, and many were night scenes, illuminated by moonlight, simulated by mother-of-pearl inlays.

The fashion for well-made automata persisted through most of the 19th century, gradually giving way to clockwork toys produced in large quantities in Germany. Until the last war a few survivals remained on seaside piers in the form of penny-in-the-slot machines, a favourite always being a depiction of a judicial hanging.

Eighteenth-century automata, especially those of fine quality, are now very rare. Nineteenth-century specimens are easier to find. Dating is according to style, and price varies with quality. No forgeries have been noticed.

AVENTURINE

A decorative hardstone. A kind of quartz, usually brown or reddish-brown, with spangles of a gold colour. The Japanese imitated aventurine in lacquer, and its appearance was simulated at Venice by mixing specks of copper with molten glass of the required colour. In the 18th century this became a speciality of the Miotti factory (Venice).

The use of Japanese lacquer of this kind is recorded in the *Livre-Journal* of Lazare Duvaux, an example being three small tables of aventurine lacquer (*verni*), whose undersides were of *vernis des Indes*, delivered to Mme de Pompadour at a cost of £60.

AXMINSTER CARPETS

The manufacture of knotted-pile carpets was established at Axminster (Devon) by Thomas Whitty in the middle of the 18th century and enjoyed considerable success. The patterns employed were European, and in keeping with the date of manufacture. The looms were acquired by Wilton in 1835.

B

BACCARAT GLASS FACTORY

There are three French factories usually identified with Baccarat—Varèche, now in Belgium, Saint-Anne at Baccarat (Lorraine), and Trelon (Nord). The very important crystal glass factory at Varèche was originally French, but the town became Belgian after the Congress of Vienna in 1813. The founder, Aimé-Gabriel Artigues, was exempted from duties on imported glass by Louis XVIII, conditional on the operation of a factory in France, which prompted Artigues to buy the Saint-Anne factory at Baccarat, founded by the Archbishop of Metz in 1765. This became the Compagnie des Cristalleries de Baccarat in 1822, and it acquired an existing factory at Trelon (Nord) in 1828. Baccarat concluded a joint merchandising arrangement with Saint-Louis (q.v.) about the same time, with Paris showrooms in the rue de Paradis, where they still are. All varieties of table and decorative glass have been made in the past, including opaline (q.v.) and paperweights (q.v.).

BACHELOR CHEST

A recent term for a kind of early 18th-century English chest of drawers of small size which has a fold-over convertible into a table.

BACK-STOOL

A stool fitted with a back, which is a step in the evolution of the single chair. First mentioned in the second half of the 16th century, the back-stool was not common until the middle of the 17th. The term was still current in the middle of the 18th century, but by then was becoming archaic.

BAHUT (French)

A term to be used with care. Originally, in medieval times, it meant a small coffer with a domed lid which fitted on the top of a large coffer. It was intended to contain articles essential for a journey, making it unnecessary to unpack the larger one. The name then came to mean a single coffer or trunk with a domed lid, and finally it was applied to almost any kind of coffer. Since the middle of the 19th century the word was at first employed to mean almost any kind of case-furniture in a medieval style—cupboards,

Baccarat. Vase of carved glass influenced by imported Japanese art and Chinese jade carving. Baccarat. Dated **1890**. *Victoria and Albert Museum.*

buffets, cabinets, or chests. Today it seems to have no fixed meaning, being applied alike to cabinets and what might be termed 'sideboards' in English, irrespective of style, which may even be completely modern. The meaning can usually be ascertained from the context.

BAKEWELL, PEARS & COMPANY

This glass-house at Pittsburgh, Penn., was founded by Thomas Bakewell and Benjamin Pears in 1808. It closed in 1882. This was America's first glass-house successfully to make lead glass, and production included everything ordinarily made in glass of this kind, crystal chandeliers first being made in 1810. Decanters, bottles, vases, table-glass of all kinds, and candelabra formed the normal output, a good deal of which was exported to South America.

BALDACCHINO (Italian)

A kind of canopy to be found over beds, thrones, altars, and statues, especially in medieval times. The most widely known is Bernini's *baldacchino* in St

Baluster. Stone balusters in the Jardins de la Fontaine, Nimes.

Peter's, Rome. A portable variety covered kings and popes in processions, and they were often employed as ornament by, for instance, Bérain (q.v.), forming part of the central motif of many designs of this kind.

BALL-FOOT

Furniture support in the form of a turned sphere to be found with English cabinet furniture of the late 17th and early 18th centuries.

BALLOON-BACK

A chair-back approximating to the profile of a balloon, rounded at the top and curving inwards towards the seat. It was derived by Hepplewhite from contemporary France, where it was termed 'Montgolfier' after the balloonist. It was especially popular during the middle decades of the 19th century in England and America.

BALLOON CLOCK

Late 18th-century mantel-clock, the case circular as to the upper part, curving inwards to form a narrow waist, and outwards again towards the base. The type originated in France with the balloon ascents of Montgolfier, and was popular in England towards the end of the 18th century.

BALTIMORE GLASS WORKS

This glass-house at Baltimore (Maryland) started making glass about 1790. Bottles and flasks were probably the principal products.

BALUSTER

An architectural term referring to one of the upright supports of the classical balustrade. Turned furniture-legs and wine-glass stems with this form are thus called. The profile is variable in shape.

BAMBOO

Furniture of bamboo was imported from China and Japan during the 18th and 19th centuries. In England the jointed appearance of bamboo was simulated in turned beechwood for various kinds of light furniture, which was often painted. Most of it was made in the early years of the 19th century, and chairs of this form are to be found in Brighton Pavilion (Sussex, England).

BANDINELLI, BACCIO (1493–1560)

Florentine sculptor, best known for his monumental *Hercules and Cacus* in the Piazza della Signoria, Florence, which was the subject of a violent attack by Cellini. A small bronze *Venus* by his hand is in the Bargello, Florence.

BANISTER-BACK CHAIRS (American)

Term employed to describe chairs, a mixture of Flemish and Spanish in style, made during the early years of the 18th century, where the back comprises a series of upright, turned spindles, the top being surmounted by a carved cresting.

BANJO CLOCKS AND BAROMETERS

Clocks with a case somewhat resembling an inverted banjo were made in America by Simon Willard from about 1800 onwards. Barometers resembling a banjo with the resonator downwards were made at about

Table decoration. Banqueting table at Apsley House, London residence of the Duke of Wellington, set with the Portuguese silver table-appointment.

Strawberry Hill, Twickenham, S.W. London. The Long
Gallery of Horace Walpole's house in the revived Gothic
style of the second half of the 18th century.

the same time. The term is not contemporary. (See *Clocks, American.*)

'BANTAM' WARE
Incised Oriental lacquer. A late 17th-century term. See *Lacquer, Coromandel.*

BARILLA
Substance obtained from a plant growing in salt marshes near Alicante (Spain), the ash of which was used in early glass-making and contained both lime and soda. It was largely exported in the 16th century to a number of glass-making centres, including Venice. There is evidence for its import into England in the middle of the 16th century.

Barley-sugar Twist. Gate-legged (q.v.) dining-table and chairs of the Restoration period (q.v.) showing the characteristic barley-sugar twist. *Ham House, Richmond (Surrey).*

BARLEY-SUGAR TWIST
A term sometimes applied to decorative turning, resembling the old barley-sugar stick, used especially in the construction of seat-furniture from the time of Charles II onwards. The design was obviously derived from the baroque architectural columns in this form, such as the posts supporting the canopy of Bernini's *baldacchino* in St Peter's, Rome.

BAROQUE STYLE, THE
This is a phase of late Renaissance classicism which followed the Mannerist style (q.v.). It was largely a product of the Counter-Reformation in Italy, and the work of Bernini (q.v.). It was current from the early part of the 17th century till the early years of the 18th, when it developed into rococo (q.v.). The architectural styles of 15th and 16th century Italy in particular were based on those of ancient Rome. The first indication of a serious abandonment of

Baroque Style. A Meissen teapot of grotesque form, probably by Georg Fritzsche, with spout in the form of a snake's head and handle in the form of human figure. The decoration is of *chinoiseries* in gold silhouette. c. 1720. Probably based on a silver prototype. *Cecil Higgins Museum, Bedford.*

classical rules as enunciated by Vitruvius (and later by Palladio (q.v.)), can be found in the work of Michelangelo, who pointed the way to the Mannerist style. The disciplines of classicism were increasingly thrown off, and the effect of the movement was to endow architecture and the decorative arts with new vitality, with, occasionally, excursions into vulgarity. The baroque architect took the supporting columns of classical architecture and twisted them like barley-sugar sticks, something to be seen occasionally in ancient Roman times, but first employed in the Renaissance for the supporting columns of Bernini's bronze *baldacchino* which covers the High Altar of St Peter's, Rome. The baroque architect indulged his fancy in the construction of terraces and great flights of steps, and when natural vistas were lacking he had them painted, like a theatre backcloth. His buildings were decorated with statuary in theatrical poses which were often strained. His fountains were posturing nymphs with water spurting from ample breasts. Bernini, who began his career as a theatre *impresario*, united the arts of architecture, painting, and sculpture in his compositions, using a variety of materials, often with coloured lighting by means of carefully placed stained glass windows.

Baroque Style. A pair of silver sauceboats of 1739 by William Kidney with grotesque pouring lip and handle, the *cartouche* being slightly asymmetrical. Late baroque/early rococo (q.v.). *Christie, Manson & Woods Ltd.*

Baroque Style. An English walnut chair of about 1740 with lion-paw feet, the splat markedly baroque in form. *Parke-Bernet Galleries, New York.*

Baroque art is nearly always dramatic in one way or another, and there is a conscious striving for unusual angles of view which had already formed part of the repertoire of the Mannerist. Much of the best architecture and much of the most significant decorative art of Germany and Austria is in this style, where it persisted well into the 18th century. It is to be found in many of the German palaces, and it inspired the early porcelain of Meissen and Vienna, the silversmith's work of Dinglinger, and the bronze sculpture and ivory-carving of the early years of the 18th century.

It had less effect in France, where the artists assembled by Colbert adhered to a more rigidly classical style, and it had hardly any effect in England, although Blenheim, built for the Duke of Marlborough by Sir John Vanbrugh, and St Martin's in the Fields (Trafalgar Square, London) by Nicholas Hawksmoor, are both examples of the baroque style. In the decorative arts, such as early silver from the hand of Paul de Lamerie, the baroque elements were largely imported from the Continent.

Before 1730 in France baroque began to give place to rococo, with which it is often confused, but baroque always differs noticeably from rococo in that the latter style makes considerable use of asymmetry in ornament. The baroque acanthus, for instance, is always symmetrically disposed; the rococo acanthus leaf often has its tip twisted to one side. In the middle of the 18th century rococo

began to give place to neo-classicism (q.v.) on the Continent. In England rococo had never reached the point of being a major style, the severely classical style of Palladio, known as Palladianism (q.v.), merging almost insensibly into the neo-classical.

Like rococo, baroque was often used as a perjorative term in the 19th century, when, influenced by Pugin (q.v.) and Ruskin, revived Gothic was much in favour, and neither style was understood or appreciated by English critics and art-historians of the day.

See *Rococo; Neo-classical.*

BARTOLOZZI, FRANCESCO (1727–1815)
Italian engraver who arrived in England in 1764. Many of his engravings are after Angelica Kauffmann (q.v.) and Cipriani (q.v.). Prints in the stipple technique by him are sought by collectors. Less often seen are engravings after drawings by Guercino. Bartolozzi was appointed Director of the Academy of Arts at Lisbon in 1802. Stipple engravings are made up of many small dots, rather than lines, and in principle somewhat resemble the modern half-tone block.

BASALTES
Name given by Wedgwood to a hard black stone-ware body introduced about 1769. A black ware, termed 'Egyptian black', had previously been made in Staffordshire, and Wedgwood's principal improvement was to make it harder, of finer grain, and more suited to the sharp reproduction of moulded ornament. Black jasper (q.v.) differs somewhat in composition from basaltes, but is equally hard. This is usually found in conjunction with reliefs in white jasper. Like jasper, Wedgwood regarded his basaltes ware as a kind of porcelain, rather than a stone-ware. A number of other Staffordshire factories made black basaltes ware in imitation of Wedgwood,

Basaltes. A moulded teapot in basaltes stoneware decorated in the neo-classical style (q.v.). By Adams of Tunstall. c. 1790.

although few succeeded in achieving a comparable quality. The best were probably those of Turner, although Mayer did some excellent work of this kind. Abroad, the factories of Königsberg and Ulfsunda copied Wedgwood's wares in this medium.

BASILISK   See *Cockatrice*

BASIN-STAND
An 18th-century bedroom stand with a circular hole in the top to hold a basin and ewer. They were sometimes triangular to fit into a corner. Basin-stands were made in a variety of forms and were often fitted with mirrors. Chippendale's *Director* illustrates examples.

BASKET-WORK
Woven wicker-work or plaited rushes were employed in the manufacture of seat-furniture from very early times. Ornament resembling such weaves to be found, for instance, as moulded decoration to porcelain plates. (See *Ozier pattern*.)

BAS-RELIEF
Carving in low relief in wood, stone, etc., or castings in plaster or metal with ornament of this kind.

BAT
The Chinese word 'fu', meaning 'bat', is also a homonym for happiness. It is therefore much used as an ornamental motif in Chinese art of all kinds. Five bats represent riches, longevity, health, love of virtue, and a peaceful death. They can be found on porcelain, rugs, embroidered textiles, and most kinds of Chinese decorative art from Ming times onwards.

BATEAU, LIT EN (French)
A term employed to describe a kind of bed produced during the First Empire and the Restoration in France because, in general appearance, it resembled a boat. Beds of this kind were usually veneered in mahogany and mounted sparsely with gilt-bronze.

BATEMAN, HESTER (fl. 1761–1793)
English woman silversmith. Hester Bateman has become one of the most popular names in silver-collecting, especially in America, not because her work was noticeably better than that of many of her contemporaries, nor because she was a woman, since women silversmiths were not uncommon in the 18th century, but because much more of her work in an identifiable form has survived to be collected. She was very prolific, and small wares especially are not uncommon. Her mark, *HB* in script, first appears in the records of the London Goldsmith's Company in 1761, when she was established at Bunhill Row, London, although very few specimens of her work exist which were made before the last quarter of the 18th century. In keeping with the period, her work was usually in the Adam style, although she made occasional pieces which were not markedly neo-classical. Most of her work was plain and simple, elegantly shaped, sometimes pierced, and often with

an engraved band, bright-cut (q.v.), which was employed in conjunction with simple beading to the rim. Hester Bateman added '& Co.' to her name in 1789, but her connection with other silversmiths of the same surname, and presumably related to her in some way, has not been satisfactorily determined. These are Jonathan, Peter, and William Bateman Senior, assumed to be her sons, with whom she may have worked in partnership. Anne Bateman was partner to Peter, and probably his wife. William Bateman was taken into partnership with them, and Anne disappears in 1805, when Peter and William continued together. It seems possible that she died in this year. William Bateman Junior was, perhaps, the son of William Senior. He never registered a mark, but his name appears in the records of the Gold-smiths' Company in 1840.

Battersea Enamel. Maria Gunning, Countess of Coventry, transfer-printed probably from a plate by John Brooks after a portrait of 1751 by Francis Cotes. Battersea Enamel Works. c. 1753. *Victoria and Albert Museum.*

BATTERSEA ENAMELS
The Battersea Enamel undertaking at York House, Battersea, London, was started by Alderman Stephen Theodore Janssen a little before 1753. It is difficult, now, to be entirely certain of what was made there, but a vast number of painted enamels (q.v.), such as inkstands, candlesticks, tea-caddies, and so forth, which are often claimed for Battersea, were not made there, but at Birmingham, or Bilston in Staffordshire. Alderman Janssen became bankrupt in 1756, and from the ensuing notice of sale in the *Daily Advertiser* it is possible to form a fairly accurate estimate of what Battersea made, and these were, to quote, 'Snuff boxes of all sizes and a great variety of patterns, of square and oval pictures of the Royal Family, History, and other pleasing objects, very proper ornaments for the cabinets of the

Battersea Enamel. Paris presenting the apple to Hibernia with Britain standing by. From a plate by S. F. Ravenet after James Gwyn. Battersea Enamel Works. c. 1753. *Victoria and Albert Museum.*

curious; Bottle-tickets with chains for all sorts of Liquor, and of different subjects; Watch-cases; Toothpick cases; Coat and Sleeve Buttons; Crosses, and other Curiosities, mostly mounted in metal, double gilt'. From this it will be seen that the manufacture could be fairly classed as toys (q.v.).

Most Battersea enamels are transfer-prints (q.v.) coloured over, and it has always been assumed that the art of transfer-printing was discovered at Battersea, attributed to the Irish engraver, and friend of Thomas Frye of Bow, John Brookes. From a remark made by Dr Pococke in August 1754, who refers to the 'china and enamel manufactory at York House, Battersea', it is possible to conjecture that porcelain may have been painted here, and that the enamel works also functioned as an outside decorating studio (q.v.). Although only one specimen of transfer-printed Chelsea porcelain is known to exist, several specimens of Battersea enamel painted by a recognizable Chelsea hand have been recorded, including some by William Duvivier. A number of Chelsea porcelain toys have enamel fittings. The possibility that the Bow and Worcester engraver Robert Hancock worked for Battersea is fairly strong. His *L'Amour* occurs on snuff-boxes, and the *Parrot and Grapes* design, familiar on Worcester porcelain, is also to be found on enamels. Simon Francis Ravenet, an engraver of considerable merit who did the plates for Hogarth's *Marriage à la Mode,* also worked for Battersea, and may have played a part in the discovery of the transfer-printing process.

The work of the Battersea Enamel Manufactory is in the rococo style. Neo-classical designs of urns, etc., occurring on English enamels are the work of either Bilston or Birmingham (q.v.).

BAUMHAUER, JOSEPH (fl. 1745–1772)

A German craftsman who became *ébéniste privilégé du roi* about 1767. His furniture is of excellent quality. He employed lacquer, wood marquetry, and the Boulle technique of brass and tortoiseshell. After 1767 his work was stamped JOSEPH between *fleurs-de-lys.* His son, Gaspard Joseph, succeeded his father and may have used his stamp.

BAYREUTH

The factory at Bayreuth is first mentioned about 1719, and was built and established for the Crown Prince Georg of Bayreuth at H. Georg-am-See. It is possible that the nomadic potter Johann Kaspar Ripp (who also worked at Nürnberg, Ansbach, Frankfurt, and Hanau), may have been connected with it. In 1729 J. G. Knoller leased it with a twelve-year privilege. In 1745 it was taken over by Adolf Frankel and Johann Schreck, and finally passed entirely into the hands of Pfeiffer. After his death in 1787 the factory was run by two painters, Oswald and Bayer. After two years a new privilege was issued to Pfeiffer's heirs by the Margraf of Ansbach, the two States then being united, but the factory declined slowly and closed in 1852.

Shapes at Bayreuth follow South German styles: pear-shaped jugs with plaited handles, tankards, candlesticks and dishes. The glaze is of a bluish tone, not unlike that of Nuremberg.

Decoration is blue-and-white, the blue speckled with white. Dishes are painted on the rim with elaborate foliate scrolls and festoons of flowers, similar to those of the *Hausmaler* (q.v.). Jugs are decorated with scattered flowers and leaves with birds between.

Bayreuth. A mounted *Enghalskrüg* (narrow-necked jug) decorated with silver and gilt ornament on a brown glaze in typical style. Bayreuth. c. 1730. *British Museum.*

Muffle-kiln (enamel) colours were used, and perhaps introduced at Bayreuth by Johann Philipp Dannhofer in 1737, after he had left Vienna (q.v.). His style is close to that of Du Paquier decoration and occasionally reminiscent of the leaf-and-strapwork done at Meissen during the Höroldt period.

Another style found at Bayreuth is that of A. F. von Löwenfinck (q.v.), who worked there after escaping from Meissen in 1736. His style is lively and free, Oriental flowers and birds being painted in very clear, bright enamels.

Also made at Bayreuth, beginning in the 1720s, was a brown glazed earthenware sometimes decorated with wheel-engraving like glass, probably imitated from Böttger's red stoneware (see *Meissen*), or with *chinoiseries* in gilt and silver silhouette inspired by early Meissen porcelain.

BEAU BRUMMEL (American)
A popular name in the United States for a gentleman's fitted toilet-table of a type made during the second half of the 18th century. The term is meaningless since such tables were in use long before George Brummell was born, in 1788. Chippendale called his version a shaving-table in the 3rd edition of the *Director*, and Hepplewhite illustrated his design in the *Guide* of 1788 as a Lady's Dressing Table.

BEAUVAIS TAPESTRY
Colbert was responsible for starting the manufacture of tapestry at Beauvais, but the looms never became part of the *Manufacture royale* (q.v.), although they received royal protection and financial assistance. The director, Louis Hinard, supplied tapestries for royal palaces and *châteaux* and to members of the Court, and according to Voltaire 600 work-people

were employed. Hinard became bankrupt in 1684, and the enterprise was taken over by Philippe Behagle until 1705, when some important work was done, including a number of tapestries to designs by Jean I Berain (q.v.) in association with the flower-painter J.-B. Monnoyer, which remained very popular for more than 20 years. In 1711 the looms were being operated by the brothers Filleul, and they were taken over in 1722 by de Mérou, when some *chinoiserie* subjects were woven. Oudry was appointed designer in 1726, and assumed the direction of the enterprise in 1734 in company with Nicolas Besnier. Oudry's own designs include his favourite hunting scenes, and Natoire designed a series illustrating the life of Don Quixote. Boucher designed a series of *Village Festivals* in 1736, and some *chinoiserie* subjects soon afterwards which remained popular for a good many years. In 1754 the looms passed into the ownership of A.-C. Charron, at which time the practice of making matching *suites* of wall-hangings, and coverings for beds and seat-furniture, became fashionable. A few carpets were also made.

The prosperity of the Beauvais looms began to decline, like those of the Gobelins workshops, with the beginning of the neo-classical style and the popularity of wallpaper, but the looms continued for some time afterwards, and a particularly popular subject of 1769 was the *Jeux Russiens*, made with matching seat-covers, as well as *Pastorals* by J.-B. Huet which illustrate the prevailing fashion for the simple life.

With the Gobelins workshops, those of Beauvais provided the finest quality tapestries to be made in France in the 18th century. (See *Tapestry*.)

Beauvais Tapestry. Tapestry after designs by Jean I Bérain (q.v.) depicting acrobats entertaining an eastern potentate. Beauvais. c. 1710. *Firle Place, Firle, Sussex.*

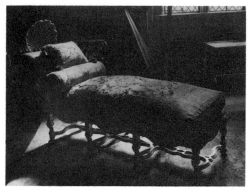

Bed, Day-. An early 17th-century day-bed with original upholstery. *Penshurst Place, Kent.*

BED, DAY-
Introduced early in the 17th century, the position of the day-bed or *lit de repos* was originally at the foot of the bed, and it was customary among ladies of fashion to recline on it during the day-time when receiving guests. It became increasingly popular in France as the century progressed, and it was occasionally to be found in England during the early decades of the 17th century, usually with an end which was of solid panelling. After the Restoration in 1660 day-beds were largely made of carved and turned walnut with caned seats and ends, like the chairs of the period. At first with loose cushions, fixed upholstery became more common after about 1680. During the Queen Anne period the turned legs and stretchers were replaced by cabriole legs. The day-bed became progressively less popular during this reign.

In France during the 18th century the day-bed developed into the *chaise longue* and remained very popular in Court circles. Mme de Pompadour, whose health was poor, made much use of it, and one of the finest of Boucher's portraits depicts her thus reclining. Generally, the style of the day-bed, both in France and England, followed that customary for chairs of the period. (See *Duchesse.*)

BED-STEPS
Beds, especially four-posters, were very high during the 18th century, due to the fact that several mattresses were piled one on the other. Bed-steps, sometimes incorporating a cupboard for a chamber-pot, were made for the purpose of climbing into bed. They were sometimes necessary, and were still being made in the first half of the 19th century.

BEECHWOOD
Beechwood ranges from light brown to reddish-brown, with a straight grain. It was widely employed during the 18th century, but principally by country craftsmen, and especially in the making of seat-furniture. In this kind of work it took the place of walnut. Beech is commonly employed in the making of so-called 'stick' furniture (q.v.), and in the

18th century it was often the foundation of japanned or gilded chairs. Like walnut and ash, it is prone to attacks by woodworm.

BEILBY, WILLIAM AND MARY
The best-known English glass enamellers, who worked at Newcastle upon Tyne. William Beilby (1740–1819) at first worked in Birmingham as a maker of enamel boxes, and was enamelling glass in Newcastle by 1762. His sister, Mary (1749–1797), was engaged in the same craft by 1767. They appear to have ceased work about 1778, when they moved from Newcastle. Their wine-glasses, usually with bucket-shaped bowls, are often painted with heraldic motifs in white monochrome and coloured enamels, but later examples of their work decorated with landscapes and other motifs of the period also include some rare *chinoiseries.*

Ale-glasses and at least one decanter painted by them have also been recorded.

Beilby. A very rare bowl painted with rococo *motifs*, and signed '*Beilby* Inv and pinx'. Dated 1765. *Victoria and Albert Museum.*

BEINGLAS (German)
A semi-opaque white glass produced by adding bone-ash to the other ingredients. Sometimes called milk-and-water glass. This type of glass, with enamelled decoration, was produced in large quantities in Bohemia and Thuringia during the second half of the 18th century and the early decades of the 19th. (See *Milch-glas.*)

BELL METAL
Bronze made of copper alloyed with 20 or 25 per cent of tin together with a small amount of zinc. Apart from being used for bells, it was employed for mortars and similar utensils.

BELLANO, BARTOLOMMEO (?1434–?1497)
A Paduan sculptor (and pupil of Donatello) who became well known for large sculpture and small bronzes. A *Saint Jerome seated* is in the Louvre and the *Rape of Europa* in the Bargello. There are examples of his work in the Staatliche Museen, W. Berlin. Bellano was also responsible for bas-reliefs, medallions, and plaquettes.

BELLARMINE

An almost pear-shaped salt-glazed stoneware wine-jug with a short, narrow neck on which is a moulded mask thought in England to be a caricature of the hated Cardinal Bellarmine (1542–1621), or of the Duke of Alva. These bottles, made in the Rhineland at Cologne or Raeren, were called *Bartmann-krüge* (bearded-man jugs) in Germany, and stoneware of this kind in Elizabethan England was generally known as 'tyger ware'. A thriving export trade was carried on by German potters with many other European countries, and specimens have been discovered as far away as America and Japan.

The appearance of a mask as ornament to Rhineland stoneware jugs goes back to before the middle of the 16th century. Dated specimens are known, the earliest being 1550 and the latest 1699. Accompanying the mask is, quite frequently, a coat of arms on a medallion applied to the centre of the body of the vessel. On examples found in England the royal arms are not uncommon, although they were obviously not made for royalty. Some arms if traced would prove to be those of towns, or even of customers, and a few are the trade insignia of merchants. Some are merely decorative rosettes, especially on the later examples. The masks degenerated considerably towards the end of the 17th century.

Bellarmines were also associated with witchcraft, and some specimens have been recovered containing objects relating to the cult.

Like most stoneware vessels of Rhineland origin the Bellarmine was cut from the wheel, after throwing, by a loop of string or wire, and the base usually usually exhibits the marks of this having been done in a series of semi-circles. It has been suggested that English copies made after 1671 by Dwight of Fulham may lack this characteristic, and certainly examples exist of this kind, but it has never been established beyond doubt that Dwight actually copied the Bellarmine, although his patent mentions copies of Cologne ware. Some examples with the arms of Charles II lacking the signs of string cutting are perhaps the most uncharacteristic of normal Rhineland production and therefore the most persuasive.

Bellarmines were copied in the 19th century by Hubert Schiffer of Raeren, who stamped his initials in the base. Specimens with a ground patch which suggests the removal of stamped initials are probably spurious, and Schiffer's handles differed from genuine specimens by being moulded instead of hand-made. (See *Rhineland Stoneware*.)

BELLEEK PORCELAIN FACTORY (County Fermanagh, N. Ireland)

This factory seems to have started in 1863, and it exhibited its wares at the Dublin International Exhibition of 1865. Its speciality was a porcelain, often remarkably thinly potted, covered with an iridescent glaze which is unmistakable. Much use was made of modelled additions in the form of shells and corals, and considerable ingenuity was lavished on open-work baskets encrusted with flowers. Some of the finest work contrasts an unglazed porcelain body (which resembles contemporary Parian bodies from the English factories) with the typical iridescent glaze by designing the plastic decoration for glazed and unglazed passages. This was taken up by the Ceramic Art Company of Trenton, New Jersey, who, after 1889, produced porcelain very similar to that of Belleek in design and decoration. Another Trenton factory, that of Ott & Brewer, was noted for its 'Belleek' porcelain made from American materials, as well as a Parian ware of fine quality.

BELLEVUE FAÏENCE (Meurthe-et-Moselle, France)

This factory, closely connected with Lunéville, was founded in 1758 by Lefrançois, and bought in 1771 by Bayard and Boyer, when it bore the title of *Manufacture royale*. Figures were made from Cyfflé's moulds, and Strasbourg wares were copied. Large painted garden figures in terracotta were made here, as well as a good deal of *faïence-fine*.

BELL-FLOWER   See *Husk Ornament*

BELLS, GLASS

The manufacture of glass bells was a speciality of the Bristol factory. From 1750 onwards an increasing quantity in both clear and opaque coloured glass was made there, and bells were popular until 1780, when production fell off. Manufacture was restarted on a fairly large scale about 1820, and most surviving examples today belong to this period, including bells of blue glass which were only rarely made before this date. Early specimens are usually in red or green glass, but those with *latticinio* decoration (q.v.) are well known, while opaque white examples belong to the last decade of the 18th century and later. 18th-century handles are plain, usually of baluster form, although they were often made in contrasting colours to the bell itself, or were given a *latticinio* decoration. Bells with handles in the form of legs or arms, or of cut-glass, are early Victorian. Manufacture was discontinued about the middle of the 19th century, although they have since been reproduced.

BELTER, JOHN H.

American cabinet-maker of the first half of the 19th century. Much of his furniture is heavily carved in a revived rococo style. His work was generally excellent in quality, and it has not uncommonly survived.

BELUCHISTAN RUGS

A mountainous area to the north-west of India, immediately south of Afghanistan. The rugs made in this area are classified as 'nomadic', and the classification includes those made by related tribes moving in Afghanistan and eastern Persia. The Sehna knot is used, and the pile is wool, with goat and camel hair. There is a wide ornamental selvedge, and the predominating colours are dark reds and browns, with usually some tan-coloured natural camel-hair. Patterns are hexagonal and octagonal medallions, while stylized floral motifs occur on some of them.

BENCH
A long seat without a back, either plain or upholstered. Those with a plain seat were often intended to complement refectory tables (q.v.). The bench is one of the oldest of all pieces of furniture.

BENCKGRAFF, JOHANNES (1708–1753)
German arcanist. Benckgraff probably gained his knowledge of porcelain-making from an early association with J. J. Ringler (q.v.). At first the two men travelled together, being at Künersberg in 1747 and Höchst in 1752. Benckgraff remained at Höchst until 1752, when a model of a porcelain-kiln mysteriously disappeared and found its way to Wegely's factory in Berlin. With the assistance of this, and some porcelain earth from the same source, manufacture was started in Berlin (q.v.) in the same year. Benckgraff left Höchst after a quarrel, and arrived in Fürstenberg (q.v.), where he died two years later.

BÉNITIER (French)
A small vessel, usually of faïence appropriately decorated, made to hold holy water. Bénitiers were commonly made in Roman Catholic countries, but rarely elsewhere.

BENNINGTON POTTERY, VERMONT
Captain John Norton began the manufacture of redware at Bennington in 1793. He was succeeded by his son, who introduced the manufacture of stoneware, and by two more generations who made redware until 1894. A grandson, Julius Norton, became interested in the Rockingham type of brown and yellow ware which was being made in New Jersey by several potteries from 1830. In 1844 he formed a partnership with Christopher Fenton, and together they founded the United States Pottery Company in 1853. As early as about 1847 Fenton had developed a porcelain body for the production of ornamental pitchers, and the ornamental wares generally in white *biscuit* porcelain now termed 'Bennington Parian'. This was largely an adaptation and simplification of English Parian.

The factory manufactured the Rockingham type of brownware with a mottled dark glaze which had been introduced by Fenton, and these products included large quantities of utility wares such as pie-plates, milk-pans, and soap-dishes. More decorative is tableware ornamented in relief, pitchers, toby jugs, teapots, sugar-bowls and book-flasks, as well as bottles in the form of figures, candlesticks, lamps, vases, and even picture-frames. Large dogs, deer, and lions are among the best of Bennington 'Rockingham' wares, and the chief modeller was an English potter from Staffordshire named Daniel Greatbach, who arrived in the United States in

1851. He was strongly influenced by English originals.

Only about half of Bennington wares were marked, which means that the unmarked examples may be either Bennington products or contemporary copies. Fenton's factory closed in 1858, but Rockingham ware continued to be made in enormous quantities, especially in the Ohio valley, up till 1900. 'Bennington' is often a generic term for wares of this type made elsewhere, notably in the region of the Ohio river, or in Pittsburgh or Baltimore.

BENT-WOOD FURNITURE
Although furniture of this kind from Scandinavia has been widely distributed in recent years, it was first made more than a century ago by Michael Thonet of Boppard-am-Rhein, who began experimenting in the 1830s. Persuaded by Prince Metternich, Thonet removed to Vienna, and there he developed the process by which wood, usually beech, was heated with the aid of steam or boiling water and bent in wooden moulds. Thonet started a factory for the mass-production of furniture in 1849, and soon developed a system whereby chairs could be made in parts for transport and assembled at their destination with the aid of a few screws. The factory achieved great success with the quantity production of chairs for cafés.

BÉRAIN, JEAN I AND II
Jean I Bérain (1640–1711) was a French designer, originally trained by Charles Le Brun, who became *dessinateur de la chambre et du cabinet du roi* in 1674. He designed not only interiors of all kinds, but settings for fêtes, banquets, theatrical performances, and royal functions generally. He is notable for a kind of grotesque (q.v.) ornament which is especially characteristic of the closing years of the reign of Louis XIV but continued to be popular until well into the following reign, especially for the decoration of faïence at Moustiers (q.v.). He influenced the engraved designs to be found on the brass inlay of Boulle (q.v.). He was succeeded as *dessinateur du roi* by his son, Jean II.

BERGAMO RUGS
A rug-making village near Smyrna. Carpets to be seen in some of Holbein's paintings came from Bergamo and from Oushak. These carpets are sometimes called 'Holbein carpets'. None of these has survived, but 18th- and 19th-century specimens are known. The Ghiordes knot is invariable, with usually a long wool pile. Red, green, blue, yellow, and white are the prevailing colours, and motifs are extremely varied and geometric. There is usually a wide and fairly elaborate border. Bergamo rugs are rare.

BERGÈRE (French)
An upholstered armchair which became fashionable in the early years of the reign of Louis XV. The high curved back was complemented by upholstered

Bérain, Jean I. A page from one of the design-books of Jean I Bérain. The design dates from the closing years of the reign of Louis XIV (d. 1715), but there are already some asymmetrical elements. See *Rococo Style.*

arms, and the seat was both wider and deeper than that of the more formal *fauteuil* (q.v.). There were several variations. The *bergère en confessionnal* was similar in general form to the English wing arm-chair; the variety termed *en gondole* (see *Gondole*) has an integral curved back and sides. The *bergère* and the *duchesse* (q.v.) often resemble each other so closely that it is difficult to separate the two.

BERLIN FAÏENCE FACTORIES
A factory flourished here about 1700 under Cornelius Funke, and some immense pieces were made. About 1740 Christian Friedrich Rewendt founded a factory at Potsdam which imitated delft to perfection. After his death in 1768 the factory was carried on by his two sons, Friedrich Wilhelm and Johann Christian. Johann Christian took up ownership in 1770, but was bankrupt by 1775. It was then taken over by a man called Sartory, and in 1790 sold to Frau von Linckersdorff. Sartory founded another factory in the same year but little is known of the wares.

A blue-and-white jar marked and dated 'Potsdam —1740' allows a whole group of pieces to be distinguished from Dutch delft. The body is reddish in tone, very different from Dutch wares, the shapes are more slender and frequently have vertical ribbing. An ornamental band of spirals and a peacock in a flowery field are motifs typical of this factory. Colours are high-temperature green, iron-red, and yellow, and some cold (unfired) colours. Occasionally the pieces are marked with a *P* and an *R* below.

BERLIN PORCELAIN FACTORY
The first Berlin porcelain factory was founded in 1752 by a merchant, Wilhelm Kaspar Wegely, who was given a monopoly by Frederick the Great. The *Modellmeister* was Ernst Heinrich Reichard, and a miniature painter from Meissen, Isaak Jakob Clauce, was one of the principal painters. This factory was forced to close in 1757.

In 1761 Johann Ernst Gotzkowsky built a second factory in the Leipzigerstrasse, which, in 1763, was bought by Frederick the Great, and the enterprise then became a royal factory. Since 1918 it has been a state factory, and is now in West Berlin. The mark was the sceptre of the Brandenburg arms. Reichard provided the secret of manufacture, and management was in the hands of J. G. Grieninger from Saxony. The *Modellmeister* was Friedrich Elias Meyer from Meissen, and painters included Karl Wilhelm Böhme (later the *Obermaler*) and Johann Balthasar Borrmann, both from Meissen. Clauce was also employed at this factory. Frederick gave the new factory many privileges, and the sale of Meissen porcelain was prohibited in the Prussian territories. From 1765 onwards both Sèvres and English influence may be noticed, and in the 1790s the effect of imports of Wedgwood's wares was extremely marked.

Berlin Porcelain. Chinese Lute Player modelled by F. E. Meyer (q.v.). Berlin Royal Factory. c. 1770. *K. A. L. Rhodes Esq.*

Wegely's porcelain is very scarce, and most surviving examples are figures in white. Most of the models were original, and probably the work of Reichard. Some well-modelled birds have since been reproduced. The colours employed for painting service-ware were few and simple, and a purple is very close to that of Höchst.

It is difficult to be certain that the rare specimens of Gotzkowsky's porcelain, made between 1761 and 1763, were decorated during this period. Much was

Berlin Porcelain. An ice-pail from the Prussian Service presented to the Duke of Wellington. The decoration represents the storming of the Ciudad Rodrigo during the Peninsular War. c. 1818. *Wellington Museum, Apsley House, London.*

taken over 'in white' in the latter year and decorated subsequently. During the early years of the royal period moulded patterns were a speciality. The Gotskowsky pattern (q.v.) was devised earlier by the Meissen factory, but the *reliefzierat mit Spalier* (relief decoration with trellis) was original, as was the *Neuzierat* (1763), and the *Antikzierat* (1767). Although *Mosaik patterns* (q.v.) were done at Meissen and Ansbach as well, they were a Berlin speciality, often used in conjunction with moulded patterns and pierced borders. A number of coloured grounds were introduced about 1770. Flowers belong to the *deutsche Blumen* category (q.v.), the early examples being pale in colouring, a much stronger palette being introduced later, and painting *en camaieu* was fashionable. In underglaze blue (not a very popular colour) the Meissen *Zwiebelmuster* (onion pattern) was imitated. Special attention was given to the quality of landscape and figure painting, the former sometimes by Borrmann and Böhme, and French engravings were often employed as a source of inspiration. Figure-subjects came from Watteau (engraved by Le Bas), with Dutch peasant scenes after Teniers, and battle-scenes either from Rugendas or from the campaigns of Frederick the Great. The *fliegende Kinder*, or flying *amorini*, were taken from Boucher, and extensive use was made of engravings by J. E. Nilson of Augsburg and Daniel Chodowiecki.

Figures came from F. E. Meyer and his younger brother, Wilhelm Christian Meyer, and there were several series of figures, such as little *amorini* representing the Twelve Months, each titled on the back. At the end of the century some excellent work in biscuit porcelain was done by the sculptor Gottfried Schadow, who executed a table-decoration in 1793 for the wedding of the Crown Prince Frederic William and the Princess Luise of Mecklenburg-Strelitz to designs by Genelli. An important service was modelled by Schadow for presentation to the Duke of Wellington in 1819. The painted decoration depicts scenes from the Duke's battles. This is now at Apsley House, London.

The factory continued throughout the 19th century, often making wares inspired by those of the 18th. Today it is the Berlin State Porcelain Manufactory, and excellent flower-painting is still one of its specialities.

BERLIN TAPESTRIES

A number of Huguenot tapestry-workers left France after the Revocation of the Edict of Nantes in 1685, and one of them, Pierre Mercier from Aubusson, settled in Berlin and was given a privilege by Elector Frederick William I. Among the most notable works of these looms was a history of the Great Elector. They later furnished a number of tapestries to the Courts of Prussia and Northern Europe, and closed in 1769.

BERLIN WOOL WORK

A kind of embroidery carried out in coloured wools on a canvas foundation to designs published in Berlin, whence the wools were often imported. The designs were printed on squared paper and transferred to the canvas as exactly as the ability of the needleworker allowed. Floral and pictorial patterns naturalistically rendered are invariable, and usually in the style current between about 1830 and mid-century. Early examples executed in silk and glass beads may date from about 1810, but these are rare. Berlin wool work was very popular in England and the U.S.A., and examples are not especially rare.

BERNINI, GIANLORENZO (1598–1680)
Born in Naples, the son of a Mannerist sculptor, Bernini attracted the patronage of the Cardinal Scipio Borghese at an early age. According to Evelyn (*Diaries*) his early activities could fairly be described as those of a theatre *impresario*, since he produced an opera in Rome in which he did virtually everything, from composing the music to painting the scenery. Much of his later work seems to have been coloured by these early excursions into the theatre, and he went on to mix white and coloured marbles with bronze, and often added stucco, painting, and light from coloured glass windows to achieve remarkable and novel effects. He is regarded, with a good deal of truth, as the creator of the baroque style (q.v.), and he was a sculptor of considerable power who greatly enlarged the scope of his art. He continued to be influential until the middle of the 18th century, as may be seen from many of the French *bronzes d'ameublement* of the period.

BERTOLDO DA GIOVANNI (?1420–1491)
Florentine sculptor, and pupil of Donatello's, who completed some of his master's work after the latter's death. He was among the first of the sculptors who made small bronzes, and his best-known work is probably the *Bellerophon* (Kunsthistorisches Museum, Vienna). His concentration on anatomical accuracy is characteristic of Florentine sculpture at the time. He executed a number of bronze plaquettes, the subjects taken from gems, either ancient or contemporary, in the Medici collections.

BERRETTINO (Italian)
Italian decoration in which the *maiolica* body is covered with a light blue glaze instead of white.

BESNIER, NICHOLAS (d. 1754)
French silversmith who became *orfèvre du Roi* in 1714 with lodgings in the Louvre. He became director of the Beauvais tapestry factory in 1724. A bowl by his hand is in the Louvre, and among his more notable works was a toilet-set for the Infanta of Spain.

BIANCO SOPRA BIANCO (Italian)
Literally, white over white. Decoration in white on a maiolica glaze tinted to a pale grey or lavender shade. Decoration of this kind is to be found on 16th-century Italian maiolica, the faïence of such

Bianco sopra Bianco. Scalloped Bristol delft plate decorated with a Chinese scene in the centre, and a border of *bianco sopra bianco* on a lavender-blue ground. c. 1760. *Victoria and Albert Museum.*

factories as Nevers and Marieberg, and in England, on Bristol delft of the 18th century.

BIDET (French)
A low stool, usually covered, holding a metal or pottery basin of violin shape, and principally used for feminine hygiene. The *bidet* had its origins in France, where it was to be found almost universally in the 18th century. Although Sheraton includes some designs for it, Arthur Young (*Travels in France*) in 1788 commended it in terms which make it plain that it was very unusual in England.

BIEDERMEIER STYLE
A German style, mainly to be seen in furniture-design, of the first half of the 19th century which was based on French Empire, but plainer and less ostentatious. Like early Victorian furniture in England it was made for the *bourgeoisie*, and the emphasis is on comfort and *Gemütlichkeit* rather than display. The name is derived from two characters in a Berlin journal, Biedermann and Bummelmeier, intended to satirize *bourgeois* philosophy. See *Philistine*.

BILLIE AND CHARLEY
Two men, William Smith and Charles Eaton, working in the middle of the 19th century who made a living as mudrakers on the Thames foreshore. Discovering a genuine medieval medallion, which they succeeded in selling to the British Museum for a respectable sum, they were inspired to make bogus medieval antiquities—medallions, vases, daggers, figures, and so forth— for which they used cock metal (an alloy of copper and lead), or lead by itself. The enjoyed a short period of success, and during this time they deceived a good many collectors. From estimates made at the time it is possible to hazard the guess that they made more than

one thousand objects, most of which were sold. Their mistakes are innumerable; in fact their productions are erroneous from beginning to end. The most obvious are inscriptions which are nonsense, and dates, around the year 1000, in Arabic numerals instead of the Roman numerals in use at the time. Today their work is regarded as an amusing curiosity, and it is sometimes collected.

BILLINGSLEY, WILLIAM (1758–1828)

Flower-painter at Derby and elsewhere: porcelain-maker. The son of William and Mary Billingsley, William II was apprenticed to the Derby factory in 1774. His father had been a japanner, and was at one time a painter of flowers at Chelsea. William II was much helped at Derby by Zachariah Boreman, one-time Chelsea painter who probably knew the secret of the gold anchor Chelsea porcelain body. This may have been the source of Billingsley's interest in the making of soft porcelain, which he attempted first at Pinxton (q.v.), and later, in 1813, at Nantgarw (q.v.). He first gained notice as a flower-painter, and, about 1784, he began to paint in a new style in which the flower-petals were first painted in full colour, and then the surplus pigment wiped off with a dry brush to form the high-lights. This new style became so popular at Derby that when, in 1796, Billingsley desired to leave, considerable efforts were made to retain his services. The style was taken up by others, and occurs, for instance, on Coalport porcelain in the early years of the 19th century. At Pinxton, Billingsley experimented with porcelain-making, going on to Mansfield in 1801, after which his formula was abandoned at Pinxton as uneconomic. In 1808, in company with Samuel Walker, his son-in-law, he arrived at Worcester, where he worked as a decorator, and perhaps experimented with porcelain-making. Leaving Worcester in 1813, we next hear of him at Nantgarw in South Wales, where he established a small factory, Billingsley and Walker being joined by William Weston Young. His kiln-wastage here was said to be in the region of

nine-tenths, and it is not surprising therefore that in 1814 the partners petitioned the Board of Trade for assistance. Lewis Dillwyn of the Cambrian Pottery, Swansea, was asked to report on their claims, and arrangements were made for the Nantgarw enterprise to be removed to Swansea, where it was placed under Dillwyn's supervision. Dillwyn insisted on modifications to the porcelain body, and Billingsley left to return to Nantgarw. In 1819 he and Walker were offered employment by John Rose of Coalport (q.v.), and in this way Rose became possessed of Billingsley's formulae. Some resemblance to Nantgarw porcelain can be observed in Coalport wares of the period.

BILSTON AND BIRMINGHAM ENAMELS

The manufacture of small objects of sheet copper covered with enamel subsequently painted was developed in Staffordshire during the 1750s. Similar problems to those which had earlier confronted the makers of Limoges enamels (q.v.) were overcome in the same way—by slightly curving the copper sheet and applying the enamel to both sides. The edges, where the greatest likelihood of damage resided, were protected with gilt-metal mounts.

A factory at Bilston, in South Staffordshire, had started to produce enamel toys, using the word in its 18th-century sense (see *Toys*), by about 1750, which means that the enamel works at Battersea (q.v.) was not the first, as has often been assumed. By 1755 Taylor of Birmingham was also making enamels in considerable quantity, although it is difficult to identify his work, except conjecturally.

The trade in both these places grew and flourished, and by 1780 there were four factories at Bilston devoted to the manufacture of enamels, one at Wednesbury, and several in Birmingham, where gilt-metal mounts were also made for the trade generally.

Enamels made in South Staffordshire and Birmingham during the 1750s are often attributed to

Bilston and Birmingham Enamels. A small collection of 'South Staffordshire' painted enamels—snuff-boxes and *étuis.* c. 1760. *Victoria and Albert Museum.*

Birmingham and Bilston Enamels. A casket decorated with landscapes in the style of the late 1750s, the relief-work surrounding them indicative of South Staffordshire manufacture. c. 1760. *Victoria and Albert Museum.*

Battersea, but large pieces such as candlesticks, and those in the neo-classical style, can only be attributed to one of the two former places. Transfer-prints were employed at Battersea and elsewhere, those of Battersea being washed over with translucent enamel through which the lines of the engraving can be plainly seen, whereas Staffordshire painting often obscures the engraving. Imitations of Continental enamel and porcelain toys, such as the *bonbonnières* of Meissen, were done in the Midlands. These include the rare *bonbonnières* in the form of human

Bilston and Birmingham Enamels. An ormolu mantel clock in the Louis XVI style made in London, and inset with enamel plaques signed by W. H. Craft. The unusually ambitious plaques were perhaps painted in Birmingham or Bilston. *Parke-Bernet Galleries, New York.*

heads and birds, the heads in particular also occurring in similar miniature form in Chelsea porcelain made about 1763. Ornament in white enamel slightly raised from the surface is an obvious derivation from the *bianco sopra bianco* of the delft painter and can first be seen about 1760. A rose-pink, derived originally from the *rose Pompadour* (q.v.) of Sèvres, was first employed about 1780.

Sources of inspiration include the *Ladies' Amusement, or the Whole Art of Japanning*, a design-book published by Sayers in 1760 with engravings taken from the work of Pillement, Boucher, and others, and early Midlands enamels often have the picture framed with rococo scrolls, and later enclosed in reserves in conjunction with a coloured ground in the manner then becoming fashionable in the decoration of porcelain. The porcelain factories frequently advertised for enamel painters, and in this way the best workmen were taken from the industry. As a result quality continually declined after about 1775, although production did not finally cease at Bilston until the 1830s.

In modern times large numbers of reproductions, often of such impressive objects as candlesticks and tea-caddies, have been made by Samson of Paris, usually marked with an 'X'. These are generally accused by the style of the painting, and by a highly polished surface unlike the surface of the genuine specimen, which is inclined to be matt rather than glossy. The mounts are also machine- instead of hand-made. Enamel being a fragile substance most old specimens have received some damage during their lifetime, and absolutely perfect examples are a cause for suspicion, although reproductions, when offered as genuine, are sometimes deliberately chipped in inconspicuous places. To anyone acquainted with genuine specimens, the reproductions are hardly dangerous.

BIRDCAGE

This term is normally employed to refer to a device fitted to 18th-century tip-up tables which allows them to revolve. The top is joined to a tripod support by an intervening 'birdcage' consisting of small turned pillars of baluster form.

The keeping of small birds in cages was very fashionable both in France and England during the 18th century, and decorative cages of fine workmanship and luxurious materials were not uncommon then, although they are now rare survivals. Small cages to contain automata (q.v.) in the form of singing birds were also popular. Seed and water boxes were often of such exotic materials as silver and Sèvres porcelain.

BISCUIT PORCELAIN

Unglazed porcelain. The fashion for *biscuit* porcelain began at Vincennes, and the notion of omitting a glaze seems first to have occurred to the art-director J. J. Bachelier. It was introduced in 1751, and soon became extremely popular. Very few glazed figures were ever made in the 18th century at either

Birdcage. A very unusual Chippendale birdcage of fret-carved mahogany and brass. Mid-18th century. *Parke-Bernet Galleries, New York.*

Vincennes or Sèvres, but most other factories avoided making *biscuit* for as long as they could. It was important that a *biscuit* figure should be perfect, without the flaws and blemishes which could be concealed by glazing and painting, and it is pertinent to remember that in the price-list of the Derby factory *biscuit* figures were, for this reason, more expensive than those conventionally finished. Such was their popularity that most 18th-century porcelain factories of any consequence made *biscuit* figures after about 1770, but other wares are less common. Vases occur occasionally, and ornamental wares, such as those from Bristol (q.v.), were sometimes additionally decorated with modelled flowers. The fashion enjoyed a revival during the 19th century, when it was called Parian ware (q.v.), which seems first to have been marketed about 1845, and, as at Sèvres in the 18th century, it was used to reproduce sculpture. Parian ware was first made by Copelands, but most important manufacturers made some kind of unglazed porcelain of this kind in the mid 19th century.

'BISQUE' PORCELAIN
Incorrect. See *Biscuit Porcelain.*

'BISHOP' BOWLS
Bowls in the form of a bishop's mitre made to contain a kind of punch called 'bishop'. They were especially produced at Scandinavian and North German faïence factories, where the drink was popular, and especially in the Schleswig-Holstein area.

BLANC-DE-CHINE (French)
The name given to a type of Chinese porcelain by Jesuit missionaries. *Blanc-de-Chine* is a fine white porcelain with a glaze richer than the normal feldspathic glaze of the Imperial factories. In appearance it has been well compared to milk-jelly. *Blanc-de-Chine* was made at Tê Hua (Fukien Province) in southern China, and it was especially popular in France during the first half of the 18th century, providing inspiration for much of the porcelain made at Saint-Cloud (q.v.). It was copied to a limited extent at Meissen during the first fifteen years or so of the factory's life, but much more at the English factories of Chelsea and Bow during their first periods. Tê Hua is especially noted for its porcelain figures, which were otherwise rarely made in China, and these were often mounted in France in gilt-bronze (see: *Mounts, Metal, to Pottery and Porcelain*). The most common figures to be made were of Kuan Yin (Buddhist goddess of Mercy) and the so-called Dogs of Fo (Buddha), but the seated, grinning figure of the Buddhist monk, Pu-tai, with bare belly, is not uncommon, and he was sometimes termed a pagod, a word of several meanings discussed under that heading. Less often seen is the Confucian god of war, Kuan Ti, and such mythical animals as the kylin. Pu-tai in particular was commonly represented in European porcelain in its early stages, some rare examples coming from Meissen where the Chinese custom of making figures with detachable heads and hands was sometimes copied. Particularly well known are cups decorated on the outside with raised branches of prunus blossom, or less often the tea-plant, and this kind of decoration on European wares is sometimes seen on such vessels as teapots and cream-jugs which were not made at Tê Hua.

Blanc-de-Chine. A fine-quality *blanc-de-Chine* figure of Kuan-ti. Tê Hua (Fukien Province) 17th century. Although Tê Hua figures were sometimes copied by early European factories, they never achieved the quality of this Chinese figure. *Bluett & Sons, London.*

BLANKET CHEST

A chest, of which the upper part was intended for blankets, and the lower part was provided with two drawers for storage. Chippendale's *Director* illustrates one in his characteristic style. The upper part of an American version popular in the early part of the 18th century had two dummy drawers at the top which concealed its true function as a chest. It is also known in the trade as a dower chest.

BLEEDING BOWLS

Small hemispherical bowls with a single, flat, horizontally projecting handle, used by barber-surgeons to contain blood taken from their patients. Bleeding was an almost universal remedy. The first English bleeding bowls date back to the first quarter of the 17th century, and they may be found in silver, pewter, and sometimes delft.

BLOCK-CUTTING

Before the introduction of the plaster of Paris mould (q.v.) into pottery-making in Staffordshire by Ralph Daniels of Cobridge, which took place about 1745, moulds were made from alabaster and other materials in intaglio (q.v.) by carving. They were used to take a clay impression of the vessel to be made. After the introduction of plaster moulds the block was sometimes employed as a master-mould from which plaster moulds could be taken for the actual work of production.

BLOCK-FRONT

Usually regarded as an American innovation, the block-front in furniture originated in Holland and Germany in the 18th century. It reached its fullest development with the case-furniture of the Townsend-Goddard family of Newport, Rhode Island, who worked in the mahogany of San Domingo. This dark, heavy, close-grained wood permitted crisp carving which is typical of this kind of furniture in which the block-front is carved with a shell. The block-front is usually found on combined desks and book-cases, desks, chests, and chests-on-chests. Without the shell the block-front was occasionally adapted to tea-tables. Though Newport block-front furniture is the finest, the same technique was employed for furniture made in Massachusetts, Connecticut, and New York, where the blocks were more fully rounded than in the Newport versions.

BLUE JOHN

This stone, a variety of fluorite, is also known as Derbyshire spar from the unique deposits at Castleton. It was especially admired during the second half of the 18th century in England. 'Blue John' was found in pieces small and large, the largest weighing up to a ton. It is usually amethyst purple in colour with striations or mottlings of lilac, cream, and almost white. The purple, when unsatisfactory, was modified by gentle heating, which made it both lighter and richer in colour. Occasional silvery veins are lead, employed by the makers to fill crevices.

Most 18th-century specimens are urns, and they are usually solid, for hollowing presented many difficulties not overcome till the early years of the 19th century. The urn was especially popular, for not only was it the most fashionable decorative *motif* of the time, but it was the easiest to make, since the stone was turned on the lathe and polished afterwards with abrasives. It is probably for this reason that all specimens postdate the introduction of the Adam style, for the numerous defects and imperfections would have made it difficult or impossible to carve into any of the shapes popular before this date. Some

Block-front. Chippendale-style shell-carved chest of drawers with block-front and claw-and-ball foot. Connecticut (America). Second half of the 18th century. *Parke-Bernet Galleries, New York.*

of the finest specimens were mounted in metal by Matthew Boulton (q.v.). William Duesbury, proprietor of the Derby Porcelain Factory, advertised in 1773 that 'a curious collection of Derbyshire fluors' were on view at his London showroom, and this may have been the beginning of the vogue.

The deposits were virtually exhausted by about 1800, but enough remained for manufacture to continue on a limited scale to mid-Victorian times, when most of the hollow examples were made by a special process. The firm of Brown & Maw, which made most of it, was apparently working on a fairly large scale in 1817. Specimens are not comparable for colour with 18th-century examples.

Other varieties of fluorite are found in America and on the European Continent.

BOCAGE (French)

A grove or thicket, from the medieval Latin *Boscus*, whence the term 'boskie', a form sometimes to be found in 18th-century England. The term is used in the decorative arts principally to describe the background of branches, bushes, and flowers of the kind to be found as part of English and German porcelain figures in the rococo style. The elaborate *bocage*, often of the maybush, is very characteristic of the best English figures of the 1760s. With the onset of the neo-classical style it became unfashionable, but it occurs again in a debased version as part of the decoration of early 19th-century Staffordshire earthenware figures, when it was usually made in a press-mould. The extension of the bocage to arch over figures in the form of a bower is to be seen as part of some very rare salt-glaze and Longton Hall porcelain groups, and similar 'bowers' were made again in the early years of the 19th century at the Worcester factory of Grainger.

See also *Flowers, Porcelain*.

BOHEMIAN GLASS

Among the most valued of semi-precious hard-stones in the 16th century was rock-crystal (German *Bergkristall*), which was carved by means of small rotating abrasive wheels. Glass bears many re-semblances to rock-crystal, approximating to it in appearance but being slightly easier to work, and it can be decorated in the same way. Among the best of the rock-crystal carvers were those of Bohemia (now Czechoslovakia), and the Prague Workshop is noted for its use of this material.

The first to decorate glass in the techniques of the rock-crystal carver was Caspar Lehmann of Prague, who was given a privilege (q.v.) by the Emperor Rudolf II for his lifetime. A remarkably fine example of his work, dated 1605, is in the Victoria and Albert Museum (London). Lehmann's privilege was transferred on his death to a pupil, Georg Schwan-hardt (1601–1667) of Nürnberg, who was also a carver of rock-crystal, and Schwanhardt introduced a technique of contrasting polished and matt carved surfaces, combining them with diamond-point en-graving (q.v.). He and his sons founded a school of glass carving and engraving at Nürnberg which did not end until the early years of the 18th century.

Bohemian carved work was, from about 1700 on-wards, the best in Europe, and the ornamental *motifs* were extremely varied, the techniques introduced by the Schwanhardts especially fostering pictorial representation. Bohemia was peculiarly suited to this kind of work, for the numerous mountain streams provided motive-power for the carving, engraving, and polishing wheels. The change to potash glass which took place about the middle of the 17th century, yielded a material much more suited to carving than the earlier soda-glass. It was not, however, until the end of the 17th century that the metal in use became entirely free of imperfections which had been due to incomplete mastery of the new process.

The Bohemian glassworkers always favoured the *pokal* (q.v.), which had originally been inspired by those in the precious metals by Wenzel Jamnitzer and others. These were made at the glass-houses and sometimes sent elsewhere for carving, one notable centre for this kind of work being Breslau. The form of the *pokal* changed with the years, the bowl gradu-ally developing from the earlier bell shape to a straight-sided funnel, the stems, knops, and covers usually being ground into facets. Today care is

Bohemian Glass. Beaker decorated with wheel-engraving on a flashed surface (see *Cased Glass*). Bohemia. c. 1840. *Victoria and Albert Museum.*

needed in examining surviving specimens of the *pokal*, which often have unmatching covers as re-placements, but the original covers matched the decoration of the remainder exactly.

Coloured glass was a diversification of the early years of the 18th century, and enamelling was also employed as decoration. Taken from the *Hausmaler*

Bohemian Glass. Pokal wheel-engraved with baroque *motifs.* Bohemia. c. 1720. *Victoria and Albert Museum.*

(q.v.) of Nürnberg was a fashion for *Schwarzlot* (q.v.) painting, and some examples are known of Bohemian glass thus decorated signed by Johann Schaper. The *Hausmaler*, Preüssler of Breslau, whose work is better known on porcelain, has also been awarded some specimens of Bohemian glass in his style, although this is uncertain. The *Laub- und Bandelwerke* (q.v.) was adopted as a motif for carved glass, sometimes in conjunction with *chinoiseries* (q.v.) at a time when these were popular on Meissen porcelain, and one such surviving example was carved at Nürnberg by Anton Wilhelm Mäuerl (1672–1737). At the beginning of the century Bohemian glass-carvers were among those who went to Dresden to help to decorate the newly-invented red stoneware of Böttger then being made at Meissen. Before mid-century Bohemian glass-workers had revived the ancient *Zwischengoldgläser* (q.v.), producing specimens of extremely fine quality sometimes with passages of red enhancing the gold, while towards the end of the century coloured enamelling of excellent quality, rivalling the best work of the porcelain factories, made its appearance. Throughout the century facet-cutting, carving, and engraving was in many cases of a quality exceeding that to be found from almost any other source.

The kind of decorative glassware made in Bohemia was ill-adapted to the neo-classical style, and little work of importance was done from about 1770 until, at the end of the Napoleonic Wars in 1815, the industry took a fresh lease of life, and many new glass-houses were opened. Lead glass of the English type was introduced and employed for elaborate facet cutting which is usually much deeper and bolder than analogous English specimens. Engraving was continued with subjects appropriate to the period, and many new coloured glasses were devised. Perhaps the most important single undertaking of the time was that of Count von Buquoy who made black glass (introduced about 1820), ruby glass, chrome green, and several other colours. Lythialine, a glass of variegated colour and a marbled surface, was patented by Friedrich Egermann. About 1830 surface staining, in which the colour was superimposed on clear glass, was introduced, and the Bohemians also attained considerable skill in the manufacture of the popular *millefiori* paperweights (see *Paperweights*). Perhaps the most familiar technique exploited at the time was that of cased glass (q.v.), and Bohemian glass-makers manufactured specimens of *crystallo ceramie* (q.v.).

After the middle of the 19th century quality gradually fell off, and the industry was eventually reduced to the point of producing little more than tourist souvenirs.

BOIS DE ROSE (French)
Tulipwood (q.v.).

BOIS NOIRCI (French)
An 18th-century term for 'ebonized' wood (usually pearwood) which was stained to simulate ebony (q.v.).

BOIZOT, SIMON-LOUIS (1742–1809)
French sculptor who studied under Michel-Ange Slodtz. Boizot married one of Oudry's daughters, and was a friend of Pierre Gouthière (q.v.). He became chief modeller to the Sèvres porcelain factory in 1775, and attempted to make a life-size equestrian statue of Louis XVI in *biscuit* porcelain which was never finished. He designed a table-decoration for Catherine the Great in 1775, but this was never paid for in full, and the debt led to international complications. As a result of his personal losses Boizot became bankrupt. He was admitted to the Academy in 1778, and during the Revolution he was appointed member of the Fine Arts Commission.

BOLOGNA, GIOVANNI DA (GIAMBOLOGNA) (1529–1608)
One of the principal Mannerist sculptors, best known for his small bronzes. Several hundred figures and groups are attributed to him, or to his workshop, and his influence was widespread during the 17th century. Some of the smaller bronzes were reductions of his larger works, and others in his style are probably by Pietro Tacca or Antonio Susini, his two best-known pupils. By far the best known among his bronzes is *Mercury* shown poised on one foot on a ball and grasping the caduceus in an upraised hand. This has since been copied hundreds of times, and 19th-century versions are common. Perhaps his most important work, the marble *Rape of the Sabines* (1579), also exists in a small bronze version which is very rare. He assisted Ammanati (q.v.) in the making of the Neptune fountain at Florence, and was responsible in 1563 for the Neptune fountain in Bologna. He was of Flemish origin.

BOLT-AND-SHUTTER
A device introduced in England early in the 18th century for maintaining the power delivered to the train of wheels moving the hands of a clock while it was being wound. This is interrupted in clocks not so fitted, and the inclusion of such a device denotes a clock of unusually good quality.

BOKHARA RUGS
The name is given to the products of several nomadic Turcoman tribes because they are sold in the market of Bokhara in Turkestan. Naturally they vary in quality, but there is no justification for calling a prayer-rug, however fine, a 'Princess Bokhara'. The term is meaningless and a dealer's invention. Characteristic of the Bokhara rug is a deep red, often called the Turcoman red, which is quite commonly seen on rugs from elsewhere in the region. Most of the best Bokharas are made by the Teke Turcomans, a tribe both numerous and widespread. The Sehna knot is used, and the pile is soft and closely clipped, sometimes with goat hair and silk added. The usual design is of octagons arranged in rows. There are several shades of red, in addition to the Turcoman red, as well as blue, green, and a certain amount of

white. Quality of both old and new rugs is excellent, but modern examples are inferior to old ones. Other types of Bokhara rugs are the Khiva Bokhara, the Beshir Bokhara, and the Yomud Bokhara. The first is made on the borders of Afghanistan, the second by more or less settled tribes near Bokhara itself, who employ a stylized tree-and-leaf motif, and the third, made near the Caspian Sea, has some affinities with Caucasian patterns (q.v.), with a characteristic brownish-red.

BOMBÉ (French)

Swelling or convex surface to be found on the front and sides of cabinet furniture in the baroque style. It is quite often a feature of French and Dutch furniture in the early decades of the 18th century, and of some later Dutch colonial furniture. The *bombé* form appears as part of the design of *commodes* in the early years of the French Régence, and its introduction was delayed because of difficulty experienced in affixing veneers to a surface with multiple curves. Its use was fairly widespread, although in Colonial America it was confined to Massachusetts. The term is actually derived from the fact that the curves are convex 'like a bomb', to quote a standard French dictionary, but is sometimes used of furniture with simple double curves perhaps more correctly described as ogee.

It is also sometimes referred to as 'kettle front' or 'kettle base'.

Bombé. A 19th-century French *commode* with *bombé* front and ends. Parquetry inlaid with star-shaped ivory medallions. Rouge and green-veined marble top. *Phillips, Son & Neale.*

BONE-ASH

Calcined ox-bones have long been known as a flux, i.e. a substance promoting fusion of the ingredients, in the manufacture of glass, but only in relatively small quantities. In 1749 Thomas Frye of Bow (q.v.) patented a porcelain body which contained a massive quantity of bone-ash, apparently with the intention of reducing the uneconomic kiln-wastage which

attended the production of the glassy artificial porcelains of the period. Bone freed from its gelatinous matter contains both lime and phosphates, and the presence of bone-ash in porcelain is revealed on analysis by a varying amount of phosphoric acid. In glass-making the percentage addition is about 5, but Bow added up to about 45 per cent to their porcelain body. This had the effect of making it more stable in the kiln, but of reducing its quality, producing a heavier, less translucent porcelain than can be seen from Chelsea during the same period. Nevertheless, the advantages were so considerable that it was speedily adopted by other factories. Lowestoft used it from the first, since they obtained their formula from Bow. Chelsea began to add bone-ash in 1755, although Duesbury had to wait until he purchased the Chelsea factory to obtain the secret. Then, in 1770, he had six bags of bone-ash sent from Chelsea to Derby. Longton Hall never acquired the secret, and the soaprock factories, with an already satisfactory body, were not attracted by this formula, although there is little doubt that they knew all about it.

True porcelain in the Chinese manner was made at Plymouth by Cookworthy, who assigned his patent to William Champion of Bristol. When Champion ran into financial difficulties in 1778 he sold the patent to a company of potters who operated a factory at New Hall, in Staffordshire. In this way the secret of making true porcelain reached Staffordshire. Josiah Spode is said to have introduced the making of porcelain into his earthen-ware factory at Stoke-on-Trent in about 1800, modifying the true porcelain of the New Hall type by adding bone-ash to it, thus producing bone-china. This has now become the standard English body, although it is little used on the Continent. The term 'china' employed in the modern English porcelain trade invariably means 'bone-china', 'porcelain' being usually reserved for true porcelain in the Chinese and Continental manner. Bone-china is also now made in the U.S.A., although preference there is largely for porcelain.

The presence of phosphates in 18th-century porcelain can be detected by a simple 'spot' test (see *Phosphate Test*), and this is sometimes employed as evidence of origin in suitable cases.

BONE-CHINA See *Bone-ash*

BONNIN & MORRIS (Philadelphia)

A factory for the manufacture of porcelain was established on Prime Street, Philadelphia, by Gousse Bonnin and George Anthony Morris in 1769. Bonnin may have learned his trade at Bow (England), and an advertisement of this date for bones suggests that the formula came from the English factory (see *Bone-ash*). In 1771 they advertised for zaffer (q.v.), for the purpose of painting in blue underglaze. About 1772 the factory ran into financial difficulties and was closed, Bonnin returning to England. Specimens of the porcelain of Bonnin & Morris are extremely rare, and much resemble Bow porcelain. An example is in the Henry Francis Dupont Museum, Winterthur, Delaware.

BOOK (or DESK) BOX (American)
In America, 17th-century joined boxes, usually of carved oak, in the Jacobean style (c. 1650–1680) for holding books, valuable papers, and writing utensils. If, as usual, its lid is slanted, it may either have been used to hold books while they were being read, or as a surface for writing. These boxes were placed on a chest or a table and are precursors of the desk on frame. The popular term 'bible box' is a sentimental Victorianism.

BORDEAUX (Gironde, France) FAÏENCE AND PORCELAIN
In 1712 a group of Montpellier potters was invited by Jacques Hustin to help him reinstate a factory founded in 1708 by Fautier. Among these men were J. B. Clerissy and Jean Collondre, though the latter soon left. Hustin's rule saw the production of drug-jars and several important services for Carthusian monasteries. Styles were those of Montpellier—*décor Bérain*, Olery's Moustiers designs, garlands, *grotesques*, and even the so-called potato-flower. The clay of Bordeaux proved excellent for making large relief-moulds—fountains, basins, and clock-cases.

In 1749 Hustin died. His son inherited the business, but he too died and left a widow in partnership with Monsau, a painter. The business closed in 1782. For a long time Hustin struggled to retain his patent, but it was finally taken away in 1750, after the workers he had brought from Montpellier left to found separate factories nearby. All used the same southern patterns of birds, roses, and carnations.

A factory that was opened in the Bordeaux suburb of Saint-Seurin by Charles-Antoine Boyer in 1765 is notable, and continued till the 19th century.

Porcelain was made at Bordeaux, at the Château de Bordes en Paludate, in 1781, using china clay from Saint-Yrieix. In 1787 the factory was taken over by Michel Vanier and Alluaud of Limoges, and continued till 1790. Porcelain was produced in contemporary Paris styles.

BOSTON, MASS., GLASS WORKS
There were a number of glass-houses in Boston established in the later years of the 18th century. The Essex Glass Works, started about 1787 by Robert Hewes and Charles Kupfer, produced large quantities of window-glass. It became the Boston Glass Manufactory in 1809, and was moved to South Boston in 1811, but here it was unsuccessful, and it closed about 1820. The premises were taken over by the American Flint Glass Works about 1850, under the direction of Patrick Slane, and here all kinds of pressed and cut glass were produced until about 1870. Several other attempts were made to establish glass-houses in the first half of the 19th century, but none was successful.

BOSTON ROCKER (American)
A type of rocking-chair based on the Windsor chair. Dating from about 1825, it is probably the most popular rocking-chair ever made, and examples have not uncommonly survived from the early decades of the 19th century.

Boston Rocker. Boston rocker of maple and pine painted black and stencilled with flowers. c. 1835. First appearing in New England about 1825, this chair became widely popular, and was manufactured by many chair-makers, including Hitchcock (q.v.).

BOTTENGRUBER, IGNAZ (fl. 1720–1730)
Hausmaler of Breslau. Bottengruber was originally a painter of miniatures and water-colours, but he emerges as a porcelain painter by 1720, and by 1723 he had become noted for his polychrome palette which exhibited, according to a contemporary, 'perfection as has not hitherto been seen'. The earliest signed and dated example known was executed in 1726. This is in excellent enamel colours, richly gilded, in the baroque tradition. Bacchic scenes were a favourite with Bottengruber, and he did some remarkable battle and hunting scenes, with excellent animal drawing. He sometimes employed violet-purple in conjunction with iron red, with gilding which is reddish in tone. In 1728, when Meissen decided to stop the sales of white ware to *Hausmaler*, Bottengruber turned to Vienna for supplies, and he probably influenced the Vienna factory styles, especially that of Jakob Helchis.

Bottengruber had one pupil, Hans Gottlieb von Bressler, whose style somewhat resembles that of his master.

BÖTTGER, JOHANN FRIEDRICH (1682–1719)

Born at Schleiz in Thuringia and apprenticed to a Berlin apothecary, Böttger began to study alchemy, and he was financed by the King of Prussia in an attempt to make gold and silver from copper and lead. When his attempts proved unsuccessful Böttger fled to Wittenberg, whence he was brought under a military escort by Augustus the Strong, Elector of Saxony, to Dresden, and set to make gold to pay for foreign wars. In 1703, when the project was on the point of failure, Böttger was imprisoned in the Albrechtsburg fortress in an attempt to sharpen his wits, but his services were begged by Ehrenfried Walther von Tschirnhausen, who discovered the secret of true porcelain-making in Europe, as a laboratory assistant. By 1708 Von Tschirnhausen was able to show Augustus specimens of porcelain of a quality good enough to warrant the construction of a factory in Dresden-Neustadt, placed under the direction of Böttger, where faïence and red stone-ware (another of Von Tschirnhausen's discoveries) were made. The latter died in October 1708, and Böttger continued his researches, first producing a successful porcelain body of his own in March, 1709, which was undoubtedly based on Von Tschirnhausen's work. The Royal Saxon Porcelain Manufactory was established in January 1710, and housed at Meissen (q.v.), some twelve miles from Dresden. By 1713 this new porcelain was offered for sale at the Leipzig Fair, and production was, by this time, on a commercial basis. Böttger remained in charge of the factory's operations under the supervision of a Commission until his death from alcoholism in 1719. The statement that Böttger actually invented the porcelain body at Meissen is a legend, although he undoubtedly did a great deal to improve it.

See *Meissen Porcelain Factory.*

BOTTLES AND FLASKS (American)

Pictorial glass flasks and bottles are an important American collectors' item. They were blown into two-piece metal moulds which gave a pattern raised in slight relief, and production began about 1808. Thirty years later they formed the staple production of many factories which were specially built for the purpose, and some have the name of the factory as part of the mould. They were made in almost every available colour, and range in size from a half-pint to a quart. Several hundred different patterns have been recorded. Later bottles of this kind were made from lime glass (q.v.). Production declined rapidly after 1870.

BOTTLES, SEALED. See *Decanter, Evolution of*

BOUCHARDON, EDMÉ (1698–1762)

French sculptor. A pupil of Guillaume Coustou, who studied in Rome and worked for a time at Versailles. His designs were sometimes employed by the porcelain factories, including Sèvres and

Böttger, J. F. Portrait of the Freiherr von Böttger. Meissen. c. 1780. *Victoria and Albert Museum.*

Meissen. At Meissen his prints entitled *Cris de Paris* (published 1737–1746) inspired a series of figures by Kändler and Reinicke.

Boucher, François. **Chinoiserie group taken from an engraving after Boucher's** *Les Délices de l'Enfance.* **Meissen. c. 1740. Boucher was a collector of Chinese porcelain.** *Antique Porcelain Company Ltd, London and New York.*

BOUCHER, FRANÇOIS (1703–1770)

French painter and designer. Boucher, who was a friend of Meissonnier's (q.v.), was elected to the Academy in 1734, and greatly influenced the course of design in the decorative arts until about 1770. A series of *chinoiserie* designs, the *Five Senses*, probably dates from about 1740, in which year he began to collect Chinese porcelain, and this was followed by the *Suite de Figures Chinoises*, which inspired porcelain figures made at both Chelsea and Meissen. Subjects from his paintings, particularly *amorini*, are to be found on the early porcelain of Vincennes and Sèvres. He designed scenery and costumes for the Paris Opèra, and in 1754 his pastoral scenes set a new fashion, occurring quite often as porcelain decoration and as the subject of *biscuit* figures from Sèvres. In the same year he was appointed designer to the factory. In 1755 he became a director of the Gobelins tapestry *atelier* in succession to Oudry (q.v.), and many of his designs were carried out in this medium. Designs for a new series illustrating the life of Don Quixote for Gobelins had been done as early as 1736 at Oudry's suggestion. Boucher was a friend of Mme de Pompadour (q.v.), who obtained for him the position of *premier peintre du roi*, and he painted erotic pictures for the King, among them a portrait of one of the King's mistresses, a girl named Murphy, immortalized by Boucher as the *Petite Morphil*. His influence on the art of his day began to wane with the death of Mme de Pompadour in 1764, and he died in 1770 while still working at his easel.

BOUCLÉ (French)

Literally, looped or curled. In its oldest form loops of metal were introduced into velvet or *brocatelle* and pulled up, giving the effect of a relief pattern on the outer side of the fabric.

BOULLE, ANDRÉ-CHARLES (1642–1732)

The most noted and influential of the French *ébénistes*, perhaps related to Pierre Boulle, a Swiss furniture craftsman who came to France in the 17th century. A.-C. Boulle was a versatile artist and craftsman in the best tradition of the Renaissance having, in addition to his talents as an *ébéniste*, a reputation for being a bronzeworker, engraver, architect, and painter. An *artisan-libre* he was appointed *ébéniste du roi* at the instigation of Colbert in 1672, and from that year onwards most of his work was for one or other of the royal palaces.

Boulle is best known for furniture decorated with an elaborate marquetry of brass and tortoiseshell, with the occasional addition of silver, pewter, ivory, and ebony. In this he was not entirely original, the fashion being inspired by Italian craftsmen imported into France by Cardinal Mazarin before 1650. Boulle's way of handling this theme, however, is strongly individual, and his work inspired *ébénistes* throughout the 18th century, and well into the 19th. He had several sons, all of whom followed their father's craft, but the best known is Charles-Joseph Boulle, who was the master of J. F. Oeben.

Boulle, A.-C. **A twin-pedestal writing-desk in the late Louis XIV style decorated with** *contre-partie* **brass and tortoiseshell marquetry in the manner of A.-C. Boulle. c. 1700.** *Wallace Collection.*

All the pieces attributed to Boulle's large workshop in the Louvre, where he employed more than twenty men, are luxurious, and among the most important works of his era. Although there is no evidence that the two men collaborated, much of Boulle's decoration seems to have been inspired by the designs of Jean I Bérain.

Few surviving examples can be definitely attributed to his workshop, but one of the best attested is in the Victoria and Albert Museum, London, and is illustrated here.

Boulle had a number of imitators in England according to contemporary records, although it is only rarely that their work can be identified. Garret Johnson (fl. 1680–1714) made arabesque marquetry and did work inspired by Boulle. Frederick Hintz of Newport Street, London, advertised furniture with brass and mother-of-pearl inlay which seems to have been thus inspired, and Peter Langlois, a French *ébéniste* working in London around mid-century with a workshop in the Tottenham Court Road, made brass and tortoiseshell inlays in the manner of Boulle. Horace Walpole was one of his customers. Best known is the work of a 19th-century *emigré ébéniste,* Louis Le Gaigneur (q.v.), whose workshop was situated in London, off the Edgware Road.

For a discussion of Boulle's technique see *Marquetry.*

BOULTON, MATTHEW (1728–1809)

English manufacturer of decorative metalwork. No real tradition of metalwork of this kind comparable to that of France and Germany existed in England before the beginning of the 18th century. Birmingham, however, had already made progress in developing the manufacture of utilitarian objects of metal, and the city considerably increased in importance throughout the 18th century. It also achieved a reputation, not entirely undeserved, for the cheap and tawdry. 'Give a Birmingham maker a guinea and a copper kettle, and he'll make you a hundred pounds' worth of jewellery', ran an 18th-century saying.

Nevertheless, there were always a few manufacturers who not only turned out sound products, but even gained for themselves an enviable reputation for decorative work. Chief among them was Matthew Boulton, of whom Wedgwood said: 'He is, I believe, the first and most complete manufacturer in England.'

Boulton entered his father's business of silver-stamper at the age of seventeen, and in 1762, three years after his father's death, he commenced to build the Soho factory. In the same year he entered into partnership with John Fothergill which was dissolved in 1781. In 1767 the Soho factory was extended, and the same year Boulton was granted royal patronage. In 1768 he met James Watt, and the two men were associated in the development of the steam-engine and its application to industrial purposes.

Boulton at first engaged in the production of small articles like steel shoe-buckles, watch-chains, snuffboxes, etc., commonly made in Birmingham at the time, but by 1762 he was making articles both of silver and Sheffield plate, the latter process perhaps learned from John Hancock who developed the invention (see *Sheffield Plate*). Becoming more ambitious, he turned to what Wedgwood called 'the ormolu business', and by 1774 the Soho works employed a thousand men making not only buttons, buckles, and trinkets in gold, silver, and base metal, but, to use the words of a contemporary, was attempting 'many other arts long predominant in France which lose their reputation in comparison with the products of this place'. The French at this time had a virtual monopoly of fine-quality bronze ornament, and the decorative metalwork of Paris included furniture-mounts and mounts for a great many exotic materials, including hardstones and porcelain. They were skilled in the making of ornamental clock-cases and lighting fixtures, the finest clock-cases especially being very considerable works of art. For manufactures of this kind at Soho we may profitably turn to the letters of Wedgwood, who visited Boulton's factory in 1776 and wrote: 'I had no conception of the quantity of d'or moulu they have sold, chiefly abroad. You remember a poor Venus weeping over the tomb of Adonis—a time-piece [see *Clocks, French, Evolution of*]. How many would you think they have sold of this single group? 200 at 25 guineas each, including the watch [equivalent to about £250 today]. They now sell as much of this manufacture as they can get up—Tripods, Vases, Groups &c.' He goes on to say that Boulton & Fothergill 'hope to supplant the French in the gilt business'.

The manufacture of ormolu (q.v.) was probably started as early as 1762, but despite a temporary success Boulton did not find it profitable, although for a time he sold a good deal to the Russian Court. We can, however, follow this attempt by English manufacturers to compete with France from contemporary trade catalogues, one of which, about 1785, refers to 'French handles' and 'Escutcheons for French handles'. Some Paris furniture in the Victoria and Albert Museum is fitted with handles closely resembling those depicted in the catalogue. Boulton followed the French in mounting various substances in ormolu, especially Blue John (q.v.) found in Derbyshire, and his mounts were comparable with the best French work. As early as 1768 he was mounting pottery and porcelain. 'Mr Boulton', wrote Wedgwood, 'is picking up vases and is going to make them in bronze. You know how old China Bowles, Jarrs, &c. are mounted in metal. He proposes an alliance betwixt the potter and metal branches, viz. that we shall make such things as will be suitable for mounting, and he will finish them with mounts.' But the project came to nothing, and Boulton thought of opening his own pottery, but this, too, was abandoned.

Like Wedgwood, Boulton bought objects in the sale-rooms of London, such as that of Mr Christie, to provide inspiration for new designs, and he sought introductions to connoisseurs of French metalwork, like the Duke of Richmond, for the same purpose. He employed a man in Italy to buy *objets d'art* suitable for copying or adapting, and in a letter to him of 1767 he mentions that the Soho factory had just started making objects of inlaid tortoiseshell, presumably in the manner of Boulle. In a letter to James Adam of 1770 Boulton refers to the employment of 700 persons in arts ancillary to metalwork, such as enamel and glass, and says that his lathes, and machinery for grinding, polishing, rolling, and turning, were actuated by water-power. It was this aspect which probably interested him in Watt's steam-engine in the first place.

It is hard to resist the conclusion that in this aspect of his business Boulton was organized on too large a scale for the available market, and he tried many expedients to popularize his manufacturers, such as ornaments for chimney-pieces and furniture of die-stamped metal which, when painted, looked like wood-carving. These are now very rare. Perhaps as early as 1774 Wedgwood's wares were being mounted at Soho, and small plaques especially made for the purpose were surrounded by a frame of cut-steel, but despite a close friendship between the two men, and many proposals from Boulton, no lasting business relationship developed.

Boulton was always ready to exploit new ideas, and in 1779 he astonished the art-world of his day with an invention for copying oil-paintings, the work of Francis Egerton who was employed at Soho as a painter of japanned ware (q.v.). This was called, at the time, the Polygraphic art, but very little is now known of it, although it seems to have involved a good deal of hand work, and it has been suggested that it was based on some kind of photographic process. However, the process was certainly used, for invoices exist, and Wedgwood bought a roundel of the Graces breaking Cupid's Bow in 1781. James Watt invented a machine for reproducing sculpture which was probably an improved kind of the pointing-machine employed today by monumental masons.

Boulton was very active in the social life of his day, and was a member of the illustrious Lunar Society of Birmingham. He was also associated in various undertakings, such as the Cornish Metal Company, with Wedgwood, Sir Richard Arkwright, and others. Like Wedgwood, Boulton made a major contribution to the Industrial Revolution in England, both in the field of decorative art and in that of heavy industry.

BOW-FRONT

When the front of a chest of drawers, a table, or a sideboard, curves outwards from either end, then it is termed a bow front. A convex curve in the middle, with two concave curves on either side, is termed a serpentine front or, occasionally, an ox-bow front. In French the equivalent term is *chantourné*.

BOW PORCELAIN FACTORY

This East London factory was established in 1744, about a year after Chelsea, when a patent was taken

out by an Irish merchant, Thomas Frye, and Edward Heylyn, a glass merchant, for a porcelain which was to contain a clay imported from America called *unaker* (q.v.). The exact location of Heylyn's glasshouse cannot be established, but it was in the region of Stratford and Bow, two adjacent areas of East London, and it was, no doubt, used for experimental firings of porcelain. In 1749 another patent was taken

Bow Porcelain. Bowl painted with flowers in the *famille rose* palette after a Chinese prototype. Bow. 1755.

out by Frye alone which, from the wording of the specification, leaves little doubt that bone-ash was intended to be part of the formula. Bone-ash is discussed under that heading, since its use was not eventually confined to the Bow factory, but it reveals its presence on analysis by a variable percentage of phosphoric acid which, with lime, forms the main constituents of bone. The earlier patent mentions fern-ash employed as a flux, and this also would give a positive reaction to a 'spot' test (see *Phosphate Test*), and although porcelain made at Bow before 1749 has not been positively identified, it is pertinent to note that both formulae would give a positive result if tested for the presence of phosphates. There are a few primitives which might be on either side of a line drawn at 1749.

In 1750 two London merchants named Weatherby and Crowther became interested in the Bow patent, and they financed a factory which was called 'New Canton'. A few circular inkwells survive from this time inscribed *Made at New Canton,* the date being either 1750 or 1751. These are important documents, and others include newspaper advertisements and the note-books of John Bowcocke, the factory's clerk. By 1755 £18,000 worth of porcelain was being sold annually, which, translated into terms of today's currency, means approximately £200,000.

Unlike Chelsea, who rarely used underglaze blue, Bow made much porcelain thus decorated from its earliest years. These are usually copies of Chinese blue-and-white patterns, since Japanese blue-and-white export porcelain had not been fashionable since the end of the 17th century. Some of the earliest Bow enamelled porcelain was undoubtedly done by Duesbury (q.v.), although attributions to his studio are conjectural. Much polychrome painting was in imitation of Kakiemon (q.v.), but Bow imitations are not of the same quality as those of Chelsea, where the resemblance is often deceptively close. The most popular pattern was the 'Quail'. Copies of Chinese

Bow Porcelain. The Fortune-teller, group by the 'Muses Modeller'. The girl shows the typical receding chin and oval face. Bow. c. 1752. *Victoria and Albert Museum.*

famille rose porcelain, not to be seen from Chelsea, are fairly common at Bow, but the quality is rarely spectacular. During 1756 and 1757, however, Chelsea artists, out of work because of the closure of the factory, came to Bow, and some of the finer Bow polychrome wares were undoubtedly painted by them. Particularly is this the case with the rare plates painted with Hans Sloane flowers (q.v.) and with *deutsche Blumen* (q.v.). A comparatively common type has a powder-blue ground with paintings in reserves of Chinese subjects, in imitation of the much valued Chinese blue *soufflé* or powder-blue. The blue ground has a granular appearance. This type was also done at Worcester, Lowestoft, and Caughley. Transfer-printing (q.v.) was done with the aid of the engraver, Robert Hancock, who left Bow for Worcester in 1757. Prints are in red, lilac, or sepia overglaze. Most blue printing is from Lowestoft, although some Bow specimens have been noted. Bow probably instituted the practice of printing in outline only to enable semi-skilled workpeople to complete the decoration by painting inside the outlines in coloured enamels. This technique for rapid production was later used by Worcester and by Wedgwood at his Chelsea decorating establishment (see *Wedgwood*). There are other subjects which fall into less well-defined categories, but these can usually be traced to a source which is German, Chinese, or Japanese, and some of them to James Giles, the outside decorator (q.v.).

From the earliest times Bow made a great deal of porcelain based on the wares of Tê Hua—the so-called *blanc-de-Chine,* decorated with prunus blossom in relief. Surviving specimens, for the most part, are plates, dishes, bowls, cups and saucers, and the like; small vases, and objects of this nature, being

a good deal rarer. Occasionally one finds decoration of this kind touched with enamel colours, which suggests painting done at Duesbury's studio.

It is, perhaps, significant that shells appear on a number of early specimens in the rococo style in conjunction with painting in the manner of Kakiemon, since these asymmetrical Japanese wares played a considerable part in the evolution of this style, and many—perhaps most—of them were probably modelled by Mr Tebo (q.v.).

Bow made many figures, variable in quality, the earlier of which are much sought. Those with a theatrical flavour include striking portraits of Henry Woodward and Kitty Clive which were very popular. Kitty Clive also occurs in a closely similar version from another factory, which may have been Chelsea or Derby. Peg Woffington, a very well-known actress, occurs as a Sphinx which is undoubtedly derived from the French fashion at the turn of the 18th century for depicting Court beauties and actresses in this form, probably inspired by the designs of Bérain (q.v.). Of Peg, the story is told that when playing a male part she incautiously remarked to Garrick that half the men in London thought her a man. 'Madam,' Garrick replied, 'the other half know you to be a woman.' The portrait Sphinx also comes from one or two German factories, and occurs in bronzes from France. An amusing, primitively modelled series of figures done about 1750–1755 can be distinguished by an oval face and a receding chin. Known models include a set of the Muses, and for this reason the man responsible for them is usually called the 'Muses Modeller', since his identity is otherwise unknown.

Bow Porcelain. Autumn, from a set of the Seasons. The model adapted from a figure forming part of a Chelsea group of about 1765. Bow. c. 1765. *Victoria and Albert Museum.*

Although much of early Bow figure-work is artless and unsophisticated some notable specimens, bearing comparison with contemporary work at Chelsea, were made around 1755, and of these, the pair of *Cooks* are representative. Although tradition has it that they were modelled by John Bacon, the sculptor and later Academician, this is not well founded. From about 1758 Bow began to employ a *bocage* (q.v.) as a background to most of their small figures which was more or less elaborate, becoming increasingly large with later specimens. Many Bow figures almost from the earliest times have a square hole pierced at the back, and these were intended to form the attachment of an ormolu mount, sometimes fitted with a porcelain candle nozzle and drip-pan, and sometimes for bronze stalks and leaves to which porcelain flowers were added. The earliest figures have plain bases, but rococo scrollwork can be observed in some of those of about 1755, and this becomes increasingly elaborate. By about 1760 these *C* and *S* scrolls (q.v.) had evolved into a kind of base with four feet, one at each corner. This was very popular. About the same time or a little later, i.e. 1760–1765, a base with a large shell in front was much used. Shells in one form or another were always a popular motif at Bow.

The Bow factory had no special mark. There are numerous workmen's marks. One, thus 丰 , which was once assumed to be the initial *F* for Frye, is simply the Chinese character for 'jade' (a mark of commendation) read upside down. Bow often simulated Chinese marks, although in a form which is nonsense, and cannot be identified as a reign-mark. The first two characters of the Ming dynastic mark sometimes appear in recognizable form. The mark of the anchor and dagger which occurs on a good deal of Bow porcelain can, with little doubt, be regarded as added by James Giles (q.v.) (the anchor of Chelsea added to a dagger from the arms of the City of London). Giles painted a great deal of Bow porcelain. Figures marked with an underglaze blue crescent are not Worcester (where figures were never given a factory mark), but Bow, and they are typically Bow in appearance.

The body of Bow porcelain is heavy for its size. It breaks with a sugary fracture, and translucency is rarely good. By transmitted light the colour is a brownish-orange. The poor translucency is often due to underfiring, and opaque pieces of Bow porcelain occur occasionally. These are so underfired that if a little ink be touched to an unglazed part the body will absorb it like blotting paper. Early Lowestoft has a body and glaze almost exactly similar to Bow, and care is needed in distinguishing early blue and white wares. The Bow factory was in financial difficulties in 1762, when it received assistance from William Duesbury (q.v.). It apparently closed finally in 1776, and what remained of the machinery, moulds, and so forth was probably bought by Duesbury. Production after 1762 seems to have been on a reduced scale, and specimens which can reliably be dated after 1770 are very rare.

BRACKET   See *Console*

BRACKET FOOT
A foot of bracket shape employed to support cabinets and chests of drawers.

BRAS DE CHEMINÉE (French)
Wall-sconces. During the 17th century these were frequently of silver in France, although gilt-bronze was much more common in the 18th century. Examples are also known in faïence, porcelain, and gilded wood. Seventeenth-century French examples are now known only from inventories, the sconces themselves having been melted for coinage during the economic troubles of the 1680s, but a few silver sconces of English make have survived. French examples in materials other than silver survive from the 18th century, usually gilt-bronze, of which there are examples in the Wallace Collection (London), the Louvre, and in the *châteaux* of Versailles, Fontainebleau, and Compiègne. A fine example in Sèvres porcelain is in the Victoria and Albert Museum (London).

Bras de Cheminée. Sconce in porcelain and gilt-bronze. Sèvres. c. 1760. *Victoria and Albert Museum.*

BRASS
Brass is primarily an alloy of copper and zinc, generally with small quantities of other metals, such as tin, added. The brass of former times contained up to about 36 per cent of zinc, although a reddish brass, very close to new bronze in colour, was made from 80 per cent of copper and 20 per cent of zinc. Quantities of zinc smaller than this probably had little effect on the appearance of the metal, which became indistinguishable from bronze.

Although zinc was unknown as a separate metal before A.D. 1000, brass was produced in ancient times by adding zinc carbonate (calamine) to copper. The whole subject, however, is buried in obscurity because of the inexact nature of the Latin and Greek words employed to describe this and kindred alloys.

Some terms seem to have been virtually interchangeable. Theophilus, the medieval writer whose *De Diversis Artibus* is very informative about technical processes of his day, describes the production of brass, but hardly throws light on the problem of terminology, and in the 17th and 18th centuries writers such as Evelyn and Martin Lister still referred to 'brazen' when they meant 'bronze' or 'gilt bronze'.

The old English *latten* (O.F. *laiton*) was undoubtedly brass. Medieval writers occasionally use the word *electrum* (strictly an alloy of gold and silver) with the same meaning. *Ormolu* (in the English sense), *pinchbeck,* and *Mosaic gold* are all brass alloys.

The manufacture of brass on a considerable scale began in England towards the end of the 17th century, a patent being taken out by John Lofting for brass-casting at this time. It increased greatly during the 18th century, at first being located in Bristol, Birmingham becoming of increasing importance after 1760. Zinc was being extracted on a considerable scale at Bristol by 1740, the manufacturer being William Champion, and production averaged about 200 tons a year. A considerable trade in zinc existed with China under the name of *tutenag,* and *tutty,* a zinc oxide deposit which formed inside Chinese zinc-smelting furnaces, was imported into England as a polishing powder. The word is derived from the old Persian *tutuya,* meaning zinc oxide. *Tutenag* is sometimes confused with *paktong* (q.v.), an alloy from China which is a kind of German silver.

Little brass has been used for the manufacture of works of art, since these are generally cast and bronze is a better casting metal, but many domestic vessels and utensils were made from brass, a notable centre for their manufacture in medieval times being Dinant, near Liège. Much brasswork also came from the Netherlands, and this was the source of a good deal of 19th-century *repoussé* brass ornament, much of it either pressed into moulds or hammered into *intaglio* moulds, the latter a very ancient method of reproducing embossed work.

BRASS FURNITURE

The fashion for brass furniture in the 19th century began with the Great Exhibition of 1851, when Birmingham manufacturers exhibited a wide variety made from drawn brass tubing (then a comparatively new technical advance) to which cast brass ornament was added. Most prominent among the exhibitors was the firm of R. W. Winfield. Some of this furniture was extremely elaborate, Winfields, for instance, showing a large four-poster bed in the 'Renaissance' style with massive openwork ends, the pillars topped first by Corinthian capitals and then by urns. The 'Angel' cot—a child's cot with a brass angel supporting the canopy—was also theirs, perhaps as revolting as anything in the Exhibition. A rocking-chair of brass, brass curtain-rod ends, chandeliers, candelabra, and many other things all conspired together to spark off a fashion in boudoir and drawing-room decoration which lasted almost

to the end of the century. In the Medieval Court of the same Exhibition was a large display of brass ecclesiastical requisites, mostly designed by, or under the influence of, A. W. Pugin (q.v.).

BRASSWORK, ENGLISH

The rise of the guilds in England considerably influenced the making of objects from brass and bronze. The manufacture of those of domestic utility—basins, ewers, mortars, candlesticks etc.—was presided over by the Worshipful Company of Founders, given a grant of Arms in 1590, and the Braziers Company who, with the Armourers, claimed a monopoly of all brasswork and copper wrought with a hammer. Defoe (*Tour of England*) refers to the manufacture of 'Battery ware, or, as 'tis called, Brass'. This was hollow-ware of hammered copper or brass, the term being derived from the French *battre*, to strike. The Companies, conservative in their outlook, exerted their influence in favour of honest work in good metal.

The manufacture of domestic utensils of tinned copper and brass increased greatly in the 17th century, copper being in great demand for saucepans and cooking-pots because of the unpleasant taste imparted to food and drink by brass, a disadvantage noted by Pliny in the 1st century A.D. Although the name of John Lofting of London is the only one we have for this date, the manufacture of small articles especially was greatly stimulated by the arrival of Huguenot refugees from the Revocation of the Edict of Nantes in 1685, and brassworkers existed in Birmingham four years later.

Many copper utensils especially were made by the journeyman-coppersmith, who set up a portable workshop wherever his services were needed, making vessels and repairing them. The best domestic vessels, however, were made in Bristol, Birmingham, and the metropolis, and among the finest specimens must be numbered imitations of silver patterns, such as the monteith (q.v.). The earliest examples of brasswork by known makers are chandeliers, the first of which date from the last quarter of the 17th century. Nearly all chandeliers of this kind are to be found in churches.

A good deal of copper and brass was employed around the hearth in the form of engraved trivets, coal-boxes, and similar appliances, and towards the end of the 18th century there was a fashion for cast chimney-piece figures, some similar in purpose to the popular pottery figures of the period, and some to be stood in the hearth. Fairly unusual are door-stops of the period, more commonly to be found in cast iron.

The 18th century saw the production of objects of copper and brass on a much greater scale than hitherto. The records of 1777 prove that thirty-odd brass-founders of Birmingham were using about a thousand tons of brass annually between them, largely made from zinc produced in Bristol. The latter town was, until the rise of Birmingham in the second half of the 18th century, the largest centre in

England for brass and copper working, and in 1833 Lewis's *Topographical Dictionary* lists brass, copper, and zinc among the principal articles of manufacture at Bristol, saying 'the brass and copper works are among the most extensive in England'. Saucepans and similar vessels were made from copper sheets in presses, and the press was adapted to the reproduction of embossed or *repoussé* ornament. The rolling-mill, invented at the end of the 17th century, was adapted to the production of Sheffield plate (q.v.) and Boulton & Fothergill at their Soho factory, just outside Birmingham, made a vast amount of decorative metalwork of all kinds in brass, some in imitation of contemporary French gilt-bronze. Boulton's mounts for vases of 'Blue John', the 'Derbyshire spar' popular in the second half of the 18th century for ornamental purposes, rival those of his contemporaries across the Channel. His clock-cases in ormolu, the design influenced by French work, sold as far afield as the Court of Catherine the Great of Russia.

It would be tedious to list all the ornamental brassware in common production, but a number of catalogues of 18th- and early 19th-century brass-founders have survived and are preserved in the Victoria and Albert Museum. One undated catalogue, probably issued in the early years of the 19th century, refers to candelabra, lamps, inkstands, flower-vases, and paperweights in bronze or 'Ormolu'. Candelabra cost 34s without glass-drops and 54s with them. Vases are listed as 'lac' (lacquered) or 'rich gold colr. also bronz.' as well as 'chamber candlesticks in Bronz.'. 'Bronz.' was obviously a commercial euphemism for 'bronzed', much in the same way as 'art. silk' means 'artificial silk'. This is evident from the description 'bronzed snuffers', which occurs in some catalogues. Another catalogue of 1811 lists lighting-appliances which include 'Etruscan lamps' (apparently stands of tripod form), and Grecian hanging-lamps for suspension from the ceiling, to be purchased 'bronzed' or 'lackered'.

Other catalogues list furniture fittings and mounts, such as handles and escutcheon plates, and the lists were intended for circulation in France and America also. One of 1785 refers to 'French handles', the illustration being in the Louis Seize style, and 'Escutcheons to match French handles'. Some French furniture in the Victoria and Albert Museum is fitted with handles closely resembling those illustrated, and they were probably exported to France as rough casts and finished there, where skilled chisellers were more numerous.

Most of the catalogues also list minor objects of utility—bolts, screws, casters, fittings for extending tables, etc.

BREAK FRONT

(French *décrochement*.) A piece of furniture, such as a wardrobe or bookcase, in which the central section projects slightly beyond the two flanking parts.

Break Front. Secrétaire-bookcase of c. 1790, the central part projecting slightly beyond the two flanking sections. The type known as 'breakfront'. *Wilfred Bull Esq.*

BRETTINGHAM, MATTHEW (1699–1769)

English architect and furniture-designer. A pupil of William Kent's, who assisted his master in the decoration of Holkham Hall (Norfolk), Kent's most impressive work. Brettingham visited Greece in company with 'Athenian' Stuart (q.v.).

BRIGHT-CUT ENGRAVING

A kind of engraving on silver, and on inserts of silver into Sheffield plate, which was popular towards the end of the 18th century in England. The line was bevelled in such a way that light was reflected from its facets, giving the engraved work an additional brightness.

Bright-cut Engraving. Helmet-shaped cream-jug in the Adam style decorated with bright-cut engraving. *Victoria and Albert Museum.*

BRISTOL DELFT

Delftware at Bristol hardly differs in methods of manufacture from other places. The history of the potteries is obscure. The first factory at Brislington was founded by Southwark potters about 1650, and the second factory developed from it in 1683. The first establishment closed down in 1750, and the second had already abandoned delftware for stoneware and creamware by 1770. The greater part of the Bristol production came from two other offshoots, St Mary Redcliffe and Limekiln Lane. After 1770 Bristol *delft* potters seem to have dispersed.

The glaze of *delft* made at Bristol is usually a bluish-white in contrast to the slightly pink hue of London wares, and the blue used for decoration is a good strong colour. Bristol artists painted with greater freedom (and occasionally less skill) than at Lambeth, and there was much imitation of similar Chinese subjects, although in most cases the treatment was rather different. Bristol had at its command the full range of high-temperature pigments. Powder-blue, purple, and manganese-purple backgrounds derived from the Chinese were painted in reserved panels, but it is easy to confuse the products of Bristol and Wincanton, while Liverpool and Bristol used blue and manganese backgrounds with identically shaped panels, and even similar decoration within them. Inscriptions at Bristol, as at Lambeth, became fewer as the 18th century advanced, although punchbowls continued with the old exhortation: 'One bowl more and then.' Commemorative plates and dishes occasionally have names in full, but initials are more common. Potters seem to have taken an interest in politics at Bristol, for inscribed and dated plates, such as 'Calvert and Martin for Tukesbury 1754' (referring to the election of that year), or 'Sir Jno Pole for Ever 1754', are known.

Although it was occasionally used in London and Liverpool, the technique called *bianco sopra bianco* (q.v.) invented in Italy is usually ascribed to Bristol. This is a decoration in white over a glaze tinted pale blue, lavender, or green, and a very typical Bristol pattern shows a repeating design on the border of a leaf spray, flowers and a pine cone. Usually the *bianco* decoration is confined to the rim with a landscape, frequently Chinese, in the well of

Bristol Delft. Punch-bowl made for the tin-miners of Cornwall in 1731. Bristol. *Victoria and Albert Museum.*

the dish standing out clearly. Flower-holders in the form of *delft* bricks, shoes, and pierced bowls, and all the normal domestic ware, were made at Bristol.

BRISTOL PORCELAIN FACTORY (CHAMPIONS)

William Cookworthy (q.v.) established a factory for the manufacture of true porcelain in the Chinese manner at Castle Green, Bristol, in 1770. In 1772 Richard Champion was licensed by Cookworthy to manufacture under his patent at Bristol, and in 1774 Cookworthy assigned the patent to him. The two men had known each other since 1764, although the extent of Champion's participation before 1772 is not precisely known.

The style of Plymouth-Bristol porcelain began to change with Champion's active participation in 1772, becoming increasingly neo-classical in form and decoration. Much inspiration was sought in the wares of Meissen and Sèvres, although this may have come at second-hand from Derby.

Much tea-ware was made at this factory, and cups and saucers are the most frequently surviving specimens. Vases were produced in considerable quantity, and many were hexagonal. This may have been due to the difficulty of firing the true (or hard-paste) porcelain body successfully, and it is noteworthy that these hexagonal forms were also used at Arita in Japan (Kakiemon porcelain, q.v.) where similar difficulties were encountered.

Excellent floral and bird painting decorates much of the production, and gilding is over a vermilion base, which was done to overcome the poor attachment of gold to the underlying glaze.

Well-modelled figures were produced in a style much influenced by contemporary work at Derby, and it is possible that John Bacon, who also provided figure models for Derby, worked for Champion. Tebo (q.v.) worked as a repairer on some of the best figures, but his own hand is to be seen sometimes. He was undoubtedly responsible for vases of

Bristol Delft. Pair of shoes. A model first introduced by the Dutch at Delft. Bristol. c. 1730.

Bristol Porcelain Factory. A set of the four Elements—Earth, Fire, Air, and Water. Bristol porcelain (Champion's factory). c. 1772. *Delomosne & Son Ltd.*

hexagonal form with masks on either side and decorated with well-modelled applied flowers. These, ultimately based on a Meissen vase of about 1745 by Eberlein, were popular at Bow in the 1750s in a rococo form with a leafy frill towards the bottom, for which reason they were often called 'frill' vases. But in the form employed at Champion's factory the 'frill' was replaced by moulded acanthus leaves. Stephan of Derby has also been suggested as one of Champion's modellers, and he probably worked for Bristol at a time when he was acting as 'free-lance'.

Underglaze-blue decoration is rare, and transfer-printing has been noted on one or two specimens, but obviously it never left the experimental stage. Most decoration is in polychrome, and a bluish-green enamel is very characteristic of the factory's wares. Coloured grounds are rare, but gold stripes used as a ground can be seen occasionally.

A special feature of Bristol porcelain is the number of tea-services made to special order, usually with initials or arms, and specimens from these are much sought.

A certain amount of porcelain, sparsely and simply decorated, was made to supply a cheaper market, probably to compete with Wedgwood's creamware, and it is often referred to as 'cottage Bristol'. Most wares of this kind, however, are wrongly attributed, and were more probably made at New Hall (q.v.).

The *biscuit* plaque, oval, with a central coat of arms or initials surrounded by a wreath of finely modelled flowers, is peculiar to Champion's factory in 18th-century England. This work has been attributed to Thomas Briand, who seems to have been the same man who probably originally supplied the formula for the Chelsea porcelain body, and then travelled on to Derby, to be connected with the early stages of porcelain-making there. Significantly enough, he is recorded at Bristol as having come from Derby.

BRISTOL PORCELAIN (LUND'S FACTORY)
See *Worcester Porcelain Factory.*

BRITANNIA METAL
A kind of pewter containing copper and antimony. It was made from about 1800 onwards as a silver substitute, and objects were often spun on the lathe (see *Spinning*). It remained popular until about 1820. Britannia metal is somewhat harder than pewter, but it has a low melting-point.

BRITISH PLATE
A very deceptive alloy, rather similar to German silver or the Chinese *paktong* (q.v.), which was made between 1830 and 1855, after which it was superseded by electroplate. It does resemble silver quite closely, but, of course, it was much cheaper, and it became very popular at the time. Silver hall-marks were often closely imitated, even, for a short period, the crowned leopard's head. When the sovereign's head occurs, the direction of the profile is reversed. Marks closely resembling genuine hall-marks are usually in a different order. Marks should be examined with care to see that they are of the usual kind used by the Assay Office, and in their correct order. No one acquainted with genuine silver of the period is likely to be deceived.

BROAD GLASS
Sheet-glass made by first blowing a bubble which was then rolled on the marver into a cylinder about 5 ft long and a foot in diameter. The cylinder was then slit down its length, laid on a flat bed of sand in a furnace, and heated until it softened sufficiently to collapse into a flat sheet. This was employed for window-glass, but it was unsatisfactory for mirror-glass because of the surface irregularities inseparable from the process. It was superseded for the latter purpose by cast glass, first made in France towards the end of the 17th century. The broad-glass process continued to be used in England during a good deal of the 18th century, and

51

old bureaux and bookcases with glazed doors of this type can be recognized by the slightly irregular surface of the panes, to be seen when light falls on them at an angle.

BROCADE (French)
A fabric which has been brocaded, i.e. ornamented with the formation of a design in relief made by introducing extra weft threads at this point.

BROCARD, JOSEPH
A French glassmaker and enameller of the second half of the 19th century who achieved a reputation for clever reproductions of Syrian enamelled glass of the 13th and 14th centuries, especially mosque lamps.

BROCATELLE (French)
Fabric similar to *lampas* (q.v.) with patterns in slight relief on a satin ground. It was often employed for furniture covering, and occasionally for wall-hangings.

BRONZE
Bronze is primarily an alloy of copper and tin, although other metals are nearly always present, either added deliberately or present fortuitously in the ores.

The most common general-purpose bronze comprises about 90 per cent of copper and 10 per cent of tin, but all kinds of variations and additions were made for special purposes, mirror-bronze, for instance, being compounded of 50 per cent of each metal.

Most objects of bronze were made by casting, and for this purpose the alloy is especially suitable. When first poured into the mould it expands slightly, forcing itself into every crevice, and then, as it cools, it shrinks, facilitating separation from the mould.

When bronze has been employed for casting, it has usually been the practice to increase the fusibility of the metal by adding a proportion of lead. As an example, the bronze-founders working for Versailles during the 17th century employed an alloy containing 92 per cent of copper, 2 per cent of tin, 5 per cent of zinc, and 1 per cent of lead, but the quantity of lead was often considerably higher when greater fusibility was sought.

Alloying metals, if present in sufficient quantity, affect the colour of the bronze. When first cast, bronze is a rich golden yellow, lighter in colour if zinc is present in significant quantities. Overmuch lead will yield a greyish-blue. The addition of alloying metals for the purpose of achieving a particular colour-effect has not been especially popular in modern times, but Pliny (*Natural History*) refers to the addition of iron in an attempt to attain red, of silver to simulate a pallid complexion, and to a flesh-coloured alloy devised by Praxiteles. Most such reports, however, are obviously gossip.

Ordinary statuary of bronze, if kept in a dry and

Bronzes. *Neptune* by Peter Visscher the Elder, Nürnberg. Early 16th century. See also illustration to Gothic Style. *Sotheby & Co., London.*

reasonably pure atmosphere free of coal-smoke, will turn first a reddish-brown, then medium brown, and finally dark brown. Few bronzes, however, are kept in such favourable conditions, and in a fairly pure atmosphere a light green surface deposit will form over a period of time if it is not protected by varnishing. Buried bronze, or bronze exposed to a polluted town atmosphere, will corrode much more readily, and to a much greater extent. Such substances as nitric, sulphuric, and hydrochloric acids, carbonic acid and ammonia, all affect the surface more or less seriously, leading to the formation of deposits of varying colours—several shades of green, blue, brown, and black, with, in the case of excavated specimens, the occasional separation of copper from tin and the formation of a whitish tin oxide.

These products of corrosion usually resolve themselves into three principal substances which are indistinguishable from the original ores of copper—cuprite, malachite, and azurite. Of the three the reddish-brown cuprite is the most important, if not the most spectacular, and there is reason to think that it always underlies the more colourful patinations. Contact with carbonic acid, present in the air and to a much greater extent in most soils, causes the formation of green malachite and the much rarer blue azurite, the latter a pigment often employed by early painters. This tends to revert to the green malachite, which is the reason why passages of blue in some Old Master paintings incline towards green today. Sulphates also yield a deep blue and a green. A bluish-green is due to interaction with nitric acid, and contact with sulphuric acid yields a dark brown or black. A saline soil, such as that to be met in Egypt, will colour the surface light green.

Bronzes. Fidélité, attributed to Falconet. The figure holds a heart in one hand and a spaniel in the other. Another version of this subject, called *L'Amitié,* was issued in biscuit porcelain by Sèvres. This was intended to represent Mme de Pompadour. *Wallace Collection.*

Most of these colour-effects will be seen on ancient excavated bronzes, but bronzes of more recent times, if they have been buried or exposed to the substances mentioned, will also show effects of this kind, but to a lesser degree.

Corrosion, when it has not affected the bronze beneath to a serious degree, is often termed *patina* (q.v.), and when sufficiently colourful is much prized. Such corrosion is a process which is largely irreversible, although new techniques have been devised which can restore the metal to some extent. It is extremely inadvisable for any but the expert to tamper with it.

It has been the custom from very early times to impart colour artificially to bronze in a variety of ways. Patination of the kind described is imitated chemically in solutions known as 'pickles'. Such bronzes are not invariably spurious, although objects thus treated always demand a considerable degree of caution. It was common practice in the 19th century among collectors, and even museum curators, to clean off a patination which was disliked, replacing it with something else. The agents recommended for this purpose ranged from sal ammoniac, known since Roman times, to smoking, using willow twigs and old shoes as fuel. Surfaces have always been varnished to protect them from contact with the atmosphere.

The best preservative was undoubtedly gilding, which interposed a protective layer of gold between bronze and the atmosphere. Gold is virtually unalterable and indestructible, except by wear and handling. The subject is fully discussed elsewhere, but it is common, in places where the layer of gold has been partly eroded, to find the exposed bronze turning green. Silver was less often employed for the same purpose, but some examples survive. Most bronzes originally silvered were later gilded, since the silver oxidized to black unless it was varnished. If gilded bronze has been buried, the combination of the two metals (gold and bronze) tends to accelerate the corrosive processes, and only in a few instances can surviving traces of gold be seen.

The casting of bronze is described below, but up to 100,000 lb of metal have been cast at a single pouring, the French especially being noted for work of this kind. The reader is also referred to Cellini's description of the casting of his Perseus in his *Memoirs.*

BRONZE AND BRASS, TO CLEAN

Add ordinary table-salt to a 5 per cent solution of acetic acid (vinegar) until no more can be dissolved.

Bronzes. Striding Horses. Workshop of Susini. 17th century. c. 1600. The horse was a favourite *motif* among Renaissance bronzeworkers. *Kunsthaus Lempertz, Köln.*

Bronze. Moulds and supports for the casting of a large bronze equestrian statue. French. c. 1700. The French were famed for their skill in casting large works as far back as the 16th century (vide Cellini). *After Diderot.*

This is an excellent cleaner for both brass and bronze. Cleaning should be followed by washing with clean water, and, when dry, by waxing or lacquering.

BRONZE-CASTING

Most of the world's great works of art in bronze, as well as the *bronzes de l'ameublement*, or furnishing-bronzes, employed to decorate interiors, are the product of casting. The principal method employed is known as the *cire-perdue* or 'lost wax' technique. This is extremely ancient, being used both by the Sumerians and the Egyptians.

There are three principal ways of casting by the 'lost wax' method. The earliest required the making of a model of solid wax over which a mould was formed of some refractory material, i.e. one which will only fuse at a considerably higher temperature than the melting-point of bronze. Fire-clay is one of the best substances for this purpose, although a mixture of plaster and brick-dust is often employed today. When the mould had been formed, the wax was melted out and the liquid bronze poured in. The resulting cast was solid.

The second method required the making of a refractory core, over which the wax was modelled to the requisite thickness. Bronze pins were inserted into the core to support the outer mould, which was then formed over the wax surface. The next step was to melt out the wax, leaving a space between mould and core which was filled with liquid bronze, after which mould and core were broken away. These casts were hollow.

The third (and latest) method was devised by the Greeks. Moulds were taken from a clay, terracotta, or wooden prototype, and the interior was covered with wax to the desired thickness, the necessary supports for mould and core being arranged at this point. The interior was then filled with a refractory substance, after which the wax was melted out to leave space for the molten bronze. The advantage of this technique is that the prototype is preserved for fresh moulds to be taken from it.

The third method especially has continued to be used through the centuries for hollow casts, but cheap decorative bronzes were made in the 19th century by electrotyping (q.v.).

It is very rare for large bronzes especially to emerge from the mould without some imperfections, and these are removed with metalworking tools—files, chisels, and so forth. Occasionally parts are missing, when the bronze fails to run into sections of the mould, and these are made afterwards and soldered into position. In France especially ornamental bronzes were usually handed to a category of craftsmen known as *ciséleurs*, who refined the details of rough castings. (See *Fondeurs, Corporation of.*)

BRONZE 'DISEASE'

When bronze corrosion is soft and porous, and the object has been buried in a saline soil, the metal tends to retain the salts, which later form disfiguring light green spots, moist and pasty in a humid atmosphere, and powdery in one which is relatively free from moisture. This has been termed, quite incorrectly, bronze 'disease' or bronze 'cancer'. The cause is well known, and all that is usually needed to check the condition is fairly prolonged immersion in several changes of distilled water to get rid of the salts which are causing it. Occasionally more expert treatment is required.

BRONZES, FORGERIES OF

Forgeries of bronzes of all kinds have been common for at least two thousand years. The Romans forged Greek bronzes, and the sculptors of the Renaissance forged Roman bronzes. These, today, are problems of attribution; some are very tricky,

Baroque style. This 17th century interior from Ham House,
S.W. London, is typically baroque in style. The furniture,
c. 1680, owes much to contemporary French design.

Tapestry. Part of a room at Osterley Park, W. London, decorated with a fitted Gobelins tapestry woven to special order in 1775 with designs by Boucher. The *canapé* and *fauteuils* are covered with tapestry woven *en suite.* The carpet is by Moore of Moorfields, London.

and most such works are interesting enough to have their own not inconsiderable value.

There are several possibilities to be borne in mind when examining a bronze. It may be completely new but inspired by old sources; it may be cast from a mould taken from a genuine specimen; and it may be a cast taken from an original work in some other material. The two latter are perhaps the most common form of fraud.

Forgeries of Renaissance bronzes, which are those that chiefly concern us here, belong to the 19th century and modern times. Some, with more than the customary amount of impudence, have been claimed for Cellini. It is these which usually provide the most stringent test of the connoisseur's discriminatory ability, for the best offer little more as a guide than style and workmanship. Perhaps the most revealing trial to which a suspected specimen can be put is to place it in company with some genuine ones for a few days. Its spurious nature will usually soon become obvious. Poor modelling and a clumsy pose are often indications, although bad craftsmanship is not entirely a prerogative of the 20th century.

Forgers rarely go to the trouble of making a complicated mould in order to take one copy from it. Identical specimens turning up in different places about the same time usually mean that, although one may possibly be genuine, the others certainly are not.

Something may be learned from patina (q.v.)— the surface appearance of old bronze—but this is by no means certain evidence, for changing one patina for another, or providing a new one, was a favourite pastime among collectors in the 19th century, and some quite scholarly works on the subject did not hesitate to give favourite recipes for 'pickles'. Some perfectly genuine bronzes have suffered in this way.

By using electrotyping (q.v.) a perfect facsimile can be obtained, down to the smallest surface blemish, but the surface appearance differs from cast bronze because the metal has been deposited particle by particle. They are not usually very difficult to detect, but in cases of real doubt, chemical or spectroscopic analysis will settle the point.

There are a few obvious points to be borne in mind. If a mould has been taken from an old bronze this may have been damaged, perhaps slightly, and the damage will appear in the copy. But there is a good deal of difference between the appearance of accidental damage and a cast of it. Old craftsmen sharpened detail by chiselling. The difference in actual tool-marks and a cast of them is usually discernible with a little experience. The use of other media as a source of inspiration is often fairly obvious if thought is given to the possibilities. For instance, a bronze figure with drapery from the waist down, or posed against a support, such as an altar or a tree-trunk, is obviously copied from a stone original, since this kind of support is unnecessary in bronze, and a bronze figure does not need drapery to strengthen it. Early bronzes were usually carefully finished, and a good deal of attention paid to the rendering of detail with punches and chisels.

Careless and slovenly work, and poor finishing, is a cause for suspicion. This also applies to furniture-mounts, and large quantities of mounts have been made in modern times, both in Paris and London, some of which are well finished. But the colour of the alloy does not resemble that of the old gilded bronze mounts, and electrical gilding is no substitute for old mercuric gilding.

Fakes are not very numerous in bronze, although a soldered line at the neck of a figure suggests that a head may have been substituted. Fake inscriptions are not unknown. Repaired bronzes can often be detected with the aid of the ultra-violet lamp (q.v.), since the repaired part will have been covered with some kind of artificial patina to disguise the joint.

Modern bronzes are often issued in limited editions, and when this has been completed the moulds ought to be destroyed. Very often they have not. Value depends on how many casts have been taken, and the buyer must rely on the honesty of the artist and the bronze-founder to limit the number of casts to the prescribed number. In a few cases it is difficult to be certain whether or not the buyer's confidence has been misplaced.

BRONZING

The term is usually employed to mean the colouring of plaster and similar materials with powder colour in imitation of bronze or copper. The pigments vary in colour, and copper is more closely simulated if a little red lead be added. Other powders, lighter in colour, imitate brass and gold. The powders are usually caused to adhere to the surface by japanners' gold size, but plaster busts are sometimes coloured with fine metallic bronze powder without the intervention of a cement. The method is often used today.

BRUNSWICK (GERMANY) FAÏENCE FACTORIES

There were two factories in Brunswick. The earliest was founded in 1707 by the Duke Anton Ulrich von Braunschweig, and directed by Johann Philipp Frantz. It was leased by a number of people with varying fortune, and during the Seven Years' War it was acquired by the Duke Karl, who kept it until 1773, when it was bought by Johann Rabe. The earliest wares were blue and white, closely copying those of Delft. Tureens in the form of grapes, asparagus, melons, etc., and figures, are in the rococo style.

A second factory was started by Rudolph Anton Chely in 1745. Vases painted in the Chinese manner, a variety of figures, and tureens in the form of ducks were produced. Chely used a mark of intertwined Cs, very like that of Custine at Niderviller, and of Ludwigsburg. Chely's factory, however, closed in 1757, and all his wares are in the rococo style, whereas those of the two latter factories are neo-classical.

Marks of the earlier factory are initial letters— VH, B&R, R&B, and R&C.

BRUSSELS CARPETS

A coarse variety of *moquette* (q.v.) was much used in France and the Low Countries as a floor-covering during the 16th, 17th, and 18th centuries. Brussels was one of the centres of manufacture, and carpets in this style became known as 'Brussels carpets'. The patterns usually follow contemporary French designs. Carpets of this kind were made in England at Axminster and Wilton (q.v.).

BUEN RETIRO PORCELAIN FACTORY

This Spanish porcelain factory, a continuation of Capo-di-Monte (q.v.), was started in 1760. It was situated near Madrid. Its products are rarely seen outside Spain. Gricci, from Capo-di-Monte, was the chief modeller until 1770, and many of the figures produced here came from his hand.

The porcelain body of the early period has been well compared with that of Saint-Cloud (q.v.), and although the first production was often in the rococo style this very quickly gave way to the neo-classical. The later body varies very much in quality, and soft paste was abandoned at the end of the century, to be replaced by a hard paste which was poor in quality. The old *fleur-de-lys* mark was, at this time, replaced by *MD* under a crown. The factory closed in 1808, but manufacture was revived in 1817 at La Moncloa and continued till 1850. During this time contemporary Sèvres styles were imitated, and some old white porcelain from Buen Retiro was decorated.

Among the earliest work to be done at the Buen Retiro factory was the decoration of a porcelain room in the Palace of Aranjuez, which includes mirror-frames and mural *consoles. Chinoiserie* figures form part of the ornament.

Buen Retiro Porcelain. Hercules resting from his Labours. Buen Retiro. c. 1770. The rock is inscribed *Non plus ultra*— Nothing beyond this.

BUFFET (French)

A very ancient piece of furniture which began as a coffer or chest. In the 16th century it was in two parts, the top sometimes being a cupboard closed by doors, and the bottom with open shelves. It was sometimes called a *buffet à armoire* (see *Armoire*). With cupboards at top and bottom, the top being for the most part somewhat narrower than the bottom, it became a *buffet à deux corps* (a *buffet* in two parts). Without the top (often missing now) it was sometimes called a *bas d'armoire* or low *armoire*, and these were made without a top in the 18th century as storage cupboards, bookcases, and so forth. *Buffets* with the top cupboard replaced by shelves become *dressoirs* (dressers). In the 17th century the two terms were synonymous. According to a 17th-century dictionary the meaning of *dressoir* was 'a *buffet* set up (*qu'on dresse*) with silver plate for show when dining'—a function of the *buffet* in Roman times. In the 18th century the *buffet* became largely a provincial piece of furniture, the best probably coming from Normandy and Arles. From Arles, the principal furniture-making centre of Provence, comes the *buffet-crédence*, a very well-carved piece of furniture in the Louis XV style which is low, and has small superimposed cupboards at the back. In appearance it is not unlike the English sideboard in design and purpose, although the proportions are different. Also provincial are the *buffets-vaisseliers,* the bottom with cupboards and the tops in the form of tiers of shelves (*étagères*), which could well be described as sideboard-dressers. The *vaisselier* is fairly common from all the provinces of France, but sometimes under a different name. Those from the Basse-Pyrénées are apt to be the largest, sometimes reaching ten feet in height. Dating is usually difficult, especially because the Louis XIII style, and that of Louis XV, lingered on in the provinces long after their currency had ended in Paris and round about.

BUHL WORK

Marquetry in the manner of A.-C. Boulle. The origin of the use of the word 'Buhl' for 'Boulle' is not known, but it may have some reference to Boulle's assumed Swiss origin.

BUN FOOT

In furniture, a turned foot of flattened globular shape commonly employed in the 17th century. In America it is termed a ball foot.

BUREAU

(American usage) The American chest of drawers is often called a bureau, whereas in Europe the term is reserved for a writing-desk. Those made in the second half of the 18th century, usually of mahogany, have not uncommonly survived.

BUREAU-BOOKCASE

A writing-desk with a sloping fall-front covering racks of pigeon holes and drawers, with drawers under, the top surmounted by bookshelves enclosed with glazed, panelled, or mirror doors. First introduced late in the 17th century, the best are in walnut or mahogany. The form appears to have been Dutch in origin, and it remained popular throughout the 18th century and into the 19th. In France as the *secrétaire-bibliothèque* it is found only among provincial furniture, and in the U.S.A. it is sometimes termed a secretary-bookcase.

BURMESE GLASS

Glass of pale greenish-yellow shading to a delicate pink first made about 1885 by the Mount Washington Glass Company, New Bedford, Mass., and used for both table-glass and decorative wares. It was made both with a matt and a gloss finish. The English manufacturing rights of the American patent were acquired by Thomas Webb & Sons of Stourbridge, who manufactured it from 1886 onwards, calling it 'Queen's Burmese'. The English version is a semi-opaque salmon-pink glass shading to a lemon-yellow.

Specimens are rare and much sought.

BURR

A burr is an excrescence on the trunk of a tree, or on the root, which, when sliced, produces a decoratively marked veneer. Usually walnut, elm, or yew. See *Oyster Veneer*.

BUSCH, CANON A. O. E. VON DEM (1704–1779)

August Otto Ernst von dem Busch was a Canon of the Seminary of the Holy Cross at Hildesheim, near Hannover, and at the age of about forty, inspired by contemporary diamond-point engraving on glass, he began to decorate porcelain in the same way as a hobby, colouring the engraved lines by rubbing black pigment into them so that, at first sight, they look a little like *Schwarzlot* (q.v.) painting. He was analogous to the *Hausmaler* (q.v.), except that he employed engraving instead of painting. A few examples of engraving from his hand on glass survive, but these are rare. Much of his work was done on porcelain (usually substandard) bought from Meissen, but a few specimens have been recorded on the porcelain of Fürstenberg. His subjects include landscapes often with buildings (usually ruined), floral sprays resembling the enamelled *deutsche Blumen* (q.v.), such birds as swans, and so forth. Technically his engraving is competent but slightly amateurish, suggesting that he was probably self-taught. A notable collection of his work, once in the Schloss Salzdahl, near Wolfenbüttel, was sold in London a few years ago. Specimens are not excessively rare, and his output must have been fairly prolific. Dated examples range from 1748 to 1775. Another Canon of the same place, probably a pupil, did similar work. His name was Johann Gottfried Kratzberg.

An isolated instance of this kind of engraving was noticed on a Worcester cup and saucer some years

Busch, Canon. Meissen bowl and cover decorated with diamond-point engraving by Canon Busch. c. 1760.

ago, but this was probably done in England by a glass-engraver. The possibility of more existing cannot be excluded, and they may be masquerading in collections as pencilled ware. The writer has seen a single example of work of this kind on Chinese porcelain, obviously done in China, and probably of 19th-century date.

Washing will often remove Busch's black pigment, and this can be renewed by rubbing lampblack or black boot polish into the incisions.

BUSTELLI, FRANZ ANTON (1723–1764)

After Kändler the work of Bustelli as a modeller of porcelain figures is perhaps the most highly valued by contemporary collectors. Bustelli was the son of a bell-maker, and was born in Locarno in 1723. He first appears in the archives of the Nymphenburg Porcelain Factory in 1754. It has been suggested that he worked for a time at the Doccia Porcelain Factory (q.v.), but this is very uncertain. He probably knew something about the secrets of porcelain manufacture, and his style was influenced by the Bavarian rococo sculptor Franz Ignaz Günther, who may also have contributed models to the porcelain factory. He was invited to work at Ludwigsburg (q.v.) in 1761, and it has been suggested that he went there for a short period, but no known porcelain figures from this factory suggest Bustelli's hand.

Bustelli's earliest models show the same fully developed style as his later ones, and it seems certain that he was a woodcarver of uncommon skill before becoming a porcelain designer. Most, if not all, his work in porcelain suggests a carved wood prototype, especially to be seen in the rendering of the drapery of some of his female Italian Comedy figures. Although he modelled other subjects, his fame largely rests on sixteen superbly modelled figures from the Italian Comedy, which today are also available in a properly marked set cast from the old moulds by the State Porcelain Factory of Bavaria, the successor to the old factory which is still housed in the grounds of the Schloss Nymphenburg on the outskirts of Munich.

Bustelli's figures are unique. They are theatrical

57

and Mannerist in their poses, and the mouths are usually open. His bases are thin, flat, and undecorated in the earliest specimens, but with slight rococo scrolls ornamenting the later ones. Especially in his later groups we find scrollwork rising from the base often to a considerable height, a development which culminated in his *Sleeper Awakened* of 1760, where the male figure is asleep inside one of the scrolls. Many of Bustelli's figures are in white, or with relatively slight passages of colour, which is especially the case with later specimens. His subjects were many and varied, and include some amusing cane-handles.

See *Nymphenburg Porcelain Factory.*

BYGONES

This is a comparatively recent term used generically of a whole group of objects which can best be described as of former utility, usually domestic, which have now been superseded or discarded. Bygones are often of wood (treen), but those of metal and other materials are common. They are sometimes decorated, and when they are the ornament is unsophisticated, and often could best be described as 'peasant' work. Included under this heading are objects of kitchen ware ranging from pot-hooks, chimney-cranes, and roasting-jacks, to butter-pats and moulds of all kinds, and wooden bowls and small gadgets, such as nut-crackers. Most domestic copper-ware—saucepans, kettles, scuttles, basins, etc.— can be regarded as bygones, as well as the brass figures discussed under the heading of *Figures, Brass.* Bygones of Sheffield plate, and even of silver, include such purely domestic items as snuffers, egg-toppers, and egg-stands. Salt and cutlery boxes of wood from the 19th-century kitchen are now sought, while the laundry supplies such simple machinery as the goffering iron and carved wood clothes-beaters. Even the older types of flat-iron are now put to new uses, becoming book-ends or door-stops.

Smoking bygones are much in demand, and range from Meerschaum pipes, tobacco-jars, pipe-stoppers, and cigar-cutters, to lighters (the table-variety first appearing about 1820) and 19th-century match boxes (some of very large size) and match-box covers. Boxes of *tole peinte,* or Pontypool ware, made for tea, biscuits, and so forth, and printed in colours, are sought, especially those commemorating such events as the Jubilee of Queen Victoria. The large painted and gilded tea-canisters which helped to furnish the Victorian grocers' shop now form part of the stock of some antique dealers. Sewing implements and needlework boxes have become increasingly popular among small collectors, especially implements of ivory and those turned from the coquilla nut.

Increasing interest is being shown in early small machinery. The phonograph is probably the most sought, with the cylindrical records which accompanied it, and these (and early gramophone records) bring good prices when by a well-known *artiste* or an historical personality. Old typewriters and cash registers are other examples of small machinery which is now in demand among collectors who realize that so much has been destroyed that these relics of the beginning of the Machine Age must eventually increase in value.

In 1969 a sudden and striking upward revaluation of the Stevengraph (q.v.), a 19th-century machine-woven silk picture, provided striking evidence of the present vogue for the bygone, and increasing interest is being taken in old tools, especially agricultural implements (already scarce) and woodworking tools. It seems no longer necessary for the antique to be also a work of art, however minor in character, to attract the collector, and other reasons, such as the collection of historical curiosities, are starting to operate. This is not entirely new perhaps, since Horace Walpole had Cardinal Wolsey's hat and Dr Dee's divining stone, which was actually a piece of coal.

Bygones offer a field for the small collector which will undoubtedly become of increasing interest in future, although it is difficult to see how it will develop.

C

C AND S SCROLLS

Ornament approximately in the form of the letters *C* and *S* which is an especial feature of the rococo style (q.v.). C-scrolls symmetrically disposed appear in England as early as the reign of Queen Anne, and both were commonly employed in the rococo designs of Chippendale. They are especially to be seen in French art of the period 1735–1760.

CABINET

A piece of case-furniture usually enclosed by doors, and containing drawers or shelves, used for the storage of valuables. It was made by cabinet-makers in England and by *ébénistes* in France. The cabinet appears first in Italy just before the end of the 15th century, and 16th-century examples are often richly and elaborately decorated with carving, painting, inlays of wood, and semi precious stones (see *Pietra Dura*). Cabinets came to France early in the 17th century, and Italian workmen were imported to make them; those of Dutch manufacture are almost indistinguishable from their more southerly proto-types. The Italian use of inlay in a wide variety of materials, which included tortoiseshell, and the vogue for mounts of gold and silver, inspired the typical work of Boulle (q.v.). In England, wood and lacquer cabinets on stands were introduced towards the end of the reign of Charles II, but they never achieved the same heights of luxury as on the Continent. By the end of the 17th century the cabinet was developing to fill specialized require-ments—a *secrétaire* or a bookcase, for instance. The cabinet as the term was understood during the 17th century, however, hardly survived the reign of William and Mary in England and Louis XIV in France.

CABINET-MAKER

In England and America, a maker of case-furniture (q.v.). The term is only approximately equivalent to the French *ébéniste* (q.v.), and it is generally employed to mean a maker of furniture of better quality than usual.

CABINETS, LACQUER

Large lacquer cabinets on stands were especially fashionable in England between the Restoration in 1660 and about 1685. The lacquer-work may be Chinese, Japanese, or European, and they were usually mounted on elaborately carved stands which were either gilded or silvered. Those of Oriental lacquer are made from the sap of the *Rhus vernicifera* (see *Lacquer, Oriental*). In the case of those of European derivation, the effect of Oriental lacquer is mimicked with oil and spirit varnishes (see *Lacquer, European; Vernis Martin*). Lacquer-work in which the design is incised is termed 'Coromandel' (q.v.).

Forgeries of cabinets of this kind are far from unknown. The lacquer was originally brilliantly coloured, and this brilliance, faded on the exterior or obscured by later coats of varnish, ought to have survived in a more or less pristine state in the interior, where it has not been exposed to the bleaching effect of light. When both interior and exterior are approximately similar, the genuineness of the work should be seriously doubted. Cabinets of this kind have large metal hinges on the outside,

C & S Scrolls. C and S scrolls are characteristic of much of the ornament of the *rococo* style. They are especially well-marked in this porcelain figure of a bird amid branches from Höchst, about 1765.

59

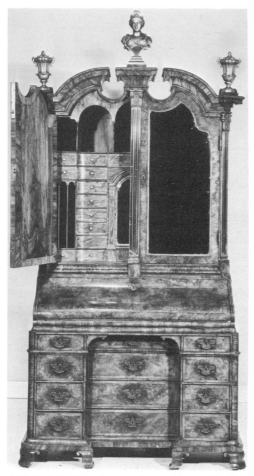

Cabinet. One of a pair of *secrétaire*-cabinets with mirror doors made in walnut for Augustus the Strong, Elector of Saxony. English. Queen Anne period. c. 1710. See also *Lacquer, European. Parke-Bernet Galleries, New York.*

and if these are removed they should reveal something like the original colour underneath.

Cabinets of Japanese origin sometimes have short feet which raise them slightly above the stand. Chinese and European cabinets lack the feet, and are recessed slightly into the stand. Oriental specimens were, however, sometimes made up from imported panels. Seventeenth-century stands, ornately carved, are very much in the Louis XIV style, and they may have been the work of immigrant French or Italian carvers.

CABOCHON (French)

An early type of cutting, of round or oval convex form, used for precious and semi-precious stones. Moulding to furniture and other materials similar in shape to the cut stone is thus called.

CABRIOLE CHAIR

An easy-chair is included under this name by Sheraton in his *Cabinet Dictionary* of 1803, where he describes it as a 'French easy chair'. It seems likely that he misunderstood the meaning of the French term '*en cabriolet*' (see *Cabriolet, En*).

CABRIOLE LEG

This, sometimes called a bandy leg, starts from just under the seat or table, curves outwards at the knee, which is often carved, and then curves backwards to the foot, tapering as it does so. Its origin is said to be uncertain, but there seems little doubt that it started with the Chinese bronze *ting*, an altar vessel on three legs of this kind, which first appeared in this form towards the end of the first millenium B.C. The *motif* was repeated as part of the design of porcelain vessels of similar form, often with painted or moulded masks on the knee, specimens of which had certainly reached Europe by the middle of the 17th century. The Dutch were the biggest importers of Chinese porcelain at the time, and the cabriole leg undoubtedly originated with them, coming to England with the accession of William and Mary. It was popular until the advent of the neo-classical style about 1760. In France it appears in a slightly modified form as part of the *Régence* and Louis XV styles, until it was replaced by the straight leg of the neo-classical period.

The word *cabriole* in French means 'to caper like a goat', and in its application to the chair-leg, the word seems to refer also to its likeness to the hind leg of a goat or satyr.

CABRIOLET EN (French)

A term introduced during the 18th century to designate chairs with a curved back which were not fixed in their position by custom or etiquette, as were chairs described as '*à la reine*' which had a fixed position in the interior scheme.

CACHEMIRE STYLE

The Delft potter, Lambertus van Eenhoorn, may have invented the style known as *cachemire*, which was also much used by his competitor, Louwis

Cabriole Leg. A Chinese bronze cauldron of the Han Dynasty (206 B.C. to A.D. 220) on three 'cabriole' legs of the type later copied in porcelain.

Cabriole Leg. Cabriole leg carved with a satyr mask on the knee and a lion-paw foot. English. c. 1730. *Mereworth Castle, Kent.*

Fictoor. The pattern appears on large, reeded *potiches*, and consists of *lambrequins, jardinières* filled with flowers, reserve painting, and scattered birds and flowers. Louwis Fictoor also painted in blue-and-white and signed his work with a monogram *LF*, not to be confused with Lambertus's *LVE*. His shapes were inclined to be bizarre, and the pieces often rather heavily decorated, but his colour sense was unequalled. On the other hand the quality of his potting falls below that of Lambertus Eenhoorn through deficiencies in the glaze and the hard dryness of his pigments.

CADDY

A small box or receptacle intended to contain tea. Porcelain and pottery versions are sometimes termed tea-jars, and, quite incorrectly, teapoys (q.v.). Caddies were made in a great variety of materials, of which silver and tortoiseshell are perhaps the most highly valued, and the best caddies were objects of fine craftmanship. Those of wood are often in the form of a casket, with two lead-lined compartments, one for green and one for black tea, and frequently a space for a circular glass mixing-bowl has been provided between them. The word probably comes from the Chinese *catty*, a weight equivalent to a pound and a quarter.

CAFFAGGLIOLO (Near Florence, Italy)

Cosimo de Medici built a country-house at Caffaggiolo, and the *maiolica* factory established in the

Cabriolet, En. Fauteuil (q.v.) *en cabriolet* (with an incurved back) of the Louis XV period, part of a suite by Lebas. *Christie, Manson & Woods Ltd.*

Cabriolet, En. For comparison: a *fauteuil à la reine* (with a flat back) of the Louis Seize period. *Parke-Bernet Galleries, New York.*

Caffagiolo. Maiolica **dish decorated with grotesques, swans, and satyrs. c. 1515. Caffagiolo.** *Wallace Collection.*

town was under the patronage of the Medici family; documents mention its existence in 1485 and 1506. The earliest pieces (bearing the mark SPR perhaps *Semper*, from the Medici motto) to be associated with Caffaggiolo are dated 1507, 1509, and perhaps 1511 in the case of the famous plate depicting the *maiolica* painter at work, now in the Victoria and Albert Museum. This factory closed in 1570, probably when the Medici withdrew their patronage.

The finest work done at Caffaggiolo is as splendid in style and execution as befitted works perhaps commissioned by Cosimo and his heirs. The subject is usually confined to the centre of dishes, while the rim is decorated with grotesques and scrolls. A strong dark blue and a brownish-red are distinctive colours. Caffaggiolo also seems to have been able to produce the lustre normally found at Deruta (q.v.).

The known wares are nearly all plates, jugs and vessels generally being very rare. After 1540 the factory declined, but there are records of work done there as late as the mid-18th century.

CAFFIÉRI FAMILY, THE

A noted family of metalworkers and sculptors of Italian origin who worked in Paris in the 17th and 18th centuries.

Philippe I Caffiéri (1634–1716): He came to France at the invitation of Mazarin and became sculptor to Louis XIV.

Jacques Caffiéri (1687–1755): Son of Philippe I; *fondeur-ciseleur* working for the King, decorating the royal palaces. His work is sometimes signed *CAFFIÉRI*. He worked principally in a well-marked rococo style, making clock-cases, furniture-mounts, chandeliers, and so on, as well as some accomplished bronze portrait busts. Perhaps his best-known work as a maker of furniture-mounts is the *commode* which was acquired by Louis Quinze for his bedroom at Versailles in 1739. (Wallace Collection, London).

Philippe II Caffiéri (1714–1774): Eldest son of Jacques C., and a *fondeur ciseleur* who assisted his father, continuing to work for the royal palaces after the older man's death. Signed *P. CAFFIÉRI*

Jean-Jacques Caffiéri (1725–92): Son of Jacques C. He became sculptor to the King, working principally in marble. A pupil of his father's, and of J. B. Lemoyne, Caffiéri was admitted to the Academy in 1757, and became chief modeller to the Sèvres Porcelain Factory in succession to Falconet.

CALLOT, JACQUES (IL CALOTTO) (1593–1635)

Born at Nancy, Callot was renowned for his etchings, producing more than 1500 plates in his lifetime. Travelling to Italy about 1608 he made etchings of fêtes and fairs, depicting beggars and hunchbacks, as well as characters in the popular Commedia dell'Arte in a very typical bizarre style. These provided inspiration for works in many other fields, 'Callot dwarfs' occurring especially in the modelling of porcelain figures in the early years of the 18th century, and sometimes as painted decoration on faïence and porcelain. Callot returned to France in 1621, and his later work is in a much more serious vein.

CAMAÏEU, EN

Decoration in several shades and intensities of the same colour. Used of painting on porcelain and wall-decoration. (See *Grisaille, En.*)

Callot, Jacques. **Cup and saucer painted with figures after the engravings of Jacques Callot. Meissen. c. 1720.** *Mrs C. B. Stout, Memphis, Tenn.*

CAMEO GLASS

Cameo cutting is cutting in relief (see *Hochschnitt*). The Portland vase (q.v.) is an example of cameo glass, and this kind of work is done on glass of one colour cased with another colour or colours, the Portland vase being white on very dark blue. The methods employed are grinding with small rotating wheels charged with abrasive such as emery (these first being used probably about the 3rd century B.C. for cutting gems of semi-precious stones), and removing surplus material with hand-held tools pointed with a diamond. (See *Hardness of Materials*.)

Due to the very high degree of skill required, and the length of time needed to complete the work, the technique is now used but rarely, if ever, but it was fairly common in ancient times, and it was revived in the 19th century by, among others, John Northwood (1837–1902), who copied the Portland vase in glass. A commission to engrave a crystal glass vase, known as the Elgin vase from its subject, took eight years to complete, which is some indication of the amount of work involved and its delicacy. The Portland vase itself took three years, but in this Northwood was probably using hydrofluoric acid as a speedier means of removing surplus glass, an acid unknown to the Romans.

Northwood's son, John Northwood junior, also employed his father's techniques, his most notable

Candelabrum. One of a set of four candelabra of bronze and gilt-bronze in the Louis Seize style. French. c. 1780. *Wallace Collection*.

Candelabrum. One of a pair of seven-light silver candelabra in the Empire style. Note winged sphinxes at base. 1812. 930 ounces. By Benjamin Smith. *Christie, Manson & Woods Ltd.*

work being a plaque of the Birth of Aphrodite. The two men founded a school of glass engravers, one member of which, George Woodall (1850–1925), did some distinguished work after having been apprenticed to the Northwoods. Joshua Hodgett (1858–1933) specialized in floral decoration done with the engraving wheel, and he, too, was similarly apprenticed.

Genuine cameo glass (sometimes termed 'overlay' glass) of this period is rare, but it was reproduced on the Continent in a glass flashed with an opal layer, on the surface of which the pattern was formed in an acid-resisting varnish, the unprotected surface then being dissolved in hydrofluoric acid and the design finished summarily with engraving tools. The painting of designs in a thick white enamel on a dark background was the method adopted for making cheap imitations of cameo glass. (See *Bohemian glass*.)

CAMPAIGN FURNITURE

Portable furniture—chairs, tables, beds, and chests especially—intended for military use, and for travelling. Most surviving examples date from the Napoleonic Wars, and were intended for high-ranking officers, although portable furniture has always been made.

CANDELABRUM

An ornamental branched candlestick, made in sets for the dining-table. It can be of silver, Sheffield plate, gilt-bronze (ormolu), or of mixed materials, such as Wedgwood's jasper mounted in ormolu, the latter often fitted with cut-glass prisms. The term is very loosely used, and is sometimes applied to multi-branched candleholders attached to a mirror, or to a wall. When glass prisms form part of the decoration the candelabrum is often termed a *girandole* (q.v.).

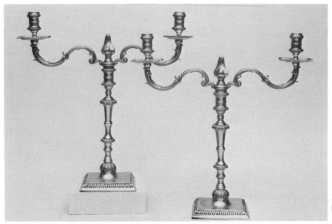

Candelabrum. **A pair of George III two-light candelabra in the Adam style. 1766. By William Cafe.** *Sotheby & Co.*

CANDLE

Candles of wax and tallow were a popular method of illumination in the great houses of former times. Rushlights, made from rushes dipped in fat, were in use in humbler homes, held in blacksmith-made holders of wrought iron. The skill of the metalworker in particular was employed to devise suitable implements for holding candles, but until the introduction of candles of a standard size in the 17th century, which led to the making of the candle-nozzle and drip-pan, most candles were very large, and the candlesticks were of the pricket variety, in which the candle was impaled on a spike. These, when intended for ecclesiastical use, were made in pairs. Candle-making was also a common village industry, and candle-moulds, and candle-boxes of wood intended to be hung on the wall to contain the domestic supply, are sometimes still to be found.

Candleholders have always been regarded as a subject for ornament, and superb examples of the metalworker's craft have been produced in great variety, ranging from the single candlestick to vast chandeliers intended to illuminate *salons,* from the simple chamber candlestick intended to light the owner to bed to multi-branched candelabra for the dining-table. They are to be found in wood, silver, brass, pewter, enamelled copper, *tôle* ware, glass, pottery, and porcelain.

CANDLE-BOX

A rectangular wooden box, often with a lid, designed to be hung on the wall and used for the storage of candles.

CANDLE-SNUFFERS

These, looking somewhat like a pair of scissors, were employed to trim wicks and extinguish candles. They were usually provided with a tray on which they stood when not in use, and in the 18th century an extinguisher in the form of a small cone-shaped cup with a handle to one side sometimes forms part of the snuffer set. They are to be found in silver and plated metal, and extinguishers occur also in porcelain.

CANDLESTICKS, METAL

Pricket candlesticks (see *Candles*) were nearly always tall, and often of wrought iron. Those of silver are a very rare survival, and some of the most famous are of bronze. These exist almost entirely in museums or cathedral treasuries, one of the finest being the Paschal Candlestick of Riccio (q.v.) in the Basilica of San Antonio of Padua. Candlesticks of silver with nozzle and drip-pan were introduced in the 17th century. They were usually made in sets of two or four, and were at first low in height. Before 1715 they were wrought, but after this date very often cast. The best of those made during the rococo period were extremely decorative; during the following Adam period the classical column was a frequent motif. Generally, the design of candlesticks follows the style of the period, but the baluster form is the one most commonly met. Variations include a slide device for ejecting the stump. Chamber candlesticks had the socket and drip-pan mounted on a saucer-shaped tray with a ring handle for carrying. A cone-shaped extinguisher was usually provided. American silver candlesticks only appear at the end

Candlesticks, Metal. **About 10 inches high. 1762.**

of the 17th century and are extremely rare. 18th-century examples are more common.

Candlesticks were also made of pewter, brass, Sheffield plate, and tôle ware, as well as wood, porcelain, and pottery.

CANNELÉ (French)
Silk fabric with a horizontal ribbing, occasionally enriched with gold or silver thread. *Côtelé* is similar, but with vertical ribbing.

CANTERBURY
The term first meant a kind of supper-tray with a tray-top, and a shelf below in three compartments to hold knives, forks, and plates. It was movable, and mounted on casters. During the 19th century the word was used to describe a music-stool with a receptacle for sheet-music, and it is often employed today to describe a variety of 19th-century stands with divisions for holding magazines.

CAPO-DI-MONTE PORCELAIN FACTORY
This Naples factory was started in 1743 under the patronage of Charles, King of Naples, who had married a daughter of Augustus III of Saxony.

The body used was a kind of soft paste porcelain, usually slightly cream in colour. Both figures and service ware are very rare, and the former bring extremely high prices. The chief modeller was Giuseppe Gricci, whose peasant figures are much sought, and his style can be recognized by the smallness of the heads. He also modelled Italian Comedy figures. Small wares include snuff-boxes and cane-handles.

A notable porcelain room (q.v.) formerly at the Portici Palace, was removed to the Capo-di-Monte Palace in 1805. This is decorated with porcelain from the factory.

Capo-di-Monte porcelain is usually unmarked, but it sometimes bears, in common with Buen Retiro (q.v.), the *fleur-de-lys*. Care is needed to distinguish between the two.

In the past a great deal of hard-paste porcelain decorated with figure subjects in relief, enamelled in colours, has been attributed to Capo-di-Monte. This is completely inaccurate. When of 18th-century date, porcelain of this kind came from the Doccia factory (q.v.). Most of it was made in the 19th century elsewhere, either in Naples, when it is usually marked with a crowned *N,* or in Germany. Later specimens are nearly always poor in quality.

The factory was removed, in 1759, to Spain, the new premises being at Buen Retiro, just outside Madrid. Spanish wares are sometimes attributed to the Italian factory, but the resemblances are generally small. (See *Doccia.*)

CARAFE
Bottle without a stopper, usually with a wider neck than customary for stoppered bottles, which was intended to hold either wine or water. Carafes were commonly made in England during the second half of the 18th century, when they were often called 'water crafts'. They were usually decorated, either with trailing or with simple wheel-engraving. They became unfashionable on the dining-table about 1800, but survived as a water vessel in the bedroom with a matching tumbler.

CARLIN, MARTIN (d. 1785)
Carlin became *maître ebéniste* in 1766, but beyond the fact that he made furniture for the royal family not a great deal is otherwise known of him. Some of his work utilizes ebony and lacquer, and he also employed the popular Sèvres plaques as a furniture

Capo-di-Monte Porcelain. The Spaghetti Eaters. Capo-di-Monte. c. 1750. *Sotheby & Co.*

Carlin, Martin. A superb Louis XVI oval *guéridon* in the style of Martin Carlin with a top of Sèvres porcelain, the legs united with a contemporary *tôle* (q.v.) tray. A type of table called, in France, *ambulante* (q.v.), and in England 'occasional'. *Sotheby & Co.*

ornament. He worked for the dealers Poirier and Daguerre, and is especially noted for the quality of his bronze mounts. Stamp: *M. CARLIN*.

CARLTON HOUSE DESK
A writing-table first made at the end of the 18th century, having drawers and pigeon-holes on the top, across the back then curving round on either side to the front. This type was first made by Gillow for the Prince of Wales, who was then living at Carlton House, London.

CARPETS, EMBROIDERED See *Embroidery*

CARPETS, EUROPEAN
Oriental carpets were known in Europe from comparatively early times, many brought back by Crusaders, but they were at first only used as bed and table covers and wall-hangings. Those used as floor-coverings were termed 'foot-carpets', and these first make their appearance in the inventory of Cardinal Wolsey (1471–1530), but it was many years before they came into general use for this purpose.

The earliest carpets to be made in Europe are termed Hispano-Moresque, and were woven in Spain during the Moorish occupation. These could hardly be called European by strict definition, and they were very much akin to Turkish carpets of the period in technique and pattern.

Manufacture of pile-carpets in Europe was started in France at the beginning of the 17th century with the establishment of looms for the purpose in the Louvre by Henri IV. This enterprise was later transferred to La Savonnerie, and was brought, in 1662, under the same management as the Gobelins tapestry looms. The workshops were removed to the avenue des Gobelins in 1826. Large pile-carpets, coarsely woven with the Ghiordes knot (see: *Rugs, Knotting of*) in the Turkish manner, were made for the Louvre and for Versailles until the end of the reign of Louis XV; most of its products were reserved for royal châteaux, and as gifts presented to foreign royalty and ambassadors. Piled coverings for seat-furniture were made, but this was rare. Knotted carpets were also made for a few years at Beauvais towards the end of the 18th century, and at Aubusson and nearby Felletin. Beauvais, Gobelins, Aubusson, and Felletin also made tapestry carpets, technically somewhat in the manner of Near Eastern Khilims (q.v.).

The manufacture of the pile-carpet was introduced into England at Kidderminster about 1750, but the most important English carpets of this kind were woven by Mr Moore of Chiswell Street, Moorfields, London. They were knotted in the Turkish manner. Moore worked for the Adam Brothers, and his carpets are to be found in some of the great houses of England, notably Syon House, Middlesex. Axminster carpets were first made in England by Thomas Whitley in 1755, and were usually designed for a particular room.

European carpets which can be dated before 1840 are extremely rare and correspondingly expensive, very high prices being asked for the few 18th-century survivals. They were hardly cheap at the time, 250 guineas being asked for a Moorfields carpet, which is equivalent to about £2,000 today.

Carpets, European. **An Aubusson carpet in the Empire style with a lettuce-green field. c. 1820.** *Parke-Bernet Galleries, New York.*

Carpets, Oriental. An Azerbaijan (S.E. Caucasian) silk rug woven with couplets praising the Sultan Nader Shah Afshar. Dated 1745. *Sotheby & Co.*

CARPETS, ORIENTAL

These are always in demand for use with schemes of interior decoration utilizing English antique furniture. They harmonize less well with French furniture, where an Aubusson carpet is usually more appropriate.

Oriental carpets come in all shapes and sizes: saddlebags, runners, prayer-rugs, and large carpets made for export to fit European room-sizes. Very few are antique, and those which are more than fifty years old are usually too valuable to put on a floor, except in places where there is no traffic. Much the same may be said of silk rugs, which are often used as wall-hangings.

There are a number of major classifications and many minor ones. The major ones are considered here under the headings of Turkish, Persian, Caucasian, Turcoman, Chinese, and Indian. The minor ones, belonging to one or other of these groups, are listed under the main headings.

Most Oriental rugs and carpets have a pile. The foundation is a large number of vertical parallel threads, crossed and interwoven with a similar series of horizontal parallel threads. The former is known as the warp, and the latter as the weft. The pile consists of short lengths of wool, camel hair, goat hair, or silk, or a mixture of them, which are looped or tied through adjacent warp threads, the ends being free and left as tufts which are afterwards clipped with scissors (see *Rugs, Knotting of*). The weft threads are used to locate the knots horizontally. The quality of a rug is partly estimated by the number of knots per square inch. Twenty is very coarse, and the finest rugs go up to 250 or more. The closest weaves are Persian. Turkeys vary from about 20 knots to the square inch to 80. Chinese average about 45, Beluchistan about 55, Caucasian up to 70, Kirman and Tabriz about 80, Bokhara about 80 (although the best Tekke Bokharas are much finer than this), Kashan about 250, and so on. These are average figures, and are not intended to be regarded as invariable. The finer the weave, the more detailed the pattern.

An Oriental rug should have the following points: the dyes must be of good colour and 'fast'; it must show few signs of wear, and certainly the pile should not be worn down to the foundation: the patterns should be pleasing and the design well balanced. Value will be increased by exceptional qualities of design. Very old rugs will naturally be worth far more than comparatively new ones. It has been suggested, as a rough guide, that the value should be doubled for each century of age. Few really old rugs exist, and wear is certainly not evidence of age. To date a rug is very much a job for the expert. It is doubtful whether any rug can be said to have a worth-while antique value unless it was made before the introduction of aniline dyes into the industry in 1870. These now largely take the place of the older vegetable dyes. Some of them are quite as good as the vegetable dyes they replaced, but others are apt to fade excessively with exposure to sunlight, or to run if wetted. A clean, wet pad rubbed on the pile should show no sign of colour if the dyes are reasonably fast. Aniline colours are inclined to make the pile brittle and to reduce wearing qualities of the rug. Rugs which are excessively bright in colour are sometimes 'washed' (q.v.) to subdue it.

When buying Oriental rugs for furnishing there are a few points worth remembering. The rug should be inspected for condition. If the foundation has been exposed to damp it may be rotten, so a suspected part should be pulled with the fingers. If it is rotten, it will tear. There is no remedy for a worn pile. If the rug is sufficiently valuable a small area can be re-piled, but this is expensive and only worth while with outstanding specimens. Holes are difficult and expensive to repair, but cuts and tears to a foundation otherwise in good condition can be sewn up inconspicuously. The pattern should be inspected to make sure that nothing has been cut away. Frayed ends are sometimes cut off and the cut edge overcast. Threads from the pile of a used rug should not come away when it is brushed vigorously. This is a fault very common with commercial Indian rugs which often persists throughout their short life. Colours must be clear and definite and should not have run into one another. If this is seen it suggests bad dyes in the first place and continued use in a damp place. Stains are usually irremovable without removing the colour from the stained area of the pile. For instance, what will remove ink will almost certainly remove the dye from the wool as well. A small stained area can be repiled, and stains are sometimes disguised with paint. If the pile of a rug is shorter than its provenance suggests it ought to be, it has probably been cut. This is sometimes done with a very dirty rug, but its life is correspondingly short, and its value much diminished.

These remarks are specifically intended to apply to rugs made within the last fifty years or so and used for furnishing. The purchase of an antique rug is something quite different, to which different criteria of judgment apply. Many old rugs are so tender that it would be impossible to put them to practical use, even if it were desirable, and if the pattern is of especial interest a degree of wear is accepted which would cause the instant rejection of a furnishing rug. Antique rugs are infinitely better in design and colour than those of more recent manufacture. With the increasing popularity of the Oriental rug in Western countries factories grew up to make them, and Western influence on sizes and patterns had a degenerative effect in many cases, although, as with the Zieglers (q.v.), European influence was sometimes salutary. The transmission of patterns has gone on through the centuries, and the various rug-making districts have developed a characteristic repertory of patterns and colours which enable their work to be identified within limits, and a tentative date awarded. As an approximate guide Turkish, Caucasian, and Turcoman designs are usually geometric, and Persian designs more naturalistic and less angular. Markedly angular *motifs* are an especial characteristic of Caucasian rugs, where the latch-hook (q.v.) is almost invariable. Religion has a considerable effect

Cartel. Cartel clock in gilded bronze case by Charles Cressent. The subject is *Love Triumphing over Time*, and the style is rococo. The subject was a popular one for clocks during the 18th century, and was employed by several bronzeworkers from Boulle onwards. c. 1740.

on the patterns used. Strongly orthodox areas such as Turkey avoid anything which might be interpreted as a representation of a living thing, plant or animal, except in a form so stylized that it is difficult to be sure of the original inspiration. The Persians, inclined to be heretical, tend to rely more on natural forms, although the technique of weaving the piled rug always leads to some stylization of design.

Rugs are of various kinds. The most important classification is the prayer-rug (q.v.), to be identified by the niche or *mihrab* (q.v.), the point of which is, in use, turned towards Mecca. The *mihrab* represents the entrance to the mosque. Some prayer-rugs, however, have three small medallions, one for each knee and one for the head, which replace the *mihrab*. Patterns which resemble a double-ended *mihrab* are often hearth or tent rugs. Grave-rugs, used to cover the dead before burial, often have a stylized cypress as part of the pattern. This is a sign of mourning sometimes used in Christian cemeteries in southern Europe in parts which were once in close contact with Islam. 'Mecca' rugs are those which, after the pilgrimage to Mecca, were offered to a mosque. Many were made at Shiraz, and they are often termed 'Mecca Shiraz' by dealers, although the term has very little meaning.

Most carpets are comparatively modern, and large ones are apt to be expensive because of the difficulty of handling them on the looms.

A type of carpet comparatively rare in the West

is the Khilim (q.v.), which is a tapestry, or pileless, rug resembling the Aubusson, the weft being used to form the pattern. The Soumac (q.v.) is also a tapestry weave, but is rarely seen in the West.

'CARRACK' PORCELAIN

Blue-and-white Chinese porcelain brought to Europe in Portuguese ships known as carracks is termed 'carrack' porcelain. The decoration is that of the period of the Emperor Wan-li (1573–1619), and the ware is thin, hard, crisp, resonant, and painted in a greyish-blue. This kind of porcelain was looted by the Dutch soon after 1600 from returning Portuguese ships, and sold by them throughout Europe. It was termed '*kraak porselein*' in Holland, where it was also copied in tin-glazed ware at Delft.

CARTEL (French)

In French heraldry the word *cartel* denotes a shield. By extension, the word was sometimes employed for objects similarly shaped, and especially, during the 18th century, for wall-clocks of this kind.

The cases of *cartel* clocks can be of gilt-bronze, faïence, or of marquetry in the manner of Boulle. Perhaps the most famous bronze *cartel* clocks are those of Cressent, with the subject of *Love vanquishing Time,* of which there is an example in the Wallace Collection (London) and another in the Louvre. Small *cartels* with watch-movements attached to the bedhead were called *cartel de chevet.* The *cartel* clock was also known as a *pendule en cartel.*

Carver Chair. Carver chair of oak. New England. c. 1650. *Wadsworth Atheneum.*

CARVER

(Generally). A man carving ornament on furniture and other objects of wood made by the carpenter (in France, by the *menuisier*). In 18th-century England the craft was combined with that of the gilder, but carvers had virtually disappeared from the furniture-trade by the accession of Queen Victoria in 1837 due to the invention of machines for this kind of work.

(English furniture). A name given to chairs with arms provided with the set of dining-room chairs. They were placed at top and bottom of the table and occupied by the person carving.

CARVER CHAIRS (American)

A chair with arms entirely made up from turned sections fitting into each other; the name is said to be derived from one in the possession of Governor Carver. A slightly more elaborate variety is sometimes termed a Brewster chair.

CARYATIDS

Female figures used in place of columns to support the pediment of a building in classical times, and, in Renaissance times in particular, as part of the decoration of certain kinds of furniture based on architectural designs. Atlantes are male statues used for

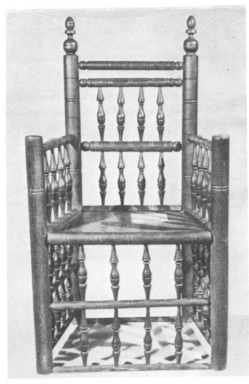

Carver Chair. Brewster chair made in New England. It may have belonged to William Bradford (1590–1657), governor of the Plymouth Colony. The front posts were originally surmounted by knobs. *Pilgrim Society, Plymouth, Mass.*

Caryatids. Caryatid supports to a chimmey-piece at Osterley Park (W. London). Osterley is a Jacobean house remodelled by the Adam Brothers.

the same purpose, and also occur, but less frequently, as furniture decoration.

CASED GLASS
The most important existing specimen of cased glass is the Portland vase (q.v.). This aptly illustrates the principle, since it began as an urn of dark blue glass which was subsequently cased with opaque white glass. The white layer was then cut away where needed to form the decoration, exposing the dark blue beneath.

Cased glass in modern times was first made in Bohemia in 1815. In the earliest variety vessels were cased with glass of several colours, and subsequent grinding yielded a marbled effect. Glass cased in a single colour, the decoration engraved on the wheel, was also made, but this was the most expensive variety. The factories specialized in transparent glass flashed with a thin film of coloured glass, usually ruby red, the flashing subsequently ground away in facets, or the decoration cut through the outer layer to reveal clear glass beneath in the same way as the cased variety. Much work of excellent quality utilized this technique.

By the 1830s cased glass was being made in England, but it did not become widespread until after the removal of the Excise Duty on glass in 1845. From 1845 to about 1870 the quantity manufactured was very great. A variety of colours and shades were employed in varying combinations, and as many as five layers were sometimes used, although three

were the more customary. The decoration was cut through the intervening layers to the clear glass beneath by the usual techniques. Vases are comparatively rare, the best by George Bacchus & Sons of Birmingham, and toilet-bottles and decanters are fairly common. Black glass overlaid with white, with added gilding, is a rare combination not often seen.

The Bohemian technique of flashing with clear glass was adopted in England in the 1850s.

CASSAPANCA (Italian)
A dual-purpose piece of Renaissance furniture, chiefly Florentine, made by adding arms and a back to a *cassoni* (q.v.), turning it into a bench (*banca*). Most specimens date from the middle to the end of the 16th century.

CASSEL (Germany) FAÏENCE FACTORY
A factory was in existence at Cassel as early as 1680 It was founded by George Kumpfe, and changed hands frequently till, in 1724, it was taken over by Johann Christoph Gilze and, after 1735, by his son Ludwig. Finally its financial difficulties were such that the Landgrave of Hesse took it over, and faïence was produced until 1766, when it was superseded by porcelain manufacture. No products from the first period are known, but the early blue-and-white wares are in the style of Delft, then of Hanau (q.v.). Some coloured wares were produced in the 'sixties, and it may also have made stoves. The mark is a monogram of the letters *HL* for Hessenland.

CASSEL (HESSE-NASSAU) PORCELAIN FACTORY
This factory was established in 1766 with the help of Nikolaus Paul (q.v.) and the patronage of the Landgrave of Hesse, Friedrich II. By 1769 it was advertising for sale coffee and tea services in blue and colours, reeded and smooth, but most surviving specimens are blue-painted. The most sought examples of the work of this small factory, however, are its figures, although it is difficult to identify the modellers. Sauerlandt illustrates a figure of Autumn and names the modeller as Johann Baptist Xaveri. Franz Josef Hess and Friedrich Künckler also modelled for Cassel, but their work has not been certainly identified. The body is a chalky-white in colour. The factory closed in 1788. The Cassel mark of the lion somewhat resembles the lion of Frankenthal, except that it has a double tail.

CASSOLETTES
Vases of porcelain or metal with a pierced cover, usually intended as pastil burners. The *cassolette* was sometimes designed to evaporate the perfume by means of gentle heat supplied by a spirit or oil lamp. In the 18th century the covers were often reversible, one side being fitted with a candleholder.

CASSONE (Italian)
A large chest or coffer, usually a marriage coffer used to store the linen which the bride brought as

part of her dowry. During the 15th century the framework of the *cassone* was comparatively simple in design. The long rectangular front panel was painted, often by artists of considerable merit, and usually there was a niche at either end in which stood a carved figure. The unpainted wood was gilded over a *gesso* ground. By 1500 carving was beginning to play a much more important part in the decoration of the *cassone,* the paintings becoming smaller and set in panels with carved work between. In some instances the painted panels were replaced by those of marquetry (*intarsia*) usually architectural in subject. As the 16th century progressed carved work became richer, and mythological subjects were sometimes done in plain wood with gold ground. The fashionable grotesques (q.v.) also made their appearance. The later *cassone* of polished wood elaborately carved is often in the form of a classical sarcophagus with lion-paw feet.

During the 16th century the *cassone* began to develop in several directions. The addition of a back and arms converted it to the practical purpose of providing somewhere to sit. In Venice the front was sometimes provided with massive doors which open to reveal drawers.

Cassoni were usually made in pairs, especially when they were marriage chests, and they bore the Arms, where appropriate, of the husband on one and of the wife on the other.

CASTEL DURANTE (Near Urbino, Italy)

Several pieces of *maiolica* are known to have been made at Castel Durante and signed by the artists before 1520, but clearly marked pieces do not occur before 1524. They are decorated with figures

Cassolettes. A pierced bronze cassolette from Venice, 16th century. The arabesques ornamenting the central part are influenced by Near Eastern sources, while the lion-paw feet terminate in acanthus leaves in the manner of contemporary grotesque ornament (q.v.).

from Biblical or classical stories, very much in the style to be found at Urbino, and possibly by the hand of Nicola Pellipario who left Castel Durante for Urbino perhaps in 1527. Many potters who later appear elsewhere seem to have started their working life at Castel Durante, especially those who went subsequently to Urbino. The mark 'da Castel Durante' does not mean that a piece was made there, but indicates rather its author's origin. If the phrase used is 'in Castel Durante', with a date, its origin is more certain.

After Nicola Pellipario (its chief figure-painter) had gone to Urbino, Castel Durante specialized in more abstract ornament, but it is difficult to say whether the embossed dishes and the *bianco sopra bianco* mentioned by Picolpasso are necessarily from Castel Durante as they were made at Faenza and other places as well. It is, however, generally agreed that trophies painted *en grisaille* were a speciality of the town.

Castel Durante dishes are of a pale, rather muddy coloured yellow clay, usually undecorated on the backs, while the rim is bordered with yellow or grey when the design is purely ornamental. Pale colours are typical.

Little is known of 17th- and 18th century production at Castel Durante. In 1635 the name of the town was changed to Urbania by Pope Urban VII, and later wares show a marked influence of Castelli (q.v.).

CASTELLI (Abruzzi, Italy)

Nothing can be certainly attributed to Castelli till the early years of the 17th century, and during the 17th and 18th centuries a number of potteries were at work here producing *maiolica* which was, for the most part, a continuation of the traditional *istoriato* style. Blue-and-white, made during the early part of the 17th century, is scarce and difficult to attribute with certainty. The best wares were probably painted by the Grue and Gentili families late in the 17th century and the first half of the 18th. Those by the Grue, for the most part, are landscapes, often with mythological figures, in a high-temperature palette. Similar work was done by the Gentili family, and attributions are largely on grounds of style. Much Castelli *maiolica* is in the form of large, decorative dishes, but drug-jars and vases with plastic decoration were also made. Specimens signed by members of both families survive, and help to attribute some of the wares. After 1750 little of importance was done, but the potteries survived here into the 19th century and imitated some of the older works.

CASTERS

Small vessels of silver, generally of cylindrical or baluster form with a pierced removable top, principally used for sugar and pepper. The piercing is often of exceptional quality and very ornamental. Casters were first made in England towards the end of the 17th century, and are at their best during the reign of Queen Anne. Eighteenth-century specimens by

Casters. A set of three silver casters by Benjamin Pyne. 1702.

American silversmiths are not excessively rare. They occur also in other metals, notably Sheffield plate, and some rare speciments in faïence and porcelain based on silver shapes have been recorded. They were made in China in porcelain to European order, but examples are very few.

CASTERS (FURNITURE)
Small wheels, fitted with swivels, attached to the feet of furniture too heavy to lift easily but required to be moved often, such as armchairs and settees. They

Casters. Caster of Chinese export porcelain based on a French silver shape. Reign of the Emperor K'ang Hsi (1662–1722).

were introduced in England early in the 18th century, and appeared in America soon afterwards. Early furniture fitted with the original casters is rare.

CATTANEO, DANESE (1509–1573)
An Italian sculptor working at Venice. He was a pupil of Jacopo Sansovino (q.v.). Among his small bronzes is a *Marine Venus* in the Louvre.

CAUCASIAN RUGS
This area of southern Russia, between the Black Sea and the Caspian, has been a rug-weaving centre for millennia, and some of the patterns are probably distantly derived from ancient Assyrian rugs known from relief sculpture. Early Caucasian rugs are rare, but since about 1929 many of new manufacture with traditional patterns have been made and exported by Soviet trading organizations. Most of these are of excellent quality, but piled on a cotton foundation instead of the wool foundation of older rugs.

The principal characteristics of Caucasian rugs generally are their severely angular patterns, which have no curving elements whatever. Prayer-rugs are woven with a stylized *mihrab* (q.v.). There are three main varieties: the Kazak, the Shirvan, and the Daghestan rug, although there are a number of other places of minor importance. Kazak rugs, made near Mount Ararat by Cossack nomads, are bright in colour with a fairly long pile. The pile of the Shirvan is shorter. The Daghestan rug is often more closely woven than either of the other two, with a short pile. All are woven with the Ghiordes knot, and the latch hook (q.v.) almost invariably appears somewhere in the pattern. (See *Rugs, Knotting of.*)

CAUGHLEY, SHROPSHIRE
This factory, near Broseley, was established soon after 1750 for the manufacture of earthenware. It becomes of interest in 1772 when, passing into the hands of Thomas Turner, the manufacture of porcelain was started. From 1775 Robert Hancock, formerly of Worcester (q.v.), was associated with it, and transfer-printing in blue underglaze became the most common form of decoration. A soaprock body was employed, and Caughley products are sometimes difficult to distinguish from those of Worcester, especially as the Caughley enterprise deliberately copied the work of the latter factory. The Willow pattern and the Broseley Blue Dragon, both in use today, are said to have been devised by Thomas Minton who was apprenticed to Turner as an engraver. Both are based on Chinese patterns, but are in no sense copies. The blue pigment employed at Caughley varies a little in shade from that of Worcester, being a brighter and somewhat purer blue than the Worcester colour, which is inclined to be blackish. A slight pattern of flower-sprigs was derived from Chantilly, and the later wares of this factory were sometimes copied. Gilding was commonly used in conjunction with blue-and-white wares, and similarly gilded blue painted wares of Chinese origin look deceptively like those of Caughley at first

Caughley, Shropshire. A blue-and-white mask-jug, the form derived from Worcester, transfer-printed with a Chinese scene. c. 1780. *Victoria and Albert Museum.*

sight. Caughley porcelain decorated in polychrome appears to have been painted at the decorating studio of Humphrey Chamberlain (see *Outside Decorators*). The commonest mark, a capital *C*, is often drawn to look like a Worcester crescent, and the crescent appears on some Caughley wares. The word 'Salopian' sometimes occurs as an impressed mark.

The factory was sold to John Rose of Coalport in 1799.

CAYLUS, ANN-CLAUDE-PHILIPPE DE TUBIÈRES, COMTE DE (1692–1765)

One of the arbiters of taste in mid-18th century France, and a firm adherent of classicism who advocated a return to classical styles during the currency of rococo. Caylus was a collector of antiquities who wrote an important book on classical and Egyptian art, the *Recueil d'Antiquités Égyptiennes, Étrusques, Grecques, Romaines, et Gauloises*, published in five volumes between 1752 and 1755, which was extremely influential. He wrote a biographical essay with Watteau as its subject in which he reveals his own taste for history-painting in the grand classical manner. (See *Neo-classical Style, The.*)

CEDAR

Cedar was especially popular during the reign of Charles II. It was valued for the making of chests and similar storage furniture because of its aromatic and insect-repellant qualities.

CELADON GLAZE

The true Chinese celadon glaze is the product of covering a stoneware body with a ferruginous slip (q.v.) before adding a feldspathic glaze. Subsequent firing produces a colour which is usually a much valued shade of green, and in that sense the term is used in this book, although true celadons can be very variable in shade, and range from putty colour, through greens of various shades, to olive, even though the technique in every case is the same. The green examples are those most commonly seen in Europe, and the first celadons to be exported were made at Lung Ch'üan during the Sung dynasty (960–1280). Most of the celadons prized in the 18th century however, and lavishly mounted in gilt-bronze (see *Mounts, Metal, to Pottery and Porcelain*), were of contemporary green glazed porcelain made at the Imperial factory at Ch'ing-tê-Chên.

Celadon stoneware was particularly sought outside China because it was reputed to have the property of changing colour or breaking if poisoned food were put into it. It probably derives its name from the fact that the Sultan of Egypt, Nur-ed-din, sent forty dishes of this ware to the Sultan of Damascus, Salah-ed-din (the Saladin of the Crusades), in 1171. It has also been suggested that the name derives from a character in the 17th-century French romance, *L'Astrée*, a shepherd whose name was Céladon and who wore a greyish-green costume. This, however, is unlikely.

Decoration is nearly always by means of incised or carved ornament beneath the glaze, although in the 18th century some large vases of porcelain were decorated with alternating panels of celadon green and white, the latter painted in underglaze blue or enamels. These are not infrequent.

Early specimens have a brown rim and foot-ring, referred to by the Chinese as a 'brown mouth and iron foot', but although the unglazed foot-ring is sometimes coloured on 18th-century porcelain specimens, the glazed rim is always white. Most late celadons of porcelain only resemble early examples superficially.

Much of the finest mounted porcelain of the 18th century consisted of vases and bowls of celadon, and the account books of Lazare Duvaux (q.v.) mention them frequently.

CELERY VASES

Tall glass vessels on a short stem and low foot for holding sticks of celery. Most were decorated with

Celadon Glaze. A pair of celadon vases of archaic jade form mounted in gilt-bronze in the neo-classical style of Louis XVI, probably to designs by Delafosse.

73

ornamental faceting and wheel-engraving. Introduced late in the 18th century, they continued to be made both in England and Ireland during the early years of the 19th. They have also been made in modern times.

CELLARET
A deep drawer in a sideboard for the storage of wine-bottles.

CELLINI, BENVENUTO (1500–1571)
Italian goldsmith, sculptor, and medallist whom Michelangelo called the greatest sculptor in the world. He was, without doubt, the greatest metalworker of the Renaissance. Cellini is especially well known for his *Memoirs*, written between 1558 and 1562, of which several English translations exist. His *Treatise* on the goldsmith's art, of which an English translation was made about sixty years ago, is indispensable for the information it gives about metalworking at the time. His best-known work is the *Perseus* (1545–54) in the Loggia dei Lanzi, Florence, and his *Nymph of Fontainebleau*, made for the château d'Anet, is now in the Louvre. A gold salt made for François I is in the Kunsthistorisches Museum, Vienna. Cellini was invited to France, to the Court of François I, in 1537, and again in 1540, when he stayed for five years.

Few of his works now survive, but a small bronze thought to be by his hand was sold at Sothebys in 1968.

CENTAUR
An animal of classical mythology with the body of a horse and the head and torso of a human being, which replaces the horse's head and neck.

CERAMICS
(German *Keramik;* French *céramique.*) From the Greek *Keramos*, a potter's earth, this term is generally employed to refer to any material made of fired clay. Pronounced *Keramic.*

CERTOSINA (Italian)
Inlaid decoration of ivory or bone, usually of arabesques and stylized ornament generally. The origin appears to have been Damascus and Cairo where the technique was popular for the decoration of furniture, and the influence of the Near East is usually apparent in Italian work.

CHAIR, CURULE
This, the Roman *sella curulis*, was originally a folding stool of X-shape, often of bronze and sometimes with a low back. The most famous survival is the 6th-century chair of Dagobert in the Louvre, which has a back and arms added in the 12th century. The type was popular among Renaissance furniture-makers, and again during the currency of the early 19th-century Empire style (q.v.).

CHAIRS À LA CAPUCIN (French)
Rush-seated chairs. At first only to be found in the provinces, but, especially in the 18th century, they came to be used even in the great houses, particularly in the servants' quarters.

CHAIRS, COUNTRY, ENGLISH
It is necessary to distinguish between country chairs and those made in the provinces to metropolitan designs. Country-made 'Chippendale' is familiar enough, and specimens distantly echoing mid-18th-century mahogany chairs in beech and similar woods are not difficult to find. The true country chair, however, is best represented by the Windsor or stick-back chair, so called because it seems first to have been made in or around Windsor (Buckinghamshire). This lent itself to mass-production methods, and assembly from components which were made, for the most part, on the wood-turning lathe. The method of manufacture necessarily dictated that few changes could be made in the basic design in response to current fashion, and apart from certain variations, such as the shape of the cresting of the back, the occasional addition of a central splat usually based on that to be found on walnut Queen Anne chairs, the disposition of the arms, and so forth, the Windsor chair altered little from the time of its first manufacture at the beginning of the 18th century to well into the 19th. The ease of manufacture, and therefore its cheapness, made Windsor chairs popular, and they first appear in America, made around Philadelphia, about 1725. Here they were especially popular, and the principle was later extended to settees and beds, as well as to small tables with turned legs and stretchers (q.v.) made to match the chairs.

Another type of chair which lent itself to mass-production was the ladder-back (or slat-back), the design based on a much more ornate type of chair popular on the Continent in the second half of the 17th century. In England the inspiration was probably Netherlandish, the idea being brought by Dutch craftsmen at the end of the 17th century. Here the back is comprised of flat, horizontal rails supported by two uprights which look rather like a ladder, from which the name is derived. The ladder-back was also popular in America, where the first examples date from the end of the 17th century, and here, too, the idea was probably brought by Dutch settlers. These were usually provided with rush seats instead of the solid wood saddle-cut seat of the Windsor chair.

The Derbyshire or Yorkshire spindle-back is also a country chair, but usually of much better quality of workmanship than either of the other two.

CHAIRS, ROCKING
This type of chair is more or less confined to America, where it seems to have originated. Perhaps the earliest are some surviving specimens of ladder-back chairs of rustic workmanship mounted on rockers which are sometimes thought

to be as early as about 1700, but the first rocking-chairs which can be certainly dated are at least a century older. The majority are almost indistinguish-able from ordinary chairs or armchairs with rockers added, but Michael Thonet (q.v.) of Vienna de-veloped a bentwood rocking chair carried on curved supports. During the late Victorian period rockers mounted on springs were introduced.

CHAIR-TABLE

A 17th-century armchair, the back of which is a circular table-top hinged on the arms which can be lowered to form a table. Today it is sometimes called a monk's seat, but without any historical justification.

In America the Jacobean chair-table was made of oak, where it had obvious popularity in houses of limited space—often only a single room.

CHAISE-LONGUE (French)

The *chaise-longue* resembling an armchair with a long seat, was upholstered and lavishly provided with cushions. A type of day-bed (*lit de repos*), the *chaise-longue* was introduced after 1740 in France, and often has the rounded end referred to as *en gondole*. The frame followed the style of seat-furniture of the period. The *chaise-longue* is com-paratively rare, and it was largely replaced after the middle of the 18th century by the *duchesse brisée* (q.v.).

CHALKWARE (1850–1890)

A name given in America to mantel ornaments made of plaster of Paris in imitation of more expensive pottery and porcelain figures popular in the 18th and 19th centuries. Chalkware was first imported from Europe, then made throughout America. In the 19th century centres of manufacture were London and New York.

Chalkware could not be glazed. The earliest examples were sized, and coloured by hand using oil or watercolours. Subjects were usually made in pairs—cats, dogs, cockerels, sheep, goats, rabbits, deer, squirrels, single or double birds, especially doves, and fruit pyramided in urns. (See *Plaster of Paris*.)

CHAMBERS, SIR WILLIAM (1726–96)

Born in Stockholm of an English father, Sir William Chambers became architect to George III and a designer of furniture. His best-known work in architecture is Somerset House (London). He was one of the last of the Palladians (q.v.), and he published an influential *Treatise on Civil Architecture* in 1759. In his youth he travelled to China as a supercargo, i.e. cargo supervisor, for the East India Company, and subsequently visited Italy. He pub-lished *Designs for Chinese Buildings, Furniture, &c.* in 1757 which were much more faithful to their inspiration than most designs of the kind, and his *Dissertations on Oriental Gardening* in 1772 was not only influential, but played a distinct part in the development of the later Romantic style. He designed

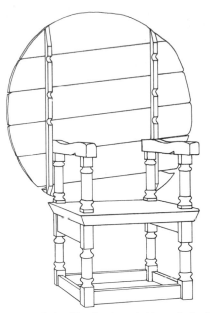

Chair-Table. Chair-table of oak, probably made in Con-necticut between 1650 and 1675. The columnar turning is rare; the baluster form is customary. Dual-purpose pieces of this type were popular in houses of limited space. *Smithsonian Institution, Washington, D.C.*

the famous Pagoda in Kew Gardens (London). Chambers employed Benoni Thacker as a cabinet-maker and Samuel Alker as carver.

CHAMPION, RICHARD (1743–1791)

English porcelain manufacturer, with a factory at Bristol. The history of porcelain manufacture at Bristol after the transference of the first factory to Worcester is very obscure, and the possibility of the existence of another factory, or factories, cannot be ruled out on the evidence. A letter written by Champion strongly suggests that a true porcelain factory existed for a short time about 1765, prob-ably doing experimental work for Cookworthy (q.v.). Cookworthy and Champion had seemingly reached a business understanding, if not a partner-ship, by 1770, since they first made each other's acquaintance in 1764. In 1772 Cookworthy retired from the Bristol enterprise, and in 1774 he assigned his patent to Champion. Soon afterwards Champion petitioned the House of Commons to extend the patent rights for a further period of fourteen years, and he was only successful after he had overcome the opposition raised by Josiah Wedgwood (q.v.) and the Staffordshire potters, who were themselves interested in porcelain manufacture. The expense of contesting this opposition proved too great for Champion's finances, and in 1778 he sought to sell his rights, when he was assisted by Wedgwood, who introduced him to a company of Staffordshire potters who, soon afterwards, started a factory at New Hall (q.v.).

Champion became Deputy-Paymaster-General of the Forces, which lasted until 1784, after which he emigrated to South Carolina, dying there in 1791.

Chandelier. An eagle surmounting a carved wood and gilt chandelier of the George II period. English. c. 1740. *Sotheby & Co.*

CHANDELIERS, GLASS

Glass chandeliers ornamented with pendant drops were preceded by those of rock-crystal (q.v.), like those which hung in the Galerie des Glaces at Versailles, and it is significant that Ravenscroft's lead-glass was said, at the time, to resemble rock-crystal in its power of light refraction. Cutting, engraving, and grinding were the customary ways of ornamenting rock-crystal, which were later taken over by the workers in glass.

Glass chandeliers were in use in Venice in the 17th century. These were not the chandeliers with which we are familiar today, but a bronze foundation almost completely covered by such ornamental *motifs* as glass flowers and leaves. In England, where the making of glass chandeliers was probably at its best, they seem to have been introduced in a simplified form before 1714, although the exact date cannot be determined. The early manufacture seems to have been in the hands of bevellers of glass mirrors, probably because they had the necessary equipment and were accustomed to the grinding of glass. The chandelier became much more in demand as the 18th century progressed, and it increased in elaboration. Branches were added about 1730, curving, and usually of faceted glass.

The foundation of the chandelier was its stem, to which curved branches with their candleholders and drip-pans were first added, followed by pendant drops cut in a variety of ornamental forms. This was followed by a type with a large central globe or bowl and an increased number of pendant drops. More deeply cut drops became common about mid-century, and with the onset of the Adam style the branches became more numerous. Neo-classicism made its appearance as part of the decoration, usually in the form of an urn, and dependant swags of lustres formed part of the design to a point where the branches were partly concealed and were therefore less elaborately decorated. The most complex examples belong in design to the end of the 18th

century, although W. B. Honey once wittily called some chandeliers of this kind a miniature history of glass over the past 150 years, so much have they been restored with drops cut at a later date. Chandeliers and lighting appliances thus decorated continued to be popular in the early decades of the 19th century, when the drops were often triangular in section.

The largest chandeliers were provided with a ceiling mechanism for raising and lowering them for cleaning, and in France during the 18th century they were commonly hired for special occasions, although this custom does not appear to have reached England so far as it is possible to judge by surviving records.

(See *Lustres, Glass.*)

CHANTILLY (Seine-et-Oise) PORCELAIN

Porcelain factory started about 1725 and closed at the end of the 18th century. The factory may originally have been started by Sicaire Cirou, perhaps from Saint-Cloud, who enjoyed the protection of the Prince de Condé. He remained director until his death in 1751. His two chief workmen were the brothers Dubois, who left in 1738 to assist in the foundation of the Vincennes factory (see *Sèvres*).

The best period of Chantilly porcelain is from its inception until the death of Cirou. Most of its work at this time was based on the porcelain of Arita (Japan) painted by Kakiemon (q.v.). The Prince de Condé had a prodigious collection of Oriental porcelain, much of it Japanese in the Kakiemon style which was then termed *premier qualité du japon*, and Cirou was granted a privilege (q.v.) for the manufacture of porcelain in the Japanese style. Saint-Cloud already had a monopoly of imitations of Chinese wares even though the line of demarcation was extremely vague, and the Chinese themselves were copying Kakiemon patterns.

Popular patterns of this derivation are the 'banded hedge' (*décor à la haie*), the squirrel, which is more likely to be a dormouse (*à l'écureuil*), the well-known 'quail' pattern (*à la caille*), the partridge pattern (*à la perdrix*), and the stork (*à la cigogne*). The dragon also appears, as well as a pair of 'phoenixes' in circular form. Figure-subjects are close derivations from those of Kakiemon.

The palette was of the characteristic Kakiemon type, and the forms often owed a good deal to Japanese inspiration. The decoration shows the asymmetrical dispositions of the Japanese style, which agreed very well with the prevailing rococo style current during most of this first period in French art generally.

The body of Chantilly porcelain at this time exhibits every sign of having been difficult to work. Of a pinkish or yellowish hue, it was invariably covered with a glaze heavily loaded with tin oxide which, at first glance, makes it almost indistinguishable from faïence. After about 1740 the style of the Kakiemon decoration began to assume more the nature of a *japonaiserie*, and direct copies are less in evidence. Towards the end of the first period European decorations became more common.

Many of the *motifs* were taken from the Prince de Condé's very extensive collection of Oriental works of art of all kinds which were made available to the factory for the purpose of copying them.

Most surviving examples are small, and usually of service-ware, although a recently discovered cartel clock-case sold at Christie's suggests the possibility of unrecognized work of greater elaboration from the 1740s. The *bourdaloue* is fairly frequent and the *écuelle* (q.v.) not uncommon. Drug-jars seldom bear more than the name of the drug. Small vases exist, and some rare specimens are mounted in gilt-bronze. Extremely interesting are knife-handles, which are often difficult to separate from those made by Saint-Cloud and Mennecy, although the use of the tin glaze helps in their identification.

From shortly before 1755 the tin-glaze was discontinued and a transparent lead-glaze substituted, the body being much whiter. Although polychrome decorations were continued, they became far less numerous because of the prohibitory edicts in favour of the Vincennes factory which, by this time, belonged partly to the King. The very existence of the factory must have been in danger, despite the protection of the Condé family. Small boxes in the former style with gold mounts as late as 1756/7 have led to the suggestion that these were perhaps continued, but it is more likely that earlier porcelain was mounted (or remounted) later. The most common decoration at this time was flower-sprigs in underglaze blue, of which the factory made a large variety, and this was probably all that was permitted. It closed finally towards the end of the century.

The mark throughout was that of the French horn (*cor de chasse*) with, in the second period, the addition of letters which are decorators' marks, and incised letters and numerals.

Some of the first period ware was sold 'in white' and painted much later by 'outside decorators'. Forgeries of the old soft-paste were made at Saint-Amand-les-Eaux, at a 19th-century factory at Chantilly owned by Pigory, and at another in the same place founded later by Michel-Isaac Aron; both used the old mark on hard-paste porcelain. Reproductions have been made by Samson of Paris (q.v.).

CHARLES X

The Comte d'Artois, who survived the Revolution and acceded to the throne of France in 1824 in succession to Louis XVIII. He reigned until 1830. Furniture styles then current include late Empire (q.v.) and revived rococo (q.v.).

CHASING

This metalworking term has two meanings. The first, and most important, is to denote the raising of ornament *from the front*, and it is, therefore, the opposite of *repoussé* (q.v.), which means raising ornament from the *back*. A pitch-block is used to support the work.

Its second meaning, less accurate and employed in describing the decoration of old jewellery and small wares in the precious metals, is strictly allied to *chiselling* (q.v.). The metal is shaped with punches, chisels, and a hammer in a manner which is partly chiselling and partly raising.

CHANCELLERIE (French)

A kind of tapestry decorated with a ground of *fleur-de-lys* with the Royal Arms, to which was added the attributes of the Chancellor, or Keeper of the Seals, framed with a border of the same attributes. They were executed principally at Beauvais and the Gobelins as royal gifts.

CHELSEA KERAMIC ART WORKS

This factory at Chelsea, Mass., was started in 1866 by A. W. Robertson. It began to make a red un-glazed ware in imitation of ancient Greek pottery in 1875, and in 1877 produced a ware noted for its floral decoration. Hugh C. Robertson, who had joined the company in 1867, attempted to discover the technique of making a number of Chinese wares, especially *sang-de-bœuf*, in which he probably anticipated Bernard Moore, the Staffordshire potter who worked to the same end. He also imitated Chinese 'crackled' glazes, which he perfected after 1895 when he moved to the Dedham pottery. Here he produced monochrome vases which compare favourably with the Chinese prototypes they imitated.

CHELSEA PORCELAIN FACTORY

This factory, situated at Lawrence Street, Chelsea (W. London), was started about 1743 by the silversmith Nicholas Sprimont, and Charles Gouyn, a jeweller, both of Huguenot descent, probably with a formula given to them by Thomas Briand, who demonstrated a fine white porcelain to the Royal Society in 1742. It is possible that Briand was a migratory workman who had worked at one of the contemporary French factories. A French reference to what was obviously the Chelsea factory occurs in 1745, when Charles Adam, concerned with the establishment of Vincennes, referred, in a communication to Louis XV, to a new factory just then established in England making porcelain more beautiful than that of Saxony. The earliest wares which

Chelsea Porcelain. Hogarth's dog, Trump. Raised anchor period. Chelsea. c. 1750–1752. *Victoria and Albert Museum.*

Chelsea Porcelain. Cup and saucer painted with *chinoiserie* figures within claret borders imitated from the *rose Pompadour* of Sèvres (q.v.). Gold anchor mark. Chelsea. c. 1763.

can definitely be dated are a series of jugs modelled in the form of goats with an applied bee, known as 'Goat and Bee' jugs, some of which have the date '1745' incised into the base, but these are so competent that they argue at least a year or two of experimental production.

Chelsea is very badly documented, and its history has been reconstructed from old rate-books, newspaper advertisements, letters, and similar records, and there are two sale-catalogues, dated 1755 and 1756, which are of great value in assessing its productions. There are also fragments recovered from the site of the old factory which throw considerable light on its productions.

From newspaper advertisements it would appear that Gouyn severed his connection with the factory about 1750, when Sprimont continued alone with the patronage of the Duke of Cumberland. The earliest productions had been based on contemporary silver, some of them bearing a strong resemblance to the designs of Meissonnier (q.v.), and these were undoubtedly inspired by Sprimont's own work as a silversmith which made use of Meissonnier's designs. From 1750 until about 1756 the principal influence was that of Meissen, and the previously mentioned Hanoverian Duke of Cumberland was the patron of the factory during this period. This is the only recorded instance of an English factory receiving royal patronage until towards the end of the century, when George III visited Worcester in 1788. In June 1751 Cumberland's secretary, Sir Everard Fawkener, wrote to Sir Charles Hanbury Williams, Ambassador to the Saxon Court, requesting that Meissen porcelain be bought and sent to Chelsea to copy. Williams gave permission to the factory to take any of his own Meissen porcelain from his London residence for the purpose.

In 1757 Sprimont fell ill, and the factory was closed for about a year. When it reopened Cumberland was no longer its patron, the Seven Years' War had started, and Sprimont turned for inspiration to styles current at Sèvres. In 1763 he again fell ill, and the factory thereafter worked at comparatively low pressure until it was sold in 1770 in a moribund condition to William Duesbury of Derby. Henceforward, until its final closure in 1784, its wares are known as 'Chelsea-Derby'.

During the earliest period, lasting from its inception till about 1749, the factory used the mark of an incised triangle, and this mark is also known in blue underglaze, although it is very rare. From 1750 to 1752 the mark of an anchor in relief raised on a small oval medallion was employed, the so-called 'raised anchor' mark. This may have been adopted to prevent William Duesbury, at that time operating an outside decorating studio, from painting and marking other wares as coming from Chelsea. The mark from 1752 to 1756 was a small anchor painted in red enamel—the 'red anchor' period. From 1758 to 1770 the mark was a gold anchor, and from 1770 onwards a combination of the gold anchor and a script letter *D*. The work of Chelsea is divided into periods according to the type of mark used, and it does fall into well-marked compartments so far as the

Chelsea Porcelain. Harlequin from the Italian Comedy, inspired by a model by Kändler at Meissen. *Victoria and Albert Museum.*

78

Chelsea Porcelain. **Hexagonal teapot painted with a Fable Scene by Jeffreys Hamett O'Neale (see** *Outside Decorators***). Chelsea. c. 1752.**

style of the productions are concerned which correspond to the mark.

A number of artists of distinction worked at Chelsea. Notable among them is William Duvivier, who may have been a faïence painter at Tournai. He was in England from 1743 till his death in 1755, and one identified specimen of his work on raised anchor Chelsea porcelain is of a harbour scene derived from those of Meissen. Jeffreys Hamett O'Neale, the Irish miniature painter who did a great deal of distinguished work on Chelsea and Worcester porcelain, started his career as a porcelain painter at Chelsea where he did a series of 'Fable' subjects. Joseph Willems, a noted modeller who came originally from the Netherlands, returned to Tournai in 1766 and died in that year.

Of later artists, Zachariah Boreman learned the art of porcelain painting at Chelsea, and went on to Derby when the London factory closed. Another Derby painter who began at Chelsea was Richard Askew, painter of cupids, who went to Derby in 1772. Nicolas Gauron, a modeller from Tournai, was at Chelsea about 1773, and Nicolas Lecreux from the same place was probably also here at this time. There were always connections between Tournai and Chelsea about which little has been discovered, but the exchanges of workmen are proof of its existence.

Up to 1750 Chelsea productions were principally inspired by contemporary rococo silver, making use of shells and crayfish, and the *blanc-de-Chine* (q.v.) of Tê Hua, to be seen in cups and the like decorated with the prunus or tea-plant moulded in relief. The acanthus appears as the moulded decoration to coffee-pots. Most of these wares are in white, but the 'Goat and Bee' jugs, and one or two other triangle period types, occur in an enamelled version, and these may properly be attributable to the end of the period. Few figures are known to have been made, and these can all be dated around 1749. The raised anchor period shows a definite change of interest. Silver-patterns were still used for dishes and a few other wares, but predominantly the octagonal and fluted wares of Kakiemon were the

most popular. Kakiemon forms and designs, and the Japanese palette, were very closely imitated to a point where they are sometimes quite deceptive. The forms alone were often employed in conjunction with European painted decoration, such as the fables of O'Neale. A series of bird models taken from George Edwards' *Natural History of Uncommon Birds* are among the most sought of the figures of the period, some painted in enamel colours by William Duesbury (q.v.) at his decorating establishment. Few figures were made otherwise, but *La Nourrice* (taken from a model originally by Palissy (q.v.)) is well known, and an Italian Comedy figure called *Isabella d'Andreini* is very much rarer.

The following red anchor period which began about 1752 shows a much greater reliance on Meissen. Fables by the young O'Neale continued, but the *deutsche Blumen* (q.v.) of Meissen began to decorate a great deal of the service-ware made at this time. About 1755 paintings of natural flowers taken from the *Gardener's Dictionary* of Philip Miller (gardener to the Worshipful Company of Apothecaries at their Botanic Garden in Chelsea) provide a much sought series. This garden was under the patronage of Sir Hans Sloane, member of the Royal Society, and plates painted in this style are are often called 'Hans Sloane' plates today. Kakiemon patterns were progressively abandoned, but there is one instance at least of a service in the Imari style (q.v.). Underglaze-blue decoration was rarely done, but when it was, it was usually marked with a blue anchor under the glaze.

Figures at this time were quite commonly derived from models by Kändler and other Meissen modellers, and some are superior in quality to the originals, principally due to the nature of the porcelain body used. By this time the factory was producing many figure models, all of which are much sought today. Especially valued are tureens in the form of fruit and vegetables, and less often

Chelsea Porcelain. **The much-sought 'Hans Sloane' decoration of plants taken from Philip Miller's** *Gardener's Dictionary***. Chelsea. c. 1754.** *Sigmund Katz Collection.*

Chelsea Porcelain. A Chelsea plate of about 1753 showing the characteristic 'moons'. Two of the three 'stilt' marks, present on Chelsea plates of all periods, have formed black patches, while the decoration on the reverse has caused dark patches to form on the left at the bottom. Photograph by transmitted light.

animals and birds. Leaf forms were also employed for plates, dishes, and sauceboats.

About 1755 styles began to undergo distinct changes, and we find gilding used for the first time. A new ground colour of blue underglaze (called Mazarine blue) was employed in conjunction with the gilding, and these styles were certainly inspired by the slightly earlier work of Vincennes rather than Meissen. By 1758, when the factory reopened and the gold anchor was first used, the reliance on Sèvres had become much more obvious, and it is at this time that we see the so-called 'claret' ground first used, which was obviously inspired by the *rose Pompadour* (q.v.) of that factory. New ground colours include turquoise, green, and yellow in conjunction with floral painting, and with a new subject from France —exotic birds. The rococo style was extremely well marked, to be seen particularly in the handles to vases, while in 1760 the painted decorations of Sèvres were influential, those after Boucher and others often comparing not unfavourably with the work of the French royal factory. Figures of the period are of fine quality, although they lack the vigour and artistry of those of the red anchor period.

From the red anchor period onwards the factory made a speciality of small 'toys' (q.v.), particularly scent-bottles, *étuis*, and *bonbonnières*, which were often inscribed in French. Those of the red anchor period have the characteristic paste and glaze, and lack gilding. The gold anchor period examples are often lavishly gilded.

Chelsea-Derby wares are in the neo-classical style, with a palette which inclines to lighter, cleaner colours than are to be found in the early period. In form most of its wares, especially vases, were based on the contemporary work of Sèvres, and painting of excellent quality was often similarly inspired. The earlier Chelsea factory had not introduced the *biscuit* figure in the manner of Sèvres, although one or two obviously experimental attempts exist. At Chelsea after its purchase by Duesbury, however, the *biscuit* figure was commonly made, and the manufacture was later taken up at Derby itself. These figures were made in two versions, unglazed, and glazed and painted, the latter being *biscuit* figures which had some defect or other. For this reason they were sold more cheaply than the unglazed figures.

Despite the fact that much of its work was derivative Chelsea porcelain is among the finest in Europe, only excelled as an artificial porcelain by that of Sèvres. Chelsea-Derby wares are hardly distinguishable from those of Derby, and there is reason to believe that, during the closing years of the factory, it was little more than a decorating establishment, painting porcelain made at the Midlands factory.

The earliest type of porcelain used during the triangle period was extremely glassy and white, resembling *milch-glas* (q.v.) rather more closely than most artificial porcelains of the period. It is highly translucent, and by transmitted light shows pinpoints of light which are fairly characteristic. By ultraviolet light the glaze exhibits a peach colour. In the raised anchor period the porcelain is still glassy, but not quite to the same extent. Plates and dishes by transmitted light sometimes show 'moons' (q.v.), while inside the footring will be found three small spur or stilt marks, similar to those found on Arita porcelain. This makes the deceptiveness of Kakiemon decorations the greater. The body of the red anchor period is still glassy, but to a lesser extent. Bone-ash seems to have been introduced about 1755. Although the exact quantity is undetermined, the reaction of some specimens of this date when tested by the normal 'spot' test is marked. In both these and the raised anchor wares fluorescence under ultraviolet light is peach in colour for the most part, although variations are sometimes to be found in which there is a distinct violet tone. During the gold anchor period the body is less glassy, with a thick and glassy glaze which, in some cases, tends to coagulate in pools, and is very often crazed. Under ultra-violet light it exhibits a violet colour, and the quantity of bone-ash present is comparable with that of Bow. The Chelsea-Derby body is a bone-ash porcelain of good quality, the translucency less marked than in the case of earlier wares, with a similar fluorescence to the gold anchor series. The resemblance is much more to contemporary Derby porcelain than to the earlier Chelsea.

CHENILLE (French)

Piled ornament of silk used on brocaded fabrics or in embroidery.

CHERRY WOOD

The wild cherry (*bois de merise*) was much used by 18th-century French *ébénistes*. In colour it is usually reddish-brown, but it can sometimes resemble a dark mahogany. The American black cherry was also much used in the Northern States for furniture-making.

CHESSMEN

The game of chess originated in the East, but the respective claims of China, India, and Persia to have invented it have never been determined. The most probable theory is that it reached Persia from India, spreading to the Western world from Persia, since some of the terms used in the game are of Persian origin—the word *rook,* for instance, which was originally *rukh.*

The chessmen customarily employed today are known as the Staunton pattern, after a well-known 19th-century player, but in former times the pieces varied very widely in form, and many are miniature works of art of considerable merit which are now widely sought. Oriental sets are especially elaborate, and are usually carved in ivory or bone. An Indian set of 1800, for instance, has a king seated in a howdah on an elephant. A German king of the 16th century is a recognizable portrait of Charles V, Holy Roman Emperor, and early European sets are no less diverse in their representation of other major pieces. The materials of which the pieces have been made are also numerous. Ivory, bone, and wood are the most commonly seen, but pottery, porcelain, Wedgwood's jasper ware, and even glass have all been employed for the purpose, as well as such materials as jade and soapstone.

It has usually been customary to carve the major pieces with a certain realism to denote their function, but occasionally some old sets made by turning represent them by different patterns and sizes.

Chess appears to have arrived in Europe about the 10th century, and by late medieval times it had become extremely popular, when it attracted the fulminations of the Church.

Complete sets of early chessmen are now highly valued, even the commoner Oriental varieties made before about 1850, and odd pieces from sets made before 1800, if well carved and representative of one of the major pieces, are well worth acquiring.

CHEST

A large rectangular box with a hinged lid, sometimes wrongly called a coffer (q.v.), which occurs in a number of forms, usually with carved decoration. The most common wood is oak or elm, but chests of cedar and mahogany can also be found. The chest is an extremely ancient piece of furniture, XVIIIth dynasty Egyptian examples having been found in the tomb of Tut-ankh-amun. Specimens survive from the 14th century, although these are excessively rare, and elaborate versions with drawers were designed by Chippendale. See *Bahut; Coffer.*

CHEST, CYPRESS

From Renaissance times onwards chests and coffers for the purpose of storing tapestries and textiles generally were made of aromatic cypress wood because it acted as a deterrent to attack from moth.

CHEST OF DRAWERS

In England the chest of drawers developed from the chest *with* drawers at the end of the 17th century, and it was at first placed on a stand. It developed into its more familiar form during the early years of the 18th century, probably under the influence of the parallel development of the French *commode* (q.v.). Chests of drawers of fine quality decorated more or less in the French manner were termed *commodes* by Chippendale in the *Director.* In the same work a low *commode* surmounted by a hanging wardrobe was described as a *commode* clothes-press (see *Clothes-press*). In these days what is occasionally described as an 18th-century chest of drawers is sometimes half of a tallboy (q.v.) fitted with a new top and, if required, new feet, usually of the bracket variety (q.v.). (See *Commodes, English.*)

CHEST-ON-CHEST   (See *Tallboy.*)

CHEVAL GLASS

A long dressing-mirror swinging between two posts, introduced into England at the end of the 18th century. Some specimens are fitted with candle-holders attached to the posts. They derive their name from the mechanism controlling the position of the mirror, which was known as a 'horse'.

CHIMERA

A mythological animal which takes several forms— a winged lion, a goat-headed lion, a lion with an additional head in the form of a goat, etc.

Chimney-piece Mirror. Chimney-piece mirror in the former hôtel de Rochechouart, Paris, now the Ministry of National Education. The marble chimney-piece is decorated with bronze. The *chenets* are in the Louis Seize style.

CHIMNEY-GLASSES

The French architect Robert de Cotte (1656–1735) is generally credited with the introduction of the chimney-glass, or chimney-piece mirror, at the beginning of the 18th century, and almost all French designers of the period produced designs for mirror-frames of this kind in great variety. English chimney-piece mirrors were usually rectangular, the longest side being parallel with the mantelshelf. They were nearly always formed in three sheets, the centre sheet being twice the width of the two on either side. Occasionally four sheets of the same size may be found in the one frame. Many have a painting incorporated in the same frame, above the mirror-glass. Frames were of gilded gesso, or of walnut carved or otherwise decorated according to the taste and style of the period. Value depends principally on the period of the frame, and on the quality of this, and of any painting which may be present. Such mirrors are now rare.

CHINÉ

Fabrics of the mid-18th century woven from irregularly dyed threads of silk, either of the warp and weft, or of the warp threads alone (*chiné à la branche*).

'CHINESE CHIPPENDALE'

A generic term for mid-18th-century English furniture in the Chinese taste when its design is based on similar designs in Chippendale's *Director* (see *Chippendale, Thomas*). Oriental lacquer made up into cabinets and screens had been popular in England since the last quarter of the 17th century, and Queen Mary had brought with her from Holland the fashion for collecting Chinese and Japanese porcelain, but it was not until the rococo style became popular in the late 1730s that Chinese designs began to be increasingly employed in the making of furniture. By the middle of the 18th century the vogue for things Chinese was at its height in England, and almost all designers of the period made use of the Oriental style. 'Chinese Chippendale' is of two kinds—the first is relatively plain, usually in solid mahogany, and the most Chinese thing about it is the use of a distinctive type of lattice-work derived from genuine Chinese furniture. A few specimens had been brought to England in the ships of the East India Company, and in 1757 Sir William Chambers (q.v.), who had been to China, published his *Designs for Chinese Buildings, Furniture, &c.,* which approached very closely to the Chinese. This was intended, as he says, 'to put a stop to the extraordinary fancies that daily appear under the name Chinese'. More often than not the style of the second became inextricably mixed with rococo, and its ornament was designed by men, such as Edwards and Darley, who were singularly ignorant of the Far East. They said of their own designs, 'Our Chinese ornaments are not only of our own manufacture but, what has seldom been attributed to the

English, of our own invention.' The Chinese taste was more or less confined to bedrooms, and it is in the bed and the mirror-frame that we find the most extravagant examples of rococo Chinese design, the mirror gilded and the bed usually japanned. Japanned furniture in imitation of Oriental lacquer was an almost invariable accompaniment of rooms designed in this style, usually in conjunction with Chinese painted wallpaper and silk hangings.

The fashion declined with the onset of the neo-classical style (q.v.).

CHINESE EXPORT PORCELAIN

Porcelain made in China and intended for export to the West. In the 18th century most decoration of porcelain intended for this purpose was based on European prototypes, but European forms were adopted at a much earlier date. Some other terms referring to Chinese export porcelain are 'Oriental Lowestoft', 'East India Company porcelain', 'Jesuit porcelain', 'carrack porcelain', and 'Nanking porcelain'.

Most Chinese porcelain intended for export was made in the Imperial factory at Ching-tê Chên. When decorated in underglaze blue it was painted in the same town, but polychrome painting was done in great part in enamelling shops set up for the purpose in the Treaty Port of Canton, where Cantonese enamels (q.v.) were also made.

Although blue-and-white porcelain was freely imported into the Middle East in the 14th and 15th centuries, and a large collection survives in the Topkapu Serail in Istanbul, Turkey, this kind of porcelain was not directly imported into the West until after 1516, when the Portuguese established trading relations with China. The ships which brought it back to Lisbon were called carracks, and about 1600 these began to be raided on the high seas by Dutch pirates. Captured porcelain of this kind, called by the Dutch *kraak porsellein*, was brought to Holland and sold to buyers in Northern Europe, among them James I of England. This was blue-and-white porcelain of the reign of Wan-li (1573–1619).

'*Chinese Chippendale*'. Governor's Palace Parlour, Colonial Williamsburg, Va. Settee and two matching chairs in Chippendale's Chinese style, c. 1760, originally the property of John Wentworth, last Royal Governor of New Hampshire. The tea-service is Worcester (q.v.), and the carpet English needlework of about 1740.

Chinese Export Porcelain. Plate decorated with the subject of Achilles being dipped in the River Styx, taken from a French engraving. Mid-18th century.

It was thin, crisply potted, and resonant, and quite commonly decorated with such subjects as deer in landscapes. The decoration was in Chinese taste, but the shapes were very commonly European, particularly plates with condiment ledges copied from those of pewter and silver.

The manufacture of European shapes with blue-painted decoration greatly expanded during the remaining years of the Ming dynasty, which terminated in 1643. Beer-mugs, ewers, goblets, vases, and so forth were imported by the various East India Companies, particularly the Dutch Company, in ever-increasing quantities throughout the 17th century, especially after the accession of the Ch'ing Emperor, K'ang Hsi (1662–1722), and by the 18th century the trade was immense. During the second half of this century much blue-and-white porcelain was shipped from Nanking. Usually blue-

Chinese Export Porcelain. A pair of neo-classical urns made in China for the Irish market. The harps have been turned sideways—a typical Chinese error of a kind frequent on this kind of porcelain. c. 1775.

and-white export porcelain has shapes derived from European prototypes, but the decoration is in Chinese taste. In the case of Nanking porcelain (q.v.), however, European *motifs* were also employed, such as the Fitzhugh border (q.v.) which, while apparently Chinese, owes a good deal to inspiration from the West.

Polychrome wares definitely made for export first appear during the reign of the Emperor K̦'ang Hsi. Like blue-and-white porcelain, the wares decorated in the *famille verte* (q.v.) were often of European shape with Chinese decorative *motifs*, although sometimes in conjunction with European armorial bearings. Such wares never bear either a reign-mark, or the double circle which commonly appears on K'ang Hsi porcelain. The *famille rose* palette, the *rose* pigment itself being of European origin, was introduced into China late in the 17th century, but the first *dated* example of its use does not occur before 1721. The best of these wares were made during the reign of Yung Chêng (1723–1735), when plates of egg-shell porcelain (extremely thin porcelain, as the name suggests) were given a ground of *rose* enamel on the reverse—the so-called ruby-back plates. The decoration, even when in native taste, begins to show signs of European influence, and by the reign of Ch'ien Lung (1735–1795) copies of European subjects were general, and the work of European porcelain factories such as Meissen provided inspiration for some export wares. At this time the prototypes for both shapes and decoration were nearly always supplied from the West, and this export trade continued until the destruction of Ch'ing-tê Chên in 1853. European shapes made during the 18th century were extremely diverse, and most of them were without any Chinese affiliations. They include in addition to the standard European plate, *écuelles,* tureens, sugar-casters, sauceboats, pepper-pots, mustard-pots, salad bowls, spoons, tea-cups (without handles), coffee-cups (with handles), teapots, tea-caddies, milk-jugs, slop-bowls, ewers and basins, *bourdaloues* (unlike those made in the West, the Chinese version had a cover), chamber-pots, *bidets,* spittoons, candlesticks, chandeliers, *torchères,* snuff-boxes, cane-handles, and *bonbonnières.* This is a very abbreviated list, but it includes the wares most frequently imported. In form these were obviously European, and they were based on pottery, porcelain, silver, or pewter, mostly patterns specially sent to China for the purpose. Sometimes one sees such curiosities as Chinese porcelain copies of European *delft* decorated with *chinoiseries* (q.v.), a subject rendered quite faithfully, and probably as meaningless to Chinese painters as most European decoration they were called upon to copy. I have also seen a blue-and-white Chinese copy of a polychrome Bow leaf-dish of 1755 painted with a Kakiemon subject. It is amusing to notice the complex influences sometimes to be found in Chinese export wares, and to trace them to their source.

Decoration was very commonly taken from European prints which began to arrive in China in the

Chinese Export Porcelain. A large punch-bowl with a view of the waterfront at Canton showing the warehouses (*hongs*) of the various East India Companies, designated by their national flags. c. 1750.

17th century. Early in the 18th century, about 1725, porcelain was produced painted in a linear style in sepia resembling European *Schwarzlot* (q.v.), with sometimes the addition of a little iron-red to the faces and hands of figures, and oil-gilding which has often worn off. This type, from the frequency with which it depicts Biblical subjects, has become known as Jesuit porcelain (q.v.). The finest specimens of export porcelain at this time, however, were probably those decorated in the *famille rose* palette, and the subjects are extremely diverse.

By far the most popular among mythological subjects was the Judgment of Paris, with nudes suggesting the existence of a Chinese pupil in Rubens' studio. One speculates on what the Chinese made of Leda and the Swan, or Achilles being dipped in the Styx. One or two examples are known apparently based on Italian *maiolica* from Urbino. Biblical subjects include Susannah and the Elders, and Bathsheba surprised by King David. The Chinese were also skilled painters of pornography, although few porcelain specimens exist. Ships are fairly uncommon, but most shipowners had a service painted for them. Punch-bowls depicting fox-hunting scenes are now highly valued, and they are usually painted in a rather 'hot' palette in which iron-red predominates.

Apart from the wares of Ching-tê Chên, export porcelain was made in the *blanc de Chine* (q.v.) of Tê Hua (Fukien Province). These kilns specialized in wares decorated with flower sprigs in relief, much copied in Europe, and in figures, such as those of the goddess Kuan Yin, who was mistaken in Europe for the Virgin. They made figures of Dutch merchants in the costumes of the period, and family groups depicting European life in China.

Although the Spaniards transhipped Chinese porcelain across the Panamanian Isthmus in the 17th century, American contacts with China were very few until after the end of the War of Independence. In February, 1784, the *Empress of China* sailed from New York for Canton, where trading connections were established. After this American ships increasingly made the hazardous journey from the East Coast, rounding the Cape of Good Hope and crossing the Indian Ocean, usually with a cargo of ginseng root which was much valued in China for its medicinal qualities. They returned with tea, silk, lacquer, porcelain, and spices. In 1788 the first

voyage in which an American ship rounded Cape Horn was undertaken, and this proved exceedingly profitable.

Among the most sought examples of Chinese porcelain decorated for the American market are those with ships flying the American flag. Specimens more conventionally decorated usually exhibit elements of the neo-classical style during the 18th and early 19th centuries, and these are similar in many respects to those intended for the European market. Of especial American interest are specimens with the Arms of the United States, those of the individual states of the Union, or with the Arms of the City of New York. Some of these were also sold directly to the European market. Among notable examples is the well-known 'Washington' service decorated with emblems of the Society of Cincinatti which is preserved in the Mount Vernon Museum, and a punch bowl dated 1802 in the Metropolitan Museum which is painted with a view of New York City. Specimens of this kind are no longer obtainable on the open market, but ship bowls, and those with armorial bearings, sometimes appear, and are very highly valued.

Chinese export porcelain of all kinds is very much sought at present, and rare specimens and large services command high prices.

CHINESE RUGS AND CARPETS

These have been made in the north-western provinces of China from the 17th century onwards. Records of manufacture before this date are unreliable. The finest carpets came from Pekin, and most examples attributed to this city have a rich blue ground.

The best Chinese carpets are much sought and command high prices. The weave is coarse, the pile long, and sometimes irregular in length. The Sehna knot is commonly employed. The Chinese sometimes clip the pile to bring out certain elements of the decoration in relief. *Motifs* of decoration are markedly Chinese, but often with signs of Persian influence. Those acquainted with the Chinese repertory of ornament for porcelain, lacquer, and so forth, will have no difficulty in recognizing the elements of carpet decoration. A few Chinese carpets based on the patterns of 17th- and 18th-century French pile carpets are known. Pillar carpets include a spirally wound variety, although these are rare.

The modern industry is centred on Tientsin, and some latex-backed pile rugs have been made in Hong Kong in recent times. The latter are artistically worthless.

CHINESE STYLE, DECORATION IN THE

In addition to the *chinoiserie* (q.v.), many fairly exact European copies of Chinese decoration were made during the 18th century, such as those to be found ornamenting some English and Dutch *delft*, and lacquer cabinets. It is, therefore, of some interest to the collector to know the original symbolism and meaning of the decoration copied. Few motifs were faithfully reproduced, and most were adapted, but nearly always an original source can be identified.

Chinese Style. A Liverpool teapot with decoration closely copying a *motif* of the reign of Yung Chéng (1723–1735). c. 1760.

The very curious shapes which sometimes accompany Chinese flower-subjects, and appear on many European derivations, are rocks. These always formed a prominent feature of Chinese landscape-gardening, and the most curiously shaped were highly valued and transported over long distances to the site. Most of them were volcanic in origin. They were also a favourite subject with Chinese painters of porcelain and landscape, but their nature was rarely understood by European copyists and they emerge in a form recognizable only with difficulty.

The Chinese had an elaborate system of flower symbolism which was also unknown to Europeans. Certain flowers are emblematic of the months and the seasons. The prunus, for instance, represented Winter; the tree-peony, Spring; the lotus, Summer; and the chrysanthemum, Autumn. The prunus was very popular, sometimes reserved in white on a blue ground. The bamboo is commonly represented, and is a longevity symbol. Simulated bamboo was employed in England in the design of chairs and small furniture towards the end of the 18th century, and some of the best specimens were made for Brighton Pavilion (Sussex) early in the 19th. The *ling chih* (*Fomes japonicus*) was a fungus which grew on tree-trunks. This also was a longevity symbol. Deer sometimes carry one in their mouths. The fruit of the peach was commonly employed in China, not only in painted form, but modelled as small porcelain winepots and waterpots for the scholar's table. As a longevity symbol it was carried by the Taoist god, Lao Tzŭ. It can be recognized in English porcelain occasionally in the form of a small sauceboat, the peach sliced vertically and placed on its side, the painted decoration usually being *famille rose* flowers. These came from Bow and Chelsea. Both English and Continental factories extensively imitated *blanc-de-Chine* (q.v.), most commonly the variety decorated with flowers raised in relief, either the prunus or the tea-plant. Imitations of *blanc-de-Chine* figures are rarer, but they occur, for instance, at Lund's Bristol factory (see *Bristol Porcelain*).

Landscapes with buildings, and interiors, were usually taken from illustrations with literary themes, probably from romances of one kind or another, and they were copied by European potters especially without any understanding of their meaning or origin. Occasionally they made up new ones, such as the Willow pattern (see *Chinoiseries*), which is a *pastiche* (q.v.) of Chinese themes, and the familiar story was devised afterwards to account for it. It is certainly not Chinese. Landscapes are commonly to be found on European japanned wares (q.v.).

The dragon takes a variety of forms in Chinese art, but only late versions are to be found on European wares of the 17th and 18th centuries. In China it symbolizes Spring, and it is a beneficent spirit of the waters, despite its ferocious appearance. It is an auspicious symbol which, from earliest times, has symbolized the Emperor when it has five claws. With four or three claws it represents princes of the blood or important officials. It has none of the ferocity and reputation for evil of the European dragon, which is quite a different animal. The *fêng huang*, sometimes called a phoenix, is the symbol of the Empress. Also known as the Vermilion Bird, it represents Spring and the Four Seasons, and, like the dragon, is an auspicious symbol.

The Eight Precious Things were sometimes copied. These, the *Pa pao*, were part of the *Po ku*—the Hundred Antiques. They are a collection of objects used in the arts, sciences, and religion.

Figures of elongated girls (*mei Jên*) appear very often on *delft* and certain kinds of porcelain, notably early blue-and-white Worcester, and from their popularity on Dutch *delft* stems the name frequently given to them—*Lange Lyzen*, or Long Elizas.

Chinese Style. Vase and cover with the AR mark in blue and European decoration. The vase closely copies a characteristic Chinese form of the early 18th century, but the shoulders are flattened in contrast with the continuous curve of the Chinese version. Meissen. c. 1735. *Kunsthaus Lempertz, Köln.*

Ch'ing Dynasty. A pair of cranes. Reign of Ch'ien Lung (1735–1796). *Christie, Manson & Woods Ltd.*

Chinese characters in simulated form appear very commonly, and sometimes they disguise dates. These are discussed elsewhere under the heading of *Reign Marks, Chinese.*

Animals appear fairly commonly. The bat (*fu*) represents happiness, since the Chinese word for both is the same. The hare is a symbol of the moon, but the rabbit has obscene connotations in China, and its appearance on Chinese export porcelain was

Ch'ing Dynasty. A large bottle decorated with peaches (Yung Chêng, 1723–1735). Similar bottles were also made during the reign of Tao Kuang (1821–1850). *Parke-Bernet Galleries, New York.*

probably intended to insult the merchant for whom the ware was made or decorated. The deer occurs with the *ling chih* fungus and is a longevity symbol. The Lion of Fo (Buddha) is usually termed the Dog of Fo in Europe, and is represented by the male playing with a ball and the female with a cub. They are often miscalled *Kylins*, a mythical animal rarely or never seen outside Chinese art, which bears no resemblance to them.

The figures known as *pagods* (q.v.) were of the monk Pu-tai (also called, in his Japanese form, Ho-tei, and there the God of Contentment), who is represented seated, with a large grin, and a bare belly. No doubt Japan inspired some of the European copies (see *Japanese Style, Decoration in the*). The Eight Immortals (*Pa Hsien*) do not appear very often on wares of European origin. They are usually accompanied by Lao Tzŭ (Shou Lao, or Old Lao), and he can be easily recognized from his large and protuberant forehead. In Japan he becomes Jurojin, and is similarly represented.

Among the more obscure symbols which were sometimes copied on European wares is the character *Shou* (longevity), which appears in a number of ornamental and conventional forms. Longevity is most frequently symbolized, and some of the other themes which bear this meaning have been noted above. The peach and the bat together mean long life and happiness.

CH'ING DYNASTY

Aso known as the Manchu dynasty. The reigning house which superseded the native Ming emperors came from Manchuria, and garrisoned China with nomad Tatar troops, the Chinese population being compelled to wear the pigtail as a way of differentiating them. The Manchu invasion began in 1644, and they retained power till 1912. The most important reigns are those of K'ang Hsi (1662–1722), Yung Chêng (1723–1735) and Ch'ien Lung (1736–1795). K'ang Hsi did much to encourage the arts, and sought the assistance of such Jesuit missionaries as Père Castiglione. An event of the first magnitude to the ceramic historian may be found in the letters of Père d'Entrecolles dated September 1712 and January 1722 respectively, which discussed the secret of porcelain manufacture and greatly influenced experiments in Europe. Jesuit reports to Europe contain much of interest, like that of Père Attiret on Chinese gardens, and they played a considerable part at the time in creating the taste for Oriental art of all kinds.

Painting on porcelain in enamel colours was brought to a high degree of perfection (see *Famille verte* and *Famille rose*) and most Chinese export porcelain (q.v.) belongs to this period. Chinese furniture, wallpaper, lacquer, textiles, and many other kinds of decoration were eagerly sought by an ever-expanding market, but throughout the 18th century the influence of European merchants in demanding decoration which appealed to Western taste, and Western notions of what Chinese art ought to be,

Clandon Hall, architect Giacomo Leoni, is notable for the
fine quality of its ornamental plasterwork by Albert Altari,
known as the 'gentleman plasterer'. c. 1720.

Andirons. Silver andirons decorate a chimney-piece at Knole (Kent), noted for its silver furniture—almost the only examples to survive from the 17th century.

Chinoiserie. Pair of silver ginger-jars decorated with chinoiseries. English. **1682. Reign of Charles II.** *Sotheby & Co.*

did much to bring about a deterioration in standards which, by the early decades of the 19th century, had resulted in the kind of triviality which also marked European art of the day. Little or nothing of importance was done after the close of the reign of Ch'ien Lung, and modern taste is much concerned with periods about which little or nothing was known until the 20th century—the Sung, T'ang, and Han dynasties, and the still earlier periods.

CHINOISERIE (French)

This term is often the cause of a good deal of confusion. It can only properly be used to mean European decoration done in the Chinese manner with a certain fantasy element. It cannot be applied to Oriental work, or to strict copies of it. In the 17th century especially many of the craftsmen of the time took their inspiration from books of travel illustrated, and sometimes even written, by those who had never made the arduous journey to the Far East, but who relied on accounts at second-hand. The elements of Oriental decoration itself were often largely meaningless to the craftsmen of the day, and it was very freely interpreted, and combined with European *motifs* and employed to ornament European forms. Chinese materials were also copied, and this began

the vogue for porcelain, which was the most sought import from the Far East, but also the imitation of lacquer, which was widely used for screens and made up into cabinets. The most notable of these imitations was the *vernis Martin* of France (q.v.), which was employed for a very wide variety of objects, from sedan chairs to furniture and snuff-boxes.

The designers of the day took Chinese *motifs* and blended them freely with European. There was, for instance, the work of Jean Bérain (q.v.), designer to Louis Quatorze, where these designs can frequently be seen. Antoine Watteau did some work of the kind which was later engraved, and inspired such things as porcelain figures. Christoph Huet was responsible for the *singeries* at Chantilly, monkeys forming part of contemporary *chinoiserie* designs. Boucher also designed in the Chinese manner. Perhaps the last *chinoiseries* worthy of notice were those of Pillement (q.v.) who, in the 1760s, did many designs for *toile de Jouy,* and whose designs also appear on English porcelain of the same period.

Chinoiserie. Teapot and two cups painted with *chinoiseries* in the manner of J. G. Höroldt (q.v.). Teapot with crossed swords and KPM (Königliche Porzellanmanufaktur). Once in the Hermitage, St Petersburg (Leningrad). *Christie, Manson & Woods Ltd.*

The most important *chinoiserie* designs on European porcelain were those of the Meissen factory, of which the best known were designed by the *Obermaler*, Johann Gregor Höroldt (q.v.), and those of A. F. von Löwenfinck (q.v.). A few of the finest examples have been attributed to the hand of Höroldt himself, and a signed engraving of a *chinoiserie* subject survives at Munich dated 1726.

In England, apart from porcelain, a great deal of imitation lacquer was made, the *motifs* of which can be described as *chinoiseries*. The tendency is especially noticeable in such things as mirror-frames in the rococo style, the *chinoiserie* being an especially common feature of rococo decoration. Chippendale, Halfpenny, and others made many designs of this kind.

From 1660 to 1770 the vogue was widespread throughout Europe, but it yielded to the increasing popularity of the neo-classical style (q.v.), and Greek and Roman *motifs* could only, with difficulty, be combined with those from China. The fantasy element gradually disappeared with the greater understanding of China, and the appearance of such books as those of Sir William Chambers who had first-hand knowledge of the country.

Even today a good deal of pottery and porcelain decoration can properly be described as belonging to this category, an example being the Willow pattern, first used in England about 1780 and probably designed by Thomas Minton. This has no connection with any known Chinese decoration.

(See *Japonaiserie*.)

Chinoiserie. Table-centre. Chinese Emperor seated on a throne in the rococo style. The figure on the left holds a scroll with pseudo-Chinese ideograms. Höchst. c. 1765. *Metropolitan Museum, New York.*

CHINTZ

A cotton cloth, usually glazed, and often printed either in monochrome or in a variety of colours. Chintz was first imported from India during the 17th century, but the name was afterwards employed for glazed, hand-printed calicoes made in Europe and America. *Toile de Jouy* (q.v.) is an example of European manufacture.

Cretonne is a French substitute for chintz, unglazed and printed only on one side. It was first introduced about 1850.

CHIP CARVING

A type of carved geometric ornament, usually based on compass-work, which was first set out and then chipped away with a chisel and mallet, much in the same way as the mason carves a soft stone. Although the technique was principally employed during the Gothic period, it was still in use during the 16th and 17th centuries for inferior work.

CHIPOLIN (French)

A very hard, brilliant varnish simulating Oriental lacquer employed in 18th-century France for the decoration of wall-panelling in designs taken from fashionable artists.

CHIPPENDALE, IRISH

Furniture contemporary with Chippendale made in Ireland from English designs. Although the designs used are often referred to as 'Chippendale', they belong, in fact, to a slightly earlier period for the most part. Irish furniture of this type was usually heavily and ornately carved, with aprons of exaggerated depth. Such decorative *motifs* as the lion-mask and lion-paw feet tended to linger in provincial Ireland after they were no longer current in London. The writer has noted an Irish chest incorporating a heavily carved front panel which was probably of Spanish origin.

Chippendale, Irish. A silver table with the type of carving associated with furniture in the Chippendale style made in Ireland. Mid-18th century. *Parke-Bernet Galleries, New York.*

CHIPPENDALE STYLE

Used of furniture based on the designs of Thomas Chippendale (q.v.) as set out in his *Gentleman and Cabinet-makers' Director*, or inspired by them. This book was published in three editions—1754, 1755, and an enlarged version in 1762. (See also *'Country Chippendale'*.)

CHIPPENDALE, THOMAS (1718–1779)

The name of Thomas I Chippendale has become a generic term for furniture in the style associated with him, largely because of the publication of a book of designs which he called the *Gentleman and Cabinet-makers' Director*. This, first published in 1754, was widely used as a source of designs by many furniture-makers of the time.

Chippendale was a member of a Yorkshire family and baptized at Otley Parish Church. He appears to have come to London about 1745, marrying Catherine Renshaw in 1748 at St George's Church, Mayfair, London. In 1755 the *Gentleman's Magazine* reported the destruction of his workshop by fire, but shortly before this date, probably in 1753, he took into partnership James Rannie, a cabinet-maker, an association which lasted until Rannie's death in 1766. Chippendale continued alone until 1771, when Thomas Haig joined him to form a partnership called

Chippendale Style. Rococo carved wood and gilded mirror of the type associated with Chippendale. The phoenix surmounting the mirror occurs both in Bow and Worcester porcelain. c. 1755. *Mallett & Son.*

Chippendale Style. The Parlour, Wythe House, Colonial Williamsburg, Va., furnished in the Chippendale style. The chairs on the right are English Chippendale, c. 1760. On the left is an American walnut chair with claw and ball feet and cabriole legs made in Philadelphia, c. 1760, which has been influenced by Chippendale's designs.

Chippendale Style. A Chippendale mahogany tripod table with a gallery of contemporary silver pattern, carved on the feet with husk ornament. c. 1755. *Park-Bernet Galleries, New York.*

Chippendale, Thomas. Chippendale carved and gilded semi-circular side-table with hardwood marquetry top made to a design by the Adam Brothers. *Park-Bernet Galleries, New York.*

Chippendale, Thomas. Top of preceding side-table. The marquetry is of typical early neo-classical ornament.

Chippendale, Haig & Co. Thomas II Chippendale, Chippendale's son, succeeded to the business after his father's death, continuing it until 1796 in association with Haig. In 1814 he opened showrooms in the Haymarket, London, which were removed in 1821 to Jermyn Street not far away. He died in 1823.

This brief review of the salient features of Chippendale's life does, in fact, include most of what is known about him. Very little of the furniture in his style, and commonly referred to as 'Chippendale', can be traced to his workshop with any certainty, and, when it can, its value is greatly increased. For his time Chippendale's workshop was a fairly large one. He was employing twenty-two cabinet-makers at the time of the fire mentioned. But it is quite impossible for him to have made all the furniture ascribed to him, and, short of an invoice from him and a history of the furniture in question in reason-able detail, attributions to the Chippendale workshop can only be conjectural.

Chippendale's designs as shown in the *Director* are drawn from three sources—rococo, revived Gothic, and Chinese. In this, he was no more than following the fashions of his time, and his rococo designs were perhaps the most influential. Most of his best furniture is made in this style, and some of it can be regarded as little more than copies of French furniture of the period. His Chinese designs are considered under the heading of *Chinese Chippendale*, and his revived Gothic under *Gothic Style, Revived.* There are a number of reprints of the *Director* (and selections from it) available at present, some of which are included in the Bibliography. From any of these the scope and nature of his designs may be seen, although if some of the more elaborate examples were ever made they do not appear to have survived. His later work, some of it done for the Adam Brothers, was in a restrained neo-classical style. Nothing is known of the work of

Chippendale, Thomas. The Combe Abbey mahogany library table by Thomas Chippendale. Mid-18th century. *Sotheby & Co.*

Chiselling and Chasing. The chiselling and engraving of metal. France. Mid-18th century. *After Diderot.*

Thomas II after 1796, but no doubt he employed the current Regency styles.

CHISELLING

The art of finishing objects of metal, usually rough casts, by removing blemishes and surplus material with metalworking chisels and a hammer. Bronze is most commonly treated in this way.

Although it is possible to cast most objects of bronze with sufficient accuracy to ensure that the details will be sharp and clear, in practice it is nearly always essential to do a certain amount of cleaning up afterwards with files and chisels. This was especially the case with the mounts of 18th-century French furniture, and they are often to be judged by the quality of the finishing. This was done by the *ciseleurs,* members of the Corporation of Ciseleurs-Fondeurs (q.v.). In works on French decorative art the word is sometimes mistranslated as *chasers,* and the process confused with *chasing* (q.v.). Apart from furniture-mounts, many Renaissance bronze figures were finished by chiselling and filing, and sometimes by drilling. Hair, especially, was often drilled.

Bronzes should always be examined for signs of chiselling, especially when the ornament is intricate. Furniture-mounts and similar small objects were often reproduced in the 19th century by electrotyping (q.v.).

Silver and gold ornament was often chiselled in the same way, and for a similar purpose, but in some cases the intention was not to remove casting blemishes, but to add small ornament which could not be cast satisfactorily. This can be seen especially in such small objects as gold boxes, where the ductile metal is 'pushed' into shape with tools like chisels and punches. This kind of work is more akin to chasing, and the latter term is often employed for it.

CHUR-BAYERN (The Electorate of Bavaria)

Chur or *Kur* is always used as a prefix and can mean either Elector or, as above, Electorate, for instance *Kurfürst,* Prince-Elector, or *Kur Brandenburg,* the Electorate of Brandenburg, Bayern, etc. From a Middle High German word *Kuren,* meaning 'to choose'.

CHUTE (French)

A long, narrow panel of relief decoration, usually of cast bronze or carved wood, which decorated walls and furniture during the 17th and 18th centuries.

Chute. Marine trophy in the form of a *chute* of the Louis XVI period. *12 Place Vendôme, Paris.*

CIPRIANI, GIOVANNI BATTISTA (1727–1785)

An Italian decorator working in London from 1753 onwards. He did ceiling and panel medallions and *arabesques* for Robert Adam, and also painted furniture (see *Furniture, English Painted*). He published the *Rudiments of Drawing* between 1786 and 1792 with engravings by Bartolozzi (q.v.).

CITRONNIER (French)

Citronwood, used as a veneer by the 18th-century *ébénistes* of France and Germany, especially in conjunction with such dark woods as mahogany. In appearance it somewhat resembles satinwood.

CLASSICAL ART

The word *classic* means an excellence which is recognized universally, or so widely that it is tantamount to universal. During Renaissance times the art of Greece and Rome was so recognized, and hence came to be termed *classical*. This was also the case in the second half of the 18th century with renewed interest in Greek and Roman art—a phase termed *neo-classical* because it followed a period in which classical ideals had to some extent been superseded by others. A feature of classical art is the formulation of rules governing artistic expression, and it can be recognized partly by its adherence to them (see *Proportion, Human*, and *Orders, The Five*). Classical art is the mainstream of European artistic tradition. The other important category, romantic art, is discussed under that heading.

See also *Adam, The Brothers*; *Gothic Style, The*; *Neo-classicism*; *Palladianism*.

CLAW-AND-BALL FOOT

A carved foot employed for chairs and tables in the early years of the 18th century in England. It was especially popular during the decade 1730–1740. It was, perhaps, derived from the claw of the Chinese dragon grasping the sacred pearl, and it first made its appearance in Holland towards the end of the 17th century. In America, however, the ball-and-claw foot had enormous popularity into the late 18th century and its variations are one of the principal clues to the region of origin of a piece of furniture.

CLAY, HENRY   See *Papier Mâché*

CLEPSYDRA

A water-clock devised in Egypt, whence it passed to Greece and Rome. It consisted of a container for water which was allowed to escape at a predetermined rate, various means of recording the flow being adopted. The Romans devised a number of ingenious mechanical elaborations. The Chinese during the Sung dynasty (960–1280) invented a water-clock which employed a mechanism that may have been the precursor of the escapement (q.v.)—the foundation of all European clock mechanisms.

The clepsydra enjoyed a revival in the 17th century, perhaps in Burgundy, and it made its appearance in Paris in 1693. Some were also made in England during the same period, although specimens are rare. Usually there is a brass cylinder from which water escapes slowly. A float in the cylinder is coupled to a single hand indicating the hour by a chain, and as it falls with the water-level it turns the hand. Such clocks ran for thirty-six hours at one filling, and were only approximately accurate.

CLERMONT-FERRAND (Puy-de-Dôme, France) FAÏENCE

The factory in this town was short-lived, and the few interesting pieces can be ascribed to a period of ten years round about 1736 to 1746. One factory, started in 1730, made rather unsuccessful domestic ware, but a man called D'Alagnat obtained a patent and the title of *Manufacture Royale* for his factory. He turned to Nevers and to Montpellier for his workers, but two of them, Antoine Dupré and his brother, must have stayed only briefly at Clermont, as they reappear at Montpellier in 1746.

Not many marked pieces exist from Clermont-Ferrand, but there are several marked either *Clermont-Ferrand* or decorated with local Coats of Arms, and with inscriptions which enable them to be identified. For instance, the ewer dated 1734 in the Bargoin Museum at Clermont-Ferrand must be one of the earliest. It is decorated in blue-and-white with an allegory of Time in the style of Jean Bérain, and *lambrequins* round the base. Blue-and-white decoration is generally uneven, and a mediocre imitation of Nevers, Rouen, Montpellier, or Moustiers.

Another factory was founded after 1775 by a man named Verdier and the name Perrier-Lauche appears on some 'revolutionary' (*faïence patriotique*) wares made at Clermont.

'CLOBBERING'

The addition of decoration in enamel colouring to Chinese blue-and-white porcelain, mainly by Dutch decorators. Similar work was done by the *Hausmaler*, Ferner (q.v.), on Meissen blue-and-white porcelain.

CLOCK-JACK

Sometimes called a roasting-jack, this was a clockwork device for turning meat hung on a hook in front of the fire. In America clock-jacks were sometimes made by the clock-makers of the time. They were sometimes used in conjunction with a chimney-crane —a wrought-iron or brass bracket attached to the wall above the hearth. Cooking-pots were suspended from it and moved to the required position above the fire.

Clock-jacks were either of brass or japanned sheet iron.

CLOCK LAMPS

These first appeared about 1730, and took the form of a glass oil-container mounted on a metal stand, with a wick-carrier projecting at right angles. Hours were marked on the outside of the oil-container, and the time was indicated by the oil-level as it was consumed.

CLOCK MOVEMENTS OF WOOD

Clock movements made of wood have been produced in various parts of the world, the best known in Europe being the cuckoo clocks of Germany's Black Forest. These have been a minor industry for many years and are still being made today, often being supplied in parts for assembly by the purchaser. Wooden movements are always weight-driven and the metal parts reduced to a bare minimum. They are reasonably good, but not highly accurate, time-keepers. In Europe they have been somewhat of a curiosity, for the most part peasant work, but a shortage of brass in America during the 18th century and part of the 19th caused clockmakers to take wood much more seriously as a clock-making material. Mostly made in Connecticut the earliest recorded specimen seems to be a long-case clock by Benjamin Cheney of 1745. A later maker was Eli Terry (q.v.) of Plymouth (Conn.), whose early clocks, beginning in 1792, were of this type. Some of these early wooden clocks are still working, but generally specimens are now rare.

CLOCKS, AMERICAN

In America from the 17th to the 19th century only the very wealthy could afford a clock, since most, if not all, of its parts had to be imported. Mostly, the wealthiest early colonists brought their own clocks with the household equipment, or imported them later. These were wall or bracket clocks.

About 1715 most clocks and known clock-makers came from England. The first established clock-maker of Philadelphia, Pennsylvania, was *Abell Cottley* (1682). *Benjamin Chandlee*, was apprenticed to Cottley in 1702. *Peter Stretch* learned his trade in England, and came to Philadelphia in 1702. *Benjamin Bagnall* (1710) was perhaps Boston's first clockmaker. *William Claggett*, at Boston, 1715, moved to Newport, Rhode Island, where he was active 1720–1740. *Gawen Brown* (1719–1801) worked in Boston, and *Isaac Pearson*, at Burlington, N.J., 1730. *Bartholomew Barwell* (active 1749) worked in New York; *David Blaisdell*, was at Annsberg, Mass. by 1740; and *Seth Youngs*, was working in Hartford, Conn. before 1740.

1750s

Most skilled clockmakers gravitated to Philadelphia. The most notable was *David Rittenhouse*, working *c.* 1750–1790, but the period otherwise produced few notable clockmakers. Each clock was made by hand, custom-built to specific order, with brass eight-day movement, and using an imported face. Clockmakers doubled as cabinet-makers, making cases for their movements. Conversely, some of the best colonial craftsmen, including *Edward James* of Philadelphia, *John Townsend* of Newport, and *Thomas Johnson* (or *Johnston*) the well-known japanner of Boston produced cases for imported movements.

1750s–1800

Tall- (or long-) case clocks were made in increasing numbers where hitherto they had been made for the very wealthy. The most revolutionary idea was the use of wood in movements to replace brass, which was both expensive and difficult to obtain. *Benjamin Cheney* and his brother *Timothy* were the earliest clockmakers in Connecticut working in wood (1745).

Benjamin Willard (*c.* 1765) headed the famous Massachusetts clock-making family, with his younger brothers, *Simon, Ephraim* and *Aaron*. They produced many different types—town, grandfather, banjo, lyre, lighthouse, girandole and shelf. They did not use wooden movements. Simon was the most notable because of his patented (1802) clock, now known as the 'banjo' (q.v.). Aaron was particularly noted for his development of the Massachusetts shelf-clock. The earliest Willard clocks are now exceedingly rare.

Eli Terry, born in 1772, had his own shop in 1793. He invented standardized or interchangeable wooden parts for his clocks. During the period 1818–1840 he was the most popular designer in the United States.

CLOCKS, ASTRONOMICAL

Clocks which record astronomical information. The first astronomical clock of which there is reliable record was that of Giovanni di Dondi in 1364. It was destroyed in 1809, but from his surviving drawings the clock was reconstructed, and this reproduction is now in the Smithsonian Institute, Washington, D.C.

Astronomical clocks give a considerable variety of information, depending on the degree of elaboration in the movement. Clocks showing the phases of the moon are common, and an addition of mechanisms of this kind to the normal movement was neither difficult nor expensive. Since tides are governed by the phases of the moon, the mechanism to record these was very similar. Much more elaborate are movements recording the annual movement of the sun, and of the planets in the Zodiac. Dials giving information of this kind occur by the middle of the 16th century as part of Augsburg table-clocks, and such clocks were of interest not only to those scientifically inclined but also to astrologers. It is probable that most such clocks were, at first, intended for astrological purposes.

There were a number of very elaborate clocks of this kind made in the 17th and 18th centuries which still survive; for instance, one now in Spain made by Thomas Hildeyard, an Englishman working in Liége. Complex astronomical clocks were popular in France towards the end of the 18th century, and they continued to be popular among those who could afford them until well into the 19th century, specimens being exhibited at the Great Exhibition of 1851. They are now infrequently made, apart from those required for special purposes.

Calendar clocks belong to the same class as astronomical clocks, the information given merely being simpler to record. Perpetual calendar clocks (very rare) allow for differences in the length of the months without alteration by hand.

CLOCKS, CALENDAR
See *Clocks, Astronomical*

CLOCKS, ENGLISH, FOR EXPORT TO THE EAST

English craftsmen from the 17th century onwards enjoyed two principal export markets of this kind— Turkey and China—although they exported also to India and south-east Asia. Clocks for China usually have ordinary numerals and are to be distinguished by the design of their cases. Clocks for Turkey have Turkish numerals. Owing to the Moslem religious prejudice against representations of the human figure the cupid spandrels were also omitted. The earliest example of a clock made for the Turkish market appears to be a hood-clock (q.v.) by Edward Stanton of about 1680, but most are much later, and are usually bracket-clocks. A maker whose clocks seem to have been in demand in Istanbul is Markwick Markham, but there were several others. Since Elizabethan times England always had trading relations with Turkey, but the period during which clocks were principally exported was from about 1750 onwards, and the trade seems to have flourished till the end of the century. Cases were usually very ornate, and profusely decorated with brass and ormolu castings which seems to have been an essential requirement of the market. Not infrequently they have elaborate chiming and musical trains. Not all of them seem to have been exported, because they are sometimes to be found in England.

Musical clocks were also in great demand in China, and decoration often makes extensive use of enamels. Automata (q.v.) of one kind or another are not unusual, and James Cox of London, who also had a shop in Canton, was probably the principal maker engaged in this trade. He held a lottery of some of his surplus wares about 1770, and that his business was on a large scale is evident from the total value of the prizes—£134,000. Some of his clocks were brought back to England when General 'Chinese' Gordon looted the Summer Palace in 1860. Cox was not the only manufacturer to trade with China, and several names are recorded. At the end of the century the trade seems to have been in the hands of a London clockmaker named Weeks. Some clocks for this market incorporated Chinese jade, ivory, and enamels in the case.

CLOCKS, EVOLUTION OF

Time, as distinct from duration, is the interval which elapses between two astronomical events of the same kind, and this (unlike duration, which is subjective) can be measured with suitable apparatus.

Clocks, Evolution of. Back-plate of bracket clock by du Chesne, early 18th century, showing customary engraving and the maker's name.

The astronomical event on which most time measurement is based is the diurnal rotation of the earth, and the day is a convenient unit which can be multiplied into weeks, months, and years, or divided into hours, minutes, and seconds. The division into hours, minutes, and seconds is purely arbitrary. There is nothing in nature to suggest it. The year, however, is the time-lapse which is necessary for the earth to complete its journey round the sun, and it therefore has an objective basis. The month was originally the time taken for the moon to travel through its phases, but this does not fit exactly with the present twelve-month year, so the present months are an arbitrary division. There is no special reason why a week should be seven days, or we should have weeks at all, apart from convenience.

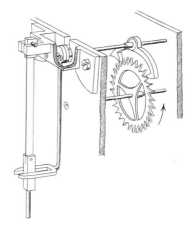

Clocks. Details of the anchor escapement, showing the top of the pendulum, and the anchor-shaped release mechanism.

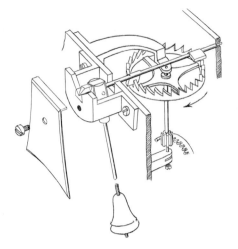

Clocks. Detail of the verge escapement, showing the crown wheel and pallets and the connection to the pendulum. The latter raises each of the pallets in turn as it swings and allows one tooth of the crown wheel to 'escape', hence the name.

The clock, which is the major time-measuring device, has evolved since the beginning of the 14th century in the direction of greater accuracy. It could hardly become much more reliable mechanically, since some of the very early clocks were so strongly made that the ancient Wells Cathedral clock only had to be replaced in 1835, and one at Rye (Sussex) is still working, having been converted to pendulum control. It boasts what is probably the world's longest pendulum.

Clock mechanisms are all the same in principle. The motive-power is provided by weights or springs, and these drive a series (or train) of meshing toothed wheels which actuate the hands that indicate the hour and sometimes provide other information as well, such as recording the motion of heavenly bodies, the times of high tides, and so forth. The power must be released in a controlled sequence, and this is done by means of an escapement (q.v.).

The inventor of the mechanical clock is unknown, but it is likely to have come from China by way of Islamic sources. Certainly clocks were known in Italy by the 14th century, and by 1364 Giovanni de Dondi was able to make an astronomical clock of considerable complexity which was destroyed in 1809. A replica is in the Smithsonian Institute (Washington, D.C.).

At first clocks were only to be found in the richest houses, but after 1400 they became fairly general. Most were made to be hung on the wall and were weight-driven. Usually they were made of iron by the locksmith or blacksmith. Brass began to replace iron for parts of the mechanism about 1550, and it had many advantages. It was easier to work, could be more accurately machined, and it was not prone to rust. Brass was extensively used by the South German metalworking cities of Ulm, Augsburg, Nürnberg, and Cassel, and by 1600 only the frame was of iron.

The first use of the spring as motive-power is attributed to Peter Henlein of Nürnberg about 1500, but this has been doubted, and a spring-driven mechanism may first have appeared in Italy. With the advent of the spring clocks came down off the wall, and spring-driven table-clocks which could be carried about were soon a South German speciality, especially at Augsburg where cases were handsomely engraved, pierced, embossed, and chased.

To the recording of the hour were added alarm and striking trains, to be followed by clocks fitted with calendar dials, and those recording the phases of the moon. One clock with a calendar dial is dated 1567, and the very elaborate Strasbourg tower-clock in the British Museum (London), which has a number of automatically moving figurines, is dated 1589. Such figurines were quite commonly added to the more elaborate clocks, usually performing movements on the hour. They later became stationary and no more than decoration, although a late 17th-century example made for Louis XIV had representations of the German Electors and Italian princes which moved on the hour, the Kings of Europe struck the hour, and a figure of Louis himself bowed acknowledgement.

Although German clocks dominated the greater part of the 17th century, by the beginning of the 18th the lead had been taken by France and England.

Clocks, Evolution of. Lantern clock in an engraved silver case by David Bouquet (d. 1665). English. c. 1650. *Victoria and Albert Museum.*

Clocks, Evolution of. Bracket clock with double-basket top and cherub spandrels showing the date, phases of the moon, etc. English. c. 1700.

Usually the French clock is the more noted for quality of its case and the English clock for the quality of its movement, but the French also made excellent movements and contributed much to the development of clockwork generally, while the English made very good but simple cases decorated with marquetry and veneering of high quality.

The best English clocks are usually those made by London members of the Clockmakers' Company, although some provincial clocks approach the London standard. Some of the more famous of the horologists working around 1700 were Thomas Tompion, Daniel Quare, Edward East, George Graham, and Joseph Knibb, but a comprehensive list is given in Britten's *Old Clocks and Watches and their Makers*, which is the essential standard work for every clock collector. Most English movements are signed usually on the dial (long-case clocks) or on the back-plate (bracket-clocks), but sometimes a signature appears on bracket-clock dials instead. Early dials are square, made of brass (usually lacquered), with a silvered chapter-ring and cast ornamental spandrels in the corners. Dials were usually engraved, and the back-plates of bracket-clocks, which, unlike those of the long-case clock, are often seen, were also engraved. The hands, of

blued steel, are more or less elaborately pierced on any but a minor specimen. A dial arched at the top was occasionally employed by Tompion before 1700, but it did not begin to be fashionable until about 1725. The arch is the usual place for the strike/silent lever on a clock with a striking and chiming train. Enamel dials were introduced about 1750 for bracket-clocks, and long-case dials were then often completely silvered. Painted dials were employed for cheap clocks, usually in oak cases, made during the second half of the 18th century. Movements usually ran for about eight days at one winding, but those intended to run for a month, or even a year, are known. The time for which a long-case clock will run can be gauged from the distance between the weights when the door is opened—the wider the distance, the longer the period, since width is governed by the size of the driving wheels.

English cases follow current fashions in furniture, marquetry being preferred during the Dutch phase of William and Mary, and the following reign of Queen Anne, with plain veneered walnut thereafter almost until the middle of the 18th century, when mahogany became the rule. Japanned cases were popular during the first half of the century, a few extremely fine but most of poor quality. These were always the work of English imitators of Oriental lacquer and not Oriental.

Bracket-clocks in ebonized or walnut cases were often given elaborately pierced gilt-metal tops towards the end of the 17th century. These are known as basket tops, and a more ornate variety as double basket tops, a term which is self-explanatory. The plain ebonized case which followed was replaced about the middle of the 18th century by the plain mahogany case. Examples of cases decorated with ormolu mounts, or even made of cast metal with sometimes the addition of enamel plaques, are rare, but they can be seen occasionally, and towards the end of the century a combination of ormolu and *biscuit* porcelain figures, or those of Wedgwood's jasper stoneware, were, like the other varieties mentioned,

Clocks, Evolution of. Spring-driven table clock, quarter striking, with steel movement. Dia. 8⅝ inches, height 3½ inches. Augsburg. c. 1585. *Sotheby & Co.*

obviously inspired by contemporary work in France (see *Boulton, Matthew*). Exceptionally ornate specimens of the second half of the 18th century were sometimes made for export to Turkey, with which country English clockmakers drove a thriving trade. Very few bracket-clocks now have their original bracket, which was attached to the wall, and it is probable that this was often dispensed with comparatively early in their existence, the clock being placed on a table or chimney-piece.

Some French cases were made by the *ébénistes* (q.v.), but long-case clocks (*régulateurs*) were not very popular in France, and most existing specimens are provincial, where they are still fairly common. Most French clocks are bracket-clocks, i.e. those made to stand on a bracket (or mural *console*) attached fairly high up on the wall; chimney-piece clocks, to stand on a mantelshelf with matching vases; those more elaborate for side-tables; and cartel clocks, which were affixed directly to the wall without a *console*, and occasionally on to the glass of a mirror about two-thirds of the way up. For the latter position we have the evidence of contemporary engravings. Some clocks, like large bracket-clocks in shape, stood on a *gaine* or pedestal, and they are, in appearance, not unlike the *régulateur* but not so tall. They lacked the long pendulum. These are called pedestal clocks. Another variety formed an integral part of a piece of furniture, usually a *cartonnier* attached to an important desk.

Clockmakers were highly regarded, and the best were given lodgings in the Louvre. Designers of the calibre of A.-C. Boulle were responsible for some of the finest cases in the early years of the 18th century, while Charles Cressent excelled as a designer of cartel clocks. Throughout the 18th century the clock-case was designed and finished with a care and skill worthy of goldsmiths' work. Many are of gilt-bronze, sometimes with the addition of marquetry in the manner of Boulle (q.v.), but combinations of materials such as silver and bronze, or marble and bronze, became more usual after 1750. To this was added the art of G. F. Strass (q.v.) in the form of 'paste' brilliants surrounding the dial, and after the introduction of the 'ring' pendulum, which swung in front of the dial, to the ring of the pendulum itself. About 1750 we find the clock partly of porcelain, sometimes with supporting figures of Meissen porcelain and added flowers of porcelain from Vincennes with leaves and stalks of bronze. By the 1760s clocks were being made from the porcelain vases of Sèvres, the clock movement being inset into the case, which was mounted in gilt-bronze. A happier way of using porcelain urns was the introduction of figures carried on a central revolving band, the hour being indicated by a stationary pointer.

Cases became so ornate—so much works of art— that the movement was almost subsidiary. For example, the famous Avignon clock in the Wallace Collection (London) designed by Boizot and executed by Pierre Gouthière (q.v.) is so much a *tour de*

Clocks, Evolution of. A long-case clock with a shell carved block-front (q.v.) by Caleb Wheaton, Providence, R.I. c. 1790. The case in the general style associated with Chippendale. *Parke-Bernet Galleries, New York.*

Clocks, French. Vase clock of Sèvres porcelain with a ground termed *œil de perdrix*, mounted in gilt-bronze. Early Louis XVI style. c. 1770. *Wallace Collection.*

Régulateur clocks, of which one was to be found in most important houses because of its accuracy, had an ornate pendulum which could be viewed through a 'window' in the door. The bob was frequently in the form of a mask surrounded by a sunburst. Pendulums were usually fitted with a suspension to compensate for variations in temperature consisting in alternate brass and steel rods, a device invented in England about 1725, where it was called a gridiron suspension.

Clocks were made in America during the 17th century, but little is known of them, and most were imported. In the 18th century records have survived of a considerable number of clockmakers, one of the most noted being David Rittenhouse (fl. 1750–1790). Most American clocks of this period were of the long-case variety, not unlike contemporary English clocks in appearance, but tending to differ in the proportions of the case, being usually somewhat wider in relation to the height. Wooden movements, like those of Switzerland and the Black Forest, were made in Connecticut in the second half of the 18th century and are now very rare. A wall-clock of banjo shape is an American innovation, patented by Simon Willard in 1802, which became

force of the sculptor's art that its time-recording function hardly seems important.

French movements, however, became increasingly elaborate. Musical clocks played a melody, or series of melodies, on the hour, employing a carillon of bells for the purpose actuated by a revolving drum studded with small pins—the same principle as that later used for the musical-box. Clocks of this kind were also made in England. The birdcage clock which set singing-birds in motion every hour was popular, and waterfalls were imitated with a revolving spiral of glass. French makers of movements directed their attention to making them smaller while preserving efficiency.

French clocks, in the design of their cases, exhibit the style of their period, but, as a general rule, until the reign of Louis XV the width of the case is invariably less than the height. Almost all cases are surmounted by a gilt-bronze figure. Cronos with his scythe was a favourite, and figures of Diana hardly less so. Apollo with the chariot of the sun is rare. We have the evidence of Mercier (*Tableaux de Paris*), writing just before the Revolution, that owners often changed the figures on their clocks for fresh ones, and isolated gilt-bronze figures which seem to have no special purpose may once have formed part of a clock. Cartel clocks are nearly always notable for the quality of their bronze-work, and they are extremely rare. Louis XVI clocks are usually a good deal wider than they are high, and the bronzework is mounted on a marble plinth. Many are topped by a classical urn with supporting figures on either side.

Clocks, French. Clock in a case veneered with Boulle (q.v.) marquetry and mounted in gilt-bronze, the movement by Thuret, Paris. The figure at the top is Diana, the huntress, and two hinds support the case from below. Although in a late Louis XIV style, the date is probably *Régence*, about 1720. *Wallace Collection.*

them more fashionable, such as hoods reconstructed to take an arched dial. An arch added to a square dial is not unusual, and is almost always quite obvious. Careful examination of the case will usually indicate when alterations have taken place to allow another movement to be substituted.

The addition of famous names to dials and back-plates is usually obvious. Not only does the quality of the movement not equal its pretensions in the vast majority of instances, but blank spaces for the addition of names rarely occur, and the faker has nearly always found it necessary to make one. Clocks with blank spaces, however, sometimes occurred, and the engraving should therefore be studied, for few forgers can reproduce 18th-century engraving convincingly. Compare the quality of the engraving with that to be found elsewhere.

Replacement of part of the original movement is inevitable, but the wear and tear of time falls more on some parts than others, and particularly on the escapement. It is doubtful whether any clocks now survive from the 18th century with their original escapement; certainly not if they have been used. Replacement of a verge with an anchor escapement may have taken place at any time from the 17th century onwards. Some clocks, however, are little more than the original back and front plates, with many new pinions and wheels substituted for the originals. If there are many vacant holes in the back-plate this is a good indication that part of the original train has been removed. Bolt and shutter mechanisms (q.v.) were so frequently removed in the 19th century that hardly any specimens survive in original condition.

Clocks, French. Clock with the hours indicated on revolving bands around a celestial globe. The figure of Time with scythe and hour-glass is surrounded by *putti* amid conventional bronze clouds. Louis XVI style. c. 1770. *Wallace Collection.*

very popular thereafter. Weight-driven clocks were virtually ousted by those deriving their motive-power from springs by 1850, and then began a period of mass-production, the products of which have little interest for the serious collector. In general, apart from a few of the finer 18th-century long-case clocks, the American contribution to clockmaking as an art was not very great.

CLOCKS, FORGERIES OF

Apart from lantern clocks, which have been quite commonly reproduced, forgeries of old clocks are almost non-existent, since it would cost as much to make them as the forger would be likely to get. But there are many in which the movement has been extensively altered, and some which have been given false signatures of well-known makers. Neither of these present much difficulty to the reasonably knowledgeable. The marriage of a movement to an incorrect case is not unusual, but this may have occurred long ago, the original case and its movement having become parted in a variety of ways. Cases especially were often altered to make

CLOCKS, NIGHT

During the second half of the 17th century English clockmakers turned their attention to the problem of telling the time at night when there were no electric switches to turn, and alarm and striking mechanisms became a frequent inclusion in domestic clocks of the period. But the bells were usually strident, and hardly an answer to the problem. The night-clock proper did not arrive until the extreme end of the 17th century. This had a continuously illuminated dial, but it must have been unsatisfactory in practice, for few seem to have been made, and one authority has suggested that they were once more numerous, but that most of them were burnt by their own lamps. Ventilation seems to have been a problem, for clocks exist where the ventilation has been increased by cutting fresh holes. The clock was provided with an oil-reservoir for the lamp, set about two-thirds of the way up the back, with burners for from one to three wicks. Dials were usually painted, and few of these clocks were fitted with a striking mechanism. Edward East made some night-clocks, including a long-case version, as did the Fromenteels, and Joseph Knibb. German clocks of the same nature exist, and they are much less rare. A few French clocks of this kind have been recorded.

CLODION (CLAUDE MICHEL) (1738–1814)

French sculptor who modelled for the porcelain factories of Sèvres and Nidervilier. Born in Nancy, he arrived in Paris in 1754. His erotic terracottas of nymphs and satyrs were especially popular then, and still are. His terracottas were widely forged in the 19th century, and most bronzes signed 'Clodion' are of this date.

CLOTHES PRESS

A large cupboard for the storage of clothes, with drawers under. The top was usually fitted with shelves and sliding trays. See *Wardrobe*.

CLUSTER COLUMN LEG

These legs, usually to be found on tables designed in the revived Gothic style by Chippendale and others, are formed from several slender columns joined together, springing from a single base and ending in a common capital, similar to those to be found in Gothic churches.

COASTER

A small, circular tray with a turned wood base covered with baize, and surrounded by a gallery of metal, sometimes pierced, which was either silver or Sheffield plate. They came into use soon after the middle of the 18th century, when it was customary to remove the table-cloth before serving dessert. Decanters and bottles were placed on the coaster so that they could be slid, or 'coasted', along the polished table-top without scratching it. They were made in pairs, sets of four, or even in greater numbers. Coasters were also made from *papier mâché*.

COALBROOKDALE, SHROPSHIRE   See *Coalport*

COALPORT, SHROPSHIRE

Porcelain factory founded about 1796 by John Rose, who had been apprenticed to Turner at Caughley. Rose purchased the Caughley factory in 1799, and operated it in conjunction with the Coalport enterprise until 1814. Billingsley (q.v.) began employment with Coalport in 1819, and the moulds and stock of porcelain in white of Nantgarw (q.v.) and Swansea (q.v.) were bought and removed to Coalport about 1822. For a period, between about 1820 to 1830, Rose employed a porcelain formula very similar to that of Nantgarw, and from this time onwards Coalport porcelain is always remarkable for its translucency.

Early Coalport and late Caughley production is almost indistinguishable, and no doubt Caughley porcelain was sent to Coalport for decoration. In 1801 the well-known Indian Tree pattern was introduced and later copied elsewhere. In 1820 the factory was awarded the Gold Medal of the Royal Society of Arts for a leadless, feldspathic glaze, since lead had been the cause of poisoning among factory operatives in the pottery industry.

John Rose began, about this time, to imitate the wares of Sèvres extensively, although these imitations are not deceptive to anyone accustomed to the earlier wares of the royal factory. Vases in the Chelsea gold anchor style were produced, and reproductions of earlier wares, such as cabbage tureens and 'Goat and Bee' jugs, are often thought to have been made here. Some copies of 18th-century Meissen wares were also made, but these are fewer since they were no longer so fashionable. Vases covered with highly modelled flowers were a Coalport speciality, as well as dessert services decoratively painted. John Rose died in 1841, and was succeeded by William Frederick Rose, when copying the wares of the 18th-century Sèvres factory was at its height. After 1862 it suffered a period of decline, but was reorganized in 1885 as the Coalport China Company, and acquired in 1925 by the Cauldon Potteries (see *Ridgway*). A mark *CBD*, for Coalbrookdale, occurring in some early Coalport porcelain cannot be satisfactorily explained. It has been assumed that it refers to a decorating studio at Coalbrookdale.

COBB, JOHN (d. 1778)

English cabinet-maker who worked for George III. Partner with William Vile (q.v.). Furniture reliably attributed to Cobb is rare, but a mahogany *commode* in the Louis XV style with marquetry ornament and English ormolu mounts (perhaps by Boulton) is in the Victoria and Albert Museum. Another of satinwood similarly embellished is at Corsham Court, Wilts. A very rococo girandole in carved and gilded wood is at Temple Newsam, Leeds.

COCKATRICE

A mythical animal with a cock's head and comb, a bird's legs and claws, and a tail ending in a spearpoint. It is similar to the basilisk, and could blast human beings with a look or with its breath. It was the product of the fertilization of a cock's egg by a serpent, and Theophilus gives directions for hatching it. It is rare in the decorative arts and is usually part of an heraldic device.

COCK-FIGHTING CHAIR   See *Reading Chair*

COCK-METAL

An alloy of copper and lead used for small castings of an inferior kind. See *Billy and Charley; Pewter*.

COFFER

(French, *coffre, bahut*.) The term 'coffer' was usually employed to designate a portable chest covered with leather and studded with nails. Like the early French *bahut*, it was employed for travelling. See *Bahut*.

COIN GLASSES

The practice of inserting a coin into the knop forming part of the stem of a wine-glass seems to date, in England, from the first quarter of the 18th century, although genuinely old specimens are very rare. The practice has continued until modern times, and has probably always been commemorative in one way or another. The ball of glass containing the coin was made separately and later inserted between the foot and the bowl. The heat consequent on this operation has often had the effect of discolouring silver coins. Obviously the glass cannot be earlier than the date of the coin, but this does not mean that it is not very much later. Each case has to be judged on its merits —by the apparent date of the glass, as well as by the certain date of the coin.

'COLD' PAINTING

The term is employed of painting in oil-colours or lacquer colours on surfaces usually enamelled. Cold painting (German *kalte malerei*) on glass and faïence is often in a very worn condition, but rare examples of red stoneware from Meissen painted in lacquer colours by Martin Schnell (q.v.) and others have fared somewhat better. There is good reason to think that much early white porcelain was painted in this way with oil-colours, especially that of Bow in England, but frequent washing has removed the paint in most cases although, on rare specimens, a few traces sometimes remain.

COLLAGE

Collage, or the making of pictures in which a variety of materials were glued to some kind of background, is not a modern invention. It has, in fact, been practised since the 17th century, chiefly as a ladies' amusement, and specimens of one kind or another not uncommonly survive. The vogue was at its height during the first half of the 19th century.

Sand-pictures (q.v.) are a kind of collage, but these were the work of professionals for the most part. At the beginning of the 18th century pictures of birds were made from plumage gummed to the background. Straw-work, or the making of pictures from straw, plain or plaited, natural or dyed, is also early, although most surviving examples belong to the 19th century. Hair-pictures, hardly collage but to be classed with pictures made in this way, were embroidered on satin from human hair, and resemble fine pencilling. Leaf-skeletons were employed decoratively in various ways in the 17th century, and rolled paperwork, in which the picture was formed by gumming tiny rolls of paper to the background, was a 17th-century technique still in use in the 19th. Finally, as the art decayed towards the end of the 19th century we find figures cut from chromolithographs and gummed to screens. There is little definite information available about this kind of amateur craftwork. Some museums have specimens, and they occur occasionally in dealers' shops. In the absence of a signature there is no way of identifying the artist.

COLONIAL FURNITURE, AMERICAN

In the 17th century there was little space in the ships of the time for such bulky cargo as furniture, and the American settlers made their own furniture from the start. The designs they followed were those with which they were familiar in their own country, but workmanship was unsophisticated, and sometimes crude. Painting was resorted to instead of polishing, and local woods were used, which in some cases helps to identify the locality of origin. As the century progressed, and the colonies began to flourish, more experienced craftsmen arrived from Europe, bringing not only new fashions but greater skill, and by the early years of the 18th century, in such centres as Philadelphia and New England, cabinet-work rivals that of England and Holland. Although the styles were those of England predominantly, many new variations were introduced which eventually culminated in the emergence of a distinctive American style.

After the Declaration of Independence furniture-makers had to supply a market which had been deprived of imported furniture by the war, and the craft was especially developed in the Philadelphia area, using the styles of Chippendale, Adam, and Hepplewhite. See *Furniture, American.*

COMMODES, ENGLISH

The term 'commode' is so often translated into English as 'chest of drawers' that it is essential to emphasize the fact that the two have little in common, and in many cases the resemblance is not even superficial. The *commode* proper as understood both in England and France during the 18th century is a highly decorative piece of furniture, low, and provided with drawers, and sometimes with cupboards

Commodes, English. Serpentine-fronted English commode in the French taste in the manner of Chippendale. Kingwood and burl-yew marquetry mounted in ormolu (q.v.). Mid-18th century. *Parke-Bernet Galleries, New York.*

Commodes, English. Marquetry top of preceding illustration.

Commodes, English. An English mahogany commode in the French taste of Louis XV mounted in ormolu. c. 1765.

as well. The term is, in fact, untranslatable, since no word has ever become current in English as a substitute. Perhaps the clearest distinction that could be drawn is to say that a chest of drawers is essentially bedroom furniture, and the *commode* was nearly always intended for the drawing-room. The word was current when Chippendale wrote his *Director*, since he describes some of his designs as 'commode tables'. Most of his designs owe much to French rococo furniture, and the addition of *chinoiseries* (q.v.) was also in accord with current French taste, although they were not usually of the same kind. But the occasional occurrence of revived Gothic *motifs* is peculiarly English, and these are not to be seen elsewhere. Perhaps inspired by the fashion current in France, a few lacquered *commodes* in the Chinese taste were made, but these are very rare. Like those of France, English *commodes* were furnished with decorative handles in brass or ormolu, and often with mounts added as well, although in England the place of mounts was usually taken by fine carving for which mahogany, not then in general use in France, was eminently suitable. The English cabinet-maker devised some variations not used by the French *ébéniste* at the time, such as the *commode* with a central cupboard flanked by narrow but deep drawers, and *commodes* which were also writing-tables, or those which combined the functions of writing-tables and dressing-tables, these facilities being concealed in a long drawer at the top. Some of the best of the *commodes* of the period were made by William Vile (q.v.), whose furniture surpassed in quality and design that attributed to Chippendale. Vile was much less influenced by the prevailing French rococo than Chippendale, and his designs are among the best of the period. Some English *commodes* catch the spirit of French rococo so well that it is sometimes difficult, at a glance, to tell where they were made. This is especially the case with finely veneered *bombé* (q.v.) specimens which are, however, later than their currency in France, most being made around 1770.

Mahogany began to go out of fashion in the 1760s for this kind of furniture, and under the influence of the Brothers Adam drawers disappeared entirely. The *commode* became half-circular (D-shaped on plan) with drawers replaced by cupboards. These were popular after 1770, and are usually of satinwood, delicately inlaid in the neo-classical style. Sometimes they have added painted decoration.

Commodes were usually made in pairs, although they have since been parted one from the other. Most are fairly large and were made to fit into the space between windows, under a tall mirror. Small examples are rare, and are valued accordingly.

COMMODE, FRENCH

A piece of furniture similar to the English chest of drawers, but much more highly decorated with gilt-bronze mounts, veneering, and marquetry, and usually with a marble top, for use in *salons* and the more important rooms. In 18th-century England chests of drawers were usually termed *commodes* when they were decorative, and French in style.

The word means 'commodious' or 'convenient', and the primary purpose was storage. It was first introduced just before the end of the 17th century, but the term does not seem to have been widely current before 1718, when the Duchesse d'Orléans described it, in a letter, as 'a large table with two large drawers'.

Although it has varied somewhat in form with the changing fashions of the time, the *commode* is still basically the same today. As a decorative piece of furniture it was at its best during the first half of the 18th century, and perhaps the most impressive are those made by Cressent and Gaudreau.

The English use of the word *commode* to denote a *chaise percée* is of 19th-century origin, and a euphemism typical of the time.

'COMPOSITION'

A casting material of whiting, resin, and size, somewhat similar to *gesso*, which is sometimes called 'compo'. While still plastic the mixture was pressed into moulds and left until it hardened, after which it could be applied by glue or panel pins to the surface to be decorated. It was first used by the Adam Brothers for making prefabricated architectural ornament in imitation of plasterwork.

In America 'composition' was a favourite device of architects of the Federal period, such as Samuel McIntire, Asher Benjamin, and Charles Bulfinch, because its use cut costs for Americans who had less money to spend on building than the English. Though 'composition' was enormously popular in New England, its use was equally essential to the elegant Adamesque interiors of Charleston, South Carolina.

CONEY, JOHN (1655–1722)

American silversmith and engraver. Coney (or Cony) worked at Boston, Mass., and his silver is among the most sought of that of the Colonial silversmiths. Relatively, his work is not excessively rare, and examples are to be found in the Metropolitan Museum, New York.

Console. Console or wall-bracket of Bow porcelain. c. 1755. The rococo style is apparent in the asymmetrical disposition of the leafage at the bottom.

CONSOLE (French)

Often applied to certain kinds of table (see *Tables, console*), the term is of architectural origin, where it is used of a corbel sustaining a superimposed load. The term is also employed of wall-brackets for the purpose of holding a clock, a vase, or something similar. Usually of carved and gilded wood, *consoles* are sometimes made of porcelain or faïence, less often of metal. In this sense the term is synonymous with the English 'bracket'.

COOKWORTHY, WILLIAM (1705–1780)

First maker of true porcelain in England, who probably received the secret from Andrew Duché (q.v.). Cookworthy was born at Kingsbridge, Devon, in 1705, and was apprenticed at fourteen to a London apothecary, returning to Devon to commence business for himself as Bevans & Cookworthy. In 1735 he married a Quaker bride who died ten years later.

In 1745 he received a visit from someone who was almost certainly Duché. All the evidence points to it, although Cookworthy does not mention his name, referring to him as the 'person who has discovered the Chinese earth', i.e. *unaker* (q.v.). In 1745 Cookworthy, who pursued the search for these materials in Cornwall, discovered *kaolin,* and soon afterwards the equivalent of the Chinese fusible rock (petuntse or *pai-tun-tzü*) on the estate of Lord Camelford. It is probable that these discoveries were preceded in or around 1748 by the discovery of soaprock, which was passed on to his fellow-Quaker at Bristol, Benjamin Lund (see *Worcester Porcelain*).

In 1765 experiments with true porcelain had reached an advanced stage, and from a letter written to Richard Champion (q.v.), it would seem that trial firings were being made at a Bristol kiln, either a *delft* kiln or perhaps a glass-house. In 1768 Cookworthy applied for a patent and opened a factory at Coxside, Plymouth (see *Plymouth Porcelain Factory*). This was transferred to Bristol in 1770, and in 1772 Cookworthy retired, giving Champion a licence to

manufacture under his patent, which he assigned to Champion in 1774.

COPENHAGEN, KASTRUP FAÏENCE FACTORY

The Kastrup Faïence Factory was fortunate in obtaining the services of master-potters from Koblenz, and from Hannong's Strasbourg factory (q.v.). It was erected in 1747 by the Court Architect, Jacob Fortling, with a very far-reaching privilege. It continued till 1777, after which it became a purely industrial undertaking. The body is greyish-buff, with a thick glaze of reddish or bluish-grey tone, and with many flaws. Painting is in enamel colours, a dull red and dark bluish-green being characteristic.

COPENHAGEN, ØSTERBRO FAÏENCE FACTORY

This factory was started by a Norwegian, but was forced to close by Gierlof of Store Kongensgade (see below). Its products, in the absence of marks and because of the presence of wares from Store Kongensgade, have only been tentatively identified.

COPENHAGEN PORCELAIN FACTORY

In 1755 deposits of china clay were found on the island of Bornholm, and the Danish Government invited Louis Fournier from Vincennes and Chantilly to attempt to establish manufacture. Fournier devised a soft porcelain body of excellent quality, but few examples survive.

In 1771 the royal factory was founded by Franz Heinrich Müller with the aid of J. G. von Langen, a mining engineer who had been associated with Benckgraff (q.v.) at Fürstenberg (q.v.). A. C. Luplau, also of Fürstenberg, was engaged as a modeller in 1776, and the Queen, Juliane Maria, was the principal shareholder.

It was probably to Luplau, more than to any other single person, that the factory owed its success, and he brought with him a number of skilled workmen from Germany. Nevertheless, financial troubles arose, and in 1780 the factory was taken over by the King and henceforward styled *den Kongelige Danske Porcelaen Fabrik.*

The porcelain made after 1780 is in the neo-classical style, and the painted decoration was much

Copenhagen Porcelain. Punch-bowl depicting the battle of Copenhagen. 1801. *Museum of Fine Arts, Boston (Mass.).*

influenced by contemporary work in Germany. In 1789 the factory started work on a service of 1602 pieces for Catherine the Great of Russia, each piece painted with an exact botanical specimen taken from a work on Danish flora. This service, the *Flora Danica,* is among the famous services of the world, and is now in the Rosenborg Castle in Copenhagen. Figures were well-modelled, and formed a large part of 18th-century production. Sources of inspiration were frequently German or French, but some figures of Norwegian peasants are novel and interesting. During the 19th century (after 1867) the factory issued a well-known series of *biscuit* figures after the Danish neo-classical sculptor, Thorwaldsen.

At the present time the factory is one of the world's principal manufacturers of fine porcelain, doing some excellent original work. Some of their recent work has been strongly influenced by Chinese wares of the Sung period.

COPENHAGEN, STORE KONGENSGADE FAÏENCE FACTORY

A privilege for a faïence factory was granted in 1722 to five shareholders with premises in the Store Kongensgade. Its first manager came from Holstein —Johann Wolff, and he is probably identical with the painter of that name at Nürnberg (q.v.). The first concession was for thirty years. It was then renewed for another twenty, and in that time there were disputes in plenty with other factories, and with merchants who ignored the prohibitions which accompanied the concession. By 1725 Wolff had been dismissed, and he later appears in Stockholm. Two years elapsed after his departure before a potter called Johan Ernst Pfau was appointed manager in his place. He stayed at Store Kongensgade from 1727 till 1749, a time of prosperity for the factory. This peaceful atmosphere was disturbed by the appearance of a new proprietor, Christian Gierlof, who fell out with Pfau and instituted proceedings against him. Pfau died before the case was settled in 1752. Gierlof went to law against all his competitors, whom he declared to be illicit, even including the Kastrup and Østerbro factories. Gierlof believed himself to be persecuted by one and all, and the factory's fortunes suffered in consequence. Finally competition, especially from Wedgwood's creamware, caused the enterprise to close.

The body of the wares is a buff, rather hard-fired clay, while the glaze, thin in places, is white, tending towards greyish-blue. There are frequent pin-holes in the glaze, similar to Dutch *delft* which greatly influenced Danish faïence. All designs are outlined in a pure blue. A mark rather like a *VP* or *JP* was used from the early Pfau period to the end.

The first five years of the factory (1722–1727) are almost a closed book, but it is clear that Pfau took up a style already established by Wolff, identifiable from a beaker bearing his initials and decorated with *motifs* which were later part of the factory's repertoire—spirals, acanthus leaves, festoons of flowers, and *lambrequins*. A second, unmarked, beaker by the same hand displays two further *motifs* which became part of the stock-in-trade—a chequer pattern, and a type of Oriental emblem within a circle. Wolff must also be held responsible for at least one Nürnberg design, i.e., the basket filled with flowers and the stars and dots interspersed between birds and flowers that had originated in Delft.

The wares are difficult to date during the Pfau period, and the decoration is, chronologically speaking, of little help, as many of the slight changes in style in European ornament seem to have passed Store Kongensgade by, and, in general, the ornament is baroque. Rococo was adopted after 1750 when Gierlof took over, and although some freshness in execution may be observed, the period of decline begins there. Some polychrome wares in high-temperature colours have been observed, but in general the production was blue-and-white.

COPERTA (ITALIAN)

A transparent lead glaze covering the tin-enamel glaze of *maiolica*. See also *Kwaart*.

COQUILLA NUT CARVINGS

The coquilla nut comes from the eastern seaboard of central South America, and its appearance after carving has been likened to boxwood. As far back as the 16th century, to judge by a few rare survivals, the nuts have been employed for carving, probably at first by seamen, and later, as more sophisticated specimens appear to show, by wood-carvers who saw in them a suitable material for small carvings. Usually carved nuts of this kind were made to serve a utilitarian as well as an ornamental purpose, and they may be found in the form of snuff-boxes, bodkin cases, and the like. They were imported in large quantities into England at the middle of the 19th century, where they were turned into pepper-pots, needle-cases, napkin rings, and similar trivia— often by turning in a lathe and by piercing. The earlier examples are attractive to the collector, but most 19th-century specimens have little merit.

COQUILLAGE (French)

Representations of shells used decoratively, such as carved ornament to furniture or the application to porcelain and silver. The *motif* belongs to the rococo period especially, although the scallop shell was an ancient classical ornament, used both before and after the currency of the rococo style.

COPPER

Gold and native copper (i.e. copper in nugget form) were the first metals to be worked by man. Copper is soft, extremely malleable and ductile, and of considerable tensile strength. It is less easily cast than its alloy, bronze (q.v.), being difficult to reduce to a sufficiently fluid state. For this reason it is usually alloyed with other metals such as lead, for casting purposes. It is easily worked in sheet form, and vessels have commonly been fashioned from copper sheet in the past. In town areas rain which has taken up carbonic acid from the atmosphere causes the formation of green copper carbonate on the surface of the metal.

Alloyed with nickel, copper yields a silvery coloured metal, and when the two metals are in the proportion of about 75 per cent of copper to 25 per cent of nickel it forms the substance from which modern 'silver' coinage is made. German silver (or nickel-silver) is brass (i.e. a copper-zinc alloy) with the addition of up to 30 per cent of nickel. Nickel-silver has been employed for a variety of purposes connected with the decorative arts which are usually of a minor character. Electroplated with silver it becomes EPNS—electroplate on nickel-silver.

COPPER WARES
Household wares of copper—kettles, saucepans, coal-scuttles, etc.—have become increasingly popular in recent years among collectors, and this has led to the manufacture of these wares by mass-production methods. It is therefore essential to know something of the old methods of production in order to differentiate between the two.

The article was usually formed by hammering a flat sheet of metal over an appropriately shaped wooden block. Hammers of varying shapes were employed, and in most cases the process was continued until hammer-marks were virtually eliminated. In the case of edges to be joined, a series of dovetails were cut along the edges, fitted together, and secured by brazing. This can be seen plainly on the bottoms of kettles and saucepans when these have been let in. Straight-sided jugs were often made by methods appropriate to the silversmith (see *Raising*), the edges being joined by folding them on either side, followed by linking together and hammering them flat. Handles were riveted rather than brazed.

Apart from saucepans and kettles, which are the most frequently met, measures for corn, ale, and wine or spirits, and beer-mullers are much sought. Corn-measures are wide-mouthed vessels varying between six and twelve inches in height, with a heart-shaped terminal to the base of the handle. They were used to scoop from a bin. The size was not standardized until 1826.

Ale-jugs (or jacks) date from the early years of the 18th century. They are like jugs in form, but the ale or spirit measures stand on bases which are about equal in diameter to the height of the vessel, which bellies out towards the base. This became too expensive to make, and the 19th century increasingly turned to straight-sided vessels which were comparatively simple and needed less skilled craftsmanship.

The old helmet coal-scuttle has been much reproduced. Old ones date from the last quarter of the 18th century, and the style and quality of workmanship—the dovetailed brazed joints and riveted handle—will serve to differentiate old from new. The base was not soldered, but folded into place with double thickness of metal at the joint. Vessels for containing liquids and for cooking were always tinned inside to prevent the formation of verdigris.

Lead seals with the initials of the reigning monarch were affixed to measures by Excise Inspectors after legislation introducing the imperial measure in 1826.

Generally, English copper is always plain. *Repoussé* or engraved decoration suggests a Continental origin—usually Dutch.

CORNER CUPBOARD
(French *encoignure* (q.v.).) Three-sided cupboards made to fit in the corner of a room. Originating in shelves permanently fixed across the angle of a wall, the corner cupboard as a separate movable piece of furniture made its début in the early years of the 18th century, usually as a completely enclosed cupboard in two parts, the upper part occasionally with a glazed door, but sometimes with tiers of open shelves. Like the French *encoignure*, the best were probably placed on a stand a few inches in height, but this has rarely survived. Soon after mid-century some elaborate specimens were designed by London makers under French influence. Corner cupboards are often found today with upper or lower part missing. Small corner cupboards were made to hang on the wall during the 18th and 19th centuries.

Especially on the Continent, elaborately decorated specimens of fine quality were sometimes made for the more luxurious interior schemes, and some from France and the Netherlands might be better termed 'corner cabinets'.

See *Encoignure*; *Étagère*.

CORNING GLASS WORKS, NEW YORK
The South Ferry Glass Works of Brooklyn, which moved to Corning in 1868, formed the basis for the present enterprise, founded in 1875. It is probably the largest factory of its kind in the world today, with an enviable reputation for decorative glass of

Corning. **Bowl engraved with the signs of the Zodiac by Stanley Waugh. Steuben Glass Company. c. 1935.** *Victoria and Albert Museum.*

Coromandel Screens. A Coromandel screen, 10 feet in height, decorated in white, red, green, and blue lacquer on a chocolate-brown ground. Reign of the Emperor K'ang Hsi (1662–1722). *Parke-Bernet Galleries, New York.*

fine quality. Since 1933 the products of the Steuben Glass Works, with Sidney B. Waugh, the sculptor, as designer, have equalled in quality much that has been done in the past, and they have specialized in blown glass decorated with wheel-engraving in a restrained style which exhibits craftmanship of the highest order.

The factory maintains a museum of glass through the ages, and publishes studies of great value to the collector of older specimens.

CORNUCOPIA

The so-called horn of plenty, from which falls fruit and flowers. As a *motif* of decoration it occurs from the Renaissance onwards, often held by the goddess Ceres. Especially in England it was made from both pottery and porcelain in the 18th century for attachment to a wall as a flower vase. Also termed a wall-pocket.

COROMANDEL SCREENS

Colourful folding screens of incised Chinese lacquer panels mounted in a wooden frame. Usually they are about 8 ft. high, and made in up to twelve leaves. They owe their name to the fact that they were transhipped on India's Coromandel coast. They belong to the 17th century and the very early years of the 18th. See *Lacquer, Oriental.*

COTTE, ROBERT DE (1656–1735)

French architect and designer, born in Paris, brother-in-law of J. Hardouin-Mansart. De Cotte became *architecte du Roi* in 1689, and director of the Gobelins tapestry looms (q.v.) in 1699. He is generally credited with the introduction into France of the chimney-piece mirror.

COTTON

A white fibrous substance enveloping the seeds of the cotton plant which, when separated from the seeds, can be spun and used to weave cloth. Cotton was first made in England about 1760, and in the U.S.A. at the end of the 18th century. It was often, at this time, decorated with printed designs. Cotton originally came from the East, one rather coarse variety being termed calico, from the city of Calicut on the Malabar Coast. Chintz (q.v.) is a glazed cotton cloth.

'COUNTRY CHIPPENDALE'

A modern dealers' term employed to describe provincial English furniture made in a plain and simple style of elm, ash, oak, or beechwood and based on the styles popularized by Chippendale (q.v.).

COURT CUPBOARD

The term seems to imply a closed piece of furniture, but it means a two-tiered open-shelved stand used for the display of silver and pewter during the early decades of the 17th century, the shelves usually resting on turned supports. Some examples have a small closed cupboard in the middle of the upper shelf. Genuine specimens are rare, but reproductions are common.

COYPEL, ANTOINE (1661–1722)

French painter, born in Paris, who became *premier peintre du roi* in 1715. He was noted for the gaily treated mythological subjects which began to be popular soon after 1700. His half-brother, Noël Nicolas Coypel (1690–1734), also painted mythological subjects.

Court Cupboard. Court cupboard of about **1680**, probably from Massachusetts. The open space below is sometimes closed with doors, when it becomes a press cupboard.

CRACE, FREDERICK (1779–1859)

An interior decorator in the Chinese style who worked for the Prince Regent at the Royal Pavilion, Brighton (Sussex). John Crace & Son of London, who first worked on the Pavilion in 1788, were importers of Chinese decoration of all kinds, including furniture, and Frederick Crace first became active in Brighton in 1802, although most of his work was done between 1815 and 1822. He helped to decorate the Music Room, the Chinese Gallery, and the South Drawing Room. Robert Jones, who worked on the Pavilion from 1817 to 1822, was associated with Crace. The decoration of the Pavilion was responsible for a minor revival of interest in Chinese decoration in the early decades of the 19th century. It had otherwise been almost moribund since the 1760s. Many of Crace's original designs are preserved in the Cooper-Hewitt Museum, New York.

'CRACKS, AGE-', IN PORCELAIN

These do not exist, although cracks are sometimes described as 'age-cracks'. They are either firecracks (q.v.) or due to damage, usually the latter.

CRAILSHEIM (Württemberg, Germany) FAÏENCE FACTORY

Little is known of the history of this factory. The owner was probably Georg Veit Weiss, a *Hafner-meister* (q.v.), and this seems the more likely as his son was owner of the adjacent glazing mill in 1769. The best period was 1751–1768, and after Weiss died his son carried on. It continued with one change of ownership till about 1827.

The wares were all kinds of soup-bowls, asparagus dishes, tea and coffee services, plates, salad bowls, etc. Crailsheim wares often have two eyes on the side of the spout on jugs or ewers. The foot-ring is unglazed, and handles have a flat thumb mark at the base with a strengthening piece over the top. The dianthus is a characteristic flower on Crailsheim designs.

CREAMWARE

(French *faience-fine*; German *Steingut*; Swedish *flintporslin*; Italian *terraglia inglese*.) This ware was also known in France as *terre de pipe* (pipe-clay), which was made at Lunéville (q.v.).

Although white-burning clays had been known from ancient times, and often used in the form of slip, it was not until English potters in Staffordshire began to refine the body employed for salt-glazed wares (see *Stoneware, English*) that a practical ware of this kind could be produced in large quantities. Whieldon employed a kind of creamware which he covered with his characteristic coloured glazes, and Wedgwood developed it by 1759 into a slightly yellow earthenware which could be precisely potted, and which he covered with a transparent lead glaze. In 1765, in consequence of an order from Queen Charlotte, he renamed it 'Queen's ware', and its popularity was confirmed by the order from Catherine of Russia for the 'Frog' service (see *Wedgwood*). Its many advantages were soon widely recognized on the Continent, and factories began its manufacture under the names given above. In 1779 Wedgwood refined it further, and increased the hardness of the body, renaming it 'pearl' ware, and this, also, was widely adopted elsewhere in England, although to a much lesser extent on the Continent.

The principal manufacture in England, apart from Staffordshire, was at Leeds and Liverpool (Herculaneum), and its first use in France was in Paris, about 1760, at a factory located at the Pont-aux-Choux.

Creamware. Leeds coffee-pot, deep cream in colour, enamelled with birds. c. 1770. *Sotheby & Co.*

CREDENCE (French) or CREDENZA (Italian)

A side-table on which food was placed, or a cupboard for the display of plate. A *buffet*. The term is generally used of Renaissance furniture.

CRESSENT, CHARLES (1685–1768)

One of the most noted French *ébénistes*, Cressent was also a sculptor and a skilful bronzeworker who did much to influence the course of design of Paris furniture in the 18th century. Cressent turned to *ébénisterie* after 1719, becoming *ébéniste* to the Regent and later working for the Marquis de Marigny, Blondel de Gagny, and the banker, Pierre Crozat. He was involved on several occasions in disputes with the Guild of *Fondeurs*, who objected to him casting his own mounts, and the best of his early work is especially noted for the magnificent quality and superb design of the elaborate bronzework. Towards the end of his life, when financially embarrassed, he turned to floral marquetry.

Although Cressent worked for many of the wealthiest men of his day he was often in financial difficulties, largely because he spent lavishly on an art-collection which he tried unsuccessfully to sell.

Work reliably attributed to him is unstamped, the stamp, C. CRESSENT, appearing on work purporting to be in his later style being regarded as dubious.

The bronze *espagnolettes* to be found decorating the stiles of some important *commodes* were probably adapted by Cressent from Watteau's designs, and mounts in the dragon forms of the *Régence* also occur on furniture reliably attributed to him.

His ability as a bronzeworker may be judged from a clock-case in the Wallace Collection (London) from his hand. This closely corresponds to an entry in the catalogue of a sale by Cressent of some of his own work in 1749.

CRESTING

Decorative ornament, usually carving, surmounting the top rail of a chair, the hood of a long-case clock, a mirror, or anything of a like nature.

CRICKET TABLE

Seventeenth-century table with a circular top on three legs, joined at the bottom by a plain stretcher. The term may have originated from a low, three-legged stool which was thus called.

CRISELLING

A progressive degeneration to which some old glass is liable. It begins as a fine network of cracks on the surface, and is due to defects in the glass itself. Its apparent cause is the condensation of water on the surface and the dissolution of some of the silicates. The remedy is to keep the specimen in a completely dry atmosphere. There is no other way to arrest the slow deterioration which will eventually destroy it. Criselling is to be found in Chinese glass made around 1700, and in the glass of George Ravenscroft in England. A report to the Glass-sellers' Company

Criselling. Bowl by George Ravenscroft (q.v.) showing the effect of criselling. *Victoria and Albert Museum.*

of 1676 states that the defect in Ravenscroft glass had then been overcome, but it can be observed in specimens made later than this.

No doubt it also occurred in glass made elsewhere before this date, but specimens no longer exist.

CROMWELLIAN CHAIR

A modern term to describe a plain chair of Spanish design slightly decorated with turning, with slung leather seat and back, the leather held in place with large-headed studs. The type was popular during the Commonwealth in England (1649–1660).

CROSS-BANDING

Narrow bands of veneer, employed especially on walnut furniture, in which the grain runs across instead of along the band. Cross-banding occurs as a border in a variety of places, and it is often seen surrounding panels of veneer.

CROWN GLASS

Broad glass (q.v.).

CRYSTAL GLASS

(Italian *cristallo*; French *cristal*.) The term is derived from the Venetian *cristallo*, meaning glass made exceptionally clear by decolorizing it with manganese oxide, and the name refers either to a fancied resemblance to rock-crystal (q.v.) or to its use as a substitute for the hardstone. A glass heavily fluxed with lead in the English manner (see *Ravenscroft, George*) was termed '*cristal*' in France, and first introduced about 1780 with the founding of the *Manufacture cristaux de la Reine* in that year. The manufacture of '*demi-cristal*', a leadless glass closely approaching *cristal* in brilliance, was introduced at the Plaine de Walsch factory in 1833.

See *Flint Glass.*

CRYSTALLO CERAMIE

Introduced into England by Apsley Pellatt (q.v.), the technique was developed in France during the 18th century. Essentially it consisted in embedding in glass some kind of ceramic ware, or anything decorative which would support a greater heat than that of molten glass. The most commonly known variety made by Apsley Pellatt took the form of portraits of notabilities in ceramic ware. Paperweights are the most common survival, but such things as vases, mugs, and decanters were sometimes decorated in this way.

Crystallo Ceramie. Glass paperweight enclosing a ceramic head of Queen Victoria. Apsley Pellatt. c. 1840. *Victoria and Albert Museum.*

In France objects of *crystallo ceramie,* usually paperweights, were made at Le Creusot, Baccarat, and Clichy, and they have also been produced in America, where they are termed sulphides. They are still being made today, some with portraits of contemporary personages.

CULLET

Broken glass with which each batch of newly made glass is mixed to promote fusion. The amount employed varies from a quarter to a half in the manufacture of lead-glass. Cullet was also employed by the early artificial porcelain factories, where the fusible substances were mainly of a glassy nature, in making the preliminary frit (q.v.).

CUPBOARD

Originally, as the name implies, a board on which were set out, either for display or use, cups and plate generally. During the 16th century the original open shelves were fitted with doors, and the word has now come to mean this kind of furniture. Closed cupboards were made in great variety, and these are separately considered under various headings.

See *Court Cupboard.*

CUT-CARD WORK

A form of ornament used by the silversmith, mostly in the 17th century. Pierced silver plates were cut with

the chisel into a variety of shapes, often based on leaf-forms, and soldered to the exterior of the vessel. Work of this kind is now done by a fret-saw adapted to metalworking. Cut-card work was introduced from France about the middle of the 17th century, and seems largely to have been practised in England by immigrant Huguenot craftsmen.

CUT-GLASS

The grinding of glass into light-refracting facets. Cut-glass probably originated in Bohemia early in the 17th century, and was employed as a method of decorating rock-crystal before it was applied to glass. English lead-glass developed by Ravenscroft (q.v.) was admirably suited to this method of decoration, but cutting did not appear in England before 1709, when an advertisement in the *London Gazette* refers to German cut and carved glasses which 'hath not previously been exposed to public sale'. By 1719 cutting was being applied to glass of English manufacture, John Akerman, a London glass-seller, being the first to advertise it in that year. He was probably employing German glass-cutters. Cut-glass chandeliers were being made before 1750, together with many other utensils such as dishes, bowls, basins, cups and saucers, sweetmeat and drinking glasses, and so on. A cut-glass teapot is in the collection of H.M. the Queen.

The Glass Excise Act of 1745 placed a tax on glass by weight, and this led to the development of much shallower cutting, since glass vessels had to be lighter and therefore thinner and less substantial, in order to save tax. In 1780 Free Trade was granted to Ireland, and this was followed by the establishment of glass-houses at Waterford, Cork, and Belfast. The effect of the Excise duty in England caused workers to leave both for Ireland and France, and a considerable export trade in cut-glass between Ireland and England grew up. Since this duty did not affect Irish glass-houses, their glass could be made heavier, and therefore the cutting could be deeper.

Cutting is done by means of revolving wheels which grind away the surface, fashioning it in such a way as to leave prisms which refract light instead of allowing it to pass directly through the glass. The principle is much the same as that of the cutting of precious stones, and the patterns were selected both for their efficiency as light-refractors and for their suitability for speedy production with the rotating wheel. For this reason diamonds and stars are by far

Cut-card Work. A pair of Victorian sauce-boats of 1850 decorated with *chinoiseries* in cut-card work.

109

Cut-glass. A pair of English cut-glass decanters and a bowl on a high foot. c. 1820.

the most common. Curved *motifs* are not so frequent, and these usually came from Ireland, especially from Waterford.

Cut-glass began to decline in popularity with the introduction of pressed glass (q.v.), and some remarks are there to be found on the differentiation between cut and pressed glass when the latter simulates the patterns to be found on the former. It must be remembered that even the most expert workman could not attain the regularity and exactness of the moulded article in cutting his patterns, and such faults are especially noticeable on early specimens, although they are far less obvious on later ones and particularly those made after the application of mechanical power to the driving of cutting wheels late in the 18th century.

Cyfflé, Paul-Louis. Gardener, after a model by Cyfflé. Niderviller (q.v.). c. 1770. *Victoria and Albert Museum.*

CYFFLÉ, PAUL-LOUIS (1724–1806)

Born at Bruges in 1724, he was later appointed *sculpteur ordinaire* to Stanislas Leczinski, father-in-law of Louis XV. Cyfflé made a kind of *biscuit* earthenware at Lunéville (q.v.) called *terre de Lorraine,* in which he modelled a series of popular figures and groups which were much copied at the time, even as far afield as Staffordshire, where his work inspired models by Ralph Wood and others. He is represented in the Musée de Sèvres, Paris.

CYLINDER

The solid semi-circular closure of writing-desks (q.v.). The French term is *bureau à cylindre,* and when the front is made up of transverse slats, *bureau à lamelles.* See also *Tambour.*

Cut-glass. A pair of 18th-century cut-glass decanters.

D

DAGLY, GERHARD (fl. 1665–1714)

Apart from the invention of *vernis Martin* (q.v.) not a lot is known of the makers of imitation lacquer furniture or the processes used. One artist responsible for some of the best European examples of such work was Gerhard Dagly who, with his brother Jacques (1665–1728), specialized in lacquer work in the Oriental manner. Dagly, of Flemish origin, worked in Berlin, and some of his surviving work which can be reliably attributed is preserved in northern palaces, including Berlin's Charlottenburg and the King's palace at Stockholm. It includes cabinets, *vitrines,* chairs, tables, mirror-frames, and a spinet. Much of it is in a distinctive Japanese style, the lacquer of Japan being the most highly valued at the time. Dagly died in Paris. See *Lacquer, European.*

DAMAS (French), DAMASK

Damask, from its supposed origin in Damascus, was a fabric with a glossy ground into which ornament of mat appearance was woven. Damask was much used for covering seat-furniture in the 18th century, and for wall-hangings and curtains.

DAMASCENING

Ornament of gold or silver wire inlaid into one of the base metals, often steel. The surface was first deeply engraved with an incised line broadening towards the bottom, and the wire was then hammered into position, the shape of the incision keying it to the base. The term is also employed to refer to steel blades having a watered appearance attained by repeated hammering. Both techniques were originally devised by the metalworkers of Damascus.

DASSON, PIERRE

Nineteenth-century French *ébéniste* who specialized in reproductions of 18th-century French furniture of fine quality. His masterpiece, a copy of the *bureau du roi Louis XV,* is in the Wallace Collection.

DAVENPORT

A small narrow desk with a writing-slope above and drawers or cupboards below. The first desks of this type were made about 1790 by Gillow to the order of Captain Davenport, but specimens are extremely rare from this period. Most are mid-Victorian.

DAVENPORT, LONGPORT, STAFFORD-SHIRE (1793–1882)

A factory making blue-printed earthenware and porcelain was established here in 1793. The date at which the manufacture of porcelain was introduced cannot be exactly determined, but about 1820 is a probable date. Much Davenport porcelain survives, although most of it is not of especially good quality. Derby was copied freely, and Thomas Steele, the Derby fruit painter, was employed. Another Derby painter, James Rouse, painted landscape plaques. Tea- and dessert-services seem to have been the staple production, many painted with Japan and so-called 'India' patterns. A celadon glaze and a *rose Pompadour* ground were both in use. An 'ironstone china' (q.v.) was made for the cheaper market. Specimens are usually marked 'Davenport', often with the addition of an anchor.

DAVID, JACQUES-LOUIS (1748–1825)

French painter who considerably influenced the development of the neo-classical and Empire styles. During the Revolution he was virtually dictator in the sphere of the arts, and he took a prominent part, with the notorious Baron Vivant Denon, in the looting of works of art by Napoleon. He died in exile after the Restoration.

DEAL

The wood of the fir and pine, frequently employed during the 18th century for the carcasses of cabinets and the lining of drawers. Baltic pine is soft, white, and straight-grained, and furniture of this wood with its original surface-finish removed is known as stripped pine, a modern term.

DEALERS

The term is generally understood to mean those who make a living from buying and selling works of art and antiques. Not all dealers maintain shops; some prefer to work from a private house. Some are prepared to supply the public generally; others sell

Dealers. Interior of the shop of the Paris dealer, Gersaint, painted by his friend, Watteau. c. 1720. *Charlottenburg, Berlin.*

only to a strictly limited clientele. Most collectors also sell as well as buy, and some fall into an intermediate class referred to as 'collector-dealers'. The line of demarcation between one and the other is often vague.

The professional dealer of standing is usually a member of an Association. Associations are usually prepared to provide lists of members to inquirers on payment of a small fee, and most of them lay down rules of conduct for their members and regulate the trade in the interests of buyer and seller.

The dealer who maintains a stock of antiques for sale is essential to the structure and well-being of the trade as a whole. By buying for stock at a time when a particular class of antique is plentiful, he helps to maintain the price-stability essential to protect the value of the collector's property. By studying the international market, he channels objects to where they are wanted, and he provides the collector with a means of disposing of unwanted items quickly in case of need.

The specialist dealer, who concentrates on one or two categories, is an invaluable collaborator in the building up of a collection, and his knowledge and experience will save the beginner from many costly errors of judgment.

Antiques are sold in a free market, and their value therefore depends on the quantity available at any given time and the current demand. Today the supply is a diminishing one, and world-demand increases continually. Price-rises, therefore, are inevitable. The collector who holds his purchases for long enough can hardly help selling ultimately at a profit. The dealer, on the other hand, takes a short-term profit on turnover in order to stay in business. Their interests are, therefore, mutual.

Like every other profession, antique-dealing includes those who are less than honest. Dealers who have been established for a considerable time, and who are members of their trade association, have obviously achieved a reputation for integrity and fair-dealing which they will not be prepared to endanger by giving the beginner less than honest treatment. The collector who has left his novitiate will be ready to join the hunt in small second-hand shops and those of minor dealers for the unrecognized antique at bargain prices, or at less than true market value, and in this pursuit he will be joined by the larger dealers and their agents in search of stock. He will discover the meaning of the phrase often used by seasoned collectors and dealers, 'profit on knowledge', but he will find also that there are no guaranteed invoice descriptions, no assurance of condition or authenticity, and that mistakes will not afterwards be rectified.

DECALOMANIA

Transfers employed to decorate furniture, etc., in the form of a picture placed face-downwards on to a piece of backing paper. This was applied to the surface to be decorated and the backing peeled off. The process was used principally in America for decorating cheap furniture and clocks, and first appeared at the end of the 18th century.

DECANTERS, EVOLUTION OF

Wine-bottles of *delft*, in shape somewhat similar to those of Rhenish stoneware, are well known, and many bear dates ranging from 1640 to 1671. Glass bottles for the temporary storage of wine appear to date from about 1623. Wine was imported in the cask, and some means of decanting small quantities, either for table use or storage, was obviously necessary. The earliest bottles probably served the dual purpose of being both a method of temporary storage and a way of serving, and might therefore be termed bottle-decanters, although until the introduction of the ornamental decanter in the

18th century it is doubtful whether any clear distinction can be drawn between one type of bottle and another on grounds of use. The storage of wine in the bottle, probably first practised with port, seems to necessitate a cylindrical bottle which could be stored on its side so that the wine would remain in contact with the cork, but it would have been just as practical to store a bottle of another shape upside down. There is some evidence that corks were first conical, and only employed to seal the bottle temporarily, whereas prolonged storage necessitated a cylindrical cork and the means for withdrawing it. Here records are unhelpful, and it can only be said that the cork-screw was known by 1700, but no information seems to be available on the exact date of its introduction. It seems likely therefore that the storage of wine in bottles was practised before 1700, whereas the cylindrical bottle, in form somewhat like the modern claret bottle, does not appear to have been introduced before about 1770. That early so-called bottle-decanters may have been used for more prolonged storage seems to be indicated by the invariable addition of a ridge immediately below the mouth of the bottle, which can only have been for the purpose of securing string employed to tie down the cork.

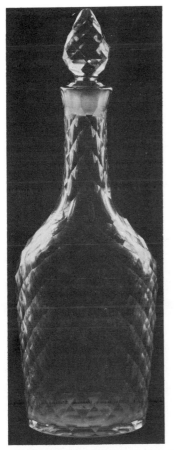

Decanter. An early decanter of club shape with a 'spire' stopper. English. c. **1755.** *Victoria and Albert Museum.*

The earliest 17th-century bottle recorded, of greenish glass, dates back to 1630, and in form it is not unlike the *delft* versions, except that its neck is longer and it lacks a handle. Later bottles were squat and almost hemispherical in shape, standing on a broad base, with a shorter neck. These evolved in the first quarter of the 18th century into a squat cylinder with a long neck, which by 1770 had become almost indistinguishable from the claret bottle, with high, sharply curving shoulders, in contrast to the burgundy bottle, which has a larger diameter and a gradual curve from neck to belly. These common bottles were of thick glass, almost black in colour, and they were usually sealed with a device on a pad of glass applied to the side. The seal is sometimes that of the owner—some, for example, of Oxford colleges—while others bear the device of a wine-merchant or an inn. Some are dated, the date being of practical use in the case of stored wine.

It is from bottles of this kind that the true decanter evolved. The earliest example is not unlike the hemispherical bottle of the late 17th century, except that it is of clear glass and has an added handle. Like the bottles, the base is deeply indented (referred to as a 'kick'), and there is provision for tying a cork. This remained in use until about 1725, and soon after this we notice a decanter very similar in general form, with the same kick in the base, but with a slightly longer and wider neck and no handle. This is a form intermediate between a decanter and a *carafe* (q.v.), and it has no provision for tying a cork, neither has it a stopper, although there is no reason to suppose that, as with the carafe, a glass was inverted over it. This type is exceedingly rare.

It was a short step from this to the balloon decanter which was almost pear-shaped, although the belly was a little more globular. These were introduced about 1745, and the survivors are either cut in facets or engraved with Jacobite motifs. Some have been ground for the fitting of a stopper, which suggests that glass stoppers were still by no means invariably supplied. By this time the provision for tying with string had entirely disappeared, and the later rings ornamenting the necks of cut-glass decanters were no more than decoration. The balloon decanter had, by 1760, evolved into a true pear-shape and was invariably provided with a stopper. The type remained popular until about 1790.

From 1750 onwards the shouldered decanter became popular, either with sides incurving towards the base, or straight and sloping slightly outwards. The former was often cut in a variety of geometric patterns, the latter were sometimes engraved (see *Label Decanters*). Most cut-glass decanters were provided with a mushroom shaped stopper, and the other variety with either a spire-shaped stopper (probably German in origin) or one of flattened oval or disc shape.

Decanters of barrel-shape were introduced about 1775 with the disappearance of the shouldered decanter; as well as a type shaped like a sculptor's mallet, and for this reason called mallet-shaped.

A decanter of sloping form, not unlike a burgundy or champagne bottle, was introduced at the same time. The first two were more or less extensively decorated by cutting, especially the mallet decanter, while the third was usually left fairly plain. The two first named had mushroom stoppers, the last, one of oval or disc shape. Similar decanters were made both in England and at the Irish glasshouses.

These types were fashionable until about 1800, but after this they were progressively supplanted by the cylindrical decanter, although the mallet-shape was revived with some variations. Square decanters were originally made for fitted boxes, usually two or more with matching glasses.

In Victorian times some of the early shapes were reintroduced, especially the balloon and the pear-shape, and variations on the mushroom stopper and the spire were both made, although they are easily recognizable as late. The metal of the 19th century, also, differed considerably from that of the 18th in being whiter and without the minor defects of earlier times. Glass of this kind was entirely commercial, and has little to recommend it apart from utility.

See *Label Decanters*; *Rodney Decanters*.

DÉCOR BOIS (French)

A form of *trompe l'œil* decoration to be found on 18th-century faïence and porcelain from France and Germany which imitates a grained wood surface, nearly always with a simulated engraving pinned to it.

DELAFOSSE, JEAN-CHARLES (1734-1789)

A leading exponent of the neo-classical style in France, who published many volumes of design and ornament.

DELFT, DUTCH

The faïence of Delft has a long tradition. There are several records of potters in the late 16th century.

Jan Floris was described as a decorator of *Aerde-werck* and 'had not his equal' in the Netherlands. Hendrik Cornelius Vroom, born in 1566, learned the craft from his father, Cornelius Hendricksz, at Haarlem, and then travelled, first to Seville, in Spain, and thence to Italy, working in Venice and Albissola. He returned to Holland in 1597. Herman Pietersz, mentioned in 1584 as a *plateelbakker* at Delft, helped to form the Guild of St Luke there, which comprised, among others, the corporation of potters. Several other names are recorded, but the question remains as to whether Dutch tin-enamel was derived originally from Spain or Italy by itinerant workers. An Italian, Guido di Savino from Castel Durante (almost certainly identical with a gallipot maker called Guido Andries), settled in Antwerp in 1512, and his family were potters there till nearly the end of the 16th century. Joris, one of his sons, established a pottery at Middelburg in 1564. Another possible relative, Jasper Andries, settled in Norwich (England) because of religious persecution and subsequently moved in 1570 to London to found the English *delft* industry. Apart from fragments and tiles, the earliest piece known to have been made in the north (though still under Italian influence) is dated 1547.

From the early years of the 17th century potters were established in a guild at Delft, but the industry grew slowly, and even in 1640 only eight master-potters were working, perhaps because most returned to their native towns after learning the craft. The only wares known from this period are painted in blue in the Chinese style, and crowded with figures and ornament. They display a lack of discrimination, because the painters were not artists and often came of very humble stock. The sudden flowering of the faïence industry at Delft in mid-17th century was directly caused by an economic crisis in the brewing industry, of which the city of Delft was an important centre. The old breweries were adapted to

Décor Bois. A cup and saucer simulating an engraving attached to a wooden background. Signed: *Rühlig fecit.* Gera. c. 1785. *British Museum.*

the needs of the pottery industry, and the change is remarkable. Between 1651 and 1660 no fewer than twenty master-potters were received into the guild, another ten the following year, and six more in each of the two years after. Now the potters became men of substance and dignity; they adopted family names instead of just adding the suffix *szoon* (son of) to their father's Christian name, as had formerly been the custom. They also named their factories, and started to use marks on their wares.

The clay used at Delft actually came from Tournai, and from Muhlheim in Germany, so the sudden rise of the industry in the town must be ascribed to Dutch trading skill, and the concatenation of events which made Holland at the same time a celebrated centre of art and the chief importer of porcelain and decoration of all kinds from China and Japan. It follows that styles at Delft divide almost naturally into two streams: Oriental and native. Landscape painting was then at its height in Holland and was adopted by the pottery painters.

In the case of polychrome wares, high-temperature colours (q.v.) were applied to the piece which had previously been lightly fired, dipped in the tin-enamel and allowed to dry. The design was out-lined in blue *trek* (q.v.) and the colours filled in on the porous and dusty surface. Colours were blue and green, with the occasional addition of pure antimony-yellow, and manganese-violet. The decorated piece was then dusted over with a lead glaze known as *kwaart* (q.v.) and fired to fuse the tin oxide, the pigments, and the lead glaze into one. *Kwaart* gave added brilliance to the wares, but it was not generally applied to the underside of a dish. The wares imitating the red and gold of Imari (q.v.) porcelain were subjected to a much longer process, because the essential iron-red had to be fired separately from the normal high-temperature colours. When a piece was to be decorated with these colours the red was not applied until the second firing had fused both the other colours and the glaze. It was then added overglaze as an enamel, and the piece fired again at a lower temperature. Only then could gilding be added, and the piece subjected to a fourth firing in an even cooler kiln. The same method was used when copying *famille verte* enamels (q.v.). No *kwaart* was subsequently applied to overglaze enamels. After 1650 many experiments were made, and by the 18th century a pink similar to the *famille rose* pigment (q.v.) had been developed.

By the end of the 17th century the faïence industry at Delft had fallen more and more into the hands of

Delft, Dutch. Dish painted in enamel colours with a central landscape. Delft (Holland). Mid-18th century. *Victoria and Albert Museum.*

industrialists, so that quality was sacrificed to quantity. Some artists tried to uphold the former standards, like Johannes van der Haagen, who, even in mid-18th century, turned back to the old designs and painted in blue monochrome. Gijsbert Verhaast, born in 1732, painted faïence panels that might well be miniature oil-paintings. The 18th century saw a continuation of many of the 17th century factories, and new ones were founded. The most important names are Zacharias Dextra, who became owner of the 'Two Ash Barrels' in 1720, and Jan Theunis Dextra, who controlled the 'Greek A' after 1759. These two men were responsible for the *renaissance* which took place at Delft at the middle of the 18th century. It is exemplified by a class of faïence imitating Meissen porcelain—all kinds of small domestic wares, such as butter-dishes, sugar-basins and so on, painted with great detail in polychrome enamels. The Dextras used a finely potted body and enamel colours. Enamel painting is considerably less exacting than free-hand painting on a tin glaze, and as the old disciplines died, and mass-production crept in, the artists of Delft lost their former skill, and by 1808 only eight factories remained, one of which was making the so-called 'English pottery'—Wedgwood's creamware in fact.

Dutch potters are rightly renowned for their painting, but they seem to have lacked plastic imagination, and when not imitating Far Eastern shapes fell to modelling bizarre, eccentric, and unlikely objects in a crude way which lacked a sense of style. Mention must be made of the production of tiles, which, in the 17th century, were at first painted with figure-subjects, ships, landscapes and flowers in blue, but later in manganese-purple, and even in polychrome. They were often made to be fitted together to form a tile-picture. When intended as single-picture tiles they were usually furnished with a border. Rotterdam, Utrecht, and Arnhem were important centres of tile-production.

See *Cachemire Style; Delft, Dutch, Forgeries of; Keizer, Aelbrecht Cornelis de.*

DELFT, DUTCH, FORGERIES OF

Dutch *delft* (or tin-enamel ware—q.v.) has been widely reproduced in Holland, in Paris, and in northern France. Samson's copies are particularly good. Forgeries are especially numerous, and by the beginning of the present century factories were established to make nothing else. J. Putten & Co. of Delft made good copies until 1850, which, perhaps, can be regarded as a continuation of traditional styles. The reproduction of Joost Thooft and Labouchére, who employed 200 people in their works in 1890, can hardly be regarded as deceptive, since although the patterns were old, the ware was earthenware covered with a transparent glaze. Similar wares are offered today as an inducement to buy Dutch bulbs.

Among the types which require especial care are those which bear the mark of such potters as Adriaen Pijnaker and Albrecht Keyser, the more highly decorated wares such as those with black grounds (*delft noir*), and plates in sets, as well as tobacco-jars. A notorious series of plates illustrating the tobacco industry once deceived an important museum.

Samson's copies are fairly dangerous, and those of northern France are not always easy to detect, although the latter sometimes suffer from a crazing of the glaze which is very rarely to be seen with genuine examples; they are also apt to be heavier.

As a test which is useful but not completely reliable, the earthenware body of Dutch *delft* is nearly always soft enough to be marked by the blade of a pocket-knife, which is rarely the case with the harder fired forgeries.

Apart from forgeries, there are many problems in attribution (q.v.) in this field, and confusion between the wares of England, Holland, and Germany is not unusual.

DELFT, EARLY ENGLISH

Before the introduction of the tin-glaze into England during the 16th and 17th centuries English potters made domestic pottery of earthenware covered in brown, green and black lead glazes. The technique of applying a tin-enamel glaze over the earthenware body was imported from Holland, whither it had come by way of Valencia (Spain) and Faenza (Italy). It was brought by two potters from Antwerp, Jasper Andries and Jacob Janson, who sent a petition to Queen Elizabeth for permission to make the new wares. They settled at first in Norwich about 1567 and used East Anglian clay.

Tin was brought from Cornwall, oxidized in the workshop, and fused with lead oxide and glass. This lump of glaze was then finely ground and mixed with water to form a solution into which the lightly-fired earthenware was dipped. The porous body soaked up the water, leaving a dry powdery surface ready to be decorated. If a painter made a mistake it could never be erased and this in part accounts for the free-flowing style and lack of detail in delftware of all kinds.

Painting was executed in the high-temperature colours, which were cobalt oxide, producing blues varying from a pale to a blackish-blue shade; copper-green, firing to a variety of translucent shades; manganese, producing a purple and purplish-black; iron, producing brick-red; and antimony, giving yellow. After 1700 these colours were more variable as the potters began to mix them, adding white glaze material for softer shades.

When the painting was finished the piece was fired again at a higher temperature and in a clay saggar to protect it from contact with the fire. Marks often seen on the back of plates are produced by stilts—the supports on which the piece rested in the saggar. The fire had to be carefully controlled, as variations in temperature, or contact with smoke, produced dull colours and discoloured glazes. Sometimes the glaze became too fluid and ran. Many firing-defects, failure of red particularly, as well as bubbling and specking, are to be seen on *delft* and may be a guide to provenance and date. Enamel-colours were used in England, particularly at Liverpool at mid-18th century, but never to the same extent as on the Continent.

The earliest known use of tin-enamel in England is on a kind of ware called 'Malling' jugs, a small group so called because one was found in the churchyard of West Malling in Kent and several others nearby. These are usually supposed to have been manufactured in or near London. They are round-bellied jugs, usually mounted in silver, and a hall-mark of 1550 on one formerly in the Swaythling collection enables an approximate date to be established. Colours are dark blue and purple and blue and black, while another group, with a blue ground flecked with orange, is called 'Tygerware' and may have been inspired by the mottled brown stoneware of Cologne also thus called (see *Bellarmine*).

Andries and Janson's petition to the Queen was presumably granted, because they set up their pottery factory by the river in London in 1571, though its exact site is uncertain. Excavation in the City of London has brought to light many dishes, pharmacy jars, vases, and jugs which may be part of the Janson product. Such wares are decorated with floral or bird motifs in blue, green, and yellow, and many small *albarellos* have been found with concentric rings or chevrons in the same colours. It is not absolutely certain that some of these pieces did not come from the Continent, but most are probably English. Since most of the potters of the 16th and 17th centuries were Flemish the wares are not easy to separate. There is a famous dish in the London Museum dated 1600 with an inscription—*The rose is red, the leaves are grene, God save Elizabeth our Queene*—which is the earliest known specimen and which is also, in its decoration, the prototype for a whole group called 'blue dash chargers' after the blue dashes round the rim. All the high-temperature colours are used, and the border design is derived from Italian *groteschi* and arabesques (q.v.).

One early dated piece painted in blue, yellow-green, orange and purple is a true 'blue dash charger' with a design of tulips and foliage, inscribed *Richard Key 1628*, and this same palette is found on a series of chargers, some with figures, others with flowers and fruit, and, about 1634, with a design of grapes, pomegranates, and foliage which derive from Venetian *maiolica*. These chargers, unlike most English wares, were probably for decoration only, and their backs are clearly designed for hanging. Although in some ways derivative, they display a native vigour which is decidedly English. Apart from flower and fruit decoration, chargers were painted with Biblical scenes, Kings of England and other popular subjects, such as ships, Coats of Arms or abstract *motifs*. Renaissance ornament was freely borrowed from Urbino *maiolica* and some have border patterns derived from Chinese porcelain. One of the most popular subjects was Adam and Eve expelled from the Garden of Eden, with a writhing serpent in a tree and a grotesque but charmingly primitive Adam and Eve below. It is not always easy to make an attribution of these chargers to any particular pottery in London or Bristol.

See also: *Bristol Delft; Dublin Delft; Glasgow Delft; Liverpool Delft; Norwich Pottery; Southwark and Lambeth Delft; Wincanton Delft.*

DELFT NOIR

Dutch *delft* with a black ground inspired by Chinese porcelain. As a type, it is much sought and highly valued, but forgeries are far from unknown. 17th-century specimens are often attributed to Adriaen Pijnacker, son-in-law of Aelbrecht Cornelis de Keizer (q.v.).

DELLA ROBBIA, LUCA (1400–1489)

Sculptor who covered large architectural reliefs with a tin-enamel glaze, at first with white over a blue ground, but later with some slight touches of colour. He was followed by a nephew, Andrea (1435–1525).

See *Tin Enamel Glazes.*

DENTIL ORNAMENT

A form of ornament common in 18th-century cabinet work, consisting of small cubes repeated at regular intervals beneath the cornice in imitation of similar architectural features of the Ionic and Corinthian Orders (see *Orders*). The term is sometimes employed to describe gilded or painted border ornament on porcelain where a *motif* is similarly arranged at intervals. This, of course, is an error, and *dentate* is intended.

DERBY PORCELAIN FACTORY

There is reason to think that Thomas Briand (see *Chelsea*) attempted to start a porcelain factory at Derby about 1745 in company with James Marchand. The late Frank Hurlbutt suggested that a group of reclining lambs marked with an incised pentagon (possibly inspired by Chelsea's triangle) might have been made by a certain André Planché about this date, but these are more likely to have

belonged to the 'Snowman' group (see *Longton Hall*). The Victoria and Albert Museum (London) has an interesting cream-jug decorated round the base with strawberries and leaves in relief which is marked 'D. 1750', and another is marked 'Derby'; it is therefore reasonable to suppose that the factory was in existence at this time, although its products were experimental. At this time there was a factory at Cockpit Hill, Derby, in which John Heath, a banker, was financially interested, and in 1756 he was joined with William Duesbury and André Planché, 'china-maker of Derby', in an agreement for the establishment of the factory which was later to be known as 'Duesbury Derby'. It is probable that the earliest Derby figures were made by Planché to Briand's formula at the Cockpit Hill factory.

A rare and important series of figures belong to the pre-Duesbury period, and these can be identified by a glaze retraction on the sides of the base, and some of the bases have a curious funnel-shaped hole into the interior. Some of these were enamelled by Duesbury at his London decorating studio. Service-

Derby Porcelain. Pair of Boars from the Florentine bronzes of Pietro Tacca. Derby. Dry-edged class. c. 1752.

Derby Porcelain. Candlestick of the 'second Dresden' period at Derby on rococo scroll base. Characteristic pale colouring. c. 1758.

ware conjecturally attributed to this period exhibits 'moons' (q.v.) by transmitted light. The modelling of the figures, often inspired by Meissen, is remarkably sophisticated and usually of excellent quality. A figure of *King Lear* exists in a 'dry-edged' form and also occurs after the establishment of Duesbury's factory, which is evidence of continuity. The porcelain is soft and glassy, and rather heavy in weight. Apart from the 'dry edge' at the base, patches bare of glaze sometimes occur. The best-known figures of this period are a pair of boars—the so-called *Florentine Boars* derived from the famous bronzes by Pietro Tacca.

1756 seems to have been the year of Duesbury's intervention, although the agreement mentioned between him, John Heath, and Planché was not ratified until later, and Planché was eventually dropped from it. From 1756 till 1758 Derby was advertising itself as 'the second Dresden', which is evidence of its source of inspiration, but some of its figures owe a good deal to Chelsea. It seems almost certain that between 1756 and the purchase by Duesbury of the moribund Chelsea factory in 1770 that his intention was to pass off his wares as coming from the latter factory. Nothing was marked, if we except a solitary figure marked *WD Co* and several instances of a forged Chelsea mark. Before the purchase of the Chelsea factory by Duesbury the only other porcelain factory consistently to mark its wares was Worcester. Duesbury's policy was a successful one, because figures made up till about

ABOVE: Finely decorated marquetry centre table (*table à milieu*) of the last quarter of the 17th century, and slightly later seat-furniture, at Ham House, S.W. London.

BELOW: Carved and turned furniture of the second half of the 17th century. English with signs of Dutch influence. *Ham House, S.W. London.*

ABOVE: The Marble Hall, Petworth, Sussex. The floor-slabs are of Sussex marble, and the chimney-piece has been carved with the arms and supporters of the Duke of Somerset by John Selden, assistant to Grinling Gibbon.

BELOW: Console table. Gilded console table at Petworth House, Sussex.

Derby Porcelain. Chamber candlestick (with carrying handle at rear) on a rococo scroll base. Derby. c. 1765.

pierced baskets, is very effective and peculiar to the factory. Richard Holdship of Worcester, who seems to have been in charge of the transfer-printing department there, was at Derby in 1764, and took the secret of transfer-printing with him. Rare examples of Derby porcelain with overglaze printed decoration are known which were made about this time, and transfer-prints on creamware made at Cockpit Hill, Derby, also exist.

With the beginning of the Chelsea-Derby period (see *Chelsea*) a factory mark was adopted both for wares made at Chelsea and at Derby. Until 1770 wares were in the rococo style, with bases showing the typical *C* and *S* scrollwork (q.v.), and much use was made of the bocage (q.v.), which perhaps owes something to contemporary stage-scenery. Although towards 1770 one or two figures where the bocage was not appropriate show concessions to the increasingly popular neo-classical style, this superseded rococo almost entirely after 1770. The forms, which were based largely on classical pottery forms, were not suited to porcelain, and Duesbury, perhaps influenced by his earlier background as an enameller, developed painting as an especial feature of Derby decoration on service-ware and vases, ably assisted by a number of artists of considerable talent, like Zachariah Boreman and 'Jockey' Hill, who painted landscapes; Richard Askew, who painted cupids, usually in *rose camaieu*; James Banford, classical subjects; George Complin, fruit and birds: and, a little later, 'Quaker' Pegg, who with great skill painted single flower sprays which are usually named on the reverse. Edward Withers was a skilful flower-painter, but most important was William Billingsley (q.v.), who introduced a completely new style to flower-painting which continued to be popular throughout the first half of the 19th century.

Among the modellers of the neo-classical period

1770 were frequently attributed to Chelsea until Bernard Rackham pointed out that both figures which could undoubtedly be attributed to Derby, and those until then awarded to Chelsea, always bore on the underside of the base three 'patch' marks which corresponded to the pads of clay on which the figure had rested during firing. While these marks are not peculiar to Derby, and sometimes appear on undoubted Chelsea porcelain, when present they can, taken in conjunction with other indications, provide fair presumptive evidence of Derby manufacture.

The early figures, made between 1756 and 1760, are notable for pale colouring and excellent modelling. These are largely copies of Meissen models by Eberlein and Reinicke rather than Kändler. The body is glassy and light in weight, and the colours almost translucent. In the following period which lasts from 1760 to 1770, when all the models have well-defined 'patch' marks under the base, the palette changed to one which was stronger and darker, and notable for what has been termed 'dirty turquoise', an impure turquoise which is not unknown on some late Chelsea figures.

During the period between 1756 and 1760 service-ware was based on that made at Chelsea, although only the less elaborate wares were copied. Some have the 'patch' marks already mentioned, although these appear on some rare specimens undoubtedly made at Chelsea during this period. *Deutsche Blumen* (q.v.) were a favourite decoration, and a decoration of large moths and other insects, often to be seen on

Derby Porcelain. Figure of a Shepherd. Model by Spengler. Derby biscuit porcelain. c. 1790.

Derby Porcelain. A Derby Tithe Pig group representing a wife refusing to part with the tenth pig unless the parson agrees to take the tenth child. c. 1770.

who had started a little before 1770 was John Bacon, R.A. There is record of payment of £75 7s 4d to him for models, and he is generally thought to be responsible for the well known figures of Milton and Shakespeare. Pierre Stephan was a relatively prolific modeller, inspired to some degree by the work of Angelica Kaufmann (q.v.). The *Three Graces distressing Cupid* is probably the best known. Jean-Jacques Spängler, son of the director of the Zürich factory, modelled *biscuit* figures for clocks in the Louis XVI style made by the London clockmaker Vulliamy, although care is needed in attributing these to his hand, since Vulliamy also purchased figures from Wedgwood in his white jasper body, which look not unlike the unglazed (*biscuit*) figures supplied by Derby for the purpose and have been so attributed.

Derby, at this time, made much use of *biscuit* porcelain for figure-modelling, inspired by contemporary work at Sèvres. These date from 1770, and among the first products of this kind were a series of three groups taken from a painting of the royal family by Zoffany, of which a complete set is at Windsor Castle. Other figures and groups were derived from French prints, although direct derivations from the models of Sèvres are rare. The earliest models have a rather waxy-looking smear glaze, probably the result of volatilization in the kiln, and later specimens have a surface which appears chalky. In his *Old Derby Porcelain Factory* of 1876 John Haslem, once employed at the factory, reprinted a list of groups and single figures, both enamelled and gilt and in *biscuit*, which gives the size, height in inches, and the prices in both versions. Those enamelled and gilt were cheaper than those made in *biscuit*, because only the most perfect specimens were left unglazed and undecorated.

The list includes figures taken from Bow and Chelsea models. Duesbury, of course, acquired the Chelsea moulds in 1770. The Bow moulds no doubt came to him in 1776, when he finally acquired the Bow factory, in which he had taken a financial interest as early as 1762. The resemblance of a few early Derby figures to those of Longton Hall (q.v.) is perhaps the result of his acquisition of some of this factory's moulds and plant when it closed in 1760. Many of the items listed, however, are difficult to identify with any surviving specimens.

After 1800 Derby productions began to decline in quality. Landscape painting remained a factory speciality, and from the last decades of the 18th century and during the early years of the 19th a speciality was the straight-sided coffee-can, derived from a popular fashion at Sèvres, which were carefully painted for cabinet display. Painters of this later period include Robert and John Brewer, who probably replaced Boreman and Hill in 1795. Robert Brewer was a one-time pupil of Paul Sandby, the Derby water-colourist, who exercised a considerable influence on some of the Derby porcelain painters, although he did not work for the factory. 'Quaker' Pegg resumed flower-painting after 1813, but had ceased by 1817. Thomas Steele did some much-sought fruit-painting; Richard Dodson painted birds; Cuthbert Lawton, hunting-scenes; George Robertson, landscapes and shipping. Throughout the latter part of the 18th century, and well into the 19th, 'Japan' patterns continued to be popular.

Duesbury died in 1786 at a time when the factory was meeting strong competition from Wedgwood's creamware and jasper. He was followed by his son, William II Duesbury, who, for a few years, took Michael Keen into partnership. William III Duesbury entered the firm in 1808, and was later in partnership with William Sheffield, whose daughter he married. The firm was then styled Duesbury & Sheffield. In 1815 the premises were leased to Robert Bloor, who had been a clerk with executive responsibility. To raise money he sold a considerable accumulation of second-grade wares which had hitherto been left in stock. He continued with a certain amount of success, although much of the production was inferior to that of the 18th century, until 1828, when, due to his failing health, the factory was placed under the managership of James Thomason. Bloor died in 1845, and about this time many of the moulds were sold to Samuel Boyle of Fenton who, in turn, sold them to Copelands (see *Spode*). These moulds, which included some belonging to the old Chelsea factory, were discovered on the premises of Messrs Spode who had inherited them in the 1920s. The writer, who saw them about fifteen years ago, was able to identify parts of the *Roman Charity*, an Italian Comedy figure, and other sections of Chelsea figures.

The later figures of the Bloor period are heavily coloured with opaque enamels with a great deal of mercuric gilding. The modellers included Edward Keys, who went to Mintons about 1826. He modelled figures of small animals, such as cats, and a set of the

Monkey Band (the *Affenkapelle* (q.v.)). His brother, Samuel Keys, modelled theatrical figures especially, including Liston as Paul Pry and Mme Vestris in *Buy a Broom*, which are now much sought. He left in 1830.

Of the later history of porcelain-making in Derby, after the closure of the original factory in 1848 another was established with the aid of some of its workmen by Locker & Company which, after 1859, was continued under the style of Stevenson & Company, and then of Stevenson & Hancock. The letters *S* and *H* were employed as a mark on either side of the old Derby marks of the crown and crossed batons, and much of their work consisted of inferior repetitions of the earlier Derby wares. The present Royal Crown Derby Porcelain Company was established in Osmaston Road, Derby, in 1877, with the aid of Edward Phillips of Worcester. Manufacture has continued until the present day by this firm, which is perhaps best known for its 'Japan' patterns, although these now form only a small part of the factory's output. Painted wares of good quality are in keeping with Derby traditions, and it now employs 140 decorators and gilders who work in traditional techniques. The factory maintains a museum of porcelain made in Derby.

DERUTA (Umbria, Italy) MAIOLICA

Deruta was one of the principal centres of *maiolica* production during the 16th century, and it has been suggested that one workshop in the town was under the patronage of Cesare Borgia. The earliest wares are difficult to separate from those of Faenza (q.v.), although some of them (which foreshadow later, more soundly attributed specimens in their decoration) are assumed to have come from Deruta. From about 1500 onwards attribution is more certain, although the so-called 'petal backs'—dishes with a kind of 'petal' pattern on the reverse—are by no means entirely confined to this centre. More certain is the manner in which profiles with which dishes of this kind are sometimes decorated are outlined with washes of blue following the contours. About 1500, probably from the Hispano-Moresque wares of Valencia, the potters of Deruta appear to have learned the secret of decoration with metallic lustre, an iridescence of the glaze which, when the metallic deposit is thick enough, exhibits a definite colour—yellow if the metal employed has been silver, and reddish or red if gold. Lustre is often associated with Maestro Giorgio Andreoli at Gubbio (q.v.), but the process was not introduced at Gubbio until 1515, although it was there developed to a considerably greater extent, and the ruby lustre (obtained from gold) was a Gubbio innovation. A feature of Deruta production is that dishes often received the tin enamel glaze only on the front, the reverse being covered with a transparent lead glaze. The high-temperature colours employed in the painting were inclined to mingle with each other, and a *sgraffiato* technique (q.v.) was sometimes employed to mitigate this fault.

Decoration is not entirely characteristic, since Deruta potters made use of most of the popular features of the Renaissance repertory of ornament, including grotesques, masks, profile portraits, borders divided *a quartieri*, etc., but a number of inscribed specimens with '*fatta in Diruta*' have survived.

Deruta began to decline after the middle of the 16th century, and its work during the 17th century is inferior. Little is known of 18th-century production, although a dish signed and dated 1771 exists.

There are still potteries at Deruta making tin-enamelled ware as tourist souvenirs.

DESPORTES, ALÉXANDRE FRANÇOIS (1622–1743)

At one time Court Painter in Poland, Desportes returned to France to become a popular painter of animal and hunting scenes. His work is sometimes confused with that of Oudry (q.v.).

DEUTSCHE BLUMEN (German)

German flowers. A type of floral decoration consisting of naturally painted flowers, either singly or in loosely tied bouquets, introduced at Meissen by the *Obermaler*, J. G. Höroldt, shortly before 1740. Mostly they were based on illustrations to the botanical works of J. W. Weidmann. A somewhat similar kind of naturalistic floral decoration was introduced a little earlier (about 1725) at Vienna.

These flowers became widely popular, and they can be seen in the decoration of many other

Deutsche Blumen. Meissen vase of about 1740 decorated with *deutsche Blumen* (German flowers).

factories, notably at Höchst, and in England on early Chelsea, Worcester, and Derby wares. They also inspired a good deal of faïence painting, especially at Strasbourg. The addition of shadows to these flowers, and to insects, was the work of a Meissen painter named Klinger and came later, about 1750. This can also be seen on derivations from Meissen made at Chelsea during the red anchor period (1752–1756).

DIAMOND-POINT ENGRAVING

Engraving glass with a diamond, or something of a near degree of hardness such as a ruby or a garnet, has been practised from Roman times, the stone being mounted in a holder, and used in much the same way as a pencil but with more pressure. The technique of glass decoration by this method in more recent times was adopted in Venice about 1560, and it soon spread to other European countries (see *Verzelini, Giacomo*). Notable work of this kind was done at Hall-in-the-Tirol, in Bohemia, and later in Holland. The technique was not much used in England after the 16th century. A well-known German glass-engraver is Anna Roemers Visscher (1583–1651).

Diamond-engraving was sometimes employed to decorate porcelain in the 18th century, although all such work was done outside the factory (see *Busch, A. O. E. von dem*). The writer has noticed a 19th-century Chinese porcelain plaque very well decorated in this way, but it seems to be exceptional. In the case of diamond-engraved porcelain, the incisions had to be filled with unfired black pigment to make the design visible. Where this has disappeared as a result of washing the remedy is to renew it with black shoe-polish.

DIAMOND-POINT ENGRAVING ON PORCE-LAIN   See *Busch, Canon A. O. E. von dem*

DIAPERS

Strictly this term should be confined to repetitive patterns of diamond or lozenge shape, but the term is often loosely used of this kind of ornament based on other geometric forms. Diapers can be found decorating furniture, usually filling in the background between more pronounced carved work, as part of the engraved decoration of metalwork, and as painted ornament on porcelain. The latter, popular in Germany in the 1760s, was called *Mosaik* (q.v.).

DIATRETARII (Latin)

The Roman term for glassworkers who decorated their vessels by means of rotating engraving wheels charged with abrasive, and diamond points mounted as a chisel. The most famous example is the Portland Vase, but showing superb technical competence are the 'cage-cups'—mostly fragmentary, although a superb and almost perfect specimen is preserved in

Diapers. Diaper ornament on a Vienna dish of about 1730. Du Paquier's factory. *Metropolitan Museum, New York.*

the Römisch-Germanisches Museum at Cologne. The work done by the *diatretarii* forms one of the two major categories into which all decorative glass may be placed. (See *Cameo Glass; Vitrearii.*)

DIETRICH, CHRISTIAN WILHELM ERNST
Porcelain-painter at Meissen, appointed art-director in 1764. A tankard initialled and dated 1730 is in the Victoria and Albert Museum, London.

DINANDERIE (French)
Vessels and other domestic objects of brass made in or near the Flemish town of Dinant, near Liége. The flourishing industry in Dinant came to an end after the sack of the town in 1466. Dinant was also a market for the supply of the raw materials of bronze and brass manufacture.

DINGLINGER, JOHANN MELCHIOR (1664–1731)
Goldsmith to Augustus the Strong, Elector of Saxony, and also an enameller. Dinglinger did some distinguished and influential work in a late baroque style, in which he was assisted by his two brothers, Georg Friedrich and Georg Christoph.

Dietrich, C. W. E. Meissen tankard inscribed *CWED im 1730,* by C. W. E. Dietrich. *Victoria and Albert Museum.*

DIRECTOIRE STYLE, THE

The style which followed the Revolution in France of 1789 has become associated with the Directory, which preceded the Consulate of 1799. In fact it had its origin in the closing years of the reign of Louis XVI, when a tendency to severe and simple lines and an increasing reliance on classical models were apparent. Very little furniture was made in France during and immediately after the Revolution, and genuine *Directoire* furniture is scarce. Most of it is in plain mahogany, relieved by isolated mounts in gilt-bronze, which are usually based on reliefs after classical models. These are decorative in intent, and often lack the accompanying utilitarian purpose of many of the earlier mounts. *Directoire* furniture inspired the early phases of what was to become the Regency style (q.v.) in England.

See also *Mounts, Metal, Furniture.*

DISH-RINGS   See *Potato Rings*

DOCCIA PORCELAIN FACTORY

This factory was founded by the Marchese Carlo Ginori in Florence about 1735, although it is doubtful whether it was more than experimental until ten years or so later. The earliest porcelain body was a type of hard paste, greyish-white in colour, very liable to firecracks (q.v.). Most of the early work is of excellent quality artistically, and in a well-marked baroque style. Johann Karl Anreiter from Vienna was present at the factory, perhaps in 1737, but did little painting here, and probably helped in experimental work. His son, Anton, was painting figure-subjects about 1740. From 1757 until 1791 the factory was directed by Lorenzo Ginori, who improved both body and glaze, and during this period started a kind of decoration in low relief, often based on Renaissance bronze plaquettes, which came erroneously to be associated in the mind of the 19th-century collector with Capo-di-Monte (q.v.). Early examples are rare, but the type was reproduced by the factory, as well as copied at Naples and in Germany in the 19th century.

Figure-modelling always formed a considerable

Dolphins. Carved and gilt side or console table in the style of William Kent. *Parke-Bernet Galleries, New York.*

part of Doccia production, and some excellent work was done, often in white but sometimes painted in a palette which included a bright iron-red peculiar to the factory. About 1770 figures were made in porcelain covered with a white tin-glaze, resembling faïence, and these were, like the earlier figures, often extensively firecracked. Inspiration for figure-modelling was taken from Meissen, from Bernini's fountains in Rome, and from the Italian Comedy. Subjects include religious and mythological figures, pastoral figures, peasants, and Orientals. In the early period many of the figures were extremely large, perhaps intended as works of small sculpture, or inspired by the large figures of Meissen in the 1730s.

The factory is still in existence.

DOLPHINS

The use of the dolphin as a decorative *motif* is very common in Renaissance times, but it is also to be seen in Greek and Roman sculpture, and in Pompeian wall-painting. It is often accompanied by tritons and nereids, especially when it forms part of the decoration of a fountain, and it frequently accompanies representations of Neptune; for instance, the well-known figure of Neptune with his trident and a dolphin, copied by the Derby Porcelain Factory from a Meissen original, which symbolizes Water from a set of the Elements. The dolphin is to be found among Renaissance bronzes in such forms as door-knockers.

The French title of Dauphin for the King's eldest son means *dolphin*, and it came originally from the Comte de Vienne Dauphiné, who gave it, with some property, to the grandson of Philip VI. The dolphin in French art usually has this significance.

DOMED TOP   See *Hooded Top*

DONATELLO (DONATO DI NICCOLO) (1386– 1466)

One of the greatest of Italian sculptors, Donatello spent most of his life at Florence, except for ten years (1442–1453) at Padua, and it is in these two places

Doccia Porcelain. Large dish perhaps painted by the Vienna painter Anton Anreiter. Doccia (Italy). c. 1740. *Metropolitan Museum, New York.*

where most of his larger works are to be found. He had very considerable influence on 15th-century painting and sculpture, and succeeding sculptors of the 15th and 16th century were indebted to him. He assisted Ghiberti on the first of the doors for the Baptistery of San Giovanni, Florence, and some of his work done for Orsanmichele is still in place. Most influential was his *David* (Bargello, Florence), which is very much in the classical style and the first free-standing nude statue to be made in Renaissance times. Perhaps the most impressive and famous of his bronzes is the Gattamelata, inspired by the equestrian statue of Marcus Aurelius in Rome, which is at Padua.

Small bronzes were made in his workshop, and are the earliest to come from Renaissance Italy, but definite attributions to his hand are difficult to sustain.

Donatello. Head of the equestrian statue of Generale Gattemalata, Padua, by Donatello. c. 1450. One of the most influential works of the early Renaissance.

DOOR-KNOCKERS

Antique brass and bronze door-knockers are still to be found in Europe fulfilling the purpose for which they were originally made, although examples of any considerable artistic merit have long ago made their way into collections of metalwork. A common early form is the lion-mask with a ring in the mouth. This was once a sanctuary-ring, to be found on the doors of ecclesiastical buildings, but it later served both as a knocker and a handle. Comparatively modern examples are fairly common.

In Renaissance times, especially in Italy, knockers were often very elaborate, frequently of *grotesque* form, and made by the foremost craftsmen of the day. They take their place in collections of Renaissance bronzework generally, and are to be judged by the appropriate criteria.

English knockers as early as the reign of Queen Anne are sometimes to be found *in situ* on old houses, and occasionally in antique shops specializing in metalwork. The lion-mask knocker was especially popular in early Georgian times, and others exhibit the influence of such contemporary designers as the Adam Brothers. The knocker in the form of a dolphin is fairly common, and in England it dates from the first half of the 18th century. In France a knocker in the form of a clenched hand is popular in some of the provinces, but it is difficult to regard these as being any earlier than the 19th century.

Miniature knockers for interior doors are usually fairly modern—probably no later than the last decade or so of the 19th century.

DOOR-STOPS

Door-stops date from 1775, following the introduction of a type of door-hinge known as the rising butt designed to close the door automatically.

The metal door-stop was made in a wide variety of ornamental forms, many of them not unfamiliar in materials such as earthenware. At first cast in the round, door-stops were made with flat backs, often deeply hollowed, from about 1800. The earliest examples are of brass, usually lacquered, and these remained popular until 1850, although they were always expensive. Production of iron stops began about 1820 in Sheffield. Some of these were painted in colours, and others were bronzed, the product of the invention of bronze powder in 1812. Most such finishes have long since disappeared under layers of black lead. After 1842 the Coalbrookdale Company were producing cast-iron stops in large quantities, and those with the name of the Company cast into the back are still to be found.

Dating is sometimes difficult, but the subject is often a good indication. *Shakespeare* was made throughout the 19th century, but *Nelson* and *Wellington* can fairly be dated to the height of their fame. *Gladstone* and *Disraeli* can be dated fairly closely, and *Edward VII* and *Queen Alexandra* in Coronation robes more closely still. *Mr and Mrs Caudle* belong to the 1840s, to the early days of *Punch*, about the same time as they first appear on stoneware gin-bottles. Many of the figures are designed so as to provide an easy method of lifting.

Door-stops of glass were made at the Bristol factory. (See *Figures, Brass*.)

DOREURS, CORPORATION DES

The 18th-century organization in Paris comprising those engaged in gilding various materials, whether by the mercuric process or by the application of leaf. See *Amalgam*.

DOROTHEENTHAL (Thuringia, Germany) FAÏENCE FACTORY

This factory was founded about 1716 under the patronage of Augusta Dorothea, a daughter of the

Duke of Brunswick. Its productions were at their best before 1750, and are principally in the baroque style, the most characteristic wares being painted usually with the typical *Laub- und Bandelwerke* (q.v.) of the period. Bright, high-temperature colours were employed exclusively. They include blue, iron-red tending to orange, greyish-green, and dark yellow. Enamels do not seem to have been used here, or at any of the Thuringian faïence factories. The mark was A B for Augustenburg, the country seat of the factory's patron.

DRAGON, EUROPEAN

This mythical animal should not be confused with the Chinese dragon, which has a quite different connotation. The European dragon owes something to the serpent, the crocodile, and the legendary hundred-headed hydra. It is usually, but not invariably, winged. To the Romans it symbolized war, and in Christian art it represented Satan, hence 'Sin'. It appears in heraldic form soon after the Norman Conquest in 1066. It is often seen in representations of St George of Cappadocia, a legend probably derived from that of St Michael, who slew Satan in this form. The classical legend of Perseus usually shows him about to slay the dragon, with the chained and naked Andromeda nearby, and in this form it occurs on Italian *maiolica*. Pistols with a dragon's head at the muzzle were called *dragons*, and were carried by dragoons. The wyvern is a dragon with two legs instead of four.

DRAW-TABLE

A table extendable by drawing out leaves at either end. The first draw-tables in England date from about 1550, and the earliest examples are simple in design. Towards the end of the century however, during the reign of Elizabeth I, more ornate specimens supported by carved bulbous legs inspired by Flemish sources became the rule. Later the draw-table yielded in popularity first to the gate-legged variety (q.v.) and then to methods of extending the size by adding additional leaves.

DRESDEN FAÏENCE FACTORY

In 1707 J. F. Böttger (q.v.), while still continuing his experiments in porcelain, decided to try to make faïence in the manner of Delft. Although Dutch workmen were given the task they failed to produce faïence, and only after the arrival of Peter Eggebrecht from Berlin was production successfully started. Böttger in the meantime had stumbled upon the porcelain arcanum (q.v.) and left the faïence factory to Eggebrecht, under whom it flourished. The latter was absent in Russia for three years, but finally returned and remained till he died in 1738. The factory was handed on to his heirs and, after passing into the hands of the Horisch family, closed finally in 1783.

This factory is famous for the monumental vases, covered jars, and flowerpots preserved in the Johanneum (Dresden), decorated with Chinese

Dragon, European. St George and the Dragon. Wood carving, polychrome. Eastern French. Early 16th century. *Sotheby & Co.*

designs, landscapes, and panels in reserve. Dated as early as 1718 are a series of pharmaceutical jars painted in blue with the arms of Saxony and the cipher of Augustus the Strong. All these wares belong to the Eggebrecht period at Dresden.

It is obvious that a faïence factory would find the competition of Meissen porcelain too much to withstand, and later products are of little interest.

(See *Meissen*.)

Dresden Faience. Two-handled vase of metal form decorated with *chinoiseries*. Faïence factory of Peter Eggebrecht. Dresden. c. 1720.

DRESSER

Originally a side-table or *buffet* which, in the 17th century, began to be provided with narrow shelves at the back, and a large shelf below supported by the legs. Drawers in the frieze followed, and before the end of the 18th century one variety was being fitted with doors and shelves in the lower part. These are known as Welsh dressers. Those with clocks incorporated are often called Yorkshire dressers, but they were also made outside that county. A type with a narrow break-front cupboard in the centre of the upper shelves, and drawers in the base flanking a small central cupboard, is sometimes termed a Lancashire dresser. The dresser in France is called a *buffet-vaisselier* or *dressoir*, discussed under the heading of *buffets* (q.v.).

(See *Court Cupboard*.)

DRESSING-TABLES

Tables equipped with the appropriate accessories and used primarily for purposes of the toilet, although both French and English specimens with additional provision for writing and reading also exist.

The earliest dressing-tables made especially for the purpose occur in England early in the 18th century. Usually these have three drawers—one long drawer at the top, and two small ones below separated by a cut-away provision for the knees. A dressing-glass in the form of a swing-mirror mounted on a base having several small drawers was placed on top to complete the *ensemble*. The bureau dressing-table was introduced about the same time, and took the form of a sloping fall-front enclosing a writing space with two long drawers under, placed on a stand supported by cabriole legs. A large swing-mirror at the back supported between two posts surmounted the whole.

Dressing-tables. A Louis XV marquetry *poudreuse* by B. Peridiez. c. 1760. The typical incurved frieze is termed a '*décrochement*'. Christie, Manson & Woods Ltd.

Dressing-tables. Carved mahogany dressing-table with claw-and-ball feet in the Chippendale style. American. New England. c. 1770. *Parke-Bernet Galleries, New York.*

At first there is little or no difference to be observed between dressing-tables intended for ladies or gentlemen, but the necessity for making provision for the daily task of shaving led to modifications. Beginning with Chippendale (q.v.), and under the influence of contemporary design in France, dressing-tables increased in elaboration. Rising tops became usual, beneath which was concealed a mirror that pulled upwards and was supported at the required angle on struts. Receptacles for toilet necessaries were placed on either side of the mirror, and pull-out slides, and drawers in the sides, or swinging out from the sides, were often included in late 18th-century specimens. Dressing-tables became extremely elaborate with the designs of Thomas Shearer (q.v.) in 1788, and those of Thomas Sheraton (q.v.).

A variant was the dressing-chest, dating from the time of Chippendale, which often had a knee-hole and a rising top concealing a mirror. The dressing *commode* was a dressing-chest in an ornate style based on contemporary French design. Special stools to accompany the dressing-table in all its forms were also made.

The French *tables à toilette* were made in great variety, some of the later examples designed to be moved to the dressing-room during the day. A type elaborately draped was a collaboration between the *tapissier* and the *menuisier*, and this was popular throughout the century, although it has not survived in its original form. Tables of *ébénisterie* were often extremely elaborate and made by the *ébéniste-mécanicien* (q.v.). They provided inspiration for the designs of Shearer and Sheraton already mentioned.

Dressing-stands are closely related to washstands in England, and date from the last half of the 18th century. They usually included a cupboard for a chamber-pot and provision for a basin filled from a ewer.

DRUGGET

A coarse woollen stuff used for floor and table coverings.

Dublin Delft. A Dublin *delft* plate decorated with a landscape in blue. c. 1760. *Victoria and Albert Museum.*

DUBLIN (Eire) DELFT

Delft was made in Dublin from about 1737 to 1776. Although specimens from this pottery are scarce, and confusion arises with Liverpool wares, it has one or two typical features. French faïence was being imported into Ireland in mid-18th century, and some of the Irish shapes reflect these models. Subjects and designs, however, were either landscapes, or adapted from Chinese blue-and-white porcelain, painted in a rather dense opaque blue which apparently affected the glaze since it is often somewhat muddy and dull.

DUBOIS, JACQUES (c. 1693–1763)

Maître ébéniste, 1742. Dubois made a good deal of rococo furniture utilizing Oriental lacquer panels and those of *vernis Martin* (q.v.). He used the stamp *I. DUBOIS*, which was also employed by his widow after his death for works produced by her son.

DUCHÉ, ANDREW

American porcelain-maker of Savannah, Ga. Duché, born in 1709, was of Huguenot descent, and a Quaker. In 1729 he started a pottery in Savannah, and by 1738 had discovered American equivalents for Chinese *kaolin* and feldspathic rock. General Oglethorpe, Governor of the Colony, wrote: 'An earth is found which Duché the potter has baked into China ware.' In the same year Duché asked for assistance from the Trustees of the Colony, and was awarded materials to the value of £12. It was probably this contemptuous gesture which prompted him to travel to England to try to sell the earth, and every effort was made to stop him leaving. Eventually he left in 1743 with a passport signed by his good friend, General Oglethorpe. Evidence suggests that Duché arrived in England in 1744, going first to Bow to see the Quaker Thomas Frye. It is evident from the patent subsequently filed that Duché was offering china clay, since feldspathic rock, or anything resembling it, forms no part of the Bow (q.v.) specification. It refers to 'virgin earth' in a purposely obscure description, but it is not stretching probabilities too far to assume that this meant 'Virginian earth'. Duché subsequently went to Plymouth to see William Cookworthy, no doubt with an introduction from the London Quakers (see *Unaker*). Little is known of Duché's activities after his return to America. One or two pieces of porcelain attributed to him are in American collections, and on the 24th November 1764 the English *Bristol Journal* carried this report: 'This week some pieces of porcelain manufactured in Georgia were imported; the materials appear to be good, but the workmanship is far from being admired.' No specimens have been recognized in England, and those in American collections are of uncertain attribution.

DUCHESSE (French)

A comfortable, well-upholstered armchair with a seat both wide and deep which was often made in more than one piece. It is probable that many surviving *duchesses* had additional pieces *en suite*, either a central stool on which the legs rested, and a foot-end (*bout de pied*) to take the weight of the feet, or the armchair to which could be added a stool and foot-end made in one piece, the whole forming a kind of *chaise-longue* (q.v.). When in more than one piece the *duchesse* becomes a *duchesse brisée*. The arms of the chair, and the back of the foot-end, were often curved in the manner termed *en gondole*. The *duchesse* is related to the *bergère* (q.v.).

DUESBURY, WILLIAM (1725–1786)

Porcelain decorator and manufacturer. Born in Cannock, Staffordshire, Duesbury had arrived in London by the early part of 1751, where he established a decorating studio (see *Outside Decorators*). Here he decorated white porcelain from Bow, Chelsea, Longton Hall, and the first Derby factory according to his surviving account-book. He also painted Staffordshire salt-glazed ware, and replacements for Meissen and Oriental services to order. This studio was closed about 1754, probably because by this time all his suppliers had established successful enamelling shops of their own, and were decorating all they could produce. Duesbury left for Derby in search of a source of white porcelain to enamel, and in 1756 we find him joining with John Heath and Andrew Planché in an agreement which led eventually to the founding of a factory at Derby (q.v.) under Duesbury's direction. This was advertised as 'the Second Dresden'. In 1764 Duesbury employed Richard Holdship of the Worcester factory, and experimented with soaprock porcelain (q.v.), but he never used it commercially. At the same time a few trial pieces of transfer-printed porcelain were made, and some have survived, but this, too, was never undertaken on a commercial scale. In 1770 Duesbury purchased the Chelsea factory, and acquired London showrooms in Bedford Street, Covent Garden, London, exhibiting, as well as Derby porcelain, alabasters and Blue John (q.v.). The Chelsea factory was run as a combined operation with

Derby till 1784. The Bow factory had been lent money by Duesbury during their financial crisis of 1763, and in 1776 he appears to have bought what remained, transferring workmen and moulds to Derby, although there is little evidence that the moulds were ever used. In 1777 he assisted James Giles (q.v.) financially, and took over his stock and premises in satisfaction of the loan soon afterwards.

DULONGMUSTER
A relief pattern applied to porcelain plates at Meissen, and first made for Jean Dulong. It has four panels surrounded by a rococo scrollwork which intrudes slightly on the centre. See *Ozier Pattern.*

DUMB-WAITER
A piece of furniture which enabled the services of a waiter to be dispensed with in the dining-room. First introduced about 1725, it consisted in a central shaft, carrying revolving circular trays, which terminated in a tripod foot. Dumb-waiters remained popular during the Regency period, undergoing several modifications. About 1820 quadruple supports replaced the earlier tripod variety. The dumb-waiter (*table servante*) was introduced in France during the reign of Louis XVI.

DUPLESSIS (PÈRE), JEAN-CLAUDE (fl. before 1733—d. 1774)
Of Italian origin, Duplessis was a sculptor, designer, and bronze-founder. He became *orfèvre du roi* in 1758, and worked for the King, Mme de Pompadour, and the Marquis d'Argenson.

Duplessis was among those appointed to supervise and administer the newly established Vincennes porcelain factory in 1745, when he was given responsibility for designing both porcelain and gilt-bronze mounts, the best of the latter probably being supplied by his workshop. He also appears to have supplied mounts for Chinese and Meissen porcelain of the kind delivered by Lazare Duvaux (q.v.) to his aristocratic customers. He held a similar post at the royal porcelain factory after the removal to Sèvres.

The most famous work by Duplessis is undoubtedly the mounts for the *bureau de roi Louis Quinze* of Oeben and Riesener.

DUQUESNOY, FRANÇOIS (1594–1647)
Called 'Il Fiammingo' from his Flemish origin, Duquesnoy spent most of his working life in Rome. He worked chiefly in marble. Little bronzes of *putti* reduced from his larger work were very popular, and reproduced in several media until well into the 18th century, inspiring a number of porcelain figures at Sèvres and elsewhere. From his hand is the much-reproduced 'manneken-pis' in Brussels.

DURLACH (Germany) FAÏENCE FACTORY
Production of faïence was successfully started in 1749 by J. A. Benchiser. Early wares are in a pale, yellowish-grey body, unglazed at the bottom, and showing marks where the base was cut from the

Dumb-waiter. Regency mahogany two-tier dumb-waiter on quadruple support. c. 1815. *Harrods Ltd.*

wheel with string. A rather faded blue on the early wares becomes stronger later and was used in conjunction with a white-speckled manganese. Green is pale and washed out, and the yellow tends towards lemon. There is also a brownish-grey and a dry brick-red. Black is used for outlines and inscriptions. Mugs are the most common shape, occasionally mounted with a cover and footring in pewter. They are decorated with slight rococo ornament round a pictorial subject—emblems of guilds or industry—and usually have an inscription. The handle often has tulips or forget-me-nots on either side. The factory was at its best in the last quarter of the 18th century, and continued till the 19th.

'DUTY DODGER'
To avoid the payment of duty imposed on silver-plate by the Act of 1719 a number of English silver-smiths, including Paul de Lamerie, took hall-marks from small objects of relatively slight value and incorporated them into much larger works for the purpose of avoiding submission to the assay office, and the consequent payment of duty. These are not to be confused with the later fraudulent practice of incorporating old hall-marks into plate of modern manufacture. See *Hall-marks, English; Silver, Forgeries of.*

DUVAUX, LAZARE (c. 1703–1758)
Paris art-dealer of the rue Saint-Honoré who supplied works of art of all kinds to the royal family, Mme de Pompadour, the French and English aristocracy, and to the financiers and *fermiers-généraux* of his day. He is especially important to the present-day student of French decorative art because of the survival of his account-books, complete except for the first volume, which list his sales to many influential clients. These were published in 1873 in two volumes edited by C. J. Courajod. Duvaux's connection with the Court began about 1747, but after

1749, when he began to be patronized by the Marquise de Pompadour, he became the principal supplier of furniture and decorative objects to the royal family, selling objects of all kinds to the King, the Queen, and the Dauphin. He gained a reputation as a connoisseur of contemporary and antique decorative art, specializing in the mounting of a variety of objects in gilded bronze, and dealing in furniture and lacquer, both Oriental and *vernis Martin* (q.v.). Appearing in his account-books is a *brûle parfum* (perfume-burner) of Chinese lacquer which was sold in 1749 to Mme de Pompadour for Bellevue. Among the many objects to be noted in his accounts are bronze-mounted porcelain baskets of Vincennes flowers, one of which he sold in 1749 to the *fermier-général*, M. de Caze, and there are entries relating to the cleaning of the flowers in similar baskets, and the replacement of missing ones. He mounted a good deal of Chinese porcelain of all kinds, especially celadon vases, in gilt-bronze, and porcelain figures from Meissen and Sèvres were similarly mounted. He supplied *chenets* (q.v.) of superb quality at high prices to many influential customers, as well as lanterns and chandeliers. Lazare Duvaux paid high prices for art-objects of all kinds at the principal sales of his day, and supplied his fellow-dealers as well as private clients.

DYOTTVILLE GLASS WORKS

This, situated at Kensington, Penn., was started as the Kensington Glass Works in 1771, and came into the possession of Dr Thomas Dyott in 1831. Dr Dyott made patent medicines, and much of his production was of bottles to be employed for this purpose, but the factory also made a speciality of bottles generally, originating many decorative designs (see *Bottles, American*). Dyott retired in 1838, but the works were continued under the name of 'Dyottville'.

EAGLE

The eagle appears as a *motif* in decorative art almost as often as the lion, and it was part of the standard of the Roman legions. It was frequently carved in the form of a lectern in Christian churches, where it represents St John the Evangelist. In classical art it symbolizes Zeus, from the form he adopted when he carried off Ganymede. The eagle is a very common feature in heraldry, and in its double-headed form (to be found as part of the arms of Austria, Prussia, and Russia, for instance) it was derived from Byzantine sources. Eagles in carved form decorate furniture during the 18th and 19th centuries, especially American furniture, and they often surmount Regency convex mirrors.

EARTHENWARE

Clay lightly fired and still pervious to liquids (see *Stoneware*). The earthenware body is covered with slip (q.v.), with a tin enamel glaze (q.v.), or with a clear glaze. With a tin enamel glaze it is usually termed *delft*, faïence, or *maiolica*, and with a clear glaze, creamware if the body is cream in colour. In France creamware is termed *faïence-fine*, and in Germany, *Steingut*, which should not be confused with *Steinzeug* (stoneware). Earthenware covered with slip, or decorated with it, is termed slipware (q.v.).

EARTHENWARE, BLUE-AND-WHITE, STAFFORDSHIRE

The blue-and-white transfer-printed earthenware extensively imported into America during the closing years of the 18th century and the early decades of the 19th has increasingly become the focus of attention among collectors in England and America. The best of it was undoubtedly made by Spode (q.v.) beginning soon after 1781, and the earliest decoration was *chinoiseries* of the Willow pattern type. Starting soon after 1800, many new patterns were introduced, some of which, such as the 'Roman' or 'Tiber' patterns of 1812, correspond to contemporary fashions in the arts generally. Much was made especially for the American market, principally after about 1820, decorated with American scenes such

Eagle. An eagle between two dolphins supporting a marble-topped table in the manner of William Kent. English. c. 1730. *Mereworth Castle, Kent.*

as views of the Hudson River, portraits of Washington, views of Mount Vernon, those of Pittsburg, and historical events. These were made by a number of Staffordshire manufacturers, and at least one, probably Rogers, employed the American eagle as a special mark on such wares. A complete list of manufacturers who exported blue-and-white earthenware of this kind to America would be impossible to compile, but among the foremost, apart from Spode, may be listed Turner, Rogers, Enoch Wood, and William Adams of Tunstall; Adams of Stoke; Stevenson of Cobridge, who worked from 1810 to 1818 and was succeeded by James Clews (to 1830); Shorthose of Hanley; Wedgwood, Davenport, and Stubbs (the latter succeeded by Mayers); J. & W. Ridgway and Lakin of Hanley, and Felix Pratt of Fenton Low. Elsewhere similar wares were made at Leeds and at Swinton (both in Yorkshire), and at the Herculaneum factory at Liverpool. Spode blue-and-white of this period is undoubtedly the most sought, and a few of the more important patterns are listed below.

Captain Thomas Williamson's *Oriental Field Sports*, with aquatints by Samuel Howitt, first published in 1805, was the inspiration of a series of transfer-prints. A series known as 'Caramanian' was taken from Mayer's *Views in Asia Minor*, and another work entitled *Views in Egypt, Palestine, and the Ottoman Empire* published in 1801. Italian patterns came in part from Merigot's *Views of Rome* of 1798; the *Tiber* pattern may be from an aquatint by Merigot and Edwards of the same year.

Most patterns of the Oriental type are *chinoiseries* such as the Willow pattern and similar derivations, but there are a few instances of very close and detailed copies of 18th-century Chinese patterns which may have been replacements for broken pieces of a Chinese service, or augmentation to one made to special order. To this class belong some rare instances of the use of the *'lange Lyzen'* (q.v.). Chinese patterns are usually termed 'Indian', recalling the earlier transhipment of Chinese wares at Indian *entrepôts*. The curious mixture of Gothic and Oriental occasionally to be seen in the middle of the 18th century (see *Gothic, Revived*) occurs again in the Gothic Castle pattern. This probably belongs to about 1830, and it has a Chinese border in conjunction with a central landscape in which a Gothic castle is incongruously mixed with Chinese trees, flowers, and a bridge. Some of these patterns can also be seen in modified versions on wares from other factories. Wedgwood, for instance, used Mayer's 'Caramanian' designs.

The best of these wares are those in which body and glaze is of good quality and the transfer-print carefully fitted to the vessel without the necessary joins being obvious.

ÉBÉNISTE

The *ébéniste* does work which is approximately equivalent to that of the English cabinet-maker, or maker of case-furniture. Generally, his work is veneered, or decorated with wood marquetry, parquetry, or some other form of inlay, such as brass and tortoiseshell. Paris *ébénisterie* usually has bronze mounts in addition.

At the end of the 18th century Paris mahogany furniture in the English style which was solid wood and not veneered was often called *ébénisterie*, and the difference between this and *menuisierie* is discussed under that heading.

See *Menuisiers—Ébénistes, Corporation des.*

Ébéniste. **An ébéniste's workshop of about 1750.** *After Diderot.*

ÉBÉNISTE-MÉCANICIEN

The evolution of furniture-design in Paris during the second half of the 18th century led increasingly to the incorporation of all kinds of mechanical devices. In Paris, where most such work was done, funiture of this kind was usually, although not invariably, intended to serve dual purposes, and for the most part it was made by the German *ébénistes*, beginning with J.-F. Oeben (q.v.). The cylinder top of the famous *bureau du roi* by Oeben and Riesener was so delicately poised that it slid open when the key was turned in the lock, and Oeben probably invented the push-pull mechanism by which the opening of a cylinder-top desk brought forward the writing-slide. He also seems responsible for the design of the combined reading-desk and toilet-table which raised the slope for holding the book when the necessary mechanism was operated. Verlet describes a bedside-table in the Louvre which looks like a *commode*, but incorporates a fall-front, a footstool which is a *prie-Dieu* (prayer-stool), and a small bookcase at the back raised into position by a handle. Roentgen (q.v.) specialized in this kind of furniture, in the design of which he was aided by Peter Kinzing, a clockmaker. A combined writing-desk and toilet-table (*escritoire-coiffeuse*) made by him for Marie-Antoinette in 1779 has swinging shelves, concealed drawers and compartments, and concealed locks. A *secrétaire* made for Catherine the Great sounded an alarm if any of the secret drawers was opened. These are but a few examples of the ingenuity which went to the making of 'mechanical' furniture, and less elaborate examples were made in England to the designs of Thomas Sheraton (q.v.) under the influence of German *ébénistes* working in Paris and at Neuwied-am-Rhein.

EBERLEIN, JOHANN FRIEDRICH (1696–1749)

Modeller at Meissen from 1735 to his death, and assistant to Kändler (q.v.). Although much of his

work was done in association with Kändler, Eberlein was a modeller of skill and originality. In association with the former he helped to create the Swan service (q.v.), the *Affenkapelle* (q.v.), and the *Cris de Paris* after Bouchardon. Among his own works may be cited a series of Chinese figures done in 1743.

EBONY

The characteristic black hardwood termed ebony is produced by several species of the *Diospryros* genus native to the tropical parts of Asia and Africa. The uniformly black wood, however, is not usually found throughout the tree, but often in irregular masses, the remainder of the timber being greyish or greenish black. It first became known in Europe during the 16th century, and its use in France towards the end of the century as a valuable cabinet wood led to the origin of the term *ébéniste* (q.v.) for men skilled enough to be entrusted with it. It was used both for veneers and inlays, and for small turned parts, as well as for borders. Falling out of fashion in France during the currency of the rococo style (q.v.), it returned to limited favour later, especially during the Empire period (q.v.). The expensive nature of the wood also led to its imitation with blackened woods such as deal and pine, known in England as ebonized wood, and in France as *bois noirci*. The use of ebony in Eastern furniture, particularly Chinese, seems to have begun during the period of the Ming dynasty (1368–1644).

Green ebony is ebony which is predominantly greenish in colour, sometimes in conjunction with an olive-brown. In 18th-century France *ébène verte*, often a fairly dark green in colour, was employed as a veneer.

ECCLESIASTICAL PLATE

From earliest times the Church was the patron of the goldsmith and of the worker in such metals as bronze, although perhaps not to the same extent in Great Britain as on the Continent. Much goldsmiths' work was melted or refashioned during the Dissolution of the Monasteries by Henry VIII, and some existing plate was converted at this time to secular uses. New ecclesiastical plate more in keeping with reformed religious notions was made during the reign of Elizabeth I, from whose reign dates much of the earliest of surviving work of this kind. Some church records provide a considerable amount of information about the history of the plate in its possession which, added to expert examination, is often extremely informative, but many important examples of fine quality are still to be found in the possession of country churches about which little has been written, and discoveries are still sometimes made of unsuspected treasures, either in former hiding places, or as the result of their coming to the notice of those able to assess their value.

Shrines and reliquaries in Great Britain hardly survived the melting-pot, although some are still to be found in Ireland. Examples of croziers and crooks

Eberlein, J. F. Meissen group of Tyrolean Dancers by J. F. Eberlein on a Louis Quinze gilt-bronze base in the manner of Duplessis. This model also occurs in Chelsea and Chinese export porcelain. *Christie, Manson & Woods Ltd.*

are in the Victoria and Albert Museum (London) and at New College, Oxford. Chalices are more frequent survivals from the 16th century, and patens (the flat, circular dish on which they stood) can both be found usually in museums and churches. Sacramental flagons, made in pairs, were intended for mixing wine with water, and were either of silver or pewter. All are occasionally found converted to secular uses. The alms-bowl or dish is an example. Censers (for incense) and chrysmatories, for consecrated oil, are now uncommon in churches, and hardly to be seen outside them. Crucifixes are rare, and are usually museum pieces.

On the Continent almost priceless ecclesiastical plate is preserved in the *Schatzkammer* of Cathedrals, although some extremely notable works of art are preserved in smaller churches. The famous 11th-century candlesticks of Bernward of Hildesheim, for instance, are preserved in the Magdalenenkirche there, and used on the altar on Sundays. Pewter was very commonly made for the poorer churches which could not afford silver, and these vessels followed silver forms fairly closely.

In dating objects made for ecclesiastical use it must always be remembered that they were not so closely subject to the prevailing fashion as those made for secular purposes, and tradition tended to dictate form and ornament. Ecclesiastical plate and church decoration generally, therefore, is by no means always as early as it may appear.

ECKERNFÖRDE (Schleswig, Germany)

Eckernförde was founded in 1765 by J. M. Otte, formerly of Schleswig (q.v.). It was first established at Criseby, and then moved to the town of Eckernförde. The factory prospered during the time of Johann Buckwald and Abraham Leihamer, but after they moved to Keil in 1769 it produced only domestic wares. The products of Eckernförde under Otte, Buckwald, and Leihamer are not very original, nor equal to their inspiration in artistic quality, but it is rather surprising that they were produced at all in the prevailing conditions. Buckwald had a checkered career, working at Holitsch, Rörstrand, and Marieberg. After leaving Eckernförde he moved on to Kiel, and finally ended in Stockelsdorff. It is not, therefore, surprising that faïence at Eckernförde has affinities with the two Swedish factories.

The most frequent colour is a strong blue, sometimes used in conjunction with manganese, and enamel colours were also employed. Many different *motifs* are found. The wares usually bear a mark containing the initials *O* (Otte), *E* (Eckernförde), and *B* and/or *L* (or a painter's mark), and below that again, the date. This practice has enabled students to pinpoint the best period, between 1766 and 1768. The body is hard-fired, greyish-green or red in tone, with a white glaze. The most important painter of the region, Abraham Leihamer, signed some pieces with his name in full; the rest in his style were probably workshop products made under his supervision. They comprise figures, flowers, landscapes, and shell decoration. Apart from its vigorous plastic sense it is difficult to select any particular style, as decoration is extremely varied.

ÉCRAN (French)
Fire-screen (q.v.).

ÉCUELLE (French)
A silver covered bowl, which also occurs in faïence and porcelain. It was originally provided with a circular stand in the form of a plate, but this has usually disappeared. The *écuelle* was used for the individual service of soup and similar liquid or semi-liquid food, and it comprised a plain bowl with two horizontally projecting handles, chiselled and sometimes pierced, and an ornamented cover which sometimes terminated in a knop in the form of an artichoke. The cover served the purpose of keeping the contents hot. The silver *écuelle* made by French provincial silversmiths is a not uncommon survival, and it is usually of excellent quality. The nearest relative in England is the porringer (q.v.), which is found both in silver and *delft*, but the *écuelle* proper

Edkins, Michael. Bristol *delft* plate bearing on the reverse the initials of Michael Edkins and his wife, Betty. Dated 1760. This plate was once in the possession of Edkins's grandson. *Victoria and Albert Museum.*

never became fashionable in England, and no specimen of English make appears to exist.

EDKINS, MICHAEL (1734–1811)
Painter of Bristol *delft* (q.v.) and enameller of glass. A *delft* plate in the Victoria and Albert Museum bears the initials *MEB* (perhaps for Michael Edkins and his wife, Betty). Generally, attributions of *delft* to his hand are uncertain. In 1762 he began to paint opaque white and blue glass made in Bristol. Tea-caddies, small vases, and cruet bottles probably by his hand have been recorded, and glass vases of a familiar porcelain shape painted in colours with Chinese figures are also sometimes thought to be by his hand. Attributions, however, are uncertain in glass as well as *delft*.

EDWARDS & DARLEY
English designers. The senior of the two was Matthias Darley (died c. 1780), a self-styled 'Professor of Ornament' who engraved plates for Chippendale (q.v.). He was in partnership with Edwards from 1741 to 1763, and the two produced,

Écuelle. Covered bowl and stand of Sèvres porcelain with a *rose Pompadour* ground and slightly raised gilding. Painted with birds in landscapes by F. Aloncle (working 1758–1781). Date letter G for 1759. Similar bowls occur in silver. *Wallace Collection.*

in 1754, the ludicrous *New Book of Chinese Ornaments*, which was very influential in the field of popular interior decoration, although its resemblance to native Chinese taste was negligible. Towards the end of his life Darley began to design in the neoclassical style. See *Chinoiserie; 'Chinese Chippendale'*.

EGG AND DART

A kind of frieze ornament, originally Greek, which formed part of the repertory of ornament of revived classical styles, sometimes appearing, for example, as carved furniture decoration. It consists of alternating egg-shaped and tongue- or dart-shaped *motifs* in relief. There are several versions.

ELECTROPLATING

The technique of covering one metal with a thin layer of another by electrical deposition. Usually copper, or brass, bronze, or German (nickel) silver, which are copper alloys, are covered with silver in this way. The technique is described under *Electrotyping* (q.v.). Invented shortly before 1840, electroplating was the subject of three patents taken out by George Elkington in 1836, 1838, and 1840. In this way objects could be plated after manufacture instead of before, as with Sheffield plate (q.v.), and this advantage caused the making of the latter to be gradually discontinued for wares of domestic utility, although it survived for some time afterwards for the making of carriage lamps.

ELECTROPLATING ON NICKEL SILVER (EPNS) See *Copper*

ELECTROTYPING

This is a method of making an accurate facsimile of objects of metal and small metal sculpture. The principle is the one used in electroplating. In electroplating, introduced by Elkington of Birmingham in 1840, the object to be plated is suspended by an electrical conductor (usually a wire) in an electrolytic solution which varies in composition according to the metal to be plated. At the opposite pole a small piece of the plating metal is suspended in the same solution. When an electric current is passed, particles of metal are taken from one pole and deposited on the other.

In the case of electrotyping a mould coated with plumbago takes the place of the object to be plated, and the metal is deposited on its surface where coated. In this way an exact duplicate of the mould-surface is obtained, the deposit varying in thickness with the amount of time the current is allowed to flow. The effectiveness of a copy taken in this way, of course, depends on the quality of the mould, and by using a piece-mould (i.e. a mould in several pieces, each of which will 'draw' from the surface of the cast) a number of copies can be made.

Although the electrotyping process is normally employed for comparatively small work, it has sometimes been used for quite large statuary. Three Berlin firms in the 19th century—Winckelmann, Sussmann, and Mohring—all possessed troughs 12 ft long and proportionate in width which could do work of this kind.

Since the metal is deposited particle by particle, its surface appearance will be unlike that of cast metal. In the case of hollow bronze statuary it will not have the same 'ring' as a cast specimen when tapped.

ELERS, JOHN PHILIP AND DAVID

The Elers brothers were silversmiths who perhaps came to England in the train of William of Orange in 1688. David Elers had learned the art of making stoneware in Cologne, and had been an employee at Fulham (see *Stoneware, English*) for three years. The Elers moved to Bradwell Wood in Staffordshire soon after 1693. Cited as defendants in Dwight's lawsuit of 1693, there is no evidence for their having made stoneware in the Rhenish style, although they admitted to making brown mugs and 'red teapots' (see *Red Stoneware*). The red teapots are an important milestone in the history of English ceramics. Like almost every other ambitious potter in Europe at the time, Dwight (see *Stoneware, English*) was much preoccupied with trying to make white porcelain in imitation of the Chinese, and he may even have been convinced of success. But the red teapots of the Elers were inspired, not by Chinese white porcelain, but by the unglazed red stoneware made at Yi Hsing which was thought to be a kind of porcelain. Böttger at Meissen (q.v.) made this red-ware before discovering true porcelain, and in Holland Arij de Milde made a soft-bodied imitation. The Elers may have heard of Staffordshire 'red clay' from Dwight, and they enticed workmen from Fulham to Staffordshire.

Elers red-ware is very rare. The two brothers seemingly remained only till 1700 in Staffordshire, after which Philip went to Dublin and David returned to London. Their products were of fine workmanship, turned on the lathe in a close-grained body varying from a deep to a brownish-red. Decoration was of *chinoiseries* (in part derived from Nieuhof's *Embassy to the Grand Tartar Cham*) and moulded in countersunk relief. Prunus-blossom and pseudo-Chinese marks are typical. Later wares have extremely confused Chinese marks. Teapots, cylindrical mugs, and pear-shaped jugs are decorated with prunus-blossom, while mugs have moulded (not reeded) bands, and a rather light-coloured body.

The Elers had considerable influence on local wares, inspiring new ideas of craftsmanship which culminated, in mid-18th century, in such excellent products as Astbury and Whieldon wares and salt-glazed stoneware.

See *Red Stoneware; Salt-glaze, English*.

ELLICOTT, JOHN (d. 1733)

English clockmaker, member of the Clockmakers' Company, 1696. He established a business near the Royal Exchange, London, which was taken over by his son, John II Ellicott (1705–1772), who was clockmaker to George III and a member of the Royal Society (elected 1736). He invented a compensated pendulum in 1752. The clocks of the Ellicotts are highly regarded and much sought.

ELLICOTT, JOSEPH (1732–1780)
American clockmaker of Philadelphia. He made a well-known musical and astronomical clock in 1769, and was a member of the American Philosophical Society.

ELM
The elm is widely distributed throughout Europe. Its wood is coarse grained and light reddish-brown in colour. In France it is termed *bois d'orme*. Elm was commonly employed for furniture-making on the Continent, especially for seat-furniture. In England it was mainly used for chair seats and table-tops in the manufacture of common furniture, but its principal use was for coffins.

EMBROIDERY
The making of patterns on a textile foundation with the aid of needlework. Usually patterns are formed by stitching in coloured wools or silks on a foundation of linen, silk, satin, velvet, and similar materials. A variety of stitches are used which are given various names, but most of them defy exact classification. *Petit point* often used in the early decades of the 18th century for covering seat-furniture is executed in silk or wool on a coarse canvas, and can be defined as patterns carried out in more than eighteen stitches

Empire Style. Sèvres ice-pail given to the first Duke of Wellington by Louis XVIII. The Egyptian *motifs* commemorate Napoleon's Egyptian campaign, and the service was made c. 1811. *Courtesy of the Duke of Wellington, K.G.*

to the inch. More than twenty-four stitches is extremely fine work. The *gros point* stitch crosses two weft threads instead of the one of *petit point*. Usually the foundation is entirely covered. Oriental carpets were copied in this kind of stitch in Europe during the 16th and 17th centuries and largely employed as table covers, since they were not sufficiently hard-wearing for use on floors. Carpets of this kind were again made in the 18th century, but with European patterns. In the U.S.A. embroidered carpets were made during the early decades of the 19th century on a ground of heavy blanket material.

Appliqué (q.v.) can also be regarded as a form of embroidery.

See *Gros point; Meubles brodés; Petit point; Stump-work.*

EMERY
A natural stone of a hardness exceeded only by the diamond much used for cutting and engraving semiprecious stones, glass, and certain kinds of pottery and porcelain (for instance, European engraved decoration on Meissen red stoneware [q.v.] and Chinese porcelain), as well as for metalworking. Large deposits exist at Cape Emeri on the Island of Naxos which were worked in ancient times, the substance being employed not only for cameo cutting and similar work, but for the shaping of statuary in the harder stones, such as basalt.

See *Hardness of Materials.*

EMPIRE, ENGLISH
The Regency style, sometimes so called in acknowledgment of its debt to the Empire style (below) of France.

EMPIRE STYLE, THE
The development of the neo-classical style in the direction of what was to become the Empire style began with the Directory (see *Directoire style*) and its rigid insistence on the copying of classical models. With the appointment of Napoleon Bonaparte to the position of First Consul those who had made money from the Revolution thought it safe to

Empire Style. Table of the Great Commanders, the top of Sèvres porcelain, the remainder of bronze and gilt-bronze. One of three ordered by Napoleon to celebrate his military prowess. This example was given to King George IV by Louis XVIII. The portrait heads are executed in Roman fashion. *By gracious permission of Her Majesty the Queen.*

Empire Style. An English *chiffonier* in the Empire style decorated with Egyptian *motifs.* c. 1810. *Wilfred Bull Esq.*

spend it, and the plain and simpler furniture of the Directory began once more to exhibit the 18th-century French love of luxury. The architects of the new style were Percier and Fontaine, in association with the painter Jacques-Louis David. Percier and Fontaine were employed to decorate Malmaison in 1798, and many commissions from the newly crowned Emperor followed. In the same way as Louis XIV before him, Napoleon came to regard art as an expression of the glory of France, and many of the old royal *châteaux* were redecorated in the new style. In England where, beginning with Sheraton, the new designs were studied and reproduced the Empire style became the Regency style, and it was also widely copied throughout the rest of Europe.

The *motifs* are predominantly classical. Sources of design were principally vase-paintings, and many of the mythological beasts of antiquity were employed as furniture-mounts. The Egyptian campaign of 1798 was responsible for the addition of sphinxes, scarabs, and zoömorphic gods. In England independently developed *motifs* include those of marine significance which commemorate the victories of Nelson.

The style remained predominant in France almost until the death of Louis XVIII in 1824, and it did not entirely disappear in England till the accession of Victoria in 1837.

See *Regency Style, The.*

ENAMELLING

Enamels employed to decorate metals are similar in principle to the enamel colours of the potter, being powdered glass mixed with a flux to promote melting and a metallic oxide pigment. Most glass used for this purpose today is lead glass, because it is easily fused and has superior properties of refraction to the other varieties, but in the past no special kind of glass was employed, and old enamels vary considerably in quality.

Enamel is an extremely ancient way of decorating metalwork, dating from well before the present era. The metal base is nearly always copper, silver, or gold, on which the enamel is placed in the form of paste or powder subsequently fused in a small kiln. There are a number of different types, classified for the most part by the way in which the powder is distributed to form the pattern. Most common is *cloisonné*, which makes use of wires soldered to the surface to contain it. Much surviving work of this kind is Chinese or Japanese, although the technique was originally derived from Europe, probably from Byzantium. The Japanese also adapted the process in the 19th century to the decoration of pottery.

Champlevé enamel is somewhat rare, although it is to be seen in conjunction with *cloisonné* quite often. Cells scooped from the metal are filled with the powdered glass which is then fused. Engraved gold and silver covered with a layer of transparent

Enamelling. Painted enamel of fine quality in *famille rose* colours and with a ruby back. Probably reign of Yung Chêng (1726–1735). A type exported to Europe in the 18th century, with decoration familiar on contemporary porcelain. Enamelled in Canton. *Sotheby & Co.*

Enamelling. A *cloisonné* enamel incense-burner supported by storks on water-lily pads and with dragon handles. The wires forming the *cloisons* can plainly be seen on the storks. *Sotheby & Co.*

Enamelling. Gold box with miniatures in the style of Charlier by Louis Roucel. Paris. 1766. *Christie, Manson & Woods.*

coloured enamel, a technique sometimes allied to *champlevé*, was especially employed by French and Italian enamellers of the 14th century, and more recently in the 19th century by Viennese craftsmen.

A rare class of enamel is made by removing the background from an object formed from wires in the *cloisonné* technique, leaving transparent and translucent enamels unsupported except by the wires. This is termed *plique à jour*, and is usually employed for jewellery.

A very large and desirable class of enamels are painted in the same way as porcelain is decorated. Here the metal foundation is covered with a thin layer of enamel, usually white, which replaces the porcelain glaze as a foundation for painting. This technique was employed in most European countries, as well as for enamels made for export and painted at Canton in China—a trade which began early in the 18th century and has continued ever since.

See *Battersea Enamels; Bilston and Birmingham Enamels; Fromery, Alex.; Limoges Enamels.*

ENAMELS, FORGERIES OF

The kind usually forged are painted enamel boxes popular among collectors today.

Samson (q.v.) specializes in reproductions, and recently quite good copies of small boxes of various kinds have reached the market which were probably made in Czechoslovakia. The collector reasonably well acquainted with old boxes is not likely to be deceived. Enamels in pristine condition always demand careful examination, for enamel is a fragile substance and some signs of the wear and tear of a couple of centuries are usually apparent. A few minor chips, a hair-crack or two, and the signs of wear at the corners might make some modern boxes more deceptive, and this possibility should be borne in mind.

Sixteenth-century enamels from Limoges (q.v.) are

not as eagerly sought as they were, but 19th-century forgeries exist, some initialled *IP* for Jean Penicaud. Piece for piece the forgeries are inclined to be heavier than genuine work. The black ground is usually poor, the blue overbright, the white defective, and the drawing weak. The best safeguard is an acquaintance with genuine enamels of this kind.

Many 18th-century English enamels are called 'Battersea' which were made elsewhere (see *Battersea Enamels*), usually at Birmingham or Bilston (Staffs.). The problem is often one of attribution, but since Battersea enamel is the more valued kind the temptation to ascribe those made elsewhere to Battersea is strong. The Battersea enamel works existed from 1753 to 1755 and production was relatively small. Anything in the neoclassical style, especially boxes decorated with an urn, cannot possibly have been made here. See also *Bilston and Birmingham Enamels.*

ENCOIGNURE (French)

A corner cupboard in one or two parts with, sometimes, a low *gradin* or base in addition, which has now nearly always disappeared. The top of the *encoignure* was sometimes a tier of shelves (*étagère*), but very often only the base now remains and has been covered with a marble top at a later date. The design of the *encoignure*, and the materials of its construction, correspond with styles of the period of its manufacture.

'END OF DAY' GLASS

Small, decorative objects usually made 'at the lamp' from left-over glass at the end of the day or in

Encoignure. An *encoignure* of the Louis XV period in *palissandre* (rosewood) and tulipwood by François Rübestück (*maître ébéniste,* 1766). *Parke-Bernet Galleries, New York.*

spare moments by glass-makers, either for themselves, as gifts, or to sell as ornaments. Usually primitive, and often amusing, glass of this kind was made universally, and it is frequently sought by collectors. In the U.S.A. it is known as 'off-hand' glass. Slag glass was a factory product, and can only be regarded as 'end of day' glass if it has been so used.

ENGHALSKRÜGE

A type of long, narrow-necked faïence jug with globular or pear-shaped body, often with a plaited handle, mounted in pewter round the foot, and with a pewter cover. It is especially typical of Hanau, Frankfurt, Nürnberg, and several other German faïence factories.

ENGINE-TURNING

The term normally refers to engraved ornament on metal incised mechanically by a special type of lathe. Two basic repetitive patterns can be cut—those of a circular or oval type, and those based on the straight line. The position of the engraved lines is controlled by the action of an eccentric cam, or by a tool called a rosette which has a series of projections. The patterns themselves have a mechanical precision unattainable by hand, but they are strictly limited in scope.

Engine-turning came into use in England soon after the middle of the 18th century, the lathe being introduced from France. It was employed for decorative metalwork by Matthew Boulton, and Wedgwood first saw it in Birmingham in 1763. He acquired one and adapted it to the decoration of pottery. Subsequently it was especially employed to decorate basaltes ware, the patterns being based on the straight line. Most existing specimens are after 1767, usually vases and bowls. The actual lathe is still preserved at Barlaston and is in occasional use today.

ENGRAVED GLASS

Glass is engraved in the same way as semi-precious stones. The cutting is done with small revolving copper wheels to the edges of which emery powder mixed with oil has been applied. The technique is a very ancient one, dating back to Roman times. Per-

Engraved Glass. Bohemian tumbler engraved with a Coat of Arms, and two figures, one of which holds a cornucopia, within a laurel wreath. End of 17th century. *Victoria and Albert Museum.*

Engine-Turning. Engine-turning lathe installed in the 1760s by Josiah Wedgwood and still in occasional use today at Barlaston (Staffs). *Josiah Wedgwood & Sons Ltd.*

haps the finest engraving was done in Bohemia in the 17th century, but it is still done today, notably at the Steuben Glass Works, New York (see *Corning Glass Works*). In the 19th century the New England Glass Company of Cambridge, Mass., had a considerable reputation for work of this kind in America. See *Emery*.

ENTRETOISE (French)   See *Stretchers*

ÉPERGNE

A recent term for an 18th-century centre-piece for the dining table. It was essentially a silver stand holding a single large cut-glass dish and several small ones for sweetmeats and so forth. Many such stands were made partly from Sheffield plate.

ERFURT (Thuringia, Germany) FAÏENCE FACTORY

There were successively three factories at Erfurt. The first was started in 1717 with a fifteen years' privilege. In 1719 another concession was granted, and this factory continued, although it was joined in 1734 to yet a third founded by Paul Stieglitz, a pewter manufacturer. The colours are all of the high-temperature variety—olive-green, bright lemon-yellow, iron-red, and blue. Manganese was used sparingly. A feathery border on plates with a central *motif* is typical, and cylindrical pewter-mounted tankards were painted with landscapes, ruins, etc. within a cartouche reserved on a manganese ground. A few figures were made here. Much of the production, where suitable, was mounted in pewter. The use of the wheel as a mark, similar to the mark of Höchst, should not be a cause for confusion since, like all Thuringian factories, Erfurt decorated only in high-temperature colours whereas Höchst used only enamels.

ESCAPEMENT

Whatever the motive-power of a clock—weights or springs— the power which drives the hands must be

Erfurt Faïence. Faience tankard decorated in high-temperature colours (q.v.), the pewter cover dated 1762. Erfurt (Germany).

tion with a long pendulum of 39·1 inches, and this led to the development of a clock with a case long enough to contain both pendulum and driving-weights. This is termed the long-case clock, or in France, the *regulateur*, and it was an extremely accurate time-keeper. The long pendulum made possible the introduction of clocks intended to run for up to a year at one winding, as well as the development of complex mechanisms for recording the movement of astronomical bodies.

Many wall-clocks (or lantern clocks) were adapted to the anchor escapement in the 17th century, but the verge was retained for bracket and chamber clocks since it was much more tolerant of being moved than the anchor escapement. Clocks on the latter principle need to be very carefully set up and maintained at a constant level. The verge was still in use in 1800, but few clocks now have their original escapement since this part of the movement is subject to the greatest wear, and the verge has nearly always been replaced with an anchor in course of repair. Holes in the backplate in the region of the escapement which cannot otherwise be accounted for are usually a sign that this has been done, although it is sometimes due to a striking-train or some other non-essential mechanism having been removed.

Replacement of the escapement is not a good reason for rejecting an antique clock. Any which now retain the original parts will be very bad time-keepers, and not the least of the charm of the 18th-century clock is the accuracy of its time-keeping when properly maintained.

ESCAPEMENT, DEADBEAT

An improved type of anchor escapement devised by George Graham in 1715. This eliminated the re-coil to be observed with the normal anchor escape-

released in a controlled and orderly sequence, allowing the same time-interval between each impulse. The device responsible, the escapement, is at the heart of any clock mechanism, and without it the clock would not function as a time-measuring device. Essentially the earliest escapement was a toothed wheel working in conjunction with an oscillating crossbar carrying pallets which alternately engaged and disengaged with the teeth, releasing one at a time. The rate at which this takes place has, from the middle of the 17th century, been regulated by the swing of a pendulum, but the earlier version (the foliot escapement) had an arrangement of small adjustable weights on the crossbar to serve the same purpose. An example of this escapement is preserved in the Science Museum, South Kensington, London.

In 1582 Galileo observed that however long a pendulum, the time taken to describe its arc was approximately the same, and Christian Huygens applied this principle to the clock in 1656, the pendulum being coupled to the crossbar of the escapement regulating the engagement and disengagement of two pallets with the teeth of a horizontally disposed crown-wheel, the name of which suggests its appearance. This is the verge escapement. About 1670, probably devised by Robert Hooke, an escapement shaped like an inverted anchor (anchor escapement) which rocked backwards and forwards was employed in conjunc-

Étagère. Hanging open shelves in the Chippendale style. c. 1760. *Harrods Ltd.*

ment. This recoil, a cause of minor inaccuracy, can be seen if the movement of a seconds hand on a long-case clock fitted with the standard escapement is studied. The hand will be seen to move intermittently, and slightly backwards at each pause. This gives the appearance of 'bouncing', which is what is happening. The seconds hand is connected directly to the anchor, and is mounted on the same arbor, or shaft, and therefore records its movements. See *Escapement*.

ESCUTCHEON
Decorative metal plate protecting key-holes in cabinet furniture.

ÉTAGÈRE (French)
A tier of shelves for the display of *bibelots* and small objects of *vertu*. It sometimes surmounted the base of an *encoignure* (q.v.). The *étagère* in Victorian times was referred to as a what-not—a term of unknown derivation.

ETCHED GLASS
Glass may be etched with the aid of hydrofluoric acid (q.v.). The glass to be decorated is first coated with wax, and the design is then produced by scratching through the coating with a sharp point to the glass beneath, or by removal of the wax where the acid is intended to etch the glass. Acid is then applied, and eats into the surface of the glass where it is un-protected. The extent to which this is done depends on the amount of time the acid is allowed to remain in contact with the surface.

EULENKRÜGE (German)
Owl-jugs. These provide one of the earliest examples of the use of tin-glaze in Germany. There are about fifteen known examples dating between 1540 and 1561. They are jugs made in the shape of owls with moulded relief feathers and sometimes Shields of Arms in oil-paint and cold gilding on their breasts. It has been suggested that they were a kind of potter's joke—a play on the word *Eulner* used in the Rhineland for potter. It seems a rather far-fetched explanation, but the alternative—that they were prizes in archery contests—is even less likely.

EVELYN, JOHN (1620–1706)
Diarist, connoisseur, and one of the arbiters of taste in 17th-century England. Evelyn's *Diaries* (various editions) contain much valuable information about the arts of his time, and he was among the earliest members of the Royal Society. He discovered Grinling Gibbons (q.v.), and brought him to the notice of Charles II and Christopher Wren. Evelyn's writings cover such subjects as architecture, painting, engraving, and numismatics, and his commentaries on journeys abroad are much concerned with works of art seen in France and Italy.

F

FABERGÉ, PETER CARL (1846–1920)

Noted Russian jeweller and designer of Huguenot descent whose family settled in Russia early in the 19th century. Gustav Fabergé, father of Peter Carl, established himself in St Petersburg as a jeweller and dealer in *objets d'art* of fine quality in 1842—an undertaking inherited by his son. Peter Carl began to manufacture *objets d'art* of the kind associated with his name soon after 1870, and in 1882 he exhibited in the Pan-Russian Exhibition in Moscow. He soon achieved an international reputation for his work, and was widely patronized not only by the Russian ruling house but by that of England, and by wealthy people throughout Europe. He became noted for the taste and skill with which he employed and combined a wide variety of precious and semi-precious materials for small ornamental works designed by him, the execution of which he supervised, although virtually nothing can be attributed to his own hand. Primarily Fabergé was a designer, assisted by his sons, and by a talented team at the head of which was a Swiss named François Birbaum. Manufacture was carried out in a number of independent workshops, the best known of which is probably that of the workmaster Michael Perchin (1860–1903). The marks of these workmasters are given in the standard work on the subject—A. Kenneth Snowman's *Art of Carl Fabergé* (Faber & Faber, London, 1963). A number of branch establishments were opened—at Moscow, Odessa, Kiev, and London, the latter in existence from 1903 to 1915. These branches were much more closely controlled by Fabergé than were the St Petersburg workshops, and, with few exceptions, no workmasters' marks appear on these products. The Fabergé enterprise fell victim to the Russian Revolution, and the intolerance of the new régime for objects of luxury. During the lifetime of the enterprise output was very considerable, and only the finest works can be regarded as exceptionally rare.

Much of the work of Fabergé owes a great deal to 18th-century France, and particularly the rococo style which, as a designer of metalwork, inevitably attracted him. With a few small works there is some Far Eastern influence, and after 1893 the *motifs* of

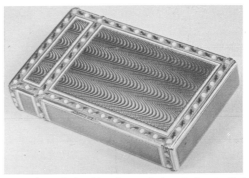

Fabergé, P. C. A gold and enamel cigarette box by Carl Fabergé *Christie, Manson & Woods Ltd.*

art *nouveau* are increasingly noticeable. Although many works are Russian in feeling and style, in general the style of most of them is basically French. Forgeries exist, and objects in the Fabergé style made elsewhere in Russia or in Germany are not uncommon.

The materials employed by Fabergé in his designs are extremely varied. He used gold in several colours (burnished and mat) which were achieved for the most part by alloying it with other metals. Silver, both of natural colour and oxidized, is slightly below the normal English standard due to the necessity for producing a metal which would take enamels successfully. Platinum was employed for some purposes. Fabergé exploited the extensive variety of Russian mineral deposits, using especially the semi-precious hardstones like rock-crystal, jade (native nephrite and imported jadeite), agate, jasper, malachite, aventurine quartz, lapis lazuli, and obsidian—the latter a natural glass of volcanic origin. Fabergé mastered the art of modifying the colour of some of these stones which were carved by highly skilled lapidaries to the designs supplied. Semi-precious stones were employed in the making of a series of naturalistically rendered and amusingly designed animals and birds, and of a series of Russian folk-types—the latter a subject already exploited by the Russian porcelain factories. These were based on prototypes supplied in wax by several modellers. Some of the animals, and most of the peasant figures,

Fabergé, P. C. A gold, enamel, and nephrite japonica flower by Carl Fabergé. *Christie, Manson & Woods Ltd.*

were made from a variety of stones carefully shaped and joined together, the colouring of the peasant costumes, for instance, being achieved by the selection of suitably coloured stones.

Some of Fabergé's most sought products consist of minute representations of objects of various kinds which were, at the time, intended to be no more than amusing toys. These often exhibit great ingenuity. Miniature sedan chairs, or drawing-room chairs distinctly echoing the Louis XVI style, and miniature case-furniture, belong to this group. Plants with flowers and leaves in variously coloured hardstones on stalks of engraved gold set in rock-crystal pots

are rarely much larger than six inches in height, and often smaller. Especially prized are Easter Eggs (also produced by Russian porcelain factories from the 18th century), the first of which was made in 1884 for the Czar Alexander III to present to the Czarina. Upon his accession in 1894 the ill-fated Nicholas II continued the custom. These eggs took a variety of elaborate forms. One is a Louis XVI clock with a case simulating Sèvres porcelain in the form of an ovoid urn, the numerals appearing on bands encircling the body—a characteristic design of the 1770s. Another is of the same general form, but inset with a clock having a conventional dial and a cock which rises from the interior to flap its wings on the hour. A number of these 'eggs' exist, but although the first was a true egg, later examples tend to become increasingly elaborate compositions built around an ovoid theme.

Perhaps the most exact comparison for the work of Fabergé would be the miniature works of the royal goldsmiths of 18th-century France, and those of the Saxon Court goldsmith, Dinglinger, with which it has an obvious relationship.

FAENZA (Emilia, Italy) MAIOLICA

The name, Faenza, is regarded as the origin of the French term *faïence* for tin-enamel wares. The earliest certainly attributed specimen dated 1500, is an *albarello* decorated with grotesques on a yellow ground but manufacture must have been established for many years before this, and was probably fully developed by 1487. One group of *istoriato* (q.v.) plates by Faenza painters exists which includes trophies and allegorical scenes in the decoration that can be dated around 1510. The earliest dated

Faenza. Albarello with medallions of heroes from Ariosto's *Orlando Furioso.* Faenza (probably Casa Pirota). First quarter of the 16th century. *Wallace Collection.*

Fabergé. Two figures in hardstones: Russian peasant woman waiting for a sauna bath. An intoxicated mujik dancing. *Sotheby & Co.*

144

specimen from the main workshop at Faenza, the Casa Pirota (which used the mark of a kind of fiery bomb), was made in 1525, and this remained a major centre of production for at least another ten years.

Faenza used a very rich and intense blue both as a ground colour and for outlining. A soft mauve ranges to a purple, and there were, in addition, orange, brown, lemon-yellow, green, and greenish-turquoise, The design called *alla porcellana* (q.v.) with blue trailing stems on a white ground is sometimes found on the backs of Faenza dishes, and blue and purple concentric rings occur, also used on the reverse side. Decorative *motifs* include *grotesques* (q.v.), arabesques (q.v.), dolphins, *amorini*, masks, foliage, and interlacing strapwork. The glaze called *a berretino* (also to be found elsewhere) was sometimes combined with *bianco sopra bianco* (q.v.). Abstract and foliate designs predominate.

The best work of Faenza had been done before 1550, but the factory continued until well into the 19th century. Emigrants from the workshops here helped during the 16th century to carry the art of *maiolica* not only to other Italian cities, but to France and the Netherlands.

FAÇON DE VENISE
Glass in the style of Venice but made elsewhere. The term is only employed of close imitations, and not in cases of mere general resemblance.

FAÏENCE BLANCHE (French)
A type of ware originating in Faenza (q.v.) in which the tin-glaze is left largely undecorated, except for a central Coat of Arms and a conventional wreath-like design round the edge.

FAÏENCE-FINE (French)
The French version of English creamware (q.v.). Earthenware, cream in colour, covered with a lead glaze and usually decorated either with painting or transfer-printing. After the commercial treaty of 1786 Wedgwood flooded the French market with creamware of excellent design and quality, seriously threatening the prosperity, and even the existence, of porcelain and faïence factories. French manufacturers began to imitate creamware in self-defence, and later adopted the English method of transfer-printing as a way of decorating it with semi-skilled labour. One of the earliest factories to produce *faïence-fine* was at Douai (Nord), operated by two Englishmen named Leigh, where the products of Leeds were imitated fairly closely and termed *faïence anglaise*. A factory at Creil produced creamware of excellent quality, rivalling the best English productions, which they decorated with transfer-printing, a series of prints of English country houses titled in French proving very popular. Other factories were situated at Sèvres, Sarreguemines (Lorraine), Apt (Vaucluse), and Chantilly (q.v.). The familiar hunting-horn mark appears also on Chantilly *faïence-fine*. These French examples of creamware are sometimes found in England, and occasionally confused with English production.

Faïence-fine. A bowl of *faïence-fine* (French creamware—q.v.) made at Creil in the early years of the 19th century. Perhaps in recognition of its origin transfer-prints of English country houses were popular. This one is of Heveningham House in Suffolk. *Victoria and Albert Museum.*

FAÏENCE, GERMAN
The earliest German tin-enamel wares (faïence) were indifferent copies of Italian *maiolica*, and the first known example is a shallow bowl dated 1526 depicting Samson and Delilah, which is coloured in pale green, manganese, yellow, and blue in the Italian style. Several other pieces—bottles, bowls, and albarellos—some decorated in blue-and-white only, are reminiscent of the styles of Venice, Faenza, and Castel Durante. They date between 1526 and 1544, but the group is a very small one. Their scarcity is probably explained by the fact that the glaze included imported and expensive tin. Some tin-enamel glaze was used by the *Hafnermeister* (q.v.) for the tiles with which they decorated their stoves, and the same glaze was used for the Owl jugs (*Eulenkrüge*, q.v.), which are exceptionally rare, only about fifteen being known. They range in date from 1540 to 1561.

Apart from the imitations of *maiolica* mentioned above, another group made at Kreussen (q.v.) may be viewed historically as among the earliest German faïence wares. The first dated piece is 1609, and it has been attributed to Lorenz Speckner's apprenticeship in Nürnberg, before he moved to Kreussen. The Kreussen group dates from 1618 and continues till 1660. It is called the 'Spiral Family' from a recurring *motif* in the design. The glaze is white over a light coloured body, with a calligraphic type of blue decoration of stylized flowers, cross-hatched, with linear foliage and the spirals that give the group its name. Coats of arms and inscriptions are also known. Although Speckner produced faïence he was working in a factory making *Hafnerware*, and his work did not lead to the development of true faïence in Germany which did not occur till mid-17th century.

Responsibility for early production of faïence in Germany undoubtedly lay with the Dutch, whose influence in the arts was widespread in northern Europe. The flourishing industry of the city of Delft was very important in the 17th century, and the huge quantities of expensive Chinese porcelain brought to Europe by the East Indiamen also served to encourage wealthy princes to embark on faïence production on their own account. The Dutch

Famille Verte. A Chinese saucer-dish painted in the *famille verte* palette. Reign of the Emperor K'ang Hsi (1666–1722). The influence of Kakiemon is perceptible, and much closer derivations have been recorded. *Bluett & Sons, London.*

entrepreneurs saw their chance, and in all the early factories Dutch craftsmen appeared, with the obvious result that many of the early wares (especially at Frankfurt, Hanau, Berlin (Potsdam), and Zerbst q.v.) closely resemble the wares of Delft and can easily be confused with them. Another point of confusion arises from the fact that some of the raw materials were used in common by both countries. Delft was unable to supply its own clay and, apart from beds at Tournai, drew extensively on German supplies.

However, it was not long before the Germans began to develop their own styles, which were also subject to the influence of Hannong at Strasbourg (q.v.) and, in a lesser degree, to that of Rouen. The numerous factories are elsewhere discussed under appropriate headings.

FAÏENCE PARLANTE (French)
A type of faïence decoration confined to local history, folklore, and emblems, very common at Nevers, but copied at Angoulême and other factories.

FAÏENCE PATRIOTIQUE
A type of late 18th-century French faïence decorated with crudely drawn Revolutionary subjects, such as the Tree of Liberty, the Bastille, etc., and generally with inscriptions like *à la liberté ou la morte.* Figures usually wear Phrygian caps. Genuine specimens are quite rare; most of those for sale are comparatively recent forgeries.

FAILLE (French)
Cloth woven to give a corded effect.

FAIRINGS
Name given to a class of small German brightly coloured hard-paste porcelain groups, and lidded boxes, which were mass-produced in moulds and given painted captions in black or gilt. They were made at the latter end of the 19th century, and well into the 20th. They are now being reproduced.

Fairings were concerned with slightly indelicate situations relating to courtship, matrimony, and domestic life; children, and their games and toys; animals behaving like human beings; and politics. There are several variations on such captions as 'The last in bed to put out the light', 'The lovers disturbed', or 'Coming home from the seaside' (a bear family in human dress). Boxes for pins, etc., had a roughened base so that they could be used as match-holders, and the lids are often decorated with the same subjects as the groups.

Fairings are much-sought, and several hundred different versions exist. Originally for sale at fairs, bazaars, and seaside stalls at prices from 1d to 1s each, they now command relatively high prices.

They were made by the firm of Conta & Böhme (founded as long ago as 1790) at Pössneck, in Saxony, and perhaps by a factory at Elbogen, Bohemia (now Czechoslovakia), called Springer, who were the successors of the original Rudolf Haidinger who founded it in 1815. Some specimens are marked 'Made in Germany', but since Bohemia was part of Germany when they were made this can be found on the products of either. Confusingly enough, both these factories used the mark of a mailed arm holding a dagger within a shield, but the Elbogen version is surmounted by a crown.

FAMILLE ROSE (French)
A distinctive palette employed in the decoration of Chinese porcelain at the end of the reign of K'ang Hsi (1662–1722). This included a rose-pink introduced from Europe, where it had been invented about 1680 by Andreas Cassius of Leyden. It was called *yang ts'ai* (i.e. foreign colour) by the Chinese. Much of the best painting in this category was done during the reign of Yung Chêng (1723–1735), when the 'ruby-backed' dishes (those of which the back, except for the space inside the footring, was covered with *rose* enamel) were first made. These, with multiple borders of great intricacy, are highly valued. Most painting in *rose* enamel was done at the Canton decorating studios, and the colour was also employed for painted enamels on a copper base. The colour varies in shade from pale pink to a brownish-red or violet according to firing temperature and quality. The best approach most nearly to a good rose-pink. Towards the end of the century the *rose* and *verte* palettes were combined (see *Famille verte*) in overcrowded decorations called 'Mandarin' (q.v.), the palette being termed *rose-verte.*

FAMILLE VERTE (French)
Enamelled Chinese porcelain made in the reign of the Emperor K'ang Hsi (1662–1722) decorated with a brilliant copper-green, manganese-purple, antimony-yellow, overglaze enamel blue, and iron-red. Some early examples exhibit underglaze cobalt-blue in conjunction with the enamels. *Famille jaune* (yellow family) is painting in *verte* enamels on a yellow

ground, and *famille noir* (black family) has a lustrous black ground in conjunction with the *verte* palette. The black ground is washed over with a translucent green enamel. The *verte* palette was sometimes used in conjunction with blue grounds which incline to purple, including powder-blue (*chui ch'ing*), the enamel painting being in reserved panels. The classification into families was first made in the 19th century by the French writer, Jacquemart.

FASHION IN ART

Fashion in art and antiques is related to style, but there are significant differences. Fashion is here intended to refer to fluctuations in taste in making purchases, while we understand by styles the various fashions in the design and making of works of art. The ability to recognize the various styles is, of course, of the utmost importance to correct dating.

Fashion in purchasing is hardly distinguishable from demand, since people will always seek to buy what is currently in vogue. Fashion always has a much greater effect on demand than standards of artistic value, which in any case can fluctuate very considerably. In the 16th century Michelangelo regarded Cellini as a far greater sculptor than himself, a verdict reversed in the 20th century, which may again be reversed in the 21st. In 17th-century France a Venetian mirror was more highly valued than a painting by Raphael. In 18th-century England Claude Lorraine and Salvator Rosa were among the most admired of painters. Today, they are Leonardo da Vinci and Rembrandt, and in a hundred years they may well be Watteau and Boucher. Taste depends on the social and economic climate of the time, rather than on intrinsic excellence which is largely a matter of opinion.

The history of the art-market is full of instances of changes in taste which temporarily depress the popularity of whole groups of objects. In porcelain, the work of the great royal factory of Sèvres costs only a fraction of what it did in the 1890s, and the later porcelain of Chelsea, inspired by contemporary work at Sèvres, is also lower in price than its early work based on the porcelain of the Meissen factory. By a vagary of taste Worcester porcelain of the 1760s and 1770s, which owes much to Sèvres, is valued more highly than that of any other period.

Fashions in antiques seem to run in cycles of about forty years. Renaissance works of art, such as Italian *maiolica* and 16th-century bronzes, dropped out of favour after the economic collapse of 1929, and are only just, in 1968, beginning to return to something like the former degree of esteem.

A good deal of Renaissance furniture, because of its large size and the current fashion for apartments and small rooms, can be bought for relatively low prices when its rarity and importance are considered, while the popularity of Renoir in the salerooms is affected at least to some extent by the ease with which his paintings blend with 18th-century French furniture styles. His nudes are a substitute for those of Boucher.

Fauteuil. Fauteuil from a suite of seat furniture signed *I. Lebas.* The incurved back is *en cabriolet* (q.v.). Louis XV period. *Sotheby & Co.*

Two subjects allied to fashion are forgery, elsewhere discussed, and rarity. If objects are extremely rare they are hardly likely to be much affected by fashion, and if demand too far outruns supply, forged works are likely to be made to supply the market.

Fashion is always closely related to social and economic conditions, and a shrewd appraisal of these two factors is helpful in assessing the future course of demand.

FAUTEUIL (French)

A chair with arms. The word is derived from the Old French *Fauldsteuil*, which meant the same as the English *faldstool*, and is derived from the Old High German *falden*, to fold. Originally a *fauldsteuil* was a folding-stool, similar to the Roman curule chair, of which an early example (the chair of Dagobert of the 7th century) is preserved in the Louvre. The word *fauteuil* came into common use in France in the second half of the 17th century to denote an upholstered chair with open arms which were either of plain carved wood or, in the 18th century, often with elbow-pads (*manchettes*), the back being flat (*à la reine*) or curved (*en cabriolet*). Strictly, there is no equivalent term in current English, and 'armchair' is only applicable in a very general sense. More nearly the *fauteuil* resembles the 'carver' from an English set of dining-chairs (q.v.). In the Middle Ages chairs without arms did not exist, and even the chair with arms (*chaise au bras*) was a very considerable rarity.

Favrile Glass. Decanter in Favrile glass engraved with the mark *LCT.* Tiffany Glass and Decorating Company, New York. 1902. *Victoria and Albert Museum.*

The chair without arms does not appear until towards the end of the 16th century in consequence of the fashion for the *vertugradin* or farthingale. The typical English armchair is more nearly analogous to the *bergère* (q.v.) in France.

'FAVRILE' GLASS
A trade name for glass in the *art nouveau* style (q.v.) made by Louis Comfort Tiffany of New York. It was given an iridescent or lustred surface by spraying it while hot with metallic salts. Some specimens are signed 'L. C. Tiffany' and others initialled 'L. C. T.' Favrile glass was first exhibited in 1893, and Tiffany was considerably influenced by the work of Emil Gallé (q.v.). Imitations were made by Lötz Witwe and the Bohemian glass-workers.

FEDERAL STYLE
An American style which began soon after the Declaration of Independence in 1776, chiefly to be seen in furniture, and current until about 1830. In its early stages it is virtually indistinguishable from the neo-classical style in Europe, and it was subject to a similar evolutionary process by way of *Directoire* to Empire. The best-known exponent of the Federal style is Duncan Phyfe (q.v.), and among those crafts-men to exhibit French influence was Charles-Honoré Launnier, who travelled to America in 1803 when he was twenty-five, and worked in the *Directoire* and Empire styles. Federal furniture is predominantly

mahogany, but curly maple usually replaces satin-wood where appropriate. *Motifs* of decoration are similar to those currently fashionable in Europe, but the eagle more commonly appears.

FELT RUGS
Although these are made extensively in Persia they are rarely exported. They are employed as a foundation for pile rugs and carpets. Felt rugs with needle-work patterns have been imported from India for many years. They are not uncommon, but are artistically negligible.

FERAGHAN RUGS AND CARPETS
These come from the plains of Feraghan, between Teheran and Isphahan. The Sehna knot is employed for old specimens, but some modern carpets are tied with the Ghiordes knot. There are from three to nine border stripes, and the Herati design (see *Herat*) is almost ubiquitous in the border. The designs often feature the Herati *motif,* and animals and birds are not uncommon. It was here that some of the weavers from Herat were settled after the conquest of the city. Vegetable dyes are almost wholly employed.

FERNER, F. J. (fl. mid-18th century)
German *Hausmaler* (q.v.). Although his work is not at all uncommon little is known of the man him-self. He commonly used the porcelain of Meissen, Berlin, and Vienna, and sometimes that of the Thuringian factories. A few signed specimens are known as a key to the attribution of others. Much of Ferner's work consists of overgilding defective Meissen blue-and-white porcelain, often with the addition of artlessly painted flowers in crude and rather dry enamel colours. He also did naively drawn pastoral figures sometimes inserted between original decoration in underglaze blue.

FERNEX, J. B. de (1729–1783)
French sculptor who also worked, about 1755, for the Sèvres Porcelain Factory. His portrait busts include Mme Favart and Mme Clairon, the actresses.

FERNS
A fashionable cult in England after 1850. The preservation of ferns, and their decorative use in the home, supplied a new *motif* for decorating a variety of objects—glass, china, needlework, wallpaper, and furnishing fabrics. A vase thus decorated by Mintons appeared in the International Exhibition of 1862. Victorian table-glass was frequently thus engraved, and fern arrangements in vases were placed under glass shades. The fashion disappeared in the 1870s.

FERRARA (Italy)
A *maiolica* factory flourished in Ferrara early in the 16th century under the protection of the Duke of Ferrara. The potters probably came from Faenza, and since no marked pieces are known it is impossible to separate the wares from those of its more southerly neighbour.

FICTOOR, LOUWIS See *Cachemire Style.*

FIDDLE-BACK

Term used to describe the figuring of some veneers, irrespective of the nature of the wood, when they resemble those usually to be found on the backs of old violins.

A Queen Anne chair with a splat somewhat resembling a fiddle in outline. Also sometimes called an urn- or vase-shaped splat.

FIGURES, BRASS

Towards the end of the 18th century, and during the first half of the 19th, figures of brass were common as kitchen chimney-piece ornaments in England, even in comparatively well-to-do houses. Some were based on popular earthenware figures of the day, themselves often copied from porcelain versions. Generally the brass figures include historical and allegorical subjects, huntsmen, animals, birds in great variety, and historical personages, such as Napoleon. The early figures were cast in simple moulds, and they usually show signs of being worked on afterwards to remove casting blemishes and to sharpen details. Modern castings imitating the old ones exist, but most are of poor workmanship with little sign of subsequent attention to finishing. See also *Door-stops.*

FIGURES, GLASS, NEVERS

Often wrongly described as 'enamel' figures, from a mistaken notion that this is the only meaning of the French *émail* (see *Glaze, French Usage*), the figures of Nevers were usually at least partially made of glass opacified with tin oxide (tin-enamel) and therefore similar to a faïence glaze (q.v.). They were made 'at the lamp', which means that they were of glass softened in the flame of the glassworker's lamp and manipulated into shape by means of various tools.

The earliest mention of glass figures from Nevers (about 100 km south of Paris) is probably one of 1605, which records that Louis XIII had several dogs and small animals of this sort. The vogue grew considerably, and at the middle of the 17th century one of the many glassworkers, Essonnes, opened a shop on the Fontainebleau road which was much patronized by Members of the Court. Still later they became so popular among collectors that some of the glass-workers migrated to Paris, where the best known was Pierre La Motte who opened his shop in 1691 and enjoyed the patronage of Louis XIV. The vogue for *verrefilé*—a contemporary term probably referring to the very thin glass rods which formed part of the materials used—continued throughout the 18th century, and into the 19th, perhaps the last of the Paris workmen being a M. Lambourd who was working in 1845.

Technically, the figures were modelled from sticks of glass, of which some had a supporting core of copper wire. The use of coloured glass for draperies and details is frequent, while the base was often of clear glass with added coloured glass to imitate rocks, grass, and so forth. This applied decoration being termed *frisé* (curly) for obvious reasons.

The earliest figures may have been inspired by similar Venetian work, and in the style of modelling they are in keeping with the period. Some are based on the popular engravings of Jacques Callot (q.v.). In the 18th century the influence of the porcelain factories is to be noted, and some were made for much the same reason as the small porcelain figures —as table-decoration (q.v.). An example in the Musée des arts decoratifs (Paris) is in the form of a group of figures on a tray with a mirror base which was made as a centrepiece. Customarily figures were depicted on a base similar to that employed for porcelain groups, and these were quite commonly made, often posed against backgrounds of paper, or sometimes with a mirror at the rear. The figures vary in height from about one inch to six inches, the larger ones being rare.

The technique was employed occasionally in Victorian England; for instance, a glass fountain decorated with peacocks in the Victoria and Albert Museum (London). Similar work was done in the 18th century at Rouen, Bordeaux, and Marseilles, although little is known of it.

FIGURES, PORCELAIN, MANUFACTURE OF

The 18th-century technique of making porcelain figures has altered very little in modern times, and the method described below is still employed by the Worcester Royal Porcelain factory for making the birds of Dorothy Doughty and other figure models.

The first step is the provision of a prototype by the designer. This can be modelled in clay or wax and is subsequently cast in lead or plaster as a permanent record. The figures of Bustelli at Nymphenburg were first carved in limewood, which can plainly be seen if they are examined for evidence of this technique.

A wax or clay prototype was dissected into component parts (head, torso, arms, legs, and any additional ornament) which were then moulded, usually in plaster. Casts or squeezes were taken from the moulds, and the figure put together by a workman known as a 'repairer' (in German, a *bossierer*). Supports (removed after firing) were put into position where necessary to guard against distortion and sagging in the kiln, and the figure was ready to be fired. After firing it was usually glazed and decorated with enamel colours fixed in the enamelling kiln. The intervention of the 'repairer' accounts for differences between one model and another, since the limbs were not always attached exactly in the same position and the added ornament could be varied at will. After use over a period of time the small moulds became blunted, and fresh moulds were taken from the preliminary cast of the prototype, which acted as a master model.

This method of producing figures in quantity is very ancient, being used by the potters of Tanagra (Greece) in the 3rd century B.C. It was also employed by bronzeworkers, especially in Renaissance Italy, for the multiplication of bronze figures. An example is the *Mounted Warrior* of Riccio, where several slightly different versions exist of which the best known is in the Victoria and Albert Museum (London).

Cheap figures in pottery and porcelain are designed so that there are no projecting parts, such as arms, which need to be separately moulded, enabling them to be cast in one operation without the intervention of a repairer. Excellent examples of this are the so-called 'flat-backs' of Sampson Smith (q.v.), earthenware figures and groups made in Staffordshire during the middle decades of the 19th century which were especially intended to be cast in an easily separated two-piece mould, thus facilitating quantity production.

Forgeries and reproductions are sometimes made from moulds taken from an original porcelain figure, and in this case, since porcelain shrinks by about one-sixth during firing, the forgeries will be smaller than the genuine examples by this amount. An excellent example of this is provided by the Chelsea figure of Doctor Baloardo from the Italian Comedy made originally about 1752. The only genuine example at present known is in the Katz Collection. It is eleven inches in height. This was restored shortly before 1914, and the restorer took a mould from it and cast twelve copies, at least one of which was sold soon afterwards as genuine. Some of the others have appeared on the market since under a more accurate designation, and a remoulded specimen is also in the Katz Collection. It measures nine and a half inches in height.

See *Firecracks in Porcelain*.

FILARETE, ANTONIO AVERULINO (?1400– d. 1469)

Italian architect and sculptor whose best-known work is a door for St Peter's, Rome. He made small bronzes, of which a reduced version of the heroic-size 3rd-century equestrian Marcus Aurelius is in the Albertinum, Dresden. This was cast in Rome, probably about 1440, and is, apparently, the earliest of the small Renaissance bronzes.

FIREBACKS

Cast-iron plates placed at the back of the hearth. The earliest known specimens, still *in situ* in some English country houses, can be dated to around 1500. These were decorated with moulded designs in great variety, the components of which, in many cases, had small relationship to each other. Since firebacks were cast in founders' sand the mould could be impressed with all kinds of objects kept for the purpose without much regard for order. Armorial bearings probably do not antedate 1600, but they grew more popular as the 17th century advanced. Biblical subjects date from Commonwealth times, and the Boscobel Oak comes after the Restoration of Charles II.

Most surviving 16th- and 17th-century firebacks were made in the foundries of Sussex and Kent, but they were also cast elsewhere in southern England,

in East Anglia, the Midlands, and Yorkshire. The industry still lingered in Sussex as late as 1939, where reproductions of old firebacks, and of wrought ironwork, were made to decorate old cottages. Firebacks were cast in moulds impressed from old ones. After a century or two of use an old fireback develops a thick, hard encrustation which is a mixture of black-lead and carbon, and the existence of this helps to differentiate it from later copies. Specimens without a coating of this kind are almost undoubtedly reproductions.

FIRECRACKS IN PORCELAIN

These are sometimes called 'age-cracks', but no porcelain cracks as the result of age. Firecracks are largely due to faulty designing, leading to unequal contraction of parts of the object during cooling after firing, although the fault seems almost inherent in some early soft porcelain bodies and may have been due to an unequal distribution of the ingredients. Firecracks are usually due to the object being made with some parts very much thicker than others. The thick parts take up the heat more slowly, vitrify a little later, and take longer to cool than the thinner ones, with the result that the inevitable cooling contraction (about one-sixth in most porcelain bodies) sets up stresses which lead to splitting. These range from quite minor splits near the edge, to massive openings underneath the base of a figure which begin and end within its confines. When a firecrack leads out to an edge the end will always be wider than the beginning, even if only a trifle, whereas a damage crack will leave the sides in contact throughout its length. Whether a firecrack is an adequate cause for the rejection of a specimen depends largely on the factory. Small factories such as Longton Hall (q.v.), working under great difficulties and with a heavy kiln-wastage, finished firecracked specimens and sold them, and usually they are now so rare that unless the crack is very unsightly it can safely be ignored, although no one pretends that the specimen would not be better without it. At factories such as Sèvres, where control was strict, such specimens were rejected, and most were probably smashed. A specimen of Sèvres which is firecracked, therefore, presents a very different problem, for it leads to the possibility that it was purloined by a workman and decorated outside the factory, perhaps at a much later date. Meissen sometimes sold their factory-rejects to decorators, scoring cuts across the mark with the engraver's wheel to indicate that this had been done.

FIRE-GILDING

A method of depositing a thin layer of gold on to silver, copper, or a copper alloy, using an amalgam (q.v.) of gold and mercury subsequently heated.

FIRE-POLISHING OF GLASS

No matter how closely the pieces of a mould for pressed glass (q.v.) fitted together, a mould-seam was invariably present on the object after casting. On the best examples this was removed by fire-polish-

ABOVE: *American furniture.* The Keeping Room from Wrentham, Mass. c. 1690. This was both a dining and living-room. The table once belonged to Peregrine White, born in Cape Cod harbour aboard the *Mayflower* in 1620. *The American Museum, Claverton Manor, Bath.*

CENTRE: *American furniture.* Painting and stencilling were commonly used to decorate American interiors and furniture, the work being executed in milk paint by journeymen. The bed is an example of the portable or 'campaign' type. From Windham, Conn. c. 1830. *The American Museum, Claverton Manor, Bath.*

BELOW: *Federal style.* Room decorated in the Federal style, and based on a New York dining-room of about 1825. The furniture is by Duncan Phyfe, except for the chairs, which are by Ephraim Haines of Philadelphia. *The American Museum, Claverton Manor, Bath.*

Chinese export porcelain. **Plaque painted in enamel
colours at Canton after a print of 1781 entitled *Le Bain* by
Bonnet. c. 1790.** *British Museum.*

ing, which involved playing the flame of a blow-lamp on to the surface for long enough slightly to melt it, thus removing the seam, and conferring a high polish on the remainder. The same process served to remove surface blemishes, and made some objects much more like cut-glass to superficial examination.

FIRE-SCREEN

(French *écran*, which distinguishes it from the draught-screen (*paravent*).)

There are several kinds of screen for this purpose. The fire-screen proper, which stood before the hearth in the form of a framed panel; the pole-screen in which the screen itself was attached to a pole carried (nearly always) on a tripod foot, and could be moved up and down as circumstances dictated; or a small screen held in the hand for the purpose of shielding the face, more popular in France than England, which is sometimes mistakenly regarded as a species of fan.

The pole-screen is the earliest of the several varieties in England, first appearing in the second half of the 17th century, when it was made of metal, the screen itself usually framing needlework. It was then called a screen-stick. It usually formed part of the hearth-furniture, all the implements being made to match. The pole-screen did not come into general use until after 1730, when it was made of wood. Both walnut and mahogany were used until about 1760, when most specimens become of mahogany or beechwood. They can be found in all the current styles—Chippendale, Adam, Hepplewhite—and the later versions often have oval or shield-shaped panels. In some late 18th-century examples the tripod support was replaced by a circular, loaded base, but this was somewhat impractical and not often used. Sheraton, under the influence of the German *ébénistes-mécaniciens* (q.v.), designed a pole-screen with a central counterweight, so that the screen slid up and down at a touch. In the early years of the Regency the screen frame was dispensed with, the screen itself being a piece of heavy material carried on a cross-bar. These were termed banner-screens. Needlework panels were the most commonly employed to fill the frame, but Hepplewhite designs in particular sometimes have a panel of ruched silk.

The fire-screen for the hearth came from Holland with William and Mary. It was a large rectangular panel supported on either side by a pair of feet. During the Queen Anne period beechwood was often used for the purpose, and the frame, like contemporary mirrors, was sometimes partly or wholly gilded. Another variety was the cheval fire-screen in which the panel tilted backwards or forwards like the cheval mirror (q.v.).

The fire-screen in France was made to match the remainder of the furniture, and was much the same in principle as the English version, although one variety (also to be found in England) had two wings, half the size of the central panel, which opened outwards to provide additional protection from the fire. Some were given leaves which moved up and down, balanced by counterweights, and others were provided with a shelf and pigeon-holes, or a reading-desk, for greater convenience. The pole-screen on a tripod support was of the English pattern, and that hand-screens were intended as fire-screens is put beyond all doubt by the name given to them—*écran à main*. These were often decorated by fan-painters.

From the days of Louis XIV, and during the reign of Louis XV, a summer hearth-screen painted in a *trompe l'œil* style was fashionable. There is one surviving example by Oudry showing a dog eating from a bowl, but the subjects were varied. The intention was to make the picture seem as though it were part of the furnishings of the room.

FIRING-GLASSES

Firing-glasses were for convivial communal drinking, and are very sturdily made of thick glass with short stems and heavy feet. The bowl was usually conical or bucket-shaped. These glasses were rapped on the table-top during toasts with a noise like a ragged volley of musketry, hence the name given to them. Glasses of this kind were much used by societies and clubs, and they occur with Masonic and Jacobite devices engraved on them, but plain specimens are the more usual. Those with conical bowls are not unlike (in general) form glasses in which ice-cream used to be sold in the 1930s, and ice-cream glasses have sometimes been sold to the unsuspecting novice as 18th-century firing-glasses. See *Toddy-glasses*.

FITZHUGH BORDER

A frequent border pattern on pottery and porcelain of the late 18th and early 19th centuries which is painted in blue underglaze. It originally decorated late Chinese export porcelain of the type often called Nanking (q.v.), and is presumed to have been first ordered from China by someone of this name. It is a complex mixture of trellis and diaper patterns, with out pomegranates and flying butterflies.

FLAGON

An elongated tankard with either a flat or domed lid and a thumbpiece for raising it. Originally a sacramental vessel, the flagon was later adapted on the Continent for the service of beer, and it can be found in silver and pewter. Specimens in Rhineland stoneware, faïence, and porcelain are usually provided with pewter or silver mounts, and a version shaped like a truncated cone in 17th-century Oriental porcelain, either Chinese or Japanese, was mounted in the same way. When used for secular purposes the term 'tankard' is the more usual. See *Schnellen*.

FLAMBÉ GLAZES

Chinese vases, bottles, bowls, etc., made during the reign of Ch'ien Lung (1736–1795) which have a lustrous crimson-purple glaze with turquoise splashes and streaks. Technically it is a reduced copper glaze, i.e. fired in a reducing atmosphere (q.v.). Glazes of this kind are often termed

Florentine Maiolica. Ewer decorated with a green washed tin glaze over a red clay body. Second half of the 15th century. *British Museum.*

'transmutation', and are also sometimes called *sang de bœuf* (ox-blood). *Flambé* glazes were first reproduced in Europe towards the end of the 19th century by the Staffordshire potter Bernard Moore, and specimens are sometimes to be found. He used a stoneware, not porcelain.

FLASHED GLASS
The technique of adding a thin film of colour to clear glass by dipping it briefly into molten coloured glass. Flashed glass was usually decorated in ways similar to those employed for cased glass (q.v.).

FLAT-CHASING
The indentation of linear ornament with a punch and light hammer especially employed to decorate Sheffield plate where, because of the nature of the metal, engraving was impossible. See *Sheffield Plate.*

FLAXMAN, JOHN, R. A. (1755–1826)
English neo-classical sculptor and designer, whose father was a moulder of plaster figures. Flaxman was admitted a student at the Royal Academy in 1769, and soon afterwards he was being employed by Josiah Wedgwood to furnish designs for pottery. In 1787 he went to Rome for seven years where he studied classical sculpture, remaining in touch with Wedgwood throughout most of this period. He was elected A.R.A. in 1797, and R.A. in 1800. His work was extremely influential, and his designs for silver were used by Rundell, Bridge & Rundell, silversmiths to the Prince-Regent, for works which had a new sculptural quality.

FLINT GLASS
The early term to describe the lead glass invented by George Ravenscroft (q.v.) in which the silica was derived from calcined flints with lead oxide as a flux. 'Lead glass', 'glass of lead', and 'crystal' are all more recent terms for the same substance.

FLINTPORSLIN (Swedish)
Creamware in the English manner: *Steingut, faïence-fine* (q.v.).

FLOOR-CLOTHS (American)
In America, a popular form of floor-covering in the 18th century made of canvas or linen heavily coated with paint. Early designs were hand-painted to imitate tiled marble floors. Later ones simulated Wilton and other manufactured carpets. Ready-made floor-cloths were also imported from England. The floor-cloth was the precursor of linoleum.

FLORENTINE MAIOLICA
Among the first centres of Tuscan *maiolica* manufacture must be numbered Florence, where the earliest wares glazed with a tin-enamel date back to about 1430. These are painted in green within outlines of manganese-purple, and are often termed the 'green family'. The type, sometimes also attributed to Orvieto (q.v.), seems to have been derived originally from wares somewhat similarly decorated and made at Paterna, near Valencia (Spain), and Spanish influence is distinctly perceptible in the Italian wares. Following this class, and first appearing just before 1450, are albarellos and drug-jars painted with Gothic oak-leaves in an inky, *impasto* blue. These, known as 'oak-leaf jars', also show signs of Spanish influence, and some of the decorative motifs are reminiscent of the patterns on Near Eastern fabrics. A green pigment also makes its appearance on a few exceedingly rare specimens, on one of which at least it has been used in an *impasto* form.

The manufacture of *maiolica* at Florence apparently did not survive the 15th century, this particular craft in Tuscany then being concentrated at Faenza and Siena, but Tuscan wares of this kind were undoubtedly the first to be made in Italy, and formed the basis for future production elsewhere.

FLORSHEIM (Germany) FAÏENCE FACTORY
In 1765 a factory was erected here by Georg Ludwig Müller, who sold it in 1773 to the Carthusian monastery at Mainz, when it was managed by Kaspar Dreste. After 1781, under Weingartner, it began to produce *faïence-fine* (q.v.) in the manner of Wedgwood. The faïence, such as it is, vaguely resembles Hanau, and is confined to peasant wares, with a very smooth glaze.

FLOWERS, PORCELAIN
Almost from the first modelled flowers have been employed as decoration in the making of European porcelain, although they are much less common from China, except on export wares. The term *millefiori* (thousand flowers) is employed for Meissen vases of the 1740s where the surface is completely incrusted with small porcelain flowers. The Vincennes factory at its inception made a speciality of such flowers, which were made into bouquets with bronze stalks and leaves. Both Louis XV and Mme de Pompadour spent large sums on them. Flowers formed part of the *bocage* (q.v.) which was especially popular with English figure-makers until 1765, and flowers until this date at least formed the knops to

teapot lids and tureen covers. In the 19th century Coalport (Coalbrookdale) and other English manufacturers specialized in delicately modelled flowers, and in our own day the late Dorothy Doughty, in her models of British and American birds for the Worcester Royal Porcelain Company, carried the art of flower-modelling further than ever before, producing faithful replicas of the most delicate blooms. The best flowers are made petal by petal in press-moulds, the petals being arranged in rest-moulds until the bloom is completed.

FLUTING

A series of narrow, concave, vertical mouldings often used as furniture decoration in appropriate places, and commonly on pilasters (q.v.). When convex, i.e. projecting above the surface instead of being below it, this type of decoration is called reeding.

FONDEURS, CORPORATION DES

The guild in 18th-century France which controlled the making of bronzework of all kinds—furniture-mounts, clock-cases, and everything comprised within the term *bronzes d'ameublement* (furnishing bronzes). In organization it was similar to that of the *Menuisiers-ébénistes*.

Generally the *fondeur* did not originate his designs. These were usually supplied by a sculptor in the form of a wood-carving or a model in wax which was converted into bronze by the *cire perdue* method. The rough cast was then finished by the *ciseleur* with chisels, files, and engraving tools. The *ciseleur* played a very important part, and the guild was later known as the *Fondeurs-ciseleurs*. The term *ciseleur* incidentally, although it is sometimes inaccurately translated as *chaser*, actually means *chiseller*. Chasing, strictly defined, is the art of raising embossed ornament *from the front*, as distinct from *repoussé* (q.v.), which means raising it from the back.

Gilding was the province of the Corporation des Doreurs, who normally employed the mercuric method (see *Amalgam*) which was known at the time

Fluting. Side-table in the Hepplewhite style, mahogany with cross-banding. The frieze is inlaid with simulated flutes. The square, tapered legs are normally fluted. *Phillips, Son & Neale.*

as *dorure d'or moulu* (literally, gilding with gold paste). Bronzes, however, were not invariably gilded. Some were lacquered, some were pickled to imitate old patination (*verde antique*), and silvering was sometimes employed, although few such specimens have survived, most having been gilded later.

The organization of the guilds into self-contained compartments was the cause of many demarcation disputes—the 'who does what' arguments familiar today. As an example we may select the sculptor and *ébéniste*, Charles Cressent (q.v.), who was in trouble on several occasions for making his own mounts. He was forbidden to do this in 1723, and twenty years or so later we find him paying a fine for the same offence. The prohibition undoubtedly often had a deleterious effect on French furniture-design, since all but the most powerful *ébénistes* were usually compelled to buy 'stock' mounts from the *fondeurs* instead of those individually designed.

Towards the end of the 18th century the *fondeurs* began to meet competition from such English makers of brass and 'ormolu' furniture decoration as Matthew Boulton (q.v.).

FONDPORZELLAN

Porcelain decorated with a coloured ground, usually with panels reserved in white for painting in enamel colours. The first ground colour to be used at Meissen—*Kapuzinerbraun* or *Kaffeebraun*—was devised by the kiln-master, Samuel Stölzel, about 1722. Underglaze cobalt-blue, introduced a little later, was employed in imitation of the Chinese powder-blue, and the same oxide supplied the pigment of the *gros bleu* of Sèvres. It was also popular with several English factories. A much-valued yellow ground was first introduced at Meissen in 1727, and this was employed in several shades. Green was also available in a number of shades, including a turquoise colour called sea-green. A rich crimson-purple of a raspberry shade is a much sought coloured ground of the period.

When the Sèvres factory (q.v.) was founded the

Flowers, Porcelain. Distinguished flower-modelling by the late Dorothy Doughty—Mexican Feijoa. Worcester Royal Porcelain Company. Examples of earlier flower modelling are illustrated elsewhere.

Fondporzellan. Meissen chocolate-pot and cover with a reddish-mauve ground painted with Harbour Scenes by C. F. Herold (q.v.). Meissen. c. 1738. *Mrs C. B. Stout, Memphis, Tenn.*

fashion for coloured grounds was well established. The royal factory was not slow to exploit their popularity. The dark *gros bleu* dates from 1749. As may be seen from its uneven appearance, it was sponged on. *Bleu céleste*, a turquoise, dates from 1752, and a yellow, *jaune jonquil*, from the same year. Violet and green were first employed in 1756, in which year the *rose Pompadour* (q.v.) first appeared, and the much-prized light enamel blue termed *bleu de roi*.

Ground colours were also much used during the 19th century by all European factories, a rather heavy maroon being popular before 1850. Especially during the middle years an imitation of the *rose Pompadour* was much employed by English factories which were copying Sèvres such as Mintons under the misnomer of *rose du Barry*. Grounds are still employed on most fine-quality porcelain today.

FORGERIES, FAKES AND REPRODUCTIONS
A forgery is a copy of a work of art made for fraudulent purposes. A fake is a genuine work of art of inferior quality altered or added to for the purpose of increasing its desirability, and therefore its value. A reproduction is an honest copy, made as decoration, which is sometimes employed for fraudulent purposes. A replica is an exact copy, often made by the original artist or craftsman, of an important work. The term is usually applied to a copy made at or about the same time as the original.

Few forgeries are really dangerous to the expert. A noted art-historian has said that the greatest mistake is to think that they ever closely resemble the genuine object, and, as a generalization, this has much to support it. Nevertheless, forgeries exist and must be guarded against, and elsewhere will be found a discussion of those which are often offered as genuine antiques by dishonest dealers and those deficient in knowledge.

Forgeries are, perhaps, the most important reason why it is wisest for the collector to buy from the reputable dealer. Although efforts are made to exclude them from reputable salerooms, they undoubtedly occur from time to time, and the conditions of sale rarely offer the purchaser any redress.

FRANCESCO DI GIORGIO MARTINI (1439–1501)
Italian architect, designer, and sculptor, who may have learned the art of bronze-casting in Donatello's workshop. Bronzes by him have previously been attributed to Pollaiuolo and Verrocchio. A small *David with the Head of Goliath* in the Museo Nazionale di Capodimonte, Naples, is regarded as coming from his hand.

FRANKENTHAL PORCELAIN FACTORY
About 1752 Paul Anton Hannong began to make porcelain at Strasbourg (q.v.) with the aid of Ringler (q.v.), but in 1754 Louix XV forbade the manufacture of porcelain anywhere within the French territories, except at Vincennes (q.v.). Hannong turned to the Elector Palatine, Karl Theodore von der Pfalz, who granted him permission to make porcelain at Frankenthal on very favourable terms. Production had started by November 1755, and had been organized on a relatively large scale by the year following. The *Modellmeister* was Johann Wilhelm Lanz, who had been brought from Strasbourg, and in consequence of the Seven Years' War, which began in 1756, a number of Meissen workers were engaged. A price-list published in the Paris *Journal de Commerce* in 1760 suggests that the factory were charging too little for their wares in relation to prices current at Meissen and Sèvres, and this supposition is borne out by increasing financial stringency which culminated in the Elector taking over the factory in 1762. The proprietor at this time was Joseph-Adam Hannong, and in consequence of the earlier edict in favour of Vincennes being allowed to go by default, he was able to return to Strasbourg to continue the manufacture of porcelain there.

Simon Feilner, from Höchst and Fürstenberg,

Forgeries, etc. One of the most notorious forgers of modern times, Han van Meegeren, painting a spurious Vermeer while in custody. *Photo: Ullstein.*

was appointed inspector at Frankenthal in 1770, and he became director in 1775. The *Modellmeister* from 1762 to 1766 was Franz Konrad Linck, the Court Sculptor, who had studied at the Vienna Academy. He is noted for some distinguished modelling in the neo-classical style. The town was occupied in 1794 by French troops, and work came to a standstill. The factory was closed finally in 1800, the moulds being dispersed to a stoneware factory at Grünstadt owned by Peter van Recum, and to Nymphenburg (q.v.).

Frankenthal is principally noted for its figure-modelling, and about eight hundred different models have been recorded. It is difficult to separate figures by Lanz made at Frankenthal from his work at Strasbourg, but examples on bases with slight rococo scrolls were probably made at the former factory. Johann Friedrich Lück probably arrived at Frankenthal in 1758, and he was perhaps *Modell-meister* in succession to Lanz. He may have remained till 1764, when he returned to Meissen. Figures attributed to him are not unlike those of Lanz in style. Karl Gottlieb Lück, presumed to be a cousin, modelled figures from 1756 to 1775, and became *Modellmeister* in succession to Linck in 1766. He was very prolific, and his figures include representations from the contemporary scene, Chinese groups (e.g. the *Chinesenhäusen*), hunting groups, and a variety of related subjects. Adam Bauer, Court sculptor to the Duke of Württemberg, was *Modellmeister* in 1775, and he provided a number of pastoral subjects and mythological figures. Melchior's work at Frankenthal differed from that at Höchst in being increasingly in the neo-classical style, although his earliest models were still in his Höchst vein. He turned largely to *biscuit* porcelain, in which medium he modelled an *Apotheosis* commemorating the fifty-year Jubilee of Karl Theodor. Towards the end of the century production was almost entirely of portrait busts and medallions.

Apart from figures, the modelled wares included

Frankenthal Porcelain. Europe, from a set of the Continents, perhaps modelled by K. G. Lück (q.v.). Frankenthal. c. 1765. *British Museum.*

clock-cases, watch-stands, *étuis*, inkstands, and large table-centres. The influence of the painter and designer Gottlieb Friedrich Riedel (formerly of Meissen) can be found in the painting of service-ware, and in the use of relief patterns, which included those closely resembling some of the Meissen *Ozier* mouldings (q.v.).

Frankenthal service-ware is especially noted for the quality of its painting. *Cabaret* sets on rhomboid or lozenge-shaped trays were a Frankenthal innovation. These were often painted with figure-subjects. Jakob Osterspei (1730–1782) did mythological figures and landscapes. Winterstein painted the same subjects, and scenes from Teniers. Johann Magnus was responsible for battle-scenes, mythological subjects, landscapes, and the popular figures after Watteau. Flower-painting was excellent in quality, and the factory also made a speciality of modelled flowers. The influence of Sèvres predominates after 1770, and gold stripes were employed over coloured grounds as a decoration for vases in the neo-classical style.

It is difficult to attribute any figures with certainty to the hand of Feilner. He was much occupied with research, and introduced a number of new colours, including a *bleu de Roi*, a light blue, and an underglaze black. Grained wood was also imitated—*décor bois* (q.v.).

Transfer-printing was used experimentally by Pierre Berthevin, who was at Frankenthal in 1769 and 1770, but only two specimens in the museum at Spires appear to have survived.

FRANKFURT (Germany) FAÏENCE FACTORY

A concession was granted in 1666 to Jean Simonet of Paris for six years. He had the backing of two

Frankenthal Porcelain. Teapot with classical figures in a landscape painted by Osterspei. Frankenthal. c. 1765. *Victoria and Albert Museum.*

Frankfurt Faience. A typical lobed jar painted with a *chinoiserie* in blue. Second half of the 17th century. Frankfurt faience is not uncommon in England, although it is sometimes confused with the somewhat similar wares of Hanau (q.v.).

merchants, Schumacher and Fehr, but by 1667 Schumacher seems to have retired. In 1673 Fehr signed a lease for life and, when he died in spring 1693, he left a flourishing business which was carried on by his widow and sons till 1723. After that date it passed from hand to hand till 1774 when production ceased.

The products of Frankfurt may be recognized by their fine, creamy glaze and brilliant blue pigment. They are very similar to the wares of Hanau (q.v.), and experts are divided as to how to separate the two. Frankfurt seems deliberately to have tried to imitate Dutch delft and probably exported to Holland, but the Germans did not use *kwaart* and attained a glaze of great brilliance without it. A black *trek* (outline) has been observed.

Frankfurt imitated blue-and-white Ming, and the Transition period of Chinese porcelain which was being imported in the late 17th century by the East India Companies, and broad-rimmed plates have panels decorated with flowers and emblems in the style of Wan-li (1573–1619). Exact, as well as imaginative copying produced an original and beautiful style. A typical *motif* is the lotus leaf pattern, and the wild goose is to be found only on Frankfurt wares.

Shapes are similar to those found at Hanau—*Enghalskrüge*, double gourd bottles, and dishes and plates with deep wells and rims. In 1693 the inventory records domestic wares of all kinds: flower vases, tiles, measuring jugs, pharmaceutical jars, and plates with a variety of different patterns. No generally recognized mark can be seen on Frankfurt wares.

'FREE' CRAFTSMEN
Although the manufacture of furniture and related things in 18th-century France was regulated by corporations or guilds, and in furniture especially members were required to stamp their work as a means of identification, certain craftsmen, usually non-members, were not permitted the privilege of so doing (*artisans libres*), or were exempted from the requirement (*artisans privilégiés*).

Those not permitted to use the stamp were often foreign craftsmen in Paris who worked in places where, by medieval tradition, non-members of the guilds were permitted to set up workshops. Such German craftsmen as Oeben established themselves in this way. Oeben become *ébéniste du roi* (i.e. to the King) in 1754, and was given the life-tenancy of a workshop by Louis Quinze. His furniture is sometimes stamped.

Oeben is, in fact, during the period from 1754 onwards an example of the *artisan privilégié* or *ouvrier de la Couronne*, much of whose work was done to the order of the King, and who was, in consequence, freed from guild supervision. Some of the finest French furniture was produced by workmen of this kind.

FRENCH PLATING
French plated wares, *cuivre argenté* (silvered copper), were made by applying up to twenty leaves of silver to the surface of the object to be plated which was first heated. This was followed by burnishing. From 1761 to 1797 wares of this kind were marked *Argent,* and from 1797, whether plated with gold or silver, they were marked *Doublé*. The process of French plating was also sometimes employed in England, usually to repair defective Sheffield plate. Gilding was done by the mercuric process. Specimens of French plating are comparatively rare outside France.

FRETWORK
Ornamental openwork, especially in wood, cut with the aid of a frame-saw. Fretwork was much used by Chippendale, especially for his Chinese style. See 'Chinese Chippendale'.

FRIT
The fusible ingredients of artificial porcelain made by the early factories were first fused, or fritted, together to form an amorphous mass, after which it was ground to powder and mixed with the clay. For this reason artificial (or soft) porcelain is sometimes termed 'frit porcelain' in some older works. See *Cullet.*

Fromery, A. Oval enamel plaque depicting the flight of Stanislas Leczinski (King of Poland and father-in-law of Louis XV) from Danzig. Signed by C. F. Herold (q.v.). Alex. Fromery, Berlin. *Sotheby & Co.*

FROMERY, ALEX.

A Berlin enameller of the first half of the 18th century whose work is on copper. His technique included raised gilding which he sometimes covered with translucent enamel, not unlike the earlier work of Christoph Konrad Hunger, the Vienna porcelain arcanist who was also an enameller. C. F. Herold, the Meissen painter, worked with Fromery from about 1740 till 1750, and an example signed by him and marked 'Alex. Fromery à Berlin' is known.

FULDA (Germany) FAÏENCE FACTORY

A factory was founded at Fulda probably by Adam F. von Löwenfinck (q.v.) some time after 1741, when the arcanist, who had already worked at Meissen, Bayreuth, and possibly Ansbach, arrived in this Hessian city with his brother, Karl Heinrich. The factory was under the patronage of the Bishop of Fulda, and attracted some talented artists whose names are familiar to all historians of German ceramic art. The Löwenfincks apart, there were G. F. Hess, his two sons, Johann Lorenz and Ignaz, J. P. Dannhofer, and Louis-Victor Gerverot. This factory only continued till the beginning of the Seven Years' War (1756), and was replaced after 1763 by a porcelain factory. The wares are few, but of fine quality. Painting, as one would expect from such a team, was very competent and original, both in high-temperature colours and enamels. There were also blue painting outlined in manganese-purple in combination with scroll-work and *lambrequins* after Rouen. Shapes were many: *Enghalskrüge* (q.v.), cylindrical mugs, tureens, and richly decorated vases.

The mark is either the Fulda Coat of Arms—a black cross on a white field—or the letters *FD*. Sometimes a painter signed with his full name, but more often only with his initials.

Fulda Porcelain. Le Panier mystérieux (The Mysterious Basket) after Boucher, based on an engraving by René Gaillard. Fulda. c. 1770. *Metropolitan Museum, New York.*

Fulda Porcelain. Flute-concert, group of figures against a rococo background. Fulda. c. 1770. *Kunstgewerbemuseum, Schloss Charlottenburg, Berlin.*

FULDA PORCELAIN FACTORY

This factory in Hesse-Nassau was founded by the Prince-Bishop Amadeus von Buseck with the aid of Adam Friedrich von Löwenfinck and his brother, Karl Heinrich, in 1741. The manufacture of faïence continued till 1756, and nothing is known of porcelain manufactured before this date which was, presumably, experimental only, and may even have been a soft paste of the kind which Löwenfinck would have met at Chantilly (q.v.) during his stay at that factory.

The first serious attempt to manufacture porcelain was made in 1757, perhaps at the instance of the Court Chamberlain, Johann Philipp Schick, whose daughter, Maria Seraphia, married Adam Friedrich von Löwenfinck. Nothing came of it at the time, but in 1764 Schick engaged Nikolaus Paul (q.v.). The factory was then under the patronage of the Prince-Bishop, Heinrich von Bibra. In 1767 the buildings were burned down, and Schick died before they could be rebuilt. Fulda was functioning again in 1768, and closed in 1790.

During the period from 1764 to 1767 figures have been attributed to the Fulda-born sculptor, Johann Valentin Schaum, and some *putti* resemble in style those carved by Schaum on the tomb of Amadeus von Buseck. Some of the figures of this period were copied from those of Strasbourg by Johann Wilhelm Lanz, and Italian Comedy figures have also been attributed.

During the second period, after the rebuilding, modelling was in the hands of Wenzel Neu, who had worked at the faïence factory, and the presence of a Höchst modeller, Laurentius Russinger, has been inferred from a close resemblance of some of the factory's figure-work to that of Höchst (q.v.). Georg Friedrich Hess, a member of a family of this name connected with the factory, functioned as a modeller.

Table-wares, of good quality, were for the most part copied from Meissen. Some landscapes in iron-red monochrome are the most frequently met.

FURNITURE, AMERICAN: BEDS

In the 17th century beds were either low-post or high-post. Though mentioned in early inventories, no high-post beds of this age have survived. They were completely draped, the frame being concealed, thus forming a room within a room. This afforded warmth and privacy in the 17th-century American 'keeping room', which combined kitchen, living-, dining-, and bedroom in one. Some beds were part-high-part low, and were folded against the wall during the day. Another device to conserve space was the trundle bed for children. This, made until the mid-Georgian period, was a low bed on wheels, which, when not in use, was 'trundled' under the larger bed. In the Queen Anne and Chippendale periods, high-post beds conformed both in elaborateness of carving and draping to the prevailing fashions, and fine-quality woods were employed.

During the currency of the Federal style low-post beds were made of such simple woods as maple and painted. High-post beds were of two kinds: those with posts of six feet or more in height with straight canopies or valances, and those with shorter posts and light upward curving supports overhead for drapery. These were variously termed 'tent', 'camp', or 'field' beds. Sheraton suggested them for low rooms, and for children or servants. In England, the field-bed was a highly elaborate form of camp-bed, with an arched tester or frame, and a framework wholly concealed by curtains and elaborate draperies. American beds of this type were generally copied from English models illustrated in the Hepplewhite and Sheraton design-books, executed in such native American woods as maple. The American tent-bed resembles a field-bed with a frame of wood or iron. It is similar to the design for a camp-bed in Sheraton's *Cabinet Dictionary* of 1803. In America exposed parts of the bed-frame were often well carved in considerable detail.

FURNITURE, AMERICAN: MAKERS OF

JACOBEAN—WILLIAM AND MARY STYLES 1640–1720

Comparatively few 17th and early 18th-century makers are known by documented furniture. Most important was *Thomas Dennis*, born in England about 1638 and trained there as joiner and carver. Dennis was a maker of wainscot chairs (see *Furniture, American, 17th century*) and richly carved chests with late Tudor and Jacobean ornament which were produced in Portsmouth, New Hampshire, and in Ipswich, Massachusetts.
Nicholas Disbrowe (1612–1683), a joiner and carver of Hartford, Connecticut. Maker of wainscot chairs and chests.

Makers of the Hadley chest type are unidentified because of the marked individuality of their product. They were scattered along the Connecticut River, from Hartford to the Vermont border.

Working in the William and Mary style, *John Gaines* (1704–1743), of Portsmouth, New Hampshire, is known for his chairs.

Furniture, American, Makers of. Press-cupboard of oak and pine perhaps made by Thomas Dennis, Ipswich, Essex County, Mass. The carved and turned decoration is characteristic of many pieces attributed to Ipswich makers. c. 1690. *Boston Museum of Fine Arts.*

QUEEN ANNE STYLE 1720–1755

William Savery (active 1740–1787), of Philadelphia. The best known American cabinet-maker in the Queen Anne style.
Job and Christopher Townsend, and John Goddard, of Newport, Rhode Island, began their activities in the period of the Queen Anne style but their important works belong to the Chippendale period.
Thomas Elfe (active before 1747) of Charleston, South Carolina, arrived from London. His best work belongs to the Chippendale period.
Thomas Johnston or Johnson (active 1732–1766), of Boston, Massachusetts, noted as a japanner.

Furniture, American. Field, campaign or tent bed of maple. Examples intended for campaigning and travelling were easily taken to pieces for transport. For domestic use, the shape of the tester was well adapted to a sloping ceiling. *Israel Sack Inc.*

Robert Crosman (active about 1730–1799), of Taunton, Massachusetts. Made the so-called Taunton chest.

CHIPPENDALE STYLE 1755–1790

Thomas Affleck (1740–1795), in Philadelphia, Pennsylvania, in 1763. Worked for many prominent Philadelphians in the most fashionable London style, including 'Chinese Chippendale' (q.v.).

Gilbert Ash (1717–1785) of New York. Established by 1756. Produced chairs, tea- and dining-tables in the London manner.

John Bachman (1746–1829) born in Switzerland, coming to Pennsylvania in 1766 as a trained cabinet-maker. His highly individual interpretation of the Chippendale style is marked by florid carving in walnut.

Thomas Burling was first active (1772–1775) in New York City. He left the city during the Revolution, but returned in 1785, and was joined by his son in 1791. His last advertisement appeared in 1796.

John Cogswell (active 1769) the maker of Boston's finest *bombé* case furniture of rococo design.

Dunlap. A family of New Hampshire cabinet-makers active in the late 18th and early 19th centuries. They worked in curly maple in the late Queen Anne style.

Thomas Elfe (active 1747–1775), of Charleston. During one eight-year period (1768–1775) he produced over 1,500 pieces, mostly case furniture, employing slaves as craftsmen.

John Elliott, Sr. (1713–1791), born in England, settled in Philadelphia. Noted for his elegant mirror frames.

Benjamin Frothingham (active 1756), of Boston. Produced desks, chests-on-chests, and desks-and-bookcases (secretaries).

James Gillingham (1736–1781). A Philadelphia cabinet-maker and chair-maker, who is best known for his chairs.

John Goddard, active in Newport from the 1740s, was the son-in-law of Job Townsend and, with him and John and Edmund Townsend, he brought the Newport block-front-and-shell style to its full development.

Jonathan Gostelowe (1745–1795) was a late exponent of the Chippendale style in Philadephia. He is known for chests of drawers, serpentine in form, with fluted, canted corners and ogee bracket feet.

Adam Hains (working till about 1815) continued the Chippendale style in Philadelphia after the Revolution. Best known for his Pembroke breakfast-tables with shaped leaves and arched cross-stretchers.

Benjamin Randolph (active c. 1760–1790). The most advanced exponent of the rococo Chippendale style in Philadelphia.

Aaron Roberts (1758–1831), of New Britain, Connecticut. Made mostly case-furniture, chiefly in cherry.

William Savery, a cabinet- and chair-maker, active 1740–1787. A labelled lowboy, one of the first American pieces to be so found, brought Savery into extraordinary prominence. This, and the long period of his activity, have combined to exaggerate his importance to the point where 'Savery' has taken on a generic connotation for much of the best of Philadelphia furniture. Since then about twenty labelled pieces have been discovered which reinforce his reputation.

Jonathan Shoemaker (active 1757). A Philadelphia exponent of the rococo style.

Job Townsend (1699–1765). His labelled desk-and-bookcase ('secretary') in the Rhode Island School of Design mark the beginning of Newport shell-carved furniture.

John Townsend (1732–1809), son of Job's brother, Christopher, was one of the leading members of the Townsend-Goddard group of cabinet-makers.

Daniel Trotter (1747–1800), of Philadelphia, worked in Chippendale and neo-classical styles.

Thomas Tufft (active before 1772), worked in the refined Chippendale style in Philadelphia.

NEO-CLASSICAL PERIOD, 1790–1830

Early Federal, 1790–1810. Hepplewhite and Sheraton styles

Mid-Federal, 1810–1820 Empire Style

Late Federal, 1820–1830. Late Empire Style

Michael Allison (active 1800–1845), of New York. He worked in the Hepplewhite, Sheraton, and Empire styles. His work is comparable to that of Duncan Phyfe.

Aaron Chapin (1753–1838), worked in East Windsor, Connecticut. His work cannot be distinguished from that of his cousin, Eliphalet.

Eliphalet Chapin (1741–1807), in East Windsor, Connecticut, 1771–1795. In a simplified Philadelphia

Furniture, American, Makers of. Mahogany silk-covered sofa in the Sheraton style by Samuel McIntire (1757–1811). Salem, Mass. *Metropolitan Museum, New York.*

style he made cherry high-chests, desks, and bookcases.

Henry Connelly (1770–1826) of Philadelphia; worked in Sheraton and Empire styles.

Matthew Egerton, Sr. (died 1802), of New Brunswick, New Jersey. Specialized in Hepplewhite and Sheraton case furniture, especially sideboards.

Ephraim Haines (1775–1811), of Philadelphia.

Lambert Hitchcock (1795–1852), of Hitchcocksville, Connecticut, established his chair-factory in 1825, and mass-produced Sheraton 'fancy' chairs. The 'Hitchcock' chair was made in other parts of New England, New York, Ohio, and elsewhere.

Charles-Honoré Lannuier (1779–1819), of New York, arrived from France in 1803. He worked in the Louis XVI and French Empire styles, making use of fine ormolu mounts, carving, and gilding.

Samuel McIntire (1757–1811) was Salem, Massachusetts' leading architect and carver. His carving, which appears on furniture by other makers, is highly individual. Favourite *motifs* include a basket of fruit, a cluster of grapes, the cornucopia, the wheat-sheaf, and alternating flutes and rosettes.

Duncan Phyfe came to America from Scotland in 1783 and established his fashionable cabinet-making shop in New York in 1795. He retired only in 1847, so that his work represents all phases of the neo-classical style, from Hepplewhite and Sheraton, to

Directoire, Empire, and Victorian. His clover-leaf card-tables with vase-shaped pedestals and brass paw feet, and chairs and sofas with sabre legs and reeded frames, are characteristic. The Phyfe style was copied so closely by others, either competitors, or workmen trained in his own shop, that positive identification is often difficult.

John Seymour arrived in 1785 from England, already a highly trained cabinet-maker, and was in Boston about 1794 with his son *Thomas*. No distinction can be made between the work of father and son. Their work is characterized by excellent craftsmanship, fine dovetailing, the use of patterned satinwood and bird's-eye maple veneers, inlaid tambour shutters, and ivory key escutcheons.

John Shaw (1745–1848) came from Scotland to Annapolis, Maryland, as a trained craftsman. He is best known for case furniture in the Hepplewhite style with pierced scrolled pediments, and shallow sideboards inlaid with ovals and conch shells.

EARLY VICTORIAN STYLE, 1830–1870

Charles A. Baudouine (active 1845–1900) of New York. A successful rival of John Henry Belter, Baudouine employed 200 men in his factory, and worked in the revived rococo style. Like Belter, he used lamination.

John Henry Belter (1804–1863) of New York. Like Duncan Phyfe and William Savery in earlier periods, Belter's name has overshadowed equally distinguished contemporary cabinet-makers. He was noted for his revived rococo designs, lacework borders of natural flowers and grapes combined with scrolls carved from layers of rosewood veneer laminated together and steamed in moulds to produce curving forms. His special methods of lamination was patented in 1856.

Elijah Galusha (1804–1871), of Troy, New York. Working in revived rococo and Renaissance styles executed in rosewood and mahogany, his finely carved furniture was as much prized as Belter's in Upper New York State.

John Jelliff (active 1836–1890), of Newark, New Jersey. Jelliff worked in the 18th century tradition and refused to employ machinery.

Joseph Meeks and Sons, of New York. This important firm, in existence for 71 years (1797–1868), produced furniture based on French designs of the 1820s, with large, plain surfaces and scroll supports.

John Needles (active 1812–1853) of Baltimore, Maryland. Like Jelliff, Needles continued to work in the 18th-century tradition, mostly in walnut and rosewood.

Anthony Quervelle (working 1835–1849) of Philadelphia. Born and trained in France, this highly competent cabinet-maker worked in the late neo-classical manner using matched mahogany veneers for high quality furniture.

François Seignouret (active 1822–1853) of New Orleans, Louisiana, was the leading cabinet-maker of the period in the South. His work is now scarce.

Furniture, American, Makers of. Mahogany chair in a late Sheraton style (c. 1805) by Duncan Phyfe of New York. *Metropolitan Museum, New York.*

Furniture, American, Makers of. Front and back of an armchair in a revived rococo style by John Belter, New York. Mid-19th century.

FURNITURE, AMERICAN: REGIONAL CHARACTERISTICS

The variety of regional variations in American furniture gives it a unique vitality and personality which serves to set it apart from other national styles. In England there was only one furniture capital—London. In France Paris not only largely set the fashion for the rest of France, but for much of Europe as well, even as far as the distant Courts of Russia. In America many cities along the Atlantic coast were centres of style for the surrounding towns and villages and in each of these furniture centres English styles were developed into a distinctively local idiom made up of individualist ideas executed by competing craftsmen. Today it is frequently possible to say whether a piece of furniture was made in New England, in which city or town, and by which cabinet-maker, simply by observing design, construction, details of carving or inlay, and the choice of woods, or from a combination of all these factors. Attribution according to area is a highly complex study which still continues.

QUEEN ANNE STYLE—1720–1755 AND CHIPPENDALE STYLE—1755–1790

Massachusetts furniture is characterized by delicacy of form and scale and a certain austerity of detail. Highboys are narrow and slender and have very thin cabriole legs. The slender lines of Massachusetts furniture is also characteristic of chairs, card-tables, pier-tables and tea-tables. The claw-and-ball foot characteristic of this area had the claws turned back to grasp tightly an almost oval ball. Newport, Rhode Island, was the centre of a very special style in the block-front. Designs were conservative and spare, with hardly any rococo details. Other characteristics include the use of heavy, dark San Domingo mahogany, and the early development of a claw-

and-ball form having slender outstretched talons, giving a pierced effect. New York furniture was sturdy, vigorous, and heavy in proportion and detail, reflecting a long-past Dutch tradition. Chair-backs are squarer and cabriole legs heavier than in examples from Boston or Philadelphia. The claw-and-ball is massive and powerful. Connecticut furniture, though influenced by Newport and Boston, retained a somewhat naïve character which is unique in flavour. The favoured wood was cherry. For decades before the Revolution Philadelphia was the largest city in America and the colonies' centre of

Furniture, American. High chest of drawers in mahogany showing strong Chippendale influence. Philadelphia, Penn. c. 1765. *Metropolitan Museum of Art, New York.*

fine craftsmanship. English influence was strong, either from the presence of London-trained cabinet-makers or from design-books. Its furniture was elaborately carved and generally ornate in the Chippendale-rococo style, the ornament taken from the latest London fashions. In the Queen Anne period Philadelphia produced the finest Queen Anne style chairs which are remarkable for their rhythmic grace. In the Chippendale period, Philadelphia chairs were the most elaborately carved of those from any centres and are closely related to the most ornate English examples. The high chest (high-boy) and low chest (low-boy), both long out of fashion in London, reached a high standard. Charleston, South Carolina, was the only Southern city with a school of cabinet-making in the Chippendale period. In Virginia and North Carolina plantation life was served by itinerant cabinet-makers working in a relatively unsophisticated style. The furniture of Charleston was aristocratic, sophisticated, and more nearly 'English' than other American cabinet-work.

NEO-CLASSICAL PERIOD 1790–1830

After the Revolution the newly established States continued to vary their interpretations of furniture styles from area to area and from city to city, though improvements in travel and communications tended to blur differences. English inspiration was still strong, either through the greater availability of design-books or a new migration of London-trained cabinet-makers, although starting about 1800 a new French influence began to make itself felt, particularly in New York.

In Massachusetts, Salem became a rival to Boston in fine craftsmanship. In Salem carving was a feature, the finest of which was executed by Samuel McIntire for various cabinet-makers. *Motifs* were elaborately carved on a punched background: baskets of fruit, the cornucopia, and garlands of grapes or fruit. In Boston the work of John and Thomas Seymour was among the most outstanding of typically American cabinet-work at any period. The Martha Washington chair was a unique New England type, as were the so-called 'Salem secretaries.' In New York French influence was strong. After the Revolution in France and the French West Indies, French immigrants settled in large numbers in this city. Duncan Phyfe and Honoré Lannuier developed a distinctive style based on French Directoire and Empire furniture. A new centre of cabinet-making, Baltimore, Maryland, came into its own after the Revolution. Its products were noticeably close to English neo-classical models, and were characterized by the use of painted glass panels (*verre eglomisé*) and gilt decoration on an inlay of light coloured wood. A unique method of pinpointing the place of origin of furniture in the neo-classical period was the popularity of inlay. Using inlay alone as a clue, cabinet-work can be assigned to Massachusetts, New Hampshire, Rhode Island, Connecticut, New York, New Jersey, Pennsylvania, Maryland, or the South.

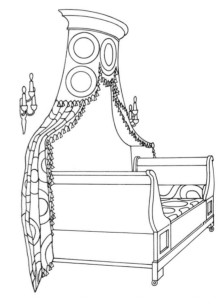

Furniture, American. Bed in the Federal style (Empire version), probably by Lannuier. Made in New York. This type is sometimes termed a 'sleigh' bed. *H. F. du Pont Museum, Winterthur, Delaware.*

Furniture, American, Terminology. Secretary in veneered mahogany and satinwood with fall-front writing-drawer. Salem, Mass. c. 1800. The glazing-bars exhibit the influence of the Gothic revival.

FURNITURE, AMERICAN, 17th Century

Large armchairs in early 17th-century homes were a status symbol and few in number, following contemporary English and Continental practice. Some side chairs, such as the so-called 'Cromwellian', were available to the well-to-do; otherwise seat furniture comprised the joint (or joined) stool, the bench, and the settle.

The most important armchairs were: (1) the wainscot, made of richly carved oak plank, (2) the Brewster, and (3) the Carver chairs, all made by the joiner. They are named from models said to have been owned by Elder Brewster (1567–1644) and Governor John Carver (died 1621). The Brewster chair consists of spindles in the back and below the arms and seat rail, forming a kind of cage for the sitter. The Carver chair has spindles in the back only, with open arms.

The two most important pieces of furniture in the Jacobean style were the court and press cupboards. In England at the end of the reign of Elizabeth, the 'court cupboard' (from the French 'court', or 'short') was provided with open shelves only. In America the court cupboard had a shelf above or below for the display of the most treasured possessions of the wealthier families—usually silver or such pottery as delftware. In addition the American version included a closed storage section for everyday utensils. The press cupboard, with drawers and cupboards was used to store clothing, the upper part being used for display.

FURNITURE, AMERICAN: TERMINOLOGY
(English and American differences)

Because of the close ties between England and her American colonies, and later, after the Revolution, with the United States, certain terms used by the designer and cabinet-maker are confusing, both because (1) they sometimes correspond *with differences*, and (2) because they may designate two or more *totally different* forms, depending on usage in the respective countries. Confusion is worse confounded by the interjection of colloquial, modern terms which were not used at the time.

England 'tallboy'
America 'double chest' or 'chest-on-chest'
England a 'dressing chest' was a four-drawer chest of drawers.
America In 1792 'bureau' was the term used to describe a chest of this kind, whereas in England a 'bureau' was a desk with a sloping top.
America In the 18th-century the term 'easy chair' was the equivalent of today's 'wing chair', and a 'corner chair' was a low, half-circular armchair to serve at a writing-desk, or to stand in a corner, which was also called 'roundabout'.
America In the 17th century and through the Queen Anne period, a 'couch' was a long chair or day-bed. In the early years of the 19th century, Sheraton's *Cabinet Dictionary* (1803) defines 'couch' as being from '*coucher*', French, to lie down on a place of repose. Hence there are seats that bear this name.
England and America 'Sofa' was a term used both by Hepplewhite and Sheraton in the 18th century. In the first years of the 19th century (Regency period in England) a 'Grecian sofa' (also called 'Grecian squab') had spirally rolled ends of unequal height and sabre legs. The design was a form of Roman banqueting couch used by Thomas Hope and modified by Sheraton. It was immensely popular in America, where it was given scrolled ends of equal or unequal height, or out-flaring ends. The term 'Récamier' is modern. Actually the couch as shown in David's celebrated portrait of Mme Récamier has equal ends and straight legs.

Furniture, American. Couch of red-painted maple or beech with anthemion ornament, and gilt striping replacing brass stringing. Attributed to P. and B. R. Thomas, or Asher and John Cowperthwaite, New York. c. 1815. The type is sometimes termed 'Récamier' from a resemblance to the couch on which Mme Récamier is reclining in David's portrait. *Brooklyn Museum.*

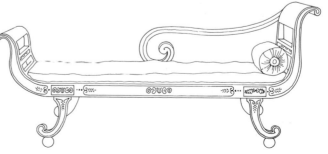

England and America A new style of bed with curved solid panelled ends designed to stand with its side instead of its head against the wall appeared in the first decade of the 19th century. At first known as 'French' beds, by the 1820s they were called 'Grecian'. They are now popularly called 'Empire' or 'sleigh' beds.

America Contrary to popular belief, there is no mention of the terms 'highboy' or 'lowboy' in 18th-century American records. Contemporary descriptions used 'high chest of drawers', and 'low chest', or 'half-chest' for which the common alternative was 'mahogany dressing table', or 'table to suit'. Though customarily each 'high chest' had a companion 'low chest', with identical decoration and finish, 'low chests' or 'dressing tables' were often made alone.

America Tall-case (or long-case) clocks are now called 'Grandfathers', a Victorian term never used during the period when they were made. Dwarf clocks of this kind are similarly termed 'Grandmothers'.

America The 'Martha Washington' chair was apparently a term used in the period. They were also called 'lolling' chairs. The so-called 'Martha Washington' work-table was a description coined in the 1890s.

England and America 'Looking glasses' was the contemporary term for what we now call 'mirrors'. In the period 'mirror' referred only to a hand-mirror.

America 'Huntboards' are sideboard tables without drawers, or sideboards with a single row of drawers, higher than usual, usually of walnut, and of simple design, made in the second half of the 18th century and early part of the 19th, in Maryland and other southern states. So-called because they were used as a table for hunters who stood to help themselves to food.

England and America The modern term 'secretary' is commonly used indiscriminately for the following different types of desks and bookcases.

England 'Bureau bookcase' (Sheraton's *Cabinet Dictionary*). A slant-top desk with book-case above.

America The same combination was called a 'desk-and-bookcase'.

America 'Secretary and bookcase' incorporated the new 'secretary drawer' described by Hepplewhite as being a type in which 'the face of the upper drawer falling down by means of a spring and quadrant produces the same usefulness as the flap to a desk'.

England 'Gentleman's Secretary' (Plate 52 in Sheraton's *Drawing Book*) was a piece intended for a gentleman to write at, to keep his accounts, and to serve as a library.

America The contemporary term was the same; now popularly called a 'Salem secretary'.

America In the late 18th century and early 19th century a 'Secretary-Escritoir' was a chest of drawers with a secretary-drawer at the top. Now called a 'butler's desk'.

America 'Tambour desk' is a modern term for a lady's writing-table with tambour shutters, a type frequently made in New England, which has no English counterpart.

FURNITURE, ENGLISH, EVOLUTION OF

A certain amount of Gothic furniture dating from the 15th century still survives, although none of it is in the original condition. What is now admired is the dark polished surface which has developed through the centuries, but much Gothic furniture was originally painted, and traces of paint still survive on some early examples. Chests and cupboards carved with the *motifs* of the period are perhaps the things which have most commonly survived, but genuine specimens are extremely rare. A little more has survived from the 16th century. The reign of Henry VIII saw the first signs of Renaissance influence in England, and Italian carvers and decorators came to work on Hampton Court, then the property of Cardinal Wolsey which was appropriated by the King in 1529. Renaissance *motifs* were at first distributed in Northern Europe by way of engravings, and therefore at the beginning of the 16th century especially we find classical ornament superimposed on Gothic forms, since the essence of the new style was thought to reside in the ornament. This persisted throughout the 16th century to a greater or lesser extent, and it was not until the true classical style was brought to England by Inigo Jones, after 1614, that the lingering traces of Gothic entirely disappeared.

During the second half of the 16th century the influence of the Netherlands is apparent in the bulbous legs common for such things as tables of the better quality, and chairs began to replace the earlier stools and benches, the first chairs being known, interestingly enough, as back-stools. Tables were now made in one piece, replacing the earlier trestle variety.

Inlaying in coloured woods was introduced during the reign of Elizabeth I, and carved ornament became more elaborate. Turning became popular about the middle of the 16th century, and continued to be fashionable in one version or another throughout most of the 17th. Turning was done on a lathe (q.v.), the wood being rotated at the same time as variously shaped cutting-tools were brought into contact with it.

The increasing prosperity and wealth of the Elizabethan period, which led to a certain amount of ostentation and vulgarity, saw a reaction in the following reign of James I. Chairs began to be upholstered instead of being given loose cushions, and chests and cabinets were made with drawers for the storage of small objects. Glass mirrors, at first small, were introduced during the reign of Charles I, and were made at Vauxhall (London) after 1670. The earlier mirrors came from Venice (see *Venetian Glass*).

The Commonwealth period was not notable for artistic innovation, but chairs with slung leather seats and backs, copied from France by way of Spain, were popular, and the Restoration marks the beginning of the influence of Chinese imports on English furniture design. As far back as 1604 James I had purchased a Chinese porcelain dinner-service

Furniture, English. Bonheur du jour in a late Louis XV style. English. c. 1765. *Sotheby & Co.*

from the Dutch, and Chinese *motifs* had influenced early delft pottery from about 1628, but lacquer panels, cabinets, and screens were rarely to be seen before the reign of Charles II, when they became popular, probably influenced by the Queen, Catherine of Braganza, who came from Portugal, a country importing Far Eastern art extensively. Lacquer cabinets made from imported panels were mounted on elaborately carved stands, and these stands were usually silvered or gilded. European craftsmen copied the Chinese panels with varnishes, and decorated them with *chinoiseries* (q.v.), the art being known as japanning (q.v.) from the fact that the panels of Japan were the more highly valued. The term, in fact, perpetuates the confusion prevailing as to the origin of Far Eastern work. India was credited with some of it—for instance, the so-called Coromandel screens.

Silver furniture, of which very few examples survive, was a fashion imported from France, but little was to be seen outside Whitehall Palace. Survivals in England include the examples at Knole (Kent) and at Windsor Castle.

Towards the end of the 17th century oak became unfashionable. The preferred wood was now walnut, and this has a more compact grain lending itself to finely detailed carving. Nevertheless, solid walnut was very costly, and large, well-figured pieces were difficult to find. This led to the introduction of veneering (q.v.). Walnut has always been valued for the quality of its figuring (the pattern formed by the grain) and thin sheets were glued to a carcass of some common wood like deal. Sheets with knot-like markings are termed burr-walnut, and a common way of using the veneers on the finer furniture is known as quartering (q.v.). In the last quarter of the 17th century chairs, settees, and day-beds (actually the last two are almost synonomous) were made with turned frames, and seats and backs of woven cane. Elaborate spiral turning was common for legs and rails, and chairs were often surmounted by a carved cresting.

The front rail was also deep and carved. A crown commemorates the Restoration, and cherub heads were frequently employed as carved ornament in addition. This type of chair was derived from contemporary France.

Marquetry (q.v.) became a fashionable kind of decoration for furniture with the accession of William and Mary. Most such work at first was done by immigrant Dutch cabinet-makers, and it is sometimes difficult to distinguish between English and Dutch work. Furniture made in Holland itself is generally larger and heavier, and cabinets often have a *bombé* (q.v.) front, with carved, outcurving feet. Marquetry was fashionable until the end of the reign of Queen Anne, when it was superseded by plain, polished wood with the figuring as the only ornament. The cabriole leg (q.v.) first appears in the reign of Queen Anne, although it was already in use in France. In its simpler versions it had a plain, rounded, club foot, or a hoof—a version of the French *pied de biche*. The claw-and-ball foot (a bird's claw grasping a ball, which may have been suggested by the Chinese dragon's claw holding a pearl) first appears about this time, and lion-paw feet occur a little later under the influence of William Kent (q.v.). The cabriole leg was often carved on the knee, usually with scallop-shell ornament which probably came from Spain by way of Holland. In a modified form the same leg was employed for cabinet stands and tables.

As in France, chair-backs tended to be lower than those of the 17th century, but were still high in comparison with the immediately succeeding styles. The splat (the centre part of the chair-back) was urn-shaped, or fiddle- or vase-shaped. The top rail was scrolled. A number of new types of furniture make their appearance, notably the bureau which had drawers and a writing-compartment below and shelves enclosed by doors above. The doors were sometimes panelled, sometimes glazed, and, very rarely, fitted with mirrors. The metal trellisage of France was never fashionable in England. Pier-glasses, and mirrors generally, were still extremely expensive, and rarely of a single sheet. The price was governed by the difficulty of manufacturing the required flat sheets, and the cost of the frame itself was usually very subsidiary to that of the whole. For this reason mirror-doors to cabinets were reserved only for the finest work, and glazed doors had small panes set in glazing-bars. Glazed doors were reserved for shelves used for the display of fine china, or for books.

At this time the typical settee was in the form of two or three chair-backs with a common seat-frame and multiple legs.

Dining-tables were relatively small, but designed to be put together to form one large table. Food was served from side-tables, and the sideboard proper did not appear until quite late in the century. Card-tables were provided with slightly sunken wells at each corner to accommodate candlesticks. Money-wells, when present, are deeper, and nearer to the centre of the table.

Furniture, Silver. Silver table and two *torchères.* English. Restoration period (q.v.). The style is decidedly Louis XIV, and these pieces help to reconstruct the appearance of French silver furniture melted about 1685. *Knole, Kent. Courtesy of the National Trust.*

The reign of George I saw a continuation of Queen Anne styles with gradual modifications. Mahogany began to replace walnut after 1733, when a tax on it was removed, and at this time the mahogany of San Domingo in the West Indies (called 'Spanish' mahogany) was the preferred variety. This was dark in colour with a slight figure, and was nearly always used in a solid form. The lighter Jamaican and Cuban mahogany, imported later in the century, was more often used in the form of a veneer.

The reign of George I saw the development of the Kent style in furniture-design (see *Kent, William*), which owed a great deal to Venice and something to the France of Louis Quatorze. Kent employed marble freely for table-tops, and the supports were massive, often elaborately carved, and nearly always gilded. The fashion for this kind of furniture owed much to the Palladian style (q.v.) in architecture, being intended for Palladian interiors. Late Kent furniture shows rococo influence. Nearly all Kent furniture is large and massive. Probably he it was who introduced the broken pediment to England for such cabinet-furniture as bookcases.

The market provided by the increasingly prosperous *bourgeoisie* of the period was catered for by Thomas Chippendale (q.v.), who published his well-known book of designs, *The Gentleman and Cabinet-maker's Director*, in 1754. Chippendale's primary inspiration was the rococo style, then at the height of its popularity in France, but carved wood replaced the gilt-bronze mounts of Paris except in rare instances. Chippendale's furniture in the Chinese style is elsewhere discussed (see *'Chinese Chippendale'*), and he made use of the Gothic style in many of his designs, such architectural motifs as cluster columns being employed for the legs of chairs and tables. He

is, in fact, best known for his chairs, the backs of which were lower than formerly, and the finest had handsomely carved openwork splats, and broad seats in the contemporary French manner. His design-book was much used during the 19th century by makers of reproduction furniture, and 'Chippendale' has become a generic term for furniture in his style, although little of it can actually be traced to his workshop. Among the furniture he introduced is the basin-stand for the bedroom.

The first signs of the neo-classical style (known in England as the Adam style) can be seen soon after 1760, when it was already evident in France. The new styles replaced the rococo of Chippendale almost completely by about 1770. Perhaps it was the Brothers Adam who first introduced the sideboard. In 1773, when it first appeared, it was a side-table flanked at either end by detached cupboards surmounted by urns. The cupboards and the table were joined a little later to form one piece of furniture, and George Hepplewhite (once apprenticed to Gillow) designed many sideboards. His *Cabinet Maker's and Upholsterer's Guide* was published in 1788.

The Adam style is notable for the use of classical *motifs* of all kinds—medallions, swags, pendants of husks, urns, the Greek key-fret, the wave pattern, and rams' heads. The urn is almost ubiquitous, appearing in all kinds of guises. Several catalogues of collections of antiquities recovered from Pompeii and Herculaneum published at this time, such as that of Sir William Hamilton (q.v.), formed part of the stock-in-trade of every designer and manufacturer.

As in France the cabriole leg was replaced by the straight and tapering leg, and chairs became lighter in weight and construction. Backs were usually oval or shield-shaped, and the lyre and the Prince of Wales's feathers often formed the splat. There was a vogue for painted furniture (see *Furniture, English, Painted*), and plaques of Wedgwood's jasper became increasingly popular as furniture decoration, although survivals are few. Satinwood was extremely popular for drawing-room furniture, but the range of exotic woods available for furniture-making had greatly increased, especially those imported from the East and West Indies and from South America. Red cedar and red deal from North America replaced deal from the Baltic for carcassing. Rosewood (q.v.), little used before 1800, became increasingly popular thereafter. Throughout this period, however, mahogany remained the preferred wood for the less frivolous side of life—the dining-room and the library.

Thomas Sheraton published his *Cabinet Maker's and Upholsterer's Drawing Book* in 1793. He was principally a designer and not a maker of furniture, and his designs were based largely on contemporary French styles. In that country they were termed *Louis Seize à l'Anglaise*. His chairs are very light in construction, and his designs make little use of carving, inlays and veneering being employed as decoration instead. Some of his later designs are in the Empire style (q.v.) of Napoleon I.

English Empire (which is indistinguishable from

Regency) includes furniture with such *motifs* as dolphins, tridents, anchors, and similar marine subjects largely inspired by the victories of Nelson. Egyptian *motifs* were popular for a time after Napoleon's Egyptian campaign in 1798. Most of the English classical *motifs*, usually based on vase-paintings and similar sources, were the same as those to be seen decorating French Empire furniture. A limited revival of the *chinoiserie* followed the decoration of Brighton Pavilion by the Prince Regent (see *Crace, Frederick*), and Gothic designs occur occasionally during the early decades of the century, although they did not become at all common until later. The Empire style eventually merged in its later phases into that known as Regency, strictly current from 1811 to 1820 but often continued until 1837 without justification. 'Regency', in common use, means anything made between 1800 and the accession of Queen Victoria.

The woods popular at the time were principally rosewood and, to a lesser extent violetwood (kingwood) and amboyna for the more expensive pieces. Imitations of the figure of rare woods, achieved by staining, can be noticed, and French polishing was introduced just before 1820. At this time and later, many 18th-century pieces were 'finished' (in more ways than one) by repolishing of this kind. Carving had fallen almost completely into disuse as a method of decorating furniture, except for a few purposes such as the central pedestals of tables. Brass stringing, introduced from France and popularized by Sheraton, became very fashionable, and inlays in the manner of A.-C. Boulle (q.v.) enjoyed a limited vogue, the best probably by Louis Le Gaigneur (q.v.) of the Edgware Road (London). Brass mounts, especially toe-caps to table-supports, were common at this time. See *Victorian Period, Style in the*.

FURNITURE, ENGLISH PAINTED

Although most furniture was painted during the Gothic period, and the Italians produced handsomely painted *cassone* (q.v.) in early Renaissance times, designers relied for a long period on plain, figured wood as furniture decoration. That mahogany should give place to satinwood undoubtedly assisted to popularize the vogue for painted furniture in the last decades of the 18th century, since the latter formed an excellent ground for decorative painting, but the Brothers Adam also made use of white wood.

The best painting on satinwood furniture was probably that inspired by Angelica Kauffmann, R.A., who also designed, and even sometimes painted, walls and ceilings for the Brothers Adam. Her work on furniture is either in polychrome or *en grisaille* (q.v.), usually in oval or octagonal panels which she especially favoured. Among the painters who also worked for the Brothers Adam were Pergolesi and Zucchi, the latter a Venetian who married Angelica Kauffmann in 1780.

The decoration of painted furniture of the period is in the neo-classical style fostered in England by Adam, and some examples are based on Wedgwood's jasper medallions with characteristic colouring. In the best work additional coats of varnish were added to the unpainted parts to bring the surface up to the level of the painting, the whole then being varnished to give the painted parts the necessary protection.

Care is needed to distinguish the best work from the painted satinwood furniture produced by minor craftsmen, and even that done by amateurs, which nearly always lacks the competence of professional execution.

Furniture of almost every kind was thus decorated, from side-tables and *commodes* to work-tables and pole-screens, and the painting ranges from classical figure-subjects to the popular wreaths and swags of flowers.

Furniture, Painted, English. Breakfront bookcase in the Sheraton style decorated with painted ornament. c. 1780. English. *Parke-Bernet Galleries, New York.*

FURNITURE, FORGERIES OF

Antique furniture is perhaps more faked and forged than any other kind of art object, although really deceptive forgeries are comparatively uncommon. Every piece of furniture must fall into one of the following categories: (1) genuine, in untouched condition, or with only minor repairs, (2) repaired more or less extensively, (3) more new wood than old, (4) faked by the addition of ornament, such as inlay or bronze mounts, to make it more desirable, (5) an honest commercial reproduction, (6) a reproduction faked with the signs of age, (7) a forgery made with old wood. Of these the serious collector of antique furniture is interested in 1 and 2. Any of the remaining classes can be utilized as interior decoration, including the forgery, provided the price paid is related to its value. Forgeries are works of good craftmanship, and this must be paid for. Even forgeries on a 'time and materials' basis are not likely to be cheap, though their true value is usually much below that of a genuine specimen. The position is a little complicated by the fact that a good deal of antique furniture in the lower and medium grades is cheaper than the cost of a really good forgery or reproduction, and reproductions of fine quality often bring high prices. One of an 18th century French *bureau plat*, made by Henri Dasson in the middle of the 19th century, sold for what it was, brought £2,000 in the London saleroom a few years ago.

Perhaps the most useful asset a collector can acquire is an eye for patina, the observable effect of time on surface appearance. This cannot be reproduced convincingly except by the most expert forger, and there are always discrepancies for the eye accustomed to judging this aspect. Wood hardens and gradually changes colour, partly due to exposure to light and air, and partly to the effect of dust-particles which are forced by cleaning into the interstices of the wood. Exposure to bright sunlight often has a bleaching effect. This modifies the transition from red to brown to be seen with old mahogany, or the golden shade of walnut. In time this leads to a variegated surface which defies exact imitation. Of course, genuine patination is often destroyed by refinishing, or by the later use of French polish which produces a smooth, characterless surface, but the specimen so treated is undesirable in any case, except as a furnishing piece, and it suggests that careful examination is required to see what else may have been done.

Forgeries are usually made from old wood, but inevitably this has previously served a different purpose. Old mahogany shop-counters are in demand among forgers for the making of furniture, but it is far from easy to eliminate the traces of their former use. Scratches and signs of damage which are perfectly natural in one position may be difficult to account for in another. Nail-holes, for example, may appear in the wrong place, and need to be stopped. This sometimes occurs when old floor-boards are adapted to oak table-tops, or old panelling is employed to make a chest. Cut edges have a different colour from the old surface, and staining to match is not a complete answer. Forgers know all about wear and patina, and take considerable pains to reproduce the effect. For instance, some Italian forgers lend chairs and tables to cafés for a few months, during the course of which they receive the wear and tear of many years of normal use. The process of faking the effects of the minor damage of a couple of centuries is known as 'distressing' in the faked furniture trade, but it is noticeable that the operation of 'distressing' invariably avoids those places which would spoil the appearance, and will be confined to the ones which are less prominent.

Forgeries tend to be confined to elaborately decorated pieces, and those which are simple in design are less likely to be false. This is not because elaborate decoration commands more money, but because specimens thus decorated are less likely to be detected. The revealing characteristics of the forgery can often be hidden under a mass of ornament. Therefore, any specimen which has more ornament than seems to be justified by its style and period is worth especially careful examination.

Worm-holes are not a sign of genuineness. They can be faked with a drill, but the old story of firing a shot-gun at newly made furniture is apocryphal. As Cecsinsky once said, a piece of worm-ridden timber will 'antique' a warehouseful of forgeries in six months.

Gilt furniture presents fewer problems to the forger, and the 18th-century methods of applying gold-leaf are perfectly well known from Dossie's *Handmaid to the Arts*, published in 1765, and similar works, but the gold on surfaces which face upwards will be found, because of dust falling on them, to be appreciably darker in old works than those places which were more protected. This is usually missed by forgers. In any case, much gilt furniture, especially mirrors, has had to be regilded at one time or another, and this does not especially affect the value. Lacquer furniture is much forged, and there are some clever and deceptive copies of 18th-century Italian lacquer made in Bologna recently, although the maker has now removed elsewhere to an unknown destination. 'Japanning' is, in any case, a vulnerable kind of surface decoration, and there are few entirely unrestored examples today. The colours of old work, European and Oriental, fade with exposure to light, and it is a good plan to remove a hinge or an escutcheon plate to see whether the colour underneath is the same as that of the remainder. If it is the chances of forgery are extremely high. Lacquer furniture was imitated in London during the 1920s, often placed on elaborately carved stands decorated with silver-leaf in the 17th-century manner. These were sold, in the first place, as decorative cabinets, but they can be puzzling to someone who does not know their origin.

Nails and screws (q.v.) are not as helpful as is sometimes suggested. The presence of old nails is probably of greater significance than that of screws of the correct type. Nails do not fall out easily. Screws sometimes become loose, and are replaced by more modern types.

Chairs need close examination when they occur in matching sets. No piece of antique furniture gets greater wear than a chair, and therefore one in pristine condition is a considerable rarity. Small sets of six are sometimes expanded to twelve by using old parts in conjunction with new. The remedy is to examine every part of every chair. Stools are sometimes fabricated from sets of old chair-legs of the cabriole type. Occasionally a forger will make serious mistakes of style, such as adding a shield-back to cabriole legs.

Perhaps the most common forgery is the small tripod table with a circular top. These are often made from discarded pole-screens or damaged *torchères* cut down, with a circular top added, the top, perhaps, from a damaged dumb-waiter, or even completely new. Half-circular satinwood *commodes* of the neo-classical period often have painted decoration added, or are otherwise 'improved'. Inlaid decoration is a fairly certain sign that the piece was not originally intended for painting.

Generally, small pieces are far more likely to be spurious than large ones. The large pieces of the first half of the 18th century have not been in great demand for many years, due to the smallness of modern rooms. The demand for small pieces, on the other hand, has outrun the available supply. Other types of furniture, such as the china cabinet, not often made until towards the end of the 18th century, are popular enough to claim a share of the forger's attention. Large pieces like the clothes-press, not particularly useful today in the bedroom, by a little careful alteration become a bookcase, the bottom being retained in its original form, and the upper part cut back, the doors being given glazing-bars and glass instead of solid panels.

French furniture is a prolific field for the faker and the forger, and it has been made on a very large scale for the antique market. The mounts do not equal those of the 18th century in quality, and this is always a point worth watching. Gilt-bronze mounts are added to plain provincial furniture, especially *commodes*, and there are shops on the Left Bank in Paris who deal in nothing but mounts for one purpose or another. Some are used for restoration; others are used for less honest purposes. It is probably true to say that spurious stamps purporting to be those of the 18th-century *ébénistes* and *menuisiers* were not used before 1882, but they have been very commonly used since. Generally, French furniture is very much a field for the expert, and the inexperienced would do well to rely on the services of a reputable dealer specializing in it.

American furniture has been forged in its country of origin, and a few specimens have found their way to Europe. The writer recently observed a forged block-front Philadelphia cabinet offered for sale in an English provincial shop. Few European dealers are competent to assess furniture of this nature.

FURNITURE, FRENCH, EVOLUTION OF

From the last quarter of the 17th century there are, perhaps, few furniture styles which did not at least owe something to France, but at the beginning of that century there was little which could be regarded as a purely French style. The origin of the style which we now recognize as French began with the building of the palace of Versailles, and the foundation of the *Manufacture royale des meubles de la couronne in* 1663, under the guidance of Charles Le Brun, to supply decorative art of all kinds to the new palace and the French Court. This encouragement, and the munificence of royal patronage, gave especial impetus to the arts of design, and one of the most influential designers of the period was Jean I Bérain (q.v.) who was the source of a great deal of the ornament employed in the decorative arts generally. His designs, for instance, certainly inspired a good many of those decorating the furniture of André-Charles Boulle (q.v.). Boulle was undoubtedly one of the most influential figures in French furniture-design,

Furniture, French. *Amoire* of ebony with marquetry of metal on tortoiseshell. The reliefs on the doors are of Apollo and Daphne and Apollo and Marysas. Late Louis XIV style, ascribed to André-Charles Boulle (q.v.). c. 1700. *Wallace Collection.*

since the decoration he introduced persisted in popularity throughout most of the 18th century and well into the 19th. Beginning with furniture decorated with marquetry of exotic woods, he turned his attention to combinations of tortoiseshell and brass, or even (but rarely) tortoiseshell and silver, the metal engraved with Bérain-like ornament. His forms were developed (probably) from the Italian furniture which had been popular during the first half of the 17th century, and from them came the custom of mounting in gilt-bronze, but most of it was very distinctively French in style. The principal difference between French and English furniture resides in the English preference for solid wood and plain veneers with carving as ornament, whereas the French not only employed decorative veneers and inlays, but a profusion of gilt-bronze and the addition of marble tops in great variety. Marble, of course, was more easily obtained in France, and was available in a wide range of colours.

Louis XIV demanded grandeur in his palaces; he wanted a style which would make an impressive outward show of his stature as Europe's most powerful monarch, and this could not but have its effect on the art of design generally.

The coming of the Regency of the Duc d'Orléans (1710–1725) brought new and more frivolous styles in its train, and new *motifs* of decoration and a fresh approach to the design of furniture are almost immediately apparent. This was, perhaps, a culmination

Furniture, French. Louis XV inlaid tulipwood and kingwood *commode.* Stamp of Adrien Faizelot-Delorme (ME1748). *Parke-Bernet Galleries Inc., New York.*

of a tendency which had started almost as far back as the 1680s, a period of financial stringency when gilt-bronze and gilded wood replaced former magnificence of which silver furniture was one aspect, a tendency which had become more marked after 1700. The principal *ébéniste* (q.v.) of the *Régence* was Charles Cressent (1685–1768), who was also a sculptor of some distinction, and he designed veneered furniture handsomely mounted in gilt-bronze which is among the finest of any made during the 18th century. Because he cast his own mounts he came into conflict with the Guild of Fondeurs-Ciseleurs (q.v.), who claimed the sole right to do this, and one of the reasons for the deterioration of the quality of mounts on some later French furniture stems from this monopoly, since the members of the Guild kept stocks of mounts which the *ébénistes* were either compelled or found it more convenient to use. Generally, the finest furniture of the period had mounts designed for it by one or other of the notable bronze-workers of the day, such as Caffiéri (q.v.).

Cressent, in his later work, turned to floral marquetry instead of the elaborate mounts of his earlier period.

Beginning with him furniture became lighter and more graceful in form, and this tendency was accentuated with the coming of the rococo style and the designs of Juste-Aurèle Meissonnier (q.v.), who designed furniture as well as silver. Curves everywhere increased in popularity, replacing the severer architectural forms of the reign of Louis XIV. This is especially noticeable in the serpentine tops to such pieces as *commodes* (q.v.), curving drawer-fronts, *bombé* sides, and in the disposition of gilt-bronze ornament which became pronouncedly asymmetrical. Mounts show greater freedom of modelling, and the more severe classical *motifs* of the earlier period were replaced by floral and foliate ornament. The influence of the metalworker is everywhere to be seen in furniture-design throughout the currency of the rococo style.

Another aspect of rococo was the influence

of the Far East. The popularity of imported lacquer led to widespread attempts to imitate it. The most successful of these imitations was undoubtedly that invented by the brothers Martin (*vernis Martin*—q.v.) which was employed to decorate many kinds of furniture, especially *encoignures* and *commodes*. It gave special impetus to the art of *chinoiserie* (q.v.), which, in its 18th-century form, had started with Watteau.

Throughout the 18th century we notice the multiplication of furniture types—the development of more comfortable chairs (such as the *bergère*), the increasing number of small tables for specialized purposes, and a noticeable decrease in size to match the smaller rooms then fashionable. Nothing to equal the English plain wooden backs of chairs is to be seen in France, except in everyday chairs for lesser apartments and for servants' quarters. Upholstered backs and seats were the rule for everything else, either *à la reine* (with a flat back), or *en cabriolet*, with a curved back. Most had handsomely carved gilded frames, or sometimes painted white and partly gilt. Polished wood was not fashionable until towards the end of the 18th century.

It is essential to remember not only the influence of the King and Versailles on furniture-design, but also that of the King's mistress, Mme de Pompadour, who furnished several *châteaux*, employing the art-dealer Lazare Duveaux very extensively, and several items are listed in his account-book as *à la Pompadour*. Her influence on the arts came not only from her purchases, but from her ascendancy with the King by which she attained support for various projects, not least the porcelain factory at Sèvres (see *Sèvres Porcelain Factory*).

Furniture, French. A very rare tulipwood *commode* in a transitional style between late Louis XV and Louis XVI, about 1775. The *ébéniste* (q.v.) was C. C. Saunier, whose stamp occurs on it twice, the second time with the letters *JME* (*jurande des menuisiers-ébénistes*). *Norman Adams Ltd, London.*

Soon after mid-century we see the influence of immigrant *ébénistes* from Germany, the first of whom was J. F. Oeben (q.v.) whose *bureau du roi Louis Quinze*, completed by J. H. Riesener (q.v.) and now at Versailles, is a masterpiece of the period. It is veneered on oak, principally with pear-wood, and with panels of holly, burr-walnut, and stained sycamore. The Germans introduced mechanical furniture—i.e. furniture ingeniously designed to serve more than one purpose (see *Ébéniste-mecanicien*).

Paradoxically, the style known loosely as 'Louis Seize' began in 1755, nearly 20 years before his accession. It is, in fact, more correctly termed the neo-classical style (q.v.). Soon after 1760 rococo curves began to disappear, and classical influence in ornament came to the fore. Cabriole legs were discarded in favour of fluted and tapered legs. Ornament included trophies of arms, musical instruments and so forth, swags of husks and medallions, and the urn once more returned to favour. The use of porcelain plaques from Sèvres in the decoration of furniture began about 1760, and was almost certainly the introduction of dealers of the period. This became very popular, particularly with Mme du Barry and the Queen, Marie-Antoinette. Martin Carlin (q.v.) did a good deal of work of this kind for the latter.

Some of the furniture of this period is not unlike that of Hepplewhite and Sheraton, and influences travelled both ways, English furniture styles becoming popular in France. The influence of Marie-Antoinette was exerted in favour of luxurious ornament and the employment of exotic woods, and some of the world's finest furniture was made at this time.

Furniture, French. One of a pair of low cabinets somewhat in a late Louis XIV style. Period of Louis XVI. c. 1780. By Étienne Levasseur. *Sotheby & Co.*

The *Directoire* style which immediately succeeded the upheaval of the Revolution is neo-classicism at its most severe. To some extent its adoption preceded the Revolution, but it was current from about 1793 to 1800. Mounts were few and simple, forms were plain, and emphasis was on quality of the wood. The period was one in which few people thought it wise to spend money on ostentation, although those who were astute enough to profit from the Revolution certainly existed. Luxury began to return with the crowning of Napoleon I as Emperor, and the work of the architects Percier and Fontaine, the principal designers in the new Empire style (which became the Regency style in England), was based largely on Imperial Roman styles which stemmed from the adoption of Roman institutions, to be seen for example in the Consulate. These designs, on the whole, had little artistic merit, but they did provide an appropriate setting for the new *régime*. The campaigns of 1798 also brought Egyptian *motifs* into favour, although there was, at the time, little understanding of Egyptian art and civilization. The use of winged lions, sphinxes, and legs in the form of a monopodium—the head and thorax of a lion continuing downwards to a single leg and paw—are all instances of Imperial Roman *motifs*. Furniture contours were copied from Greek and Roman sources, especially from vase-paintings.

The defeat of Napoleon, the accession of Louis XVIII, and then of Charles X, saw a continuation and gradual modification of the Empire style. A brief Gothic revival took place about 1830, but it did not become important as it did in England. The marquetry of Boulle continued in favour, and had a brief vogue during the reign of Louis-Philippe, as well as a revived rococo which, curiously enough, became fashionable a few years later than it did in England. The Second Empire (1852-1870) is notable

Furniture, French. *Bonheur du jour* decorated with marquetry of tulipwood and harewood by Léonard Boudin. Louis XV style. c. 1760. *Parke-Bernet Galleries, New York.*

for a revival of Renaissance and Louis Quatorze designs which were copied in a modified form, and this, also, has its parallel in England (see *Victorian Period, Style in the*).

So far the progression of style in Paris furniture has been discussed, but French provincial furniture (or *Regionale*) differs in many respects from that of Paris. It made very free use of native woods, such as oak, walnut, beech, and elm, with cherry as a substitute for mahogany, the latter wood being principally employed by the *ébénistes* of Bordeaux. Until well into the reign of Louis XIV the designs of Louis XIII remained popular, and provincial craftsmen always lagged considerably behind Paris in the adoption of current fashions. Perhaps this can nowhere better be seen than in the *armoire* (q.v.), where the characteristic carving of the Louis XV period still lingered until well into the 19th century. Designs vary from province to province, but the *armoire* is always an excellent indication of the prevailing local style.

FURNITURE, STEEL, FRENCH

Steel furniture was first made in France during the Louis XVI period, although nearly all surviving examples belong either to the *Directoire* or the Empire. Built up largely of steel rods, furniture of this kind was principally employed for campaigning during the Napoleonic wars. Beds, chairs (often with slung seats and backs), settees, and tables, the latter sometimes with marble tops, have all been recorded. Examples with added decoration of gilt-bronze exist.

FÜRSTENBERG PORCELAIN FACTORY

The first attempt to make porcelain here was in 1746, but it was not until the autumn of 1750 that porcelain of saleable quality was produced, and it was not until Benckgraff (q.v.) arrived from Höchst

Fürstenberg Porcelain. Porcelain picture in rococo gilt frame signed by J. G. Eiche. Fürstenberg c 1767. Framed pictures seem to have been peculiar to this factory in the 18th century. *Mrs. C. B. Stout, Memphis, Tenn.*

that any real success was achieved. The principal modeller in this early period was Simon Feilner, noted for some figures of *Miners* of excellent quality. Satisfactory enamelling was not achieved until about 1763, after the close of the Seven Years' War, and underglaze blue remained poor until 1767. Until 1770 the porcelain was yellowish in colour, with a greyish glaze very apt to speck during firing. To disguise these defects relief patterns were popular, and those of Meissen and Berlin were copied. Engravings were particularly popular as inspiration for painted decoration, and flowers were often in purple monochrome or iron-red. *Tableaux*—pictures in porcelain, with or without a moulded rococo frame—were done between 1767 and 1768, and these were usually signed. J. G. Eiche (at the factory between 1760 and 1795) was a painter of figures and landscapes who did a number of them.

The first *Modellmeister* was Simon Feilner, whose *Miners* have been mentioned. He was also responsible for some Italian Comedy figures. He was discharged in 1768, but a smaller version of some models by his hand were issued about 1775. J. C. Rombrich (at the factory from 1762 to 1794) copied the figures of Meissen as well as ivory-carvings, and towards the end of the century he was responsible for portrait medallions in *biscuit* porcelain. A. C. Luplau (1765–1776) worked in a rather similar style to Rombrich. Best known is his *Flohsucherin* (*The Flea Search*), depicting a woman pursuing her search for a flea to fairly intimate lengths. Desoches (1769–1774) was influenced by Sèvres, and was perhaps inspired by Chardin and Greuze. K. G. Schubert (1775–1804) copied ivory-carvings by Permoser and others, artisans from Höchst, and street-vendors from Berlin. He did *biscuit* reliefs in the manner of Wedgwood, and both jasper and basaltes were copied (see *Wedgwood*).

The factory still exists, and has reproduced some of its old models.

FUSEE

A device fitted to many watch and spring-driven clock movements to ensure a continually even supply of power from the spring to the going train, which is connected to the spring-barrel through a cone-shaped drum with spiral grooves. The spring-barrel drives the fusee by a length of gut or a fine steel chain, thus ensuring that the weaker the spring becomes as it unwinds, the less power is required to drive the train of wheels. It is, in fact, an infinitely variable gear. The device was perhaps first employed in Bohemia early in the 16th century, although it was probably invented about 70 years before in Italy. It was developed and improved in France.

G

GALLÉ, EMIL (1845–1905)

It has been well claimed for Gallé that he initiated a renaissance of the art of glass in France, and he was one of the moving spirits of the *art nouveau* style (q.v.). Among his many technical innovations was *Mondscheinglas* (moonlight glass), which was the product of adding cobalt oxide to the molten metal. He employed hydrofluoric acid extensively to etch patterns, and he began, in 1884, to make cased glass (q.v.) in two or three layers, sometimes alternating translucent and opaque glasses, which he used to imitate hardstones. He introduced metallic foils between the layers, as well as air-bubbles, for special effects. Those specimens he made himself bear his signature in relief; those he only supervised are marked '*cristallerie d'Emil Gallé*'. He had a number of followers, notably Rousseau and Léveillé, who devised a method for colouring glass by distributing coloured glass powder over the surface and firing it. He also gathered round him a group of craftsmen in other fields, notably furniture-designing and book-binding, who shared his ideas.

GALLERY

An ornamental railing of wood or metal, usually fretted or pierced, especially to be found round the edges of tables, or the tops of cabinets in the Louis XVI style; anything of this nature and appearance employed as ornament to objects of silver, etc. Galleries were most popular during the second half of the 18th century.

GALLOON

Braid of variable width in a variety of materials employed to cover the junction of wood and fabric in upholstered furniture.

GAMES-TABLE

A small table fashionable during the 18th and early 19th centuries which was equipped for the playing of a number of games. The top was usually inlaid as a chess-board, and upon removal, a backgammon board was disclosed below. Tables were fully equipped with chess and draughtsmen, backgammon dice, etc.

Gallé, Emile. Vase of blown and cased glass with decoration etched with hydrofluoric acid. Emile Gallé, Nancy, France. c. 1885–1900. *Corning Museum of Glass, Corning, N.Y.*

GARDE-MEUBLE, JOURNAL DE

The Garde-Meuble was the royal French furniture repository. It is of special interest to the scholar engaged in historical research because all but the most minor pieces of royal furniture were recorded, described, and given an inventory number in the *Journal* which, started in 1685, had run to eighteen volumes by the time of the Revolution. The *Journal* also gives the name of the maker or dealer who supplied a particular piece, the royal palace or residence for which it was intended, and its position therein. This enables furniture bearing royal inventory marks to be closely identified, and for this reason the history of 18th-century French furniture in particular is much better documented than that of

England, where it is rare for any piece of furniture to be traceable with certainty to a particular maker.

Marks on furniture were branded, painted, or stencilled, but rarely struck with a stamp. The royal mark is usually the *fleur-de-lys* in conjunction with a crown, but the double-L monogram was sometimes used during the reign of Louis XV.

> *BV* under a crown refers to the Château of Bellevue.
>
> *CP* under a crown refers to the Château of Chanteloup.
>
> Interlaced *C*s under a crown mean Compiègne.
>
> *F* or *FON* with a crown or the *fleur-de-lys*, or *GR* or *F* beneath a crown, refers to the Garde-Meuble de Fontainebleau.
>
> *MA* under a crown refers to the Garde-Meuble de la Reine (Marie-Antoinette).
>
> *SC* under a crown refers to Saint-Cloud.
>
> *CT* or *T* means the Palais de Trianon, and *GT* means Grand Trianon.
>
> *T* or *TH* under a crown refers to the Tuileries.
>
> *V* means Versailles.
>
> *MRCV* within a shield and under a crown is the mark of the Mobilier Royal of the Palais de Versailles.
>
> *GM* means Garde-Meuble.
>
> *MLM* refers to Malmaison.

These stamps, of course, are additional to those of the *ébéniste* or *menuisier* responsible for manufacture, and were added subsequently, when the entry was made in the *Journal*.

GARDEN CARPETS

Persian carpets made from the 16th to the 19th century, the pattern of which represents the flower-beds, paths, streams, etc., of a formal garden seen from above.

GARNITURE DE CHEMINÉE

Term applied to sets of vases as chimney-piece decoration, usually in porcelain or *delft*, but also to sets of vases in other materials which sometimes included a central clock. Sets usually consisted of three, five, or even seven alternating covered vases and beakers, and they were principally of Chinese porcelain or Dutch *delft*, although *garnitures* were also made elsewhere. In France, where the fashion was at its height soon after 1700, *garnitures* of Chinese porcelain were especially prized. The fashion began to wane with the onset of the rococo style, for this kind of symmetrical disposition was no longer fashionable. Later *garnitures* of Sèvres porcelain, unlike early Delft examples usually of Chinese design, were purely European in style. Many isolated beakers and vases of appropriate shape to be seen today once formed part of a *garniture de cheminée*.

GATE-LEG TABLE

A type of folding table which first appeared at the beginning of the 17th century. Two semi-circular flaps were hinged to the fixed central part and carried, when raised, on 'gates' pulled out from the centre support, on which they were pivoted. Early examples are simple in construction, but later ones are often much more elaborately designed, sometimes as many as four 'gates' being provided instead of the normal two. Turned legs are invariable. Such turning as the barleytwist (q.v.) is to be found with the finest specimens. Seventeenth-century tables were usually of oak, but an oval mahogany version, sometimes on cabriole legs with ball-and-claw feet, survived well into the 18th century. These differ in their design from the 17th-century types, but the principle remains the same.

Seventeenth-century specimens are scarce, but tables of this kind have been reproduced in large quantities to furnish country cottages.

A mid-19th-century version, which has rectangular flaps instead of semi-circular ones, and is usually on turned legs, was termed a Sutherland table.

GAUDREAU, ANTOINE-ROBERT (c. 1680–1751)

Appointed *ébéniste du roi* in 1726, Gaudreau worked also for other members of the royal family and for Mme de Pompadour. His furniture is unstamped. A remarkably fine *commode* by him, with mounts in the rococo style by Caffiéri, is in the Wallace Collection.

GAUFRAGE (French)

A technique for producing relief ornament in textiles, especially velvet, by pressure, the material being passed between heated metal rollers suitably provided with relief designs on one and matching intaglio designs on the other. The same process was employed for stamping paper and leather. The principle is the same as the English goffering iron.

GENOA (Liguria, Italy)

Faïence-making at Genoa flourished at the same time as at Savona (q.v.), in the late 17th and 18th centuries, but work is less flamboyant, and painted with greater care and restraint. Style is, generally, very similar. See *Savona*.

GERA PORCELAIN FACTORY

Founded by two faïence workers with the aid of Graf Henry of Reuss in 1779, this factory passed to Johann Georg Wilhelm Greiner and Johann Andreas Greiner a year later. The two Greiners were already working at Volkstedt, and Gera became a branch of this factory until 1782, when the Greiners continued alone. The ownership of the factory became the subject of a complicated dispute after the death of J. G. W. Greiner in 1792.

The work of Meissen was much copied, and the crossed swords were freely added. Both the *Zwiebel-muster* ('onion' pattern) and the *Strohblumenmuster* (strewn-flower pattern) were copied in a blackish underglaze blue. A few figures have rococo bases, but these all appear to be subsequent to 1795. Views of Gera, and a painted imitation of grained wood

Gera Porcelain. Small tureen in the form of a bundle of asparagus—a typical rococo *motif* still in use at a provincial factory. Gera (Thuringia). c. 1785. *Antique Porcelain Co. Ltd.*

(the so-called *décor bois*), are both to be found. The more ambitious service-ware sometimes has a coloured ground.

GERMAIN FAMILY, THE
French silversmiths. Pierre (1647–1684) made silver *guéridons* and chandeliers for Louis XIV. Thomas (1673–1748) was, perhaps, the greatest of all French silversmiths, who became Master of the Guild in 1720, with lodgings in the Louvre. He did much notable work for the French Court, and for foreign Courts, especially that of Portugal. He was also noted as a sculptor, bronzeworker, and *ciseleur*. François-Thomas Germain (1726–1791) replaced his father, Thomas, as *orfèvre du Roi*, and worked principally in the rococo style. A pair of candlesticks made for Mme de Pompadour is in the Musée Nissim de Camondo, Paris. Another Pierre Germain, born in Avignon in 1716, appears to have been related to Thomas. He published two books of designs of rococo ornament in 1748 and 1751 respectively.

GESSO (Italian)
A composition material made of whiting, linseed oil, and size widely used in England and on the Continent in the 18th century especially. Mirror and picture frames, and some kinds of furniture, were covered with a thin layer of *gesso* as a preliminary to gilding, painting, lacquering and japanning. It was employed for partially attached modelled or carved ornament forming part, particularly, of mid-18th-century mirror-frames, when it was supported by stiff iron wire. Towards the end of the century ornament to furniture which would at one time have been carved from solid wood was moulded from *gesso*, and specimens are obviously of lesser quality than those which are carved.

Modelling of low relief ornament in *gesso* subsequently gilded formed part of the decoration of some English furniture from about 1690 onwards. Table-tops thus treated can usually be referred to the reign of Queen Anne, when *gesso* was also used to decorate mirror-frames. See '*Compo*'.

GHIORDES RUGS
Ghiordes is the Gordium of antiquity where Alexander the Great cut the Gordian knot. It is not far from Smyrna. The Ghiordes knot is used invariably, and the pile is of wool clipped short. The border is quite often wide and elaborately patterned, and most of the production has been of prayer-rugs. Quality varies with age. Many modern Ghiordes rugs are very poor.

GIBBON, GRINLING (1648–1721)
English woodcarver, first discovered by John Evelyn, who brought him to the notice of Charles II (*Diary*, 18 January 1671), and then to that of Christopher Wren, His Majesty's Surveyor. He is best known for his woodcarving, although he was also a designer of merit. Most of his surviving work is in limewood, pine, or fruit wood, and is to be found decorating chimney-pieces, overdoors, and other architectural features. Attribution to his hand, unless there is good supporting evidence, should be accepted with reserve. He is generally credited with far more than he could have completed in his lifetime. His name is often mispelled 'Gibbons'.

GILDING, COLD
Early glass and porcelain glazes were gilded by applying gold-size, oil-size, gum-water, or varnish to the surface, followed by laying on of gold-leaf which could afterwards be burnished if required. The process was employed in England for cheap glasses simulating those imported from Germany on which the gilding was fired and therefore permanent. Size-gilding has either worn off altogether, or survives as traces only.

GILDING, WOOD
The principal kinds of 18th-century gilding are oil-gilding, varnish-gilding, and japanners' gilding. These were employed not only for gilding wood (especially carved work) but also for metal or any other rigid substance, although metal was usually gilded by one or other of the methods described under that heading. A different treatment was also accorded to paper and leather, both of which are pliable.

In the 18th century gold-leaf was procurable in several different colours, the best ranging from a full yellow to a leaf with a slightly reddish cast. Inferior gold alloyed with copper and silver was sometimes passed off as pure leaf. One variety, known as Dutch gold, contained far more copper than gold. This, of good colour when laid on, in time became

Gilding, Wood. An 18th-century wood carved and gilt model of a wolf. Length 23½". *Sotheby & Co.*

Gilding, Wood. A gilder's workshop of about 1750, showing the application of gold-leaf to picture- and mirror-frames and mouldings. *After Diderot.*

disfigured with green spots unless it was protected by lacquer or varnish.

Since oil-gilding was the cheapest and easiest method of applying the leaf it was the most often employed. It was so called because it was caused to adhere to the surface to be gilded by fat oil, made from linseed oil exposed to the atmosphere for several weeks in the summer. The surface was first primed with a drying oil mixed with yellow ochre to which a little vermilion was added, and when this priming coat was dry the surface was coated with fat oil, also ground with a little yellow ochre, on which, when tacky, the leaf was laid and pressed into place with a squirrel's tail. It was then brushed over to remove any loose gold-leaf. Varnish gilding was done in much the same way, varnish replacing the fat oil.

Japanners' gilding was done with gold powder (or imitations of it) cemented to the ground with gold-size—an adhesive having a base of drying oil, the ingredients of which were often ground with vermilion. This process was frequently employed to imitate the gold grounds of imported Japanese lacquer. Gold powder was made by grinding leaf-gold in honey, the honey afterwards being removed from the gold by dissolving it in water.

Gilding on wood was usually burnished, especially carved work. Burnishing was done with a dog's tooth, or with an agate or flint burnisher.

Gilding of paper was done by using gum-water as an adhesive, usually gum arabic and gum senegal dissolved in water with the addition of a little sugar candy. Gilding on leather was often done in the same way, but in the decoration of book-bindings japanners' size was sometimes employed.

See *Silvering.*

GILDING, METAL

The most commonly employed technique for gilding metal before 1840 was with the aid of mercury (see *Amalgam*). This method, owing to the poisonous nature of the fumes evolved, is rarely employed today except for restoration, and gilding by electrical deposition has been the preferred technique since its introduction (see *Electro-plating*). Metal has always been covered with gold or silver in leaf-form (see *French Plating*), but this has not been so widely popular as the mercuric process, which was well known to the Romans. Parcel (or partial) gilding is the use of gold to decorate selected parts of an object, and the term is also employed of the partial gilding of woodwork. Silver-gilt (French: *Verneuil*) refers to the gilding of silver, usually to prevent tarnish, and this was sometimes employed before the introduction of glass liners to protect the inner surface of silver salts from contact with the salt, which induces the formation of silver chloride.

Giles, James. Chelsea vase of the gold anchor period painted with exotic birds in the manner associated with James Giles. Similar birds occur on blue-scale Worcester porcelain. See *Outside Decorators. Victoria and Albert Museum.*

GILES, JAMES (fl. 1760–1770)

Outside decorator (q.v.) of English and Chinese porcelain. The first definite date we have is 1760, when Giles advertised that he was able to procure and paint Worcester porcelain 'to any or in any pattern'. Much of the best Worcester porcelain of the 1760s came from his studios, but his work may also be found on Chelsea and Bow porcelain, and occasionally on Chinese porcelain. He maintained a studio and a staff of painters, and it is probable that he was connected with O'Neale, and perhaps with Donaldson.

GILLOT, CLAUDE (1673–1721)

A French artist, noted also as a designer. He was especially fond of the Italian Comedy (q.v.), and he employed the popular grotesques, as well as satyrs and monkeys. Watteau became his pupil in 1704.

GIRANDOLE (French)

From the Italian *girandola*. This is a term with a variety of meanings. It can be an elaborate wall-sconce, usually with several branches; a table-chandelier made from a variety of materials but, when the term is correctly used, having a decoration of faceted pendant drops of glass or rock-crystal; or a large ornamental candelabrum with two or more branches. It also exists entirely in glass. Lyre-shaped wall clocks made in America about 1820 by Lemuel Curtis of Massachusetts are also sometimes thus called. See *Lustres, Glass; Chandeliers, Glass.*

'GIRL IN A SWING' PORCELAIN

At one time attributed to the Chelsea factory (q.v.), it is now accepted that this porcelain was made at a separate factory not far away, which was founded probably by Charles Gouyn after the dissolution of the partnership between Gouyn and Sprimont in 1749. It received its name from the first model to be identified, a *Girl in a Swing*, of which examples are to be found in the Victoria and Albert Museum

Glasgow Delft. Delft bowl with an inscription to Robert Gilchrist, Lord Sheriff of Hamilton. Dated 1761. Glasgow. *Victoria and Albert Museum.*

'Girl in a Swing' Porcelain. The *Girl in a Swing* made about 1752 at the breakway Chelsea factory probably belonging to Charles Gouyn. *Victoria and Albert Museum.*

(London), and the Museum of Fine Arts, Boston, Mass. On chemical analysis the porcelain body employed proves to be very similar to that of Chelsea triangle wares (q.v.), except that the proportion of lead oxide included is very much greater—often as large as 18 per cent. Of documentary examples, a *Britannia mourning the Death of the Prince of Wales* is the most valuable, since this event took place in 1751. Many new models have been attributed within recent years, as well as scent bottles which were formerly thought to have been made only at the Lawrence Street Chelsea factory.

It is thought that those principally engaged in this manufacture were some potters from Staffordshire who came to London to start on their own account just before 1750. The factory appears to have closed towards 1760. Its service-ware has not yet been convincingly identified, although several likely examples exist.

GLASGOW (Scotland) DELFT

Founded in 1748 by potters from Lambeth called Dinwiddie, Findlay, and Nisbet, this factory produced nothing satisfactory till the following year, 1749. It continued only till 1770, when it turned to creamware.

Pieces are very rare, only six being hitherto definitely accepted. The character of the painting is rather linear, giving a delicate effect on pieces shaped in the forms of Chinese export ware. The glaze is greyish, with bubble-holes, as if firing had given trouble, and the colours are soft manganese, a rather dull lime-yellow, grey-blue, bluish-green, and dark violet-blue.

GLASS, AMERICAN

Wistar, Caspar. The first American successfully to operate a glass manufactory over a lengthy period of time. Established in 1739 in Salem County (New Jersey), Wistar, born in Germany in 1695, imported four glassmakers from his homeland. His Wistarberg

Glass, American. Creamer of glass pressed in one piece. L. B. Curling & Sons, Fort Pitt Glass Works, Pittsburgh. c. 1829–1833. *Corning Museum of Glass, Corning, N.Y.*

Works produced the usual bottles and window panes as products of domestic utility in steady demand. In addition, the workmen turned out individual pieces of excellent quality, free-blown and probably intended for family or friends. These were usually made from ordinary amber, olive, or green glass, left over at the end of the day, and they followed generally Continental glassmaking traditions. Objects of this type were produced in many glasshouses during the 18th century and well into the 19th. They comprise a distinct group of American glass termed, generically, 'South Jersey.' Early American glass-makers were practical rather than master-craftsmen, and their products represent individual expression, not industrial organization. The objects made for their own use were generally simple, and related to pewter and furniture of the period; occasionally naïvely ornate with swan-chicken shaped finials and tiers of crimped glass handles.

Henry William Stiegel, self-styled 'Baron' of Manheim, Pennsylvania, created a second American glassmaking tradition between 1765 and 1774 with the aid of German, English, and Irish workmen. In contrast to 'South Jersey' glass, the Stiegel-type is generally made either from clear or artificially coloured glass. The principal manufacture was bottles and window glass, but tableware was a standard part of the factory's output, and was usually decorated by enamelling, engraving, or pattern moulding. The market was a colonial society dominated by English taste, and Stiegel-type glass included many elegant objects made in the English style, in addition to large quantities of glassware in German peasant styles. In the absence of evidence of American manufacture these are virtually indistinguishable from European peasant glass but some patterns seem to have originated in the colonies. The diamond-daisy mould is an example. Stiegel's factory was bankrupt in 1774.

John Frederick Amelung, a German emigrant from Bremen, founded his factory at New Bremen, Frederick County, Maryland, in 1784 with the aid of German glass-workers who came with him. His

attempts to achieve a clear, colourless metal, and his interest in wheel-engraving, led him to make some of the most historically important glass of fine quality produced in America before 1800. He was the only American glassmaker of the time who left inscribed and dated examples of his work, and his craftsmanship was superior to that of any contemporary. Though his factory produced utility glass, his table ware, flip-glasses, decanters, and so on, are his most prized wares. Amelung glass is now excessively rare, but signed and dated examples exist in America's principal museum collections. The factory failed in 1796.

Baltimore Glass Works. This glasshouse in Baltimore, Maryland, was founded about 1790. Its workmen comprised craftsmen from Amelung's New Bremen factory and some from Stiegel's workshop. It produced pattern-moulded and engraved wares in the Stiegel tradition, as well as bottles and flasks.

Glassboro Glass Works a glasshouse founded *c.* 1780–1781 at Glassboro, New Jersey, by two former employees of Caspar Wistar. In 1840 it was purchased by the Whitney Bros., when bottles and flasks were its principal production, one of the most popular being a globular bottle with a long neck decorated with a relief portrait of Jenny Lind, which was made in 1850. The factory still continues as the Owens Bottle Company.

After the War of Independence, glass-making in the United States continued to suffer from lack of support, both public and private. Glasshouses in the East closed down and workmen migrated, many to the Midwest, where the economic importance of the liquor trade assured bottle manufacturers of a market, and where transportation difficulties made competition difficult. The growing national fervour which culminated in the War of 1812 brought a short era of prosperity, and encouraged the establishment of many new glasshouses. But with the signing of the Treaty of Ghent a flood of English glass poured into the United States. By 1820 more than half of the American glass companies had failed. The final establishment of the American glass industry on a sound financial basis came only with the development of mechanical production.

South Jersey Glass. During the first slump, in the late 18th century, a number of small glasshouses were established in southern New Jersey by former employees of Caspar Wistar. Pieces were individually blown, of good quality, often bearing a marked resemblance to Wistar specimens, which, especially when workmen migrated to the Midwest, confuses both attribution and date. Some decorative devices, such as the so-called 'lily-pad', had no European prototypes. The colours of South Jersey glass were usually light—aquamarine of a green or yellow tone, and clear sea-greens. Amber and olive tones, and blue (such as deep cobalt), were less common.

Pitkin Glass Works. The first glasshouse to operate in the State of Connecticut, it was established by Captain Richard Pitkin and his two sons in 1783, and produced bottles and flasks of olive-amber and olive-green glass. Very few specimens can be reliably attributed. A ribbed flask, often referred to as the 'Pitkin type', was made later in several widely scattered factories, such as the Keene Glass Works in New Hampshire, and the Coventry Glass Works in Connecticut. Bottle makers at Mantua and Zanesville, Ohio, and elsewhere in the Midwest, turned out examples in brilliant greens, aquamarines, and golden ambers. The original Pitkin Works closed about 1830.

Pittsburgh (Pennsylvania) Glass Works. The first of these was the O'Hara & Craig Pittsburg Glass Works started in 1797, an early cylinder and bottle house. It was the first in the United States to use coal as fuel. Many factories, large and small, opened during the first half of the 19th century, and the Pittsburg area became known for pressed glass of such excellent quality that it was difficult to differentiate from cut-glass.

New Geneva Glass Works. Founded by Albert Gallatin in 1797 in Fayette County, Pennsylvania, it was the first glasshouse west of the Allegheny Mountains. No glassman himself, Gallatin employed a well-trained German family of craftsmen named Kramer. Chief of these was Baltzer Kramer, who had been employed by Stiegel at Mannheim, and by Amelung at New Bremen. Another glassworks across the river at Greensboro was established about 1807 by Christian Kramer. Collectively the output is sometimes called 'Gallatin-Kramer' glass or 'Kramer family' glass.

Glass, American. Pokal (goblet) of clear glass with wheel-engraved decoration and inscription. c. **1784–1791.** J. F. Amelung. The New Bremen (Maryland) Glass-house. *Metropolitan Museum, New York.*

The principal products were window-glass and bottles, but in addition there were pitchers, sugar bowls, flip-glasses, tumblers, goblets, footed bowls and milk-bowls—both free-blown and pattern-moulded—which were made till about 1850.

White Glass Works. This factory, established in 1815 at Zanesville, Ohio, by Isaac van Horne, continued until 1851. They made bottles and flasks, of which those decorated with Masonic emblems and the Eagle are perhaps the best known.

Boston, Mass. Glass Works. There were a number of glass-houses in Boston established in the later years of the 18th century. The Essex Glass Works, started about 1787 by Robert Hewes and Charles Kupfer produced large quantities of window-glass. It became the Boston Glass Manufactory in 1809, and was moved to South Boston in 1811, but here it was unsuccessful, and it closed about 1820. The premises were taken over by the American Flint Glass Works about 1850, under the direction of Patrick Slane, and here all kinds of pressed and cut-glass were produced until about 1870. Several other attempts were made to establish glass-houses in the first half of the 19th century, but none was successful.

Blown Three-Mold Glass. In the early 19th century, fine Irish, English, and American cut-glass was scarce for any but the very wealthy. To meet the insistent demand for less expensive but elegant glass tableware, three-mould models began to be made about 1812. The glass was made at glass-works in different sections of the country in quantity between 1820 and 1830. It has the charm of early glass, the mark of the individual workman, and the irregularities of hand craftsmanship. Blown three-mould glass became outmoded by the advent of pressed glass and mass-production.

CUT-GLASS

Bakewell and Company (1808–1882) of Pittsburgh was the first company to make cut-glass commercially in the United States. The early output at Bakewell included decanters, compotes, pitchers, tumblers, wines, salts, cruets, sweetmeat jars, flasks, candelabra, candlesticks, chandeliers, and lamps.

New England Glass Company. Founded in 1818 at Cambridge, Massachusetts, with a cutting department having 'twenty-four glass cutting mills operated by steam.' Cutting experts were brought over from Ireland, and the decanters, wine glasses, and tumblers made by these workmen can hardly be distinguished from Waterford glass. From 1818–1888, the factory produced cut and engraved wares that in quality, purity and design were unequalled by any in the world.

PRESSED GLASS

The mechanical production of decorative glass in press-moulds was developed in America in the early decades of the 19th century, although moulded glass was being produced in Europe at the turn of the century.

The first record of pressed glass in America is to be found in a patent granted to John Robinson of the

Stourbridge Flint Glass Works at Pittsburgh for 'making pressed-glass door-knobs', and this was followed in the next two or three years by other patents relating to improvements both in moulds and in the method of pressing molten glass into them. The earliest presses were hand-operated, and a steam-operated press was first patented in 1864, to be followed in 1871 by a patent for a revolving block carrying a number of moulds for the mass-production of suitable objects. The latter principle is still in use today for the manufacture of utility glassware on a large scale.

Two principal methods of making pressed glass are distinguishable. The first is the simplest. Molten glass was placed in the mould and a plunger brought down to force it into contact with the mould-walls, and to form the interior. The second, for more elaborate shapes such as vessels with handles, required a mould in several parts, the mould-sections being taken apart to release the object after cooling. In both cases the plunger had to be of a shape which would withdraw from the object when it had been formed and had solidified. In 1865 a new kind of blowpipe was patented by William Gillinder of Philadelphia which enabled an object to be pressed and blown in one operation. This was an adaptation to semi-automatic production of the age-old technique of blowing into a mould. Further patents on the same principle followed during the second half of the 19th century.

The production of press-moulded glassware was large, and the patterns extremely diverse. Most were adapted from techniques already familiar (cutting and engraving), but the forms were often new and the designs governed by the need for ease of pressing. Some new kinds of decoration were devised, such as a basket-weave moulding which could not be produced by traditional means, and some vessels were in forms familiar in 18th century *faïence* and porcelain, such as tureens and covered dishes in the shape of animals and birds. Nor was technical progress elsewhere entirely neglected as a source of inspiration. A covered dish in the form of a railway-car was produced in 1886. As might be expected oil-lamps were made in great variety, the reservoirs often surmounted by female figures. Glass *compotiers* also occur similarly upheld—a design probably based on the work of contemporary porcelain factories. In the second half of the 19th century mould-blown bottles in the form of human and animal figures became popular, and manufacture continued into the early decades of the 20th century. Unlike many kinds of pressed glass, these are usually difficult to trace to a place of origin.

Many new shades and colours were devised by the many pressed-glass factories, including the shading of one colour into another. Much of the best coloured glass came from Hobbs, Brockunier & Co. of Wheeling, Va., while silvered glassware was a speciality of Dithridge & Co. of Martin's Ferry, Ohio.

Nineteenth century press-moulded glassware of American origin is not often seen outside America, and the subject is much too vast to be discussed adequately here. It has been exhaustively treated by Albert Christian Revi (*American Pressed Glass and Figure Bottles*) to which the reader is referred for detailed information.

Pressed glass is very attractive to the small collector, although purists are inclined to date the decline of glass as an art to the abandonment of traditional methods in favour of mass-production techniques. The fact that patterns which were formerly engraved and cut by lapidaries could be so easily imitated is perhaps the reason why many collectors of earlier glass today tend to regard the best blown glass as superior in artistic qualities to engraved specimens. The separation of wheel-cut glass from moulded copies is discussed under *Pressed glass, English.*

Lacy Glass. Pressed glass with a stippled background between the patterns producing an effect not unlike that of old lace. It was manufactured extensively in the United States by the Boston and Sandwich Glass Company (see below) and also by the New England Glass Company, in Pittsburgh, Pennsylvania, West Virginia, New Jersey, in New York at the Brooklyn Flint Glass Works, and in Maryland and the Midwest. More cup-plates and salts with lacy glass designs were made than any other articles. Lacy glass is now a much sought collectors' item.

Sandwich glass. Glass made at Sandwich, Mass., by the Boston and Sandwich Glass Company, established by Deming Jarves in 1825. It closed in 1888. under the pressure of imminent financial collapse and union demands. The principal production was lead glass of fine quality. Pressed glass (see above) was introduced about 1828. Glass of this kind where the patterns were given a stippled background became known as lacy glass. The making of opaline glass (q.v.) began about 1830, and an excellent ruby colour is now much sought. Wheel-engraving, cutting, and etching were also practised as methods of decoration. Often sought in these days are cup-plates from Sandwich. These were in addition to the ordinary cup and saucer of pottery or porcelain, and were employed as cup-stands when tea was poured from the cup into the saucer to cool it, a custom which was prevalent in polite circles in 18th-century England. Cup-plates of pressed glass, either translucent or transparent, were ornamented with a variety of designs. Over 1,000 patterns have been recorded and their popularity among collectors has led to their imitation in modern glass.

The Westmoreland Glass Company of Grapeville, Penn. are said to have some of the original Sandwich moulds which they have used to make reproductions.

HISTORICAL FLASKS

A strong national pride which ran high from 1815–1870 created an enormous demand for this type of flat mould-blown bottle. Known collectively as

American pictorial flasks, they were decorated with a wide variety of subjects—Masonic symbols, national heroes, presidential candidates, visiting dignitaries, such patriotic emblems as the flag and the eagle, and the more mundane aspect of national enthusiasm implicit in 'Success to the Railroad.'

Pictorial glass flasks and bottles are an important American collectors' item. They were blown into two-piece metal moulds which gave a pattern raised in slight relief, and production began about 1808. Thirty years later they formed the staple production of many factories, which were specially built for the purpose, and some have the name of the factory as part of the mould. They were made in almost every available colour, and range in size from a half-pint to a quart. Several hundred different patterns have been recorded. Later bottles of this kind were made from lime glass. Production declined rapidly after 1870.

LATE 19TH CENTURY 'ART' GLASS
Foremost among the types described as 'art' glass is 'Peachblow', which resembles a Chinese porcelain glaze known as 'peach-bloom', and in colour shades from ivory to deep rose-red. 'Peachblow' glass was made by the New England Glass Company and by Hobbs, Brockunier & Company of West Virginia. Specimens are rare. A variation of 'Peachblow' which exhibited a mottled effect on a glossy surface was called *Agata* and was made by the New England Glass Company. Another glass of pale amber shading to ruby was called *Amberina* and made by the New England Glass Company and by the Mount Washington Glass Company.

So-called 'Burmese' glass originated in 1885 at the Mount Washington Glass Company. It was made in a dull or glossy finish, and its colours range from a pale greenish-yellow shading to a delicate pink. The factory, having patented their ware, sold a licence to manufacture to Thomas Webb & Sons of Stourbridge, England, who marketed it under the name of 'Queen's Burmese.' 'Pomona' glass was patented by the New England Glass Company about 1885. It was a clear blown glass with a surface treated by etching, tinting, or staining with a straw colour.

'Hobnail' was originally called 'Opalescent Dewdrop'. It was pressed in full-sized moulds, the tips of the nodules being of opalescent glass in various colours. It was produced about 1886.

'Favrile' glass was a trade name for glass in the *art nouveau* style made by Louis Comfort Tiffany in New York in the 1890s. It was given an iridescent or lustred surface in imitation of long buried ancient glass by spraying it while hot with metallic salts. Its colours were bluish green and gold, a light mother-of-pearl and red and such unusual variations as mazarine, aquamarine, turquoise, and Samian red. Specimens are signed 'L. C. Tiffany-Favrile', 'L.C.T.', 'Louis C. Tiffany', and 'Louis C. Tiffany, Inc., Favrile'. Favrile ('hand wrought') glass was first exhibited in 1893, and was considerably influenced by the work of Emile Gallé (q.v.). Imita-

tions were made by Lôtz Witwe and the Bohemian glassworkers.

PUBLIC COLLECTIONS
The following public collections in America are available for study: The Metropolitan Museum of Art, New York, The Corning Museum of Glass, Corning, N.Y. The Henry Francis du Pont Museum, Winterthur, Delaware.

GLASS, BLUE, ENGLISH
Although coloured glass had been made in England from the beginning of the 18th century, demand for it on a considerable scale only came at mid-century. The predominant colours were then red and green, and blue glass at this time was difficult to make because of the unreliability of available supplies of the necessary pigment, cobalt oxide, which did not yield a sufficiently stable colour, tending to incline to purple. The finest cobalt came from Saxony, where the available supplies went to the Meissen porcelain factory, and it was not until about 1760, when Dresden was captured during the course of the Seven Years' War, that supplies became available for export. From then until 1780 blue glass of exceptional quality was made at Bristol, but from 1780 until 1820 supplies from Saxony became difficult to procure, and the glass of this period has a distinctly purplish tinge. In the 18th century blue glass was made principally at Bristol, but some came also from London and Stourbridge. Imitations of old Bristol blue glass are very common at the present time.

Glass, Blue, English. Finger-bowl of coloured glass decorated with a key fret in gilt. Probably Bristol. c. 1700. *Victoria and Albert Museum.*

GLASS, COLOURED
Coloured glass was made before the colourless variety. The principal colouring oxides are copper, manganese and cobalt, all of which were known to the Egyptians.

Blue glass is made with both cobalt and copper, cobalt blue tending to have a slightly reddish tinge, whereas the copper blues are greenish. A very pure blue results from a combination of the two. Cobalt is a very common pottery colour which is also employed for colouring glazes.

Copper blues incline to be turquoise in colour, but under certain conditions—a high lime content in the glass and by heating in a reducing atmosphere (q.v.) —copper yields a red, which is the basis of the very rare underglaze pottery colour first employed in

Glass, Coloured. Three pieces of ruby glass made by Johann Kunckel of Berlin. The example on the left is decorated with simple wheel-engraving. *Kestner-Museum, Hannover.*

China during the latter part of the 14th century, and again in the early part of the 18th.

Iron is capable of producing blue when the glass is heated in a reducing atmosphere, which is responsible for the bluish cast of some pottery and porcelain glazes. It can also, under certain conditions, yield green, a colour which varies from sea-green to olive, and is the basis of the Chinese and other celadon glazes (q.v.). Green is also obtained from chromium oxide, a colour introduced after 1795. The use of this substance as a colouring agent in glass, or in the preparation of pottery colours (either green or maroon), is therefore subsequent to this date.

Most of the colours yielded by manganese are purples of one shade or another resembling the colour to be obtained by dissolving crystals of permanganate of potash, but in sufficient concentration it can produce a black. In small quantities manganese was formerly employed as a decolorizer —that is, it neutralized unwanted traces of colour arising from impurities, the most frequent of which was iron, in the raw materials used to make glass.

Although a good ruby colour can be obtained from copper under reducing conditions, an especially rich shade of ruby was devised about 1679 by Johann Kunckel, director of a Berlin glass-house under the patronage of the Great Elector. Kunckel employed gold chloride for the purpose, following Andreas Cassius of Leiden who invented the *rose* pigment employed to decorate late 17th-century German enamelled faïence and some contemporary Chinese porcelain termed the *famille rose* (q.v.).

White translucent glass, often called *Milchglas*, was made by adding oxide of tin to the other ingredients. This is indistinguishable from the maiolica and delft glazes on pottery. Glass of this kind was often employed as a porcelain substitute.

Uranium oxide is a modern colouring agent, but it seems to occur naturally in minute quantities in certain glasses of the 18th century and earlier since, under ultra-violet radiation (q.v.), they exhibit a strong orange fluorescence.

Glass. English wine-glasses with opaque twist stems. *Left:* the popular thistle-shaped bowl wheel-engraved with flowers. *Right:* a funnel-shaped bowl engraved with a basket of flowers; folded foot. *Victoria and Albert Museum.*

Glass, Cut. Sweetmeat glass with a cut bowl and a Silesian stem. c. 1735. *Victoria and Albert Museum.*

European lacquer. Bedroom in Brighton Pavilion, Sussex, the furniture decorated with *chinoiseries*. The armchair to the right is carved to simulate bamboo. c. 1815.

Painted and gilded compartmented ceiling at Chiswick
House, W. London, the interior design by William Kent.
The house has now been restored to its original condition,
and the grounds are in course of restoration to Kent's
design.

GLASS, ENAMELLED, GERMAN

The earliest enamelled glass to bear decoration recognizably intended for the German market is Venetian in origin, and goes back to the early decades of the 16th century, but it is very difficult to be sure with specimens of this date whether the glass was made and decorated in Venice, whether the glass is Venetian but painted in Germany, or if both glass and decoration are German. Enamelling certainly went out of fashion in Venice about 1530, and any glasses made subsequently with this kind of decoration were probably to fulfil an export order. From the 16th century onwards it was a German custom to add a date to much of their work both in pottery and glass, and this helps to establish a stylistic sequence by which undated specimens can be placed to an approximate year of manufacture. Care, however, is essential in dating, since tradition was strong in Germany at this time, and late pieces sometimes look deceptively early.

Enamelled glass was made principally in Bohemia, Silesia, Franconia, Thuringia, Saxony, Hesse, Brunswick, and Brandenburg. Bohemia (q.v.) was an especially prolific glass-making area, and a good deal of enamelled glass can be safely attributed to it, not only from the Coats of Arms of Bohemian families, but from peculiarities in decoration and technique generally. But even this cannot be regarded as certain, since Bohemian glassworkers helped to found glassworks in, for instance, the Franconian area of the Fichtelgebirge, presumably influencing these factors there also. Bohemian enamels are apt to be the most brilliant, and ornamental borders include patterns of varied dots and white dashes round the base. Attributions to Franconia are helped by glasses decorated with a mountain on which an ox-head has been superimposed, and this refers to the mountain called the Ochsenkopf in the Fichtelgebirge range. Kreussen (q.v.) is in this area, and here stoneware was painted with enamels of the kind found on glass. The production of enamelled glass in

Thuringia is recorded by 1571, and workshops in Silesia, Hesse, Saxony, and Brandenburg were all in production by the early years of the 16th century. Coats of Arms and similar ways of identifying locality are useful, the Brandenburg eagle being an example.

Perhaps the greater number of surviving glasses are *Humpen* (q.v.)—tall, cylindrical, covered tankards, of which one variety is termed *Wilkommen*, from the inscriptions on them to welcome guests. *Stangengläser*—tall and slender cylindrical glasses (the name means 'pole-glass')—occur with enamelled decoration, and the *Passglas*, a cylindrical glass intended for communal drinking and ringed with glass or enamel threads, was similarly painted.

Decoration is extremely varied. Some of the more important themes are discussed under *Humpen* (q.v.), but family and hunting scenes, commemorative symbols, guild devices, armorial bearings, and allegorical subjects are all to be found, usually dated. Glasses termed the *Halloren*, the enamelling depicting a procession, were made for salt-workers at Halle-an-der-Saale, the earliest recorded being dated 1679. *Hofkellerei* (Court cellar) glasses usually bear Saxon arms, and were presumably made in that region. These are analogous to Meissen porcelain marked *KHC* (*Königliche Hofconditorei*) for Royal Court Confectionery. Portrait glasses are rare, and usually depict Kings and Electors.

During the 18th century taste changed considerably, and the discovery of the art of porcelain-making undoubtedly had its effect on the enamelled glass industry, which turned to the cheaper market. Bottles, small tankards, and beakers, in clear, blue, or *Milchglas* (q.v.), continued to be made, principally in Bohemia, and in the 1750s at Basdorf. *Motifs* of decoration are principally floral, primitive figure-painting, and animals, with some continuation of guild subjects. Basdorf imitated porcelain painting, but without achieving the same quality. Much important enamelling on glass was done by the *Hausmaler* (q.v.).

Reproductions of 16th- and 17th-century enamel glass were made in the second half of the 19th century in Germany. In general, the glass is too green and lacks the bubbles and striations of the earlier specimens. In the case of the *Humpen*, the most frequently copied, the walls of the vessel are too straight, the originals bulging slightly in the middle, and they invariably have a cover, which few old specimens retain. The enamels come very close in shade to the old ones, but they show no sign of wear or flaking, and the glass generally has a newly made appearance, unmistakable to anyone acquainted with the old ones. The decoration itself, especially that of the *Reichsadlerhumpen*, closely resembles the originals.

GLASS, FORGERIES OF

Like most other things of antique value, glass has not escaped the attention of the forger, and this kind of chicanery is rife in the field of old wine-

Glass, Enamelled, German. Beaker painted in enamels by Gottlob Samuel Mohn of Dresden. c. 1812. *Victoria and Albert Museum.*

glasses, among the most popular subjects for the glass-collector.

Enamelled glass from Germany, particularly the *Reichsadlerhumpen* (q.v.), was copied in the early years of the 19th century. The metal shows distinct differences from that of the 17th century, but the enamelling is very close to the original. Enamelled glasses with defective decoration have been restored by partial repainting in cold colour, since it would be impossible to fire fresh enamels on to the surface without damaging those already existing. Forgeries of the rare *Hausmalerei* (q.v.) exist, some on plain glasses of the period.

It is essential, when examining old glass, to be sure that *everything* is right—colour, type of metal, form, decoration, and the small idiosyncrasies inseparable from manufacture at a particular place and time. The colour of glass can be examined against a background of white paper, if possible alongside an attested specimen of similar provenance and date.

Wine-glasses with air-twist, white twist, or coloured twist stems have all been forged, and the twist usually seems to be more deeply embedded than in genuine specimens, where the twist is much nearer to the surface. Threads in forgeries sometimes lack continuity, and are not so symmetrically disposed. In general, the diameter of the foot of an old wine-glass is always greater than that of the bowl, whereas the reverse is the case with most modern glasses. A 17th-century glass is usually lighter in weight than one of the 18th century of comparable size.

Although it is difficult for the forger to imitate the metal of old glass successfully, he does turn old glasses worth a few pounds into something very much more valuable by adding engraved decoration, and caution should be exercised in buying glasses with Jacobite emblems made in England in the middle of the 18th century. Where there are mat areas—the 'frosted', unpolished effect which forms part of the pattern and comes from the removal of the polished surface—these parts should be inspected carefully, for an old glass which has been frequently handled may have patches where contact with the fingers has repolished the surface. But the best way of detecting a fraud of this sort is to put it beside a genuine glass of the same kind and compare the two.

Scratches should always be examined with care. Dust is abrasive, and when it settles in the bowl of a wine-glass, subsequent polishing leaves scratches behind, and these become increasingly multiplied with the passing of time. Scratches under the foot come from moving the glass on a table-top on which there are minute particles of grit. Over a century and a half these become extremely numerous, but they leave behind a well-defined effect, for no two scratches are ever in the same direction. This appearance is difficult to imitate. Forgers do it with emery powder, but the fake scratches are usually too deep, and too many of them run in the same direction, or in a noticeable pattern.

Paperweights (q.v.), such as those made by Bac-

carat, are now being made in Czechoslovakia, America, and even, if one report is accurate, in China. Those from Czechoslovakia are offered for a few pounds to English antique dealers. The decoration is usually fairly coarse and the workmanship inferior to genuine specimens, and this is, perhaps, the best safeguard.

Irish cut-glass has been reproduced in recent times both in Bohemia and America, and in the best specimens the colour has been well imitated, although it is usually, perhaps, a trifle too blue. It is essential to be alert for signs of recutting in specimens with a scalloped border, perhaps to disguise a chip, and in bad cases the scalloping is sometimes ground away altogether and the edge repolished. Honey-jars of cut-glass often have replacement covers, and these do not have the same value as those with the original covers. Occasionally specimens of modern Venetian glass resemble that of the Renaissance period fairly closely, and these could be deceptive to anyone insufficiently acquainted with old ones.

Among the more ambitious forgeries recorded is one of a Verzelini (q.v.) goblet and those of *Zwischengoldgläser* (q.v.). These are especially worth while to the forger, for if they are accepted they will obviously fetch a very high price.

GLASS, FRENCH

Although the art of making stained glass was brought to a high degree of excellence, France did not excel in the making of table and decorative glass until the 19th century. In medieval times simple glasses, analogous to the *waldglas* of Germany, were made in France, and this type was called *verre de fougére*, or fern glass, because fern-ash provided the potash flux. Italian workmen from Altare brought the influence of Italy to France, but only at Nevers did the industry gain any real foothold (see *Figures, Glass, Nevers*).

Mirror-glass was being made in Lorraine in the 14th century, but it was of a primitive kind, and the mirrors of the Galerie des Glaces at Versailles were supplied from Venice. The invention of a process whereby mirror-glass could be cast in sheets on a flat bed (plate-glass) is attributed to Bernard Perrot of Orléans in 1688, and a company was founded by Abraham Thévart in the same year to exploit the invention. This factory, located at Saint-Gobain, in Picardy, became the *Manufacture royale des grandes glaces,* a company which is still the largest manufacturer of mirror-glass in France. Table-glass for much of the 18th century was imported from Bohemia and England, although factories for its manufacture were started in Lorraine as early as 1738. In 1780 the *Manufacture des cristaux de la Reine* was started by Philippe-Charles Lambert to make table-ware of crystal glass, but because of the Revolution beginning in 1789, no considerable progress was made until the early years of the 19th century, although glass of excellent quality produced at an earlier date is sometimes mistaken for

English. Napoleon I encouraged the manufacturing arts, and France soon began to overtake England in the quality and variety of its products, especially in wares based on the technical advances of the Bohemian industry (see *Bohemian Glass*). English manufacturers were invited to start factories in France towards the end of the 18th century, a proposal the more attractive because the glass industry in England was then labouring under the handicap of a vicious tax which had already forced some manufacturers to turn to Ireland. French chemists made several useful discoveries, and machinery was increasingly pressed into service for quantity manufacture. Opaline glass (q.v.) was an early introduction, and before mid-century French manufacturers were rivalling Bohemia in the production of coloured glasses. In 1833 a new type of glass, between crystal and ordinary domestic glass, was introduced at Plaine de Walsch and termed 'Demi-crystal', which bears much the same relationship to crystal as ironstone china does to porcelain. Unlike crystal (q.v.) this is not fluxed with lead oxide. Cased glass, *latticino* (or filigree glass), and *millefiore* (q.v.) were produced as the result of the experiments of Georges Bontemps of Choisy-le-roi, beginning about 1845, and this was followed by agate glass (analogous to the Italian *calcedonio*: see *Venetian Glass*), and the so-called *pâte de riz* (q.v.). Mechanical glass blowing into moulds was an innovation of 1824 by Robinet, and the technique of press-moulding was imported from the U.S.A. (see *Pressed Glass, American*) in the 1820s. This process was employed for the manufacture of bottles, principally wine-bottles, and after 1830 these were made in large numbers and a great variety of forms especially for the makers of liqueurs—historical personages, monks, nuns, buildings, all kinds of subjects, which are now collected. This fashion no doubt inspired the vogue for pictorial flasks in the U.S.A. Many of these bottles were made at Trelon (Nord), a branch of the Baccarat factory (q.v.). Paperweights (q.v.) of fine quality were made from 1845 till about 1851 at Saint-Louis, Baccarat, and Clichy, and there is special demand for those made before 1850. After this date production became inferior in quality and the interest of collectors diminishes. A process for the continuous production of plate-glass was invented about 1854 by Hutter, and in 1873 Baccarat bought the patent of a furnace invented by Siemens for the continuous production of glass. A machine for blowing glass bottles was developed in 1894, making production in large quantities possible. Towards the end of the century Emil Gallé (q.v.) contributed greatly to the birth of *art nouveau* (q.v.), and the 20th-century work of René Lalique (q.v.) is also much sought.

GLASS, NATURE OF

Glass is not, as might be supposed, a true solid. It comes into a category referred to by physicists as super-cooled liquids, which means that it passes from a liquid to a rigid state without any noticeable structural changes. It has been well described as a congealed solution of several substances, of which silica and alkali are invariables. This is true up to a point, but for certain scientific purposes glasses are now made of silica only, and this is fused at the exceedingly high temperature of 1,600° C.

This exception apart, the actual fusion temperature is governed by the amount of alkali present, since it acts as a flux which lowers the melting point of the silica. The usual source of silica is sand, although crushed rock is sometimes employed, and the alkali in old glass was derived from two sources—wood-ash inland and burnt sea-weed near sea-coasts. The first is called potash-glass, because wood-ash contains potassium carbonate which is the fluxing material; the second is termed soda-glass, because the fluxing substance is sodium carbonate. The latter comes especially from the Mediterranean littoral and includes the glass of Syria and Venice. Lead as a flux (first employed in pottery glazes in very early times) was first introduced into ordinary glass by the English maker Ravenscroft (q.v.) in 1676. It was added in the form of red lead.

These three varieties have very different properties. Potash-glass passes very quickly from a liquid to a rigid state as it cools, and it allows little time for manipulation while it is still plastic. Therefore it was more usually cut and engraved. Soda-glass becomes rigid more slowly and remains plastic for a greater length of time, allowing the workman to manipulate it in this state. The differences between the two can be well seen in early Bohemian work, where potash-glass was used, and Venetian glass, which is a soda-glass, since manipulative techniques were very largely practised in Venice. Lead glass was originally intended as a substitute for rock-crystal (q.v.), and because of its superior light-refracting qualities, it was at its best when cut into light-refracting facets (cut-glass, q.v.).

All sands contain impurities of one kind or another, and iron is nearly always present. This discolours glass made with it, giving it a bluish or yellowish tinge, and it is the cause of much of the distinctive colour of some old glasses. The Egyptians discovered that they could neutralize this effect by adding a small amount of manganese, which was normally used as a colouring agent, yielding, in larger quantities, violet, purple, or brown. The Venetians rediscovered this in the 15th century, and were able in this way to produce their 'cristallo' glass. The term 'crystal' for a clear and colourless glass of good quality has been current ever since. Originally it was used to compare it with the much-prized rock-crystal.

Apart from man-made glasses, there are a few naturally occurring glasses, usually of volcanic origin, of which obsidian is the best known.

GLASS PICTURES

The term refers to a technique popular from the last years of the 17th century onwards. The actual process of making fell into several stages. An ordinary print, line engraving or mezzotint, was laid down on a sheet of glass with Venice turpentine or mastic varnish as an adhesive, and it was then rubbed with the fingers while damp in such a way as to remove all but the thinnest layer of paper, just sufficient to carry the engraving, and this was then varnished. At this stage the lines of the engraving were easily perceptible from the back, and this formed the guide for the subsequent painting in colours, usually with varnish as a medium, which was done on the back of the print. The most difficult part of the process was the removal of the surplus paper, which needed great care if it was not to be rubbed into holes. The effect obtained in the best specimens was that of a delicately tinted engraving. Most glass pictures were based on mezzotint, although some made use of line-engraving, and few of aquatint.

The earliest glass pictures go back to the last years of the 17th century, and they are discussed in a book published in 1700 by Dr William Salmon entitled *Polygraphice: or the art of Drawing, Engraving, Limning, Painting, Varnishing, Japanning &c.*

Specimens are extremely variable in quality, and crudely coloured examples are fairly common, many produced in the 19th century. The finest examples were undoubtedly produced in the 18th century, when the exercise of a considerable degree of skill is usually apparent. Forgeries are not uncommon, but most are accused by the glass, which does not have the slight surface irregularity and occasional striations of 18th-century glass, added to which the colouring is generally poor and the execution crude. The smell of new paint is a sign of a recent forgery, or at best of restoration, but most forgeries in these days are old enough for this to have disappeared. Few forgeries are likely to deceive those well acquainted with genuine work.

The range of subject is very wide, but portraits are perhaps the most common, and these include almost all the notabilities of the day. The stage is well represented, some pictures being scenes from plays and others portraits of well-known players. Sporting scenes range from duck-shooting to fox-hunting, and there are portraits of famous racehorses in the tradition of the late 18th century. Purely decorative pictures depict scenes from rural life, allegorical subjects such as the Months, the Seasons, the time of day (morning, afternoon, evening, and night), the Elements (earth, fire, air, and water), the arts and sciences, and many more. These form a very desirable group. The work of all the well-known engravers of the time was employed in this way, and many pictures are after oil-paintings by noted contemporary artists. See also *Mirror and Glass Painting*.

GLASS, PRINCIPLES OF DECORATION

Some ways of decorating glass are also employed for other substances, notably enamelling, which is to be found on pottery, porcelain, and metal.

Those methods more or less confined to glass (and to closely related substances such as rock-crystal) fall into two principal categories, a separation established in Roman times when the two groups were called *vitrearii* (from *vitrearius*, a glass-worker), and *diatretarii* (from *diatreta*, which were vases or drinking-cups engraved, carved, and pierced, made from either glass or hardstones).

The *vitrearius* made vessels by blowing, moulding, or blowing into moulds, and also decorated them with trailed ribbons of glass. He manipulated the form while the vessel was still in a plastic stage, and added handles where required.

Perhaps the best known example of the art of the *diatretarii* may be found in the Portland vase (British Museum), which was copied in the 1870s by John Northwood of Stourbridge in glass, and in jasper stoneware by Wedgwood. A remarkable example of the type known as cage-cups is in the Römisch-Germanisches Museum in Cologne.

The division between the two techniques in glass-working has persisted since Roman days, and it has been strengthened by the properties of the two principal types of glass, soda-glass and potash-glass (see *Glass, Nature of*). Soda-glass remains in a plastic state over a wider temperature range than potash-glass, and it was therefore more easily manipulated. This variety, made principally along the sea-coasts of the Mediterranean and especially at Venice, is noted for the virtuosity displayed in manipulative decoration. Potash-glass, passing from the plastic to the rigid state more quickly, was nevertheless harder and more brilliant than soda-glass, and much more suited to carving and engraving. Glass fluxed with lead ('lead' or 'flint' glass) is also especially suitable for carving, and it is particularly noted for the property of light-refraction. Hence it has often been ground into facets with the property of refracting light, a variety termed 'cut' glass, the facets acting in much the same way as those employed in the finishing of precious stones.

The likeness to the cutting of precious stones is especially close in the cutting of glass pendant drops forming part of the decoration of *chandeliers* and *girandoles* which replaced those originally of rock-crystal.

Especially in the 16th century, glass-engraving and carving was inspired by the much-valued carvings and engravings in rock-crystal (q.v.), and the earliest examples of engraved glass were the work of hard-stone carvers. Caspar Lehmann, who worked in Prague for Rudolf II, was the first since Roman times to employ deep engraving on glass. The art of glass-engraving became increasingly popular during the first half of the 17th century, and after 1650 the industry especially flourished in Bohemia and Silesia, the numerous mountain streams of the area providing ample motive-power for the *Schlief- und Polier mühle*, the polishing and grinding mills, which were necessary for doing work of this kind on a commercial scale.

Bohemia also made cut-glass, but the fashion for this was largely developed by English glass-workers in the early decades of the 18th century following the introduction of lead-glass in 1676 by George Ravenscroft.

The categories referred to still exist today in glass made by hand. The techniques are more closely described under the appropriate headings.

See *Bohemian Glass*; *Cameo Glass*; *Acid Engraving*; *Wheel Engraving*; *Diamond-point Engraving*; *Stippling*; *Sand-blasting*.

GLAZE, CRAZING OF
(French *craqueleure*.) The cracking of a ceramic glaze, nearly always due to a disagreement in the rate of shrinkage of glaze and body during cooling. The Chinese discovered a method of controlling the crazing of porcelain glazes, and employed it decoratively, colouring it a faint brown or black which gives an appearance of a fine network of lines covering the whole surface.

GLAZE, FRENCH USAGE
The terms employed in French to describe ceramic glazes are a little confusing, especially as they are used in older works. *Vernis* (varnish) is generally employed of low-temperature glazes covering common earthenware and fine earthenware (the so-called *faïence-fine*). *Émail* (enamel) is sometimes used of the glazes of common pottery, but it nearly always denotes a tin-enamel glaze (see *Faïence*). *Couverte* is sometimes employed of the high-temperature glaze of porcelain fired at the same time as the body, and of the glaze of some high-fired stonewares. *Émail* also means enamel colours employed for overglaze painting, as well as enamels proper. To be sure of the exact meaning it is often necessary to look carefully at the context.

GLAZING-BARS
The wooden tracery into which glass panes were fitted in the doors of 18th-century cabinets and bookcases; sometimes inaccurately termed Astragals.

GLOBES
Although globes mounted on stands were known exceptionally in 16th-century England, it was not until the 18th century that they became fashionable. They were made in pairs, celestial and terrestial, the most noted 18th-century manufacturer being George Adams. There are rare examples of globes made in unusual materials. One of Rouen faïence by Pierre Chapelle of 1726 is in the Musée des Beaux-Arts, Rouen.

GOBELINS TAPESTRY
The old-established workshops of the Gobelins family formed part of the organization of the *Manufacture royale des meubles de la couronne* (q.v.), and these were removed in 1662 by Colbert and grouped with a number of other looms, notably those of the Louvre, to supply tapestries for Versailles. The enterprise was placed under the direction of Charles Le Brun (q.v.), and it was protected from foreign competition, employing about 250 workmen. It also had the right to take orders from private persons and from abroad. It closed in 1694 as a consequence

of financial difficulties, but reopened in 1699. It was under a number of directors after Le Brun retired in 1683, of whom the most prominent were Robert de Cotte (architect to the King) from 1699 to 1735, Jean-Baptiste Oudry (q.v.), François Boucher, and Jacques Neilson (1761–1788). An example of the work done under Neilson is to be found at Osterley Park (West London) in the form of a room with furniture coverings *en suite*; another is in the Metropolitan Museum (New York).

The earliest Gobelins tapestries were influenced by the paintings of Raphael in their subjects, but an important early series commemorated events in the reign of Louis XIV, of which one depicts his visit to the Gobelins workshops and is now at Versailles. Most of the tapestries of this period are distinctly influenced by either Italian or Flemish sources in their style, but a more purely French style is to be seen after the reopening in 1699, and more direct imitation of painting became the rule under Oudry, even to the inclusion of a semblance of the frame. The attempt at this time to render oil-painting into terms of textile weaving led to the multiplication of colours, and to a considerable increase in the number of dyes, and these had a deleterious effect on design generally, a defect which Neilson strove to overcome.

The tapestries of the Gobelins workshops reflect all the changes in fashion and design of the period, and notable artists and designers provided cartoons. Many during the first half of the 18th century show the interest then being taken in exotic subjects inspired by the Far East and the Americas, the two sometimes being mingled in a manner slightly incongruous.

Tapestries became increasingly unfashionable with the introduction of wallpaper, and they declined in popularity very considerably after 1770. There is always a time-lag to be noticed between the date of tapestry subjects and the actual beginning of a fashion for the subject in question due to the length of time that tapestries took to weave. For this reason we find Boucher subjects still coming from Gobelins in 1770 after they had ceased to be fashionable elsewhere. During the period from 1770 to the Revolution oil-paintings were a popular subject, at the same time as they were also being employed for plaques of Sèvres porcelain.

Like Beauvais and Aubusson, Gobelins made *suites* of tapestries which included wall-hangings, *portières*, and *entre-fenêtres*, which were sometimes accompanied by coverings for seat-furniture woven to the same design, and carpets were sometimes designed for the same purpose, although the tapestry carpet was much more a 19th-century product, and most surviving examples are of this date.

See *Tapestry*.

GOBLET
Strictly a wine-glass, with a cover, holding more than four ounces of liquid (one-fifth of a pint). In practice the term is employed much more loosely to mean any

large wine-glass which has no other specific name. The term is also applied to wine vessels of rock-crystal or of one of the precious metals. (See *Pokal.*)

GODDARD, JOHN
American cabinet-maker of the second half of the 18th century, whose workshops were at Newport (Rhode Island). He is credited with the introduction of the block-front (q.v.). Ogee feet are a fairly common feature of his furniture. He worked with his son-in-law, John Townsend. (See *Furniture, American: The Makers.*)

GODWIN, EDWARD WILLIAM (1833–1886)
English architect and designer of furniture and interior decoration whose work also influenced design in Germany and Austria.

In his designs Godwin was largely unaffected by earlier styles so widely copied at the time, but he did draw inspiration from Japanese furniture then becoming known in the West, and much of his furniture is in what has come to be known as the Anglo-Japanese style. He worked in collaboration with Whistler, and influenced the development of *l'art nouveau* in Glasgow. He can fairly be regarded as one of the precursors of modern furniture design.

GÖGGINGEN (Near Augsburg, Bavaria) FAÏENCE FACTORY
A factory was erected here in 1748 with a privilege, but was transferred to Friedberg. In 1749 Joseph Hackl was appointed modeller, and in 1752 he bought the business. Göggingen faïence is painted in high-temperature colours in quiet tones with floral European as well as Chinese designs. Blue monochrome was used, and some of the diaper patterns on the rims of plates are reminiscent of Rouen (q.v.). Marks are the initials *CB* (Chur-Bayern) (q.v.), with or without a crown indicating the patronage of the Prince-Bishop of Augsburg, and the initials *JH*.

GOLD
A yellow metal, soft, extremely malleable, ductile, and very heavy. Gold was known to man in nugget form from the earliest times. It can be cast, when it shrinks considerably on cooling. It can be chiselled and shaped with metalworking tools. Since it does not tarnish it has often been employed to cover and protect other metals which are subject to this kind of deterioration, a process known as gilding (q.v.). It can be beaten into leaves which are about one two-hundred thousandth of an inch in thickness, and alloyed with mercury it forms a pasty mass known as an amalgam (q.v.). At present its cost is prohibitive for the manufacture of works of art, except for those intended to be employed as an anti-inflation hedge, which usually take the form of medallions.

Gold, being soft, needs to be alloyed with another metal, usually copper, and the proportion of gold to the alloying metal is expressed in carats. Pure gold is 24 carats, and the most usual alloys contain 9, 14, or 22 carats of gold. Gold coins are usually 90 per cent gold and the remainder copper.

GOLD, DUTCH
Gilders' leaves beaten from gilded copper and used, in the 18th century, as a cheap substitute for gold-leaf. German gold was a powdered metal prepared from leaves of Dutch gold in the same way as gold powder was prepared from gold-leaf (page 175).

GOLD, MOSAIC
An 18th-century gold substitute, an alloy of tin, mercury, sulphur, and sal ammoniac which, when calcined, yielded a flaky gold-coloured powder known as *aurum Mosaicum.*

GOLD, SHELL
Gold powder prepared with gum-water for painting on paper. Eighteenth-century water-colours generally were put into mussel-shells, and this practice gave its name to gold made to be used in the same way as water-colour.

GONDOLE, EN (French)
The term refers to the inwardly curving arms of certain armchairs and settees in the Louis XV style, or to the low curving back of the footstool which formed part of the *duchesse* (q.v.). Seat-furniture of this kind is principally to be dated between 1740 and 1770, although the type also occurs up to about ten years later.

GORGE-DE-PIGEON (French)
A type of opaline glass (q.v.).

GOTHA PORCELAIN FACTORY
Situated at Gotha in the Thüringerwald, the factory was founded in 1757 by Wilhelm von Rotberg with the aid of the arcanist, Nikolaus Paul (q.v.). For some years it survived precariously, and almost nothing is known which can reliably be dated before 1763, but by 1767 the buildings were extended and, after 1772, porcelain of a much better quality than hitherto began to be made. By 1780 it was admittedly producing the best porcelain then being made in Thuringia. The work of the larger factories was very freely copied, especially that of Fürstenberg (q.v.), and *biscuit* figures appear after 1770. The rococo style was little used, and most specimens are markedly neo-classical. The factory specialized in small coffee-sets. A painter, Gabel, who was a pupil of Tischbein's, painted landscapes, historical scenes, and flowers; Rüger painted landscapes and flowers; and Frey was responsible for flowers and arabesques. The factory became the property of Prince August von Gotha in 1802, and in 1805 it was removed to the Sieberlehn Allee.

The factory continued to operate during the 19th century, making porcelain of good quality. Morgenroth & Co. of the same town was established in 1866, Fr. Pfeffer in 1892 for the manufacture of faïence and porcelain, and Gebr. Simson in 1883. These are still working today. Gotha is now in East Germany.

Gothic Revival. The first Gothic revival of the middle of the 18th century shows the style at its most fantastic. The engraving shows Walpole's version of it in the staircase at Strawberry Hill (q.v.). *From a guide to the collection printed at Strawberry Hill.*

Gothic Revival. An English porcelain church of about 1830, intended as a pastil burner, which owes its form to the contemporary vogue for revived Gothic.

GOTHIC REVIVAL, THE

Despite the general turning towards classical styles which came with the Renaissance the Gothic tradition in England was never entirely discarded. Christopher Wren disliked Gothic, but he used it occasionally when circumstances demanded, and William Kent, a Palladian, built a Gothic villa. But the most influential revivalist of the Gothic style was Horace Walpole, who began to gothicize his villa at Strawberry Hill (q.v.) in 1750. About the same time we notice the use of the pointed arch in the design of furniture by Chippendale, and Batty Langley (q.v.), who tried to gothicize the Five Orders (q.v.) and invented a style which Walpole called 'Batty Langley Gothic', published his *Gothic Architecture Improved* in 1742.

The fashion in the middle of the 18th century did not last for more than a few years, during which it became confused both with rococo and the vogue for Chinese ornament, and it gave way before the pressures of neo-classicism, but it persisted here and there, mostly in country districts, until towards the end of the century, when it began once more to revive. At this time it became caught up with the Romantic movement (q.v.), and Walpole's 'plaything house' gave way to James Wyatt's Fonthill Abbey, built for William Beckford, which was of cathedral-like proportions. Until about 1820 the Gothic revival was principally confined to houses, but in 1818 the Government granted a million pounds to be spent on church building, and from this date Gothic increasingly became the only conceivable style for ecclesiastical architecture, although many new churches were roundly condemned as being

'pure Batty Langley'. The style received its accolade when it was selected for the new Houses of Parliament, to replace those destroyed by fire in 1834, and by 1835 the widely disseminated designs of Pugin were affecting the design of furniture, metalwork, and even, although not frequently, porcelain. Revived Gothic persisted in one form or another throughout the 19th century, and it had temporary currency in France during the 1830s as the Troubadour style, although it was not taken very seriously. It had greater impact in Germany, but greatest of all in England, where even public lavatories and railway stations were built in the style of 15th-century churches and cathedrals. Nineteenth-century Gothic had some influence on the *art nouveau* style.

See *Gothic Style, The.*

Gothic Revival. The beginning of the 19th-century version of the Gothic revival was marked by a pseudo-grandeur vastly different from Walpole's small house at Strawberry Hill. Of cathedral-like proportions is this interior of the Great Hall of Fonthill Abbey built by James Wyatt for William Beckford. *From Rutter's 'Delineations of Fonthill'.*

Gothic Style. The Tomb of Saint Sebaldus by Peter Visscher and his sons. 1508–1519. Mainly Gothic in style, this tomb also has elements of the new Renaissance style then just reaching Southern Germany. This can especially be seen in the figures. *Nürnberg Old Town, Church of Saint Sebaldus.*

GOTHIC STYLE, THE

The Gothic style in Europe predominated from the later years of the 12th century to the beginning of the Renaissance, when classical styles once more became the rule. The origin of Gothic has always been disputed, but there seems little doubt that it had its origin in Islamic architecture, and probably made its way northwards from Spain, where the pointed arches which are characteristic of the style were being employed in the 9th century by the Moors. Classical architecture made small use of the arch, which was always semi-circular. The principle of post and lintel (column and entablature) meant that the weight of the roof and the pediment imposed direct thrusts acting vertically downwards, transmitted in this way to the foundations. Such thrusts are termed

'dead loads'. Gothic architecture, however, is based primarily on the pointed arch, for which reason it was termed by Pugin the 'pointed Christian style'. The overhead thrusts are transmitted diagonally rather than vertically, and the number of arched windows pierced into walls soon exceeded the capacity of the flanking masonry to support them. The Gothic architect, therefore, devised methods of balancing one thrust with another, often transmitting them across arcades to specially built buttresses which led them to the ground. The Gothic cathedral in particular, therefore, is a building in which the loads are balanced against each other, and these are termed 'live' loads. This, of course, is opposed to the classical principle of 'dead' loads, and the new style was noted for pinnacles and towers, the weight of which was used to balance diagonal thrusts of one kind or another. Classical architecture is made up of horizontal and vertical lines, the greatest accent being on the horizontal. Gothic architecture principally exhibits vertical lines, and gives an impression of soaring.

These two ways of thinking about architecture led to different ways of thinking about the decorative arts generally, and the Renaissance (q.v.) is principally a return to the earlier classical themes of Greece and Rome. Early works such as furniture, in northern countries especially, often show a mixture of Gothic and classical *motifs*, particularly the employment of pointed arches as a carved *motif* in conjunction with others of recognizably classical origin. Works purely in the Gothic style are too early to warrant inclusion here, and the style, which never made much headway in Italy, had almost disappeared there before the end of the 15th century. It lingered until almost 1600 in northern countries such as Germany, France, and England, although with continual modifications towards a more purely classical vocabulary of ornament.

Gothic Style, The. Gothic fan-tracery in Henry VIII's chapel at Hampton Court (Surrey), 16th century. For an 18th-century revival applied to secular purposes see the colour plate of the gallery at Strawberry Hill.

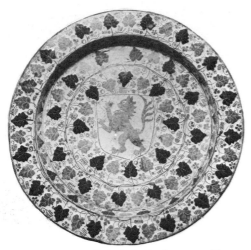

Gothic Style, The. Typical Gothic lion on a Hispano-Moresque dish of the mid-15th century. *Sotheby & Co.*

GOTZKOWSKY PATTERN

A moulded pattern applied especially to plates, and introduced at Meissen in 1744. It has four narrow panels left plain, alternating with four wide panels decorated with moulded flowers which also encroach on the centre of the plate. These were termed *Gotzkowsky erhabene Blumen.* They were copied elsewhere, notably at Chelsea about 1754. See *Ozier Pattern.*

GOURGOURAN (French)

Loosely employed to refer to Indian silks of various kinds, the term was also employed of silks imitating Oriental varieties made in France.

GOUTHIÈRE, PIERRE (1732–1814)

Maître doreur and *ciseleur*; the most celebrated bronzeworker of his day.

Gouthière had moved to Paris before 1758, in which year he married the widow of François Cériset, a *maître doreur* to whom he had been apprenticed. He was first employed by the Court about 1769, working especially for Mme du Barry, whose spending was conspicuous even in an age of magnificence. She is reputed to have spent a million *livres* with Gouthière alone (about £500,000 in today's money). Much of the furnishings and paintings of the Pavillon de Louveciennes were bought with Gouthière's advice. Although he made a great deal of money, Gouthière's expenditure was lavish, and Mme du Barry owed him a large sum of money which he was unable to collect. Perhaps because of this he became bankrupt in 1788, and he eventually died in poverty.

Work which can reliably be attributed to his hand is very rare, and no confirmation exists of a presumed connection between Gouthière and Riesener, or with Weisweiler. The Avignon clock in the Wallace Collection is exceptionally well documented, and the case is signed: *Boizot fils sculpsit et exécuté*

par Gouthière cizeleur et doreur du roy a Paris Quay Pelletier à la Boucle d'or 1771 (model by Boizot the younger, and executed by Gouthière, chiseller and gilder to the King, at the Golden Knocker on the Quay Pelletier, Paris, in 1771).

For this work Gouthière was paid 9,200 *livres* (about £4,600 today), Boizot receiving 1,500 livres for the model and moulds, and the clockmaker, Lunazy, 360 *livres* for the movement.

GRAINING

Trompe l'œil (q.v.) painting on furniture which imitates the colour and figure of a rarer and more costly wood. It was first employed in England during the 16th century.

GRANDFATHER CLOCK

A comparatively recent term for the long-case clock (see *Clocks, Evolution of*).

GRANITE

Granite, a plutonic rock, is a crystalline mixture of quartz and feldspar with, usually, another mineral, such as mica, hornblende, or muscovite. It is extremely hard, and was largely worked with the aid of abrasives. The most usual colours are grey and red, and it is capable of taking a very high polish. In the 18th century granite was used in France for table-tops in place of marble, and for chimney-pieces.

GRANDMOTHER CLOCK

A term of very recent origin employed to describe a rare type of long-case clock, about two-thirds of the normal size, made during the first half of the 18th century. Reproductions are fairly common.

Gouthière, Pierre. The Avignon clock, original model by Boizot, executed by Gouthière in 1771. One of the finest French clocks still in existence. *Wallace Collection.*

Greek Revival. An engraving of c. 1765 satirizing the *neo-grec* phase which marked the beginning of the neo-classical style (q.v.).

GREEK REVIVAL

A *néo-grec* phase marked, about 1760, the opening of the neo-classical style in France, to be seen particularly in the adoption of such ornament as the wave-pattern, often called the Vitruvian scroll (q.v.). In England a Greek revival, started by such men as 'Athenian' Stuart (q.v.) at mid-century, became exceptionally well marked about 1795. It extended into the opening decades of the 19th century, and did not finally yield to revived Gothic until the early 1840s. Regency designers, like Thomas Hope (q.v.), often produced 'Grecian' designs, which are first to be seen in the later work of Sheraton (q.v.).

GREENSBOROUGH (Penn.) GLASS WORKS

This enterprise was established about 1807 by Christian Kramer, who had previously been employed by Amelung (q.v.). Before its closure in 1849 the factory produced some excellent coloured glassware which is sometimes called the 'Kramer family' glass. (See *Glass, American.*)

GRÉGOIRE, GASPARD (1751–1846)

Grégoire devised a method of decorating velvet by painting on the warp before the weft threads were passed through it, which gave a very distinctive appearance to the design.

GREGORIAN CALENDAR

The Julian calendar, based on one introduced by Julius Caesar, was slightly inaccurate in its determination of the length of the year. The Gregorian calendar, introduced in 1582 by Pope Gregory XIII, removed an accumulated error of ten days. This calendar was not adopted in England till 1752, when the error had become eleven days. It was

eliminated by following 2 September by 14 September. Minor discrepancies in dates can sometimes be thus explained. For instance, 10 September 1583 on the Continent would have been 1 September in England.

GRÈS DE FLANDRES See *Rhineland Stoneware*

GRIFFIN (or GRYPHON)

The griffin has the head and wings of the eagle (the beak somewhat longer and more sharply hooked) and the body of a lion. It symbolizes strength, agility, and the destroying power of the gods. It is fairly common in styles founded on classical art, and may sometimes be seen during the currency of the Empire and Regency styles (q.v.).

GRIS TRIANON

A soft grey colour to be found on certain old French chairs, usually in the Louis XV style. The term had its origin in the chairs painted in *blanc de plomb* (lead white) for the Petit Trianon which dust and time turned to grey.

GRISAILLE, EN

Painting in several shades and intensities of grey or stone-colour. Painting *en grisaille* is to be found on porcelain, but the term also refers to *trompe l'œil* (q.v.) wall-painting imitating bas-reliefs in stone, which was especially popular during the early years of the 17th century.

Griffin. A silver griffin from the 'Portuguese Service' presented to the Duke of Wellington by the King of Portugal. It commemorates the battle of Badajoz in 1812. *Apsley House. London.*

GROS DE TOURS (French)

A cloth much used for covering seat-furniture in the 18th century, although it was well known in the second half of the 17th. It was corded, and sometimes embroidered.

GROS POINT

Embroidery stitch. See *Petit Point*.

GROSZBREITENBACH PORCELAIN FACTORY

This Thuringian factory was founded by Major Anton Friedrich Wilhelm Ernst von Hopfgarten in 1777, and it was later sold to Gotthelf Greiner of Limbach, of which it became a branch establishment, remaining in the Greiner family until 1869. It is difficult to distinguish its work from that of Limbach, and both factories used the same mark. Another factory, Bühl & Söhne, was founded here in 1869.

GROTESCHI (Italian)   See *Grotesques*

GROTESQUES

A form of ornament characterized by fantastic shapes based on a combination of human, plant, and animal forms. The origin is Roman, and it became popular after the excavation of Nero's Golden House (buried under the ruins of the Baths of Titus) at the end of the 15th century, where grotesques occurred in the form of frescoes. Raphael adapted them to the decoration of the *loggie* of the Vatican and after publication in engraved form in 1507 they became immensely popular with craftsmen of all kinds, and were especially fashionable as decoration to Italian *maiolica*. They continued with popularity unabated throughout the 17th century, forming part of the designs of Jean Bérain (q.v.), and into the 18th when they were more often termed *arabesques* (q.v.). Grotesques figures were variations on such themes as a winged human figure (male or female), the wings replacing arms, which terminated in acanthus foliage, or perhaps in the hind legs of a satyr-like animal. Masks, which owed more than a little to Roman theatrical masks, were often decorated with foliage,

Grotesques. Dish depicting women bathing in a landscape by Maestro Giorgio at Gubbio (q.v.), dated 1525. The border is decorated with grotesques of the period. *Wallace Collection.*

acanthus (q.v.) sometimes taking the place of the beard. Dolphins were given foliate tails, and are sometimes little more than a head, the remainder being acanthus scrolls. The *maiolica* of Urbino exhibits the characteristic form taken by grotesques during the 16th century, and many of the bronzes of Riccio are based on ornament of this kind.

GROUND COLOURS ON PORCELAIN, See

Fondporcelain

GUARANTEES

Some dealers guarantee the correctness of their invoice description in writing as a matter of course. While this is a sign of their confidence in what they are selling it is strictly unnecessary if the description is reasonably detailed, since if the object is wrongly

Grotesques. Bronze lamp by Riccio (q.v.) in the grotesque style. c. 1520. *Victoria and Albert Museum.*

Grotesques. An Urbino plate of about 1570 showing the later form taken by grotesque ornament. See also *Berain, Jean,* for 17th-century grotesques. *Wallace Collection.*

Gubbio. A lustred plate of about 1530 with a distinctly archaizing decoration. Gubbio. *British Museum.*

described a guarantee adds nothing to the buyer's legal right to recover his money.

A guarantee, however, can be worthless if the invoice description is vague or misleading since it relates to the description, and it might, in the event of legal action, be difficult to link description satisfactorily with the object itself.

GUBBIO

Gubbio belonged at the height of its fame to the Dukes of Urbino. It had been a pottery centre since the Middle Ages. Gubbio's reputation is founded entirely on the work of a master potter, Giorgio Andreoli, an exile from Pavia, who became a citizen of the town. He had been a sculptor and is said to have worked in the manner of the della Robbia (q.v.). He is famous for his use of gold lustre, though it

is not known how he acquired the secret, but he certainly brought it to a high point of perfection and, in addition, developed the ruby-red lustre. It was to Maestro Giorgio that other factories (Castel Durante and Urbino) sent their *maiolica* to be lustred. Gubbio was, however, productive on its own account. It is possible to distinguish between wares made at Gubbio and designed to be lustred, and those made elsewhere in which the lustre was perhaps an afterthought, for in such pieces no parts remained uncoloured for a later application of lustre, nor were the colours designed to harmonize with it, whereas at Gubbio a plate to be lustred was painted over with a thin layer of yellow-ochre and spaces reserved for the lustre. Maestro Giorgio produced works of great delicacy, whereas some of the work of masters from Urbino or Castel Durante gains nothing, artistically speaking, from the addition of the lustre.

Maestro Giorgio was closely influenced by Deruta for the first fifteen years of his period at Gubbio, but the reddish tone of his lustre enables us to distinguish between the two. His early wares are larger, heavily potted, and enamelled only on the upper side. After 1517 they become thin and elegant and are decorated with bold *groteschi* (q.v.) mixed with trophies, festoons, dragons' heads, human masks, dolphins, etc., all reserved on a dark blue ground, and resembling the work of Castel Durante. At Gubbio even quite ordinary pieces are lustred, and many of them must be considered only as coming from Maestro Giorgio's workshop, not from his own hand. After 1530 the wares began to decline. Maestro Giorgio died in 1552.

GUILLOCHE (French)

Neo-classical ornament based on interlacing circles. It varies considerably in degrees of elaboration.

Guilloche. Vase with brilliant blue enamel ground and gilt-bronze mounts, said once to have belonged to Horace Walpole. Sèvres. c. 1766. The gilt bronze base is decorated with guilloche ornament. *Victoria and Albert Museum.*

H

HAAS, GEORGE LEWIS (fl. c. 1780)

A maker of sand-pictures who is especially noted for bright colouring, and for the use of low-relief. He was particularly fond of animal studies. Originally from Germany, Haas worked as a table-decorator to George III, and he decorated a ceiling in the Queen's Lodge, Windsor (demolished 1823), with a sand-picture after Benjamin West.

HACKWOOD, WILLIAM (d. 1839)

Principal modeller to Wedgwood from 1769 to 1832. Apart from his work in preparing and adapting busts and reliefs from antique sculpture for reproduction in jasper and basaltes ware, Hackwood was responsible for a good many of the portrait medallions which were extremely popular at the time, one of which is a portrait of Josiah I himself. Several of these are either signed on the face or initialled without Wedgwood's consent.

HAEMATITE

A black, red, or brown stone very rich in iron which is sometimes used for decorative carvings and inlays.

HAFNER WARE (German)

A *Hafner* is a stove-maker. The principal production of the *Hafner* potters was lead-glazed stove-tiles decorated in a variety of ways. By extension the term is also applied to vessels made by the *Hafner* in similar techniques to those employed for stove-tiles. The tiled stove, usually green glazed, goes back at least to the 14th century, but no stoves and few tiles survive which can be dated to much before 1500. Nürnberg and Lübeck were considerable centres of stove-tile manufacture, and a handsome specimen from Villingen in the Black Forest, signed by Hans Kraut, is in the Victoria and Albert Museum (London). The vessels associated with the *Hafner* potters are usually jugs, for the most part round-bellied, with a short, cylindrical or funnel-shaped neck. Mouldings outline relief decoration, and keep the coloured lead glazes with which they are covered from mingling with each other. These glazes are commonly blue, green, brown, and violet-purple, the two latter colours coming from manganese. The occasional use of tin-enamel (q.v.) is also to be observed in some

instances. The subjects of the ornament are varied; mostly Biblical in a late Gothic style, Coats of Arms, or portraits of rulers and notable personages. The occasional influence of early Renaissance ornament occurs on some, such as the semi-circular arch replacing the Gothic pointed arch. Among the most notable of the potters to be associated with these wares is Paul Preuning of Nürnberg. Related to the *Hafner* wares is a series of dishes from Silesia, ranging in date from about 1550 to 1600, which have the designs incised into the clay before firing, the incisions serving to keep the coloured glazes from running together. The technique is often termed *halb-fayence* (see *Mezza-maiolica*).

HALB-FAYENCE (German) See *Mezza-maiolica*

HALDE, JEAN-BAPTISTE DU (1674–1743)

A Jesuit who collated the letters and reports of French missionaries sent from China. Subsequently he published the *Description Geographique, Historique, &c. de la Chine* which appeared in 1725 and was published in English translation soon afterwards. The work was extremely influential and much

Hafnerware. Wall-cistern decorated with coloured glazes by a Nürnberg *Hafner* potter. Nürnberg. First quarter of the 16th century. *British Museum.*

used towards the middle of the 18th century by manufacturers and craftsmen in search of information about Chinese manufacturing processes. It is referred to by William Cookworthy (q.v.), and Josiah Wedgwood possessed a copy.

HALFPENNY, W. & J.

William Halfpenny, 'Carpenter and Architect', worked during the first half of the 18th century in London, being joined by his son at an unknown date. Together they produced the fantastic *New Designs for Chinese Temples, Triumphal Arches, Garden-seats, &c.*, which was published in 1750/2. This, a work in execrable taste, was hardly taken seriously at the time, but they became among the leaders of what was then known as the 'Chinese taste' in popular circles.

HALL-MARKS

Stamps in the form of punch-marks indicative of the quality of precious metals, and conveying such information as the name of the maker and the date of manufacture. The practice of adding hall-marks to gold and silver is very ancient, and examples of Greek silver with the maker's name go back at least to the 5th century B.C. The Romans stamped gold and silver ingots as a guarantee of the purity of the metal. The use of several stamps, each conveying a specific piece of information, probably began in Byzantium about the same time as it became the capital of the Eastern Roman Empire.

The necessity for a measure of control involving assay to determine the proportion of precious metal to alloying metal became evident in Western Europe towards the end of the 13th century. It was common at this time for the more unscrupulous among the goldsmiths to add excessive quantities of base metal, and the scandal became so notorious that some way of protecting both the public and the honest trades-man had to be found. The method adopted was to require each manufactured object to be taken to an assay hall or office to be assayed and, if found to be of the requisite quality, stamped with a device. This proved so successful in controlling fraudulent alloying of precious metals that by the middle of the 14th century very few European countries were without some organization for marking manufactured objects of gold and silver, although the systems adopted, and the information conveyed by the various punches, differed from one country to another. Records now are nearly always incomplete, and it is not always possible to identify stamps with certainty, or to say precisely what they mean. Usually, however, hall-marks are of great value in establishing date and provenance.

English Hall-marks

The earliest definite legislation in England on the subject of hall-marks dates back to 1300 when the standard for silver was laid down as 925 parts of silver to 75 parts of alloying metals. When tested and found to be of this fineness the object was marked with a crowned leopard's head. This mark later came to be regarded as the London Assay Office mark, the lion passant guardant being substituted as an indication of quality. The crown was omitted from the leopard's head after 1820.

From 1363 a mark denoting the maker was added. At first this was a device, of which a record was kept at the Assay Office, but by the 17th century the use of the initial letters of Christian and surname, either alone or in combination with a device of some kind, had become customary. In 1697 it was laid down by legislation that the first two letters of the maker's surname should be used, and devices alone were discontinued at this time. In 1738, in consequence of a new Act, the maker's mark became the initial letters of Christian and surname once more, and the silversmith was compelled to use a different type of lettering from that formerly employed.

In 1478 the practice of marking with a date-letter, changed yearly, was started, and these have run in twenty-year cycles ever since, from *A* to *U*, omitting *J*. The London date-letter was changed on 29 May.

The lion passant guardant crowned as evidence of the fineness of the metal was first used in 1544, but the crown was omitted after 1550. By this time the customary London marks comprised the leopard's head crowned (the London Assay Office mark), the lion passant guardant (the assay mark), the maker's mark, and the date-letter, but all these were by no means invariably added, and a statute of 1575 apparently released the goldsmith from the obligation of doing more than add his own mark. Some surviving late 16th- and 17th-century silver bears only the maker's mark.

The Wrought Plate Act of 1697 laid down a new and compulsory standard of 959 parts of silver to 41 parts of alloying metal, which was known as the Britannia standard. The lion passant guardant was replaced by a figure of Britannia, which is not to be confused with the figure of Hibernia on Irish silver which was added from 1729 to acknowledge payment of duty imposed on wrought silver. At the same time as the Britannia stamp was added the London leopard's head was changed for a lion's head erased, the leopard's head returning as the assay-office stamp in 1720 when the former sterling standard was restored. The Britannia standard, however, remained optional, and it is still sometimes employed. The similarity of modern marks of this kind to those used in the early years of the 18th century has led to confusion, and to modern work being sold for old.

The Act of 1719 which restored the sterling standard also imposed a duty of 6d an ounce on wrought silver. The addition of the sovereign's head to acknowledge payment of duty took place in 1784, and it was discontinued in 1890, although the sovereign's head has since been added in 1935 for the Jubilee of George V and Queen Mary, and in 1953 for the Coronation of Queen Elizabeth II. The *standing* figure of Britannia (very rarely seen) denoted *repayment* of duty when silver was exported.

For provincial hall-marking the reader is referred to several excellent books of silver-marks listed in the Bibliography. Among the earliest Assay Offices were Chester, Bristol, and Norwich, and the latest were Sheffield and Birmingham, established in 1773. There were also several minor offices, the mark of which is seldom seen, such as King's Lynn. A number of provincial offices used the London leopard's head as a sterling mark, and the lion's head erased as a mark of the Britannia standard.

French Hall-marks

A system of hall-marking was introduced into France early in the 14th century, although a Paris mark existed by 1300, as may be seen from the inventory of the English Edward VI, which refers to spoons marked with a *fleur-de-lys*, stating that this was the Paris mark. Hall-marking as a legal requirement dates from 1313 with an order from Philip the Fair that gold should be tested for purity and stamped accordingly in Paris. Soon afterwards this was extended to other provincial centres. By the end of the century 186 French cities had been empowered to test and mark gold and silver.

The exact meaning of the marks employed is not always certain, but a system of date-lettering was in use which is not especially reliable. The maker's mark surmounted by the *fleur-de-lys*, and the assay mark impressed by the Guild, were the earliest. Date-lettering came later, and the letter was changed each year with the appointment of the new Guild-master (*garde de métier*). From 1789 to 1797 no stamps were added at all, and in the latter year the old standards were re-established and new punches introduced.

Eighteenth-century gold and silver usually bear the mark of the *fermier* (a man who bought the right to levy duty on plate). At first the goldsmith brought his work to the Maison Commune for the Guild stamp to be added, and he then paid duty to the *fermier*, who added his mark in discharge of this obligation. Later the system was changed and at a certain stage in the manufacture the *fermier* stamped the work with a *charge* mark, entering it in his records, adding the *discharge* mark when the work was completed and the duty paid. In 1765 all articles of silver-gilt were required to be stamped *Argent* (silver), and the discharge mark stamped over the letter *A*.

HAMADAN RUGS AND CARPETS

Hamadan itself is a Persian marketing centre for rugs woven in the surrounding district. The Ghiordes knot is used, and there are several borders, the outside one usually being of camel-hair. Natural, undyed camel-hair is frequently employed, in conjunction with green, pink, blue, and red. Since the 1880s aniline dyes have been increasingly used. The pole-medallion (a medallion with a projection at either end) is very common, together with floral designs. Hamadans are usually coarsely woven, and 'runners' of varying lengths and widths are a fairly common production.

Hamburg. **Characteristic Hamburg faïence ewer decorated with Coat of Arms.** *British Museum.*

HAMBURG (Germany) FAÏENCE

No documentary evidence exists as to the origin of the wares which have been grouped together under this heading either because they were found in or near the city of Hamburg, or because they bear other distinguishing marks—the arms of the city, or of private citizens, for instance. However, the later faïence stoves of Hamburg clearly continue a local technical and artistic skill, which argues the existence of an organized system of production during the period of the earlier wares, the latest of which is dated 1656. Among these jugs predominate, and are of characteristic shape. Like a rather squat pear they have a wide foot and a short neck, usually with a pewter lid. The body is yellowish, with a well-fused, thinly applied glaze, and the painting a bright blue with occasional touches of yellow, green, and brownish-red. Nearly all have a reserved panel, or a shield of arms and a decoration of flowers, leaves, and branches. The faïence of Hamburg in the 17th century, although influenced by Oriental designs, seems to have been an isolated development, perhaps induced by the sturdy independence of the great Hanseatic city. About fifty years later Hamburg began to make stoves tiled in faïence, painted in blue with all manner of designs composed in a rich baroque or rococo style—Biblical subjects, land- and seascapes, and views of the city. There was much fine painting which can be safely attributed to individual painters. After about 1750 stoves painted in this way gradually went out of fashion, and plain neo-classical styles supervened.

HAMILTON, SIR WILLIAM (1730–1803)

Grandson of the third Duke of Hamilton; Knight of the Bath, 1772; Ambassador to the Court of Naples,

1764–1800; husband of Lord Nelson's mistress, Emma Hamilton. Sir William took an active part in the excavations then being carried on at the newly discovered Herculaneum and Pompeii, and his collection of Greek and Roman antiquities, especially vases, was published in 1766/7 by d'Hancarville (q.v.) as *Antiquités étrusques, grecques, et romaines*, a work which was very influential, since it was consulted by manufacturers such as Wedgwood and Boulton, and by contemporary designers generally. Hamilton's influence on Wedgwood was especially strong, and a number of letters written by the latter to Sir William are preserved at Barlaston. Many Wedgwood designs were inspired by published drawings of Hamilton's collection of vases—a collection which later passed to the British Museum. The publication of Hamilton's collection did much to popularize the neo-classical style (q.v.). Hamilton purchased the Barberini vase in Italy and sold it to the Duchess of Portland. This later became the 'Portland' vase (now in the British Museum) and is discussed under that heading.

HAMMONTON GLASS WORKS (New Jersey)
This factory, which specialized in bottles and flasks, started operations about 1820 and closed about 1858. Their flasks are excellent in design and often aquamarine in colour.

Hanap. The Great Seal of Ireland silver cup of 1592. *Christie, Manson & Woods.*

Hanau. Enghalskrug (narrow-necked jug) painted with the arms of the Counts of Hanau. Hanau. Behagel's factory. End of the 17th century.

HANAP
A large standing cup and cover of silver important as an accessory of the dining-table in the 16th and early 17th centuries. The hanap was sometimes an ostrich egg or coconut shell, then both exotic rarities, mounted in silver.

HANAU (Germany) FAÏENCE FACTORY
After Hamburg, Hanau is the oldest faïence factory in Germany. Essentially Dutch in its beginnings, the town of Hanau had a settled Dutch community which had grown steadily from mid-16th century, and Daniel Behagel founded the factory in 1661. In conjunction with his son-in-law, Jacobus von der Walle, he applied for a concession to start a factory in Frankfurt. When they did not immediately receive a favourable reply they turned their attention to Hanau. Permission was granted and the factory was soon established, but in 1679 the original concession expired and the enterprise fell into the hands of the manager, Johannes Bally. He died in 1688 and it passed to his widow, but in 1693 reverted to Daniel Behagel, one of its founders, in company with the widow of Van der Walle. After repeated changes of ownership it belonged in 1726 to Heinrich van Alphan, between 1740 and 1745 to his son, Hieronymus, and later (after 1787) to a company, Martin, Dangers & Co., with a privilege of twenty years. After only seven years it changed hands yet again, and was owned by Daniel Toussaint, who sold it to the last owner in 1797, Jacob Achilles Leisler, who kept it going till 1806 when it seems finally to have succumbed. Hanau wares show a bewildering

similarity to those of other places, particularly Frankfurt.

First period (1661–1700). At this time Dutch styles were dominant—blue monochrome painting, outlined with blue, not black, and lacking *kwaart* (q.v.). Typical shapes, which are also found at Frankfurt, are the *Enghalskrug* (q.v.), a long-necked jug with a slight lip, oviform body and broad foot, often mounted in pewter, and a second form of jug with a spirally fluted body, horizontally reeded neck, and a plaited handle. Plates are often concave with radial ribbing. Decoration on the *Enghalskrüge* is generally a shield of arms on the plain models, while the spiral jugs have scattered flowers with sets of interspersed dots, or birds, both very typical of Hanau.

Second period (1700–1740). by this date long-necked jugs and the spiral jugs were an established speciality. This whole family was made to the day the factory closed. Decoration changed, the groups of dots becoming closer together, sprigs of flowers smaller, and the birds more numerous. Another *motif* from the first period had been a large and irregular bouquet of Chinese flowers. This now became asymmetrical, formal, and stiff. Chinese figure subjects were Europeanized in the 18th century. Lobed plates with a small landscape, and fruit or flowers in the centre, had a radial design to the rim. Colouring is blue and white or a combination of the four principal high-temperature colours, while the glaze is rather grey, greenish, or bluish.

Third period (Hieronymus von Alphen). The flower decoration becomes symmetrical and stylized, accompanied by 'German' flowers (see *Deutsche Blumen*) and rather poor experiments with enamel colours. Jugs are usually unglazed on the base. The only mark to be generally recognized is an incised crescent shape, and it has been observed on many jugs. Other marks are almost legion.

D'HANCARVILLE, BARON

Pierre Germain Hugues was a French adventurer who assumed the title of Baron d'Hancarville. He was associated with Sir William Hamilton (q.v.) in the publication of the latter's collection of Greek and Roman vases, and later published a highly inaccurate work entitled *Recherches sur l'origine, l'esprit, et les progrès des arts de la Grèce* (1785).

HANDS

Models of hands in a variety of materials were popular in Victorian England. Perhaps the most common, and the best, are those in Parian porcelain made by Copeland, Minton, and others, but specimens in carved wood, cast-iron (from the Carron Ironworks, Stirling), alabaster, marble, slag glass, and brass have all been noted. They are to be found holding a small vase as paperweights, as ring-holders (the fingers outspread), clenched as door-knockers (common in France), and adapted to many other uses. The writer has observed a pair of hands in the form of pottery gin-flasks which were taken from moulds cast from life.

The origin of the fashion is obscure, but it has been suggested that it was influenced by the cult of spiritualism, then just attracting public curiosity, in which the 'materialization' of spirit hands played a part.

HARBOUR SCENES

A type of porcelain decoration introduced at Meissen about 1724 and popular through the 1730s. The best known are depictions of exotic port scenes in which Oriental figures (Turks and Chinese) mingle with European merchants on a quayside surrounded by bales of merchandise (sometimes with marks which may be significant), and with ships and lifting spars in the background. Obviously most are intended to represent Venice, which was the principal European entrepôt of the Oriental trade. They were frequently derived from Augsburg engravings of Italian ports (Venice and Genoa) by Melchior Kysell after Johann Wilhelm Baur. A Meissen service depicting Dutch ports and harbours was painted by Johann Balthasar Borrman (1725–1784), subsequently at Berlin, for the Stadtholder of Holland about 1763. Very rarely Italian harbour scenes were copied elsewhere, notably at Chelsea soon after 1750, and one such example in the Katz Collection bears initials on a bale apparently denoting the painter, William Duvivier, together with the date 1751. Christian Friedrich Herold (q.v.) painted harbour scenes, according to Marcolini, and this record also suggests, without being definite on the point, that they were also painted by Johann Gregor Höroldt, but no specimens have been attributed.

HARDNESS OF MATERIALS

It is sometimes necessary to find the exact nature of certain substances, particularly hardstones, which are used in the making of works of art. Materials vary very much in hardness (their resistance to being scratched) and a harder substance will always scratch one which is softer. A table of relative hardness of the commoner substances was constructed by the Austrian chemist Mohs, and this is given below. Substances, listed in numerical order, will always be scratched by one of a higher number. For instance, jade, which is often confused with steatite or serpentine, will scratch glass, but both steatite and serpentine will be scratched by glass. Both the latter substances when drawn across the surface of glass will leave a narrow line which can be rubbed off with the finger, and this should not be confused with a scratch. A steel knife-blade which has not been especially hardened will have a hardness ratio of about 5.

1.	Steatite, soaprock, talc.
2.	Gypsum
2·5.	Amber.
3.	Alabaster.
4.	Serpentine.
5.	Coral, soft porcelain.

5·5. Glass, lapis lazuli, obsidian.
6. Haematite, turquoise, opal feldspar, hard porcelain.
7. Agate, amethyst, flint, rock-crystal, jade (nephrite and jadeite), chalcedony, cornelian.
7·5. Beryl, emerald, tourmaline, zircon.
8. Topaz, spinel, chrysoberyl.
9. Sapphire, ruby, emery (carborundum).
10. Diamond.

In making this test select a part where a minute scratch will not matter. Only slight pressure is needed, and if the substance used to do the scratching is felt to 'bite' nothing more is required, but tests on either side of the estimated number may be necessary to establish its nature with certainty. Usually the physical appearance of a substance will be sufficient to suggest its identity, and the test is only needed for confirmatory purposes.

The test for hardness can also be applied to metals. Resistance to scratching is measured by the depth of a scratch made by a diamond-point to which a fixed weight is applied. A list of the relative hardness of metals most commonly employed in the decorative arts is appended:

1. Lead.
2. Pewter.
3. Tin.
4. Aluminium.
5. Gold.
6. Silver.
7. Zinc.
8. Copper.
9. Nickel.
10. Platinum.
11. Iron.
12. Steel (about 5 on Mohs' scale).

HÄUER, BONAVENTURA GOTTLIEB (1710–?)

Porcelain painter at Meissen from 1724. According to the factory-list he was painting figures and landscapes of good quality in 1731. His work is not unlike that of Heintze and Herold (q.v.), and it is difficult to separate them. A service bearing the initials *BGH* was sold in London in the 1960s.

HAUSMALEREI (German)

The word means, literally, 'home painting', and the *Hausmaler* were men who obtained white wares from the factories and painted them at home. The practice began in the 17th century with the decoration of glass and faïence in Germany, and the earliest of the *Hausmaler* were glass-painters skilled in the use of enamel colours. The faïence factories themselves used high-temperature colours applied before firing, and fired in one operation with the glaze. They supplied glazed wares without decoration to the *Hausmaler*, and probably much *Hausmalerei* at first was specially commissioned; at least, this much seems probably from the occurrence of Coats of

Hausmalerei. Faïence dish enamelled with fruit and flowers and a central panel of figures by an unknown *Hausmaler.* Late 17th century. The dish is a silver pattern, and the border decoration reminiscent of 17th-century *repoussé* decoration. Nürnberg faïence.

Arms. The *Hausmaler* sometimes signed their work, either in the decoration itself, or just below a handle where present. One of the first of them, Johann Schaper who died in 1670, worked in *Schwarzlot* (q.v.) on faïence. He was a Nürnberger who had been a stained-glass worker, and his painting features detail scratched in with a needle-point in the manner of the stained-glass painter. He it was who introduced, in faïence painting, the addition of touches of iron-red and gilding to the *Schwarzlot* colour-scheme, already in use in glass-painting. Perhaps a pupil, John Ludwig Faber, painted landscapes and flowers in *Schwarzlot*. Two dated examples of his work exist, one of 1683 and the other of 1689. Hermann Benckert of Nürnberg painted on both glass and faïence, an octagonal glass bottle attributed to him being in the Victoria and Albert Museum (London). Translucent enamels were probably introduced by Faber, but Abraham Helmhack (1645–1724) made more extensive use of them, and a lantern-slide painted by him is in the Victoria & Albert Museum. Helmhack was also a faïence painter who was

Hausmalerei. Porcelain bowl enamelled by J. F. Metzsch of Bayreuth. c. 1750. The border framing the painting is characteristic of some of the work of this *Hausmaler.*

200

Hausmalerei. Cup and saucer of Meissen porcelain amusingly painted with figures within a border of baroque ornament. c. 1720. The style is uncharacteristic of factory decoration of the period and is probably the work of a Dresden or Augsburg *Hausmaler. British Museum.*

probably the first to employ a polychrome enamel palette. Two signed pieces are known, but a good many others survive which are initialled, but without dates. He painted mythological, Biblical, and pastoral scenes, usually on white faïence from Frankfurt. Helmhack and Rössler were among the first to use the newly invented purple of Cassius devised by Andreas Cassius of Leyden, and later to become the *rose* enamel of China (q.v.). Many examples of *Hausmalerei* on faïence are signed only with initials, some of which can be identified. *IH* is Johann Heel and *MS* is probably Mathias Schmidt. *BS, IBF, HBF, IMG,* and *W* are, so far, unidentified.

After the introduction of porcelain at Meissen the *Hausmaler* turned their attention to a more promising material. In the first years of the factory's life they caused a certain amount of trouble by painting porcelain in lacquer colours, because these speedily wore off, and hardly any specimens now survive, but they must have been a very different kind of home painter from men like Schaper, Faber, and so on. The earliest *Hausmaler* of note whose work has survived to be identified on porcelain is Johann Aufenwerth of Augsburg, who, assisted by his daughter, Sabina, was working before 1720. Typical of his style are figures in a landscape painted in iron-red and lilac with a framing of baroque scrollwork. This he did very commonly, principally on tea and coffee ware. He used *Schwarzlot* occasionally, but examples are rare. Perhaps the earliest *chinoiseries* in gold silhouette, probably by him, are to be dated back to 1715, although this date is that of the porcelain on which they were executed, and the decoration could possibly be later.

Slightly later is Bartolomäus Seuter, also of Augsburg, some of whose work is on Meissen porcelain made before 1720 which was sold by the factory in 1730. Some of Seuter's painting is of Watteauesque subjects in *Schwarzlot* with touches of iron-red. He also did *chinoiseries* in gilt silhouette (see also *Porcelain, German, Forgeries of*). and he may have added gilding to the rare early Meissen examples of underglaze blue decoration.

The work of Ignaz Bottengruber of Breslau is to be found both on the porcelain of Meissen and Vienna. Most of his work falls between 1720 and

1736, and artistically he is probably the most important of all the *Hausmaler.* He commonly used a purple monochrome, but occasionally a more extended palette, and he specialized in battle and hunting scenes, as well as mythological subjects. Signed and dated pieces exist.

Daniel and Ignaz Preussler (father and son) were Bohemian decorators whose work is to be found on glass, and on European and Chinese porcelain. Ignaz worked between 1720 and 1730. Daniel worked only in *Schwarzlot*; his son also used a polychrome palette and a purple monochrome. Another Bohemian decorator, Franz Ferdinand Mayer of Pressnitz, worked between 1745 and 1770. He was extremely versatile, doing landscapes, mythological scenes, figure-subjects, and so forth. A good deal of his work survives, most of it on Meissen porcelain. Little is known about J. F. Ferner, working about 1750, and much of his work is no more than the over-gilding of defective blue-and-white Meissen porcelain. Some fairly crude pastoral scenes on cups and saucers are also regarded as by his hand.

A good deal of excellent work of this kind was done by Johann Friedrich Metzch of Bayreuth, both on faïence and on porcelain from Meissen and China. He had probably been employed at Fürstenberg (q.v.). Landscapes, figure-painting, and *chinoiseries* have been attributed to him. Probably working in his studio was Joseph Philipp Dannhofer of Vienna.

Several Meissen painters were accused of painting at home, among them C. F. Herold and J. G. Heintze, the latter suffering a term of imprisonment in 1749 for this offence.

Defective pieces sold during the years after the Seven Years' War ended, from 1763 onwards, which were scored across the mark, often fell into the hands of some of the later *Hausmaler* whose names have not been recorded, and the quality of the painting is variable.

Little is known about Dutch decorating studios which, at the beginning of the 18th century, were painting Oriental porcelain, especially Japanese, which had been sent to Europe in white. This ranges from the simple lettering of condiment bottles to quite elaborate painting. A good deal of their work

Headboard. Headboard of a bed designed by Robert Adam and now in Osterley Park. The original drawing is in the Soane Museum, Lincoln's Inn, London.

was inspired by the Far East, subjects from Kakiemon or the Chinese *famille rose*, and occasionally landscapes and Italian Comedy scenes. All these are rare. Much more common are specimens of Chinese blue-and-white porcelain overpainted with flowers in colours and gilding—work sometimes termed 'clobbering'.

Although *Hausmalerei* was largely confined to Germany and Bohemia, decorating establishments also existed in England, the most notable of which was owned by James Giles at Clerkenwell, London, who for some years did most of the more elaborate decorations on Worcester porcelain, as well as painting some examples of Chelsea and even Chinese porcelain. He is elsewhere discussed (see *Giles, James*). The equivalent term to *Hausmaler* in Vienna was *Winckelmann*, and in France, where the practice was uncommon, *chambrelan*.

HEADBOARD

(French *chevet*.) The panelled head of a bedstead, usually supported on either side by posts which were, in appropriate cases, extended to carry the tester (or canopy) at the back.

HEINTZE, JOHANN GEORG

Porcelain-painter at Meissen from 1712 to 1749.

Heintze painted both harbour scenes and landscapes. In the case of the latter, milestones bearing a date or the distance from Dresden are probably his, and a cup and saucer have been recorded with JGH on an inn sign. He was relatively prolific, and was imprisoned in 1749 for painting as a *Hausmaler*, after which he left Meissen and was later at Berlin and Vienna. His work is sometimes confused with that of C. F. Herold (q.v.).

HENRI DEUX WARE See *Saint-Porchaire, Faïence of*

HEPPLEWHITE, GEORGE (d. 1796)

Little is known of Hepplewhite's life. He was first apprenticed to Gillow of Lancaster, a family of carpenters and cabinet-makers who established themselves in London about 1760. Hepplewhite's book of designs, *The Cabinet-maker and Upholsterer's Guide*, was published posthumously in 1788 by his widow, Alice, who continued the business under the style of A. Hepplewhite & Co. Further editions were published in 1789 and 1794. Many contributions to the vocabulary of furniture ornament were made by Hepplewhite. Chairs with shield- and heart-shaped backs are carved with wheat-ears, honeysuckle (anthemion), swags of drapery, and Prince of Wales's feathers. Hepplewhite was somewhat less indebted to the French than Sheraton, but nevertheless adapted a number of French designs, one of which was the *duchesse* or *bergère*, which, in England, was given vaguely phonetic spelling of 'Barjier'. Hepplewhite made greater use of mahogany than Sheraton, who was much attracted to satinwood. A great deal of the furniture in his style is carved. He made some quite elaborate mechanical furniture (see *Ébéniste-mécanicien*), and specialized in settees, both upholstered and with a splat back, the latter being of the two, three, or four chair-backed type. Some of Hepplewhite's furniture may be regarded as transitional between the rococo of Chippendale and the neo-classical of Adam, and Hepplewhite occasionally used the French cabriole leg for early settees or for pier-tables. Like Chippendale, his designs include those for ornamental chests of drawers which were, at the time, termed *commodes* (q.v.).

Heintze, J. G. Cup and saucer painted by J. G. Heintze with river scenes and landscapes. Meissen. 1743. The monument is thus inscribed. *British Museum.*

HERAT RUGS AND CARPETS
This one-time capital of Afghanistan was, until the middle of the 18th century, the centre of a very large carpet industry. The Herat carpet of commerce is made by Persian weavers in the province of Khorassan. The Ghiordes knot is generally used, and the border has from three to seven stripes. Medallion centres are not common. The pear pattern is fairly general, and the Herati design (which originated in Herat), a rosette between two lanceolate leaves, is almost invariable. There is a general resemblance to Khorassan rugs and carpets from elsewhere in the province, and especially to those of Feraghan.

HERAZ CARPETS
Name given to carpets from an area south-east of Tabriz. They were made in villages in this district, commonly with the Sehna knot, and some are very large. There is usually a central medallion, and modern productions are noted for the angularity of the ornament. The weave is coarse, but quality is good and the pile hard-wearing. The classification includes rugs made at Bakhshis, Gorevan, and Serapi. See *Rugs, Knotting of*.

HERCULANEUM (LIVERPOOL) POTTERY
This factory was started in 1794 by Richard Abbey, formerly an engraver in the employ of Sadler & Green (q.v.). It was taken over in 1796 by Worthington, Humble and Holland with the aid of workmen from Staffordshire, when it first became known as Herculaneum. Most of the wares being produced in Staffordshire at the time were made here—creamware, basaltes, lustred earthenware, and terracotta. After 1800 there was a limited production of porcelain. The factory flourished especially between 1806 and 1833, and it closed finally in 1841.

The most frequent survival is creamware, blue painted, transfer-printed, and very occasionally in polychrome. Creamware painted with blue *chinoiseries* in a summary manner is especially common. Jugs of creamware transfer-printed in black, and sometimes slightly coloured over the print with enamels, are the most sought, especially those with named ships forming part of the decoration.

Much of the early production was unmarked, but *Herculaneum* impressed and printed is found on some early wares. Later wares (after 1822) are marked *Herculaneum pottery*. The Liver bird is a late mark (after 1833).

Generally, Herculaneum wares are imitations of those of Staffordshire, and creamware owes a good deal to that of Wegwood (q.v.).

HEREKE CARPETS
A factory here was owned by the last Turkish Sultan, Abd-ul Hamid II. The designs were based either on 18th-century carpets from the Savonnerie (q.v.) or from those of Persia. The pile was often clipped to produce a relief effect. A few carpets were produced which are literally enormous, perhaps the largest being woven for the Yildiz Kiosk, Istanbul.

HEROLD, CHRISTIAN FRIEDRICH (1700–1779)
Porcelain-painter at Meissen from 1725 to 1777; probably a cousin of J. G. Höroldt (q.v.). The subjects most reliably associated with C. F. Herold are harbour scenes and landscapes. He worked as a painter of enamel on copper for Alex Fromery of Berlin (some specimens are signed 'Herold fecit'), and was in trouble with the factory management for working independently as a *Hausmaler* (q.v.). There is a signed cup and saucer dated 1750 in the British Museum which may be *Hausmalerei*. It is not safe to take the letter *H* in gold appearing on some Meissen wares as his signature.

HERREBØE (Norway) FAÏENCE FACTORY
In 1758 a faïence factory was established at Herrebøe by Peter Hofnagel, and although several others were started only the products of this factory are known. The wares are of considerable interest, displaying an independence of style unusual in the northern factories. By 1760 the factory was fully productive, and the man probably responsible was a painter from Berlin called H. C. F. Hosenfeller, who arrived about that time. The marks used combine the monogram *HB* with the initials of workers, but they are more than a little uncertain and can be discounted, as the wares themselves are recognizable without them. The style remained rococo throughout the twelve years of the factory's life, starting in a rather restrained manner which was soon discarded in favour of a bold and vigorous style.

The body is a lightly fired, fine-grained, buff, rather porous clay, while the glaze is either a cool bluish-white or ivory in tone. It has a tendency to craze, and has somewhat the appearance of thick white oil-paint. It lies unevenly, and the body shows a reddish tone through it. Blue and manganese high-temperature pigments are the only colours used at Herrebøe, and they are never combined. The painting is generally done with a full brush, while shapes are accented in a linear, graphic style. The effect is daring, lively, and vigorous compared with similar styles from Germany.

Herrebøe leant towards plastic decoration, with many spirals and twists to break the smooth line. A famous centrepiece in the Kunstindustriemuseum in Christiania is a fine example of the style. A fat, smiling *putto* wreathed in flowers stands amidst shells and delicate pots arranged, as it were haphazard, amid writhing coils. This was probably one of the most ambitious products of the factory, but many cisterns and tureens are also known. 'Bishop' bowls (q.v.) were made here. Designs include Chinese landscapes, figures, European landscapes, animals, naturalistic flowers and Biblical scenes. Unfortunately the factory could not be made to pay and after repeated attempts to revitalize it it closed in 1772.

High-temperature Colours. The high-temperature palette which decorated faience was more colourful than that of porcelain. This dish, part of a service made at Urbino for P. Pucci, is painted with Aeneas slaying the deer. 1532. *Christie, Manson & Woods.*

HIGHBOY
An American term for the English tallboy (q.v.).

HIGH-TEMPERATURE COLOURS
The term is usually employed of those colours used in the manufacture of faience which were painted on the raw glaze before firing, and fixed during the same firing as the one which fused the glaze. By this means a piece could be glazed and decorated in one operation, but difficulties were experienced in other directions, notably erasures were impossible, and painting had, therefore, to be in a broad and simple style. Very accomplished painters, such as those decorating the best of Italian *maiolica*, were capable of doing fairly detailed work in these colours, but this is exceptional.

The high-temperature colours are relatively few, and are metallic oxides of one kind or another. The most useful is cobalt-blue, which was also employed to decorate porcelain before the glaze was applied forming the class known as underglaze blue. This was the only underglaze pigment in use for porcelain decoration in 18th-century Europe, if we exclude a few exceptional specimens where manganese-purple was employed for this purpose. The Chinese

High-temperature Colours. Underglaze blue is the principal high-temperature colour employed on old porcelain, and Meissen experienced great difficulty with it at first. This ice-pail of about 1735, decorated with *indianische Blumen* (q.v.), belongs to a period when this colour had been mastered.

used both cobalt-blue and copper-red underglaze during the 18th century, usually by themselves. In the comparatively rare instances where the two were used together either the cobalt-blue or the copper-red failed to develop properly, since the two colours needed different temperatures to attain the best result.

Of high-temperature colours used for faience decoration cobalt-blue and manganese-purple are commonly seen, with the addition of copper-green, and orange and yellow from iron and antimony. Variations in shade were obtained by simple mixing, but this was done only to a limited extent. Red was an exceptionally difficult colour, and was usually employed over the glaze as an enamel. Painting in high-temperature colours was a factory operation, and it is not therefore to be found as part of 'outside' painting (*Hausmalerei*). These colours are also known as colours of the *grand feu* when employed to decorate faience.

HIPPOCAMPUS
A legendary water-animal with the body and fore-legs of a horse but a dolphin's tail.

HISPANO-MORESQUE POTTERY
Pottery made by the Moors in Spain, or under Moorish influence. The term is usually employed to refer to pottery decorated with metallic lustre of a pale straw colour on early examples, and a coppery

Hippocampus. Neptune with a Hippocampus. Bronze by the Venetian Alessandro Vittoria. c. 1575. *Victoria and Albert Museum.*

Hispano-Moresque. Tazza decorated with bryony foliage in blue and lustre. Valencia. Mid-15th century. *British Museum.*

red on the later specimens, but wares not so decorated, made under Moorish influence, are also thus called. The earliest specimens known cannot be reliably dated before the 14th century. Some came from Malaga, but by far the greater number came from the district around Valencia. The usual combination is lustre and blue, and the most widely known, and one of the earliest surviving examples, is an amphora-shaped vase with large 'wing' handles preserved at the Alhambra in Granada.

Motifs of decoration include bryony and vine leaves, superbly drawn heraldic beasts (often found on the reverse of dishes), inscriptions in the *neskhi,* Kufic, or Gothic scripts, and arabesques and interlacing strapwork.

The Moors were finally driven from Spain in 1609, but the industry was continued at Valencia, the *motifs* of decoration employed becoming increasingly European in style without ever quite losing their original Moorish flavour. Pseudo-Arabic inscriptions done by Christian potters are usually meaningless and unreadable. Manufacture of peasant wares based on the older types still continues.

In the 19th century, due to the fact that fragments of 17th- and 18th-century wares were dredged from a dock at Bristol, the suggestion became current that they were actually made there. This, of course, is quite erroneous.

HITCHCOCK, LAMBERT (fl. 1820-1850)
A Connecticut furniture-maker who manufactured Sheraton-style chairs painted black and stencilled with floral patterns in gold, popularly known as 'Hitchcock' chairs. The name is also given to a type of clock, often with a wooden movement, the case of which is decorated with stencilling, made in several places about the same time as the chairs. (See *Furniture, American, The Makers.*)

HOADLEY, SILAS (1786–1870)
American clockmaker working at Plymouth; for a time with Eli Terry (q.v.). His clocks were of excellent quality, but specimens are now rare.

HOCHSCHNITT (German)
Literally, high cutting; glass-carving in relief resembling ancient cameo carving. The technique

was employed in 17th-century Germany for the finest glass decorated in the manner of the rock-crystal carver. Examples are the work of Friedrich Winter at Petersdorff and of Martin Winter and Gottfried Spiller at Potsdam. The term can equally be used of similar cutting in hardstones.

HÖCHST (Germany) FAÏENCE FACTORY
This factory was started by two Frankfurt merchants, Göltz and Clarus, who may have been inspired by the enamel-painter A. F. von Löwenfink (q.v.), for together they applied for a privilege (q.v.) for a period of fifty years, and the first wares were fired in December 1746. Besides Adam Friedrich von Löwenfinck, several other artists worked at Höchst who reappear at other faïence-porcelain factories— Zeschinger, a painter in enamel colours, G. F. and Ignaz Hess, and Joseph Philipp Dannhofer (see *Bayreuth, Vienna*). There are also some unidentifiable initials. Höchst is noted for its production of tureens and covered vessels modelled life-size in the shapes of barndoor fowl and turkeys, as well as game pheasants, boars' heads, etc., all decorated in natural colours. There were also many vessels made in the shape of vegetables and fruit.

Most of the painters in this factory were employed alike on porcelain and faïence, and in consequence they used enamel colours as a rule. The high-temperature palette was exceptionally good and varied— red, green, and celadon (q.v.), cobalt-blue, yellow, a pale lemon-yellow, and a straw colour, with outlines in black, to which were added overglaze enamels.

After Löwenfinck's departure a new style, the so-

Hitchcock, Lambert. Chair by Lambert Hitchcock of Connecticut with typical decorative stencilling of flowers. On some specimens Hitchcock's name is stencilled on the back edge of the seat.

called *Deutsche Blumen* (natural flowers), took the place of the *Indianische Blumen* (Oriental flowers). The glaze is a brilliant milky-white. If it is marked Höchst faïence bears the wheel that forms part of the Electoral Arms of Mainz (see *Höchst Porcelain*), but the faïence painters usually added a signature.

Johann Benckgraff took over in 1750, but his attempts to make porcelain failed until J. J. Ringler's arrival in 1750/51. It is possible that at this time till 1757, when production of faïence ceased, the same kilns were being used for both wares.

HÖCHST PORCELAIN FACTORY

The porcelain factory at Höchst is first recorded in 1746 when Johann Christoph Göltz, Johann Felicien Clarus, and Adam Friedrich von Löwenfinck (q.v.) were given a privilege by the Elector of Mayence (Mainz) to organize a porcelain factory here. They were unsuccessful, and von Löwenfinck left for Strasbourg in 1749. More successful attempts were made in 1750 with the aid of Johann Benckgraff (q.v.) and Johann Jakob Ringler (q.v.). By 1757, when Göltz died, the factory was considerably in debt, and it was continued with difficulty by a Court official until 1765, when it became the *Churfürstliche-Mainzische privilegierte Porzellan-Fabrique* (porcelain factory privileged by the Elector of Mainz). In 1788 it was entirely taken over by the Elector, and it deteriorated slowly until 1798, when it was sold for 1,700 florins. Some of the moulds went to Müller of Damm, near Aschaffenburg, who reproduced Höchst figures, using the wheel mark from the Electoral Arms with the addition of the letter *D*. The moulds have been used at one time or another ever since for the making of reproductions.

The earliest Höchst porcelain is very primitive in appearance. It is greyish in colour, and the translucency is poor. Figures were heavy and solidly made, resembling primitive soft-paste porcelains. Enamel colours tended to flake off. Improvements had been made by 1753, and about the same time rococo scrollwork first appears on the bases of figures. A great deal of table-ware was made, and a crimson monochrome enamel is both characteristic

Höchst Porcelain. Teapot painted in the characteristic puce monochrome. Figures in a landscape within rococo scroll borders. Höchst. c. 1760. *Victoria and Albert Museum.*

of a good deal of the painting and very effective. Subjects after Teniers and those taken from the Berlin engraver Chodowiecki are among the best of the work of the time.

It is difficult to attribute figures to some of the modellers known to have worked here. Simon Feilner, better known for his modelling at Fürstenberg, has been awarded figures which do not stylistically resemble his work at Fürstenberg very closely. Laurentius Russinger, who arrived in 1758 and was *Modellmeister* in 1762, has been given some large *chinoiserie* groups. Best known and most prolific of the Höchst modellers was Johann Peter Melchior (q.v.) who has been estimated to have executed about 300 models for the factory.

HOGARTH CHAIR

A late Queen Anne chair of walnut with a pierced splat (see *Splat*), hooped back, and a fairly straight cabriole leg (q.v.) heavily carved on the knee. It is to be seen in Hogarth's engravings, hence, presumably, the name.

HOLITSCH (Hungary) FAÏENCE FACTORY

This was started in 1743 with the aid of Francis of Lorraine, husband of Maria-Theresa. Management and inspiration were predominantly French, the styles of Strasbourg being especially copied. Most sought are the well-known tureens in the form of birds and vegetables which have since been forged. The mark is either *H* or *HF*. After 1786 the factory turned to *faïence-fine*, some of which was painted by workmen from the Vienna Porcelain Factory (q.v.). The mark was the factory name in full.

HONEYSUCKLE See *Anthemion*

HOOD

That part of a long-case clock which is detachable by sliding forwards or upwards, and which encloses the movement. It is superimposed on the trunk, which protects the pendulum.

Höchst Porcelain. Shepherd and Shepherdess by the *Modellmeister,* Johann Peter Melchior. Höchst. c. 1770. *British Museum.*

HOOD-CLOCKS

The precursor of the long-case clock proper (q.v.), which resembles that part of the early long-case clock which houses the movement. It was hung on the wall, the ropes from which the weights were suspended and the pendulum both being exposed.

HOODED TOP

The semi-circular arched top of certain early 18th-century English cabinets, sometimes wrongly called a domed top.

HOOPED BACK

A chair of the Queen Anne period, the uprights of which form a continuous curve with the top rail.

HOP

The hop plant (leaves and flowers) often appears as engraved or etched decoration on ale-glasses, and sometimes on pottery vessels intended for this or a similar purpose.

HOPE, THOMAS (1770–1831)

Architect and furniture-designer of the Regency who was much influenced by the French Empire style (q.v.) of such designers as Percier and Fontaine. His *Household Furniture and Interior Decoration* (1807) refers to 'the pure taste of the antique reproductions of ancient Greek forms'.

HORN

This material is derived from the horns of cattle and related species. Small objects such as snuff-boxes were quite frequently made from horn, and, softened by gentle heating, it can be pressed into shape (see *Obrisset, John*). Horn is transparent, and its use in the making of horn-books is discussed under that heading. Beakers of horn are not uncommon. As an organic material, horn is prone to the attacks of insects.

HORN-BOOKS

A piece of wood, or some substance like pewter, brass, leather, ivory, or even silver, having on the front a printed sheet protected by a thin sheet of horn secured in place by brass strips or nails. Those of ivory and silver are very rare and fetch comparatively high prices. They date back to the 16th century and must be regarded as exceptional. Most horn-books are of wood, and the printed sheet is usually headed by the alphabet and followed by the Lord's Prayer. They were intended to teach children to read, and some have a hole in the handle so that they could be attached to the child's belt. Some later examples were open at the top to allow the insertion of fresh sheets of paper as the child progressed with his studies. Forgeries are known. One is in the British Museum, purporting to be medieval but actually made in 1835. Recent pewter forgeries, if not common, exist in fair numbers. Horn-books of pewter marked 'St. Paul's AD 1729' need especially careful examination.

Horoldt, J. G. Silver-mounted tankard decorated with a *chinoiserie* in the manner of Johann Gregor Höroldt. Meissen. c. 1725. The figure in the foreground is persuading a monkey to jump through a hoop. Baroque scroll framing round the scene, with scattered *indianische Blumen. Boston Museum of Fine Arts.*

HÖROLDT, JOHANN GREGOR (1696–1776)

Born in Jena, and probably a pupil of C. K. Hunger's. As a young enameller Höroldt came to Meissen in 1720, and in 1723 he was appointed *Hofmaler* (Court Painter) to Augustus the Strong, and *Obermaler* (chief painter) to the Meissen porcelain factory when he introduced a new and much more colourful palette than had been employed hitherto. In 1731 he was appointed manager of the factory workers, but he quarrelled frequently with J. J. Kandler (q.v.) and, perhaps in consequence, he left the factory for Frankfurt-am-Main at the beginning of the Seven Years' War, returning to the factory after the end of the war in 1763. Two years later he was awarded a pension. He is best known for his development of a distinctive type of *chinoiserie* (q.v.) very popular at Meissen from about 1725 until 1730, although there is no reason to suppose that the greater number were executed by Höroldt himself. That he provided the patterns for the painters to work from cannot be doubted, and a number of engravings by his hand of this subject survive, of which one in Munich is inscribed '*J. G. Höroldt inv. et fecit 1726*'.

HORSE-BRASSES

Amulets once attached to the harness, latterly as a form of ornament but in earlier times to ensure good luck. Genuinely old specimens are now scarce, most being recently-made copies of traditional designs. From the collector's viewpoint it is desirable that brasses of this kind should originally have been made for their proper purpose and not for sale merely as ornamental brassware, but since designs were continually being added until the custom fell out of favour with the passing of the horse as a means of traction, it is difficult to say where the line of demarcation is to be drawn. Nineteenth-century brasses have such subjects as the steam locomotive.

Houdon, J.-A. The well-known bust of Voltaire by J.-A. Houdon dated 1781. *Victoria and Albert Museum.*

Horse-brasses are usually circular in shape with an upper pierced rectangular piece through which a strap was passed. The custom of ornamenting horse-harness with pierced metal plaques is undoubtedly of great antiquity, to which some of the subjects such as the crescent moon testify. Others have arisen in a variety of ways. For example, a barrel was obviously once worn by a brewer's dray-horse. Estimates of the number of subjects existing vary between 1,000 and 1,500.

It is very difficult to distinguish between old and modern brasses, especially when the subject is a traditional one, but those accustomed to appraising old metalwork can often make a fairly reliable judgment. Perhaps the most obvious sign of age is the presence of wear from cleaning, since brasses of this kind were usually polished frequently, but this is by no means to be regarded as a certain guide.

HOUDON, JEAN-ANTOINE (1741–1828)
French sculptor, who studied in Rome and became an Academician in 1777. His work was reproduced by the porcelain factories of his day, especially by Sèvres. His bust of Voltaire was copied in porcelain at Derby, and in Staffordshire earthenware.

HOWARD, EDWARD (1813–?)
American maker of clocks and watches who founded the E. Howard Clock Company in 1861. He was apprenticed to Aaron II Willard (q.v.).

HUBERTESBURG (Saxony, Germany)
Although a faïence factory was founded here in 1770 by J. F. Tännich, it made little headway owing to competition from Meissen. It later came under the direction of Count Marcolini of Meissen, and then copied English creamware which was sometimes marked 'Wedgewood'. Notice the intrusive median 'e'! Leeds pierced ware was also imitated. The factory continued until well into the 19th century. Faïence from the Tännich period is extremely rare, and mostly in museum collections.

HUGUENOTS
The adherents, in France, of the reformed religion: French Protestants. They were granted freedom of worship by Henri IV in 1598 by the Edict of Nantes, but this was revoked by Louis XIV in 1685, and many Huguenots emigrated from France and settled in neighbouring countries. Since many of them were excellent craftsmen, and for this reason had been encouraged by Colbert, their persecution resulted in the loss of many of France's most skilful workers, who took their skill as craftsmen and designers elsewhere. Many silversmiths and weavers came to England, and, during the first half of the 18th century, Huguenot silversmiths were among the best of those working in London.

The Revocation of the Edict of Nantes in 1685 sent some of the best craftsmen in France to America, either by way of England, or directly from Holland. Apollos Rivoire, silversmith, anglicized his name to Paul Revere, settled in Boston, and became the father of a famous son of the same name (q.v.). Many Huguenots were highly regarded as silversmiths in New York. The best known was Bartholomew Le Roux (1663–1713). Other large Huguenot settlements were in Rhode Island, Pennsylvania, and Charleston, South Carolina.

HUMPEN (German)
An almost cylindrical tall glass beaker or tankard of German origin, the domed cover of which is usually now missing. These remarkable vessels, normally decorated with enamel colours but occasionally with diamond-engraving, take several forms, of which the rarest and best known is the *Reichsadlerhumpen* (Imperial eagle tankard). This is decorated with the Arms of the Holy Roman Empire—a double-headed eagle with outstretched wings, the wings consisting in overlapping shields of Arms of the Electors. Less elaborately decorated the *Kurfürstenhumpen* bears the Arms of the Electors alone. The *Apostelgläser* depict the Twelve Apostles, and the *Walzenhumpen* was commonly painted with the Arms of the nobility and gentry.

Large numbers of tankards, usually smaller in size, were made to commemorate marriages and other events among prosperous merchants, tradesmen, and artisans, the latter often with the tools of the owner's trade, and these have not uncommonly survived.

Many *Humpen* are dated, and they range from the second half of the 16th century to the early years of the 18th.

Forgeries of the more impressive examples, especially the *Reichsadlerhumpen*, were made in the 19th century. The enamelling in both colour and quality is very close to the original, but there are

Humpen. *Humpen* of the type referred to as the *Reichsadlerhumpen* decorated with the arms of the Holy Roman Empire and the Electors. Probably Bohemian. 1594. See *Glass, German, Enamelled. Victoria and Albert Museum.*

differences in the glass itself, which in 19th-century specimens is thicker, the colour (a greenish or yellowish tinge) is more pronounced and uniform in shade, and it lacks the bubbles, striations, and imperfections normally associated with early glass. Forgeries are quite commonly found with their covers, which have rarely survived in the case of genuine specimens.

In addition to enamel painting glass of this kind is also to be found painted in unfired colours (*kalte malerei* or cold painting), sometimes with the addition of gilding, and even of diamond-engraving. Specimens are known with painting on a gold or silver ground, but these are very rare. Nürnberg and Hall-in-the-Tirol seem to have been the principal centres of manufacture of these.

HUNTING CARPETS
A rare type of Persian carpet decorated with hunting scenes amid floral *motifs*, and made from the early part of the 16th century till towards the middle of the 17th.

HUSK ORNAMENT
A conventional flower of bell-shape used in the form of a chain, either vertical or as a swag (q.v.), during the neo-classical period.

HYDROFLUORIC ACID
This is the only known acid which will attack glass and silica products generally, including pottery and porcelain glazes. It is supplied in non-vitreous containers, and should be kept carefully stoppered, since the vapour will cloud the surface of any glass kept near it. This acid is used by fakers of old pottery and porcelain to remove sparse decoration in preparation for re-enamelling in more sumptuous and expensive styles. It is extensively employed in the decorative etching of glass, and it is also used in the phosphate test (q.v.) to determine the provenance of certain early English porcelains.

Hydrofluoric acid was first discovered in 1771 by the German chemist Scheele. This has led to some doubts with regard to the earliest known piece of etched glass, done by Schwanhardt, the Bohemian glassworker, about 1670. It is possible that fluorspar in the glass reacted with an acid, which he called *aqua fortis* (literally, strong water), with the production of a weak hydrofluoric acid, but the reason was not recognized, and the discovery remained undeveloped.

See also *Bone-ash.*

I

ILMENAU PORCELAIN FACTORY

Founded about 1777 by Christian Zacharias Gräbner with the aid of the Duke Karl August of Weimar. The Duke took over the factory in 1783. Goethe, who was a Privy Councillor and President of the Chamber of Finance, supported the leasing of the factory to Gotthelf Greiner in 1786, and in 1792 Greiner's place was taken by Christian Nonne, with Ilmenau as a branch of the factory at Volkstedt (q.v.). The porcelain of Gräbner was very poor in quality, and Goethe wrote that it was 'worse than any in the neighbourhood'. Both body and glaze were considerably improved with the advent of the arcanist Franz Josef Weber, who had been at Ludwigsburg, Frankenthal, and Höchst, and was the author of a treatise on porcelain-making. Until the advent of Greiner figures were produced in considerable variety, many the work of Johann Lorenz Rienck. After this they were discontinued. Under Nonne Wedgwood's blue jasper ware was freely imitated, including portrait medallions and cameos. It is difficult to identify anything with certainty before 1800.

Nonne & Roesch was founded in 1808, and other porcelain factories founded subsequently include Metzler Gebr. & Ortloff (1875), Galluba & Hoffmann (1888), and Arno Fischer (1907).

IMARI PORCELAIN

Japanese porcelain, with painted decoration based on textile patterns, which was so called from the port of shipment, Imari, in the province of Hizen, not far from Arita, where the porcelain was made and decorated. It is an overcrowded decorative scheme painted in a number of colours, of which a blackish dark blue and a strong dark red predominate. It was first made soon after 1700, probably at the suggestion of Dutch merchants, and the earliest specimens were well painted, but quality deteriorated as the 18th century progressed, and by far the greater number of examples to be found today were made in the 19th century, when quality was extremely poor. The general decorative scheme was copied in China at the beginning of the 18th century, and these wares are often called 'Chinese Imari'. It was also copied in Europe by a number of the porcelain

Imari Porcelain. An Arita jar of c. 1700 with 'textile' decoration on the shoulders and floral decoration below.

factories. Worcester is an example (Queen Charlotte's pattern).

IMPASTO (Italian)

The application of paint or pigment so thickly that it stands out from the surface in low relief. Usually employed of painting, it is sometimes used to describe such decoration as that of Florentine *maiolica* oak-leaf jars where the pigment was thickly applied.

INCE, WILLIAM & MAYHEW, JOHN (fl. 1758–1810)

Ince & Mayhew are notable among furniture-makers of the second half of the 18th century in London. Their design-book, *The Universal System of Household Furniture*, was published between 1759 and 1768, and it was to some extent based on Chippendale's *Director*. Attributions have been made on the strength of similarity to designs appearing in this book, or because of the presence of their trade label. They were importers of French furniture, and they supplied this to the Prince of Wales for his residence at Carlton House (London) between 1783 and 1789 through the agency of Dominique Daguerre.

INDIAN, AMERICAN

The American Indian with feathered headdress appears quite frequently in the decorative art of the

211

Indianische Blumen. Bowl decorated with *indianische Blumen* and elements of the Kakiemon pattern called the 'Banded Hedge'. Meissen. c. **1725.** *Boston Museum of Fine Arts.*

first half of the 18th century, even in incongruous juxtaposition with Chinese as in the early *chinoiseries* of Meissen. Sometimes an Indian mask with head-dress appears carved on the knees of cabriole legs (q.v.) during the decade between 1730 and 1740. The Indian occurs as a *motif* in some French tapestries, and in works allegorical of the Continents he usually represents America.

INDIAN CARPETS

India acquired a very considerable reputation for the making of fine carpets in the 16th and early 17th centuries, the best coming from Lahore and Agra, but the art thereafter declined. Carpets are still made and exported in large quantities, but they are no longer hand-woven, and the wearing quality is poor. Pink often predominates in the patterns, which are usually distantly based on Persian *motifs*.

INDIANISCHE BLUMEN (German)

India flowers. Stylized floral decoration usually derived from the porcelain-painting of the Japanese, Kakiemon (q.v.), and used at Meissen in the early years of the factory's life, particularly between 1720 and 1740. They often accompany European subjects. These flowers were very popular and widely copied elsewhere, for instance, at Höchst, at Chelsea on early wares (1750–1752), and occasionally at Worcester. They occur quite commonly on enamelled faïence.

INFLATION AND DEVALUATION

Antiques are often referred to as a 'hedge' against inflation or devaluation, which means that those holding them will be largely protected against the consequences of either of these two forms of currency depreciation because the value of their property will move upwards more or less in ratio to the extent of the depreciation of currency. Inflation is the progressive devaluation of money which results from the printing of excessive amounts of paper currency, or the creation of credit beyond the capacity or willingness of a nation to produce the equivalent value in goods. Distrust of a government's ability or desire to maintain the value of currency leads to an increasing demand for such objects as antiques, gold, diamonds and real property, or to a lesser extent,

shares, all of which retain a real value which is independent of currency depreciation. For our present purpose, devaluation acts in much the same way as inflation by reducing the value of currency, except that it occurs at once and to a fixed extent. A nation is compelled to devalue when the internal value of its monetary unit becomes markedly lower than the rate at which it is exchanged into foreign currencies. Price-rises after devaluation are usually greater than the amount by which the currency has been devalued because the demand for objects of value increases as confidence in currency diminishes.

Some degree of inflation has nearly always been present, and it is impossible to understand the prices formerly given for antiques unless due allowance is made for the intervening depreciation. The following table gives factors by which prices of former times should be multiplied to bring them to terms of today's currency:

1760–1815	× 15
1815–1850	× 12
1850–1914	× 8
1919–1930	× 6
1930–1939	× 4

From this it will be seen that an object sold for £100 in 1939 has *not* appreciated in real value in the meantime if it sells today (1968) for £400.

See *Investment, Antiques as.*

INKSTANDS

The inkstand, once called a standish, is rarely seen before the last decades of the 17th century, but they were popular throughout the 18th, and included receptacles for ink, sand, and wafers, as well as a pen-stand. Many have provision for a taperstick. Glass bottles for containing ink appear soon after the middle of the 18th century. Inkstands were made of silver, Sheffield plate, and pewter, but porcelain and faïence examples are far from unknown. They were made by Sèvres, Derby, and Worcester, to name only three factories.

INLAYING

A kind of ornament in which a recess is cut into the surface to be decorated which is then filled with such materials as woods of different colours, ivory,

Inkstand. Inkstand (*encrier*) of Sèvres porcelain, perhaps a gift from Louis XV to his daughter Madame Adelaide. Dated **1758.** *Wallace Collection.*

212

mother of pearl, or metal. In its effect it is similar to marquetry (q.v.), but it is technically different.

INTAGLIO (Italian)
A form of incised ornament in which the design is sunk below the surface. Seals are commonly cut in this way, and *moulds* for bas-reliefs are of the same kind.

INTARSIA (Italian)
Inlaying in coloured woods, at its best from about 1475 to 1525 in Italy, and first developed at Siena. Designs became increasingly elaborate, and landscapes, interiors, figure-subjects and arabesques decorated the finest furniture of the period. After 1525 its popularity declined in favour of carved ornament. See *Marquetry*.

INVESTMENTS, ANTIQUES AS
Antiques have become a popular international investment as a result of an almost world-wide distrust of currencies. The tendency to invest in this way is first to be noted among the financiers of 18th-century France as a reaction from the instability of the *livre*, and it has been common in that country ever since as the upper- and middle-class version of the peasant's sock. In most other countries antiques have only become a popular investment since 1945, and the movement has gathered especial momentum during the 1960s.

The belief that antiques and works of art generally are a much sounder investment than more conventional outlets for spare money is, on the whole, well founded, and there are particular reasons why this should be so today. Apart from increasing demand for a diminishing supply, the art-market is in a unique position. In former times decorative furnishings were relegated to the attic when they became unfashionable because skilled designers and craftsmen existed who were able to replace outmoded things with those of an equivalent quality in the new styles. In modern times when furniture is made by mass-production methods from synthetic materials, and there is virtually no parallel to the earlier *objets d'art et vertu*, antique works acquire an enhanced value in consequence. It is noteworthy that in the rare cases where modern craftsmanship is comparable prices obtained parallel and even exceed those obtained for antiques. An example is to be found in the porcelain birds designed by the late Dorothy Doughty for the Worcester Royal Porcelain Company (q.v.), which were issued for the first time in 1931.

Although values fluctuate between comparatively narrow limits today as a product of fashions in interior decoration, prices as a whole can, in the foreseeable future, only move in an upward direction.

See *Inflation and Devaluation*.

INVOICING
It is important for a number of purposes—insurance, the maintenance of records, as a protection against error, and so forth—that purchases should be accompanied by an invoice setting forth the correct description of the object bought, its approximate date, and its price.

The description of the object should be read carefully to see that it accords with the dealer's verbal description. 'In the style of' is not the same as 'by'. A piece of porcelain, for example, described as being 'in the style of Chelsea', is certainly not Chelsea in the opinion of the seller, whatever else it may be.

If the invoice description is correct and unequivocal and as agreed between the parties, then further guarantees are unnecessary, since if the facts prove later to be otherwise, the buyer can, at his option, return the object and reclaim his money.

In the case of a dispute with a member of the British Antique Dealers' Association, the Association are prepared to act as arbitrators on request. In the case of non-members it may be necessary to take legal action, but most dealers of standing who make a genuine error will welcome an opportunity to rectify it.

In the case of purchase from second-hand dealers and small antique dealers, it is obviously impracticable to expect a detailed and accurate invoice, since they do not know enough to give one. Here the buyer must be his own expert, and the situation ought to be reflected in a lower price to compensate for the risk.

In the absence of an invoice any action to recover the price paid for an object wrongfully described verbally would be very difficult to sustain, but in the case of a reproduction worth very much less than a genuine piece, it is possible that the court would take into account the price paid, and if this were the price of a genuine piece, they would deem it to have been sold for what it purported to be. In all matters involving deception in this and related fields, such as art-forgery, English law is apt to demand a degree of proof difficult to provide, although on the Continent and in the U.S.A. a more serious view is taken of such cases. French law is inclined to be lenient in matters of fraud which would not have deceived a man of ordinary prudence. The remedy is to buy from established dealers who are members of their trade associations.

IRON
A metal with a high melting point, which can be hammered, welded, or twisted into shape while at red or white heat. Works of decorative art are made in this way, a technique termed wrought iron. Iron is not a good casting metal. It shrinks considerably as it cools, and this tends to blur ornamental detail. For this reason iron in its cast form has been little used, except for such objects as firebacks (q.v.) and stoves.

IRONSTONE CHINA
Stone china, an extremely hard, partially fused earthenware containing the same feldspathic rock as

Iron. Part of a wrought-iron stair-railing. Queen's House, Greenwich (S.E. London). Architect, Inigo Jones.

was commonly employed for true porcelain and bone-china (q.v.), was introduced by Josiah I Spode of Stoke-on-Trent, Staffordshire, about 1805. It was usually decorated with Japan patterns. In 1813 C. J. Mason (q.v.) patented his 'Ironstone China' which was supposed to contain iron slag, and this became very popular with the cheaper market. Its manufacture later spread considerably and Ridgeways (q.v.) made it in large quantities.

ISPHAHAN CARPETS AND RUGS
Isphahan was the Persian capital under Shah Abbas, and in about 1600 a very important royal carpet factory was located here where hunting carpets were made. As in the case of pottery of the period, carpet design was influenced at this time by Chinese *motifs*, and at a later date, in the 18th century, Herati designs (see *Herat*) sometimes occur. The industry was revived in the 1920s, and productions are now purely commercial.

Istoriato. Urbino saucer of 1535 decorated in the *istoriato* style with the subject of Jupiter visiting Semele.

ISTORIATO (Italian)
Literally, history-painting. The term is employed to refer to scenes from history, the Bible, mythology, etc., usually copied from contemporary paintings and engravings, to be found on 16th-century Italian *maiolica*, and wares influenced by it. *Istoriato* decoration was first employed in its most characteristic form, in which it completely covers the surface of plates and dishes without a border pattern, at Urbino (q.v.) in the middle of the 16th century. The engravings of Marcantonio Raimondi (q.v.) were frequently employed as sources of inspiration.

ITALIAN COMEDY, THE
(Italian *Commedia dell'Arte.*) The Italian Comedy, very popular as a decorative theme during the first half of the 18th century, had its roots in the old Roman theatre. It was played by strolling groups of actors, and it had no fixed form, the dialogue and action being extemporized around a *scenario*, of which there were a number of popular versions. The principal characters were Harlequin, Pierrot (or Pedrolino), Pantaloon, the merchant, the Doctor (Boloardo, Balvarel, Balanzani), the Lawyer (Avvocato), Mezzotino, the swashbuckling Captain, and numerous women, of whom Columbine (or Isabella) is the best known. The names were often varied, and subsidiary characters were introduced to suit a particular *scenario*. The Italian Comedy was a favourite subject with such painters as Watteau and Gillot, and the characters appear commonly in porcelain from most of the German factories. Kändler (q.v.) modelled a very important series of Harlequins for Meissen, and no less important is a series of sixteen figures done for Nymphenburg by Bustelli

Isphahan Carpets. A fine-quality Isphahan carpet in the Herati style (q.v.). Note the border pattern. *Parke-Bernet Galleries, New York.*

Palladian style. A Palladian doorcase surmounted by a pediment, from Chiswick House, W. London. The architect was the Earl of Burlington, and the interior decoration by William Kent. The colour scheme is in distinct contrast to the paler colours of the Adam version of the classical style.

Wrought iron balustrade from Chiswick House, W.
London. c. 1725.

(q.v.). Among other factories to produce figures of this kind may be numbered Höchst, Fürstenberg, Kloster-Veilsdorf, and Mennecy. Those from the English factories of Chelsea and Bow are usually based on Meissen originals. The Italian Comedy was often used as a theme of painted ·decoration, especially in Germany.

IVORY

Most ivory comes from the tusks of the elephant, the best from the African elephant, but the tusks of the mammoth, walrus, narwhal, and boar, and the teeth of the hippopotamus, are sometimes employed for decorative carvings. Only the tusks of the mammoth and the elephant are large enough for anything but small-scale work. Those of the mammoth, found in considerable quantities in Siberia, are the largest.

Ivory has been employed from the earliest times as a material for small sculpture. It is not an easy material in which to work, although it can be filed, cut with small knives, and sawn. It is polished with pumice powder, followed by whiting. The harder ivories, such as those from East Africa, are inclined both to warp and to crack, and objects of ivory need to be kept in a humid atmosphere. In conditions of excessive dryness moistening (but not wetting) with water may be an advisable precaution. When new, ivory is yellow on the surface and white within, but the white layers uncovered by carving yellow with age. Ivory can be softened by immersion in phosphoric acid, and it will regain its natural hardness after drying. It can be freed of grease on the surface with benzine, and bleached with hydrogen peroxide.

Forgeries of objects of ivory are far from unknown, but are usually limited to those of consider-

Italian Comedy. Harlequin from a series of Harlequins modelled by Kändler. Meissen. c. 1740. *Christie, Manson & Woods.*

able rarity and value, such as the consular diptychs—late Roman writing tablets. These, and other early and medieval ivories, were forged both in France and Germany during the 19th century. Forgeries of the *vierge ouvrante,* a figure of the Virgin hinged at the back and opening to reveal miniature carved scenes, are also well known. The Japanese especially stain new ivory to resemble old work, and cracks are sometimes simulated by immersing the object in boiling water followed by rapid drying before a hot fire. Objects of ivory are restored with new carving, and are sometimes altered and recarved to make them more desirable. Ultra-violet radiation (q.v.) is especially useful in detecting work of this kind.

Ivory has always been valued as an inlay, often in conjunction with ebony, and *certosina* is an Italian form of inlay, originally from the East, of cypress or walnut, ebony, and ivory.

During the 15th and 16th centuries the use of ivory as a material for small sculpture largely yielded place to bronze in Italy, although exceptionally some small and decorative objects occur which are of fine quality. Generally, work of this kind was limited to what might well be called *objets d'art.* Ivory-carving survived to a much greater extent in Germany and France, and it returned, in both these countries, to considerable popularity with the growth of the baroque style. Among the noted sculptors to work occasionally in this medium in the 17th century may be numbered François Duquesnoy (q.v.). In Germany Balthasar Permoser (1651–1732) is among the best known, and his *Seasons* were copied in porcelain at Fürstenberg (q.v.). Ivory-carvings of the late 17th and early 18th centuries frequently provided inspiration for the porcelain-modellers, and Von Lücke, the Meissen *Modellmeister,* was also an ivory-carver. Many porcelain figures of the early decades of the 18th century were taken either from this source or from Renaissance bronzes. In France from early times Dieppe was an especially notable centre of ivory-carving, and in the 18th century snuff-graters were a minor but decorative product. Perhaps the

Ivory. Chair from the Indo-Portuguese colony of Goa. 18th century. *Soane Museum, Lincoln's Inn, London.*

Ivory. A pair of ivory tankards with silver-gilt mounts. German. Mid-17th century. *Christie, Manson & Woods.*

most outstanding of 18th-century German ivory-carvers was Simon Troger (1693–1769), who often combined carving in wood and ivory. There is an important *Crucifixion* from his hand in the Victoria and Albert Museum (London). He, too, inspired porcelain figures. Much ivory-carving was done during the 19th century, but little of it was of serious consequence, and a good deal were forgeries and reproductions of earlier work.

Ivory has been employed for *objets d'art* of all kinds. Notable are mounted tankards carved with figure-subjects in relief, which came from the Netherlands in the 17th century. Eighteenth-century products include snuff-boxes, fans, cane-handles, bodkin-cases, embroidery implements, etc. Embroidery and sewing accessories of turned ivory commonly furnished 19th-century sewing-boxes.

Well-carved ivory figures as well as many small objects, such as *netsuké*, have come from China and Japan.

JACKFIELD (Shropshire) POTTERY

An old-established pottery was operated at Jackfield from about 1750 to 1775 under the direction of Maurice Thursfield. The principal ware made seems to have been a red earthenware body covered with a black glaze which was decorated with oil-gilding and cold painting. Both have frequently worn off, more or less, although an occasional specimen is still found in reasonably good condition. Jacobite inscriptions and emblems are not uncommon. The cow milk-jug in ware of this kind is traditionally termed 'Jackfield', although most were, in the absence of such indications to the contrary as oil-gilding, probably made in Staffordshire. Wares decorated with applied floral sprigs are definitely Staffordshire, and perhaps Whieldon. Nineteenth century black glazed ware is sometimes erroneously called 'Jackfield'.

JACOB, GEORGES (1739–1814)

Menuisier and *ébéniste* working in Paris, probably trained by Louis Delanois. Jacob specialized in seat-furniture of all kinds, and was among the first of the *menuisiers* to adopt the Louis XVI style. His work is probably the most notable of that period. Jacob was perhaps the first to employ mahogany for the making of seat-furniture, possibly influenced by some of the more prominent English designers of the day. The sabre-leg was probably one of his innovations. His later work was in an early version of the Empire style.

Jacob did a great deal of work for the French royal family, and he is represented in the English royal collections at Windsor Castle. His business was taken over in 1796 by his two sons, who achieved a considerable reputation as *ébénistes* under the name of Jacob-Desmalter, an undertaking much favoured by Napoleon which survived the fall of the First Empire.

Jacob's stamp was *G * IACOB*.

JACQUARD, JOSEPH-MARIE (1752–1834)

Inventor of a device for speeding the operation of weaving which allowed the weaver to carry out the whole operation without assistance. The device was first demonstrated at the Paris International Exhibi-

Jackfield. Red earthenware jug covered with a black glaze and decorated in oil gilding with a man holding a decanter and wine-glass. Inscribed 'The Duke's Health'. Jackfield. c. 1760. *Hove Museum and Art Gallery.*

tion of 1800, and was later adapted to the power-loom. It achieved immediate success, and greatly cheapened the cost of textile production at the time, enabling much larger quantities to be produced.

JAPANESE STYLE, DECORATION IN THE

Early European works closely copying those of Japan can be put into two principal categories—porcelain decorated in the Kakiemon (q.v.) and Imari (q.v.) styles, and japanned furniture copying Japanese lacquer panels. The closest copies of Kakiemon porcelain undoubtedly came from Chelsea (q.v.) soon after 1750, and these wares are sometimes so accurate that even those accustomed to Arita porcelain with this decoration are momentarily deceived. The palette is almost exactly the same, and the three 'stilt' marks on the back are common to both Chelsea and Arita. The copies of Meissen and Chantilly are

Japanese Style. Chelsea covered octagonal bowl in imitation of the forms popularized by Arita (Hizen Province), with closely copied decoration. Chelsea. c. 1752. *Victoria and Albert Museum.*

not so close. The same ware was imitated on Dutch delft, and there are some rare Chinese plates with Kakiemon decoration. The so-called Imari painting, largely based on textile patterns, was imitated very closely at Chelsea, and to some extent at Worcester, where it is not deceptively close. It appears less frequently on Continental porcelain.

Some of the best 17th-century lacquer panels were closely imitated from Japanese originals, and the value attached to those of Japanese manufacture is sufficiently indicated by the word 'japanning' which served to describe the copies. Stalker and Parker, in their *Treatise of Japanning and Varnishing* of 1687, wrote: 'The glory of one country, Japan alone, has exceeded in beauty and magnificence all the pride of the Vatican at this time and the Pantheon before. . . .'

Japan was reopened to Western trade (and Eastern, with the U.S.A.) by Commodore Perry in 1853. Exact copies were seldom made after this date, although Japanese influence was often strong, and this is considered under the heading of *Japonaiserie.*

Japan has some *motifs* of decoration in common with China, such as the dragon and the *fêng huang* (or phoenix), which is called the *ho-ho* bird in Japan, but only the latter seems to appear on Kakiemon porcelain where the painting is mostly floral, with occasional figures, and animals such as the tiger and the squirrel (or tree-rat). The chrysanthemum occurs on Imari wares, and it is the Imperial *mon*, or badge of rank.

JAPANISCHE PALAIS, DRESDEN

Augustus the Strong, Elector of Saxony and King of Poland, was an avid collector of porcelain, and the owner and patron of the Meissen Porcelain Factory (q.v.). In 1717 he acquired from the Graf von Flemming the Holländische Palais in Dresden-Neustadt to house his extensive collection of porcelain. This he renamed the Japanische Palais, which is some indication of the popularity of Japanese porcelain at the time, and he displayed his personal collection of Oriental wares on the ground floor, the upper floor being reserved for the products of his own factory. The Japanische Palais eventually housed nearly 40,000 pieces which were put into store in 1775, and later transferred to the Johanneum, where they formed part of the porcelain collection there. One of the most ambitious projects for the Meissen porcelain gallery was the modelling of almost life-size birds and animals by Kirchner and Kändler (q.v.), which was started about 1727 and abandoned about 1733 after many failures due to technical difficulties. Kändler then began modelling figures of much smaller size (*Kleinplastik*) which were principally intended for table-decoration.

JAPANNED SHEET-IRON WARE

The principal centres of production in England were at Pontypool, Bilston, and Wolverhampton. These are discussed under the heading of Pontypool Ware. French *tôle peinte* was similarly made. See *Tôle.*

JAPANNING   See *Lacquer, European*

JAPONAISERIE (French)

Much early European porcelain painted with designs after Arita (Hizen Province) cannot legitimately be described as *Japonaiserie* since they were copied exactly and often deceptively. They are further discussed under the headings of *Kakiemon* and *Japanese Style* (q.v.). Actual *japonaiseries*, or Japanese decoration with a fantasy element similar to *chinoiseries* (q.v.), occur comparatively rarely in the 17th and 18th centuries, although they appear on some Dutch *delft*. The Dutch were the principal (and almost the only) importers of Japanese art at the time.

Japonaiseries are to be seen after Commodore Perry opened up Japan to Western trade in 1853, and they were a feature of art in Paris in the 1860s. Such things as wood-block prints, fans, fabrics, furniture, and metalwork were being imported in large quantities and influenced the manufacture of many kinds of European decoration, such as that of porcelain at Worcester. Artists influenced by

Japanische Palais. Two bowls sold as surplus from the Johanneum soon after the First World War. The inventory mark is incised into the glaze with a diamond just below the mark. The mark on the left is Japanese, that on the right a rare Meissen factory mark. Both are decorated in the Kakiemon style (q.v.). c. 1725. *British Museum.*

Japanese art at the time include Manet, Monet, Degas, Whistler, and Van Gogh.

See *Art nouveau Chinoiseries.*

JARDINIÈRE (French)

A stand or container for flowers and plants of wood, porcelain, faïence, or metal. It is an essential part of the love of flowers to be found in the 18th century, especially in France, and some of the finest small *jardinières* were made of Sèvres porcelain. The *jardinière* crossed the Channel to England soon after 1750. In porcelain, *câche-pots* and wine-coolers are sometimes misdescribed as *jardinières*, and cellarets which have lost their liners are also sometimes erroneously so called.

JARVES, DEMING (1791–1869)

American glassmaker. See *Sandwich Glass.*

JASPER

Jasper is a variety of quartz which occurs in several colours—dark green, reddish-brown, yellow, and (rarely) blue and black. It is opaque. Jasper has been used for small works of art, often in combination with metal mounts.

JASPER-WARE

Name given by Wedgwood to the hard, fine-grained stoneware he introduced in 1775. Wedgwood had been experimenting with high-fired materials for some time before this year in a way which leaves little doubt that he was attempting to find the secret of porcelain manufacture. He referred to basaltes as 'black porcelain' and to jasper as his 'biscuit porcelain'. The latter contained an unusual ingredient in the form of barium sulphate, found in Derbyshire and referred to by Wedgwood in his letters to Bentley as 'cawk' or 'spaith fusible'. Jasper is normally opaque, but hardfired specimens may be translucent to some degree. Bentley evidently considered this a defect, since it might be interpreted as an infringement of Champion's patent for the manufacture of porcelain contested by Wedgwood and the Staffordshire potters in 1775, and he urged Wedgwood to avoid firing it to this point.

Uncoloured jasper is white, but it could be coloured with the usual metallic oxides used in the pottery industry, and a palish blue is the most frequent, although a darker shade of blue was used. Lilac, sage-green, yellow, and black were not uncommonly employed, but other colours are much rarer. They can properly be termed 'pastel colours', and match the colour-schemes favoured by the Adam Brothers to be seen, for instance at Osterley Park (West London).

The earliest jasper is coloured throughout ('solid'), but after 1780 the colour was usually applied as a surface wash, such wares being termed 'jasper dip'. Jasper was widely imitated in Staffordshire and on the Continent. Perhaps the best of the imitations are those of William Adams of Greengates (Staffs), who used a violet-toned blue, and John Turner of Lane End whose ware was even more porcellaneous than that of Wedgwood.

Jasper was employed for reliefs, portrait medallions, vases decorated with applied reliefs, cups and saucers and teapots, cameos, and a wide variety of ornamental wares, including chimney-piece friezes and furniture-mounts. It is still being manufactured, and the designs available include many 18th-century ones.

JENSEN, GERRIT (fl. c. 1680–1715)

Apparently an immigrant from the Netherlands, Jensen (Gerrard Johnson) was a member of the English Joiners' Company in 1685. Much of his furniture appears to have been of painted lacquer, but he also employed marquetry, including metal inlay, the latter perhaps under the influence of Boulle. He supplied furniture to Kensington Palace and Hampton Court, as well as chimney-piece and pier-glass mirrors. He is recorded as working at Chatsworth (Derbyshire) in 1688.

JEROME, CHAUNCEY (1793–1860)

American clockmaker of Bristol, Conn., who started in 1821, and developed the brass movement which replaced the wooden movement for shelf-clocks. This was exceedingly successful, and Jerome's clocks were extensively exported to Europe. Specimens of these, and other Connecticut clocks of the period, are occasionally to be found in England, especially in East Anglia.

JESUIT PORCELAIN

Chinese export porcelain decorated with religious subjects, usually in *Schwarzlot* (q.v.) or sepia monochrome with slight gilding. Polychrome examples are rarer. The most frequent subjects are the birth of Jesus, His baptism, the Crucifixion, the Resurrection, and the Ascension. Most surviving specimens were made between about 1730 and 1750. They appear

Jesuit Porcelain. Plate of Chinese porcelain decorated in Canton with the Crucifixion. The outer border is a type of *Laub und Bandelwerke* (q.v.) inspired by European porcelain. *Victoria and Albert Museum.*

219

to have been copied from European line-engravings to the order of Jesuit missionaries.

One of the first Jesuit missionaries to reach China was St Francis Xavier, but Matteo Ricci, who arrived about 1600, was much more influential. He was invited to the Court of the Emperor Wan-li (1573–1619), and this began a period when Jesuits were rarely absent from the Chinese Court, except during the closing years of the Ming dynasty. Louis XIV encouraged French Jesuits to settle in China, and they became extremely influential at the Court of the Emperor K'ang Hsi (1662–1722). Father Castiglione founded a school for painters at Pekin, and taught the Chinese the craft of painted enamels, later to become a popular export ware at Canton. Father d'Entrecolles wrote his famous *Edifying and Curious Letters* which, among other things, discussed porcelain-making and were known to every aspiring manufacturer in Europe. Father du Halde wrote his famous history of China, Father Attiret wrote about Chinese gardens, Father Amiot made clockwork for the Chinese Court, and Father Benoist was a hydraulic engineer. When the Order became involved in the events which led to its suppression in France its missionaries in China continued to be supported by the Emperors, and they were exempted from the harassment of Christians which took place during the second half of the 18th century. During the early period of their influence in China, the Fathers wrote long reports of Chinese life and conditions to France which survive in a 19th-century edition of some forty volumes.

JEVER (Oldenburg, Germany) FAÏENCE FACTORY
A factory was established here by J. Tännich in 1760, but its existence was precarious and it closed after sixteen years. The wares are plastic in character and it has been suggested that this was due to the influence of Zerbst (q.v.). Butter-dishes modelled as swans, and tureens decorated with flowers and foliage in relief, are among some of the excellent pieces made here.

The mark, very rare, is *Jeve* or *Jever*, with a painter's mark.

JEWELLED PORCELAIN
Although precious stones, such as turquoise, were occasionally inset into Böttger's red stoneware (q.v.), the term is usually employed to refer to a type of decoration invented about 1781 at Sèvres by Cotteau,

in which drops of translucent enamel were applied over gold foil. A similar process was, in fact, in use in Germany at an earlier date, and it was revived at Worcester in 1865 for a service made for presentation to the Countess of Dudley, the jewelled work being by Samuel Ranford.

JEW'S PORCELAIN
Frederick the Great, to assist his Berlin factory, compelled his Jewish subjects to buy 300 thalers' worth of porcelain before they were allowed to marry or deal in property. The provision was finally abolished by Frederick William II. A similar expedient was adopted at Kloster-Veilsdorf (q.v.).

JOINT STOOL
A 17th-century small rectangular wooden stool with a plain seat supported by four turned legs which are joined near the bottom with stretchers. The components were fitted together with mortice and tenon joints held in place with dowel pins. Sometimes wrongly called coffin stools because they were thought to have been used to support coffins, joint stools have been widely reproduced, but 17th-century specimens are very rare.

JOHNSON, THOMAS
A mid 18th century English carver and designer of furniture who had premises at Grafton Street, Soho, London. He designed in a mixed rococo and Chinese style, and his work, especially mirror-frames, is often wrongly attributed to Chippendale. Johnson had a considerable effect on the design of the more extravagant 18th-century mirror-frames and *chinoiserie* furniture.

See *Chinoiserie*; 'Chinese Chippendale'; Edwards & Darley.

JOSEPH (ÉBÉNISTE)   See *Baumhauer, Joseph*

JOUBERT, GILLES (1689–1775)
Maître ébéniste soon after 1715, Joubert achieved eminence as *ébéniste* to the Crown, supplying much furniture to the royal palaces. He was succeeded as *ébéniste du roi* by Riesener in 1774, the year of the King's death. The output of Joubert's workshop was very large, and he may also have been a dealer in furniture. He often worked in association with other *ébénistes*, such as Marchand, for whom he probably provided designs. His own furniture, of excellent quality, was always in the rococo style.

KAKIEMON, SAKAIDA

Twelve members of the Sakaida family named Kakiemon have been recorded, the first member of this name working in the early part of the 17th century, the last being born in 1879. The first member of this widely known family was born in 1596, and he painted porcelain in underglaze blue, reputedly learning the art of enamelling in polychrome in 1644, three years after the Dutch gained their trading monopoly with Japan. The painting of the Sakaida Kakiemon family at this time was on the porcelain of Arita (Hizen Province), where the shapes are very characteristic. Octagonal and hexagonal vases and bowls are usual and those of square section not infrequent. These shapes may have been adopted originally because of difficulties experienced in firing the natural mixture of clay and feldspathic rock used here. The wares were given a light firing first, and then glazed and subjected to the full heat of the kiln. This has the effect of giving the surface of the glaze a slightly musliny appearance, an effect which also occurs on some early Chinese porcelain, where it is termed 'chicken skin'.

The wares particularly associated with the Sakaida Kakiemons are painted in a very distinctive palette which includes iron-red, a bluish-green, light blue, and yellow. In the earlier specimens the light blue is replaced by underglaze blue. Rarely, some gilding is present.

The designs of the best period, between about 1680 and 1720, are asymmetrical, leaving plenty of empty space, and are rather better known from European copies such as those of Meissen, Chantilly, and Chelsea than from the actual Japanese wares themselves. The well-known 'Quail' pattern is an example, and the 'Tyger and Wheatsheaf', actually derived by the Japanese from Korea, is another. The so-called 'Hob in the Well' was a favourite at Chelsea. The palette of these wares was copied very faithfully in Europe, and some Chelsea copies are so close at first glance that it is difficult to tell them from those of Japan especially as both have the same 'stilt' marks within the footring.

Early Kakiemon wares are much collected and have now become very scarce, but a few early 19th-

Kakiemon. Meissen ewer and basin of silver shape painted with the 'Flying Fox' pattern after Kakiemon. c. 1730. *Newman & Newman (Antiques) Ltd.*

century repetitions are very close to the early ones. Colours introduced about this time include reddish-brown, purple, black, yellow, and a lilac-blue.

See *Chantilly*; *Imari*; *Meissen*.

KÄNDLER, JOHANN JOACHIM (1706–1775)

Kändler was born at Fischbach near Dresden in 1706, and was apprenticed to the Court Sculptor, Benjamin Thomae, in 1723. Augustus the Strong conferred on Kändler the honour of being sculptor to the Saxon Court in 1730, and a year later he began to model for the Meissen Porcelain Factory, becoming *Modellmeister* (q.v.) in 1733, a position he retained for forty years. Kändler sometimes had as many as a hundred workers under his control, among them modellers of talent and skill such as Eberlein, Reinicke, and Meyer (q.v.). He created a number of important services especially notable for their plastic decoration, such as the Sulkowski service, the Swan service (q.v.), and several others. Kändler, who began by modelling large figures of animals for the Japanische Palais of Augustus, was always attracted to large-scale projects, and he was for many years engaged on one to make a life-size equestrian statue of the Elector which was never finished. But he is best known for the many small figures (*Kleinplastik*) originally intended as table-decoration, and the actual

Kändler. Group of Freemasons by Kändler. Meissen. c. 1744. The Electors of Saxony were Grand Masters of the Order. *Newman & Newman (Antiques) Ltd.*

number has been put in excess of a thousand different models. These were the inspiration for many other European porcelain factories, and they were quite commonly copied in England, notably at Chelsea. After the Seven Years' War, Acier (q.v.) was appointed joint *Modellmeister* with Kändler, who consistently worked in the baroque and rococo styles and did little work of consequence in the neo-classical styles of the post-war period. The Kunstgewerbemuseum at Dresden has the only signed example of his work, a *Triumph of Galatea*, modelled in 1773.

KAS (or KAST)

The kas (from *kast,* the Dutch name for cupboard) was more of a wardrobe than a cupboard. The American version was made by Dutch descendants of early settlers in New York in the second half of the 17th century and throughout the 18th. They were found in the region which was, until 1665, the Dutch colony of New Netherlands, and is now New Jersey, New York, Connecticut, and parts of Massachusetts and Vermont. Some are very large, and they are usually on bun feet. Some were fitted with shelves behind the doors, and some had a drawer, or drawers, below the cupboard space. The oak kas was carved with heavy baroque mouldings, or decorated with marquetry in the Dutch manner, but more often it was of pine, with painted decoration of pendant fruit, birds, and flowers simulating what would have been carved decoration in Holland.

KASHAN CARPETS

Kashan is one of the centres of the silk carpet industry in Persia. The famous Ardebil carpet was probably woven here, and a number of old Hunting Carpets (q.v.) can be assigned to these looms. Kashan is a large city between Teheran and

Isphahan, and since the 19th century it has also produced carpets with a wool pile with floral *motifs* and connecting vines, usually with a central medallion. Modern silk rugs and carpets are hard-wearing and of good design, but the quality is not equal to that of old specimens.

KAUFFMANN, ANGELICA (1741–1807)

Swiss painter who was in London from 1766 till 1781. She was a friend of Reynolds, and a founder-member of the Royal Academy in 1768. She designed and painted panels for the Adam Brothers, although most work in her style was not from her hand and examples actually painted by her are very few. Her history-painting inspired much neo-classical decorative painting both in England and on the Continent, although, needless to say, Vienna porcelain plates of the 19th century signed 'Angelica Kauffmann' are not by her. She married Antonio Zucchi, who designed the frontispiece of the *Works in Architecture* for the Adam Brothers.

KAZAK RUGS

Caucasian rugs (q.v.) made by Cossack nomads.

KEENE (New Hampshire) GLASS WORKS

This was established in 1816, but production was small for some years until it came under the managership of Justus Perry. In the early stages it produced amber and olive-green glass blown into moulds, and bottles and flasks formed a considerable part of the output. It closed about 1850. Another factory started here about the same time, and surviving until 1855, is noted for 'off-hand' (q.v.) glass of excellent quality, although specimens are rare. See *Glass, American.*

Kas. A painted *kas* with decoration of fruit *en grisaille.* Dutch style, from Hardenbergh House, Ulster County, New York, which was built in 1762. *H. F. du Pont Museum, Winterthur, Delaware.*

222

KEIZER, AELBRECHT CORNELIS DE

Dutch potter who joined the Guild of St Luke in 1642, and was made an elder. He was a man of some consequence and his mark *AK*, in monogram, was copied by his contemporaries, as well as by his successors. They also imitated his style, and only the finest pieces should be considered as perhaps being actually by his hand. He painted in blue-and-white and polychrome, and took the whole field of Chinese and Japanese ornament for his model. Delft painting developed into fanciful variations on Oriental themes, which, freed from the conventions and symbolism of the East, produced a more picturesque effect.

Aelbrecht de Keizer was followed by his son, Cornelis, and two sons in law, Jacobus and Adriaen Pijnacker. They founded a partnership, but Adriaen later abandoned his share to become a master-potter on his own account. He used a red monogram, *APK*, which has been much copied. Known principally for his Imari (q.v.) style, and particularly for paintings of Japanese women in landscape, he was very skilful also in the use of blue-and-white and a green pigment. He also produced the very rare black *delft* (*delft-noir*). Pijnacker used a bluish glaze, and the blue pigment and gilding were thinly applied.

KELLINGHUSEN (Holstein) FAÏENCE FACTORY

In 1760 Carsten Behrens engaged workmen from Saxony to start a porcelain factory. When he was forced to turn it instead into a faïence factory he formed a company, and in 1765 the factory received its privilege, and a technical manager called Sebastian Kirch from Jever was installed. Kirch left after three

Kashan Rugs. A cut-silk Kashan prayer-rug woven for presenting to a Shah. *Sotheby & Co.*

years, and Behrens was forced to carry on alone. His heirs were faced with competition from two of Behrens' workers who had obtained a privilege to make white wares in the same town. These two factories seem partially to have merged. In 1787 a third enterprise was begun in the town by Georg Geppel, and there was considerable competition for the excellent clay of the neighbouring Overdorf.

Most of the faïence produced here was peasant ware well decorated with conventional flowers painted in high-temperature colours.

KELSTERBACH (Germany) FAÏENCE FACTORY

A factory was founded at Kelsterbach in 1758 by Johann Christian Frede. In 1760 he shared his privilege with Kaspar Maritz. The faïence seems to have been confined to domestic wares, some in the late Hanau style and some imitating porcelain in blue-and-white. The factory was probably the same as the one which made porcelain slightly later.

KELSTERBACH PORCELAIN FACTORY

This factory, founded in 1761, was situated in Hesse-Darmstadt, on the left bank of the Rhine between Frankfurt and Mainz. It was the property of the Landgrave, Ludwig VIII, and was for the first three years of its existence under the direction of Christian Daniel Busch of Meissen. The principal modeller in the early period was Karl Vogelmann, assisted by Peter Antonius Seefried. By 1766 about

Kelsterbach. Two soldiers agreeing on a truce. Probably modelled by Vogelmann. Kelsterbach. c. 1765. *Metropolitan Museum, New York.*

223

131 models were listed, of which perhaps 75 were by the hand of the former. It has been suggested that the art of producing porcelain figures in quantity (see *Figures, Porcelain, Manufacture of*) was not mastered by Vogelmann, and that each figure was separately moulded from a lead master-model, although this is very uncertain. Surviving examples do, however, suggest that some hand-modelling took place. Seefried's style was much influenced by that of Bustelli, as well as by Vogelmann. Seefried had been at Nymphenburg (q.v.) during Bustelli's lifetime, and he returned there in 1767. His models, like Bustelli's, sometimes have half-opened mouths. The factory survived precariously until the 1790s.

KENT, WILLIAM (1684–1748)

English architect, landscape gardener, painter, interior decorator, and designer of furniture. Kent was one of the principal arbiters of taste in England during the first half of the 18th century. After studying in Italy for some years he met the Earl of Burlington in Rome. Burlington became his patron and employer, and, as an architect, Kent adopted the Palladian style (q.v.) especially favoured by the Earl. As a landscape gardener Kent was much esteemed. He broke away from the current rigid styles of the French and Dutch, and his informal arrangements based on natural landscape considerably influenced the course of the art in England and on the Continent, a later example of this influence on Continental design being the gardens of the Petit Trianon at Versailles. According to Horace Walpole he was unsurpassed in the management of water. Kent's reputation as a painter was low, even at the time, and Walpole records that his father, Sir Robert

Walpole, who employed Kent as a mural and ceiling painter at Houghton Hall (Norfolk), refused to allow him to work in colours. But, adds Walpole, to compensate for his bad painting he had excellent taste in ornament. Apart from Houghton, an example of Kent's interior decoration is to be seen at Chiswick House, on the western outskirts of London, the exterior design being the work of Lord Burlington. In recent years a start has been made here on the careful reconstruction of the grounds to Kent's original plan.

A recent critic, Sacheverell Sitwell, has written that the gilt furniture at Houghton, designed by Kent, must be among the wonders of English interior decoration, and this is hardly an exaggeration. Kent is renowned for massive furniture, movable only with difficulty, lavishly carved in an Italian style based on Venetian models, and superbly gilded. Like some wines Kent's furniture does not travel well. Most of it was designed for a particular setting, in the same way as most contemporary French furniture, and it matches the fixed interior decoration.

Most of Kent's furniture was carried out to his designs by talented Italian workmen, and it is sometimes difficult to be certain whether the origin is English or Italian. His side-tables on massive carved supports, usually with tops of marble or *scagliola* (q.v.), were often in the form of an eagle with outstretched wings or intertwined dolphins. At his best Kent can only be matched for magnificence by the contemporary furnishings of Versailles.

His cabinet-furniture, such as bookcases, was based on the prevailing severely classical architectural styles, and he made use of the broken pediment, if, indeed, he did not introduce it. Picture-

frames designed by him are massive, with supporting classical columns topped by a pediment, the colouring usually white and gold. It is probable that the taste for picking out the mouldings of mahogany doors with gold was originally due to his influence.

KEYBOARD INSTRUMENTS

Under this heading may be grouped the virginal, spinet, clavichord, harpsichord, and pianoforte, which are all the same in principle. There are, however, certain differences between them. In the case of the virginal, spinet, and harpsichord the strings are plucked when the keys are depressed, the plucking being done by plectra of quill, metal, whalebone, or even leather. The harpsichord has more strings for each note which are operated by a larger number of plectra with the object of providing a greater range of intensity and quality of tone. The harpsichord was provided with keyboard stops, like those of an organ in appearance, which varied the number of strings plucked at any one time, and the strings themselves were tuned to normal pitch with one set an octave lower and the other an octave higher. On later versions of the instrument the keyboard stops were replaced by foot-pedals. The clavichord, which existed in the 16th century, had strings at a right angle to the keyboard, and the sound was produced by a kind of copper hammer falling on the string when the key was depressed. It is a rare survival.

The pianoforte was invented in Italy in 1709, and the earliest surviving example was made in 1720. Here the strings are struck by a felt-covered hammer, and musically this arrangement has much to commend it. Especially after 1750, when Mozart introduced a new style of melody and accompaniment for which the pianoforte was particularly well suited, the harpsichord began to lose favour, and production ceased about 1800.

Virginals date from Elizabethan times. The spinet was largely developed on the Continent in the 17th century, the Ruckers family of Belgium being the most noted makers at that time. Rubens is known to have painted some of their cases. The harpsichord was developed during the 18th century, the best-known maker being Burkhardt Tschudi, a Swiss who made them in London. He was reputed to have made 1,200 by the time of his death in 1773. He was succeeded by Broadwood, who made the new pianoforte.

The harpsichord and the early pianoforte are not uncommon survivals, and their value is largely governed in these days by the decorative qualities of the case, although the harpsichord, and even the spinet, are still to be heard for appropriate music. Restoration of old keyboard instruments to playing order is possible and is quite often undertaken.

KHILIM (Turkish)

A type of rug made in Turkey and parts of Persia and Central Asia which has no pile. The technique is a kind of tapestry weave (see *Tapestry*), in some ways similar to the Aubusson rugs and carpets of France, and the pattern is alike on both sides. Khilims also resemble Soumakh rugs, but the latter are even more akin to European tapestries in the way in which they are woven. Khilims are often termed 'double-faced' because the pattern is the same on either side, and designs are geometric, predominantly rectilinear, and in bright colours. Most such rugs have a *mihrab* (q.v.), since they are light and portable and therefore in demand as prayer-rugs. Due to their light weight they are unsuitable as a floor-covering except in places which are little used, and in the East they are employed to cover divans, or as hangings. The Khilim most often found in the West comes from Shirvan, and has a basic pattern of broad stripes interspersed with narrow ones. Kurdish Khilims, from the Lake Van area, often have yarn ends left loose on the underside. The *mihrab* is present on nearly all of them. Khilims made in the Merve district have a diagonal pattern, usually with a narrow border. Anatolian Khilims generally are of excellent quality, and usually have a *mihrab*. Large rugs of this kind are often in two parts, sewn together from top to bottom down the centre.

These rugs are sometimes erroneously termed 'Kelims' in the catalogues of the English provincial auctioneer.

KHORASSAN CARPETS AND RUGS

So called from their place of origin—the Persian province of Khorassan. The Sehna knot is used, and there are from three to seven border stripes, with the Herati design (see *Herat*) usually present. The pear design is common in the field, and animals and birds are frequently represented, together with variations of the Herati pattern. Plain fields also occur. The dyes are not always good.

KIDDERMINSTER CARPETS

The manufacture of carpets and rugs at Kidderminster (Worcestershire) goes back at least to the early decades of the 17th century, although no specimens of this age are known. The early productions were smooth-faced. The *moquette* (q.v.) carpet in the Brussels manner was introduced in 1753, and production thereafter was on a very large scale.

KIDNEY-TABLE

A dressing- or writing-table of kidney-shape first introduced in the Sheraton period. The concave curve faces the sitter, and in the case of a writing-table there are often tiers of drawers on either side of a kneehole.

KIEL (Holstein) FAÏENCE FACTORY

In 1758 a factory was founded in the city of Kiel by Peter Grafe which was soon bought by the ducal house and, under the direction of J. S. F. Tännich, it produced some good quality pieces. However, it proved to be as unprofitable as many others, and was sold in 1766 to Renners and Newman who employed Buchwald and Leihamer from Eckernförde (q.v.) who were incompetent as business men, but they

Kidney-table. **A very rare Sheraton kidney-table (reniform) in amboyna cross-banded with rosewood. c. 1800.** *Phillips, Son & Neale.*

left their artistic mark at Kiel. They reappear after 1769 at Stockelsdorff. The factory closed some time before 1793. The faïence is lightly fired, and of a pale buff (sometimes almost white) clay. Although the glaze is a smooth, cold white, its variable thickness causes considerable changes in tone. Sometimes there are many small pin-holes, but it can be almost flawless.

Kiel followed Marieberg (q.v.) in the use of enamel colours, and its standard was equal to the German factories. In style it resembles Strasbourg, Marseilles, and Sceaux, and although the crimson is dryer than that of Strasbourg, and French elegance is lacking, there is nevertheless a certain freedom which makes up for these defects. Kiel dishes with a wavy rococo rim usually have a brown edge. Much painting was done from nature, and this factory's *repertoire* of flowers was far wider than any other in the north, and second only to France.

There are several marks: usually a *K* followed by, for instance, a *T* in the Tännich period, and painters' marks or numerals.

KINGWOOD   See *Violetwood*

KIRCHNER, JOHANN GOTTLOB (1706–?)
Kirchner was one of Meissen's most distinguished modellers, entering the factory's service in 1727, becoming *Modellmeister* in 1731, and leaving in 1733 after a quarrel with Kändler. He was a sculptor of considerable talent, and contributed extensively to the early development of the art of the porcelain figure in Europe, originating the Meissen 'model book' in which the styles, shapes, sizes, and so forth were listed and described. He was much occupied with modelling large figures of animals for the Japanische Palais, and his work is, in many ways, superior to that of Kändler. The Saint-Nepomuk of 1731 is an example of his smaller work.

KIRMAN RUGS AND CARPETS
Kirman is a large city in the south of Persia from which some of the best rugs and carpets are procured. They are especially popular in England. The industry appears to have existed from the 18th century, although very few specimens of this date have survived. The Sehna knot is used, and colours are inclined to be much lighter than those to be found with Persian rugs generally. They include a light blue and rose. Designs are more naturalistic than those of rugs from elsewhere, and the medallion centre is common.

KLINGER, JOHANN GOTTFRIED (1711–1781)
Porcelain-painter at Meissen to whom is attributed the practice of adding shadows to flowers and insects, which can also be seen at Chelsea (q.v.) during the red-anchor period. A Meissen example of shadowed flowers dated 1742 is in Berlin. Klinger was apprenticed at Meissen in 1731, and remained until 1746. He was at Vienna until his death in 1781, and may have functioned as a *Hausmaler.*

KLOSTER-VEILSDORF PORCELAIN FACTORY
One of the largest of the Thuringian factories, Kloster-Veilsdorf was founded by Prince Wilhelm Eugen von Hildburghausen about 1760, using clay from Passau. A privilege was granted in 1765, the factory director being the Court Sculptor, Friedrich Döll.

Using various expedients the Prince assisted the factory to expand, one of them being to compel his Jewish subjects to take porcelain instead of money.

Kirchner, J. G. **Harlequin from the Italian Comedy, probably modelled by Kirchner. Meissen. c. 1730.** *Sotheby & Co.*

Nevertheless, it ran into financial difficulties. It later passed to the Greiner family, who operated it until 1822, when it was reorganized on a commercial basis. It is still in existence.

Service-ware often copied Meissen, and a good deal of it was well painted, use being made of Nilson's engravings as inspiration. Döll himself was probably the chief painter. Figures were manufactured on an increasingly extensive scale after about 1777, the best-known modeller being Franz Kotta, who was perhaps apprenticed here in 1777, leaving for Volkstedt in 1783. Several complaints were received from Meissen that the mark of the crossed swords was being imitated, a charge which, though refuted, no doubt had substance.

KNIFE-BOXES
A box with a sloping top and serpentine front, the interior fitted with small partitions into which knives and forks were inserted for storage. These were made in England from about 1760 onwards. They were in pairs, and placed at either end of the side-table in the eating- or dining-room. They were commonly veneered in mahogany and very often inlaid with shell ornament and stringing in a lighter coloured wood. Many of the less ornamental specimens have had the interior removed during the 19th century and a letter-box slot cut into the lid. Some of the finest Adam knife-boxes were in the form of classical urns.

'KNOCK-OUT'
This method of determining the ultimate value of property bought at auction probably goes back to Roman times. After the public sale a private auction is held between dealers who have agreed to buy beforehand on joint account. Further bidding takes place, the property going to the dealer who offers the highest price, the difference between public and private prices being distributed among those present.

Although this practice has been illegal in England since the passing of the Auction (Bidding Agreements) Act, 1927, prosecutions under the Act can only be instituted with the consent of the Solicitor-General, a clause apparently inserted by the judge responsible for drafting the Act because it was then intended to apply only to bloodstock sales, and not to those of antiques. No prosecutions involving antique dealers appear to have been instituted since the Act was passed, but an undertaking not to participate in a 'knock-out' is required from all members of the British Antique Dealers' Association as a condition of membership.

It is argued by its opponents that the 'knock-out' works against the interests of the seller by reducing competition among buyers, thus depriving him of part of the value of his property. This argument overlooks the fact that the auctioneer, who is the vendor's agent, has a duty to protect his client by fixing a suitable reserve price below which his property may not be sold. If the auctioneer makes a mistake, and fixes the reserve price at too low a level, then the dealers present have no duty in law to correct the auctioneer's mistakes. To assume the contrary would lead to ludicrous situations if the principle were extended.

The 'knock-out' can only be very profitable to the dealer if the seller is badly advised, and the employment of a reputable auctioneer with knowledge of the value of the property he is selling is the obvious safeguard. In those cases where there has been a considerable difference between public and private prices the object must have been badly catalogued, and no buyers can have been present outside the members of the 'knock-out' who knew enough to offer a price nearer its market-value. This is an infrequent combination of circumstances.

See also *Auctions, Sales by*.

KNOP
A knob, such as that forming the handle of 18th-century teapot lids, which took various ornamental forms—a flower, a fir-cone, or a pineapple. The word is employed principally in referring to silver or porcelain.

KÖNIGSBERG (East Prussia, Germany) FAÏENCE FACTORY
After establishing the factory of Marieberg in 1758, Johann Eberhard Ludwig Ehrenreich, a German born in 1722 at Frankfurt, left Sweden, via Stralsund, to go to Königsberg, where he obtained a privilege for a new factory which was in production by 1772. It never really prospered, and was sold by auction in 1788, changing owners several times till about 1810, when it closed.

Apart from its imitations of English creamware, this factory made predominantly blue-and-white wares with some manganese painting. The glaze inclines to grey or greyish-blue, and the blue is very intense. The faïence is marked in the Swedish manner with the day, month, and year, a painter's mark, and a monogram *HE* (Hofrat Ehrenreich).

A factory founded here in 1775 by Paul Heinrich Collin, who had spent a good deal of time in England, specialized in copies of Wedgwood's basaltes wares, making a number of portrait medallions. One of the philosopher, Kant, is the best known. The factory closed in 1785.

KRAAK PORSELEIN (Dutch) See *Carrack Porcelain*

KREUSSEN (Bavaria)
German centre for the production of stoneware which started at an unknown date, and developed from an existing manufactory of stove-tiles (*Hafnerware*). The earliest 17th-century wares, which were decorated in relief, were made in a greyish clay covered with a thin brown glaze (see also *Rhineland Stoneware*), but by 1618 the factory had developed its characteristic technique of painting stoneware in bright enamel colours, a practice undoubtedly derived from contemporary glass-enamelling (see *Glass, German, Enamelled*). Some of the

later Kreussen subjects suggest a relationship with the glass-painters, as well as the use of a dense white enamel which is common to Kreussen stoneware and Franconian glass. Squat tankards with pewter lids are a fairly common survival in this group, and flasks often have pewter screw-stoppers. Manufacture continued till the end of the 17th century, and most surviving specimens were made after 1640.

KUFIC SCRIPT

An angular, formal Arabic script sometimes to be found as part of the decoration of Near and Middle Eastern carpets and rugs, and on pottery from the same region. It also occurs on Hispano-Moresque pottery (q.v.). Like all Arabic scripts, it is read from right to left. Most such inscriptions are verses from the Korān, dedicatory, or giving the year of manufacture.

KÜHNEL, CHRISTIAN FRIEDRICH (1719–1792)

Porcelain-painter at Meissen from 1740 to 1780. Kühnel specialized in battle-scenes, and one specimen in the British Museum (London) depicts scenes from the Russo-Turkish War of 1775.

KÜNERSBERG (Bavaria, Germany) FAÏENCE FACTORY

The factory was built about 1745 by a man called Küner, who had recently been ennobled by Charles V. He acquired property at Bergersbad, renamed it Künersberg, and applied for a faïence privilege which was granted. He was able to secure a good many skilled workers from other factories, Sperl, Leinfelder, Busch, etc., none of whom stayed long in one place. The faïence was of a high standard, with luminous colours on a very milky glaze. Some imitations of Rouen in a strong blue, yellow, and green; heraldic plates and flower-decorated ewers; and still-lifes and hunting scenes all date from mid-18th century. The painting is original in invention and skilled in execution.

Marks are either *Künersberg* in full, or *KB*.

KWAART

Covering of lead glaze applied to 17th- and 18th-century Dutch *delft*, and to some English *delft* inspired by Dutch techniques. After the pigments had been laid on to the tin-enamel the piece was dusted with lead glaze in powder form and fired, fusing all together in one operation. The same process in Italy was termed *coperta*.

L

LABEL DECANTERS

Shouldered decanters of English flint glass (q.v.), made from about 1755 onwards, lettered with the name of the contents, and usually with a floral and foliate design in addition. The wheel-engraved design was mat on clear glass. Most were intended to hold a quart, and some rare examples three pints or more. The usual height is eleven inches. Floral patterns varied with the label, those for containing wine having the vine-leaf and grapes; those for ale, the hop-vine; and those for cider, apples. Slight cutting of the stoppers was usual by 1760, and more elaborate cutting from about five years later. Care should be taken in acquiring specimens that the stopper belongs to the decanter and is not a replacement.

Label decanters are also to be found lettered in white enamel, but these are rare (see *Beilby, William and Mary*). Those of blue glass from Bristol, made in the early years of the 19th century, are lettered in gold, and lack the pronounced shoulder of the clear-glass versions. Labelled carafes (q.v.) are also to be seen occasionally, but lack the floral ornament.

LACE, GOLD AND SILVER

In France the manufacture of gold and silver lace was located at Lyon, Paris, and at Aurillac in the south-west. Manufacture at Lyon appears to have been established in the early years of the 16th century, and it expanded greatly in the 17th, when lace of a metal simulating gold (*l'or faux*) was also made. The industry was transferred to Geneva in 1685, after the Revocation of the Edict of Nantes. The best laces of this kind were made in Paris, in a factory belonging to Simon Châtelain, a Huguenot who died in 1675. He specialized in a lace called *Point d'Espagne* which achieved a considerable reputation. This workshop, too, was closed in 1685. The lace of Aurillac was of gold foil wound on silk thread and was principally exported to Spain. The period of the greatest popularity of these laces was the reign of Louis XIV, but they were still popular at the middle of the 18th century. A lace of mixed silk, gold, and silver threads was made at Caen and Bruges during the 19th century.

Gold thread was being made in England as early as 1238, and 'passments' (*passementeries*) of gold and silver are referred to in Queen Elizabeth's time, when they were sometimes adorned with pearls. The best were imported from Venice, which was a considerable centre of manufacture. Gold lace was popular during the reign of James I, and under the Duke of Buckingham, who was granted a monopoly of its manufacture, much lace of a very debased quality was produced. The drawing of silver wire having a copper core was started in England in 1637 but was soon discontinued. Spinners of gold and silver thread, and lace and spangle workers, were well established in London during the reign of Charles II, when a contemporary record speaks of 'many thousands' thus employed. Both Queen Anne and George II prohibited the import of foreign lace of this kind, and English makers drove a thriving export trade with India. The fashion eventually disappeared at the end of the 18th century, to be retained only for military uniforms.

Sicily was once celebrated for its gold laces, and manufacture on a considerable scale existed in Zurich.

See *Threads, Metal, in Textiles*.

LACEWORK IN PORCELAIN

This was introduced shortly before 1770 at Meissen (q.v.) and is first to be seen applied to figures by Michel-Victor Acier, chief modeller from 1764 to 1779. Actual lace was dipped into porcelain slip (i.e. body diluted with water to the consistency of cream) and applied to the figure. Subsequently the lace burned away in the kiln, leaving its simulacrum in porcelain. At first confined only to small additions to costume, figures were produced in the 19th century with elaborately flounced lace skirts. Lacework of this kind is, of course, extremely fragile, and hardly in the best tradition of porcelain designing.

Its introduction is also attributed to Joseph Hannong at Strasbourg (q.v.).

LACQUER, EUROPEAN AND AMERICAN

The gum obtained from the *Rhus vernicifera* (see *Lacquer, Oriental*) was unexportable to Europe, and

Lacquer, European. Tea-caddy decorated with simulated Oriental lacquer. French. 18th century. *Victoria and Albert Museum.*

European lacquer is therefore an imitation made with different substances. Although there were several ways of simulating the true Oriental lacquer the commonest was a varnish made from resin obtained from an insect, *Coccus lacca*, dissolved in 'spirits of wine' (alcohol), to which a pigment was added. The resin was known under several names—shellac, seed-lac, and gum lac. This varnish was painted over a wooden foundation, several coats being applied. Parts in low relief were built up either from gesso (q.v.), or from a mixture of gum and sawdust. The surface was then decorated with painting in varnish colour, and sometimes dusted with gold powder, or gilded with applied gold-leaf. This is the underlying principle of all European imitations of Oriental lacquer-work.

Although a few specimens of Oriental lacquer arrived in Europe in the early years of the 16th century, it was not imported on a large scale until just before 1600. The first attempts to imitate it belong to the opening years of the 17th century in France, where Oriental lacquer was very fashionable. The first English lacquer may have been produced soon afterwards, although it did not become generally popular until the publication of the well-known *Treatise of Japanning and Varnishing* by Stalker and Parker in 1688. In the first half of the 18th century lacquer became popular in Europe for the decoration of wall-panelling, an excellent example being a well-known room in Rosenborg Castle, Copenhagen.

By the end of the 17th century imitations of Oriental lacquer of excellent quality were being made almost throughout Europe. Holland, which imported much lacquer from Japan, produced some extremely close imitations, and it has been suggested that Japanese lacquer-workers were imported for the purpose of teaching Dutch craftsmen. Particularly valued is some of the lacquer-work from Germany by Gerard Dagly (q.v.) and others. German lacquer furniture continued to be made during the early years of the 18th century at Dresden by, among others, Martin Schnell (q.v.). Hamburg and Augsburg were also notable centres for this kind of work.

Lacquer remained fashionable in France throughout the 17th century, and specimens of European furniture were even sent to the Far East to be decorated in this way. During the 18th century, from 1730 onwards, a simulated lacquer invented by the brothers Martin (see *vernis Martin*) was much prized, and some of the finest *ébénisterie* of the period was decorated with lacquer panels, Oriental and European (see *Pagods*). Japanese lacquer was especially prized for this purpose.

Italian lacquer, the subject of a considerable number of contemporary forgeries, came mostly from Venice. Nearly all surviving specimens are of 18th-century date. Here, the simulation of the Oriental product was not so close as many other European varieties managed to achieve, but the Venetians did some excellent gold *chinoiseries* (q.v.) on coloured grounds, and later, well-painted European scenes such as miniature landscapes and bouquets of flowers.

A good deal of English lacquer survives. Stalker and Parker's *Treatise* was mainly designed to appeal to the amateur decorator, and the art was even taught in young ladies' academies of the day. No doubt they lacquered existing household furniture rather than that specially made for the purpose. The best work was done by professionals, and at the end of the century it was possible to obtain almost any item of household furniture, including chimney-pieces and mirror-frames, thus decorated. Temporarily unfashionable in the early decades of the 18th century, except for long-case clocks, lacquer returned to favour a little before mid-century, at the same time as it was at the height of its popularity among French *ébénistes*. Some of Chippendale's Chinese designs were intended to be lacquered, and beds and bedroom furniture were often thus decorated and used in conjunction with Chinese painted wallpaper. The fashion persisted, largely among amateur decorators, throughout the second half of the century, and it was freely employed in the decoration of Brighton Pavilion in the early years of

Lacquer, European. French *secrétaire* decorated with lacquer panels of the *vernis Martin* type. The decoration of landscapes was termed *à la pagod* (see *Pagods*). Period of Louis XV. Signed *Dubois JME. Sotheby & Co.*

the 19th century. Lacquer colours were also used to decorate *papier mâché* made by Henry Clay of Birmingham and others.

In America, using simplified methods, the japanner confined his ground colours to black or 'tortoiseshell.' His designs were suggested by imported lacquer, Oriental porcelain, delftware, East Indian painted cottons, or from Stalker and Parker's treatise and design-book already mentioned. Boston was the centre for American japanned furniture beginning in 1712, the most important name being Thomas Johnston (active 1732). Japanning was also done in New York and Philadelphia.

See *Pagod Papier Mâché*.

LACQUER, ORIENTAL

True lacquer is a gum exuded by a tree known botanically as the *Rhus vernicifera*, which becomes extremely hard after exposure to the air. Before hardening it is coloured with a variety of pigments, of which true scarlet (derived from cinnabar) and green are the most sought. Yellow lacquer is comparatively rare, and black and reddish-brown the most common. Decoration is carved and incised, and some of the finest specimens consist of several layers of different colours built up on a wooden foundation, the ornament being carved down to expose the various layers according to the requirements of the pattern. Decorative cabinets and panels of lacquer (rarely of the highly carved variety) were much prized during the 17th century, cabinets sometimes being made up from imported panels. Objects in native taste include cabinets, boxes, trays, vases, and table-screens, but occasionally much larger objects have survived. Notable among them is the 18th-century throne of Ch'ien Lung, now in the Victoria and Albert Museum (London). Carved lacquer fell into disuse in China towards the end of the 18th century, and does not seem to have been made since. Although most lacquer is on a wooden foundation, a very rare variety (*kanshitsu*) made in both China and Japan is laid on successive layers of hemp or fabric.

There is contemporary evidence that Japanese

Lacquer, Oriental. A fine-quality Japanese lacquer box, 18th century. *Sotheby & Co.*

lacquer was preferred to Chinese in the 17th century. The practice of carving was introduced into Japan from China about this time, but specimens are coarse and distinctly rare. Designs incised into lacquer, and enhanced with a dusting of gold powder, was originally a Chinese technique, but the best specimens came from Japan. Japanese lacquer furniture includes stands with shelves on different levels and cupboards closed with sliding doors. These are not especially rare, and most were imported after 1853. In native taste the Japanese specialized in lacquer boxes, often exquisitely worked. These are usually either writing-cases or medicine boxes (*inrō*). Designs are asymmetrical—a distinctive feature of Japanese work. They are difficult to date, but most were made in the 19th century.

See *Coromandel Screens*.

LACQUERING

By this is meant the laying of clear or coloured transparent varnishes on to metals, either to colour the surface or to preserve them from rusting or oxidization. Lacquering was an especially common way of preserving brass and iron. Brass door furniture, and clock-dials before the introduction of silvering, as well as metals of a silver colour, were sometimes coated with a lacquer tinted yellow, the pigments being

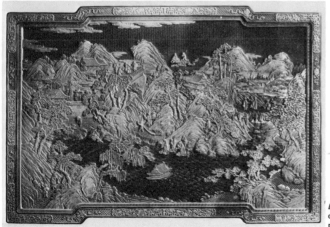

Lacquer, Oriental. In Imperial cinnabar, carved lacquer panel depicting the Taoist paradise. 18th century. *Sotheby & Co.*

Lambrequins. Rouen faïence plate of about 1720 elaborately decorated with a border pattern of *lambrequins* of the *style rayonnant* variety. *Musée des Beaux-Arts, Rouen.*

turmeric, saffron, or gamboge often reddened with a little dragon's blood, the latter being a bright-red gum obtained from the fruit of a species of palm. Dragon's blood was also occasionally added to clear lacquer used to protect brass with the object of softening the harshness of the colour of the metal.

To make a suitable lacquer add an ounce and a half of shellac and an ounce of gum sandarac to a quart of alcohol. This should be stored in a light-proof container. It can be coloured if desired.

LACY GLASS
Pressed glass with a stippled background between the patterns producing an effect not unlike that of old lace. It was manufactured extensively in the U.S.A. by the Boston and Sandwich Glass Company (see *Sandwich Glass*), and is now much sought by collectors. See *Glass, American.*

LADDER-BACK CHAIR
An English provincial chair with a back having horizontal slats between the uprights, suggestive of a ladder. Originally these chairs had rush seats. Chippendale made fine-quality mahogany chairs with transverse slats of carved and pierced mahogany.

See *Slat-back Chairs.*

LADIK RUGS
Ladik is the ancient town of Laodicea, now in Turkey. Among the most sought of its products is the prayer-rug with a triple *mihrab* (q.v.), and a row of stylized hyacinths or tulips immediately above. The Ghiordes knot was used, and the wool pile is very short. Colours are good, and there is a characteristic magenta which is combined with red, green, blue, yellow, and white. Ladiks are always prayer-rugs.

LALIQUE, RENÉ (1860–1945)
Lalique started as a designer, and exhibited jewellery at the Salon des Artistes Français towards the end of the 19th century. Subsequently he became inter-

ested in rock-crystal (q.v.), and then in architectural glasswork. The Lalique glass works at Wingen-sur-Moder (Alsace-Lorraine) was acquired in 1920, and Lalique exhibited his new designs with great success at the Paris Exhibition of 1925. The factory was continued after his death by his son, Marc. A good deal of Lalique glass deserves to be classified as 'antiques of the future'. The best is signed 'Lalique' in diamond engraving.

LAMBETH DELFT   See *Southwark and Lambeth (London) Delft*

LAMBETH PORCELAIN FACTORY
The wares of this South London factory are, as yet, unidentified, but a letter exists in the Wedgwood Archives addressed to Josiah Wedgwood by Matthew Horn of Lambeth claiming to have made figures, and vases four or five feet high, as well as dishes which were translucent, and offering to come to Staffordshire without pay to demonstrate his knowledge. The offer was not accepted, and nothing else seems to be known about Lambeth. Like the factories of Limehouse, Stepney, and Greenwich, its wares may exist but there seems no way of identifying them.

LAMBREQUINS
A type of ornament most commonly to be seen on Rouen faïence at the beginning of the 18th century, and on early porcelain from Saint-Cloud (q.v.). The word originally referred to certain bed-draperies, but it came to mean an abstract ornament based on pendant lacework, scrollwork, and the decoration of book-covers. *Lambrequins* adapted to a central position and radiating outwards were termed *style rayonnant.* The origin of this kind of pattern was

Lambrequins. A covered jar decorated with *lambrequins* in underglaze-blue porcelain of Saint-Cloud. c. 1700. *Victoria and Albert Museum.*

certainly not bed-drapes, but rather the engraved designs of *ornamenistes* such as Virgil Solis and Jean Bérain, where they were called *broderies*, which suggests that they were originally derived from embroidery patterns. *Lambrequins* began to disappear with the *Régence* (1715–1725), but the *style rayonnant* lingered until the middle of the 18th century.

LAMÉ (French)
Cloth woven from metal threads, usually gold and silver.

LAMERIE, PAUL DE (1688–1751)
The best known of the rococo silversmiths working in England, de Lamerie was born in the Netherlands of French parents. He was brought to England in 1691 by his father, and apprenticed at the age of fifteen to Pierre Platel, another Anglo-French silversmith. He entered his mark at the Goldsmiths' Hall in 1712, when he had premises at Windmill Street, near Piccadilly Circus. His mark at that time, in accordance with the rule of using the first two letters of the surname, was *LA*, but this he changed to *PL* in 1732, when he was still at Windmill Street, although Sir Charles Jackson suggests that this mark may have been entered as early as 1724. Since examples of his work thus marked exist which are earlier than 1732, we can fairly assume that he occasionally employed this stamp before it was officially entered. An Act of 1739 compelled all goldsmiths to enter a new mark consisting of the initial letters of their Christian and surnames, and that of de Lamerie shows his initials, *PL*, in script, with a crown above and a pellet below. He was then at Gerrard Street, not far from his original premises.

De Lamerie was a silversmith of exceptional skill, much influenced by the prevailing rococo style in France, and there is often more than a hint of both Bérain and Meissonnier in his designs. He was especially master of the art of engraving and flat-chasing.

De Lamerie was prolific, despite the fact that he employed only two assistants, and his work was much sought at the time by noble families. Today it not undeservedly commands the highest prices of all 18th-century English silversmiths in the saleroom.

LAMPAS
A type of patterned satin somewhat resembling damask, which was sometimes brocaded or ornamented with gold and silver thread.

LAMPS, GLASS
The earliest English glass lamps were of the 'float-wick' type, in which a small hempen wick floated in train-oil (whale-oil) in a cup on a low stem and foot. These date from about 1680, and were in use throughout the 18th century with various improvements to the wick. Soon after their introduction an improved lamp was introduced which was a container for oil with a small handle, and a central cover through which the wick passed, the lower part being

Lamerie, Paul de. A helmet-shaped ewer reminiscent of late 17th-century French ewers of faïence from Nevers. By Paul de Lamerie. London. 1736. Silver-gilt. *Sotheby & Co.*

immersed in the fuel. It was not until the 1780s that the flat ribbon wick was introduced, but this gave considerably better illumination. Eighteenth-century lamps of candlestick form were provided with a spherical chamber to which a small cylinder was attached. The chamber contained the oil and wick, the cylinder fitting into the candle socket in place of a candle. The lacemakers' lamp is somewhat similar in appearance, but a great deal rarer. This could burn either oil, with the aid of the device described, or a candle. The stem is hollow, with an opening in the foot closed with a cork, and midway it broadens out into a sphere. The stem and the sphere were intended to be filled with water, which was retained by the cork, and, when lit, the sphere formed a low-power magnifier.

Few American glass lamps can be dated, even tentatively, to the closing years of the 18th century, but after about 1825 those of pressed glass were produced by the New England Glass Company (q.v.) and the Boston and Sandwich Glass Company (see *Sandwich Glass*) and became widely popular. The oil-reservoirs were made of both clear and coloured glass, at first for whale-oil, and from about 1865 for kerosene (paraffin oil). The shades were often of glass decorated with cutting and engraving.

LANCASTER (NEW YORK) GLASS WORKS
A group of Pittsburgh workmen established a glass works here in 1849. It made bottles and flasks in amber, aquamarine, green, and transparent glass. 'Success to the Railroad' is a Lancaster flask which is much sought. See *Glass, American*.

LANCRET, NICOLAS (1690–1743)
French painter, pupil of Gillot (q.v.), who worked so much in the style of Watteau that their landscapes are often almost indistinguishable one from the other. He later painted *Fêtes Galantes*, and these, like those of Watteau, commonly inspired porcelain-painting from about 1740 onwards. 'Watteau scenes', in fact, can usually be described as 'Lancret scenes' with as much accuracy.

Lange Lyzen. A 'long Eliza' on a Worcester vase of c. 1758. The shape of the vase is Chinese, and goes back to the 1st millennium B.C.

LANGE LYZEN (Dutch)
'Long Elizas.' Figures of women copied from Chinese porcelain by European faïence and porcelain painters (nearly always in blue), in which height and slenderness have been exaggerated. They can be seen quite often decorating early Worcester blue-and-white porcelain. The prototypes are to be found on Chinese porcelain exported during the reign of Wan-li (1573–1619).

LANGLEY, BATTY (1696–1751)
Architect and interior designer. The son of a gardener, Batty Langley seems to have been largely self-taught as an architect. He is notable for his influence on mid-18th-century design, but in any capacity he was always a joke to the *cognoscenti* such as Horace Walpole. Although his first essays in architecture were in the classical style, he later turned to Gothic, which Walpole dismissed summarily as 'Batty Langley Gothic'. His *Gothic Architecture Improved* (the Five Orders [q.v.] gothicized) appeared in 1742. His opinions on landscape gardening may be gathered from the following quotation of 1728: 'No three trees to range together in a straight line . . . Nothing more shocking than a stiff, regular garden. . . . Ruins of Buildings, after the old Roman manner to terminate such walks that end in disagreeable objects; which Ruins may be either painted on canvas, or actually built in that Manner with brick and covered with plastering.' His books now have only antiquarian interest.

LAPIDARIES
Workmen skilled in the cutting and engraving of precious and semi-precious stones, with the aid either of rotating wheels of varying sizes charged with abrasive, or with hand-tools pointed with a ruby or diamond. Lapidaries often worked in glass, notably during Roman times and later in Germany. See *Bohemian Glass*; *Diatretarii*; *Hardness of Materials*.

LAPIS LAZULI
A rare semi-precious stone of mixed composition. The rich deep azure colour is due to the presence of the mineral lazurite, and, in colour, this much resembles the prized azurite patination of some old bronze. Lapis lazuli can be either opaque or slightly translucent. It has been used in the past for small decorative objects, and for inlaying in conjunction with other stones. It is also the source of the natural ultramarine pigment of the painter, but it is rarely used today owing to its cost.

LA ROCHELLE (Charente-Inférieure, France) FAÏENCE
The city of La Rochelle is one of several western towns (Angoulême, Saintes, Cognac, and Marans) which were influenced by workers from both north and south (Rouen and Nevers, Montpellier and Moustiers) all of which had some influence on the faïence of the Charente region. The first attempt to produce faïence was in 1721, but it failed. Pierre Roussencq started a more successful business at Marans in 1740, taking in, in 1749, a shipowner of La Rochelle called Henri Brevet. On the dissolution of this partnership some time before 1754 Brevet opened another factory at La Rochelle. In 1789 the same company under the name of Piaud et Crespin recorded 20,000 pieces in its storehouse. The influence of Rouen and Nevers is so great as to cause difficulties of attribution. One of the Borne family is mentioned in the records, as well as Laurent Boissier and Jacques Dupré. They came from Montpellier in 1753. Decoration is therefore derivative, but some original designs, in the neo-classical style, of local scenes framed in swags and garlands do occur, to be followed by revolutionary designs. Enamelling was introduced by Piaud, and he subsequently used naturalistic flower-patterns derived from Marseille and Meissen. Some crudely potted pieces have Chinese figures in green and red who wear big hats.

La Rochelle. Four plates of La Rochelle faïence. Second half of the 18th century. *Musée Régional Dupuy-Mestreau, Saintes, Charente-Maritime.*

Rococo pieces encrusted with shells were made at La Rochelle, and these are being reproduced today.

LA SALLE, PHILIPPE DE (1723–1805)
An influential designer and weaver of silks and velvets at Lyon. La Salle was a friend of Boucher, and his fabrics were so highly regarded that he received many commissions from the French, Spanish, and Russian Courts. His work is represented in the Textile Museum at Lyon, where many of his original designs can still be seen.

LATCH-HOOK
An almost invariable ornamental element of the Caucasian and some West Asiatic rugs, which also sometimes occurs on Chinese rugs. It is formed as follows:

Lattice-work. Lattice-work forming the backs of chairs in the Soane Museum, once the residence of Sir John Soane. *Lincoln's Inn, London, W.C.*

LATHE
The lathe is a device for rotating the material to be shaped while bringing a cutting-tool into contact with it. It has been aptly described as the 'queen of machine-tools', and it is certainly the most versatile. The earliest known picture of a lathe is to be found on the wall of an Egyptian tomb of the 3rd century B.C., but it was probably in use before 1000 B.C., and may have been suggested by the potter's wheel which is considerably older. The spring-pole and treadle drive may have been known before the present era, but it was certainly common by medieval times. This, however, had many drawbacks, notably that it was difficult to guide the cutting-tool and work the treadle at the same time, and that the work revolved backwards and forwards. By the middle of the 16th century at the latest a continuous drive had been devised, by which a second man turned a driving-wheel which was weighted to enable the work to proceed smoothly. The first screw-cutting lathe, by which the position of the tool was governed mechanically, dates from the end of the 15th century, and Leonardo designed a number of improvements to it. Various improvements were made subsequently, and by 1701 the turning of iron is mentioned by Charles Plumier (*L'Art de Tourneur*) although it was rarely done. Plumier himself designed an improved lathe for this purpose. An iron-turning lathe driven by water-power was in use in Sweden by 1710.

The engine-turning (q.v.) lathe was developed in France before the middle of the 18th century, and by 1770 an advanced design utilizing a 'rose' to guide the tool was in use. In England Henry Maudslay, apprenticed at Woolwich Arsenal, devised notable improvements, producing his first screw-cutting lathe in 1797 which could handle work three feet long and six inches in diameter. It was on these later developments that the Industrial Revolution was largely based, and by 1800 most of the features of the modern lathe had already appeared, although they still needed to be perfected.

Until the end of the 18th century most of the simpler operations, such as wood-turning for furniture-makers, were still being done on primitive lathes, and until about 1750 the lathe was principally being used for wood-turning, for decorating such soft metals as pewter, and for making parts for clocks and scientific instruments from brass where precision was needed.

See *Engine-turning*.

LATTEN
Old English term for brass (q.v.); from the Old French *laiton*.

LATTICE-WORK
A criss-cross arrangement of wood or metal. In wood, lattice-work is part of the design of some Sheraton chair-backs, and in metal it is used instead of wood for the panels of doors to cabinets and bookcases, usually with a backing of silk. See *Fretwork*.

LATTICINIO GLASS   See *Venetian Glass*

LAURAGAIS, LOUIS-LÉON-FELICITÉ BRANCAS, COMTE DE
An enigmatic figure about whom little is known. Shortly before 1763 he made some rather primitive hard porcelain from clay found near Alençon, and a few specimens of uncertain attribution survive. He took out an English patent in 1766, and it has been said that he was also acquainted with Cornish kaolin. This antedated the patent of Cookworthy of Plymouth (q.v.) by two years. Most surviving specimens attributed to the Comte de Lauragais are in the

Laub und Bandelwerke. **Leaf and strapwork surrounding a landscape on Meissen porcelain of about 1740.** *Hastings Museum and Art Gallery.*

Musée de Sèvres, although some ascribed to him were exhibited in a loan collection at the Alexandra Palace (North London) in 1873 and destroyed by fire while on exhibition.

LAUREL
The leaves of this plant appear quite commonly in the 18th century as an element of neo-classical decoration. It was originally sacred to Apollo.

LEAD
A silvery grey metal, soft, inelastic, malleable, very plastic, and of relatively great weight. Lead is extremely soft and can easily be cut with a knife. It can be fashioned in sheet form with ease, and edges can be joined by soldering at low temperatures. It soon breaks under stress, but it is a useful casting metal owing to its low melting-point (327° C.), although it possesses the disadvantage of shrinking considerably during cooling. Lead corrodes quickly with exposure to the weather in industrial areas, with the formation of a whitish lead carbonate which may eventually destroy it entirely, although rain in country areas rarely has a serious effect.

Lead has always been used for garden-ornaments —statuary, vases, *jardinières,* and fountains. During Tudor times it was employed for rain-water down-pipes to houses, and in sheet-form it was used for bas reliefs in the making of architectural sculptured ornament.

If it is necessary to protect lead from the effects of weather an application of grease, such as vaseline or water-pump grease, is effective, or waxing or lacquering (q.v.) can be used instead.

Lead is alloyed with tin, when it forms solder or pewter (q.v.) according to proportion. Added to bronze it increases the fluidity of the metal in its molten state. Alloyed with copper it becomes cock-metal (q.v.).

Objects of lead subsequently gilded have sometimes been passed off as gold. Superficially the resemblance is fairly close, and the weight is comparable.

LE BRUN, CHARLES (1619–1690)
French painter and designer; pupil of Simon Vouet; studied in Italy, 1642–1646. In 1648 Le Brun took a leading part in the formation of the French Academy, and was appointed director of the Gobelins factory (the *Manufacture royale des meubles de la couronne* —q.v.) in 1662, becoming thereafter virtual dictator of art in France until the death of Colbert. His most important work was the Galerie des Glaces at Versailles.

LE CREUSOT GLASS FACTORY
This factory was originally situated in the grounds of the *château* of Saint-Cloud, near Sèvres, and it was under the patronage of Marie-Antoinette. It made crystal glass in the English style. The undertaking was removed to Le Creusot in 1785 to be near the source of coal fuel. In 1806 it became the *Manufacture de leurs Majestés Imperiales,* but it was bought by Baccarat (q.v.) and Saint-Louis (q.v.) in association in 1831 and suppressed. Le Creusot was noted for lustres for lighting-fixtures, crystal glass, cut-glass, and *crystallo ceramie* (q.v.).

LEEDS POTTERY FACTORY
It is believed that a pottery was being operated near Leeds (Yorkshire) during the 1750s. The partners were John Armitage, William Green, and Henry

Lead. **Lead figure of a Shepherdess. 17th century. Figures of this kind were commonly used as ornaments in the gardens of great houses.** *Christie, Manson & Woods Ltd.*

Ackroyd, the latter reappearing in a list of partners in 1781. Henry Ackroyd died in 1788 and his share was inherited by his widow and daughter.

William Hartley joined the firm in 1776 and the new style of the pottery was Humble, Hartley, Greens & Co. Hartley's advent brought prosperity and a change of style. He seems to have intended to develop the factory as a competitor for Wedgwood, and he was very talented and produced lively, individual wares. The business was very prosperous during the last quarter of the 18th century. In 1781 William Humble resigned and the firm traded as Hartley, Greens & Co, and in 1806 the Leeds pottery relinquished its interest in Greens, Hartley & Co. of Swinton, which continued as Brameld & Co., subsequently becoming the Rockingham China Works (q.v.).

At that time decline seems to have set in at Leeds, the partners were in dissent, and the increase in Continental creamware reduced its export markets. It became bankrupt in 1820, after which it was carried on in a halting way, and with several changes of ownership and name—Samuel Wainwright; the Leeds Pottery Company; Stephen and James Chappell; Warburton & Britton, after 1850; and in 1872, Richard Britton, till 1878, when he too became bankrupt.

In mid-18th century the wares produced by Leeds were largely made in imitation of Whieldon. They include white salt-glaze; glazed and unglazed red stoneware; red earthenware; black earthenware; creamware, plain, painted or with coloured glazes; and coloured bodies with applied designs in cream-coloured clay. Some of these pieces may be certainly recognized as Leeds, since they have handles and terminals of a kind made only in the Yorkshire factory. Clay came from Poole and flint from Sussex, apart from some local white clay mentioned in the records.

Salt-glaze ware was made at Swinton and other south Yorkshire factories as well as Leeds, though it is not always easy to recognize it. Tea- or coffee-pots of this kind with a feathered pattern on the spout may be Leeds. Red stoneware (q.v.) needed no glaze as it was hard-fired. Engine-turning was practised, and it was given pseudo-Chinese marks, occasionally to be found on other Leeds pieces.

Creamware was made of clay from Poole, white clay from local beds, and flint from Kent and Sussex, with grit in the form of local sand. The wares are original in form, and often fluently and well painted. The glaze is rather yellowish and uneven in application, with crazing in the hollows. Attempts to control this led to very thin applications of glaze and dry patches on the body. After the fashion for crabstock handles had passed, Leeds used a form typical of its wares—a double, reeded, intertwined handle with applied terminals. Early knops were acorns, flowers, or mushroom-shaped.

After 1775 Champion's (q.v.) patent was partially overruled, with the result that Cornish stone and clay were available to all earthenware potters. These raw

Leeds Creamware. A teapot of typical form enamelled with flowers. Leeds creamware. c. 1770. *Hove Museum and Art Gallery.*

materials completely changed the body, which became much more brittle and paler. To achieve the pale colour was every potter's ambition, and refinement to match the neo-classical style naturally followed. William Hartley was responsible for the new patterns. There was much pierced work in the style of contemporary silver, whilst rococo forms gave way before the swags, urns, husks and acanthus leaves of the Adam style. Between 1790 and 1800 many figures were produced, but mostly in pearlware. These figures may all have been modelled by one man, John Smith. The glaze in conjunction with a white body produced a greyish tone of the kind called pearlware by Josiah Wedgwood, which is a form of creamware glazed with a bluish tint rather than the usual yellow or greenish tones. In the early period coloured glazes of the Staffordshire type were made at Leeds; they preceded enamel-painting and were still in use in 1820.

Creamware made at Leeds was enamelled by outside decorators called Robinson & Rhodes (q.v.). After 1768 the factory probably did its own enamelling, but the style altered very little. Much of David Rhodes's enamelling is black and red, with blue, green, yellow, or rose-pink flower knops. Figure-painting in landscape was free and natural in style. These men were also responsible for stylized bird- and flower-painting, and a diaper design they called chintz. After 1775 the palette was enlarged with the addition of green, blue, purple, pink, yellow, and sometimes gilding, with some red monochrome painting of flowers and figures in landscapes. A great quantity of creamware was shipped to the Continent and decorated in Holland. The Dutch palette is brick-red, pale green, blue, flesh-colour, yellow and black. The enamels are very dry, and Biblical and political subjects were popular.

Transfer-printing was in full swing at Leeds by 1780, though it was not so competent as at Liverpool. Colours were brick-red, jet-black, and a purplish black, and, after 1800, blue-black and grey.

The Modern Pottery at Leeds, founded by Slee in 1888, used the old Leeds moulds and patterns for creamware bearing an imitation of the old mark. In general, these forgeries are lighter in weight than the old ware, and the mark has been added with a suspicious evenness. The glaze is slightly more lustrous, and the finish too precise. It is difficult to describe adequately the many slight variations which add up to the recognition of the spurious specimen, but anyone acquainted with the old ware ought not to be deceived. Medallions in black basaltes ware, and creamware decorated with silver lustre, were also made here in imitation of the original factory. Contemporary Continental imitations, sometimes very close, were made at Douai by an Englishman named Leigh.

LE GAIGNEUR, LOUIS

Owner of the Buhl Manufactory with a workshop at Queen Street, Edgware Road, London, Le Gaigneur was one of the best of the 19th-century craftsmen to work in the style of A.-C. Boulle. Little is now known of him, and it is probable that he was an *emigré ébéniste* who came to London during the Revolution. The Prince Regent bought Boulle furniture from him in 1815, and a table from his hand is in Windsor Castle. His prices—£250 for a table, equivalent to about £2,500 in 1968—are related to those charged in Paris for work of good quality before the Revolution, and his work should not be confused with the many inferior imitations of Boulle furniture made later in the 19th century in Paris, and probably in London also.

His stamp was *LE GAIGNEUR*, or *LOUIS LE GAIGNEUR FECIT*, although it is not known whether he employed it invariably.

LELEU, JEAN-FRANÇOIS (1729–1807)

Leleu received his training in the workshop of J. F. Oeben, but left after his master's death in 1763 in consequence of a violent quarrel with Riesener. Leleu, who became *maître ébéniste* 1n 1764, worked for the Court, the Prince de Condé, Mme du Barry, and Marie-Antoinette. His furniture designs are varied. Some examples are decorated with plaques of Sèvres porcelain, but he also worked occasionally in the style of A.-C. Boulle. Influenced by Oeben, he produced dual-purpose furniture of complicated mechanical design. Stamps: *J. F. LELEU* or *JFL*.

LEMOYNE, JEAN-BAPTISTE (1704–1778)

Sculptor, son of J.-B. Lemoyne *aîne* (1679–1731). Lemoyne *fils* became an Academician in 1738, and was noted for his portrait busts. Some of his work was reproduced by the porcelain factories; for instance, his *Hercules and Omphale* by Vincennes and Chelsea.

LEONI, LEONE (1509–1590)

Italian sculptor working in Milan. He was also a goldsmith and medallist, and there are several small bronzes by him in Vienna. He worked in Spain where he was assisted by his son, Pompeo (1573–1608).

LE ROY, JULIEN

One of the most noted of French clockmakers, Le Roy became *maître* of the Guild in 1713. He was

responsible for many improvements to clock-movements, and made a number of important innovations. Le Roy wrote several books on the craft of clock-making, and gained a contemporary European reputation.

LES ISLETTES (Meuse, France) FAÏENCE

In 1737 a factory was founded in this village near Lunéville which was run by the Bernard family till the middle of the 19th century. Its faïence was successful, due to its popular appeal and topical subjects, many of which were copied from magazines. They include military scenes, contemporary events, and decorations of birds, flowers, trophies, and *chinoiseries*. A few figures and groups imitating those of Lunéville were made.

LESUM (Hannover, Germany) FAÏENCE FACTORY

This factory was established at Lesum in 1755 by J. C. Vielstich (see *Wrisbergholzen*). Apart from the usual useful wares, Vielstich seems to have made many kinds of boxes in the shape of vegetables and fruit, as well as baskets, ink-stands, pot-pourri vases, wall-tiles, and stoves. Some pierced baskets and tankards in manganese with reserves of flowers or galloping horses are of good quality. Outstanding, however, is a large blue-and-white stove, and stove-tiles were very similar to work done in nearby Hamburg. The body is reddish, with a yellow or blue-toned glaze. Blue is used in combination with a dull manganese, insipid green, and various yellows. The mark is *V* with a stroke and a painter's mark below.

LIBBEY GLASS COMPANY

This company, located at Toledo, Ohio, was founded by W. L. Libbey, who leased the works of the New England Glass Company (q.v.) in 1878. The Toledo factory is noted for cut-glass of exceptional quality. See *Glass, American*.

LIBRARY STEPS

Steps made for the purpose of reaching the topmost shelves in libraries. Chairs were sometimes made to serve a dual purpose, unfolding in the middle to form three or four steps for this and kindred purposes. Most are English, made towards the end of the 18th century and in the early decades of the 19th.

LIGNUM VITAE

A very hard dark brown or greenish-black wood from South America used in the 17th century, especially by the Dutch, for chests and cupboards, or for objects where hard wear had to be resisted.

LILLE FAÏENCE

Jacques Feburier, a merchant-potter of Tournai, and Jean Bossu applied to build kilns at Lille in 1696. The two men quarrelled and Feburier returned to Tournai, but he came back in 1700, took over the enterprise from the inefficient Bossu, and made it prosper. Feburier worked intentionally in the style of Dutch delft, and his clay came from the same place, near Tournai, which causes confusion, but the wares are light, with a good-quality glaze made from lead and tin brought from England. In 1729 Jacques Feburier died, and was succeeded by his widow and son-in-law, François Boussemaert. The business was a great success and only began to decline after 1776, when Boussemaert's interest turned to a glass factory at Lille and a porcelain factory at Arras. The faïence factory at Lille continued till 1802. Marks were fairly common in the Boussemaert period: entwined script letters *JBF*, accompanied by the *fleur-de-lys* and the dolphins from the City's Coat of Arms.

The first period produced a rich blue and polychrome *style rayonnant* (q.v.) and *genre* scenes in blue *camaieu* in the manner of Delft. These were followed by rococo pieces in a palette of purple, yellow, and yellowish-green. The red is very opaque and muddy. There are several series of jugs and other wares with designs depicting local crafts and bearing the emblems of the guilds—coopers, weavers, tanners, etc. Figures were popular, and Lille made jugs in the shape of *gendarmes,* women in aprons, nurses, and so on, somewhat in the manner of English Toby jugs. Other factories were also working at Lille, and one, run by Barthelemy Dorez, started in 1711 and subsequently made porcelain. Other small enterprises manufactured mostly tiles.

A mark, *Lille 1767,* surmounted by a crown, with foliate designs on either side, has been extensively used on reproductions of snuff-boxes, wall-plaques, etc., within recent times. The actual place of manufacture is uncertain.

LIMBACH PORCELAIN FACTORY
This factory was founded by Gotthelf Greiner, a glass-maker, in 1772, who established a flourishing concern which, after his death in 1797, became Gotthelf Greiner Söhne. The earliest mark of crossed *L*'s was deliberately adopted to simulate the

Limbach Porcelain. Virgin and child. c. 1775. *British Museum.*

crossed swords of Meissen, but in 1787, after strong protests from the royal factory, the mark of the clover leaf was adopted, although the crossed *L*'s mark was still employed at Groszbreitenbach (q.v.) which was a branch establishment.

Service-ware was well painted both in monochrome and polychrome enamels, often in imitation of standard Meissen patterns. Landscapes and figures with ruins occur in purple monochrome.

Flowers were a particular favourite until 1790. Painters were drawn both from Kloster-Veilsdorf and Ludwigsburg. Figures were commonly made, and although naive in modelling they have a character and charm of their own. Large heads are a distinctive feature. The signatures *Heinrich Haag* and *J. Haag* appearing on some specimens of Limbach porcelain are those of Johann Jakob Heinrich and Johann Friedrich Haag, factory painters who also functioned as *Hausmaler* between 1767 and about 1800.

LIME GLASS
A substitute for lead-glass discovered in America in 1864 by William Leighton, a chemist in a glass factory at Wheeling, West Virginia. It was especially used in the manufacture of bottles, and provided severe competition for many of the manufacturers of lead-glass at the time. It had the advantages both of cheapness, and of cooling much more quickly than lead-glass, enabling manufacturing processes to be speeded up. It was noticeably lighter in weight.

Library Steps. A pair of library steps which, when not in use, fold to form a low table. English. Late 18th century. *Wilfred Bull, Esq.*

Limewood. The *Gänsemännchen* (Man with a Pair of Geese). Limewood model by Pancraz Labenwolf for a bronze fountain in the Obstmarkt, Nürnberg (1540–1545). *Germanisches National Museum, Nürnberg.*

LIME (LINDEN) WOOD

A soft, finely textured wood without a well-marked grain, ivory-white when first cut, but darkening with age. Lime has always been one of the most prized woods for carving since it does not split when chiselled. It has been extensively employed for the carved decoration of furniture, and mirror and picture frames, as well as for small sculpture. In England, Grinling Gibbon (q.v.) relied on it almost entirely, and much of the carved wood sculpture of southern Germany and Austria is in this medium. The original models for Bustelli's (q.v.) porcelain figures at Nymphenburg were carved in limewood, and bronzes often started life in this way. Limewood was also employed in England as a foundation for japanning.

LIMEHOUSE PORCELAIN

A factory for the manufacture of porcelain existed at Dick (or Duke) Shore, Limehouse, East London, from 1747 or before till 1748. Its existence is recorded by Dr Pococke in his references to visits to Newcastle-under-Lyme and Bristol, and it is confirmed by several contemporary advertisements, the last of which, on 3 June 1748, called a meeting of creditors. It is possible that a soaprock porcelain (q.v.) was made, but no certainly attributed specimens so far have been identified.

LIMOGES (Haute-Vienne, France) FAÏENCE

Famous for its porcelain production in the late 18th and 19th centuries, Limoges also made faïence, but of an entirely derivative kind. The enterprise was founded in 1736 by a man named Massié, and one or two rare pieces marked *Limoges,* and dated between 1738 and 1741, confirm the factory's existence. Shards found on the site are nearly all domestic ware, octagonal or chamfered plates, jars, and circular ink-stands with blue-and-white *lambrequins* in the southern style.

LIMOGES (Haute-Vienne, France) PORCELAIN FACTORIES

France's principal deposits of clay and china stone are at Saint-Yrieix, not far from Limoges. An inferior kind of faïence was made here from 1736, and at least some of the production was in the style of Moustiers (q.v.). A manufacture of hard-paste porcelain was established here in 1771 by two brothers named Grellet, with the aid of André Massié, who founded the faïence factory, and a chemist named Fournérat. It was under the protection of the King's brother, the Comte d'Artois (later Charles X). The mark *CD* was used, and when this appears in conjunction with the Sèvres mark, it denotes a date after 1784, when the King seems to have acquired the factory as a branch of Sèvres, and Darcet, later a Sèvres director, was placed in charge. Decorations are principally those current at Sèvres, and in Paris generally. Mostly table-services were made, and it is possible that some Limoges white porcelain may have been sent to Sèvres for decoration.

Beginning in 1797 with a factory started by Baignol, new enterprises began to spring up, and much porcelain was exported to the United States in the 19th century under the name of Haviland ware. This is now also manufactured in the U.S.A. The greater part of the production was of service-ware of good quality, usually fully marked.

Limoges Faïence. Wall-fountain of Limoges faïence. 1793. *Musée National de Céramique Adrien-Dubouché, Limoges.*

LIMOGES PAINTED ENAMELS

The painted enamels of Limoges range in date from the beginning of the 16th century to the end of the 17th. The subject is not well documented, and the art seems to have been largely the secret of a few families and passed on from father to son. Best known are the Penicaud family, of which the first was Nardon (Léonard) who died about the middle of the 16th century. There were several others of the same name, chiefly three called Jean who succeeded each other, and one named Pierre. The Limousin family started with Léonard Limousin in the early years of the 16th century, and he later became enameller to François I. The work of other enamellers of this name is less well known and inferior to that of Léonard. The work of his brother Martin, two of his sons (both named François), and two Jeans (Jehan) has been tentatively identified. The Nouaillier family, of whom the best known is Nicolas, worked in the 16th century, but their work is artistically unimportant. Of better quality are the enamels of Pierre Reymond, who flourished in the second half of the 16th century. He appears to have worked for German patrons, and was influenced by such painters as Dürer. Unlike the others, it is probable that he organized his work on almost factory lines, and inferior contemporary copies of his more important work exist initialled by him. These were probably made by workmen under his supervision. The Laudin family continued to practise the art during the 17th century.

Enamelling of this kind may have been practised in Poitiers, in Vienne, not far from Limoges, since Lister (1698) refers to the ancient vases of Poitiers, which were not at that time any longer to be had. Attributions to individual families working in Limoges during the 16th century are very uncertain, and are based on a relatively small number of signed or documented examples.

The early technique of Nardon Penicaud was to

Limoges Enamel. **Limoges painted enamel plaque with the subject of the Crucifixion. 16th century.** *Sotheby & Co.*

prepare a flat plate of copper a little thicker than that which later became customary, which he covered, front and back, with a layer of enamel opacified with tin oxide on which the design was outlined in black and given a light firing. Coloured enamels were then applied to the surface within the outlines and also fired. The palette was a simple one. Blue from cobalt oxide; turquoise-blue and green from copper; a mustard-yellow; violet from manganese, and a brown from the same source. A wash of very pale manganese-violet provided flesh tints, and gold, in the form of honey-gold, was employed fairly extensively, although this has largely disappeared in many instances. The enamel covering at the back of many early specimens is fissured, probably the result of unequal contraction rates of the enamel and the metal base.

Later in the 16th century painting *en grisaille* (q.v.), often on a black ground, became fashionable, and a red pigment derived from gold was employed for flesh-tints. Painting *en grisaille*, or in black, with flesh-tints in red, a little gilding being added, was the basis for the later faïence colour-scheme known as *Schwarzlot* (q.v.), which probably had its origin in enamelling of this kind.

The earliest designs to be found on Limoges enamels are religious, and taken from illustrations to devotional works. The style is late Gothic. During the reign of François I (acc. 1515, d. 1547) classical themes of the Renaissance were first in favour, and Léonard Limousin (d. 1575) was among the earliest of the enamellers to accept the new influence. Some examples of his early work have been identified as based on Raphael, after engravings by Marcantonio Raimondi (q.v.). This enameller was relatively prolific, and survivals attributed to him are fairly numerous. Pierre Reymond was much influenced by Renaissance themes, and he employed *motifs* which reveal considerable similarity to the grotesques (q.v.) popular as decoration on contemporary *maiolica*. Perhaps the closest to Italian *maiolica* in the use of classical themes and grotesque ornament was Jean Court, called Vigier, whose work is represented in the Salting Collection (Victoria and Albert Museum).

The origin of painted enamels is uncertain. Until the beginning of the 16th century enamel on metalwork had been executed in either the *champlevé* or *cloisonné* techniques (q.v.), and difficulty was at first experienced in laying an enamel ground without these aids, especially as the base metal could not be thick enough to utilize the customary method of deeply scoring the surface to key the enamel to the metal. It was eventually found that a metal plate held between two layers of enamel, one on either side, gave satisfactory results. Thin, flat plates, however, were insufficiently rigid to protect the enamel from cracking, and later specimens are therefore convex on the upper surface and concave on the lower which greatly strengthened them. Many Limoges enamels were framed in cast brass mouldings, and were originally in wooden cases.

Neglected by collectors in recent times, Limoges enamels were much in demand between 1880 and 1914. In the 1850s they were imitated on Worcester porcelain by Thomas Bott, it is said at the suggestion of the Prince Consort, who collected them.

The making of enamels was started at Limoges at a much earlier date than that discussed here, and *chasses* and reliquaries in the *champlevé* technique are much sought today.

LINCK, FRANZ KONRAD (d. 1793)

Court Sculptor to the Elector-Palatine, Linck studied at the Vienna Academy, and subsequently at Berlin and Potsdam. He was *Modellmeister* to the Frankenthal porcelain factory (q.v.) from 1762 to 1766, and provided it with models for some years after. He worked in an early version of the neo-classical style, and his modelling is excellent in quality. His figures have slightly smaller heads than is usual, and the features are uncommonly expressive. He made considerable use of the nude, and most of his subjects were taken from classical mythology.

LINENFOLD (English)

Ornament carved to simulate folded linen, which was especially popular during Tudor times but can sometimes be found decorating later work. Linenfold carving was generally employed for wall-panelling and for chests. Primarily a Gothic *motif*, it may be seen soon after 1500 combined with medallions enclosing heads. Most linenfold panelling was at one time painted, and in rare instances traces of paint can still be detected.

LINEN-PRESS (English)

A cupboard with shelves for storing linen, sometimes fitted with flat boards for pressing the linen operated either by weights or by a screw mechanism. The linen-press was introduced about mid-17th century to replace the earlier chest employed for the purpose.

LINNELL, WILLIAM AND JOHN

William Linnell (fl. 1720–1763) was a carver and gilder, and the sale of his effects in 1763 included pier-glasses, carved terms, brackets, and *girandoles*, as well as Derbyshire and Italian marble tables. This suggests the kind of work he was doing. He was succeeded by John Linnell (d. 1796), perhaps a son, who was a carver, cabinet-maker, and upholsterer. John Linnell worked at Osterley Park (West London), both to his own designs and to those of the Adam Brothers.

LION

The lion has been a popular ornamental *motif* from the earliest times, much used by the Greeks and Romans. It occurs frequently in Renaissance art, and is a common heraldic emblem. In Christian art Christ is represented as the Lion of Judah, it is an attribute of St Mark, and was used as a moulded mask on Venetian glass for this reason. It also' symbolizes St Jerome. The lion head with the ring in its mouth is employed as a knocker, a door-handle,

Lion. Lion forming one of the handles of an English wine-cistern 4½ feet long. Cistern by the Royal Goldsmith, Thomas Heming. Made in 1770.

a furniture handle, or as a ring handle to vessels of bronze. It is carved as an ornament on furniture, and in England it occurs as a carved *motif* on the knees of cabriole legs (q.v.) to chairs and settees made between 1720 and 1735 so often that this is sometimes called the 'Lion period'. The lion-mask is also found in conjunction with lion-paw feet. In Regency times it again appears as cast ormolu ornament, the paws as the feet of tables and chairs. In heraldry the lion *couchant* represents sovereignty; *rampant*, magnanimity; *passant*, resolution; *guardant*, prudence; *salient*, valour; *sciant*, counsel; *regardant*, circumspection.

LIOTARD, JOHN STEPHEN (1702 to after 1776)

Miniaturist in enamel and water-colour, born in Geneva. He studied in Paris (1725), was in Rome in 1738, and afterwards visited Istanbul where he adopted Eastern costume. He twice visited England, the second time in 1772 when he brought glass-pictures painted in enamels which were admired but judged too expensive. An enamel self-portrait in Eastern costume was in the Strawberry Hill (q.v.) sale of 1832.

LISTER, DR MARTIN (fl. c. 1700)

Dr Martin Lister was physician to Queen Anne. He journeyed to Paris in 1698 in the train of the Duke of Portland, who was taking part in the negotiations for the Peace of Ryswick. Lister's importance is in a short book written by him entitled *A Journey to Paris in the Year 1698*, published in that year. In it he records visits to several artists and collections, as well as to the Saint-Cloud porcelain factory (q.v.) and the manufactory of mirror-glass in the Faubourg

Saint-Antoine. Lister was a man of many interests, who was a keen observer, and his book is of considerable interest to students of the period.

LIT DE PARADE (French)

The *lit d'apparat*, or state bed, was usually that of the King, and from the earliest times it was always the focus of great luxury. It was, in France, at one time called the *lit de justice*, because the King literally dispensed justice from it. It was also here that he died in state.

The *lit de parade* had the most elaborate curtaining and canopy, and it was situated in a large room which was one of common resort, where the King gave audiences and transacted state business. The French kings, in particular, usually had many beds. Louis XIV had more than four hundred, in a kind of descending scale of luxury, and these were of many different types, being named principally from the presence or absence of headboards, and pillars, and differences in the form of the canopy and the drapes, or in the method of suspending the canopy. Where the canopy was upheld by four posts (*quenouilles*) the bed was termed *lit à la française*; if from the back only, *à la duchesse*; and suspended from the ceiling, *d'ange*. In the form of a pitched roof it was *à pavillon*, and in the form of a crown, *à la couronne* or *impériale*. The curtains, which were moved on rods, were masked at the top by drapes, usually scalloped but sometimes straight. When scalloped they were termed *lambrequins* (q.v.). The corner posts were sometimes decorated at the top with ornamental *pommes* (apples), a term which is self-explanatory, and with plumes termed *panaches*, from those decorating medieval helmets. The bed-drapes were of silk, satin, damask, brocatelle, and velvet, and were often bordered with gold *passementeries* (q.v.) and fringes embroidered with gold lace (q.v.).

Beds of this kind began to go out of fashion with the beginning of the 18th century, and few now survive. Examples can be seen in England at Knole, in Kent.

Lion. Bow porcelain lion and lioness of c. 1752.

Lit de Parade. Bed at Osterley Park, W. London, designed by Robert Adam. The chair is French, *en cabriolet* (q.v.), period of Louis XVI.

Lit de Parade. Robert Adam's original design for the bed at Osterley illustrated here.

LIT DE REPOS See *Bed, Day-*

LITHOPHANES

Usually flat plaques of fine-quality *biscuit* porcelain with moulded *intaglio* decoration intended to be viewed only by transmitted light. By ordinary light it is extremely difficult to see what the subject is intended to be, and the lithophane looks like porcelain with an irregular surface on one side. Lithophanes of circular section are comparatively rare, but they are sometimes to be found as the decoration of lamp-shades and of *veilleuses* (q.v.).

Of uncertain origin lithophanes were first made around 1830 and continued to be produced until about 1900. The best were made by Continental factories, especially those of Germany, but some Wedgwood intaglios are translucent, and have been adapted for this purpose. Lithophanes of excellent quality came from Berlin, made at the Royal Factory, and from Meissen, and they appear to have been made by some 19th-century English porcelain factories, although a marked specimen has not so far been recorded.

Lithophanes range in size from miniatures about one inch by one and a half inches to relatively large specimens about twelve inches square, and very occasionally even more. The latter were usually intended for framing and were hung with a light behind them, but the principle was obviously suited to lanterns of one kind or another, such as hall-lights, when the plaques were set in metal frames. Other uses include table-screens, candle-shields, and hand-screens which served a similar purpose to 18th-century screens of *papier mâché*. Small circular lithophanes were quite commonly set in the bottom of tankards, to be seen when the vessel was drained, and less often they can be found in the bottoms of

cups and mugs of one kind or another. They were, in fact, adapted to most purposes where they could be viewed by transmitted light. Most are white, some are slightly tinged with colour, and a few have the addition of translucent enamels.

Lithophanes were first modelled in translucent wax, the object of the craftsman being to remove sufficient wax to give the desired amount of light transmission, building up his picture from dark and light passages. The subjects employed are extremely varied, although it is unlikely that many were original, and most were probably taken from contemporary prints.

The largest collection of lithophanes is to be found in the Blair Museum of Lithophanes, Toledo, Ohio, which is especially rich in the rarer varieties.

A method of making lithophanes from press-moulded opal glass was patented by Hobbs, Brockunier & Leighton of Wheeling, Virginia, in 1871. The production consisted principally of lamp-shades with decoration similar to that familiar on the porcelain variety.

LIVERPOOL (Lancashire) DELFT

Delftware was first manufactured in Liverpool by Southwark potters about 1710. Trade must have flourished, because no fewer than twelve factories were working about 1760. After that date competition from Staffordshire, and particularly from Wedgwood's creamware, became so intense that all the best potters left Merseyside, and the *delft* industry declined. At Liverpool the glaze is more variable than at either Bristol or Lambeth, the result presumably of so many different potteries. It ranges in tone from clear blue to a very pure white. Unfortunately neither the colour, nor the body, offers a clue to origin, though one Liverpool pottery must have fired at a higher temperature than normal, because a tin-glazed mug in the Victoria and Albert Museum ascribed to Liverpool about 1750 is certainly as hard as stoneware.

Liverpool made quantities of punch-bowls, some of immense size, and, as is to be expected, many are decorated with ships and inscriptions on a streaming pennant. Bristol, however, also utilized ships. Large jugs and ornamental vases were very skilfully done, the latter deriving both in shape and decoration from Chinese originals. Like the painters at Bristol, Liverpool artists were inclined to work sketchily, with less attention to detail than at Lambeth. Liverpool and Bristol used similar templates for reserves in conjunction with blue and manganese grounds. These were laid on the piece to be decorated, covering the part which was to be left white, and the pigment sponged on to the rest of the surface. The artist then added the painting within

Liverpool Delft. A rare survival. Liverpool *delft* teapot decorated with a pseudo-Chinese scene in red and yellow. c. 1750. *Victoria and Albert Museum.*

Liverpool Delft. A rare pill-slab bearing the arms of the Apothecaries' Company, a type more frequently seen from Lambeth. c. 1750. *Sotheby & Co.*

the reserves. Towards the end of the 18th century enamel-painting was tried at Liverpool, but specimens are rare. A bottle of about 1760 with Chinese figures is in the Glaisher Collection. Letters and numbers, generally in blue but occasionally in colour, as well as a *prunus* blossom scroll, appear fairly frequently on the backs of plates from Liverpool.

Transfer-printing (q.v.) at Liverpool was developed by two men, John Sadler and Guy Green (q.v.), who also decorated porcelain and Wedgwood's cream-ware in this manner. It became very popular after 1755, but sounded the death-knell of *delft* decoration. Enamel-colours had to be used, usually black or red, and the method was naturally most effective for flat objects, such as tiles or plates.

Liverpool was responsible for a decoration in a special palette associated with Thomas Fazackerley, and now called 'Fazackerley colours'. These comprise dark and light purple, brilliant blue, green,

russet-red and yellow, but their tone is infinitely variable, as are the designs. Flowers are common, with dark purple veining to petals and leaves.

LIVERPOOL PORCELAIN FACTORIES

There were several factories in this city, the earliest being that of Richard Chaffers at Shaw's Brow which made a soaprock porcelain similar to that of Worcester (q.v.) from a formula brought by Podmore in 1756. Chaffers' porcelain has many resemblances to that of Worcester, but the body is greyish, and the glaze is slightly blued. Chaffers died in 1765, and the factory passed to Philip Christian. The wares made here have often been confused with those of Worcester, and in recent years many changes in attributions have taken place as a result of closer study of the productions of this factory.

James, John, and Seth Pennington had a factory at Shaw's Brow which Jewitt (*Ceramic Art of Great Britain*) describes as 'very large', where they made *delft* ware and porcelain. Porcelain bowls painted with ships in a style reminiscent of *delft* bowls similarly decorated probably came from here, and a blue described as 'sticky' has been regarded as a Pennington colour. A factory operated by Zachariah Barnes may have been responsible for a jug in the

Liverpool Porcelain. Teapot of typical form. The broad blue band decorated with gilding is characteristic, and the base, in sloping inwards, differs from similar bases at Worcester, with which Liverpool porcelain is sometimes confused. Chaffers' factory. c. 1760.

245

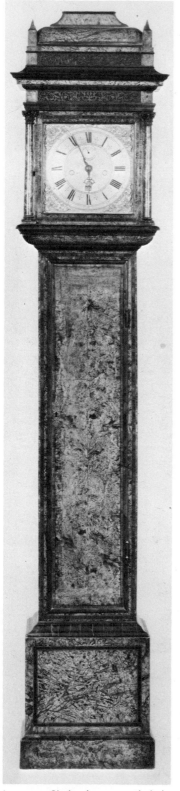

Long-case Clocks. **Long-case clock by Thomas Tompion. London. c. 1705.** *Parke-Bernet Galleries, New York.*

British Museum inscribed 'Frederick Heinzelman Liverpool 1779', and Samuel Gilbody, William Read & Co. made porcelain, although it has not been certainly identified. Gilbody was associated with Sadler & Green (q.v.). See also *Herculaneum*.

LIVERY CUPBOARD (English)
An early type of free-standing cupboard designed for food-storage. Surviving specimens belong to the late 15th/early 16th centuries.

LOCK, MATTHIAS (fl. c. 1740–1769)
A carver and designer who published ten books of ornament between 1740 and 1769. He was one of the pioneers of the rococo style in England who considerably influenced the designs of Chippendale. It has been suggested that he was employed by Chippendale as a designer.

LONG-CASE CLOCKS, ENGLISH
Following the hanging lantern clock we have a kind of wall-clock mounted on a bracket called a hood clock which somewhat resembles the upper part of the long-case clock with the weights and pendulum both exposed. This allowed dust to penetrate to the movement and was generally unsightly, so the addition of a trunk enclosing both pendulum and weights was a rational development, and some of the early hood clocks actually had a trunk enclosing this part added later. The first long-case clocks date back to about 1670, the reign of Charles II, and they had a square hood, sometimes with an added pierced and carved cresting which has usually disappeared. These early hoods were designed to be lifted upwards to permit winding, and at a later date pulled forward. The addition of a door to give access to the dial did not take place until 1695. About this time, also, the domed hood made its appearance, although it did not become general till a few years later. The arched hood and dial date from about 1720, and at the same time the door to the trunk, originally rectangular, was also arched at the top, repeating the lines of the hood. A combination of domed hood and arched dial is sometimes to be seen around 1720.

The width of the trunk was to some extent governed by the length of time the clock would run at one winding. The standard time for a clock of good quality was eight days, but exceptionally clocks ran for a month, and, more exceptionally still, a few were made, especially by Thomas Tompion, which would run for a year. This demanded heavier weights, and larger driving-wheels which spaced the weights farther apart, with a consequent increase in the width of the trunk. One can see at a glance how long a clock will run by looking at the distance separating the weights. A 'bull's eye' in the centre of the door through which the pendulum can be seen starts about 1710, and occasionally it was added to plain doors later.

Early long-case clocks were about seven feet in

Chandelier of Meissen porcelain. c. 1750.
W. A. Coolidge, Esq.

Centre-piece from the Portuguese service at Apsley
House presented to the first Duke of Wellington in 1816
to commemorate his campaigns. Made in the Lisbon
Arsenal, and designed by Domingos Antonio de Sequeira,
there are about one thousand separate pieces.

height, but medium-quality clocks have sometimes been altered to reduce the height. This may take the form of removal of the cresting, and an indication of its former presence will be found on the top of the hood. Or the case may have been cut down at the bottom, quite often done if it became worm-eaten or rotten from a damp floor. The base, which broadens out from the trunk and on which the clock stood, was usually decorated with a veneered panel cross-banded on all sides. After cutting down, the lower border will be missing entirely or reduced in width.

There are many indications of date, apart from the name of the maker. The columns on either side of the hood were given a barley-sugar twist until 1700. Georgian long-case clocks differ in their proportions from earlier specimens, the trunk usually being wider, and the base square instead of rectangular. The size of the dial is an indication. The very earliest clocks have a dial eight inches square, which had increased to ten inches by 1680, and by 1705 was sometimes eleven inches. After 1720 dials are almost invariably twelve inches, necessitated by the increasingly elaborate nature of many of the movements.

The first dials were of undecorated brass, although the surface was matted and gilded. Engraved ornament decorated them from the reign of James II, at first a simple Tudor rose. The reign of Queen Anne saw the introduction of the silvered chapter-ring on which the numerals were engraved, and the greater use of engraving as ornament generally. Silvered dials with numerals in black began to displace brass dials about 1755, and enamelled dials were introduced a little before 1800. Painted iron dials on cheap clocks in oak cases, usually 36-hour clocks with weights suspended from ropes or chains instead of gut lines, began about 1800 also. Exceptionally, painted dials of unusually fine quality are to be seen earlier. The painter, Zoffany, did dials of this kind for Stephen Rimbault, a well-known clock-maker, in the 1760s. The spandrels at the corners of the dial were the winged cupid's head before 1700, the kind of ornament one sometimes sees on Lambeth *delft*, and this was followed by a pair of cupids supporting a crown. After 1750 fresh devices came into fashion, some elaborate, and on fine-quality clocks the spandrels were always carefully chiselled after casting.

It is very rare to find a first-quality movement in an oak case, and, when this occurs, almost invariably the two did not start life together. The best clocks in the early period had cases of walnut or lacquer. Walnut cases were often handsomely decorated with marquetry (q.v.), parquetry (q.v.), or quartering (q.v.). Only exceptionally is this to be found on the sides of the case. The richest marquetry, of flowers, foliage, and birds, was influenced by contemporary work in France and the Netherlands, and a good deal of it was probably done by immigrant workmen, some of them doubtless of Huguenot origin. This phase is especially to be seen in the reign of William and Mary and Queen Anne. One of the many designs is termed 'seaweed' marquetry, from a resemblance to certain kinds of marine plants. Some of the woods used for this purpose include ebony, violetwood (later to be called kingwood), laburnum, olivewood, yew, holly, sycamore, various fruitwoods, and amboyna. English and Dutch lacquering is to be found decorating clock-cases; English lacquer usually based, however distantly, on Chinese work, and Dutch on Japanese lacquer, more inclined in treatment to resemble the Kakiemon painting on porcelain (see *Kakiemon, Sakaida*). Mahogany became fashionable with the rise of the Chippendale style (q.v.), often as a veneer on oak or pine, and marquetry disappeared. This continued to be the normal way of making long-cases until about 1820. Chippendale designed a good many cases for clocks, but one rarely sees an example which owes very much to him, although all are in the general furniture-style of their period.

Until 1680 the long-case clock had only an hour hand, for clocks in general were so inaccurate that close approximation was impossible. The anchor escapement, however, by increasing the accuracy of the clock, made a minute hand desirable. Hands of blued steel, cut and pierced, often provide useful information about dating when they are original. The arched dial became the usual position for the seconds hand when this was introduced, and often for the strike/silent lever. Moving figures in the arch, usually a rising or waning moon, date from after 1730, and twenty years later even more elaborate motions were introduced. Clocks often indicate the date. Occasionally they give astronomical information as well, but this is rare. See also *Clocks, Evolution of.*

LONGTON HALL (Staffordshire) PORCELAIN FACTORY

For many years little was known about this factory, and attributions were almost entirely conjectural, based on very slight evidence. The discoveries of Dr Bernard Watney, both those of a documentary nature and those arising from excavation on the site, have turned this into one of the best documented of the smaller English factories, and it is notable that almost all the earlier conjectural attributions were later sustained by evidential proof of one kind or another.

The factory was founded by a salt-glaze potter named William Littler (c. 1724 to after 1760), and some of the Longton productions resemble, often quite closely, existing specimens of salt-glazed ware. A fine blue decorating some rare examples of stoneware, referred to as 'Littler's blue', also occurs on some Longton porcelain. One example of salt-glaze in the British Museum bears the mark of crossed *L*'s (? for Littler, Longton) which also appears occasionally on Longton porcelain. Although this mark is almost invariably in blue, the writer has identified one specimen with the *L*'s incised underglaze.

Production included both figures and service-ware in considerable variety, a good deal of it free

Longton Hall. Rare figure of a woman. Longton Hall. c. 1755. *Sigmund Katz Collection.*

adaptations from the work of more sophisticated factories. Among the rarities is an arbour group, obviously based on a then-existing salt-glaze group, which was modified to form a candlestick. This is in the Katz Collection (Boston Museum). Very unusual are some models which seem to have been based on earlier Italian bronzes, and some candlestick groups with rococo scrollwork similar to that appearing slightly later (!) at Frankenthal, and perhaps taken from a common source. A factory speciality was a large variety of dishes, as well as sauceboats, teapots, and small tureens, modelled in the form of overlapping leaves, and although the inspiration came from elsewhere the adaptations have much of the charm of novelty.

There was obviously some connection between Longton Hall and the Plymouth (q.v.) factory of Cookworthy (q.v.), since some years after Longton had closed in 1760 almost identical models to those made earlier at Longton can be seen from Plymouth. It is often thought that in some way Cookworthy managed to acquire Longton moulds, and it is difficult in some cases to see how else the resemblance could have come about otherwise.

Limited use was made of transfer-printing, done by Sadler & Green (q.v.) at Liverpool, and some excellent topographical painting based on French prints came from the hand of a workman called the 'Castle Painter', who was probably John Hayfield.

The factory appears to have been started in, or slightly before, 1750, and among the early figures once known as 'Snowmen' (q.v.) are one or two which resemble contemporary work at Bow and

Chelsea. It closed in 1760, but it is possible that very little was done after 1758, since in this year the Derby factory engaged a number of hands from Longton Hall. The connection between Duesbury (q.v.) and Longton is not clear. In 1751 he was enamelling figures at his London studio which are recorded in his account-book as coming from Staffordshire. This must have meant Longton, since it was the only porcelain factory existing there at the time. When Duesbury left London he moved first to Longton before going to Derby, and he appears in some contemporary records of the time as though he were working at, or for, the factory. There seems no evidential confirmation that he bought part of the Longton stock and machinery when it closed in 1760, although there is a tradition to this effect.

The wares of this small factory are much sought and highly valued. Its history is very adequately summarized, and the newly discovered documents reprinted, by Dr Bernard Watney, *Longton Hall Porcelain* (Faber & Faber, London, 1957).

LOUIS XIV (1638–1715)

Louis XIV acceded to the throne in 1643, and came under the influence at an early age of his minister Cardinal Mazarin, one of the most noted art-collectors in the Europe of his day. After the death of Mazarin in 1661, Louis ruled as an absolute monarch with the aid of Jean-Baptiste Colbert (1619–1683), his Finance Minister, and conceived the plan of making art contribute to the glory of France. Colbert founded a Fine Arts Commission in 1663, and the Academy of Architecture in 1671, and the *Manufacture royale des meubles de la couronne* (q.v.) was established for the purpose of supplying works of art of all kinds to the royal palaces. This was based on the acquisition of the Gobelins tapestry factory (q.v.), and the *Manufacture* was placed under the general direction of Charles Le Brun (q.v.). Louis disliked Paris, and began a series of major additions and alterations to a hunting-lodge at Versailles built by Louis XIII in 1624. These, when completed, made Versailles the largest and most sumptuous palace in Europe, much envied and copied by other princes, and the King transferred his Court there in 1684. These works, and the furnishing of the King's other palaces, such as Marly,

Longton Hall. Teapot painted with a topographical scene probably based on a contemporary French engraving. By the 'Castle Painter' (John Hayfield?). Longton Hall. c. 1755.

created a definite style in French decorative art which swept Europe, continuing, with the modifications of time and fashion, to be among the most important today.

The style which is usually termed 'Louis Quatorze' falls into three fairly definite parts. The earliest, which lasts until about 1665, is largely based on that of the preceding reign. The middle period, which lasted until about 1700, was of the utmost luxury, but rigidly symmetrical, and the French version of the international baroque style. After 1700 the first signs of the approaching rococo period (q.v.) may be seen in an increasing element of fantasy, based to a considerable extent on the current popularity of Chinese and Japanese art, which, in the reign of Louis XV, culminated in the asymmetrical rococo style. Many of the elements of the middle period are to be found in England in the design of Restoration (q.v.) works of decorative art, which gave way to a Dutch style with the advent of William and Mary.

LOUIS XV (1710–1774)

The name of Louis XV is intimately associated with the development of the rococo style (q.v.), which he did much to encourage. Louis acceded to the throne of France on the death of his great-grandfather, Louis XIV, in 1715. Until he reached his majority in 1725, France was governed by a Regent, the Duke of Orléans, a period during which the *Régence* style was current. As Louis grew older he began to devote much attention to the arts, and, after his great-grandfather, he proved to be the most notable art-patron in modern history. In this he was assisted by his mistress, Mme de Pompadour (q.v.), who influenced the arts of her day to a marked degree and was the principal patron of the Sèvres Porcelain Factory. Rococo, with which both are associated, is commonly called the Louis Quinze style, but sometimes, in France, the *style Pompadour*.

Louis XV. Above all, the reign of Louis XV was the age of rococo, and although this style was superseded before his death in 1774 by the neo-classical, it is rococo, nevertheless, which is meant by the expression *style Louis Quinze.* Illustrated is a copy of the *bureau du roi Louis Quinze* in the Louvre, made by Pierre Dasson after Oeben and Riesener (q.v.). *Wallace Collection.*

Louis XIV. Few men so well expressed the spirit of the later years of the reign of Louis XIV in the decorative arts as André-Charles Boulle (q.v.). This writing-desk from Petworth (Sussex) is an excellent example of his style.

Especially after the death of Mme de Pompadour in 1764 rococo began to give way noticeably to the neo-classical style (q.v.) which, in its later phases, is often termed the Louis Seize (q.v.) style, and these movements are discussed under the appropriate headings.

Under Louis XV many changes took place in French decorative art in the direction of greater freedom of expression, and a lessening of the strict insistence on etiquette and protocol which had marked the reign of Louis XIV. The tendency of the period to favour smaller rooms, and therefore smaller and more mobile furniture, started with the building of the Petits Cabinets at Versailles by Louis XV, who was far less conventional in outlook than his predecessor.

LOUIS XVI

Born in 1754, Louis XVI, grandson of Louis XV, ascended the throne of France in 1774. He married Marie-Antoinette, daughter of the Empress Maria-Theresa, in 1770. Of a retiring disposition, Louis was much inclined to leave affairs of state to ministers of very uneven quality. Marie-Antoinette loved pleasure and luxury, and, unlike her husband, was a patron of the arts on a considerable scale. Much of the finest furniture by such *ébénistes* as Riesener (q.v.) was made for her, or with her encouragement, and the neo-classical style, at first fairly plain and simple, developed under her influence in the direction of a luxury comparable with that of the two previous reigns.

The neo-classical style itself is known in France as the *style Louis Seize*, although it had its beginnings fifteen years or so before he commenced to reign. In its early phases it exhibits elements of the rococo style, especially abroad and in such departments of the decorative arts as porcelain. Towards the initial outbreak of the Revolution in 1789 styles tended once more to become simpler, culminating a few years later in the *Directoire* style (q.v.).

Louis XVI was executed in January, 1793, and Marie-Antoinette a few months afterwards.

Louis XVI. The neo-classical style, often termed the *style Louis Seize*, began fifteen years or so before the death of Louis XV. This small mahogany writing-desk by J. H. Riesener, who made much furniture for Marie-Antoinette, is an excellent example of the style. The strictly symmetrical, classically based ornament and the straight and tapering legs are characteristic. c. 1775. *Sotheby & Co.*

LOUIS SEIZE À L'ANGLAISE (French)
A term sometimes used in France to refer to the designs of Sheraton, which were well known in Paris towards the end of the 18th century.

LOUISVILLE (Kentucky) GLASS WORKS
This factory was in existence for a few years after 1856, making flasks, some of which are marked. Several colours were used, including amber, brown, aquamarine, and olive-green, as well as transparent glass. See *Glass, American*.

LOVE–SEAT
A chair wide enough for two people to sit side by side; a small settee. Introduced during the second half of the 17th century, it was first called a courting chair. Other terms for chairs and settees of this kind include the *tête-à-tête* and the *causeuse*, or conversation-chair. Later versions are sometimes shaped, in plan, like the letter *S*. See *Marquise*.

LOVE-SPOONS
Carved wooden spoons with large handles, nearly always openwork, which often have hearts pierced as an essential motif. The spoon may have one or two bowls attached to the same handle. The woods used are varied, but sycamore and birch seem to have been favourites.

Most love-spoons come from Wales, although specimens from Scandinavia and Switzerland have been noted. In Wales they were the equivalent of an engagement-ring, and they were, presumably, carved by the donor, often with little more than a pocket-knife. Some are elaborately decorated with skilful workmanship, but the best can hardly be regarded as more than peasant work. Apart from the heart, which is obvious, much of the symbolism of the ornament is obscure. The National Museum of Wales has a representative collection.

LOWBOY (American)
A low chest of several drawers on cabriole legs, usually made to match a highboy (see *Tallboy*).

LÖWENFINCK, ADAM FRIEDRICH VON
Born in 1714, von Löwenfinck was apprenticed at Meissen at the early age of thirteen, working as a painter of flowers in colour, according to the factory-list, until the end of his apprenticeship in 1734. In 1736 he fled to Bayreuth, becoming a flower-painter at the faïence factory there. Pursued by the Meissen directorate, he fled to Chantilly, in France, accompanied by his brother, Karl Heinrich. He returned to Germany about 1740, obtaining employment at Ansbach, and went thence to Fulda (1741) and Höchst (1749). While at Fulda he married Maria Seraphia Suzanna Magdalena, daughter of the Court Chamberlain, Johann Philipp Schick. In 1749 he travelled to Strasbourg (q.v.) accompanied by Karl Heinrich and a still younger brother, Christian Wilhelm. He was made director of the Haguenau Faïence Factory, an offshoot of Strasbourg, and died in 1754, being succeeded by his wife.

Von Löwenfinck's two brothers were both flower-painters. Adam Friedrich began his career as a flower-painter, but his attributed work at Meissen also includes some much-sought '*chinoiseries*' in a slightly humorous vein which owe their inspiration to the painting of the Japanese, Kakiemon (q.v.). rather than to Chinese sources. Subjects include animals with trifid tails and sometimes sharply pointed noses. Signed examples of his work on faïence seem all to be flower-paintings, although it has been suggested that some Meissen decoration assumed to be by his hand is signed with initials

Löwenfinck, A. F. von. Teapot, spoon-tray, and tea-jar painted with fantastic animals by A. F. von Löwenfinck. Meissen. c. 1735. Animals of this kind may have influenced O'Neale at Chelsea. (q.v.). *Mrs C. B. Stout, Memphis.*

concealed in the painting. His work elsewhere is on faïence.

LOWESTOFT PORCELAIN FACTORY

Porcelain made at Lowestoft (Suffolk) is very similar to that of Bow (q.v.), since it contains bone-ash in much the same proportions, and specimens decorated in blue underglaze are often a little difficult to separate from those made at the London factory. Like Bow, the degree of translucency by transmitted light is variable.

The factory was first proposed when Hewlin Luson discovered clay on his estate in 1756, but it was not until 1757 that a company consisting of Philip Walker, Robert Browne, Obed Aldred, and John Richman succeeded in producing a saleable porcelain to a formula provided by Browne, who appears to have got it from Bow. Robert Allen joined the factory in 1757 as manager, and when it closed towards 1800 he continued to decorate porcelain in his own muffle-kiln. A teapot of Chinese porcelain signed by him was possibly the cause of Chaffers's error in attributing the vast amount of armorial Chinese export porcelain to Lowestoft. In America 'Oriental Lowestoft' is still a common and erroneous term for porcelain made and decorated in China for the European and American markets.

By far the greater amount of surviving Lowestoft porcelain is decorated in blue underglaze, both painted and transfer-printed (q.v.). That early production was influenced by Worcester is apparent both from the patterns employed, and from the later Worcester crescent mark which appears not infrequently on Lowestoft porcelain of this kind. In contrast to Worcester, however, Lowestoft wares are thicker and less neatly potted, the greenish or bluish glaze being full of minute bubbles. Inscribed

Lowestoft Porcelain. Jug painted with a scene representing a cricket-match. Lowestoft. c. 1780. *Victoria and Albert Museum.*

wares form an important group. These often bear the name of the owner as well as the date, and the words 'A Trifle from Lowestoft' are not uncommon. Belonging to this group are birth-tablets, which record the name and date of birth of a child.

About 1770 the use of enamel colours became common. A mauve-pink is more or less peculiar to this factory, and was used with patterns derived from the Chinese 'Mandarin' decoration after about 1775. There were several artists named Redgrave working here, and they gave their name to the 'Redgrave' pattern, a derivation from the Chinese of rocks and peonies in blue and red.

A few figures were made at Lowestoft—*putti* and small animals—and portions of the moulds were found when the factory-site was excavated in 1902.

LOW-TEMPERATURE COLOURS

Colours of the *petit feu*; those fired in the muffle or enamelling kiln at a lower temperature than the fusion point of the glass or glaze to which they were applied—hence the name. Low-temperature colours are generally known as enamel colours, and were widely used to decorate porcelain and, to a lesser extent, faïence during the 18th century. One of the advantages of colours of this kind is that they do not need to be applied in the factory at which the wares are made, and it is, therefore, not surprising that the earliest examples we have of their use are specimens of faïence painted by *Hausmaler* (q.v.) (home-painters) in the second half of the 17th century. The faïence factories themselves did not use enamel colours until later, during the second quarter of the 18th century, since to do so meant another manufacturing operation (a second firing) which added to the cost of production. They did so primarily because of competitive pressure from the porcelain factories, where this method of decoration was extensively used, especially at Meissen which experienced considerable difficulties in satisfactorily firing the principal high-temperature colour—cobalt-blue. Soft porcelains, fired at a lower temperature, were usually decorated with cobalt-blue underglaze from the first.

Enamel colours were also employed to decorate

Low-temperature Colours. Low-temperature colours, first used on pottery by the stoneware makers of Kreussen early in the 17th century, were often employed on faïence of the 18th century for imitations of porcelain (known in Germany as *fayence-porzellan*). This plate is from Ansbach (q.v.), and is a member of the 'green family' which imitated Chinese porcelain. c. 1730. *Germanisches Nationalmuseum, Nürnberg.*

small boxes and other wares of metal, being painted on a ground of enamel, usually white, fused to the metal base (see *Battersea Enamels*).

Glass enamelling was done in Germany (see *Glass, German, Enamelled*), where enamels were first applied to pottery and porcelain decoration, in Venice (see *Venetian Glass*), and in England (see *Beilby*).

LOZENGE
A diamond-shaped figure especially used in heraldry. It was frequently employed both in carving and inlay on 17th-century oak furniture.

LÜCK, JOHANN FRIEDRICH (mid-18th century)
J. F. Lück is presumed to be a relative of C. L. von Lücke (q.v.). He was a modeller at Meissen in 1757, but left to work at Frankenthal. What he did at the latter factory is uncertain, but Hofmann thought him to be the *Modellmeister* in succession to Lanz. He remained until 1764. In the latter year he returned to Meissen in the somewhat subordinate position of *Oberbossierer*, or chief 'repairer', a 'repairer' being a man who put figures together from moulded components. J. F. Lück's attributed work is somewhat in the manner of J. W. Lanz of Strasbourg and Frankenthal (q.v.) and he worked in a marked rococo style.

LÜCK, KARL GOTTLIEB (mid-18th century)
Presumed to be a cousin of J. F. Lück (q.v.), K. G. Lück was at Frankenthal as both a 'repairer' and modeller from about 1756 to 1775. There seems no doubt of his contemporary reputation, since he was asked to go to Meissen to assist with Kändler's attempt to make a life-size equestrian statue of Augustus. In 1766 he became *Modellmeister* at Frankenthal in succession to Linck (q.v.), by whom he was influenced. Among the many models attributed to his hand are Chinese figures, pagodas with Chinese figures (*Chinesenhäuser*), and those depicting contemporary life. One of his best-known models is a group called *The Good Mother* after the painting by Greuze engraved by Laurent Cars.

Lück, K. G. Le Bouquet (after an engraving by Eisen) by K. G. Lück. Frankenthal. c. 1765. *British Museum.*

Lücke, C. L. von. The *Hofnarr* (Court Jester) Fröhlich, a later version of a model traditionally attributed to von Lücke. Meissen. c. 1740. *British Museum.*

LÜCKE, CHRISTIAN LUDWIG VON (?–1780)
Modeller at Meissen from 1728 until 1729. From 1750 he was a modeller at Vienna, and subsequently an arcanist (q.v.) at Fürstenberg. He was also at Copenhagen. The son of an ivory-carver of Dresden, von Lücke's figure-modelling was sometimes based on ivory-carving if tentative attributions are accepted. These include a figure of Augustus the Strong, and one of the *Hofnarr* (Court Jester) Fröhlich. The two modellers J. F. Lück and K. G. Lück (q.v.) are assumed to have been related to him.

LUDWIGSBURG (Germany) FAÏENCE FACTORY
Faïence was made in this town after 1763, but pieces are exceptionally rare. A large white bust of Duke Charles is in the State Collections at Wurtemberg, and a jar in the Sèvres Museum is decorated in enamels and cold-gilding. The dishes in the Hamburg Museum, and in the Victoria and Albert Museum (London), have floral monograms in the centre and four blue *cartouches* containing groups of fruit on a black ground, painted in high-temperature colours.

LUDWIGSBURG PORCELAIN FACTORY
The first successful attempt to make porcelain at Ludwigsburg (Württemberg) was made in 1756 by an architect, B. C. Häckher. The factory was taken over in 1758 by the Duke Karl Eugen. J. G. Ringler (q.v.) became Director in 1759, a post he retained for the next forty years, and G. F. Riedel, a designer

Ludwigsburg. Group of *Diana and Nymphs* by J. W. C. Beyer. Ludwigsburg. c. 1760. *Cecil Higgins Museum, Bedford.*

Ludwigsburg. Teapot of characteristic form painted with a battle scene. Ludwigsburg. c. 1765. *British Museum.*

from Meissen, was appointed *Obermaler*. The latter was responsible for painted decoration and plastic design. The Duke had considerable enthusiasm for his factory, visiting both Sèvres and Wedgwood in search of ideas. After his death in 1793 it declined, and closed finally in 1824.

Ludwigsburg porcelain was poor at first, greyish in tone, with an imperfect glaze. Nevertheless, it had very superior plastic qualities, and the factory not only became known for its figures but for groups of considerable size. The first are attributed to a collaboration between Riedel and Göz, the factory's *Oberbossierer* (see *Figures, Porcelain, Manufacture of*), and these are of mythological subjects. The *Modellmeister* from 1762 to 1772 was Jean-Jacob Louis, whose figures sometimes have an 'L' scratched into the base. Apart from rococo dancers, a *Turk*

Ludwigsburg. A Lady's Toilet, group satirizing hair-fashions of the time. Ludwigsburg. c. 1775. *British Museum.*

Leading a Horse, and some Chinese figures reminiscent of Bustelli (q.v.) in style, he was probably responsible for unusual models of booths at a fair, a series started about 1767. The modeller of a series of figures from the streets, illustrating life among the common people, is unknown, although the influence of J. W. C. Beyer is perceptible. Possibly Beyer provided engravings from which they were copied. For want of a name this man has been termed the *Modeller der Volkstypen* (Modeller of Folk-types). Domenico Feretti, Court Sculptor, was at the factory from 1764 to 1767 after decorating the Residenz at Stuttgart and the Ludwigsburg Palais. On grounds of style he has been awarded some Chinese figures, and small versions of his sculpture in stone (a *River God*, a *Nymph*, and so on) were no doubt by his hand. Another Court Sculptor, Pierre-Francois Lejeune, worked at the factory, but his models have only doubtfully been identified by Balet (*Ludwigsburger Porzellan*).

During the latter part of the 18th century the modelling varied from the 'sentimental to the academic pseudo-antique' to borrow a phrase from Hannover, and this period is represented by the work of P. J. Scheffauer and J. H. Dannecker.

A factory at Amberg, in Bavaria, reproduced Ludwigsburg models in the 19th century, and these are principally accused by noticeable differences in colouring. Before 1770 Ludwigsburg colours are soft, and a great deal of the figure is left in white, with flesh tones only slightly indicated. Colours became stronger as the century advanced, and some later reissues have this new colour scheme.

As at Fürstenberg the body was not very suitable for service-wares, and the same device of relief patterns was adopted. Painting was of good quality, and the subjects are inclined to be large in relation to the size of the piece on which they are painted. Sources of inspiration include engravings by Riedel, and those after Boucher, Watteau, Rugendas, and J. E. Nilson.

253

LUNÉVILLE (Meurthe-et-Moselle, France) FAÏENCE

This factory was founded by Jacques Chambrette and inherited by his son-in-law, Charles Loyal, in 1758. It was given permission to use the title *Manufacture royale* by Stanislas Lezcinski, the father-in-law of Louis XV and exiled King of Poland. Business declined however, and Chambrette was declared bankrupt. The factory was taken over by his son-in-law, who, in 1788, sold it to Sebastian Keller and Guérin, which, as the firm of Keller & Guérin, continued until well into the 19th century.

At first Chambrette used high-temperature colours (q.v.), particularly blue, but he soon adopted the enamelling technique. Much of his faïence seems to have been imitated from the work of Strasbourg, Niderviller, and even Sceaux, and Lunéville painted wares are difficult to attribute. From this factory came the large models of lions and dogs which were used as garden ornaments, often placed on pillars on either side of the bottom of flights of steps. These were repeated later by Keller & Guérin.

Perhaps the principal manufacture here was figures in a body called *terre de pipe* (a kind of unglazed *faïence-fine*—q.v.) modelled from 1755 onwards by Paul-Louis Cyfflé (q.v.). It was a soft white earthenware, somewhat resembling *biscuit* porcelain (q.v.), at least superficially. Cyfflé later operated a true porcelain factory here for the manufacture of similar figures, which was authorized by the Sèvres management conditionally upon them being sold as *terre cuite*. They were apparently marketed at the time under the name of *Terre de Lorraine*, since this appears on one specimen as an impressed mark, although the name was also used for figures in *terre de pipe*.

The factory made *faïence-fine* in the English manner perhaps as early as 1765, since some specimens are in the rococo style.

LUSTRE DECORATION

(French *décor à réflets métalliques*.) Decoration by means of the deposition of a thin film of metal on a pottery glaze, or, much more rarely, on glass. The metals employed were silver, gold, copper, and platinum. Only platinum yields a silver colour. Silver itself gives a straw colour, gold a ruby-red, and copper a colour which ranges from yellowish-red to a deep coppery red. Some of the best lustre pottery on which copper was used is to be found among that termed Hispano-Moresque (q.v.), of which specimens are known from the late 14th century onwards. Gold (i.e. ruby-red) lustre was employed both at Deruta (Italy) and at Gubbio not far away by Maestro Giorgio Andreoli from about 1515. Lustre decoration can also be found occasionally on Tuscan *maiolica*, particularly that from Caffagiolo. A purple-toned lustre occurs on early Meissen porcelain, beginning in the Böttger period and remaining in use till about 1735. Platinum was first employed in England towards the end of the 18th century. It was often used entirely to cover the ware,

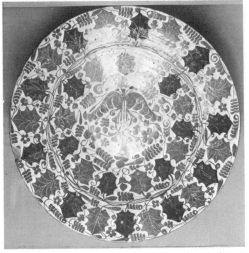

Lustre. Dish in brownish lustre decorated with formal flowers and bryony foliage. Valencia. 16th century. *British Museum.*

when it is sometimes termed 'poor man's silver'. 'Resist' lustre of this period was executed by first covering the part of the object not required to be decorated with a cut-paper stencil, after which the lustre was applied. The paper burned away in the kiln, leaving its simulacrum in white against a silver ground. The same effect was sometimes achieved by painting the glaze with a varnish which 'resisted' the application of the lustre. Gold (red) lustre of poor quality occurs on the early 19th-century pottery of Sunderland, and copper-lustre wares otherwise decorated in a variety of ways were commonly made at various potteries in England during the 19th century.

LUSTRES, GLASS

The term at the beginning of the 18th century was generally applied to cut and faceted glass decorating chandeliers and lighting appliances generally. At this early date the term 'fire-lustre' was sometimes employed, which is reasonable proof that cutting as a means of decoration already existed. 'Crystal cut lustres' to be found in 1728 is more positive, suggesting cutting in the manner of rock-crystal (q.v.), which was the origin of the fashion for work of this kind. By 1738 the word had, by extension, come to refer to the chandelier itself, much in the same way as 'the China ware' for Oriental porcelain became 'china' about the same time. The word was also sometimes applied to other lighting appliances; for instance, the *girandole* (q.v.). See *Chandeliers, Glass*.

LYON (Rhône, France) FAÏENCE

Faïence was originally made in this city by Italians, probably from Liguria and Florence. Several workshops are recorded, notably those of Tardessir and Gambini, who later became the partners of Conrade at Nevers (q.v.). Apart from *faïence blanche* (q.v.) the style followed the *istoriato* (q.v.) manner of Urbino. The *coperta* (q.v.) is also lacking. Although the kilns probably never entirely closed down, little is recorded after the first period till mid-18th century (about 1733), when Joseph Combe and Jacques Marie Ravier acquired a patent and the coveted title of *Manufacture royale*. The business changed hands several times, and was finally declared bankrupt in 1770. Since Combe came from Moustiers it is natural that this style should predominate; blue-and-white Bérain decoration (q.v.) and grotesques in yellow ochre are typical of this factory. Enamel colours were not well developed.

It is difficult to attribute pieces to individual factories at Lyon, though the work of an Italian, Pierre Mongis, has been recognized by tufted foliage growing from rocks on the borders (as well as the centre) of dishes and plates. There are river-gods and other classical figures and, exceptionally, the occurrence of red, though this was later displaced by the more usual yellow. Lyon faïence has a thick, heavy body with the glaze gathering round the footring.

Lyon was also the centre of the silk-weaving industry in France from the 15th century, although it did not become important until the industry was encouraged by Colbert during the reign of Louis XIV. It was the home of one or two notable provincial *ébénistes* in the 18th century.

M

MAGIC LANTERN

An optical device for the projection of painted glass slides and silhouettes invented by the German Kircher in the second half of the 17th century. Circular slides were the earliest to be made, and some very rare examples were painted by the *Hausmaler* (q.v.) Abraham Helmhack, of which there is an example in the Victoria and Albert Museum.

The magic lantern was often carried from place to place by itinerant showmen, and porcelain groups depicting it were made at Sèvres, Derby, and elsewhere.

MAHOGANY

The most popular of all cabinet woods, coming principally from the West Indies, especially Honduras, Jamaica, and Cuba. 'Spanish' mahogany came from San Domingo. In colour mahogany is a rich but variable brown, and most varieties are prized for their figure. It is used both as a veneer and as solid wood. Mahogany from San Domingo was renowned for the beauty of its colouring, even though its figure was not so well-marked as the Cuban variety. The latter, paler in colour, was handsomely figured, and it began to replace the San Domingo wood about 1750. Mahogany from Honduras was popular towards the end of the century. It is paler in colour, and, in certain conditions, has faded to a golden brown with grey tints. It was sometimes used in solid form and veneered with Cuban wood. African mahogany first arrived in Europe about 1830. It is light brown in colour, with a pronounced figure, but it has never been employed for work of high quality. Despite its hardness mahogany is an excellent wood for carving, and English furniture-makers of the 18th century made good use of this quality.

Although mahogany was known in England in Elizabethan times, apart from a few isolated instances no use was made of it until the duty on timber from the West Indies was abolished in 1721. Thereafter it was very popular, and was extensively employed for all but inferior work until the beginning of the Adam style, when satinwood (q.v.) and rosewood (q.v.) became fashionable. Mahogany, however, always remained the preferred wood for libraries and dining-rooms.

Under the name of *bois d'acajou* mahogany came into use in France about 1750, principally as a veneer, but it did not become widely popular until towards the end of the century. Chairs of solid mahogany were made during the 1780s, but often by *ébénistes* rather than *menuisiers*.

MAIOLICA, ITALIAN, FORGERIES OF

Forgeries of 16th-century Italian *maiolica* are not in the least unusual, and some are very deceptive. A 19th-century authority in this field, M.-L. Solon, once rashly remarked that no forgery of this kind was skilful enough to deceive an expert, and he accompanied his remark by an illustration of a particularly obvious one. During the 19th century, Italian *maiolica* was much sought, and high prices were given for good specimens, but fortunately for the collector today all the most ambitious forgeries were done then, and most are now much easier to recognize than they were. It is essential to remember that the forgery of one's own day is always the most difficult to detect, for the persistent idiom of the time, which inevitably creeps into the drawing, passes unnoticed, whereas it becomes immediately apparent a few years later.

Technically, the production of tin-enamel ware presents few serious difficulties, and a great deal is known about the processes of the time, so much greater reliance must be placed on the style of drawing and decoration than is normally required. There can be few things easier to recognize than the 19th-century style in drawing, with its all-pervading sentimental approach, and this is as evident in forgeries of Renaissance drawing as it is in the avowed work of the period. It is here that a close acquaintance with the genuine object serves the collector well, and an acquaintance with the 19th-century idiom, as evinced in its art, is also essential.

It must be remembered that a good deal of spurious *maiolica* was not at first intended to be sold as old ware, but as interior decoration to ornament the kind of fake Renaissance *buffet* beloved of the 19th-century furniture-maker. These are easy to detect, but the neophyte must not imagine, because

Maiolica, Italian, Forgeries of. Part of a large 19th-century dish in the *istoriato* style. It is notable for the clumsiness of the seated female figure in the foreground, and the obviously 19th-century style in the drawing.

he has some initial successes in detecting them, that nothing more deceptive awaits him. For example, there is a perfectly genuine Deruta dish in the possession of the Victoria and Albert Museum (London) from which the glaze in the centre has been removed and a portrait of Perugino substituted, thus enormously increasing its value were it genuine.

In the early years of the 19th century *maiolica* was termed 'Rafaelle ware' because Raphael was thought to have painted some of it. Actually these Raphael subjects were only contemporary copies of his works, usually after engravings by the 16th-century Marcantonio Raimondi, who, incidentally, was perhaps the earliest forger of the engravings of Dürer. It is not, perhaps, surprising that the first forgeries are of this kind, and they are of a type termed *istoriato*, or history-painting, because the subject was usually of this nature. There followed a vogue for portrait heads of women accompanied by an amatory inscription. These are called *coppe amatorie*, and the rather terse inscription, *Silvia Bella*, occurs on a genuine dish from Castel Durante (q.v.) in the Victoria and Albert Museum painted about 1520 by Nicola Pellipario. This type is very rare, but the forger has provided us with a bevy of pseudo-Renaissance beauties with a variety of names. The *albarello* (q.v.) was an especial favourite with the forger for portrait decoration, although the genuine *albarello* with a true portrait is rare.

The reliefs of Luca della Robbia (q.v.) are strictly sculpture rather than pottery. They are terracottas covered with a tin-enamel glaze (q.v.), and they are very highly valued. They were copied at Bologna about 1850 by Angelo Minghetti, who also copied the *istoriato* styles of Urbino. Cantagalli of Florence (whose wares are sometimes marked, appropriately, with a crowing cock) reproduced della Robbia sculpture, as well as the *maiolica* of Urbino, Faenza, Deruta, and Gubbio (q.v.), all of which they

exhibited at the Paris Exhibition of 1900. The Doccia factory (q.v.) also began to imitate 16th-century *maiolica* in the 1840s, particularly the ruby lustre pigments of Deruta and Gubbio, and for these they received awards in the Great Exhibition of 1851. The same lustre pigments were imitated by Carocci, Fabbri & Co., represented at the International Exhibition (London) of 1862. At Pesaro a factory belonging to Magrini was copying 16th-century wares in the 1870s, as was Feruccio Mengaroni in the same place. Some of the best copies were done by Torquato Castellani, son of the art-dealer Alessandro Castellani, whose collection of Italian *maiolica* was dispersed in a well-known sale in Paris in 1878. Some of the son's work was signed, but some unsigned specimens were accepted as genuine. Some very deceptive forgeries, which have now disappeared, were marketed by a dealer in Rome in 1913, and may have come from this source.

When considering apparently important specimens careful attention should be paid to the painting and the nature of the ornament. To bring the high prices, which make a really clever forgery worth while, the decoration must be of a rare type and of apparently similar quality to other highly valued specimens. To make an exact copy, or even a near-copy, of a well-known piece would be much too dangerous. It would not be long before someone recognized it. Nor it is possible for a forger to produce something entirely new, for this would cause too much speculation and unusually close examination—something he wants to avoid. Most forgeries therefore are of the nature of a *pastiche* (q.v.)—a combination of the elements of several genuine specimens—and this should be borne in mind.

It is essential to remember that genuine specimens of 16th- and even 17th-century Italian *maiolica* are very rare in comparison with the vast number of later copies and reproductions on the market, and there are few subjects for the collector where greater caution is essential.

MALACHITE

A bright copper-green stone which can be either slightly translucent or opaque. Normally it has well-marked veinings. It has been much valued in the past for making small works of art, and it was a favourite stone with Fabergé (q.v.). The principal source of supply is the U.S.S.R., and columns of malachite are to be found in the Hermitage, Leningrad. Poor-grade malachite is a source of metallic copper, and in colour it much resembles the green patination of certain excavated bronzes.

'MANDARIN' PORCELAIN

A kind of Chinese export porcelain with elaborate figure-subjects mainly in rose-pink, red, and gold, set in panels framed in underglaze blue, which was popular at the end of the 18th century. It was frequently copied by English potters after 1800.

MANNERISM

Style in art, particularly Italian art, current from about 1520 to 1580, and affecting painting and sculpture principally, although its influence can be observed in the decoration of such other things as furniture, the form and painting of *maiolica*, etc. The style can be particularly well seen in small bronzes such as those of Gian da Bologna (q.v.) and his pupils. Mannerism was the product of a new approach to classicism which began with Michelangelo. Mannerist sculptors posed their figures in often strained or distorted poses, the figure was elongated in defiance of classical theories of proportion (see *Proportion, Human*), and anatomical details, such as musculature, were unduly emphasized. The purpose was to heighten the dramatic effect of the work and its emotional content. The subjects popular were those which lent themselves to this kind of treatment, and *Hercules and Anteus* and the *Rape of the Sabine Women* were both popular.

MANUFACTURE ROYALE DES MEUBLES DE LA COURONNE

An organization set up by Jean-Baptiste Colbert, French Finance Minister, in 1667 to supply works of art to royal palaces and the Court, and especially to the Palace of Versailles. It was under the general direction of Charles Le Brun (q.v.). The foundation was the tapestry workshops of the Gobelins family, with which were grouped other Paris looms, including those of the Louvre. A decree of 1667 establishing this enterprise refers to 'painters, high-warp tapestry weavers, gem-cutters and jewellers, metal-founders, engravers, *ébénistes* and *menuisiers* in wood and ebony (*sic*), dyers, and other workmen in all manner of arts and crafts'. Protection was granted from foreign competition and the enterprise given special terms otherwise. The work of the *Manufacture royale* played a very great part in establishing the distinctively French style in the arts.

The rise of new industries outside this organization (such as the manufacture of mirror-glass), the practice of granting privileges (q.v.) and subventions to other enterprises, changes in fashion, and the completion of Versailles, led to a gradual diminution of the activities of the *Manufacture royale*, which concluded with the death of Oudry (q.v.), director of the Gobelins workshop, in 1755.

MAPLE

A tree found in both Europe and America yielding a wood with highly decorative figuring when cut into veneers (see *Fiddle-back*). As a furniture wood it was particularly popular in Central Europe during the 18th century, but it was largely favoured in France during the first half of the 19th century, where it is termed *bois d'érable*. American furniture veneered with maple dates from the end of the 17th century. Bird's-eye maple is a figure with dark spots in the lines of the grain.

MARCANTONIO RAIMONDI (1487–1539)

The art of printing from engraved copper-plates was introduced about the middle of the 15th century, probably in Germany. Marcantonio Raimondi, a pupil of Francesco Francia of Bologna, showed his talent as an engraver at an early age, and he began by imitating Dürer to the point of forgery, since he added the *AD* monogram. Furiously angry, Dürer complained to the Signoria at Venice, where Marcantonio was then working, and later reproductions were issued without the monogram. Arriving in Rome, Marcantonio came into touch with Raphael, and began to make copper-plate engravings of Raphael's drawings. These were very popular. Pornographic illustrations to an especially lewd sonnet by Aretino earned him a spell in prison, but his release was procured by Cardinal de' Medici, and he afterwards worked on engravings after Bandinelli. Primarily an engraver of the work of others, Marcantonio's work was extremely popular, and his engravings were widely disseminated. They inspired craftsmen in several media, notably the painters of *maiolica*, and much of the *istoriato* painting of Urbino and elsewhere after the work of well-known painters of the day was taken from Marcantonio's version. He played a considerable part in disseminating the revived classical themes of the Renaissance in Germany and France.

MARCOLINI, COUNT CAMILLO (1736–1814)

Director of the Meissen factory from 1774 until 1814, Marcolini was appointed at a time when all porcelain factories were meeting with great difficulties, partly the product of the introduction of the neo-classical style to which porcelain was ill-suited, and partly the increasing competition of Wedgwood's creamware (q.v.). Many new ideas were tried at this time, including imitation of Sèvres *biscuit* figures, and copies of Wedgwood's jasper (q.v.) in porcelain, known as *Wedgwood-arbeit* (q.v.). Despite many expedients the factory had incurred enormous debts by 1799. Marcolini attempted to resign, but he was persuaded to stay. He was dismissed in 1813, after the bombardment of Dresden by Napoleon's armies, by a commission set up to consider ways of reviving the factory. During Marcolini's directorship the customary mark was the crossed swords with a star between the hilts.

MARIEBERG (Sweden) FAÏENCE FACTORY

The Marieberg factory was founded on the island of Kungsholmen near Stockholm by Johann Ehrenreich (v. Königsberg) with the aim of making porcelain. His privilege was granted in 1759. The newly erected buildings having been burned down it was decided to manufacture faïence only, entirely in the tradition of Strasbourg and Marseilles and using only enamels. By 1762 the factory had 148 workmen and a large turnover, but in 1766 its activity was curtailed by economic troubles, and Ehrenreich was forced to leave. A Frenchman, Pierre Berthevin from Mennecy, directed the factory from 1766–1769,

Marieberg. Figure of a boy somewhat in the manner of Mennecy. Marieberg. c. 1769.

followed by Henrik Sten under whose direction faïence gave way to English creamware (*Flintporslin*), Marieberg was bought in 1782 by Rörstrand, and in 1788 ceased production.

From the outset Marieberg concentrated on plastic models, birds, and flowers, and these far outstripped the factory's competence in painting. They also attempted to produce a violet-coloured glaze, perhaps in competition with Rörstrand's *bianco sopra bianco*, but it gathered in uneven pools, was not successful, and was probably abandoned about 1765. Marieberg used a very brilliant blue with success for flowers such as convolvulus and cornflowers. The plastic element at Marieberg holds equal place with painting, and was fully developed by 1765.

Berthevin made few changes, though towards the end of his stay transfer-printing was introduced and carried on by his successor, Sten, who saw its possibilities in relation to the neo-classical style, using it with skill and taste in black or brown monochrome.

Marieberg faïence is marked with the three crowns of Sweden above a stroke, followed by the letters *MB* and an *E* or *B*, the date, and possibly a painter's mark.

See *Rörstrand.*

MARIEBERG (Sweden) PORCELAIN FACTORY

The manufacture of porcelain at the Marieberg factory was a later extension of the faïence undertaking (q.v.). It was started by Pierre Berthevin, who had previously been employed at Mennecy

(q.v.), and from 1766 to 1769 when he went to Frankenthal, the styles of Mennecy were copied. During these years the use of transfer-printed decoration was started, but was employed to a far greater extent in the following period, when Anders Stenman was in charge of production. The porcelain made at Marieberg until 1777 was a soft-paste, but in that year experiments were conducted with a hard-paste body with the aid of Jean-Jacques Dortu, who came from the small Swiss factory at Nyon. Marieberg closed in 1788.

The porcelain of Marieberg is rare and largely derivative. The two principal influences were Mennecy in the early period and Copenhagen in the later.

MARKS ON POTTERY AND PORCELAIN

The custom of placing a mark to indicate the factory or workshop of origin on pottery is a very ancient one. Roman potters quite commonly marked such wares as Samian pottery with their name, and sometimes the place of origin. The first European ware to be marked fairly consistently was Italian *maiolica*, sometimes only the initials or the name of the painter, and sometimes more extended information. Only wares of special significance, however, were marked at this time. With the rise of the porcelain factories in the 18th century marking became customary, and the first to adopt a regular factory mark was Meissen (q.v.), who used the crossed swords from the Electoral Arms of Saxony to denote patronage by Augustus the Strong. The Vincennes-Sèvres factories employed the royal monogram of Louis XV for the same purpose. The absence of marking, if this is sufficiently noticeable to appear a matter of deliberate policy, is also significant. Very little porcelain made in England was marked for the first fifteen years or so, except from Chelsea where marking was fairly consistent, and this suggests that the factories hoped to pass off their wares as coming from Chelsea, from China and Japan, or from Meissen. It is worth noting that the Derby factory at its inception called itself 'the second Dresden', and it also imitated the wares of Chelsea. Worcester employed pseudo-Chinese marks for wares decorated in imitation of the Oriental, and the crossed swords of Meissen can be found on some Worcester vases. Among the smaller factories, Lowestoft pirated both the crescent mark of Worcester and the crossed swords of Meissen. Of all the factory marks that of Meissen was the most abused, particularly by the Thuringian factories, who employed such marks as crossed *L*s and crossed hayforks with deceptive intent.

English pottery was rarely marked, and then only with pseudo-Chinese seal-marks, until the advent of Josiah Wedgwood. He instituted a system of impressed marks which serve to identify his wares with reasonable certainty, although false marks have been noticed. His competitors however, making much the same kind of ware in imitation, rarely marked them.

Apart from factory marks, either painted or impressed, many wares of both pottery and porcelain carry workmen's marks of one kind or another which are often of unknown import, and we notice the occasional addition of marks *after* manufacture, such as the 'Johanneum mark' of Meissen (see *Johanneum*) which was done for a special purpose.

The late Emil Hannover once remarked that the surest way to get together a bad collection is to rely on marks, and these can cause a great deal of confusion if taken at their face value. If all the characteristics of a specimen taken together are in favour of a certain attribution, then a confirming mark is a valuable piece of clinching evidence. By itself, and without the essential characteristics, a mark guarantees nothing.

Some of the principal marks to be found on European pottery and porcelain are included in the Appendix. This list, however, is by no means exhaustive. Marks are far too numerous to include even in a book of this kind, and the reader is referred to books devoted to marks, especially to those by W. B. Honey and John Cushion. For an explanation of the meaning of Chinese reign-marks see *Reign-marks, Chinese*. Japanese porcelain is not consistently marked, and the ideograms appearing on occasional specimens can only be read by someone acquainted with the language. Long inscriptions appearing as part of the decoration of Chinese porcelain are usually poems.

MARLBOROUGH LEG (also formerly spelled 'MALBROW' and 'MARLBORO'.)

A trade term used by cabinet-makers in the 18th century for a leg of square section often ending in a block (plinth) of similar section. The term may have

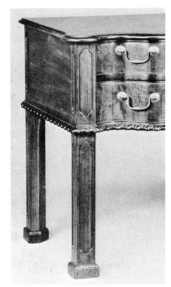

Marlborough Leg. Detail of mahogany writing-table with Marlborough leg. Philadelphia. c. 1770.

originated as a compliment to George Spencer, fourth Duke of Marlborough, to whom Ince and Mayhew dedicated their book, *The Universal System of Household Furniture* (1762). Chippendale also adapted the square leg from the Chinese, and characteristically mixed decorative *motifs*, using classic or Gothic to relieve the plainness of the simple form.

In America, especially Philadelphia, the Marlborough leg gained popularity over the fashionable *cabriole* leg with claw-and-ball feet. Thomas Affleck was the most prominent colonial user of the Marlborough leg.

MAROT, DANIEL (d. c. 1718)

Member of a French Huguenot (q.v.) family of architects and designers, and a one-time pupil of Jean Lepautre. Driven from France by the persecution which followed the Revocation of the Edict of Nantes in 1685, he was appointed architect to William of Orange, later William III of England. Marot worked extensively at Hampton Court, which was William's favourite residence, as a designer both of furniture and interior decoration, and he made a speciality of elaborately draped beds. Here, he had the assistance of Dutch and French Huguenot craftsmen. Marot considerably influenced design during the early years of the 18th century, before the revival of Palladianism.

MARQUETRY

A kind of surface ornament in which patterns are formed from sheets of coloured veneers (q.v.), or such materials as brass, tortoiseshell, ivory, etc., which are clamped together and fret-cut in one operation. The discarded parts, after the marquetry has been assembled, are sometimes employed to form similar patterns with the materials in a different order. In the case of Boulle furniture (see *Boulle, A.-C.*) a sheet of brass and of tortoiseshell were clamped

Marot, Daniel. An exceptionally fine state bed in the manner of Daniel Marot (c. 1700) from Clandon Park (Surrey). The style of the chairs is contemporary, and based on the Louis XIV style.

261

together, cut out, separated, and put together with tortoiseshell predominating (termed *premier partie*) and then applied to the furniture to be decorated. The remainder was put together with the brass predominating and employed for a similar purpose. This was known as *contre partie*. Patterns formed in marquetry were often enhanced by dyeing and engraving woods, and with related techniques.

MARQUISE

An upholstered armchair similar in many ways to the *bergère* (q.v.), but with a seat wide enough for two. It is a French version of the English love-seat (q.v.). The *marquise d'alcove* was a corner chair with an unusually wide seat. The term is also employed in other ways, notably to describe a type of blind.

MARROW SCOOP

A kind of silver spoon shaped like a large scoop at one end, with the handle in the form of a smaller scoop, for the purpose of removing marrow from bones. First made late in the 18th century.

MARSEILLE (Bouches-du-Rhône, France) FAÏENCE

From the late 17th to the end of the 18th century Marseille was a flourishing faïence centre, where at least seven factories were producing wares in the manner of Rouen, Nevers, and Moustiers till independent styles evolved. The production at this period is difficult to separate from the work of Nevers or Montpellier, but even more from Moustiers (q.v.), because Joseph Clerissy remained on good terms with his brother, Pierre I Clerissy. The development of enamel colours at Marseille in the second half of the 18th century is its greatest contribution to the art of faïence.

Saint-Jean-du-Désert

This factory was founded in 1679 by Joseph Clerissy, who rented a pottery from Joseph Fabre. In 1680 he engaged the two sons of François Viry (a painter at Moustiers), and died in 1685 deeply in debt. His widow married François Viry, who probably managed the factory till he, also, died in 1697. Antoine II Clerissy—Joseph's eldest son—was now of an age to take over, and remained at Saint-Jean-du-Désert till 1733, when the enterprise moved to La Joliette in the centre of the city. The designs of Joseph Clerissy at Saint-Jean, and of his brother Pierre I at Moustiers, are easily confused, and the presence of Viry in both places only adds to the difficulty. However, decorations after Antonio Tempesta in blue with purple outlines are attributed to Saint-Jean-du-Désert by analogy with pieces marked *FVF, EVF, OVF* assumed to be signatures of members of the Viry family. Moustiers, Nevers, and Savona had great influence, and ornamental drug-jars, Chinese scenes, and *galanteries* may easily be confused if the typical Saint-Jean purple outline has been omitted.

Joseph Fauchier—Clerissy

This factory lay in the Bourgade Saint-Lazare, just outside the city, and was owned by Anne Clerissy, daughter of Joseph I of Saint-Jean. She died in 1711 leaving the business to her daughter, Madeleine, and her son-in-law, Louis I Leroy, who was not a potter. Joseph Fauchier was manager, and Madeleine learned enough from him to train her son, Louis II Leroy, who became a partner in 1731, and head of the factory in 1741. He inherited on Madeleine's death in 1749. Fauchier left in 1724. While still at this factory Joseph Fauchier made a famous centre-piece, now in the Limoges Museum, signed *Fauchier à la Bourgade*. He was also responsible for figures of saints, and reliefs with a thick white glaze, similar in type to the work of Della Robbia (q.v.).

The Pentagon—Joseph Fauchier

Fauchier continued to make figures in his own factory. Several of them are signed (for instance, a *Virgin and Child*) *Fauchier 1735*. He taught his craft to his nephew, Joseph II Fauchier, who carried on the factory very successfully for forty years. It continued into the 19th century. The Fauchier family, although they must have known the enamelling technique, always used high-temperature colours (q.v.), adapting them to new designs, and gradually the influence of Rouen and Moustiers was left behind. The yellow ground, often forged today and sometimes attributed to the Veuve Perrin, was in fact invented by Fauchier. It is either painted with naturalistic flowers, or with designs in white reserves. This factory also produced quantities of tureens in the shape of fruit, vegetables, and birds fully equalling the models of Strasbourg.

Enamel-painting—Colours of the Muffle-kiln (Petit-feu)

Claud Perrin started a factory about 1740, but probably did not use enamel colours so early. After his death in 1748 the enterprise was carried on by his widow, always known as the *Veuve Perrin*. She reorganized the enterprise, and was largely responsible for the development of the enamel colours and brilliant faïence that made Marseille famous. In 1755 the Veuve Perrin engaged Honoré Savy, a former potter in the Leroy factory, who is said to have invented a dark green enamel used *en camaieu* at Marseille. He remained till 1770, though after 1764 he had his own workshop. His work was good, and he was a man of considerable prestige, but he died without means several years before the Revolution. In 1775 Veuve Perrin was in partnership with Abellard, a former Clerissy workman from Saint-Jean-du-Désert. Joseph Perrin, her son, succeeded in 1793, and kept the factory open till early in the 19th century.

Joseph Gaspard Robert, a native of Marseille, founded a factory in 1750 with his stepfather, André Estieu. Business flourished, and after 1759 he also made porcelain. His faïence is very smooth and finely painted.

Antoine Bonnefoy was apprenticed in 1756 to Joseph Gaspard Robert, and left in 1762 to go into partnership with his brother, Joseph Bonnefoy. At first he was unsuccessful, but after Joseph retired the business prospered. There were many other minor factories producing faïence in Marseille, at one time perhaps as many as twenty.

The early wares of the Saint-Jean-du-Désert factory are painted in blue with manganese outlines, and with subjects after Tempesta, such as we have seen at Moustiers (q.v.). The Bérain style of Moustiers was also used in the same way, as well as shapes and designs in the manner of Nevers, Rouen, and Savona. The plastic specimens follow the style of Nevers rather than of Moustiers. Painting on faïence at Marseille generally is far better in technique and style than almost any other French factory, with the possible exception of Strasbourg, and this can, in part at any rate, be accounted for by the School of Painting established in 1756, on which the factories drew for talent. The directors of this school broke from tradition by teaching its pupils to paint directly from nature, avoiding conventional formulae. The result is the dazzling faïence-painting seen especially from the factory of the Veuve Perrin, where flowers, fish, seaweeds, and all kinds of natural scenes are brilliantly represented. The Veuve Perrin factory produced the most varied types of enamel decoration, and seems to have had an unlimited supply of subjects, which were rendered in a sophisticated technique. A yellow ground was adopted from Montpellier and used over glaze, while a deep blue-green was invented by Honoré Savy. The Veuve Perrin made excellent imitations of Chinese export porcelain, and also used designs based on French engravings. *Chinoiseries* and the designs of Pillement (q.v.), the 'India' flowers of Strasbourg, and naturalistic bouquets all appear at Marseille with a new, unusual freedom. The Veuve Perrin liked bunches of wild-flowers on a white ground, while Robert preferred small bouquets and birds. Decoration drew on all subjects popular in the mid-18th

Marseille Faïence. Pot pourri vase. Marseille. c. 1760. Factory of the Veuve Perrin. Marked *VP. Musée de Sèvres.*

century; landscapes with ruins, harbour-scenes, marine-subjects, and flowers everywhere, scattered or arranged in festoons or garlands. Forms were rococo, inclining towards the Louis Seize style, and finally at Bonnefoy's factory, they become neoclassical.

Savy is thought to have invented a dark bluishgreen, and on early pieces it sometimes has dark outlines and black shading. The yellowish-green monochrome is usually attributed to Robert, but the products of his factory are difficult to separate from those of the Veuve Perrin, though Robert's faïence was a very pure white with a rich glaze. His *motifs* are similar to those of the Veuve Perrin, and he was fond of insects, as well as marine-subjects, birds, and *scènes champêtres*.

The faïence of Marseilles has been much forged, and the mark of the Veuve Perrin especially should be viewed with extreme caution.

MARSEILLEMUSTER

A kind of moulded ornament for the decoration of plates introduced at Meissen in the 1750s. It has six panels, each surrounded by rococo scroll ornament which also encroaches on to the centre of the plate. The panels were used for painted ornament, principally *deutsche Blumen* (q.v.) and birds. This, like other Meissen moulded patterns, was copied elsewhere at many contemporary factories. See *Ozier pattern.*

MARTHA WASHINGTON (American)

Either a chair with a high stuffed back and open wooden arms, in late 18th-century style; or a small

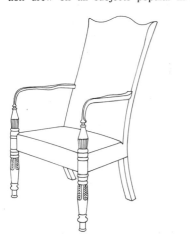

'Martha Washington'. 'Martha Washington' chair in mahogany, reflecting Sheraton influence. c. 1800. By Joseph Short, Newburyport.

Masks. Door-knocker of bronze. The masks at top and bottom are separated by a cartouche; the two satyrs on either side are mounted on dolphins with scrolling tails; the whole with intertwined serpents. Late 16th-century grotesque style. Italian. *Victoria and Albert Museum.*

worktable containing sewing implements—from 1780 onwards. See *Furniture, American.*

MARTINIÈRE, ANTOINE NICHOLAS
A mid-18th-century Paris enameller, some of whose work was done for Mme de Pompadour.

MARTINOT FAMILY
Clockmakers to the French Court who began working in the 16th century. Balthazar Martinot (fl. 1679–1708) was clockmaker to Louis XIV, and a prominent member of the Clockmakers' Guild. Jean Henri Martinot and Jerôme Martinot were also clockmakers to the same King.

A well-known clock by Jerôme Martinot in the Victoria and Albert Museum has a case signed *'Fait par* [Jacques] *Caffiéri'.*

'MARY GREGORY' GLASS
Blown, tinted glass decanters, bottles, wine-glasses, etc., in ruby (cranberry), green, pink, blue, turquoise, and amber glass decorated in opaque white enamel with Victorian children at play—a girl or boy on each glass. These were made and exported about the middle of the 19th century by Hahn of Galonz (Jablonec), then in Bohemia and now in Czechoslovakia. They were sent to America, where (it is said) a real-life Mary Gregory copied the designs while working for the Boston and Sandwich Glass Works (see *Sandwich Glass*).

MASK
The human face in mask form. A popular ornament from early Renaissance times onwards, and no doubt suggested by Roman theatrical masks. The mask took many forms. The Medusa head (q.v.) was popular among metalworkers, and the fashion for grotesques (q.v.) gave rise to the mask with distorted features, often in conjunction with foliage, to be found decorating *maiolica*. It sometimes occurs in the early part of the 18th century with American Indian feathered head-dress. The many variations include the satyr mask (q.v.).

MASONS, FENTON (Formerly Lane Delph), STAFFORDSHIRE
A porcelain factory at first making wares somewhat in the style of New Hall was established here about 1802. Specimens of porcelain, sometimes impressed *M. Mason*, are rare. About 1813 C. J. Mason patented a kind of stoneware which he called 'Ironstone China', and this was principally decorated with transfer-prints in underglaze blue, or with gaudy Japan patterns. Nearly all Mason's wares are marked. Most familiar are moulded jugs in several sizes, but service-ware of all kinds was made. The business was purchased in 1851 by Francis Morley, and later it was taken over by two brothers named Ashworth.

MATTED
The term is applied to a flat, sunk background of both woodcarving and metalwork which is dotted with punch-marks. The tool used for the purpose was called a matting-punch.

MAYER, FRANZ FERDINAND (fl. mid-18th century)
German *Hausmaler* (q.v.) working at Pressnitz in Bohemia. A relatively large amount of work by Mayer, and in his style, has survived, and it is possible that he maintained a studio. A plate painted with an Italian Comedy scene is dated 1747, and a record exists of his house being struck by lightning in 1776, which suggests a working life of thirty

Mayer. Porcelain plate painted with a landscape and river scenes by Franz Ferdinand Mayer of Pressnitz (Silesia). c. 1750. Meissen porcelain. *Victoria and Albert Museum.*

years. Much of his work is on defective Meissen porcelain, some of it of the 1720s, which implies he was buying outmoded ware. Flowers are a common border decoration, and his enamel colours are dry, lacking in brilliance, and of poor colour. Insects commonly cover faults in the glaze, although this was a universal practice.

MAZERS

Mazers are wooden bowls for use as food-containers. They seem to have originated in Germany at an early date, and were certainly known in England by the reign of Edward III. Mazers are nearly always of maple (q.v.). The earliest are shallow, but later examples are deeper. In England mazers of maple were known in the 16th century according to contemporary records. Silver rims with engraved decoration, sometimes inscribed, were an early addition, and a silver foot was probably first added about the same time. A few known examples have the addition of inset precious stones. A very rare type is the double mazer, which takes the form of a small bowl inverted on a larger one which has a single handle, the whole being mounted in silver. One of 15th-century date with gilded silver mounts is in the Germanisches Museum, Nürnberg.

MECCA RUGS

Wealthy Mohammedans took prayer-rugs of the finest quality on the pilgrimage to Mecca, after which they were presented to a mosque and hung upon the wall. Many were made at Shiraz (q.v.), and are termed 'Mecca Shiraz'. This is a dealer's term, however, to be used with considerable care.

MECHANICAL FURNITURE

Furniture fitted with mechanical devices for various purposes. See *Ébéniste-mécanicien*.

MEDICI FAMILY, THE

A Florentine family of merchants and bankers who became noted as patrons of the arts. They first emerge in the 13th century, but they did not achieve wealth and fame until the time of Giovanni de' Medici (b. 1360), who was succeeded by his son, Cosimo (1389–1464). Cosimo laid the foundations of Medici political power and influence, and encouraged the revival of art and literature, making Florence the centre of learning at the time. Lorenzo the Magnificent (1448–1492) was a munificent patron of the arts who did much to encourage the art of printing. In 1513 Giovanni de' Medici was elected to the Papal chair as Leo X, and Florence became a Papal dependency. Catherine de' Medici became the wife of Henri II of France in 1533. Cosimo I (1519–1574), also called 'the Great', was a member of a cadet-branch of the family, descending from the earlier Cosimo, and he, too, was a patron of art and literature. The family became extinct in 1737.

Medici Porcelain. Ewer of Medici porcelain influenced both by contemporary *maiolica* and Chinese porcelain. The gadrooning at the base, for instance, is reminiscent of painted ornament to be found on certain late Ming vases (q.v.). Florence. c. 1580. *Metropolitan Museum, New York.*

MEDICI PORCELAIN

By the 16th century Chinese porcelain was comparatively well known in Europe, but the first attempt to copy it was not until 1575, when an artificial porcelain was made under the patronage of Francesco Maria de' Medici, Grand Duke of Tuscany, for which reason it is termed 'Medici' porcelain. Attempts to copy Chinese porcelain had been made at least a century earlier in Persia, where the adoption of Chinese styles for faïence painted in blue had already taken place. To judge by surviving specimens, some of which are very slightly translucent, glaze material was mixed with the clay. Any kind of chemical analysis being out of the question, early potters working on this problem had to experiment by trying to find the composition of Chinese porcelain from external appearances, and principally the difference between pottery and porcelain to them was one of translucency. There was only one man-made translucent substance—glass—and an opaque white glass, not unlike porcelain superficially, had already been made by adding tin oxide to clear glass. It is possible that experiments had been made at Venice in the utilization of glass of this kind to make a porcelain substitute, for there is a record in 1508 of seven bowls of *'porcellana contrefacta'*, which suggests something of the kind. But these could not have been made in any of the ways open to the potter, and Chinese porcelain was obviously a product of the potter's wheel. To add ground glass to white clay, forming the mixture by the accepted pottery techniques, was an obvious solution, and it has been suggested that the first experiments towards the making of Medici porcelain were the work of Orazio Fontana, a *maiolica* potter of Urbino (q.v.), assisted by a Levantine. As a *maiolica* potter Orazio Fontana would have been acquainted with glass opacified with tin oxide, for this was the *maiolica* glaze. The presence of a 'Levantine' assistant suggests knowledge of the experiments apparently made in Persia already referred to.

From surviving documents it would appear that the Medici porcelain body included sand, glass, powdered rock-crystal (silica), and the white earth of Faenza (a centre for *maiolica* production), together with a proportion of Vincenza clay. The glass and other fusible ingredients were probably fused together, ground to powder, and mixed with the clay, the latter conferring cohesion and plasticity on the mixture and providing the required refractory quality. The glaze is hazy, full of minute bubbles, and gives the impression that a little tin oxide was included. It is, in fact, not unlike the glaze of some early Ming porcelain, and in the past specimens have been mistaken for Chinese.

For the most part Medici porcelain forms were inspired by those of China, the pottery of Persia, and the native *maiolica*. All these styles were sometimes combined in one piece, although the mixture is rarely incongruous. Decoration is nearly always in blue alone, but sometimes in blue and maganese. An example in polychrome is of uncertain attribution.

About forty pieces are known still to exist, almost all of them in important museums. Further discoveries are possible, but hardly likely.

See *Porcelain*.

MEDUSA HEAD

The head of a woman with hair in the form of writhing serpents. Medusa could turn men to stone with a glance, and she was slain by Perseus, who observed her reflection in his polished shield. For this reason her head frequently appears as an ornament to shields and breastplates, and in painted depictions of them.

MEILLONAS (Ain, France) FAÏENCE

A small factory was founded in 1759 in the grounds of his château near Bourg-en-Bresse by Hugues de Marron. A potter named Gautherot managed the factory. De Marron was guillotined in 1794, and although the factory did not close until 1830, its wares were no longer of artistic importance. Its products were inclined to be heavily potted, and painted with high-temperature colours in the southern style. Some excellent work was done during the stay of Protais Pidoux (see *Aprey*), probably between 1762, when he left Aprey, and 1766, the date of his appearance in Mâcon. Among the decorations from here are *genre* scenes, landscapes, and natural flowers, often surrounded by a heavy yellow scrolling imitating picture-frames.

MEISSEN PORCELAIN FACTORY

This, by far the most important 18th-century factory in Europe, was the first to make true porcelain in the Chinese manner, and was arbiter of fashion in porcelain-making from its inception in 1710 to the beginning of the Seven Years' War in 1756. It was established in the fortress of the Albrechtsburg in the small town of Meissen, some twelve miles from Dresden in Saxony, and its porcelain was, until recently, called 'Dresden' in England. It has always been called 'Saxe' in France. The factory is still working, and producing wares of extremely good quality. It is now in East Germany.

Two principal types of ware were made at Meissen. A very hard red stoneware (separately considered under the heading *Red Stoneware*) which was produced from 1710 to 1730, and white porcelain. A limited amount of faïence was made early in the 18th century at a factory at Dresden (operated in conjunction with Meissen) which is also separately considered (see *Dresden Faïence*). Both the red stoneware and the porcelain body were discovered by the Graf von Tschirnhausen and his assistant, J. F. Böttger (q.v.). The first porcelain to be made at Meissen was exhibited at the Leipzig Fair in 1710 and offered for sale in 1713, by which time production was well established. Until 1719 this is usually called Böttger's porcelain (*Böttgerporzellan*). The body was hard but with a slightly yellowish cast, and a glaze notable for the number of minute bubbles in suspension in it. A good deal of the production was probably decorated in one way or another with 'cold' colours (*kaltemalerei*), which were either oil-colours, or, more likely, lacquer colours, such as those employed by Martin Schnell (q.v.). These have since disappeared, although specimens of red stoneware thus decorated have sometimes survived. Enamel colours were primitive—yellow, blue, green, rose-pink, iron-red, and violet. A lustre (q.v.) of purplish hue was discovered in 1715, and very occasionally used as a ground colour. Oil-gilding was employed occasionally, and limited use was made of silvering which has now oxidized to black. Both applied and moulded decoration can be observed from the first, usually of flowers and foliage, and reticulated, or 'pierced', porcelain imitated a well-known Chinese type. Twig handles, and masks surrounded by foliage, occur also on red stoneware. Gold was employed as a ground, and some of the earliest *chinoiseries* in gilt silhouette probably belong to the end of the

Meissen. Porcelain teajar (*Teebüchse*) of Böttger's porcelain, the moulded floral decoration in panels taken from Oriental sources. Meissen. c. 1715. *Boston Museum of Fine Arts.*

Böttger period, although many of those obviously later are the work of *Hausmaler* (q.v.) who bought outmoded Böttger porcelain at a later date. A few figures were made at this time, including some of Augustus the Strong, Chinese figures intended as pastil-burners, and dwarfs after Callot (q.v.) which were perhaps modelled by Georg Fritzsche. Some models appear alike in red stoneware and porcelain, notably a small bust intended to represent Vitellius.

A new period began with the advent of J. G. Höroldt, often termed the *malerische Periode* (or painter's period), which lasted from 1720 to about 1735. A much whiter porcelain body was introduced, together with a new and more colourful palette of stronger and cleaner colours. Limited use of underglaze-blue pigment was made after 1720, but the factory experienced difficulty with this colour for several years afterwards, which was not overcome until 1732, when such patterns as the *Zwiebelmuster* ('onion' pattern) the *Blaublümchenmuster* (blue-flower pattern, based on the Chinese late Ming 'aster' pattern), and others became popular, the first named being commonly used today at several factories.

Chinoiseries were probably the most popular decoration of the 1720s. Among the earliest was the gilt silhouette—some factory work, some by the *Hausmaler* Seuter, and perhaps some also by Aufenwerth. The best of the polychrome *chinoiseries* were based on designs engraved by Höroldt, of which signed and dated specimens exist, and these are relatively numerous. A later type of *chinoiserie* (which might better be called a *japonaiserie*) attributed to A. F. von Löwenfinck (q.v.) is now much sought. Practically every painter of competence turned his hand to the *chinoiserie*. Japanese porcelain from Arita, of which Augustus the Strong was very fond,

Meissen. A characteristic tea and coffee service of about 1730 decorated with *chinoiseries* after Höroldt (q.v.) which shows the most popular contemporary forms for the various items. Meissen. *Antique Porcelain Co. Ltd.*

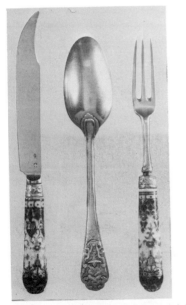

Meissen. Silver-gilt dessert knives and forks. Porcelain handles from Meissen mounted in Augsburg silver. c. 1735. *Christie, Manson & Woods Ltd.*

inspired much Meissen porcelain at this time, even to the extent of copying the characteristic Japanese shapes, and the palette approached that of Kakiemon (q.v.) very closely. Most such work was based on Kakiemon types, but copies of the variety termed 'Imari' (q.v.) were made, although these were not nearly so popular. A number of painters are recorded in 1731 as doing '*Japannischen Figuren*'. *Indianische Blumen*, floral decoration which also accompanied many European subjects, were based on Japanese flower-painting.

Landscape and topographical painting began soon after 1720 with river-scenes on the Elbe and views of the countryside around Dresden. Some were in *Schwarzlot* (q.v.), but most were in polychrome, extremely well painted. Harbour-scenes (q.v.) began to appear in 1724, but these were much more popular in the 1730s. Battle-scenes came into vogue early in the 1740s, and scenes from the Italian Comedy (q.v.), many after Watteau, towards 1750, although very rare instances of characters from the Comedy can be seen much earlier—for instance, a Harlequin about 1724. Also in the 1750s, pastoral subjects and scenes of gallantry after Watteau become much more frequent, together with little *putti* obviously inspired by Boucher. It is well known that prints were imported from Paris both as inspiration for the painters

Meissen. Miner (Bergmann) from a series by Kändler depicting members of the Court in this guise. Meissen. c. 1745. *Cecil Higgins Museum, Bedford.*

and the modellers. The earlier *indianische Blumen* were replaced by *deutsche* Blumen (q.v.) after 1735, and these developed into a style of painting known as the *ombrirte deutsche Blumen*—shadowed German flowers, introduced by Klinger (q.v.). Flowers were employed both as subsidiary decoration, and as the principal form of decoration. Framing painting, both European and *chinoiserie* subjects, at least until the early 1740s, was an elaborate scrollwork, symmetrical and baroque in style, known as the *Laub und Bandelwerke* (q.v.) (lit. leaf and strapwork).

The first use of ground colours (*Fondporzellan*) is to be found early in the 1720s, when Stölzel (the kiln-master) invented the *Kapuzinerbraun*, a coffee-brown which imitated the so-called 'Batavian' porcelain imported by the Dutch from China. Other ground colours followed. A much prized yellow ground dates from 1727, and was to be had in several shades. Sea-green, apple-green, pale grey, lilac-blue, lavender, a greyish-blue called *clair de lune* (of Chinese origin), and a rich crimson-purple followed. The factory knew how to make a celadon glaze (q.v.), but it was very rarely used, although there is an example in the British Museum. Meissen was the only 18th-century factory to reproduce this much-valued Chinese glaze colour reasonably successfully. Experiments in the 1730s utilized coloured bodies decorated with white relief-work. When ground colours fell into disuse after the Seven Years' War they were replaced by *Mosaik* patterns (q.v.). From 1735 onwards moulded patterns were developed for service-ware which had plain panels for painting (see *Ozier Patterns*).

The Academic period (*die Punktzeit*, or 'Dot' period, from the dot placed between the hilts of the crossed swords mark) began in 1763, and painters

were sent to Paris to seek inspiration from Sèvres. They were especially charged with finding the secret of the Sèvres enamel blue called *bleu de roi*. Dietrich (q.v.), who was in charge of painting, encouraged the use of paintings in the Dresden Gallery as models, and plaster-casts of classical statues were provided as inspiration. Hunting- and battle-scenes, pastoral scenes, silhouette portraits, and miniature portraits and medallions were popular between now and the end of the century. Topographical painting returned to favour, but in a different style from the earlier use of this subject. Vertical gold stripes on either a white or blue ground were a new introduction for vases, a fashion later copied by the English Derby factory. Stripes were extremely fashionable towards the end of the 18th century both as porcelain decoration and for furnishing fabrics generally.

The *plastische Periode* (the plastic period) began soon after 1733 with the advent of Kändler. It is true that a few figures had been made as far back as the Böttger period, and Kirchner (q.v.) had done some remarkably fine work during the years between 1728 and 1733. Kirchner was, in many ways, a better sculptor than Kändler, but he did not have the same appreciation of the potentialities of porcelain. Apart from the large animals done for the Japanische Palais, where Augustus housed his collection, by Kirchner and Kändler, large figures were also made for ecclesiastical purposes, such as a set of *Apostles* (of which a *St Paul* survives at Leipzig), as well as altar-furniture, Madonnas, and at least one very large Crucifixion. This was continued by Kändler, and among his larger works may be numbered a mirror and a console table, given by Augustus III to Louis XV, which Kändler took to Paris in 1750, but which did not survive the French Revolution.

The *Kleinplastik*—the small figures popularized by Kändler— were originally table-decoration made in sets to replace those formerly made of wax or sugar (see *Table-decoration*). *KHC* is a mark sometimes found on early Meissen figures, and it simply means *Königliche Hof Conditorei*—Royal Court Confectionery—where they were once stored until

Meissen. A 'crinoline' group by Kändler depicting a trinket-seller. Meissen. c. 1741. *British Museum.*

Meissen. Rococo table-appointments. A group of Meissen Swans, perhaps from the Swan service (q.v.) or inspired by it, of the type employed to decorate the table. Meissen. c. 1740.

required for the dessert table. *KHK* refers to the Court kitchen. All the figures in the set contributed to a central theme, which was usually allegorical, and they were dotted about among the service-ware, which was often matching in its decorative theme. An example is the Swan service (q.v.). The centre-pieces of these decorations were often extremely elaborate. Kändler made one—the *Ehrenpforte*, or Temple of Honour—for Augustus III which was eight feet high, and comprised 127 pieces which were set up when required. One made for the factory director, the Graf von Brühl, contained 264 pieces.

The earliest of Kändler's figures were painted in strong colours, sometimes with *indianische Blumen* over a gold or black ground. This scheme was particularly used for the well-known 'Crinoline' groups. Most of these were made between 1740 and 1745. The palette is, in fact, very useful in judging the date of Meissen figures, because just before 1750 it was altering very considerably and becoming much paler. This change marks the ending of the baroque tradition, and the rise to popularity of rococo styles from Paris, first to be seen in 1737 with the Swan service. The earlier brilliant reds change to pink, black gradually disappears except for hats and shoes, the earlier rich buttercup-yellow becomes a primrose, and so on. And hand in hand with this change we see an alteration in the shape of the bases which, during the baroque period, had been plain and simple, usually without any kind of scrollwork. Gradually the scrolls become evident, and by 1755 they are invariable. Kändler was able to assimilate the rococo style, but not the following neo-classical, and some of his last models done about 1770 still have bases with rococo scrollwork, at a time when Acier (q.v.) was producing flat oval or circular bases with such ornament as the Greek key-fret. Kändler had a taste for satire, which he never entirely lost, and he was incapable of model-ling the kind of sentimental group which was Acier's speciality. Of this kind is the well-known model of von Brühl's tailor riding on a goat, the companion model of his wife being by Eberlein. *Alte Liebe* is another satirical group depicting a youthful gallant kissing the hand of a crone, while Cupid holds a telescope to his eye. No doubt this had its origin in some piece of Court scandal. Figures in sets allegorical of almost anything lending itself to such treatment poured from Kändler's studio, and those of his many assistants, such as Eberlein, Reinicke, Meyer, Punct, *et al.* Typical of this type are *The Five Senses, The Four Elements, The Four Seasons, The Twelve Months,* and *Liberty and Matrimony.* Hunting subjects were popular, in sets with huntsmen, hounds, and the quarry; and masquerades, a popular diversion, probably account for such sets as those which comprised members of the Court dressed as miners. The theatre was also an influential source of figure-models, especially the Italian Comedy, and Kändler's series of *Harlequins* are especially sought and among the best of his work. The *Affenkapelle* (q.v.), or Monkey Band, was very popular at the time, and so were the *Cris de Paris*, which was a set based on engravings by the Comte de Caylus after Bouchardon. Of the work of Acier, little need be said beyond that its sentimental style is not particularly in the taste of today, and his work is not very much sought. Schönheit and Jüchtzer were responsible during the last twenty years or so of the 18th century for some *biscuit* porcelain figures in the neo-classical style.

MEISSONNIER, JUSTE-AURÈLE (1695–1750)

Born in Turin, Meissonnier worked principally as a goldsmith and *ornemaniste*, becoming *orfèvre du roi* in 1724. He became *dessinateur du cabinet du roi* in succession to Jean II Bérain in 1726. Virtually nothing can now be certainly attributed to Meissonnier apart from his design-books, but these were extremely influential and largely responsible for the

Meissonnier, J.-A. A page from the design-book of Juste Auréle Meissonnier showing silver tureens in the rococo style. The asymmetry is very pronounced, and water is well represented in the one shown at the top left. The crayfish knop appears at Chelsea (q.v.) before 1750 in the form of salts.

development of the rococo style. Many of his designs were done for foreign royalty and nobility, and they helped to promote the fashion abroad. Among Meissonnier's designs for silver were those with marine subjects, including rocks and shells, and these inspired not only goldsmiths, but also the porcelain factories. The shell salts of Chelsea and Bow are examples.

Meissonnier was among the first to make use of asymmetry in his designs, which was later to become the most distinctive feature of the rococo style.

MELCHIOR, JOHANN PETER (1742–1810)

Melchior was born at Lindorf, near Düsseldorf, the son of a peasant, and his early years were spent as a cowherd. He was apprenticed to a sculptor in Düsseldorf, and proved an apt pupil. He came to Mainz in 1765, and soon afterwards was offered the post of *Modellmeister* at the Höchst porcelain factory. His appointment as Court Sculptor followed in 1769. He was on terms of friendship with Goethe, who was godfather to one of Melchior's sons. In 1778 Melchior went to Frankenthal, which he left in 1793 to go to Mannheim to escape the French armies. In 1796 he was appointed joint *Modellmeister* with Auliczek at Nymphenburg, and his most important work was done here between 1800 and 1810. He is especially noted for his pastoral figures and groups modelled when he was at Höchst. He did little modelling at Frankenthal, and his work at Nymphenburg was mainly in the current Empire style.

MELES RUGS

Made not far from Smyrna, the Meles rug is coarsely woven with the Ghiordes knot, the pile being of wool.

A golden yellow is fairly characteristic, and designs are very close to those of the Caucasus (q.v.). There is usually a fairly elaborate border. Meles rugs are rare.

MELTING-POINT

The temperature at which metals pass from the solid to the liquid state. Those commonly used in the making of antiques and works of art generally are as follows, with their melting-point in degrees centigrade:

Copper	1082°	Zinc	650°
Tin	232°	Gold	1062°
Lead	327°	Silver	960·5°

Mercury becomes liquid at −39° (i.e. it is liquid at ordinary temperatures) and its boiling-point, when it vaporizes, is 357° (see *Amalgam*).

These figures relate to pure metals. The melting-points of alloys depend on their constituents. The higher the tin-content of bronze, for instance, the lower the melting-point.

MENNECY PORCELAIN FACTORY

Louis-François de Neufville, Duc de Villeroy, owned a small faïence factory as early as 1734. A specimen in the manner of Rouen is in the Musée de Sèvres. The manufacture of porcelain, at first in the ruc dc Charonne, Paris, was transferred to the Neufville estates at Mennecy, on the northern outskirts, about 1735. It was under the managership of François Barbin. This factory was started and operated without royal permission, and in 1748 Barbin was forbidden to copy or imitate the porcelain of Vincennes, or to employ any of its workmen. Barbin was joined by his son in 1751, who became a partner in 1758. Both men died suddenly in 1765. In 1766 the factory was bought by Joseph Jullien and Symphorien Jacques, a painter and a sculptor respectively, who already owned an existing faïence factory at Sceaux (q.v.). The Mennecy factory was moved to Bourg-la-Reine in 1779, and came under the patronage of

Mennecy. Putto after Boucher on a rockwork base. Mennecy. c. 1745.

the Comte d'Eu. It is doubtful whether any porcelain was made after 1780, and the last years, after Charles-Symphorien Jacques (son of the original proprietor) joined the factory, were probably occupied with making creamware in the manner of Wedgwood (faïence-fine, q.v.). In 1778 a complaint was made to the Minister of Commerce about the damage being done to the factory's business by imports of English creamware. There are one or two other factories having connections with Mennecy, particularly Crépy-en-Valois.

The early porcelain of Mennecy is similar in many ways to that of Saint-Cloud (q.v.), but the body has a dark ivory tone which is unmistakable. A good deal of early ware was painted with the fashionable Oriental patterns, and forms were copied from blanc-de-Chine. Knife-handles were a popular manufacture, and some have been excavated in the rue de Charonne. By far the commonest survival are small custard cups and covers with a spiral moulding painted with little flower-sprays in imitation of Meissen deutsche Blumen (q.v.), for which a pinkish-purple, and a purple-brown which is unmistakable, was used. Attempts were made to copy the wares of Vincennes-Sèvres (See Sèvres, Porcelain of), but these are rare. The use of the royal monogram in conjunction with the customary mark, DV incised (for de Villeroy), has been recorded. Small boxes were a fairly common item of manufacture, and today these are much sought. Some are in the form of animals.

Numerous figures were made, and one of the best-known modellers is Nicolas-François Gauron, who may have worked also for Vincennes in 1754. He became chief modeller at Tournai in 1758, remaining until 1764, and there is evidence of his activity in England. At Tournai a likely class of figures may be found in groups of children similar to those made at Mennecy, and these are again similar in style to some groups of the same subject modelled at Derby

(England). One recorded group of this kind, however, is marked DV Mo, and this seems to have been the work of Christoph and Jean-Baptiste Mo, although they may have functioned as 'repairers' rather than as modellers. It is also possible that they were repeating earlier models by Gauron. By another hand are well-modelled Italian Comedy figures, and adaptations from Meissen. Some rare figures of uncertain provenance, but with Mennecy colouring, may properly be attributable to this factory. Biscuit figures were made, inspired by those of Vincennes-Sèvres, and some portrait medallions. White glazed figures unmarked are difficult to separate from those made at Crépy-en-Valois, and the wares of Bourg-la-Reine are a continuation of those of Mennecy. Not much porcelain was made at Bourg-la-Reine, but some was marked with B R incised.

MENUISIERS (French)

The word used to describe those French craftsmen who made furniture and interior fittings of all kinds from solid wood. They prepared work such as chairs and boiseries for the carver, which, according to Roubo (a menuisier of the 18th century who wrote a treatise on his art), was not very satisfying work.

Originally, the menuisier (who is approximately equivalent to the English carpenter and joiner) was the sole maker of furniture, and in the 16th century he began to practise the highly skilled craft of inlaying, then newly introduced from Italy. Certain materials, especially ebony (ébène), were extremely rare and precious at the beginning of the 17th century, and they were therefore given only to the most skilful menuisiers, who in consequence were called menuisiers en ébène. Eventually this was contracted to ébénistes, and the craft became divided between those who made chairs, beds, boiseries, and so forth,

Menuisiers. View of a *menuisier's* workshop, showing the manufacture of furniture. Bottom left is a chair ready for delivery to the upholsterer. *After Diderot.*

Menuisiers. Carved detail from a folding chair probably made for Queen Marie Leczinska's bedroom in 1738. *Mr and Mrs Charles B. Wrightsman, New York.*

and those who decorated furniture with veneers and marquetries, as well as the rarer applied work in semi-precious stones and metals.

The distinction is occasionally finely drawn. An *armoire*, however well carved, is usually *menuiserie* if it is in solid wood, and *ébénisterie* if it is inlaid or veneered, but towards the end of the 18th century certain chairs and pieces of small furniture made in solid wood of exotic or expensive varieties came to be called *ébénisterie*, since they were made by *ébénistes* to the standard to be expected from them.

See below.

MENUISIERS-ÉBÉNISTES, CORPORATION DES

The craft guilds, founded in medieval times, survived in France until the Revolution, and they were especially powerful in Paris during the greater part of the 18th century. The *menuisiers-ébénistes* were concerned with woodwork of all kinds, both furniture and interior fittings such as *boiseries*, door-cases, window-cases, built-in furniture, and shutters. *Menuisiers* were mainly concerned with work in solid wood, and *ébénistes* with veneered furniture, but the terms are more closely defined under these two headings.

Maîtres (or masters) of the guild took apprentices at the age of twelve or fourteen for a term of from three to six years, after which the pupils became eligible as *maîtres* in their turn. Before an apprentice could be accepted he had to submit a specimen of his work which was good enough to pass the very high standards laid down. The King had the power to create *maîtres* of the guild without these formalities, a right occasionally exercised by Louis XV, principally in favour of foreign craftsmen working for the Court.

Beginning in 1741 every *maître* was required to possess a stamp which was used to strike his name on pieces made by him, and on those he repaired. A committee of the guild was charged with the duty of preserving the quality of its members' work, and to this end they visited every workshop several times a year. Any work considered to fall below the necessary standard was seized and sold for the benefit of guild funds. Approved specimens were struck with an additional stamp—the conjoined letters *ME* for *menuisiers-ébénistes*.

The guilds were finally dissolved in 1793, and the use of stamps was then no longer compulsory, although they were still employed occasionally. Throughout the 18th century guild membership rarely fell much below a thousand craftsmen.

See *Artisans-libres*.

MESHED RUGS AND CARPETS

Capital city of Khorassan, and one-time capital of Persia, Meshed is also a well-known centre of pilgrimage in the Islamic faith. It is a marketing centre for rugs produced in the province, including those of the Beluchi tribes from the east. The Sehna knot is generally employed, the weave is coarse, and the colours are nearly all of vegetable origin. Patterns include the pear design, the Herati *motif* (a rosette with two lanceolate leaves on either side), and sometimes animals and birds, usually with a medallion in the centre. Some carpets from here are very large.

MEUBLE (French)

Literally, movable. The word is used in France in the same sense as 'furniture' in English. *Ameublement* means 'furnishing', as in *bronze d'ameublement*— a furnishing bronze, as distinct from one of especial artistic value. Houses and real estate in France are termed *immeubles*, that is, immovables, the two words forming a logical distinction of a kind which one expects from the French.

Menuisiers. Stages in the upholstery of a *fauteuil* (q.v.). At the bottom is shown a chair with detachable seat and back, enabling the upholstery to be changed quickly. *After Diderot.*

MEUBLES BRODÉS

These, an impressive feature of the decoration of Versailles in the 17th century, no longer exist, and are known only from records and one or two drawings. They were very large embroidered panels in high relief, the subjects of which sometimes included figures with faces and hands of silver. Pillars were also thus ornamented. Work of this kind was executed over a wooden foundation, and cabinets were sometimes constructed of embroidered panels. Gold and silver thread was extensively employed, which largely accounts for the fact that specimens have not survived.

MEUBLES PRÉCIEUX (French)

It is desirable to distinguish between objects which, while decorative, were made primarily for utility, and those which, while serving a practical purpose with difficulty, were made principally for their decorative value. The latter are termed, in French, *meubles précieux*, and they were especially popular in France during the second half of the 18th century, when dealers encouraged a vogue for small, luxuriously fitted and decorated pieces of furniture, such as the *table à ouvrage*—the work-table—which was coveted by every woman who aspired to be thought fashionable.

MEYER, FRIEDRICH ELIAS (d. 1785)

Born at Erfurt in Thuringia, Meyer was at first Court Sculptor at Weimar, becoming a modeller at Meissen under Kändler (q.v.) in 1746, and remaining until 1760. Meyer worked in a rococo style rather than Kändler's customary baroque, and, unlike Reinicke and Eberlein, the *Modellmeister* does not seem to have influenced him. Attributions to Meyer, in the absence of documentary evidence, are a little uncertain. He is often awarded figures with disproportionately small heads and long limbs, but this characteristic is not part of the *Malabar* figures which he is known to have modelled, and he later repeated the same theme at Berlin, where he became *Modellmeister* in 1761, in a figure of a *Chinese Lute Player*. His brother, Christian Wilhelm, was a somewhat better modeller, and both were at Berlin together. Christian Wilhelm modelled allegorical groups and figures. To F. E. Meyer the factory attributes a *biscuit* porcelain bust of Frederick the Great done in 1778.

MEZZA-MAIOLICA

Wares, usually dishes, with a red pottery body covered with a white slip through which the outlines of the decoration were incised. They were then painted and covered with a lead glaze, the incisions serving to keep the colours from intermingling during firing. These wares were made in Italy throughout the 15th century, and were discontinued with the rise of the taste for more elaborate painting made possible by the development of the *maiolica* glaze. In Germany a technique called *Halb-fayence* is very

Meyer, F. E. Chinese woman modelled by F. E. Meyer. Berlin porcelain. c. 1768. *Schloss Charlottenburg, Berlin.*

similar, and it is to be found decorating wares made in Silesia during the second half of the 16th century. See *Tin-enamel Glaze.*

MICHELOZZO DI BARTOLOMMEO (1396–1472)

Florentine sculptor who collaborated with Donatello. Michelozzo was an excellent bronzeworker, but only one small bronze has hitherto been tentatively attributed to him, a *St John the Baptist* in the Bargello, Florence. He also had a considerable reputation as an architect.

MIHRAB (Persian)

In Near and Middle Eastern rugs, a prayer niche with a pointed arch at the top which varies in form from one district to another. In use the top of the arch is pointed towards Mecca. The *mihrab* itself can be found in tile-work decorating the walls of mosques, and it sometimes occurs as a decorative *motif* in other kinds of Islamic art.

MILAN (N. Italy) FAÏENCE

Faïence was made in this city in the 18th century by Felice Clerici, who founded a factory about 1745. It is to be distinguished by a very white tin glaze, thin potting, and decoration in imitation of Japanese Imari porcelain (see *Imari*). Some faïence copies of Meissen porcelain painted in panels reserved on coloured grounds are attributed to a factory belonging to Pasquale Robati which was started in 1756.

MILCHGLAS

Glass opacified with oxide of tin. In appearance it is white and translucent, resembling milk in colour, which gave rise to the name. The first instance of glass coloured in this way is to be found at Venice

Ming Dynasty. A large wine-jar decorated in underglaze blue. Yüan/Ming dynasty. 14th century. *Christie, Manson & Woods.*

in the early years of the 15th century, at the same time as the introduction of the *maiolica* glaze on pottery, which is glass similarly treated. Because of the demand for Chinese porcelain at this time, which had to remain largely unsatisfied until the opening of the sea-routes to China by the Portuguese in the early years of the 16th century, there is little doubt that this kind of glass was employed in attempts to make a porcelain substitute. A Venetian record of 1508 refers to seven bowls of *porcellana contrefacta* which may be evidence of these experiments. In the 18th century Venice produced glass plates of this kind in the manner of porcelain.

At Potsdam, where *Milchglas* was also made, it was significantly called *Porcellein-glas*, and its production in the early years of the 18th century was more or less synchronous with the development of Meissen porcelain which superseded it. A factory at Basdorf produced this kind of imitation porcelain towards the middle of the 18th century, and production of wares decorated with enamelling was still continuing in the early years of the 19th century at some North German factories. Similar wares, some imitative of porcelain, were produced in Bohemia and Holland, and in England the Bristol glass-houses made wares some of which were strongly influenced by Chinese porcelain.

Sheets of *Milchglas* were very occasionally used as a support for elaborate enamel paintings in the manner of easel-pictures.

MING DYNASTY

Chinese reigning house which came to power in 1368 and continued till 1644. It was during this period that exports of Chinese art to the West first assumed importance, and it was then that Chinese porcelain was first made in its familiar form, both enamel and underglaze colours being an early development. Exports of porcelain to the West were at their largest during the reign of Wan-li (1573–1619), when it first became known as 'carrack' porcelain (q.v.). *Cloisonné* enamel was developed

during the Ming dynasty, although specimens are rare, and most belong to the following Ch'ing dynasty. Great caution is necessary in accepting Ming reign-marks as authentic. They were commonly added to objects made in the 18th century and later.

MINTON'S (Stoke-on-Trent, Staffordshire) POTTERY AND PORCELAIN

Thomas Minton was born in 1765 and apprenticed to an engraver (perhaps Hancock) at Caughley. He is credited with the invention of the 'Willow' and 'Blue Dragon' patterns. His factory, started in 1796, first made earthenware, especially the blue-printed variety which Staffordshire largely exported to America. Soft-paste porcelain was made from about 1798 till 1811, but was discontinued in the latter year. Production started again about 1821, probably with the help of workmen from Derby, and bone-china (q.v.) soon became the principal ware to be made here. Many of the wares before 1850 were largely based on those of Sèvres, and to a lesser extent Meissen and Chelsea, the style being a revived rococo (q.v.). Workmanship was extremely good and fine-quality wares were produced, even though the designs were derivative. Many figures and groups were made, although in the absence of a mark they are often attributed elsewhere, sometimes to Rockingham. Parian figures (q.v.) first appeared about 1845. Some rare Gothic designs can probably be awarded to the influence of A. W. Pugin (q.v.).

In 1817 the style was Thomas Minton & Sons, and in 1836, after the death of Thomas Minton, his son took John Boyle into partnership, the style then being

Minton's. Ewer and stand of Minton's so-called *'maiolica'* (pottery decorated with coloured glazes, not tin-enamel ware), the ewer based on Renaissance metalwork painted with classical deities; the stand decorated with the Labours of Hercules. The ewer signed by *Thos. Allen.*

Minton & Boyle. Boyle withdrew in 1842, and was replaced by Michael Hollins in 1845. The firm then became Minton & Co. In 1849 they were joined by Colin Minton Campbell, and, when Herbert Minton died in 1858, it became Hollins & Campbell. The present company was founded in 1883.

For some years after 1854 the factory's chief modeller was the French sculptor Carrier-Belleuse, who left to become director at Sèvres, and Marc-Louis Solon, formerly of Sèvres, introduced the *pâte-sur-pâte* decoration (q.v.), which had been developed at Sèvres from a technique introduced by the Chinese in the 18th century. Specimens of his work are sometimes initialled *MS*.

The factory is still in existence and is noted for fine porcelain.

MIOTTI, VINCENZO (fl. 1711–1747)

A glassworker of Murano (Venice). The Miotti glass-house actually dates from the early years of the 17th century, and was especially active between the dates noted above, when Vincenzo and his sons specialized in enamelling opaque white glass, usually in imitation of porcelain. Dated specimens are well known, ranging from 1731 to 1747. Some are marked in enamel on the base with the name Miotti, Al Gesu (the name of the glass-house), and Murano. An impressed mark of Daniel Miotti has also been recorded. See *Milchglas*; *Venetian Glass*.

MIRROR AND GLASS PAINTING

Most surviving mirror-paintings are Chinese and belong to the 18th century, but the technique probably originated in England towards the end of the 17th century. Generally, the silvering was scraped away from the area which it was desired to paint and replaced by painting in oil. Obviously mirror-painting, being on the back of a sheet of glass, meant working in reverse, what would ordinarily be the final touches being put on first, followed by the foundation colours. The technique seems to have reached China early in the 18th century, the mirrors being sent from Europe. The best are of Chinese scenes and are extremely well painted. In the second half of the 18th century some painting on plain glass was done in China, often of European subjects, and this kind of work was continued into the 19th century when specimens are usually inferior in quality. English painting on clear glass in the 19th century is not uncommon, and often of shipping scenes. Most of it is unimportant, and the subjects have been much reproduced in recent years. Pictures on glass done with the aid of engravings are discussed under *Glass Pictures*.

MODELLMEISTER (German)

Man in charge of the design and modelling of porcelain figures. The *Modellmeister* in the 18th century was often the Court Sculptor, and it was his duty to oversee the design and execution of the figures produced by modellers employed by the factory, and to provide original designs of his own. Some of the *Modellmeister* were very prolific. Kändler (q.v.) is reputed to have modelled more than a thousand original works for reproduction at Meissen, as well as those which he did in conjunction with Reinicke and Eberlein (see *Meissen*).

MOIRÉ

A closely textured silk with a 'watered' appearance, very fashionable during the 18th century and the early decades of the 19th.

MONOPODIUM

From the Greek, meaning (literally) a single foot, the term is applied to certain small tables of the Regency and Empire period which have a three-sided support usually terminating in brass claws at the bottom corners. Tables of this kind were designed in England by Thomas Hope (q.v.).

MONTAUBAN (Tarn-et-Garonne, France) FAÏENCE

The town of Montauban had already been a pottery centre for many years when, in 1761, David Lestrade (see *Ardus*) founded a faïence factory which he ran until he died in 1791. His colleague at Ardus, Arnaud Lapierre, also came to Montauban, dying there in 1772. His business was carried on by his widow and children, and finally by his son-in-law, Jean Quinquiry. High-temperature and enamel colours were used in this factory. Six other factories were in competition about the same time, and the wares are not easy to distinguish. Research into Lapierre's accounts, and pieces from the Lestrade family, help in attributing certain designs described as *à fleurs*, *à personnages*, or *à la Chine*. The products of these small southern factories are almost impossible to separate as workers moved indiscriminately from one to another.

MONTEITH

An oval or circular deep bowl with a scalloped rim made to hold iced water for cooling the bowls of wine-glasses which were suspended by the foot from the scalloping. Usually English, the monteith also made its appearance in France fairly early in the 18th century, although I have been unable to trace the whereabouts of a surviving specimen.

The exact year in which the monteith was first introduced is known from a reference to it in 1683 by the Oxford diarist, Anthony à Wood, who records the derivation of the name, which came from a Scotsman called Monteigh who wore the bottom of his cloak thus scalloped.

The earliest monteiths are of silver, and one or two are known in gold. While in the early period it took a fairly standard form, the introduction of the detachable rim in 1694 gave it a more or less dual purpose, since it could serve also as a punch-bowl. Early example are without handles, and some have had the handles added at a later date. Decoration follows that customary at the time.

The monteith remained popular throughout the

Monteith. Monteith of 1700 by John Jackson. It has a detachable rim, turning it when desired from a glass-cooler to a punch-bowl. *Garrard & Co. Ltd.*

18th century, one of the last examples recorded being hall-marked for 1790. This has scallops based on the Greek wave-pattern, and handles in the form of rams' heads.

Monteiths also occur in English delft ware from the last years of the 17th century, and in porcelain and creamware at a later date. The two latter, it is to be assumed, were accompanied by wine-coolers, and formed part of the dinner-service. One or two glass examples still exist, and monteiths of Sheffield plate were made during the last quarter of the 18th century.

MONTPELLIER (Hérault, France) FAÏENCE
Faïence was made in this southern city at the end of the 16th century, and particularly by two potters, Pierre Estevé (1590), and his son, Jean, who succeeded him in 1596 in partnership with Pierre Ducoin. They are thought to have made drug-jars in the Faenza style, some decorated with leaves and some with historical figures. Three other families, Favier, Ollivier, and Boissier, were responsible for the drug-jars made for the two important local

hospitals. None of these wares is marked, but they have been separated from the work of Marseilles, Nevers, Moustiers, and Lyon by M. Thuile (*La Céramique ancienne de Montpellier*), who thus proved the importance of Montpellier in mid-17th century. Shortly after the beginning of the century Montpellier advanced from the simple *faïence blanche* (q.v.) to original and vigorous designs of flowers and fruit. Seventeenth-century spouted syrup or wet-drug-jars made in Montpellier are distinguishable from their Italian models by having a small ring between the body and the spout. A yellow ground has been much reproduced recently.

The city's factories continued to produce without interruption for about two and a half centuries, the same families controlling the industry—Favier, Boissier, Ollivier, and Collondre. Pierre and Ollivier sent workers from Nevers to their brother, Jacques, in Montpellier. The factory of Jacques Ollivier gradually developed into the most important in the city, and in 1725 became a *Manufacture royale.* André Philip came to Montpellier from Marseille as a young man of twenty-four, and died there in 1805. In 1767 he succeeded Antoine Dupré in the former Boissier factory, which remained prosperous into the 19th century, long after others had closed because competition was too great. Many potters from Montpellier reappear in minor south-western factories, such as Toulouse, Ardus, Bordeaux, and La Rochelle. Nearby factories were at Beziers, Pezenas, and Ganges (Hérault).

MOORFIELDS CARPETS
Thomas Moore of Moorfields, Clerkenwell, London, began to make carpets about the middle of the 18th century which were coarsely knotted in the Turkish manner. Moore's carpets were undoubtedly the best English-made carpets of his day, and some of them were designed by Adam. A number have survived,

Moorfields Carpet. Room at Osterley Park, West London, showing a Moorfields carpet in the Adam style. c. 1765.

notably at Osterley Park and Syon House, West London. The specimen from Ingestre Hall was sold in London about ten years ago for a price rivalling those obtained for 18th-century Savonnerie carpets.

MOQUETTE
A coarse imitation of silk velvet with a pile of wool which was used in France especially for table-covers, wall-hangings in servants' rooms, floor-coverings, and as coverings for the kind of seat-furniture intended to stand hard wear. It also existed in a cut variety.

Floor-coverings of *moquette* were made at Brussels and elsewhere, including Axminster and Wilton (q.v.)

See *Velvet*.

MORRIS, WILLIAM (1834–1896)
English poet and designer. Morris was educated at Marlborough and Oxford, and was first a painter, turning to poetry later, and publishing his first book of poems in 1858. He became one of the earliest socialists, writing a defence of his theories which was notable more for his sympathy with the poor than for any kind of profound knowledge of their economic consequences. He was among the first to recognize the damaging effect of industrialization on the contemporary arts, and he proposed a return to the hand-craftsmanship of former times opening, in 1863, an establishment for the making of wall-paper, stained glass, tiles, and other forms of household decoration. In his designs he was influenced by Ruskin, and he also came under the influence of a group of artists calling themselves the pre-Raphaelite brotherhood. He was much under the influence of the Gothic revival (q.v.), and his circle included the designer and decorator Walter Crane, and the potter William de Morgan. Together with Burne-Jones, Rossetti, and Philip Webb they organized the Arts & Crafts Society which opened the way to the 'Modern Movement' and the style known as Art Nouveau (q.v.). Morris's work in this field was perhaps his most substantial contribution, leading as it did to a reassessment of popular attitudes to the arts generally, and was a valuable corrective to the surge of bad taste which marked the period beginning with the Great Exhibition of 1851. In his closing years Morris became interested in typography and devoted much of his time to the Kelmscott Press from 1890 to his death in 1896. A fine edition of Chaucer is an important example of his work during this period.

MOSAIK
Repetitive ornament on porcelain consisting of a network of geometric forms, sometimes of lozenge-shape (diaper), used to fill spaces between panels painted with flowers or figures and usually surrounded by painted or moulded scrollwork. The network is often painted over a coloured ground. This kind of ornament is first to be seen at Vienna at a comparatively early date. It was introduced at Meissen soon after 1760, and it is also to be found

Mosaik. Berlin plate of c. 1770 decorated with a mosaik pattern of overlapping scales.

on the porcelain of Ansbach (q.v.). It was, however, a speciality of the Berlin porcelain factory, especially during the 1760s, although it became progressively less fashionable thereafter. *Mosaik* patterns sometimes occur on other kinds of European porcelain under the influence of German production.

MOSBACH (Germany) FAÏENCE FACTORY
The factory in Mosbach was founded by Pierre Berthevin (see *Marieberg*) under the patronage of the Elector-Palatine, Carl Theodor (see *Frankenthal*), and by Johann Tännich who worked at Meissen, Strasburg, and Kiel. After two years Berthevin retired and, two years later, Tännich became manager. He also failed to make the factory pay, and Carl Theodor handed the direction of it to J. G. F. List. Tännich moved to Mannheim and Frankenthal about 1781.

No wares from the first period are known. Some Tännich wares have been identified by a *T*, and from pieces bearing the monogram *MB* and an Electoral hat. In List's time the monogram *CT* (Carl Theodor) was used, but without the crown found on Frankenthal porcelain. After 1806 the mark was *CF* (Carl Friedrich).

One or two pieces have polychrome landscapes, and a rococo clock is dated *Mossbach 1774*. Domestic wares, jugs, tankards, and plates are similar to those of Durlach, with rather indifferent painting. Production of faïence was discontinued here in favour of *Steingut* (q.v.).

MOTHER-OF-PEARL
The iridescent lining of the shell of the oyster and other molluscs, usually employed as an inlay to furniture and small objects generally. Mother-of-pearl was sometimes added to marquetry, and it was inlaid into *papier mâché* in the 19th century. It was occasionally inlaid by the Japanese into lacquer panels. A lustre pigment described as 'mother-of-pearl' occurs on early Meissen porcelain.

Mounts, Metal, to Furniture. **Rococo** *commode* **by Gaudreau with mounts by Jacques Caffiéri (see** *Caffiéri Family***) after a design by Slodtz. A superbly mounted example of French** *ébénisterie.* **c. 1740.** *Wallace Collection.*

MOULINS (Alliers, France) FAÏENCE

This factory in the centre of France had a strongly independent style. Its history is not well documented, but is mentioned as early as 1730 in the Clermont-Ferrand records (q.v.). However, it only really developed after Louis Dubourg's foundation of 1757 had been taken over by Joseph Chambon. At one time there were several factories working in Moulins, though by 1793 they were producing only domestic wares.

Faïence of Moulins is closely related to that of Nevers: small religious figures were produced, one dated 1736 and another 1741 bearing the signature *Chollet*, which suggests that he may be the same person as the man who signed a Nevers group of *St Anne and the Virgin* dated 1735. There was a brief period at Moulins when models derived from Rouen and Sinceny were freely and imaginatively handled. Moulins faïence is grouped by analogy with an octagonal plate decorated with *chinoiseries* and signed 'à moulins' now in the Musée Nationale de Céramique at Sèvres, and a figure of St Roch in the Moulins museum. The *chinoiserie* (q.v.) decoration is very fanciful, and designs could be interchanged, used together, or separately, and seem frequently to be by the same hand. Pagodas, exuberant vegetation, long-tailed birds, and strange insects inhabit the design, right up to the rim. The composition, despite its derivation from Sinceny, is handled in a very original way. There is another group in the European taste which shows rococo scrolls framing birds, *galanteries,* and *genre* scenes.

The palette is stronger than at Nevers. Apart from blue, it has two yellows, one almost orange, a heavy olive-green, and red applied rather sparingly as at Rouen. Plates have a slightly conical, often notched, rim, and the body is thick, with a thin glaze. The base has no footring, but large stilt-marks.

MOUNT WASHINGTON GLASS COMPANY

This was founded in 1837 with a factory at New Bedford, Mass. Peachblow glass was among the more important of its productions, and the so-called 'Burmese' glass was developed here and patented by the factory. It was used both for table-glass and decorative wares. The factory sold a licence to manufacture this glass to Thomas Webb & Sons of Stourbridge (England), who marketed it under the name of 'Queen's Burmese'. See *'Burmese' Glass; Glass, American.*

MOUNTS, METAL, FURNITURE

Mounting in bronze, brass, gilded bronze, and even the precious metals dates back to very early times, and it was extremely fashionable in Rome. It became once more popular in 17th-century France and Italy, being introduced into France by Italian craftsmen, but it was during the 18th century that the custom of mounting furniture in this way reached its height, to be seen especially in the furniture of the Paris *ébénistes* (q.v.). In France this is to be dated to the 1680s, when, owing to a shortage of the precious metals, gilded wood and bronze began to replace them for many purposes in the royal palace of Versailles. Boulle (q.v.) and Cressent (q.v.) were among the most prominent of the early makers of furniture thus mounted, which continued to increase in popularity during the 18th century, and is to be seen on 19th-century furniture of the period, and ever since on reproductions.

It must be remembered that these mounts are not only decorative but also serve a utilitarian purpose. Much furniture of the time was veneered and decorated with marquetry, and the mounts protected the edges of veneers from being lifted by accidental contact. Mounts on the corners of pieces of furniture strengthened them at this point; metal mouldings to the edges of tables protected the edge from being bruised; escutcheon plates to keyholes prevented the key from scratching the woodwork; on leather-covered table-tops a *filet* of bronze covered the join between two sheets of leather; at the bottom of the legs *sabots* or *chaussures* protected the toes from contact with feet and brooms. In fact, when traced to their original purpose, very few mounts are purely decorative and with no other function.

The custom of mounting in this way is one in which the designing of furniture by metalworkers, such as Meissonnier (q.v.), undoubtedly played a large part, and both Boulle and Cressent were also sculptors and bronzeworkers.

Similar mounts were used in England on furniture in the French style during the 18th century, but for the most part carved wood as decoration replaces the metal mount on English furniture of the period. Matthew Boulton (q.v.) made furniture-mounts, and the brassworkers of Birmingham during the latter part of the 18th century made handles, escutcheon plates, and similar small wares, as well as furniture-mounts of a simple kind, some of which were probably exported to France.

Handles and Escutcheons

In England the drop handle was the principal type used during the period of the Carolean and William and Mary style. The small backplate to which the handle was attached was commonly circular, oval, or lozenge-shaped. The shape of the drop itself was most commonly the so-called 'tear-drop.' In the

ABOVE: A Lambeth delft dish of c. 1680 decorated with Adam and Eve in high-temperature colours. This belongs to the group termed 'blue dash chargers' from the border decoration.

BELOW: *Bocage. The Dancing Lesson,* after Boucher. A superb Chelsea porcelain group of the gold anchor period (c. 1760) depicting a couple teaching a monkey to dance, with a flowering maybush in the background.
The London Museum.

ABOVE: A saltglaze jug painted with a pastoral scene in enamel colours and dated 1764. English. Staffordshire. *Victoria & Albert Museum.*

BELOW: Gilded brass lantern in the neo-classical style from Osterley Park, W. London.

Wedgwood blue jasper vase surmounted by a figure of Pegasus. c. 1785. *Colln. Sir John Wedgwood.*

Chinoiserie. **Beaker-shaped vase decorated with chinoiseries by J. G. Höroldt, and signed** *'J. G. Höroldt fec. Meissen'.* **Dated 1726.**
Dresdener Porzellansammlung. Dresden.

American colonies the drop handle was the fashion from about 1690 to 1720.

In the first half of the 18th-century the style changed to a loop or bail handle mounted on a solid, flat plate with bevelled edges. The surface of the plate was sometimes ornamented by punch work in the period from 1710 to 1730. A more elegant development led to the centre of the solid backplate being cut out to give the effect of flat scrollwork. Still later, with the advent of the rococo style, backplates were elaborately pierced and chiselled in this manner. Escutcheons (keyhole-plates) were usually made to match.

It has now been established that the vast majority of furniture 'brasses' used by American cabinet-makers in the 18th century and later were imported from England, the principal source being Birmingham. The catalogues of Birmingham factories providing essential information for American cabinet-makers.

About 1750 a new variety of handle was introduced in keeping with the trend towards lighter construction in English furniture. The loop handle now had no backplate, and was fastened to two rosettes, one at either end.

For *commodes*, cabinets, sideboards, pedestals, and other furniture in the neo-classical or Adam style brass mounts in the form of rams' heads, festoons of husks, and similar classically based ornament were provided. Matthew Boulton's factory in Soho, near Birmingham, began to manufacture 'ormolu' mounts, finely chased, of a rich and golden colour, in 1762 utilizing Adam designs.

During the last quarter of the 18th century starting about 1775 the backplate was again introduced, this time made of sheet brass ornamented by die-stamping. Marcton and Bellamy, Birmingham brass-founders, patented their process in 1779. In America, brasses were stamped with favourite patriotic subjects such as stars and eagles, as well as acorns, flowers, and cornucopias.

From about 1800 small brass knobs, ornamented or plain, superseded the familiar loop-handle on tables, chests of drawers, and small pieces of furniture. In America knobs were stamped with patriotic *motifs* such as the eagle or a head of Washington. Those either of pressed or cut glass were much used from 1815–1840, and wooden knobs were employed on Late Empire or Early Victorian furniture.

The simplest loop handle was the loose ring handle attached to a circular plate in the Sheraton style. Later, during the Regency period, the most common form was the lion's mask with the ring in its mouth. The new pulls or knobs projected about an inch from the surface.

See *Ormolu*.

MOUNTS, METAL, TO POTTERY AND PORCELAIN

The earliest recorded European example of mounting pottery in metal appears to be the Chinese vase (now preserved in Dublin, but lacking its mount) which

Mounts, Metal, to Pottery, etc. Meissen vase of the *mille-fleurs* type mounted in gilt-bronze in Paris. c. 1750. *Wallace Collection.*

was mounted in silver in the 14th century. The mount can be dated accurately, since it bore the arms of Louis the Great of Hungary, and it must have been almost contemporary with the vase. The mount itself is known from a drawing in the Bibliothèque Nationale in Paris. It was removed during the 19th century and has now been lost. There are other rare mounted specimens still preserved which date to before the opening of the Chinese trade by the Dutch East India Company in the early years of the 17th century, and these were probably brought back by Portuguese or Arab traders on the old caravan route. A celadon bowl mounted in silver was given by Archbishop Warham to New College, Oxford, in 1580, and is particularly well known.

The Near East is well represented by a number of examples of Isnik pottery mounted in silver in the second half of the 16th century. Isnik (the old Nicaea) is not far from Istanbul, and the Elizabethans imported a good deal of Turkish pottery of this kind which for many years passed under the misnomer of 'Rhodian' under the impression that it had formerly been made at Rhodes.

Bellarmines (q.v.), and other vessels of Rhenish 'tyger ware', were mounted in silver during Elizabethan times, and examples of Rhineland stoneware (q.v.) thus mounted exist from the 17th century. The early English 'Malling' jugs (see *Delft, English*) are known with silver mounts.

Much 17th- and early 18th-century Chinese and Japanese porcelain was mounted in silver in England, Holland and Germany, including such things as mustard-pots, lemonade-jugs, and barrel-shaped tankards. In fact, most vessels needing a cover of some kind were mounted, both as ornament and to provide the cover. Porcelain knops were sometimes removed and replaced with an ornamental knop in silver in the European taste.

Meissen porcelain tankards, and those of German faïence, were often mounted in silver, silver-gilt, or

Mounts, Metal, to Pottery, etc. Höchst tankard mounted in silver at Nürnberg, probably by Jacob Pfaff. c. 1755. *Mrs C. B. Stout, Memphis, Tenn.*

pewter, sometimes with inscriptions. It was customary to mount porcelain in silver, and some much-sought Meissen *chinoiserie* tankards were thus embellished by Elias Adam of Augsburg. Faïence mugs were usually provided with a hole in the top of the handle to which a pewter cover was attached, although those of porcelain are sometimes mounted by means of strapping.

But mounting was at its most elaborate in 18th-century France, when gilt-bronze mounts of the highest quality were added to Chinese, Japanese, and European porcelain alike. Mounting in gilt-bronze was not confined to France. It was also done in Germany and England (see *Boulton, Matthew*), but the finest work came from Paris, particularly during the reign of Louis XV (see *Duvaux, Lazare*). The designs of mounts made outside France were nearly

Mounts, Metal, to Pottery, etc. Pair of Chinese *blanc-de-Chine* (q.v.) porcelain Dogs of Fo mounted in gilt-bronze as candlesticks in Paris. c. 1750. *Christie, Manson & Woods.*

always in the French taste, although with minor differences which reveal their origin and sometimes give rise to controversy.

The earliest European porcelain figures were small, and since at the time no one thought of making a display of them in a glazed cabinet, they needed something to set them off, and make them larger and more impressive. They were, therefore, put on a bronze base of typical rococo scrollwork, sometimes with the addition of a bocage (q.v.) of flowers and leaves, the flowers usually from Vincennes and the leaves of bronze, either green or gilt. The figure, often from a set intended originally for table-decoration (q.v.), was adapted to a variety of decorative purposes which were at the same time practical. There are, for instance, figures mounted with a candleholder and a handle, becoming in this way chamber-candlesticks. The mounters also exercised great ingenuity in grouping several pieces of porcelain within one mount, such as a central vase of *blanc-de-chine* (q.v.) with flanking European figures, perhaps as an inkstand, or for some less well-defined purpose.

Metal mounts were usually so designed that they protected and partly enclosed the porcelain, preserving it from damage, and it was, wherever possible, affixed by screws, or set into the metal with hard wax. Although the finest work was of cast and chiselled bronze, mercurically gilt (*dorure d'or moulu*), some less important specimens were set in bronze covered with a coloured lacquer which preserved the metal from corrosion.

Mounts were designed by some of the best bronze-workers of the day—people like Caffiéri, and the brothers Slodtz. Duplessis, responsible for the mounts to the famous *bureau du roi Louis XV* (see *Duplessis*), was also a director of the Sévres porcelain factory, and some of the best French mounts to be found on Meissen and Sèvres porcelain were probably by his hand, or designed by him.

The custom of mounting porcelain in the old style was continued in France during the 19th century, but the date of manufacture is usually obvious from the style of the mount, and these do not have the value of earlier work. Care must be taken to see that

mounts and porcelain belong together. Figures have sometimes been put on mounts to which they did not originally belong, and odd sets of vase-mounts, or silver mounts of the kind employed during the 17th century, are sometimes adapted to fit new objects. The signs are usually fairly apparent to anyone looking for them.

MOUSTIERS (Basses-Alpes, France) FAÏENCE

Moustiers is one of the most important faïence centres of France, equal to Nevers and Rouen. The town had known many potters, who were attracted by the clay deposits in the mountains nearby, but how the potters became tin-enamellers, unless it was through Italians who had settled in the town, is unknown. However, in the early days, before 1679, Antoine Clerissy (who founded the most important factory in the town) was known only as a maker of earthenware. The title *faïencier* came after this date to his son, Pierre. Pierre I (so called to distinguish him from his grandson who followed) directed the Clerissy factory till 1728, while his brother, Joseph, went to Marseille (q.v.). After Pierre I, came Antoine II (to distinguish him from his grandfather), who had been a partner since 1710, and on his retirement Pierre II, his eldest son, took over. This was the period of greatest prosperity, enabling this last Pierre to retire with a barony in 1774. The factory was sold to Fouqué in 1783, and the Clerissy family no longer held sway in Moustiers.

Several other factories competed in the early 18th century with Clerissy: Jean-Baptiste Ferrat, Clerissy's nephew by marriage, from 1718 to 1791; Pelloquin and Fouqué, till 1783 when Fouqué acquired Pierre Clerissy's factory; Joseph I Olerys, 1738–1749; Jean-Baptiste Laugier, in company with Joseph II Olerys, till 1790; and Jean-Gaspard Ferraud, from 1779 till 1874. There were also many small workshops in the surrounding region started by absconding and itinerant potters who used the patterns they had learned at Moustiers.

Early wares at Moustiers (and, until 1730, new designs) all come from Pierre I Clerissy's factory. Nevers and Rouen played their part in influencing both shapes and decoration, but Moustiers had a finer body and a more brilliant glaze than either. Later wares are very difficult to classify, and the best possible 'outline' history is that of Damiron, who has provided our knowledge of the factories at Moustiers.

1680–1710. Clerissy, Antoine I, Pierre I

Italian influence lasted longer at Moustiers than elsewhere. Decorations were inspired by Antonio Tempesta and the Flemish engraver, Floris. Shapes are rather plain, with some pretty dishes derived from Rouen, and more rarely from drug-jars and pieces in Italian style made at Nevers. Borders were borrowed from the Rouen *style rayonnant*, with *lambrequins* and *ferroneries*, but they were more delicately handled, and some of the best work was

Moustiers. Dish painted in high-temperature colours with a pastoral scene within rococo scroll borders. Moustiers faïence. Laugier and Olerys. c. 1740.

done by Gaspard Viry, who was also perhaps responsible for fine borders of hunting-scenes, scrolls, chimeras, and masks.

1710–1740. Clerissy, Pierre I, Antoine II, Pierre II —The Blue-and-white Bérain Style

Only blue-and-white was made before 1739, in which year Olerys returned from Alcora (q.v.). The designs of Jean Bérain spread from the Court of Versailles to the south and are especially characteristic of Moustiers. They are delicate in effect, and their fantasy makes them easy to recognize. The centre of a large dish, for instance, was painted with a classical scene in an elaborate frame. This frame was then surrounded by grotesques (q.v.), terms, festoons, urns, birds, and portraits, all seemingly hanging in space. Although more plates and dishes have survived than anything else, all the normal shapes produced in faïence—wall-fountains, sugar-casters, helmet-jugs, etc., must have been made here as elsewhere. The glaze is of a fine milk-white colour, and the potting thin and light.

1740–1793. Olerys, Joseph I, Joseph II—High-Temperature Polychrome Painting

A native of Marseille, Joseph Olerys may have been apprenticed as a boy to Pierre I Clerissy. In 1723 he was in Marseille, whence he travelled to Alcora to found a factory under the patronage of the Duke of Aranda. He remained till 1738. Having mastered the techniques of high-temperature colours and learned much from Spanish painters, Olerys returned in 1738 to found a factory at Moustiers. It flourished till 1749 when Joseph died, but did not close till 1793, though competition had greatly increased, with twelve other factories working in the town.

Olerys introduced high-temperature polychrome colours, and after 1740 the Bérain style was painted in orange, purple, and a soft green as well as in blue. Many imitations are found at all the smaller southern factories and even at Marseille and Lyon. Olerys' first style at Moustiers naturally reflects Alcora, especially the bordered plaques and dishes with mythological subjects and polychrome designs after Bérain. Moustiers could boast no red at this point, but we find brown, purple, green, yellow and

Moustiers. Dish decorated in high-temperature colours with isolated fantastic figures and 'potato flowers' (probably nightshade). Moustiers. The factory of Laugier and Olerys. c. 1750. *Victoria and Albert Museum.*

blue which were often used for stock patterns with self-explanatory names: *à guirlandes; à medaillons; à grotesques* (q.v.), and chinoiseries (q.v.). There was also an Alcora pattern called *à la fleur de solanée* (potato-flower) and some military *motifs*. The usual mark was *OL* (Olerys Laugier), but it was much abused.

1770. Jean-Baptiste Ferrat Factory—Period of Enamel Decoration
Enamel colours were introduced about 1770, causing the factory to prosper. The grandsons of the founder imitated Strasbourg, Marseille, and Aprey, though the colours were stronger and the drawing less subtle. Birds, flowers, and *chinoiserie* designs were handled with considerable skill.

1779–1874. Jean-Gaspar Feraud—High-Temperature Colours
This factory was started by a man trained by Fouqué, and although the colours of the *grand feu* (see *High-temperature Colours*) were · then gradually being superseded, he succeeded in creating new designs which fall into a category now known by his name. The colours, a soft yellow and green, were applied in conjunction with a smooth glaze and subjects included natural flowers, birds, garlands, grotesques, medallions, and butterflies. He also produced a yellow ground, and may sometimes have used enamel colours.

MUGS
These were similar in purpose to the tankard (q.v.), but lack the cover and are generally smaller. They can be found in a straight-sided or baluster-shaped version. They occur in silver, pewter, delft, creamware, and porcelain. In either pottery or porcelain the straight-sided mug is the most common, the baluster shape being distinctly rare.

MULE CHEST
A storage chest dating from about 1650 which was placed on a base fitted with drawers.

MÜNDEN (Hannover, Germany) FAÏENCE FACTORY
Faïence was made here in 1746 on the site of a workshop making clay pipes which lay slightly outside the town. In 1775 it started to make English-style creamware also. Of the faïence produced here, the most characteristic pieces are pierced, double-walled vases, and dishes and plates with pierced rims having a small flower in relief set at the intersections. Colours are manganese-purple, dull green, blue (usually by itself), and yellow, but no enamels. One group is decorated in green and purple with landscapes in reserves in the manner of Meissen. The mark is either an *M* or three crescents.

MUSICAL-BOXES
The musical-box, which enjoyed a tremendous vogue in the 19th century, was based on a very simple principle. A steel comb, the teeth tuned to scale in a variety of ways, was plucked by pins projecting from a revolving cylinder, the pins set in such a position that they came into contact with the teeth of the comb at precisely the right moment. The principle was a very old one, having been used in watches made at Nürnberg in the early years of the 16th century (see *Watches, Evolution of*). It was then in the form of a revolving disc with teeth on the periphery, and the device was employed for the same purpose in watches made during the 18th century, as well as in some musical clocks. The separation of the musical part of the clock from the timekeeping train took place in the early years of the 19th century with improvements to the revolving cylinder, although a simple version had been used to operate hammers striking bells in musical clocks of the last quarter of the 18th century. The development of the cylinder so that it could take a greater number of pins enabled longer and more complicated pieces of music to be played with an enlarged repertoire.

The first musical-boxes proper had appeared in

Mugs. Porcelain mug decorated with a *chinoiserie* from Vienna, Du Paquier's factory. c. 1725. *Metropolitan Museum, New York.*

England by 1820, usually driven by clockwork, though sometimes operated by hand-turning. They became so popular that all kinds of improvements were soon devised, such as the introduction of dampers to prevent the teeth from vibrating excessively, which was essential if the same one was to be struck again almost at once. Nicole-Frères of Geneva, one of the best and most prominent makers, introduced the two-comb box which allowed variations in the intensity of the sound, and soon afterwards as many as five combs were being employed for special effects. Cylinders of nearly two feet in length made their appearance, and a drum and bell accompaniment was possible by 1850. About the same time air-vibrated reeds were used to give the effect of wood-wind.

The interchangeable cylinder as a means of augmenting the repertoire still more dates from 1850, and by 1870 a series of cylinders had been incorporated into a single box, any one of which could be selected at will. By 1870 musical-boxes able to reproduce chords had appeared, and five years later came the first long-player, able to give a three-hour programme. Methods of setting the pins in the cylinders automatically had already been devised.

By 1885 a machine utilizing circular discs of card had been made at Leipzig and marketed as the Symphonion, and the card disc was followed by the metal disc (the polyphone) before 1890. The career of the musical-box was ended by the invention first of the phonograph, and then of the gramophone.

Although many of the cases were plain, elaborately decorated cases were provided for the better-quality mechanisms, and a few specimens, probably

Myers, Myer. **Early American two-handled silver cup by Myer Myers (1723–1795).** *Parke-Bernet Galleries, New York.*

made to special order, have cases and ornament which put them into a class of their own.

MYERS, MYER (1723–1795)

Noted American silversmith working in New York. Of Jewish descent, Myers made the plate for the synagogue at Newport, R.I. He was president of the New York Silversmiths' Society in 1776.

(See *Silver, American.*)

NAILS AND SCREWS

These are sometimes suggested as a test for the authenticity of a piece of old furniture, but it is one which needs care. Until about 1790 nails were hand-cut. Screws were first introduced about 1675, and therefore should not be present in anything made before this date unless they have been employed subsequently during the course of repair or addition. The earliest screws have hand-filed threads with a shallow spiral, practically no taper, and no point. The slots are nearly always slightly off-centre. The modern pointed screw was not introduced until 1851. If screws of this type in a piece of furniture are original, then it is evidence of manufacture after 1851, but screws fall out and need to be replaced, especially those securing locks and hinges. Generally, screws should not be missing from parts which ought not to have been disturbed, but some furniture was made to take apart, and it was secured by screws, some of which may have been lost and replaced. Nails sometimes fall out, and the forger usually manages to find a supply from the demolition of old houses. In practice, it is only rarely that anything of importance can be determined in this way.

'NANKING' PORCELAIN

Chinese blue-and-white porcelain made in the second half of the 18th century (and later) for export. It was made at Ching-tê Chên, the Imperial factory town, and shipped from the port of Nanking. Decoration is often of nondescript Chinese landscapes and pagodas, with usually a little gilding. It sometimes has the Fitzhugh border (q.v.), or something closely resembling it. 'Nanking' decoration (called *Macao* by the Portuguese) was extensively copied and adapted by English potters. The Willow pattern is one example adapted from this source.

The most sought examples of the *genre* have blue-and-white borders (especially the 'Fitzhugh') in conjunction with enamelled designs (usually armorial bearings) in the centre. This was done at Canton, not Nanking, and these cannot strictly be termed 'Nanking'. The term, in fact, is of very little value, and owes its existence to 19th-century dealers.

'Nanking' Porcelain. A 'Nanking' dish with blue floral borders and gilt enrichment of the Fitzhugh type (q.v.), the centre with a Coat of Arms in *famille verte* enamels. c. 1780. *Phillips, Son & Neale.*

NANTES, EDICT (AND REVOCATION) OF

See *Huguenots*

NANTGARW PORCELAIN FACTORY

This South Wales factory was founded by William Billingsley (q.v.) in 1813, using an extremely glassy artificial porcelain with a thick, soft glaze. It contained bone-ash, and the formula may have come to Billingsley from Zachariah Boreman, who had worked as a painter at Chelsea in the 1760s and was a colleague of Billingsley's at Derby. In 1814 Billingsley was experiencing kiln-wastage amounting to about nine-tenths, although his wastage on flat-wares such as plates may have been very much less, and most of the surviving examples of Nantgarw porcelain are of this form. It is probable that the factory was established to supply a considerable London demand for porcelain resembling that of Sèvres, since stocks of white porcelain from the French factory, coming from the accumulated stock sold by Brongniart soon after 1800, were becoming exhausted, and the decorating studios of London were seeking supplies of something comparable. Much Nantgarw porcelain was decorated in these London studios, especially by Baldock. W. D. John has pointed out that the enamel colours used by the London decorators induced a halo in the glaze immediately surrounding the painting, which can be seen

Nantgarw. Plate painted with an aquatic bird within a border of shells and restrained rococo scrolls. Nantgarw. c. 1815.

if light falls on it obliquely. Factory painting is simple and of excellent quality. The more elaborate paintings are likely to have been executed in London.

The Nantgarw factory was removed to Swansea (q.v.) in October 1814, but Billingsley and his partner, William Weston Young, returned to Nantgarw in 1817, and continued until 1819, when the two men were offered employment by John Rose of Coalport (q.v.). Some Coalport porcelain made about this time closely resembles that of Nantgarw, and it is possible that limited use was made of Billingsley's formula. William Weston Young continued at Nantgarw until 1822, where, in company with Thomas Pardoe, he was occupied in decorating accumulated stocks of white porcelain. Nantgarw porcelain is scarce and much sought.

See *Swansea*; *Outside Decorators.*

NAPLES (ROYAL) PORCELAIN FACTORY

This was started in 1771 by Ferdinand IV in an attempt to revive the earlier porcelain of Capo-di-Monte (q.v.), and there is a resemblance between some of the early wares and those of its predecessor, due to the presence of the same workmen. The style adopted was the neo-classical, and *biscuit* figures were commonly produced. The factory was sold in 1806 to a French company, and some of the moulds were acquired by the Doccia enterprise (q.v.). The mark was an *N* surmounted by a crown, sometimes with the initials *FRF* (*Fabrica Reale Ferdinandea*). Later, the factory was in the hands of various private owners, closing in 1834. An incised signature, *Giordano*, is probably that of a modeller working in the later years of the 18th century.

NEF

Silver casket in the form of a ship which, in medieval times, was a table centre-piece for containing salt and spices. The nef is exceptionally known in other materials than silver, notably Venetian glass. It continued to be made until the 18th century, although it is rare after the 16th century.

NEO-CLASSICAL STYLE, THE

The classical (q.v.) styles which were revived with the onset of the Renaissance underwent several extensive modifications during the centuries which followed, such as that termed baroque (q.v.), which in turn led to rococo (q.v.). The purest version was Palladianism (q.v.), which was based ultimately on the works of Vitruvius (q.v.), and this was the most admired style in England from the beginning of the 18th century until the advent of the Adam Brothers (q.v.). Despite the circumscribed popularity in England of rococo, revived Gothic (q.v.), and the Chinese taste around the middle of the 18th century, there was no really serious break in the English classical tradition which began with Inigo Jones (1573–1652), and neo-classicism in England may be regarded merely as a different aspect which had its roots in Pompeii, Herculaneum, and Spalato rather than in metropolitan Rome.

Herculaneum, near Naples, was found accidentally in 1719 by Prince Elbeuf, and this discovery can, perhaps, be regarded as the starting-point of the later classical revival, although no very serious interest was taken in the new discovery until the middle of

Nef. The Burghley Nef. Nautilus shell mounted in silver, parcel-gilt, made by Pierre Flamand. Paris hall-mark for 1482. *Victoria and Albert Museum.*

Neo-classical Style. The 'Etruscan' room at Osterley Park designed by Robert Adam about 1776 with furniture to match. Decoration in this style was an early phase of neo-classicism.

the 18th century, when excavations were started at Pompeii. The principal influences at work in the dissemination of the new discoveries were Johann Joachim Winckelmann (q.v.), the Comte de Caylus (q.v.), and Sir William Hamilton (q.v.), English Ambassador at Naples.

In 1748 a mission consisting of the Marquis de Marigny (Directeur des Bâtiments, an arbiter of taste in mid-century France, and brother of Mme de Pompadour), the architect Jacques-Germain Soufflot (1713–1780), and the engraver and designer Cochin le jeune left Paris to study ancient art in Italy, and this was followed by a series of attacks on rococo. To their influence must be added that of Giovanni Battista Piranesi (1720–1778), a Venetian architect who recorded the antiquities of Rome in a number of etchings which were very popular, as well as his writings in favour of Roman architecture, and, in painting, Giovanni Paolo Pannini (1692–1768) specialized in ruins, influencing both Piranesi and such later artists as Hubert Robert ('Robert des Ruines').

The new designers in France were largely unknown, since those most outstanding worked in the rococo style, to which Louis XV always preserved an unswerving loyalty, but Mme de Pompadour made tentative essays towards acceptance of the new style in her private apartments, and the fashion

was taken up by some of the *fermiers-généraux* such as Grimod de la Reynière. The first reaction from the exuberant curves of rococo is to be found in France soon after 1750, but by 1760 the transition was well marked. Falconet's *Baigneuse* of 1757 was aimed at a taste less subject to changes of fashion (to use his own words), which implied a concession to the prevailing reaction. Swags (q.v.), urns (q.v.), plaited cable ornament, and the Vitruvian scroll (q.v.) all made their appearance about this time. Curves began to disappear, and the straight and tapering chair-leg was introduced. The repertory of ornament began to show marked changes from that popular during the currency of the rococo style to something more obviously classical. This, in France, is termed the Louis Seize style, despite the fact that it began long before Louis XVI acceded to the throne, and it is contemporary with the beginning of the Adam style in England.

At the end of the Seven Years' War in 1763 the new style made its appearance in Germany, and here, as in France, it became inextricably mixed with the developing ideas of the Romantics (q.v.), until the antithetical term 'romantic classicism' becomes not unjustified. The period marks the emergence of such painters as Greuze, whose *genre* painting extolled the simple annals of the poor with mawkish sentimentality. Neo-classicism in France also came to be identified with political and philosophical ideas propounded by Rousseau, Diderot,

287

Neo-classical Style. Armchair with splat in the form of a lyre and caned seat. Neo-classical design made by Thomas Chippendale the Younger. *Christie, Manson & Woods.*

and others, and it was vigorously promoted by those who disapproved of the laxities of Court Life and government under Louis XV, especially the part played by Mme de Pompadour in state affairs. The earlier phases of the style were notable for restraint and simplicity, which again becomes evident when it enters its *Directoire* phase (q.v.), but from 1780 onwards, under the influence of Marie-Antoinette and the Comte d'Artois (later Charles X), neo-classical furniture and decoration reached a degree of luxury hardly less than that of the earlier rococo phase of the reign of Louis XV.

After 1770 a new kind of ornament, such as bee-hives, baskets of ozier work, and agricultural implements, owed their popularity to the *hameau* of Marie-Antoinette at Rambouillet, which was designed by Hubert Robert. This had rustic thatched cottages occupied by real peasants engaged in the normal activities of farming, and milk from the cows was made into butter and cheese by the Queen in a dairy furnished with vessels of Sèvres porcelain. The prevailing sentimentality of the age was responsible for such amorous *motifs* as hearts pierced with arrows, quivers, flaming torches, garlands of roses, and others of like nature. *Motifs* of decoration generally owed much more to the suburban villas of Pompeii than to metropolitan Rome, and this can especially be noted in the arabesques, which are very different from the grotesques (q.v.) of Nero's Golden House that had inspired Raphael and earlier generations of designers.

In England, Robert Adam, who had spent four years in Italy and Dalmatia (now Yugoslavia), returning in 1758, began to propagate the new gospel. There was a time-lag between England and France, and it was not until 1765 that the neo-classical style began to make headway in popular favour, although within a few years Adam's version began to influence the development of neo-classicism in France. Outside, his buildings diverged little from the accepted Palladian style, but inside he introduced pastel colours and delicate *stucco* tracery in the old Roman manner which was very different from Palladian interiors as exemplified by the work of William Kent. It is worth quoting from the *Architectural Works* of Robert and James Adam which clearly set forth the difference: 'The massive entablature, the ponderous compartmented ceiling, the tabernacle frame [i.e. an ornamental frame surrounding a niche or recess], almost the only species of ornament formerly known in this country, are now universally exploded, and in their place we have adopted a beautiful variety of light mouldings, gracefully formed, delicately enriched, and arranged with propriety and skill. We have introduced a great diversity of ceilings, friezes, and decorated pilasters, and have added grace and beauty to the whole by a mixture of grotesque [i.e. arabesque] *stucco* and painted ornaments, together with painted reainceau [i.e. *rinceau*—scrolls] with its fanciful figures'. This did not go uncontested. It was disliked by Sir William Chambers (q.v.). Walpole wrote in 1773, 'from Kent's mahogany we are dwindled to Adam's filigree', and in 1785 he refers to 'Mr Adam's gingerbread and sippets of embroidery'. The Torrington Diaries refer to 'the modern frippery, Adamatic style' in 1789, and in 1799 George III, to whom Adam had been appointed architect in 1762, said 'that the Adams have introduced too much of neatness and prettiness'. As a

Neo-classical Style. White figure slightly touched with gold representing John Milton leaning on a classical column. Derby. c. 1775. The simple base, the absence of colouring, and the column used to support the figure are all in the classical style.

student of architecture in his youth the King was certainly entitled to his opinion.

In furniture Chippendale (q.v.) worked to designs by the Adam Brothers, and both Hepplewhite and Sheraton designs were strongly influenced by the style. Perhaps its greatest exponent was Wedgwood (q.v.), and the pastel colours of jasper ware were no doubt inspired by the palette adopted for mural and ceiling decoration by Adam. Ceiling roundels and murals were painted by Pergolesi, Cipriani, and others. Angelica Kauffmann provided designs, and in a few cases executed the work herself. In metalwork Matthew Boulton was strongly influenced by the new classical style from the first. Over 9,000 drawings by Adam are preserved in the library of the Soane Museum, Lincoln's Inn Fields, London, once the residence of the architect Sir John Soane who bought the drawings after Robert Adam's death. These include many drawings of furniture.

Later phases of the neo-classical style include the *Directoire*, Federal, the Greek Revival, Empire, English Regency, and *Biedermeier*, all of which are discussed elsewhere.

NEREID

A sea-nymph, usually to be found in conjunction with a Triton, and often with a hippocampus (q.v.); sometimes the subject of porcelain figures during the rococo period, and quite often of marine mythological painting.

NESKHI SCRIPT

A cursive Arabic script, read from right to left, sometimes decorating rugs, and such pottery as Hispano-Moresque.

NEVERS (Nièvre, France) FAÏENCE

Nevers was one of the earliest and most important centres of production of faïence in France. Greatly influenced at first by the Italians, who founded it, the wares gradually evolved into a French style, and the factories flourished till late in the 18th century. They have never entirely ceased production, though many have closed down.

In the middle of the 16th century the Duke of Gonzagues acquired the Duchy of Nevers by marriage, and many artists and craftsmen followed him to Nevers from Italy. In 1588 an Italian called Gambini, possibly a relative of Gambini of Lyons (q.v.), joined the Conrade brothers in founding the first factory, which was granted a privilege of fifty years in 1603 by Henri IV. Gambini had learned his craft either at Faenza or Urbino, and early pieces from Nevers are difficult to distinguish from those of Lyon, which was also founded and run by Italians trained in the *maiolica* tradition. Conrade and Gambini's production extended for about thirty years, and greatly influenced the artists of the city. The first wares are truly Italian; for instance, a dish in the Louvre dated 1589 showing *The Triumph of Galatea*, and several others, all in the *istoriato* (q.v.) style developed at Urbino. At the end of the first

Nevers Faïence. A Nevers faïence plate with decoration in white, orange, and yellow on a ground of *bleu Persan.* c. 1650–1680. *Victoria and Albert Museum.*

period, about 1674, the style had become much more French. It can be recognized by its classical or Biblical subjects, and the very characteristic blue wavy lines for a sea bearing dolphins and swans bestridden by laughing cherubs. Figures are outlined in manganese, and the colours are robust, chiefly a vigorous blue, yellow, and manganese used for drapery, tree-trunks, rocks, etc. The palette lacks red, and its place is taken by a warm orange. Blue *camaïeu* is to be seen with manganese outlines. There are some large sculptural figures with a thick, white, satiny glaze which were perhaps made by the Conrades about 1640. Towards the middle of the century a different style is apparent as the artists began to copy French engravings instead of Italian ones. The works of Simon Vouet in particular were used as inspiration for scenes decorating the centres of dishes. The rims were treated separately, unlike the original *istoriato* of Italy where the painting covered the whole of the dish.

In 1630 another Italian, Pierre Custode, founded a factory called *The Sign of the Ostrich*, and he has been credited with the invention of the decoration described as *bleu Persan* (Persian blue). At this period there were at least four factories in Nevers, and Pierre Custode was the founder of a dynasty of potters. The *bleu Persan* was not exactly a French invention (the Venetians used a colour very like it) but in the manner of its use it is entirely French. There were two kinds of coloured glaze; a blue and a yellow, both extremely rare today. Of the blue wares, the objects were dipped in a deep blue glaze and the decoration painted over it in white enamel, sometimes heightened with gilding. The yellow type was painted in white, and blue over white. It is extremely rare. Decoration on these wares is sometimes a splashed or marbled effect, as well as the more usual flowers and Oriental figures. Figures and landscapes were gradually discarded in favour of a decoration of leafy stalks and flowers, especially tulips and carnations. Custode's production of blue-ground faïence is justly famous. Large dishes, wall-fountains, ewers, and pilgrim bottles were all thus glazed with deep blue and decorated in white.

At this period Oriental porcelain was arriving at European ports in large quantities, and the effect on potters everywhere was immediate. The baroque style, and late Renaissance survivals, were replaced by Oriental shapes—baluster vases, double-gourds, long-necked bottles, and *potiches*. They were copied everywhere, and at Nevers a European scene sometimes appears on an Oriental shape, or a Chinese landscape on a baroque shape, for the two styles seem to have been interchangeable.

At the beginning of the 18th century production was at its height. The Conrades had gone long since, and other potters, such as Nicolas Étienne, had replaced them. But the beginning of the decline was at hand. Louis XIV's need for money led in 1685 to the melting down of France's silver-plate, which was replaced by services of faïence. The steep rise in demand was followed by an increase in production, and production-line methods meant a diminution of quality. In 1743 eleven factories were working in the city.

At mid-18th century the climate of fashion was changing; faïence was old-fashioned, and porcelain, with its delicate colours, all that was desirable. Potters began to experiment, and there was much imitation, not only of Rouen, but also of the enamel colours of Strasbourg. Probably many of the factories only survived by their production of useful and popular wares: *faïence parlante* (q.v.), wares with scenes from popular folklore, and *faïence patriotique* (q.v.), quite obviously made for a new *clientèle*. The Revolutionary wares are primitive and decorated with slogans—*vive les bons citoyens*, and so on, where spelling was an approximate art, being presumably as rare an accomplishment as reading. There has been much forging of these Revolutionary wares, which are often collected today. By 1797 six factories in Nevers had closed down, and the town's great days were over, although it continued to produce useful wares throughout the 19th century till today.

NEVERS GLASS FIGURES See *Figures, Glass, Nevers*

NEW ENGLAND GLASS COMPANY
Founded 1818 at Cambridge, Mass., by Edmund H. Monroe and associates, with a glass-house on a site formerly occupied by the Boston Porcelain and Glass Company, this firm continued to operate until 1888, when it was removed to Toledo, Ohio, to become part of the Libbey Glass Company (q.v.). The general manager was Deming Jarves, who founded the Boston and Sandwich Glass Company in 1825 (see *Sandwich Glass*). Pressed glass of excellent quality was manufactured at both places. The New England Glass Company is noted for lead glass of excellent quality, and for engraved work. (See *Glass, American*.)

New Hall Porcelain. Teapot of characteristic silver pattern sparsely painted with simple sprigs of flowers. New Hall. c. 1790.

NEW HALL PORCELAIN FACTORY
This factory at Shelton, Staffordshire, was founded about 1781 by a company of potters who bought Richard Champion's (q.v.) patent for true porcelain which had been assigned to him by Cookworthy (q.v.). They made simple wares of true porcelain, usually with a decoration of floral sprays or copies of simple scenes based on contemporary Chinese export porcelain. The more elaborate Cantonese patterns known as 'Mandarin' appear on wares which are very similar in style to the porcelain being made at the time by Miles Mason (q.v.). The manufacture of true porcelain continued from 1781 to 1810, after which a kind of bone-china (q.v.) was substituted.

NICKEL
A silvery metal, occasionally used as a casting medium, but more often as an alloying metal in association with copper (q.v.).

NICKEL-SILVER See *Copper*

NIDERVILLER (Moselle, France) FAÏENCE
This factory was founded in 1754 by Baron Jean-Louis de Beyerlé, director of the Strasbourg Mint. He enticed workmen from the Hannong factory, and also introduced artists from Meissen. Both Beyerlé and his wife were people of culture, and the products were luxurious and finely executed. In 1774 the factory was bought by the Comte de Custine, when the excellent German painter, Anstett, was replaced by Lanfrey. After the Count's execution in 1793 Lanfrey became proprietor of the factory, and it subsequently lost its artistic character.

Early wares at Niderviller are very similar to those of Strasbourg. The glaze is, if anything, finer, though somewhat yellowish. The flower-painting is extraordinarily elegant, though the colours are not so fresh—for instance the purplish-red—as at Strasbourg. Niderviller made a speciality of a *trompe l'œil* effect (q.v.) in which wares are painted to look like grained wood with a white section in reserve resembling a piece of paper painted with a landscape in crimson *camaïeu*. Sometimes green monochrome was used for natural flowers, and bird patterns were copied from Sceaux, as well as landscapes. Cyfflé's models were used after his moulds were acquired by this factory in 1780.

NIDERVILLER PORCELAIN FACTORY

Although a faïence factory was established here in 1754 by the Baron Jean-Louis de Beyerlé, the production of porcelain did not begin before 1765, and only in 1768 was it put on a commercial basis. The factory passed to Adam Philibert, Comte de Custine, in 1770. It passed again to L. W. Dryander, early in the 19th century, when it began to make *faïence-fine* (q.v.). It is still in existence. One of the modellers during the 18th century was Charles-Gabriel Sauvage (q.v.), later chief modeller at Sèvres, who was associated with Paul-Louis Cyfflé (q.v.). Niderviller was probably the only factory seriously to compete with Sèvres in the quality of its figures, those of Sauvage (also called Lemire) being neo-classical in style. Cyfflé preferred *genre* subjects. *Biscuit* porcelain of good quality was produced, and the wares include some elaborately ornamented vases. The decoration of table-wares followed contemporary fashion. Subjects include the *décor bois* (q.v.), and some well-painted *Fables* after La Fontaine.

NIELLO

An alloy, Byzantine in origin, which was used especially in Russia for inlaying objects of silver, and less often of other metals. It ranges in colour from black to grey, and its constituents are lead, silver, and copper with the addition of a little borax and sulphur. The line incised into the metal is triangular in section, the apex usually opening on the surface as a narrow line. In this way the alloy was locked into position. The same technique is employed to inlay other metals. See *Damascening*.

NILSON, JOHANN ESAIAS (1721–1788)

German engraver of Augsburg who worked in the rococo style, and whose engravings were both copied on to porcelain and faïence as decoration, and adapted to the modelling of figures at Nymphenburg, Berlin, Fürstenberg, Ludwigsburg, and elsewhere.

'NIPT DIAMOND WAIES'

This term, referring to glass decoration, dates from the end of the 17th century, and means a process by which vertical ribs spaced round a vessel were drawn together with pincers at regular intervals to form lozenges while the glass was still soft.

NOMAD RUGS

Much rug-weaving is done by wandering tribes living in tents, and these are often termed 'nomad rugs' in consequence. The nomads are widely distributed throughout Central Asia, and their work can easily be recognized by certain well-marked characteristics. Nomad rugs are never exactly symmetrical, and they rarely lie entirely flat. A woven selvedge and fringe at either end is customary. It can often be noticed that a field colour will end abruptly, to begin again with a slightly different shade. This is due to the work being done with two separately dyed batches of wool, and is certainly not a detraction. The Bokhara (q.v.) is a typical nomad rug.

'NONSUCH' CHESTS

Late 16th- and early 17th-century chests, the surface inlaid with views of Henry VIII's palace of Nonsuch. The term is sometimes used of inlaid decoration generally in the same style. Built by Henry VIII, Nonsuch, in Surrey, was Queen Elizabeth's favourite summer residence. It was given by Charles II to his mistress Barbara Villiers, Countess of Castlemain and Duchess of Cleveland, who had it pulled down in about 1670

NORTHWOOD, JOHN See *Cameo Glass*

NORWICH (Norfolk) POTTERY

When Jasper Andries first arrived in England he settled in Norwich, where he founded a pottery about 1567 which remained in production till about 1696. It is therefore the earliest pottery to make *delft* in England. Some wares which differ slightly from Lambeth—posset-pots, white ware, and some puzzle-jugs decorated with a flower—may have been made here, though some claim that they are Continental.

NOVE (Venice, Italy) FAÏENCE FACTORY

A factory was established here in 1732 by Giovanni Battista Antonibon for the manufacture of faïence. By 1762 it was employing 150 men. The faïence is finely potted, with a brilliant glaze, and Meissen and Sèvres porcelain were imitated.

NOVE (Venice) PORCELAIN FACTORY See *Venice Porcelain*

NÜRNBERG (Germany) FAIENCE FACTORY

The factory at Nürnberg was founded in 1712. A potter from Hanau (and other places) called Johann Caspar Ripp was appointed manager by three glass and pottery merchants, Christoph Marx, H. G. A. Hemmon, and the guardians of a minor named J. C. Romedi. Romedi died in 1720 and his share fell to J. J. Meyer. Hemmon's share had previously been transferred to J. A. Marx, one of the best painters in blue and foremost in other ways. Painters whose names also appear elsewhere are mentioned in the records, and on some recorded pieces: Johann Wolff (see *Copenhagen, Stockholm*), Valentin Bontemps, Wenzel Ignaz Proschen, Adam Schuster, G. M. and A. Tauber, J. A. E. Gluer, Strobel, Possinger, G. F. Grebner, Georg Friedrich Kordenbusch, Caspar Neuner, and Andreas Kordenbusch. The factory passed from the hands of Marx to G. S. Kess and the G. F. Kordenbusch mentioned above. They were followed by J. T. Eckert towards the end of the century, and his successor, J. H. Stuntz, who remained till the closure of the factory in 1840. Many

Nürnberg. A ewer decorated in coloured enamels with a landscape. Nürnberg. First half of the 18th century. Probably *Hausmalerei* (q.v.). *British Museum.*

painters signed their name or initials at Nürnberg, but it is rare to find the monogram of the city, *N* or *NB*.

In face of severe competition from Hanau and Frankfurt the factory at Nürnberg retained its individuality, and developed a style of mixed Chinese *motifs*, German flowers, and plants. A feather leaf is a recurring element, and decoration on plates is often radial or, at any rate, symmetrical. A central *motif* of a basket of fruit with flowers is often found. Small narrow-necked jugs with plaited handles painted in blue on a greyish-blue glaze with birds and flowers are considered to be a Nürnberg speciality, though they were made just as frequently at Frankfurt, Hanau, and Ansbach. Local landscapes, Biblical scenes, and *genre* scenes, are perhaps peculiar to Nürnberg in style. The foliate strapwork (*Laub und Bandelwerke*—q.v.) of the baroque style was employed during the factory's best period. The colours were good, with a clear, brilliant blue and lemon-yellow, a rather dull green, and variable shades of manganese. The glaze, bluish or a very pure white, is sometimes glassy in appearance. Forms are similar to those of Hanau and Frankfurt, but a speciality of Nürnberg seems to have been a small circular dish with a sunken six-pointed star in the centre and heart-shaped depressions between, known as *Stern-*

schussel. A kind of jug with pierced Gothic rosettes in the body is also peculiar to Nürnberg.

NUTMEG GRATER
Small cylindrical silver box designed to contain a nutmeg, and to be carried in the pocket. When the lid was opened a steel grater was revealed. This was intended for grating the nutmeg into hot toddy (see *Toddy-lifters*). Most specimens were made c. 1770 to c. 1830.

NYMPH
A female spirit inhabiting the sea, rivers and streams, fountains, woods, and lonely plains. Nymphs accompany satyrs (q.v.), and often attend the goddess Diana.

NYMPHENBURG PORCELAIN FACTORY
Athough the first attempts to make porcelain at Munich were undertaken in 1729, nothing was actually achieved until 1747, when, with the aid of the Elector Maximilian III Joseph, Franz Ignaz Niedermayer succeeded in making porcelain, a task in which he was assisted by some workmen from Vienna. The new enterprise was at first housed at Neudeck. In April 1761 it was removed from Neudeck to buildings in the grounds of the Schloss Nymphenburg, to the north-west of Munich, where it still remains as the Bavarian State porcelain factory. From 1751 the factory was under the general direction of the Graf Sigismund Von Haimhausen, a skilful and competent administrator, and a better porcelain body was employed after 1753 when Ringler (q.v.) first arrived in Munich. Even this, however, proved unsatisfactory, and Ringler was discharged in 1757, his place being taken by Johann Paul Rupert Härtl, a chemist who had studied mining

Nymphenburg. Count Sigismund von Haimhausen, portrait-bust in porcelain by Bustelli. Nymphenburg. c. 1760. *Bayerisches Nationalmuseum, Munich.*

Nymphenburg. The Stormy Wooing. Group by Bustelli (q.v.). Nymphenburg. c. 1760. Antique Porcelain Co. Ltd.

and geology. Bustelli (q.v.) was first employed as a modeller in 1754, his place being taken as *Modell-meister* in 1764, after his death, by Dominikus Auliczek.

From 1754 onwards the factory was very success-ful, and by 1761 it was exporting to Turkey and the Levant by way of Venice, as well as supplying porcelain to Brussels, Vienna, and Amsterdam, since, unlike Meissen, it was not seriously affected by the Seven Years' War. The economic recession of 1766 threatened the factory's existence, and the appoint-ment of Auliczek as factory inspector in 1773 at first resulted in an improvement. But the War of Succession in 1778 created new difficulties, and by 1780 cheap English creamware was already making severe inroads into the German porcelain factories' markets. Auliczek, himself, became increasingly incompetent, and ultimately had to be removed.

Maximilian III Josef died in 1770, to be succeeded by Karl Theodor of the Palatinate, who already had his own porcelain factory at Frankenthal. For a time Nymphenburg took second place to Franken-thal, but when the Frankenthal factory was closed in 1799 its moulds were removed to Nymphenburg, and they are still being used today for properly marked reproductions of old Frankenthal figures and groups. The *Modellmeister* and chief overseer from 1797 to 1810 was Johann Peter Melchior (q.v.), formerly of Höchst and Frankenthal, who did some excellent work during the early years of the 19th century.

Table-wares from Neudeck are very rare, and do not seem to have been of great importance artistic-ally. Some of the early wares may have been sent to Augsburg, not far away, for decoration by one of the *Hausmaler*, and it was not until 1756 that a painter from Vienna organized the enamelling shops on a successful basis. Underglaze-blue painting was attempted for the first time in 1762, but specimens are rare. Much of the painting consists in naturally depicted flowers similar to the Meissen *deutsche Blumen*, but landscapes, figures, and animals were painted by Lindmann, Zächenberger, Lerch, Klein, and others. A factory speciality was the *rechaud* or *veilleuse* (q.v.).

To a far greater extent the reputation of the factory rests on its figures. The earliest to be identified are those of Josef Ponnhäuser, a modeller from Vienna who worked between 1754 and 1755. To judge from the figure of a goose modelled in the former year Ponnhäuser had little experience as a designer and the porcelain body was giving trouble, since his goose, standing erect, has been supported fore and aft by tree-stumps and foliage. Bustelli had a much greater grasp of the principles of design, and there are no solecisms of this kind. From his hand is a remarkable portrait of the Graf von Haimhausen which is now in the Bayerisches Nationalmuseum. In addition to his Italian Comedy figures he did some notable *chinoiserie* groups characterized by rococo scrollwork. Auliczek's work is competent but often pedestrian, and he suffers to some extent from having followed a modeller of Bustelli's stature. Melchior's modelling is characterized by his adoption of a classical style in keeping with the pre-vailing Empire style (q.v.) of the early years of the 19th century.

O

OAK

In England the oak was used both for furniture and architectural purposes from very early times, but this wood was also very commonly employed throughout Europe. In France it is *bois de chêne*, and in the north-western provinces, as may be seen from Normandy *armoires*, it approaches the appearance of English oak fairly closely. There are a number of European varieties which are very widely distributed. Irish oak was especially esteemed in medieval times, and was used in England for furniture-making. The holm oak (or ilex) is the evergreen oak, originally from southern Europe, which was introduced into England during the reign of Elizabeth I. Bog-oak, very closely approaching black in colour, was found in peat bogs where it had lain for long periods. There are two main varieties of American oak—red and white— but it is often difficult to say from which species any particular specimen of wood came originally. As in Europe, oak was employed in America for furniture-making.

Oak was commonly used in England for furniture until towards the end of the 17th century, when it was largely superseded by walnut for better-quality work, and in the 18th century by mahogany. Most oak furniture is the work of the carpenter rather than the cabinet-maker. It was also employed as a carcass wood, as in the 18th-century Dutch marquetry furniture.

During the currency of the Regency style pollard oak was occasionally used as a veneer for fine furniture.

OBERMALER (German)

Man in charge of the design and painting studios in 18th-century German porcelain factories. He was expected to contribute designs of his own, and he was usually a colour chemist as well. The best-known *Obermaler* is Johann Gregor Höroldt at Meissen, who introduced a new palette soon after his arrival in 1720, and was responsible for the finest *chinoiserie* designs (see *Meissen*). *Obermaler* were usually Court Painters, or held some similar position.

OBRISSET, JOHN (fl. 1705–1728)

A French Huguenot who settled in London and acquired a reputation for the excellence of his snuff-boxes and other small objects made of pressed horn and tortoiseshell.

OBSIDIAN

A hard, brittle, volcanic glass, black, green, or reddish in colour, which, in appearance, resembles a coloured bottle-glass, especially if it is chipped. Obsidian can only be shaped and polished with abrasives (q.v.). It is used in works of decorative art occasionally.

OEBEN, JEAN-FRANÇOIS (c. 1720–1763)

A German craftsman who arrived in Paris before 1749, in which year he married the daughter of François Vandercruse (called La Croix). Oeben became a pupil of Charles-Joseph Boulle in 1751, and after Boulle's death was made *ébéniste du roi* with lodgings in the Gobelins (Paris). He became *maître ébéniste* in 1761 in consequence of his work for the King, despite the fact that he had not completed a formal apprenticeship.

Oeben numbered both Leleu and Riesener among his own pupils, and Mme de Pompadour was among the earliest of his patrons. He began his masterpiece, the *bureau du roi Louis Quinze* (finished by Riesener) in 1760, the mounts being supplied by Duplessis.

Oeben was among the first to associate furniture with mechanical devices which either made it more efficient as furniture or enabled it to serve a number of purposes. A notable example of this is the *bureau du roi* itself, and it was no doubt Oeben's reputation for work of this kind which brought him the King's commission in the first place.

Oeben died in 1763, and his workshop was continued by his pupil Riesener until 1768, in which year Riesener was made *maître* of the guild and married Oeben's widow. It was an 18th-century custom for the chief assistant or apprentice in the workshop to marry the widow of his dead master to ensure continuity. It was generally observed, and may also be found in the history of the many faïence factories.

Furniture made between 1763 and 1768, although it may bear Oeben's stamp, was doubtless either made by or under the supervision of Riesener. His stamp, *J. F. OEBEN*, occurs on some examples of furniture almost certainly made by Riesener.

He is not to be confused with Joseph Oeben (or Open), an *ébéniste* of Tours, who also stamped his furniture, adding the name of the city.

OETTINGEN-SCHRATTENHOFEN (Bavaria, Germany) FAÏENCE FACTORY

Established at Oettingen in 1735, this factory was transferred in 1737 to Schrattenhofen. The factory employed an artist called Johann Ulrich Sperl, who is later encountered at Künersberg (q.v.), and a painter in blue-and-white called Gottfried Leinfelder. Wares are chiefly tankards, but brown ware in the manner of Bayreuth was also made. Marks are either *Oettingen*, or an *L* over the *O* which has been ascribed to Leinfelder.

OFF-HAND GLASS See *'End of Day' Glass*

OLIVE

A tree sacred to Athene, wreaths of which are emblematic of peace. The foliage in Christian art symbolizes the Virgin.

ONOLZBACH See *Ansbach*

ONYX MARBLE

A lime carbonate which is not to be confused with the semi-precious hardstone termed onyx. Onyx marble is a water-deposited limestone found in the form of stalactites and stalagmites. It is sometimes miscalled alabaster.

OPALINE GLASS

The word is mainly applied to glass of French origin, or to glass made elsewhere in a similar way. It means glass entirely or partially opacified by the addition of suitable agents. Often milky-white in appearance, it is frequently coloured. Some opaline glass is virtually indistinguishable from the earlier *Milchglas* (q.v.), the difference being largely one of terminology. The word itself seems not to have been in use before 1823 when Baccarat (France) coined the word 'opalin' for glass of this kind, which at Saint-Louis was termed *pâte de riz*. By 1838 'opalin' seems to have been in fairly general use, and six years later there is reference to 'opalin bleu'. By the early years of the 20th century 'opaline' was firmly established.

The opaline glasses of France were derived from the coloured glasses of Bohemia, where a black opaque glass was first made in 1820, a marble glass in 1825, and then a whole range of translucent and opaque colours. The manufacture of opaline was at its most popular between 1840 and 1870, after which it declined in popularity. A good deal of opaline was produced by blowing into moulds and later by pressing (see *Pressed Glass*). Pressed opalines are usually of poor quality.

The first glass which can, perhaps, correctly be termed 'opaline' was made between 1810 and 1820 in forms influenced by the Empire style. Production included such things as vases and carafes, as well as candlesticks and similar useful objects. After 1820 production increased, although quality was no longer as good, and many objects of domestic utility were made at this time, including even *veilleuses* (q.v.). Relief and painted patterns can both be seen, and some designs show traces of the influence of the Gothic revival. Before 1835 painted designs were often in cold colours, but after this date enamels were the rule. About the same time the earlier gold-leaf used for gilding was superseded by gold powder.

The three main sources of opaline in France were Baccarat, Saint-Louis and Le Creusot, but there were a number of other factories making it, notably Choisy-le-roi and Bercy. Colours were varied. The rarest and most sought is the *gorge-de-pigeon*, translucent and faintly tinged with mauve, of which examples are to be found in the Musée des arts décoratifs (Paris). The *bulles de savon* (soap-bubbles) introduced about 1822 were opal glasses of several colours with a misty appearance, like a rainbow, as the name implies. Yellow opaline from antimony is exceptionally rare, first made about 1810. Turquoise is another rare colour, and dates from about 1825. The purple of Cassius, which is also the *famille rose* pigment of Chinese porcelain, was employed for pinks, which tend to be distinctly reddish in the early period and lighter in colour after about 1825. The very rare violet opalines date from 1828. The commonest colours are greens and blues, of which sky-blue, after 1835, was very popular. Black opaline is to be found occasionally, and a white variety which is almost opaque was popular for lamp-shades.

OPAQUE TWIST STEMS

Wine-glass stems in the 18th century were often decorated with threads of white and, less often, coloured glass in the interior of the stem which were twisted into more or less elaborate patterns. The technique was inspired by, and derived from, Venetian *latticinio* glass (see *Venetian Glass*), and the method employed was similar to that of the air-twists (q.v.), blobs of white glass replacing the tear. The earliest opaque twists were simple and sometimes crude, but they later became much more elaborate, and a large number of intricate patterns were produced. Forgeries are far from uncommon. These are more often of the opaque-twist variety than the air-twist. Generally, the spurious twist seems much more deeply embedded in the stem than in genuine glasses, where the twist is inclined to be near the surface; the threads in forgeries sometimes lack continuity; and they are not so symmetrically disposed as in most old specimens.

In the 18th century the technique was also employed in Holland, but English white opaque twists are generally much whiter than contemporary Dutch work.

Opaque Twist Stems. Two English wine-glasses wheel-engraved with sailing ships, each with a different style of opaque twist in the stem. c. 1760. *Sotheby & Co.*

OPPENORD, GILLES-MARIE (1672–1742)
French architect, draughtsman, and engraver who considerably influenced the development of the rococo style with his published series of engraved ornamental designs. He influenced Cressent's (q.v.) furniture, and is perhaps best known for his rococo wrought ironwork designs, including staircase rails, balcony rails, gates, and iron furniture.

ORDERS, THE FIVE
An 'Order' is an architectural term which comprises the classical column with its capital and super-imposed entablature. Vitruvius described four such Orders, or groups of columnar composition, which he called the Tuscan, the Doric, the Ionic, and the Corinthian. A fifth was added later—the Composite, formed from the Ionic and the Corinthian. Vitruvius laid down very strict rules governing the relationship of the whole to the parts of each Order, although these rules were often so obscure as to be open to interpretation. Book III of the *Ten Books of Architecture* is partly devoted to a description of the numerical basis of the proportional system, and of the rules governing the diameter and height of columns, the proportions of intercolumniation, and so forth.

These things were taken very seriously, not only by the Palladians (q.v.), but by artists generally. Leonardo da Vinci made a famous drawing of Vitruvian man based on human proportions laid down by Vitruvius (Book III, Chap. I), and Dürer also studied the subject and wrote a treatise on it. A notion grew up that perfection in art could be attained by rules, and by the discovery of a system of ideal proportions such as that which the Greeks had earlier laid down for figure-sculpture.

Although not well understood outside an enthusiastic few (and not always by them), the Five Orders exercised a considerable fascination, even if sometimes indirect, on craftsmen of all kinds, apart from architects and interior decorators. For instance, Chippendale (q.v.) thought it necessary to preface his *Gentleman and Cabinet Maker's Director* of 1754 with a disquisition on the Five Orders, and Batty Langley (q.v.) attempted to create five new Orders adapted to the Gothic architectural style.

The interest in proportional systems, if it did not always create great art, had the merit of preventing a good deal of bad art, especially architecture, from seeing the light of day.

See *Proportion, Human*

'ORIENTAL LOWESTOFT'
A term often used of Chinese export porcelain decorated with armorial bearings. It is completely inaccurate and owes its existence to Chaffers (*Marks and Monograms*), who ascribed certain Chinese export wares to this small East Anglian factory on evidence which was, to say the least, tenuous. This type of ware is here correctly discussed under the heading of *Chinese Export Porcelain* (q.v.).

ORMOLU
A much-abused word, which it is better to avoid when accuracy is essential (and possible). It first appeared in the English language about the middle of the 18th century, and when Josiah Wedgwood used it in a letter of 1770 he spelled it 'Or-moulu'. This is an intermediate form, taken from the original French which is *dorure d'or moulu*—literally, gilding with gold paste. This refers to gilding bronze with an amalgam of mercury and gold which, when combined together, form a pasty mass. An illustration in Diderot's *Encyclopédie* shows a gilder's

Orders, The Five. From left to right: Tuscan, Doric, Ionic, Corinthian, and Composite. The relationship between base and entablature to column and capital is also shown. Chippendale discusses the subject in the introduction to his *Gentleman and Cabinet Maker's Director. After Diderot.*

shop, and the method of applying the amalgam with a brush. Firing drove off the mercury, leaving the gold adherent to the bronze. This, sometimes called fire-gilding, is further discussed under *Gilding, Metal* (see also *Amalgam*).

The term 'ormolu' was employed in England not only to denote bronze gilded in this way, which was not often done, but an alloy similar to brass, of a light golden colour, which could be used for similar purposes to French gilded bronze without additional gilding. See *Brass* and *Pinchbeck*.

ORVIETO (Umbria, Italy)
Many 14th-century wares were found at Orvieto and this town established a type which has also been found in Rome, Siena, Perugia and Faenza, much akin in style and obviously of early date. The body is usually red and hard-fired, roughly potted, and the decoration painted over a thin, mat layer of tin enamel. Some relief moulding has been noticed, but it is not in the least clear-cut or sharp. Colours are copper-green and manganese-purple, with very occasional additions of pale blue and yellow. Ornament is Gothic with animals, usually heraldic, or consists of primitive linear patterns. Flat washes were avoided, their place being taken by cross-hatching, a characteristic noticeable in the whole group. Some jugs are only partially glazed with tin-enamel and, even in the 15th century, dishes still had only a lead glaze on the back, from which we must assume a necessary economy in the use of tin. In mid-14th century, hospitals began to equip their pharmacies with earthenware vessels, and drug-jars and pitchers are perhaps the most common survival.

OTTOMAN
A long, low, stuffed seat without a back designed to seat several people. Appearing in England in the early years of the 19th century, it developed circular or corner forms, and a type which allowed people to sit back to back. Later in the 19th century it was also made in sectional form with arms dividing it into compartments. The centre support was often topped by a *jardinière* (1845). It should not be confused with the 18th century French *ottomane*, which was primarily a small settee, usually with an oval seat, and arms the curves of which were integral with the back, for which there were several variations—*ottomane à la turque, ottomane russiens, sopha en ottomane*, etc. All these were probably dealer's terms.

OTTWEILER (Nassau-Saarbrücken) PORCELAIN FACTORY
A factory was started here in 1763 with the patronage of Prince Wilhelm Heinrich, the arcanist being Étienne-Dominique Pellevé. Faïence was also made. Pellevé left in 1767, and the factory was then leased to two Frenchmen who brought workers from France. A tureen in the Hamburg Museum painted with figures after Nilson (q.v.) is signed *Wolfart Prinxit* (sic)—probably Friedrich Karl Wolfart who was at Frankenthal in 1766, at Pfalz-Zweibrücken in 1767–1768, and at Höchst in 1771. There is a figure dated 1766 at Hamburg. Polychrome mythological and Italian Comedy scenes, some after Nilson, have been recorded, as well as decoration in underglaze blue and purple monochrome. Specimens are rare.

OUDRY, JEAN-BAPTISTE (1689–1755)
French painter, designer, and director of the tapestry looms of Beauvais and Gobelins. He was especially fond of animal subjects, and many of his paintings are scenes from the chase. These inspired not only tapestries, but many other works of decorative art, including porcelain painting. His work is sometimes confused with that of Desportes, a slightly earlier painter of the same subjects.

OUSHAK RUGS
Sometimes called Ushak. In the 16th century Oushak was one of the great centres for the making of rugs and carpets in Anatolia, and a few rugs from here, usually employed as table and bed covers, began to reach Europe late in the 16th century. Carpets depicted in Holbein's paintings, and often called 'Holbein carpets', came from here and from Bergamo (q.v.). Survivals of these early carpets are exceedingly rare. More recent Oushak products are coarsely tied with the Ghiordes knot, the pile is of wool, and the designs are usually of medallions and geometric *motifs*. Contemporary production is usually specially designed for export. Colours are bright, and include red, brown, green, and blue.

OUTSIDE DECORATORS, ENGLISH
Outside decorators in England occupied a position similar to that of the *Hausmaler* in Germany, buying porcelain in white from the factories and painting it in their own workshop, but some of them seem to have worked in closer co-operation with the factories than was the case in Germany. The first

Orvieto. Dish of the green and manganese family depicting a bird in the Gothic style. 'Orvieto type.' c. 1460. *Victoria and Albert Museum.*

Outside Decorators. Chelsea plate of the gold anchor period painted with sliced fruit in the Giles (q.v.) studio. c. 1760.

English outside decorator was William Duesbury, later a manufacturer of porcelain at Derby, who had a workshop in London between 1750 and 1753. His account-books survive, and from them we know that he painted porcelain from nearly all the factories then in existence, and especially the 'dry-edged' Derby factory, as well as salt-glazed wares from Staffordshire. Thomas Hughes is little known, but there is a specimen signed by him in an American museum, and he seems to have worked during the 1750s. The first outside decorator whose work can be certainly identified is James Giles of Clerkenwell, London, who seems to have started work just before 1760 and to have continued until 1776. Presumably he functioned as a painter himself, but he employed a number of artists. There are four plates in the Victoria and Albert Museum, London, presented by a descendant, Mrs Dora Grubbe, which are of certain attribution. W. B. Honey attributed to his workshop some colourful 'dishevelled birds' to be seen alike on Chelsea and Worcester porcelain. A decoration of sliced fruit which appears on the wares of both these factories came from the Giles studio, and some landscapes pencilled in black and washed with green from the same source, although the fashion was an established factory-decoration at Chelsea in 1756, where it may have been done by O'Neale. The hand of Giles, however, can be inferred for some of them by analogy with rare specimens of Chinese porcelain decorated in England in this manner.

Many coloured ground decorations on Worcester porcelain may have been the work of Giles, particularly opaque colours such as green. By strong transmitted light a few specimens reveal a sparse underglaze-blue decoration under the coloured ground. A claret ground, the English version of the *rose Pompadour* (q.v.), may be attributable to Giles when it occurs on Worcester porcelain. Somewhat overdecorated Bow figures bearing the anchor and dagger mark were probably done in the Giles work-

shop, and there is record in 1760 from Thomas Craft of Bow of a bowl which he had 'burned in Mr Gyles' Kiln' at a cost of 3s. Transfer-printed Worcester porcelain enamelled over the transfer seems to have been the work of Giles rather than the factory, and a consequence of the curtailment of his supplies in 1768, when Worcester engaged painters from Chelsea. In 1767 the factory advertised 'an enamelling branch in London' which could only have referred to Giles, and the latter's account-book lists purchases from William Davis & Co. of Worcester, from which it may be deduced that Davis was in charge of this aspect of the company's business.

Some of the Kakiemon patterns, such as the *Quail*, on both Worcester and Bow porcelain were undoubtedly painted by Giles, and his account-books suggest an extremely large turnover between 1760 and 1768, his most prosperous years. In 1777 Giles was forced to ask Duesbury for a loan, and his workshop seems later to have been taken over by this Derby entrepreneur.

Giles employed a number of marks. A brown anchor appears on Chelsea porcelain in conjunction with decoration which can reasonably be attributed to him. The anchor and dagger on Bow porcelain is also probably a Giles mark. A gold crescent on Worcester, and occasionally a gold anchor on the same porcelain, must be the work of Giles, since these marks always occur in conjunction with decoration in his style. Marks on Worcester porcelain in overglaze red are also likely to be those of Giles. 'Blanks' with a scale-blue ground supplied to him by the factory bear the normal factory mark, and these blanks can sometimes be found in an undecorated state, probably outmoded stock sold off in the 18th century either by Giles or the factory.

Some Chelsea porcelain painted by O'Neale while he was still employed at the factory is signed with a concealed signature, usually in an inscription on an obelisk which is part of ruins in a landscape.

Outside Decorators. Worcester plate by Jeffrys Hamett O'Neale painted with the fable of the Raven and the Waterjar. Worcester. c. 1765.

Outside Decorators. A Worcester vase painted with a Teniers subject by John Donaldson. c. 1765. *British Museum.*

Some of his work for Worcester is signed in full. Donaldson occasionally signed his work with the monogram *JD*.

Fidelé Duvivier, member of a family who were Chelsea painters, decorated for several factories, including Chelsea, Worcester, Derby, and New Hall. Some of his work has the subject of children playing, with a pot-works, identifiable by a beehive kiln, in the background.

Wedgwood had a decorating studio in Chelsea where James Banford was employed before he left for Derby, and Zachariah Boreman worked as an outside decorator at the end of the century. It has been said that none of his work for Derby was ever signed, but the writer has identified one mug painted with a landscape initialled *ZB* by his hand, and this may have been done for an outside decorating workshop.

In the 19th century a number of china-dealers maintained decorating studios. Best known are those of Baldock, Mortlock, and Robins & Randall of London. Some of them bought supplies of outmoded white ware from Sèvres, and when these came to an end they turned to Nantgarw (q.v.), which provided an acceptable substitute. Robins & Randall were established in Spa Fields, London, and they decorated the porcelain of Coalport, Nantgarw, and Swansea in Sèvres styles. Randall was especially skilled in the imitation of the wares of the royal French factory, and specimens were referred to in the trade at the time as 'Quakers'—an allusion to Randall's religion. Randall started a small factory at Madeley (Shropshire) in 1825 which lasted until 1840

for the purpose of making porcelain suitable for imitations of Sèvres.

Independent modellers are less frequent than painters. John Bacon, R.A., perhaps modelled for Bow. He was first apprenticed to Crispe of Bow Churchyard, who taught him the art of modelling for porcelain. He later supplied models to Wedgwood and Derby, and probably to Champion at Bristol. Pierre Stephan may have started as a modeller at Chelsea during the gold-anchor period. He was at the Derby factory between 1770 and 1774, and later worked for Wedgwood, but he also worked for Derby as a free-lance, providing models after Angelica Kauffmann (q.v.). It is possible that Louis-Francois Roubiliac supplied a few models to his friend, Sprimont, at Chelsea. Perhaps from his hand are a set of the *Senses* produced during the red-anchor period, but later gold-anchor figures bearing an impressed *R* are erroneously attributed. These may have been done by Mr Tebo, since the writer has noticed a Chelsea group of about 1763 in the style of those often marked *R* which bore the impressed *To* mark. It is possible, however, that Tebo was here functioning as a 'repairer', i.e. a man who put the moulded components of figures together in preparation for firing.

Generally, the work of the outside decorators is much sought, and provides an interesting and colourful aspect of English porcelain manufacture during the 18th century.

See also *Hausmalerei.*

OVERLAY GLASS See *Cased Glass*

OYSTER VENEER

Veneer obtained by transverse slicing of roots and branches of certain trees, especially walnut, the shape and marking bearing some resemblance to the oyster shell. Veneers of this kind are principally to be found on late 17th-century English walnut furniture.

Outside Decorators. A rare Worcester dessert plate painted by Fidelé Duvivier. The beehive kiln in the background occurs in other examples of this painter's work. c. 1780.

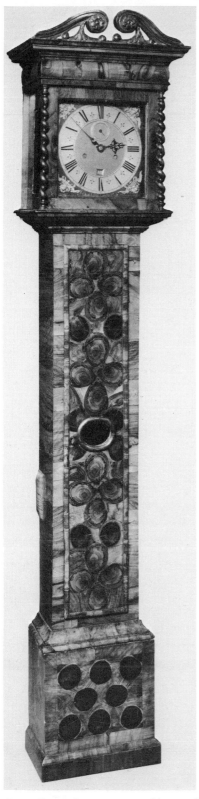

Ozier Pattern. Meissen coffee-pot of c. 1745 decorated with an all-over moulded basket-work (ozier) *motif* except for small reserved panels.

OZIER PATTERN

A moulded basket-work pattern introduced in the early 1730s by J. G. Höroldt at Meissen. The first, simple version was termed the *ordinair-Ozier* and was used to decorate a service made for Count Sulkowski about 1735. This has ozier mouldings in sets of four, divided at intervals by a moulded radial rib which was confined to the ledges of plates. The *Altozierrand* (old ozier pattern) is also a basket-work moulding divided by radial ribs, and confined to the ledge of the plate. The *Altbrandensteinmuster* (old Brandenstein pattern) was developed in 1741. It has panels divided into sets of three, one narrow and plain, one narrow with dotted squares, and one wide with circumferential mouldings, crossed by ribs which are a segment of a spiral. The ribs encroach on to the centre of the plate. The *Neuozierrand* (new ozier border) introduced in 1742 had an outer border of basket-work moulding and a plain inner border confined by a moulded line of scroll form which extended towards the centre of the plate. In addition there were four sets of spiralling ribs giving twelve narrow panels and four wide ones. The *Neubrandensteinmuster* (the new Brandenstein pattern) was similar to the old one in having the plain narrow panel, and the panel with dotted squares, but in other respects it was similar to the *Neuozier*. The *Brühlsches Allerlei-Dessin* ('Brühl's various' design) was a complex pattern of basket-work, moulded flowers, shells, and similar *motifs* confined by rococo scrollwork, no two panels being alike; this was confined to the ledge. Some items of service ware, such as coffee-pots, were covered with a plain moulded decoration of basket-work. These *ozier* patterns were quite commonly reproduced by other European factories, including Chelsea.

See *Dulongmuster; Gotzkowsky pattern; Marseille muster; Vestunservice.*

Oyster Veneer. Oyster veneer on the case of a clock by Joseph Knibb. First quarter of the 18th century. *Sotheby & Co.*

P

PADAUK WOOD
This wood from the Adaman Islands and Burma, usually a well-marked red in colour, and sometimes with a distinct figure, was somctimes uscd by 18th-century English cabinet-makers. It was also the wood of some Far Eastern furniture and cabinets. Padauk (or padouk) was usually employed in solid form, and only rarely as a veneer.

PAGODA
The many-storeyed Chinese pavilion, thc roof curved at the eaves, which was described and illustrated by Sir William Chambers (q.v.), who designed the pagoda in the Royal Botanical Gardens at Kew, S.W. London. The characteristic roof was employed by Chippendale and others in the design of furniture.

PAGODS or PAGODES (French)
No doubt originally two words, the terms are often used interchangeably. There are three principal meanings:

(a) Early seated porcelain figures of the Chinese monk, Pu-t'ai, with grinning face and bare belly. These usually came either from China, or from Meissen during the Böttger period and immediately afterwards. The same design also appears as part of *chinoiseries* by Bérain (q.v.) and others.

(b) The familiar, many-storeyed Chinese building known as a pagoda.

(c) A *Pagodes* (applied to furniture) meant case-furniture of Oriental lacquer panels with landscape subjects. Duvaux invoiced two *commodes à pagodes* to Mme de Pompadour.

PAJOU, AUGUSTIN (1730–1809)
Pupil of J.-B. Lemoyne *fils*, Pajou was a French sculptor who also modelled for the Sèvres Porcelain Factory. His portrait of Mme du Barry was done in 1770.

PAKTONG
An alloy of copper, zinc, and nickel from China closely resembling the 'German silver' or 'nickel-silver' discovered in Europe in 1849. The Chinese

Pagod. Small *chinoiserie* figure of the type known in the 18th century as a pagod. Böttger's porcelain. Meissen. c. 1715. *Mr and Mrs Henry Stern.*

metal, which was well known in the 18th century, and discussed by J.-B. Du Halde in his *General History of China* (1738), was probably the result of smelting a naturally combined copper-nickel ore to which zinc was added. *Paktong* is a Cantonese word, the Mandarin being *pai t'ung*, meaning 'white copper'. It is white in colour, tinged with yellow, and seems to have come from Yunnan Province in the south.

The Chinese employed *paktong* for such purposes as making hinges for the doors of cabinets of lacquer or wood, and for the decoration of furniture generally. In Europe (especially in England) it was sometimes employed to make candlesticks and other small objects of domestic utility. Occasionally larger things, such as grates and hearth-furniture, were made of it, since it is a very tough metal which does not corrode easily.

It is sometimes confused with *tutenag* (see *Brass*).

PALLADIAN STYLE, THE
A severe version of the classical styles of ancient Rome based on the designs of the Italian architect

Palladian Style. Coved ceiling at Mereworth, Kent, painted in panels. Architect: Colen Campbell. c. 1720. Walpole wrote in 1752 after a visit: '(Mereworth) is in so perfect a Palladian taste that I must own it recovered me a little from the Gothic.'

Andrea Palladio (1518–1580). Palladio based his own work largely on the *Ten Books of Architecture* of Vitruvius, architect and military engineer to Augustus, which seem to have been written about 15 B.C., although both date and authorship have been questioned. Palladio's *Quattro Libri dell' Architettura* of 1570 greatly influenced his successors, including the English Inigo Jones (1578–1652), first truly classical English architect and surveyor of royal buildings to James I, whose Banqueting House at Whitehall (London), and the Queen's House at Greenwich (S.E. London) built for Queen Henrietta Maria, are surviving testimonies to his genius.

In Europe the severities of Palladio gave way to baroque (q.v.) and in England the style of Inigo Jones was superseded by that of Sir Christopher Wren, which owed its inspiration to France rather than Italy. Palladianism appeared once more after Wren's fall from royal favour, when it was adopted by an influential group of architects, headed by Lord Burlington, which included William Kent (q.v.), Colen Campbell, and others almost equally eminent.

Inigo Jones's designs were republished, and the characteristics of his work can often be traced in the decoration of great houses built around 1730. Two English masterpieces of the style, both based on Palladio's Villa Capra at Vincenza (Italy), are Chiswick House, London (Burlington), and Mereworth Castle, Kent (Campbell).

The essence of Palladio's architectural theory lies in strict adherence to theories of proportion and design enunciated by Vitruvius, in which the Orders (q.v.) played an essential part. This necessarily led to the acceptance of a fairly rigid scheme of proportion and ornament into which designs had to be fitted —a kind of discipline which did not permit much variety, although it had a salutary effect on design.

Apart from Italy, Palladianism in the true sense is hardly to be found on the Continent, but the designs of Perrault for the façade of the Louvre, which were preferred to Bernini's baroque, perhaps come as near to its spirit as anything. In any case the Academy of Architecture established by Colbert in 1671 imposed its own discipline on the individual architect's designs.

In interior decoration and general furnishings the influence of the Palladian style in architecture is strongly apparent in the work of William Kent, Giacomo Leoni, Isaac Ware, and Sir William Chambers (q.v.). Palladian classicism in England merged into the neo-classicism (q.v.) of Robert Adam without any well-marked break in the tradition such as had occurred in France during the currency of the rococo style (q.v.).

PALISSY, BERNARD (1510–1590)

Palissy was a man of many talents, and in the realm of the arts he was a potter, glassworker, and a glass enameller. Only his work as a potter can be identified. He became a potter about 1540 after seeing a dish which was probably Italian *maiolica*. He settled at Saintes, in the Charente, and for many years pursued researches which left his family almost destitute. After fifteen years of experiment he began to produce his rustic ware—large dishes, nearly always oval, with a yellowish white clay body, the reverse covered with a mottled glaze not unlike the tortoiseshell wares of Whieldon in Staffordshire, but peculiar to Palissy in its colouring. This is, in fact, one of the best tests of the genuineness of a specimen. Decoration was with coloured lead glazes, and he used only a few simple colours —cobalt blue, copper green, manganese violet, and yellow. The obverse at this time usually represented a stream of water arranged to leave an island in the centre of the dish in and around which are reptiles, plants, shells, insects, and similar natural history subjects modelled in relief, some of which are obviously casts from life. These became extremely popular as decoration, placed on *dressoirs* and *buffets*, and Palissy was later granted the use of a kiln and workshop in the gardens of the Tuileries which was under construction at the time. He then greatly extended his range of subjects, and produced ornamental dishes decorated in the manner of contemporary pewter and silver, and in some instances took his inspiration from reliefs in ivory. A few very large pieces survive, such as the enormous cistern in the Victoria and Albert Museum (London). His work was continued by the Avon pottery, whence comes the figure of a nurse and child which is often called the 'Palissy nurse'. It was copied in porcelain by the English Chelsea factory about 1750.

Palissy's pottery is sometimes termed 'faïence', but it is strictly earthenware covered with coloured glazes. It was very popular with collectors in the 19th century, when it realized high prices. Forgeries and reproductions were also numerous, the best being those of Georges Pull of Paris, which usually bear his impressed mark. Another imitator was Charles Avisseau of Tours, and Minton's employed a comparable technique in the second half of the 19th century. Particularly common are crude versions of the rustic ware made by Mafra of Caldas, in Portugal, which are hardly likely to be mistaken for the genuine ware, even by a novice.

PALLISANDRE (French)   See *Rosewood*

PALM LEAVES

In classical times these were awarded to visitors to the Olympic Games, and they were borne in Roman triumphal processions. Gabriel bears a palm branch in representations of the Annunciation. The formalized version is termed a palmette, and the palmette divided vertically downwards is called a half-palmette.

PANTIN, SIMON (père et fils)

The Pantins were among the numerous Huguenot *émigré* craftsmen to settle in London. Simon Pantin was a member of a family prominent among Paris goldsmiths and clockmakers. He was not, however, the first to come, since Nicolas Pantin, a clockmaker, settled in London as early as 1651, and Samuel Pantin was Master of the Irish Goldsmiths' Company in 1679. Simon Pantin entered his mark at the Goldsmiths' Hall in 1701, setting up his workshop at the Sign of the Peacock in St Martin's Lane, London. His mark shows a peacock spreading its tail over his initials.

Much of Pantin's work was in a plain style associated with Queen Anne, but which is, perhaps, at least as much French Provincial in origin. Most of his surviving work is domestic silver noted for its excellent proportions and only slightly decorated with engraving.

The younger Simon Pantin entered his mark in 1731, on succeeding to his father's business. He died two years later, in 1733, when the workshop, now at Green Street, Leicester Fields (now Leicester Square), was continued first by his widow, and then by Lewis Pantin, the last of the family and perhaps a younger brother, who entered his mark in 1739.

PAPERWEIGHTS, GLASS

The production of decorative glass paperweights began in France in the 1840s, but was soon taken up elsewhere, especially in England. The principal centres of manufacture were situated at Baccarat, Saint-Louis, and Clichy in France, and at Stourbridge, Birmingham, and London in England. Weights similar in style were made in the 19th century in America, at the Milville factory, New Jersey, with the aid of workmen from Saint-Louis and Baccarat, while weights somewhat differently decorated were made in Germany.

Paperweights, Glass. Millefiori glass paperweight. A minute letter *B* and the year **1846** occurs on one flower. Baccarat. **1846.** *Victoria and Albert Museum.*

Paperweights. Rare Saint-Louis pink encased overlay weight. *Sotheby & Co.*

Paperweights can be divided into several main groups according to the technique of manufacture and the kind of decoration. Most of them are based on the old *millefiori* technique of Alexandria which dates back to Imperial Roman times. Coloured glass canes were first fused together into a cylinder about three inches across, and this was then heated and drawn out into a cane about ten feet long, obviously becoming much thinner in the process but retaining the original disposition of the canes. The canes were then cut across into sections and embedded into clear glass. This formed the basic technique of the decoration of most weights, French or English.

The method of embedding was to arrange the cane-sections forming the pattern in an iron mould which was heated to a point where the glass began to soften. A little fluid glass was poured in so that the canes became incorporated with it, after which it was covered with clear glass and then shaped by successive dipping into the molten metal. By another method, particularly when the background was to be of the *latticinio* type, the sections were arranged on a bed of glass and fused at the lamp, the remainder being added as before. When finished the added clear glass had a magnifying effect. Finally the base was smoothed by grinding, and sometimes a simple radiating pattern cut into it.

Nearly all surviving weights fall into one or other of the following categories:

1. An even disposition of the *millefiori* pattern over the whole surface.
2. A geometric pattern arranged from contrasting *millefiori* sections.
3. Isolated *millefiori* sections against a background of some kind, often a *latticinio* type (q.v.). This group includes the so-called carpet weights.
4. Decoration consisting in flowers, bouquets, animals, reptiles, and so forth formed in a mould and incorporated into the weight, sometimes in conjunction with the *millefiori* decoration, or against a background of *latticinio*.
5. Weights flashed with opaque coloured glass subsequently ground in facets to reveal the clear glass beneath and, through these 'windows', the decoration of the interior. The most frequent colours employed were pink, turquoise, dark blue, a version of the rare *rose Pompadour* (q.v.), and an apple-green. These are termed overlay weights.

Incorporated into some of the *millefiori* weights are canes in the form of tiny silhouettes of animals, flowers, and similar motifs.

Most French weights are a variation of the *millefiori* type, but single sprays of flowers or fruits are not uncommon, although bouquets are rare. Weights with such subjects as reptiles and butterflies are very rare and command high prices. Overlays are also extremely rare; they were made at Baccarat, Saint-Louis and Clichy, perhaps the least common being those of Baccarat, and the best those of Saint-Louis.

The most usual diameter is about three inches, but miniature weights of slightly less than two inches occur, and the largest are in the region of four inches.

Baccarat seems to have made paperweights from 1846 to 1849, because one or other of the dates between these years is often incorporated in the design, the most usual being 1848 and the rarest 1849. Some have what are probably workmen's initials incorporated, the letter *B* being the most frequent. Saint-Louis weights are less commonly dated, specimens of 1847 and 1848 being the most often seen. The earliest recorded is 1845, and the latest 1849. The initials *SL* are present on some dated weights, and occasionally on undated ones. Clichy weights sometimes bear the letter *C*, and more rarely the name, *CLICHY*, in full.

French weights are much sought by collectors, overlays and weights decorated with a single subject, especially a reptile or a bouquet, being the most valued. Dated weights are preferred to undated, and those before 1847 or after 1848 are especially desirable. The colour of the decoration should be good, and the surrounding glass what is termed 'water white', which is self-explanatory.

The first English weights came from Stourbridge about 1845, but the *millefiori* weight seems to have been introduced by Apsley Pellat (q.v.) who employed French workmen, and he describes the process of manufacture in his *Curiosities of Glassmaking* (1849). The first English manufacture was crude, and weights of good quality were not made before 1848, the most usual pattern being known at the time as 'Venetian star work'. The weights made at Stourbridge somewhat resemble those of Clichy, which has led to the supposition that French workmen were employed there. Stourbridge manufactured many other things besides paperweights, the most frequently seen perhaps being an inkwell with a *millefiori* decoration in the base, but scent-bottles, seals, and similar small items exist. An English weight with the letters *IGW* incorporated was made at the Islington glassworks.

Paperweights are still being made today. Imitations of French styles come from America, and excellent weights, not unlike the earlier weights of Stourbridge, from North London. Weights are still made in

Birmingham, and at Perth in Scotland, the latter sometimes being marked *PY*, for Paul Ysart, the son of the Spanish founder. Copies made in Bohemia of old French weights have been on the market for some time, and even those from China. Care is therefore necessary in acquiring specimens.

Recently attempts have been made to identify French paperweights by means of fluorescence under ultraviolet radiation (q.v.). It is possible at present to give only preliminary indications, but investigation suggests that the normal colour exhibited by Baccarat weights is a soft blue, those of Saint-Louis a peachy pink, and of Clichy a soft green. It is not yet possible to say whether or not this result is sufficiently invariable as to be reliable on all occasions.

PAPIER MÂCHÉ

The process of making papier mâché was invented in France, and first came to England during the 1670s, but little use was made of it until the middle of the eighteenth century. Paper was pulped, mixed with glue or gum mastic and chalk, and varnished when dry. By another process sheets of paper were caused to adhere to each other by a paste formed of flour and water and size. In either case formation was by pressing into wooden moulds, after which the completed object was finished by sizing. Papier mâché was, at this time, principally employed for making imitations of stucco and plaster ornament to be applied to ceilings and walls, a fashion which seems to have started in France just before mid century reaching England about five years later. Chamber's *Cyclopedia* (first published in 1753) refers to its use for 'frames for pictures, fine embossed work, and other parts of furniture'.

In 1772 Henry Clay of Birmingham, a japanner, patented a type of papier mâché subsequently japanned which became extremely popular, leading to his appointment as Japanner-in-Ordinary to the King and the Prince of Wales. His wares were built up of successively laid sheets of paper pressed on to a wooden mould until the desired thickness had been attained, after which the object was stoved, carefully smoothed, and coated with japan and varnished. The colours employed were black, crimson, and green—the most sought lacquer colours from the Orient. Clay largely produced panels for screens, furniture, and so forth, and trays, the latter sometimes being painted to special order. Vases were a little exceptional, and were formed over wooden moulds.

Decoration with bronze powders of several colours dates from about 1802, green bronze being employed for foliage and graphite as shadowing. After 1843 stencils were sometimes employed for parts of bronze pictorial decoration, such as landscapes. Mother-of-pearl was introduced into the industry by Jennens & Betteridge of Birmingham about 1825, being at its best before 1840.

Papier-mâché furniture was made in England and France, but English production was on a very large scale, the industry being located at Birmingham and Wolverhampton. In the former city the principal makers were Jennens & Betteridge. The best furniture was made in the 1840s, and there is a noticeable deterioration in taste in the specimens exhibited at the Great Exhibition of 1851. Almost everything was made in this material, from small boxes and teapoys to firescreens, chairs, settees, footstools, tables, beds and even cabinets and *secrétaires*. Much was exported to America, and Jennens & Betteridge even maintained a New York office for a time.

Decoration was elaborate, and often of good quality. Edward Haselar and George Neville were well known for their flower-painting, and David Sargent for ferns. The Oriental style was developed in the 1830s in Birmingham by Edwin Booth, and this work is usually of high quality. Fine painting on trays of this date, to be found occasionally, often took its subjects from such popular artists of the day as Landseer.

In America the Litchfield Manufacturing Company started, in 1850, to make papier-mâché screens, boxes, small tables, and especially clock-cases, the latter being their speciality. They employed artists from England, and used a process similar to that of Henry Clay, but their products were not so well finished.

Care is needed in buying papier mâché, for some of it has been very cleverly restored and redecorated in modern times.

PARCEL-GILT

Partially gilt. Gilded decoration to be found on mahogany furniture (or, more rarely, walnut) is sometimes thus called. The term is also applied to the partial gilding of metal.

PARIAN WARE

Copeland & Garrett (q.v.) of Stoke-on-Trent introduced a type of porcelain extensively used for figure modelling which, because of its marble-like appearance, became known as Parian. It is very similar to hard-paste *biscuit* porcelain, such as that used at Sèvres from about 1770 onwards, although it was fused at a slightly lower temperature. It was especially suitable for casting in moulds and was therefore very popular for decorative wares. In 1845 the Art Union of London determined to reduce some fine statuary to small size which they proposed to issue in limited editions to be manufactured by Copeland & Garrett. Copelands had already manufactured a number of figures in this material in 1844, but the decision of the Art Union undoubtedly gave Parian considerable impetus, and it was soon being manufactured by all the principal factories of the day, some of the best examples being by Mintons (q.v.). After 1851 an enormous number of different models were produced by a large number of factories, one at least, Robinson & Leadbetter, making nothing else. Towards the end of the century Parian delicately coloured and gilded made its appearance, but this

Parian Ware. Emily, from Wordsworth's White Doe of Rylstone. W. T. Copeland. c. 1850. Victoria and Albert Museum.

was more extensively manufactured on the Continent, especially in Thuringia, than it was in England.

Parian was much admired at the New York Exhibition of 1853, and was soon a favourite with American manufacturers, chiefly for portrait busts and parlour ornaments. American Parian was slip-cast (q.v.), and it was first introduced at Bennington, but was eventually made from Vermont to the Carolinas, and to Ohio.

PARIS FAÏENCE

Although the foundation of potteries was encouraged by Henri IV, and statutes protecting the *faïenciers* were drawn up in 1659, the history of the Paris faïence factories is obscure, partly owing to the confusion between shops and actual potteries.

Claude Révérend, for instance, was granted a privilege in 1664 which ran optimistically, *'de faire la faïence, et contrefaire la porcelaine, aussi belle et plus que celle qui vient des Indes Orientales'* (to make porcelain and faïence surpassing in beauty that of the East Indies). It is more likely that he was an agent for Dutch delft, and no faïence has been attributed to him. He had a warehouse at Saint-Cloud. Most of the Paris potters worked in the suburb of Saint-Antoine, François Dezon in the rue de Charonne and Hébert and Digne in the rue de la Roquette. A man called Ollivier appeared at mid-18th century and became famous for making faïence stoves. Factories were also at Sceaux (q.v.), at Meudon, Passy, Poissy, and Longjumeau.

See *Saint-Cloud Porcelain.*

PARIS, PORCELAIN OF

Nearly all the early French soft porcelain factories were located in and around Paris. Many faïence factories were in the same area, and imitations of

Wedgwood's creamware (*faïence-fine*) came from such places as Creil and Pont-aux-Choux. Hard paste porcelain was first introduced at Sèvres just after 1770, and at the same time various interdictions in favour of the royal factory were relaxed. As a result a number of small factories grew up in and around Paris with the object of making porcelain of this kind, mostly under the protection of a member of the royal family or someone almost equally eminent. Their productions were in the Louis Seize or Empire style until after 1814, when those surviving adopted one or other of the styles current at the time. They are listed below.

Fabrique de Gros Caillou, Vaugirard les Paris
Not much is known of this factory. There is reason to think that porcelain might have been made as early as 1762, but nothing has been identified. In 1773 Advenir Lamarr (or perhaps Advenier et Lamare) applied to use the mark *AD*, but little has been identified. In 1784 the factory is mentioned in a decree as belonging to Veuve Jullien at Bugnau de Gros Caillou.

Fabrique du Comte d'Artois, (probably) faubourg Saint-Denis
First founded by Pierre Antoine Hannong about 1770, who registered the letter *H* as a mark. He was replaced by Barrachin as director in 1776. In 1779 it came under the protection of the King's brother, the Comte d'Artois (later Charles X), with the mark of *CP* under a coronet. Louis-Joseph Desplanches became proprietor in 1782. Desplanches used coal for firing for the first time in Paris. The factory copied the jasper of Wedgwood in a blue *biscuit* porcelain body, and in 1785 permission to make *biscuit* figures was applied for and conditionally granted in 1787. In its later work it copied Sèvres more or less directly, and the two factories maintained a connection of an indeterminate nature. After 1802 it was owned by Marc Schölcher and closed in 1828.

Fabrique du faubourg Saint-Antoine
Although an application was made by Sieur Morelle in 1773 for permission to make porcelain, with the mark *MAP*, nothing has been identified.

Fabrique de la rue de la Roquette
For the first factory here see *Saint-Cloud.* A factory for the manufacture of faïence also existed before 1750. A porcelain factory was started by Souroux in 1773, and he registered the letter *S* as his mark. This may be the same as one called Les Trois Leverettes, in existence about 1774, and owned by Vincent Dubois. The mark is a pair of headless arrows (obviously a simulation of the Meissen crossed swords), and these should not be confused with the crossed torches of De la Courtille adopted for the same reason. *Biscuit* figures were made here.

Fabrique de la Courtille
In the rue Fontaine-au-Roy, this factory was founded by Jean-Baptiste Locré de Roissy, originally from

Leipzig, in 1773, and managed by Laurentius Russinger of Höchst (q.v.) from 1774. It was at first known as the Manufacture de Porcelaine Allemande, and its early wares are very German in style. Figures were made on a considerable scale, some models by Christoph Mô (see *Mennecy*), and Meissen was imitated. Extremely well-painted vases are not uncommon, some with tooled gilding, and *biscuit* figures were imitated from Sèvres. An important group allegorical of the birth of the Dauphin in 1781 is in the Victoria and Albert Museum (London). The mark of the Locré period was a pair of crossed torches. In 1800 it came into the hands of Pouyat of Limoges, and the date of its closing is unknown.

Fabrique de la rue de Reuilly, faubourg Saint-Antoine

Started by Jean-Joseph Lassia of Strasbourg who registered the mark *L*. Henri-Florentin Chanou (registered mark *CH*), formerly of Sèvres, may have been associated with this factory, and he was certainly at the Barrière de Reuilly from 1779 to 1784. Few specimens have been identified.

Fabrique de Clignancourt

This factory, started by Pierre Deruelle in 1771, was under the protection of the Comte de Provence (later Louis XVIII). Porcelain made here was of excellent quality, and not unlike that of contemporary Sèvres. The first mark was that of a windmill, alluding to the nearby windmills of Montmartre, and later the letters *LSX* in a monogram. The letter *D* below a coronet has also been recorded. A great deal of the decoration was of flower-sprays in polychrome, but

Paris, Porcelain of. **A Paris dessert-service painted with birds and flowers. End of the 18th century.** *Phillips, Son & Neale.*

some landscapes in a brownish-yellow monochrome were the work of Georg Lamprecht. A few *biscuit* figures were made, but they are very rare.

Fabrique de la Reine, rue Thiroux

This factory was founded in 1778 by André-Marie Lebeuf with the protection of Marie-Antoinette. Its products are still known as *porcelaine de la reine*. The Queen's patronage dates from 1779, and the mark is the letter *A* with a crown above. Much of the decoration consisted in small sprigs of cornflowers and the daisy. The rose was also a favourite flower. A certain amount of good quality bird-painting was done, and gilding was usually slight. In 1797 the factory was sold to Charles Barthélemy Guy who had a decorating studio in the rue de Petit-Carrousel. He originally had a small factory on the corner of the rue d'Échelle, about which almost nothing is known otherwise. The factory at rue Thiroux was still working in the middle of the 19th century, but seems to have closed soon afterwards.

Perché (fl. 1795–1825)

An independent decorator who worked for Guy in the rue Thiroux (above), and also for the Fabrique du Comte d'Artois. He sometimes used a perch as a mark.

Fabrique du Duc d'Angoulême, rue de Bondy

This factory enjoyed the patronage of the Duc d'Angoulême, eldest son of the Comte d'Artois. It was founded by Dihl in 1780 and Guerhard was taken into partnership in 1786. Much of the production was decorated with a pattern of strewn cornflowers ('Angoulême sprig'), and also with large naturalistic flowers. Some good *biscuit* figures were made, and Dihl probably introduced the fashion for

portraits painted on porcelain. The factory was transferred to the rue du Temple in 1796. Marks: the monogram *GA* on early wares. Later *Dihl, Guerhard & Dihl*, or *rue de Bondy*.

Fabrique de la rue Popincourt
Lemaire (see *Vincennes*) founded a factory in the rue Popincourt which came into the possession of Johan-Nepomuc-Hermann Nast, of German origin, in 1782. In 1784 it was removed to the rue des Amandiers-Popincourt. This factory eventually became one of the largest in Paris, and painting was of excellent quality. Flowers were popular, ranging from strewn cornflowers to more elaborate mixed bouquets. The mark is usually *Nast à Paris*, occasionally abbreviated to *N*.

Also from this factory are some excellent *biscuit* figures, clock-cases, and imitations of Wedgwood's jasper in *biscuit* porcelain with a blue or lilac ground.

Fabrique du Duc d'Orléans, rue Amelot
This factory, started in 1784, passed to a partnership between Montarcy, Outrequin, and Toulouse in 1786, when it came under the protection of the Duc d'Orléans, the mark being *LP* under a coronet. The factory, at first in the rue des Boulets, faubourg Saint-Antoine, was removed to the rue Amelot, near the Pont-aux-Choux, at the same time. It later passed through a number of hands. Scattered single roses appear on some surviving examples.

Rue Saint-Pierre (Pont-aux-Choux)
A factory here was regarded as one of the most important in Paris in 1798, and almost nothing is now known of it.

Fabrique de 'Prince de Galles', rue de Crussol
This, called the Prince of Wales's factory, was started in 1789 by an Englishman, Christopher Potter, who is thought to have been the first in Paris to decorate porcelain with transfer-printing (q.v.). No specimen survives. The factory passed to E. Blancheron in 1792, and was afterwards in several hands. Porcelain by Potter, marked *Potter à Paris*, is very rare. Decoration is usually slight. Gold stars were sometimes used, and a little painting in the fashionable *grisaille*. Blancheron's mark was *EB*. Potter owned the Chantilly factory for a year or two, but in consequence of his financial difficulties it was closed in 1800. Little is otherwise known of him.

Fabrique de petit rue Saint-Gilles, boulevard Saint-Antoine
Founded about 1785 by François Maurice Honoré who was in partnership with Dagoty, both here and in the boulevard Poissonière. The factory was under the patronage of the Duchesse d'Angoulême. Production was on a fairly large scale, and some vases were made in imitation of Wedgwood.

Darté Frères, rue de Charonne (later rue de la Roquette)
This factory was founded about 1795. It employed a *bleu de roi* (enamel blue) ground, and some good polychrome landscapes were done. Some plates with portraits of Roman emperors imitate ancient cameos. Mark: *Darté Frères à Paris*.

Decorating Studios
There were a number of studios in Paris which specialized in the painting of porcelain made elsewhere. After the sales of white porcelain by Brongniart (see *Sèvres*) a good deal of old Sèvres porcelain was decorated by them.

Generally, there is sufficient similarity between the products of most of the Paris factories (especially in their use of strewn flower sprays) to make them easily recognizable. Much was fairly lavishly gilded, but with the brassy mercuric gilding which differs considerably from that of the Sèvres factory in its early period. In the absence of a mark it is often difficult to differentiate between factories. Paris porcelain is in considerable demand for interior decoration, but a great deal of it is of small interest to the serious collector.

Parquetry. A Louis XV *commode* of kingwood decorated with parquetry. Rouge marble top. Stamp of the *ébéniste* E. Doirat. *Phillips, Son & Neale.*

PARQUETRY
The term was originally applied in France to the design of wood-block floors, where blocks of the same wood were laid in such a way as to contrast the grain—for instance, the 'herring-bone' or *point d'Hongrie* pattern. It has since been employed for furniture veneers of the same wood, applied on a similar principle of contrasting the grain to form a pattern. It is also applied to a pattern of cubes in light and dark coloured veneers. See *Marquetry*.

PASGLAS (German)
Usually from the Rhineland, the *pasglas* is a cylindrical beaker encircled with a notched spiral thread, or by equidistant threads. Such vessels were for communal drinking, the threads serving to mark the amount to be consumed by each drinker. Plain cylindrical beakers of this kind were often decorated with enamel painting. See *Glass, Enamelled, German.*

PASSEMENTERIE (French)
Ornamental fringes and braids. Galoons. The word appears as 'passment' in some English Tudor records.

Interior at Uppark, Sussex. The chairs (c. 1750) are English
in the Louis XV style, and covered with Beauvais tapestry.

The dinning-room at Clandon Hall, redecorated in 1801.

Passementerie. Making *passementerie.* France. Mid-18th century. *After Diderot.*

'PASTE'

Artificial gemstones and jewellery made from them. See *Strass, Georges Frédéric.*

PASTICHE

A forgery composed of the elements of several genuine works not necessarily by the same hand, and not always of the same period. Several examples spring to mind, but perhaps the best is the notorious tiara of Saitaphernes made by Isaac Rouchomowsky and sold in 1896 to the Louvre. This purported to belong to one of the Scythian Kings, and to have been excavated at Olbia on the Black Sea coast, with a date of the 3rd/2nd century B.C. The ornament was actually taken by Rouchomowsky from several different sources which varied considerably in date, and attention was first drawn to this fact by Adolf Furtwängler of Munich, who actually traced one of them. His view eventually proved to be correct. Perhaps the greater number of forgeries are pastiches of one kind or another, which is one reason why acquaintance with genuine works is the best safeguard.

The term is also used of works of art for decorative purposes comprising passages taken from various sources and recombined in such a way as to suggest an original work by a particular artist. These occur chiefly in the field of painting, and the line of demarcation between legitimate and spurious is a narrow one.

PASTIGLIA (Italian)

A kind of *stucco* ornament in low relief, nearly always gilded and sometimes painted, to be found decorating early Italian furniture and woodwork.

PÂTE DE RIZ (French)

Glass produced by firing glass-powder in a mould. The process was first employed by a sculptor, Henri Cros (1840–1907), who began, about 1884, to imitate

antique cameos, *intaglios*, and plaquettes in this way. He was awarded a gold medal for a bas-relief called *The History of Fire* at the Paris Exhibition of 1900. He also modelled figures, the appearance of which recalls in many ways that of certain hardstones or wax in their translucency and colouring. Albert Dammouse employed a somewhat similar technique from about 1898, and soon afterwards Francis Décorchement began to make moulded bowls and vases, either faceted or with relief decoration, which also resemble hardstones. Henri Cros and his son, Jean, influenced the development of the *art nouveau* style (q.v.). Glass of this kind was also termed *pâte de verre.*

Pastiche. Pastiche by Van Meegeren of a de Hoogh in the collection of H.M. the Queen. The changes are comparatively minor, and principally confined to such points as seating standing figures, and standing those which were seated. The woman holding a wine-glass is copied from a Vermeer at Dresden. *Photo Ullstein.*

Pâte-sur-pâte. Pilgrim bottle with *pâte-sur-pâte* decoration. Mintons. c. 1890. *Victoria and Albert Museum.*

PÂTE-SUR-PÂTE (French)

Literally, paste on paste, the technique is essentially the painting of designs on the unfired, unglazed body of porcelain in liquid white slip. It was first employed in Europe at Sèvres soon after 1850, although it was hardly new then, since it had been used by the Chinese in the 18th century. It was perfected by Marc-Louis Solon, who did some very much sought work for Mintons (q.v.). It was also employed by the Rookwood factory of Cincinnati (Ohio).

PATINA AND PATINATION

Surface changes occurring as the result of the passage of time are usually referred to as patination. The term includes a certain amount of wear and tear, although not accidental damage, and it strictly refers to the result of the operation of such factors as sunlight, impurities in the atmosphere, and similar agents having a long-term effect on surface-appearance. Good patination enhances value; defective patination, or its removal, depresses it. Patination should not be confused with dirt; there can be nothing against the removal of dirt, whereas patination should not be tampered with unnecessarily.

In the case of furniture patination arises from several causes. Wood hardens with age and it gradually changes colour. This is only partly caused by exposure to the air; it is also a product of dust-particles falling on to the surface which are forced by cleaning and polishing into the interstices of the wood itself. Colour is modified by the kind of polish used and how often it is applied, but the general tendency of these factors is to darken the colour. Where a surface is exposed to bright sunlight, however, a bleaching effect will occur, modifying the

colour of mahogany from red to brown, and walnut first to a golden shade, and eventually to a greyish colour. Usually the colour is variegated, for the factors mentioned do not operate equally over the whole surface, and sunlight falls on a table-top, or on the front or side of a cabinet, not equally over the whole of it. The top of a table gets the most dust and the most polishing, so it will differ in colour from the legs or the frieze.

During the 19th century, however, a good deal of old furniture was stripped of its patination and the surface french-polished, which destroys a great deal of its charm. French polish is a kind of varnish thickly applied in successive coats to give a feature-less, highly polished surface which depresses the value even of a perfectly genuine piece otherwise.

Patina presents the forger with his greatest difficulty, for it is almost impossible to reproduce in a way which will deceive those who have studied the subject. This has led to a considerable trade in old wood for the making of forgeries of antique furniture, but if wood has once served another purpose, then traces of the original purpose are almost certain to remain. Cut edges, for instance, will have a different colour, and these will have been stained to match. But stain never quite reproduces the effect of age, and itself changes colour after a while. Since it started by matching the remainder, after it has begun to change colour its nature soon becomes fairly obvious. Attempts to disguise the fact that old wood has been used can often be seen if a lock-plate is unscrewed from a drawer, for if the piece is genuinely old the colour of the wood under the plate, where it has been protected from sunlight and polishing, should differ from the exposed parts. If it does not, either the piece is spurious or it has been refinished recently. For the same reason the outside of a lacquer cabinet, exposed to light and air, will exhibit a colour more faded than that of the interior, and old lacquer cabinets always have the same ground colour inside as they do outside. So far as the outside is concerned, a lock-plate or a hinge removed ought to show something like the original colour underneath.

Handsomely patinated bronzes are much sought. Some of the effects which are termed patination ought really to be referred to as corrosion, because they are the product of chemical changes in the metal wrought by various factors. But this kind of patina is usually only to be seen on excavated bronzes and do not concern us here, except that the effects of burial, much valued among collectors of ancient bronzes when colourful, were sometimes imitated later for their decorative appearance. An example of this is the *verde antique* finish (a green varnish) sometimes employed in 18th-century France for bronze mounts. Generally, the kind of corrosion which affects Renaissance and post-Renaissance bronzes is termed air-patination, and it is a light green of powdery appearance which forms over the surfaces of a bronze exposed to the weather. This affects only the surface and is the product of contact with water-borne acids in the atmosphere. When bronze is first cast it is usually golden brown in colour, and this deepens with exposure to air to a reddish or deep brown, due to the formation of cuprite on the surface. Both the green and the brown are natural patinations. But collectors have never been content with the natural colour of bronze. In Roman times many attempts, some successful, were made to modify the colour by altering the alloying metals or their proportions. The Romans treated the surface with mercury to simulate silver, or plated it with molten tin for the same purpose. They also 'pickled' it in various solutions, and this practice has gone on ever since. It was common in Renaissance times. It is to be seen in 18th-century France, where bronze mounts, usually gilded, were used for many purposes. In the 19th century it was quite common for collectors, and even museum curators, to clean off patination not to their taste and replace it with something else. One quite scholarly handbook of the period recommends several substances for the purpose, ranging from sal ammoniac, well known to the Romans, to smoking with green willow twigs and old shoes for fuel. The patination of later bronzes, therefore, raises many difficulties and problems; that of excavated specimens is much easier to assess.

Gold is very little affected by the agents which alter the surface appearance of other metals, but silver does develop a fairly distinctive colour with age, although cleaning with abrasive substances, and mechanical devices such as rotating mops, will remove it by removing the surface. Generally, however, it has a soft greyish colour, very different from the over-bright surface of new work. Genuine silver is an alloy, and however small the proportion of alloying metal, it does tend to alter the colour slightly. Silver repaired or refurbished by electro-plating differs quite distinctively in colour, for electroplating deposits pure silver. The colour of old silver could, perhaps, legitimately be referred to as patina, since it is a surface appearance conferred by the effects of time.

Ivory is a substance on which age leaves its traces. Apart from the dirt which fills minute surface cracks, the colour changes to something which ranges from pale yellow to dark brown. Newly carved ivories are often stained to imitate these colours, but this can usually be detected by ultra-violet light (q.v.), an old surface exhibiting a mottled yellow, while a newly carved and stained one will usually show a purple reflection. As an instance of the forger's ingenuity, girls have been given small forgeries of ivory to wear between their breasts for a few months, the oily secretions of the skin imparting a deceptive patination, but fats and oils fluoresce brilliantly under ultra-violet radiation, and any such effect from what purports to be old ivory ought to be questioned.

Although burial affects certain kinds of pottery and glass the specimens to which it applies are too old to be considered here. This apart, no really helpful indications exist. Pottery and porcelain are virtually indestructible, and any serious changes in their outward appearance can only be produced by contact with circumstances unlikely to affect post-Renaissance specimens.

Forgeries of wood sculpture are aged in various ways, and given a spurious patination which is usually incapable of surviving expert examination. Potassium permanganate is employed as a stain, and various strong alkalis are used. In the case of the latter, a white powdery appearance on the surface suggests recent staining in which soda has been used, the excess coming to the surface and remaining as a white deposit. New gilding on wood is 'aged' by staining it with liquorice juice or rubbing it with burnt paper. Gilding is nearly always over a *gesso* ground (q.v.), and in the case of spurious furniture the underlying wood is often deal. This shrinks after a while leaving minute cracks in the overlying gilding. Gilding is darker on the parts of a genuine surface facing upwards than it is elsewhere, for dust has fallen on it over the years. In the case of a tall mirror very often the gilding is more defective on the lower part, which can be reached by a duster, than on the upper which seldom receives this attention. It is points of this kind which are always important in considering whether a particular specimen is genuine or spurious.

There is nothing more valuable to a collector than a knowledge of the effects of time on the things in which he is interested, and this can be especially important in the detection of spurious work of many kinds.

PAUL, NIKOLAUS
Porcelain arcanist who assisted in the foundation of a number of German factories in the 18th century. He is thought to have received the secret from Reichard, who worked at Wegely's Berlin factory (q.v.), and there is record that he was subsequently at Fürstenberg, Fulda, Cassel, Gotha, and Kloster-Veilsdorf. There is some evidence that he assisted Gotzkowsky to revive the Berlin factory in 1761. Paul, about which little is otherwise known, is typical of the wandering arcanists of the period. See also *Benckgraff, Johannes*, and *Ringler, Josef Joachim*.

PEACHBLOW GLASS
The name is derived from a resemblance to the Chinese porcelain glaze known as 'peach-bloom'. The colour shades delicately from cream or bluish-white to pink or violet-red, the pigment being related to that used for the Chinese *rose* enamel. Peachblow glass was made by the New England Glass Company of Cambridge, Mass., and the Mt Washington Glass works at New Bedford (q.v.). Specimens are rare.

PEARL WARE
An earthenware body, introduced by Wedgwood towards the end of the 18th century, the glaze of which is white or bluish-white in appearance. It was later extensively manufactured in Staffordshire,

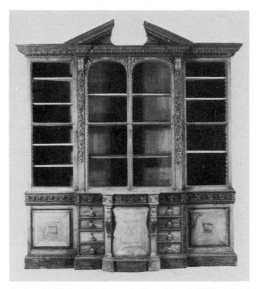

Pediment. Walnut bookcase in the style of William Kent showing the broken pediment. c. 1735. *Christie, Manson & Woods Ltd.*

Leeds, and elsewhere, superseding the earlier cream-ware.

PEASANT WARE

The term is used of pottery made by unsophisticated communities in contact with metropolitan civilization; for instance, the wares of rustic communities made for sale in local markets. Much early Stafford-shire porcelain, such as slip-ware, could be so described.

PEDIMENT

Architecturally, the triangular part which surmounts a portico to be found in classical buildings of all kinds, for instance, Palladian (q.v.). The pediment is also to be found as decoration of furniture designed from late Renaissance times onwards under the influence of the classical revival in architecture. A broken pediment is one in which the two ascending sides of the triangle do not meet at the apex, and the space left between the two sides is utilized for a socle on which to place a bust or an urn. In English furniture at the end of the 17th century, and during the early decades of the 18th, the ascending sides were often curved inwards in the shape of a letter *S* —Hogarth's line of beauty—and this is known as a swan-neck pediment. It is especially to be found surmounting bureaux-bookcases of fine quality.

PELLAT, APSLEY (1791–1863)

A 19th-century manufacturer of decorative glass who introduced a number of processes into the industry in England. He was associated with French glassmakers, and developed the *millefiore* paper-weight, as well as the type called *crystallo ceramie* (q.v.).

PELLETIER, JOHN (or JEAN) (fl. c. 1690–1710)

Carver and gilder. London maker of carved and gilt stands, table-supports, *guéridons*, screens, mirror-frames, and the like, who worked in the contemporary style of Louis XIV. Some of his furniture survives at Hampton Court, executed for William and Mary.

PENNSYLVANIA GERMAN FOLK ART (also called PENNSYLVANIA DUTCH)

An original colony in 1683 was followed by successive waves till the time of the Revolution. The immigrants, Rhineland Germans and Swiss, continued the way of life of their European forebears, largely because they were isolated by language barriers. For this reason they produced a folk-art unique in America.

In furniture the period of the finest examples was the second half of the 18th century, though they appear older than this because form and ornament are based on the traditions of 17th and early 18th century pieces in the homeland. Most striking were the dower chests of tulipwood in background colours of medium blue, dark green, brown, or black. Superimposed were elaborately painted designs, the owner's name or initials, and the date in Roman numerals. Other utilitarian items of furniture in walnut, oak, or yellow pine were dressers and cupboards, and wardrobes (called *schrank*), some of which had painted decoration.

The Pennsylvania Germans employed a standardized, traditional vocabulary of decorative *motifs*, whether applied to furniture, pottery, or iron. Favourite of all *motifs* was the stylized tulip, and secondly the heart. Designs also include the pomegranate and floral forms, paired and single birds

Pediment. Swan-neck pediment to an American secretary-cabinet of mahogany made in Philadelphia in the second half of the 18th century. *Parke-Bernet Galleries, New York.*

314

Pennsylvania Dutch. A dower chest of tulipwood and pine with painted decoration of horsemen, unicorns, birds, and stylized flowers. Pennsylvania German. Berks County, Penn. c. 1780. *Metropolitan Museum, New York.*

(doves, parrots, and peacocks), vases and urns with flowers, the tree of life, and an enormous variety of geometric stars. Heraldic subjects were immensely popular (the crown, lion and unicorn) as were medieval symbols—cock, mermaid, stag and horseman, pelican and fish.

Also in the same folk tradition was Pennsylvania pottery using local red clay covered with a transparent lead glaze and decorated simply with yellow slip or with incised designs.

Another unique product of the Pennsylvania Germans was their *Fracturschriften* (usually called *Fractur*) which were certificates recording vital statistics—births, baptism, and marriage, done in freely-drawn Gothic lettering and illumination in the medieval tradition.

In the same tradition was the work of an itinerant whittler carver, William Schimmel (c. 1865), who produced great quantities of Pennsylvania German eagles in the round. Other subjects were parrots, cockerels, squirrels, owls, and dogs.

PERGOLESI, MICHELE–ANGELO
An Italian artist working in England who did ceilings and panels for Robert Adam and other neo-classical architects. He also designed furniture and chimney-pieces. A work, *Designs for Various Ornaments*, which was dedicated to the Duke of Northumberland, was published in parts between 1771 and 1801, and included designs for ornamental plasterwork, etc.

PERSIAN RUGS AND CARPETS
The geographical term 'Persia' is employed to denote so large an area, and so many varieties of both rugs and carpets were woven within its confines, that it is impossible to do more than generalize briefly here. Some of the more important centres are discussed elsewhere. Rugs have always been an important aspect of Persian decorative art, and in the 16th century the Shah offered large prizes to encourage the best of the weavers. Attempts were made, in the 19th century, to prevent the use of aniline dyes, first introduced about 1870, but these were unsuccessful, and artificially synthesized dyes

Pennsylvania Dutch. Slip-covered dish of red earthenware with *sgraffiato* decoration. Probably by Henry Roudebuth, dated 1793. Montgomery County, Penn. *Metropolitan Museum.*

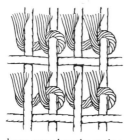

have now largely replaced the older vegetable dyes. The chief drawbacks of aniline dyes, apart from the colour itself which is not always as pleasing as that of the older dyes, is that they are apt to fade in sunlight, to run when wetted, and to make the pile brittle, reducing the wearing qualities of the rug. Some vegetable dyes, however, are apt to fade in strong light, even though not to the same degree. In 1934 the Persian Government made regulations preventing the export of rugs of poor quality, especially those arising from inferior workmanship, dyes, or materials.

Both the Sehna (or Persian) knot and the Ghiordes (or Turkish) knot are used. The areas from which most of the rugs seen in the West are imported are Isphahan, Tabriz, Kirman, Kashan, Herat, Meshed, and Heriz. Productions are discussed briefly under those headings.

PESNE, ANTOINE (1683–1757)

French painter. He became an Academician in 1730 and was invited to Berlin, where he was appointed chief painter to Frederick the Great and director of the Berlin Academy. A portrait of Frederick by him was engraved and used as transfer-printed decoration on Worcester porcelain.

PETIT (Jacob et Mardochèe) PORCELAIN FACTORY

This factory was established at Fontainbleau (Seine-et-Marne) in 1795, and was bought by J. & M. Petit about 1830. A great deal of decorative porcelain was made here, mostly in early 19th-century styles. It specialized in figures of one kind or another, but especially the *veilleuse* (q.v.) in the form of figures (the *personnage*). Some clock-cases surmounted by figures are very large and well painted. The initials *JP* have been commonly employed as a mark.

PETIT POINT (French)

Embroidery in which the pattern is made up of short stitches, usually employed in the 17th century and early part of the 18th as an upholstery covering, put on to a frame to be used as a pole-screen, or glued down on to the top of a card-table. Examples of the latter use are very rare, and those which depict playing-cards as part of the pattern should be seriously questioned. The table may be genuine, but the embroidery will have been added later. Embroidery in long stitches is often termed *gros point*, but for the most part there is no clear line of demarcation between the two. Reproductions and forgeries of early *petit point* needlework were made in England,

Petit, Jacob. Porcelain clock in the form of an Arab mounted on a spirited steed. Jacob Petit. c. 1830. *Harold Newman Esq.*

France, and Belgium towards the end of the 19th century. Old needlework feels harsh to the touch, because the stitches were pulled tight, and palpable softness is a sign of relatively modern work.

As a general rule *petit point* crosses only one warp or weft thread of the coarse canvas foundation, and consists in eighteen or more stitches to the inch. *Gros point* crosses two threads, and the stitching for this reason is more obvious.

PETITOT, JEAN (1607–1691)

Huguenot enameller who, born in Geneva, worked mainly in France. Petitot was noted especially for miniature portraits in painted enamel, and many

Petit Point. Settee, carved and gilt, and covered with rose *petit point*. First quarter of the 18th century. English. *Parke-Bernet Galleries, New York.*

survive. The Louvre (Paris) and the Victoria and Albert Museum (London) have a large number of examples, and there is an extensive collection at Windsor Castle. Petitot painted most of the celebrities of his day, including Louis XIV, the Prince de Condé, Christina of Sweden, and the Cardinals Richelieu and Mazarin.

PEWTER

The term 'pewter' is applied to an alloy of varying constituents. Lead, tin, copper, zinc, antimony, bismuth, and even small amounts of silver, are among the metals which have been used for the purpose. Britannia metal and cock-metal (q.v.) are really classifiable as a kind of pewter. Fine pewter in medieval times especially consisted largely of tin with the addition of about 25 per cent of copper to harden it, and traces of silver have sometimes been noticed in the pewter of this period. Alloys were varied to fulfil several purposes—colour, hardness, ease of working, etc.—and they were governed by a number of factors. For instance, tin can be alloyed with approximately 25 per cent of copper, and this was the proportion used for such flat-ware as dishes, porringers, etc. Other things, especially hollow-ware (e.g. tankards, mugs, and bowls), were of tin alloyed with slightly less than 25 per cent of lead. These proportions held good till about 1700, when alloys became more varied. Not all of the metals first mentioned were deliberate additions. It was undoubtedly the custom to melt suitable scrap vessels from several sources, and of different kinds, to provide metal for new work, and these may not have been of the same alloys. Also, metals in early times were not refined to high standards of purity, and other metals were probably associated with the ores from which they were derived. Pewter of raw materials from different sources, therefore, is likely, on analysis, to yield different results.

In Great Britain the makers of pewter formed themselves into a Guild in 1348, and one of its objects was to maintain the standard of the metal, since lead was often included in larger quantities than was desirable. Lead-poisoning from the metal dissolving out of the alloy was a frequent result of using too much lead, and the prevalence of lead-poisoning in ancient Rome was due to the lack of appreciation of its poisonous properties when made into waterpipes.

The Pewterer's Company seem to have taken their responsibilities seriously, and rigidly to have main-

Pewter. French pewter tankard decorated with classical scenes in medallions and strapwork. The influence of Augsburg silver is perceptible. First half of the 17th century. *Victoria and Albert Museum.*

tained standards of purity in the alloys and in workmanship. From 1503 it became compulsory to mark all pewter vessels (see *Touch-marks*). Manufacture was widespread in England, but London, York, Bristol, and Exeter may be selected as among the chief sources. The pewterers of the larger cities in Scotland and Ireland also achieved a good reputation for their wares.

Pewter generally can be divided into ecclesiastical and domestic wares, and some of these are described elsewhere under various headings.

Pewter tends to discolour and constant cleaning was therefore necessary, usually with abrasives. When these were harsh, such as silver sand, the relatively soft surface was often scored. These signs of age occur on a good deal of genuinely old metal.

PEWTER, DECORATION OF

Engraving as a method of decorating pewter dates at least from the second half of the 16th century, but most work of this kind is crude in comparison with the engraving to be found on contemporary silver. Also the engraved line is not very effective on the surface of pewter, and this led to the introduction of wriggle-work (q.v.) as a method of decoration, a technique sometimes found on silver of the later years of the 17th century.

Pewter was often decorated with ornament impressed into the surface with the aid of steel dies. Ornament of this kind is repetitive, and is often to be found round the ledges of plates and dishes. It was struck either with a single punch, or with several different ones used in combination.

Hollow-wares (tankards and bowls) were often cast in moulds, and the moulds were sometimes

Pewter. Pewter porringer. English. Late 17th century. *Victoria and Albert Museum.*

Pewter. Pewter canister with a screw top in an early Renaissance style. German. 16th century. *Victoria and Albert Museum.*

given *intaglio* ornament which, on the cast, appears as relief-work. This is rare, and perhaps more likely on Continental rather than English pewter. Most English specimens belong to the early years of the 17th century, and late 17th-century examples bearing royal portraits and illustrating historical events in relief are on record. These, perhaps, owe their origin to immigrant Dutch craftsmen.

Engraved inscriptions and monograms are unusual, but they occur occasionally.

PEWTER, TO CLEAN

Much old pewter is a dull grey in colour, and some collectors prefer to bring it back to its original brightness. This is not entirely justified in the sense that its colour today may fairly be regarded as patination, and a sign of age which it would not necessarily be wise to remove.

For those who wish to do it, unless there is corrosion present fine abrasive powders, or a fine steel wool, will usually be sufficient. Powders can be applied with buffers and polishers supplied with electric drills. Harsh abrasives such as coarse emery powder or emery cloth should be avoided. They will leave unsightly scratches which will be difficult to remove. Fine emery cloth, 000 grade, or very fine steel wool, are both safe, and can be used as a preliminary treatment, followed by polishing with increasingly fine abrasives—a domestic scourer, followed by jeweller's rouge, or a good metal polish. When corrosion is present which it is difficult to remove otherwise hydrochloric acid may be tried, either diluted two to one with water or, if this is

insufficient, pure acid. Petroleum jelly or automobile grease will protect parts which it is desired to keep from contact with the acid. Oxide softened in this way should be easy to remove with fine emery cloth. The surface after cleaning with acid will be dull and can be repolished as outlined above.

PFALZ-ZWEIBRÜCKEN PORCELAIN FACTORY

This factory was established in 1768 under the patronage of the Duke Christian IV, and housed in the castle of Gütenbrunn. Laurentius Russinger of Höchst was artistic and technical director until he was succeeded by Jakob Melchior Höckel, also of Höchst, who was later at Kelsterbach. The factory closed in 1775. There are two qualities, for the poorest of which a local clay was used, but Passau clay was employed for the finest work. Most surviving examples are service-ware decorated with polychrome flowers, but landscapes in purple with gilt rococo framing occur occasionally. Figures have not been identified, but one in the Spires Historical Museum has been attributed to this factory.

PHILISTINE

Probably from the German *philister*, a term once used at some universities to signify an outsider. An uncultured or commonplace person. One who, like some provincial aldermen, loudly proclaims that he knows nothing of art but knows what he likes.

PHOENIX

A mythical bird, the only one of its kind, which immolated itself every few centuries on a funeral pyre, rising from the ashes with youth renewed to live another cycle. It is usually represented as rising from flames, and it occurs not infrequently in decorative art of all kinds. The *fêng huang*, a bird sacred to the Empress of China, is sometimes erroneously termed the phoenix. See *Chinese style, Decoration in the.*

PHOSPHATE TEST

To test porcelain for the presence of phosphates, choose an unglazed part of the base, or carefully

Phoenix. Phoenix in flames. Petworth, Sussex.

clean away the glaze from an inconspicuous part with a carborundum stone. Apply a drop of hydrofluoric acid with a wax-taper (hydrofluoric acid attacks glass and glaze), and leave for five minutes. Then wash the spot with water from a small syringe into a test-tube containing a small quantity of warmed ammonium molybdate in nitric acid. A yellow precipitate will form if phosphates are present. This test is employed when the nature of some early English porcelains, especially Bow, is in doubt. Bow porcelain of all periods will show a positive reaction.

The substances mentioned can be purchased from any industrial chemist. Hydrofluoric acid gives off irritant fumes. Since it attacks glass, it comes in non-vitreous containers. It should be stored in a locked cupboard, and not near glass, since a slight leak of vapour past the stopper will etch a glass surface. Porcelain to which it has been applied should be washed in running water to remove all traces.

PHYFE, DUNCAN (1768–1854)

American cabinet-maker of Scottish descent whose name was originally Fife. He first worked as a joiner in New York in 1789. Later he had a flourishing business as a maker of case-furniture and chairs. His early work was influenced by Sheraton, and his later furniture by the French Empire and English Regency styles, and especially by the Regency designer, Thomas Hope. Phyfe's furniture is much sought after and highly valued.

See *Furniture, American.*

PICCOLPASSO, CIPRIANO (1524–1579)

At one time a potter at Castel Durante, Piccolpasso wrote an account of the making of *maiolica* between 1556 and 1559 entitled *Li tre libre dell' arte del vasaio.* It gives instructions how to procure and treat the clay, with recipes for preparing pigments and glazes and notes on kiln-design and firing-techniques. It is preserved in the Victoria and Albert Museum (London), and was edited and translated into English in 1934 by Bernard Rackham and A. Van der Put.

PICTURESQUE

This term is now defined by the *O.E.D.* as 'fit to be the subject of a striking picture', but it was not its meaning in the 18th century. Then it meant an arrangement of nature, such as a landscaped garden, imitating a painting by the admired Claude Lorraine or Salvator Rosa. It was still used in this sense by Uvedale Price (*Essay in the Picturesque*) in 1794. He regarded the study of pictures as the means whereby 'we may learn to enlarge, correct, and refine our view of nature and by that route become good judges of scenery'. This notion had a considerable impact on the course of art in the later decades of the 18th century, influencing the development of Romanticism. In its earlier phases it affected the design of landscape gardens by William Kent (q.v.) and others, as well as the development of rococo

(q.v.) in England. Gardens of this kind were, in France, known as *Anglo-chinois*, in recognition of the influence of Chinese gardening which is also strong, and an example is to be found in Marie-Antoinette's garden of the Petit Trianon.

PIERCED WORK

A method of decorating English silver and Sheffield plate during the second half of the 18th century, which may have been introduced from Ireland since potato-rings (q.v.) are among the first objects to be thus treated. Potato-rings occur also in Sheffield plate. The pierced ornament was cut with a small piercing saw, not unlike a fret-saw in principle, on the best work, but stamping was also employed, especially in the making of Sheffield plate. The fashion was extended at the time to the popular creamware, some of the wares of Wedgwood and Leeds being decorated in this way. The same technique was sometimes employed for porcelain in England and on the Continent. Pierced covers and necks to vases mean that they were intended for *pot-pourri.* In more recent times George Owen (d. 1917) made elaborately pierced or reticulated porcelain for the Worcester Royal Porcelain Company. Owen perhaps owed his inspiration to Oriental ivory-carving, and to the popularity of wares in the Japanese style introduced at Worcester in 1872.

PIER-GLASSES

(French *trumeaux.*) Tall, rectangular mirrors designed to be placed on the piers between windows. The purpose of the pier-glass was to lighten the dark space between windows, and the proportions of any particular mirror are a fair indication of its period because of the variation in the width of piers. Narrow glasses are the earlier. The actual mirror-glass of early specimens is usually in at least two pieces. The frames are nearly always of carved gilt wood, or of gilded *gesso,* and style is in keeping with period.

Pierced Work. Pierced work in an inkstand from Du Paquier's Vienna factory. c. 1730. *Cecil Higgins Museum.*

Pier-glasses. Pier-glass, the frame in the style of William Kent, above a console table. *Chiswick House.*

PIER-TABLE
A late 18th-century table, usually semi-circular, intended to be placed against the piers between windows, taking the place of a *commode* in France. Above it was a pier-glass (q.v.).

PIETRA DURA (Italian)
A kind of inlay employed especially for cabinets and table-tops of coloured marbles and semi-precious stones. It was at its most popular during the first half of the 17th century, but the high cost of the materials caused many inferior imitations to be made, either from common materials (see *Scagliola*) or by *trompe l'œil* painting (q.v.).

PIGALLE, JEAN-BAPTISTE (1714–1785)
French sculptor, member of the Academy in 1744, Pigalle was much in favour with Louis XV, and he was official sculptor to Mme de Pompadour. He modelled for the Sèvres Porcelain Factory.

PIJNACKER, ADRIAEN (fl. 1680–1707)
Dutch delft potter. See *Keizer, Aelbrecht Cornelis de.*

PILASTER
Like the column, the pilaster has a base and a capital, but it has a flat surface normally fluted, is rectangular in section, and is usually employed in a form which projects only slightly from the building or piece of furniture of which it forms part. Unlike the column it is architecturally ornamental rather than load-bearing, and it usually forms part of a wall. It was frequently part of the decoration of English case-furniture in the 18th century, and in France during the neo-classical period.

Pigalle. Portrait of Louis-Florent Chéron—an original plaster model by J.-B. Pigalle. *City of Birmingham Art Gallery.*

PILGRIM-BOTTLE
A circular bottle flattened at the sides with two perforated handles on the shoulders through which a cord could be passed. Pilgrim-bottles of pottery

Pilgrim-bottle. Pilgrim-bottle of Böttger's red stoneware mounted in silver. Meissen. c. 1715. The form is found in a variety of materials, including glass. *Boston Museum of Fine Arts.*

go back to Roman times, and they are also to be found from China at the beginning of the Ming dynasty (1368–1644). Most of those made more recently, whether of metal, porcelain, pottery, or glass, were usually intended to be decorative and not for practical use. Some are decorated on the sides with relief ornament, while others, especially those of faïence, are often well painted.

PILLAR CARPETS
Carpets originally intended to cover pillars. Most are from Chinese Turkestan, but the practice is a very ancient one, carpets being used for this purpose in Imperial Rome. The long sides of pillar carpets have no borders, and on examination it will be seen that the pattern when wrapped round a cylindrical object is more or less continuous. A rare variety of Chinese pillar carpet is made to be wound spirally round the pillar.

PILLEMENT, JEAN-BAPTISTE (1728–1803)
French designer of ornament, born in Lyon. His designs were principally in the rococo style, and chiefly *chinoiseries* and *singeries* (q.v.). They occur on *toile de Jouy* (q.v.), on porcelain from several factories, and on faïence, enamels, and *objets d'art* generally. Pillement also painted landscapes in the manner of Boucher.

PINCHBECK, CHRISTOPHER (1670–1732)
Throughout the ages cheap alloys resembling gold and silver have been made, either for deceptive purposes, or as cheap imitations of more valuable objects. Pinchbeck introduced an alloy of copper and zinc (a kind of brass) for the manufacture of jewellery and small objects of *vertu* which was sometimes given a wash of gold to increase its deceptive appearance, and his name has passed into the language as a common term for work of this kind. He was succeeded by one of his sons, Edward Pinchbeck.

Pillement. Worcester mug transfer-printed with a subject from a design by Pillement after Boucher. c. 1758.

Similar alloys were made in France, the best by Leblanc of Paris.

Pinchbeck was also a clockmaker, and a member of the Clockmakers' Company.

PINEAU, NICHOLAS (1684–1754)
Architect and designer, and a pupil of the architects J.-H. Mansart and G. Boffrand. After a period of ten years during which he worked in Russia, Pineau returned to Paris in 1726 and became one of the earliest and most influential designers to work in the rococo style, although most of his designs were comparatively restrained. They earned the approbation of J.-F. Blondel, who was an early critic of rococo extravagances.

PINXTON (Derbyshire) (1796–1812)
A small porcelain factory working principally in the Derby tradition. It was started in 1796 by Billingsley (q.v.) and situated on the estate of John Coke. Production was small and specimens are rare. Decoration was principally of flowers painted in the contemporary Derby style, but some landscapes are attributed to John Cutts who continued the factory after Billingsley left it in 1799. Under his managership the quality of the porcelain produced deteriorated considerably, the body becoming almost opaque. Table-services and small vases formed the greater part of the production, and straight-sided coffee-cans resemble those then being made at Derby. No figures were made. The hand of Billingsley as a painter does not seem to have been positively identified on these wares, and no doubt he devoted his attention to the production of porcelain.

PIPE-STOPPERS
Small implements for pressing down tobacco while smoking. In a strictly utilitarian form these, combined with other gadgets for the convenience of the pipe-smoker, are not unknown today, but in the past they took many ornamental forms. The earliest seem to date from the middle of the 17th century, and they continued to be popular in decorative form at least until 1850. They are to be found in a wide diversity of forms and materials, the latter ranging from silver and porcelain to ivory, bone, and wood. Some are in the form of natural objects, such as a boar's tusk mounted in silver. Those of wood (often boxwood) are usually well carved, and specimens said to have been made from the Boscobel Oak, which sheltered Charles II after the Battle of Worcester in 1651, have been noted. Brass stoppers date from the 17th century, but are more common from the 18th, especially those in the form of figures.

Stoppers sometimes serve a dual purpose, with perhaps a spike for loosening the tobacco, or combined with a seal or a corkscrew.

Although most pipe-stoppers are not expensive, those of porcelain often command high prices, the most highly valued perhaps being the unique Worcester specimen in the form of the head of the figure of the well-known female gardener modelled about 1770 by Mr Tebo. Examples from Meissen are also known, although those from the minor German factories are distinctly rare.

PIQUÉ (French)

The art of inlaying gold and silver either in the form of strips of metal or dots into tortoiseshell or ivory. The art is predominantly French, and belongs principally to the 17th and 18th centuries. It was once entirely French until the Revocation of the Edict of Nantes in 1686 drove Huguenot craftsmen abroad. Some came to England, and the best English work of this kind falls between 1740 and 1760, when the designs somewhat resemble those of Chippendale, a contemporary. Later work in the Adam style is also excellent in quality with typical motifs of the period. The art continued into Victorian times, but later examples are usually poor in quality and design.

In France the finest specimens belong to the reign of Louis XIV, when the familiar decorative *motifs* of the day occur in miniature. The rococo scrolls of Louis XV inevitably occur on work done at the time, while the work of the following Louis XVI period has all the familiar neo-classical *motifs*.

Objects thus decorated are always small, and comprise chiefly snuff-boxes, *bonbonnières*, scent bottles, etc. Jewellery of appropriate forms was often thus decorated. All are much sought today.

PITKIN GLASS WORKS

A factory was established at Manchester, Conn., by Captain Richard Pitkin and his two sons in 1783. It produced bottles and flasks of amber and olive-green glass, but very few specimens can be reliably attributed. A ribbed flask, often referred to as the 'Pitkin type', was made later at several factories. The Pitkin works closed about 1830. See *Glass, American.*

PITTSBURGH (Penn.) GLASS WORKS

The first of these was the O'Hara factory started in 1797, and this was also the first in the U.S.A. to use coal as fuel. Many factories, large and small, opened during the first half of the 19th century, and Pittsburgh became known for pressed glass of such excellent quality that it was difficult to differentiate from cut-glass. See *Glass, American.*

PLASTER OF PARIS

Gypsum, a mineral, of which alabaster is one form. Plaster of Paris is the product of calcining gypsum to remove the water of crystallization. It is then a fine powder of the appearance and consistency of flour. When added to water the powder first forms a semi-liquid mass, and then sets rapidly into a rigid substance which is both soft and porous. For this reason it has always been much employed for mould-making and casting. When plaster sets there is a distinct rise in temperature, followed first by slight expansion and then by contraction, which facilitates the separa-

tion of mould from cast. The use of plaster for this and other purposes connected with the decorative arts is very ancient, although it declined after Roman times until the Renaissance. Much fine ornamental plasterwork decorates houses of the period between the 16th and 18th centuries. The porous properties of plaster led to its use in the manufacture of fine earthenware and porcelain for slip-casting (q.v.). Plaster is sometimes carved with chisels and rasps, although it is rarely used as a medium for modelling. As *tesso duro* it has been used for the making of bas-reliefs for ornamental purposes, and in this form is gauged with glue water and boiled linseed oil. Plaster is sometimes employed as a moulding material for casting in bronze and other metals, when it is mixed with a refractory material such as brick-dust or pumice powder. Plaster casts can be coloured to imitate bronze (see *Bronzing*), and are sometimes coloured to imitate silver. Films of silver or gold can be deposited on a plaster surface which is first covered with graphite by electroplating methods. The surface of marble can be imitated by repeated applications of milk, and plaster is often employed to 'load' candlesticks made of sheet silver.

Plaster varies in fineness, hardness, and setting time according to methods of manufacture and additives.

PLUM WOOD

(French *bois de prunier*.) A fruitwood sometimes employed by the best of the French *ébénistes* especially for tables. In England it occurs as part of the inlay of Tunbridge ware (q.v.).

PLYMOUTH PORCELAIN FACTORY

A factory was opened at Coxside, Plymouth, Devon, for the manufacture of true porcelain in the Chinese manner by an apothecary, William Cookworthy (q.v.), in 1768. This was transferred in 1770 to another factory at Castle Green, Bristol.

The early wares of the Plymouth factory are often primitive and inclined to show many manufacturing faults. The glaze is variable in thickness, often specked, and sometimes with a slightly pitted surface resembling the effect which the Chinese so well call 'chicken skin'. Plates and saucers are very rare, and this points to difficulties with flat wares generally.

Plymouth Porcelain. **A set of three mugs in sizes painted with exotic birds in the manner of M. Soqui. c. 1770.** *Christie, Manson & Woods.*

The most frequent survivals are leaf-shaped pickle trays, sauceboats of silver pattern, mugs, both baluster-shaped and straight-sided, and tea and coffee pots. Shellwork was a common form of decoration, perhaps brought to Plymouth by Mr Tebo (q.v.). The most usual variety is the salt in shell form mounted on a pile of small shells and corals.

Like the saucer, the cup is a considerable rarity, and, like those of Bristol, both cups and saucers show a spiral 'wreathing' in the body which can only be seen on wheel-thrown pieces. It seems likely that the body was a difficult one to throw, and that it tended to 'unwind' slightly in firing. Because of this handles on both Bristol and Plymouth porcelain are nearly always slightly askew, and these are useful tests for the nature of the ware.

Much Plymouth porcelain is in forms familiar from elsewhere. Some of it much resembles Bow porcelain of about fifteen years previously, and some Longton Hall figures are almost duplicated by Plymouth models, strongly suggesting that Longton moulds were employed. Some of the stock of the Longton factory was sold at Salisbury (Wiltshire) in 1760, and it is possible that moulds or prototypes of Longton figures were sold at the same time. It is possible that Cookworthy bought some and used them later, or he may have bought some of the figures and had casts taken from them for fresh moulds by Mr Tebo, to whose presence the Bow influence is no doubt due. Apart from Tebo, there were one or two other artists of talent, notably M. Soqui, reputed to have come from Sèvres, who painted exotic birds in the Sèvres style, later going to Bristol to continue the kind of bird-painting he originated at Plymouth. He also did similar work at Worcester in the 1770s. Henry Bone, later a member of the Royal Academy, was probably apprenticed to Cookworthy as a painter, and some workmen perhaps came from Worcester or even Chelsea, although this is speculation. In 1770 the Castle Green factory certainly advertised for painters in a Worcester journal.

Decoration in underglaze blue occurs quite frequently, the blue usually blackish in tone. Polychrome decoration often reaches a high standard, and much of the decoration is Chinese in style. Enamels stand out palpably from the glaze in a way common to most true porcelain, and the colours have, in some cases, partially flaked off.

Figures are not plentiful, and most are derived from Bow and Longton originals. A series of bird models based on those of Meissen are scarce but much sought. Although made when the neo-classical style was well advanced, most of Cookworthy's figures retain the rococo scroll bases of five or ten years earlier.

Unless a specimen is primitive it is difficult to say which were made at Plymouth and which at the Castle Green factory before Champion took it over in 1772, but after this date the style begins to differ very noticeably, conforming increasingly to the fashionable neo-classical forms and decoration.

POKAL (German)

A covered wine goblet or cup on a high baluster stem of silver, rock-crystal, or glass, usually handsomely decorated.

POKERWORK   See *Pyrography*

POLE-SCREEN   See *Fire-screen*

POLISH CARPETS

Brightly coloured silk carpets made in Isphahan (Persia) during the 17th century for export to Poland. Some were still in private possession in Poland before 1939, but their subsequent fate is unknown. Eighteenth-century carpets in the French style made in Poland are also sometimes thus called. The factory of Prince Radziwill is reputed to have employed Persian weavers.

POMANDER

Aromatic perfumes, and vessels to contain them, have always been considered indispensable as a mark of refinement. The pomander was a portable container for such perfumes, the finest of which were of silver or gold. They were usually provided with a wooden case which has now disappeared.

Generally spherical, the sides pierced to allow the perfumes to escape, pomanders were often divided into two parts, hinged to open in the middle, with one or more compartments inside. The earliest record of the pomander under this name in England goes back to the beginning of the 16th century, although there are earlier references to what seems to be a kind of pomander under the name of musk boxes. From frequent references throughout the 16th century, and their depiction in contemporary portraits, it is obvious that the pomander became extremely popular in the England of the day, especially as a way of combating the numerous malodours which the sensitive nose could hardly escape. Pomanders of the 17th century on the whole tend to be smaller, some less than an inch in diameter.

The pomander was regarded as an article of adornment sometimes, in the case of women, to be hung from a girdle or a necklace. It was always of fine workmanship, and frequently enriched with pearls and a variety of precious stones. Although it was usually spherical in shape, some examples of vase or bottle shape exist, and the forms are variable according to the purpose for which the pomander was intended, those with several compartments departing from the spherical for obvious reasons.

Pomanders were also extremely popular in Italy and France. In the former country they existed at least as early as the 14th century.

See *Pouncet Box; Vinaigrette.*

POMONA GLASS

A rare decorative glass made by the New England Glass Company (q.v.), partly etched with hydrofluoric acid and partly stained a straw colour. See *Glass, American.*

POMPADOUR, MARQUISE DE (1721–1764)

Born Jeanne-Antoinette Poisson, the Marquise de Pompadour was, after the King, the most noted patron of the arts of her period. She was a member of a circle of well-known financiers and *fermiers-généraux*, and she married the nephew of one of the latter class, Le Normant d'Étioles, Director of Public Works. She became the King's mistress in 1745, and in this way brought the influence of the financial classes into royal circles. The rococo style in France is sometimes known as '*le style Pompadour*'; this is unjustified by the facts, but certainly she patronized the arts extensively during its currency. Although Louis XV remained faithful to rococo to the end of his life in 1774, Mme de Pompadour was attracted to the neo-classical style before 1760, although only in her private apartments. Her influence on furniture-design may be seen from Duvaux's (q.v.) account-books in which there are several pieces invoiced as '*à la Pompadour*', and the Sèvres Porcelain Factory was largely her creation. She built and decorated a number of houses, her favourite architect being Lassurance, with Jacques Verberckt responsible for some of the interiors. Many of the most famous artists and craftsmen of the day worked for her, and Boucher was a friend who owed much of his success to her. Her health was always poor, and she died in 1764 after several months of illness. Of her Voltaire wrote: 'Her lively gait became a regal carriage; her roguish glance became majestic; her voice acquired royal dignity; and her mind rose with her rank.'

She procured for her brother, Abel-François Poisson, the post of Directeur des Bâtiments, and he subsequently became the Marquis de Marigny. This was a singularly successful appointment, and he, too, exercised considerable influence on the arts of his day, especially in the introduction of the neo-classical style (q.v.).

PONTIL MARK

A roughened circular area found on the bottom of old blown glass, particularly drinking-glasses, which marks the spot where it was joined to the pontil rod during the operations of finishing. When these were completed the glass was severed from the rod. On early glasses this mark usually remains intact, but during the second half of the 18th century it was often ground smooth on glasses of good quality, leaving a smooth circular area to mark its position. After about 1850 it disappeared altogether. Reproductions of old glasses have a rough pontil mark, but this is nearly always much smoother than in old specimens. The pontil is sometimes referred to by the old English name of 'punty'.

PONTYPOOL WARE

Japanned sheet-iron used for the manufacture of a wide variety of useful and decorative objects at a factory at Pontypool (Wales). Manufacture was at first based on a heat-resisting varnish invented by John Allgood about 1680, although a factory was not established until soon after 1730, when Edward Allgood (1681–1763) founded the Pontypool Japan Works. The first wares appear to have been decorated only in gold with Chinese subjects on black, crimson, and chocolate-brown grounds. Die-pressed openwork patterns decorate the borders of early trays, some of which were extremely large. Much early work was primitive in the methods employed, trays being shaped by hammering.

After 1760 the original factory came into the possession of one of the sons, the other two establishing a rival factory at Usk, not far away, although the wares produced were very similar and differentiation is not easy. At Pontypool painted decoration under the new dispensation became more elaborate and of better quality, and Benjamin Barker, a journeyman-painter specializing in sporting scenes, was employed. His sons, Thomas Barker (of Bath) and Benjamin, acquired reputations as landscape painters and decorated some trays with rustic scenes. The factory was inherited by William Allgood in 1776, when Pontypool ware began to be exported to France (see *Tôle peinte*) and Holland. Improvements in the heat-resisting varnish used enabled production to be extended to such things as tea and coffee urns, and kettles with charcoal braziers, the forms often based on either contemporary silver or Sheffield plate. The same period saw the addition of cast-metal finials, lion-masks for ring handles and the like, which were often gilded. Both factories made a great diversity of domestic ware of all kinds, from snuff-boxes to candlesticks, and from cake-baskets to letter-racks. The Pontypool factory continued until about 1820, the one at Usk continuing until 1860.

To be considered with Pontypool is the japanned tin-plate industry of Bilston (Staffordshire) and Wolverhampton (Warwickshire). Bilston began to produce wares of this kind about the middle of the 18th century, and specialized in 'blanks'—undecorated things like trays and tea-caddies which were painted elsewhere. Much of the production was poor in quality and, when decorated, painted summarily in crude colours (red, blue, and yellow). A large export trade was done, especially with the United States, for which trays were painted to appeal to contemporary American taste.

Production at Wolverhampton began in the 1760s, a factory belonging to Taylor & Jones being under the direction of a one-time Pontypool workman named Jones. The wares were termed 'Pontipool', which became a kind of trade description among the numerous factories which grew up in the town. Trays were a Wolverhampton speciality. Soon after 1812 the use of bronze powders was introduced (see also *Papier Mâché*), and patterns depicting tigers, also extensively exported to India, became popular. A method of applying a block-printed decoration was devised about 1850, and transfer-printing (q.v.), similar to the technique in use in the pottery and porcelain factories, helped in quantity production. Stencilling was also employed to speed production of cheaper trays. Edwin Booth (whose work also occurs on papier mâché) did some of his characteristic Oriental scenes.

The peak year of export to America was 1889, and an American industry on Wolverhampton lines was established soon afterwards. The industry was still in being at Wolverhampton at the beginning of World War II. Pattern-books are preserved at the Wolverhampton Museum.

PORCELAIN

Porcelain is the most recently introduced type of ceramic ware. Although wares definable as porcelain were made in China in the 8th century of the present era, it was not until the Yüan dynasty (1280–1368) that porcelain appeared in its most familiar form. Three categories are distinguished—true (or 'hard') porcelain, artificial (or 'soft') porcelain, and bone porcelain (bone-china). The first was made in China and then in Europe and the U.S.A., the last two were made only in Europe and the U.S.A. True porcelain and bone-china are still being manufactured; artificial porcelain was discontinued in the early decades of the 19th century.

True Porcelain

It is correct to classify as true porcelain all bodies made of clay and a fusible rock. In China it was made from kaolin (china clay) and a fusible feldspathic rock termed *pai-tun-t'zü*, the latter usually written in the form employed by 18th-century French missionaries, who called it *petuntse*. The word means a white stone. Kaolin is plastic; it takes and retains any shape imposed upon it by the potter. It fuses at a temperature of approximately 1700°C. *Petuntse* fuses at a lower temperature, about 1450°C., into a kind of natural glass somewhat analogous to obsidian. *Petuntse* in powdered form is mixed with kaolin, and vessels formed from the mixture are fired at the lower of the two temperatures. The kaolin, being the more refractory of the two substances, holds the vessel in shape during firing, while the fusion of the *petuntse* is taking place. If kiln temperatures are allowed to rise to something near the fusion point of the kaolin the vessel sags out of shape and becomes what is technically known as a 'waster'. It may even end as a vitreous puddle on the floor of the kiln.

True porcelain nearly always has a glaze of powdered feldspathic rock dusted over the surface and fused into a layer of natural glass during the firing process.

True porcelain was first made in Europe soon after 1700 in Germany, at the Meissen factory (q.v.), the manufacture being extended to Vienna about 1720, to France about 1770, and to England (at Plymouth and Bristol) about the same time. The wares of these factories are discussed under the appropriate headings. The principle of its manufacture was well known in England before the first appearance of Plymouth porcelain in 1768. Robert Dossie in his *Handmaid to the Arts* of 1758 discusses it at length (Vol. II, p. 333). He also records

the remaking of ground-up Chinese porcelain, which was mixed with gum-water and refired, but no specimens exist.

A kind of true porcelain utilizing soaprock (a form of steatite) instead of *petuntse* was made at Bristol (before 1750), the factory later being transferred to Worcester. Soaprock porcelain was also made at Liverpool and Caughley. It was finally discontinued at Worcester about 1823.

Artificial Porcelain

Chinese porcelain began to arrive in Europe in appreciable quantities in the Middle Ages, and it was extremely highly valued. So great was the desire to possess this exotic substance that European potters tried to reproduce it without knowing what materials were employed by the Chinese. In the absence of reliable chemical knowledge potters could only try to reproduce the Chinese ware on the basis of its general resemblances to substances known at the time. Chinese porcelain is translucent when held up to the light, and the only known manufactured substance to possess this property was glass, which the glassmakers had learned to opacify with tin oxide (see *Tin-enamel*). This kind of glass was being used to glaze the earthenware known as *maiolica*, and was therefore well known to earthenware potters of the time, who attempted to make a substitute for Chinese porcelain by mixing white clay with powdered glass.

The first artificial porcelain was made in Italy about 1575 under the patronage of Francesco Maria de' Medici, Grand Duke of Tuscany (see *Medici porcelain*). This brief experiment was perhaps based on what seem to be attempts to make artificial porcelain by the Persians in the 14th century, who mixed clay with glaze material, and was probably the work of Orazio Fontana, a *maiolica* potter of Urbino.

A more successful attempt was made to establish manufacture in France towards the end of the 17th century, and much 18th-century porcelain made in France and England was on this principle.

Artificial porcelain was very difficult to fire successfully, since the critical temperature range (about 1200° C.) was extremely narrow and difficult to maintain. Comparatively minor variations, upward or downward, often spoiled the entire contents of a kiln. Beginning with the Bow factory (q.v.), which started manufacture on a commercial scale in 1750, English factories progressively adopted the practice of including massive quantities of bone-ash (calcined animal bones) with the other ingredients. This, by increasing the permissible temperature range, made it possible to fire the artificial body employed with fewer 'wasters', but chiefly at the expense of quality. Bone-ash was not employed on the Continent, where the artificial body was largely abandoned soon after 1770 in favour of true porcelain.

Bone-china

This is, today, the standard English porcelain body, although it is little used elsewhere. Bone-china is a true porcelain modified with the addition of bone-ash, and the formula was reputedly devised by Josiah

Spode and introduced soon after 1800. It was extensively adopted during the early years of the 19th century, the 18th century formulae being progressively abandoned.

PORCELAIN, ENGLISH

The manufacture of porcelain was started in England somewhat later than on the Continent. Although Bow, in East London, was at one time thought the first factory to be established, there now seems little doubt that Chelsea, in West London, preceded it by a year or two, working to a French formula brought probably by a workman from Chantilly. The porcelain made at Chelsea is almost indistinguishable from early French soft paste, except for a few characteristics noted under the heading *Chelsea Porcelain Factory*. Bow, on the other hand, seems to have worked to a formula which included both bone-ash and, in the early stages, Cherokee china clay imported under the name of unaker (q.v.). Chelsea was established in 1743, and experimental work was probably being done at Bow in 1745. Very soon after the latter date William Cookworthy began to experiment with porcelain in the Chinese manner (i.e. clay and fusible rock), probably as a result of conversations with Andrew Duché of Savannah, Georgia (q.v.), and these experiments continued over many years, culminating in the establishment of the Plymouth factory in 1768. It is possible that the experiments of Cookworthy played a part in the establishment of a factory at Bristol about 1748 which used what is, for all practical purposes, a true porcelain, since it was made from clay and fusible rock, although in this case the rock was soaprock, and not the feldspathic rock of the Chinese and the later Plymouth factory. This first Bristol factory was transferred to Worcester in 1752, and soaprock porcelain was settled in a successful career which only came to an end in 1823. Other West of England factories used the same formula, and porcelain often closely resembling that made at Worcester also came from Caughley and Liverpool. A small quantity of soaprock was introduced into porcelain made at Swansea for a year or two just before 1820.

The porcelain of the 18th century in England, therefore, falls into three distinct categories. An artificial porcelain which is fundamentally clay and ground glass made at Chelsea till 1755, Derby till 1770, and at Longton Hall; bone-ash porcelain in the manner of Bow which was employed by this factory throughout its life, by Chelsea after 1755, by Derby after 1770, and by Lowestoft from about 1756 to 1800; soaprock porcelain first made at Bristol about 1748, at Worcester from 1752 till 1823, at Liverpool by Richard Chaffers from 1756, and at Caughley from 1772.

Although all these porcelains possess characteristics which make it possible to differentiate one from the other without chemical analysis, the bone-ash and soaprock groups can both be identified in this way by the amount of phosphoric acid and magnesium oxide they contain. See *Bone-ash* and *Soaprock*.

English porcelain, in both form and decoration, was largely derivative during the 18th century, and for much of the 19th. The sources of influence were Meissen, Sèvres, and Oriental. From 1750 to 1760 the influence of Meissen undoubtedly predominates, both in figure-modelling and service-ware. That of Sèvres is apparent at Chelsea after 1756. Among the Oriental wares the finest and most sought at the time were probably those based on porcelain decorated in the manner of Kakiemon, and these were copied very deceptively at Chelsea, but perhaps in some cases from Meissen derivations. The Chelsea palette is, however, a much closer approximation to the Japanese ware than that of Meissen. Chinese styles were very popular with almost every factory except Chelsea, and they are at their best on Worcester porcelain where the Kakiemon patterns are seen comparatively rarely. At Chelsea the *indianische Blumen* of Meissen were followed by the *deutsche Blumen* of the same factory, even to the extent of adding shadows to flowers and insects which had first been done at Meissen by a decorator named Klinger. Meissen *chinoiseries* occur on some rare early Chelsea wares, and the harbour scenes of the same factory were also copied, probably by William Duvivier.

Sèvres rococo styles began to gain a foothold at Chelsea as early as 1755, and they were firm favourites by 1758. Later they were much favoured at Worcester, and lingered there long after the neo-classical style had brought considerable changes to the porcelain of Derby. The Derby factory of William Duesbury began by calling itself the 'second Dresden', only adopting the neo-classical style after Duesbury purchased the almost moribund Chelsea factory in 1770.

The small true porcelain factory at Plymouth founded by Cookworthy certainly brought nothing new in the way of form or decoration to porcelain, and much of its work bears a fairly strong resemblance to the earlier work of Bow and Longton Hall, reasons for which are advanced under the appropriate heading. But the second Bristol factory which grew from it, and was under the direction of Richard Champion, did make extensive use of the neo-classical style, although it was too short-lived ever to develop it to any considerable extent.

The early 19th century saw a fashion for well-painted landscapes which can justifiably be termed 'topographical', and these were often continued round vases and similar objects without a formal frame or border. Many of them were titled underneath, a type usually called 'named views'. Feathers, shells, and fruit were popular, and flat plaques painted with landscapes achieved considerable popularity.

Chinese designs came back to favour, although they had never been entirely discarded, and the styles of Sèvres still predominated in the luxury market. A great deal of the porcelain of Nantgarw and Swansea owes much to the French factory, and Mintons, Worcester, and Coalport produced porcelain which closely followed its designs. Before 1870 a revival of interest in Japanese art was having its effect on porcelain design and decoration, but this time ivory-carving was the primary inspiration rather than Japanese porcelain. The styles of the Renaissance could be seen in such objects as an imitation nautilus cup in porcelain on a foot which owed a good deal to the real nautilus shells mounted in silver-gilt by the goldsmiths of Augsburg in the early years of the 17th century.

The Sèvres fashion for modelling figures in unglazed porcelain (*biscuit*) in the 18th century came back to favour with the introduction of the Parian body, extensively used for the making of figures in the 19th century. This, at the time of its introduction about 1845, was termed 'statuary porcelain', which is sufficient indication of the purpose for which it was intended.

During the 19th century Staffordshire was, apart from Worcester, the principal centre of porcelain manufacture, and its products became increasingly commercial. During the early years of the 20th century porcelain fell from favour as a result of changes in taste, but it has since largely returned to its original popularity, led by the Worcester factory with a distinguished revival of figure-modelling to be found in the birds of Dorothy Doughty and the horses and cattle of Doris Lindner.

PORCELAIN, ENGLISH, FORGERIES OF

Apart from the Plymouth and Bristol factories, all 18th-century English porcelain—the kind which is forged and reproduced—is a soft porcelain, in practice if not by definition. There is reason to regard Worcester as a true hard porcelain in the sense that the principle of manufacture (clay, plus a fusible rock) was the same as the Chinese, but when tested it reacts in the same way as the soft porcelains. It will file as easily. (See *Porcelain, Tests for.*)

The principal target of forgeries, as distinct from fakes, is Chelsea. Worcester is faked as well, but Chelsea fakes are rare. Samson makes many reproductions of Chelsea and Bow figures, and sometimes confuses the two factories in one figure, but these are always in hard porcelain and, despite a conspicuous gold-anchor mark, are not deceptive for that reason. The colouring is inaccurate, and it could hardly be otherwise, since the enamelling is on a very different type of glaze. Where Samson copies are especially faithful in the modelling they seem always to be smaller than the originals. The anchor mark is always of gold, probably because the 19th-century belief that a gold anchor denoted quality and not period still dies hard on the Continent. The anchor is usually large and conspicuous, whereas the true Chelsea anchor is small and inconspicuous. Pseudo-Chelsea plates which lack the 'stilt' marks within the footring may have been made at Saint-Amand-les-Eaux; this peculiarity is almost invariably present on old Chelsea. There is, however, the possibility that a specimen of this kind might be a near-contemporary replacement for a broken part of a Chelsea service, perhaps made at Derby or one of the other factories of the time, and this is always to be reckoned with, although it is unusual.

Turning to ambitious forgeries, there are not many that are very dangerous, but some white soft porcelain figures of birds purporting to be Chelsea of the raised-anchor period, which first appeared on the market about fifteen years ago and deceived for a time a famous auction-room and some expert dealers, may still be around and could possible reappear. I viewed the first in company with a well-known authority on Chelsea porcelain, and while we both rejected the specimen offered as Chelsea, we considered it might conceivably be a very early Derby production—a variety about which little is known. Neither of us believed it to be Bow for a number of good reasons, although when I later had an opportunity of testing one of them chemically I discovered the porcelain from this aspect to be almost indistinguishable from Bow. These birds illustrate an important point which the collector would do well to bear in mind. Since they seemed to be fairly primitive in modelling and production the possibility of a modern origin was not at first suspected. Although they did not strictly resemble a first-period Derby figure we were tempted to advance this supposition simply because less is known about these wares than any others of the period, and therefore unusual objects were more possible. This is a weakness of the eliminative process unless the possibility of forgery is borne in mind (see *Attribution*), and every type of forgery has to appear on the market for the first time. It is then that it is most likely to deceive. The birds were later traced to their source, and it is believed that the original number (quite small) has not been added to, but if accepted as genuine they could bring several hundreds of pounds apiece.

A factory in the West of England has made a few fairly deceptive forgeries of early English porcelain. It has probably now closed. A well-known figure of the 'Girl in a Swing' class (q.v.) of 1752—a girl holding out a skirt—is one of them, and these need careful examination. From the same source have come some lop-sided rococo vases decorated with applied flowers of the kind made at Longton Hall and Derby. Like nearly all the originals the cover is missing, probably because it would have been too much trouble to make.

Chelsea was certainly copied in the 19th century. Its wares are said to have been reproduced at Coalport, which is likely, since Mintons during the same period quite often copied Chelsea designs and listed them as such in their pattern-books. One design in particular is very close to an important rococo vase of the gold-anchor period but has a 19th-century painting in the reserved panels. Attributed to Coalport are some forgeries of the small

'Goat & Bee' jug (see *Silver, Forgeries*), the original design based on a silver pattern which does not now exist in a genuine version, although some silver forgeries have been made to provide a prototype for the Chelsea porcelain jugs. Coalport is also credited with cabbage tureens copying those of the red-anchor period, a chocolate cup and saucer with a claret ground (the Chelsea version of *rose Pompadour*—q.v.), and 'Derby' figures purporting to belong to the 1760s with the characteristic Derby 'dirty turquoise' as part of the colouring. Certain bird tureens, very rare from Chelsea and belonging to the red-anchor period, may have been made by Randall at Madely (Shropshire), and it is not impossible that the 'Goat and Bee' jugs and cabbage tureens usually credited to Coalport actually came from here.

Worcester porcelain has been extensively imitated. This nefarious practice goes back to the 18th century when Lowestoft pirated the mark, and Caughley's mark was intentionally very close to that of Worcester. Hard porcelain forgeries with the scale-blue ground do not present a problem, and positively common are copies in fine earthenware by Booths of Tunstall, which are superficially quite close to the appearance of Worcester specimens. Attention should be paid to the scale ground which, on reproductions, is often lightly printed and then painted, and this can be seen from the mechanical precision of the pattern which is quite different from the 18th-century hand-painted scales. The scale-blue ground was also copied at Coalport, and old Worcester blue-and-white has been reproduced in Staffordshire.

None of these should deceive the collector with a little experience.

So far as the more valuable kinds are concerned, Worcester has always suffered much more from the faker—the addition of coloured grounds and expensive types of decoration to plain specimens by re-enamelling. Worcester always produced a large quantity of sparsely decorated wares, and these have sometimes been suitable for the purpose, since the decoration can be covered by a dense, opaque ground colour, such as an imitation of the prized apple-green, with an expensive type of subject added within its confines. If a Worcester plate of this kind be held to a strong light the original decoration can sometimes be seen underneath the ground. As a rule the process of re-enamelling leaves behind black specks in the glaze, and signs of a certain amount of sputtering due to the glaze having remelted, and these should be watched for. Unfortunately much Worcester porcelain was decorated outside the factory in the 18th century, particularly by James Giles (q.v.) of Clerkenwell, and although he was, for part of the time, supplied with 'blanks' by the factory, some of his work is in the form of over-decoration, and these are quite genuinely collectors' pieces, sometimes worth a good deal of money. The period of time which has to elapse between manufacture and enamelling before the defects referred to are likely to appear is unknown, but there is evidence that it might have been relatively short in some instances, and due to some factor other than time.

Sparse enamel decoration has also been removed from the Worcester glaze by hydrofluoric acid, and the specimen repainted in sumptuous and expensive styles. This was a speciality of an Italian named Cavallo in the 1870s. His painting is poor in quality and the ground colours dense and opaque. This was once known among wise collectors as 'Cavallo's Worcester'. Old tea and coffee services were a favourite with him, and a claret ground with Watteau figures needs careful examination.

It must be remembered that Barr, Flight & Barr made some copies of the First Period wares, and these are not always marked. The problem is one of attribution. The modern factory has reproduced a few of the older wares, particularly Hancock transfer-prints in blue, but these are on modern porcelain and properly marked.

Among the more unusual types of forgery is a Lowestoft mug in underfired porcelain inscribed *Abr. Moore August 29th 1765*, which even has the smudged underglaze blue so often seen on genuine specimens. This has a crazed glaze, which is rarely or never seen on genuine Lowestoft. There are several in existence.

Samson has made copies of Champion's Bristol porcelain, and both reproductions and originals are in a hard porcelain body, but the spiral wreathing to be seen in many such Bristol wares is absent on Samson reproductions, this being a manufacturing idiosyncrasy that it is impossible or extremely difficult to copy.

Forgeries of 19th-century English porcelain are unusual. Most of the factories were in the business themselves, copying Sèvres, Meissen, and Chelsea. Much Swansea and Nantgarw porcelain was painted in London decorating-studios, and the same studios used French porcelain—old Sèvres wasters and new ware from such manufacturers as Nast of Paris —for similar patterns. This has probably given rise to the assumption that Paris plates of this kind were forgeries.

PORCELAIN, FRENCH

Very little is known of early attempts to make porcelain in France, but Claude Révérend of Paris (q.v.), an importer of Dutch faïence, attempted to make artificial porcelain, for which he was granted a privilege by Louis XIV. Louis Poterat of Rouen also applied for a privilege in 1673, which was granted without reference to the earlier one of Révérend's, and a faïence manufacturer of Saint-Cloud, Pierre Chicanneau, may have discovered a formula for the making of artificial porcelain before 1700. The history of this factory before 1700 is obscure, and the records contradictory. Numerous small factories sprang up in the early decades of the 18th century, protected by members of the aristocracy, of which the most important were at Mennecy and Chantilly. Both Saint-Cloud and Chantilly relied heavily on Oriental sources of inspiration. The wares of the

Porcelain, French. View of a porcelain factory showing enamellers and figure-modellers. *After Diderot.*

former were often based on those of Tê Hua which were termed, by the French, *blanc-de-Chine* (q.v.). From Chantilly came extremely accurate copies of Kakiemon wares. Mennecy developed a more purely European style which owed something to Meissen, and something also to the later wares of Saint-Cloud.

In 1738 the first attempts were made to produce porcelain at Vincennes, but these were not entirely successful until 1745, when Meissen wares were copied. Vincennes achieved success with modelled flowers of porcelain, and then went on to produce wares in the rococo style which owed little or nothing to the German factory. The factory was removed to Sèvres in 1756, and in 1753 it came under the protection of the King and Mme de Pompadour which, after the removal, culminated in the purchase of the enterprise by the King. Because of this royal interest various edicts were promulgated which led to the virtual suppression of porcelain manufacture elsewhere in France, even the factory at Strasbourg in Alsace having to move across the border to Frankenthal in the Palatinate. The established factories of Mennecy and Chantilly, with one or two other minor enterprises, were able to continue by manufacturing sparsely decorated wares almost clandestinely.

The distinctive Sèvres style was progressively developed during the 1750s and 1760s, much influencing the course of porcelain design elsewhere in Europe, even to some extent at Meissen, and a number of innovations included the making of plaques for furniture and urns for mounting as clocks.

The interest of Louis XV ensured the predominance of the royal factory, but Louis XVI took less interest in it, and new porcelain factories began to spring up in Paris patronized by members of the royal family like Marie-Antoinette and the Comte d'Artois. These multiplied towards the Revolution. Sèvres itself obtained the secret of making true porcelain in the Chinese and German manner in 1770, and all the new Paris factories used this type of body exclusively. The character of French porcelain started to change, not only in response to the

new classical style, but because of the difference in the porcelain body used, and the superb quality of the early wares of Sèvres, with a rich glaze, sumptuous ground colours, and soft enamel painting was superseded by comparatively undistinguished wares which, although decorated with skill, lacked the charm of the soft pastes.

Little was made during the Revolution and, with the rise of Napoleon, Sèvres adopted the Empire style, which was as little suited to porcelain as the neo-classical style before it. Among the concessions made to the influence of Wedgwood may be found the prized *biscuit* porcelain (q.v.) employed to make reliefs in the manner of Wedgwood's jasper ware.

During the 19th century a great deal of table-ware of good quality was made at Limoges, and one factory started by an American produced considerable quantities for export to the States under the name of 'Haviland'. This ware is still produced today, both in France and at a factory in America, where it is extremely popular.

PORCELAIN, FRENCH, FORGERIES OF

Forgeries of Sèvres porcelain are discussed under that heading, since these are especially numerous. For the rest, many are hardly more than problems in attribution, and, apart from a few not very deceptive specimens from Saint-Amand-les-Eaux, there are no recorded forgeries of the porcelain of Saint-Cloud, although there is confusion between this, the early wares of Chelsea, and *blanc-de-Chine* which should hardly trouble the seasoned collector. Mennecy porcelain has been forged in a hard porcelain with *DV* incised as the mark, but the nature of the porcelain makes detection fairly simple.

Sèvres apart, most forgeries of French porcelain are of the wares of Chantilly (q.v.) which have always been much sought. A later factory at Chantilly owned by Pigory added the hunting-horn mark, and yet another factory in the same place founded by Michel-Isaac Aron used the mark on hard porcelain. Paris reproductions thus marked also exist. Forgeries have come from Saint-Amand, which also bought old white ware from Sèvres, Chantilly, and Tournai for decoration.

PORCELAIN, GERMAN

That Germany was the first to make true porcelain in the Chinese manner can, perhaps, be traced directly to the Elector of Saxony's passion for Chinese and Japanese wares. He often paid enormous sums for specimens, and is reputed to have spent 100,000 thalers (perhaps about £200,000 today) on his collection of porcelain during the first year of his reign. This passion led him to support Ehrenfried Walther von Tschirnhausen and Johann Friedrich Böttger in their efforts to discover the secret of porcelain-making, which eventually resulted in the foundation of the Meissen factory (q.v.) in 1710. The intense demand for porcelain in Europe could not be met by imports from the Far East, and in 1716 experiments were started at Vienna by Claudius Innocentius du Paquier, who was given a privilege (q.v.) by the Emperor, Charles VI, in 1718. By 1719 wares of good quality were being produced, the essential secret being provided by Samuel Stölzel, a kiln-master from Meissen. Many of the German factories later established owed their existence to workmen from Vienna rather than Meissen, who took the secret of manufacture with them. Two of the principal arcanists who came from Vienna are Ringler and Benckgraff (q.v.). It was not until the middle of the 18th century that other German factories were started, and then within a few years of each other, and usually with the support of a royal or aristocratic patron, such enterprises as Höchst-am-Main, Berlin, Nymphenburg (Munich), Fürstenberg, Frankenthal, and Ludwigsburg came into existence.

From its inception till the beginning of the Seven Years' War in 1757, when the factory was occupied by Frederick the Great, Meissen took the lead, and its wares were wildly fashionable throughout Europe. In England the Chelsea factory relied heavily on imports from Meissen for inspiration during the red-anchor period (1752–1755), even proposing to buy porcelain from Germany for the purpose of copying it. From about 1757, however, the lead began to pass to Sèvres in France, and to the other German factories, and ultimately imports of Wedgwood's creamware made such inroads into the markets supplied by Meissen and most other German factories that they all experienced considerable financial difficulties, many closing at the end of the 18th century.

The early wares of the Meissen factory were inspired especially by Japanese porcelain decorated in the Kakiemon style, but under the direction of the *Obermaler*, J. G. Höroldt, a distinctive European style was soon developed, miniature landscape painting of various kinds decorating a great deal of the wares of the period. Figure-modelling, at first much dependent on ivory-carving for inspiration, developed, under J. J. Kändler, into an important aspect of the decorative arts of the time. At the time this small sculpture (*Kleinplastik*) was primarily intended as table-decoration (q.v.), and most such figures belong to a set with a common theme. Many of the other German factories took their inspiration from Meissen, sometimes to the point of copying Meissen models and adding a deceptive mark, but Vienna developed a style of its own, and some remarkable figure-modelling was done at Nymphenburg by F. A. Bustelli (q.v.).

During the 19th century Meissen, Berlin, and Nymphenburg continued to produce porcelain of fine quality, although much of it was based on former styles. All these factories are still working today, and producing high-quality wares. Berlin and Nymphenburg are in West Germany, and Meissen in East Germany.

Towards the end of the 18th century many small factories sprang up in Thuringia, and this became a centre for the manufacture of large quantities of cheap decorative porcelain in the 19th century, made by such factories as that of Voigt Brothers of Sitzendorf. The 19th-century wares are very common, but of poor quality. Those of the 18th century have a good deal of interest for collectors of German porcelain.

A special feature of German porcelain is distinguished painting done by *Hausmaler* (q.v.)—painters who bought their porcelain in white from the factories and decorated it at home in enamel colours.

PORCELAIN, GERMAN, FORGERIES OF

The wares to which the forger has principally devoted his attention are those of Meissen (q.v.), and most are obvious to those well acquainted with genuine specimens. The present Nymphenburg factory, with the inestimable advantage of possessing the old moulds, cannot produce an Italian Comedy figure by Bustelli which is not perfectly obvious to expert eyes as modern work. It is therefore hardly likely that, however well equipped, a forger will be able to do better. The Nymphenburg products, incidentally, have impressed identifying marks under the base.

Nevertheless, not everyone is an expert, and the collector wants to know what the possibilities are. To begin with the most obvious, there are a large number of wares on the market, usually cups and saucers but a few vases, marked with the *A R* monogram of Augustus the Strong and his successor, Augustus III. These should deceive no one. They are decorated with Watteau subjects and panels of flowers on a yellow, maroon, or turquoise ground alternately, and this is a scheme used by the factory itself in the 1750s, but never with an *A R* mark which was reserved for important wares and not used otherwise. All are the work of Mme Helena Wolfsohn of Dresden, against whom the factory took action in the 1870s, forcing her to change her mark to a crown with 'Dresden' immediately underneath. This is the 'Crown Dresden' of the provincial auctioneer. Meyer and Sohn used the Meissen crossed-swords mark with the letter *M* between the hilts about the same time.

The firm of Karl Thieme of Potschappel made some not very dangerous copies, but they later became the Sächsische Porzellanfabrik and copied the highly valued crinoline groups of Kändler, including the one often said to be a portrait of Countess Kösel (one of Augustus the Strong's many mistresses), well enough to deceive several collectors before World War I. Some of them figured in the notorious case of Dickins v. Ellis early this century, wherein was proved the old aphorism: there are three kinds of liars—liars, damned liars, and expert witnesses. Very deceptive forgeries were made by Weise of Dresden, and Samson (q.v.) has always reproduced Meissen figures, especially birds, and has also copied the work of other German factories. There seems no doubt that, in the 19th century, the Meissen factory itself was prepared to supply reproductions of old figures from moulds in its possession.

Some very dangerous forgeries have been made in recent years in Berlin. These are *chinoiseries* in gold silhouette, a very highly valued type, which are on genuine porcelain of the Böttger period. They are especially difficult to detect for this reason, but genuine gold-silhouette work always shows signs of wear from rubbing, whereas one examined by the writer was in pristine condition, which was, to say the least, a cause for grave suspicion.

Dressel, Kister & Co. of Passau have made dangerous copies, not only of Meissen figures, but those of Ludwigsburg, Frankenthal, and Höchst. Those of Höchst have been given the old 'wheel' mark from the electoral arms. Poor copies have been made by Voigt Brothers of Sitzendorf, in Thuringia, and these should deceive no one but a novice.

In many cases old moulds survived. The present Nymphenburg factory has those of the 18th-century factory, and of Frankenthal, and uses them to make legitimate reproductions which are properly marked. The moulds of Höchst after the closure of the factory in 1796, and especially those of figures by Melchior, found their way to Müller at Damm, near Aschaffenburg, who used them, early in the 19th century, to make earthenware copies. They may later have come into the possession of Dressel, Kister & Co. at Passau. Old Ludwigsburg moulds were used at Amberg (Bavaria) to reproduce figures, and the Württembergische Porzellanfabrik at Schorndorf has used the old marks of this factory with the addition of *WPM*. At Fürstenberg the old moulds have also been used, and the mark *A.a.M* added—*aus alten Model* (from an old model).

There are many contemporary and near-contemporary copies of Meissen porcelain. There is, for instance, Kändler's well-known *Lovers* (c. 1745) copied fairly accurately at Ludwigsburg about twenty years later (see *Attribution*). The Greiner family, who owned a chain of factories in Thuringia towards the end of the 18th century, had numerous disputes with Meissen on the subject of pseudo-Meissen marks, such as the crossed hayforks of Rudolstadt drawn so that they resembled the crossed swords of Meissen.

In general, reproductions of old figures, unless they come from the original moulds, are accused by the modelling as well as by the porcelain, which differs from that of the 18th century in a fairly distinctive manner, and although colouring sometimes approaches the original it very rarely duplicates it. It has been said that all 18th-century figures have brown eyes, and those of the 19th century blue. This is a generalization on which it would be unwise to rely, but to say that blue eyes are a mark of 19th-century manufacture proves so invariably true in the writer's experience that any figure with this colouring should not be accepted as older than this without very serious consideration. The manner in which the mouth has been painted can be very revealing, as comparison of a few specimens of differing dates will show. The expression of the mouth, incidentally, is the place where most forged bank-notes fail, and this is one of the reasons why a portrait is incorporated in most of them.

Restoration is not a sign of great age. Plenty of later figures have been broken and restored, and this has sometimes been done deliberately, although always where it least matters. The forger calculates that, preoccupied with the amount of restoration present, the buyer will overlook the other defects.

Production at Meissen was divided into three categories—*gut, mittel, und auschuss* (good, middle quality, and rubbish). The two latter were often sold to outside decorators. The practice of scoring cuts in the glaze across the mark to indicate that the piece was less than the acceptable quality was started in 1763. The precise meaning is not known, but one cut seems to denote sold undecorated, and two cuts, second quality decorated at the factory. An inventory mark thus:

N–294

W

was incised into the glaze of specimens preserved in the Johanneum, Dresden, and a few duplicates were sold from this collection soon after the World War I. Naturally specimens from so distinguished a source command a higher price, and spurious Johanneum marks have been scratched in subsequently with varying degrees of persuasiveness.

At Vienna it is said that a letter *A* denoted a factory reject, and that *X* meant sold undecorated. But these letters do not appear on white ware sold after the factory closed in 1863, which was bought by Ludwig Riedl and others and decorated with subjects calculated to appeal to the taste of the time. The 'signature' of Angelica Kauffmann appears on some of them.

Finally, the porcelain 'toys' of Meissen, which are popular among collectors, have been deceptively forged, the size contributing to the difficulty of detecting them. A scent-flask in the form of a seated pug, the head forming the stopper and the body the flask, and a *bonbonnière* in the shape of a pug's head, have both appeared on the market and these are probably the commonest examples of a deceptive type.

Generally, forgers avoid the unusual, for these are likely to send the collector to an expert dealer or a museum in search of help. They tend to concentrate on things illustrated in popular handbooks which the collector is likely to have. Seeing it illustrated, he is less likely to question what is offered.

PORCELAIN, ORIGIN OF THE TERM

The usual explanation is that the word 'porcelain' was derived from the term *porcella* or *porcellana* first applied by the Portuguese to cowrie shells, the back of which was thought to resemble that of a little pig. The appearance of the inside of these shells is not unlike that of Chinese porcelain.

This explanation is by no means certain, however. The word appears in a French inventory of 1360, long before the Portuguese reached China, when an object is referred to as '*de pierre de pourcelaine*'. The same term is employed in an inventory of Charles V. It did not, however, necessarily refer to Chinese porcelain, the only known variety at the time. In Florio's Italian dictionary of 1598 'porcellana' or 'porcelane' is defined as 'a kind of earth whereof they make fine China dishes', but 'China' is defined as 'a Venice basin', leaving us to infer that the word was employed to describe a *maiolica* basin in the Chinese style, since there is no reference to contemporary attempts to make porcelain in Venice, if we leave to one side attempts to make glass opacified with tin oxide as a porcelain substitute. In a Spanish dictionary of 1599 'China metall' is defined as 'fine dishes of earth, such as are brought from Venice', which seems to exclude glass, although the word 'metal' is commonly applied to glass.

Probably 'pourcelaine' in its 14th-century sense was some kind of hardstone, such as chalcedony, and when Chinese porcelain was first imported by the Portuguese it received its name from a resemblance to the material thus called by the French. Chinese porcelain, however, was certainly known in Europe in the 14th century, although only as a very rare and precious substance. In any case, the generally accepted derivation first given above seems open to very serious question.

PORCELAIN ROOMS

Few of these now survive, but they were once frequent in palaces and castles throughout Europe during the middle years of the 18th century. Many such rooms contained only suitably displayed collections of porcelain vases, dishes, and figures, both Oriental and European, but in some rare instances the actual furnishings and fittings of the room itself were wholly or partly of porcelain. An example is the room from the Dubsky Palace now in the Österreichisches Museum für angewandte Kunst in Vienna. This has a chandelier, candle-sconces, and chimney-piece of Vienna porcelain (q.v.) of the du Paquier period, the walls, mirror, clock, and furniture being inset with porcelain plaques. From the style of the painting, the porcelain can be confidently ascribed to the years between 1725 and 1735, and the

fashion for using porcelain plaques as furniture decoration therefore antedates the use of Sèvres plaques by the French *ébénistes* by about twenty-five years.

An especially notable room of this kind, decorated with Capo-di-Monte porcelain (q.v.), was once in the Portici Palace, Naples, but is now in the Capo-di-Monte Palace, whence it was removed in 1805.

PORCELAIN, RUSSIAN

The most important Russian porcelain factory was the Imperial Factory at St Petersburg, although its products are rarer than those of Moscow. This was founded in 1744 with the aid of the arcanist C. C. Hunger, who obtained the secret from Böttger at Meissen, but his knowledge was deficient, and actual production was started with the aid of Dimitri Vinogradov. Production was certainly established by 1750, since by this time the factory was able to produce snuff-boxes inscribed with the names of the owners, or painted with portraits, battles scenes, and so on. After 1762 it was on a considerable scale. The inspiration of Meissen is to be seen in table-services, as well as that of Sèvres. Snuff-boxes were a favourite item of production during the reign of Elisabeth I, and were often produced as royal gifts. During the reign of Catherine the Great vases were made, some extremely well decorated. Figures include those representing folk-types, which later inspired similar figures from the Moscow factories. Table-services continued to be produced during the reigns of Paul I and Alexander I, when the neo-classical style was adopted, and very elaborate vases survive, lavishly gilded and extremely well painted. Paintings from Catherine's collection at the Hermitage were frequently a source of inspiration for painted decoration on porcelain. Under Nicholas I the eclecticism which was a notable feature of 19th-century European art can also be observed in the productions of this factory. It still survives as a state enterprise.

The actual date of the founding of Gardner's factory near Moscow (at Verbilki) is uncertain, but it may have been as early as 1758. Service-ware, extremely well decorated, was an early production, and Meissen was copied in a less expensive style. A speciality was a series of figures of Russian peasants, and realistic representations of beggars, wrestlers, and folk-types generally in national costume, often very well modelled. Marks are occasionally in English as well as Russian.

State protection for the industry in 1806 caused a number of other private factories to be established, notably that of Alexei Popoff, also at Moscow, and its products are often not unlike those of Gardner. The military scenes of 1812 are peculiar to the Popoff factory, and are rarely seen. The wares of Popoff were copied at another factory established by Kozlov in 1820.

There were a number of other, smaller factories of less importance. Kornilov's factory, founded in 1832, produced wares comparable for quality with those of Gardner. That of the Novy brothers, founded in 1830, produced tea-services usually decorated with floral *motifs* as well as figures. The factory of Prince Youssoupov near Moscow mainly worked for the Prince himself. Some work of very high quality was done, mostly with the aid of foreign craftsmen. This was started in 1811, and specimens are very rare. Batenin in St Petersburg produced large tea-cups and saucers lavishly gilt and painted with views of the city.

Production of porcelain in Russia began to decline in 1861, with the abolition of serfdom, since the cost of paying workmen made many of the smaller factories unprofitable.

The Russian porcelain usually seen in the West comes either from St Petersburg, or the factories of Gardner or Popoff in Moscow. Wares from the Kozlov factory are seen very occasionally.

PORCELAIN, TESTS FOR THE NATURE OF

It is often essential to ascertain whether a particular specimen of porcelain is of the soft or hard variety (see *Porcelain*). There are a few simple tests which can be applied, and these will establish its nature beyond doubt.

Soft porcelain is nearly always slightly porous. Dirt on a unglazed part will be difficult to remove, and it may be impossible to wash off. Some soft porcelain which has been slightly underfired will absorb ink like blotting-paper, and this will be accompanied by poor translucency (see *Porcelain, Translucency*) and even by opacity, since firing has not proceeded to the point of vitrification. This is a feature of some Bow porcelain. Dirt on hard porcelain will wash off at once.

Soft porcelain glazes are a kind of glass applied to the body after a preliminary firing and then fired again. They will be altogether more glassy in appearance than the thin, glittering glazes apt to characterize hard porcelain, and they may even have run into pools in hollows, and, on primitive wares, are apt to collect in drops near the base. It was often essential to grind a footring where present, since soft porcelain glazes sometimes run underneath it, and much the same applies to figures. The flat, even, close-grained base of some Chelsea figures is the result of grinding. These glazes are also soft, and multiple scratches which are the result of wear will often be seen (see *Glass, Forgeries of*). The feldspathic glazes of most hard porcelains are much tougher and less liable to damage.

Enamels used on soft porcelain glazes often sink into them to some extent, most noticeable on old Sèvres (q.v.). Enamels on hard porcelain glazes lie on top, palpable to the finger-tips. Chinese porcelain enamels show this effect very well. Most European enamels are opaque and mat, whereas Chinese enamels are sometimes translucent.

Chips should be examined with great care. Those to soft porcelain will have a granular texture, looking rather like fine sugar; those to hard porcelain will be conchoidal and look like chips in thick glass.

Porcelain, Russian. Peasant breaking ice. Moscow. Gardner's factory. Early 19th century. *British Museum.*

Finally, a file drawn firmly across the unglazed surface of soft porcelain will cut it. In the case of hard porcelain, it is much more likely to take metal off the file. This is a test rarely required.

PORCELAIN, TRANSLUCENCY IN

When porcelain is held up to a source of light, such as an electric-light bulb, the light is transmitted through it with an intensity varying with the power of the bulb, the thickness of the porcelain, its degree of vitrification, and its composition.

Vitrification depends on the attainment and maintenance of an optimum temperature during firing. Underfired porcelain may be opaque, or almost so, and semi-porcelains (which are strictly a kind of stoneware—(q.v.) are always opaque. Bow porcelain is often virtually opaque because the factory had a tendency to underfire their wares. Chinese porcelain of the early variety, or that from provincial kilns, is opaque when it exceeds 5 mm. in thickness, and wares of the 18th century from the Imperial kilns when more than 10 mm.

Certain kinds of artificial porcelain, notably that made at Chelsea and Chantilly, exhibit circular patches of greater translucency when held to the light, and these are termed 'moons', but 'moons' also occur occasionally in some early Meissen true porcelain. The earliest Chelsea (q.v.) wares of the triangle period are remarkable for points of light, usually termed 'pinholes', and these occur occasionally in other wares of a primitive kind.

Early wares also vary in the colour to be observed when examined in this way. By transmitted light some porcelains exhibit a distinctly greenish shade, especially the soaprock body of Worcester, but the

Porringers, etc. Charles II silver caudle cup of 1661, and a tazza of the same date, with *repoussé* decoration. *Parke-Bernet Galleries, New York.*

natural colour of these is usually orange, and this, regarded as a drawback, was modified by the addition of a little cobalt blue. The greenish tinge of Worcester was probably induced artificially with cobalt blue because, while it is always present in early blue-painted wares, it it not invariably so in those decorated in overglaze colours, especially the transfer-printed variety.

Some of the early bone-china, especially that from Spode and Minton, exhibits a very high degree of translucency which has been likened to the appearance of sodden snow in colour. This is not seen before the 19th century, but was fairly common thereafter.

PORCELLEIN-GLAS (German)

Glass decorated in the manner of porcelain. See *Milchglas.*

PORPHYRY

A volcanic rock of red and white feldspar crystals in a matrix of red stone. It is rare, except in small blocks, although large masses sometimes occur. It has been employed in the past for small works of art, and as an inlaying stone. See *Pietra Dura.*

PORRINGERS, POSSET-CUPS AND CAUDLE-CUPS

These three terms are often confused, and it is difficult sometimes to say what is a porringer and what a caudle-cup. In general form the caudle-cup is a vessel of swelling globular shape below, curving inwards above, and then outwards to the rim. It has a handle on either side, and looks somewhat like the prototype of the later loving-cup. It should have a cover, although this is often missing. The porringer is a vessel similar in general form, also with two handles and a cover, but with straight sides. The division, in these days, between the two is a conventional one, and the purpose of either is to some extent doubtful. Porringers may have been used to serve porridge of one kind or another, and caudle was a thin gruel mixed with wine and spices. The posset-cup was used to serve posset, a blending of milk with hot sack

(sherry) and spices. It is not unlike the porringer in form, and all three are slight variations on the same theme. They occur in silver and pewter, and occasionally in London delft in the 17th century. The posset-pot is similar to the covered porringer or caudle-cup, but it has the addition of a spout. This was made in London and Bristol delft, and specimens are much sought. A vessel known as a porringer in America was made from the 17th century onwards until about the middle of the 18th. In form it resembles the English bleeding bowl (q.v.), and it occurs in pewter and silver.

Beginning with the Chelsea factory during the gold-anchor period, covered cups with two handles and a saucer, known as caudle-cups, were very popular for presentation, particularly at births and christenings. They served a similar purpose in England to the 'confinement cups' of the German factories. Porcelain caudle-cups continued to be made until well into the first half of the 19th century.

PORTERS   See *Door-stops*

PORTLAND VASE, THE

The Portland vase (also known as the Barberini vase), which is now in the British Museum (London), is the finest example of Roman cameo glass known to survive. It cannot be precisely dated, although the first century A.D. is barely possible, and the subject-matter of the decoration has not been satisfactorily intepreted. The vase is of cased glass, the relief work being white on a very dark blue ground. The vase came into the possession of the Barberini family in Rome before 1642, when it was the subject of the first written record. It is likely that it was found about sixty years earlier. In 1780 the family sold it to a Scottish art-dealer living in Rome, James Byres, who had a mould taken from it from which James Tassie cast sixty plaster copies. It was then sold to Sir William Hamilton (q.v.) about 1783, but he, in need of money, was compelled to sell it again to the Dowager Duchess of Portland in January 1784. At this time it was drawn by Cipriani and

The Portland Vase. Copy by Josiah Wedgwood. c. 1790. The actual number made of this first issue is not known. Twenty-eight were ordered, but not all the orders may have been fulfilled. Thirteen numbered copies are known, and seven unnumbered. Further copies have been made in the Wedgwood factory from time to time. *Josiah Wedgwood & Sons Ltd.*

engraved by Bartolozzi. When the Duchess died in the following year the vase was auctioned for 980 guineas (about £12,000 today) and was bought by her son, the third Duke of Portland, who lent it to Josiah Wedgwood to copy in 1785. The Duke then deposited it with the British Museum on loan, and in 1845 it was smashed to fragments by a drunken man. It was repaired with great skill and was again on exhibition in the same year, remaining on loan until 1945 when it was bought by the Museum. It was then taken to pieces and restored again with a considerable improvement in its appearance.

It has been the subject of two accurate copies—one in jasper by Josiah Wedgwood, and another in cased glass, in 1873, by John Northwood of Stourbridge. This task occupied Northwood for three years, but since he had the advantage of hydro-fluoric acid to clear away some of the unwanted glass the work probably took longer originally.

The first Wedgwood edition, of which about sixteen survive, was issued in 1790, but there have been several subsequent editions.

PORTRAIT MEDALLIONS, IVORY
Portraiture in all media was very popular during the latter half of the 17th century and most of the 18th. Portrait medallions in ivory first became popular at the end of the 17th century. Many of the surviving examples are French, and some English portraits in this medium are by migratory French carvers. David La Marchand (d. 1726) worked in both countries, probably coming from Dieppe where there was a flourishing school of ivory-carving. He initialled a portrait of the Duke of Marlborough now in the Victoria and Albert Museum (London). Another carver, Michel Molart (d. 1713), also came from Dieppe and was a *graveur des medailles du roi* with lodgings in the Louvre. He did a notable portrait of Louis XIV wearing a helmet crowned with Apollo

and his chariot as the emblem of the Sun King. Giovanni Pozzo (d. 1752) was carver to Prince Eugen of Savoy. Mostly he worked in Rome and carved one or two English notabilities visiting the city. Ivory medallions of this kind are often unsigned, but identification of the portrait is often certain, for the subject is named. The fashion declined before the end of the 18th century, and there are no forgeries.

PORTRAITS, MINIATURE, IN PAINTED ENAMEL
The fashion for painting miniature portraits in enamel on copper began early in the 17th century with the work of Jean Petitot (q.v.), and it continued until the middle of the 19th century, fostered no doubt by patrons who appreciated the permanent nature of the medium. The principal centres of the art were, at first, Paris and Geneva, to which were added London and Dresden in the 18th century. One of the first to practise this kind of enamelling in London was a Frenchman, Charles Boit, who enjoyed a certain amount of success, despite a deficiency in technique. Christian Zincke (q.v.) from Dresden was appointed cabinet painter to the Prince of Wales. A self-taught Irishman, Nathaniel Hone (1718–1784), enjoyed considerable success, and Henry Bone, later elected to the Royal Academy, learned to enamel as a boy at Cookworthy's Plymouth porcelain factory. He painted one of the largest enamels recorded, a *Bacchus and Ariadne* after Titian, which measured 18 × 16 inches. This was sold in 1825 for £2,310, not a great deal less than the sum paid for the original Titian in 1806. Bone is said to have executed upwards of 500 enamels in his lifetime, many of which are titled on the back. His son, Henry Pierce Bone, also practised as an enameller. William Essex was an English 19th-century enameller who painted portraits, as well as executing enamels after well-known artists such as Wouvermans. He was appointed enamel painter to Queen Victoria in 1839.

PORTRAITS, WAX
Miniature portraits in wax, either painted or left plain, were very popular in England during the 18th

Posset-pot. Posset-pot of London *delft* decorated with Chinese subjects. Dated 1673. *British Museum.*

century and the early part of the 19th. An original model was carved in hard wax and this was then cast in plaster. It was from this mould that the portrait was taken, and after the final touches, which sometimes include painting, it was mounted on a variety of backgrounds: a dark coloured wax; velvet over some material like slate; polished slate; glass with a dark backing; Wedgwood's black basaltes ware, etc. After this, the tablet and its portrait was placed in a circular oval frame which was sealed at the back. Convex glasses indicate a date after about 1780. Most wax portraits are in profile in comparatively low relief, but very occasionally three-quarter or full face poses are in much higher relief.

The earliest wax portraits were probably those by Frederick Motley done in the 1730s, but the finest in this medium were undoubtedly those by Samuel Percy (1750–1820), some of his portraits being in high relief. He often initialled his work. Catherine Andras, appointed modeller in wax to Her Majesty in 1800, is another well-known name. Peter Rouw (Sculptor and Modeller of Gems and Cameos to H.H. the Prince Regent) was active between 1787 and 1840, and his output seems to have been large. It is amusing to note that the last modeller of this kind worth comment was Richard Cockle Lucas (1800–1883), who owes his fame far more to the wax bust of Flora attributed by Wilhelm von Bode to Leonardo da Vinci, and bought by him for the Kaiser Friedrich Museum, Berlin, in 1909. Lucas apparently copied it from a Leonardo school-piece.

POT-LIDS   See *Pratt & Co., Fenton, Staffs.*

POTATO RINGS

These are better called dish rings, since there is no certainty that their use was limited to holding dishes containing potatoes. They are of Irish silver, and appear to have come into use about 1740. It is supposed that many were sold during the famine of 1847 as scrap metal. This, of course, was the Irish potato famine, and the circumstance may have something to do with the name often given to them. They are, in any case, now very rare, although reproductions are common, both in silver and in copper plated with silver. The hall-marks should be carefully checked. The best are massive in weight and deep. The workmanship is of fine quality, and they are noted for excellent pierced work.

Examples are also known in Sheffield plate (q.v.), which were made about 1760.

POTTERY AND PORCELAIN (AMERICAN IMPORTS)

The American colonists of pre-Revolutionary times who came from most of the principal European countries brought the current techniques and styles of their homeland pottery industry with them. Thus the wares made in their new country were in the European tradition. This is the case with the so-called Pennsylvania Dutch pottery (q.v.) and slip-

wares. The making of stoneware inspired by the Rhineland was also started by German immigrants in the same region. The more sophisticated wares, such as porcelain, were imported from Europe in the 18th century, and it was not until the 19th century that both pottery and porcelain were produced in America in sufficient quantity to supply an appreciable part of the home-market demand. These remarks are principally concerned with wares imported for use at the time of manufacture. In more recent times relatively large quantities of old pottery and porcelain of interest to collectors have been imported, and some of the finest and most important collections of this kind have been made in the United States—those of the late Sigmund Katz of Covington, Louisiana, or Judge Irwin Untermyer of New York, to name but two.

The wares of Meissen and Sèvres were not imported into the United States during the 18th century except to a very limited extent, and in the 19th century much of the French porcelain imported came from Limoges, where an American, David Haviland, established a factory about 1840 (see *Limoges*). Sèvres made one or two allegorical groups of American interest, and portraits of Benjamin Franklin, perhaps the most depicted of all American statesmen. English porcelain factories sent a good deal more, but this was, perhaps, to be expected, since connections with the colonies were numerous, and the establishment of the porcelain industry in England owes much to an American potter, Andrew Duché (q.v.) of Savannah, Georgia. It seems certain that he inspired the founding of the Bow factory (East London), where the patent specification refers to the inclusion of Cherokee clay from Virginia under the name of unaker (q.v.). Josiah Wedgwood also imported this clay for the manufacture of jasper ware. No recorded confirmation of its employment in France can be found in that country, although Wedgwood in one of his letters states that it was known there, and it may have been used by Sèvres for experimental purposes. There is no record in England of the export of Chelsea porcelain, although it was probably sent to the Governors of colonies, and specimens are employed in the decoration of the interior of the Governor's Palace at Colonial Williamsburg. The West of England factories, such as Bristol, Worcester, and presumably Liverpool, who were in touch with the colonists, probably sent considerably more, no doubt through either Bristol or Liverpool which were the principal ports of western trade. Specimens of American porcelain manufacture arrived in Bristol in 1764, and were probably the work of Duché, since the Philadelphia factory of Bonnin & Morris (q.v.) was not founded until 1769, when Gousse Bonnin, obviously of French extraction but probably a Bow workman, helped to start a factory which made porcelain similar to that of Bow. This factory lasted only for about three years.

Although Staffordshire wares such as the mottled glazes of Whieldon, saltglaze, creamware, and so forth were exported on a fairly large scale, no especial decoration for the American market seems to have been done until after the War of Independence, but very soon afterwards blue-printed pearl ware was in great demand in the United States, although it was not until 1840 that the process was first employed in America by the Jersey City Pottery. This period marks the introduction of the 'historical pottery' decorated with 'American views', portraits of statesmen, and so forth, at first in blue, but later, in the 19th century, in lavender, pink, and green. Ridgways of Stoke-on-Trent (q.v.) produced a series entitled 'Beauties of America'. From Herculaneum (q.v.) came jugs with American subjects printed in black, sometimes with ships flying the American flag.

The delft potteries of Bristol and Liverpool also sent their wares, including painted tiles, to America, and from Liverpool those printed by Sadler & Green. But records are so scanty that reliable information as to the extent of these exports is impossible to find. The characteristic pottery of Castleford in Yorkshire (closed 1820) was made in large quantities for export to America.

English potters as an industry strongly favoured the American side during the War of Independence, and later they did not hesitate to depict British defeats as decoration. Chief among the supporters of the American cause was Josiah Wedgwood, who exported creamware, basaltes, jasper, and pearl ware. From his letters we learn of American potters from Charleston who came to the Potteries to recruit workmen for their own factories, and this was but the beginning of a movement westward of men rather than pots. When, during the 19th century, Tucker of Philadelphia (the first, after Duché and Bonnin, to make porcelain in America) needed skilled workmen to help in the manufacture of porcelain in the manner of Sèvres he imported European workmen. James Bennett, an Englishman, established a factory at East Liverpool (Ohio), and Charles F. Binns, a relative of R. W. Binns of Worcester, founded the New York State College of Ceramics.

Among 19th century wares to be popular in America were Parian, ironstone china (or semi-porcelain), Gaudy Dutch and Gaudy Welsh (peasant wares with patterns of naively stylized flowers and lustre), and 'sponged' or 'spatter' ware (an earthenware stippled or sprayed with bright colours which was made in the early years of the 19th century by, among others, Adams of Greengates). From Staffordshire came unsophisticated figures and groups, some of which were portraits of American personages of all kinds who were in the public eye, from boxers to evangelists, and transfer-printing on service-ware was superseded by lithographic processes, the better specimens of which are even now being collected.

A popular 19th century export was Belleek porcelain, made at a factory founded in 1859 on the borders of Donegal, in Ireland, and much of the production was sent to America. A similar ware was made by the Ott & Brewer Co, at the Etruria Pottery, Trenton, New Jersey.

The early colonists of New York (once New Amsterdam) were Dutch, and they were supplied by the homeland with the tin-enamelled wares of Delft, including tiles. The Dutch were masters of the Far Eastern trade, and Chinese porcelain of the reign of K'ang Hsi (see *Ch'ing dynasty*) was sent from Holland to America. Chinese porcelain was also being transhipped in the 17th century on the west coast by the Spaniards, brought over the isthmus of Panama, and sent to Spain and Portugal from the east coast, to which the presence of Chinese porcelain in a recently discovered wreck off the Florida Keys testifies. This was not, however, the earliest Chinese porcelain to be found in America. Some fragments of Ming wares (see *Ming dynasty*) were found on a California beach where Sir Francis Drake is believed to have careened his ships. No early Japanese porcelain is known with subjects remotely connected with America, and it is probable that little or none was ever imported. Porcelain of the 'Imari' type painted with Dutch ships is not uncommon, but these are the only western subjects to occur.

In modern times English potters have continued to export extensively to America, and Dorothy Doughty designed her 'American Birds' series for the Royal Worcester factory from her studies of birds in their native surroundings, travelling extensively in America for the purpose.

POTTERY, ENGLISH, FORGERIES OF
Forgeries of English pottery are far from unknown, and some are extremely deceptive and require very great caution.

Spurious Lambeth delft posset-pots have been recorded, but otherwise no forgeries of English delft are known to me, and this does not seem likely to prove a very fruitful field for the forger. In general, except for such rarities as the posset-pot mentioned, prices are not high enough to tempt the really skilful forger, and nothing short of work of this kind is likely to deceive. Delft collectors, because of the nature of the ware, certainly study their possessions more closely than is usual, and therefore are more likely to notice discrepancies. They are, moreover, much more seriously interested than those who buy porcelain as decoration.

There are, however, some very dangerous forgeries of Astbury-Whieldon types in existence, and special caution is required in buying specimens from any but an expert source. One shown to me of Whieldon tortoiseshell ware, done by a studio-potter as a curiosity, was so close to the original that it made me wonder how much Whieldon of this type is genuine and how much spurious and done by an even more skilful hand. Some deceptive copies of Whieldon figures with a glaze of this kind have been recorded, perhaps made in Portugal, in which the colour of the earthenware body was darker than the

Pottery, English, Forgeries of. Left: Toby jug in pale pastel colours. Porcelain. Probably German. c. 1900. Right: Toby jug of earthenware decorated in enamel colours. Late Staffordshire copy of an Enoch Wood model.

usual primrose-yellow of the originals, but this is a hazardous guide.

Wallace Elliot (*Trans. E.C.C.*) illustrates a forgery of a salt-glaze 'Pew' group with Wedgwood's impressed mark. Here it was found impossible to make the reproduction entirely faithful to existing 'Pew' groups of this kind, and Wedgwood could conceivably have made them, although it was very unlikely and no genuine specimen is known, so 'Wedgwood' was added to explain the differences. Among the forgeries of salt-glaze is a cat of solid agate ware, and enamelling done later on plain salt-glaze specimens to enhance the value of something otherwise worth only a few pounds. Decoration of Jacobite significance requires special care in this as in other fields.

Creamware was manufactured at several English factories—Wedgwood, Derby, and Leeds, to name a few—and it was also made on the Continent in the 18th and 19th centuries; in France as *faïence-fine*, and in Germany as *Steingut*. This is a problem of attribution. A pottery founded at Leeds in 1888 by Slee has used the old factory's moulds and patterns for creamware bearing the old mark. The same pottery has made black basaltes reliefs similarly marked.

Wedgwood's products were frequently copied, not only by his friendly rivals, Adams of Tunstall and Neale of Hanley, but by Josiah's cousin, Ralph Wedgwood, in 1792, at a factory at Ferrybridge (Yorkshire) where the copies were stamped 'Wedgwood & Co'. J. Smith & Co., of the Stockton Potteries, marked imitations 'Wedgewood'. Notice the intrusive median 'e'. There were many contemporary copies of both jasper and basaltes made on the Continent, a few of which are mentioned elsewhere, but none, in my experience, were ever marked 'Wedgwood'. Unmarked specimens of this kind were almost certainly not made by Wedgwood, since the factory marked its wares 'Wedgwood' from

its inception, apart from the ornamental wares of the Wedgwood & Bentley period, which are so marked.

POTTERY, FRENCH, FORGERIES OF

The wares of Bernard Palissy (q.v.) were especially copied in the 19th century. Those of Minton in England and Mafra of Caldas (Portugal) are hardly worth considering, since they are not in the least deceptive. Very close are those of Georges Pull, a Paris naturalist who began to imitate Palissy in 1856, but these are usually marked. Charles Avisseau established a factory at Tours in 1842 for this especial purpose, and his nephew, M. Landais, also imitated Palissy at the same place. I have elsewhere remarked that copying of Palissy became a 19th-century industry, but very few copies are deceptive to anyone who has taken the trouble to study genuine examples closely. The so-called Henri Deux ware presented too many technical and marketing problems to be a favourite target with the forger, but it was copied by Mintons, and Avisseau displayed specimens at the International Exhibition (London) in 1862.

Much more dangerous are reproductions and forgeries of French faïence, which are common, the chief source of reproductions being Samson of Paris. Large oval Strasbourg dishes painted with the popular flowers probably come from here, and few English or American dealers know enough about French faïence to detect them. A good many French dealers are in the same position. The vivid carmine of old Strasbourg has never, to my knowledge, been reproduced successfully, and Samson's copies are not difficult to detect to anyone with knowledge of the old ware. The old faïence of Nevers, especially that with the *bleu Persan* ground and white enamel painting, was being copied in the 19th century by Montagon, and since. The faïence of Rouen, especially that decorated with *lambrequins* (q.v.), has been reproduced, although some dishes have a footring, which never occurs on old wares. Some were done at Nevers, at a factory founded in 1850, and others at Quimper (Finistère), especially after 1872. When a red enamel is employed to decorate genuine Rouen ware it will be found to have a 'burst bubble' effect, which is one way of being reasonably certain of the attribution.

Marseille is an especial target, and in these days much of what one sees with the *VP* mark of the Widow Perrin is spurious. The copper-green enamel of Honoré Savy has also been copied, but less frequently. The wares of Moustiers have not escaped attention, and the mark of Lille, with the date, 1757, is a positive danger-sign. The making of faïence was revived at Aprey from 1806 to 1885, and reproductions of 18th-century wares were undertaken, sometimes from the old moulds. Mugs painted in blue with an Oriental horseman and a palm tree, which are not uncommon in England (I have seen several for sale), came from here. Samson has also copied old Aprey faïence.

The figures of Niderviller and Bellevue modelled by Cyfflé were being reproduced in the 19th century and later from old moulds, and a special caution is necessary against the large figures of lions, once garden-ornaments, which have been copied quite cleverly. They are usually accused by a condition which is too pristine.

Above all, most examples of the so-called *faïence patriotique*, decorated with Revolutionary emblems such as the Tree of Liberty, the Bastille, and so forth, and sometimes inspiring inscriptions such as *'à la liberté ou la morte'*, are spurious more often than not. They represent a difficult type of which to be certain, but they are far too common for most to be genuine.

POTTERY, GERMAN, FORGERIES OF

Forgeries and reproductions of old Rhineland stoneware are very common, most belonging to last century when these wares were much more popular than they are today. The most obvious are commercial reproductions made in thousands in the 19th century, the intricately moulded decoration of the grey body often touched with blue. These have serial numbers stamped on the base, and their nature is therefore obvious, and since the numbers are deeply impressed it would be impossible to remove them without leaving obvious traces. Makers of this kind include Dümler of Hohr, Merkelbach und Wick of Grenzhausen, and Villeroy und Boch of Mettlach. Much more deceptive are copies done by Hubert Schiffer of Raeren, who employed both the brown and the grey clay. The drab white stoneware of Siegburg was copied by Peter Löwenich, and some of his copies are very faithful to their origin, since the clay is the same, and the decoration comes from old moulds. Careful comparison of the bases of one of these copies with that of a genuine specimen will reveal the difference, since the old ones were cut from the potter's wheel with a loop of string, and this always leaves characteristic and unmistakable marks. The bases of Löwenich have a footring slightly recessed underneath, and one can only assume he did this deliberately as a means of differentiation.

The red stoneware of Meissen, introduced about 1709 by J. F. Böttger, was copied at the time at a number of places, notably at Plaue-an-der-Havel, where it was called 'Brandenburg porcelain'. Reproductions were made in the 19th century at several factories, notably Kamenz in Saxony, which are particularly deceptive, rivalling the Meissen product in hardness, which the others rarely do. A very rare black-glazed type painted with gold and lacquer colours has been imitated in Bohemia (now Czechoslovakia). Specimens with engraved decoration, done in the 18th century by glass-engravers, have been forged in modern times.

The faïence of Hanau, Frankfurt, Nürnberg, and Bayreuth has been reproduced, although most examples will not trouble anyone with expert knowledge. The *Eulenkrüge* (the rare owl-jugs) are said to have been copied by Fleischmann of Nürnberg,

and the work of the 17th-century *Hausmaler* (q.v.) on faïence have been forged.

Spurious bird-tureens in the manner of Höchst, and tureens in the form of fruit and vegetables made at Holitsch in Hungary, have also been recorded.

POUNCET-BOX

Like the pomander and the *vinaigrette* (q.v.) the pouncet-box was designed to contain aromatic substances, usually a sponge soaked in some kind of essential oil or perfumed vinegar. Ebony walking-sticks often had pouncet-boxes mounted at the top, and these survived from Elizabethan times almost to the middle of the 18th century. In shape the pouncet-box was usually circular, flattened, with a domed, pierced lid.

POWDER-BLUE

Chinese porcelain ground colour in which the pigment has been *blown* on to the surface of the vessel through a bamboo tube closed at one end by a silk screen. This gives a characteristic granular effect. The same effect was mimicked by European porcelain manufacturers (Worcester, for instance) by sponging.

PRATT & CO. (Fenton, Staffordshire), POTTERY MANUFACTURERS

Felix Pratt started a factory about 1780 which made a moulded earthenware decorated with orange, blue, and green glazes, or painted with underglaze colours of the high-temperature variety (q.v.). This type of ware, however, was made elsewhere in Staffordshire, and attributions to Pratt are uncertain. The same firm, under the designation of F. & R. Pratt, made many of the pomade-pot lids, and those for fish and meat paste jars, which have since become a popular collectors' item. By 1851, the year of the Great Exhibition, a process of transfer-printing in colour had been perfected, probably by Jesse Austin. This was done by utilizing accurately placed transfers, each of which was of a different colour. Small dots or circles can be found at the edge of the designs, and these were intended to ensure accurate location.

A very large number of different designs exist, the earliest, perhaps, being of bears—a reference to the

Pratt Ware. A jug in the manner of Felix Pratt with a portrait of Nelson. Staffordshire. c. 1800. *Hove Museum and Art Gallery.*

contents, which was bear-grease then particularly valued as an application for the hair. This kind of pomade, and the hair-preparation known as Macassar oil marketed by a firm named Rowlands, were the reason for the 'antimacassar' which protected the upholstery of Victorian chair-backs. Rural scenes, historic events, and a wide variety of other subjects, include reproductions of popular oil-paintings of the time. Pot-lids were popular until the 1880s. They are now being reproduced for the collectors' market, sometimes from original plates, but the material of these spurious examples is much harder than the relatively soft earthenware employed to make the old ones. Similar lids were made by the firm of T. J. & J. Mayer.

PRAYER-RUGS

Rugs employed by Moslems to cover unclean ground during prayer. They are characterized by a niche or *mihrab* (q.v.), which in one form or another appears on all of them. Prayer-rugs are made in Persia, Anatolia (Turkey), the Caucasus, and the Turkoman area to the east of the Persian border, and they can be differentiated one from the other by their colouring and the nature of the pattern. The Persian rug has a *mihrab* curved at the top and borders woven with pious texts from the Koran. The floral, foliate, and even animal decoration is fairly naturalistic. The Caucasian rug is notable for angular, geometrically based *motifs*. The Anatolian types are typically Turkish (see *Carpets, Oriental*), and the distinctive dark red and browns of the nomadic Turkomans are not easily confused.

Prayer-rugs are not uncommon in the West, and few of them are very old, but the Saph, or communal prayer-rug, with a number of niches side by side, is distinctly rare. These are mostly Anatolian, and were first produced in the 17th century in the Oushak district; they are still sometimes made today. A few rugs of this nature were made in Chinese Turkestan at the end of the 18th century, but they are very unusual.

PRESS CUPBOARD (American)

Large cupboard made as a clothes press (q.v.). The lower part was given either drawers, or a cupboard enclosed by two doors. Press cupboards were made from the end of the 17th century onwards, and later versions were often in the styles of Chippendale or Heppplewhite. See *Furniture, American.*

PRESS-MOULDS

Moulds of fireclay or plaster of Paris used in the manufacture of pottery and porcelain, and especially of porcelain flowers. The porcelain body while plastic is pressed into the moulds (see *Flowers, Porcelain*).

PRESSED GLASS, AMERICAN

The mechanical production of decorative glass in press-moulds was developed in America in the early decades of the 19th century; moulded glass was first produced in Europe about 1800.

The first record of pressed glass in America is to be found in a patent granted to John Robinson of the Stourbridge Flint Glass Works at Pittsburgh for 'making pressed-glass door-knobs', and this was followed in the next two or three years by other patents relating to improvements both in moulds and in the method of pressing molten glass into them. The earliest presses were hand-operated, and a steam-operated press was first patented in 1864, to be followed in 1871 by a patent for a revolving block carrying a number of moulds for the mass-production of suitable objects. The latter principle is still in use today for the manufacture of utility glassware on a large scale.

Two principal methods of making pressed glass are distinguishable. The first is the simplest. Molten glass was placed in the mould and a plunger brought down to force it into contact with the mould-walls and to form the interior. The second, for more elaborate shapes such as vessels with handles, required a mould in several parts, the mould-sections being taken apart to release the object after cooling. In both cases the plunger had to be of a shape which would withdraw from the object when it had been formed and had solidified. In 1865 a new kind of blowpipe was patented by William Gillinder of Philadelphia which enabled an object to be pressed and blown in one operation. This was an adaptation to semi-automatic production of the age-old technique of blowing into a mould discussed earlier. Further patents on the same principle followed during the second half of the 19th century.

The production of press-moulded glassware was large, and the patterns extremely diverse. Most were adapted from techniques already familiar (cutting and engraving), but the forms were often new and the designs governed by the need for ease of pressing. Some new kinds of decoration were devised, such as a basket-weave moulding which could not be produced by traditional means, and some vessels were in forms familiar in 18th-century faïence and porcelain, such as tureens and covered dishes in the shape of animals and birds. Nor was technical progress elsewhere entirely neglected as a source of inspiration. A covered dish in the form of a railway-car was produced in 1886. As might be expected, oil-lamps were made in great variety, the reservoirs often supported by female figures. Glass *compotiers* also occur similarly upheld—a design probably based on the work of contemporary porcelain factories. In the second half of the 19th century mould-blown bottles in the form of human and animal figures became popular, and manufacture continued into the early decades of the 20th century. Unlike many kinds of pressed glass, these are usually difficult to trace to a place of origin.

Many new shades and colours were devised by the pressed-glass factories, including the shading of one colour into another. Much of the best coloured glass came from Hobbs, Brockunier & Co. of

Wheeling, Virginia, while silvered glassware was a speciality of Dithridge & Co. of Martin's Ferry, Ohio.

Nineteenth-century press-moulded glassware of American origin is not often seen outside America, and the subject is much too vast to be discussed adequately here. It has been exhaustively treated by Albert Christian Revi, *American Pressed Glass and Figure Bottles*, to which the reader is referred for detailed information.

Pressed glass is very attractive to the small collector, although purists are inclined to date the decline of glass as an art to the abandonment of traditional methods in favour of mass-production techniques. The fact that patterns which were formerly engraved and cut by lapidaries could be so easily imitated is perhaps the reason why many collectors of earlier glass today tend to regard the best blown glass as superior in artistic qualities to engraved specimens. The separation of wheel-cut glass from moulded copies is discussed under *Pressed Glass, English.*

See *Glass, American; Lacy Glass.*

PRESSED GLASS, ENGLISH

Glass pressed into moulds was principally made in England in the 19th century by Sowerby & Co. of Gateshead-on-Tyne in a factory largely devoted to the manufacture of domestic wares; they used the mark of a peacock's head in relief. Geoffrey Godden has investigated their production and lists the kinds of decorative glass made as vitro-porcelain, patent Queen's ware, tortoiseshell, rubine, *giallo, blanc-de-lait* (milk-white), aesthetic(!) green, enamelled opaque, stained *blanc-de-lait*, and malachite. It would be tempting to identify these descriptions with surviving specimens, which are fairly numerous, but some of them are meaningless. It would be interesting to discover what precisely was meant by 'aesthetic' green, although this was the period of the aesthetes, and malachite was, apparently, sometimes blue or even brown, whereas true malachite is always copper-green. This glass was also called 'sorbine'. Vitro-porcelain partook in appearance of both glass and porcelain, and it recalls that opaque glass had always been employed as a porcelain substitute (see *Milchglas*). The patent Queen's ware was glass of an ivory colour, recalling that of Wedgwood's creamware. It contained uranium as a colouring agent, which suggests that it could be identified with a Geiger counter, and it was probably inspired by the contemporary ivory porcelain bodies then being introduced by the Royal Worcester Porcelain Company. Godden records that the 'enamelled opaque', which was an opaque glass with an enamel ground in imitation of porcelain, was unsatisfactory, with dull, dry-looking colours. The period of its greatest popularity fell between 1870 and the turn of the century.

A large variety of small decorative objects were made in these types of glass, and the basket-weave was a popular moulded pattern.

Apart from Sowerby's, similar kinds of glass were manufactured by Greener & Co. of Sunderland, who used a lion crest mark, and George Davidson & Co. of Gateshead (a turret and lion crest mark), while Sowerby's employed a moulded peacock's head. After 1872 the Patent Office Registration mark (see *Appendix*) is also frequently present.

Pressed glass in imitation of cut-glass was also made in large quantities inexpensively, although it did not match the finest French imitations for quality. It is not usually difficult to differentiate between cut-glass and moulded imitations. The faceting of cut-glass is done in the same way as precious stones are cut, by means of an abrasive wheel, and the cut facets have sharp edges easily perceptible to the finger-tips which can be seen under a magnifying glass. In the moulded imitations the edges of the facets are blunt, although some of the best reproductions are first moulded and then the more prominent facets sharpened on the wheel. The whole of a piece should therefore be examined, and if the characteristic appearance of pressed glass can be seen anywhere, then the whole has been pressed. The presence of mould-seams is an immediate condemnation to the seeker after cut-glass, but these were often removed by fire-polishing (q.v.). Cutting on the wheel also leads to slight irregularities in the disposition of the faceting, no matter how skilfully it has been done, whereas the facets of pressed glass have an exactness which might well be called monotonous.

PREUSSLER, DANIEL & IGNAZ

These *Hausmaler* were members of a family of glass-workers, painters, cutters, and polishers, and Daniel (1636–1733) and his son, Ignaz (christened 1676), are the best known. Much of the work attributed to them was done in *Schwarzlot*, in red and purple monochromes, and sometimes *en grisaille*. They worked in Breslau and Kronstadt in Bohemia. It is probable that the elder Preussler worked mainly on glass and Chinese porcelain, and that, although Ignaz worked on Chinese porcelain occasionally, he employed European porcelain to a far greater extent. Landscapes, hunting scenes, battle

Preussler, Ignaz. Teapot of Meissen porcelain decorated in *Schwarzlot* (q.v.) by Ignaz Preussler. c. 1725. *British Museum.*

scenes, and mythological subjects have been attributed to them, as well as *chinoiseries*, but an element of uncertainty is frequent.

PRIE-DIEU (French)
A chair with a high back and a seat low enough for kneeling, often with a broad upholstered shelf instead of a top rail. As the term implies, it is a prayer-stool or devotional chair.

PRINCE OF WALES'S FEATHERS
Three ostrich feathers; the badge of the Prince of Wales. These feathers were often used as a carved motif on the backs of chairs designed by Hepplewhite (q.v.).

PRIVILEGE
It was common in Continental Europe especially during the 17th and 18th centuries for ruling princes to grant what was virtually a monopoly for a period of years to a person or persons introducing new and improved manufactures. This was usually termed a privilege, and it frequently conveyed the sole right to make a particular article on very favourable terms. Sometimes buildings rent-free, or almost so, formed part, together with exemption from fiscal imposts, and the imposition of protective duties on imports. In appropriate cases permission might be given to take wood as fuel. Sometimes sources of raw materials were reserved to the holder of the privilege, and subsidies were occasionally given in addition. The terms varied according to the needs of the particular case, and where an industry was successful permission might be given to the holder's heirs or assigns to continue on the same terms. The custom was not followed in England in quite the same way, but some instances occur of monopolies granted in the 16th and 17th centuries which were, in most respects, similar to the privilege. Instances of favourable legislation to protect certain industries are rather more numerous, and these also occur on the Continent.

PROPORTION, HUMAN
Systems of ideal proportion in the modelling of the human figure were first devised by the ancient Greeks. Definite rules were laid down by Vitruvius (q.v.), who probably took them from the writings of the Greek, Pamphilus. The subject was extensively studied by Renaissance sculptors in the 16th century, and the more classically based sculpture of the time, including small bronzes, was sufficiently influenced by it to require discussion here.

'Vitruvian man' was represented many times during the Renaissance, but is probably best known from the drawing by Leonardo. Vitruvius laid down that a man with his legs apart and his arms extended to form an X should be contained in a circle of which the navel is the centre. A man standing upright, his arms outstretched at right angles to his body, ought to fit exactly into a square, so that the length of the two arms added to the width of the body equals his height. The head was a unit of measurement. The entire body was divided into two exact halves at the pubic bone, and the part from the top of the shoulder-blade to the bottom of the inner ankle was divisible into three—from the shoulder-blade to the top of the ilium, one-third; from the ilium to the knee-cap, one-third; from the knee-cap to the bottom of the ankle, one-third. From the pubic bone to the bottom of the knee-cap should be two heads; from the knee-cap to the sole of the foot should also be two heads, but half the length of the nose was sometimes allowed to be added to the legs. There were also a number of minor rules hardly needing discussion, such as the one which laid down that the breadth of the wrist should equal the length of the nose. There were some departures from these rules in depicting the female figure, the shoulders being narrower and the buttocks broader. A fairly well-marked departure is to be seen in the case of Hercules, who is depicted as broader than was otherwise customary, and Silenus, who is often dwarfed.

The sculptors of the Renaissance steeped themselves in Greek notions of how the human figure should be depicted, and it is therefore worth recording a few of them here. The face was oval, with a rounded forehead, and any angularity in the shape of the upper part of the head was regarded as disproportionate and ugly. The hair often came down low on the forehead, or was curved about the temples. The style of the hair, in fact, helped to identify the personage portrayed. Jove has curling hair and beard, sometimes with locks combed upward from the temples to give the appearance of small rams' horns. Pluto has hair which is longer and straighter, and falls low on the forehead. Neptune's hair often appears to be saturated with water. Apollo has long hair tied on top and hanging down at the back. Both Venus and Diana have their hair tied on top, but sometimes knotted at the nape of the neck.

The eyes were large and, in the case of virgin goddesses, modestly lowered. The eyes were somewhat deeper than is natural, and the eyebrows fairly prominent. The mouth was given a full lower lip above a rounded chin. In representations of gods and goddesses the lips were sometimes parted, but closed in depictions of human beings. The teeth were hardly ever shown, except in figures of satyrs and sileni. In men the pectoral muscles tended to be enlarged and made prominent, especially in broad-shouldered figures of Hercules, whose hair is usually woolly (a style termed *mallos* in Greek—literally, *wool*). In women the breasts tended to be small, almost virginal, and pointed. In men the belly was flat, with well-marked muscular development. In women it was rounded, and in both sexes the navel was deeply sunken. The knee-joint was rarely well defined, but the hands and feet were always carefully modelled.

Although these remarks apply principally to Greek sculpture, much sculpture of the 16th and 17th centuries noticeably conforms to Greek ideals as they had been transmitted to posterity by the Romans.

See *Mannerism*.

French tapestry commemorating the ending of the
American War of Independence, and showing Minerva
triumphing over Britain. Its presence in an English gallery
is evidence of the unpopularity of the war with large
sections of British opinion. *Osterley Park, W. London.*

Regency style. Furniture of the early years of the 19th century at Brighton Pavilion, Sussex, which was built by the Prince Regent. The table on dolphin supports in the foreground was inspired by Nelson's victory at Trafalgar. The mirror is earlier, about 1750.

PRUNTS

Medallions or pads of glass employed as decoration, especially on the stems of early roemers. They often have a raised pattern of dots, when they are referred to as 'raspberry prunts' from a resemblance to the surface of the fruit. Early prunts conical in shape and ending in a point are known, and a few in the form of a lion-mask were no doubt inspired by Venice.

PUGIN, AUGUSTUS WELLBY (1812–1852)

Architect and designer in the revived Gothic style. Born the son of Auguste Charles, Comte de Pugin, who fled from France during the Revolution and obtained employment with John Nash, architect of Buckingham Palace and Regent Street. A. W. Pugin had unusual opportunities for familiarizing himself with the Gothic style. Nash disliked Gothic, and gave his assistant the task of studying it, so that the Comte de Pugin became an authority on it, a taste he passed on to his son, who developed an obsession for Gothic at an early age. At fifteen he was employed by a goldsmith to make designs for plate, and he also designed furniture in the Gothic taste for Windsor Castle, where even the footstools had crockets. During a period as a designer of scenery at Covent Garden Opera House he had the opportunity to produce the stage-sets for an opera based on Scott's *Kenilworth*, and in 1833 he built a Gothic house for himself near Salisbury. A year or two afterwards he began a long series of decorative designs in the Gothic style, and he received many commissions for churches, colleges, and houses. The year 1837 saw his appointment as Professor of Architecture at the Roman Catholic college of Oscott, and about the same time he assisted Sir Charles Barry, whose own taste leaned rather more to the classical, to design the new Houses of Parliament. Between 1849 and 1852 he designed tiles for Minton's porcelain factory, and at the Birmingham Exhibition of 1849 they showed 'Pugin's bread-tray' and 'Pugin's garden seat'. Pugin wrote to Minton in 1852: 'I think my patterns and your workmanship go ahead of anything.' Pugin arranged the Medieval Court at the Great Exhibition of 1851, where his influence was everywhere apparent. He died in 1852, the most influential figure in the mid-century Gothic revival in England. See *Gothic, Revived*.

PUNCH AND ITS SERVICE

Punch was a drink compounded of brandy, aqua vitae, or rum, with the addition of the juice of oranges and lemons, and sugar, together with spices such as nutmeg. It became fashionable in England during the reign of William III, and it remained popular throughout the 18th century. Its popularity led to the establishment of clubs for the drinking of punch, and private houses were equipped to serve it, much in the same way as houses today have fitted cocktail cabinets, and sometimes miniature bars. Among the necessities were punch-bowls, which were of silver, delft, or Chinese porcelain. English porcelain was used later, but most kinds, Worcester apart, would not bear heat without cracking, and Chinese porcelain or earthenware of one kind or another was preferred for this reason.

Long-handled punch-ladles served to lift the punch from the bowl to the glass, and sugar-bowls, sugar-dredgers, spice-dredgers, and graters for nutmeg, as well as the glasses themselves, all formed part of the necessary equipment. Punch-pots of porcelain or earthenware, looking like outsize teapots but lacking the strainer at the base of the spout, were probably used to carry ready-made punch from the tavern, as well as for the service of hot punch, since glass was too prone to crack under heat to be trusted. For the same reason small mugs, such as those made at Longton Hall and Worcester, may have been used to replace glasses for use with hot punch. In the second half of the 18th century punch-barrels on stands, and urn-shaped vessels fitted with silver cocks to draw off the liquid, were made in porcelain, earthenware, silver, Sheffield plate, and even glass. Continental porcelain barrels, such as those from Meissen, and the familiar Dutch delft boy astride a barrel, were for wine or spirits, and are not to be confused with punch vessels. Punch-glasses, like tumblers but with handles and specially treated to withstand hot liquids, were sold from about 1770 onwards. The usual form of punch-glass had a conical straight-sided bowl on a baluster stem, and some bear appropriate inscriptions, although the greater majority are plain and undecorated for obvious reasons.

See *Toddy Glasses*.

PURDONIUM

A closed coal-scuttle, the 19th-century invention of Mr Purdon, which has a removable sheet-metal container for coal.

PUTTI (Italian) See *Amorini*

PYROGRAPHY

The art of producing pictures on wood by charring it with heated tools. At its best the art demanded a high degree of skill. The pictures were executed with heated points on close-grained hardwood. No pigments were used, and the gradations of tone, from light brown to black, were a product of the heat of the tool and the time it was allowed to stay in contact with the wood. Blowpipes were employed to simulate the effect of washes in painting, and the same effect was sometimes achieved with sulphuric acid. Lines were also incised with a cold point through dark areas.

The first such pictures go back at least until the early years of the 17th century, and work of the kind sometimes decorated furniture, the underside of coffer-lids often being treated in this way. Most finely detailed pictures belong to the 19th century, and the artists are generally unknown, although signed panels by Ralph Marshall exist dated around 1840.

Q

QUAICH (Scottish)

From the Gaelic word *cruach*, meaning a cup. The quaich is a drinking vessel with two plain handles, one on either side, intended to contain spirit. The bowl is usually almost hemispherical, but the diameter is greater than the depth. Most examples are set on a low foot. The handles project at right angles from the top, being disposed much in the same way as with the *écuelle* (q.v.), which the quaich somewhat resembles. The handles are nearly always turned over at the end.

The earliest quaiches were probably carved from solid wood, but by the 17th century they were being turned on the lathe. Some were made of staves, like a miniature barrel, with a silver rim and foot, and some silver examples have vertical lines engraved on the outside reminiscent of the appearance of the staves. By the end of the 17th century wooden quaiches were being mounted with silver, and the interior was sometimes lined with the same metal.

Examples entirely of silver are often decorated with engraved floral patterns, including the Jacobite rose, but rarely the thistle. The pewter quaich is very rare.

Few were made after the middle of the 18th-century, but there was a brief revival under the influence of Walter Scott's medievalism at the beginning of the 19th century, and a few have been made more recently. The hall-marks should be checked.

QUALITY

The quality of any object nearly always determines its real value. Age and rarity are usually secondary considerations. Good quality may be said to consist in a general excellence of design, allied to a high level of craftsmanship and materials carefully chosen for their suitability for the purpose, taken in this order.

The ability to estimate quality comes with experience, and it is the product of seeing and comparing carefully many examples of the same kind, both good and bad. This can be done in museums, salerooms, dealers' showrooms, and country-houses open to the public.

Understanding of true quality also comes from the acquisition of knowledge which will enable comparisons to be made intelligently.

The collector is wise always to buy the best quality he can afford. Objects of this kind, although more expensive in the first place, are more satisfactory to own and easier to sell. They also appreciate in value more quickly and to a greater extent than those of poor quality.

QUARE, DANIEL (?1632–1724)

Noted English clockmaker, perhaps second only to Tompion (q.v.). He was a member of the Clockmakers' Company in 1671, and Master in 1708. He became clockmaker to George I, and invented a repeater watch mechanism. Barometers by Quare are also much sought. Like Tompion he made a long-case clock, now at Hampton Court, which goes for twelve months with one winding.

QUARTERING

A method of ornamenting flat surfaces with sheets of veneer. Two of the sheets from a set of four which had been sliced successively, and therefore had the same figure, were reversed and juxtaposed with the other two. This gave a large panel of four sheets, of which two of the quarters were mirror-images of the other two. It was usually employed for comparatively large surfaces, such as fall-fronts to writing-cabinets and bureaux, especially in England at the beginning of the 18th century, although it also occurs on furniture from elsewhere.

QUARTETTO TABLES

A nest of four small tables fitting one under the other. The design appears to have originated with Thomas Sheraton (q.v.).

QUARTIERI, A (Italian)

A design used on Italian *maiolica* (and in France, at Lyon and Nevers) in which the decoration on a plate is divided on the rim radially into six or eight panels filled in with a scale pattern, foliate ornament, etc.

QUIMPER (Loc Maria) FAÏENCE

In Britanny the factory of Quimper was second only to those of Rennes. It was founded by a Marseille worker, Jean-Baptiste Bosquet, in 1690, and continued by his son. The factory was at Loc Maria. Pierre Bosquet's daughter married a potter from Nevers called Belleveaux who had been employed in the factory since 1722. He became director, and invited Pierre Caussy (son of the original Caussy at Rouen—q.v.) to join him. After 1749 Caussy was responsible for the factory's development. Loc Maria was bought by Antoine de la Hubaudière at the end of the 18th century. In 1872 its director, Fouqueray, began to make 18th-century-style faïence, using Caussy's documents and designs. These accurate copies of Rouen faïence were marked with the monogram HB. The factory's history defines its style: first the influence of Provence, then Nevers, finally Rouen, when it was doubtfully described as 'making products indistinguishable from the originals'. Some blue-and-white wares painted with florettes were actually found at the factory and serve as a guide. Copies of Rouen are close, but the paste is thick, and the colours, especially the red, defective. Faïence is still being made at Quimper.

R

RAISING

Raising is the process of hammering a vessel into shape using a single sheet of metal. It is applicable to the precious metals, and to such malleable base metals as copper. The sheet metal is usually roughly shaped by hammering it with a round-faced hammer into a circular depression cut into a piece of hard wood. The work is then transferred to a kind of T-shaped anvil called a stake, employing a variety of differently shaped hammers and mallets having striking-faces which are either curved or flat. The work is finished by planishing with a flat-faced hammer to remove the grosser hammer-marks left during the preliminary shaping, and it is then annealed to remove any stresses and distortions in the metal. Elaborate vessels, such as bowls on stands, were raised in parts and subsequently soldered together. Raising has been largely employed for making silver and gold vessels, but some are partly raised, and partly constructed by other methods. A typical brass jug, for instance, began as a flat cone-shaped piece of metal (Fig. *a*). This was bent round and seamed as in Fig. *b*, the seam being closed by hammering. The pouring lip was then raised, and the jug was completed by soldering on a handle and a bottom (Fig. *c*).

RAMS' HEADS

Form of ornament of Roman and Etruscan origin much employed during the neo-classical period both in England and France, either in carved wood or cast in metal.

RAUENSTEIN PORCELAIN FACTORY

This Thuringian factory was founded in 1783 by Johann Georg, Johann Friedrich, and Christian Daniel Greiner with the aid of the Duke of Saxe-Meiningen. For the most part production consisted in inferior copies of Meissen with a greyish glaze. Porcelain was also made here during the 19th century bearing a mark intended to simulate the crossed swords of Meissen with the addition of *R - n*, the 18th-century mark.

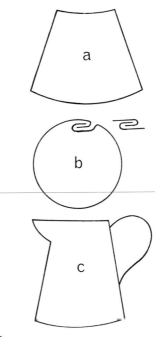

Raising.

RAVENSCROFT, GEORGE (1618–1681)

Ravenscroft succeeded in devising the first practical glass employing lead as a flux. This was added in the form of litharge (protoxide of lead), although red lead is just as suitable. Glass made in this way is heavier, bulk for bulk, than soda-glass or potash-glass (see *Glass, Nature of*), and in its property of light-refraction it is considerably superior to the other kinds mentioned. It was at first regarded as a substitute for rock-crystal (q.v.), and the application of the technique of grinding it into light-refracting facets (cut-glass) was doubtless suggested by the earlier technique of the rock-crystal workers.

Ravenscroft first set up a glass-house in the Savoy, London, but by agreement with the Glass Sellers' Company this was later transferred to Henley-on-Thames. Some of his glass is marked with the seal of the raven's head, but few specimens survive. His glass-houses were taken over, for some

Ravenscroft A rare Ravenscroft showing signs of criselling (q.v.). Lead glass. 17th century. *Sotheby & Co.*

reason unknown, by Hawley Bishopp in 1678, and Ravenscroft died three years later.

A particular difficulty experienced by Ravenscroft was the criselling (q.v.) of his early production, and a number of specimens still survive showing this defect. Ravenscroft's invention entirely changed the course of English glass-production, which, until his time, had been largely based on that of Venice, even to the extent of using a similar soda-glass.

READING-CHAIR

An 18th-century chair with high, semi-circular arms, and a reading-desk fitted to the back, the seat broad in front but curving sharply inwards. The user sat facing what would normally be the back of the chair, his book open on the reading-desk, and his elbows on the arm-rest. These chairs are, quite erroneously, sometimes called cock-fighting chairs. Chairs for a similar purpose in French furniture, but without the reading-desk, were intended for spectators at card games.

RED STONEWARE

When tea was first imported into Europe in the 17th century it also became customary to send with each chest a spouted red stoneware winepot made at Yi-Hsing (Kuangtung Province) which had been found very effective for infusing the new beverage. These soon became extremely popular and they were extensively imitated, beginning in Holland soon after the middle of the 17th century with the red wares of Arij de Milde of Delft, whose factory was called 'De gekroonde Theepot'. The factory of John Dwight of Fulham (London) probably made what he called in his patent application 'red porcelane' towards the end of the 17th century, although no specimens are certainly identifiable. The Elers Brothers (q.v.), once silversmiths of Cologne, were manufacturing red

teapots at Fulham from about 1690 to 1693, and afterwards at Bradwell Wood in Staffordshire. A few reliably attributed specimens still survive. The first production at Meissen under Böttger was of an exceptional hard red stoneware, some specimens of which are actual casts of Yi-Hsing pots. Böttger's products were imitated at Plaue-an-der-Havel (Brandenburg) from 1713 to about 1730. German red stoneware was not confined to teapots, and figures and such decorative objects as vases based on contemporary silver designs in a late baroque style were also made. New methods of decoration based on the glass-engraver's wheel, which included faceting, were introduced, and some specimens were inset with precious stones. Red stoneware continued to be made in Staffordshire throughout the 18th century by Astbury and others. Wedgwood called his version *rosso antico* (ancient red), by which time the original derivation from China appears to have been completely lost sight of and the material regarded as a kind of terracotta or Samian ware.

REDUCING ATMOSPHERE

When a kiln used for pottery or glass-making has an atmosphere which contains a heavy concentration of carbon monoxide it is said to be 'reducing'. Some metallic oxides used as colouring agents yield a very different result when heated in the presence of carbon monoxide than when they are fired in an atmosphere containing oxygen. Copper oxide is an excellent example, yielding turquoise or light green in the presence of oxygen, and a purplish-red when fired in an excess of carbon monoxide. This is the basis of several important pottery and glass colours. The effect can be well seen in the Chinese employment of underglaze copper-red as a porcelain colour, but

Red Stoneware. An extremely rare Harlequin from the Italian Comedy (q.v.) in red stoneware. Meissen. c. 1715. *Museum für Kunsthandwerke, Frankfurt.*

the use of underglaze blue and copper-red in conjunction (which calls for an atmosphere alternately rich in oxygen and carbon monoxide) is very rarely successful. The same principle was employed in the 18th century for the so-called *flambés*, which are a purplish-red and sometimes streaked with a vivid copper-blue where the colouring agent has reacted with oxygen. This remained a Chinese secret until towards the end of the 19th century, when it was reproduced by the English potter, Bernard Moore. The Chinese method of attaining a reducing atmosphere was to throw wet wood into the furnace.

A number of glass colours owe their existence to the same principle.

REEDING See *Fluting*

REGENCY STYLE, THE

The Regency style is sometimes termed 'English Empire' in recognition of the debt it owes to the French Empire style (see *Empire Style*) of Percier and Fontaine. Strictly the term 'Regency' refers to styles fashionable between 1811 and 1820, when the Prince of Wales was Regent, but the term in popular use has been extended to mean almost anything designed between 1800 and the accession of Queen Victoria in 1837. There is one important point of difference between the neo-classical style of Adam (q.v.) and that of the Regency. The Adam style made fashionable a fresh variety of classical ornament principally derived from provincial Pom-

Red Stoneware. Teapot (*Teekanne*) of baroque metal form. Polished red stoneware. Meissen. c. 1710. *British Museum.*

peii, then in course of excavation, rather than metropolitan Rome, and this was without a great deal of influence on the actual forms of furniture, apart from ornamental details. During the Regency period, however, furniture design was often closely based on actual Greek and Roman models taken from a variety of sources, but principally from red-figure vases (both Greek and Italian) which were being excavated in ever-increasing quantities. Naturally, a great deal of furniture did not fit easily into this scheme of things, although designs for chairs were to be come by without difficulty. Sideboards, for instance, had to be designed to reconstruct what a Roman sideboard might have looked like had the Romans possessed them.

The beginnings of the Regency style can be seen in the Greek revival (q.v.), and in the work of the architect Henry Holland (1745–1806) in the last decade of the 18th century which was inspired by the French *Directoire* style (q.v.) that first appeared just before the Revolution. Holland, however, was by no means a copyist, and he contributed a great deal which was original to the movement. He was followed by Thomas Hope (q.v.) and his *Household Furniture* of 1807, which showed reproductions of classical furniture from the sources mentioned. The severe and simple lines of the best Regency furniture, which was in the *Directoire* tradition, were lost in George Smith's *Collection of Designs* of 1808, which enlarged the cabinet-maker's repertory of ornament without adding much of value.

Regency furniture makes considerable use of inlaid brass stringing, a late 18th-century French innovation introduced into England by Sheraton, and bronze mounts which were in the form of lion masks and paws, rams' heads, winged sphinxes, griffins, and so forth. These were put on furniture of dark, well-figured rosewood (q.v.), in a colour-scheme which contrasted with Adam's earlier use of light-coloured satinwoods.

Inspired by Napoleon's campaign in Egypt of 1798, the employment of Egyptian *motifs* in the decorative arts, considerably evident in France and to a lesser extent throughout Europe, can also be seen in England, probably under the influence of Vivant Denon's (q.v.) book, *A Journey to Upper and Lower Egypt*, which was, despite the events of the time, available in translation. Decoration of this

Regency Style. Brighton Pavilion (Sussex). Interior with circular table and chairs in the Regency style. The general scheme of decoration otherwise might well be termed Chinese Gothic. Notice (centre) the column terminating in pseudo fan-tracery.

Reign-marks, Chinese. A Derby openwork basket of 1778 with pseudo-Chinese reign-marks in blue. The date is disguised in the mark. *Ex Ainslie Collection.*

kind was employed by Thomas Hope, including zoömorphic gods and the Egyptian lotus. Occasionally, such exotic motifs as the crocodile can be found. Marine subjects, like anchors and ropes, were inspired by Nelson's naval victories.

Taste in the Regency period did not confine itself to classical models. Under the influence of the Prince of Wales, to whom patriotism, expediency, and the Napoleonic Wars dictated a suppression of his own taste for Paris furniture, there was a limited revival of the *chinoiserie*, to be seen both in his Chinese drawing-room at Carlton House, and to a much greater extent in Brighton Pavilion, 'Hindoo' outside and Chinese inside. Japanning also returned to favour. Towards 1820 revived Gothic made its appearance in both exterior and interior decoration, a movement fostered by the contemporary Romantic revival in literature. An early Renaissance revival termed 'Elizabethan' also enjoyed a considerable vogue. All these opposing trends survived to a greater or lesser extent until the Great Exhibition of 1851, which was the turning point in Victorian taste (see *Victorian Period, Style in the*).

REICHSADLERHUMPEN (German)
Tankard of enamelled glass. See *Humpen.*

REIGN MARKS, CHINESE
Marks consisting of four or six characters to be found on many kinds of Chinese decorative art, and commonly on porcelain. They were also imitated on European wares, rarely with much fidelity, and they were sometimes employed to disguise dates, or identifying marks of one kind or another. The seal mark is square in shape, and it embodies the characters in conventionalized form. This, too, sometimes occurs on European wares, although hardly in a deceptive simulacrum of the original. An example of this mark is to be found on Worcester porcelain in the 18th century. Apart from reign marks, other characters with a variety of meanings were copied on to European porcelain without understanding of their significance. One as follows 玉 which means *jade* (a mark of commendation) was used on Bow porcelain, where it was read upside down by later authorities, and for a long time was referred to as

the *F* mark, and thought to refer to the manager, Thomas Frye.

The full six-character mark gives the dynasty and the emperor's name, and they read from the right downwards, thus:

(4)	Hsi	Ta	(1)
(5)	in the	Ch'ing	(2)
(6)	reign of	K'ang	(3)

that is to say, made in the reign of the Emperor K'ang Hsi of the Ch'ing dynasty. The reign-marks of other emperors can be ascertained from the list of marks to be found in the Appendix. Caution should be exercised in dating Chinese works from reign-marks. They were frequently added not to indicate the date, but as a mark of commendation when an earlier reign was particularly noted for the excellence of similar wares. Vast quantities of 18th- and even 19th-century Chinese porcelain in particular bear Ming reign-marks, and these were sometimes copied on to European imitations.

REINICKE, PETER (fl. 1743 onwards)
Reinicke was one of Kändler's (q.v.) principal assistant modellers at Meissen, and, with Eberlein (q.v.), was responsible, under the *Modellmeister's* direction, for many well-known figures and sets of figures. He was engaged in 1743, remaining until his death in 1768, and like Eberlein helped with the

Reinicke, Peter. The Night Watchman. Model by Kändler and Reinicke in association. Meissen. c. 1753. *K. A. L. Rhodes Esq.*

Renaissance. If it were desired to select a work of art more characteristic of the early Renaissance than almost any other, undoubtedly the famous Porte del Paradiso of Ghiberti from the Baptistery of San Giovanni at Florence would have a very strong claim to pre-eminence. Commissioned in 1425, the ten panels occupied Ghiberti and his assistants for twenty-seven years. *From an electrotype in the Victoria and Albert Museum.*

Affenkapelle, the *Cris de Paris*, and some of the Chinese figures of the 1740s. In association with Kändler he modelled a white bust of Albert II for Maria Theresa in 1744, and some portrait busts of the Popes.

RENAISSANCE, THE

The revival of the art and learning of Greece and Rome which followed the Gothic period in European art is termed the Renaissance; literally, the rebirth. It is hardly possible to define it closely since the term means different things to different people, and there is also no general agreement as to its beginning or its end. For present purposes it is sufficient to say that it began in the 14th century, and it is usual to divide it into two fairly distinct parts—the Early Renaissance from about 1420 to 1500, and the High Renaissance which, in the case of painting and sculpture, ended about 1530. Thereafter the styles current in these two arts were Mannerism (q.v.) and then Baroque (q.v.). In the case of the decorative arts, however, the period from 1530 to about 1600 is probably better termed the Late Renaissance.

Until the onset of the Gothic style at the end of the 12th century, Greek and Roman models had largely provided the vocabulary of Western European art. Gothic was embraced much more enthusiastically in the northern countries than in Italy, and its duration in the latter country was shorter, since it did not gain the same hold as it did in France, Germany, and England.

The old classical traditions had persisted in Greece and the Near East, as they had in Italy, and beginning in 1204 with the looting of Byzantium by the Crusaders, artists, craftsmen, and scholars began to make their way to Italy. Allied to this was a growing revolt against the power of the medieval Church, and an awakening of interest in the antique world as a result of Italian excavations. By the early part of the 15th century these ideas were beginning to crystallize, and the new classical influence may be especially seen in the bronze doors designed by Ghiberti for the Florentine Baptistery in 1420 which Michelangelo called the 'Gates of Paradise'. The Renaissance came later to the northern countries, being first discernible soon after 1500.

Throughout the 15th century classical ideals in Italy gathered strength, and architects increasingly

351

based their designs on old Roman models. Gothic motifs were progressively abandoned, and the repertory of classical ornament increasingly employed. This, however, was more restricted than that available to the designers in the revived classical style of the second half of the 18th century which followed the discoveries at Pompeii and Herculaneum (see *Neo-classicism*).

The Renaissance style developed principally in Florence, where it was fostered by the banking family of Medici (q.v.) and the merchant guilds of the time, but notable contributions came later from Ferrara, Mantua, Urbino, Milan, and, in the 16th century, from Rome. Venice, the centre of Near Eastern trade, brought to Italy many new techniques, materials, and designs from this source, including the practice of inlaying furniture with ivory and coloured woods, termed *certosina* (q.v.) and *intarsia* (q.v.) respectively.

The Renaissance saw the rise of tin-enamel pottery in Italy (there termed *maiolica*—q.v.), and the return to favour of the small bronzes (q.v.) popular in Roman days, some of which were frank reproductions of excavated Roman specimens even to the damage inflicted by time and burial. The glasshouses of Murano (Venice) were doing some of their most important work, and surviving goldsmiths' work is remarkable for the richness of its ornament and for skilful craftmanship.

The Renaissance is the most prolific and fertile period of European art, and Italian craftsmen especially were remarkable for their versatility. It was customary for them to maintain studios or workshops where assistants and apprentices were employed, and in some cases it is very difficult to differentiate between the work of master and assistant. Italian craftsmen migrated to the northern countries taking the new styles with them, and many northern craftsmen came to Italy to study.

Unlike the neo-classical period which favoured pastel shades, the Renaissance interior was decorated in bright colours, and much use was made of rich fabrics woven either in Italy or the Near East.

RENDSBURG (Holstein) FAÏENCE FACTORY
In the face of protests from Schleswig and Eckernförde a concession was granted at Rendsburg to two burgesses, Clar and Lorentzen. Although a comprehensive inventory of the faïence produced there was issued in 1767, the business seems not to have prospered, and it turned to creamware. The first period of the factory lasted only from 1765 to 1772, and so few specimens have been preserved that it is impossible to discern an outline or general scheme. Early wares were painted in blue or manganese with floral *motifs*. Towards the end of the 18th century the factory imitated Wedgwood's basaltes ware as well as his *rosso antico*.

RENNES (Brittany, France) FAÏENCE
Although faïence tiles may have been made here in the 17th century by Italian potters, the first factories of which definite records survive were not established until the 18th century. The first was at the pavé Saint-Laurent, started in 1748 by a Florentine named Forasassi. In 1756 it came under the managership of J.-B.-A. Bourgouin, from whose hand several signed pieces have survived, among them an inkstand in the Musée de Sèvres. A copy of the statue of Louis XV in the market square also came from here.

Another factory, in the rue Huë, was started in 1749 by François Alexandre Tutrel, and marked specimens survive in the Rennes Museum.

For the most part surviving faïence from these factories is difficult to attribute. Wares were influenced by Rouen, Moustiers, and Marseille, while in the moulded wares and figures the influence of both Italy and Provence can, perhaps, be traced. Red was not used among the high-temperature colours, the green is dark, the manganese inclined to 'bubble', and the general colour-scheme is more sombre than that of French faïence generally. Another factory started by Jean Vaumont in 1820 continued until 1878.

REPAIRS AND RESTORATIONS
The condition of every work of art begins to deteriorate from the moment it leaves the craftsman's hand, however slow the process may be. This is speeded by the accidents of time, and sooner or later, in the case of many, restoration and repair become inevitable. Whether to restore, and to what extent, are always difficult questions to answer. It is legitimate to put an object back nearly enough into its original condition, provided no substantial alteration is made to it as a whole. For instance, to put a leg on a chair which has only three is sensible; to smother the whole chair with french polish to disguise the repair is not. To replace a missing arm on a porcelain figure is justifiable; to cover the whole figure with paint or a varnish to conceal what has happened is indefensible. Dirt ought to be removed if it is safe to do it; dirt is not an improvement, and it should not be confused with patination. But it is not advisable to remove dirt if this can only be done by damaging the object itself.

In the case of porcelain, specimens which are cracked, but with decoration of fine quality, are best left as they are. The crack will still be there after restoration, and it can only be disguised effectively by an excessive amount of overpainting. Chips, if inconspicuous, are not very important, but a restorer can fill them without trouble if they are really unsightly. Some things, such as old tin-enamelled ware, are so prone to chipping that a perfect specimen would be a cause for suspicion. In the case of porcelain figures, hands and fingers are frequent casualties, and a good restorer can replace them so that the repair is almost imperceptible. A figure which has been broken and put together again without very much replacement of missing parts is hardly to be despised if rare and of good quality otherwise, and although the old prejudice against a figure which

352

has had the head broken off and replaced dies hard, this is no more serious, if restoration is not called for, than a similar accident to an arm. On the other hand, if the head has been heavily restored, or even a replacement, this is a much more serious matter than a restored or replaced arm, since it can fairly be regarded as the most important part.

Repair, restoration, and alterations to old silver are the subject of several Acts of Parliament in England. It is illegal to add any substantial quantity of metal to something which has previously been hall-marked without resubmission to the Assay Office for the additions to be assayed and marked. It is not an offence to remove decoration, nor to remove dents and make similar small repairs, but the character of the object must not be altered. For example, it is illegal to make a mustard-pot out of a small mug.

Furniture nearly always needs repair, although the extent varies. Replacement of missing pieces of veneer or marquetry, the relining of drawers, and work necessary to maintain structural stability are essential and legitimate. An object must be preserved, it must be sightly, and it must be serviceable. But if the piece is extensively repaired and is subsequently sold, then the dealer in England must consider the position arising under the Misrepresentation Act of 1967 and the Trade Descriptions Act of 1968. A chest made up out of pieces of old wood cannot be regarded as properly described if this fact is not stated, and to make a set of twelve chairs by cannibalizing six or eight old ones and adding fresh parts is not a legitimate repair.

Modern central-heating is very dangerous to much old furniture, and it poses many problems, especially with veneered and mahogany specimens. The reason is the excessive dryness of the atmosphere which this form of heating engenders. Glue completely dries out, it crystallizes as can be seen if a joint is pulled apart, and it becomes brittle, losing its adhesive qualities. As a result glued joints become loose and veneers lift, to be caught by a careless duster and broken off. They rise from the carcass in bubbles. Warping of panels and table-tops sometimes takes place, and all this needs specialized and expensive professional attention. In the case of warping and loose joints, immediate removal to a normally humid atmosphere in the very early stages will sometimes cure it, but professional help is often required.

If warping is allowed to proceed beyond the initial stages then it is quite often irreversible, and in any case the affected part usually needs to be refinished after it has been straightened with loss of the patina. Effective humidification is often the answer to the problem, but damage still sometimes occurs unless the furniture is subjected to the new conditions gradually, so that moisture present in the wood is not dried out too quickly, or to an excessive and dangerous degree. Furniture which is principally prone to suffer in this way is that of the 18th century, and especially veneered case-furniture. Warping can also occur as a result of leaving furniture

exposed to strong sunlight through a window. Generally, moisture is less of a problem, although furniture which has taken up a considerable amount needs to be dried out slowly over weeks or months, and the surface appearance is sometimes affected by it.

Skilled restorers are not always easy to find, and the best are necessarily men of a high degree of skill in several associated arts. Their charges may sometimes seem high, but what is apparently a simple job is often difficult and time-consuming. As a rule, plain pieces are much more difficult to repair satisfactorily than those with a lot of elaborately modelled or carved work, where the new work can more easily be blended with the old. Such is the demand for their services at present that many amateurish restorers are setting up in business. It is safest to rely on recommendations, and most dealers will arrange for repairs to be done, or recommend a reliable man to undertake them.

REPLICA

An exact copy of a work of art, either made at the time or at a later date. An example is the replica of the *bureau de roi Louis Quinze* by Dasson in the Wallace Collection, the original, at Versailles, being by Oeben and Riesener.

REPOUSSÉ

The art of raising ornament in low relief *from the back*, usually in copper or one of the precious metals, using punches of various shapes and a hammer. The metal is supported on a yielding pitch block during the process. The making of relief ornament in this way is extremely ancient, and such objects have been mass-produced, especially in copper and brass, by hammering a flat sheet into the hollows of an intaglio mould carved from hard wood.

Forgeries of *repoussé* work have been produced, mostly in the 19th century, by electrotyping, using a mould taken from a genuine original. These are not difficult to detect, since the back only imperfectly follows the front.

RESTORATION, THE

By this term is understood the reign of Charles II in England, from 1660 (the end of the Commonwealth) to 1685. The accession of Charles II brought an immediate revulsion from the plainness and severity of the Puritan styles of the Commonwealth. Walnut began to replace oak; the Queen, Catherine of Braganza, brought Portuguese and Chinese influence; and imports of works of art from the Continent, as well as the Far East, greatly increased. Silver became very fashionable, and silver toilet-services were in the room of every maid of honour at Court. Silver furniture (q.v.) was made in emulation of the furnishings of Louis XIV, and plans were drawn up for the rebuilding of Whitehall Palace (destroyed by fire in 1698) in imitation of Versailles. This project came to nothing because Parliament refused to vote the necessary money. The Revocation of the Edict of Nantes in 1685, which brought Huguenot work-men to England, and the accession of William and Mary, who brought Dutch workmen in their train, helped to modify and develop the Restoration style towards the creation of that of Queen Anne. Jacobean, Carolean, or Late Stuart are all terms used to describe the Restoration period.

REVERE, PAUL (1735–1818)
American silversmith working at Boston who suc-ceeded his father Paul I Revere (1702–1754) at the latter's death. Of Huguenot descent, Paul II Revere was very active politically, and took part in the Boston Tea Party in 1773. In 1775 he rode from Charleston to Lexington, rousing the minute-men as he went, and in so doing inspired Longfellow's poem. He became a lieutenant-colonel of artillery, reverting to his trade of silversmith with the coming of peace in 1780.

See *Silver, American.*

RÉVÉREND, CLAUDE AND FRANÇOIS
In 1664 a privilege (q.v.) was granted to these two men for the manufacture of porcelain in France. They seem to have been Paris merchants who im-ported delft from Holland, and the privilege gave them the sole right to manufacture porcelain in the Chinese manner in and around Paris for a term of 50 years. There is record that François Révérend employed Dutch workmen in 1667 at a factory near Saint-Cloud on the western outskirts of Paris, whence came some of the tiles in all probability for the Trianon de Porcelaine built three years later. This factory was under the direction of one Morin, almost certainly to be identified with François de Morin who read a paper on the manu-facture of porcelain to the Académie des Sciences in 1692. In 1698 Dr Martin Lister (*A Journey to Paris*) described visiting a porcelain factory at Saint-Cloud making 'chocolate cups and the furniture of tea-tables' in porcelain, and he records seeing M. Morin, who for 25 years had experimented with porcelain, reaching a successful conclusion three years before. From Lister's description it appears to have been a soft porcelain primarily composed of clay mixed with ground soda-glass (see *Glass, Nature of*). Morin was apparently a member of the Académie des Sciences, for elsewhere Lister records visiting him at home, and describes him as a man 'very curious in minerals'. This has led the writer to postulate the existence of a second factory at Saint-Cloud (q.v.), and to suggest that a few surviving pieces marked with the initials *A.P.* and a star might be his work.

See *Saint Cloud, Porcelain of.*

RHINELAND STONEWARE
The German term for stoneware is *Steinzeug*, and Rhineland stoneware is much more familiar from 19th-century reproductions which are common in the shops of small antique dealers. Early examples, however, still exist in fair numbers, and are some-times found among the reproductions. Most examples are tankards, jugs, and bottles intended for the service of beer or wine. The decoration of early examples takes the form of moulded pictorial reliefs, and inscriptions are common at all periods. Later decoration is often impressed or incised. The ware was fired to a high temperature which fused a natural mixture of clay and silica in one form or another to an impervious stoneware which is un-usually hard (see *Hardness of Materials*). Although manufacture began as far back as 1300 the most sought specimens belong to the 16th and 17th centuries, and were made at Cologne and Frechen, Siegburg, Raeren, and in the Westerwald (Höhr, Grenzhausen, and Grenzau). Rhenish stonewares were wheel-thrown, and they were cut from the wheel with string, leaving a flat base which, in firing, became slightly concave. The string-marks are usually apparent. Some later reproductions, made in clay from the same beds and decorated with reliefs from some of the old moulds, are accused by a slightly recessed footring, and this is always a danger-signal. Glazing was with salt (see *Salt-glaze*).

Exceptionally important 'finds' have been made during excavations at Cologne in the course of re-building after the last war, and this was one of the principal centres of the industry. The Elers Brothers (q.v.), who may have introduced stoneware to England, came originally from Cologne, and many of the large, round-bellied jugs with a bearded mask on the neck were made here. These were called Bellarmines (q.v.) in England, and *Bartmannkrüge* (bearded-man jugs) in Germany. Cologne stoneware was covered with a brown glaze over a grey body.

At Siegburg the industry was virtually brought to an end in 1632 after the town was looted by the Swedish army, but many of the finest examples of Rhenish stoneware came from here. A white clay was used, and the best known of Siegburg potters was Anno Knütgen, whose work is generally in a late Gothic style with some elements of Renaissance ornament. He was later at Höhr in the Westerwald. White stoneware in the Siegburg manner was made at Höhr by Knütgen and his sons. Among the most impressive of Siegburg wares are *Schnellen*, tall, tapering tankards decorated with elaborate relief-work covering the whole surface. These are known with dates between 1528 and 1631.

The wares of Raeren are of considerable interest. The early specimens are brown-glazed, and the later grey ware from this source, which sometimes has touches of blue pigment added, is hardly of very much consequence. A number of early potters from here are recorded whose work was outstanding. Jan Emens belonged to the second half of the 16th century, although his mark also occurs on much later repetitions of his early wares. He is especially remarkable for large, handsome jugs some of which are decorated with friezes of classical ornament. Working in a somewhat similar style his contem-porary, Baldem Mennicken, was one of several potters of the Mennicken family.

The wares of the Westerwald (Höhr, Grenzhausen, and Grenzau) were of a fairly standard type—grey stoneware with the addition of blue pigment to enhance plastic decoration, but in the later wares of the 17th century, and the early years of the 18th, manganese sometimes replaces blue. A good deal of the production was exported, and jugs with crude portraits of William and Mary, Queen Anne, and even George I were commonly made for the English market. Those with portraits of Louis XIV were intended for France.

Factory reproductions of the Westerwald stonewares in particular were made in large quantities during the 19th century, and most of them have a serial number stamped into the base. They came from Dümler of Höhr, Merkelbach & Wick at Grenzhausen, and Villeroy & Boch at Mettlach.

German stoneware was much sought by collectors in the 19th century, and especially substantial prices were paid for specimens with contemporary silver mounts. More recently it has fallen out of favour, except among a few collectors, for no apparent reason.

Rhineland Stoneware. A Rhineland stoneware jug of characteristic form made for export to England, and mounted in silver about 1590. *Sotheby & Co.*

RIBBON BACK

Ribbons of carved wood tied in bows decorating the splats of chairs designed by Chippendale (q.v.), and illustrated in the *Director.* They are among the most sought of all Chippendale's designs.

RICCIO-ANDREA BRIOSCO (1470–1532)

A Paduan bronzeworker who made a very large number of small bronzes, many of them based on grotesques (q.v.) taken from frescoes in the then newly-discovered Golden House of Nero, of which engravings were published in 1507 subsequently playing an important part in the grammar of Renaissance ornament. Many bronzes have been attributed to Riccio. Two in the Victoria and Albert Museum (London)—the *Satyr and Satyress* and the *Shouting Horseman*—are both important examples of his work. Riccio made many small decorative objects, usually of grotesque form, such as oil-lamps, door-knockers, etc., and his animal sculpture is unusually fine.

RIDGWAY, JOB

Ridgway, in association with his sons, established a pottery at Hanley (Staffordshire) in 1794, and this was removed to Cauldon Place Works at Shelton, not far away, in 1802. Here they manufactured pottery, porcelain, and 'stone' china. From 1814 to 1830 the firm was conducted by John and William Ridgway, Job Ridgway's sons, but this partnership was dissolved in 1830, John remaining at Cauldon Place and William removing to Bell Bank. They made 'stone' china in large quantities. Their porcelain was good in quality and well painted, often with coloured grounds and gilding. Wedgwood's basaltes and jaspers were imitated occasionally. The enterprise was taken over by 1855 by T. C. Brown-Westhead, Moore & Co., and in 1932 it passed to the Coalport China Company. The group were acquired in 1936 by George Jones & Son Ltd and moved to the present position—Crescent Works, Stoke-on-Trent.

RIESENER, JEAN-HENRI (1734–ret. 1801)

The most noted *ébéniste* of the second half of the 18th century, Riesener began his career in the workshop of Oeben in 1754. Upon his master's death in 1763 he took charge for Oeben's widow, which was the cause of violent quarrel with Leleu, a fellow-workman. In 1768 he became *maître* of the guild and married Oeben's widow, and in the year following he completed the *bureau du roi Louis Quinze,* started by Oeben in 1760 who designed it. In

Riesener, J. H. Secrétaire made by J.-H. Riesener for Marie-Antoinette at Versailles. French. 1780.

Rock-crystal. Carved ewer and stand, the ewer mounted in silver-gilt and the handle representing a triton struggling with a sea-monster. Probably Italian. 16th century.

1774 Riesener was appointed *ébéniste du roi* in succession to Gilles Joubert, and for the next ten years he enjoyed outstanding success and an extraordinary degree of favour at the Court, executing many commissions for the royal palaces. His prices were exceedingly high, and this led to his eventual replacement by G. Benemann, although Riesener continued to enjoy the patronage of Marie-Antoinette. His work, in the full tide of the Louis Seize style, became unfashionable after the Revolution.

Riesener's furniture is especially noted for the superb quality of its mounts, although the suggestion that these were the work of Pierre Gouthière are without confirmation. Verlet has suggested that Riesener employed his own bronzeworkers.

He customarily stamped his furniture *J. H. RIESENER*, but false stamps with the name mis-spelled have been noticed.

RINGLER, JOSEF JOACHIM (1730–1804)
German arcanist who learned the secret of porcelain-making while employed at Vienna. He was at Künersberg in 1747 in company with Benckgraff (q.v.), and in 1752 the two men were at Höchst (q.v.), where Ringler was an adviser on kiln-design. In 1753 Ringler went on to Strasbourg and became technical director at Nymphenburg in the following year, staying till 1757. Two years later he became director of the Ludwigsburg factory (q.v.), where he remained until his retirement forty years later.

ROBINSON & RHODES
A firm of enamellers in Leeds (Yorkshire), who 'enamelled, gilded, and repaired china'. They sometimes worked on Staffordshire wares, but especially on Leeds creamware (q.v.). By 1768 the partnership had broken up. Robinson became an independent painter, Rhodes working for Wedgwood as his chief enameller in London. See also *Outside Decorators*.

ROCK-CRYSTAL
A clear transparent mineral somewhat resembling glass. Rock-crystal is a pure quartz, and it has always been very highly valued as a material for cutting and engraving, and for making into vessels by mounting in the precious metals. Rock-crystal carvers always had considerable influence on glass-engraving. Some, like Caspar Lehmann (1570–1622) whose workshops at Prague had the Emperor Rudolf II as a patron, worked in both media, and 18th-century Bohemian glass-engravers were also influenced by rock-crystal carving. Early chandeliers like those of Versailles in the 17th century were fitted with pendant drops of rock-crystal, and it was only later that glass was employed for the purpose.

ROCKINGHAM (Swinton, Yorkshire) POTTERY AND PORCELAIN
This pottery may have been established as early as 1745, and it closed in 1842. It was on the estate of the Marquis of Rockingham. When Earl Fitzwilliam became the patron of the factory in 1826 it became known as 'Rockingham', and the crest of the family, a griffin, was adopted as the mark.

The earliest production was a brown stoneware, but in 1778 John and William Brameld, in association with Thomas Bingley, took over the factory, and from 1788 to 1806 it was closely associated with the Leeds pottery (q.v.). Brameld wares at this time very closely resemble typical Leeds productions. A rich manganese-brown glaze was developed which became known as the 'Rockingham glaze', and among the characteristic products thus decorated is the Cadogan teapot—derived from a Chinese wine-pot of peach shape which, lacking an opening at the top, was filled through the bottom. This enjoyed the minor popularity of novelty, even though it was inefficient for its Western purposes, and it was subsequently also made elsewhere.

Porcelain was introduced in 1826, the proprietors then being Thomas Brameld and his two brothers. The styles were principally a revived rococo in imitation of current production at Coalport, and 'named views', which were popular at the time. Coloured grounds were commonly employed for service-ware. Cottages and castles in porcelain are much sought but of doubtful attribution, and a few figures were made. Small vases modelled in the form of tulips are rare. An infamous 'rhinoceros' vase, surely the ugliest ever to be made and one of the largest, is preserved in the Victoria and Albert Museum (London).

There was once a quip current among dealers: 'When you buy it, it's Coalport; when you sell it, it's Rockingham', which records not only the similarity between the work of the two factories, but also the difference in value. It is often difficult, in the case of unmarked wares, to be certain at which factory they were made. There is, of course, no difficulty in the case of those which are marked.

ROCKINGHAM WARE

This, in the U.S.A., differs from the wares termed 'Rockingham' in England (see above).

American Rockingham is a yellow body covered with a dark brown glaze which is usually mottled in consequence of the glaze having been spattered before firing. It was made at a number of factories, notably Bennington, Vermont (q.v.), and at East Liverpool (Ohio).

ROCOCO STYLE, THE

It has been said that rococo began when the scrolls stopped being symmetrical (see *C and S Scrolls*), and as a rule-of-thumb guide to the recognition of this important style this could hardly be bettered. Nevertheless, it is superficial, and there are many aspects of rococo as important as asymmetrical scrollwork.

It is often said that rococo had its origin in Italy, but this, too, is a superficial judgment. The earliest and most influential of French rococo designers, Juste-Aurèle Meissonnier (q.v.), was born in Turin, although he had become *orfèvre du roi* in Paris by 1724, but the beginning of the elements of the style can be traced in the designs of Jean I Bérain (q.v.) a good many years earlier. Asymmetry in rococo design was very much more a product of Japanese and Chinese influence than anything European, and this had begun back in the late 17th century with imports of asymmetrically decorated Kakiemon (q.v.) porcelain by the Dutch. This was especially popular in France and Germany, being much more highly esteemed than Chinese porcelain. In England the notion of asymmetry goes back to the late 17th century—a time when Sir William Temple first introduced the idea of *Sharawadgi* (q.v.). This, for all the obscurity of its origin, was undoubtedly one of the starting points of rococo, and we find it used again in 1750 by Horace Walpole at the height of the imported rococo style. It is, perhaps, not without significance that rockwork, an essential feature of Chinese gardening so often depicted in Chinese art of all kinds, should also be an important feature of the rococo style, which, in France, is often termed *rocaille* (rockwork). Chinese gardening had great influence on English gardening of the early decades of the 18th century which was certainly rococo in spirit, and gardens of this kind were laid out in France and termed the *goût Anglo-chinois*. They are inextricably bound up with yet another rococo feature, the concept of the picturesque (q.v.). Add to this the enormous popularity of Oriental art generally during the currency of the style, and the very great influence on the path it took becomes obvious. Although European art had previously to this (and excepting occasional excursions into asymmetry during the currency of the alien Gothic style) been rigidly symmetrical in the classical manner, minor excursions into asymmetry had already been made by Bérain, and by the beginning of the Regency of the Duc d'Orléans in 1715 a new lightness and frivolity in the decorative arts was

Rococo Style. Commode in the rococo style of kingwood and tulipwood. Stamp of the *ébéniste* Nicholas Grevenich (*maître* 1768). *Parke-Bernet Galleries, New York.*

apparent. Designs by Meissonnier done as early as 1724 are asymmetrical, and soon afterwards this had become a well-defined feature of the new and rapidly evolving style in the decorative arts which was to sweep Europe, from Sweden in the north to Italy in the south, arriving in England perhaps by 1735, but certainly a very few years later. Bavarian rococo, both in architecture and the decorative arts generally, is an exceedingly important aspect (see *Nymphenburg Porcelain Factory* and *Bustelli, F. A.*).

Perhaps the most important theme in rococo art was water. The popularity of shell-collecting in the 18th century suggested the ornamental use of a variety of colourful shells as well as rockwork, and these can be seen as early as 1737 as a *motif* of a very important service made at Meissen for Count von Brühl, and known from one of its most frequent *motifs* as the 'Swan' service (q.v.). The larger pieces, such as tureens, were decorated with nymphs and nereids and other minor water deities.

Flowers were popular throughout the 18th century, but never more so than during the currency of the rococo style, and they were employed to decorate almost every conceivable object — painted, carved, woven, modelled, cast, and embossed. Nothing, perhaps, was more characteristic of the rococo use of flowers than those of porcelain with bronze stalks and leaves which came from Vincennes. Sèvres porcelain, with that of Nymphenburg, best expressed the spirit of rococo, just as Meissen did its finest work in the baroque style (q.v.).

In French furniture the asymmetrical mounts of *commodes*, the serpentine curves of table-tops, the luxuriance of carved acanthus, and the scrolls of panelling (*boiserie*) and seat-furniture, are all typical of the rococo style, which in England is to be seen in the furniture of Chippendale and his contemporaries. In England, too, the fantastic curves and convolutions of mirror-frames designed by Thomas Johnson and Matthias Lock, with their exotic birds and *chinoiseries*, are characteristically rococo.

Nevertheless, *rococo* was not universally accepted. Designers like Jacques-François Blondel (1705–1774) made only minor concessions to contem-

Rococo Style. Swedish *commode* in the rococo style. Mid-18th century. *Dorotheum Kunstabteilung, Vienna.*

Rococo Style. Venetian painted *commode* in the rococo style. Mid-18th century. *Christie, Manson & Woods.*

porary taste, often excusing themselves for so doing, and Charles-Nicolas Cochin le jeune (1714–1790) attacked the prevailing asymmetry in the *Mercure de France* as early as 1754. Men like these laid the foundations of the following neo-classical style (q.v.).

In England rococo themes are especially to be seen in Chelsea porcelain of the triangle period (1745–1749), when the influence of the silversmith predominates. No doubt the designs were those of the factory's manager, Nicolas Sprimont, whose surviving silver often suggests the design of his factory's porcelain at this time, but many of them were obviously influenced by the design-books of Meissonnier with which Sprimont must have been well acquainted. The second period of the red-anchor mark (under the influence of the factory's Hanoverian patron, the Duke of Cumberland) was partly influenced by the baroque designs of Meissen. This period lasted from about 1750 to 1755, after which there was a return

Rococo Style. Lovers in a rococo arbour from a design by G. F. Riedel. Höchst. c. 1760. *Mrs C. B. Stout, Memphis, Tenn.*

to the wholly rococo themes of Sèvres. In English porcelain, rococo influences may be seen in the fondness for dishes of leaf-form, tureens in a variety of shapes suggested by natural forms, the scrollwork of bases to figures, and the *bocage* (q.v.) which often ornaments them. In English silver, Paul de Lamerie (q.v.) may be selected as one who worked in the rococo style for part of his career.

A revival of rococo took place in the early years of the 19th century, and it is especially to be seen in the porcelain of the period. It was again revived in the early years of the 20th century (Edwardian rococo), a characteristic example of this revival being the decoration of the Ritz Hotel, Piccadilly, London.

RODNEY DECANTERS

These are not earlier than 1780, the year in which Admiral Rodney defeated the French fleet at the battle of Cape Saint-Vincent. They were first made for the cabins of ships' officers, and the shape was governed by the purpose, for they broaden out from the neck into a large flat base, necessary for stability at sea. The line of the sides is a slope from neck to base sometimes cut with concentric steps distinguishing them from ships' decanters which followed normal practice more closely, although the bases were always broader than those intended for use on land. Rodney decanters are, in general, the more profusely ornamented.

ROENTGEN, DAVID (1743–1801)

David Roentgen, *ébéniste-mécanicien* (q.v.), was the son of a furniture-maker, Abraham, who had a factory at Neuwied-am-Rhein. David became proprietor of this in 1768, and he was soon noted for furniture in the rococo style of Louis XV, even before he paid his first visit to Paris in 1774 in company with Peter Kinzing, a clockmaker who also made musical and mechanical devices. From this period onwards the furniture made at Neuwied was essentially in the Paris style then prevailing—the neo-classical.

Roentgen became especially noted for marquetry of superb quality and the many mechanical devices incorporated into his furniture. His marquetry subjects included the popular trophies representing such subjects as the arts and sciences, Italian Comedy scenes, and *chinoiserie* (q.v.) landscapes with figures in a later style recalling the designs of Pillement (q.v.). He soon attracted the attention of Marie-Antoinette, and in 1780 he opened a *depôt* in Paris, joining the guild of *menusiers-ébénistes* (q.v.) in the same year. In 1783 he received his first commission from Catherine the Great of Russia, for whom he did a great deal of work in a simple classical style which was a precursor of the later Empire style. He also made a considerable amount of furniture for King Friedrich Wilhelm II of Prussia, and in 1791 he opened a factory in Berlin under the name of David Hacker, one of his workmen who was designated manager. In 1795 he moved his Neuwied factory to Cassel under the name and management of another workman, Christian Härder, as a precaution against a French military invasion, returning to Neuwied in 1802.

Some of his furniture made for Catherine the Great, and once in the Hermitage (Leningrad), was sold in 1928 by the Soviet Government at Rudolph Lepke's Berlin saleroom.

ROETTIERS, JACQUES (b. 1707, retired 1772)

French silversmith. Master of the Paris Guild, 1737. Roettiers married the daughter of Nicolas Besnier (q.v.) and, after 1765, was associated with his son Jacques-Nicolas as *orfèvre ordinaire du roi*. He was among the earliest to adopt the neo-classical style.

Rococo Style. The rococo revival of the early years of the 19th century produced this overdoor at Apsley House, London, W.1, the residence of the Duke of Wellington.

ROGERS GROUPS (American)

Plaster statuary reproducing John Rogers' patented story-telling groups, *genre* sculptures produced in New York from 1859 to 1893. The subjects and treatment were excessively sentimental, using themes from the Civil War, domestic life of the time, and popular legends, and they were an indispensable part of the American Victorian parlour. The New York Historical Society, New York, has a large collection.

ROLL-TOP DESK

A desk with a curved closure made on the tambour (q.v.) principle. In French it is termed a *bureau à lamelles*, the semi-circular solid closure being a *bureau à cylindre*.

ROMANTIC ART

The term 'romantic' has almost as many meanings as there are writers on the subject, but it is possible to reduce most of them to a fairly plain statement of its significance. European art can be divided into two principal categories or traditions—the classical, which is the mainstream, and the romantic. Classical art is based on that of Greece and Rome, and it is governed by rules first laid down at this time, even through they have been subject to interpretation ever since (see *Classical*). The origin of romantic art can be traced as far back, but not to the lands bordering the Mediterranean. It is sufficient to go back to the Gothic phase (q.v.) of European art, when classical rules were abandoned for several centuries. Romantic art is really art which is an expression of the emotions ungoverned by rules, to which is sometimes added a love of the exotic. This is not entirely absent from some art which might otherwise be termed classical, but the rules were never seriously transgressed, and the influence of the emotions was never allowed to override other considerations. In Europe the post-Gothic romantic movement began in the 18th century, and, curiously enough, developed alongside the neo-classical phase, and was almost part of it. It is also to be seen in such movements as the Gothic revival in England, to some extent in the

Romantic Art. Gothic art, because of its primary appeal to emotion, can fairly be described as romantic. This view of Strawberry Hill (q.v.) is intended to evoke emotive responses.

Romayne Work. This Scottish oak chair, a curious mixture of Gothic and classical *motifs*, is decorated on the back with Romayne work. *Victoria and Albert Museum.*

rococo style in France, and in the the revival of *chinoiserie* at the Brighton Pavilion (Sussex) (see *Crace, Frederick*). It can be seen in the sentimental approach of the late 18th century; for instance, in Goethe's romance *The Sorrows of Werther,* which was especially influential, and in the modelling of some porcelain figures, like those of Michel-Victor Acier at Meissen. In the middle of the 18th century men abandoned the rules of classical art with difficulty, and Batty Langley (q.v.) endeavoured to find or formulate rules governing the Gothic style—a singularly unprofitable occupation. By 1830 the romantic movement was at its height—in the arts, literature, and music—but by the 1870s it was in retreat. It survives today particularly in the popular arts, such as the film and cheap literature, and in such movements as Surrealism.

See *Classical Art.*

ROMAYNE WORK
Ornamental motif, Italian in origin, also occurring on early Renaissance furniture from England, and the Netherlands. It consists in roundels carved in low relief with a human head.

RÖMER (or ROEMER) (German)
A type of wine-glass, usually green in colour, made principally in the Rhineland and the Netherlands from the 16th century onwards. The bowl is spheroidal and the wide stem ornamented with prunts (q.v.). The stem is expanded towards the bottom to form the foot, which was at first made by winding glass rod over a conical former, the bowl being welded to it. The hollow blown foot and stem is a little later, and in the 18th century rod was wound over an already blown stem. In the 17th century the *römer* was often employed for distinguished engraved decoration from such workers as Anna Roemers Visscher (1585–1681).

A few English *römers* of the 17th century survive, both those of soda-glass and in the lead-glass of Ravenscroft (q.v.). In general design they resemble the German version but lack the spirally wound foot. In the 18th century English *römers* (by now called 'rummers') departed so far from the original German *römer* that the origin is hardly perceptible. Bowl forms are varied, the stem is short, and the foot is sometimes square. Glasses of this type are usually thick and heavy.

RÖRSTRAND (near Stockholm) FAÏENCE FACTORY
Johann Wolff (see *Copenhagen* and *Nürnberg*) is reputed to have left Copenhagen (Store Kongensgade) under a cloud. Accusations of luring away its workers, and even of downright theft, drove him away. He appeared before the Chamber of Commerce in Stockholm seeking a faïence concession, and armed with a quantity of raw cobalt blue, bought, he declared, at Elsinore. This was in September 1725, and the Chamber of Commerce was so convinced of his technical skill that a company was soon formed and a factory at Rörstrand erected. The privilege was granted in 1729, but Wolff was dismissed before that date on the grounds of negligence, dishonesty, and even of having taken bribes from competitors. His place was taken by A. N. Ferdinand, who was joined by Christoph Conrad Hunger (of Meissen, Vienna, and Venice), a porcelain-worker, and another German called Thelot. Hunger was dismissed in 1733, and Ferdinand promoted manager, in which position he remained for six years. He was followed by J. G. Taglieb, painter of Ansbach (q.v.), who directed the factory till 1741. Although business was good, the enterprise was administratively weak and economically unstable. A Swede called Anders Fahlstrom was appointed manager in 1741, and production improved in quantity and quality but was never sufficient to make the factory profitable, even with State support. In 1753 one of the shareholders, Elias Magnum Ingman, moved out to Rörstrand to reorganize the factory, increasing the number of hands so that production also increased. Quality was maintained however, and even improved, until 1758 when Marieberg (q.v.) was founded. Johann Buchwald worked at Rörstrand and is thought to have introduced high-temperature colours. He left for Marieberg in 1758, as did other workers from Rörstrand. Anders Stenman, who developed the art

of transfer-printing on faïence independently of England, also moved to Marieberg. Ingman died in 1773. The sole remaining owner of Rörstrand, he had been ennobled in 1758, and his son now bore the title Nordenstolpe. Under this name in 1782 he bought Marieberg which was closed down soon afterwards. Faïence had long ceased to be made at Rörstrand when it was sold in 1797. It has been replaced by English-style creamware. The factory is still working.

Styles at Rörstrand were subject to a combination of many traditions—French, German, Chinese and Dutch—but were often completely original. No pieces from the very early days have been recognized, but Wolff's hand can be detected on several pieces marked *Stockholm*. Hunger's name appears on a tray dated 1733, done in a very South German style. Figure-painting in the beginning seems to have been a deliberate attempt to break away from Wolff's German baroque, though with no great success, as both the ordinary *Laub- und Bandelwerk* (q.v.) and Wolff's own peculiar style continue through the following years.

Painters of blue-and-white at Rörstrand looked to Delft, Rouen, and Chinese export porcelain (q.v.) for inspiration, though the last was no direct inspiration till the 1740s, when wares in this style became an integral part of production. There was a long-tailed bird on a flowering spray; a pavilion and weeping willow; a flower-spray with a broken, twiggy stem; and a dead bird and parasol, possibly inspired by Pillement (q.v.). French and German engravings were used as elsewhere, especially the work of Oudry and Boucher.

The Rörstrand glaze was a variable white, but the factory also looked back to the earlier *bianco sopra bianco* by colouring the white glaze to a bluish-grey found at Delft (rarely), and at Bristol, and also associated with Saint Amand-les-Eaux. It is possible that Rörstrand used it first. The factory was fairly inventive, producing several original *motifs*: the scattered trefoil; the blue leaf and Pole star; the so-called 'Rehn' pattern, consisting of a rococo border containing different themes. Styles followed European developments, and can be arranged chronologically. Till the foundation of Marieberg in 1758 painting at Rörstrand was almost entirely in blue, manganese and yellow being applied very sparingly. The change to enamels began in 1758, undoubtedly to compete with Marieberg, but it was soon realized that it would be more profitable to extend the range of the high-temperature colours. No red was ever successful and the manganese, purple, green, and yellow are pallid and tend to separate. The blue is powerful, brilliant, and sparingly used. There was a good deal of copying of the Marieberg plastic styles, but Rörstrand ranks as the most important of the northern factories. Till 1773 Rörstrand faïence is marked with the name of the place, and the day, month, and year; often, too, with a painter's mark and the price. In the early period it was marked *Stockholm*, and after 1758, *Rörstrand*.

Flintporslin (q.v.), an imitation of Wedgwood's creamware, was made here towards the end of the century, largely copied from English sources.

ROSE

The rose is commonly employed as ornament in all kinds of decorative art, and is the attribute of several Christian saints. The rose and thistle in combination, sometimes to be found on glass, denote Jacobite sympathies. The rosette is a conventionalized rose.

ROSE POMPADOUR

A ground colour first introduced at the Sèvres porcelain factory in 1757 and said to have been devised by the painter, Xhrouet (Chrouet), although this is uncertain. It was discontinued after the death of Mme de Pompadour in 1764. *Rose Pompadour* is a rose-pink related to the purple of Cassius and the Chinese *famille rose* (q.v.). A version of it was employed in England during the 19th century under the misnomer of *rose du Barry*, although the colour was originally discontinued at Sèvres six years before Mme du Barry became the mistress of Louis XV. Variants have sometimes been used on other materials apart from porcelain, such as on glass as a flashing or overlay.

Porcelain decorated in *rose Pompadour* has always been in great demand, and it was imitated at the time at Chelsea and Worcester, where it was termed 'claret'. The colour as used at Sèvres is opaque, but faked grounds of this kind often utilize a pigment which is much more transparent. The original shade is very rarely even approached in copies from elsewhere, or in later reproductions, so acquaintance with genuine examples is the best safeguard.

ROSEWOOD

A wood obtained from the species *Dalbergia*. It is thus related to violetwood (q.v.). In France it is termed *pallisandre*. It can range in colour from a brownish-yellow to a dark purplish-brown, and the figure is usually well marked. It was probably known in the early part of the 17th century as an exotic wood from South America, and became much more popular on the Continent in the second half of the same century. It was fashionable in France during the *Régence* period under the name of *bois de Sainte-Lucie*. In England it was, perhaps, first used by Chippendale, but did not become popular until towards the end of the 18th century, when it was widely fashionable, especially for drawing-room furniture.

East Indian rosewood comes from the *Dalbergia latifolia*, and is often known as blackwood. The wood is a purplish-brown in colour with black veining. A good deal of Chinese furniture is of this wood.

ROSSO ANTICO

This, as the name implies, was an imitation of the red pottery of Greece and Rome, and was Wedgwood's (q.v.) version of the body elsewhere considered under the heading of *Red Stoneware*. Designs are

Rouen. Dish decorated in blue and yellow ochre. A version of the *style rayonnant.* c. 1720. *Victoria and Albert Museum.*

in 1685 and its replacement by faïence. All the metal shapes appear in pottery. From the first period of the Poterat factory, 1646–1696, several pieces of *faïence blanche* (q.v.) are known, dated and inscribed *faict a Rouen,* done in the blue and yellow of Faenza, or perhaps Nevers since the presence of a man called Custode is recorded in Rouen in 1646. Chinese styles also appear during the Poterat first period, and Louis's patent actually described wares 'like to those of China'.

Rouen's classic period coincides with the new century when the famous *style rayonnant* and *à lambrequins* (q.v.) was first devised. It lasted till about 1735. The *rayonnant* style is easily recognized. On large, flat surfaces such as plates or dishes a close-knit pattern radiates from a focal point. The pattern of *lambrequins* is a symmetrical design with spirals or scrolls, either in silhouette or in white reserve against blue. The design is partly derived from patterns engraved by Bérain, Solis, Marot, and Delaune

very similar to those of the black basaltes body, and it is sometimes found decorated with black figures in imitation of Greek 'black figure' vases. In the 19th century it was sometimes enamelled with Chinese flowers in the *famille rose* palette. A buff ware made from a similar kind of body was termed cane ware.

ROUEN (Normandy, France) FAÏENCE AND PORCELAIN

Rouen, the capital city of Normandy, was already producing faïence in mid-16th century under Masseot Abaquesne, described in the records as *esmailleur de terre.* In 1542 he supplied faïence tiles to Anne de Montmorency, High Constable of France, for the Château d'Écouen, and probably also decorated drug-jars in the manner of Faenza till about 1570. Many Italian potters were summoned to France by François I, among them Girolamo della Robbia, who worked in terracotta and enamels.

It was not until 1644 that Nicholas Poirel sought a privilege for a factory in Rouen, and in 1648 it was granted for fifty years, at which point he sold the business to Edmé Poterat, who erected kilns at Saint Sever-les-Rouen, on the road to Elbeuf. Edmé's two sons, Michel and Louis, were also potters. Michel inherited his father's factory, and Louis set up on his own account in 1673. This latter business was sold in 1720 to Nicolas Fouquay, who became Rouen's leading *faïencier.* The original Poterat undertaking was sold to M. de Villeray in 1726.

Poterat's monopoly expired in 1696, and eighteen new factories were founded, the most famous being those of Levavasseur and Caussy. Poterat never regained his monopoly, and other factories established their rights. Competition was intense and fuel very scarce, and in 1723 it was divided by law between the various factories. No new kilns were allowed till 1757 when a new order was made relaxing the rule so long as coal or charcoal, not wood, was used for firing. Much of Rouen's prosperity arose from the melting-down of French silver ordered by Louis XIV

Rouen. Life-size bust of Apollo. Rouen faience. Nicholas Fouquay's factory. c. 1740. *Victoria and Albert Museum.*

known as *broderies* (lace). The effect can sometimes be dry and monotonous, but in good examples it well reflects the austere dignity of the last years of Louis XIV. Rouen clung to this style long after most other places had adopted the rococo.

Till the late 17th century blue-and-white was dominant, but the palette was gradually augmented by blue, green, yellow, and red. A yellow ochre ground was developed by 1725 painted with figures in reserve, the *bleu Persan* of Nevers was copied but decorated with *motifs* popular at Rouen rather than the 'Persian' flowers of Nevers, and after 1740 the style was fully polychrome. Figures were made at Rouen, outstandingly by Pierre Chapelle (for example, the *Apollo* in the Victoria and Albert Museum, London), and after mid-century Chinese porcelain was widely imitated. Attempts were made to copy the muffle-kiln enamels, possibly by Guillibaud first mentioned in 1720, who imitated all kinds of Chinese and Japanese (Kakiemon) *motifs* —dragons, pagodas, cornucopias, and so on—in the vivid high-temperature colours of blue, green, brick-red, and lemon-yellow. After 1745 Rouen at last accepted the rococo style, symmetry became a thing of the past and shapes irregular. Plates now have wavy rims with familiar *motifs* for decoration—pastoral scenes after Watteau, Boucher, and Lancret; the cornucopia (*à la corne*), arrows, and quiver, composing a kind of trophy called *au carquois*; and of course *chinoiseries* (q.v.).

Enamel colours brought the inevitable degeneration, and only the factory of Levavasseur used them successfully, though even his wares never approached the work of Strasbourg or Marseille. After 1770 Rouen faïence declined, at first owing to competition from the creamware of Josiah Wedgwood (q.v.), and later because of the Revolution. Wares were still produced in the 19th century, particularly in imitation of earlier styles such as the popular cornucopia.

Many imitations of Rouen faïence were made in 18th-century factories, such as Sinceny, Quimper, Saint-Cloud, Lille, Liége, Brussels, and Ansbach, all of which copied the Rouen designs. These pieces, however, have a value in their own right. Those made recently by Samson and La Hubaudiére are a different matter, and caution should be exercised. The old Rouen designs are being reproduced today, but they are not difficult to distinguish from the originals.

Louis Poterat applied for a privilege to make porcelain in the Chinese manner in 1673, but little or no use was made of it. At an inquiry in 1694 it emerged that although Poterat knew how to make porcelain, he was actually producing very little, and this is stated in the preamble to the privilege granted to Chicanneau at Saint-Cloud (q.v.). The attribution of a few specimens to Rouen is probably a matter of local patriotism, and although the mark of *A P* has been claimed for Poterat's factory, it is more likely to denote *à Paris*. There is a mustard-pot in the Musée de Sèvres with the arms of a Rouen family which, quite probably, was made there. In general, attributions are very doubtful.

Rustic Furniture. A table in the rustic style of the second half of the 18th century. Mereworth Castle. Specimens are also to be found in the Victoria and Albert Museum.

ROUNDEL

Ornament occupying a circular space. Roundels enclosing a portrait carved in low relief sometimes decorate Renaissance furniture. See *Romayne Work*.

RUGS, HOOKED

Rugs popular in the U.S.A., and made by hooking lengths of wool or strips of cloth through a canvas foundation. Patterns are unsophisticated, and essentially hooked rugs are a kind of folk art.

RUGS, KNOTTING OF

Pile rugs are made by twisting a short length of yarn round two warp threads. This leaves two free ends which are clipped with scissors to the required length, either uniform, or with emphasis on parts of the pattern, done by cutting the pile to slightly different heights. The characteristic Turkish knot, the Ghiordes knot, is employed alike in the making of Anatolian and some Persian rugs, and for most early European hand-made carpets, such as the Savonnerie (q.v.). The yarn is twisted round the warp threads in such a way that the free ends lie side by side on the same plane. The other knot commonly used is the Persian Sehna knot which is twisted in a different way so that one of the two ends lies slightly behind the other. Usually the quickest way of deciding which knot has been used is to ascertain the direction of the nap. If it runs vertically from top to bottom it has been woven with a Ghiordes knot; if diagonally, with a Sehna knot. The information is sometimes useful in attempting to ascertain the most likely place of manufacture of a particular rug. For pileless rugs see *Khilims*.

RUMMERS   See *Römer*

RUNNERS

Oriental rugs and carpets which are much longer than they are wide. In Europe they are employed for halls and corridors, but in the East they are laid along the sides of the room or tent. See *Hamadan*.

RUSTIC FURNITURE

Furniture (chairs, benches, and tables) made to resemble the branches of trees. It dates from the Gothic revival of about 1750. In Victorian times it was also made in cast iron.

SABRE LEG

A curved chair-leg of the Empire or Regency period (q.v.) copied from ancient Greek or Italian vase-paintings. Later examples, belonging to the 1830s and early 1840s, have legs of sabre form at the back of the chair in conjunction with turned legs in front. The term seems to be derived from the shape of the cavalry sabre of the period.

SADDLEBAGS AND SADDLE-COVERS

Near and Middle Eastern pile carpetings, almost square, in sizes ranging from 18 in. to 5 ft., are usually saddlebags, the smaller sizes for the ass and the larger for horses and camels. Saddle-covers, also nearly square, have a hole at one end to take the pommel of the saddle.

SADLER, JOHN (and Guy Green)

Independent discoverer of the art of transfer-printing on pottery and porcelain, who was in partnership with Guy Green as Sadler & Green. The first record we have is an affidavit made in 1756 to the effect that the two men had printed 'upwards of 1200 earthenware [delft] tiles of different patterns' at Liverpool. Sadler did not manufacture pottery himself, but printed pottery and porcelain for a number of manufacturers, especially for Wedgwood. He retired in 1770 and died in 1789, the firm being continued by his partner. Sadler's notebook, with details of a variety of ceramic processes, is in the Liverpool Public Library. See *Battersea Enamels, Transfer-printing.*

SAINT-AMAND-LES-EAUX (Nord, France) FAÏENCE AND PORCELAIN

Two factories flourished at Saint-Amand, the one founded by Dorez in an old pottery, and that of Pierre Joseph Fauquez who opened a second factory (his first was at Tournai) in 1718, and finally settled there himself. After his death in 1740 his son followed, and his grandson till 1793. At first Fauquez imitated the styles of Rouen and the soft-paste porcelain of Tournai, but the family fame rests on his introduction of the old *maiolica* technique of *bianco sopra bianco* (q.v.), literally, white over white, which

Sadler & Green. Liverpool *delft* tile printed by Sadler & Green with hunting scenes surrounding a central Coat of Arms within a rococo scroll border. c. 1760. *British Museum.*

is really white flowers or figures over a pearly grey ground. It is also found from Bristol, and sometimes from Delft and Tournai. Fauquez used enamels with great originality in conjunction with this technique, adding coloured flowers to lacework designs. Some naturalistic flowers in the style of Strasbourg also occur on a white ground. The factory, which survived into the 19th century, is artistically of considerable importance.

Saint-Amand passed to J.-M.-J. de Bettignies of Tournai (q.v.) after 1793, and began to make soft porcelain during the early years of the 19th century. This was much used for forgeries of Chelsea, Sèvres, and other 18th-century factories, including Chantilly. Copies of Sèvres sometimes bear the royal monogram. 'Chelsea' plates purporting to belong to about 1758–1760 which lack the customary 'stilt' marks probably came from here.

SAINT-CLEMENT (Meurthe-et-Moselle, France) FAÏENCE

Saint-Clement, an off-shoot of Lunéville (q.v.), was also unsuccessful financially. Charles Loyal, who followed Chambrette, took as partners Richard

Saint-Cloud. Pot-pourri jar, the rabbit in white porcelain, the vase coloured with a wash of green, mounted in gilt-bronze. Saint-Cloud. c. 1735. *Victoria and Albert Museum.*

Miqué and Paul Louis Cyfflé (q.v.), but the partnership did not last, and the factory was finally absorbed by Keller and Guérin of Lunéville. Saint-Clement was of little importance until 1772, when Miqué adopted a Louis Seize style for the products and used the fine *terre de Lorraine* (q.v.) underneath a tin-enamel glaze.

SAINT-CLOUD (Seine-et-Oise, France)
FAÏENCE

In 1675 Chicanneau, who came originally from Rouen, was director of the factory at Saint-Cloud, a fact recorded in a commission he was given for the Trianon de Porcelaine. When he died his widow married Henri Trou, who managed the factory and was followed by his son in 1746. Disputes between the Chicanneau and Trou descendants brought the factory to bankruptcy in 1766.

Saint-Cloud was always greatly under the influence of Rouen. It supplied faïence to most of the hospitals, and domestic wares to the Royal Palaces which were specially marked *BV* (Bellevue), *CR* (Choisy-le-Roi) and *T* (Trianon). Imitations of Nevers, Rouen, and Delft were all produced at Saint-Cloud. The palette contained no red, and black replaced blue outlines. See *Saint-Cloud Porcelain.*

SAINT-CLOUD PORCELAIN

A factory for the making of faience (q.v.) under the direction of Henri Charles Trou, bailiff to the Duc d'Orléans (the Regent), existed here in 1679, in which year Trou married Berthe Coudray, widow of Pierre Chicanneau. In 1702 Louis XIV granted a privilege (q.v.) to Berthe Coudray, and to her children by Pierre Chicanneau, for the manufacture of faïence and porcelain at Saint-Cloud. This superseded a privilege granted to the Révérends (q.v.) and to Louis Poterat at Rouen (q.v.). As a result of a family quarrel in 1722 Marie Moreau, widow of Pierre Chicanneau *fils* (one of the children mentioned above), founded a porcelain factory in Paris at the rue de la Ville l'Évêque, faubourg Saint-Honoré, leaving the original factory to Henri II Trou, and Trou became proprietor of both factories in 1742. A factory is reputed to have been conducted by the husband of Marie-Anne Chicanneau, one François Hébert, in the rue de la Roquette, Paris, and it has been suggested that some rare specimens of this date marked with crossed arrows (from the hôtel des Arbalétriers not far away) may be his manufacture. Hébert, a dealer in pottery, appears to have been connected with Gilles Dubois, a Chantilly workman who also worked abortively at Vincennes. This seemingly inextricable tangle was no doubt the result of the French law of *heritage*, which often leads to similar complications today in the division of property.

At this factory a great deal of surviving porcelain was made, minor specimens of which are not very rare. The body is a frit porcelain covered with a thick greenish-toned glaze. Much of the decoration, when it was not Oriental, was derived from the faïence of Rouen, especially the *lambrequins* (q.v.) in underglaze blue, as well as the *style rayonnant* discussed under the same heading. These remained fashionable until at least 1735. Fairly direct copies of Chinese *blanc-de-Chine* occur at all periods, and copies, some fairly accurate, of Chinese decoration in enamel colours were undertaken, although since these copies sometimes contain elements of the Kakiemon style (q.v.) it is possible that they were derived from Chinese imitations of Japanese porcelain made about 1700.

A large group of wares are moulded with an imbricated pattern based on the artichoke, and these overlapping leaves are to be found on cups and saucers. Teapots were given animal and bird heads to both spout and handle in imitation of metalwork, and forms generally often owe a good deal to contemporary silver. Specimens mounted in silver also occur. A number of figures were made, perhaps the best known being a smiling Chinese in the Victoria and Albert Museum (London), and some of the later figures are copied from Meissen. The factory specialized in the making of 'toys' (q.v.)—snuffboxes, cane-handles, and so forth—and these were often mounted in silver. They form a very desirable category of surviving wares.

The early unpainted wares have sometimes been confused with those of Chelsea of the raised anchor period, which they somewhat resemble. Usually they are heavily potted, as with most experimental soft porcelains, and slight firecracks and a certain amount of warping can sometimes be observed. The later wares are inferior to the earlier. One of the marks used, a sun-face, obviously refers to Louis XIV. It has been said that this implies a date before 1722 when Trou took over the factory, but it is more likely that it implies before 1714—the death of Louis XIV and the beginning of the Regency. The factory closed in 1766.

There are no recorded forgeries, but quite a few problems of attribution.

See *Révérend, Claude and François*.

SAINT-LOUIS GLASS FACTORY

This Lorraine factory, near Munsthal, was founded in 1767, but the production of crystal glass was not fully established until 1782. It was, however, almost immediately successful, with a large and increasing turnover. In 1829 it became the Compagnie des Verreries et Cristalleries de Saint-Louis, and it was among the first to adopt the press-moulding technique. It also made opaline glass (q.v.) and paperweights (q.v.) in great variety, now much sought. From 1831 to 1857 it had a marketing agreement with Baccarat (q.v.), and shared showrooms in Paris, in the rue de Paradis, where it still is.

SAINT-MAUR (France)

This factory for the manufacture of velvet was started by a *lyonnais*, Marcelin Charlier, soon after the middle of the 17th century. It made velvets of exceptional quality, some of which were sold for 1,000 *livres* (£500) an *aune*, a unit of measurement slightly greater than a metre. Charlier supplied Versailles with *portières* according to a contemporary source decorated with designs 'after Sieur Bérain' (q.v.). Damask and *lampas* were made at the same factory. See *Velvet*.

SAINT-OMER (Pas-de-Calais, France)
FAÏENCE

In 1751 Louis Saladin was granted a privilege to work in Saint-Omer and 'for three leagues roundabout' for 20 years. Although purporting to be in the style of Delft, the influence was actually that of Rouen, as the director of this factory, Jacques-Adrien Levêque, came from there. The enterprise was successful, but finally declined in 1775 through litigation. Levêque's training at Rouen resulted in the repetition of Normandy designs, but with considerable originality. Some services imitating silver-patterns, and sculptural wall-cisterns decorated with Chinese scenes and rococo *motifs* of exotic and decorative flowers, are in the Saint-Omer Museum. Levêque made a speciality of themes of peasant women in blue or purple *camaïeu*, and also manufactured exceptional coloured grounds in yellow and a blue deeper than that of Nevers, with decoration of opaque colours and *bianco sopra bianco*. He also made animal and vegetable tureens in the style of Hannong at Strasbourg.

SAINT-PORCHAIRE 'FAÏENCE'

Known as Henri II ware, faïence d'Oiron, and Saint-Porchaire faïence, this ware is not faïence, was once mistakenly thought to have been made near Oiron, near Thouars, and it has no special connection with Henri II beyond being made in his reign. Very little

Saint-Porchaire 'Faïence'. Salt of inlaid earthenware based on a silver prototype. The so-called *Henri Deux* ware. Saint-Porchaire. c. 1550. *Victoria and Albert Museum.*

is known about this ware, and few specimens have survived. It is thinly potted, covered with a lead glaze, and the decoration is by means of the very unusual technique of inlaying. Ornament was indented into the soft clay, the indentations being filled with clays of a contrasting colour, brown and black being the most usual, but green, violet, blue, and even iron-red not unknown. It was made from about 1525 to 1565, during the reigns of François I and Henri II, and salts are perhaps the most frequent survival. Ewers, candlesticks and *tazze* are also known. Forms were usually based on contemporary metalwork, and the more elaborate specimens exhibit a great deal of intricate applied modelled ornament. Inlaid decoration strongly resembles contemporary bookbinding ornament, and it has been assumed that bookbinders' stamps were employed to make the preliminary indentations. The scarcity of surviving specimens has led to the suggestion that only one or two men were responsible for manufacture, and that their output was mainly for members of the Court. Certainly the nature of the ware seems to preclude manufacture on a considerable scale. Mintons and others made reproductions about 1875, when the ware was the subject of keen competition among wealthy collectors, and these are to be seen occasionally. They are not deceptive, and collectors today are hardly likely to meet a genuine example outside a museum. About 70 specimens are known to have survived. See *Toft, Charles*.

SAINTES (Charente-Inférieure, France)
FAÏENCE

The kilns at Saintes were worked by Louis Sazerac for two years after 1731. In 1738 a potter from Montpellier, Jacques Crouzat, left Bordeaux and installed himself in Saintes. The products were very similar to those of Nevers. See *La Rochelle*.

SALT-GLAZE See *Stoneware*.

SALT-GLAZED WARE, ENGLISH, ENAMELLED See *Stoneware, English*

Samadet Faience. Melon-shaped tureen and stand and a plate, decorated in a Chinese style. Samadet. c. 1775.

SALT-GLAZED WARE (SCRATCH BLUE)

Staffordshire salt-glazed ware, often dated, which is decorated with incised patterns, usually flowers, the scratches being filled with blue pigment. See *Stoneware, English.*

SALTIRE CROSS

In heraldry, a cross formed by a bend and a bend sinister, i.e. a diagonal line from left to right, crossed by another from right to left, like an *X* on its side. Saltire stretchers are stretchers (q.v.) in this form which originated in Italy, and came to England from France in the reign of William and Mary.

SALTS

Salt is not only essential to human existence, but it has always been the subject of ceremonial, and salt-containers have often been among the principal table-appointments. A salt of impressive size marked the difference, in the great houses, between the lord, his family, and friends, and his servants and retainers who sat 'below the salt'. A particularly splendid example from Italy is the gold salt by Cellini (q.v.) which is preserved in the Kunsthistorisches Museum at Vienna, made for François I of France. In England the great (or standing) salt was of silver, although few examples survive, and those usually in museums, or among the college plate of the old universities.

In the 17th century the standing salt became less fashionable, and some were doubtless melted during the Civil War for coinage, when much early English silver was destroyed. They were replaced by trencher salts, triangular or square in form, low in height, and simply designed. These occur also in rare specimens of Lambeth delft. Trencher salts of circular form rather than square came with the first decades of the 18th century, and by the reign of George II small salts with a circular bowl having an inverted rim were placed on three or four small feet. These are also to be found in enamel on copper. With the neo-classical period the boat-shaped salt, the earliest often pierced, became popular, and these are sometimes to be found on a high foot. When they have handles they look like small sugar-basins. Salts in this period also occur in oval and octagonal form. Early 19th-century salts are either reversions to earlier shapes or, quite often, they were

designed to match the remaining parts of a dinner-service.

Salt has a corrosive effect on silver, especially when damp, leading to the formation of silver chloride (see *Silver, Tarnish on*). To overcome this George II salts were often gilded in the interior (silver-gilt), and Adam period salts were given blue glass liners. Silver salts are usually marked on the bottom.

SAMADET (Landes, France) FAÏENCE

This factory was founded in 1732 by Abbé Roquépine with a twenty-year privilege. It was very successful, and remained in the family's hands till 1785, when it was bought by Jean d'Yze. It closed in 1836. Some marked pieces (*S* or *Samadet* in full) help to identify a group of blue-and-white faïence in the manner of Bérain, mostly spittoons, candlesticks, and wig-stands. The earliest polychrome example is painted with *chinoiseries*, and marked *Samadet 1732*. Slightly later come pieces decorated with flowers and insects on a white or yellow ground. A design of grotesques in green and white outlined in purple and a stylized flower-pattern, more Chinese in style than the grotesques of Moustiers, is a speciality of Samadet, though not peculiar to it.

SAMARKAND RUGS

Some nomadic Turcoman rugs, such as those made at Kashgar and Yarkand, are termed 'Samarkand' because they are taken there to be sold. No carpets have been made at Samarkand for many years.

SAMPLE CORNERS

The corner of an Oriental carpet woven to show border patterns and part of the field design. Specimens are rare.

SAMPLERS

Embroidered designs on linen usually, especially after the 17th century, of a juvenile character. The first English samplers were merely a record of the needle-worker's skill in executing a variety of stitches and simple patterns. The foundation was coarse linen. The earliest surviving examples date from the first decades of the 17th century, although they were being made a good many years before this, but by the second half of the 17th century much more elaborate and decorative samplers embroidered with considerable skill are to be found. By the 18th century the making of samplers had become a juvenile pastime or task, and increasingly they had an educative purpose, the subjects being the letters of the alphabet, and pious mottoes and verses which become more and more sickly and sycophantic as the 19th century is approached. Many bear the name of the executant and the date, and they continued to be made until the middle of the 19th century. In America samplers seem to have been made almost from the beginning of colonial days, and those of the 18th century are very similar to English samplers in their subject matter. Samplers were also produced in Germany, Holland, and Spain, the two former being not unlike those of England and America.

SAMSON, EDMÉ, ET CIE (Paris)

This is a name which soon becomes very familiar to the collector of old pottery and porcelain. Samsons reproduce almost every variety, and their products are often seen in the shops of less knowledgeable dealers as antique. The firm was founded in 1845 and at first specialized in replacements for services, but subsequently excellent reproductions of Chinese and Meissen porcelain were made, but those of English porcelain are less deceptive. Samsons have also reproduced both French faïence and Dutch delft, making excellent copies of the wares of Strasbourg (q.v.), although their glaze is whiter than the greyish tone of genuine specimens.

Samson reproductions of English soft-porcelain figures give little trouble, since they are in a standard Continental hard-paste body. Most dangerous are their copies of Chinese 'armorial' porcelain (see *Chinese Export Porcelain*), Continental hard porcelain, and faïence. Samsons state that all their reproductions are marked with a letter *S*, which often accompanies a well-known factory mark, or, in the case of Chinese porcelain, forms part of a simulated seal mark. There is no reason to doubt the accuracy of their statement, but such marks can quite obviously be removed by the unscrupulous with a grindstone or hydrofluoric acid. Samsons are credited with far more than they actually make, and the name has become almost a generic term for a clever reproduction.

Apart from pottery and porcelain, the firm make reproductions of Battersea, Bilston, and Birmingham enamels, the two latter often offered under the generic name of 'Battersea'. See *Bilston and Birmingham Enamels*.

SAND-BLASTING

Sand-blasting was invented in 1870, and it has a number of uses in connection with a variety of materials. It consists in directing a stream of particles of sand, impelled by air-pressure from a gun, at a high speed towards the surface to be treated. It is often used in the decoration of glass, especially plate-glass, the design being cut from a sheet of specially prepared paper which protects those parts of the surface required to be left untouched. It is, in fact, a form of stencilling. The effect can be controlled by the size of the nozzle of the gun, the degree of fineness of the sand, and the length of time the jet is directed on to any particular spot.

SAND-PICTURES

The use of differently coloured sands to form pictures was not a particularly new idea in the 18th century, and it was frequently employed as a kind of table-decoration in the reign of George III. Nevertheless, these decorations did not become permanent until someone, perhaps Zobel, conceived the notion of glueing grains of sand to a suitable foundation, probably towards the end of the 18th century.

The best-known practitioners of this minor art were Benjamin Zobel, G. L. Haas, and Frederick Schwiekhardt. Apart from the work of Zobel, sand-pictures are rarely signed, and must be identified from their characteristics.

Small sand-paintings of the Isle of Wight were done about 1830 with sands of varying colours found at Alum Bay, with occasionally the addition of artificially coloured sand. The workmanship is apt to be primitive, and the subjects are principally local views.

SANDWICH GLASS

Glass made at Sandwich, Mass., by the Boston and Sandwich Glass Company, established by Deming Jarves in 1825. It closed in 1888. The principal production was lead-glass of fine quality. Pressed glass (q.v.) was introduced about 1828. Glass of this kind in which the patterns were given a stippled background became known as lacy glass. The making of opaline glass (q.v.) began about 1830, and an excellent ruby colour is much sought. Wheel-engraving, cutting, and etching were also practised as methods of decoration. Often sought in these days are cup-plates from Sandwich. These were in addition to the ordinary cup and saucer of pottery or porcelain, and were employed as cup-stands when tea was poured from the cup into the saucer to cool it, a custom which was also prevalent in polite circles in 18th-century England. Cup-plates of pressed glass, either translucent or transparent, were ornamented with a variety of designs. Over 500 patterns have been recorded, and they are much sought by collectors, which has led to their imitation in modern glass.

The Westmoreland Glass Company of Grapeville, Penn., are said to have some of the original Sandwich moulds, which they have used to make reproductions. See *Glass, American*.

SANG, ANDREAS FRIEDRICH (before 1719 to after 1747)

Thuringian glass-engraver, and Court engraver to Duke Ernst August of Saxe-Weimar. He is first recorded at Erfurt in 1719. He was working in Weimar from 1723 to 1732, and went to Ilmenau until 1747. After this he worked in Holland, where he influenced Dutch glass-engraving. He was noted for finely detailed landscapes decorated with *Laub- und Bandel-*

werke (q.v.). A signed specimen of his work is in the Kunstgewerbemuseum, Cologne.

SANSOVINO, JACOPO TATTI (1486–1570)

Italian sculptor and architect, and pupil of Andrea Sansovino. He began his career in Florence and Rome, and went to Venice in 1527, where he became architect to the city. Of his small bronzes, a *Jupiter* of about 1550 is in the Kunsthistorisches Museum, Vienna.

SARCOPHAGUS

Cellaret. A large rectangular box popular from about 1800 onwards, of mahogany or rosewood, designed in imitation of the ancient stone sarcophagus. As wine-coolers they had a lead lining, but they are sometimes misdescribed today as log-boxes, when the original lead lining is usually missing. They can, of course, be used for the latter purpose, but this was not their original function.

SATIN

A silk which originated in the East having a smooth and glossy surface on one side and a mat surface on the other. Its first appearance in France was in the 14th century.

SATINADE (French)

A cheap variety of satin made in the 18th century at Bruges.

SATINWOOD

A lustrous golden-yellow wood, finely figured, which was very popular among English furniture-designers, Sheraton especially, towards the end of the 18th century for all kinds of cabinet-work, small decorative tables, and side- and pier-tables. It was termed in France *bois satiné*, but it was not so often used there, its place being taken for marquetry and decorative veneering by *citronnier* (citronwood—q.v.).

Two varieties of wood are recognized as satin-

wood—one from the West Indies, and one from the East Indies, the latter belonging to the same family as mahogany. East Indian satinwood was first used by the Dutch in veneered cabinet-work, and in England it was mainly employed for small veneered surfaces and cross-banding (q.v.). Satinwood was rarely used as a solid wood, although chairs of this kind occur, made about 1800. Birch and chestnut sometimes provided substitutes for satinwood.

SATYR

A woodland deity in human form, either with horse's ears and tail as represented by the Greeks, or with goat's ears, tail, and hind legs in the Roman form. Satyrs became noted for their lust, and they occur quite frequently in 18th-century erotic works, such as the sculpture of Clodion and Fragonard.

SATYR MASK

This was popular as the carved detail of the knees of English cabriole legs from about 1730 to 1740, and it probably came to England from Germany in the wake of George I. See *Lion-masks*, which were employed for the same purpose. In the second half of the 18th century the satyr mask was popular in moulded form as the subject of Staffordhire pottery jugs. It appears as an ornamental detail to some kinds of porcelain, usually German and commonly from Höchst (q.v.). Mask spouts occur on jugs modelled as overlapping leaves from Worcester, made about 1760.

SAUVAGE, CHARLES-GABRIEL (1741–1827)

Born at Lunéville, in Alsace, Sauvage worked as a modeller at Niderviller not far away in the porcelain

and faïence factories. He was at Sèvres as chief modeller in 1808. He was also known as *Lemire père*.

SAVERY, WILLIAM (1721–1787)
American cabinet-maker of Philadelphia, whose furniture, mainly in a highly carved Chippendale style, is much sought by collectors. Like Chippendale, Savery's name has tended to become a generic term for fine-quality furniture in this style made in Philadelphia of mahogany and maple. See *Furniture, American.*

SAVONA (Liguria, Italy)
Savona flourished as a centre of faience manufacture in the late 17th and 18th centuries, following the new fashions of Chinese porcelain rather than trying to imitate the earlier *maiolica* tradition. Decoration is nearly always blue-and-white, and painting is inclined to be summary. Bowls, basins, flasks (sometimes mounted with pewter), and large dishes are not infrequent. There were many painters, and as many marks, but the principal factory mark is probably the Arms of the City, combined with numerous initials of unknown or doubtful import.

SAVONNERIE, LA
The origin of the Savonnerie carpet factory must be sought in the popularity of the Near Eastern pile carpet and the desire to produce a substitute. The first privilege of 1627, granted to Pierre Dupont whose workshop was in the Louvre, refers to the manufacture of carpets in the manner of the Levant, and the technique of Turkish carpets was especially imitated. The undertaking was later removed to a disused soap-factory (hence the name) where some extremely fine pile carpets were made under the general direction of Charles Le Brun (q.v.), and decorated in a style which owed no more than the technique to the Orient. For many years carpets were woven only for the King, for his immediate family, and for those few whom he desired to honour,

Savona. Lobed jar decorated in pale blue with a pewter screw-top. Savona. c. 1700.

so that the ownership of a Savonnerie carpet became a much-sought mark of distinction. During the 18th century, however, royal commissions became fewer, and private persons were given permission to buy carpets from these looms, although they were so expensive that it was a privilege of which advantage was rarely taken. The factory barely survived the Revolution, and in 1825 it was amalgamated with the Gobelins tapestry workshops.

The factory did not confine itself to carpets, but produced coverings for seat-furniture, and even decorative panels for screens. The carpets especially lent an air of magnificence to the French royal palaces of the 17th and 18th centuries, and about 30 of the finest are known to survive, of which 11 are in the possession of Paul Getty and 13 in the Rothschild collection.

La Savonnerie. Carpet-weaving looms. Mid-18th century. After Diderot.

Sceaux. Pot-pourri vase of faïence painted in the manner of porcelain. Sceaux. c. 1780.

The designs follow those customary during the period of manufacture, and the royal monogram frequently forms part of them.

See *Rugs, Knotting of.*

SAWS

Frame saws and those used for cutting veneers were introduced in England during the last quarter of the 17th century. The circular saw was in use by about 1790, and the band-saw by 1858. The curved marks on sawn, unplaned boards left by the circular saw, sometimes put forward as a sign of forgery or a reproduction, can only apply as a certain test on furniture made before about 1790.

SAXE, PORCELAINE AU (French)

Just as the English have always misdescribed Meissen porcelain as 'Dresden', so the French have referred to it as 'Saxe' (Saxon). *Saxe au point* means *die Punkzeit*, or 'dot' period, during which a dot was placed between the hilts of the crossed-swords mark (1763–1774), and *Saxe à l'étoile* to the Marcolini period when an asterisk was put in the same position (1774–1814).

SCAGLIOLA (Italian)

An imitation brecciated marble made by embedding marble chippings of appropriate colours in a cement. It was employed during the 18th century, both architecturally and for such purposes as table-tops.

SCEAUX (Seine, France) FAÏENCE

A faïence factory was established after 1748 by Jacques Chapelle on the site of a pottery that had been in existence since 1735 and situated opposite the castle at Sceaux. Chapelle was a skilful potter, and must have been successful in making porcelain, because in 1749 Vincennes enforced its monopoly to stop production at Sceaux. Chapelle, forced to abandon porcelain, decided to produce as close imitations as he dared and, using enamel colours, sold '*faïence japonnée*' in a shop in Paris in 1754 which he boasted could be mistaken for porcelain.

He bought out his partner, de Bey, in 1759 and ran the business alone till 1763. Marks of the period are *CS* (Chapelle-Sceaux), or a *fleur-de-lys*—part of the Coat of Arms of the Duchesse du Maine. Meissen, Chantilly, and Strasbourg all exerted their influence on the wares, and Strasbourg provided workers for the factory. Between 1745 and 1750 the Sceaux palette was less brilliant than that of Strasbourg, the colours being rather dull.

Chapelle retired in 1763 and leased the factory to Charles-Symphorien Jacques and Joseph Julien, who had worked together at Mennecy (q.v.) and Bourg-la-Reine (q.v.). Both painted with equal ease on porcelain and faïence, and Sceaux faïence has much in common with soft-paste porcelain of the period. In 1772 Chapelle sold the factory to Richard Glot, who had the Duc de Penthière as patron. At this period the marks are *SP* or *OP*. After the death of the Duke in 1793 Glot was arraigned for misuse of funds, and the factory was bought by Cabernet in 1796 and continued into the 19th century. The late 18th century saw excellent workers at Sceaux, and the wares are of very high quality. The factory's fame enabled it to command the best painters, who came from Sèvres, Mennecy, and Strasbourg, and from Aprey, whence came a painter of birds called Jarry.

Decoration of every kind is to be seen on Sceaux faïence: flowers, birds, landscapes, and animals, as well as animal and vegetable tureens and figures deriving from Niderviller and Strasbourg. The fine paste covered with a lead glaze used at Sceaux made the tin-enamel wares competitive in quality with creamware, but in the end even the refined work of Sceaux was superseded by the cheapness and popularity of imported wares from England.

For later Sceaux porcelain, see *Mennecy.*

SCHLESWIG FAÏENCE

The factory of Schleswig was started in 1755 through the enterprise of Ludwig von Lücke (q.v.), the Meissen

Sceaux. Faïence plate decorated in enamel colours with the fashionable exotic birds. Sceaux. c. 1760. *Victoria and Albert Museum.*

modeller, who obtained a privilege of 20 years for a company, the most important members of which were Otte, Burgomaster, his two brothers, and Johann Rambusch, a customs official. Lücke left after a year and, after 1758, Rambusch became the sole proprietor of the factory, which passed to his son when he died in 1773.

The best period was before Rambusch took over. Afterwards he had great competition from other Schleswig factories, as well as from English creamware. Rambusch applied for another 20-year concession in 1795—the third—but was granted only 15 years. In 1800 he leased the factory to Lachmann and Wolff for three years, and then sold it to a judge of the Supreme Court. After years of decline it finally succumbed.

The Schleswig factory is remarkable chiefly for the plastic quality of its wares and a decoration in manganese-purple. The body is often a pale buff, tending towards white, while the glaze is inclined to a dirty grey. The general effect is very uneven, sometimes light, but occasionally thick, heavy and crude, and depressingly provincial, although one would conclude from the use of manganese that the wares were made specially to be sold in Copenhagen, where blue-and-white wares were prohibited.

The mark of the early period—monogram *S O* and *L* below—has been observed on some pieces decorated chiefly in manganese and heightened with blue, but marks are not always present. Rambusch added a greyish-green and yellow to the palette, and he occasionally also used enamels for flowers in the style of Meissen. The grey-green is characteristic, and especially the way it tends to disintegrate on firing into its components. It is nearly always outlined in manganese. There is also a yellowish-green which is used in conjunction with manganese.

Schnell, Martin. Black-glazed stoneware pilgrim flask decorated in lacquer colours with a Chinese scene by Martin Schnell. Meissen. c. 1715. *Metropolitan Museum, New York.*

The products of the Schleswig factory are not well known, and only the pieces most commonly found are immediately recognizable, such as the type of manganese-painted plate with relief moulding and softly painted flowers and foliage in the centre; apple-tureens with leaves in relief on the cover, and a dark manganese decoration of flowers; and plates, cream-jugs, etc., painted in manganese, the typical greyish-green, and occasionally blue. Although usually rococo in style, some of the wares made about 1775 incline towards the neo-classical style.

SCHNELL, MARTIN (fl. 1703–1740)
German maker of imitation Oriental lacquer. A pupil of Gerhard Dagly (q.v.), Schnell produced some extremely competent lacquer work, especially trays, and furniture by him is preserved at Dresden. He also executed murals in this technique. He provided designs for porcelain, and is perhaps best known outside Germany for the specimens of Meissen red stoneware decorated in lacquer colours (i.e. *kalte malerei*) with Oriental subjects which are often ascribed to his hand.

SCHNELLEN (German)
Tall, tapering tankards, usually in Rhineland stoneware (q.v.), the best coming from Siegburg. They often still retain their pewter or silver covers. Sixteenth-century *Schnellen* were usually decorated in relief in a late Gothic style.

SCHREZHEIM (Germany) FAÏENCE FACTORY
A factory was built in 1752 by Johann Baptist Bux, and went slowly downhill after the first period till 1872. The factory's reputation rests on its large, finely modelled pieces; for instance, the faïence altar-tabernacle at Schrezheim, a large statue of St Nepomuk now at Würzburg, and a Madonna formerly in the Igo Levi Collection, as well as candlesticks, wall-plaques and wine-barrels. It also followed the fashion for making tureens and boxes shaped as fruit, vegetables, turkeys, and tortoises. In the high-temperature colours the decoration is nearly always blue, manganese, green, and yellow. Enamel painting in luminous red, greens, browns, and purple are of Oriental flowers, German flowers, and more rarely Rouen-style baroque ornament. The body is reddish-brown and the glaze bluish. The mark is a *B* below a small arrow, or, some say, a branch of box, referring to Bux the founder.

SCHWANHARDT FAMILY, THE
Glass-engravers of Prague and Nürnberg. Georg Schwanhardt (1601–1667) was a pupil of Caspar Lehmann in his Prague workshop (see *Bohemian Glass*), and his wheel-engraving, of the highest quality, is usually of landscapes surrounded by baroque scrollwork with passages of diamond-point engraving. Signed specimens are known. His sons, Georg (d. 1676) and Heinrich (d. 1693), were also wheel-engravers, and the latter is reputed to have discovered a method of etching on glass. There is

a panel done in this way dated 1686 in the Germanisches Museum (Nürnberg) which is the earliest example of etched glass known. There were a number of 17th-century Nürnberg engravers who worked in a style similar to that of the Schwanhardts, of whom the most noteworthy is Hermann Schwinger (1640–1683).

SCHWARZLOT (German)

Painting in black monochrome on porcelain, faïence, and glass in a style usually inspired by line-engravings. Much work of this kind is on German porcelain of the first half of the 18th century, and more often than not it is the work of one of the *Hausmaler* (q.v.). At Vienna (q.v.) during the du Paquier period painting of this kind was combined with touches of iron-red (usually employed for the faces and hands of figures) and a certain amount of gilding. The same colour-scheme can be found on more or less contemporary Chinese porcelain made for export—the so-called 'Jesuit' category, from the subjects which are usually (but not invariably) religious, and inspired by Jesuit missionaries in China. The *Hausmaler* (q.v.) Aufenwerth and Seuter of Augsburg did similar work, usually on Meissen porcelain. The work of the Bohemian *Hausmaler*, Ignaz Preussler, can be found on both European and Chinese porcelain, the latter obviously imported 'in white' for later decoration. Worcester pencilled ware can be regarded as a kind of *Schwarzlot*, although properly *Schwarzlot* subjects should be European and not Chinese.

SCHWIEKHARDT, FREDERICK

Of Dutch origin, Schwiekhardt probably arrived in England as a young man in 1786. As a maker of sand-pictures he was much influenced by Dutch painting, doing winter scenes and flower-pieces in characteristic style. The colouring of much of his work was enhanced by the use of water-colour. Specimens are rare.

SCONCES

Candle-holders, usually with two or more branches, made to be hung on the wall. Silver sconces became popular in England during the last half of the 17th century, and some particularly fine examples were made during the first half of the 18th by Paul de Lamerie (q.v.) and others. They can also be found made of brass, in *tôle* ware, and in faïence.

SCRIMSHAW

A kind of American folk-art developed by New England whalemen in the early decades of the 19th century. The term is used to describe both the object created and the process of etching or carving on whale's teeth or whalebone. Scrimshaw is a peculiarly American form of folk-art, though it is occasionally seen from elsewhere. Early whalebook logs refer to it as 'scrim shouting' and Melville's *Moby Dick* refers to 'skrim shander articles'.

Scrimshaw was a product of the boredom attending voyages lasting from three to five years. Engraving or etching, using primitive instruments like penknives and ships' tools, the whaler varied his designs or pictures according to his material—the ivory teeth of the sperm whale, or whalebone of both the right and sperm whale. Most popular were scenes of ships and whales, flags, and eagles, as well as figures of ladies and gentlemen.

The two most common of the scrimshaw products were the busk (bodice stay) and the jagging or

Worcester porcelain vase of c. 1770 painted in reserves with a sheep-shearing scene by John Donaldson and signed with a monogram. The cover is, perhaps, by O'Neale. *Lady Ludlow Collection, Luton Hoo.*

Hausmalerei. Jug painted in enamel colours with a hunting scene by Mathias Schmid. Nürnberg faience. c. 1722.

Of the many styles competing for attention during the Victorian period, the Near Eastern was perhaps the newest and most exotic. This is not a harēm, but a room in the house of Lord Leighton in Holland Park, W. London, now a public museum. The tiles to be found on the walls are a mixture of genuine Persian and Isnik (Turkish) specimens, and copies by William de Morgan. It was made during the last quarter of the 19th century.

crimping wheel (for laying a design along the edge of a pie). Other forms were yarn-winders, work-boxes, rolling-pins, napkin-rings, spool-holders, clothes-pins, and ivory heads for canes.

Scrimshaw was made exclusively for gifts to those most loved by the craftsman—mothers, fathers, sisters, sweethearts—and for this reason it has a personal charm unique in American folk-art.

SCULPTURE, GLASS
Pliny the Elder refers to glass sculpture in Roman times without giving details, but presumably it was carved from a solid block of glass using the techniques of the *diatretarii* (q.v.). In the 20th century Aristide Colotte has revived the practice, making similar sculpture in France.

SEALS
Although exceptional examples exist from very early times the seals likely to interest the collector can hardly be earlier than the later years of the 17th century. There are several kinds—desk seals, which were often elaborate; seal rings; and watch-fob seals.

The part used to make the impression in wax was often carved in *intaglio* (q.v.), usually by processes not dissimilar from those used by the old Roman gem-cutters or by contemporary glass-engravers. This is the case with seals of semi-precious hardstones, such as agate or cornelian, and even of such soft materials as English marble. The glass seals of James Tassie (q.v.), and the basaltes and jasper seals of Wedgwood and others, were formed in ways appropriate to the material. Perhaps the most expensive of 18th-century seals today were those made of porcelain at Chelsea (London) discussed under that heading, and the factory made a speciality of small work of this kind from about 1755 to its purchase by Duesbury in 1770.

Seals usually bear monograms or devices, many of the latter being stock-patterns bought from dealers, such as Mrs Chenevix, the toy-woman (see *Toys*). The best usually give some indication of the former owner's identity, such as his initials or a crest, and these were ordered directly from seal-engravers.

Most seals are mounted in metal—gold, silver, brass, steel, or pinchbeck—although porcelain seals from Chelsea usually have only a slight gold band when they are mounted at all.

Seals are difficult to date, but the more massive examples are likely to belong to the 19th century rather than the 18th.

SEAT-FURNITURE
The term comprises all furniture for sitting—chairs, settees, sofas, etc., made singly or in *suites*. It is particularly used of 18th-century French furniture in *suites*. In France it was customary to award a fixed position in the interior scheme to certain sets of chairs, etc., which fall under this heading, and these were frequently carved to match the *boiseries*, and door- and window-cases. They were also usually covered with fabrics closely harmonizing with, and

Seat-furniture. George I walnut shell-carved settee with ball-and-claw feet covered in *petit point* needlework. c. 1740. *Parke-Bernet Galleries, New York.*

often matching, the rest of the interior drapes, including the curtains. The tapestry-looms, like those of Beauvais or Gobelins, wove *suites* of tapestries which included fitted wall-hangings, pelmets, etc., and coverings for the seat-furniture intended for the particular room were woven to match. Rooms of this kind can be seen at Osterley Park (London, England) and the Metropolitan Museum, New York.

Chairs and *fauteuils* (q.v.), when they had a flat back, were termed *à la reine*, and were always accorded a fixed position. Those with a curved back, referred to as *en cabriolet*, were moved to various positions as required. Many new varieties of chair were introduced during the 18th century, more luxuriously upholstered and intended for relaxation, such as the *bergère* (q.v.), which itself developed several sub-types—the *bergère en confessionnal* (a wing armchair) or the *bergère en gondole*, with two integral incurving arms, and so on. These rarely had a fixed position, although they were often found near the chimney-piece. Elsewhere one can hardly find a parallel to the French etiquette of the chair, except in circles influenced by the French Court.

The line of demarcation between seat furniture proper and that made for reclining, such as the day-bed and the chaise-longue, is difficult to draw, and the latter are sometimes included in this category.

SEAWEED MARQUETRY
A scrolling foliate pattern owing something to the appearance of certain marine plants, hence the name, which was carried out usually in holly or boxwood against a background of walnut. It is seen at its best on English long-case clocks of the late 17th and early 18th centuries. It perhaps owes its origin to the influence of Boulle and Bérain (q.v.).

SEDAN CHAIR
A covered chair slung on poles, borne by two men, which was used in the 17th and 18th centuries as a substitute for wheeled transport in urban areas. Probably originating in the East, and arriving in Europe by way of Venice, the sedan chair (which seems to have nothing to do with the town of that name) was introduced into London from Naples in

Settee, Chair-back. Twin chair-back settee in the Sheraton style covered with the fashionable striped material of the period—a French style. English. c. 1790. *Strawberry Hill, Twickenham, S.W. London.*

1634. In this year Sir Sanders Duncombe was granted a licence to keep 50 chairs for hire. Sedan chairs are a not-uncommon survival. Rarest are those licensed to ply for hire, which are plain, and usually covered with black leather. Extremely luxurious specimens made for private use are actually more common, since they were more carefully preserved. Decoration in England includes carving, gilding, silvering, and panels painted by artists of repute. In appropriate cases the chair sometimes had an added crown or coronet. A lift-up top was intended to accommodate the high *coiffeure.* In France, panels of *vernis Martin* (q.v.) and inset panels of Sèvres porcelain were employed to decorate the more luxurious examples.

SEHNA KNOT   See *Rugs, Knotting of*

SELLING ANTIQUES
There are several avenues open to the collector who wishes to sell all or part of his collection. The two principal methods are by auction, or to a dealer, all of whom are willing to buy privately.

In the case of the saleroom, subject to the reserve price the collector has no choice but to take what is offered, since the sale is to the highest bidder. In selling to a dealer the collector will usually be asked to state his price, and it is then for the dealer to accept or reject the offer. The dealer will take into account what an object is likely to fetch in the saleroom, and unless he has a compelling reason for wanting it, he will expect to buy at the same price-level, or a little below. The collector does not have to pay saleroom commission, and he gets his money at once instead of waiting for it.

When the collector is well known, and not anxious for an immediate sale, he may find, if the dealer is willing, that he will get a higher price if he suggests that the dealer sells it for him, taking a commission for his trouble. Since the dealer does not need to lay out capital he will be content with a lower rate of profit.

This suggests that anyone taking up collecting seriously would do well to cultivate the acquaintance of a dealer, or dealers, of repute. Once he is on good and mutually profitable terms with them he will find many of his problems of buying and selling solved. He will usually buy on better terms, interesting objects will be saved for his inspection, and he will be helped to dispose of unwanted items.

SERPENTINE
A magnesium silicate, green in colour and easily carved, which is sometimes called *verde antique.* It is not unlike marble in appearance. Serpentine has mostly been used for making small works of art and, in China, as a medium for imitating jade.

SETTEE, CHAIR-BACK
An 18th-century English settee with a back formed from two or three chair-backs. Both Chippendale and Hepplewhite designed settees in this style.

SETTEE, KNOLE
An upholstered settee with a high straight back and arms, the arms of which are constructed to drop down to form a reclining couch. The first Knole settee is to be found at Knole, in Kent (England), and it dates from the first half of the 17th century. The arms are lowered by a rack mechanism. The type enjoyed renewed popularity in the 1920s and 1930s.

SETTLE
A bench, usually of oak, for two or more persons which has a high back and arms. It often has a hinged seat which opens to form a storage chest (box-settle).

SEUTER, BARTHOLOMÄUS (1678–1754)
Hausmaler of Augsberg, who painted on porcelain, faïence, and glass. Much of his work is on the faïence of Nürnberg and Bayreuth and the porcelain of Meissen, and he is established as a porcelain-painter before 1729 by a contemporary reference which says, 'Seuter buys the best porcelain ware which he has sent mostly in white from Dresden.' There is also a record that he purchased outmoded white ware in 1735. Seuter painted both in polychrome and *Schwarzlot* (q.v.), and his subjects range from *chinoiseries* to those inspired by Watteau. The best of his painting is extremely competent, and was much valued at the time, as well as today. A border of C-shaped scrolls with a central dot are thought to be a Seuter characteristic, and it occurs on some very rare specimens of enamelled glass. It is probable that Seuter maintained a workshop which worked in the same general style, and overgilding of defective blue-and-white Meissen porcelain may have been done by his assistants, as well as by Ferner (q.v.).

SÈVRES PORCELAIN FACTORY, THE
This factory, started with the aid of workmen from Chantilly (q.v.), was first housed in the fortress of

Vincennes, to the south-east of Paris, and was removed to Sèvres in the south-west in 1756. Although experimental work was being done as early as 1738, no practical results of consequence were achieved before 1745.

The factory was intimately connected with the French Court, and in 1759 it became the sole property of Louis XV. Thereafter, it remained royal property until the coming of the Republic, when it became a national undertaking, which it still remains. The Musée de Sèvres, which has a fine collection of ceramics generally, as well as of Sèvres porcelain, is open to the public. The early wares are termed 'Vincennes', and they become 'Sèvres' after 1756. When the exact place of manufacture is doubtful they are sometimes termed 'Vincennes-Sèvres'.

The mark of the factory is the double *L* monogram of Louis XV and Louis XVI. There is a system of date-lettering, the letters nearly always appearing inside the monogram, which fix the date of a specimen to a particular year. This was started with A in 1753, while the factory was still at Vincennes, and it finished with Z in 1777, omitting W. It started again in 1778 with AA, and finished in 1793, during the Revolution, with PP. A specimen without a date-letter ought to mean *before 1753*, but this is far from being invariably the case, and it usually means made in the 19th century. Also present are various small marks and devices outside the monogram which identify painters and gilders, and these can be checked against any good book of marks. Forgeries are always well marked, usually with an early date-letter (commonly 1753), which has little to do with the type of decoration. For marks adopted during the Revolution, and those of the 19th century, books of marks can be consulted. For part of the time in the 19th century a system of indicating date of manufacture existed. Production in 1745 largely consisted in the manufacture of artificial flowers in porcelain, and these

Seuter, B. Coffee-pot painted with a hunting scene in *Schwarzlot* with touches of iron-red, and richly gilt. *Hausmalerei* on Meissen porcelain by Bartholomäus Seuter. c. 1735. Note the dotted scrolls level with the top of the spout. *Cecil Higgins Museum, Bedford.*

Sèvres. *Vaisseau à màt* after a design by Duplessis and painted with birds in landscapes by J. Ledoux. This, the most famous of all Sèvres vases, is in the form of a sailing vessel with mast. Several 19th-century factories, including Minton and Herend (Hungary), made copies. Vincennes. c. 1755. *Wallace Collection.*

were immensely popular. By 1749 they formed the greater part of the manufacture, and had become so fashionable that the Marquis d'Argenson wrote of the King's expenditure on them, that it was 'a great scandal'. At the same time the factory was making copies of Meissen (q.v.) painted decoration, and some Japanese designs based on those of Sakaida Kakiemon (q.v.) which were already extremely popular at Chantilly. These are very rare, and hardly exist outside museums.

Considerable changes in design took place in 1752 with the introduction of vases designed by the goldsmith to the King, Duplessis (q.v.), who was a director of the factory, and a number of vases of great importance were produced, notably the *vaisseau à màt*, a boat-shaped vase, of which there is a specimen in the Wallace Collection (London). These are extremely rare. Vases of fine quality soon became among the factory's most characteristic products, in pairs, or in sets of three, four, or five. The latter were termed a *garniture de cheminée* (q.v.). The factory at this time was especially noted for the quality of its soft porcelain body, the finest ever produced, and for coloured grounds and painting of especially remarkable quality, as well as for gilding richly tooled and chased.

An intense lapis-blue, introduced at Vincennes in 1753, was employed to border the edges of many things, from dishes to *cachepots*, and to outline moulded ornament. It also occurs as a monochrome for *en camaïeu* (q.v.) figure-painting, flesh-tints being added in pink. The earliest ground colour was the *gros bleu* (later imitated at Chelsea as mazarine-blue). This is dark in colour and was sponged on before glazing. Because of its intensity it was nearly always covered with patterns of gilt lines, and it was,

Sèvres. Tray painted by Vieillard (working 1752–1790), the border with an apple-green ground. Sèvres. 1758.

at Vincennes, sometimes used as a ground on which exotic bird decoration in gold silhouette was superimposed, a fashion adopted at Chelsea some ten years later. Gold, thickly laid on and carefully tooled, is to be found on many of these early wares. *Bleu celeste*, a fine turquoise, was first produced in 1753, and it was reproduced at the Sèvres factory in 1887. This colour has always been a favourite target with the forger, but nearly always it inclines too much to green rather than to the blue of the original. The *jaune jonquil*, a very rare ground colour, was first used in 1753, and violet and green in 1756. Many colours were already in existence in 1753, and were listed in a book compiled by the factory's chemist, Hellot, but some of them are difficult to identify from the descriptions, and many were probably little more than experimental. The famous *rose Pompadour* (q.v.) was invented in 1757 and discontinued in 1764 after the death of the Marquise, who was greatly interested in the factory.

Painting of flowers, birds, and figure-subjects greatly increased after about 1750 with the recruitment of some of the fan-painters of Paris who were skilled in the execution of miniature decoration, many of them being flower-painters. Flowers at first were decorative rather than naturalistic, but they later began to lose some of their earlier spontaneity, probably under the influence of the *deutsche Blumen* (q.v.) of Meissen. Birds, at first of the exotic variety, gradually became more realistic, being based after 1775 on Buffon's *Natural History of Birds*, the particular species sometimes being named on the reverse. The children of Boucher were a favourite subject for monochrome painting, but painting in polychrome was not common at Vincennes until a year or two before the removal to Sèvres. Most Boucher subjects are, in fact, subsequent to the removal. Once the factory became established at Sèvres much more elaborate painting was undertaken, including subjects after the popular Teniers the Younger. Morin, at the factory from 1754 onwards, did some very distinguished paintings of shipping and harbour scenes inspired by those of Meissen.

Complete services were not made until 1753, but plates and similar articles of service-ware were made and bought by dealers, who put services together from them. The financial crisis of 1757, which compelled the King and his Court to send their silver to the Mint for conversion into coin, increased the demand for porcelain services which could not entirely be supplied from the much tougher porcelain of China and Meissen, and towards 1760 we find that the output of services from Sèvres greatly increased. The first of the outstanding services made here was for the King and had a *bleu celeste* ground and polychrome flower-painting. This was started in 1753, and it became increasingly the custom for both the King and Mme de Pompadour to give services to foreign royalty and ambassadors. Porcelain became popular also for toilet-ware of all kinds, from *bidets* to chamber-pots, as well as cosmetic jars, and toilet-tables were provided with porcelain containers.

The particular soft-paste porcelain employed by the factory did not lend itself easily to complex and detailed modelling such as that to be seen from Meissen, but its place was taken by elaborate mounts of gilt-bronze, many designed, perhaps, by Duplessis,

Sèvres. Sèvres *biscuit* porcelain. Model after Falconet. Stand of glazed porcelain with a *bleu de roi* ground enriched with enamelled flowers and gilding. 1762. *Wallace Collection.*

Sèvres. Ewer and bowl with a myrtle-green ground decorated with gilt spots, and painted by Asselin (fl. 1750–1794) with children after Boucher. Sèvres. 1767. *Wallace Collection.*

and the best are usually attributed to him. Mounts were applied both to vases and to the *biscuit* figures later discussed.

The factory made a speciality of small sets of tea, coffee, and chocolate things which usually comprised a porcelain tray, one or two cups, a teapot, cream-jug, and sugar basin, teapots being by far the most common. These were listed as a *déjeuner* if intended for one cup, and as a *cabaret* if with two cups.

Plaques for the decoration of furniture became an important item of the factory's production. They were first made about 1760, perhaps at the suggestion of the dealer, Simon-Philippe Poirier, and several *ébénistes* like Martin Carlin (q.v.) specialized in this kind of work. Especially popular were tops for small tables which were usually made with a fretted bronze gallery, and these are among the most valued of all tables of this kind. Plaques were also employed

Sèvres. A Louis Philippe *bonheur du jour* inset with plaques of Sèvres porcelain. A 19th-century repetition of a Louis XV style. c. 1830. *Phillips, Son & Neale.*

to ornament such large furniture as *secrétaires*, being inset in a framework of gilt-bronze.

Clock-cases were a later speciality of the factory, although one of the earliest, a rococo case with figures of Zephyrus and Flora in the British Museum, dates back to about 1750, and came from Vincennes. Later, clocks were inset into pillars and vases of porcelain, or mounted in a combination of porcelain, gilt-bronze, and marble, one such clock being made for Marie-Antoinette by Thomire, who replaced Duplessis at Sèvres in 1783.

Much sought are boxes from this factory, usually made from small plaques set in a gold frame, although some were made in one piece with a metal-hinged cover. 'Toys' (q.v.) were made in very great variety, from sword-hilts (purely for ornament) to seed-trays for canaries.

Despite the amazingly high quality of these products in soft porcelain, it was expensive to make and fragile in use, and the factory assiduously sought a formula for hard porcelain in the Saxon manner. They achieved this in 1770, although for several years afterwards it was only used for figures. The new body offered many manufacturing advantages, not the least that fewer firings were needed to fix the enamel colours, but it was done at the expense of quality. Its employment for wares other than figures at first brought many difficulties, but by 1783 it was possible to make a vase 5 ft high which, with its companion, is now in the Louvre. New ground colours were devised for the hard porcelain body, including brown, black, and a dark blue, as well as a tortoiseshell ground which had been introduced somewhat earlier. An innovation of 1781, probably the invention of Cotteau, was a combination of raised gilding and translucent enamels, sometimes put over gold foil, which imitated rubies, emeralds, and so forth. This was later imitated at 19th-century English porcelain factories, notably at Worcester for the Dudley service.

The decoration at this time was purely in the neo-classical style, the earlier rococo of soft porcelain having been entirely abandoned. Etruscan friezes, medallions, and friezes *en grisaille* (q.v.) adapted from classical sources were frequently employed. Flower-painting was entirely naturalistic, and a decoration of scattered cornflower sprigs (*décor barbeau*) was devised to please Marie-Antoinette, and was much used by some of the other Paris porcelain factories (see *Paris, Porcelain of*), particularly the Fabrique de la Reine of the rue Thiroux, which enjoyed her patronage and used her monogram as a mark.

A new departure was the production of large plaques of porcelain, some almost 2 ft square, intended to be hung on a wall. These imitated oil-paintings, of which hunting scenes by Asselin after Oudry are fairly typical.

Just before the Revolution the competition of Wedgwood persuaded the factory to imitate his blue-and-white jasper ware in *biscuit* porcelain, and a number of examples survive. The modelling is in much higher relief than Wedgwood's and the style typically French.

Very little was made during the Revolution, and much of it was decorated with Revolutionary emblems. In 1800 Alexandre Brogniart was appointed director, and financial assistance was given by the new government. In 1806 Napoleon I took the factory under his protection, and the factory's products began to conform to the prevailing Empire style (q.v.). Brogniart entirely discontinued the manufacture of soft porcelain and sold off some of the old stocks (see *Sèvres Porcelain, Forgeries of*).

The earliest figures made at Vincennes were glazed, although very few painted examples have ever been recorded. Glazed figures are extremely rare, most having been made in an unglazed porcelain termed *biscuit* which was introduced by the art-director, Jean-Jacques Bachelier, in 1751. Bachelier was doubtless looking for a novelty which would enable the factory to compete on better terms with the glazed and painted figures of Meissen, and *biscuit* seems to have been popular from the first. Perhaps more important than the modellers themselves to a cursory review such as this were the designers. Boucher was among the earliest; so also was Pigalle. Boucher's designs were especially popular, and continued to be made for many years. Most influential of all in the making of figures was Étienne-Maurice Falconet, whose *La Nymph qui descend au Bain* (popularly known as *La Baigneuse*) which began as a marble exhibited in the Paris Salon of 1757, is probably the best known of all Sèvres figures. It was copied in porcelain at Meissen, Ludwigsburg, Zürich, Berlin, and Copenhagen, but not in England strangely enough. A companion, *La Nymph qui sort du Bain* (sometimes called *The Nymph with the Sponge*), was executed in 1762.

Figures of all kinds poured from the factory. The subjects were taken from every conceivable source—the drama, *fêtes*, dances, romances, designs by painters, and illustrated books—and all were modelled with a sophistication and elegance unknown elsewhere, not even at Meissen. *Biscuit* is a very demanding medium, for it requires perfection in casting and firing. The English Derby factory, which also tried its hand at making *biscuit* figures, glazed and painted the slightly imperfect ones and sold them for less.

Falconet left in 1766 to make the great equestrian statue of Peter the Great at St Petersburg (now Leningrad), and his place was taken by the bronze-worker Jacques Caffiéri (see *Caffiéri Family*) whose portrait of Voltaire was praised by the sitter, someone notoriously difficult to please. It was at this time that *biscuit* began to be used for reproductions of sculpture in miniature, and it loses some of its earlier charm in consequence.

In 1770 Louis-Simon Boizot took over the direction of the sculpture and modelling studios from Bachelier, who remained art-director, and Boizot modelled a number of important allegorical groups. In 1779 Catherine the Great ordered about 40 models by Boizot as table-decoration (q.v.), for which most of the *biscuit* figures were always intended.

Long before this, first perceptible in fact during the period in which Caffiéri was chief modeller, the neo-classical style had made its appearance, and it increasingly influenced the production of figures. The general atmosphere of Court life also brought changes. In 1782 Pajou scandalized the Court (although probably not very seriously) by modelling an allegorical group of an almost-nude Venus carrying the newly born Dauphin symbolizing love. But his Venus was an unmistakable portrait of Marie-Antoinette. He was ordered to alter the features and remove the *fleur-de-lys* from the drapery.

Almost every sculptor of importance contributed, men such as Lemoyne and Pajou, Houdon and Clodion; almost every event was commemorated and every conceivable subject represented, allegorically or otherwise. When Montgolfier made his first balloon ascent in 1784 Sèvres produced a *Groupe de l'Aerostat*, representing a balloon on a pedestal while a winged Genius passed the torch of truth and light to a figure symbolizing Physics. The year 1785 saw the first reliefs in the manner of Wedgwood—a little belated, for many of the Paris factories had been producing them for some years before this.

During the Revolution portrait busts of Danton, Marat, and Robespierre made their appearance, as well as some of the Revolutionary generals, including Napoleon Bonaparte. At this time many of the old moulds were smashed, and figures and groups in stock representing royalty were also destroyed.

Manufacture of figures was revived in the 19th century, but nothing of the earlier quality was made.

SÈVRES PORCELAIN, FORGERIES OF

These are especially numerous. Indeed, there are a far greater number of forgeries and reproductions existing than genuine specimens, and, more than any other, porcelain purporting to be old Sèvres requires very careful examination.

Of the reproductions, the factory revived its own soft porcelain in 1887 under Théodore Deck at a time when *vieux Sèvres* was fetching very high prices in the contemporary saleroom. This was usually decorated with a turquoise ground in imitation of the old *bleu celeste*, and Watteau-esque figures in panels, the drawing characteristic of the sentimental approach of the 19th century. The gilding is much poorer than 18th-century work. The copies of Randall of Madeley (Shropshire) were close, and at the time deceptive, but he refused to add the Sèvres mark. Those of Coalport and Minton were also fairly close. In some cases factory marks which would identify the origin otherwise have been removed. Coalport used the *bleu de roi*, a rich and prized enamel blue of 1756 onwards, which in the 18th century was peculiar to Sèvres. Samson (q.v.) copies are in hard paste, and Moritz Fischer at Herend in Hungary also used hard paste to copy the *vaisseau à mât*, to which he added the Sèvres mark.

Sèvres porcelain in the 18th century was always of the finest quality, and imperfect pieces were rejected. No doubt many were smashed, but after 1756 they were allowed to accumulate, and some found their way outside the factory to be decorated in small kilns. Catrice, a factory flower-painter, was arrested and charged with using the royal monogram on pieces purloined by him. Starting in 1804 the accumulated 'wasters' were offered by Brogniart in several sales, the last one in 1815. Much was bought by Peres & Ireland of Paris, and some was exported to London for decoration by Baldock of Bond Street, Mortlock of Oxford Street, and Robins & Randall of Spa Fields. The porcelain of the Nantgarw factory (q.v.), which made a soft porcelain not unlike that of Sèvres, was employed by the same decorators when supplies of Sèvres 'wasters' ran short, and Randall eventually started his Madeley factory in 1825 to remedy the deficiency.

Peres & Ireland employed a decorator named Soiron, formerly of Sèvres, who did some work in the earlier expensive styles, sometimes imitating the jewelled work of Cotteau (see *Sèvres Porcelain Factory*). He painted medallion portraits of Louis XV and Mme du Barry which were not subjects used as painted decoration in the 18th century, although *biscuit* porcelain portraits exist. Carelessly he added the date-letter for 1761 to one such specimen. Some of his work is signed, which the factory did not permit in the 18th century.

'Wasters' of this kind were probably confined to such wares as cups and saucers and plates, and these are precisely the kind of fakes one sees, especially cups and saucers. No doubt defective vases were smashed, as is still the custom at factories making expensive ornamental porcelain.

A good deal of old Sèvres was decorated sparsely, and this has sometimes tempted the faker to clean off the old decoration with hydrofluoric acid and substitute something much more expensive. These are rarely successful, and the tampering is nearly always obvious on superficial examination. The surface of the glaze is uneven due to remelting, and this is apparent to the finger-tips if not to the eye. Sometimes there is a 'burst bubble' effect in the glaze, and often black specks in addition, which are always a danger signal. Attempts have been made to add enamel ground colours to plain specimens, but those I have seen have always been conspicuously unsuc-

Sèvres Porcelain, Forgeries of. A plate of soft-paste Sèvres porcelain (probably old stock sold in 1804) decorated with cupids after Boucher and a green ground. Refiring the glaze has resulted in an orange-peel effect over the surface of the green ground—typical of the troubles which beset the faker in redecorating soft porcelain.

cessful, the new ground being uneven and irregular. It is said that *gros bleu* has been successfully melted through the glaze, but this is very unlikely. Forgeries of 18th-century hard porcelain from Sèvres are extremely unusual. It has never been valued sufficiently highly, and there are plenty of close contemporary copies from the Paris factories.

The factory made very few glazed and painted figures, and anything purporting to come from Sèvres of this nature requires especially careful examination, bearing in mind the possibility of glazing and painting a *biscuit* figure. I have only seen one attempt, and this was obvious. The *biscuit* figures themselves were never marked in the 18th century, and a mark suggests a 19th-century factory reproduction or a forgery. Unmarked figures of this kind were made at many 18th-century porcelain factories at one time or another, and these are not forgeries. Many are models not made at Sèvres at all.

Few fakes or forgeries of old Sèvres are really dangerous, and most of the legend which has clustered around reproductions is false, such as John Rose of Coalport buying one of his own factory's vases in the London saleroom as Sèvres to show his workmen what a Sèvres vase really looked like. This can only reflect on his judgment and knowledge if true. In examining old Sèvres special attention should be paid to the painting, for if there has been any tampering, or if the object is a forgery, this is where it will be at its most obvious. Genuine examples may be studied in most of the world's great museums, and for this there is no substitute.

See *Rose Pompadour*.

SGABELLE (Italian)

Italian Renaissance chair without arms, the early examples on three legs, with a solid seat and a board back. The carving of the back later became very elaborate, and seats were sometimes made as small

Shaker Furniture. Shaker cupboard-chest of pine with a rose-red stain from Watervliet, N.Y. c. 1840. *The Shaker Museum, Old Chatham, N.Y.*

coffers with a lid, or with a drawer under. This type was given two solid supports, front and back, often elaborately carved, which took the place of legs. Stools somewhat of this form lack the back.

SGRAFFITO (Italian)

Literally, 'scratched'. The term (though more usually *graffiti*) is often applied facetiously to untutored drawings to be found on the walls of public lavatories, and this practice is of very considerable antiquity, as the ruins of Pompeii prove. Applied to pottery, it means ware which has been washed over with a differently coloured slip to the body itself, through which the decoration has been incised. See *Mezza-maiolica*.

SHAGREEN

The untanned skin of the shark (or sometimes of the horse) which was given a granular finish and usually dyed green. It was popular in the 18th century as a covering for small boxes, *étuis*, etc.

SHAKERS, AMERICAN

One commentator has said: 'For the sheer beauty of the direct solution, elemental but not primitive, there is little in America to surpass their designs.' The Shakers, originating in Manchester, England, are a sect founded in 1758 by Ann Lee. As 'Shaking Quakers' they were declared heretical and emigrated to America in 1774. The first colony was established in 1780 at Watervliet, near Albany. Eventually there were 18 communities or societies in New York, Massachusetts, Connecticut, Maine, New Hampshire, Ohio, and Kentucky. The movement

reached its greatest popularity about the time of the Civil War when membership totalled 6,000.

The Shakers separated themselves from the 'world' to seek a more spiritual way of life. They repudiated private property, marriage, the bearing of arms and all worldliness. Living in semi-monastic communities they were almost completely isolated. Their belief in a doctrine of order and use meant that products should serve as perfectly as possible their appointed purpose. Purpose predetermined design. Communal function influenced craftsmanship. Much furniture was suited to group use—long trestle tables and benches, built-in drawers, large cupboards and chests, and multiple-purpose kitchen and office furniture. Furniture for a specialized purpose might have marked individuality. There were rocking-chairs with arms for the aged, chairs for invalids, children's chairs, weaving and tailoring chairs, and footstools and settees for visitors. Furniture was designed to allow for the difference of sex—tables, chairs, and desks for the sisterhood were lower in height and more delicate in construction than those for the brethren. The key tenet of all craftsmanship was simplicity. Anything considered superfluous or useless was discarded. Carvings, inlays, veneers, mouldings, excessive turnings, and surface decoration added nothing to their feeling for harmony of proportion and refinement of line. The slightest accessory was given the status of an art, delicate poplar basketry, fine hand-made ironware, coloured silk kerchiefs, hand-loom rugs and clothing softly glowing with natural dyes—all were products of a kind of religious functionalism.

See *Furniture, American.*

SHARAWAGGI

Sometimes spelled *Sharawadgi*, this word of unknown derivation was first employed under the impression that it was Chinese by Sir William Temple in 1685, who thought it meant the studied beauty of irregularity, one of the key concepts of the rococo style (q.v.). Walpole also employed the word in 1750 to mean Chinese want of symmetry in buildings and gardens.

SHEARER, THOMAS

A contemporary of Sheraton and Hepplewhite about whom little is known. He contributed plates to the *Cabinet-makers' London Book of Prices and Designs* in 1788, and is generally credited with the invention of the sideboard (q.v.) as an integral piece of furniture.

SHEET-GLASS

Glass in sheet form for mirrors, glazing, and other purposes was formerly made by first blowing a globe which was rolled into a cylinder, after which the ends were cut off with shears, the side slit open, and the sheet flattened out. Glass made by casting on a flat bed was a technique introduced into France towards the end of the 17th century, but it did not arrive in England for almost a hundred years afterwards.

Sheet-glass made by the first-mentioned process

Shaker Furniture. Dining-room in the Shaker Museum, Old Chatham, N.Y. The chairs are low-backed to slide under the table-top. Pegs were also provided to hang them on the wall, as may be seen here. *The Shaker Museum.*

Shaker Furniture. Sisters' visiting room in the Shaker Museum, Old Chatham, N.Y. The table and chest are of maple. *The Shaker Museum.*

can be recognized by imperfections in the metal, and by slight surface irregularities when viewed from an angle. It was employed not only for mirrors and windows but for glazing the doors of bookcases and cabinets, although it is comparatively rare to find either today in which the old glass is entirely intact.

Blown sheet-glass is thinner than old cast glass, or modern glass, and this can be well seen in most 18th-century mirrors. If a coin be laid on the surface, the distance between it and its reflection is the thickness of the glass. Because it was thin, when 18th-century glass is bevelled the bevels will be much wider and shallower than is the practice today, and in some cases will be almost imperceptible.

SHEFFIELD PLATE

Copper sheet sandwiched between two sheets of silver foil; French *cuivre argenté*. Thomas Bolsover of Sheffield discovered a process in 1743 which led to the fusion of thin bars of silver on to much thicker bars of copper, the bars then being passed through a rolling-mill to flatten them into sheet form. The sheets were from one-sixteenth to one-third of an inch thick, and they could be employed for most of the purposes for which sheet silver was used. It was not until Bolsover's apprentice, Joseph Hancock, developed the invention, and started the necessary rolling-mills, that Sheffield plate was launched on its successful career, but it was, in fact, the growth of this industry which produced a demand for solid silver made in Sheffield, and this led to the establishment of the Sheffield assay-office in 1783. The Act necessary for this to be done was amended in 1784 to allow makers of plate to register their names and devices, and when the manufacture of Sheffield plate was established in Birmingham (see *Boulton, Matthew*) manufacturers there were compelled, to their chagrin, to register their marks at Sheffield.

By 1765 the manufacture of Sheffield plate was on a rapidly increasing scale for most of the wares which had hitherto been made of silver. Boulton's factory at Soho, Birmingham, was making Sheffield plate, and producing wares made from it, on a con-

Sheffield Plate. Pierced salt with glass liner. Sheffield plate. Late 18th century. *Victoria and Albert Museum.*

siderable scale by 1764, and eventually manufacture was established in several cities, like London, Nottingham, and Dublin. Similar wares were also made on the Continent in several countries. After 1800 various attempts were made to improve on the base metal, including the use of German silver (a nickel-copper alloy), and manufacturers producing these wares were known as 'platers on white metal'.

Most of the copper employed for the 18th-century manufacture of Sheffield plate was alloyed with a little zinc, making it technically a brass. The thickness of silver was one-twelfth that of the base metal, and rolling was done at red heat. On early specimens the silver after rolling often slightly overlapped the copper, and when turned over at the edge it covered the intervening base metal. Generally, however, the nature of the metal can be plainly seen at a sheared edge, where copper can be discerned lying between two sheets of silver. For certain vessels the silver sheet on the inside was thinner than that on the outside, and in some early wares, one silver sheet was omitted altogether, the interior of the vessel being tinned instead. The earliest wares were always single-plated.

Defects in plating were at first disguised by a process known as French plating (q.v.) in which silver leaf was laid on in successive layers and burnished, and later by electroplating, although the latter is to be found as part of the manufacturing process only on the very latest wares. See *Electroplating*.

Much Sheffield plate was made by raising (q.v.), and in the case of objects like teapots, spout and handle were soldered into position with silver solder in the manner of the silversmith. The use of dies was a comparatively early method of manufacture for such objects as candlesticks which were made in a number of parts and assembled, as well as for ornament to be attached to such raised work as teapots and coffee-pots. Early specimens of die-stamped work were often finished by hand. A special tool, the swage, was used to raise bands on hollow wares and the edges of salvers, and this ornament is commonly to be found towards the end of the 18th century.

In the decoration of Sheffield plate flat-chasing took the place of engraving, since an incised line would obviously cut through the silver to expose

Sheffield Plate. Cream jug of Sheffield plate. English. Late 18th century. *Victoria and Albert Museum.*

base metal. Designs were indented into the surface from the front, and embossing from both front and back occurs on early pieces (see *Repoussé*). Fluting and gadrooning was done in the same way. Flat-chasing, which can be found occasionally on 17th-century English silver, more closely imitated engraved ornament, and was described as 'denting in'. As with silver, pierced work (q.v.) decorated some of the best Sheffield plate, especially cake-baskets and similar articles which were also thus decorated by the silversmith.

It is rare to find specimens of Sheffield plate which can reliably be dated before 1770, but a very few survive which are embossed with rococo (q.v.) designs in the manner of the silver of the 1750s, and these are obviously about 1760 or perhaps slightly later. Some plain specimens, by their shape, suggest a similar dating. In many ways these early pieces are comparable with contemporary silver in the fact that they were made by a single craftsman. Later wares intended for quantity production were often die-stamped in parts, or made by several hands and then assembled. Dating of pieces in the neo-classical (q.v.) style is usually easier, and this was, in many ways, more suited to the material than the preceding rococo. For this reason it was speedily adopted, but the popularity of bright engraving (q.v.) on the silver of the time taxed the ingenuity of the makers of Sheffield plate. By about 1780 it had become customary to add bands and other kinds of ornament of silver to the plated ware to provide a suitable metal for bright cutting, and on the best work handles were frequently of silver, or of copper especially heavily plated to withstand wear. Silver shields were inset on articles like *entrée* dishes and salvers to enable crests and monograms to be added in bright cutting after about 1800.

By this time output was enormous, and comprised almost everything normally to be found in contemporary silver. Quality also began to deteriorate, and silver additions became much thinner and lighter in weight. The copper revealed by a sheared edge was sometimes covered with soft solder on the cheaper wares, instead of being disguised by silver wire, a method which had first been employed in 1787. Great pains, however, were still being taken with articles of the best quality to make them deceptively like silver, even to marks, which at first sight seem to be assay marks.

The best Sheffield plate of the later period was burnished by hand, and gilding occurs on some rare specimens, usually the interiors of salts, sugar-basins, and cream-jugs. As with silver, gilding was soon abandoned in favour of blue glass liners. Specimens gilded on the exterior are very rare.

It is doubtful whether Sheffield plate made before 1784 bore any kind of mark. Although marks had to be registered with the Assay Office it was not compulsory to use them. Many pieces after this date were marked, however, and the marks were often so disposed as to resemble those on contemporary silver. Retailers sometimes added their own mark. From registered marks preserved in Sheffield Assay Office it is possible to say that in 1824 there were seventy-seven makers in Birmingham and fifty-one in Sheffield, but very few new names were registered after this date. Marks generally to be found on Sheffield plate are listed in Frederick Bradbury's handbook of silver marks. See *Bibliography*.

SHEFFIELD PLATE, FAKES AND FORGERIES OF

Objects made of Sheffield plate on which the silver has worn away to reveal the base metal beneath are sometimes electrically replated, but this has the effect of destroying the original colour, which inclines slightly to yellow or to a leaden tinge, replacing it with a spurious brightness. In the case of a piece so worn as to be unsightly there is something to be said in favour of replating, but it certainly reduces value.

It is important, in the case of replated wares, to be certain that they were Sheffield plate to start with. The popularity of old Sheffield plate at the beginning of the present century led to the manufacture of reproductions which were electroplated from the first, some of which were struck from old dies. Many old pieces were raised by methods appropriate to the silversmith, but modern imitations are often spun for cheapness and have no seams, although the recognition of seams on an old piece is sometimes a little difficult if it has been subsequently plated. Spinning was employed occasionally in the making of Sheffield plate after 1802. The signs of replating are not difficult to find as a rule. Old pieces will always show signs of wear somewhere, leading to the base-metal appearing through the silver, and these can be found especially where it has been handled often, on the edges of cast ornament, and where cleaning has left its mark. Where this cannot be seen, the whole being covered with silver, replating should be suspected, especially if any chasing present is obscured by the deposition of new metal. Seams, likewise, tend to disappear. When in doubt as to the nature of the silver, scraping in an inconspicuous position is often revealing. If base metal appears at once then electroplating is almost certain, since the coating of silver deposited in this way is always very thin. If several scrapes are needed, Sheffield plate is much more likely. Marks closely resembling those properly belonging to Sheffield plate were sometimes copied on electroplated wares, and authenticity should not be assumed on this evidence alone.

SHELLAC

A resinous substance obtained from the insect, *Coccus lacca*. It is sold in the form of thin, small plates which are soluble in alcohol. It is the basis of a number of varnishes (q.v.). Shellac was well known in the 18th century.

SHELLWORK

Shells of all kinds, but especially exotic varieties, were much sought by collectors throughout most of the 18th century, both in England and France. Martin

Shells. Shell-carved block front to a mahogany chest of drawers in the Townsend-Goddard style. American. Newport, R.I. Second half of the 18th century. *Parke-Bernet Galleries, New York.*

Lister in his *Journey to Paris* (1698) mentions visiting collections of this kind, and instances later of large shells being mounted in gilt-bronze as orna-

ments are not uncommon. High prices were paid for fine specimens, and shells as a *motif* of the rococo style are elsewhere discussed (see *Rococo*).

Occasionally one finds examples of shells used to form or decorate small ornamental objects of one kind or another. As examples, the Victoria and Albert Museum (London) has a vase with a large bouquet of flowers made up of a variety of shells, and a plaque ornamented with them.

The use of shells for ornamental objects of this kind was always the work of amateurs, and they were never the subject of commercial production. Good specimens are rare.

Shells were also used to ornament the walls of grottoes, and a few examples have survived in England.

SHERATON, THOMAS (c. 1750–1806)

Sheraton began his career as a journeyman cabinet-maker, and did not come to London until about 1790, spending most of his earlier life in and around his birthplace of Stockton-on-Tees, if we accept the publication of religious pamphlets, the last of which is dated 1782, as evidence of his presence in the town of publication. No piece of furniture which can

Shellwork. Grotto with the walls decorated with shellwork. 18th century. *Goodwood House, Sussex.*

be proved to come from the hand of Sheraton exists, and he is only known as a designer. His principal works are *The Cabinet Maker and Upholsterer's Drawing Book* (published in parts between 1791 and 1794), and the *Cabinet Dictionary* of 1803.

Sheraton designs are often strongly influenced by contemporary French neo-classical styles, and in France Sheraton furniture is called *Louis Seize à l'Anglaise*, which is a fair description of much of it. A good deal of his furniture, especially dressing-tables, is of the multi-purpose type introduced by the German *ébénistes* of Paris (see *Ébéniste-mécanicien*). Sideboards were, in Sheraton's day, a comparatively recent introduction, and he designed many extremely elegant versions. His beds were very strongly influenced by current French fashions, especially in the canopies, and a design entirely his own of a summer bed has two single beds, with a centre passage between them, covered by one draped canopy. He made designs for painted furniture, and for interiors, including pelmets and curtains. His own description of a *commode* which appears in one of the interiors refers to a tablet inset in the centre of the frieze 'made of an exquisite composition of statuary marble', to be had 'of any figure, or on any subject, at Mr Wedgwood's near Soho Square [London]'. By this time Wedgwood plaques were occupying much the same position in the decoration of some English furniture as Sèvres plaques were in France.

The essentials of the Sheraton style are straight lines rather than curved, a notable lightness and delicacy of form and ornament, and a preference for satinwood veneers and inlays. His later work owes much to the prevailing Empire style in France, but this was neither so popular, nor so influential, as his earlier designs.

Sheraton, Thomas. A Sheraton *secrétaire*-bookcase in inlaid satinwood and mahogany with clock and candle-holders. **Late 18th century.** *Parke-Bernet Galleries, New York.*

SHEVERET

An English term current about 1790 for the lady's writing-desk called in France the *bonheur du jour* (q.v.), from which it was doubtless derived. Also *Cheveret*.

SHIELD-BACK CHAIR

A chair with the back in the shape of a shield, a favourite with George Hepplewhite (q.v.). This form of back became increasingly popular after 1785.

SHIRAZ RUGS AND CARPETS

These were made largely by the tribe of the Kashkais and sold in Shiraz. They are nomad carpets (q.v.). The Sehna knot is nearly always employed, but the Ghiordes knot occurs occasionally. Designs include the pole-medallion (in which the medallion has a projection at either end), the pear pattern, and scattered flowers throughout the field. Birds and animals are common. The prayer-rug of this type is often called 'Mecca Shiraz' (q.v.). Many saddlebags come from here.

SIDEBOARD

Although the term 'side board' was employed for the kind of side-table which served the same purpose before the introduction of the piece of furniture thus designated today, the first sideboard designed with flanking cupboards starts with the onset of the Adam style, and Adam is credited with the innovation. The sideboard began as a side-table to which had been added a separately constructed matching cupboard on either side, usually in the form of a pedestal surmounted by an urn. The urns were knife-boxes. Later, urns gave way to a continuous top on the same level, with cupboards or deep drawers on either side. These were intended to hold wine-bottles, and there was often provision for a chamber-pot. Lead-lined drawers held water for washing glasses, which was done between courses, although these have rarely survived in original condition.

Hepplewhite, Shearer, and Sheraton designed

Sideboard. Regency sideboard in the Egyptian style, the legs surmounted by a bust and terminating in human feet. Between the central drawers a winged scarab. c. 1815. *Wilfred Bull Ltd.*

many sideboards in a light and elegant style, often with curving fronts. Those which curve inwards in the middle allowed servants to pass each other in a confined space. Many had a brass rail at the back to display large dishes, and as a support for candle-holders.

During the Regency period sideboards became considerably larger, and separate pedestal cupboards, or those integral but clearly defined, enjoyed a return to favour. The pedestals were usually wider at the top than the bottom, supported on paw-feet, and the same tapering shape was employed for the now square knife-boxes and bottle-containers, which replaced the urns of the earlier period. A sarcophagus (q.v.) often stood beneath, between the pedestals.

Backs and mirrors came into vogue with the opening years of Queen Victoria's reign, and the mirrors, small at first, rapidly multiplied, or became much greater in size. There was a fashion, also, for 'Elizabethan' sideboards in carved oak which could better be termed *buffets*. The 'art furniture' movement of the 1860s and 1870s engendered sideboards with painted panels, or those ornately carved either in a revived late Gothic style or something purporting to be Early Renaissance.

SIENA (Italy)
Siena is one of the first recorded Italian pottery-centres. It mastered the tin-enamel glaze at an early date, and was in full production by 1500. Two famous tile-pavements made at this factory contain almost the complete *repertoire* of ornamental design, full of the inventiveness and variation of the Renaissance, and these tiles have enabled other pieces to be classified by analogy.

Dominant ground colours are orange, a red known as *terra di Siena*, orange-yellow, copper-green, and deep blue, all very brilliant in hue. Wares are *albarellos*, vases, dishes, and plates, all of which are extremely rare today. Siena plates and dishes are decorated with blue and orange floral decoration on the back, and these are sometimes termed petal-backs. Profile portraits are thrown into relief by a blue shadow behind; these usually occur on the wells of dishes, or on *albarellos*, often enclosed by close-knit leafy wreaths, sometimes accompanied by waving ribbons. Another pattern of palmette flowers

on thin blue stems is reminiscent of Hispano–Moresque-inspired designs at Florence. Plates have large numbers of concentric borders, sometimes plain but often filled with very varied ornament.

After 1525 Siena seems to have been more or less overwhelmed by Faenza, and the factory remains in semi-obscurity till an 18th-century revival, but the potters never returned to the early brilliance, following rather the manner of Castelli. No wares are known after 1747.

See also *Deruta*.

SILHOUETTE PORTRAITS
Profile portraits, usually in black paper affixed to a background which is generally white. The word itself is derived from the reputation for parsimony gained by one of Louis XV's Finance Ministers, Étienne de Silhouette, but the earliest silhouettes go back to the end of the 17th century. In England they were sometimes termed 'shades'.

Basically, the silhouette portrait was the outline of the shadow of the sitter's profile, the shadow being thrown on to oiled paper by means of a suitable source of illumination and the outline drawn in pencil. This outline was sometimes filled in with black pigment, and sometimes cut from white paper and mounted on black board. Portraits cut from black paper are not unusual. Sometimes, especially when they are half- or full-length, a background was sketched in more or less detail. Rarer are portraits which are partly in black and partly painted in colour. These are usually French, are commonly portraits of naval and military officers, and are often full-length. Silhouettes are sometimes black with the hair in a lighter shade and hair-ornament in gold. Glass silhouettes are those painted on glass on the reverse side; they are often French, and very similar to *verre eglomisé* (q.v.). Many are on the reverse side of oval convex glasses, usually with a flat white background. Rarely, examples are found in black on a background of a material like plaster of Paris. Although the techniques mentioned were all hand-work, a mechanical contrivance for taking silhouettes was introduced early in the 19th century in the form of a rod pivoted to provide one long arm and one short. The long arm was fitted with a pointer which followed the outlines of the sitter's face, and a pencil attached to the short arm traced the outline, which was filled in

Silhouette Portraits. Silhouettes used in the decoration of an English dinner-service of c. 1820. *Sotheby & Co.*

with black pigment, probably lamp-black. Dickens, in *Pickwick Papers*, mentions a profile machine which executed a complete portrait in two and a quarter minutes.

Occasionally some quite elaborate scenes in silhouette may be found, such as one done by Auguste Edouart in 1835 of field sports, and from Germany came book-illustration in the same medium. Such profile portraitists as Miers of the Strand, London, kept all original sketches, and could supply replicas to order. Those who cut their profiles from paper with scissors took pride in the speed with which this part of the operation could be completed, since this aspect is often alluded to in old advertisements.

There is space to mention only a few of the better-known practitioners of the art. Rare, and much sought, are the cut-paper silhouettes of Francis Torond (1743–1812). J. Buncombe of Newport (Isle of Wight) from about 1745 onwards painted silhouettes of military men with uniforms in colour in the French style. Edward Foster of Derby often made silhouette portraits in colours other than black. Foster, who came from London, also employed a machine for taking profiles which, in 1811, was then 'newly invented', and this machine was also, according to his advertisement, capable of making an etching on a copper plate from which any number of profiles could be reproduced. Isabella Beetham was at work soon after the middle of the 18th century, and did profiles on convex glass. John Miers (1758–1821) is perhaps the best known of all profilists. The silhouette enjoyed renewed popularity in the 19th century, and the work of August Edouart, who published a treatise on the subject in 1835, is the most distinguished. Another 19th-century profilist named West specialized in miniatures for mounting in rings and brooches. Among the many who worked abroad was a Parisian, A. Forberger (1762–1835), who often employed a background of gold-leaf.

In America the art of the silhouette was well established soon after the middle of the 18th century, but in the first half of the 19th it reached the period of its greatest popularity, before it was ousted from favour by the newly emerging art of photography. Here, also, a profile machine was in use in the early years of the 19th century, perhaps the best known being that of William King (fl. 1785–1805). The techniques employed in Europe are all to be found in America, Charles Polk (1767–1822), for instance, using the gold ground. Edouart spent about ten years in America, producing a great deal of work of excellent quality.

SILK

This lustrous filament obtained from the cocoon of the silkworm (*Bombyx mori*) was first woven into a textile fabric in China long before the present era. The Romans traded with China for silk, and the Byzantines bought it in such vast quantities that the city was almost bankrupted by the expenditure. It was here that the silkworm was first introduced, according to legend, by some monks who secreted the eggs in a slip of bamboo. The trade in silk flourished especially after the Renaissance, Venice being one of the principal ports of import, and it was a staple of the East India Companies' trade. Silk was widely used in France during the second half of the 17th century, and throughout the 18th century, as a furnishing fabric.

SILK, PAINTED

(French *soierie peint*.) Silk as a support for painted decoration was employed in France during the second half of the 18th century, but surviving specimens are rare.

Silk. **Silk-weaving loom. French. Mid-18th century.** *After Diderot.*

SILK RUGS

Rugs with a pile entirely of silk are rare, although silk and wool mixtures are not uncommon in the making of fine rugs. They are very closely knotted, usually on a cotton foundation.

Silk rugs were first made in China, later in northern Persia, and then in Anatolia, following the course of the Old Silk Road. In former times silk rugs were usually specially commissioned, and the task given only to weavers of proven skill. These are now virtually unprocurable, but modern examples from Kashan (q.v.) in northern Persia are not unusual, although expensive. Inferior copies have come from Kasarieh in Asia Minor, usually with a *mihrab* and a hanging mosque lamp towards the top of the niche, and these are fairly common. There are numerous silk and wool imitations.

Needless to say, the best rugs of this kind are not suitable for floor-coverings.

SILVER, AMERICAN

The earliest silversmiths in the American colonies generally worked with coins brought to them by their customers, who, in the absence of banks, regarded wrought silver as a kind of insurance. American silver was customarily stamped with the individual maker's mark, either initials or name, which was unlike the more closely regulated English system, where each year had its stamp, and the maker and assay office could readily be identified. In colonial days silver was a rare and much prized possession, available to very few, though silversmithing flourished at a surprisingly early period. In Massachusetts before 1650 a prosperous mercantile middle-class supported silversmiths who worked in simple and vigorous English fashions of Charles I, and later of the Commonwealth. Robert Sanderson (1608–1693), the 'father of [American] silversmiths', and John Hull (1624–1683), made most of Boston's earliest silver. Others were Jeremiah Dummer (1645–1718), and John Coney (1656–1722), an extremely versatile and productive craftsman. Edward Winslow of Boston (1669–1753), whose working years were largely in the 18th century, was, like Hull, a leader in the colony. He is chiefly famous for elaborately wrought sugar-boxes. Winslow worked intimately with John Coney on private commissions.

From 1660 to 1697 American silversmiths worked in late Stuart and William and Mary styles. Typical products were the two-handled cup, porringers, the great or standing salt, small trencher-salts, tankards, mugs, and beakers, candlesticks, either simple Doric columns or cluster-columns, spoons, vessels for drinking tea, coffee and chocolate, and boxes for sweetmeats.

New forms during the Queen Anne period were baluster and bulbous shapes, and octagonal forms, several inspired by Oriental porcelain. New items were casters for pepper and sugar, braziers or chafing dishes, and stands or salvers.

Silversmithing in New York, originally a Dutch settlement, began a generation later than in New England, and at first differed markedly in style. A number of wealthy Dutch families insisted on models taken from their homeland. The majority of New York silversmiths were Dutch, or of Dutch descent. Jacob Boelen (1654–1729), Hendrik Boelen (1684–1755), Koenraet Ten Eyck (1678–1753), and Jacob Ten Eyck (1705–1793); Cornelius Kierstede (1675–1757), of Albany; Peter Van Dyck (1684–1750), Adrian Banker (1703–1772), and Benjamin Wynkoop (1675–1751). New York silversmiths made wide use of embossed, engraved, and cast ornament, and their products were distinctly more generous in proportion, and more massive, than Boston silver. Characteristic were bowl-shaped cups directly derived from Dutch silver and ornamented with bold *repoussé* and flat-chased flower *motifs* in reserved panels. These wide bowls might be simpler or smaller, but they found universal favour in New Amsterdam as New York then was. Tankards and beakers were also favourites. A secondary influence on New York silver was the work of such Huguenots as the Le Roux family and Simeon Soumain (1685–1750).

Towards the close of the century other silversmithing centres arose in cities with cultured and wealthy patrons. In Newport Samuel Vernon was especially well known, and in Charleston, South Carolina, the Huguenot, Solomon Legare, set up shop in 1691. In Philadelphia, Philip Syng (1670–1739) arrived from Ireland to found a distinguished family of silversmiths before moving on to Annapolis.

Prominent in the second generation of native-born craftsmen was John Burt of Boston (1693–1745). John trained three sons, William (1726–1751), Samuel (1724–1754), and Benjamin (1729–1805). But it is Jacob Hurd (1702–1758) whose work, like Coney of a generation earlier, today exceeds in quantity and variety that of any of his contem-

Silver, American. Two-handled silver bowl with floral decoration by Cornelius Kierstede. New York. 18th century.

poraries. Hurd taught his sons Nathaniel (1729–1777) and Benjamin (1739–1781) to be silversmiths. In New York Myer Myers (1723–1795) was a prominent Jewish silversmith who made silver for Protestant churches as well as extraordinary ritual pieces for the Newport synagogue. His domestic forms are much collected today. In Philadelphia Francis Richardson (1681–1729) headed the most illustrious family of that city's silversmiths, Joseph Sr. (1711–1784), Joseph Jr. (1752–1831), and Nathaniel (1754–1827). From 1750 to 1825 Philadelphia was the largest city in America. Philip Syng, Jr. (1703–1789) is chiefly famous for his silver standish made in 1752 for the assembly of Pennsylvania which was used by the signatories of the Declaration of Independence.

The classical revival of about 1765–1800 introduced new *motifs* in silver—slender columns, friezes, drapery, pendant husks, acanthus foliage, laurel leaves, swags, masks, rosettes, and medallions. A new technique was 'bright cutting' (q.v.).

Unquestionably today the patriot, Paul Revere, is America's most famous silversmith, who worked during the period just before and after the Revolution. He was a copper-plate engraver, wood carver, cannon- and bell-founder, a maker of such utility items as andirons, an engraver and a supplier of dental accessories. Unfortunately, the sentimental poem by Longfellow has long distorted his value as a silversmith. His work is of varying quality, much quite distinguished, and much of only average quality.

Of the public collections available for study of American silver the ten following are the foremost.

The Cleveland Museum of Art; Colonial Williamsburg; Henry Ford Museum; The Henry Francis du Pont Winterthur Museum; The Metropolitan Museum of Art, New York; Minneapolis Institute of Arts; Museum of the City of New York; Museum of Fine Arts, Boston; Philadelphia Museum of Art; Yale University, Garvan and Related Collections.

SILVER, ENGLISH

English silver made before the Restoration (q.v.) is exceedingly scarce. The commonest survivals are specimens of ecclesiastical plate (q.v.), and of plate in the possession of some of the older colleges. Although objects of silver were always quite frequently melted for coinage, or to make new ones in more up-to-date forms, the Civil War was the most disastrous episode in the history of English silver, when very large quantities of plate were melted to provide metal for coinage to pay the troops of both King and Commonwealth.

Coevally with the vogue for silver in massive quantities at the Court of Louis XIV in France, a similar fashion is to be observed at that of Charles II in England. The English silversmiths of the early Restoration period leaned heavily on Continental design-books, principally those of Holland which, in turn, were largely influenced by Italian fashions. The silver furniture of the period has not survived except

Silver, English. One of a pair of candelabra by Nicholas Dumé. 1776. *Christie, Manson & Woods.*

in very rare instances, of which the most notable is that of Knole in Kent. Decoration of the period includes embossed animals amid flowers as large as themselves, and large embossed flowers only, both of which were of Dutch origin. The acanthus (q.v.) was a favourite kind of ornament which can be noticed frequently in the decorative arts of the period. Also largely of Dutch origin are Chinese *motifs*, both engraved and embossed, which are much more in the nature of *chinoiseries* (q.v.).

As in France so much silversmiths' work was produced at this time that a shortage of the metal for other purposes was eventually experienced, and in 1697, with the object of freeing supplies for coinage, the new Britannia standard containing 95·8 parts of pure silver was introduced, instead of the 92·5 parts of the sterling standard, with the intention of making it difficult to melt silver coins for manufacturing purposes. In 1685 the Revocation of the Edict of Nantes brought Huguenot (q.v.) silversmiths to England, and since they were mostly provincial craftsmen French provincial influence began to replace that of Holland. The plain silver of the Queen Anne period, and cut-card work (q.v.), were both Huguenot innovations produced side by side with the *chinoiseries* of the native silversmith. Elaborately

Silver, English. George IV soup tureen and cover of c. 1825, with reeded and gadrooned ornament, and feet and handles ornamented with acanthus leaves. *Sotheby & Co.*

Silver, English. Silver dish by Paul de Lamerie. *Sotheby & Co.*

pierced work of fine quality, such as may be found in the tops of sugar-casters, are also an example of Huguenot innovation.

The styles of the closing years of the reign of Louis XIV, and the *Régence* period which followed, arrived in London towards the end of the reign of George I (d. 1727), and Paul de Lamerie (q.v.) executed some splendid examples in this *genre* a little later. The early years of the 18th century were also remarkable for some very large so-called wine-cisterns (usually refrigerators for wine-bottles), and the glass-coolers termed Monteiths (q.v.). The reign of Queen Anne saw the development of the teapot, coffee-pot, and chocolate-pot. These had all made their appearance in the reign of William III, the earliest teapots being conical, and of the 'cut out and soldered' variety. The silver kettle, with stand and spirit lamp, made its appearance about the same time, and tea-caddies were introduced during the reign of Queen Anne in sets of either two or three for containing different varieties of tea for blending purposes, for which a locked case was provided.

The early signs of rococo influence (q.v.) occur in England around 1740, and the designs of Meissonnier (q.v.) arrived about the same time. Rococo asymmetry first occurs in the work of Paul de Lamerie, and he is perhaps the acknowledged master of the style in English silver, although excellent work in this style was done by Nicolas Sprimont, originally from Liége, who was later manager of the Chelsea Porcelain Factory (q.v.). His designs owe a good deal to Meissonnier, and some of them were later trans-

lated into porcelain during the factory's first period. About 1745 a German influence begins to appear with the work of Charles and Frederick Kändler, and their version of the style differs from that of the Huguenot silversmiths, being more akin to South

Silver, English. Wine-cistern of 1794 by James and Elizabeth Bland. The legs of acanthus form terminate in lion-paw feet. The frieze immediately below the gadrooned edge is of bell-flowers. *Christie, Manson & Woods.*

German rococo. Some of Charles Kändler's silver shows all the fondness for elaborate and finely executed ornament of the Augsburg metalworker. Figure-subjects of rococo *chinoiserie* appear around 1750, contemporary with gilt-wood mirror-frames of the same subject. At this time the larger objects of

Silver, English. The Sutherland wine-cistern by Paul de Lamerie, 38 inches wide. 1719. *Christie, Manson & Woods.*

silver, such as *chenets*, vases, and wine-cisterns which had been popular earlier, went out of fashion, perhaps for much the same economic causes as limited the production of decorative silver in France. The influence of the Italian Comedy (q.v.), popular in the porcelain of the period, may be seen in rare taper-sticks, the candle-nozzle and drip-pan supported by a figure of Harlequin. Little or nothing is to be seen of the fashion for revived Gothic in silver.

Neo-classicism (q.v.) began to influence silver design soon after 1760, and the simpler styles of Adam were much favoured by such silversmiths as Matthew Boulton (q.v.), who had a taste for quantity production. The absence of any surviving specimens of classical silver caused both form and decoration to be based on bronzework excavated plentifully at Pompeii and Herculaneum, and made available in an increasing number of illustrated works which had started with the Comte de Caylus (q.v.) and Sir William Hamilton (q.v.). To a lesser extent classical pottery provided the silversmith with models, and much was decorated with the popular swags, rams' heads, etc. Bright-cut engraving (q.v.) replaced the earlier plain engraving, and pierced work (q.v.) was quite commonly employed for the larger centre-pieces known as *épergnes* (q.v.). The most elaborate came from Thomas Pitts of Air Street, Piccadilly, London, who specialized in them. The vogue for pierced work can also be seen in Sheffield plate and contemporary creamware from Wedgwood and Leeds, and salts and sugar-containers in this form were given blue glass liners. Many new utensils of silver for table use first appeared about this time.

Such designers as Flaxman (q.v.) began to design in a more severe style than 'Adam filigraine', and this new severity is more or less contemporary with the Greek revival (q.v.) and the *Directoire* period (q.v.). The Empire style (q.v.) in France became more or less the English Regency style (q.v.), and much massive plate in this manner came from Paul Storr (q.v.) and Rundell, Bridge & Rundell, silver-smiths to the Prince Regent, towards the end of the Regency period. It introduced a sculptural style into English silver which had not been seen hitherto.

During the 1820s a revival of the rococo style in silver, as well as in porcelain, is to be noticed. Flowers were a favourite *motif*, and they occur in conjunction with asymmetrical scrollwork. Flowers of this kind

Silver, English. An engraved silver tray of 1738. London. Maker unknown. The 'piecrust' border is also found on contemporary tables. The asymmetrical engraving denotes an early example of the rococo style in England. *Parke-Bernet Galleries, New York.*

were also embossed on plain silver of the early decades of the 18th century, which loses a good deal of its value in consequence.

Victorian silver is the expected hotch-potch of styles, but at the end of the 19th century some interesting designs in the *art nouveau* manner were made by such men as C. R. Ashbee, the translator of Cellini's *Treatise on Goldsmithing*.

SILVER, FORGERIES OF

This is one of the few fields in which the collector really has the law on his side, for to forge objects of gold and silver has for centuries been an offence visited with very heavy penalties. The system of hall-marking (q.v.) is also a considerable protection, although, as will be seen, not an entirely reliable one. When a silversmith submits his work for hall-marking the metal is tested to see that it contains only the permitted amount of alloy. The reason is not difficult to see. At the time of writing pure gold is worth about £12 an ounce troy. Therefore the value of the metal alone in a cup weighing five ounces is £60. To add an ounce of alloying metal worth a few pence would bring an additional profit to the maker of £12. Silver is worth less, but, of course, objects of silver are often much heavier. The temptation to add alloying metals for one reason or another has always been strong.

Hall-marks make life difficult for the forger, for, no matter how good his work may be otherwise, these must still be added. It is true that occasionally specimens are found bearing only the maker's mark but they are very rare, and anything of this kind is certain to be subjected to a great deal of expert scrutiny. Marks are sometimes taken from old pieces which are too damaged to be anything but scrap-silver and transposed to a newly made piece. They can be inserted in various ways, but the forger likes best of all to find the marked bottom of a coffee-pot or a teapot, for this can be soldered into a newly made piece in a manner which is almost indetectable. Size is not very important, for this can always be

Silver, English. A George I octagonal sugar-box and cover, c. 1730, the form influenced by immigrant Huguenots. *Sotheby & Co.*

extended a little by hammering. It may make the metal thinner, but it is always inserted over the real bottom since the intention is only to provide marks.

It is a serious offence in England to possess false punches; in the United States it is not even a misdemeanour. Many falsely marked pieces of silver purporting to be English are therefore in circulation there, and some might find their way to England. Genuine punch-marks were added one at a time, and they are not evenly spaced or exactly in line. The maker's mark will be at either end; the remainder were added by the Assay Office. An ingenious fraud was discovered because an American forger made a single stamp carrying all the punch marks, and these were precisely in line, with the same distance between each one. New punches, of course, will give a much sharper impression than those which have had some wear, and forgers are not so active that this is likely to happen to any they may have. Also, a genuinely old mark will always have some wear from cleaning. Although forgers know this and act accordingly it is difficult to simulate wear convincingly to someone who is experienced in looking at old silver-marks. Sometimes the new ware is submitted to the Assay Office to be marked, and then the marks, except for that of the Office, are heavily blurred. This is done with silver of the Britannia standard (q.v.) which is still used occasionally, and the presence of the Britannia mark makes silver purporting to belong to the turn of the 18th century more convincing.

The position of marks is of some importance, although this was not observed so invariably that it is a certain indication. The usual position is given below, and if marks are out of position it suggests more than usual care is needed.

Side-marks (near the top)	Bottom-marks
Early tankards	Tankards (later)
Porringers	Trencher salts
Caudle-cups	Jugs
Coffee-pots	Dishes
Teapots (rarely)	Punch-bowls
Chocolate-pots	Coffee-pots
Sauceboats	Teapots (usually)
	Chocolate-pots
	Sauceboats
	Casters
	Tea-caddies

Early pieces are most likely to have side-marks; later ones, bottom-marks, either in line or arranged radially, but position was, to some extent, a matter of convenience, and there are some things which lend themselves more easily to one position than the other. Early spoons may be marked on either bowl or stem, but from the last decades of the 17th century only on the stem.

Much more common is an alteration in the whole character of a genuine piece to make something more in demand, and therefore more valuable. These have a genuine set of hall-marks, and this aspect presents no problem. It is comparatively easy to make a mug into a jug by adding a pouring lip, and the jug is much rarer. An oval teapot with handle and spout removed can become a tea-caddy. A caster without a top can be reshaped into a cream-jug; saucepans become posset-pots and caudle-cups; spoons can be converted into the much rarer forks; and valuable spoons can be cast in moulds which will reproduce the hall-mark, although this is not a fraud which the knowledgeable collector will find difficult

Silver, Forgeries of. Late 19th-century silver-gilt Goat and Bee jug with the transposed mark of T. Penfold, London, 1724/5. This was made at a time when such collectors as Lady Charlotte Schreiber were collecting early English porcelain to provide the lost silver prototype of the porcelain jug for which they were searching. Since it is in the rococo style the date-mark quoted is much too early for the design. *Victoria and Albert Museum.*

Silver, Forgeries of. Chelsea porcelain Goat and Bee jug of c. 1745 (see *Chelsea Porcelain*) for comparison with the illustration opposite. The form is based on a contemporary silver pattern.

Silver, Forgeries of. A genuine tankard of 1729 altered into the much rarer jug by the addition of various parts. *Worshipful Company of Goldsmiths.*

to detect. All these things will bear genuine marks, although they may not be in the usual place.

Both silver and gold are malleable metals—that is, they can be shaped, and reshaped, by hammering, and a great deal can be done by a skilful workman. But hammering makes the metal thinner, and this helps in the detection of fraud. Thin places are not unusual, especially in trays, and they are often the result of removing an unwanted engraved inscription, usually one of comparatively recent date made to a presentation piece of silver before it had achieved its present value. Holes are sometimes patched, and both this kind of repair, and thin places due to removal of inscriptions, can be thickened up by electro-plating. This deposits metal of a different colour, and it means that the whole piece must be buffed to correspond (see *Putina*). Gilding is sometimes employed to cover faults of colour of this kind, since the gilding of silver was frequently practiced.

Some very fine plain silver was embossed with bastard rococo decoration in the 19th century, which completely spoils its value. Attempts are sometimes made to hammer this out, but only with disastrous effects on the shape. These things are not difficult to detect, for the style of the ornament and the quality of the workmanship are obviously Victorian. The amount of embossing is usually excessive, and often takes in the mark. It must be remembered however, when the mark is sometimes a good deal earlier than the decoration suggests, that a few pieces are known which were embossed with ornament of this kind in the 18th century.

Foreign silver needs to be carefully watched. The number of spurious specimens of Dutch silver on the market is high, and marks are not reliable. Silver purporting to belong to the reign of Louis Quatorze in France also needs careful examination, and a lot of scepticism. Much silver was sent to the Mint in the 1680s, and surviving specimens are very rare. Workmanship of forgeries is poor, and such *motifs* as baroque strapwork often diverge very considerably from surviving specimens of the period. An example which recently came to my notice had a profile portrait of Louis Quatorze on one side, and that of an unidentifiable woman who bore a strong resemblance to Marie-Antoinette on the other. The

decoration, had it been genuine, would have placed it to about 1700, when the Queen of France was dead and Mme de Maintenon was hardly likely to be represented in such a way. Wine-tasters of silver-gilt with a gold coin of Louis XIII inset were made in Paris during the last century. Generally, forgeries of French silver are not as numerous as those of the Dutch variety, probably because little of it, apart from provincial work, has survived.

Occasionally one sees much more ambitious forgeries made on the Continent. I remember a large silver-gilt charger which had the outer border elaborately decorated with *repoussé* work in the manner of the Dutch silversmiths of the mid-17th century and the centre with a silver medallion in the manner of Cellini, but things of this kind need very expert examination and, if genuine, are beyond the reach of most collectors.

There is very small chance of buying forged silver from a reputable and expert dealer, although even the best sometimes make mistakes. In fact the expert dealer is among the most active in stamping out forgeries, and the British Antique Dealers' Association co-operates with the Goldsmiths' Company in England in so doing.

SILVER, FRENCH

Relative to the quantity produced, very little French silver has survived. For the finest it is necessary, for the most part, to look outside France, to the museums of Lisbon and Leningrad, to the Munich Residenz, and to owners abroad who bought when it was contemporary, such as the Berkeley Castle dinner-service sold at Sotheby's in 1960 for £207,000. The reasons for this scarcity may be sought in the economic crises which afflicted the reigns of Louis XIV and Louis XV, and finally the catastrophe of the Revolution. Of these, the first was probably the most destructive, since the splendid silver furnishings of Versailles were among the objects melted for coinage, but Louis XV sent his plate to the Mint in cartloads, and members of his Court were subjected to a great deal of pressure to do likewise. The same crises produced various sumptuary laws designed to limit the amount of silver used for decorative work. Because of this we have lost the work of Claude I Ballin, who made many of the silver tables and *jardinières* for Versailles, and of his nephew, Claude II Ballin, although from the latter a basin and casket survives in the Residenz at Munich, and two *surtouts de table* (table-centres) are in the Hermitage (Leningrad).

Much of the appearance of silver at this time, and in the 18th century, can be deduced from the gilded bronze which took its place. In the second half of the 18th century silver became, to some extent, almost an antiquarian taste, rococo tending to linger as the preferred style well into the neo-classical period. In England the work of such silversmiths as Paul de Lamerie and Nicolas Sprimont may be regarded as characteristic of much rococo French silver which no longer survives, since they

Silver, French. **A silversmith's workshop. Mid-18th century.**
After Diderot.

worked from contemporary French design-books, such as those of Meissonnier (q.v.). Silver was extensively looted in France during the Revolution, and melted for the value of the metal. The movements of Napoleon's armies accounted for the loss of a great deal of European silver generally, since it was looted by his troops and hammered flat for ease of transport. The smallest things tended to survive. Those which were easily portable, such as highly decorated snuff-boxes, *étuis*, and the like made with superb craftsmanship, and French gold boxes especially, are much sought today. French provincial silver has more commonly survived than that of Paris, and specimens are to be found at prices comparable with those of English silver of the same period. These are usually plain in style and of domestic utility.

Hall-marking was introduced into France in the 14th century, although it was never so systematic as that of England and the method of date-lettering not so clear. At first there were two marks—the maker's mark in the form of an emblem surmounted by the *fleur-de-lys*, and the assay mark of the Guild in the form of a letter of the alphabet which was changed yearly with the appointment of a new guildmaster. In the 18th century the charge and discharge marks of the *fermier* of the tax are to be found, which, as to the first, denotes the entry of liability to tax in the *fermier*'s accounts, and the second, the payment of it. From 1765 all articles of silver-gilt (*vermeil*) were stamped *Argent*, with the tax discharge mark over the letter *A*. From 1789 to 1797 no stamps were added at all, and in the latter year the metric system was adopted and new punches decreed. In 1789 no fewer than 186 towns in France were empowered to test and stamp gold and silver. As in England, gold and silver marks were heavily protected by law, and death was the decreed penalty for forgery or the transposition of marks from one object to another.

Some of the more prominent of Paris silversmiths are noted elsewhere in this work, but surviving examples of their work are few and mostly in museums.

SILVER FURNITURE

Very little silver furniture now survives, although Louis XIV once had an impressive display at Versailles, which included tables, mirror-frames, *jardinières*, *torchères*, and so forth. Usually the large pieces, such as tables, were plated over a wooden foundation. A rare table preserved at Knole (Kent) is made in this way, but the quoted weight of one table at Versailles, melted in 1685 when the royal silver was sent to the Mint, suggests that it was solid. The silver furniture of Louis XIV was copied at the Court of Charles II, although on a more modest scale. Nell Gwynn, however, had a silver bed, which was made in 1676. The silver *chenets* of France were also to be found in England; although survivals are now very rare a silver fender and hearth furniture may be seen at Ham House (Ham, S.W. London).

During the same period carved wooden furniture and metal mounts were often covered with silver leaf. Lacquer cabinets were usually placed on stands decorated in this way.

SILVER, TARNISH ON

A thin greyish or blackish film which forms on neglected silver. It is usually silver sulphide, but in a saline atmosphere it is quite often silver chloride. With excavated objects the formation of silver chloride sometimes proceeds to the point of perceptible corrosion. Tarnish can usually be removed quite easily with a good metal polish.

SILVERING

Silvering by leaf or powder was occasionally employed in the 18th century on a variety of materials, including pottery and porcelain glazes and glass. In France and southern Germany silvered *boiseries* were combined with yellow to make a very attractive colour-scheme.

Nevertheless, because silver easily oxidized to black, and in leaf or powder form was difficult to clean, it never became as popular as gilding, and it could only be satisfactorily employed if the surface were protected by varnish or lacquer. It also seems to have been prone, when used on wood or metal, to develop unsightly spots, although this may have been the product of excessive adulteration of the metal with others. Protective varnishes were generally mastic, copal, or sandarac.

A metal simulating silver was called *argentum musivum*. A contemporary recipe for its manufacture calls for tin, bismuth, and quicksilver (mercury). Sizes for laying silver-leaf were usually mixed with white pigment, either flake white (white lead) or whiting, to which a little lamp-black was added.

Silvering occurs most commonly in the case of glass on the *Zwischensilbergläser*, and in ceramics on a notable series of brown glazed wares from Bayreuth (Germany) in the first half of the 18th century. This has usually oxidized to black, but the colour can sometimes be restored with a little gentle cleaning. Great care is essential.

There is reason to think that silvering was more common in the 18th century than surviving specimens suggest, and that a good deal of it was subsequently gilded because of the drawback referred to. Silvered work in the 18th century, especially picture-frames, was sometimes given a coat of coloured lacquer to bring the appearance nearer to that of gilding.

See *Zwischengoldgläser*.

SILVERING FOR MIRRORS

Mirrors in the 18th century were 'silvered' with tin foil over which a layer of mercury was spread very evenly with the aid of a hare's foot. Upon this the glass was laid, and pressed down firmly until glass and backing adhered. Mercury was sometimes combined with an alloy of tin and lead to which bismuth was added.

SINCENY (Aisne, France) FAÏENCE

Founded in 1737 by Pierre Pellevé, Sinceny built its reputation by using workmen and designs from Rouen. Pellevé was succeeded by Mériat, though the date is in doubt. Strasbourg painters introduced enamel decoration under Chambon in 1775, and the factory continued till 1864. Sinceny was virtually an offshoot of Rouen, and the quality of the wares sometimes surpassed that of the original factory. Pierre Pellevé's first workers all came from Rouen, and Mériat was a well-known Rouen potter.

A small quantity of blue-and-white was made before the arrival of the workers from Normandy, but in general Sinceny's evolution followed Rouen with *lambrequins*, polychrome *chinoiseries*, and rococo designs. The palette in the early stages was

Sinceny Faïence. **A plate of Sinceny faïence. c. 1740.** *Musée de Sèvres, Paris.*

rather uneven, and the red-brown thick, although it improved as time went on. Sinceny red does not exhibit the 'bubbling' which is typical of that of Rouen. The artists of Sinceny were very versatile and painted water-plants and reeds, as well as a peculiar duck-like bird, in a fresh, naturalistic style. The Sinceny glaze is a more bluish-white than that of Rouen, and a brilliant lemon-yellow on Chinese figures is typical. Although many details remain to remind one of Rouen, there are differences. After 1760 Sinceny relied less on Rouen designs, developing stylized flower-patterns such as the yellow rose, and bunches of tulips. The factory took on a new lease of life when enamel colours were introduced in 1755 and workers arrived from Lorraine.

Singeries. Boiserie (panelling) at the Château de Chantilly decorated with *singeries* by Christoph Huet. See also *Affenkapelle. Musée Condé, Chantilly, Oise.*

Enamelling was quite successful in Sinceny, though it never achieved the inspired freedom of Strasbourg.

SINGERIES (French)
Decoration, usually mural, of the first half of the 18th century in which monkeys play the principal part (French *singe*—monkey or ape). They are often dressed in pseudo-Chinese costume, and the *singerie* is closely related to the *chinoiserie* (q.v.). Best known are the *singeries* of Christoph Huet at Chantilly, where hunting scenes, tea-parties, and so forth are depicted with monkeys in the Chinese taste wearing the livery of the Prince de Condé. These, until the discovery of Huet's account for the work rendered in 1741, were often attributed to Watteau.

SLAG GLASS
Glass, variable in colour, so called because a proportion of slag from iron foundries was added to the other ingredients. Slag glass is notable for the variations in colour to be found in each piece, although this was largely under control. It was extensively manufactured in the second half of the 19th century.

Slag glass is termed agate glass (q.v.) in the U.S.A. A variety of a golden agate colour was manufactured there about 1900.

SLAT-BACK CHAIRS (American)
Chairs similar in design and construction to those called ladder-backs in England. The seats were, as in England, usually of woven rushes. Shaker (q.v.) chairs of the 19th century are very similar in form, although the earliest slat-backs in America were made in the 17th century. See *Furniture, American*.

SLIP
Clay diluted with water to the consistency of cream. It is employed to disguise the colour of an earthenware body in the same way as a tin-enamel glaze, with which it is sometimes confused. Decoration is incised through the slip to the body underneath (see *Sgraffito*), and is also trailed on to a contrasting surface like icing on a cake. Slip is used for combed wares. As a casting material it is discussed under the heading of *Slip-casting*. See *Slipware, English*.

SLIP-CASTING
The formation of objects of fine earthenware and porcelain by casting with liquid slip (q.v.) into moulds of plaster of Paris (q.v.). The moulds are filled with liquid slip, and plaster, being absorbent, extracts water from it, leaving a firm coating of clay adherent to the walls of a thickness proportional to the length of time the slip is allowed to remain in contact. When the desired thickness has been achieved the surplus liquid is poured off, the clay remaining behind allowed to dry to leather hardness, and the moulds removed, dried, and used afresh. Vessels made in this way can usually be identified from the shape, which is not the usual circular shape of the potter's wheel, and from slight traces (mould-marks) on the surface of vessels in the position of the mould joints, although such seams were carefully removed from wares of fine quality.

SLIPWARE, ENGLISH
Slipware is pottery decorated with slip (q.v.). It had its beginnings in medieval pottery, but specimens are extremely rare. The earliest wares of this nature to exist in any numbers date from the 17th century, and come mostly from Staffordshire. Some rare specimens can still be found from Wrotham in Kent, and from London.

An especially important Staffordshire variety is known as Toft ware, because dishes elaborately decorated in trailed slip are found inscribed with the name of Thomas Toft. At one time it was assumed that the Toft family were potters, but there is no record of the name in this connection, and a solution advanced by Frank Falkner is that they were made *for* Thomas Toft rather than *by* him, and for others whose names they bear. Those with the name of Thomas Toft bear dates in the 1670s, and a Ralph Toft posset-pot is as late as 1683. Other names in the same class include Ralph Simpson and Ralph Turnor. Several different kinds of trailed slipware were once grouped together under the generic term of 'Toft ware', but in recent years attempts have been made to separate them, based on the variety of techniques employed. The trailed slip was applied very skilfully, but in a naive and unsophisticated style which can be classified as peasant art. Most known wares of this type are dishes with such designs as a rampant lion; amusing mermaids; Adam and Eve, no less amusing; the Pelican in her Piety, a survival from medieval times; Charles II in the Boscobel Oak, with the lion and unicorn on either side; and boldly executed inscriptions. There is often the addition of slips of reddish-brown, dark brown, and olive-green. Posset-pots are much rarer than dishes, and perhaps the earliest is dated 1683. The type was discontinued soon after 1700.

Feathered and combed slip was introduced early in the 18th century, and continued to be made for many years afterwards, in some places till recent times.

Devonshire was the source of the white clay employed by Staffordshire slipware potters, and, especially at Bideford, slipware has been made in Devon since the 17th century, usually with *sgraffito* decoration (q.v.). Other potters worked at Fremington and Barnstaple making similar wares. Perhaps the best known are harvest jugs, and large, yellow-glazed loving-cups crudely decorated with figures. Slipware came from potteries in Somerset, Glamorgan, Wiltshire, and the north of England. Especially noteworthy are the potteries of Sussex— Rye, Dicker, Chailey, and Burgess Hill—which made simple, warm-coloured wares with applied, trailed, and inlaid patterns of foliage, stars, and so forth, with inscriptions which were often inlaid by impressing the raw clay with bookbinders' type. These range in date from late in the 18th century till

Slipware, English. Three-chambered slip trailer, probably from the old Rye pottery. *Hastings Museum.*

the middle of the 19th. Many of these small centres of slipware production were still working late in the 19th century, especially those making feathered, marbled, and combed slipwares for domestic use.

Slipware was made in London during the 17th century, and authenticated pieces date from 1630 to 1670. The Puritanical temper of the period affected the decoration, and slip is used for such pious, trailed exhortations as 'Fast and Pray', which appears, most unsuitably, on a porringer. The boldest flights of fancy produced only plain flowers and coils. This pottery factory may have been destroyed in the Great Fire of 1666.

The small Kentish village of Wrotham was the site of a pottery in the late 17th century. Very little evidence exists for its having been in production in the 16th century, and the first well-authenticated dated piece is a tyg of 1612 marked *IL* (perhaps for John Livermore). Two potters appear in the Parish register, George Richardson (died 1687) and Nicolas Hubble (died 1689), and a pot with Richardson's initials is dated 1642. Another dated piece from Wrotham (1614) is a large, globular jug in the Victoria and Albert Museum with a grotesque mask on the front touched in with clay, the rest covered with a dark brown glaze. The same initials, *IL*, recur. Wrotham wares are usually a warm deep red-brown or yellow. Early pieces are tygs, cups, posset-pots, and some candlesticks not found elsewhere. A unique jug of 1649 is in the Department of Ceramics, Smithsonian Institution, Washington, D.C. Later pieces date to 1721. Decoration was of applied pipeclay. This clay was stamped into flowers, stars, rosettes, and shapes taken from the Rhenish stoneware (q.v.) imported into England in large quantities in the 17th century. Wrotham ware is characterized by slip applied in strokes, known as 'stitching', round the reliefs and on the handles, the latter sometimes inlaid with ropes of twisted red and white clay. The decoration of trailed slip was applied in a viscous state not always with a successful artistic effect, and as time went on it lost its vigorous character.

SMITH, SAMPSON

Potter of Longton, Staffordshire, who made earthenware figures. His work is discussed here under the heading of *Staffordshire Figures, 19th*

Century. He appears to have been working soon after 1851.

'SNOWMAN' PORCELAIN

Porcelain figures covered with a thick, semi-transparent glaze. Most of them have counterparts either in salt-glaze (q.v.) or Whieldon ware (q.v.), and in some cases both. They were made at Longton Hall during the first years of that factory's existence, although, in the past, they have often been attributed to Derby during its earliest period. See *Longton Hall Porcelain.*

SNUFF-BOXES

The practice of taking snuff was first noticed about 1496 among the natives of the newly discovered American continent. It became extremely fashionable at the Court of Louis XIV, despite that monarch's dislike of the habit, and it came to England at the time of the Restoration of Charles II in 1660. For many years the actual smoking of tobacco was unusual and regarded as a social *gaffe*, and the taking of snuff was the most common way of using the leaf. At first powdered snuff was not on general sale, and the addict bought tobacco in the form of a long roll of tobacco-leaves called a *carotte* from the shape, and this he rubbed on a tobacco-grater, which for some time did duty as a snuff-box as well. Some of these graters are small works of art in themselves.

The snuff-box was at the height of its popularity in the 18th century, and the earliest cannot be dated to much before 1700. They were made of almost

Snuff-boxes. Porcelain snuff-box painted by Georg Heinrich Holtzmann after Boucher. Fürstenberg. c. 1760. *Sotheby & Co.*

Snuff-boxes. Snuff-box of gold and enamel. French. c. 1735. *Wallace Collection.*

every conceivable material, the finest being of gold or silver, handsomely worked, sometimes jewelled, and often inset with painted enamel medallions. The gold boxes in particular bring very high prices indeed today. Most Continental factories made boxes of porcelain, usually mounted in gold and delicately painted. Enamel boxes were popular, the best with gold mounts, but they were also fragile. Boxes of hardstones such as agate and rose-quartz set in gold mounts are of high quality. Horn and tortoise-shell boxes, also in metal mounts, were popular. *Vernis Martin* (q.v.) provided the decoration for some very decorative boxes, while those of papier mâché are positively common, the best by the English Samuel Raven of Birmingham, or by the German Stobwasser which are signed inside the lid. Pewter boxes are to be found without difficulty, and wooden boxes also occur. Neither of these two was once so rare as they now seem, for they must have been made in large quantities. They were not valued sufficiently to make preservation worth while.

Another variety is the Chinese snuff-bottle, intended for home-consumption but also exported to Europe. These occur in a variety of materials, from porcelain to jade or glass, and are commonly shaped like a miniature *rouleau* vase. The best are decorated with great skill, and some examples of glass are quite elaborately painted on the *inside* of the bottle, the brush being inserted through the narrow neck. The best date from the early part of the reign of Ch'ien Lung (1736–1796), although they existed at a much earlier date. Manufacture was discontinued in the early years of the 19th century with a decline in the fashion for snuff-taking. They should have a small spoon attached to the stopper for extracting the snuff, but this is often missing.

Snuff-boxes in the 18th century came to be regarded as status symbols, and much fine craftsmanship was lavished on them. Most people of consequence owned several at least, and Frederick the Great is reputed to have had 1500, while Mme de Pompadour had one for every day of the year, many of Sèvres porcelain. Towards the end of the century the quality of snuff-boxes began to decline.

Curiosities in snuff-boxes—those in the form of boots, human heads, animals heads, etc.—were made after 1800.

Value is according to workmanship and materials.

SOAPROCK PORCELAIN

The Chinese refer to clay as the bones of porcelain and to feldspathic rock, which forms the other major ingredient, as the flesh. The reason for this is the refractory nature of clay, which fuses at a far higher temperature than does the rock. The aim of the porcelain-maker is to raise the temperature of his kiln high enough to fuse the rock into a kind of natural glass, but not high enough to fuse the clay. The Chinese use a feldspathic rock to produce hard porcelain fusing at about 1450°C., but it is not the only fusible rock suitable for the purpose. Soaprock is a kind of steatite which fuses at a lower temperature than the rock used by the Chinese and by Cookworthy in England, but the principle involved is essentially the same. Soaprock reveals itself on analysis by a quantity of magnesium oxide which reaches 16·50 per cent in Worcester porcelain equivalent to an addition of soaprock equal to 50 per cent of the whole.

The origin of the use of this rock is unknown, but it is possible that the soaprock body was originally discovered by William Cookworthy, the Plymouth apothecary who, in 1745, received a visit from an American, Andrew Duché of Savannah, Georgia, who had been making porcelain experimentally in America since 1738. Duché was in England in 1744 and 1745. It is virtually certain that it was he who visited the Bow factory with samples of Cherokee clay known as *unaker* (q.v.), and although he is not named in Cookworthy's well-known letter of 1745, when Cookworthy refers to the discovery of Chinese earth in Virginia, his identity can reasonably be inferred. There is the probability that Cookworthy, who immediately began to search for similar materials in England and eventually found them in Cornwall, first discovered soaprock and gave or sold the formula to Benjamin Lund. There is an interesting connection between Duché, Bow, Cookworthy, Lund's Bristol, and the Worcester factory—Duché, Thomas Frye of Bow, Cookworthy, Benjamin Lund of Bristol, and Josiah Holdship of Worcester were all Quakers. Lund was granted a licence to exploit the soaprock deposits of Cornwall in 1748, and manufacture of soaprock porcelain began in Bristol either in this year or the one following. It is possible that soaprock was employed at Limehouse in London (q.v.), since one of the undertakers here was, according to Dr Pococke, also present at Bristol.

When the Bristol enterprise was transferred to Worcester Dr Wall and William Davis were given an additional amount equivalent to their own shareholding in exchange for the secret of making soaprock porcelain, and no doubt these two men were entrusted with the technical side of the transfer. Robert Podmore may have been the man at Bristol who actually mixed the porcelain body used, because in 1756 he defected to Liverpool and sold the secret to Richard Chaffers, who used it to make porcelain at Shaw's Brow. This closely resembles Worcester porcelain, and is still frequently confused with it. The Derby factory was in possession of the secret by 1759 when Richard Holdship of Worcester defected to sell the soaprock and transfer-printing processes to Duesbury. The soaprock body reached the newly established Caughley factory in 1775 with the arrival of Robert Hancock from Worcester, and it continued to be used until 1799 when the factory was sold to John Rose. To overcome an excessive kiln-wastage factor soaprock was added to the porcelain body used at Swansea (q.v.), starting about 1815 and continuing until 1823. This, known as the trident body, contained a smaller quantity than it was customary to add at Worcester. With the introduction of the English bone-china body (q.v.) the use of soaprock was progressively discontinued, and it disappeared entirely soon after 1820.

Soaprock porcelain was extremely practical in the circumstances of the 18th century. It lent itself to precise and neat potting—one of the distinguishing features of old Worcester particularly—and it would withstand hot water without cracking, which made it especially suitable for teapots. Soaprock porcelain varies in translucency from green to orange, but it is almost certain that the green translucency, to be seen commonly at Worcester, was actually the product of adding a little cobalt-blue to the paste.

Soaprock was used to a very limited extent in some Italian porcelain bodies, but the suggestion that it was used in China under the name of *hua shih* (slippery stone) does not seem to be well founded. Magnesium oxide has never been identified in the body of Chinese wares of this kind, although the unusual appearance of the glaze suggests that it might have been used for glazing purposes.

SOAPSTONE

Like serpentine, soapstone (otherwise steatite or talc) is a magnesium silicate. The stone has a greasy feel, and it is easily carved. It occurs in a variety of colours—green, reddish-brown, light grey, and yellow—alone or in combination. It has been extensively used for small carved ornaments by the Chinese, but less frequently in Europe. Crushed soaprock (q.v.) replaces feldspar in some 18th-century English porcelains, notably those of Worcester.

SOUMAC RUGS See *Khilims*

SOUTH JERSEY GLASS

A number of small glass-houses were established in the southern part of New Jersey late in the 18th century by workmen who had formerly been employed by Caspar Wistar (q.v.). Pieces were individually blown, of good quality, and sometimes decorated with coloured glasses combined in the same vessel. Early specimens resemble those made by Wistar, and are a frequent cause of confusion. South Jersey glass-houses continued into the 19th century, and probably most surviving examples were made after 1800. See *Glass, American*.

SOUTHWARK AND LAMBETH (London) DELFTWARE

Some time between 1620 and 1625 a new pottery was established in St Olave's parish at Southwark by Christian Wilhelm. Perhaps he had some kind of royal patronage since he styled himself 'Gally-potter to King Charles I'. His successors all seem to have been English, and the pottery was still working at the end of the 18th century. Potters from this workshop founded another in the next parish, St Saviour's, Southwark, and these two establishments, with the original Aldgate pottery, are the origin of subsequent potteries at Lambeth, Bristol, and Liverpool. The wares that have been attributed to Southwark (that is, the first truly English tin-enamel ware) comprise barrel-shaped jugs, wine-bottles, straight-sided posset-pots, and dishes. Several specimens are dated. The decoration is in blue and manganese, usually imitating Chinese Ming dynasty blue-and-white porcelain, with *motifs* of birds, insects, and rocks to which a date is added. A pottery seems to have been established at Lambeth about 1665, but the wares are scarcely to

Southwark and Lambeth (London) Delft. A London *delft* tankard decorated in blue with pseudo-Chinese *motifs* derived from Ming porcelain of the reign of Wan-li (1573–1619)—the so-called 'carrack' or 'kraak' porcelain (q.v.). Southwark. c. 1630. *Victoria and Albert Museum.*

Southwark and Lambeth (London) Delft. A dish of 1665 with an outer border of blue dashes, and an inner floral border reminiscent of some Continental faïence. London *delft. British Museum.*

be distinguished from those of Southwark, and after the middle of the 17th century the whole group of London or Lambeth *delft* is difficult to separate as there were about 20 potteries working in Lambeth and Vauxhall alone. Seventeenth century London wares are, in the main, sparsely decorated in blue-and-white. The glaze is a good white, sometimes pinkish, and contrasting well with the pale blue of inscriptions, dates, and Coats of Arms, which are found more frequently from London than from other factories.

Wine-bottles, mugs, and posset-pots are among the most important examples, many of them dated, but there are silver shapes as well as goblets shaped like Venetian glass, and puzzle-jugs, tygs, punch-bowls, apothecary's pill-slabs, candlesticks, bleeding-bowls, and barber's basins. Bottles, taking the place of stoneware bottles from Germany, were decorated with descriptions of their contents: 'Sack', 'Renish wine', or 'Whit'. Most bottles are dated between 1640 and 1650, but they seem to have continued till about 1671.

The first mugs were barrel-shaped, but this form was gradually superseded by a globular form with a short cylindrical neck which, like the bottles, may have been derived from a stoneware model. About 1660 there appears a kind of wine-cup, some straight-sided and others rounded, dated, and with the arms of one of the City of London Companies, or perhaps with a portrait of the King. Cups, goblets, and chalices were all based on silver-forms, sometimes appearing very clumsy in the different medium. Plates and dishes were moulded in the style of contemporary pewter and silver, and deep lobed vessels were made as finger-bowls to hold rosewater or some other perfumed water at table. A whole group of wares is devoted to drinks of one kind or another: spouted posset-pots, for instance, to hold the reviving drinks known as caudles and syllabubs.

These became more and more elaborate, starting with straight sides and a flat cover, like the specimen in the Glaisher Collection dated 1731 which is inscribed *Stephen Gardner.* They developed bulbous, curving sides and covers, culminating in a very rare late 17th-century type with a crown on the cover. Almost contemporary with the posset-pot was the punch-bowl which became very common in the 18th century, especially at Bristol. Drug-jars, both dry and wet, bleeding-bowls, and pill-slabs were also made throughout the century, as well as barber's basins with a wide rim from which a section was cut to fit the neck. Bleeding-bowls (q.v.) may be distinguished from porringers since they have only one handle or lug.

Foreign influence had its effect all through the 17th century. Apart from the period of the Commonwealth when decoration was very sparing, Chinese, Dutch, and French styles had their effect on English delftware. Obviously the accession of William III encouraged connections with Holland, but the influence of the Dutch was more or less continuous and particularly occurs in the manufacture of tiles and small objects such as cats, books, and shoes sometimes intended as flower-vases. French influence is discernible in some oval dishes based on that most unlikely forerunner—Bernard Palissy (q.v.). These are nearly all in moulded polychrome *delft,* copies of an allegorical dish known as *La Fécondité* depicting a naked woman with five children. Another Palissy inspiration was a dish in high relief with a design of frogs, shells, snakes, plants, and lizards. These dishes date from 1633 to 1697. A fashion copied directly from France towards the end of the century was the so-called *bleu Persan* of Nevers (q.v.). Lambeth copied this dark blue ground, decorating it in white with Chinese Ming dynasty subjects and floral designs,

Southwark and Lambeth (London) Delft. One of a pair of foodwarmers (*veilleuses*). Lambeth *delft.* c. 1760. These appear to be among the earliest *veilleuses,* and the type may have been introduced a year or two before. See *Veilleuses. H. F. du Pont Winterthur Museum.*

including the popular Chinamen among grasses. About 1690 Lambeth *delft* had developed its poly-chrome palette, and at this period, too, a new kind of plate with a deeper well appeared which was painted boldly with simple themes.

Chinese *motifs* dominated English 18th-century production, but as the wares of K'ang-hsi (1662–1720) began to arrive in Europe the derivative style changed from that of the 17th century. Dutch and English potters used identical models and shared a common inspiration, yet, although there are similarities, the two are not difficult to distinguish. The careful Dutch copies of elaborate Oriental specimens are unique, and no English craftsman attempted to copy this type of ware but confined himself to the simpler models which allowed him freedom to paint in his own lively manner. Certainly some English interpretations of Chinese subjects are remarkable for their lack of understanding, but this in no way detracts from the unsophisticated artistry of the decoration.

English potters of the 18th century did not look to Holland for shapes, and the only real Dutch con-tribution seems to be a limited use of *kwaart* (q.v.) for a short period between 1720 and 1730. Lambeth also used the Continental method of outlining a design (called by the Dutch, *trek* (q.v.)) usually in a dark blue or green; Dutch potters, and those of Frankfurt (q.v.) and Hanau (q.v.), used either a blue or black pigment. European subjects are especially prized today, but they rarely appear in pure form, as Oriental *motifs* had become inextricably mixed with them at the turn of the century. Delftware did not lend itself to moulded rococo ornament decorating the porcelain of the period, and only a few moulded pieces are typical of the style. The neo-classical style in turn superseded rococo and is to be discerned in formal swags and borders, laurel, and acanthus leaves. Its final adoption as a European style coin-cided with the collapse of the *delft* industry in England.

In the early 18th century the new fashion for tea-drinking created a demand for teapots, cups, saucers, caddies, sugar-bowls, and so on. Tea and coffee ware was based on silver and pewter models of the period and all tableware, however unsuitable, was made in *delft*. Apart from bowls, all these are exceedingly rare.

Many 17th-century forms continued into the 18th century—puzzle-jugs, punch-bowls, bottles, and jugs. Plates are of several sizes up to about 18 in., and of varying depth. Dishes are round or oblong, with plain or scalloped edges. With the rise of the glass industry *delft* bottles became much less common and eventually disappeared.

SPANDRELS

Small cast-brass ornaments found in the four corners of clock-dials beginning about 1680. They take a number of forms, but cherub heads surrounded by formal acanthus foliage are fairly common. The best were carefully finished before being affixed to the dial, and this is a test of quality.

Spandrels. Dial of a bracket clock by Joseph Knibb, c. 1700, showing spandrels in the form of winged cherubs. *Sotheby & Co.*

SPANISH OR BRUSH FOOT (American)

A variation of the scroll foot said to have originated in Spain in the 17th century. The foot is an upright scroll turning backward, the knuckle being the point where it touches the floor. Flemish examples reverse the scroll and bring it forward.

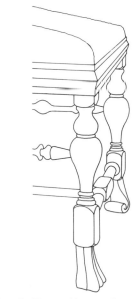

Spanish Foot. Upholstered stool with turned legs terminat-ing in the Spanish foot. c. 1700. Stools in American furniture are distinctly rare. *New Hampshire Historical Society.*

SPARTA CARPETS

Turkish carpets woven at Izmir (Smyrna) and round about, notably at Isparta. They are the Turkey

Sphinx. Stone sphinx in the garden of Chiswick House (W. London), architect, the Earl of Burlington. c. 1720. See also *Bérain, Jean I.*

carpets of commerce, and the older ones especially have a longer pile than is customary with Persian carpets. More recently the pile has been cut to a closer approximation to Persian practice. Persian rugs, such as the Feraghan and the Serabend, are also imitated in this area. Sparta carpets have always been made for export, and the designs often show European influence. The colours are soft, and the carpets were made in sizes suitable for Western rooms, although they are usually large.

Carpets not unlike the Sparta in appearance, but with open, plain fields, were made in Greece during the 19th century by Turkish weavers, principally for the English market. These are also usually termed 'Sparta' carpets.

SPELTER   See *Zinc*

SPHINX

A mythological animal to be found both in Egyptian and Greek art. It has the body of a lion (sometimes winged in Greek and later Egyptian versions) with the head of a human being. Early sphinxes are male; the female with human breasts is later. The ram's-head sphinx is to be found occasionally, but it is rare. Sphinxes were commonly represented during the 17th and 18th centuries, being a favourite with Jean I Bérain (q.v.). Actresses and members of the Courts of the day were sometimes modelled in this form in terracotta, bronze, or porcelain. An example in English porcelain is the Bow model of Peg Woffington, done about 1752.

SPINNING

Much metalwork formerly raised (q.v.) is now spun, but spinning as a method of making bowls and similar vessels of circular section is very ancient, almost as old, in fact, as the lathe which is indispensable to the process. Spinning is done by bringing a revolving circular sheet of metal held in a lathe into contact with a former of hard wood which is the same shape as the interior of the vessel it is proposed to make, at the same time pressing the burnisher against what is to become the exterior of the bowl, so that the metal is gradually forced into

contact with the former and compelled to take its shape. A variety of shapes can be made in this way, and these are not confined to simple bowls from which the former can be withdrawn when the operation has been completed, since formers can be made in several pieces and taken apart for withdrawal. Vessels are often partly spun and partly formed in other ways, with cast ornament soldered into position. The method can be employed to shape any malleable metal. It is possible for a skilled craftsman to spin an oval, but this is rare.

SPIRAL TURNING

Wood turned in a lathe to form a progressive and non-re-entrant curve—a barley-sugar twist (q.v.).

SPLAT

That part of the chair-back which lies above the seat and between the uprights on either side. Splats were occasionally solid but most often pierced, and it was customary to ornament them with marquetry or carving.

SPODE (Stoke-on-Trent, Staffordshire)

Josiah I Spode was apprenticed to Thomas Whieldon (q.v.), and later founded a factory for the manufacture of earthenware. This was taken over by his son, Josiah II Spode (1754–1827), who added the manufacture of porcelain about 1800 and is generally credited with the introduction of bone-china (q.v.) into Staffordshire. In 1805 he began to make stone china. William Copeland became a partner about 1813, and the firm was styled Spode & Copeland.

Splat. Walnut English dining-chair of c. 1740 with carved vase-shaped splat. *Parke-Bernet Galleries, New York.*

Josiah III Spode died in 1829, and in 1833 the style became Copeland & Garrett, Thomas Garrett having been taken into partnership. About 1847 the style was changed to Copeland, late Spode, and then to W. T. Copeland & Son. The company still manufactures fine china in Staffordshire.

The early productions include vases and table-services in the Empire style, and new ground colours were introduced, among them turquoise, vermilion, and 'Sardinian green'. Japan patterns were a factory speciality. Later in the century Spode porcelain was apt to be excessively and gaudily decorated with gilding, jewelling, and moulding. The Parian body (q.v.) was introduced about 1846, but soon passed beyond the Spode factory to Staffordshire generally. Spode production in this body was excellent in quality, and in better taste than a good deal of their glazed and enamelled porcelain of the period.

'Stone china' was usually decorated with Chinese designs painted over outline transfers (see *Transfer-printing*). The 'Mandarin' patterns of early 19th-century Chinese export porcelain were copied, and vases were often decorated with applied flowers in addition. These productions often resemble the work of Miles Mason (q.v.). The factory also specialized in blue-printed earthenware.

SPOON-BACK

A chair-back curved to fit the back of the sitter which was introduced from Holland late in the 17th century, remaining fashionable till almost the middle of the 18th. It was especially popular during the Queen Anne period, and the splat is sometimes decorated with marquetry.

Sprimont, Nicholas. Portrait of the Duke of Cumberland, the 'Butcher' of Culloden, and patron of the Chelsea factory. Raised anchor mark (see *Chelsea Porcelain*). c. 1752. *Sotheby & Co.*

SPRIMONT, NICHOLAS (1716–1771)

English silversmith of Huguenot descent; manager of the Chelsea Porcelain Factory (q.v.) from ?1745 to 1749 in partnership with Charles Gouyn, from 1750 to 1756 under the patronage of the Duke of Cumberland, and proprietor from 1756 to 1769, when the factory was sold to James Cox and transferred to William Duesbury. Sprimont's porcelain is considered under the heading of *Chelsea Porcelain*. As a silversmith he was one of the leading exponents of the rococo style (q.v.), much influenced by Meissonnier (q.v.). Silver from his hand is in the collections of H.M. the Queen and the late Sigmund Katz Esq. of Covington, Louisiana.

SPUN-GLASS

The manufacture of glass fibres fine enough to be woven was started towards 1840. It was employed for weaving imitations of silk brocade. A life-size lion by the glass-maker Hazard with spun-glass fur is in the Conservatoire des Arts et Métiers, Paris.

STAFFORDSHIRE FIGURES, 19TH CENTURY

The Victorian era was especially notable for the large numbers of earthenware figures produced by the potters of Staffordshire, and a smaller number in Scotland, which commemorated popular, famous, or notorious personages, and national and international events. These simple white earthenware portrait-figures, designed by unknown artists, represent the peasant art of Victorian England.

Spoon-back. Spoon-back chairs of about 1740. English provincial. The Little Dining-room, Governor's Palace, Colonial Williamsburg, Va. The silver chandelier is English, by Daniel Garnier; the clock American, Philadelphia, by Edward Duffield; and the silver-mounted knife-boxes in cases covered with shagreen (q.v.). The handles of the knives and forks are of Worcester porcelain. The punch-bowl on the table is Lambeth *delft*, c. 1700.

Staffordshire figures, 19th century. An early portrait of Queen Victoria. Staffordshire, c. 1840. *Constance Chiswell.*

Since photographs were hardly available before the 1860s, crude likenesses of real people were taken from engravings from the *Illustrated London News,* music-covers, etc. Some Shakespearean personages were based on engravings in Tallis's *Shakespearean Gallery* of 1852–1853.

There were numerous makers in the Potteries, but very few specimens were marked, although the names of Sampson Smith of Longton (Staffs.), Lancasters of Hanley, and Unwin do occur rarely. From the figures based on Tallis's *Shakespearean Gallery,* and others with similar characteristics, come the category termed the 'Tallis' factory, which is otherwise unidentified, and another category, known as the 'Alpha' factory, was responsible for well-modelled portraits painted all round with additional passages of underglaze blue. Indistinguishable from Staffordshire productions were the Scottish earthenware figures of fisher-girls from the Prestonpans Pottery or Rathbone's Pottery at Portobello. Probably large portraits of Scottish national heroes (Wallace, Bruce, and Rob Roy) are of Scottish origin.

The Staffordshire figures here discussed were introduced about the time of the marriage of Victoria, a new and young Queen, to Albert, the Prince-Consort, in 1840, and this marriage excited the potters' imaginations. From it came numerous groups of the couple themselves, and the children of the marriage were later potted in almost infinite variety, many figures bearing no titles but easily identifiable. The opening of the 1851 Exhibition inspired large portraits of Victoria and Albert. The 'Royal' group is very large, since it includes relations of the royal family and foreign rulers. Other sources of inspiration were military and naval events, commanders of the armed Forces, statesmen, notable contemporary sportsmen, personalities of the stage (probably aimed at a more sophisticated public), the circus, and crime. The trade at which the potters aimed was not purely local, except for preachers (for instance, the Reverends Christmas Evans and Jon Elias), as may be seen from the portraits of famous people of all countries. America is well represented by figures of Washington; Franklin; Lincoln; John Brown (1800–1859), who advocated the abolition of slavery; the Cushman sisters, Charlotte and Susan, actresses who came to England in 1845 and played in *Romeo and Juliet*; James Henry Hackett (1800–1871), an actor who made frequent visits to England and appeared as Falstaff; Mrs Amelia Bloomer (1818–1894), who introduced the reformed style of dress for women popularly known as 'bloomers'; Isaac Van Amburgh (1811–1865?), animal-trainer, who appeared at Drury Lane (London) with a mixed cage of lions, leopards, and a lamb, a performance Queen Victoria attended three times; John Solomon Rarey (1827–1866), horse-tamer, who appeared before Victoria and Albert at Windsor; John Carmel Heenan (1835–1873), boxer, whose 37-round match against Tom Sayers in 1860 was declared a draw; Moody and Sankey, revivalist preachers, who came to England in the last quarter of the 19th century; and characters from Harriet Beecher Stowe's *Uncle Tom's Cabin.*

The figures were cast in simple plaster moulds in two parts, only a few needing a greater number or the addition of hand-modelling. Clay was pressed into each part of the mould and removed when sufficiently dry. Not more than perhaps two figures (three in the summer) could be made from each mould in a working day due to the time which had to be allowed for drying. The separate parts were joined (or 'luted') with slip by a workman known as a 'repairer' or 'sticker'. The open bottom was closed by pressing it into a one-piece mould, which gave the figure a slightly domed base. The clay figure was then ready for the various firing processes necessary to convert it to glazed and coloured earthenware. From 20 to 200 figures could be taken from each mould, so sharpness of detail has been lost in some of the later ones, and unintended variations occur. The height of the figures varies from a few inches to two feet.

From a catalogue issued by William Kent, who had many of the so-called 'Tallis' moulds, in the early 1900s the current wholesale price of many figures can be ascertained, and as prices of industrial pottery varied little between 1850 and 1910 it is safe to assume that these differed but little from the original prices. Up till 1910 the figures were sold to the retail trade for as little as 2½d each for a small and simple five-inch figure of Wellington, to 5s or more for larger and elaborate portraits, such as that of Garibaldi.

Production from 1840 to 1865 was very great,

Cartoon Gallery at Knole (Kent). The cartoons are after Raphael by Daniel Mytens, and the ceiling plasterwork is by Richard Dugan, plasterer to James I. The walls are hung with rose-red Genoa velvet, and the furniture is of the period of Charles II.

The Renaissance style in England did not become well-marked before the early years of the 17th century, and Knole (Kent), redecorated in 1607, is an outstanding example of the grafting of the new style on to an older building.

and on these early models large areas of underglaze blue occur. Later, a considerable amount of space was left white and the detail picked out in gold. At first 'best' gold was used, but this needed to be burnished after firing, and it was also apt to wear off. 'Bright' gold, which did not tarnish, was invented by Johnson Matthey & Co. in the early 1880s, and forms a useful means of dating, as any figures with this kind of gilding cannot have been made before that time. Figures less charming, and in smaller quantities, came from the Potteries until about 1900.

There are a number of reproductions in existence made from the old moulds, some of which are still in the hands of Staffordshire potters. A fairly reliable test of authenticity is that the glaze is 'crazed' on most old productions, whereas this does not occur on those manufactured today. The way in which the mouth is painted is almost invariably recognizably 20th century in style, and this is an idiosyncrasy which it seems beyond the power of the painter to correct.

STAINED GLASS
The staining of glass by covering the surface with a thin film of metallic oxide subsequently fixed by a light firing was first practised for the decoration of table-glass in Bohemia. The stain was applied either to the inside or the outside, and light engraving was often employed as decoration. Ruby, yellow, amber, green, blue, violet, and rose-pink were the principal available colours. Staining was first practised in England at Stourbridge during the 1840s, probably invented by Thomas Wood. Ruby and green were the most popular colours.

STANDISH
An inkstand (q.v.).

STANGENGLÄSER
'Pole' glasses, so called from their tall cylindrical form. They are related to the *Humpen* and the *Pasglas*.

Stevengraphs. An early Stevengraph woven for the York Exhibition of 1879.

STEINGUT (German)
Earthenware with a transparent lead glaze made in the German territories; the German version of English creamware and French *faïence-fine*.

As in France, imports of Wedgwood's creamware seriously affected the prosperity of both the porcelain and faïence factories, and many of the latter in particular turned to the making of earthenware of this kind towards the end of the 18th century. Hubertusburg (q.v.), belonging to the Elector of Saxony, was one of the first, and *Steingut* was made almost exclusively from 1776 onwards, both enamel painting and transfer-printing being used as decoration. This factory copied Wedgwood's impressed mark and his designs fairly closely. Königsberg (q.v.) was certainly making what they called 'English ware' of a deeper cream or yellow colour than English creamware by 1779, and Münden (q.v.) was producing it shortly afterwards. The *Steingut* of Durlach (q.v.) is markedly buff in colour. The Holitsch (q.v.) factory on the frontiers of Hungary and Moravia, which was noted for its faïence tureens in the form of animals and vegetables, made *Steingut* from 1786 onwards, and Proskau, in Poland, was engaged in a similar manufacture from 1796, when transfer-printing was first used. The same wares were made at several centres in Scandinavia, where they were called *flintporslin*, and by the end of the century creamware had become very widely distributed throughout Central and Northern Europe.

STEINZEUG (German)
Stoneware, sometimes salt-glazed (q.v.) as in the case of the Rhineland wares (q.v.), or unglazed, like Meissen red stoneware (see *Meissen*).

STEVENGRAPHS
A trade name for mounted silk pictures made on a modified form of the Jacquard loom by Thomas Stevens of Coventry. The weaving of bookmarks was started by Stevens in 1862, and of silk pictures in 1879. Manufacture was later taken up by W. H. Grant of Coventry and, to a lesser extent, by others,

STEPHENSON'S "TRIUMPH,"
SIXTY MILES AN HOUR.

WOVEN IN THE YORK EXHIBITION, 1879.

The FIRST TRAIN ran on September 27th, 1825, From STOCKTON to DARLINGTON.
REGISTERED.

THOMAS STEVENS, INVENTOR & MANUFACTURER, COVENTRY & LONDON.

but contemporary examples by other makers seem rarer than genuine Stevengraphs.

Stevengraphs, now a popular collectors' item with an American society devoted to their study, were made with many different subjects, among them portraits of royalty and notable persons including politicians like Gladstone; commemorative exhibitions; notable buildings like a view of the Crystal Palace; historical subjects, including the Declaration of Independence, depicting its signing in the Pennsylvania State House; sporting subjects of all kinds, especially racing and hunting; Lady Godiva's quasi-historical attempt to reduce the incidence of taxation on the citizens of Coventry by riding naked through the streets—a method which was popular with at least one of its citizens, Peeping Tom, who is also included; bicycle races; boats and ships; and mail-coaches, railway trains, and fire-pumps. A popular series of bookmarks included birthday and Christmas greetings, and many with inspiring texts and messages of the kind beloved by Victorian piety. Many of these silk pictures, which are very finely detailed, are devoted to American subjects, so they were obviously popular exports. Most were provided with cardboard mounts with the title on the front and Stevens's name on the front and back, although this practice may not have been invariable since some have been noted without them. Those pictures in the original mounts are the most sought. The printed caption in its most extended form reads 'Woven in silk by Thomas Stevens, inventor and manufacturer, Coventry and London (Registered)'. The simple 'woven in silk' or 'woven in pure silk', without the name, also occur.

Thomas Stevens died in 1888, but the firm continued weaving silk pictures, often in the form of calendars, until at least 1938. The works were destroyed by bombing in 1940. A comprehensive list of subjects, with some indication of comparative rarity, was published by Sprake and Darby in 1968, and a new work on the subject by Geoffrey A. Godden is in the press as I write.

STICK-BACK
A chair-back made up from turned 'sticks' socketed into the top rail and the seat. See *Windsor Chair*.

'STICK' FURNITURE
This term is employed to describe chairs, stools, settees, and tables made from turned and straight spindles which, in the case of chairs, are socketed into the seat and solid top rail. Examples are the Windsor chair (q.v.) and the cricket table (q.v.).

STIEGEL GLASS
This was made at Manheim, Pennsylvania, between 1765 and 1774 by Henry William Stiegel, with the aid of English, German, and Irish workmen. The principal manufacture was of window-glass and bottles, but domestic and table glass was of fine quality and sometimes coloured blue, amethyst, green, amber, and opaque white (*Milchglas*). Decora-

Stipple Engraving. **English wine-glass with a baluster stem stipple engraved in Holland with the portrait of a man holding a *römer*. Frans Greenwood. Signed and dated 1720.** *Victoria and Albert Museum.*

tion included engraving and enamelling, as well as moulding. Survivals are few and attribution difficult. See *Glass, American.*

STIPPLE ENGRAVING
A method of decorating glass by building up the desired ornament with minute dots made with a diamond point. Occasionally lines were drawn with the diamond as part of the design, but for the most part the artist relied on density, close spacing giving the effect of highlights and wide spacing of shadow. This technique was confined to 18th-century Holland, and English glasses were usually employed for the purpose. The best-known practitioners of the art are Frans Greenwood (1680–1761), David Wolff (fl. 1784–1795), and Aert Schoumann (1710–1792). Some of their work is signed.

Stipple engraving as applied to printing plates became fashionable towards the end of the 18th century, and the work of Bartolozzi (q.v.) employs this technique. Stippled plates were also employed in the transfer-decoration (q.v.) of pottery and porcelain, the impression usually being taken on 'bats' of soft glue, and for this reason termed 'bat-printing'.

STOBWASSER, JOHANN HEINRICH
Stobwasser had a workshop at Brunswick in the second half of the 18th century where he achieved a considerable reputation for small lacquered wares, such as snuff-boxes, furniture, etc. About 1770 he also devised a process for lacquering papier mâché, of which he made small boxes, many of which bear his name inside the lid.

STOCKELSDORFF (Nr Lübeck, Germany) FAÏENCE FACTORY

The factory of Stockelsdorff was situated on the property of a nobleman, Georg Nicolaus Lubbers, near Lübeck, and it evolved from a stove-tile factory. Its founder is probably identical with the founder of the Kiel factory (q.v.), Peter Grafe. The privilege to make faïence was granted in 1771. After 1773 Buchwald and Leihamer were working here, but they left after a brief stay, and a painter called Creuzfeldt took their place. Lubbers died in 1788, when the factory was continued by Buchwald's son, but the production is no longer of artistic interest.

Stoves and tea-trays were its most important products. Stoves were either rococo or in a transitional neo-classic style, decorated in enamels with figures, *genre* scenes, or landscapes, and usually signed by the painter, though sometimes they are without any kind of mark. Colours typical of Stockelsdorff are a pale and a clear blue-green with black shading, a yellow similar to that found at Kiel, a soft violet, and mat red. High-temperature colours were also used, and can be seen on several tea-trays, especially blue and manganese. The blue-and-white wares, being unmarked, are difficult to distinguish from Eckernförde (q.v.), though the body at Stockelsdorff is a pale, yellowish white and is lightly fired in contrast to the hard-fired greyish body of Eckernförde.

STOLLEWERKE, MICHEL

Master of the French clockmakers' guild in 1746, Stollewerke achieved a great reputation for his clocks with astronomical trains which marked the movements of the sun, moon, and planets. An elaborate clock of this kind by him is in the Wallace Collection, (London). This appears to have been designed by the astronomer Alexandre Fortier.

STONEWARE

(French *grés*; German *Steinzeug*.) Earthenware is clay fired to a degree where its particles are lightly joined together, a state known as point-to-point sintering. In this state it is pervious to liquids unless it is glazed. Stoneware is impervious, and to achieve this the clay is mixed with some kind of fusible rock. Firing takes place at a temperature of about 1200°C. which fuses the rock, and for this reason it may be regarded as a kind of coarse, opaque porcelain, usually either grey or red. Stonewares of good quality were made in the Rhineland (see *Rhineland Stoneware*), at Meissen, and at Kreussen. In England stoneware was made at Fulham by Dwight, and at Hammersmith and Bradwell Wood (Staffordshire) by the Elers Brothers. From about 1720 onwards various potters in Staffordshire made a white stoneware glazed with salt which is usually termed salt-glaze ware, and this method of glazing, done by adding a shovelful of salt to the kiln while red hot, was commonly used in the manufacture of most ornamental stonewares. The finest white salt-glazed stoneware was regarded as an acceptable substitute for porcelain, and some

of it in the 1750s was enamelled in the porcelain manner. Wedgwood's jasper ware (q.v.) is strictly, by definition, a kind of stoneware, although specimens fired at a slightly higher temperature than normal are faintly translucent, and Wedgwood himself regarded it as a kind of *biscuit* porcelain (q.v.). See also *Red Stoneware*.

STONEWARE, ENGLISH

Stoneware is a hard-fired vitreous ware impervious to liquids, and it was first imported into England from the Rhineland (see *Rhineland Stoneware*) in the form of the tall, greyish-white jugs from Siegburg known as *schnellen*, and the mottled brown jugs from Cologne termed 'tyger ware'. A common survival among the latter is the Bellarmine (q.v.). In 1671 John Dwight (1637–1703) of Fulham took out a patent for manufacture of stoneware in imitation of that of Cologne, but specimens are now very rare. Dwight also tried to refine his stoneware until it approached the colour of that of Siegburg, attempting, in addition, to achieve the translucency of porcelain. A few specimens of this kind which can reasonably be attributed to him are slightly translucent in places. In addition his notebooks refer to a red porcelane' (imitating the wares of Yi-Hsing—see *Red Stoneware*) and a 'mouse coloured porcelane with white specks'. There is no doubt, therefore, that some of these wares were experimental discoveries made during the course of attempts to make porcelain. Dwight's notebooks were discovered in 1869. They have since been lost again, but the British Museum has a copy.

The most important and best-documented of Dwight's surviving wares are a number of figures, once in the possession of his descendants, which are for the most part in the Victoria and Albert Museum and the British Museum (London). They are of exceptional quality, and seem to have been individually modelled. The name of Grinling Gibbon (q.v.) has been associated with them in the past as the modeller, but without any evidential justification. Notable is an effigy of Dwight's daughter inscribed 'Lydia Dwight, dyed March 3, 1673'. Two small busts of Charles II and James II are in the Victoria

Stoneware, English. Moulded saltglaze teapot commemorating Admiral Vernon's victory at Portobello in 1739. Staffordshire. *Victoria and Albert Museum.*

and Albert Museum, and a magnificent large bust of Prince Rupert in the British Museum. A number of classical figures covered with a brownish wash survive. All Dwight's productions are glazed with salt.

Dwight probably made Bellarmines (q.v.), but these are difficult to separate from those made in the Rhineland. In 1676 he contracted with the London Glass-sellers' Company to supply them with English instead of German stoneware, so the two kinds must have been comparable. During the 18th century the Fulham pottery made beer-jugs and large tankards, the lower part drab-coloured and the upper part brown, decorated with a variety of applied reliefs usually crude and unsophisticated of which hunting-scenes are the most common. These were sometimes mounted with a silver band round the rim. Manufacture of stoneware of this kind continued until well into the 19th century, when the factory passed into the ownership of Doulton. Gin-flasks in several sizes, decorated in relief with a variety of subjects and often inscribed with the name of the tavern for which they were made, came principally from Fulham during the first half of the 19th century, and some from the factory of Stephen Green which are often marked with the name impressed. Collectable drab-coloured stoneware of the later period, from near the end of the 18th to about the middle of the 19th century, includes teapots, tobacco-jars in various guises, mortars, jelly-moulds, puzzle-jugs, and storage jars, sometimes mottled in a manner similar to that of the old 'tyger ware'.

Red stoneware (q.v.) made by Dwight, which he termed 'red porcelane', has only been conjecturally identified. That of the Elers Brothers (q.v.) has survived in greater quantity. Dwight's drab-coloured ware was developed in Staffordshire into a much whiter ware intended to rival porcelain. Staffordshire manufacturers had been making a kind of brown stoneware since the end of the 17th century which was not unlike that of Fulham, and similar wares with a dark brown glaze having a metallic sheen came in considerable quantities from Nottingham. By about 1725 experiments towards the elimination of iron, which coloured the finished ware in varying shades of brown, were showing useful results, and by about 1740 biscuit-coloured wares decorated in relief, glazed with salt, were being produced in considerable variety. From about 1740 (the earliest specimen is dated 1742) a simple incised decoration was used on a greyish stoneware, the incisions being filled with blue pigment. This is termed 'scratch blue' and dated examples occur till 1776.

The production of relief decorated stoneware received considerable impetus from the invention of slip-casting (q.v.) in plaster moulds (see Block-cutting), and production was soon on a considerable scale. At first uncoloured, salt-glazed stoneware of this kind was being decorated with enamel colours just before 1750, and the glaze gives the enamel colours a brilliance not always to be seen on contemporary examples of English porcelain. Enamelling is reputed to have been introduced by a Dutchman

named Willem Horologius, who worked at Hot Lane near Burslem, but this has not been established, although the possibility that Dutch decorators from some of the independent studios in Holland established themselves in England is a fairly strong one. By 1751 William Duesbury (q.v.) was enamelling salt-glazed ware of this type at his London studios, and figures of swans in this ware have been associated with him as a result of an entry in his account-book recording 'swiming swans done all over'. Figures from his hand are assumed to be those enamelled thickly in red, turquoise, and purple. Another enameller, who may have been employed by Duesbury, painted chinoiseries in a free and vigorous style. Yet another, probably an English painter working in Staffordshire between 1750 and 1760, had a naive approach and an equally free and vigorous manner.

Almost everyone in Staffordshire made salt-glazed wares of this kind. Some are marked Wedgwood. Littler of Longton Hall (q.v.) made wares covered with a rich blue glaze which also occurs on porcelain and is termed 'Littler's blue'. Some Longton Hall porcelain often has obvious affinities with contemporary salt-glazed pottery.

Although plates and dishes form the bulk of surviving wares, the invention of slip-casting in plaster moulds brought many novelties in its train, such as teapots in the form of horses and camels which are much sought. Sauceboats are a fairly common survival. Decoration in relief was the rule and this often covers the whole surface. Wares, such as plates, were also pierced in imitation of contemporary silver. Most of the ornament was in the rococo style (q.v.) which was then current.

The advent of creamware and the rise of the porcelain factories in England ultimately caused the manufacture of stoneware of this kind to be discontinued, but Wedgwood introduced fine unglazed stonewares, black basaltes and jasper, which were well adapted to the forms demanded by the neo-classical style and became very popular for this reason. See Basaltes, Elers Bros., Jasper, Red Stoneware, Wedgwood.

STONEWARE, NOTTINGHAM
James Morley of Nottingham made stoneware which was the subject of a lawsuit with Dwight in 1693. Pieces resemble those of Fulham in shape. Nottingham ware exhibits various shades of reddish-brown, thinly and delicately potted, and decorated with incised designs of formal flowers and inscriptions. Dates range from 1700 to 1799. It is particularly noted for puzzle-jugs, and vessels in the form of bears. The Nottingham tradition was continued in the Midlands and North at Belper, Brampton, Chesterfield, and Denby, where stoneware is still made.

STORR, PAUL (fl. 1797–1821)
The principal English Regency silversmith. Storr first registered his maker's mark at the Goldsmiths'

Storr, Paul. Tea-urn in the Regency style. Paul Storr. 1809–1810. *Victoria and Albert Museum.*

Stralsund Faïence. A Stralsund 'terrace' vase painted in enamel colours. Mid-18th century. Similar vases were made at Rörstrand and Marieberg (q.v.). *Sotheby & Co.*

Hall in 1792, when he was in partnership with William Frisbee. The partnership seems to have been dissolved soon afterwards, and Storr joined Rundell & Bridge with retail premises at Ludgate Hill in London, Storr working at Dean Street, Soho.

Storr became a partner in Rundell & Bridge, an association which included William Theed, the sculptor, who designed the figure-decoration then popular. By 1805 the firm had become Rundell, Bridge & Rundell, goldsmiths to their Majesties, and they were also extensively patronized by the Prince Regent. From 1803 to 1819 Paul Storr was largely concerned with princely commissions, not only as a craftsman but as a designer as well, although some of the designs were Flaxman's (q.v.).

The plate designed and made by Paul Storr is the epitome of the Regency style, decorated largely with classical *motifs* based on those of Imperial Rome, but with an occasional excursion into Egyptian subjects inspired by Napoleon's campaign there of 1798, and Nelson's victory of the Nile.

In 1820 Storr left Rundell, Bridge & Rundell to enter into partnership with John Mortimer under the style of Storr & Mortimer, with a joint mark entered at the Goldsmith's Hall in 1821. Storr retired from active work in 1839.

STRALSUND (Pomerania, Germany)
FAÏENCE FACTORY

A factory in this then Swedish possession was working from 1757. Ehrenreich (of Marieberg) and Buchwald (of Copenhagen) took over the management, and it became entirely Swedish in style. The factory was damaged by an explosion in 1770. It was re-started, but limped along financially till 1792 when it was closed.

Stralsund faïence has a buff body with a greenish tone. The glaze is grey and cold, with colours drier and harder than those of Rörstrand or Marieberg, but otherwise it is similar, and patterns were borrowed unscrupulously. It is marked in a manner

similar to the two parent factories, allowing accurate dating but leaving doubt as to the hand of the artist.

STRAPWORK

Ornament consisting chiefly of flat, interlacing bands, perhaps derived in part from the wrought-

Strapwork. Engraved strapwork on a standing cup of silver-gilt. English. c. 1585. *Christie, Manson & Woods.*

411

iron strapping of ornamental chests, and partly from Near Eastern sources. Designs for strapwork were popular among 17th- and early 18th-century designers of ornament, and it occurs in England as carved ornament to some mid-18th-century furniture. See also *Laub- und Bandelwerk*.

STRASBOURG (Alsace, France) FAÏENCE

Strasbourg was one of the most important centres of faïence production in France. Charles-François Hannong, originally Dutch, came to Strasbourg in 1709, where he established a small factory for the manufacture of clay-pipes. In 1721 he took Johann Heinrich Wachenfeld, a painter from Ansbach, as a partner, but this lasted only till 1722, when Wachenfeld returned to Germany. Even at this early date the inventory of the factory shows that armorial dishes, drug-jars, and *garnitures* for chimney-pieces were being made, and after Wachenfeld left Hannong's genius asserted itself. He enlarged the original building, built a mill to grind materials for glazing, and in 1724 constructed a second workshop at Haguenau. After 1732 Paul-Antoine and Balthasar Hannong (Charles François's two sons) managed both factories, enlarging the buildings and the range of wares. In 1739 Balthasar took over Haguenau, while Paul retained Strasbourg, though finally Paul acquired both. He was a member of the City Council, as had been his father before him, and a man of standing in the town. Notable painters from Germany were employed by Paul Hannong at Strasbourg. In 1748 Carl Heinrich and Christian Wilhelm von Löwenfinck arrived, followed in 1749 by their brother, Adam Friedrich (q.v.) who became director of the Haguenau factory. Paul Hannong may have learned the secret of making porcelain from the much-travelled Löwenfincks, and he was thereby inspired to found his porcelain factory, later moved across the river to Frankenthal (q.v.) in Germany. At this period Johann Wilhelm and Johann

Ludwig Lanz, both sculptors, worked for Hannong, producing figures and all kinds of sculptural wares. Paul Hannong died in Strasbourg in 1760.

The two Alsatian factories were now managed by Paul's son, Pierre-Antoine, while Joseph remained at Frankenthal. Pierre brought Haguenau and Strasbourg to the point of ruin in two years, and in 1762 Joseph had to sell the porcelain factory at Frankenthal to try to save them. He was a remarkable man who ran his business with an understanding of commerce and art, at the same time concerning himself with the social welfare of his workers. He published a new catalogue of the factory's wares in 1771 which has enabled scholars to classify the production. Joseph died a poor man, due to litigation and unwise experiment with porcelain.

Early styles at Strasbourg in the time of Charles-François and Paul Hannong were derived from Rouen, at first almost always in blue-and-white and later in high-temperature polychrome. Examples are very rare. Paul Hannong introduced the enamel decoration known as 'India flowers' about 1745, adapted from Japanese porcelain (see *Kakiemon*) by way of Chantilly. In turn, these developed into natural bouquets of European flowers as control of the enamels improved. They were very freely painted, and tulips, roses, and carnations bloomed profusely on the tin-enamel glaze—flower-painting which was perhaps only equalled by that of the Veuve Perrin at Marseille. In the time of Joseph, the French artists Monnoyer, Pillement, and Ranson produced original designs which replaced the botanical engravings that had been used as models at Meissen. There are some landscapes, usually in crimson-purple and white, and a well-known Strasbourg series is a variation on a *chinoiserie* theme. In these a single Chinese figure in a landscape fishes, smokes, or serenely contemplates the view. A carmine-purple enamel is highly characteristic of much Strasbourg decoration, and this was widely copied elsewhere at the time. It is

Strasbourg. An octagonal plate painted with a typical *chinoiserie* after Pillement in characteristic colours. Period of Joseph Hannong. Mark *JH*. c. 1765. *Victoria and Albert Museum.*

Strasbourg. A Strasbourg silver-pattern dish decorated with a pattern derived from Rouen. c. 1735. *Victoria and Albert Museum.*

Strasbourg. A boar probably modelled by J. W. Lanz as part of a hunting series. Strasbourg. c. 1750. *Victoria and Albert Museum.*

also a characteristic of many forgeries at present circulating, but it does not achieve the quality and shade of the colour on old wares.

Paul Hannong brought techniques to perfection, and created designs in collaboration with his brilliant team of technicians, painters, and sculptors —the Löwenfinck and Lanz brothers, and the Anstetts—which ensured the factory's fame throughout Europe. Everything was successfully attempted at Strasbourg, and at mid-century rococo designs had superseded the baroque—vases, shields, groups, and many vigorous, small figures of huntsmen, peasants, and dogs used for table-decoration, and, most famous of all, the large tureens in the shape of turkeys, geese, and other birds. Gradually rococo gave way to more restrained styles in the manner known as *façon d'argent* (silver-pattern) or *façon de Paris.*

STRASBOURG PORCELAIN FACTORY

Paul-Antoine Hannong established a porcelain factory as an extension of the existing faïence factory. He secured the aid of J. J. Ringler (q.v.), Adam Friedrich von Löwenfinck and his wife, Maria Seraphia, née Schick (see *Fulda Porcelain Factory*), having arrived in the previous year. Although experimental work was started in 1745, porcelain was not made commercially until 1751, but little trouble was experienced, and production was soon considerable in quantity. It rapidly attracted the attention of the Vincennes administration however, and by 1755 Hannong was forced to transfer his porcelain undertaking to Frankenthal (q.v.). Paul-Antoine's son, Joseph-Adam, acquired the Frankenthal undertaking from his father in 1759, but because of financial difficulties it was bought by the Elector-Palatine in 1762. Joseph-Adam returned to Strasbourg, and in consequence of the easing of previous prohibitions in favour of the Sèvres factory he was able to recommence porcelain manufacture in 1766, when it was soon again on a considerable scale. Financial misfortunes culminated in the death of his patron, the Cardinal de Rohan, in 1779, and he was pursued for payment of debts to the Cardinal by Louis de Rohan, the heir. In 1781, impossibly

Strasbourg Porcelain. Group of children playing. Period of Joseph Hannong. Strasbourg. c. 1770. *Cecil Higgins Museum, Bedford.*

burdened by debt, Joseph-Adam fled to Munich, and died a few years later in straitened circumstances.

The porcelain made at Strasbourg during the first period much resembles that made later at Frankenthal. Figures by the modeller Lanz and others are much sought, and it is thought that those with a base in the form of a grassy mound instead of rococo scrollwork should be awarded to Strasbourg rather than Frankenthal. Notable are figures of huntsmen, and the colouring resembles that of the enamelled faïence produced by this Alsace factory.

The porcelain of Joseph-Adam is identifiable without much difficulty. The marks are extremely lengthy—workmen's marks, pattern numbers, and so forth—but all of them include an *H*. Porcelain is in the Louis Seize style, and the designs inclined to be clumsy, especially a fluted, tapering leg to some table-vessels which is reminiscent of those to be seen on furniture of the period. *Chinoiseries* somewhat similar to those appearing on Strasbourg faïence, which owe something to Pillement (q.v.); excellent flower and bird painting; and *genre* painting after Teniers, Van Ostade, and others, are all to be seen. A strong, violet-toned carmine, similar to the carmine to be found on enamelled faïence, occurs also on porcelain. A number of figures were made influenced by Sèvres, Niderviller, and Frankenthal, some perhaps modelled by Valentin Gusi. It has been suggested that Joseph Adam, rather than Meissen, first introduced the use of lacework (q.v.) on porcelain figures.

STRASS, GEORGES FRÉDÉRIC (fl. 1719–1773)

Maker of imitation precious stones. Strass came to Paris from his native Strasbourg in 1719 and established himself on the Quai des Orfèvres a little later. He became Court Jeweller in 1734. Strass established himself at a time when fashions in jewellery were changing. Hitherto mainly a combination of the precious metals and enamels, pearls had been the customary addition. Diamonds in larger quantities than hitherto, principally from India, had begun to reach Europe, and the lapidaries of Holland evolved ways of cutting and polishing them, although for many years only the simplest operations could be undertaken and the settings had to be adapted to fit the stones. Diamonds, of course, had been known in the past as stones of such hardness that they would cut and engrave anything else—glass, gems, and hardstones—but they could be cut and polished only by diamond itself. In the early years of the 18th century first diamonds and then other gemstones began to replace enamel as the preferred way of decorating jewellery, and the value set on work of this kind was so great that jewel robberies became commonplace. It was for this, among other reasons, that imitation gems approaching, and even excelling, the real stones in appearance became extremely fashionable.

Ravenscroft, the English glassmaker, had already invented his lead-glass, which approached the diamond in its power of light-refraction, and Strass made use of this cut into appropriate shapes, each stone with a backing of silver foil to increase refraction. This is the jewellery often known as 'paste', which, of course, has continued to be made ever since, although techniques have varied and modern work is no longer of 18th-century quality. The technique devised by Strass was not new, for the Romans had imitated gem stones by backing glass with coloured foil during the Imperial Roman period, as Pliny records. Other makers of imitation gem stones turned to rock-crystal (q.v.), but it had a less spectacular appearance; this kind of jewellery was principally made in Spain.

Some of the features of 18th-century 'paste' jewellery are, first, the setting, which is always of high quality, as carefully made as though the 'stones' were diamonds, but because of the necessity for providing a recess for the piece of silver foil the back of the stone was closed. Open, or 'claw', settings were never used. The metal is almost always silver, and the use of gold suggests a later date than the 18th century. If a 'stone' is removed from its setting, usually a difficult and inadvisable operation, the foil will be seen to be separate from it. 'Stones' with silvered backs denote a date of mid-19th century or after. In some cases a tiny black spot will be noticed in the centre of the 'stone', which was done to improve light refraction and was discontinued during the 19th century. Apparent yellowing of the 'stones', a feature of some 'paste' jewellery, is not due to discoloration of the glass itself but to that of the backing foil. This suggests that the mount was, in the first place, of inferior quality, since the setting should have been sufficiently air-tight to obviate this kind of discoloration. The best 18th-century 'paste' is as brilliant as the day it was made.

The settings of 18th-century jewellery were never cast but built up with the same techniques as the settings of genuine stones. Due to the ease with which 'paste' could be worked it was possible to make it in a much greater variety of shapes, and because of this it often excels genuine diamond jewellery in appearance. Due to ease in cutting it was easier to design jewellery with the Strass 'stones' mounted closely together, whereas the techniques of diamond cutting available at the time tended to force the designer to space stones more widely apart.

The best 'paste' jewellery of the 18th century was the work of Strass, and it was as much sought at the time for its decorative value as for its power of simulating the genuine stones, but there were many other makers at the time who cannot now be identified. A good deal of 'paste' of excellent quality was made in England and rivals the best French work, although it is inclined to be simpler in design and more confined to such things as shoe-buckles. Today, really good specimens of 18th-century 'paste', even early 19th-century examples, tend to be rare, and are much sought.

The term 'paste', both for the stones and as a generic term for the jewellery of which it forms part, is English. On the Continent 'paste' is still referred to as 'Strass'.

STRAWBERRY HILL

The residence at Twickenham (S.W. London) of Horace Walpole (1717–1797), collector, connoisseur, and one of the arbiters of taste during the 18th century. He bought Strawberry Hill in 1745 from Mrs Chenevix and transformed it from a small villa, built in 1698 for the Earl of Bradford's coachman, to what he called a 'castle' in the revived Gothic style. In this he had the active aid of two friends, Richard Bentley and John Chute, and the encouragement of many more. To Walpole, Strawberry Hill was an amusing conceit to be enjoyed rather than criticized, and he regarded Palladianism as the true beauty. He began to alter the villa in 1750, writing to his friend, Horace Mann, in Florence, 'I am going to build a little Gothic castle at Strawberry Hill. If you pick up any fragments of old painted glass, arms, or anything, I shall be excessively obliged to you.' To Walpole, much of the charm of Strawberry lay in its small size. Of its Gothic staircase, he wrote to Mann that it was so pretty and so small 'that I am inclined to wrap it up and send it to you in my letter'.

Walpole gathered a large and varied collection of works of art at Strawberry, ranging from a magnificent bust of the Emperor Vespasian in basalt with drapery of agate marble, bought at Cardinal Ottoboni's sale for £22, to Cardinal Wolsey's hat. He was also among the first collectors of Italian *maiolica*, and his French furniture included a pair of ormolu-mounted *encoignures* lacquered in black and gold. A *Description of the Villa*, including its contents, was printed at Strawberry for the use of visitors, the first edition (very rare) being dated 1760.

The contents of Strawberry were sold by the auctioneer, Robins, in 1842, and the house itself is

Strawberry Hill. Photograph of the library today. *Strawberry Hill, Twickenham, S.W. London.*

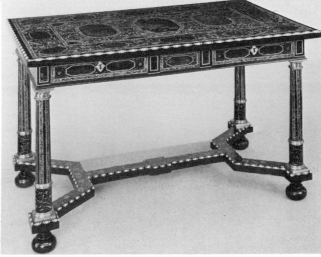

Stretcher. A Dutch table, made in Antwerp about 1640, showing a stretcher of the period. The table is of oak veneered with tortoiseshell, and inlaid with ivory and ebony—a forerunner of the Boulle (q.v.) technique. *Victoria and Albert Museum.*

now a training college belonging to the Congregation of St Vincent and St Paul. The interior decoration is carefully maintained as nearly as possible in its original state.

STRETCHER
Rails, often turned, curved, or decoratively carved, which were placed between the legs of chairs and tables to reinforce them. The X-shape came to England from France, and was originally inspired by Italian furniture-design. Especially well-carved stretchers occur on French furniture during the early years of the 18th century, where the central ornament, on which much skill was lavished, was termed by the *menuisiers* the 'nut'. Stretchers are also the frame, the size adjustable by means of wedges, on which the canvases of oil-paintings are nailed. See *Table, Console; Saltire Cross.*

STRINGING
A narrow strip of inlay, usually about one-third of an inch wide, of contrasting colour, either wood or metal, used as an ornament in furniture-making. Stringing of brass, popular during the Regency in England, was first introduced in France soon after 1770.

STRIPPED PINE   See *Deal*

STUART, JAMES ('ATHENIAN'), 1713–1783
Antiquary, painter, architect, member of the Dilettanti Society (founded 1734), F.R.S., F.S.A., author of the *Antiquities of Athens* (4 vols. fol.). His influence on the decorative arts of the day may be

Stripped Pine. Cupboard of pine, originally painted, and now stripped to bare wood in the modern taste. English country furniture. c. 1820. *Wilfred Bull Esq.*

deduced from the fact that his friend, Josiah Wedgwood, subscribed to the volumes mentioned as they were published.

STUMP-WORK
Needlework in relief employed in the form of panels used decoratively as a covering for small caskets, and as decoration for mirror-frames during the 17th century, principally in the reign of Charles II. Stump-work was obviously a small-scale version in an unsophisticated style of the sculptural *meubles brodés* (q.v.) of Versailles in the days of Louis XIV. The *meubles brodés*, worked in gold and silver, have long since disappeared; stump-work has occasionally survived to the present day. The design is padded, and the faces and hands of figures, sometimes carved from wood, are covered with silk or satin which was painted and pencilled. Tiny seed-pearls and sequins often form part of the design, and mica was used to represent windows in buildings. This kind of work was usually executed on a foundation of cream-coloured silk which, when original, is usually in a very poor state, tender and fragile. Specimens in which the *appliqué* work has been transferred to a new silk background will show either an absence of the needlework scrolls which filled the intervening spaces between the figures, or replacement by new work. Large cabinets on stands were sometimes covered with *appliqué* needlework of this kind during the 17th century, especially in France, but these have now almost entirely disappeared.

STYLE RAYONNANT (French)
See *Lambrequins*

SULPHIDES   See *Crystallo Ceramie*

SULPHUR, CASTING IN
Sulphur mixed with a small proportion of iron filings is employed for taking moulds of coins and medals, which are then used for taking plaster-casts.

SULTANABAD CARPETS AND RUGS
Once a centre of pottery industry, Sultanabad now manufactures carpets and rugs so extensively that it is the principal occupation. There has been considerable European interest in the industry which is almost wholly commercial. In this district carpets are manufactured for export with a much longer pile than is customary with Persian carpets, and these are often termed 'Mahadshiran'. There are three border stripes commonly with the Herati design (see *Herat*), and the field has large, scrolling, floral patterns, usually with the Herati *motif*.

SUTHERLAND TABLE   See *Gate-legged Table*

SWAG
A suspended festoon of foliage, fruit, flowers, or drapery of classical origin very popular among such neo-classical designers as the Adam Brothers in

The Swan service (*Schwanengeschirr*) of 1737–1741 was not the first of the series which helped to make the factory famous throughout Europe, but it is certainly the most widely known. Made for the Count von Brühl, director of the factory, it comprised over a thousand pieces. It was also the first truly rococo service to come from Meissen, and marks a new phase in porcelain design at that factory.

Based on the familiar rococo theme of water, swans in various guises are the predominant *motif*, but nereids, tritons, dolphins, shells, and so forth are to be seen as part of the richly modelled decoration. The service was designed by J. J. Kändler and his assistant, J. F. Eberlein. Sources of inspiration are obscure, and no doubt much was original, but the influence of J.-A. Meissonnier (q.v.) is perceptible.

SWANSEA PORCELAIN FACTORY

In 1814 William Billingsley (q.v.) and his partner, William Weston Young, petitioned the Board of Trade for assistance with their Nantgarw (q.v.) enterprise. Sir Joseph Banks, President of the Royal Society and a member of the Board, referred the matter to Lewis Dillwyn, proprietor of the Cambrian Pottery at Swansea (South Wales), for an opinion on their claims. Dillwyn, who had hitherto manufactured only earthenware, thought that Billingsley's porcelain could be made a commercial success, and the Nantgarw factory was removed to Swansea in October 1814. The first production utilized Billingsley's formula, but the kiln-wastage factor was still so high that Dillwyn insisted on modifications. The first

Swag. Swags decorating the front of a cabinet in the Adam style. *Temple Williams Ltd.*

England, and commonly to be seen as part of the ornament of the Louis Seize style in France.

SWAN SERVICE

Meissen (q.v.) was the first European porcelain factory to make large services for table-decoration.

Swan Service. Dish from the Swan Service made at Meissen for the factory director, Count von Brühl. This is one of the key pieces of the rococo style in Germany. Meissen. c. 1737. *Antique Porcelain Co. Ltd.*

Swansea. Cup and saucer decorated in a version of a well-known late 18th century Sèvres style. Swansea porcelain. c. 1817.

417

Swansea Porcelain. A bowl with a deep blue ground painted with flowers in the manner of Billingsley. Swansea. c. 1817.

of these produced the 'duck-egg' body, of good quality with a well-marked green translucency. This no longer contained the bone-ash added at Nantgarw. Nevertheless, the new body was not commercially profitable, and in 1817 another change was made to a body containing a percentage of soaprock (q.v.). The result was a porcelain inferior in appearance to either of the two varieties previously mentioned, with a glaze which has been likened to pigskin from the minute depressions to be seen in its surface. This is sometimes called the 'trident' body, because the porcelain made from this formula was often marked with an impressed trident.

The venture came to an end in 1817, when Dillwyn transferred his interest to Timothy and John Bevington who continued to make the soaprock body till 1823. Billingsley returned to Nantgarw and continued to make his porcelain till 1819, and in the latter year sold his interest to John Rose of Coalport, going to Coalport as an employee.

As in the case of Nantgarw, a good deal of Swansea porcelain was decorated in London. Painting was in keeping with contemporary styles, and some of it is of excellent quality, although a certain amount of simply decorated ware intended for a cheaper market was also made. Fine specimens are much in demand.

See *Nantgarw Porcelain Factory.*

SYCAMORE

(French *bois de sycomore.*) A tree of southern and central Europe which was introduced into England in the 16th century. The wood varies from cream-coloured to yellowish-brown, and it often has a very decorative figure of the type described as 'fiddle-back' (q.v.). Sycamore veneers were popular in England during the Adam period, both naturally coloured and in the brownish-grey dyed form known as harewood. Sycamore was also a favourite with Dublin cabinet-makers. On the Continent it was employed by David Roentgen (q.v.).

SYLLABUB GLASSES

Syllabub was a favourite dessert during the 17th and 18th centuries, and although it changed a little as time passed it remained basically the same, the common ingredient to all recipes being milk or cream. During the 17th century it was quite often made from milk, cider, sugar and various spices, but in the 18th century whipped cream, sherry, lemon juice and sugar was a fashionable preference. The syllabub had to be frothing, hence the glasses made for its service have bowls much larger than those of wine-glasses, although they are otherwise fairly similar. The bowls are very wide at the top, narrowing abruptly about half-way down to a small cup-shaped depression. In the 1770s the old syllabub glass, which was always on a stem and a foot, became unfashionable and was replaced by a stemless glass. Decoration and form follow, more or less, those customary for wine-glasses of the period. Syllabub became unfashionable as a dessert during early Victorian times.

SYNG, PHILIP (1703–1789)

American silversmith, son of Philip Syng (1676–1739), who emigrated to Philadelphia from Ireland in 1714. Philip II Syng was the best of the Philadelphia silversmiths of his day, and a friend of Benjamin Franklin. He made the inkstand in the State House at Philadelphia which was used in the signing of the Declaration of Independence.

See *Silver, American.*

T

TABLES, BUTTERFLY

A small table with turned legs and stretchers and deep leaves held up by swinging brackets curved like a butterfly wing. They may have square, oval, or rectangular tops—circular tops are rare. Butterfly tables are essentially an American form, unknown in England. They first appeared about 1670.

Table, Butterfly. A table with turned legs and two flaps, the latter held in the raised position by wing-like supports on either side. The type is confined to America.

TABLE-DECORATION

Great attention has always been paid to the decoration of the dining-table, although much table-decoration has been ephemeral, especially figures of confectionery which adorned Roman banqueting tables in the 17th century, or those of wax—a substance quite commonly employed. State occasions demanded extremely elaborate decorations, and these, whatever the material, were usually based on a single theme of one kind or another.

In wealthy countries such as 17th-century France, especially before the economic difficulties of the 1680s, table-decorations were sometimes of silver, although such luxury was confined to the tables of the King and the aristocracy. Hardly anything has survived, apart from an odd piece or two, since the scarcity of the metal made it essential to send them

to the Mint. The same thing happened again in France in the middle of the 18th century, when vast quantities of silver were melted, and the King sent his plate to the Mint in cartloads.

After the invention of porcelain in Europe at the beginning of the 18th century this substance took the place of confectionery and silver in the decoration of the table, although silver candlesticks and vessels were often retained for important occasions.

The small figures made at Meissen and designed by J. J. Kändler and his talented assistants, which are now treasured in cabinets, were nearly all intended for table-decoration, being produced in sets to illustrate a central theme. They were usually grouped round a large centre-piece which has only rarely survived. These sets were sometimes so large, and took so long to set out, that dessert was served

Table-decoration. The Temple of Love. The centre of a table-appointment by Kändler. Meissen. c. 1750. *Museum für Kunsthandwerke, Frankfurt-am-Main.*

Table-decoration. Tureen with the arms of the *Kurfürst* (Elector) Philipp Karl von Mainz painted with views of Boppard and Mainz. Meissen. c. 1735. *Museum für Kunsthandwerke, Frankfurt-am-Main.*

at a separate table. An inventory mark sometimes to be found on Meissen figures, *KHC*, testifies to this custom, for it means *Königliche Hof Conditorei* —royal court confectionery.

In a Meissen inventory of 1753 there is reference to such architectural compositions as churches, temples, town-houses, peasants' cottages, and so forth, with rocks, grottoes, pools, and fountains. A Temple of Honour comprised 264 pieces, with 74

Table-decoration. Silver-gilt table-centre with the Arms of Queen Victoria and the Prince Consort. Designed by Prince Albert and exhibited in 1849. Maker, Robert Garrard, 1842. Queen Victoria's four favourite dogs are part of the decoration. *By gracious permission of H.M. the Queen.*

figures, and was nearly four feet in height and three feet in width. Table-decorations of this kind were *en suite* with the plates, dishes, tureens, condiment vessels, and even knife-handles, an excellent example being the Swan service (q.v.) in which the ornament is based on the theme of water.

Porcelain table-services of this kind continued to be designed from time to time by all the great porcelain factories. Two examples are the famous Berlin service presented to the Duke of Wellington in 1819 by Frederick William II to commemorate Wellington's victories (this is now in Apsley House, London), and the Shakespeare service made by the Worcester Porcelain Company in 1852. Also in Apsley House is the famous 'Portuguese' silver table-decoration presented by the King of Portugal to the Duke in commemoration of the Iberian campaign.

More ephemeral kinds of table-decoration were to be seen in England during the reign of George III, done by men called table-deckers, who often used coloured sands and similar substances for work which did not survive the occasion for which it was done. One table-decker was Benjamin Zobel (q.v.), better known for his sand-pictures.

TABLE CONSOLE See *Table-supports.*

TABLE, OCCASIONAL See *Ambulantes*

TABLE, PEMBROKE
An occasional (or breakfast) table perhaps so called because it was first ordered by the Countess of Pembroke. It is small, with two hinged flaps for extension on either side. The design of the support varies according to the style and period of manufacture.

TABLE, REFECTORY
A table, long and narrow like the trestle-table which it replaced, that was to be found in the refectory or dining-hall of monasteries, and later in large houses where diners were numerous. Early tables have two solid supports, one at either end, which are joined by stretchers, the top being made of long planks. Occasionally, when the table is relatively small, the top is a single piece of wood. At the beginning of the 16th century in Italy tables of this kind, especially those in large houses, were increasingly decorated with carving appropriate to the period, and the solid supports were discontinued in favour of legs, either turned or carved. An extending version made its initial appearance in Italy towards the end of the 16th century. This had two half-leaves which pulled out from beneath the centre and doubled the length.

Refectory tables were made in most European countries. Italian, Spanish, and English specimens are perhaps those most frequently met.

TABLE SERVANTE (French)
The term has various meanings—side-table, dumb-waiter, or what would now be called a dinner-wagon. The inventory of Mme de Pompadour mentions

Table, Dining. Sheraton three-pedestal dining-table of c. 1800 showing two additional leaves in position between the pedestals. *Wilfred Bull Ltd.*

tables of this kind which were, apparently, small, and placed conveniently to hold bottles and glasses. Those mentioned also had leaden buckets (*'sceaux de plomb'*) as containers for ice. The dumb-waiter (q.v.) proper was introduced from England during the reign of Louis Seize.

TABLE, SOFA-

The sofa-table is about five feet long and two feet in width. It was given drop-leaves at either end, and a central drawer or drawers in the frieze, with dummy drawers on the other side. Pedestal supports terminate in three or four feet, and a rarer type has end-supports, usually of lyre form. The sofa-table was introduced towards the end of the 18th century to stand either in front of the sofa or along the back. Intended for the drawing-room it was usually of fine workmanship, some of the best belonging to the English Regency period (q.v.). The sofa-table was made in America until about 1840, the best being in the Federal style (q.v.).

TABLE-SUPPORTS

Pierre Verlet has adduced evidence to show that the word 'table' in 17th- and 18th-century France referred only to the top, especially when this was of marble or some decorative stone. The supports, of carved and gilded *menuiserie* (q.v.), were

Table, Sofa-. Interior at Petworth (Sussex), showing a sofa-table in position behind the sofa—a customary position.

regarded as expendable, to be changed to suit the prevailing fashion, and no doubt some of the marble tops were recut to the shape then in vogue. There is contemporary evidence to prove that the word 'table' was employed with a similar meaning in England towards the end of the 17th century.

The earliest table-supports were in the form of folding trestles, allowing the table to be taken down and stored when not in use, and these persisted in France until fairly late in the 18th century for occasions when very large tables were needed. For the most part, however, the trestle-table was superseded by the refectory table (q.v.) in the 16th century, especially in Italy where the top was at first supported by two solid supports at either end, usually elaborately carved and always joined by stretchers for stability. These were later replaced by four or more legs, either turned or carved, which were similarly reinforced by a stretcher.

Table-supports after the 16th century were usually in the form of legs, but the finest examples often take other forms. An example may be found in the eagle and dolphin supports of William Kent in England, which are paralleled by contemporary Italian supports.

The *console* table was strictly a fixture, being supported only in the front and attached at the back to the wall. Side-tables, which in England preceded the development of the sideboard in the second half of the 18th century, are on four or more legs and movable, although sometimes with difficulty owing to the size and weight. Tables generally, other than dining-tables, are divided into side-tables (a category which includes the *console* table) and centre-tables (*table à milieu*). This classification, however, does not take into account the numerous small tables which became fashionable during the second half of the 18th century, few of which had a fixed position. These, in France, were often called *ambulantes* (q.v.).

TABLES À TOILETTE (French)
Dressing-tables (q.v.).

TABLES, BREAKFAST
Dating from about 1750, these were so called by Chippendale in his *Director*. They are small tables on four legs with two hinged flaps opening out on either side when required for use.

TABLES, GAMING
Throughout the 18th century, and during the early decades of the 19th, a veritable passion for gambling existed, both in England and on the Continent, and tables for this especial purpose were made in great variety. Most were card-tables, but those for more specialized purposes, such as backgammon and chess tables, were not infrequent, and occasionally specimens intended for the playing of several games, can be found, usually including the pieces (such as chessmen). In England during the early years of the 18th-century flap-tables of mahogany with cabriole legs, the movable flap usually supported when re-

quired on the gate-leg principle (q.v.), the inside of the top covered with baize, were often of exceptional quality, since they were made largely for the great houses. A few dating from about 1730 had what is now called a 'concertina' support for the flap, in which part of the frame, to which two of the legs were attached, pulled out in a manner suggestive of a concertina action, providing a firmer support than the gate-leg principle. In some later tables the top, after being opened out, swivelled to allow the frame to which the legs were attached to act as the support. Early examples, usually of mahogany, were dished in the corners to hold candlesticks, and these dishings are sometimes mistaken for money-wells. The latter were towards the centre when provided, in the naturally convenient position, and deeper. Corners were generally rounded on early and late examples, but square corners can be seen from about 1730 till past mid-century. Carved ornament follows that of the period. Specialized tables include those for the game of *ombre*, popular in France, and the later loo table, a game popular in the first half of the 19th century, is circular, with a central stem resting on a base with either three or four carved feet in the Regency or Empire style. In France, *tables à jouer* were produced in great variety for a large number of different games, and some of them served for the playing of several. The passion for gaming in Paris is commented on in a letter written from that city by Horace Walpole.

TABLES, HARLEQUIN
An English table of the last quarter of the 18th century, designed under the influence of the French

Tables, Library. **A Regency library table in rosewood. c. 1820.** *Sotheby & Co.*

ébéniste-mécaniciens (q.v.), which could serve several purposes. Usually it was a combined dressing- and writing-table.

TABLES, LIBRARY

These are among the most handsome examples of English furniture, and are to be found in a variety of forms. At mid-18th century library-tables were usually large flat-topped desks, the surface leather-covered, with two pedestals of drawers which were sometimes replaced by cupboards for containing folios. Between the pedestals was a large kneehole with a long drawer above. Similar tables with drawers on either side are often termed partner's desks. Towards the end of the century, under the influence of Sheraton and Hepplewhite, the circular library-table became fashionable. This provided space for several persons to work at the same time, and a super-imposed drum-shaped part in the centre of the top served to contain books, with small drawers and cupboards for writing accessories and the like. Library-tables are sometimes furnished with pull-out writing-slides, and pull-up reading-desks are not uncommon. These convenient additions probably reveal the influence of the German *ébénistes* working in Paris, where they were customarily provided for many types of furniture. See *Ébéniste-mécanicien*.

TABLES, SIDE-

These, in the 17th century, were originally serving-tables placed against the wall, and this remained one of their purposes until the introduction of the side-board (q.v.). They were not, however, designed solely for the eating- (or dining-) room, and elaborately decorated examples, such as the carved and gilt side-tables of William Kent, were for the *salon*. Both in England and France the best side-tables belong to the first half of the 18th century. See also *Table-supports*.

TABLES, TEA- AND SUPPER-

The portable table, the top of which, when not in use, could be tilted so that it might be stood against a wall out of the way was something in which the English cabinet-maker excelled, and they were popular in England long before such conveniences were thought of in France. Mme de Pompadour, who died in 1764, had a tea-table on a carved support 'of English make' at her château of Saint-Ouen, but this was very exceptional.

The nature of such a table, the top on a pillar terminating in a tripod support often carved and turned—something which the 18th century called a 'claw' support when the feet terminated in a ball and claw—was not possible until a suitable wood could be found which was available in sufficient quantities, but the increasing supplies of mahogany imported by about 1730 provided an eminently suitable material. The planks were often wide enough for the top to be turned from one piece, tables in walnut always needing a top of two or more pieces, and mahogany was strong enough for the table to be designed to withstand normal usage. Mahogany, moreover, was an excellent wood for carving, although uncarved examples intended for a cheaper market were made in large quantities.

The top of carved tables always had a moulded border, and these are tea-tables or, with a fretted gallery, silver-tables. The moulding and gallery served much the same purpose as the fretted brass galleries of small French tables—they helped to save precious china from being swept off the top on to the floor. Tables with a plain top, without moulding, were intended to be spread with a cloth, and are therefore supper-tables. Usually the tripod support is plain as well, since it was hidden from sight by the cloth, and, when not in use, by the top.

The best of these tables had a top which could either be tilted, revolved, or removed altogether, being mounted on a 'bird-cage', a support consisting of an upper and a lower platform joined by four turned pillars. A simpler arrangement, which was merely hinged onto a single platform, limited the movement to tilting only.

The tripod table went out of fashion in 1770, when satinwood began to replace mahogany in the drawing-room, its place being taken by a new kind of portable table with hinged flaps, like the Pembroke table (q.v.).

TABOURET (French)

A low, stuffed stool. Seating at the French Court until well into the reign of Louis XV was governed by strict etiquette, and the right to sit on a *tabouret* when the King was present was a privilege of birth and rank. Although the etiquette governing their use was less strict, *tabourets* were to be found in England at the Court of Queen Anne, but after this they were superseded by chairs.

TABRIZ RUGS AND CARPETS

This Persian city has always been an important centre of carpet manufacture. Considerable deterioration in design and colour has been noticeable during the last fifty years or so, and quality has become markedly poor in some recent imports. Much weaving has been done for export, some of it under European supervision, and this did much to revive the industry at the turn of the present century. Some authorities hold that the carpet from the Ardebil mosque (Victoria and Albert Museum, London), perhaps the best known of all Persian carpets which is dated 1539, came from Tabriz. This has been rejected on the grounds that it is woven with the Sehna knot, while the standard knot of the region is at present the Ghiordes knot, but this is not certain evidence. Tabriz is also the source of some of the finer silk rugs of commerce.

TALLBOY

Essentially this piece of furniture is one chest of drawers on top of another, and tallboys were made in two parts. First introduced towards the end of the 17th century, they continued to be made until the end of the 19th.

Tallboy. Tallboy decorated with Chinese scenes. English japanned work (see *Lacquer, European*). c. 1755. *Wilfred Bull Esq.*

TAMBOUR

A flexible shutter used as a closure for cabinets, desks, bedside cupboards, etc. It was made by gluing strips of wood, inserted at either end into a groove, to strips of linen or canvas. Shutters of this kind are referred to in France as *à lamelles*. They are most familiar as closures of roll-top desks (q.v.).

TAMBOUR WORK

A kind of embroidery popular during the 18th and 19th centuries which takes its name from the hoop over which the foundation material was stretched.

TANKARD

Drinking vessel, usually for beer, with a hinged lid and a thumbpiece for raising it. Tankards are usually of tapering cylindrical shape, lower in height and of a greater diameter than the flagon (q.v.). The earliest English silver tankards are of 17th-century date, when the proportions noted above are especially marked. They have a flat lid, but a domed lid derived from Continental sources made its appearance about the time of Queen Anne. The earlier shape is the

Tankard. A Charles II *chinoiserie* tankard of 1669. *Sotheby & Co.*

most common in American silver. Smaller drinking vessels without a lid are termed mugs (q.v.).

Tankards occur also in pewter, stoneware, faïence (often with pewter or silver mounts), and occasionally in porcelain, including Chinese export porcelain.

TAPESTRIES, AMERICAN

The making of tapestries was introduced into New York in 1893 from France. With the aid of workmen from that country copies of old tapestries were produced.

TAPESTRIES, ENGLISH

The first English tapestries of which there is any record were woven at Barchester in Warwickshire by William Sheldon about the middle of the 16th century, at a time when tapestries were being extensively imported from the Low Countries. The manufacture of tapestry on a larger scale was started at Mortlake (S.W. London) in the reign of James I, and Charles I caused weavers to be brought from Flanders. From 1620 to 1636 the director was Sir Francis Crane, who died in the latter year, the looms then being known as the King's Works. Some examples have the initials *FC*, and others *Car. Re. Reg. Mortl.* (Carolus Rex Regnans Mortlake). Very little work was done during the Commonwealth, but the looms continued until the time of Queen Anne. Quality is generally good. During the 18th century tapestries were made at Lambeth, Fulham, and Soho (London).

TAPESTRY

The word is so often loosely used to refer to embroidered fabrics with pictorial subjects that it needs to be closely defined. A classic example of misuse is the so-called Bayeaux 'tapestry', which is needlework and does not in the least resemble true tapestry. A tapestry is a textile in which the pattern is formed by coloured weft threads as they are woven into the warp. These terms are defined under the appropriate headings. The effect of this method of weaving is to leave a vertical slit along the margins of the various parts of the pattern which are drawn together by stitching. Tapestry was first made in ancient Egypt. The technique was well known to the Romans, and tapestries formed an essential part of interior decoration during the Middle Ages, both for wall-hangings and canopies. They continued to be extremely popular during the 17th century and for the greater part of the 18th, although towards the end of that century they began to give way in popularity to patterned fabrics and wall-papers. Tapestries were principally woven as wall-hangings, and a full *suite* comprised *portières* (for the doors) and *entre-fenêtres* (for the space between the windows). Matching sets as coverings for seat-furniture were also supplied for important *suites*, although this was an 18th-century development. The three great French centres of tapestry-weaving were Aubusson and Felletin, Beauvais, and the Gobelins, but there were

Tapestry. Tapestry-weaving. A workman at the loom. France. Mid-18th century. *After Diderot.*

looms in Italy, Germany, and England which are discussed under the appropriate headings (see below).

Tapestry carpets were made at Beauvais and the Gobelins (rarely), and Aubusson (commonly). Nearly all surviving examples are of 19th-century date. In the Near East the technique is to be seen in the Khilims and Soumacs (smooth-faced carpets).

The prepared cartoon for the weaving of a tapestry was placed under the warp threads as a guide to the weaver (low-warp weaving), or the design was outlined on the warp-threads themselves (high-warp weaving)

TAPISSIER (French)

The term not only means a tapestry-weaver but those generally concerned with the soft-furnishings of the house. It is analogous to the English 'upholsterer', although this is not an exact translation. The word *tapisserie* is also employed to refer to soft-furnishings generally.

TAPPIT HENS

Scottish pewter chalices which are variable in size, the largest holding about three quarts. They were originally made for ecclesiastical purposes.

TASSIE, JAMES (1735–1799)

Born at Pollokshaws, near Glasgow, Tassie began life as a stonemason, going to Dublin in 1763 hoping to become a sculptor. Here he met Dr Henry Quin, who was engaged in reproducing gems and precious stones, and in copying antique cameos. Working with Quin in his laboratory, Tassie produced a white material having the appearance of porcelain from finely powdered glass. This substance could be softened by heating, and in this state pressed into moulds of plaster of Paris. The plaster moulds were taken from original wax models.

Towards 1770 Tassie came to London where he obtained financial help from the Society for the Encouragement of the Arts, and he took premises in Great Newport Street, not far from Wedgwood's showrooms. Here he produced replicas of ancient engraved gems in his glass paste, both opaque white and coloured, as well as making occasional use of sulphur casts. By 1769 his work had become extremely fashionable, and his gems were mounted as jewellery by London jewellers. He also supplied moulds of cameos and intaglios to Wedgwood for reproduction in the latter's basaltes body. His fame as a maker of plaster moulds was sufficient to cause him to be commissioned to take the first casts of the Portland vase (q.v.).

By 1775 he had issued a catalogue of 3,000 items,

Tapestry. One of a set of four Brussels tapestries illustrating the story of Venus and Adonis. By de Vos after Albani. Mid-18th century. *Perez (London) Ltd.*

and received a commission from Catherine the Great to supply her with a complete collection of his 'pastes in imitations of gems and cameos'. A catalogue of 1791 made by Rudolf Raspe, Keeper of the Museum of Antiquities at Cassel, which was devoted to his work in coloured pastes, white opaque glass, and sulphur casts, numbered 15,800 examples of reproductions from the antique.

But the most important part of his work was the production of relief portraits in glass paste or wax, the latter material very popular during the last part of the 18th century. Many of these were modelled from life, and about 500 different portraits are known. Undoubtedly he influenced Wedgwood in the production of his portrait medallions in jasper and basaltes ware.

James Tassie was succeeded after his death by his nephew William (d. 1860), who chiefly produced casts of engraved gems. Few portrait reliefs have been identified as coming from this period.

TEAPOY

Strictly, a small tray-top table of the Regency period with a central stem set on a tripod support which was used in the drawing-room for the individual service of refreshment generally, but the term is also employed of large tea-caddies on supports of a similar type.

TEARS IN GLASS

The tear is to be found in the stems of many wineglasses both English and foreign, as well as glasses for other purposes made on the same plan. The workmen indented the softened metal with a tool and covered the depression thus made with a layer of molten glass. The trapped air in expanding produced a bubble which assumed the characteristic tear- or inverted pear-shape when the stem was drawn out in the final stage of manufacture.

TEBO, MR

Itinerant porcelain modeller. Little is known of him, but he was probably of Huguenot descent, and his name is likely to have been Thibaud. A reference in the *Daily Advertiser* (London) for 13 November 1747 refers to a Mr Teboe, Jeweller, which, while it may not be the Tebo here referred to, is evidence for the name itself. Attention was first drawn to his existence by a group of figures made at Bow, coherent in style, which are marked *To* impressed into the body. The modelling of all marked examples is obviously by the same hand, and many of the earlier have shell-encrusted bases. Shellwork of this kind may have been one of Tebo's specialities, since we find it again at Plymouth when it was decidedly unfashionable elsewhere, and Tebo was at this factory about 1768. He appears to have worked at Bow from soon after 1750 to about 1763, when he went to Chelsea. A group in the Winterthur Museum, Delaware, bears the *To* mark, and the subject is of *putti* modelled in a somewhat similar style to that of Tebo at Bow, but of better quality. In 1768 he was in Plymouth, and at Bristol in 1770. He arrived at Worcester soon afterwards, and was responsible for perhaps all of the surviving figures, some of which strongly resemble his style at Bow, and one, a *Gardener*, is like a Plymouth model which can fairly be assumed to have come from his hand. Several of them are marked *To*. He joined Wedgwood in Staffordshire about 1774, but Wedgwood had a poor opinion of his capabilities, and he left within a year. He went to Dublin where he finally disappears into obscurity. It is probable that he also functioned as a 'repairer'—a man who put together porcelain figures from moulded components. Apart from specific references by Wedgwood, which definitely prove his existence, most of our conjectures concerning him are by deduction from stylistic evidence taken in conjunction with his characteristic mark. His output was prolific.

TERMINOLOGY, FURNITURE   See *Furniture, American* (English and American differences).

TERRACOTTAS

Unglazed objects made from natural ferruginous clay. These, after firing, vary in colour from brick-red to buff. Terracottas vary in hardness according

Tebo, Mr. A rococo coffee-pot based on a silver prototype (perhaps Continental) in the Tebo style. Bow. c. 1756. Sotheby & Co.

Terracotta. Bacchante and Cupids. Terracotta by Joseph Marin (1759–1834). French. 1793. *Victoria and Albert Museum.*

to firing temperature, but most are comparatively soft. They are quite often painted. Florentine terra-cotta portrait busts of the 15th century are important works of art, and a good deal of small sculpture was later executed in this medium by such artists as Clodion (q.v.). See also *Rosso Antico*.

TERRAGLIA INGLESE (Italian)
Creamware. *Faïence-fine*. Creamware in the English manner was made at Naples at the Del Vecchio and Giustiniani factories early in the 19th century. The body is a deep cream, and the wares somewhat more heavily potted than those of England.

TERRE DE LORRAINE (France)
A kind of *faïence-fine* (q.v.) made at Lunéville (q.v.). The body employed here for figures modelled by Cyfflé (q.v.).

TERRE-DE-PIPE (French)
Pipeclay. *Faïence-fine*. An earthenware body used at Lunéville (q.v.).

TERRY, ELI (1772–1852)
American clockmaker of Plymouth, Conn., many of whose early clocks were of wood, both long-case and shelf-clocks of the thirty-hour variety. Many later Connecticut clockmakers were at one time apprenticed to him, and he did much to influence their work. See *Clocks, American*.

TESTER
A bed canopy, either supported on four posts, two at either end, or on posts only at the head, the foot being suspended from the ceiling. See *Canopies*.

TEXTILES, OLD, IDENTIFICATION OF
In this frequently difficult task nothing can be of greater assistance than a comprehensive knowledge of the history and techniques of the past. Only a few hints and suggestions of a general nature can be given here. For instance, width is sometimes revealing. In France after 1666 nearly all fine-quality French textiles have a width of $21\frac{1}{4}$ inches, whereas those of Italy and Spain are more usually $20\frac{1}{2}$. La Salle (q.v.) occasionally made silks of from $27\frac{1}{2}$ inches width up to $31\frac{1}{2}$ inches, but this was exceptional.

Attention should be paid to faults in the weave. Those in hand-woven materials will be irregularly dispersed; those made on modern machine looms will recur at fixed intervals.

Until the 19th century was well advanced only animal and vegetable (organic) dyes were employed, the inorganic dyes (made from coal-tar) first coming after the discovery of mauve by Perkins in 1856. The organic dyes employed during the 18th century, although of a colour superior to the later synthetic dyes, were, apart from indigo, often fugitive, fading with exposure to light, and they were not usually very fast, tending to wash out.

Wear is not a very safe guide, since it can be

Theatre in Pottery and Porcelain. Polito's Menagerie. Staffordshire. c. 1840. *Hanley Museum.*

simulated, although this will usually be obvious to anyone accustomed to examining old fabrics. The presence of dirt indicates nothing at all.

Some French silk factories are able to copy old designs still existing in their archives, and one sometimes sees seat-furniture which has been re-covered in this way, but it is extremely expensive.

THEATRE IN POTTERY AND PORCELAIN, THE
The theme has always been an unfailing source of inspiration for figure-modelling, and the Italian Comedy is considered under that heading. In the 1750s both Vincennes and Sèvres (q.v.) produced figures inspired by contemporary theatrical productions, and the German factories were not slow to follow the lead. Contemporary with these French figures may be numbered English porcelain figures of popular actors and actresses, such as David Garrick, Henry Woodward, Peg Woffington, and Walpole's Twickenham neighbour, Mistress Kitty Clive. In the 19th century the Derby Porcelain Factory produced many figures depicting actors and actresses in characteristic parts, and Staffordshire figures and groups with this subject were extremely popular throughout the first half of the 19th century.

THOMAS, SETH (1758–1859)
American clockmaker associated with Eli Terry (q.v.). Starting on his own account in 1812, Thomas rapidly built a large business which, in 1853, became the Seth Thomas Clock Company. A section of his native town of Plymouth was named Thomastown in his honour. Many of his early clocks had wooden movements. See *Clocks, American*.

THONET, MICHAEL (fl. 1830–1871)

Thonet was a cabinet-maker of Boppard-am-Rhein who later moved to Vienna. He was a 19th-century pioneer of mass-produced furniture, and was the inventor of the bent-wood chair. After his death in 1871 his business was continued and greatly expanded by his sons. See *Furniture, Bent-wood*.

THREADS, METAL, IN TEXTILE-WEAVING

The metal threads customarily employed in textile-weaving were silver and gold with the occasional use of copper, and finely drawn gold wire has been employed for this purpose from very early times. Silver wire was being employed in France in the 14th century, and, as in the case of gold, weaving of this kind was at its most popular during the reign of Louis XIV in the 17th century. Tapestries were also woven with gold and silver thread from very early times and occasionally enhanced with pearls. Almost nothing has survived of this kind of work, however, because during the French economic troubles of the 17th and 18th centuries most was burned to extract the metal. Tapestries burned in France in 1743 yielded about £25,000 worth of gold and silver.

In the case of gold, thin strips of metal in the form of foil were sometimes wound round a silk or linen thread, and gold foil was also employed occasionally in the form of strips of varying widths. Silver has the drawback of oxidizing to black, and about 1800 attempts were made in France to overcome this by employing silvered copper wire. The age of a fabric woven partly of this metal can be established by rubbing it against a mildly abrasive surface when the characteristic glint of copper will provide the information required.

See *Lace, Gold and Silver*.

THUYA WOOD

Thuya (or thuja) wood comes from the sandarac tree growing in the Atlas Mountains of North Africa. It was much esteemed by the Romans for furniture-making, and has always been rare and expensive. Thuya was employed by the French *ébénistes* of the 18th century, and occasionally in England after about 1760. It is reddish-brown in colour with a very well-marked grain.

TIEFSCHNITT (German)

Literally, deep-cutting; glass carving in intaglio, resembling in technique the intaglio gems of ancient times.

TIFFANY GLASS   See *Favrile Glass*.

TIGER WARE (or TYGER WARE)

A 16th-century English term for stoneware jugs imported from the Rhineland (q.v.) which have a mottled brown glaze. The classification includes the Bellarmine (q.v.). Early English delft jugs, called 'Malling' jugs, were made in imitation of this ware.

Tiger Ware. 'Malling' jug imitating tiger ware, with Elizabethan silver mounts. c. 1560. *British Museum*.

TIN

A white metal, silvery in colour, very weak and brittle. Tin is often employed as a casting metal, and it fuses at a relatively low temperature. It is commonly employed as an alloying metal in combination with copper (bronze), and lead (solder). When bent, tin emits a peculiar squeak which has become known as the 'cry' of tin. Tin-plate is thin sheet iron covered with a layer of tin as a protection against rusting. Both copper and brass vessels are washed in the interior with molten tin to prevent contact of food with the copper or brass surface, and vessels have also sometimes been dipped in molten tin to simulate the appearance of silver, although the resemblance is superficial.

TIN-ENAMEL GLAZES

These characterize a type of pottery known as *delft*, *faïence*, or *maiolica*. The glaze is essentially glass opacified by the addition of tin oxide, which is white unless it has been coloured deliberately.

The earliest use of tin oxide for the purpose goes back to the days of Babylonian brick-reliefs decorated with this glaze (about 1000 B.C.), but nothing of the kind is to be seen between about 500 B.C. and the eighth century, when this glaze was rediscovered by Persian potters. Moslem conquests spread the knowledge along the northern coast of Africa into Moorish Spain, whence it passed to Italy by way of the island of Maiolica (now Majorca), and to France by way of the provinces bordering the Pyrenees. It did not, however, gain a firm foothold in France until later, when the early centre at Lyon was much influenced by the potters of Faenze in Italy, and in this way the ware gained its name of faïence. Later still, the industry was established in the city of Delft in Holland, and wares made here and in England came to be called *delft*.

All these, therefore, are technically the same ware, and the use of the three terms is regional. 'Faïence' is applied to wares made in France, Germany, Spain, and Scandinavia. '*Maiolica*' refers to Italian wares, and 'delft' to those of Holland and England. But there are other complications. It has been customary to refer to wares made predominantly in an Italian style as *maiolica*, and some early Dutch wares are thus confusingly termed. In Germany, when faïence was decorated in the enamel colours of porcelain, it became the rule at the time to call it *fayence-porcelain*, and the term 'faïence' is applied to certain wares from Egypt and the Near East which are not faïence at all, and, in the case of Egypt, cannot even be classified as true pottery. Finally, the French call earthenware with a transparent glaze, (made in imitation of Wedgwood's creamware) '*faïence-fine*'.

The wares themselves are discussed under the appropriate headings, but essentially they are the same from a technical aspect. The fritted glaze material was ground to a fine powder and made into a suspension with water. Into this the ware was dipped so that the glaze material was deposited on the surface in the form of a fine powder. When this had dried the decoration was painted on in blue, or in a limited range of colours which would develop in the kiln at the same time as the glaze was fired, and for this reason erasures were impossible. This leads to the style in which much tin-enamel ware is painted —broadly, and with washes of colour, without much attention to detail. These colours are known as high-temperature colours, or colours of the *grand feu*, to distinguish them from enamel colours (a later technique) painted over the glaze after firing, which are known as colours of the *petit feu*.

Since tin oxide was fairly scarce and expensive some dishes were covered with glaze only on the front, and the practice grew up, particularly in Italy and Holland, of covering the fired tin-enamel glaze with a further layer of transparent glaze (termed *coperta* in Italy and *kwaart* in Holland).

Painting in enamel colours began in Germany with the work of the *Hausmaler* (q.v.) in the second half of the 17th century, but it was later taken up by the factories. Much of the most valued tin-enamel ware of the 18th century is decorated in this way.

European tin-enamel ware is usually made of local clay which varies between pale buff in colour to a brick-red, the opacity of the glaze serving to disguise this otherwise undesirable effect. The ware itself is very soft, since it was fired at a relatively low temperature, and it is rare to find a specimen entirely undamaged unless it is a showpiece which has always been carefully preserved—the case with some Italian *maiolica*. Factories making tin-enamel ware were usually small and their activities not well documented. For this reason attribution is often very much a matter of opinion.

TINSEL PICTURES

Tinsel was a glittering metal foil made in sheets and cut into strips to give a sparkling effect to fabrics used for dresses and for decoration generally during the 19th century. Most tinsel pictures are of theatrical subjects of the 'penny plain, tuppence coloured' variety, which show actors and actresses in rôles and postures full of vitality, and in costumes of fabric plentifully adorned with tinsel. Pictures of this sort are a kind of *collage* (q.v.), and they are especially interesting to collectors of objects associated with the early theatre. The makers' names do not seem to have been recorded.

TOAST-MASTERS' GLASSES

The toast-master had to remain sober, and glasses of this kind, while seeming to hold as much as an ordinary glass, had a bowl thickened in such a way that it only held a fraction of the normal amount. Similar glasses were popular among tavern-keepers for serving drinks to coach passengers making a temporary stop outside an inn. By the time the deception was discovered it was too late to do anything about it. See *Firing-glasses*.

TOBY JUGS

Always popular with collectors of English pottery, the Toby Jug in the form of a man seated holding a tankard of beer and a pipe was introduced soon after 1760 by Ralph I Wood (see *Wood Family, The*). The idea seems to have come from a character named 'Toby Philpot' in a popular song of 1761 called 'The Brown Jug'. Jugs of this kind were soon being made in considerable quantities by a number of manufacturers in Staffordshire, and those of Enoch Wood have survived in the greatest numbers. There are many variations, some consistent enough to have received distinctive names. Not all are of Toby Philpot. The *Night Watchman* of Enoch Wood

Toby Jugs. Toby jug by Ralph Wood. c. 1760. *Burnap Collection, William Rockhill Nelson Gallery, Kansas City, Mo.*

depicts a man seated with a lantern, and a woman is usually termed 'Martha Gunn', who was a bathing attendant at Brighton, then becoming a popular watering-place. Toby Jugs have been much reproduced and copied, not only in earthenware but sometimes even in porcelain, of which material no early and genuine examples exist. Detection is usually very easy.

TODDY-GLASSES

A particular difficulty in the way of serving hot drinks in the 18th century was due to the imperfect annealing after manufacture which left objects of glass with unrelieved stresses that often caused them to break if anything much hotter than warm was put into them while still cold. Improvements in the process of annealing were made about 1780 and to some extent made this less risky. No doubt this was the reason for the increasing popularity of hot toddy. Toddy glasses were thick and without stems, somewhat like the firing-glass (q.v.). Toddy rummers are larger, with usually a bucket-shaped bowl and a short stem. Some have heavy square feet instead of the usual circular variety. The best have wheel-engraved decoration, usually of sporting scenes, although masonic emblems, initials, and inscriptions have all been noted. See *Firing-glasses; Toddy-lifter.*

TODDY-LIFTERS

Toddy was a drink allied to punch (q.v.) which was usually made from hot grog (a mixture of rum and water, and less often of whisky or brandy and water) with the addition of lemon juice, nutmeg, and sugar. The toddy was served from a bowl, like punch, sometimes with the aid of a toddy-lifter. This is about six inches long, made of glass, and not unlike a small decanter in shape. It has a long neck, and a hole at top and bottom, the lower part holding about a glassful of liquid. The toddy-lifter was dipped into the bowl and allowed to fill through the hole in the bottom. The thumb was then placed over the upper orifice, air-pressure keeping the contents from flowing out. The toddy was released into the glass by removing the thumb, which allowed air to flow into the top. Toddy-lifters, rare today, were popular novelties at the time, and they were made to match sets of glasses. The best are handsomely cut, and the necks are ringed to allow a firm grip.

TOFT, CHARLES (1832–1909)

Modeller at the factory of Mintons, in Staffordshire, who was employed in the 1860s in making reproductions of Saint-Porchaire (q.v.) or Henri II ware. His work was regarded at the time as so close to the appearance of the very few surviving examples of the early ware as to be difficult to distinguish. He used the same methods as the original makers, and signed his copies 'C. Toft. Mintons', to which a date was sometimes added.

TOILE DE JOUY (French)

Linen of Jouy. *Toile peinte* (q.v.). The first attempts to imitate hand-decorated Oriental cottons and linens in Europe by means of block-printing came at the end of the 17th century, and it is probable that the industry would have developed quickly but for an edict of 1686 which forbade the wearing either of the Oriental fabrics or their European imitations as a measure of protection for the silk-weavers of Lyon and Tours. This remained in force until 1759, and similar restrictions existed in England to protect the wool-manufacturers.

In 1759 a factory was established at Jouy, near Paris, by Christophe-Philippe Oberkampf, a Bavarian, for the manufacture of printed linen which received the name of *toile de Jouy*. Two notable designers were Jean-Baptiste Huet and Jean Pillement (q.v.), the latter specializing in *chinoiseries* (q.v.). Until 1770 printing was in monochrome utilizing wood-blocks, and wood-blocks were retained for some time afterwards for printing in colours, but printing from copper plates started about 1770, and before the Revolution in 1789 a method of printing in several colours with the aid of engraved rollers had been devised.

Printed linens were made elsewhere in France during the 18th century, notably at Rouen, Montpellier, Orléans, and Beautiron. The fashion, at the time of writing, has just been revived in France.

TOILE PEINTE (French)

Literally, painted linen or cotton, although the term also embraces printed fabrics of the same kind. First imported from the East, these fabrics were generally termed chintz (q.v.) in English, and often *indiennes* and *perses* in France. See *Toile de Jouy.*

TOKENS, TRADE

Tokens resembling coins of copper or bronze were made and circulated in England by tradesmen and other private persons to supplement the official coinage during many centuries, the first record of the practice going back to the reign of Edward I. Tokens were only accepted at their face value locally, and they were redeemed on presentation to the person issuing them, either in coins of the precious metals or in goods. Tokens were essential because the Mint failed to issue sufficient copper coinage for small transactions, and the position which thus arose in consequence was regularized in 1613 by royal proclamation. They were rendered unnecessary in 1672 by the issue of large numbers of farthings and halfpennies from the Mint, but copper coinage again became scarce in the 18th century, when they returned to favour especially for the payment of wages.

The invention of improved coin-presses by Matthew Boulton, who produced official coins in large quantities at his Soho factory in Birmingham, helped to make the further issue of tokens unnecessary, and towards the end of the 18th century they were even regarded as counterfeit money. The demand for coin grew, however, and even silver money became excessively scarce, which led to the first issue of silver tokens in 1811, in which year the Bank of England also began to circulate silver tokens valued at 1s 6d and 3s 6d.

The Mint, however, was newly equipped by Matthew Boulton, who installed a steam-engine as motive power, and the making of tokens was forbidden in 1817, those circulating being called in and exchanged for coin from the Mint.

Tokens exist in great variety. Most existing specimens belong to the 18th century or the early years of the 19th. Some bear portraits of personalities of the time, such as Nelson and Wellington, with the addition of a political slogan or a pious wish: retailers' tokens often bear advertising material in addition to the name of the firm issuing them; many depict factories and mines, while others bear views of canals and pictures of stage coaches.

The token became a subject for the collector as early as 1795, and the dies for obverse and reverse were varied by the makers to provide new varieties and rarities for the cabinet, known as 'mules'. These were never circulated. Perhaps from this date onwards many of the tokens struck were primarily for the collector.

Tokens in other materials are rare, but they exist. The Worcester Porcelain Company in the 18th century issued tokens of porcelain which are sought by collectors today.

TÔLE (French)

Sheet-iron. *Tôle de cuivre* is sheet copper. *Tôle peinte* refers to objects of sheet-iron made for decorative purposes during the second half of the 18th century in France which were ornamented by first covering them with a kind of varnish and then adding painted decoration of variable quality, some extremely good.

The origin of *tôle peinte* in its familiar form can be traced to the 1740s with the development of a heat-resisting varnish, but manufacture was on a very small scale until a factory was founded by Clément in 1768. After this objects made in this way became extremely popular, although the greater quantity of surviving specimens belong to the early part of the 19th century.

Several coats of a special paint were applied to the object to be decorated, the surface being blackened when required by smoke from a resinous torch. The painted surface was smoothed, and several coats of varnish superimposed. The decorative painting was then executed in coloured varnishes on this ground, often in the manner of Sèvres porcelain on the best specimens, and the gilded borders and surrounds so popular at the royal porcelain factory were also imitated. Usually the earlier examples are the finest. A few specimens survive which were sent to the decorating studios at Canton (China) for painting, and imitations of Oriental lacquer done in France are not uncommon.

The forms are diverse, but many are *jardinières* and containers for pot-plants and bulbs. Inkstands, *verriers* (the English monteith, q.v.) for cooling glasses, *rafraîchissoirs* (ice-pails), *cassolettes* (urns used as perfume-burners), *pots-pourris* or containers

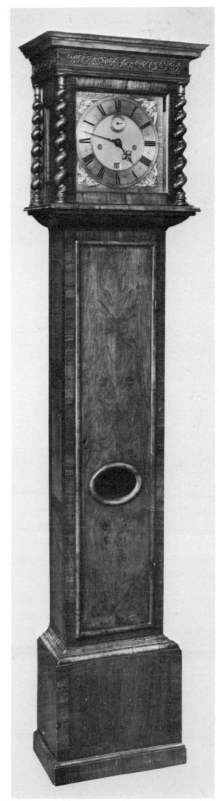

Tompion, Thomas. Long-case clock by Thomas Tompion. c. **1690.** *Sotheby & Co.*

for sweet-smelling herbs for scenting rooms, wall-fountains and *bénitiers*, lanterns, candlesticks, lighting fixtures generally, and food-warmers (*veilleuses*, q.v.), have all been noticed.

See *Pontypool Ware*.

TOMPION, THOMAS (1639–1713)

Noted English clockmaker who was admitted to the Clockmakers' Company in 1671. He was associated with Dr Robert Hooke, who devised the balance spring of watches and the anchor escapement of clocks. Tompion, who saw the development of the long-case clock in England, made many improvements to the clock mechanisms of his day, and his work is the most highly valued of all English clockmakers.

TORCHÈRE (French)

A flat-topped stand, often of considerable height, intended to hold a candelabrum. It was usually ornamented with carving and gilding.

TORTOISESHELL

The horny back-plates of (usually) the hawk's-bill turtle. When required to be of large size these plates can be joined by heat and pressure, and they can also be dyed. Tortoiseshell was much used for small articles such as snuff-boxes, usually with silver mounts, and as a veneer for furniture and caskets. See *Boulle, A.-C.; Horn.*

TORTOISESHELL WARE

A term sometimes applied to the earthenwares of Thomas Whieldon and others which were covered with mottled coloured lead glazes, usually manganese-brown with touches of blue. An imitation tortoiseshell ground (*fond écaille*) was introduced at Sèvres late in the 18th century but specimens are rare.

TOUCHMARKS ON PEWTER

These are analogous to the hall-marks on silver, but they do not have the same authority. They indicate usually the maker and place of manufacture, but information about them is lacunary, and it is not always possible to associate marks with either of these two things. Touches are extremely varied, and they never became standardized in the same way as silver-marks, although they often resemble them closely.

The London Pewterers' Company from very early times used the mark of the lilypot (three lilies growing from a vase) and the portcullis or strake. These denoted provenance, and probably quality as well. The rose and crown was employed for fine-quality wares, and there is evidence that at the end of the 17th century it was probably used on wares made for export. It appears on similar wares in both French and Dutch pewter. The crowned X came into use late in the 17th century as an indication of hard metal of good quality, but it was later much more widely used and lost its original connotation. This mark also occurs on Continental pewter.

The practice of using a maker's mark seems to have been fairly general by about 1503, and by 1550 a record was kept of each member's touch on a large plate at the Pewterers' Hall. These early touchplates were destroyed during the Great Fire of London in September 1666, and new touchplates were struck beginning in 1668, five now being in the possession of the Company, which perhaps record craftsmen working since 1640, because those working before the Fire struck their touches afresh. These are illustrated in Cotterell's *Old Pewter, its Makers and Marks*, London, 1929.

America's makers of pewter also employed touches which were intended to identify the maker. Some early specimens bear such English devices as the lion rampant and the rose and crown, but these were largely replaced by the American eagle after the War of Independence. Nineteenth-century American pewter often bears the maker's mark in full.

Marks on Continental pewter have not been systematically investigated in the majority of cases. Forgeries of English pewter with simulated touchmarks have recently appeared on the market.

TOULOUSE (Haute-Garonne, France) FAÏENCE

A factory was founded in Toulouse by Guillaume Ollivier and Claude Favier in 1676. In 1721 Henri Collondre left his father's factory in Montpellier (q.v.) to go to Toulouse, accompanied by his grandson, Théophile, who was granted a patent in 1725. His cousin, Michel Collondre (son of Gilbert), was still running it in 1750 against strong foreign competition from Marseille and Ligurian faience. One or two pieces—a candlestick in the Limoges Museum signed *Mo Collondre*, and a bottle in the Victoria and Albert Museum (London) with the word *Toulouse*—act as guides to the products, which were probably decorated in a derivative blue-and-white Bérain style.

TOURNAI (Belgium), PORCELAIN OF

Faience had been made at Tournai since the last years of the 17th century, and in 1751 François Peterinck, a potter from Lille, took over the faience factory and began to make soft porcelain about the same time with the aid of Robert Dubois, a workman from Chantilly who had been at Vincennes when the factory was first founded. In 1752 Peterinck was granted a privilege by the Empress Maria Theresa, since Tournai was situated within her territories. By 1762 the factory was employing 200 people. The body was essentially clay mixed with a glassy frit, and among the processes used in manufacture was the comparatively new one of slip-casting (q.v.). The earliest porcelain was greyish in colour, and the first figures were inclined to sag, but, especially after 1762, the colour was much improved and most of the earlier troubles otherwise seem to have been overcome.

The earliest painting was in blue underglaze, and

Tournai. **Pastoral group, perhaps by Nicholas Lecreux. Biscuit porcelain. Tournai. c. 1765.** *Victoria and Albert Museum.*

these wares were especially popular in northern France. The patterns were usually Oriental in derivation, with the 'onion' pattern of Meissen making an occasional appearance, as well as moulded basket-work patterns to the borders of plates (see *Oziermuster*). Early polychrome decorations include the Meissen *deutsche Blumen* and exotic birds, and after 1756 painting was also influenced by Strasbourg faïence (q.v.). In 1763 the factory appointed Henri-Joseph Duvivier from Chelsea to be chief painter, and decorations of a more ambitious kind owing a good deal to Sèvres begin to appear. Duvivier was especially noted for his exotic bird painting. Coloured grounds, with such additions as the *œil de perdrix* gilding of Sèvres, are to be seen, and *pot-pourri* vases are among the most important examples of work of this kind. The Louis Seize style of Paris was adopted about 1780.

Tournai made figures of excellent quality after 1762, both in *biscuit* and glazed porcelain. Nicolas Gauron from Mennecy (q.v.) was at the factory from 1758 till 1764, and Joseph Willems of Chelsea, who died in 1763, also worked here. Nicolas Lecreux was among the best of the factory's modellers, working until 1780, and Antoine Gilles did a figure of Saint-Theresa which was presented to the Empress Maria Theresa.

Peterinck retired in 1796, leaving the factory to the management of his son-in-law, Jean-Maximilien-Joseph de Bettignies, whose sons bought it in 1817. After 1830 it was mainly occupied with service-ware.

It is often said that Tournai made forgeries of Chelsea porcelain, but there is no direct evidence of this, and it may be derived from the fact that they employed the same artists. On the other hand, there is much better evidence for forgeries of several kinds

being made at Saint-Amand-les-Eaux (q.v.), which was an associated factory.

TOYS

The word 'toy' in the 18th century did not have the same meaning as it does today, and it was generally used of small decorative objects of one kind or another which were sometimes known as 'gallantries'. These small objects are now rare. They comprise scent-bottles, *bonbonnières, étuis,* small caskets for containing miniature implements or scent bottles, tobacco and snuff-boxes, cane-handles, pipe-stoppers, buttons, bodkin-cases, thimbles and other needle-working accessories, toothpick-cases, knife-handles, and porcelain flowers made to be attached to bronze stalks and leaves.

Toys. **Polish hussar. Miniature figure by Kändler & Reinicke. Meissen. c. 1750.** *K. A. L. Rhodes Esq.*

This list is not intended to be exhaustive. It includes the objects most commonly seen. Boxes of one kind or another were usually given lids decorated with detailed miniature painting on both sides, and the best were mounted in gold. Cane-handles and scent-bottles were frequently modelled in the form of human figures, and *bonbonnières* as human heads. Scent-bottles are often in the form of human or animal figures, the head removable to act as a stopper. Others are in the form of small flasks often decorated in miniature with great skill.

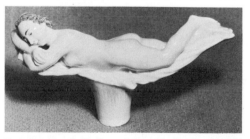

Toys. **Cane-handle by Simon Feilner. Fürstenberg. c. 1755** *Señor Jose M. Mayorga.*

433

Porcelain toys are perhaps the most frequent survival, although those of enamel on copper are common. They also occur in silver and glass.

A well-known dealer in small wares of this kind in mid-18th-century London was the 'toy woman', Mrs Chenevix, from whom Horace Walpole bought Strawberry Hill (*vide Letters*, 8 June 1747: 'It is a little play-thing house I got out of Mrs Chenevix's shop, and is the prettiest bawble you ever saw'.)

TRACY, EBENEZER (1744–1803)

Chair-maker of Norwich, Conn. He specialized in Windsor, or stick-back, chairs, and his mark was *E B TRACY* branded under the seat.

TRANSFER-PRINTING

A method of decorating pottery and porcelain first employed in England and not often used elsewhere until the 19th century. It appears to have been developed by an Irish engraver, John Brooks, about 1753, although there are other claimants, notably Sadler & Green of Liverpool, who may have developed the process independently. An engraved copper plate was inked with ceramic colour and a print taken from it on paper. While the ink was still wet this was pressed on to the glazed surface, leaving behind an impression of the design in monochrome.

Blue underglaze was very commonly employed, but overglaze colours include black, red, and sepia. An attempt was made in the 18th century to print in polychrome at Liverpool, but surviving specimens are very few, and the process was not fully developed until the 19th century.

The earliest transfer-prints closely resemble a line-engraving, but, under the influence of Bartolozzi (q.v.), a stipple process became popular at the end of the 18th century. Prints of this kind were often transferred to porcelain on 'bats' of soft glue instead of paper, and the technique is therefore referred to as 'bat' printing.

Transfer-printing. Enlargement of part of *The Milkmaids*, showing Hancock's signature. Worcester porcelain. c. 1760.

Outline transfer-prints to be filled in with colour by hand were first introduced at Worcester about 1760, and enabled porcelain to be decorated by semi-skilled labour. The same technique was later adopted by Wedgwood at his Chelsea Decorating Establishment, and its introduction there is discussed by Wedgwood in his letters to Bentley.

In the 18th century the most important transfer-printed porcelain comes from Worcester, where Robert Hancock was engaged in 1757. A few specimens are to be seen from Derby, but they are distinctly rare. On creamware transfer-printing was employed by Wedgwood, Leeds, and the Cockpit Hill factory at Derby. Transfer-printing in gold was invented by Peter Warburton in 1810, and stipple-prints in colours, such as those decorating 19th-century pomade pot lids, were developed by Pratt of Fenton. Lithographic transfers came into use after 1851. Some of the best transfer-printing on the Continent is to be found on the *faïence-fine* (cream-ware) of Creil, near Paris, in the early years of the 19th century.

TRAYS

The English tray made its appearance towards the end of the 17th century. Trays were of wood (plain of lacquered), papier mâché, and silver. Silver trays were sometimes circular, but those of other materials were basically oblong, or oval during the Sheraton period. They were fitted with handles or pierced hand-holds, and a gallery was provided for most of them to prevent the contents from sliding off. Butlers' trays, plain oblong trays of mahogany, were intended to be placed on an X-shaped stand. There were many specialized small trays, such as the comb-tray for the dressing-table, and the spoon-tray which

Transfer-printing. A Bow plate printed in outline only, subsequently filled in with enamel colour. c. 1756. The same technique was employed at Worcester and by Wedgwood at his Chelsea decorating studio.

formed part of the porcelain tea-service. The tray-top table had a small gallery round the top, and the term, 'trays', is also extended to mean sliding, shelf-like drawers within wardrobes or sideboards.

TREEN
Name given in England to early wooden household utensils commonly made of sycamore, such as bowls, trenchers (platters), plates, etc. which preceded pewter, as pewter preceded earthenware, porcelain and silver, for table use. The word, treen, is apparently derived from the medieval use of the word *tre* or tree. Treenware, as a term, may never have been used contemporaneously. In the first 50 years of the American colonies wooden trenchers, platters, bowls and mugs were customary.

TREK (Dutch)
Outline in black, cobalt or manganese oxide used on Dutch delft and other tin-enamel wares to indicate the design to be followed.

TRIPODS
Ornately carved three-legged stands for candelabra or vases based on the old Roman bronze tripod. They first appear during the currency of the Adam style. See *Athénienne*.

TRITON
A son of Poseidon (Neptune) and Amphitrite; minor sea-gods, usually represented as men with the tails of fish.

TROMPE L'OEIL (French)
The use of such techniques as perspective and fore-shortening in painting to deceive the eye into mistaking the apparent for the real. Painting for this purpose was done during the Imperial Roman period, but it was at its most elaborate and deceptive during the currency of the baroque style (q.v.) in the 17th century, when painted landscapes and vistas were often employed to increase the apparent size of interiors. Other examples may be sought in summer firescreens (*écrans*) in 18th-century France, and in the use of such *motifs* as engravings pinned to grained wood imitated as the decoration of faïence and porcelain. Italian *quadratrure*.

TROPHIES
In early times trophies were the arms of a beaten enemy which were hung up in a tree to celebrate a victory. Later weapons were grouped together as a popular *motif* for sculptured and painted ornament, and the notion was extended to groupings of other objects symbolizing a variety of ideas—musical instruments as emblematic of music, for example. In 18th-century France trophies of this kind arranged in the form of *chutes* (q.v.) were a common form of mural decoration.

TROUBADOUR STYLE, THE   See *Gothic Revival*

Trophies. Trophies of arms. Mural painting at Hampton Court, S.W. London.

TROY, JEAN-FRANCOIS DE (1679–1752)
French painter who spent many years in Italy. In France he enjoyed a special reputation as a history, genre, and portrait painter and he produced cartoons for tapestries.

TUCKER PORCELAIN FACTORY (American)
William Ellis Tucker started a kiln in Philadelphia about 1825 to produce bone-china and pottery. In 1828 the mark was 'Tucker & Hulme, Phila.', frequently with 'China Manufacturers' added. William Tucker died in 1832 and from 1833 to 1836 the factory continued with Joseph Hemphill and Thomas Tucker (William's younger brother) as manager.

The Hemphill period was distinguished by a rich taste, with enamel painting in the Sèvres style and a lavish use of gilding. The avowed aim was to imitate Sèvres porcelain, and workers were imported from Europe. Tucker decoration includes portraits of famous men such as George Washington, family coats-of-arms, and monograms.

TULIPWOOD
Wood from the species *Dalbergia*, and related to rosewood and violetwood. Misleadingly, it is known in France as *bois de rose*, while rosewood is called *pallisandre*. The principal source of supply was Brazil. It is usually a light brown in colour with pinkish streaks variable in intensity. The finest examples of veneering with tulipwood occur on the work of the French *ébénistes* from about 1750 onwards, who frequently employed it in conjunction with amaranth (q.v.).

TUNBRIDGE WARE
The term is applied for the most part to a kind of wood-mosaic made for the most part at Tunbridge (now Tonbridge) or Tunbridge Wells in Kent (England), and records show that the industry was already in being at the end of the 17th century, although the finest mosaic pictures belong to the 18th and early 19th centuries. The method of making the mosaics was to glue long strips of variously coloured woods together and then to slice them transversely. The thin slices were glued to brown paper to support them, and transferred to the object to be decorated. Both native and imported woods were used to achieve the desired range of colours, and about 160 different woods were employed, some of which were dyed chemically. Mosaic patterns were very often

combined with marquetry (q.v.), and they sometimes form only a subsidiary part of the decoration.

Many small objects, mostly boxes of one kind or another, were decorated in this way. Much 18th-century work was of fine quality, the patterns being closely detailed and built up of many small pieces of carefully selected colour. One of the finest surviving examples, a picture of the Pantiles, Tunbridge Wells, has 20,000 pieces in an area measuring nine inches by seven inches.

After 1850 the quality of the workmanship considerably deteriorated, and the industry came to an end about 1900. There is an important collection in the Museum at Tunbridge Wells.

TURCOMAN RUGS AND CARPETS

These rugs come from Turkestan, an area of Russian Central Asia lying to the north of Persia and Afghanistan, bounded on the west by the Caspian Sea and on the east by the Chinese province of Sinkiang. They are woven by nomads, and the classification includes rugs from Kashgar and Yarkand, towns which are strictly in China. They are also related in both design and colour to Afghan rugs. The Sehna knot (see *Rugs, Knotting of*) is used almost invariably, and the predominant design is a series of octagon medallions. A rich brownish-red is characteristic of the region, and is termed 'Turcoman red'. Some of the principal types are noticed elsewhere—Bokhara, Samarkand, Kashgar, and Yarkand.

TURIN (Piedmont, Italy)

A faïence factory was at work here during the 17th century painting in a blue-and-white style somewhat resembling that of Savona (q.v.). Another was founded by Giorgio Rosetti in 1725, where the wares produced were influenced by Moustiers (q.v.) and the southern French factories.

TURKEY-WORK

Turkey-work as a kind of needlework came into fashion in England in the late 16th century. It simulated the pile rugs being imported from the Near East for the houses of wealthy Europeans. Turkey-work was made by pulling heavy wool through canvas or coarse linen, knotting it and cutting the ends to form a pile (see *Rugs, Knotting of*). Turkey-work carpets were used as table-covers, in the same way as Oriental rugs during this period. Turkey-work was also used for cushions and upholstery, and when used for the latter purpose doubled the cost of those covered in leather.

In America Turkey-work was noted in inventories and wills as being in general use for cushions and furniture coverings from 1646.

TURKISH RUGS AND CARPETS

The principal rug-weaving districts of Turkey are situated in western Anatolia (Asia Minor) and in Kurdistan to the east, in the Lake Van area. The Ghiordes knot (see *Rugs, Knotting of*) is invariable, and the pile, like the foundation, is of wool or goat hair. The pile is nearly always longer than that of the Persian rug. In colouring a deep purplish-brown is characteristic, and the designs are geometrical, often closely resembling those of Caucasian rugs (q.v.). The Turks, who incline to orthodoxy in religion, take the proscription against the representation of living things seriously, and do not include birds, animals, or figures of any kind in their repertory of ornament except in a very stylized version, and if naturalistically rendered ornament is to be seen, then the rug is much more likely to be Persian. Most of the large carpets of commerce are woven near Smyrna (Izmir), and are discussed under the heading of Sparta carpets. Some of the more important Turkish rug-making centres noticed elsewhere are Oushak, Ghiordes, Bergamo, Meles, Kereke, Sparta (Isparta), and Ladik.

TURNING

The shaping of metal, wood, or stone in a lathe (q.v.). Turning was especially used in the design and construction of furniture from Tudor times onwards until the early years of the 18th century, and again towards the end of the same century. It was also used for a whole range of chairs known as stick-backs (q.v.), of which the best-known example is the Windsor chair.

U

ULTRA-VIOLET LIGHT

Ultra-violet light is finding increasing use in the examination of works of art of all kinds where forgery or restoration is suspected. Often called 'black' light, true ultra-violet radiation cannot be seen by the human eye. It is propagated by a quartz tube containing mercury vapour which provides an intense illumination rich in ultra-violet radiation as well as visible light. The visible light is screened off by a filter of dyed glass, although in practice a little red and violet light still passes. Examination is carried out in a darkened room, and the observed effect will be either a reflection of the visible light passing the filter, or a true fluorescence. True fluorescence is a glow, similar to phosphorescence, except that it will disappear immediately the exciting radiation is shut off, whereas phosphorescence will continue to persist for a while.

The explanation is that when ultra-violet light falls on certain materials these are able to transform the short-wave, invisible radiation into one of a longer wave-length which is visible. The colour of the subsequent fluorescence depends on the wave-length to which the ultra-violet radiation has been transformed. Substances capable of exhibiting fluorescent effects are by no means numerous, and they often appear in the object itself in only minute traces, and when two objects apparently made of the same substances to ordinary appearances in normal light exhibit the same fluorescent effect under ultra-violet radiation it may be safely concluded that they are made from the same materials. If an object be added to in the course of restoration it is virtually certain that the new substances employed will give a different effect from the remainder. For instance, varnishes sometimes employed to simulate glaze in restoration of pottery and porcelain will fluoresce yellow, whereas the glaze will probably yield some shade of violet. The restored area will therefore be perfectly obvious. A few restorers have endeavoured to defeat this kind of examination by spraying the whole object with a glaze substitute, but in this case the fluorescence, while being perfectly even, differs from that of a genuine glaze, and can be seen by comparison. One or two restorers recently have employed substances in their work which yield comparable effects with the glazes of pottery and porcelain, but careful examination nearly always reveals sufficient difference between the two to trace the restored area. Painted enamels are similarly restored, and ultra-violet radiation is no less useful in this case.

Experience has suggested, however, that this kind of radiation may have other uses, apart from the detection of restoration. For instance, some figures by Samson (q.v.) proved to have a substance in the porcelain body or the glaze which caused it to give a mustard-yellow fluorescence. It is impossible to say to what section of their production this applies, but several such figures examined gave the same result, and it depends on which material is responsible, and for how long it was used, whether this can be regarded as a useful test of origin. In any case it is rarely required, for Samson reproductions are not usually deceptive enough to require this kind of examination. Early Chelsea porcelain, made before about 1755, fluoresces with a well-marked peach colour, and this observation is so firmly established that it is regarded as definitive test in the case of porcelain otherwise agreeing with known Chelsea characteristics. After 1755 the fluorescence changes to a violet colour, but this is to be expected, since the factory changed its formula at this time, and probably its source of raw materials as well. The colours exhibited by other English factories are not so well marked, but enough has emerged to show that they are often fairly characteristic. Examination should be carried out alongside a specimen of certain attribution.

Some old glass, particularly lead-glass, merely exhibits a characterless violet reflection from which nothing can be learned. In leadless glass, however, an orange fluorescence is not uncommon, and this may, perhaps, mark the presence of traces of uranium oxide. The same effect is to be seen in some modern laboratory glass. This orange fluorescence in old glass goes back for many centuries, the effect having been observed in 14th-century Syrian glass. Generally, not much work has been done on the fluorescence of old glass, but the chances are that a fluorescent effect will be observed with some old glasses, perhaps as the result of degenerative changes in the material itself.

In furniture fluorescence cannot be used to tell the difference between an old piece and a new one, but it does quite often reveal repairs and alterations, usually as the result of the difference in the effect exhibited by new and old varnish. In the case of stone sculpture, repairs and alterations can often be seen fairly easily, but the best results have been obtained from the softer stones, such as marble and alabaster. Marble gives a uniform purple colour when freshly cut, and a mottled white when the surface has been undisturbed for a long, but undetermined period. The effect of examining old ivories in this way is mentioned under patina (q.v.), but generally old ivory, the surface of which has been undisturbed, will exhibit a mottled yellow, while a freshly worked surface will give a purple reflection. Repairs to textiles—rugs, tapestries, and so forth—can often be detected by the difference between new work and old.

The ultra-violet lamp cannot be expected to give results which can be set down in black-and-white. The effects cannot be recorded in such a way as to make them useful. Colour photographs have been made, but they have never been successful in reproducing the observed effect. This kind of radiation could, perhaps, best be described as a new kind of vision, with a language of its own which has to be learned. Differences in the observed effects are never meaningless, but exactly what they mean has to be interpreted, and experience can only be gained by practice. The lamp is a personal tool, because the information it gives cannot be recorded objectively, and it is only possible to give the beginner some general guidance. It is impossible to say beforehand exactly what is to be expected from any material, and in any case filters differ slightly in the results they give, not only from maker to maker, but even from batch to batch. To use the lamp properly it should be employed in conjunction with a study of the materials and processes employed in the making of works of art, but, in general, both collector and dealer who would like a more effective way of detecting restorations in particular with much greater certainty than can be expected from the unaided eye can hardly be without it. It is now used by all the major museums and auction-rooms, and by many dealers. Suitable apparatus is made by Engelhard Hanovia Lamps of Slough. The most useful filter is one designed to pass maximum radiation at 3,660 Ångstrom units. There is also a short-wave filter available passing 2,537 Å.U. which is principally for laboratory and experimental work.

UNAKER

Virginian china clay. This substance played an influential part in the development of the porcelain industry in England. It was used by a number of factories, notably Bow and Wedgwood, and in June 1950 a marker was placed on Highway 28, five miles north of Franklin, North Carolina, to indicate the site

of a pit from which supplies of this Cherokee clay were drawn by Wedgwood for use in the making of jasper (q.v.).

Unaker is an interesting aspect of Anglo-American ceramic history which begins in 1744, when a man from the then colony of Virginia arrived in London with samples of china clay which the Cherokee Indians called *unaker*, and almost certainly with specimens of china stone—the feldspathic rock necessary to make true porcelain. Although his name has not been recorded, all the evidence incontrovertibly points to the traveller being Andrew Duché of Savannah, Georgia (q.v.).

The source of the china clay used by the first English porcelain factories has always been somewhat of a mystery, since most of them had been established for at least a year or two before china clay was discovered by William Cookworthy in Cornwall. There is an old tradition that Chelsea used Chinese clay, or *kaolin*, brought by East Indiamen as ballast, and a discovery some years ago of a Spanish galleon wrecked off the Florida Keys has demonstrated that it was Chinese practice to pack porcelain for export in barrels otherwise filled with powdered china clay. The possibility that the East India Company sold clay of this kind to Chelsea is fairly strong. In a letter to a friend of 1745 Cookworthy, who had been visited by Duché, wrote: 'He [Duché] is gone for a cargo of it. . . . They can import it for £13 a ton, and by that means afford their china as cheap as common stoneware; but they intend to go only about 30 per cent. under the Company.' Since the East India Company was the only enterprise likely to be referred to as 'the Company' in this context, it is clear that Cookworthy either knew, or surmised, that they were importing Chinese clay. The Chinese themselves, well knowing the principles of porcelain manufacture, were always prepared to sell china clay, although they kept the part played by feldspathic rock a secret.

In December 1744, Heylyn and Frye at Bow registered a patent for the manufacture of porcelain, and referred in the specification to 'an earth, the produce of the Cherokee nation in America, called by the natives *unaker*', which was essential to their formula. Duché did not at once return home. In 1745 we find him in Plymouth, waiting for a ship, and here he visited Cookworthy, who was convinced that his samples were equal to Asiatic porcelain. Cookworthy refers to his visitor's acquaintance with the *History of China* written by du Halde, a French missionary, in which the process of porcelain-making is described. Like Cookworthy and Frye, Duché was a Quaker. It seems an inescapable conclusion that Cookworthy, who began an intensive search for the materials of porcelain-making in England as soon as his visitor left, discovered soaprock as a substitute for feldspathic rock, and conveyed the secret to his fellow-Quaker, Lund, at Bristol, and through him to the Quaker Holdships at Worcester (see *Soaprock*).

With the discovery of Cornish clay the subject of

Chimney-piece in the Palladian style at Clandon Hall, Surrey. The architect, Giacomo Leoni, published a revised edition of Palladio's *Four Books of Architecture* in 1725.

Chinoiserie. The Music-room at Brighton Pavilion, Sussex, decorated in the Chinese taste of the early decades of the 19th century.

Unicorn. A silver unicorn forming a handle of the wine cistern shown on page 243. Maker: Thomas Heming. 1770.

unaker was not pursued any further by Cookworthy, but Richard Champion, who succeeded to Cookworthy's 1768 patent at Bristol, received a letter from his brother-in-law in South Carolina and a box of Cherokee clay to be used for experimental purposes. A similar box was sent to Worcester, but no record exists of what was done with it. In 1767 an attempt was made to sell American clay to Wedgwood, perhaps an approach from the captain of a ship trading between Liverpool and America. Wedgwood arranged to import an experimental quantity in this year, and employed Thomas Griffiths to journey into the interior of South Carolina in search of clay. Griffiths returned in 1768 with five tons, but at prohibitive cost.

Hitherto *unaker* had only been used in the making of porcelain, and Wedgwood was prevented by the patent of Cookworthy and Champion from making true porcelain. In 1773, however, he found a use for it in the manufacture of 'Gems and Cameos'. This, no doubt, refers to his new jasper-ware which was in production by the early part of 1775, and Wedgwood himself refers in his letters to jasper as his

'biscuit porcelain'. The Cherokee clay must have been widely known at the time because, in 1777, Wedgwood wrote to Bentley that 'it may not be a bad idea to give out that our jaspers are made of Cherokee clay'. There is little doubt that Cherokee clay continued to form part of the finest quality jasper-ware during Wedgwood's lifetime, and in 1785 he wrote a long letter to William Constable giving the history of his own connection with it. In the course of this letter he mentions he had since learned that a Frenchman, who may have been Duché, had sent the clay to one or more of the porcelain manufactories of France where they could make nothing of it. No record of the import of Cherokee clay into France appears to survive, but Sèvres were experimenting with a wide variety of earths during the 1760s with the object of discovering the secret of true porcelain in the Chinese and Meissen manner before the discovery of suitable deposits at Saint-Yrieix.

UNICORN

(French *licorne.*) A mythological animal in the form of a horse with a single straight horn growing from the centre of its forehead. It is depicted in some early French tapestries, and occasionally in other media, but it was not often used. Said to be a native of India, it was thought that it could only be captured by a virgin which no doubt accounts for the lack of specimens in captivity.

URBINO (Italy)

The *maiolica* of Urbino became so popular that it suppressed the inventiveness of its competitors and stifled their individual styles. In common with other Italian cities, Urbino must have been producing pottery from the early years of the 15th century, but no record appears in the city's archives before 1477, and it was really Nicola Pellipario called da Urbino (who actually came from Castel Durante) who introduced the style that made the city famous. This is the style to be seen in the Gonzaga service made for Isabella d'Este, wife of Gian Francesco Gonzaga, Marquis of Mantua. The dishes are decorated in a

Urbino. Urbino armorial dish painted in the *istoriato* style with high-temperature colours by Francesco Xanto Avelli da Rovigo. 1532. From a service made for Piero Maria Pucci. Subject: Aeneas slaying the deer. *Christie, Manson & Woods.*

well in the centre with the impaled arms of the two families, and the rim is painted with mythological and Biblical subjects. The colours are brilliant and produce fine harmonies on the white enamel ground. This service was painted before Nicola left Castel Durante, but is proof, if need be, that he was responsible for introducing and developing the style at Urbino. Nicola's son Guido, who took the name Fontana, had three sons, Orazio, Camillo, and Nicolo, of whom Orazio Fontana shares the honour, with Xanto Avelli, of being one of Urbino's two most famous masters. Xanto Avelli signed many of his works which are dated between 1528 and 1542, though probably these dates do not exactly correspond with his working life. He was an *istoriato* painter and borrowed more or less accurately from almost every source, but his work nevertheless bears a personal stamp, arising perhaps from the restrictions of the medium on which he worked. He was a very prolific painter, but his sense of colour is less sure than that of Nicola and his style more stilted. He made large services commissioned by the Dukes of Urbino, and some very imposing pieces, but much of the work was done in his studio and cannot certainly be attributed to his hand. Probably his workshop was the most important in the town, and its influence was far-reaching.

Urbino painting seems based on an intention, above all, to disguise the material. This had many defects, for decorative feeling was often thrown to the winds in the speed and skill—rather than artistry—by which the colours were applied. The *istoriato* style must have been a godsend to the studio workers, whose training embraced all its elements. It required considerable skill but little inventiveness.

Orazio Fontana, who was really responsible for the wide dissemination of the style, left his father's workshop in 1565 and died in 1571. During these years he took up the style known as *grotesques* (q.v.), from Raphael's revival of Roman ornament in the Loggie of the Vatican, a purely ornamental style fundamentally much more suited to the decoration of *maiolica* than *istoriato* painting. The *motifs* were to become common currency in European ornament —terminal figures, those with foliate limbs, masks, medallions with miniature scenes either in blue *camaieu* and *en grisaille*, or in rich colours on the white ground, in contrast to *istoriato* painting which had been intent on covering the entire surface. At first the new decoration was used merely as a frame to a scene in the older style, but development of plastic feeling at Urbino lent itself to this kind of ornament, and it was after 1560 that Urbino produced the snake-handled ewers, birds' and lions' heads on salts, and many different plastic forms filled with the fantasy of the High Renaissance. These *grotesques* continued in vogue till well into the 17th century, and became fashionable almost everywhere. During the later years of the 17th century *maiolica* painting degenerated rapidly at Urbino, the wares became coarse and the decora-

tion crude. Production, however, continued, and, in 1770, a Frenchman named Rolet set up a faïence factory, but of this little is known. See *Raimondi, Marcantonio*.

URN

A kind of vase based on forms first employed by the Greeks for pottery about the 5th century B.C. The urn was especially employed as an ornamental device during the 18th-century neo-classical period, both by the Adam Brothers and the designers of the Louis Seize period in France. The large wooden vases standing at either end of the Adam sideboard intended for cutlery, and vessels of silver or Sheffield plate of similar shape with a tap, are termed urns. Urns were also employed in two-dimensional form as inlay, or as the splats of chairs during the Adam period. In France they occur as part of the decoration of clock-cases, lighting fixtures, etc. The early Queen Anne fiddle-back (q.v.) chair splat is sometimes referred to as urn- or vase-shaped.

URNS, TEA-

Nearly always of Sheffield plate, the purpose of the tea-urn was not unlike that of the Russian samovar, except that it held only boiling water which was drawn through a tap at the base into the teapot, for, contrary to popular belief, tea was neither made nor stored in it.

The earliest tea-urns were heated by charcoal, which was followed about 1794 by the employment of a lump of iron brought to red heat in the stove and inserted in a socket in the base. About the same time an improved version was patented which boiled water in an upper compartment and allowed it to flow, on the turning of a tap, on to tea-leaves beneath. Tea-urns heated by spirit-lamps were first made about 1790, but they did not immediately become popular, for fuel-alchohol, produced by the distillation of wine (spirits of wine), was scarce and expensive.

Urn. A bronze urn after a marble urn for the gardens of Versailles by Girardon for Colbert. *Wallace Collection.*

Urn. Silver wine-cooler in the form of the Greek *krater*, a vessel for mixing wine and water, of the type usually termed an urn. English, by Robert Garrard. 1816. *Christie, Manson & Woods.*

The first tea-urns were usually of the classical ovoid shape popularized by the Adam Brothers, although an almost globular version was introduced early in the 19th century. A number of variations occur, one being a combined tea and coffee maker, in which boiling water from a large urn could be directed into either of two smaller ones. This first appeared about 1797.

The decoration of tea-urns generally is appropriate to the period.

See *Sheffield Plate.*

VALUE

Contrary to popular belief, antiques and works of art do not have a monetary value which can be stated in precise terms, except within limits. An automobile has a fixed value, which is the result of adding to production-cost a margin of profit related to demand and to the price fixed by competitors for a similar vehicle. While a competitor's price for a related object might influence an antique dealer in the price he asks, he is, in fixing his price, usually actuated by current demand as far as he knows it, and in some cases, and to some extent, by potential demand.

The value of any object can be defined as what a willing buyer will pay to a willing seller, but this implies that the value cannot be known until buyer and seller have agreed on a price. Broadly this is correct, and until an object is sold its value is guess-work. It is true that the guesses may have an objective foundation, such as prices realized in the saleroom for similar objects, but there are a number of factors in any particular case which may lead to a higher or lower price at the time of sale.

In estimating value it is essential to look first at what objects of the same kind have realized in the saleroom within a year or two of sale, and then to consider carefully the genuineness, quality, age, rarity, and condition of the object it is proposed to value, as well as any changes in demand or circumstances which may have taken place in the interim. A major difficulty in the way of using saleroom prices to arrive at a basic figure is that, unless the object sold was inspected by the valuer, its quality and condition must be largely unknown and the circumstances of the sale difficult to estimate.

For this reason any object can legitimately be valued at several different levels. For insurance purposes value should be fixed at what the object would cost to replace with a reasonable equivalent in unfavourable circumstances. For estate duty purposes it is legitimate to estimate what it might fetch at a forced sale, and there is a considerable difference between the two figures.

The value of any object is enhanced in certain circumstances, notably inclusion in a sale of high quality, or as part of a collection which has become well known for containing pieces of unusual interest. The reputation of the collector himself as an authority on a particular subject has a similar effect.

Inclusion in a poor sale will depress value, since fewer people willing and able to pay a high price will be present, and, mixed with inferior objects, even one of unusual quality will often suffer from its company. Bad cataloguing has the same effect, since in these days many people are inclined to rely on catalogue descriptions when buying from large salerooms. If most dealers were asked where they would be most likely to find a bargain they would answer: In a small provincial saleroom, in a sale largely composed of rubbish, where the important lot is inaccurately catalogued.

Fashion can depress or enhance value, although not in these days to a very serious extent. Obviously the time to sell is when the demand for a particular class of antique is at its height.

It is fair to say that there are as many values as there are valuers, and even the most expert rarely estimate within 10 or 20 per cent of the eventual price realized in the saleroom. Quite often, because of unforeseeable circumstances, the discrepancy is even wider. As an example, a fine-quality piece of furniture was included in a sale in a famous auction-room a few years ago. It was estimated to realize about £2,000 and brought £10,000, simply because two private collectors who detested each other were both determined to have it. No valuer could forsee circumstances of this kind, nor would the same piece bring anything like a comparable price again, unless, in the meantime, furniture of the same kind had appreciated in value to this extent—by no means an impossibility.

Valuation is an art and not a science, and the ability to value with a reasonable degree of accuracy is the product of long experience. In the case of antiques only experienced dealers, saleroom experts, and collectors of long standing are likely to be able to forecast with reasonable accuracy the price at which any specimen is likely to sell.

The difficult question of artistic value is not here discussed. It is not a factor which has any very special effect on price in many cases, since it is usually a matter of opinion. Many of the entries in this *Dictionary*, however, will help the reader to assess this aspect. It is also allied to Fashion in Art (q.v.).

VANBRUGH. SIR JOHN (1664–1726)
One of the few English baroque architects, whose works include Castle Howard and Blenheim Palace. Pope wrote an epitaph:

> Lie heavy on him, earth, for he
> Laid many a heavy load on thee.

He was also a furniture-designer in the tradition of the time.

VAN EENHOORN, SAMUEL AND LAMBERTUS
Two sons of a Delft potter (q.v.), who made their mark in the 17th century. Samuel painted Chinese subjects in blue-and-white and occasionally manganese-purple on a rather bluish glaze. His hand has been recognized on several large and finely decorated *potiches* and vases. See also *Cachemire Style*.

VAN LOO, CARLE (1705–1765)
French painter, born in Nice. He became an Academician in 1735, and was made *premier peintre du roi* in 1763. His work sometimes inspired Sèvres porcelain painting.

VAN RYSSENBURGH, BERNARD (fl. 1735–1765)
Van Ryssenburgh (or Risen Burgh) was a Flemish *ébéniste* working in Paris towards the middle of the 18th century. He specialized in lacquer furniture and floral marquetry, and supplied furniture to Mme de Pompadour through Lazare Duvaux (q.v.). He seems to have become *maître ébéniste* about 1736, and to have died, or ceased working, about 1765. His stamp was *BVRB*.

VARNISH
Varnishes are a solution of resin in a solvent, such as alcohol. When varnish is exposed to the air the alcohol evaporates, leaving a thin film of resin on the surface of the object to which it has been applied, usually furniture or paintings. Resins are numerous —copal, mastic, dammar, amber, etc. Varnish provides a protective film which can usually be removed with alcohol, although occasionally other, more powerful solvents are required.

During the 16th and 17th centuries furniture was protected with oil and wax, and in the 17th century an oil varnish—a solution of a gum or resin in linseed oil—was employed which sank into the wood. In the 18th century the usual surface treatment for wood was lac dissolved in spirits of wine (alcohol) which imparted a thin, lustrous film to the surface of the wood. Early in the 19th century an unpleasantly shiny varnish known as French polish was introduced, which is also lac dissolved in alcohol, and a good deal of 18th-century furniture was later re-

polished with it. It is often better to remove this and repolish in a way which is closer to the original surface-finish of the 18th century.

VAUXHALL GLASS
A glass-house for the manufacture of mirror-glass established at Vauxhall (or Foxhall), S.W. London, in 1670 by George Villiers, Duke of Buckingham. Mirrors were given a broad but shallow bevel, which is often hardly perceptible. Evelyn saw the glass-house in 1676, when he records '. . . looking-glasses far larger and better than any that come from Venice'.

VEILLEUSE (French)
Literally, night-lamp. The *veilleuse* is a tea- or food-warmer, also known as a *réchaud*, which means strictly a dish-warmer. *Veilleuses* are to be found in earthenware, stoneware, and porcelain, some of the most interesting being in tin-enamelled ware. The date of origin appears to be about the middle of the 18th century, the earliest known probably being those of Lambeth delft. They were made in most countries, from Russia to England, and from Sweden to Italy. In general form they consist of a base on which is placed a cylindrical chimney, pierced towards the top to allow hot air to escape, and surmounted by a covered food-container at first, and later by a teapot. The chimney has an aperture at the bottom to allow for the insertion of a lamp, the *godet*, which is a small cup containing oil with a floating wick. Many porcelain examples are very well painted, and designed to allow the transmission of light by which the painting is seen at night. A particularly interesting type is the porcelain *personnage*, the *veilleuse* in the form of a figure, usually with the arms so disposed that one forms the spout of the teapot and the other the handle, the body from the waist upwards being a teapot, and from the waist downwards the chimney. These seem mostly to have been made in France and Bohemia, and the best were the work of Jacob Petit (q.v.).

Veilleuse. A *veilleuse* or food-warmer decorated with figures in a landscape. Nymphenburg. 1755–1760. *Señor Jose M. Mayorga.*

VELVET

(French *velour*.) A fabric with a close, standing pile on the outer surface. Velvet is woven with additional warp threads taken over thin metal rods in the form of loops which are subsequently cut (cut velvet). The withdrawal of the rods without cutting results in uncut velvet (*épinglé* or *frisé*). *Ciselé* velvet refers to the formation of patterns by leaving some of the loops uncut. Some velvets, such as Genoese velvet, were made with a silk pile, and these were the best. Others, like the hard-wearing Utrecht velvet, had a pile of wool. Silk velvet was extremely expensive in 18th-century France, and the cost of covering a normal *fauteuil* was about 50 *livres* (£25). See *Moquette*.

VELVET, GENOESE

Cut satin velvet, often with large stylized floral designs of Near Eastern origin. These velvets were later made in France, especially at Lyon, Tours, and Saint-Maur (q.v.).

VELVET, MILANESE

One of the luxury materials of the 17th century. Cardinal Mazarin possessed a *suite* of hangings of this velvet decorated with *grotesques* after Raphael and with medallions representing scenes from the life of François I, each piece bearing his Arms at the top. See *Velvet*; *Velvet, Genoese*.

VENEERS AND VENEERING

Veneers are thin slices of rare exotic woods employed to decorate carcasses of common wood, such as deal, oak, or pine. The use of veneers as furniture decoration can be traced back at least to ancient Egypt, but the practice was especially popular during the 17th, 18th, and early 19th centuries, principally because many new woods were being imported from both East and West.

Many woods suitable for furniture-making, especially the cheaper ones, have a monotonous and uninteresting surface, whereas the most decorative woods have usually been expensive and obtainable only in small quantities. Veneering, therefore, was an economical way of making use of available supplies. Although veneers today are machine-cut to about $\frac{1}{64}$ of an inch in thickness, in former times they were sawn by hand and vary in thickness from about $\frac{1}{16}$ inch to about $\frac{1}{8}$ inch for burr-walnut. Care was taken to select only those pieces with a decorative grain.

By *grain* we mean the normal surface-markings or figure of wood, and this varies from being well marked to hardly perceptible, from markings of almost geometrical accuracy to a random figure. Certain characteristics, such as burrs, curls, and so forth, which form part of the figure of some woods, are much prized for their decorative value, and the figure known as 'oyster-shell' was obtained from transverse slices taken from certain branches which yielded a circular pattern. Successive slices were sometimes opened out like a folded sheet of note-paper, one being the mirror-image of the other, and when this was done with four successive slices at the top and bottom of a panel the result was termed quartering. The latter arrangement is often to be seen on fall-fronts to English writing-desks of the early years of the 18th century. Great ingenuity was brought to the arrangement of veneers, and a variety of decorative patterns could be achieved in this way. Some of the woods more commoly employed as veneers are listed below:

Acacia—A rich brown with a well-marked grain which was a favourite with the French *ébénistes*.

Acajou—See *Mahogany*.

Amboyna—Reddish-brown with a well-marked grain, often with burrs. Also a favourite with the French *ébénistes*.

Blackwood—A West Indian wood, varying from greenish-black to brown in colour.

Coromandel—An Indian wood, black, mottled, and striped in a yellowish shade.

Holly—White in colour, with a close and even grain. Most often employed for stringing and inlaying.

Mahogany—Although quite often employed in solid form, mahogany was also popular as a source of veneers. The usual colour is a rich reddish-brown, which is darker in the Cuban variety. The latter variety is noted for its figure.

Padauk—A Far Eastern wood, dark red in colour, sometimes used as a source of veneers. More often it was employed in solid form, and is sometimes mistaken for mahogany.

Palissandre—See *Rosewood*.

Purplewood—Close-grained and purple in tone, with very little figure. Principally employed by the French *ébénistes*.

Rosewood—A wood, reddish-brown in colour, with darker markings, often with a well-marked figure.

Satinwood—The colour ranges from yellowish to almost golden. Satinwood often has a well-marked figure which is much valued.

Snakewood—Not often seen, snakewood is a chestnut-brown in colour with darker mottlings.

Sycamore—Popular in France. Sycamore veneers are white, but the wood takes stain well, when it is termed harewood, and it is rarely found in an uncoloured state.

Thuyawood—Yellowish in colour with a curly figure, thuya comes from North Africa, and it was particularly valued by the French *ébénistes*, although it is not often seen. As a furniture wood it has been highly valued since Roman times.

Tulipwood—Reddish-brown with yellowish and grey stripes. The wood is related to rosewood, and it is called *bois de rose* in France.

Violetwood—The predominant 18th-century wood in France for fine work. It is hard, close-grained, and a dark purple in colour with darker streaks. Since the 19th century it has been called kingwood in England.

Walnut—A dark brown wood much valued for the cutting of veneers. There are several European varieties, of which Italian walnut is used extensively. American walnut is also much used. This is darker than most European walnuts, but it exhibits a good figure.

Zebra wood—Reddish-brown with dark stripes.

Ebony was employed only to a very limited extent after the 17th century, and maple, yellowish-white in colour and often with a curly mottled figure, became popular during the 19th century, especially in America.

This does not pretend to be exhaustive, but it lists the woods principally used. The subject is discussed under the related headings of *Marquetry* and *Parquetry* (q.v.). The woods mentioned are also separately considered.

VENETIAN GLASS

Venice was a glassmaking centre in the 11th century, but nothing has survived which can be accurately dated before 1450. Venice was in a particularly favourable position to develop a glassmaking industry, since it not only had a plentiful supply of suitable sand and quartz pebbles, but it was the principal trading port between Europe and the Near East and it was in touch with the glassmakers of Syria and Alexandria. Venetian glass-workers may actually have learned their craft in Damascus, for some of its earliest productions owe more than a little to Islamic enamelled glass from Syria. Venice also received several influxes of skilled workers from elsewhere, notably from Damascus and Byzantium when these cities were captured by invaders. At first production was located in Venice itself, but by 1291 it seems to have been on so large a scale that the Senate became apprehensive of the danger of fire from the numerous furnaces, and decreed that the industry should be removed to the island of Murano where it still remains. One result of the concentration of the industry here was that it became a State monopoly giving its craftsmen a high social status, and to preserve the essential secrets of manufacture severe penalties were enjoined for any workman absconding. These

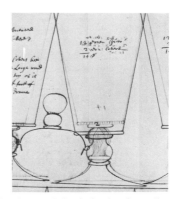

Venetian Glass. Drawings made by the London glass-seller, John Greene, when sending an order to Alessio Morelli, master glassmaker of Murano (Venice). 1677. *Harleian MSS, British Museum.*

included the imprisonment of near-relatives, and finally, if the absconder still proved obdurate, assassination. These restrictions and penalties still existed in the 18th century, and when Colbert imported workmen from Venice to make the mirrors for the Galerie des Glaces, during the building of Versailles, they died in mysterious circumstances. Some workmen, however, escaped to join the rival centre at Altare, near Genoa (q.v.), which had been started originally by glass-workers from Normandy, and here no restrictions were placed on their movements. It is probable, since similar things were made both here and at Venice, that many early glasses from northern parts of Europe described as *façon de Venice* (q.v.) could, with equal truth, be regarded as *façon d'Altare*, and that workmen from Altare rather than Venice founded many of the industries farther north.

The Venetians employed a soda-glass made from sand or ground pebbles, lime, and soda, the latter obtained from burning seaweed. This was later replaced by *barilla* (q.v.) from Spain, an ash containing both lime and soda. These substances yielded a glass which especially lent itself to manipulative techniques (see *Glass, Nature of*), and this property is to be well seen in some of the more elaborate Venice productions of the 17th century.

The glassmakers of Venice made many technical advances of the utmost importance, some of which, despite precautions, found their way to other centres of the industry. One of the most notable was the rediscovery in the middle of the 16th century of the use of small quantities of manganese as a decolorizer, for neutralizing unwanted tints which were the result of such impurities as iron in the raw material. At first not entirely successful, the resultant greyish glass was nevertheless still very much better than anything being produced elsewhere, and its lack of a pronounced colour made it extremely popular. The Venetians termed it *cristallo* because of a fancied resemblance to rock-crystal, and in considering the productions of Venice at this time one must always bear in mind the value placed on semi-precious hardstones of all kinds, of which rock-crystal was but

Venetian Glass. Dish of enamelled glass decorated with a Coat of Arms. Venetian glass. c. 1500. *Victoria and Albert Museum.*

one. Others which the Venetians attempted to imitate in glass include onyx, agate, and chalcedony, and they even called this kind of glass *calcedonio*. Later on, at the beginning of the 17th century, they began to imitate aventurine (q.v.), which they did by including minute copper scales in a suitably coloured glass.

Since the days of Marco Polo in the middle of the 14th century a certain amount of trade with China had been done by Venice, probably by way of Syrian ports which were one of the terminals of the Old Silk Road. There is no reason to doubt that Chinese porcelain was known there in the 15th century, and in the second half of that century the *maiolica* glaze, which is glass opacified with oxide of tin, became well known. In the early years of the 16th century there is record of bowls of *porcellana contrefacta*, which were probably glass of this kind, and experiments with it were perhaps being made as early as 1470. It seems likely that it was regarded as a porcelain substitute at the time, although not a satisfactory one (see *Medici Porcelain*), but in the 17th and 18th centuries it was undoubtedly so regarded, and it was painted with enamels in the manner of porcelain. Quite a number of specimens of this kind survive, some, now in the Victoria and Albert Museum (London), brought back by Horace Walpole in 1741 and kept at Strawberry Hill (q.v.).

Perhaps the most important of surviving Venetian glasses are the early specimens with enamelled decoration, and one of these, the Barovieri cup in the Museo Civico Correr at Venice, is probably the earliest known piece of Venetian glass to survive, since it was made about 1450. This technique began in Syria in the 13th century, and perhaps the best known are lamps (or lamp-shades) made for the mosques of Cairo in the 14th century. Most surviving Venetian work of this kind can be dated to the last quarter of the 15th century, and the technique is unmistakably related. The earliest specimens are pictorial, but shields of Arms and simpler decorative *motifs* made their appearance in the early years of the 16th century, when bands of coloured dots in enamel were sometimes the only decoration. It is, perhaps, a little surprising that enamel decoration on *maiolica* did not make its appearance at this time, since it was technically quite possible using the glassmakers' methods, and the secrecy which always surrounded the industry is probably the explanation. By the middle of the 16th century enamelling had passed out of fashion, but a few pictorial glass dishes after Raphael painted in cold colours (that is, unfired oil-colours) were done in the second half of the same century, and in this case there can be little doubt that they were inspired by contemporary *maiolica*.

Perhaps the most characteristic of all Venetian work is the *latticinio* technique, of which the more elaborate versions were called *vetro de trina*, or lace glass, and this, beginning a little before 1550, persisted into the 18th century. It consisted of threads of opaque white glass embedded in clear or coloured glass, and convoluted to produce either simple

Venetian Glass. A 'winged' goblet with *latticinio* bowl. Venice. Early 17th century. *Victoria and Albert Museum.*

patterns, or those which were intricate and interlacing. The simplest example of *latticinio* is to be found in the opaque white twist (q.v.) stems of 18th-century wine-glasses, but the Venetians carried the technique to far greater lengths, not only employing the white glass in the form of threads and ribbons, but even producing a combed version not unlike that to be seen decorating some early Egyptian glass.

There were a number of other techniques employed in Venice, one of which, diamond engraving, was used towards the end of the 16th century, but soon abandoned, probably because the nature of the metal made it hazardous. But it did become popular in the German territories, particular at Hall-in-the-Tyrol, and about 20 years later it made its appearance in England with the glasses of Verzelini (q.v.). Nothing like wheel-engraving or carving was ever attempted before the 18th century, since the type of glass made it impossible. At their best the Venetian diamond-engravings are examples of fine craftsmanship.

There remain one or two minor techniques to be noticed which were, at first, peculiar to Venice. Ice-glass, which has a rough surface not unlike that of ice, was made by plunging hot glass into water and then reheating it. A similar effect was the result of rolling the glass while soft on to fragments which were then subsequently melted in. Like the elaborately convoluted glasses, with which Venice is always associated, these processes prove the tractable nature of the metal.

Very little important glass was made much after 1650, although Venice remained for many years one of the principal sources of mirror-glass. The Venetians also produced mirror-frames and chandeliers, and the later 18th-century productions were decorated both with engraving and cutting.

More recently, particularly after 1850, Renaissance styles have been revived, and if some of them are not in the taste of today, at least they proved that the Venetian glass-worker had lost none of his skill. More recently still the imperfections of Renaissance glass have been imitated, and this forms a trap for the unwary.

Despite the efforts of the early glassmakers, Venetian styles and techniques soon passed to other parts of Europe, but especially to Germany and the Netherlands. Not all such glass can be attributed to defecting Venetians. The glass-centre at Liége, which was in existence soon after the middle of the 16th century, owed its inception to workers from Altare. Some of the work produced in these various centres can only be told apart from Venetian glass with great difficulty.

VENICE MAIOLICA
Venetian *maiolica* cannot be attributed with any kind of evidential basis until about 1525, although the glassmakers of Murano were including tin oxide in glass to make it white and opaque before the end of the 15th century. Imitations of *maiolica* by means of cold painting on glass occur at about the same time as Venetian *maiolica* can first be attributed. The earliest *maiolica* shows very clearly the influence of the Orient, especially the kind of Ming porcelain (see *Ming Dynasty*) commonly exported from China to Persia, and there imitated on large faience dishes. The trade with Germany in enamelled glass was also extended to *maiolica* if specimens with the Arms of German families can be accepted as a guide. The influence of both Faenza and Urbino is perceptible in wares made before 1580, those in the latter style probably being by itinerant Urbino painters recorded as having been in Venice. Ewers, globular vases (perhaps suggested by Chinese porcelain), and drug-jars were all made before 1580, and a decoration of fruits perhaps influenced the early faience painting of the Netherlands and, indirectly, that of 17th-century England.

Venetian *maiolica* is glazed with a semi-transparent tin-enamel, suggesting that tin was not in plentiful supply. The glaze is bluish-grey, the colours employed are strong and of the high-temperature variety, and the backs of dishes are usually plain, although the use of several concentric circles in yellow pigment seems to have been peculiar to Venice.

During the 18th century a pottery belonging to the Bertolini brothers produced a hard-fired, thin, almost resonant ware, with a decoration of landscapes on a pale blue or greyish ground.

VENICE PORCELAIN
Noted for its glass, Venice never developed a flourishing porcelain industry. As early as 1508 attempts had been made to make a substitute for the rare specimens of Chinese porcelain which were then finding their way into Europe by using opaque white glass, but the first porcelain factory was not started until 1720, when one was founded by Giuseppe and Francesco Vezzi, who made a hard porcelain resembling that of Böttger at Meissen (q.v.). Form and decoration are related both to early Meissen and Vienna wares. A native of Dresden, named Hewelcke, made porcelain about 1758, but the factory was short-lived, and little can now be identified with even reasonable certainty. A factory belonging to Gemiano Cozzi was started in 1765, closing in 1812. The porcelain made was a kind of soft paste, and Meissen was commonly imitated. This factory used the mark of an anchor (also used at Chelsea and Sceaux). A factory at Nove, not far from Venice, was established about 1728 by Giovanni Battista Antibon to make faience, and the manufacture of soft porcelain was added in 1752. It later experimented with hard porcelain, but specimens are of doubtful attribution. Painted decoration is chiefly floral.

VERNIS MARTIN (French)
Literally, Martin's varnish. A varnish invented about 1730 by two brothers, Guillaume and Étienne-Simon Martin, for the imitation of Oriental lacquer. It was very popular at the time, and plaques made with this varnish were incorporated into some of the best furniture of the period. The Martins were patronized by Mme de Pompadour, and by Queen Marie Leczinska to whom they supplied an *encoignure* for Versailles in 1738. Apart from furniture, *vernis Martin* was employed to decorate wall-panelling (*boiseries*), the panels of sedan chairs and coaches, musical instruments, *étuis*, snuff-boxes, hand-screens, and many like objects. They were quite frequently painted by, or in the manner of, the

Venice Porcelain. Plate painted with a classical scene. Venice. Vezzi factory. c. 1735.

Vernis Martin. Commode decorated in vernis Martin.
Louis XV style. c. 1755. *Christie, Manson & Woods.*

popular artists of the day. The varnish was supplied
in several colours, of which green was the most
sought.

VERRE EGLOMISÉ (French)

The term is employed to describe sheet-glass ornamented with engraved silver and gold leaf, with
sometimes the addition of painting. The term itself
seems to be derived from Jean-Baptiste Glomy (d.
1786), a French dealer in picture-frames who employed the technique for decorative borders surrounding prints and mirrors, and its extension to
more ambitious work took place in the 19th
century. The technique, however, is much older, and
mirrors decorated in this way occur in French
inventories towards the end of the 17th century.
Even then, there was nothing particularly novel about
it since it was merely a development of an existing
practice (see *Zwischengoldgläser*). Work of the
same kind was done by a Dutch artist named Zeuner
(fl. 1775), who painted views of Holland with passages of gold and silver leaf. In America, in the
late 18th century, during the period of the Federal
style, *verre eglomisé* was especially popular as
decoration to the panels of Sheraton type mirrors,
to the cases of wall and shelf clocks, and on the
panelled doors of so-called 'Salem' secretaries.
Designs were usually in black or white and gold.

VERROCCHIO (Andrea del Cione) (1435–1488)

Florentine sculptor, goldsmith, and painter, perhaps
a pupil of Donatello's and the master of Leonardo
da Vinci. He maintained a workshop specializing in
sculpture, painting, and goldsmiths' work, and is
noted for large sculpture in bronze, of which perhaps
the best known is the *David* (before 1476) in the
Bargello, the equestrian statue to the *condottiere*,
Bartolommeo Colleoni, at Venice (c. 1479), and the
Incredulity of Saint Thomas (c. 1480) for Orsanmichele, Florence. Vasari mentions him as having
executed small bronze figures, and a small *Love
Weeping* in the Louvre is usually attributed to him.

Verzelini, G. A goblet of Verzelini's glass, the bowl decorated
in gilding by Anthony de Lysle with the arms of the Vintner's
Company. Dated 1590. *Sotheby & Co.*

VERZELINI, GIACOMO (fl. 1575–1592, d. 1606)

Verzelini was originally from Murano (see *Venetian
Glass*). He escaped to London, and was granted a
patent or privilege (q.v.) by Queen Elizabeth for
the making of drinking glasses in the style of Murano
for a term of 21 years. This glasshouse was first at
Crutched Friars in the City of London, and later at
Broad Street not far away. Verzelini became natural-
ized in 1576.

Glass attributable to Verzelini is very rare and
extremely highly valued. About eight glasses
decorated with diamond-point engraving survive,
one of which, in the Musée de Cluny (Paris), is of
doubtful provenance. The metal is grey with many
imperfections inseparable from glass of this period.
The *motifs* of decoration are somewhat reminiscent
of those of the Middle East, perhaps to be expected
from someone of Venetian origin. All are dated and
bear names or initials. The engraving is thought to
have been the work of Anthony de Lysle, who is
recorded as an engraver on pewter and glass.

Verzelini's glasshouse was continued after 1592
by Sir Jerome Bowes, who enjoyed the remaining
years of the privilege, and it is possible that production continued into the early years of the 17th
century.

VESTUNSERVICE

The Festoon service made at Meissen for Frederick
the Great in 1760. It has a border of moulded
flower-garlands and a band of pierced 'chain' ornament around the rim.

VEUVE PERRIN See *Marseilles Faïence*

VICTORIAN PERIOD, STYLE IN THE

It would be an over-simplification to say that the Victorian period had no style of its own. It imposed its own imprint on those it borrowed, but, throughout the reign of Queen Victoria, style was largely influenced by the demands of machine production, and the notion of eclecticism—the idea that one style was as good as another and that they could be jumbled together without regard for the historical verities. Nor did these ideas begin with the accession of Victoria; they were apparent long before George IV yielded place to William IV.

At the beginning of the 19th century two principal styles are apparent—the Grecian, and the related Empire style (q.v.) of Napoleon I which, in turn, was a development of the neo-classical style (q.v.), represented in England by that of the Adam Brothers (q.v.).

Perhaps by 1830 four principal styles may be noted as prevailing: the Grecian; revived Gothic (q.v.); 'Elizabethan', which was Renaissance ornament superimposed on late Gothic; and the first indications of a style which, for the want of any more definite term, we may call 'Louis XIV', although the resemblances were always superficial. Alongside these four we have revivals of limited currency, such as revived rococo (see *Rococo*), which affected principally the design of porcelain and

Victorian Style. Cabinet of painted and gilded wood, designed by William Burges, made by Harland & Fisher, and painted by E. J. Poynter. c. 1858. *Victoria and Albert Museum.*

silver, and a fashion for *chinoiserie*, very limited in scope, which was confined largely to such trivia as papier mâché and japanned tin-ware (see *Pontypool Ware*).

Although the Grecian style was admired, especially in architecture, until almost 1840, it had before this date given pride of place to revived Gothic. In furniture, design still owed something to the Grecian style, which lingered until the 1840s in dining-room chairs with sabre legs, but revived Gothic had gained ground rapidly since 1834, when the style was adopted for the new Houses of Parliament to replace the building destroyed by fire in that year. By 1845 any other style, except for secular buildings, was unthinkable, and even those, from railway stations to urinals, blossomed forth with pointed arches and artificial stone crockets. Soon cabinet furniture of all kinds in revived Gothic was in great demand, and some ornate examples were shown at the Great Exhibition of 1851, such as a cabinet designed by J. G. Crace and now in the Victoria and Albert Museum (London). Crace was an interior decorator very much under the influence of A. W. Pugin (q.v.), and the latter's medievalism found very full opportunity for expression at the Great Exhibition, where he was responsible for the Medieval Court.

The late classical styles of the early part of the 19th century are discussed under the heading of Empire (q.v.), of which they form a continuing part, and most true Gothic works fall outside the scope of this book, although the style itself is briefly discussed (see *Gothic Style*). Perhaps the most obvious feature of Gothic architecture is the use of the pointed arch instead of the semi-circular arch of the classical styles. Pugin, in fact, referred to Gothic as the 'pointed Christian style', and this motif constantly recurs in all kinds of things. For instance Mintons about 1840 produced a classical Greek *krater* set on a pedestal which was decorated with a Gothic pointed arcade in relief, thus introducing Graeco-Gothic to the Victorian world, although it was not taken up with much enthusiasm anywhere else. This puts one in mind of Horace Walpole's garden seat—Chinese at one end, and Gothic at the other.

The first Gothic revival, which came shortly before the middle of the 18th century, was popularized (but not started) by Horace Walpole (q.v.), who began to Gothicize his villa at Strawberry Hill (Twickenham, S.W. London) in 1750. Walpole's villa, and his art-collection, in which many medieval and pseudo-medieval works were included, became a resort for the fashionable, and a catalogue (now exceedingly rare) was printed for the use of friends and visitors. Batty Langley (q.v.), an architect of garden pavilions, attempted to relate the Gothic style to the proportional system of the classical architect (see *Orders, The Five*), which was a singularly fruitless pastime, and by mid-century deliberately constructed Gothic ruins, either of stone or of wood and plaster, were popular as garden ornaments, one of which Walpole

Victorian Style. Centre-piece representing the Business Duties of the Goldsmiths' Company (part of a suite of plate in their possession). Design and maquette, Alfred Brown. Makers: Hunt & Noskell, London. 1855–1856. *The Worshipful Company of Goldsmiths.*

thought 'had the true rust of the barons' wars'. The fashion for Chinese ornament also current occasionally actually produced the curious hybrid 'Chinese-Gothic' already referred to.

The fashion for 'Gothic' declined with the onset of the Adam style (q.v.), but it was not entirely dead, and it returned reinvigorated with the building of Fonthill Abbey (Wiltshire) by William Beckford (architect, James Wyatt) which was first planned in 1796. Strawberry Hill, to Beckford, was a 'Gothick mousetrap', and Fonthill itself was conceived as a building of cathedral-like proportions. The popular romances of Sir Walter Scott, and the building of his house at Abbotsford in 1812, inspired romantically crude versions of medieval furniture which, made around 1820–1830, were said to be in the Abbotsford style. Allied to these influences was a vogue for the 'Elizabethan' style, which could be anything from Tudor to English Renaissance, although it could easily mean a mixture of both. The 19th-century Gothic revival received its greatest impetus from the work of A. W. Pugin, for whom the Gothic style assumed the proportions of a crusade. Largely responsible for the ornament of the present Houses of Parliament, he also designed furniture for Windsor Castle. For a time he designed porcelain for Minton's in Staffordshire, and had a high opinion both of their porcelain and of his own designs.

Beginning in England about 1830, and in France about five years later, was a revival of the 18th-century rococo style, but the shells and the *C* and *S* scrolls are a long way from those of Meissonnier's design-book. The style was well represented at the Great Exhibition of 1851, and it was partly the

product of the development of machinery, here and in America, which made possible the mechanical cutting of scrollwork. 'Everyone connected with cabinet-making', wrote one contemporary, 'is aware of the difficulty of obtaining good and novel designs of furniture. When such designs are obtained, everyone is equally aware of how comparatively easy it is to adapt them to the kind of work required; they may, in fact, be multiplied indefinitely by engrafting the decorations of one on the forms of another.' The implications of this statement are perfectly clear —the Victorian manufacturer was free, if he so desired, to graft Gothic ornament on to classical forms. Ralph Wornum, who certainly should have known better, wrote about the same time: 'Ornament is not a luxury, but in a certain stage of mind an absolute necessity.' The rococo style of the 1830s onwards is an example of this statement in action, and an example of the first, if it be needed, has already been quoted—the Minton classical vase on a Gothic pedestal.

The so-called Louis XIV style became really fashionable about 1860, and perhaps the most striking examples are vast and ornate cabinets in the worst of taste made by people like Jackson & Graham and Wright & Mansfield. The Victoria and Albert Museum (London) preserves a specimen. Since little of the kind survives from the period in question, it is probable that the designers had had their brains addled by reading Louis Quatorze's inventories, which describe some of the cabinets of the time in considerable detail. It was in 1850 that an American furniture-maker referred to 'the rich and ornate style known as "Louis Quatorze" . . . which is now one of those in supreme public taste', and some cabinets appeared in the New York Exposition of 1853 replete with an anachronism in the form of marble tops.

Victorian Style. The Hare and Pheasant. Carving in limewood by Thomas Henry Kendall, Warwick. A popular mid-Victorian *motif. Warwick County Museum.*

It is, indeed, difficult to see in most examples of this style anything much resembling the furniture of 17th century France.

The opening of Japan to international trade by Commodore Perry in 1853 brought a new influence to the scene, both in furniture and such materials as porcelain. Edward Godwin (q.v.) designed some excellent furniture in the Anglo-Japanese style, but the French were traditionalists, and Franco-Japanese furniture of the reign of Napoleon III harked back to the lacquer furniture of the 18th century, but hardly matched it for elegance. Emile Reiber designed an *encoignure* for the Emperor of ebony, rosewood, and lacquer replete with ormolu mounts, which is now in the Musée des arts decoratifs (Paris). This was the period of the *japonaiserie* (q.v.). In the 18th century furniture to Oriental designs had been made in wood turned to simulate bamboo, but the fashion for Japanese decoration produced furniture of actual bamboo, which was extremely fashionable from about 1870 onwards, eventually reaching the drawing-room.

A few people of taste were not satisfied with the course of events, among them Charles Eastlake and William Morris (q.v.). Eastlake wrote *Hints on Household Taste of 1868* (one of his less serious works) which was widely read in England and America, and Morris, with rare temerity, founded a factory in 1862 to offer to the public models for good taste. But even he did not avoid pseudo-medievalism, although he returned to the 13th century which was a little earlier than most Gothic revivalists cared to go. Moreover, he was no mere copyist, but based his designs on these early forms instead. He disliked the machine, and tried to make much of his furniture by hand, which put it out of the reach of most people. Nevertheless, he did considerably influence others, and later he inspired many designs in other fields—wallpaper, textiles, pottery, and so on. Some of Morris's furniture was painted

by the Pre-Raphaelites—Rossetti, Burne-Jones, and Madox Brown, and it is among the best of its period. The principles he laid down were developed by Bruce Talbert, whose *Gothic Forms Applied to Furniture* was published in 1867, although Talbert's versions were more ornate.

This hotch-potch of styles which characterized the 19th century ended with the coming of *art nouveau* (q.v.) which, owing something to Gothic, was nevertheless the last European style in its own right.

VIENNA PORCELAIN FACTORY, THE

This was the second true porcelain factory to be established in Europe, the first being Meissen. It was started by Claudius Innocentius du Paquier, a Court official, in 1719, with the aid of the Meissen kiln-master, Samuel Stölzel. The latter returned to Meissen in the following year taking with him a young enameller, Johann Gregor Höroldt. After several years of financial difficulties du Paquier was able to establish the factory on a sounder basis, and production was varied and of excellent quality, showing a good deal of originality. In 1744, in consequence of further financial trouble, the factory was taken over by the Empress Maria Theresa, and became a State enterprise. This began the State Period (1744–1784) during which it had varied fortunes culminating in yet another financial crisis, and the appointment of the Freiherr Konrad von Sorgenthal as director. From 1784 to 1805 von Sorgenthal guided the factory's fortunes through its greatest period of prosperity, but the 19th century saw yet another slow decline, and it closed finally in 1864, when a good deal of white ware was sold to decorators in the city, prominent among whom was Ludwig Riedl who repeated some of the styles which had met with success during the Sorgenthal period.

Vienna Porcelain. Bowl and cover painted with a topographical scene. Note the onion-shaped domes and steeply pitched roofs typical of Central European architecture. Vienna. Du Paquier's factory. c. 1730. *British Museum.*

Victorian Style. A plate painted in a coppery lustre pigment in the Deruta style. Fulham. William de Morgan's factory. c. 1880.

Vienna Porcelain. Neptune and Amphitrite, modelled by J. J.
Niedermayer. Vienna. c. 1760. *Victoria and Albert Museum.*

Vienna Factory. Perfume vase with animal supporters based
on a silver prototype. Vienna. Du Paquier's factory. c. 1725.
Cecil Higgins Museum, Bedford.

Du Paquier porcelain is much sought, but is now
extremely rare. The porcelain itself somewhat
resembles that of Böttger at Meissen. Most of these
early wares were moulded silver-patterns, those
which are wheel-thrown being distinctly rare. Far
Eastern wares had a relatively slight effect on
decoration and forms, and *chinoiseries* did not attain
the same popularity as at the Saxon factory. Of those
which exist, the derivation seems to have been
lacquer rather than porcelain. *Laub- und Bandelwerk* (q.v.) was often elaborate and a favourite
theme; *indianische Blumen* (q.v.) were replaced by
deutsche Blumen (q.v.) about 1730, a few years
earlier than at Meissen.

A great deal of Vienna painting at this time was in
Schwarzlot (q.v.), and animals and hunting scenes
were especially popular in this colour-scheme, some
taken from the engravings of Riedinger. Battle-scenes
were based on the work of Rugendas, engraved by
Bodenehr, and landscapes, topographical scenes,
Biblical scenes, and mythological subjects were taken
from a variety of contemporary sources. Among the
more important of the painters may be mentioned
Johann Karl Wendelin Anreiter von Zirnfeld, who
painted landscapes with figures usually in *Schwarzlot*, and who left signed examples. Joseph Philipp
Dannhöffer, who worked at several other factories
in the German territories, probably did landscapes
and Biblical subjects, and perhaps *chinoiseries*, but
his hand has not been certainly identified. The most
important was Jakob Helchis, who may have been a
pupil of the *Hausmaler* Bottengruber (q.v.). His
painting, usually in *Schwarzlot*, is of uncommonly
fine quality. Figure-modelling occurs principally as
the handles of tureen-covers and as ornament to
candlesticks. Free-standing figures for table-decoration are very rare and much sought. No marks were
used before the beginning of the State period, but a
few dated pieces exist. Since some of the known factory painters also functioned as *Hausmaler* it is
difficult to be sure in what capacity they signed
some of the documentary specimens in existence.

Vienna Porcelain. Group by Anton Grassi. Vienna. c. 1785.
Victoria and Albert Museum.

With the opening of the State period in 1744 new artists were engaged, including the painters Christian Daniel Busch and Johann Gottfried Klinger from Meissen. Joseph Jakob Ringler (q.v.) was also at the State factory in its early years, and he is considered in more detail elsewhere. Figure-modelling was undertaken on a much greater scale, and Johann Josef Niedmayer was appointed *Modellmeister*. The factory attempted to adopt many of the most successful developments elsewhere, trying to copy the *bleu de roi* and the *rose Pompadour* of Sèvres, and sending a modeller to Rome and Venice to study the initial stages of the neo-classical movement. In 1780 an Englishman offered to sell the secret of making porcelain with a coloured body, which may have been an imitation of Wedgwood's jasper, and the factory later used this kind of body for imitations of Wedgwood's new ware. Rococo made small impact on the Vienna Porcelain Factory, which clung to the late baroque style until neo-classicism had been well established in France. In 1778 Anton Grassi succeeded Niedermayer as *Modellmeister,* and he is probably the most important German modeller in the revived classical style of Louis Seize.

During the Sorgenthal period a fruitful collaboration developed between Philipp Ernst Schindler, the *Obermaler* who had arrived from Meissen in 1750, and Josef Leithner, a colour chemist. Leithner devised a new blue of fine quality, termed *Leithner-blau,* and discovered how to simulate bronze in porcelain. In 1796 he produced a black and a light orange-yellow pigment, and a *biscuit* porcelain body. Georg Perl invented a method of gilding in relief.

A very popular decoration at this time consisted of careful copies of paintings in Viennese galleries by such artists as Titian, Rubens, and Raphael, and Angelica Kauffmann inspired a number of similar copies. Occasionally works by such English painters as George Morland were also used for this purpose. The figures of the period by Grassi or his pupils, Johann Schaller and Elias Hütter, are often in *biscuit* porcelain, and in 1792 Grassi journeyed to Italy to view excavations at Herculaneum. He sent back to Vienna a new illustrated work on the subject which was much used thereafter, as well as a large number of casts, engravings, and drawings.

VILE, WILLIAM (d. 1767)
Partner with John Cobb (q.v.), and also a royal cabinet-maker. Vile's work is of exceptional quality, and some of his furniture at Buckingham Palace and Windsor Castle can definitely be attributed. In his furniture-design Vile seems almost to have passed from Palladianism to Adam neo-classicism without being influenced by the rococo which affected such designers as Chippendale and his own partner, Cobb, although specimens of this kind of work from the hand of Vile may not have survived. A secretary made in 1761 for Queen Charlotte shows an earlier Dutch influence, and a jewel-cabinet also made for the Queen and now at Windsor Castle is in what is a virtually symmetrical Louis XV style, but this is exceptional and may have been due to Cobb's influence.

VINAIGRETTE
A later development of the pomander (q.v.) which contained a sponge soaked in aromatic vinegar. The perfume was vinegar blended with such essential oils as those of lavender and cloves. *Vinaigrettes* were made of gold, silver, and enamel in the 18th century, and in Victorian times many were produced in mother-of-pearl and gilded pinchbeck (q.v.). They are variable in size, some comparable with a snuff-box, and others little more than half an inch in diameter.

The *vinaigrette* has a pierced inner lid through which the perfume escaped, and an outer lid which, in silver examples, should have an interior surface of silver-gilt to prevent the tarnishing action of vinegar on unprotected silver. Most *vinaigrettes* are rectangular, but some are oval or circular, and sometimes they were made in more decorative forms, such as shells. Decoration is in keeping with their period, silver examples of the 18th century often being handsomely engraved. In Victorian times there was a fashion for decorating the lid with famous abbeys and castles in relief.

The *vinaigrette* seems to have disappeared with the Great Exhibition of 1851.

See *Pomander; Pouncet Box.*

VINCENNES, FRANCE
Vincennes is a little to the south-east of Paris. The first factory here, and the most important, was started in 1738 and removed to Sèvres in 1756 (see *Sèvres Porcelain Factory*).

A small factory for the manufacture of faïence was started here by Pierre-Antoine Hannong, formerly of Strasbourg (q.v.), in association with de la Borde, *valet de chambre* to Louis XV. A small quantity of hard porcelain was made, probably clandestinely, but Hannong was forced to relinquish his interest in 1770, and in 1774 the enterprise came under the patronage of the Duc de Chartres, managed by a man named Séguin. Hannong then founded a factory, probably in the faubourg Saint-Denis, Paris, under the patronage of the King's brother, the Comte d'Artois (see *Paris, Porcelain of*).

VIOLETWOOD
The *bois violet* of France, a wood much esteemed among *ébénistes* from the beginning of the 18th century onwards. The term *bois du roi* or kingwood became current in the early years of the 19th century. *Bois violet* came from Guiana or Brazil. It belongs to the species *Dalbergia*, and is thus related to rosewood. The wood is striped with dark brown or purplish-brown veinings. It was principally used in the form of veneers, and in England in the second half of the 18th century for banding.

VITREARII (Latin)
Glass-workers in ancient Rome who formed their vessels by blowing and moulding, often decorating

them with trailed glass added in a semi-molten state. This is one of the two major categories in which all glass can be placed, the best later example being much of the work of Venice (see *Diatretarii*).

VITRUVIAN SCROLLS
A decorative *motif* resembling stylized waves used in neo-classical architecture, and as a frieze ornament for furniture and other objects. It is also termed the Greek wave-pattern.

VITRUVIUS
Marcus Vitruvius Pollio was an architect and engineer who is said to have been given charge of military engines and public buildings by Augustus (63 B.C.–A.D. 14). His *Ten Books of Architecture (De Architectura)* was the first work of its kind to be written in Latin, and in so doing Vitruvius made use of Greek manuscripts now lost. It is the only work on the subject to be preserved from ancient times, and was therefore much consulted by Renaissance architects. The first published edition appears to be one without date or name of place which probably appeared in Rome before 1490.

VIVANT DENON, BARON DOMINIQUE
An associate of Jacques-Louis David (q.v.) and later Inspector-General of French Museums, who, with David, helped to organize the plundering of European art-collections, especially those of Germany and Austria, an activity which earned him the soubriquet of 'The Packer'. Most of his nefarious acquisitions were returned after Waterloo. In 1802 he published a *Journey to Upper and Lower Egypt*, the illustrations to which formed an inspiration for ornament in the Egyptian manner during the currency of the Empire style (q.v.).

VOLKSTEDT PORCELAIN FACTORY
This factory was first established at Sitzendorf in Thuringia by Georg Heinrich Machelheid, with the patronage of Prince Johann Friedrich zu Schwarzburg-Rudolstadt. It was moved to Volkstedt in 1762. The mark adopted was that of the hayfork from the Schwarzburg arms. Originally the body used was a soft paste, perhaps the only certain instance of the employment of this type of body in Germany, but it was discontinued by 1767 when the factory was taken over by Christian Nonne. In 1787 Nonne was involved in a quarrel with Meissen over the deceptive use of the crossed hayforks mark. The factory passed to the ownership of the Prince in 1797, who disposed of it two years later to Wilhelm Heinrich Greiner and Carl Holzapfel, and it later became the Älteste Volkstedter Porzellan-Fabrik.

The porcelain of Volkstedt is naive and provincial in its design, and it often copied the products of Meissen. Much service-ware is decorated with flowers and fruit, and landscapes and figure-subjects were executed in either polychrome or purple monochrome, occasionally inspired by the Berlin engraver, Daniel Chodowiecki. Figures were of good quality, although a little stiffly modelled, and relief portraits painted in colours in rococo frames were done by Franz Kotta, who arrived in 1783 and later became *Hofmaler* (Court Painter). A modeller, Friedrich Künckler, came originally from Fürstenberg and was later at Cassel and Berlin. His work cannot now be identified with certainty.

A number of porcelain factories were established here in the 19th century, including Eckert, Richard & Co. (1895), Karl Ens (1900), Müller & Co. (1907), and Schäfer & Vater (1890). A number are still in existence.

VULLIAMY, BENJAMIN (d. 1820)
English clockmaker employed by George III. His date of birth is uncertain, but during the last quarter of the 18th century he was producing clocks in the Louis Seize style ornamented with *biscuit* figures of Derby porcelain. At least one specimen is known with jasper figures by Wedgwood, the mark impressed on the sole of the foot. His son, Benjamin Lewis Vulliamy (1780–1854), Master of the Clockmakers' Company, was Court Clockmaker.

W

WAINSCOT

Oak of superior quality employed for panelling and furniture-making in the 16th and 17th centuries. Panelling is sometimes termed wainscotting for this reason.

WALDGLAS (German)

Literally, *forest glass*. In the Middle Ages glass of good workmanship but poor metal was made in small glass-houses in the German forests where fuel was plentiful. Production increased in the 15th century, when the *Igel*, or hedgehog beaker, decorated with blobs of glass drawn out to a point, is a characteristic survival. Other vessels of *Waldglas* are referred to in contemporary records as *Krautstrunk* ('cabbage stalk' glasses), and *Warzenbecker* ('wart' or 'nipple' beakers), the origin of the *roemer* (q.v.). *Waldglas* appears in a variety of decorative forms, but all are products of manipulation of the glass in its plastic stage. Specimens are very rare.

WALLENDORF PORCELAIN FACTORY

The date of the foundation of this Thuringian factory is unknown, but the first attempts to make porcelain were conducted about 1751. In 1764 a privilege was granted to J. W. Hamman, and Ferdinand Friedrich, Johann Georg, Johann Gottfried, and Gotthelf Greiner, members of a family considerably interested in porcelain manufacture in the Thüringerwald. Only common wares were produced, as well as a few naively modelled figures reminiscent of those of Limbach (q.v.), which was founded by Gotthelf Greiner. Meissen wares of the less ambitious type were freely imitated, the mark being drawn to imitate the crossed swords of this factory. Kaempfe & Heubach founded a factory here late in the 19th century using the same mark.

WALNUT

The walnut tree is widely distributed throughout Europe, and its wood was extremely popular for furniture-making in the 17th century, both solid and as a veneer. In England the tree was probably introduced by the Romans. In colour it varies from light to dark brown with blackish veining, and it has always been valued for the beauty of its figuring. The European tree is the *juglans regia*. American walnut is the *juglans nigra*, and this ranges from light to very dark brown, being not unlike mahogany in appearance. The figuring is usually much less well marked than that of the European variety. Virginian walnut was occasionally imported into England during the 17th and 18th centuries, although it was regarded as inferior to native supplies and generally employed for solid work as a mahogany substitute. Continental walnut was imported during the 17th century when the technique of veneering was first introduced by Dutch craftsmen. With the appearance of Huguenot refugees from the Revocation of the Edict of Nantes in 1685 French walnut from the Grenoble area (among the best in Europe) began to be used in England. Burr-walnut is a veneer cut from the burrs to be found on the trunk, and the best probably came from Italy.

Walnut was especially valued in England from the reign of Charles II to that of George I principally as a veneer (q.v.), and this period is often termed 'the Age of Walnut'. For a long time afterwards it was valued principally for gunstocks, but it returned to favour to a limited extent towards the end of the 18th century. It is an excellent carving wood, but prone to attacks of woodworm.

WALPOLE, HORACE (1717–1797)

Horace Walpole, third son of Sir Robert Walpole, and, from 1791, Earl of Orford, was a noted collector, connoisseur, and arbiter of taste in England in the 18th century. Walpole popularized the revived Gothic style of the middle years of the 18th century in the reconstruction of his villa at Strawberry Hill (q.v.), and he wrote voluminously on many aspects of the arts, providing the art-historian of today with valuable commentaries on the events of his time. His works in this *genre* include the *Anecdotes of Painting* (first edition, 1761–1771) largely from notes compiled by George Vertue; *Catalogue of Engravers* (1763); and the *Essay on Modern Gardening* (1785).

His *Letters* are an extremely valuable source of information about 18th-century taste in collecting. There is an edition edited by Cunningham (1857–

Walpole, Horace. The Cabinet at Strawberry Hill, where many of the more important items in Walpole's art-collection were kept. *From the guide to Strawberry.*

1859), and a more complete and useful one by Mrs P. Toynbee (16 vols., 1903 *et seq.*). Mrs Toynbee's edition is thin paper, and has an especially useful index. There are also a number of abridged and selected editions which are not nearly so useful, since no editor has yet thought of selecting only those letters dealing with the arts.

WARDROBE
The term is derived from the French *garde-robe,* a small closet adjoining a bedroom, used as a dressing-room and for the storage of clothes. In England it came to be called a wardrobe, although the term was not in general use until the second half of the 18th century. During the early decades of the 17th century the wardrobe took the form of an oak cupboard made in several sizes, the height invariably being greater than the width. Drawers were provided in the base, and less often at the top, in the frieze. Little change took place in the construction of the wardrobe until the later years of the 17th century, when veneered walnut specimens, some of which were decorated with marquetry in contemporary styles, were made for a few of the great houses.

Chippendale designed clothes-presses with two doors above, and two short and one long drawer below. His more elaborate designs featured a serpentine front, the doors decorated with rococo mouldings, and with carved canted corners. The Hepplewhite clothes-press was characterized by the familiar features of the neo-classical style, and Sheraton was the first to design a wardrobe with two long, narrow cupboards flanking the large central one which usually had three long drawers in the base. Hepplewhite popularized the term 'wardrobe', which

began to take the place of the earlier 'clothes-press' about this time.

WARMERS, HAND- OR FOOT-
These, when hand-warmers, are spherical metal boxes (usually brass) in two parts, in the interior of which is a container for hot charcoal or a piece of hot iron. Foot-warmers are somewhat larger and vary in shape, but the principle is the same. Hand-warmers are usually plain; foot-warmers are often well-decorated, sometimes with *repoussé* ornament. The latter were probably imported from the Netherlands. Both kinds were in use in the 17th century, but they are probably much older. They served to supplement the primitive heating arrangements of former times.

WARMING-PAN
A pan of brass or copper with a hinged cover to which a long wooden handle is attached. The pan was filled with hot charcoal and passed over the bed-sheets to warm and air them on cold nights. Some rare early specimens have an iron handle. Perhaps the earliest dated example to survive was made in 1616, and several exist which date from the first half of the 17th century. Well-decorated early examples are much prized, especially when dated, but the popularity of the warming-pan as an ornament in old country cottages has led to their reproduction on an extensive scale, and old ones are not often seen.

WARP
(French *chaîne.*) The vertical threads running from top to bottom of a piece of cloth or a tapestry (q.v.). They are intersected by the weft threads which run from side to side and usually pass alternately over and under those of the warp, although this arrangement is varied in the manufacture of certain kinds of textiles, notably tapestry and satin (q.v.). With the latter the characteristic smooth surface is achieved by passing the weft threads under one warp thread and over three.

'WASHED' RUGS
Some modern Near and Middle Eastern rugs have colours which are too bright for present-day taste. Such rugs are often washed and chemically treated for the purpose of subduing and mellowing the colouring. The practice began in London a little before the First World War, introduced by an Armenian carpet dealer, but it is now fairly general with new pieces of colours which are deemed too harsh. The effect is to wash out any surplus dye and to bleach the remaining dye slightly.

WATCHES, EVOLUTION OF
Watches could not be made before the invention of the spring, and the first mechanical time-keeper to be truly portable has been attributed to Peter Henlein of Nürnberg about 1510, although the Romans employed portable sun-dials, and these had, in the

Watches. Watch signed on the back-plate *Johannes Bayesa, Londini.* English. Third quarter of the 17th century. *Victoria and Albert Museum.*

keys. Watch-cocks, the bracket covering and protecting the balance-spring, were carefully engraved, and they have even formed the subject of collections, apart from the movement of which they originally formed part.

Cases were decorated by engraving, embossing and chasing, chiselling, damascening, and even in the case of some rare specimens, with *niello,* all techniques discussed elsewhere under these headings. Cases partly of such hardstones as agate and rock-crystal are known, and although the dial was at first protected by an elaborately pierced and engraved cover rock-crystal sometimes provided a transparent cover for the dial before 1630, and glass became increasingly common afterwards. The first watches had only a single hand, but a second hand was added by about the end of the 17th century, at which time repeater watches which struck the preceding hour when a lever was depressed first made their appearance.

The art of the enameller embellished a few of the earliest cases, especially those of German make, but in the 17th century, and especially from France, some extremely fine enamel work is to be seen, and this method of decoration became increasingly fashionable. The earliest use of enamel employed the *champlevé* technique (see *Enamels*), and by the middle of the 17th century a mixed technique of

11th century, been improved by the addition of a compass. French and German watches survive from about 1550, usually spherical in form.

By the end of the 16th century the watch was nearly always circular, about two inches in diameter and half an inch thick, although exceptionally watches were made in forms such as that of a skull, in quatrefoil, octagonal, and square shapes, and even in forms suitable for such purposes as insetting into the hilt of a rapier. Even though the motive-power provided by the spring was constant, early watches were very inaccurate time-keepers until about 1675, when the balance-spring was invented either by Christian Huyghens or Robert Hooke.

It has been well said that, from the beginning, a constant feature of the watchmaker's character has been a desire to complicate the problem, and as early as the beginning of the 17th century watches were often fitted with strike mechanisms, some had alarms, and some included a mechanism indicating the date. Much more rarely some told the day of the week, or showed the sign of the Zodiac.

But watches have always been collected more for the cases than for the complexities of movements, and from the first they were small objects of decorative art, made of gold, silver, or gilded metal and usually worn outside the clothing as an ornament, like jewellery. Both dials and backplates were handsomely and minutely engraved, and much care and skill were lavished even on such details as winding-

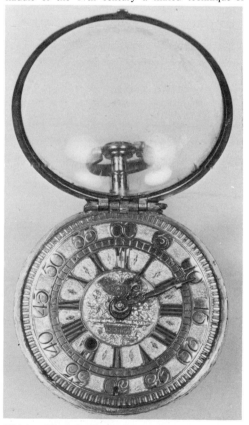

Watches. Watch in gilt metal case pierced and engraved. German. Signed *Benedick Firsten Felder.* Early 18th century. *Victoria and Albert Museum.*

459

champlevé and *cloisonné* can be noticed occasionally. Relief enamelling, in which a slightly raised floral design is a feature of the decoration, has been noted on a case fitted with a movement by the English horologist, Edward East. A combination of relief enamelling with jewelled work and painted enamel occurs on a case with a movement by David Bouquet, member of the English Clockmakers' Company in 1632 who died in 1665. It is probable that cases of fine quality were made on the Continent, in France or Holland, and fitted with movements in London, where makers had achieved a considerable reputation for accurate work.

Painted enamels of the highest quality were common in the 17th century, especially in France, the back of the cases being decorated with a variety of subjects—portraits, landscapes, religious and mythological figures, and scenes of gallantry. Early dials sometimes have painted landscapes, and those of a slightly later date, figure-subjects. Because of the quality of the work lavished on the cases, and their general fragility, watches were often provided with outer cases which were plainer but still decorated with considerable care.

Less ornate work is characteristic of watches made at the end of the 17th century, and embossed cases were fashionable during the first half of the 18th. More rarely they were enamelled, but enamel dials superseded those of metal about 1720. Enamel watch-cases were made in England at Battersea, in South Staffordshire, and at Birmingham in England, but they did not become fashionable, probably because of their general fragility, the enamel being easily chipped away from its copper base. Watches made for the Turkish market have Turkish numerals on the dial, and this was a flourishing export market, as it was in clocks. By the end of the 18th century we find engine-turning (q.v.) increasingly employed to decorate cases.

Most of the best English clockmakers also made watches—Tompion, Quare, Graham, East, and many others—but the most notable watchmaker of the 18th century, Abraham Louis Breguet, worked in Paris. His movements were, perhaps, the finest which had been made until that time, and examples of his work are much sought. It has been said that no two watches by him are alike, either in case or movement. His cases are plain and simple and in excellent taste, and he devised many improvements and refinements to the movement, including a self-winding mechanism operated by the motions of walking.

Early watches were wound by a key. The first keyless watch, wound by means of a knob at the top of the case which moved up and down, was made about 1790, and the first watch wound by turning the knob was the work of Breguet's grandson, C. L. F. Breguet, about 1840.

Many early American clockmakers also made watches, but those of the 18th century are extremely rare. It is undecided whether they imported the parts and assembled them, or actually made them in their workshops. The first undoubted manufacture of watches seems to have been by Luther Goddard of Shrewsbury, Massachusetts sometime after 1809. Quantity production of watches began in 1850 when Edward Howard and Aaron Dennison started an enterprise which grew eventually into the Waltham Watch Company. The development of cheap watches, such as those popularized by Ingersoll, began about 1890. As with clocks, America has made little contribution to the watch as a work of art.

WATER COLOURS
Colours for which water is the medium of transfer to the surface to be painted, usually a specially prepared paper. Water-colours are now obtainable in cakes made largely of gum acacia, and in moist form in collapsible tubes, when a little glycerine is added to preserve the consistency. Most water-colours are transparent, and from the early years of the 19th century they have usually been applied in washes. There are some opaque colours, of which Chinese white is an example (see *Gouache*). Delicate effects are sometimes obtained by glazing with transparent colours over opaque ones. Although water-colours are principally used for drawings, they can be found on such decorative objects as fans.

WATTEAU, JEAN-ANTOINE (1684–1721)
French painter and designer, and a pupil of Gillot (q.v.) and Audran (q.v.). Although best known for his painting, Watteau was a talented designer of arabesques, which were an inspiration for a number of craftsmen of the time, and he was among the earliest to use the popular monkeys as decoration. Huet's *singeries* at Chantilly were at one time thought to be by his hand. Watteau considerably influenced the art of decorative design throughout the first half of the 18th century, and in the 1750s characteristic subjects from his paintings were much used in the decoration of porcelain, perhaps from the *Recueil Jullienne*—engravings of about 700 of his paintings made for his friend Jean de Jullienne. Much of his work foreshadows the rococo style (q.v.) which immediately followed his death.

WEDGWOOD, JOSIAH (1730–1795)
Historians of pottery and porcelain are agreed that Josiah I Wedgwood was the man who, in the 18th century, changed the whole course of the European pottery industry. The popularity of Chinese porcelain in the 17th century was so great that numerous attempts were made to imitate it. The earliest successful attempt was at Meissen in Saxony (q.v.), and this factory set the fashion for porcelain manufacture till the beginning of the Seven Years' War in 1756. The initiative then passed to Sèvres (q.v.), owned by the King of France, and here a style was created which governed porcelain manufacture elsewhere for many years. But the neo-classical style (q.v.) was unsuited to porcelain, especially the classical vase-forms, and factories making porcelain began to get into financial difficulties. Most of the ordinary

demand for table-ware had been supplied for many years by the makers of faïence—pottery covered with an opaque white glaze and painted in blue, or in a limited range of high-temperature colours (q.v.). This was soft and easily damaged, and more expensive to make than transparent glazed earthenware. It was also unsuited to the new classical forms, which looked incongruous in ware thus glazed. This was the situation when Josiah Wedgwood, member of a family with a long tradition of pottery-making in Staffordshire, put aside his partnership with Thomas Whieldon (q.v.) and started his career as an independent potter.

Wedgwood was the last of twelve children, and he belonged to the fourth generation of a family of potters, who continued in the same occupation for another five generations. His own skill as a potter may be seen from a vase which he threw personally to commemorate the opening of the factory he called Etruria in 1769.

He was first apprenticed to his brother Thomas, to learn the art of throwing on the wheel, and then went on to form a partnership with Thomas Whieldon. Here he was fortunate, since Whieldon agreed that while the results of experiments made by Josiah I should be for the benefit of both, he should not be required to disclose his methods. It was at this time that he began to keep his *Experiment Book*, devoting himself largely to improving the earthenware body employed at Whieldon's factory at Fenton Low (Staffordshire), and by 1763 he had developed a creamy white earthenware covered with a transparent glaze (creamware) which, after Queen Charlotte had ordered a tea-service in 1765, he called Queen's Ware. This ware was something new, a substitute alike for porcelain and tin-enamelled pottery. It was decorated with transfer-printing (q.v.) by Sadler & Green of Liverpool, and later with enamel painting. This marked the beginning of the end for the tin-enamel industry, which began progressively to decline as creamware became more popular, and by the end of the century only three factories survived at Delft, in Holland, once the greatest centre for the manufacture of this type of pottery. For a time creamware was kept from the market in France by royal decree, but even before the Revolution French manufacturers were turning to *faïence-fine* (q.v.), as creamware was known in that country. The victory of creamware was complete when Catherine the Great ordered the famous 'Frog' service, so called because it was intended for the palace of La Grenouillère in St Petersburg. This, completed in 1774, was decorated with English views, and the cost was about £2,250—equivalent to £18,000 in today's money. It is still preserved in Leningrad.

Creamware was only one of Wedgwood's many innovations. Experiments with a black ware, which he refined and hardened, produced a dense black stoneware that he called basaltes. This was an extremely popular material for vases especially.

The classical vases collected by Sir William Hamilton, English Ambassador at Naples, and illustrated in his catalogue, popularized the type of Greek and Roman pottery, then thought to be Etruscan, painted with figures in red on a black ground—the 'red-figure' type. Ancient vases of this kind were in demand for decorating Adam interiors, and Wedgwood supplied new ones hardly distinguishable from the old. Wedgwood patented a red enamel for the figures which he called 'encaustic', and in 1769 he opened a decorating studio in London, at Chelsea, to which the finest of his Staffordshire wares were sent for painting. The demand eventually became so great that defective vases were furnished with wooden covers and bases and sold to eager buyers.

Wedgwood saw that both creamware and basaltes could easily be adapted to the forms and decorations demanded by the interior styles of the Brothers Adam (q.v.), and increasingly he captured the market supplied by the porcelain factories with 'Etruscan' vases which cost from two to five guineas. All his wares were stamped plainly with his name, a new departure for Staffordshire where marks had been little used. Most important of all, he introduced new principles into the manufacture of pottery which he may have culled from Jean-Baptiste du Halde's *Description of China*, translated into English about 1725. This book was in his library, and du Halde described the production-line system in operation at the Chinese Imperial factories at the end of the 17th century, where the processes of manufacture, from the raw clay to the finished product, were broken down into many separate operations, each of which was the responsibility of a man skilled in that particular section. Wedgwood was quick to realize that herein lay the secret of cheap, large-scale manufacture, and in 1772 we find him analysing his costs on an almost modern basis. In many ways his solution of the problem differed from that of the Chinese, but it led to a reduction in costs and the establishment of methods of manufacture which were the forerunner of those of today. He was thus enabled to lower his prices, and to supply a vastly larger market, bringing his products within reach of many people who formerly could not have afforded them.

Despite a keen interest in porcelain there are many reasons why Wedgwood did not make it. At first excluded from the process by Champion's patent, which he helped to contest in 1775, he had lost interest by the time Champion was prepared to sell his rights three years later. Porcelain was then going out of fashion, and he had, in the meantime, perfected his own fine stoneware which he called jasper. This is almost indistinguishable from unglazed porcelain and was, in fact, termed by Wedgwood his 'biscuit porcelain'. The first mention of objects manufactured in jasper occurs in 1774, but Wedgwood went on improving on it until 1780, adding to the original white body a number of excellent colours. Much jasper was in the form of white reliefs on a blue ground, a typical Adam colour-scheme. Lilac, yellow, sage-green, and black are among the other colours used. Much jasper after 1780 was employed to make vases and

Wedgwood, Josiah. Top left: Jasper drum made as a base for ormolu candelabra with Waterford cut-glass drops. c. 1790. Below: Jasper salt-cellar decorated with the 'Dancing Hours' of John Flaxman. Late 18th century. Broken classical column with the ravages of time imitated in jasper is decorated with Greek winged sphinxes of the type favoured by Adam with a lyre between. Late 18th century. *Josiah Wedgwood & Son.*

Wedgwood's fame was assured. Meissen, in a desperate attempt to stave off financial disaster, introduced a variety of novelties, not the least the so-called '*Wedgwood-arbeit*', an imitation of jasper. The Thuringian factories closely simulated jasper medallions, factories in Scandinavia made basaltes, and everywhere creamware (*faïence-fine* in France and *Steingut* in Germany) was being produced. His influence on the design and production of European porcelain by about 1780 was comparable with that of Meissen at the beginning of the century, and of Sèvres in the middle of it.

Much of Wedgwood's ornamental production was done in association with a friend, Thomas Bentley, who became his partner in 1767, and in 1769 Bentley agreed to live in London and take charge of the business there. In September of that year the Chelsea decorating studio was opened, and business began to expand. The year 1773 saw the first catalogue of ornamental wares, which included medallions, cameos, intaglios for seals and for mounting as jewellery, busts and figurines, lamps and candelabra, Etruscan tea-ware, flower-pots, vases (some imitating such hardstones as agate and porphyry), and tablets for chimney-pieces and furniture-mounts. In 1774 the 'Frog' service was completed, followed by its exhibition in his new showrooms in Greek Street, Soho, London, the first catalogue of Queen's Ware was produced, and jasper was developed to a point where Josiah was ready to start producing it for the market, the first specimens being sold in 1775. Not only was Wedgwood exporting to almost the whole of Continental Europe, but he investigated the possibility of selling vases to the Turks, which he started to do in 1774. In the American War of Independence Wedgwood supported the cause of the colonists at a time when it was unpopular in England generally, and the company has retained close connections with the U.S.A. ever since that time.

medallions, but it enjoyed increasing popularity for other purposes, such as the decoration of furniture, and as plaques for the ornamentation of chimney-pieces. Towards the end of the century Wedgwood exported his plaques to France for furniture decoration, and his jasper was imitated by Sèvres in *biscuit* porcelain. Plaques for insetting into chimney-pieces were first inspired by plaster reliefs designed by the Adam Brothers, and in 1771 Wedgwood wrote to his partner with the suggestion that he should show creamware reliefs to 'the Mr Adamses'.

Wedgwood often exchanged ideas with his friend Matthew Boulton (q.v.) of Birmingham, where he first saw the engine-turning lathe, which he later employed to decorate vases of basaltes ware (q.v.). Boulton exported to France, and employed Wedgwood's jasper medallions mounted in ormolu to decorate clock-cases and vases in imitation of contemporary French styles.

After his initial success in obtaining the order for the 'Frog' service from the Empress Catherine,

Wedgwood's wares, and his methods, became so widely known that many attempts were made to recruit his workmen by American and Continental potteries. Finally, in an attempt to dissuade them from accepting apparently tempting offers, Wedg-

Wedgwood. Josiah. Three plates of creamware. Left and centre are identical with the 'Frog' service made for Catherine the Great, but lack the frog within a shield which appears on the rim of the service proper. *Sir John Wedgwood.*

wood published a pamphlet entitled *Address to the Workmen in the Pottery on the subject of entering into the service of Foreign Manufacturers.* Several Continental potters endeavoured to gain employment with Wedgwood for the purpose of learning his manufacturing secrets, among them Louis Gerverot, who later started a creamware factory at Cologne. Etruria was visited by the Duke Karl Eugen who owned the Ludwigsburg factory in 1776, where some of the later wares were in the style of Wedgwood.

Bentley died in 1781, and Wedgwood suffered a severe loss. He turned to scientific pursuits, inventing a pyrometer in 1782, i.e. a thermometer capable of measuring very high temperatures. Until this time the only method of judging kiln-temperatures was to pull out a plug and look at the colour of the fire. In consequence of his invention Wedgwood was elected to the Royal Society.

Wedgwood was friendly with the painter George Stubbs, who first asked for creamware palettes, and later for large tablets of creamware on which to paint. The very rare paintings by Stubbs on this support are the only examples known of its use. Wedgwood was also in touch with Joseph Wright of Derby (the 'Candlelight Painter'), who provided him with some drawings for use as designs for pottery-making. Flaxman (q.v.) began to design for Wedgwood in 1775, when he provided a pair of vases and a series of bas-reliefs for jasper, and in 1784 Wedgwood began his copy of the Portland vase (q.v.) for which Flaxman provided preliminary information. While he was in Rome Flaxman continued to supply Wedgwood with models, and Thomas Banks, the sculptor, also promised to employ all the time he could spare in making models for pottery. In 1789, in a letter to Lord Auckland, Wedgwood refers to keeping several modellers in Rome, and to getting designs from Paris. In 1789, in a letter to Flaxman, he refers to the new prudery of the time as affecting the ornament of jasper, making some of Flaxman's designs unsuitable. In the same year (1790) the first copies of the Portland vase were exhibited and greatly praised by Sir Joshua Reynolds.

After 1790 Wedgwood went increasingly into retirement, leaving the pottery to be managed by his sons, one of whom, Josiah II, married in 1792. Josiah I died in 1795, universally mourned. In the words of Gladstone, 'he converted a rude and inconsiderable manufactory into an elegant art and an important part of National Commerce'.

Josiah II and Thomas Byerley, the latter a partner before the death of Josiah I, took Wedgwood pottery into the 19th century. Byerley died in 1810, and Josiah II in 1843. There was little immediate change. The popular 'Pearl ware' (q.v.), introduced by Josiah I about 1780, continued to be made. Perhaps from as early as 1792, and until 1810, platinum (i.e. silver-colour) lustre, either painted or resist (see *Lustre Decoration*), was made at Etruria, as well as a pink lustre which ornamented shell-shaped dishes. Some very well painted Chinese flowers appear on black basaltes ware, and more rarely on red ware. Jasper-

'*Wedgwood-Arbeit.*' *Solitaire* in blue *biscuit* porcelain imitating Wedgwood. Grossbreitenbach, Thuringia. c. 1794. *Kestner-Museum, Hannover.*

ware enjoyed a revival in the 19th century and is still being made, and a series of busts in black basaltes by the sculptor Wyon include some contemporary notabilities, as well as reissues of old models. Much sought today are the wares painted by Emil Lessore (1805–1876), who had worked for Sèvres as an outside decorator in France, and for Wedgwood from 1858 to 1875. The English Wedgwood Society and the American Wedgwood Society are both devoted to the study of Wedgwood's pottery and porcelain.

Wedgwood's pottery was commonly marked from the first, either *Wedgwood* impressed, or *Wedgwood & Bentley* on ornamental wares from 1769 to 1780. 'Useful' wares, i.e. those of domestic utility not decorated exceptionally were marked *Wedgwood* only during this period. Very few wares are signed by the workman responsible, an exception being the signature of Hackwood (q.v.) on portrait reliefs, either in full or initialled, but workmen's marks are not uncommon. 'England' or 'Made in England' appears on wares manufactured after 1891.

Some of these, notably the 'Fairyland Lustre' of the 1920s, are now much sought by collectors.

'WEDGWOOD-ARBEIT'

Copies of Wedgwood's jasper-ware (q.v.) made at the Meissen factory towards the end of the 18th century.

WEFT

(French *trame*). Threads which run from side to side of a piece of cloth, usually passing alternately under and over those of the warp (q.v.). The weft is sometimes called the woof.

WELSH DRESSER   See *Dresser*

Whieldon, Thomas. Horseman and pillion rider decorated with coloured glazes. Whieldon. c. 1750. *Colonial Williamsburg, Va.*

WESTERWALD STONEWARE

German stoneware from the Westerwald region—Höhr, Grenzhausen, and Grenzau. See *Rhineland Stoneware.*

WESTMORELAND GLASS COMPANY

This factory at Grapeville, Penn., is said to have some of the original moulds of the Sandwich Glass Company, which they have used to make reproductions. See *Glass, American.*

WHAT-NOT

The term was first used about 1808–1810 in the Regency period for a small, rectangular stand with shelves designed to stand against a wall, and intended to display a variety of objects, ornaments, curiosities, books, and papers.

The what-not in its Victorian form came into general use only in the 1840s, grew in height, and, by the 1850s, was often designed for a corner.

When made on a larger scale and combined with mirror panels and marble the what-not was often called an *étagère* (q.v.). See *Étagère.*

WHEAT–EARS

These sometimes occur as carved decoration on Hepplewhite chairs. See *Hepplewhite, George.*

WHEELBACK CHAIR

A chair of the English neo-classical period, the back in the form of a wheel, the spokes radiating from a central plaque which was sometimes painted. Caning occasionally replaced the spokes. Oval backs on the same principle were also made.

WHEEL-ENGRAVING

Engraving by means of small copper wheels charged with an abrasive (see *Emery*) and rotated by a treadle has been employed since the 3rd century B.C., at first for carving hardstones and then for the decoration of glass. Some very finely detailed and important work has been done in this way, and it was employed especially as a technique of glass decoration in the 17th and 18th centuries. Wheel-engraving is also to be found on the red stoneware of Meissen before about 1720, and specimens are highly valued. The Dutch engraved Chinese porcelain with a brown glaze (the so-called 'Batavian' type) in this way, cutting through the glaze to the white body beneath. Specimens are rare. See *Cameo Glass; Meissen; Portland Vase.*

WHEELING GLASS WORKS

There were several glass works in and around this West Virginian town from about 1814 onwards. The largest was that of Hobbs, Brockunier & Co., where William Leighton discovered lime glass (q.v.) which provided an excellent metal, lighter in weight than lead-glass, at about one-third of the cost. This factory produced excellent glass of all types. See *Glass, American.*

WHIELDON, THOMAS (1719–1795)

One of the most influential potters in 18th-century Staffordshire, Thomas Whieldon started a factory at Fenton Low in 1740 for the manufacture of knife-handles, and agate (q.v.) and tortoiseshell (q.v.) ware. Although it is difficult to identify his wares with certainty, he made salt-glaze, and most other wares current in Staffordshire in his day. A number of potters who later made their mark started as apprentices at Fenton Low; Josiah Wedgwood (q.v.) was Whieldon's partner from 1754 to 1759. Whieldon's products were never marked.

Most of the ware associated with his name is covered with a characteristically mottled or 'clouded' glaze of a type first to be seen on the backs of dishes by Bernard Palissy (q.v.). Green, yellow, dark brown, manganese-purple, and grey were dusted on to the body in the form of powder, and when the glaze was

Whieldon, Thomas. Plate with moulded border decorated with characteristic mottled coloured glazes. Whieldon. c. 1750. *Victoria and Albert Museum.*

fired they mingled with it irregularly to produce an effect which, at its simplest, is often termed 'tortoise-shell'. Wedgwood developed these coloured glazes, perfecting green and yellow glazes which were used to decorate teapots and similar wares moulded in the form of cauliflowers and pineapples. It is always uncertain whether any particular specimen was made at Fenton Low during his partnership with Whieldon, or later, at his own factory. Whieldon coloured glazes appear on a number of figures, including some which are also found in the typical 'Astbury' technique (q.v.) and which are therefore termed 'Astbury-Whieldon'.

Whieldon wares are usually thinly and precisely potted, and from the body normally employed here Wedgwood eventually developed his creamware.

Whieldon, Thomas. Teapot of creamware decorated with moulded patterns and coloured glazes. Whieldon. c. 1755. *Hove Museum and Art Gallery.*

WHITE GLASS WORKS

This factory, established in 1815 at Zanesville, Ohio, by Isaac van Horne, continued until 1851. They made bottles and flasks, of which those decorated with Masonic emblems and the Eagle are perhaps the best known. See *Glass, American.*

WHITNEY GLASS WORKS, GLASSBORO', NEW JERSEY

This factory was started about 1780, and was purchased by the Whitney Bros. in 1840. Bottles and flasks were the principal production, one of the most popular being a globular bottle with a long neck decorated with a relief portrait of *Jenny Lind*. This was made about 1850. The factory now belongs to the Owens Bottle Company. See *Glass, American.*

WILLARD, AARON (1757–1844)

Clockmaker, and brother of Benjamin and Simon I Willard (q.v.). He was hardly less noted at the time than Simon. His son, Aaron II Willard (1783–1863), took over his father's business in 1823, retiring in 1850. He is supposed to have introduced a fashion for clocks with cases of lyre-shape made between 1820 and 1840. These are now rare. See *Clocks, American.*

WILLARD, ALEXANDER (1774–?)

Clockmaker of Ashby, Mass., who is said to have made long-case clocks with wooden movements. See *Clocks, American.*

WILLARD, BENJAMIN (1740–1803)

American clock-maker born at Grafton, Mass. He worked as a maker of long-case clocks at Grafton, Lexington (1768), and Roxbury (1771). He was the elder brother of Simon Willard (q.v.). See *Clocks, American.*

WILLARD, SIMON (1753–1848)

Simon I Willard was a noted American clockmaker, born in Grafton, Mass. From 1788, when he moved to Roxbury, he was the undoubted leader in the field of American clockmaking. Between 1780 and 1802 he appears mainly to have been engaged in the mak-

ing of long-case clocks, but in 1801 he patented the 'banjo' clock (q.v.), which was soon being widely imitated, although Willard did not take action for infringement. He retired in 1839, selling his business to Elnathan Taber (1784–1854) who was also a clockmaker of distinction. His son, Simon II Willard (1795–1874), was a watch and chronometer maker of distinction. He sold clocks and his name sometimes appears on the dials, but these appear to have been made by someone else. See *Clocks, American.*

WILLOW PATTERN

A pseudo-Chinese pattern introduced at Caughley about 1780, and said to be the work of Thomas Minton. The type was copied with extensive variations at many other English factories, and versions made to order were done in China. The legend attached to this pattern is of English origin, not Chinese. One version appears in the Kai-lung stories of the late Ernest Bramah. The Caughley version of this pattern differs considerably from those made elsewhere, and the most familiar one is of 19th-century origin. The *Broseley Blue Dragon* pattern, also said to be the work of Thomas Minton, is still in use today.

WILTON CARPETS

The manufacture of *moquette* (q.v.) carpeting dates from about 1740 at Wilton (Wiltshire), when it was introduced by Lord Pembroke. The loops of the velvet (q.v.) weave were cut, a development probably introduced here. Woven in narrow strips, Wilton carpeting was very popular during the 18th century. The Axminster (q.v.) looms were acquired in 1835, when the manufacture of knotted pile carpets was started.

WINCANTON (Somerset) DELFT

The delft pottery at this small Somerset town, 34 miles from Bristol, was founded some time before 1737, the year of the earliest known dated specimen. It is very difficult, if not impossible in most cases, to separate wares made here from those of Bristol, but those decorated with manganese, especially those with a manganese ground and reserved panels in white, are often attributed to Wincanton. Polychrome wares were not, apparently, made, and none have been attributed. The date of closure is not known.

WINCKELMANN, JOHANN JOACHIM (1717–1768)

German art-historian and one of the most influential figures in the development of neo-classicism (q.v.). Once librarian to Count von Bünau at Dresden, he became librarian to Cardinal Albani in Rome. He took great interest in the excavations at Herculaneum, Pompeii, and Paestum, publishing his very influential *Geschichte der Kunst des Altertums* in 1764, and the *Monumenti Antichi Ineditii* in 1766. Made Superintendent of Antiquities in Rome in 1763, he was murdered in an inn at Trieste in 1768.

WINDSOR CHAIRS

Stick-back chairs (q.v.), nearly always with arms, with turned legs and a solid seat. The best are of yew wood, the seat usually being of elm. These were largely made around High Wycombe (Buckinghamshire), and probably date from the end of the 17th century. They were, however, made elsewhere in England, and regional variations occur. One rare 18th-century version is based on the Chippendale chair, with pierced splat and elementary cabriole legs, and two additional 'stick' stays helping to support the back. Backs take a variety of forms, of which the rounded hoop-back is the most sought. Early American Windsors belong to the period 1760–1800, though they were apparently first pro-

'Windsor' Chair. An American 'Windsor' chair of 1795–1800, lighter and more graceful than its usual English counterpart. In the best American examples hickory or ash replaced the English yew wood. The Windsor chair in America was usually painted green or black.

duced in the Philadelphia area about 1725. After 1800 designs were influenced by Sheraton and the best examples belong to a period before about 1825.

Windsor chairs are catalogued according to the style of the back: comb-back, bow-back (or hoop-back), fan-back, low-back, and the New England armchair (with continuous arm and back). With the addition of a shelf the form was termed a writing-arm Windsor. Saddle-seats were of pine, legs were turned from maple, birch, ash, or chestnut. Spindles were steamed and made of ash, hickory, and oak. Unlike the English versions, American windsors were usually painted, green (most popular), red, yellow or black. They were used inside as hall-chairs in homes, or publicly, in inns and public buildings. They were frequently sold as garden-chairs, and as such were used on lawns and porches. Though originating in Philadelphia, other centres were New England, New York, and the South.

WINE AND DECANTER LABELS

When the decanter first replaced the bottle labels bearing the name of the contents, with a small chain for suspension round the neck, came into popular use. It was a product of the necessity for identifying the contents, and an extension of the custom of the Lambeth delft potters who named the contents of their bottles and often dated them. With the introduction of the glass bottle labels of wood or parchment were attached to the neck, and it was only when the clear glass decanter became popular that anything more decorative was called for. Silver labels of this kind date from about 1740, although many, especially the early ones, bear only the maker's mark, and prior to 1790 a fully hall-marked label is rare. These are ornamented in the style of their period. With the establishment of the Battersea Enamel Works in 1753 wine-labels of painted enamel made their appearance, and seemingly were much sought at the time. Enamel labels were also made at Bilston (South Staffordshire) and in Birmingham. Wine-labels of porcelain were made, but they are very rare survivals. Those of creamware from Liverpool are more common, and examples in pinchbeck and Sheffield plate also exist. Wine-labels continued to be made until well into the 19th century, and many of this date are electroplated with silver on base metal.

Forgeries of 18th-century enamel wine-labels exist, but should not deceive an experienced collector of enamels, since the painting is too coarse to be of the period.

WINE-BOTTLES, GLASS   See *Decanter, Evolution of*

WINE-GLASSES, ENGLISH

Until the advent of George Ravenscroft (q.v.) England imported nearly all its wine-glasses from Venice, and the few native products were imitations of the Venetian style in soda-glass. From about 1690, however, wine-glasses were made in England on a much greater scale, and the influence of Venice gradually disappeared.

The earliest stems were of baluster shape (q.v.), at first thick and heavy, but later, by about 1720, of a much lighter and slenderer type termed balustroid which was principally associated with glasses made at Newcastle. The so-called 'Silesian' stem, ribbed and shouldered, was popular for a few years following 1715, but these are more often found as part of sweetmeat glasses rather than of wine-glasses. Until 1730 almost every glass has the edge of the foot folded under for additional strength, a practice derived from Venice and termed a 'folded foot'. Stems, at first simple, became more elaborate technically with the introduction of the air-twist (q.v.) in the 1730s which, by the 1750s, was beginning to be replaced by the opaque twist stem (q.v.). Towards 1780 the latter was made with both white and coloured twists in varying degrees of complexity.

Bowls are to be found in great variety—bell-shaped, conical (or funnel-shaped), the round funnel which was curved at the bottom instead of straight-sided, trumpet-shaped, thistle shaped, ogee shaped, and several variations on these themes.

It would be impossible to list the permutations and combinations of foot, stem, and bowl which went to make up the 18th-century English wine-glass in sufficient detail to be useful, but this has been done by E. Barrington Haynes, *Glass through the Ages*—a Pelican book which has been reprinted several times.

Most 18th-century glasses are undecorated, but engraved glasses form a very desirable group, and those denoting Jacobite sympathies bring especially high prices. Some rare glasses are enamelled by the Beilbys (q.v.), and glasses with faceted stems instead of the types mentioned above are not un-common during the latter part of the 18th century.

WIRE

Metal drawn out into a thread of variable thickness, which may be round, flat, square, or triangular in section. Gold and silver especially was drawn through a series of holes in a draw-plate, each hole being smaller than the preceding one. In this way the desired gauge (or thickness) was attained. The technique was known in England during the 14th century, but wire fine enough for weaving into cloth or lace was not made until the 17th century. Such wire was employed for purposes like making gold and silver lace (q.v.). Heavier-gauge silver wire is sometimes to be seen as part of silver made towards the end of the 18th century, and a process for plating wire of base metal with silver or gold, employed to a limited extent in the making of Sheffield plate, was first patented by Whately in 1768. Sugar-baskets with blue glass liners are an example. The use of wire for this purpose was discontinued soon after 1800.

WISTAR, CASPAR

German glassmaker, who started to make glass in Salem County, New Jersey, in 1739 with the aid of glass-workers brought from Germany. After his death in 1752 the enterprise was continued by his son, Richard, closing about 1780. Bottles, drinking-glasses, and window-glass were the principal products, and glasses which were aquamarine, blue, green, amber, and brown in colour were made, sometimes two or three colours combined in one example. Very few specimens survive to authenticate this information, but examples are to be seen in the Metropolitan Museum (New York) and the Pennsylvania Museum (Philadelphia). Decoration of reasonably well-attested specimens consists in super-imposed designs carried out in threads of coloured glass, and in the metal itself. Wistar's glass is often termed 'Wistarberg', but the term is very loosely used for apparently early glass in his style. See *Glass, American*.

THE WOOD FAMILY

This famous Staffordshire family of potters produced much earthenware of all kinds during the second half of the 18th century. Ralph I Wood (1715–1772) is probably the best known, and his products the most widely sought. He specialized in figures which were excellent in quality, and include some of the best 18th-century Staffordshire work of this kind. They were covered with coloured lead glazes in yellow, green, brownish-purple, green and grey, but applied in a manner which gives them an effect of enamelling rather than the clouded, mingled appearance achieved by Whieldon. Many of his models were adapted from the work of Cyffié (q.v.) at Lunéville, but the Toby Jug is purely English in design, and one of the finest of the Wood models, an equestrian figure of Hudibras, owes nothing to Continental sources. Jugs with decoration in low relief inscribed 'Fair Hebe' were probably modelled in the first place by a Frenchman, Jean Voyez (fl. 1740–1791) who had originally worked for Wedgwood, and later made reproductions of some of Wedgwood's wares. A few items of service ware, such as sauceboats and other decorative pieces, are occasionally attributed to Ralph I Wood, but, in most such cases, Whieldon, or some other manufacturer of the period working in his style, can also be regarded as a possible attribution. Figures are the most certainly ascribed. Ralph II Wood (1748–1795) continued to make figures of excellent quality, often much resembling the earlier work of his father, but these were decorated in enamel colours, and the introduction of this kind of painting is usually regarded as having been due to his influence.

A brother of Ralph I Wood, Aaron Wood (1717–1785), achieved fame as a block-cutter, and was reputed to be the best in Staffordshire. Probably many of the blocks made for salt-glazed wares decorated in relief were from his hand, although those bearing the initials of Ralph Wood have also survived. A signed block by Aaron Wood is in the British Museum.

Enoch Wood (1759–1840), son of Aaron Wood, was perhaps the most prolific manufacturer of the

Wood Family. The Drunken Parson being escorted home by his Clerk. A popular satirical group. Enoch Wood. c. 1790.

whole family, although his wares do not rival those of Ralph I Wood for quality. He was, for a time, in partnership with Ralph II Wood, but in 1790 entered into another partnership with James Caldwell which continued until 1818. Here almost every variety of wares current in Staffordshire were made, but as very few were marked identification is very difficult. As an example, the writer has noticed an oval creamware dish painted with the cornflower sprig of the Marie-Antoinette factory in Paris (see *Paris Porcelain*) which bore the mark *Wxxx*, associated with Enoch Wood, and to be found on rare specimens of Staffordshire porcelain in the form of figures based on those of Ralph Wood. He also made a good deal of blue-printed earthenware.

Enoch Wood specialized in figures. A relief plaque, *The Descent from the Cross* dated 1777 in the Victoria and Albert Museum (London), is signed by him, and the British Museum has a self-portrait in the form of a life-size bust which has a long inscription on the back recording some of the family history and his strong objections to the high taxation of his day. Some of his figures and groups are extremely large, notably his *Demosthenes* (sometimes known as *Saint Paul Preaching to the Athenians*), one of which is in the Victoria and Albert Museum. Enoch Wood's figures are invariably decorated in enamel colours. He appears to have done some work for Wedgwood, since figures from the identical mould have been noted with his mark and with that of *Wedgwood* impressed, although not both on the same piece. Enoch Wood figures are still relatively common.

WOODWORM

The furniture-beetle (*Anobium punctatum*) is a particular enemy of the softer furniture woods, especi-

ally walnut. This wood, seemingly fairly sound to the eye, will sometimes be honeycombed with worm-tunnels below the surface to an extent where it will crumble under pressure. The beetle lays its egg in a crack or crevice, and the worm, after emerging, immediately starts to burrow into the wood, leaving a circular entrance-hole. It emerges as an adult beetle to start the life-cycle afresh. During its passage through the wood it excretes a kind of fine wood-dust, and if this is seen when the wood is tapped it is a sign that the larva is active. There are a number of reasonably effective methods of killing active larvae, but it is always essential to examine affected woodwork carefully to estimate the damage which has taken place, which is usually proportional to the number of holes to be observed and the distance between them. Numerous holes near to each other suggest an infestation which is likely to have seriously weakened the structural qualities of the timber.

A furrow, or half-tunnel, opening lengthwise on the surface is a danger-signal. Worms do not make half-tunnels, and either the specimen has been repaired with old, worm-eaten wood, or the very unlikely supposition must be accepted that the specimen was originally made of wood thus affected. The faker sometimes uses worm-eaten wood because the presence of worm was once regarded as an infallible sign of age, and worm-holes were simulated by drilling. Stories of worm-holes imitated with a shot-gun are apocryphal. This would be simple to detect, since the lead shot would still be present at the bottom of the hole, and those which did not penetrate would bruise the wood. As one authority once remarked: An old worm-eaten piece of wood, left in the dark with a store full of modern furniture, will 'antique' the lot between February and June so far as worm-holes are concerned.

WORCESTER PORCELAIN FACTORY

This Worcestershire porcelain factory is the only one in England which can point to an unbroken line of descent from a mid-18th-century beginning. Wedgwoods have only added the manufacture of porcelain to their other wares comparatively recently. The Worcester Royal Porcelain Company celebrated its bicentenary in London with an exhibition of early wares in 1951, and an impressive collection is maintained at the Dyson Perrins Museum which is attached to the factory. Recent excavations (1969) on the original site have added considerably to the available information about this factory.

The undertaking from which it grew was established in Bristol about 1748, at Redcliffe Backs on a site which is now part of Bristol Docks. The factory was originally a glass-house owned by William Lowdin who, according to Dr Pocock, had formerly been connected with Limehouse (q.v.). in London. Also connected with the enterprise was William Miller, and a Quaker, Benjamin Lund, who in 1748 obtained a licence to dig and search for soaprock (q.v.) in Cornwall. Soaprock formed the basic substance of both Bristol and Worcester porcelain, replacing the feldspathic rock of Chinese, Meissen, and Plymouth (q.v.) porcelain. The wares from Bristol made at this time are termed 'Lund's Bristol' to differentiate them from the later wares of Richard Champion whose factory was established in the same city.

It is very difficult in most cases to separate early wares made at Worcester from those of Bristol. There is a rare figure of a Chinese Immortal in porcelain imitating the *blanc-de-Chine* of Tê Hua (q.v.) which bears on the base the inscription in relief *Bristoll 1750*. There are also some early sauceboats marked *Bristoll* in the same way. The transfer took place in 1752, negotiations beginning in the previous year. And some very rare small sauceboats made at Worcester immediately afterwards are similarly marked *Wigornia* in relief, this being the Latin form of Worcester. The general characteristics of both are extremely similar. The glaze of some wares which seem more entitled to be termed Bristol than Worcester sometimes has the appearance of containing a small amount of tin oxide which has slightly opacified it. A Bristol attribution is not unreasonable if we remember that Bristol was also a flourishing centre for the making of *delft*. The hand of the painter is not a certain guide, since some were undoubtedly transferred to the new factory. The shapes are silver-pattern, the decoration executed with a very fine brush with almost pencilled lines, and there is often a noticeable recession of the glaze from the inside of the footring, which later becomes a characteristic of almost all Worcester porcelain made before 1770. This is not, as has so often been said, a retraction of the glaze. The workman, after glazing, ran a small tool round the inside of the footring to clear it of surplus glaze which might otherwise have run down under the base, necessitating subsequent grinding. Although grinding of footrings was a common necessity at almost every other factory, and hardly a piece of Chelsea is to be seen without some indication of this having been done, only isolated examples of it can be found from Worcester until at least 1770, and not often thereafter.

The most important names among the partners who signed the deed of partnership which inaugurated the Worcester enterprise on June 4th, 1751, were Dr John Wall, Richard and Josiah Holdship, Edward Cave, editor of the *Gentleman's Magazine*, and William Davies. William Bayliss, a signatory, does not appear to have had much influence on day-to-day operations, although he was the largest single shareholder. Of all these people, Wall and Davis were selected for special treatment, the two being awarded an additional amount equivalent to their shareholding in exchange for the secret of making soaprock porcelain, from which it would appear that they were entrusted with the task of acquiring the necessary manufacturing processes from Bristol. Payment was also made to Robert Podmore and John Lyes of Bristol, and it was Podmore who later defected and went to Liver-

pool to sell the soaprock secret to Richard Chaffers.

It now seems probable that the moving spirit at Worcester until 1772 was Josiah Holdship, and until 1772, when Wall became the effective head of the factory, the term 'First Period' is more in accord with the facts. Although he died in 1776, the second period, more justifiably termed 'Wall', can be extended until 1783 when the factory was sold to Thomas Flight, who bought it for his sons, Joseph and John. The break with the past is the more definite because a new porcelain body and glaze were introduced which differ somewhat from the old ones. The wares are usually termed 'Flight' Worcester. In 1793 Martin Barr joined the firm, and wares were then styled 'Flight & Barr' until 1807. From the latter year to 1813 the style was 'Barr, Flight & Barr', and from 1813 to 1840, 'Flight, Barr & Barr'. Porcelain of these periods is often marked with the name in full, or initial letters impressed, and the approximate date of manufacture can be deduced from the style of the firm. In 1783 Robert Chamberlain, one of the factory's decorators, started business in partnership with his brother, Humphrey, an outside decorator. At first they merely ran a decorating establishment painting porcelain supplied by Caughley in white, and to some extent by Worcester itself. They turned to the manufacture of porcelain with a factory at Diglis, Worcester, in 1792 with such success that, in 1840, they were able to amalgamate with the original company to form the foundation for the present Worcester Royal Porcelain Company. In 1811 they introduced their 'Regent' body which was first employed to make a service for the Prince Regent. A relative of the Chamberlains, Thomas Grainger, founded a factory about 1812 to make porcelain. He, too, started as an outside decorator about 1800. The firm was Grainger, Lee & Co., with a factory at St Martin's Gate, and this amalgamated with the Worcester Royal Porcelain Company in 1889. The principal factory was run by W. H. Kerr and R. W. Binns from 1852 until the foundation of the Worcester Royal Porcelain Company ten years later. James Hadley, chief modeller to the factory, founded a small factory of his own in 1896 in the Bath Road, and after his death in 1903 it was purchased by the Worcester Royal Porcelain Company, his sons and their staff returning to the parent enterprise in 1905. Worcester is currently noted for porcelain of extremely fine quality, and it has revived the art of figure-modelling with the fantastically successful American Birds of Dorothy Doughty (q.v.), the later British Birds, the work of Doris Lindner, and the models of Ronald and Ruth van Ruyckevelt.

The inspiration for the forms of early Worcester porcelain is fairly equally divided between contemporary silver and Chinese porcelain. Those based on silver patterns were moulded, and those on Chinese porcelain were thrown on the wheel. The earliest wares, including those which can reasonably be attributed to Lund's Bristol factory, were

469

Worcester Porcelain. An early Worcester vase of Chinese form enamelled with birds and flowers in a mixed Chinese and Kakiemon style. C. 1752. *Sigmund Katz Collection.*

painted in enamels, but underglaze blue soon became very popular for wares based on those imported from China. The blue is often blurred, but the porcelain itself is finished with exceptional neatness, the glaze is well fitting and never crazed, and because of the nature of the porcelain, which was unlike the glassy porcelain in use elsewhere, teapots never cracked as a result of pouring boiling water into them. It is very exceptional to see a Worcester teapot which has a hot-water crack (i.e. one which does not lead out to an edge), whereas they are very frequent in the rare surviving Chelsea and Derby teapots.

Many of the early wares were decorated with underglaze blue in a variety of patterns based on late Ming and K'ang Hsi porcelain, some with pseudo-Chinese marks which can be related to Ming marks. Neither Japanese shapes nor decorations were very popular at Worcester, and some of the rare Kakiemons, such as the *Quail*, were probably the work of James Giles (q.v.) rather than the factory. The Queen Catherine pattern is a factory decoration based on an Imari pattern, and these were a little more popular. Comparatively early, and certainly by 1760, a Worcester version of the Chinese *famille verte* palette (q.v.) was in use, as well as a *rose* enamel employed for some of the floral patterns, and these were being executed with the aid of outline transfers by about 1760 or soon afterwards. Transfer-printed wares (q.v.)—one of the factory's most popular products—were first made in 1757 with the employment of Robert Hancock who had been at Bow and the Battersea Enamel Works in London. There appears to have been a considerable amount

of friction between Hancock and Richard Holdship, who was in charge of the printing department, and this led to the latter's defection in 1759, when he went to Derby to sell the soaprock and transfer-printing secrets to Duesbury. Many of the earlier examples of transfer-printing are signed by Hancock in full, or with the initials *RH*, to which was added an anchor—the rebus of Richard Holdship.

The rococo style was adopted particularly in the popular leaf forms which include a series of moulded dishes, some of which were undoubtedly stands for small tureens; the rare cauliflower tureens are surviving examples. Jugs moulded as overlapping cabbage-leaves with a mask under the pouring lip were very popular, and frequently copied at Lowestoft, Caughley, and Liverpool. The influence of Meissen is to be seen in the adoption of *deutsche Blumen* (q.v.) before 1760, and the leaf dishes mentioned may have been imitated directly or by way of Chelsea.

No doubt transfer-printing inspired black pencilling, a type of painting done with a very fine brush in a technique not unlike that of the engraver. Much rarer are painted versions of transfer-prints.

A good deal of the more elaborate decoration done in the early 1760s can undoubtedly be attributed to the outside decorating studio of James Giles (q.v.). The factory supplied Giles with 'blanks' already partly decorated in underglaze blue for this purpose. Typical are scale-blue dishes—a basic pattern of overlapping scales in underglaze blue with white panels which the factory left unpainted. These panels Giles decorated with exotic birds, flowers, and fruit. More rarely the scale ground occurs in enamel colours—yellow, red, pink and light blue—and it is probable that Giles was responsible for at least some of them. Assigned in the past to the factory

Worcester Porcelain. Mask jug transfer-printed with a portrait of the King of Prussia and dated 1757. England was allied with Prussia in the Seven Years War (1756–1763). *Victoria and Albert Museum.*

Bookcases in the revived Gothic style at Strawberry Hill,
Twickenham, S.W. London—Horace Walpole's house. They
date from the 1750s.

The Palladian style. Mereworth House, Kent, c. 1722.
Architect, Colen Campbell. The plan is based on Andrea
Palladio's Villa Rotunda at Vicenza, N. Italy.

was an enamel blue of a 'dry' appearance, but this, also, seems to have been a Giles colour. A number of Kakiemons, such as the Quail pattern, also seem to have been by Giles by analogy with similar patterns on Bow porcelain. The explanation could be either a migratory painter who went from Bow to Worcester, or a common origin in the Giles workshop, and of the two alternatives the latter seems the more likely. Transfer-prints in black later coloured with enamels seem almost certainly the work of Giles, and a sale-catalogue survives which records his purchase of this kind of porcelain at auction. Apart from Giles some of the much-valued work of Jeffryes Hamet O'Neal and John Donaldson on Worcester was done outside the factory (see *Outside Decorators*)

About 1768 Worcester engaged some of the Chelsea painters, and this begins a period in which the styles of Sèvres much influenced the factory's work. This influence was particularly strong between 1770 and 1784, and it shows itself in a wide variety of rich ground colours, and often elaborate but restrained gilding. Much of its best work is worthy to stand beside that of the French factory.

Worcester figures are few in number, and have only been identified with certainty in recent years, although the fact that figures were manufactured was known from contemporary records. Perhaps the most frequent survival is a *Turk and Companion* and a *Gardener and Companion*, and these are not unlike earlier Bow models in style. The impressed letters *To* occur on some of them, and from this the hand of Mr Tebo (q.v.) may reasonably be deduced. Other models have been identified, including a group of canaries amid branches which have a rococo scroll base, although they seem to have been produced as late as 1770. These, also, were no doubt the work of Tebo, especially since they bear a strong resemblance to well-known earlier Bow birds.

During this period till 1784, Worcester porcelain is very precisely and sometimes extremely thinly potted, closely resembling some of the finer-quality Chinese wares in this respect. The glaze is of variable thickness, but early and late wares are apt to have a thicker glaze than those of the middle period. An area bare of glaze immediately inside the footring can be found on many of them, which can be well seen if a lead pencil is run round the inside of the footring. This will mark the unglazed part but will slide over the glaze. Worcester glazes are never crazed, and if crazing is present the origin must be sought elsewhere. Most wares are exceptionally free from firecracks, although these occur occasionally to a minor degree. The colour by transmitted light is often green but, especially with transfer-printed wares, sometimes orange. The natural translucency seems to have been orange, and the green due to the addition of a little cobalt blue to the body to modify it.

The early wares of the Flight period differ from those of the productions prior to 1784. The body has a greyish hue. Fluted shapes were popular, and slight gilding and scattered flowers in imitation of current Paris fashions are common. This was followed by a much whiter body, not unlike the one then in use at Derby.

The style current during the early Flight period was the neo-classical, and this can be seen especially in the vases and refrigerators (ice-pails) which often follow contemporary silver-patterns. Some of the patterns employed for service-ware at this time are still popular, notably the 'Blue Lily', renamed the 'Royal Lily' after it had been chosen by George III during his visit in 1788 when the factory was first styled 'Manufacturers to their Majesties'. The current fashion for topographical painting was adopted towards the end of the 18th century, and this included many views of Worcester and the neighbourhood. Some of the more notable painters of the time were John Pennington, Thomas Baxter, and perhaps William Billingsley (q.v.).

Robert Chamberlain was probably director of the Worcester enamelling workshop before he left to found a workshop of his own in King Street in 1783. The wares he made on his own account after 1792 much resemble those of the Flights at first. Two important services manufactured by Chamberlains before the introduction of the improved 'Regent' body in 1811 are the Nelson service of 1802 and one for the Duke of Cumberland in 1806. 'Regent' porcelain was of exceptional quality, expensive to produce, and employed only for special orders. One, for example, produced for Princess Charlotte cost £1,050 at the time, which is equivalent to about £9,000 today.

Under Kerr and Binns the factory made strenuous attempts to revive a flagging trade with considerable success. *Biscuit* porcelain which had been revived in Staffordshire under the name of Parian (q.v.), was used for figure-modelling by Kirk for part of a very well-known service of the 1850s based on the *Midsummer Night's Dream* of Shakespeare. A richly decorated service made for the marriage of the Earl and Countess of Dudley utilized the jewelled decoration (q.v.) of Sèvres, with gilding and jewelled work by Samuel Ranford and panels of female heads by Thomas Callowhill. Thomas Bott did some notable work inspired by the painted enamels of Limoges, probably at the suggestion of the Prince Consort. During the second half of the 19th century Worcester assumed the lead in the manufacture of ornamental porcelain which it has since maintained, and many new bodies and decorative themes were introduced, among them wares based on Japanese styles. Excellent work was done from 1875 onwards by James Hadley which is now collected. From 1912 to 1953 the factory was under the guidance of Charles William Dyson Perrins, whose collection formed the basis for the present Works Museum, and during his chairmanship services were made for royalty in all parts of the world. The first pair of the American Birds of Dorothy Doughty were issued in 1935, and these represent a degree of technical achievement

Worcester Porcelain. Chiff-chaff on Hogweed, from the British Birds series of Dorothy Doughty. Worcester Royal Porcelain Company. Modern production.

undreamed of in the 18th century. Their designer is one of the few who became almost a legend in their own lifetime, and the fantastic success which her work achieved in America led to the issue of the British Bird series currently in production. But Dorothy Doughty was only one of the factory's talented designers, and Worcester now leads the world in the production of high-quality figures which are already collector's items. Grainger's factory, later to be absorbed by the Worcester Royal Porcelain Company, began by copying the wares of both Flight and Chamberlain, but they later branched out into the manufacture of ornamental wares in Parian, and of 'bower' groups, which were, perhaps, inspired by similar groups made in salt-glazed ware, and in porcelain by Longton Hall (q.v.), in the middle of the 18th century. A small group of figures are surrounded by an overarching bower of delicately modelled flowers and leaves.

Worcester porcelain is, perhaps, the most easily recognized of all 18th-century wares, and there are no forgeries which are deceptive to the reasonably knowledgeable collector. For this reason, perhaps, this factory's wares have always been greatly in demand, and it is still the most popular of all the 18th-century English factories internationally.

WRIGGLE-WORK
A kind of engraving used on silver, especially during the late 17th century. It is also very common on pewter, where line engraving was not so effective. It was in use till about 1725, but occasionally occurs later on both silver and pewter. The line took the form which follows:

WRISBERGHOLZEN (Hannover, Germany) FAÏENCE FACTORY
A factory was probably started here about 1737 and managed by a man named Vielstich. It continued into the 19th century, and was at one time controlled by L. V. Gerverot (see *Fürstenberg Porcelain Factory*). The early wares are the most interesting. Influenced by Delft, they are painted with bluish-white flowers, and are a combination of Dutch and Chinese shapes. Polychrome was also used: blue, yellow, and green. No enamel colours are known.

The mark is a monogram *WR* with painter's marks and numbers.

WÜRZBURG (Franconia) PORCELAIN FACTORY
This factory was started in 1775 by Johann Kaspar Geyger and closed about five years later. A few specimens of service-ware have been identified, and figures have sometimes been ascribed to Würzburg on fairly inadequate evidence.

WYVERN   See *Dragon*

Y

YARD-OF-ALE

Slender English ale-glass about three feet in length which has a spherical bulb at one end and a trumpet shaped orifice at the other, the two being joined by a tubular section. In general appearance the shape is similar to that of a long coaching-horn. Yards-of-ale are first recorded in the 17th century, and the capacity is usually about a pint, or slightly more. Drinkers were required to empty the vessel without taking a breath or removing the glass from their lips. It is very difficult to do this without being deluged with ale when air eventually reaches the liquid in the bulb. Few genuine examples now survive. Most are comparatively recent reproductions.

YEW WOOD

(French *bois d'if*). A close-grained yellowish-brown hardwood which sometimes exhibits a purplish-brown colour. It comes from a tree widely distributed throughout Europe. Yew was always popular as a furniture wood in England in the form of veneers and inlays, and for Windsor chairs in conjunction with an elm seat. In France it was principally employed for the former purposes.

YORKSHIRE CHAIRS

Originally a mid-17th-century design from Yorkshire (England) with turned legs and stretcher, and carved crescent-shaped rails at the back. Reproductions are common, genuine specimens scarce.

Z

ZAFFER

Term current among 18th-century English potters for cobalt blue used for painting underglaze. The word was derived from the Italian *zaffare* (Arabic *zafre*) meaning cobalt in the form of a glass frit (q.v.) obtained from Venice. This was finely powdered and used as a pigment.

ZERBST (Anhalt, Germany) FAÏENCE FACTORY

A factory was established here by J. Caspar Ripp (who also worked at Frankfurt, Nürnberg and Ansbach), a man who wandered from place to place even more than was usual for 18th-century potters. The wares are blue-and-white and polychrome of so varied a character that it is difficult to distinguish any one definite characteristic, apart from a grey-green colour on a bluish base, and yellow used in conjunction with red, a practice rare at other factories in the North. Applied and painted flowers, and a flower knop on lids of tureens, are also typical.

The mark is *Z*, combined with a variety of letters which are probably painter's marks.

ZIEGLER & CO.

A Manchester firm engaged from the 1860s onwards in an import and export trade in Persia. Zieglers played a considerable part in expanding European trade in this part of the world in rugs and carpets, and especially in influencing the production of those of a suitable size for Western rooms. They commissioned carpets of excellent quality which were made in and around the Sultanabad area, and those made in the Persian style, but designed by an Englishman, were once known in the trade as 'Ziegler carpets'.

ZINC

Although zinc is principally alloyed with copper to make brass, it was commonly used, under the name of spelter, to make small casts of sculpture and imitations of *bronzes d'ameublement* from about 1850 onwards. These, much inferior to bronze, were

produced mainly in Berlin by a number of firms, and a process employed for bronzing the surface was invented by a man named Geiss. Many clock-cases in the French style were thus produced, and have not uncommonly survived.

ZINCKE, CHRISTIAN FRIEDRICH (c. 1684–1767)

Enameller. Born at Dresden, Zincke came to England in 1706 and studied there. He soon achieved a reputation as a prolific enameller of great skill. Zincke was noted for painted enamel miniatures of portraits in oils. He did work of this kind for the royal family, and he was appointed cabinet painter to the Prince of Wales. For a time he had so much work that he was forced to raise his prices from 20 to 30 guineas. He retired in 1746 but was afterwards commissioned by Mme de Pompadour to paint a small enamel miniature of Louis Quinze. Zincke spent most of his working life in England, and he was well represented at the Strawberry Hill sale of Horace Walpole's collection in 1832.

ZOBEL, BENJAMIN (b. 1762; d. after 1800)

Zobel, the best-known maker of sand-pictures, was born in Germany and trained as a confectioner. He studied painting in Amsterdam, and came to London in 1783 where, through the influence of Louis Weltje, *chef* to the Prince of Wales, he obtained employment decorating the royal dining-table.

His sand-pictures, which are not an infrequent survival, are hardly original in their subject-matter, and most are derived from the works of well-known contemporary artists such as Abraham Cooper, George Stubbs, James Northcote, Benjamin West, and George Morland, as well as from old masters, one sand-picture of Daniel in the Lion's Den being recorded as signed 'B. Zobel after Rubens'. Another is inscribed 'designed by Morland for B. Zobel while in the Isle of Wight 1793'—evidence of collaboration between the two men.

Zobel's son, James, who lived in Norwich adopted his father's profession, but his work is neither so competent nor so well known as that of his father.

Zurich. A pair of Zurich figures, marked 'Z'. c. 1770.

ZÜRICH (Switzerland) FAÏENCE AND PORCELAIN FACTORY

This factory was established in 1763, one of the founders being the Swiss poet and painter, Salomon Gessner. Adam Spengler was director, and his son, Jean-Jacques Spengler (or Spängler), came to England as a modeller to the Derby factory. After Spengler's death in 1790 the manufacture of porcelain seems to have been discontinued in favour of faïence and *faïence-fine*. From 1793 onwards the factory was in a number of hands, closing towards the end of the 19th century.

A soft-paste porcelain was made until 1765, but specimens are exceedingly rare. A hard paste was introduced in this year, and thereafter porcelain of excellent quality was produced, specimens of which are much sought. Figures of the highest quality, many inspired by those of Ludwigsburg (q.v.), were probably modelled by Johann Valentin Sonneschein who came from that factory, and Jean-Jacques Spengler (later of Derby) may also have modelled some of them. Service-ware is well painted with miniature Swiss landscapes and figure subjects, perhaps to designs supplied by Gessner, and one example exists signed by him. Earlier Meissen styles were also copied, both the *indianische Blumen* (q.v.) and the *deutsche Blumen* (q.v.), and some of the later wares show distinctly the influences of Berlin and Sèvres.

The earlier faïence, made before 1793, is usually decorated in much the same style as contemporary Zurich porcelain. In addition, transfer-printing was done, and this is also to be seen on the later *faïence-fine*.

ZWISCHENGOLDGLÄSER

'Gold sandwich' glasses. Technically *Zwischensilberglas* is the same, except that silver replaces gold.

Vessels of this kind, usually conical tumblers, are double glasses, one fitting precisely into the other. The outer surface of the inner glass was decorated with gold or silver leaf, after which it was inserted into the outer glass, the rim being sealed with lacquer. Occasionally the interior of the outer glass was painted with oil or lacquer colour, and the exterior of the inner glass covered with gold or silver leaf to form a ground against which the painting can be seen.

The technique is extremely ancient, the origin perhaps to be sought in Alexandria. It was also employed by Islamic glass-workers, some rare Fatimid specimens from Egypt (969–1164) having survived. In more recent times most such work has come from Bohemia, Silesia, and Austria. Specimens are rare.

Zwischengoldglaser. A *Zwischengoldglas* of c. 1730 from Bohemia. *Victoria and Albert Museum.*

APPENDIX OF MARKS

ENGLISH PORCELAIN

Factory Marks

CHELSEA. 1745–1749. Incised. Known in underglaze blue.

CHELSEA. 1745. Incised.

CHELSEA. 1749. In underglaze blue.

CHELSEA. 1750–1770. Raised on medallion, red, blue, lilac, brown, and gold.

CHELSEA–DERBY. 1770–1784. Red and gold.

DERBY. ?1750. Incised.

DERBY. 1750. Incised.

DERBY. c. 1760. Incised. Unique mark.

DERBY. c. 1764. Mark of Richard Holdship on transfer-printed mug.

CHELSEA–DERBY. 1777. In gold.

DERBY. 1780–1784. In blue or purple.

DERBY. 1784–1810. In red, blue, and gold. Incised on base of *biscuit* figures.

DERBY. 1795–1796. Duesbury & Kean.

DERBY. 1820–1848. Bloor period.

DERBY. Copy of Meissen mark.

PINXTON. In gold.

PINXTON. In red.

PINXTON. Workman's mark. In red.

BOW. 1749–1753. Incised.

BOW. 1749–1753. Incised.

BOW. 1749–1753. Incised.

BOW. 1758–1775. In red. Possibly a Giles mark.

BOW. 1755–1760. In underglaze blue.

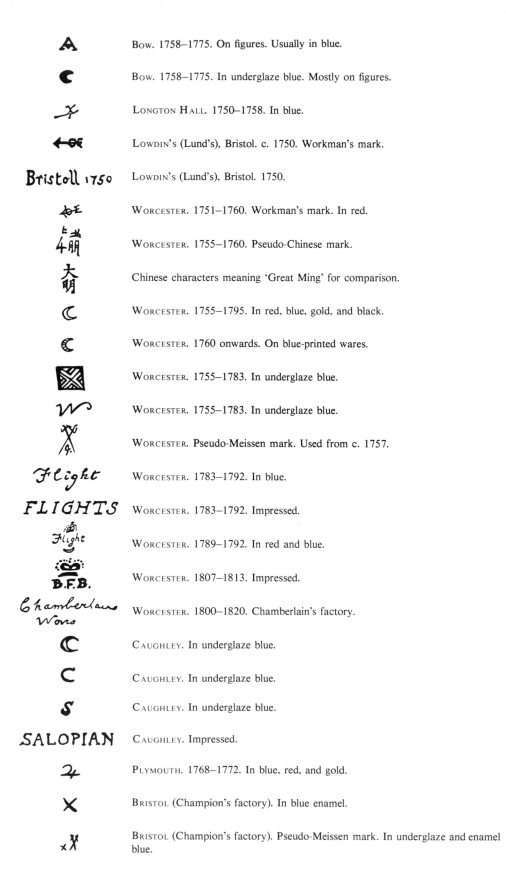 **A**	Bow. 1758–1775. On figures. Usually in blue.
C	Bow. 1758–1775. In underglaze blue. Mostly on figures.
✗	Longton Hall. 1750–1758. In blue.
⟵	Lowdin's (Lund's), Bristol. c. 1750. Workman's mark.
Bristoll 1750	Lowdin's (Lund's), Bristol. 1750.
丄王	Worcester. 1751–1760. Workman's mark. In red.
4明	Worcester. 1755–1760. Pseudo-Chinese mark.
大明	Chinese characters meaning 'Great Ming' for comparison.
ℂ	Worcester. 1755–1795. In red, blue, gold, and black.
ℭ	Worcester. 1760 onwards. On blue-printed wares.
▨	Worcester. 1755–1783. In underglaze blue.
𝓌	Worcester. 1755–1783. In underglaze blue.
✗/9.	Worcester. Pseudo-Meissen mark. Used from c. 1757.
Flight	Worcester. 1783–1792. In blue.
FLIGHTS	Worcester. 1783–1792. Impressed.
Flight	Worcester. 1789–1792. In red and blue.
B.F.B.	Worcester. 1807–1813. Impressed.
Chamberlain Wors	Worcester. 1800–1820. Chamberlain's factory.
ℂ	Caughley. In underglaze blue.
C	Caughley. In underglaze blue.
S	Caughley. In underglaze blue.
SALOPIAN	Caughley. Impressed.
4	Plymouth. 1768–1772. In blue, red, and gold.
X	Bristol (Champion's factory). In blue enamel.
×X	Bristol (Champion's factory). Pseudo-Meissen mark. In underglaze and enamel blue.

B6 — BRISTOL (Champion's factory). In blue enamel.

SWANSEA — SWANSEA. 1814–1817. Impressed. A similar mark known painted in red and other colours.

NANT-GARW C.W — NANTGARW. Impressed.

Artists' Marks

Z B — ZACHARIAH BOREMAN. On a Derby mug c. 1780.

JOHN DONALDSON. On a Worcester vase c. 1765–1770.

* — ISAAC FARNSWORTH, repairer. On Derby *biscuit* figures and groups.

△ — JOSEPH HILL, repairer. On Derby *biscuit* figures and groups.

JEFFREY O'NEALE. In a disguised form as part of an inscription. Chelsea c. 1754.

To — TEBO. 1749–1780(?). The mark of a migratory repairer who worked at a number of factories. Impressed into body. See *Tebo, Mr.*

Wedgwood

WEDGWOOD
WEDGWOOD

Mark upon Queen's Ware from 1769 until the present, and upon ornamental jasper, black basalt and terracotta, from 1780 until the present. Latterly the words Etruria and Barlaston and the name of the pattern have often been added.

ETRURIA · WEDGWOOD & BENTLEY

Mark found inside the plinth of old basalt vases and sometimes on the pedestal of a bust or large figure.

WEDGWOOD & BENTLEY: ETRURIA

Mark placed round the screw of basalt, granite, and Etruscan vases.

WEDGWOOD
& BENTLEY
Wedgwood
& Bentley

Marks used from 1769–1780. After Bentley's death, WEDGWOOD only was used. Found on busts, vases, figures, plaques, medallions, and cameos.

WEDGWOOD
(in red or blue)

Mark upon bone china or porcelain 1812–1815, printed in red, blue, or gold.

WEDGWOOD
BONE CHINA
MADE IN
ENGLAND

Mark upon fine bone china from 1878 until the present, printed in sepia and other colours.

OF ETRURIA
WEDGWOOD
MADE IN
ENGLAND
& BARLASTON

Mark upon Queen's Ware from 1940 to the present, with the name of the pattern often added.

French and Belgian Porcelain

 S.ᵗ C
T

SAINT CLOUD. In blue. Used separately, but known in conjunction. The latter mark sometimes incised.

CHANTILLY. In red or blue. The usual mark, with several variations.

D.V.

MENNECY. In blue, red, black, and incised.

SÈVRES. Mark for the year 1753. Nearly always in blue enamel.

SÈVRES. Mark for the year 1788.
The Royal Monogram of the crossed L's was in use at Vincennes before 1753. The letter in the centre of the Monogram was added from 1753, and represents the year of manufacture. The letter A stands for 1753, B for 1754, and so on. The letter W was omitted. In 1778 the date letters were doubled, the first being AA. The system was discarded in 1793, finishing with PP. The letters A, B, and C refer to pieces made at Vincennes, the letter D onwards to those made at Sèvres. Letters and devices added outside the mark usually refer to artists who can, in some cases, be identified therefrom. Figures in soft *biscuit* porcelain were *never* marked.

R.F
Sevres.

SÈVRES. Period of the first Republic.

SÈVRES. Period of Charles X. 1824–1828. The last two figures of the year were usually added.

s v.⊕P.48.

SÈVRES. Louis Phillipe. 1845–1848.

sN54

SÈVRES. Period of Napoleon III.

Ḣ
•

STRASBOURG. Paul Hannong. 1752–1755.

NIDERVILLER. 1770–1793.

⚓

SCEAUX.

Χ

PARIS (de la Courtille). In blue underglaze, and incised.

N ꞉ ꞉
Paris

PARIS (Rue Popincourt). For Nast of Paris. Nast is sometimes written in full.

PARIS (Clignancourt).

PARIS (Rue Thiroux). In underglaze blue.

FONTAINEBLEAU. Jacob Petit.

TOURNAI (Belgium). In various colours.

German Porcelain

German porcelain is usually well-marked. Nevertheless, a mark is neither a safe nor satisfactory test of genuineness. At best it can only provide confirmatory evidence. This list includes all the more usual marks to be found, but, for the sake of brevity, it omits workmen's marks, and marks which are self-explanatory, e.g. 'Gera', which is sometimes used in full under topographical paintings of this town. For a more detailed list the reader is referred to Honey (*Dictionary of European Ceramic Art*) or Cushion (*German Ceramic Marks*), where the various ancillary marks are recorded in full.

MEISSEN. 1723–1724. For Königliche Porzellan Manufaktur. Also 'K.P.F.' (Königliche Porzellan Fabrik) and 'M.P.M.' (Meissner Porzellan Manufaktur).

MEISSEN. 1723 onwards. The caduceus (*Merkurstab*) used principally on coffee-cups for the Turkish market.

MEISSEN. 1725 onwards. Date of cessation doubtful, but prior to 1763. The monogram of Augustus, for Augustus Rex. Used generally on pieces intended for royal gifts or for the Elector's personal use.

MEISSEN. An early version, about 1725. The mark was introduced about 1724. The crossed swords from the Electoral Arms of Saxony.

MEISSEN. The usual type of mark appearing in the 1740s.

MEISSEN. 1763–1774. The Academic Period (*Die Punktzeit*)

MEISSEN. 1774–1814. The Marcolini Period. The asterisk between the *points* at an earlier period on blue painted ware is a workman's mark.

VIENNA. Du Paquier Period. 1719–1744. An imitation Chinese seal-mark. Other imitations of Chinese marks have been recorded.

VIENNA. 1744–1749. Impressed. An early version.

VIENNA. 1749–1820. Painted in blue. The impressed shield was used again after 1820.

NYMPHENBURG. 1754–1765. The early variety.

NYMPHENBURG. c. 1765–1780.

NYMPHENBURG. Used from 1763 to 1767 on some specimens. The hexagon mark. This was painted in underglaze blue.

HÖCHST. 1750–1796. In crimson or purple. Slight variations from time to time. The mark also occurs (rarely) in an impressed form.

HÖCHST. Probably between 1765–1774. The wheel surmounted by the Electoral Crown.

FRANKENTHAL. Impressed. Mark of Paul Hannong. Also to be found on Strasbourg porcelain.

FRANKENTHAL. 1756–1759. Lion from the Arms of the Palatinate. Sometimes found in conjunction with 'IH' impressed, for Joseph Hannong, who owned the factory from 1759 to 1762.

FRANKENTHAL. c. 1756. In blue. From the Electoral Arms.

FRANKENTHAL. With slight variations from 1762 to 1793. The commonest mark. The monogram of the Elector, Carl Theodor.

BERLIN. Wegely's factory. Impressed and in blue.

BERLIN. 1761–1763. Gotzkowsky's factory. In blue underglaze.

BERLIN. 1765–1770. The sceptre mark.

BERLIN. 1770–1800.

FÜRSTENBERG. In blue. This, and the following mark, are early. Later, it was added much more sketchily.

FÜRSTENBERG. In blue.

LUDWIGSBURG. 1758–1793. The monogram of Carl Eugen, Duke of Württemberg. Usually in blue.

LUDWIGSBURG. Another version of the mark listed above. Late marks are often crudely drawn.

LUDWIGSBURG. Late 18th century. Stag's antler from the Arms of Württemberg.

ANSBACH. The 'A' is for the Markgraf, Alexander. In blue.

ANSBACH. Impressed.

ANSBACH. Sometimes found with the 'A' beneath.

KELSTERBACH. From 1768 to the end of the century. In blue or manganese. For Hesse-Darmstadt.

KELSTERBACH. From 1766, but usually a late mark. In blue or impressed.

FULDA. From c. 1780. For Fürstlich Fuldaisch. The *Heinrichsmarke.*

FULDA. From c. 1765 to 1780. An early mark.

HESSE-CASSEL. In blue.

TETTAU. From 1794 onwards.

GOTHA. From at least 1783.

GOTHA. From 1783 to 1805.

GOTHA. From the end of the 18th century. A late mark.

WALLENDORF. c. 1778 onwards. This should not be confused with the mark of Wegely's Berlin factory.

WALLENDORF. An early mark imitating Meissen.

VOLKSTEDT. 1760–1799. A pseudo-Meissen mark.

VOLKSTEDT. 1799 onwards.

KLOSTER-VEILSDORF. 1760–1797. The commonest mark.

KLOSTER-VEILSDORF. Probably before 1765. Rare.

KLOSTER-VEILSDORF. From 1797 onwards. Also used at Limbach, Groszbreitenbach, and Ilmenau from about 1788.

LIMBACH. 1772–1788.

LIMBACH. An imitation Meissen mark.

LIMBACH. After 1788. Clover-leaf. Also used at Kloster-Veilsdorf, Groszbreitenbach, and Ilmenau.

ILMENAU. c. 1792.

GERA. The name is sometimes inscribed in full.

RAUENSTEIN. This, and the following mark, from about 1783 onwards.

RAUENSTEIN.

Italian Porcelain

FLORENCE. On Medici porcelain. Several variations known.

CAPO-DI-MONTE. A similar mark was used at Buen Retiro.

NAPLES (Royal Factory). 1771–1806. In blue, red, and impressed.

DOCCIA: In blue, red, gold, or impressed.

NOVE (Venice) in red, blue, or gold.

VENICE (The Cozzi factory).

VINOVO (near Turin). In blue and incised. Some variations observed.

Spanish Porcelain

BUEN RETIRO. Incised.

BUEN RETIRO. Incised. A late mark.

Other European Factories

COPENHAGEN (Denmark). From 1775.

MARIEBERG (Sweden). In several forms. From about 1766. Incised, in blue, and in red.

ST PETERSBURG (Leningrad), Russia. In blue. 1762–1796. The monogram represents Ekaterina (i.e. Catherine II).

The letter 'P' representing the Emperor, Paul. 1796–1801.

MOSCOW (Russia). Impressed. Gardner's factory. Early 19th century.

'AP'. Popoff's factory, Moscow. Early 19th century.

ZÜRICH (Switzerland). In blue.

NYON (Switzerland). In underglaze blue.

WEESP (Holland). In underglaze blue. 1759 onwards.

OUDE LOOSDRECHT (Holland). Incised, enamel colours, and underglaze blue.

OUDE AMSTEL (Holland). In blue and black.

THE HAGUE (Holland). In underglaze blue. In overglaze blue the mark usually denotes Tournai porcelain decorated at The Hague.

CHINESE CHRONOLOGY

c. 3500–2000 B.C.	Neolithic culture. Decorated pottery recovered from graves.
c. 1766–1122 B.C.	Shang-Yin Dynasty. Period of finest ritual bronze vessels.
1122–255 B.C.	Chou Dynasty. Ritual bronzes and jades. Early pottery.
c. 481–205 B.C.	Period of the Warring States.
221–206 B.C.	Ch'in Dynasty. Great Wall of China constructed.
206 B.C.–A.D. 220	Han Dynasty. Pottery, stoneware, bronzes, jades.
220–589	The Six Dynasties.
	386–535: Period of the Northern Wei (pottery and tomb figures).
	506–556: Period of the Liang.
581–618	Sui Dynasty.
618–906	T'ang Dynasty. Fine pottery, tomb figures, metalwork, jades, etc.
960–1280	Sung Dynasty. Pottery, porcelain, stonewares with coloured glazes, jades, etc.
1280–1368	Yüan Dynasty. First blue-and-white porcelain.
1368–1644	Ming Dynasty.

1368–1398: Hung Wu.
1399–1402: Chien Wên.
1403–1424: Yung Lo.
1425: Hung Hsi.
1426–1435: Hsüan Tê.
1436–1449: Chêng T'ung.
1450–1456: Ching T'ai.   Decoration in coloured enamels. Fine blue-
1457–1464: T'ien Shun.   and-white porcelain. *San tsai* decoration. Jades.
1465–1487: Ch'êng Hua.   Enamels. Lacquer. Development of painting on
1488–1505: Hung Chih.   porcelain.
1506–1521: Chêng Tê.
1522–1566: Chia Ching.
1567–1572: Lung Ch'ing.
1573–1619: Wan Li.
1620: T'ai Ch'ang.
1621–1627: T'ien Ch'i.
1628–1643: Ch'ung Chêng.

1644–1912   Ch'ing Dynasty.
1644–1661: Shun Chih.
1662–1722: K'ang Hsi.   *Famille verte, famille rose,* most Chinese export
1723–1735: Yung Chêng.   porcelain, Canton enamels, furniture, laquer, etc.
1736–1795: Ch'ien Lung.
1796–1820: Chia Ch'ing.
1821–1850: Tao Kuang.
1851–1861: Hsien Fêng.
1862–1873: T'ung Chih.
1874–1908: Kuang Hsü.
1909–1912: Hsüan T'ung.
1912 onwards: The Chinese Republic.

CHINESE REIGN MARKS

The following marks are found on Chinese works of art of all kinds, and record the dynasty and the name of the emperor. Great caution is necessary in accepting them at their face value, however, since the Chinese often add early reign marks to things made in the style of the period, and sometimes even without this much justification. Unless the other factors present are sufficient to justify an acceptance, such marks should not be used as evidence of age.

The marks given are in standard form. Slight differences in calligraphy will be observed between (say) marks drawn in the Ming period and those done later, but some acquaintance with Chinese calligraphy is necessary before this can be used as evidence of date.

It is possible to say, fairly definitely, that if the mark was done in the Ming period, then it will have been done in the reign of the emperor given. Examples of the later use of Ming reign marks usually occur in the following (Ch'ing) dynasty, not later in the Ming Dynasty.

Marks can be interpreted as follows:

(4) Hua	Hua		(1) Ta	Great
(5) nien	} period made		(2) Ming	Bright (dynasty)
(6) chih			(3) Ch'eng	Ch'êng

The characters are read from the top right, downwards.

Ming Dynasty

年 洪
製 武
Hung Wu
(1368–1398)

德 大
年 明
製 正
Chêng Tê
(1506–1521)

年 永
製 樂
Yung Lo
(1403–1424)

靖 大
年 明
製 嘉
Chia Ching
(1522–1566)

德 大
年 明
製 宣
Hsüan Tê
(1426–1435)

慶 大
年 明
製 隆
Lung Ch'ing
(1567–1572)

化 大
年 明
製 成
Ch'êng Hua
(1465–1487)

曆 大
年 明
製 萬
Wan Li
(1573–1619)

年 成
製 化
Ch'êng Hua
(1465–1487)

啟 大
年 明
製 天
T'ien Ch'i
(1621–1627)

治 大
年 明
製 弘
Hung Chih
(1488–1505)

年 崇
製 楨
Ch'ung Chêng
(1628–1643)

Manchu, or Ch'ing Dynasty

治 大
年 清
製 順
Shun Chih
(1644–1651)

光 大
年 清
製 道
Tao Kuang
(1821–1850)

熙 大
年 清
製 康
K'ang Hsi
(1662–1722)

豐 大
年 清
製 咸
Hsien Fêng
(1851–1861)

正 大
年 清
製 雍
Yung Chêng
(1723–1735)

治 大
年 清
製 同
T'ung Chih
(1862–1873)

隆 大
年 清
製 乾
Ch'ien Lung
(1736–1795)

緒 大
年 清
製 光
Kuang Hsü
(1874–1908)

年 嘉
製 慶
Chia Ch'ing
(1796–1820)

The square seal marks sometimes replace the more usual characters.

ENGLISH SILVER MARKS

London

The mark of the *Leopard's Head* was introduced in 1300 and the *maker's mark* in 1363.

A letter, changed annually to mark the year of manufacture, was first incorporated within the mark of the *Leopard's Head* from 1463 to 1478. Thereafter a separate *date letter* has always been punched. Thus from 1478 to 1544 three marks were used (viz., *Leopard's Head*, *maker's mark*, and *date letter*). In 1544 the *Lion passant* was added, making a total of four thenceforward, except for (i) the temporary or optional changes made by the Acts of 1696 and 1719 respectively, and (ii) from 1784 until 1890, when a fifth mark, the *Sovereign's Head*, was punched.

In each of the tables below and on the next page, the twenty letters of the reduced alphabet used at Goldsmith's Hall are columnated on the left and against them in the following columns are placed the years which the letters signify. It should perhaps be emphasized that the letter was changed on 19 May in the period covered by the upper table and 29 May in that by the lower; thus one letter served from, for example, 19 May 1550 until 18 May 1551; in these tables (and in similar cases in the succeeding pages) only the first of the two calendar years in question is placed against the appropriate letter.

In the table below, which embraces the eleven cycles from the introduction of the separate *date letter* until the break in sequence in 1696–1697, only the marks from 1558 onwards are included. The regularity of the London cycles has allowed two lines to be ruled across the tables at ten-year intervals to aid reference. The letter *A* of each alphabet with the *Leopard's Head* is shown: no *makers' marks* are shown, and information about them should be sought in Sir C. J. Jackson's *English Goldsmiths and their Marks*.

A	1478	1498	1518	1538	1558	1578	1598	1618	1638	1658	1678
B	1479	1499	1519	1539	1559	1579	1599	1619	1639	1659	1679
C	1480	1500	1520	1540	1560	1580	1600	1620	1640	1660	1680
D	1481	1501	1521	1541	1561	1581	1601	1621	1641	1661	1681
E	1482	1502	1522	1542	1562	1582	1602	1622	1642	1662	1682
F	1483	1503	1523	1543	1563	1583	1603	1623	1643	1663	1683
G	1484	1504	1524	1544[1]	1564	1584	1604	1624	1644	1664	1684
H	1485	1505	1525	1545	1565	1585	1605	1625	1645	1665	1685
I	1486	1506	1526	1546	1566	1586	1606	1626	1646	1666	1686
K	1487	1507	1527	1547	1567	1587	1607	1627	1647	1667	1687
L	1488	1508	1528	1548	1568	1588	1608	1628	1648	1668	1688
M	1489	1509	1529	1549	1569	1589	1609	1629	1649	1669	1689
N	1490	1510	1530	1550	1570	1590	1610	1630	1650	1670	1690
O	1491	1511	1531	1551	1571	1591	1611	1631	1651	1671	1691
P	1492	1512	1532	1552	1572	1592	1612	1632	1652	1672	1692
Q	1493	1513	1533	1553	1573	1593	1613	1633	1653	1673	1693
R	1494	1514	1534	1554	1574	1594	1614	1634	1654	1674	1694
S	1495	1515	1535	1555	1575	1595	1615	1635	1655	1675	1695
T	1496	1516	1536	1556	1576	1596	1616	1636	1656	1676	1696
U	1497	1517	1537	1557	1577	1597	1617	1637	1657	1677	——

1. The *Lion passant* introduced in 1544.

	🛡	🛡	🛡	🛡	🛡	🛡	🛡	🛡	🛡	🛡	🛡	🛡	🛡
A	1697[1]	1716	1736	1756	1776	1796	1816	1836	1856	1876	1896	1916	1936
B	1697	1717	1737	1757	1777	1797	1817	1837	1857	1877	1897	1917	1937
C	1698	1718	1738	1758	1778	1798	1818	1838	1858	1878	1898	1918	1938
D	1699	1719	1739	1759	1779	1799	1819	1839	1859	1879	1899	1919	1939
E	1700	1720[2]	1740	1760	1780	1800	1820	1840	1860	1880	1900	1920	1940
F	1701	1721	1741	1761	1781	1801	1821[4]	1841	1861	1881	1901	1921	1941
G	1702	1722	1742	1762	1782	1802	1822	1842	1862	1882	1902	1922	1942
H	1703	1723	1743	1763	1783	1803	1823	1843	1863	1883	1903	1923	1943
I	1704	1724	1744	1764	1784[3]	1804	1824	1844	1864	1884	1904	1924	1944
K	1705	1725	1745	1765	1785	1805	1825	1845	1865	1885	1905	1925	1945
L	1706	1726	1746	1766	1786	1806	1826	1846	1866	1886	1906	1926	1946
M	1707	1727	1747	1767	1787	1807	1827	1847	1867	1887	1907	1927	1947
N	1708	1728	1748	1768	1788	1808	1828	1848	1868	1888	1908	1928	1948
O	1709	1729	1749	1769	1789	1809	1829	1849	1869	1889	1909	1929	1949
P	1710	1730	1750	1770	1790	1810	1830	1850	1870	1890[5]	1910	1930	1950
Q	1711	1731	1751	1771	1791	1811	1831	1851	1871	1891	1911	1931	1951
R	1712	1732	1752	1772	1792	1812	1832	1852	1872	1892	1912	1932	1952
S	1713	1733	1753	1773	1793	1813	1833	1853	1873	1893	1913	1933	1953
T	1714	1734	1754	1774	1794	1814	1834	1854	1874	1894	1914	1934	1954
U	1715	1735	1755	1775	1795	1815	1835	1855	1875	1895	1915	1935	1955

1. The *A* of the first sequence lasted only from 27 March till 29 May 1697.

2. After 1 June 1720 the marks of the old standard were resumed, as in the third column, while those of the new standard were used concurrently, with the same date letter, on such plate as was made of the higher standard required.

3. The *Sovereign's Head* mark was added on 1 December 1784 to show the payment of duty and continued until 30 April 1890.

4. The *Leopard's Head* is no longer crowned after 1821.

5. The *Sovereign's Head* mark was not used after 1890.

Birmingham

The Assay Office was established at Birmingham in 1773, with the *Anchor* as its distinguishing punch. When the duty was doubled in 1797, the *King's Head* was duplicated for a short time(†). The sequences are of twenty-five, omitting *J* or *I*, or twenty-six letters.

	1773	1798	1824	1849	1875	1900	1925	1950
A	1773	1798	1824	1849	1875	1900	1925	1950
B	1774	1799	1825	1850	1876	1901	1926	1951
C	1775	1800	1826	1851	1877	1902	1927	1952
D	1776	1801	1827	1852	1878	1903	1928	1953
E	1777	1802	1828	1853	1879	1904	1929	1954
F	1778	1803	1829	1854	1880	1905	1930	etc.
G	1779	1804	1830	1855	1881	1906	1931	
H	1780	1805	1831	1856	1882	1907	1932	
I	1781	1806	1832	1857	1883	1908	——	
J	——	1807	——	1858	——	——	1933	
K	1782	1808	1833	1859	1884	1909	1934	
L	1783	1809	1834	1860	1885	1910	1935	
M	1784[1]	1810	1835	1861	1886	1911	1936	
N	1785	1811	1836	1862	1887	1912	1937	
O	1786	1812	1837	1863	1888	1913	1938	
P	1787	1813	1838	1864	1889	1914	1939	
Q	1788	1814	1839	1865	1890[1]	1915	1940	
R	1789	1815	1840	1866	1891	1916	1941	
S	1790	1816	1841	1867	1892	1917	1942	
T	1791	1817	1842	1868	1893	1918	1943	
U	1792	1818	1843	1869	1894	1919	1944	
V	1793	1819	1844	1870	1895	1920	1945	
W	1794	1820	1845	1871	1896	1921	1946	
X	1795	1821	1846	1872	1897	1922	1947	
Y	1796	1822	1847	1873	1898	1923	1948	
Z	1797†	1823	1848	1874	1899	1924	1949	

1. The *Sovereign's Head* mark was added on 1 December 1784 to show the payment of duty and continued until 30 April 1890.

Chester

There seems to have been a succession of moneyers at Chester from Saxon times and of goldsmiths from the 13th century. The omission of any mention of Chester in early Acts has been explained on the ground that both the city and county were under the Earls of Chester and not under the Crown until the time of Henry VIII. There were *makers' marks*, but no regular assay office marks until 1686; a sequence of date-letters began in 1701 with cycles of irregular lengths.

A	1701	1726	1751	1776	1797	1818	1839	1864	1884	1901	1926
B	1702	1727	1752	1777	1798	1819	1840	1865	1885	1902	1927
C	1703	1728	1753	1778	1799	1820	1841	1866	1886	1903	1928
D	1704	1729	1754	1779	1800	1821–2	1842	1867	1887	1904	1929
E	1705	1730	1755	1780	1801	1823	1843	1868	1888	1905	1930
F	1706	1731	1756	1781	1802	1824	1844	1869	1889	1906	1931
G	1707	1732	1757	1782	1803	1825	1845	1870	1890[1]	1907	1932
H	1708	1733	1758	1783	1804	1826	1846	1871	1891	1908	1933
I	1709	1734	1759	1784[1]	1805	1827	1847	1872	1892	1909	1934
K	1710	1735	1760	1785	1806	1828	1848	1873	1893	1910	1935
L	1711	1736	1761	1786	1807	1829	1849	1874	1894	1911	1936
M	1712	1737	1762	1787	1808	1830	1850	1875	1895	1912	1937
N	1713	1738	1763	1788	1809	1831	1851	1876	1896	1913	1938
O	1714	1739	1764	1789	1810	1832	1852	1877	1897	1914	1939
P	1715	1740	1765	1790	1811	1833	1853	1878	1898	1915	1940
Q	1716	1741	1766	1791	1812	1834	1854	1879	1899	1916	1941
R	1717	1742	1767	1792	1813	1835	1855	1880	1900	1917	1942
S	1718	1743	1768	1793	1814	1836	1856	1881	——	1918	1943
T	1719	1744	1769	1794	1815	1837	1857	1882	——	1919	1944
U	1720	1745	1770	1795	1816	1838	1858	1883	——	1920	1945
V	1721	1746	1771	1796	1817	——	1859	——	——	1921	1946
W	1722	1747	1772	——	——	——	1860	——	——	1922	1947
X	1723	1748	1773	——	——	——	1861	——	——	1923	1948
Y	1724	1749	1774	——	——	——	1862	——	——	1924	1949
Z	1725	1750	(1775)	——	——	——	1863	——	——	1925	1950

1. The *Sovereign's Head* mark was added on 1 December 1784 to show the payment of duty and continued until 30 April 1890.

Dublin

Goldsmiths were working in Dublin at least as early as the 13th century. In 1605 the City Council required that each maker strike his mark, and that three others, *Lion*, *Harp*, and *Castle*, be stamped, and in 1637 the goldsmiths were granted a charter. Three cycles of date-letters are found from 1638 into the 18th century, but so little plate survives that the table below does not begin until 1720; the figure of *Hibernia* was added in 1731(†); the duty stamp of the *King's Head* was not punched till 1807(*).

A	1720	1747	1773	1797	1821	1846	1871	1896	1916	1942
B	1721	1748	1774	1798	1822	1847	1872	1897	1917	1943
C	1722	1749	1775	1799	1823	1848	1873	1898	1918	1944
D	1723	1750	1776	1800	1824	1849	1874	1899	1919	1945
E	1724	1751	1777	1801	1825	1850	1875	1900	1920	1946
F	1725	1752	1778	1802	1826	1851	1876	1901	1921	1947
G	1726	1753	1779	1803	1827	1852	1877	1902	1922	1948
H	1727	1754	1780	1804	1828	1853	1878	1903	1923	1949
I	1728	1757	1781	1805	1829	1854	1879	1904	1924	1950
K	1729	1758	1782	1806	1830	1855	1880	1905	1925	1951
L	1730–1 †	1759	1783	1807*	1831	1856	1881	1906	1926	1952
M	1732	1760	1784	1808	1832	1857	1882	1907	1927	1953
N	1733	1761	1785	1809	1833	1858	1883	1908	1928	1954
O	1734	1762	1786	1810	1834	1859	1884	1909	1929	etc.
P	1735	1763	1787	1811	1835	1860	1885	1910	1930–1	
Q	1736	1764	1788	1812	1836	1861	1886	1911	1932	
R	1737	1765	1789	1813	1837	1862	1887	1912	1933	
S	1738	1766	1790	1814	1838	1863	1888	1913	1934	
T	1739	1767	1791	1815	1839	1864	1889	1914	1935	
U	1740	1768	1792	1816	1840	1865	1890¹	1915	1936	
V	——	——	——		1841	1866	1891	——	1937	
W	1741–2	1769	1793	1817	1842	1867	1892	——	1938	
X	1743–4	1770	1794	1818	1843	1868	1893	——	1939	
Y	1745	1771	1795	1819	1844	1869	1894	——	1940	
Z	1746	1772	1796	1820	1845	1870	1895	——	1941	

1. *Sovereign's Head* discontinued.

Edinburgh

The goldsmiths of Edinburgh were associated with the other hammermen there and their records date from 1525. In 1457 a deacon and other officers were appointed by statute and the *deacon's mark* and the *maker's mark* had to be stamped. The town mark, a *Triple-towered Castle*, was added in 1485. In 1681 a variable *date-letter*, changed in September, was adopted and the *Deacon's mark* was replaced by the *Assay-master's mark*; in 1759 this last was replaced by the *Thistle*.

A	1681	1705	1730	1755	1780	1806	1832	1857	1882	1906	1931
B	1682	1706	1731	1756	1781	1807	1833	1858	1883	1907	1932
C	1683	1707	1732	1757	1782	1808	1834	1859	1884	1908	1933
D	1684	1708	1733	1758	1783	1809	1835	1860	1885	1909	1934
E	1685	1709	1734	1759	1784[1]	1810	1836	1861	1886	1910	1935
F	1686	1710	1735	1760	1785	1811	1837	1862	1887	1911	1936
G	1687	1711	1736	1761	1786–7	1812	1838	1863	1888	1912	1937
H	1688	1712	1737	1762	1788	1813	1839	1864	1889	1913	1938
I	1689	1713	1738	1763	1789 }	1814	1840	1865	1890[1]	1914	1939
J	—	—	—	—	1789 {	1815	—	—	—	—	—
K	1690	1714	1739	1764	1790	1816	1841	1866	1891	1915	1940
L	1691	1715	1740	1765	1791	1817	1842	1867	1892	1916	1941
M	1692	1716	1741	1766	1792	1818	1843	1868	1893	1917	1942
N	1693	1717	1742	1767	1793	1819	1844	1869	1894	1918	1943
O	1694	1718	1743	1768	1794	1820	1845	1870	1895	1919	1944
P	1695	1719	1744	1769	1795	1821	1846	1871	1896	1920	1945
Q	1696	1720	1745	1770	1796	1822	1847	1872	1897	1921	1946
R	1697	1721	1746	1771	1797	1823	1848	1873	1898	1922	1947
S	1698	1722	1747	1772	1798	1824	1849	1874	1899	1923	1948
T	1699	1723	1748	1773	1799	1825	1850	1875	1900	1924	1949
U	——	1724	1749	1774	1800	1826	1851	1876	1901	1925	1950
V	1700	1725	1750	1775	1801	1827	1852	1877	1901	1926	1951
W	1701	1726	1751	——	1802	1828	1853	1878	1902	1927	1952
X	1702	1727	1752	1776	1803	1829	1854	1879	1903	1928	1953
Y	1703	1728	1753	1777	1804	1830	1855	1880	1904	1929	1954
Z	1704	1729	1754	1778 1779	1805	1831	1856	1881	1905	1930	1955

1. The *Sovereign's Head* mark was added on 1 December 1784 to show the payment of duty and continued until 30 April 1890.

Exeter

Goldsmiths were working at Exeter from the 14th century onwards, but it was not until the Act of 1701 that eleven of the small number of goldsmiths working there established a sequence of date-letters. The amount of plate produced declined in the 19th century and little was assayed after 1850. The office was closed in 1883. The *Leopard's Head* was not used after 1777(*).

	A	B	C	D	E	F	G	H	I
A	1701	1725	1749	1773	1797	1817	1837	1857	1877
B	1702	1726	1750	1774	1798	1818	1838	1858	1878
C	1703	1727	1751	1775	1799	1819	1839	1859	1879
D	1704	1728	1752	1776	1800	1820	1840	1860	1880
E	1705	1729	1753	1777*	1801	1821	1841	1861	1881
F	1706	1730	1754	1778	1802	1822	1842	1862	1882
G	1707	1731	1755	1779	1803	1823	1843	1863	
H	1708	1732	1756	1780	1804	1824	1844	1864	
I	1709	1733	1757	1781–2	1805	1825	1845	1865	
K	1710	1734	1758	1783	1806	1826	1846	1866	
L	1711	1735	1759	1784[1]	1807	1827	1847	1867	
M	1712	1736	1760	1785	1808	1828	1848	1868	
N	1713	1737	1761	1786	1809	1829	1849	1869	
O	1714	1738	1762	1787	1810	1830	1850	1870	
P	1715	1739	1763	1788	1811	1831	1851	1871	
Q	1716	1740	1764	1789	1812	1832	1852	1872	
R	1717	1741	1765	1790	1813	1833	1853	1873	
S	1718	1742	1766	1791	1814	1834	1854	1874	
T	1719	1743	1767	1792	1815	1835	1855	1875	
U	——	1744	1768	1793	1816	1836	1856	1876	
V	1720	——	——	——	——	——	——	——	
W	1721	1745	1769	1794	——	——	——	——	
X	1722	1746	1770	1795	——	——	——	——	
Y	1723	1747	1771	1796	——	——	——	——	
Z	1724	1748	1772	——	——	——	——	——	

1. The *Sovereign's Head* mark was added on 1 December 1784 to show the payment of duty and continued until 30 April 1890.

Glasgow

The Glasgow goldsmiths were incorporated with other metalworkers there as early as 1536, and a minute-book covering the period 1616–1717 survives. Although a cycle of date-letters has been tentatively traced from 1681 to 1705, when the *Fish, Tree, and Bell* mark (from the burgh arms) was used, it was not until as late as the Act of 1819 that the Glasgow Goldsmiths' Company was constituted a body corporate and the *Lion Rampant* mark (from the Royal Standard of Scotland) was introduced. A regular sequence of date-letters began in that year and the sixth cycle of twenty-six letters is now in progress.

A	1819[1]	1845	1871	1897	1923	1949
B	1820	1846	1872	1898	1924	1950
C	1821	1847	1873	1899	1925	1951
D	1822	1848	1874	1900	1926	1952
E	1823	1849	1875	1901	1927	1953
F	1824	1850	1876	1902	1928	1954
G	1825	1851	1877	1903	1929	1955
H	1826	1852	1878	1904	1930	etc.
I	1827	1853	1879	1905	1931	
J	1828	1854	1880	1906	1932	
K	1829	1855	1881	1907	1933	
L	1830	1856	1882	1908	1934	
M	1831	1857	1883	1909	1935	
N	1832	1858	1884	1910	1936	
O	1833	1859	1885	1911	1937	
P	1834	1860	1886	1912	1938	
Q	1835	1861	1887	1913	1939	
R	1836	1862	1888	1914	1940	
S	1837	1863	1889	1915	1941	
T	1838	1864	1890[2]	1916	1942	
U	1839	1865	1891	1917	1943	
V	1840	1866	1892	1918	1944	
W	1841	1867	1893	1919	1945	
X	1842	1868	1894	1920	1946	
Y	1843	1869	1895	1921	1947	
Z	1844	1870	1896	1922	1948	

1. The *Sovereign's Head* indicates payment of duty.
2. The *Sovereign's Head* was discontinued in this year.

Newcastle

Goldsmiths were working at Newcastle at least from the middle of the 13th century, although no extant plate made there seems to date from before the middle of the 17th century, when the mark of the *Three Castles* stood alone with that of the maker. The Newcastle Assay Office was re-established in 1702, with an erratic cycle in gothic capitals, and closed in 1884.

A	1721	1740	1759	1791	1815	1839	1864
B	1722	1741	1760–8	1792	1816	1840	1865
C	1723	1742	1769	1793	1817	1841	1866
D	1724	1743	1770	1794	1818	1842	1867
E	1725	1744	1771	1795	1819	1843	1868
F	1726	1745	1772	1796	1820	1844	1869
G	1727	1746	1773	1797	1821	1845	1870
H	1728	1747	1774	1798	1822	1846	1871
I	1729	1748	1775	1799	1823	1847	1872
J	—	—	—		—	1848	—
K	1730	1749	1776	1800	1824	1849	1873
L	1731	1750	1777	1801	1825	1850	1874
M	1732	1751	1778	1802	1826	1851	1875
N	1733	1752	1779	1803	1827	1852	1876
O	1734	1753	1780	1804	1828	1853	1877
P	1735	1754	1781	1805	1829	1854	1878
Q	1736	1755	1782	1806	1830	1855	1879
R	1737	1756	1783	1807	1831	1856	1880
S	1738	1757	1784[1]	1808	1832	1857	1881
T	1739	(1758)	1785	1809	1833	1858	1882
U	—	—	1786	1810	1834	1859	1883
W	—	—	1787	1811	1835	1860	
X	—	—	1788	1812	1836	1861	
Y	—	—	1789	1813	1837	1862	
Z	—	—	1790	1814	1838	1863	

1. The *Sovereign's Head* mark was added on 1 December 1784 to show the payment of duty and continued until 30 April 1890.

Sheffield

The assay office was instituted at the same time as that at Birmingham, with the *Crown* as its town mark. The first two cycles are complicated because the letters are jumbled and not in sequence.

A	1779	1806	1824	1844	1868	1893	1918	1943
B	1783	1805	1825	1845	1869	1894	1919	1944
C	1780	1811	1826	1846	1870	1895	1920	1945
D	1781	1812	1827	1847	1871	1896	1921	1946
E	1773	1799	1828	1848	1872	1897	1922	1947
F	1774	1803	1829	1849	1873	1898	1923	1948
G	1782	1804	1830	1850	1874	1899	1924	1949
H	1777	1801	1831	1851	1875	1900	1925	1950
I	1784[1]	1818	——	1852	——	1901	1926	1951
J	——	——	——	——	1876	——	——	1952
K	1786	1809	1832	1853	1877	1902	1927	1953
L	1790	1810	1833	1854	1878	1903	1928	1954
M	1789–94	1802	1834	1855	1879	1904	1929	etc.
N	1775	1800	——	1856	1880	1905	1930	
O	1793	1815	——	1857	1881	1906	1931	
P	1791	1808	1835	1858	1882	1907	1932	
Q	1795	1820	1836	——	1883	1908	1933	
R	1776	1813	1837	1859	1884	1909	1934	
S	1778	1807	1838	1860	1885	1910	1935	
T	1787	1816	1839	1861	1886	1911	1936	
U	1792	1823	1840	1862	1887	1912	1937	
V	1798	1819	1841	1863	1888	1913	1938	
W	1788	1814	——	1864	1889	1914	1939	
X	1797	1817	1842	1865	1890[1]	1915	1940	
Y	1785	1821	——	1866	1891	1916	1941	
Z	1796	1822	1843	1867	1892	1917	1942	

1. The *Sovereign's Head* mark was added on 1 December 1784 to show the payment of duty and continued until 30 April 1890.

York

Being the second city in England during the Middle Ages, York had a mark as early as 1411 and a cycle of date-letters is thought to have begun in 1559 with the town mark—*'the halfe leopard head and half flowre-de-luyce'*; the former half may have been a half *rose* crowned from 1632–1698, but there seems to be no record of a change until the re-establishment of the office in 1700, when the *Cross charged with five Lions passant* (from the city arms) was introduced, with the *Leopard's Head erased* and *Britannia*, and a new but short-lived cycle. After an interval of seventy-three years another incomplete cycle has been noted, followed by two cycles, each of twenty-five letters, omitting *J*, and part of a third which brought the series to an end when the office was closed in 1857.

A	(1559)	1583	1607	1631	1657	1682	1700	(1776)	1787	1812	1837
B	(1560)	1584	1608	1632	1658	1683	1701	(1777)	1788	1813	1838
C	(1561)	(1585)	1609	1633	1659	1684	1702	1778	1789	1814	1839
D	(1562)	(1586)	1610	1634	1660	1685	1703	1779	1790	1815	1840
E	(1563)	1587	1611	1635	1661	1686	(1704)	1780	1791	1816	1841
F	1564	(1588)	1612	1636	1662	1687	1705	1781	1792	1817	1842
G	1565	(1589)	1613	1637	1663	1688	1706	1782	1793	1818	1843
H	1566	1590	1614	1638	1664	1689	——	1783	1794	1819	1844
I	(1567)	(1591)	1615	1639	1665	1690	——	——	1795	1820	1845
J	——	——	——	(1640)	——	——	——	1784	——	——	——
K	1568	1592	1616	1641	1666	1691	——	1785	1796	1821	1846
L	1569	1593	1617	1642	1667	1692	——	1786	1797	1822	1847
M	1570	1594	1618	1643	1668	1693	——	——	1798	1823	1848
N	(1571)	1595	1619	1644	1669	1694	——	——	1799	1824	1849
O	1572	1596	1620	1645	1670	1695	——	——	1800	1825	1850
P	1573	1597	1621	1646	1671	1696	——	——	1801	1826	1851
Q	1574	1598	1622	1647	1672	1697	——	——	1802	1827	1852
R	1575	1599	1623	1648	1673	1698	——	——	1803	1828	1853
S	1576	(1600)	1624	1649	1674	1699	——	——	1804	1829	1854
T	1577	1601	1625	1650	1675	——	——	——	1805	1830	1855
U	——	——	1626	1651	1676	——	——	——	1806	1831	
V	(1578)	(1602)	——	1652	1677	——	——	——	1807	1832	1856
W	(1579)	(1603)	1627	1653	1678	——	——	——	1808	1833	
X	(1580)	1604	(1628)	1654	1679	——	——	——	1809	1834	
Y	(1581)	(1605)	1629	1655	1680	——	——	——	1810	1835	
Z	1582	(1606)	1630	1656	1681	——	——	——	1811	1836	

CLOCK CHARTS

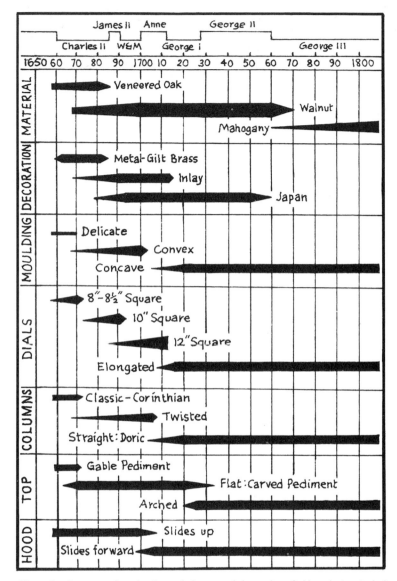

Chart showing approximately the periods covered by various fashions in horological materials, techniques and styles from 1650 to 1800, for domestic clocks.

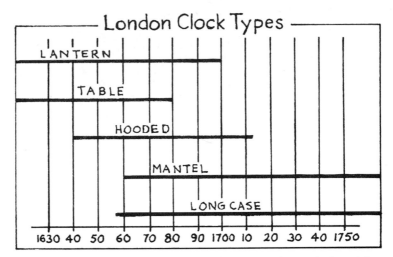

Chart showing the periods and progressions of popular clock types in demand from London makers, *circa* 1630–1750. Provincial styles followed.

ABOVE: The Kakiemon style. A pair of Meissen porcelain bottles decorated with characteristic Japanese subjects. *Left:* Decorated at Meissen. *Right:* Painted in Dutch decorating studios. Both c. 1725. The Dutch also imported Japanese porcelain 'in white' for enamelling.

BELOW: Tureens in the form of gamecocks. Chelsea. Red anchor period. c. **1754.** *Fitzwilliam Museum, Cambridge.*

ABOVE: English dish decorated with trailed and coloured slips, c. 1680, depicting the medieval legend of the Pelican in her Piety, in which she is feeding her young with drops of blood pecked from her breast. *Glaisher Collection, Fitzwilliam Museum, Cambridge.*

BELOW: Moulded dish decorated with mottled coloured glazes of the 'tortoiseshell' type. Whieldon ware. c. 1755. *Glaisher Collection, Fitzwilliam Museum, Cambridge.*

ABOVE: A Chinese saucer-dish decorated with fowls in the *famille rose* palette. The *rose* pigment covers the back, except for the space inside the footring—the so-called 'ruby-back' group. Reign of Yung Ch'eng (1722-1736).

BELOW: Chinese export porcelain. Figures of a Dutch merchant and his wife decorated at Canton. c. 1770. *Mme Espirito Santo Collection, Lisbon.*

SELECT
BIBLIOGRAPHY
AND
READING
LIST

Note: Publishers' names are given for books that were known to be in print and available for purchase when this work went to press. Some of the books for which publishers' names are not given may have been reprinted since then; otherwise they may be consulted in libraries or purchased through sellers of antiquarian and second-hand books.

AMERICAN ANTIQUES
(see also under *Furniture, American*; *Glass, American*, etc.)

GENERAL

Dow, George F.	THE ARTS AND CRAFTS IN NEW ENGLAND, 1704–1755, Topsfield, Mass., 1927.
Davidson, Marshall B.	LIFE IN AMERICA, two vols., Houghton Mifflin, New York, 1951.
Hummel, Charles F.	Samuel Rowland Fisher's Catalogue of English Hardware. WINTERTHUR PORTFOLIO I, Winterthur, Delaware, 1964.
Kimball, Fiske, and Donnell, Edna	'The Creators of the Chippendale Style', Metropolitan MUSEUM STUDIES, New York, 1928–1930.
Larkin, Oliver W.	ART AND LIFE IN AMERICA, Holt, Rinehart & Winston, New York and London, rev. ed., 1960.
Lipman, Jean	AMERICAN FOLK ART IN WOOD, METAL AND STONE, New York, 1948.
Prime, Alfred Coxe	THE ARTS AND CRAFTS IN PHILADELPHIA, MARYLAND, AND SOUTH CAROLINA, vol. I, 1721–1785; vol. II, 1786–1800, Walpole Society, 1932.
Susswein, Rita Gottesman	THE ARTS AND CRAFTS IN NEW YORK, 1726–1776, The New York Historical Society Collections, 1938. THE ARTS AND CRAFTS IN NEW YORK, 1777–1799, The New York Historical Society Collections, 1954.

ART AS INVESTMENT

Baynton-Williams, Roger	INVESTING IN MAPS, Barrie & Rockliff, London, 1969; Clarkson Potter, New York, 1970.
Cumhaill, P. W.	INVESTING IN CLOCKS AND WATCHES, Barrie & Rockliff, London, and Clarkson Potter, New York, 1967.
Delieb, Eric	INVESTING IN SILVER, Barrie & Rockliff, London, and Clarkson Potter, New York, 1967.
Falkiner, Richard	INVESTING IN ANTIQUE JEWELLERY, Barrie & Rockliff, London, and Clarkson Potter, New York, 1968.
Lloyd, Ward	INVESTING IN GEORGIAN GLASS, Barrie & Rockliff, London, 1969; Barnes & Noble, New York, 1970.
Morley-Fletcher, Hugo	INVESTING IN POTTERY AND PORCELAIN, Barrie & Rockliff, London, and Clarkson Potter, New York, 1968.

Rush, Richard	ART AS INVESTMENT, Prentice-Hall, New Jersey and London, 1961. ANTIQUES AS INVESTMENT, Prentice Hall, New Jersey, 1968.
Woodhouse, C. Platten	INVESTMENT IN ANTIQUES AND ART, Bell, London, 1969.

THE ART MARKET

Allen, F. L.	THE GREAT PIERPONT MORGAN, New York, 1949.
Beard, Miriam	A HISTORY OF BUSINESS, New York, 1928.
Chambers, F. P.	A HISTORY OF TASTE, New York, 1932.
Behrman, Samuel N.	DUVEEN, London, 1962; Peter Smith, Massachusetts, n.d.
Carter, A. C. R.	THE YEAR'S ART, 1882–1947, London and New York, published annually.
Christie, Manson & Woods	Annual Review of Sales, London.
Duvaux, Lazare	LIVRE-JOURNAL DE . . ., 1748–1758 (Ed. C. J. Courajod), Paris, 1873.
Graves, Algernon	ART-SALES, London, 1922.
Marillier, H. C.	CHRISTIE'S, 1766–1925, London, 1926.
Reitlinger, Gerald	THE ECONOMICS OF TASTE, two vols., Barrie & Rockliff, London, 1961 and 1964; Holt, Rinehart & Winston, New York, 1964 and 1965.
Rheims, Maurice	LA VIE ÉTRANGE DES OBJETS, Paris, 1959.
Rush, Richard	ART AS INVESTMENT, Prentice-Hall, New Jersey and London, 1961.
Roberts, W. L.	MEMORIALS OF CHRISTIE'S, 1766–1896, two vols., London, 1896.
Saarinen, Aline	THE PROUD POSSESSORS, Random House, New York, 1958.
Savage, George	THE MARKET IN ART, Institute of Economic Affairs, London, 1969.
Sotheby & Co.	Annual Reviews of Sales, London.
Sutton, Denys	CHRISTIE'S SINCE THE WAR, 1945–1958, London, 1959.
Taylor, Francis H.	THE TASTE OF ANGELS, London, 1948; Little Brown, Boston, 1948. PIERPONT MORGAN AS COLLECTOR AND PATRON, 1837–1913, Pierpont Morgan Library, New York, 1957.

ART NOUVEAU

Amaya, Mario	ART NOUVEAU, London, 1966; Dutton, New York, 1966.
Battersby, Martin	ART NOUVEAU, Hamlyn, London, 1969. THE WORLD OF ART NOUVEAU, Arlington, London, 1968; Funk & Wagnalls, New York, 1969.
Madsen, Stephen Tschudi	SOURCES OF ART NOUVEAU, Wittenborn, New York, 1957. ART NOUVEAU, Weidenfeld, London, and McGraw Hill, New York, 1967.

| Musée National d'Art Moderne | LES SOURCES DU XXe SIÈCLE (Exhibition Catalogue: Les Arts en Europe de 1884 à 1914), Paris, 1960. |

Musée National d'Art
Moderne

LES SOURCES DU XXe SIÈCLE (Exhibition Catalogue: Les Arts en Europe de 1884 à 1914), Paris, 1960.

Rheims, M.

THE AGE OF ART NOUVEAU, Thames & Hudson, London, and Abrams, New York, 1966.

Schmützler, R.

ART NOUVEAU, London, 1964; Abrams, New York, 1964.

Selz, P., and Constantine, M. (Eds.)

ART NOUVEAU, London and New York, 1960.

BRONZES

Barth, Hans-Martin

DIE SEBALDUSKIRCHE IN NURNBERG, Königstein-im-Taunus, n.d.

Benezit, E.

DICTIONNAIRE CRITIQUE ET DOCUMENTAIRE DES PEINTRES, SCULPTEURS, etc., Paris, 1911–1923.

Bode, Wilhelm von

FLORENTINE SCULPTORS OF THE RENAISSANCE, London, 1908; New York, 1909.
ITALIAN BRONZE STATUETTES OF THE RENAISSANCE, London, 1907–1912.

Cellini, Benvenuto

TRATTATI DELL'ORIFICERIA E DELLA SCULTURA (English translation by C. R. Ashbee, 1898).
MEMOIRS (various editions).
TREATISES ON GOLDSMITHING AND SCULPTURE (English translation by C. R. Ashbee, 1898), Dover, New York, 1966.

Düsseldorf Kunstmuseum

Exhibition Catalogue, DEUTSCHE BRONZEN DES MITTELALTERS UND DER RENAISSANCE, 1960.

Fortnum, C. Drury

BRONZES, London, 1877.

Guiffrey, J. J.

LES CAFFIÉRE, SCULPTEURS ET FONDEURS-CISÉLEURS, Paris, 1877.

Hill, A. A.

CORPUS OF ITALIAN MEDALS OF THE RENAISSANCE BEFORE CELLINI, 2 vols., Oxford, 1930.

Hill, G. F.

RENAISSANCE MEDALS (rev. by Graham Pollard), Phaidon, London and New York, 1967.

Mackay, J.

THE ANIMALIERS, Barrie & Jenkins, London, 1971.

Niclausse, J.

THOMIRE, FONDEUR-CISÉLEUR, Paris, 1947.

Oman, Charles

THE GLOUCESTER CANDLESTICK, Victoria and Albert Museum, London, 1958.

Planiscig, Leo

PICCOLI BRONZI ITALIANI DEL RINASCIMENTO, Milan, 1930.
DIE BRONZE PLASTIKEN, Kunsthistorisches Museum, Vienna, 1924.

Pope-Hennessy, John

ITALIAN RENAISSANCE SCULPTURE, London and New York, 1958.
ITALIAN HIGH-RENAISSANCE AND BAROQUE SCULPTURE, three vols., Phaidon, London and New York, 1963.
RENAISSANCE BRONZES, Phaidon, London and New York, 1965.

Radcliffe, A.

EUROPEAN BRONZE STATUETTES, Michael Joseph, London, 1966.

Rich, J. C.

MATERIALS AND METHODS OF SCULPTURE, Oxford University Press, New York and Oxford, 1947.

Sauerlander, W.	DIE SKULPTUR DES MITTELALTERS, Berlin, 1963.
Savage, George	CONCISE HISTORY OF BRONZES, Thames & Hudson, London, and Praeger, New York, 1968.
Tavernor-Parry, S.	DINANDERIE, London, 1910.
Vasari, Giorgio	LIVES OF THE PAINTERS, SCULPTORS AND ARCHITECTS (various editions).
Victoria and Albert Museum	Catalogue of an Exhibition of Italian Bronzes, London, 1961. Catalogue of Italian Plaquettes, E. Maclaglan, London, 1924.
Wallace Collection	Catalogue of Sculpture, J. G. Mann, London, 1931.
Young, W. A.	OLD ENGLISH PATTERN-BOOKS OF THE METAL TRADES, Victoria and Albert Museum, London, 1917.

CHALKWARE

McClinton, K. M.	A HANDBOOK OF POPULAR ANTIQUES, New York, 1946.

CLOCKS AND WATCHES, ETC.

ENGLISH AND AMERICAN

Baillie, G. H.	WATCHES: THEIR HISTORY, DECORATION AND MECHANISM, London, 1929. WATCHMAKERS AND CLOCKMAKERS OF THE WORLD, N.A.G. Press, London, 1951.
Britten, F. H.	OLD CLOCKS AND WATCHES AND THEIR MAKERS (various editions), London.
Bruton, E.	CLOCKS AND WATCHES, 1400–1900, Praeger, New York, and Barker, London, 1967.
Cescinsky, H., and Webster, M.	ENGLISH DOMESTIC CLOCKS, London, 1913; New York, 1914. OLD ENGLISH MASTER CLOCKMAKERS AND THEIR CLOCKS, London, 1938.
Clutton, C., and Daniels, G.	WATCHES, Batsford, London, and Viking, New York, 1965.
Cumhaiil, P. W.	INVESTING IN CLOCKS AND WATCHES, Barrie & Rockliff, London, and Clarkson Potter, New York, 1967.
Cuss, T. P. C.	THE BOOK OF WATCHES, Country Life, London, 1967.
Daniels, George	ENGLISH AND AMERICAN WATCHES, Abelard-Schuman, London and New York, 1967.
Drepperd, Carl W.	AMERICAN CLOCKS AND CLOCKMAKERS, Branford, Massachusetts, 1958.
Hayward, J. F.	WATCHES, ENGLISH, Victoria and Albert Museum, H.M.S.O.
Hoopes, P.	CONNECTICUT CLOCKMAKERS OF THE EIGHTEENTH CENTURY, Hartford, 1930.

Hume, A. W. J. G.-O.	COLLECTING MUSICAL BOXES, Allen & Unwin, London, and Crown Publishers, New York, 1967.
Jerome, C.	HISTORY OF THE AMERICAN CLOCK BUSINESS FOR THE LAST SIXTY YEARS, New Haven, Conn., 1860.
Palmer, B.	BOOK OF AMERICAN CLOCKS, Macmillan, New York and London, 1950. TREASURY OF AMERICAN CLOCKS, Macmillan, New York and London, 1967.
Symonds, R. W.	MASTERPIECES OF ENGLISH FURNITURE AND CLOCKS, London, 1940. A HISTORY OF ENGLISH CLOCKS, London, 1947. THOMAS TOMPION, Spring Books, London, reprint, 1969.
Tyler, E. J.	EUROPEAN CLOCKS, Ward, Lock, London, 1969.
Ullyett, K. R.	BRITISH CLOCKS AND CLOCKMAKERS, London, 1947. IN QUEST OF CLOCKS, Dover, New York, 1950; Spring Books, London, reprint, 1969.
Webb, Graham	THE CYLINDER MUSICAL-BOX HANDBOOK, Faber, London, 1968.

AUSTRIAN AND GERMAN

Jordan, E. V. B., and Bertele, H. von	BOOK OF OLD CLOCKS AND WATCHES (English translation by Alan Lloyd), Allen & Unwin, London, and Crown Publishers, New York, 1964.

DUTCH

Hanna, W. J.	KLOKKEN, van Dushoek, Bussum, 1961. FRIESA KLOKKEN, van Dushoek, Bussum, 1964.

FRENCH

Gélis	L'HORLOGERIE ANCIENNE, Paris, n.d.
Lengelle, H.	LA PENDULE FRANÇAISE, Paris, 1963.

ITALIAN

Morpurgo, E.	DIZIONARIO DEGLI OROLOIAI, 1950.

ORIENTAL

Mody, N. H. N.	JAPANESE CLOCKS, Kegan Paul, London, and Charles Tuttle, Rutland, Vt, 1968.
Chapuis, A.	LA MONTRE CHINOISE, Paris, 1919.

SWISS

Chapuis, A., and Jaquet, E.	TECHNIQUE AND HISTORY OF THE SWISS WATCH, Boston Book, Mass., 1956

DESIGN BOOKS

The following is a select list of key design books which have influenced international architecture and furniture design, especially in England and America.

MID-1600s

Stalker, J., and Parker, G.	TREATISE ON JAPANNING AND VARNISHING, 1688. Reprint, Transatlantic, Levittown, New York, and Tiranti, London.

1700–1755

Chippendale, Thomas	GENTLEMAN AND CABINET-MAKER'S DIRECTOR, 1st ed. 1754, 2nd ed. 1755, 3rd ed. 1762. Reprint, Dover, New York, and Constable, London, 3rd ed.
Edwards and Darly	NEW BOOK OF CHINESE DESIGNS, 1754.
Gibbs, James	A BOOK OF ARCHITECTURE, 1728. Reprint, Blom, Bronx, New York.
Halfpenny, William	NEW DESIGNS FOR CHINESE TEMPLES, 1750.
Hogarth, William	ANALYSIS OF BEAUTY, 1753.
Langley, Batty and Thomas	CITY AND COUNTRY BUILDER'S AND WORKMAN'S TREASURY OF DESIGNS, 1740.
Lock and Copland	NEW BOOK OF ORNAMENTS, 1752.
Lock, Matthias	NEW DRAWING BOOK OF ORNAMENTS, 1740.

1755–1800

Adam, Robert	RUINS OF SPALATRO, 1764.
Adam, Robert and James	WORKS IN ARCHITECTURE, issued in sets, 1773–1778. Second vol. 1779. Third vol. 1822. Reprint, Blom, Bronx, New York, three vols.

CABINET-MAKER'S LONDON BOOK OF PRICES, 1788, with plates by Thomas Shearer, Hepplewhite and others.

Chambers, Sir William	DESIGNS OF CHINESE BUILDINGS . . ., 1757. Reprint, Blom, Bronx, New York.
Halfpenny, William and John	THE MODERN BUILDER'S ASSISTANT, 1757.
Hepplewhite, George	CABINET-MAKER AND UPHOLSTERER'S GUIDE, 1788. Reprint, Dover, New York, and Constable, London.
Ince and Mayhew	UNIVERSAL SYSTEM OF HOUSEHOLD FURNITURE, 1759–1762. Reprint, Transatlantic, Levittown, New York, and Tiranti, London.
Manwaring, Robert	CABINET AND CHAIR-MAKER'S REAL FRIEND AND COMPANION, 1765. Reprint, Transatlantic, Levittown, New York, and Tiranti, London.
Piranesi	DIVERSE MANIERE D'ADORNARE I CAMINI, 1769, showing Etruscan, Egyptian, Greek, and Roman ornament. Immediately translated into French and English.
Sheraton, Thomas	CABINET-MAKER AND UPHOLSTERER'S DRAWING-BOOK, 1791–1794. Reprint, Praeger, New York and London.

Stuart and Revett	ANTIQUITIES OF ATHENS, 1762.
Swan, Abraham	DESIGNS IN ARCHITECTURE, 1757.
Tatham, Charles	ETCHINGS OF ANCIENT ORNAMENTAL ARCHITECTURE, 1799.
Ware, Isaac	COMPLETE BODY OF ARCHITECTURE, 2nd ed., 1756.
Winckelmann, Johann	HISTORY OF THE ARTS OF ANTIQUITY, 1764. Reprint, Ungar, New York, 1968. Translation by A. Gode. UNKNOWN MONUMENTS OF ANTIQUITY, 1767.

1800–1830

Ackermann, Rudolph	REPOSITORY OF THE ARTS, 1809–1829.
Hope, Thomas	HOUSEHOLD FURNITURE AND INTERIOR DECORATION, 1807. Reprint, Tiranti, London, 1970.

LONDON CHAIR-MAKERS' AND CARVERS' BOOK OF PRICES, 1808.

Mesangere, Pierre la	MEUBLES ET OBJETS DE GOÛT, 1802–1830.
Moses, Henry	DESIGNS OF MODERN COSTUME, 1823, with drawings of furniture in the best style of Thomas Hope.
Nicholson, Peter, and Michael Angelo	THE PRACTICAL CABINET-MAKER, UPHOLSTERER AND COMPLETE DECORATOR, 1828.
Percier and Fontaine	RECUEIL DE DÉCORATIONS INTÉRIEURES, 1st ed., 1801.
Sheraton, Thomas	CABINET DICTIONARY, 1803. Reprint, Praeger, New York and London, n.d. (recent).
Smith, George	COLLECTION OF DESIGNS FOR HOUSEHOLD FURNITURE, 1808. Reprint, Praeger, New York and London. CABINET-MAKER'S AND UPHOLSTERER'S GUIDE, DRAWING BOOK AND REPOSITORY, 1826–1828. Reprint, Praeger, New York and London.
Vivant-Denon, Baron	VOYAGE DANS LA BASSE ET HAUTE ÉGYPTE, 1802.

1830–1870

Eastlake, Charles	HINTS ON HOUSEHOLD TASTE, 1868. Reprint, Dover, New York, and Constable, London, 4th ed.
Fildes, George	ELIZABETHAN FURNITURE, 1844.
Jones, Owen	PLANS . . . OF THE ALHAMBRA, 1842.
King, Thomas	CABINET-MAKER'S SKETCHBOOK, c. 1835.
Lawford, Henry	CABINET OF PRACTICAL? USEFUL AND DECORATIVE FURNITURE DESIGNS? 1855.
Liénard	SPECIMENS DE LA DÉCORATION . . . AU XIXe SIÈCLE, Liège, 1866.
Loudon, J. C.	ENCYCLOPAEDIA OF COTTAGE, FARM AND VILLA ARCHITECTURE, 1833.
Pugin, A. W. N.	GOTHIC FURNITURE IN THE STYLE OF THE FIFTEENTH CENTURY, 1835.

Talbert, Bruce	GOTHIC FORMS APPLIED TO FURNITURE, 1867.
Whitaker, Henry	PRACTICAL CABINET-MAKER, 1847.
Wood, Henry	A SERIES OF DESIGNS OF FURNITURE DECORATION, 1845.
Wyatt, Digby	REPORT OF THE FURNITURE AT THE PARIS EXHIBITION OF 1855, 1856.

FORGERIES

Bonaffé, E.	COMMERCE DE LA CURIOSITÉ, Paris, 1901.
Cescinsky, Herbert	THE GENTLE ART OF FAKING FURNITURE, London, 1913. Reprint, Dover, New York, 1967.
Demeure, F.	L'IMPOSTURES DE L'ART, Paris, 1951.
Eudel, Paul	TRUCS ET TRUQUEURS, Paris, 1907.
Mailfert, André	AU PAYS DES ANTIQUAIRES, Flammarion, Paris, 1935.
Savage, George	FORGERIES, FAKES AND REPRODUCTIONS, Barrie & Rockliff, London, 1963; Praeger, New York, 1964.
Symonds, R. W.	THE PRESENT STATE OF OLD ENGLISH FURNITURE, London and New York, 1921.

FURNITURE
(see also under *Design Books*)

Many of the books listed under other headings contain information about forgeries.

GENERAL

Bode, W. von, and Herrick, Mary E.	ITALIAN RENAISSANCE FURNITURE, New York, 1921.

CATALOGUS VAN MEUBELEN EN BETIMMERINGEN HET RIJKSMUSEUM, Amsterdam, 1962.

Cescinsky, H.	CHINESE FURNITURE, London, 1962.
Edlin, H. L.	WHAT WOOD IS THAT? (with 40 wood samples), Thames & Hudson, London, and Viking, New York, 1969.
Falke, Otto von	DEUTSCHE MÖBEL: DES MITTELALTERS UND DER RENAISSANCE, Stuttgart, 1929.
Fitzgerald, C. P.	BARBARIAN BEDS: THE HISTORY OF THE CHAIR IN CHINA, Canberra and London, 1965.
Hayward, H. (Ed.)	WORLD FURNITURE: A PICTORIAL HISTORY, Hamlyn, London, and McGraw, New York, 1965.
Hinckley, F. Lewis	DIRECTORY OF THE HISTORIC CABINET WOODS, Crown Publishers, New York, 1960.

Holzhausen, W.	LACKKUNST IN EUROPA, Cologne, 1958.
Jonge, Dr C. H.	HOLLÄNDISCHE MÖBEL UND RAUMKUNST, 1650–1780, 's Gravenhage, 1922.
Kates, George	CHINESE HOUSEHOLD FURNITURE, Dover, New York, and Constable, London, 1962.
McClelland, N.	DUNCAN PHYFE AND THE ENGLISH REGENCY, New York, 1939.
Moraizoni, Giuseppe	IL MOBILIO ITALIANO, Florence, 1940. NEO-CLASSICO ITALIANO, Milan, 1955. IL MOBILE VENEZIANO, Milan, 1958.
Philippe, J. F. E.	LE MOBILIER LIÉGOIS: MOYEN ÂGE–XIXe SIÈCLE, Liège, 1962.
Schmitz, H. (Ed.)	DEUTSCHE MOBEL DAS BAROK UND ROKOKO, Stuttgart, 1923.
Schötmuller, Frida	FURNITURE AND INTERIOR DECORATION OF THE ITALIAN RENAISSANCE (in English), Stuttgart, 1929.
Shapland, H. P.	PRACTICAL DECORATION OF FURNITURE, three vols., London, 1927.
Singleton, E.	DUTCH AND FLEMISH FURNITURE, London, 1907.

AMERICAN

Andrews, E. D., and F.	SHAKER FURNITURE, Dover, New York, and Constable, London, 1950.
Bjerkoe, E. H.	THE CABINETMAKERS OF AMERICA, Garden City, New York, 1957.
Burroughs, P. H.	SOUTHERN ANTIQUES, Richmond, Va, 1931.
Burton, E. M.	CHARLESTON FURNITURE, 1700–1825, Charleston, Va, 1955.
Comstock, Helen	AMERICAN FURNITURE: A COMPLETE GUIDE TO SEVENTEENTH, EIGHTEENTH AND EARLY NINETEENTH CENTURY STYLES, Viking, New York, 1962.
Cornelius, C. O.	MASTERPIECES OF DUNCAN PHYFE, New York, 1922.
Downs, J.	AMERICAN FURNITURE: QUEEN ANNE AND CHIPPENDALE PERIODS, Collier-Macmillan, London, reprint, 1962; Viking, New York, rev. ed., 1967.
Hinckley, F. L.	DIRECTORY OF ANTIQUE FURNITURE, New York, 1953.
Kettell, R. H.	PINE FURNITURE OF EARLY NEW ENGLAND, Dover, New York, and Constable, London, 1954.
Lockwood, L. V.	COLONIAL FURNITURE IN AMERICA, New York, 1926.
Miller, E. G.	AMERICAN ANTIQUE FURNITURE, Dover, New York, and Constable, London, new ed., 1966.
Montgomery, C. F.	AMERICAN FURNITURE OF THE FEDERAL PERIOD (1788–1825), Viking, New York, 1966; Thames & Hudson, London, 1967.
Nagel, Charles	AMERICAN FURNITURE, 1650–1850, New York, 1949.

Nutting, Wallace	A WINDSOR [Chair] HANDBOOK, privately printed, 1917.
Ormsbee, T. H.	EARLY AMERICAN FURNITURE-MAKERS, New York, 1935 THE STORY OF AMERICAN FURNITURE, New York, 1935.
Otto, C. J.	AMERICAN FURNITURE OF THE NINETEENTH CENTURY, Viking, New York, 1965.

ENGLISH

Allsopp, Bruce	DECORATION AND FURNITURE, Pitman, London, 1953; New York, 1953.
Aslin, E.	NINETEENTH CENTURY ENGLISH FURNITURE, Faber, London, 1962; Taplinger, New York, 1966.
Bell, J. Munro	CHIPPENDALE, SHERATON AND HEPPLEWHITE FURNITURE DESIGNS, London, 1900 and 1922.
Brackett, Oliver	ENCYCLOPAEDIA OF ENGLISH FURNITURE, London, 1927. ENGLISH FURNITURE ILLUSTRATED, London and New York, rev. ed., 1950.
Cescinsky, H.	ENGLISH FURNITURE OF THE EIGHTEENTH CENTURY, London, 1907.
Fastnedge, Ralph	ENGLISH FURNITURE STYLES FROM 1500 TO 1830, Penguin Books and Jenkins, London, 1962.
Harris, E.	THE FURNITURE OF ROBERT ADAM, Tiranti, London, reprint, 1963.
Hayward, H.	THOMAS JOHNSON AND ENGLISH ROCOCO, Tiranti, London, reprint, 1964; Transatlantic, Levittown, New York, n.d.

HEPPLEWHITE'S CABINET-MAKER AND UPHOLSTERER'S GUIDE, 1788, New York and London, reprint, 1963.

Jourdain, M.	REGENCY FURNITURE, New York, rev. ed., 1948; Country Life, London, rev. ed., 1949. WORK OF WILLIAM KENT, Country Life, London, 1948; New York, 1949. ENGLISH DECORATION AND FURNITURE OF THE EARLY RENAISSANCE, 1500–1650, Batsford, London, 1924; New York, 1924.
Jourdain, M., and Edwards, R.	GEORGIAN CABINET MAKERS, New York, 1945; Country Life, London, 1948.
MacQuoid, P.	HISTORY OF ENGLISH FURNITURE, London, 1938; Dover, New York, 1968.
MacQuoid, P., and Edwards, R.	DICTIONARY OF ENGLISH FURNITURE FROM THE MIDDLE AGES TO THE LATE GEORGIAN PERIOD, three vols., London, 2nd rev. ed., 1954.
Musgrave, C.	REGENCY FURNITURE, 1800–1830, Faber, London, rev. ed., 1970.
Pugin, A. W.	GOTHIC FURNITURE IN THE STYLE OF THE FIFTEENTH CENTURY, London, 1835.
Read, Brian	REGENCY ANTIQUES, London, 1953.
Roe, F. G.	ENGLISH COTTAGE FURNITURE, London and New York, 1950.

Symonds, R.	FURNITURE-MAKING IN SEVENTEENTH AND EIGHTEENTH CENTURY ENGLAND, Connoisseur, London, 1955. VENEERED WALNUT FURNITURE, Tiranti, London, reprint, 1959; Trans-atlantic, Levittown, New York, 1948. MASTERPIECES OF ENGLISH FURNITURE AND CLOCKS, London, 1940. PRESENT STATE OF OLD ENGLISH FURNITURE, London and New York, 1921. OLD ENGLISH WALNUT AND LACQUER FURNITURE, London and New York, 1923.
Truman, Nevil	HISTORIC FURNISHINGS, London and New York, 1950.
Wenham, Edward	OLD FURNITURE FOR MODERN ROOMS, London, 1939; New York, 1940.
Wills, Geoffrey	ENGLISH LOOKING-GLASSES, Country Life, London, 1965; American Book Co., New York, 1966.

FRENCH

Bemrose, W.	MANUAL OF BUHL [sic] WORK AND MARQUETRY, Bemrose, London, 1872.
Boulanger, G.	L'ART DE RECONNAÎTRE DES MEUBLES RÉGIONAUX, Paris, 1966.
Courajod, L. (Ed.)	LIVRE–JOURNAL DE LAZARE DUVAUX, two vols., Paris, 1873.
Devinoy, P., and Janneau, G.	LE MEUBLE LÉGER EN FRANCE, Hartmann, Paris, 1952.
Dilke, Lady	FRENCH FURNITURE AND DECORATION OF THE EIGHTEENTH CENTURY, London, 1901.
Havard, Henri	DICTIONNAIRE DE L'AMEUBLEMENT, four vols., Paris, 1889.
Liénard	SPECIMENS DE LA DÉCORATION ET DE L'ORNAMENTATION AU XIXᵉ SIÈCLE, Liège, 1866.
Ricci, Seymour de	LOUIS XIV AND REGENCY FURNITURE AND DECORATION, London, 1929.
Roubo	L'ART DU MENUISIER, Paris, 1774.
Salverte, Comte François de	LES ÉBÉNISTES DU XVIIIᵉ SIÈCLE, various editions, Paris, 1st ed., 1922.
Savage, George	FRENCH DECORATIVE ART, Allen Lane, The Penguin Press, London, and Praeger, New York, 1969.
Verlet, P.	LES MEUBLES DU XVIIIᵉ SIÈCLE: VOL. 1 MENUISERIE, VOL. 2 ÉBÉNISTERIE, Presses Universitaire de France, Paris, 1956. FRENCH ROYAL FURNITURE, Barrie & Rockliff, London, and Clarkson Potter, New York, 1963. FRENCH FURNITURE AND INTERIOR DECORATION OF THE EIGHTEENTH CENTURY, Barrie & Rockliff, London, and Charles E. Tuttle, Rutland, Vt, 1967.
Watson, F. J. B.	CATALOGUE OF FURNITURE, Wallace Collection, London, 1956. LOUIS XVI FURNITURE, Tiranti, London, 1960; New York, 1961.

514

GARDENS

Dutton, Ralph	THE ENGLISH GARDEN, Batsford, London, 1937; New York, 1938.
Erdberg, E. von	CHINESE INFLUENCE ON EUROPEAN GARDEN STRUCTURE, Cambridge, Mass., 1936.
Gromort, G.	JARDINS D'ITALIE, Paris, 1922. L'ART DES JARDINS, two vols., Paris, 1934.
Jellicoe, G. A.	BAROQUE GARDENS OF AUSTRIA, Benn, London, 1932.
Jourdain, Margaret	THE WORK OF WILLIAM KENT, Country Life, London, 1948; New York, 1949.
Manwaring, E. W.	ITALIAN LANDSCAPE IN EIGHTEENTH CENTURY ENGLAND, Russell, New York, 1925.
Rémon, Georges	LES JARDINS (DE L'ANTIQUITÉ A NOS JOURS), Flammarion, Paris, n.d.
Repton, H.	LANDSCAPE GARDENING, London, 1803.
Sirén, Osvald	CHINA AND THE GARDENS OF EUROPE IN THE EIGHTEENTH CENTURY, New York, 1950.
Southwark, J. S.	VAUXHALL GARDENS, New York, 1941.
Stroud, Dorothy	'CAPABILITY' BROWN, Country Life, London, 1950; New York, 1951.
Walpole, Horace	Essay on Modern Gardening, Strawberry Hill Press, 1785. Included in the three-volume edition of ANECDOTES OF PAINTING of 1857, with additional material by Dallaway.

GLASS

GENERAL

Bergstrom, E.	OLD GLASS PAPERWEIGHTS, Crown, New York, 1947; London, 1948.
Buckley, Wilfrid	THE ART OF GLASS, London, 1939. EUROPEAN GLASS, London, 1926.
Davies, D. C., and Middlemas, K.	COLOURED GLASS, Jenkins, London, and Clarkson Potter, New York, 1969.
Dillon, E.	GLASS, London, 1907.
Elville, E.	DICTIONARY OF GLASS, Country Life, London, 1961.
Garnier, E.	HISTOIRE DE LA VERRERIE, Tours, 1886.
Haynes, E. B.	GLASS THROUGH THE AGES, Penguin Books, Harmondsworth, 1948.
Janneau, G.	MODERN GLASS, London and New York, 1931.
Jiřík, F. X.	GUIDE TO THE GLASS COLLECTION IN THE MUSEUM OF INDUSTRIAL ART OF THE PRAGUE CHAMBER OF COMMERCE, Prague, 1934.

Metropolitan Museum of Art	Catalogue of an exhibition of glass, New York, 1936.
Middlemas, K.	CONTINENTAL COLOURED GLASS, Barrie & Jenkins, London, and Doubleday, New York, 1970.
Nesbitt, A.	GLASS, South Kensington Museum Handbook, London, 1878.
Pazaurek, G.	GLÄSER DER EMPIRE- UND BIEDERMEIERZEIT, Leipzig, 1923.
Rackham, B.	KEY TO POTTERY AND GLASS, London, 1940; Brooklyn, New York, 1941.
Rogers, F., and Beard, A.	5000 YEARS OF GLASS, New York, 1948.
Savage, George	THE ART OF GLASS, Weidenfeld & Nicolson, London, 1965; New York, 1965.
Schmidt, R.	DAS GLAS, Berlin Museum Handbook, Berlin and Leipzig, 1922.
Wilkinson, R.	HALLMARKS OF ANTIQUE GLASS, Madley, London, 1968.

AMERICAN

GLASS FROM THE CORNING MUSEUM OF GLASS, Corning, New York, 1965.

Knittle, R. M.	EARLY AMERICAN GLASS, New York, 1927.
McKearin, G. S., and H.	AMERICAN GLASS, New York, 1941. TWO HUNDRED YEARS OF AMERICAN BLOWN GLASS, Crown, New York, rev. ed., 1966. THE STORY OF AMERICAN HISTORICAL FLASKS, Corning Museum, Corning, N.Y., 1953.

ENGLISH AND IRISH

Bickerton, L. M.	ENGLISH DRINKING GLASSES OF THE EIGHTEENTH CENTURY, Barrie & Jenkins, London, 1971.
Bles, Joseph	RARE ENGLISH GLASSES OF THE SEVENTEENTH AND EIGHTEENTH CENTURY, London, 1925.
Buckley, Francis	A HISTORY OF OLD ENGLISH GLASS, London, 1925.
Davis, D.	ENGLISH AND IRISH ANTIQUE GLASS, Barker, London, and Praeger, New York, 1965.
Francis, G. R.	OLD ENGLISH DRINKING GLASSES, London, 1926.
Hartshorne, Albert	OLD ENGLISH GLASSES, London and New York, 1897.
Honey, W. B.	GLASS. A HANDBOOK AND GUIDE TO THE MUSEUM COLLECTION, Victoria and Albert Museum, London, 1946.
Lloyd, Ward	INVESTING IN GEORGIAN GLASS, Barrie & Rockliff, London, 1969; Barnes & Noble, New York, 1970.
Powell, H. J.	GLASS-MAKING IN ENGLAND, Cambridge University Press, England and New York, 1923.

Thorpe, W. A.	A HISTORY OF ENGLISH AND IRISH GLASS, Black, London, 1929; Boston, 1930. ENGLISH GLASS, Black, London, 1935; Barnes & Noble, New York, 3rd ed., 1961.
Warren, Phelps	IRISH GLASS, Faber, London, 1970.
Winbolt, S. E.	WEALDEN GLASS, Hove, 1933; New York, 1933.
Westropp, M. D.	IRISH GLASS, London, 1920; Philadelphia, 1921.

FRENCH AND BELGIAN

Baar, A.	RETROSPECTIVE DE LA VERRERIE ARTISTIQUE BELGE, Liége, 1930.
Chavance, R.	LA CÉRAMIQUE ET LA VERRERIE, Paris, 1928.
Frémy, E.	HISTOIRE DE LA MANUFACTURE ROYALE DES GLACES DE FRANCE AU XVIIᵉ ET AU XVIIIᵉ SIÈCLES, Paris, 1909.
Gerspach, E.	L'ART DE LA VERRERIE, Paris, 1885.
Janneau, G.	LE VERRE ET L'ART DE MARINOT, Paris, 1925.
Rosenthal, L.	LA VERRERIE FRANÇAISE DEPUIS CINQUANTE ANS, Paris, 1927.

GERMAN

Hudig, F. W.	DAS GLAS, Vienna, 1925.
Pazaurek, G.	KUNSTGLÄSER DER GEGENWART, Leipzig, 1925. MODERNE GLÄSER, Leipzig, 1901.
Rademacher, F.	DIE DEUTSCHEN GLÄSER DES MITTELALTERS, Berlin, 1933.
Saldern, Axel von	GERMAN ENAMELLED GLASS—THE BEINICKE COLLECTION, Corning, N.Y., 1965.
Schmidt, R.	BRANDENBURGISCHE GLÄSER, Berlin, 1914. DAS GLAS, Berlin and Leipzig, 1922. DIE GLÄSER DER SAMMLUNG MÜHSAM, Berlin, 1914 and 1926. 100 JAHRE OESTERREICHISCHES GLASKUNST: LOBMEYR: 1823–1923, Vienna, 1925.

ITALIAN

Cecchetti, B., and Zaretti, V.	MONOGRAFIA DELLA VERTRARIA VENEZIANA E MURANESE, Venice, 1874.
Lorenzetti, G.	VETRI DU MURANO, Rome, 1931.

NETHERLANDS

Buckley, W.	NOTES ON FRANS GREENWOOD AND THE GLASSES HE ENGRAVED, London, 1930. NOTES ON AERT SCHUMANN AND THE GLASSES THAT HE ENGRAVED, London, 1931. NOTES ON D. WOLFF AND THE GLASSES HE ENGRAVED, London, 1935.

Frothingham, A. W.   HISPANIC GLASS, Hispanic Society, New York, 1941.

HERALDRY

Fairbairn's   BOOK OF CRESTS OF THE FAMILIES OF GREAT BRITAIN AND IRELAND, Dover, New York, and Constable, London, reprint; Prentice-Hall, New York and London, reprint; Heraldic Book, Baltimore, Md, 4th ed., 1968.

Fox-Davies, A. C.   THE ART OF HERALDRY, London, 1905.
COMPLETE GUIDE TO HERALDRY, London, 1925.

Franklyn, Julian, and Tanner, John   AN ENCYCLOPAEDIC DICTIONARY OF HERALDRY, Pergamon, Oxford, 1970.

IVORIES

Kunz, G. F.   IVORY AND THE ELEPHANT IN ART, Archaeology and Science, New York, 1916.

Maskell, Alfred   IVORIES, Prentice-Hall, London, and Tuttle, Rutland, Vt, 1966.

Victoria and Albert Museum   Catalogue of Carvings in Ivory, London, 1927–1929.

LACQUER

(The subject is also discussed in general works on old furniture.)

Holzhausen, W.   LACKKUNST IN EUROPA, Cologne, 1958.

Stalker, J., and Parker, G.   A TREATISE ON JAPANNING AND VARNISHING, 1688, Tiranti, London, reprint, and Transatlantic, Levittown, New York, reprint, 1960.

Strange, E. F.   Catalogue of Chinese Lacquer in the Victoria and Albert Museum, London, 1926.
CHINESE LACQUER, London, 1926.
Catalogue of Japanese Lacquer in the Victoria and Albert Museum, London, 1924.

Symonds, R. W.   OLD ENGLISH WALNUT AND LACQUER FURNITURE, London, 1923.

METALWORK

(For Sheffield Plate, see *Silver.*)

Ayrton, M., and Silcox, A.   WROUGHT IRON AND ITS DECORATIVE USE, London and New York, 1929.

Bell, Malcolm   OLD PEWTER, London and New York, rev. ed., 1913.

Blum, W., and Hobaboom, G. B.   PRINCIPLES OF ELECTROPLATING AND ELECTROFORMING, McGraw, London and New York, 3rd ed., 1949.

Bonnin, A.	TUTENAG AND PAKTONG, New York, 1924; Oxford, 1925.
Burgess, F. W.	CHATS ON OLD COPPER AND BRASS, Benn, London, 1954.
Cotterell, H. H.	OLD PEWTER: ITS MAKERS AND MARKS IN ENGLAND, SCOTLAND AND IRELAND, Batsford, London, new imp., 1968; Tuttle, Rutland, Vt, 1963.
Gardner, J. S.	ENGLISH IRONWORK OF THE XVIITH AND XVIIITH CENTURIES, Batsford, London, 1911; New York, 1911.
Graeme, A. V. S.	OLD BRITISH PEWTER (1500–1800), London, 1952.
Hoever, Otto	AN ENCYCLOPAEDIA OF IRONWORK, London, 1927.
Kerfoot, J. B.	AMERICAN PEWTER, Boston, 1924.
Laughlin, L. I.	PEWTER IN AMERICA, two vols., Boston, 1940.
Massé, H. J.	PEWTER PLATE, Bell, London, rev. ed., 1911. CHATS ON OLD PEWTER, Benn, London, rev. ed., 1949; Dover, New York, 1969. THE PEWTER COLLECTOR, New York, 1921; Barrie & Jenkins, London, rev. ed. by R. F. Michaelis, 1970.
Michaelis, R. F.	ANTIQUE PEWTER OF THE BRITISH ISLES, Bell, London, 1955.
Price, F. G. Hilton	OLD BASE METAL SPOONS, Batsford, London, 1908.
Richards, H. S.	ALL ABOUT HORSE BRASSES, privately printed, England, 1944.
Somm, A. H.	EARLY AMERICAN WROUGHT IRONWORK, three vols., New York, 1928.
Weaver, Sir Lawrence	ENGLISH LEADWORK, London, 1909.
Welch, Charles	HISTORY OF THE WORSHIPFUL COMPANY OF PEWTERERS OF LONDON, London, 1902.
Wood, Lindsay Ingleby	SCOTTISH PEWTERWARE AND PEWTERERS, Morton, Edinburgh, 1907.

POTTERY AND PORCELAIN

GENERAL

Burton, W.	PORCELAIN: ITS NATURE, ART AND MANUFACTURE, London, 1906.
Cox, Warren	BOOK OF POTTERY AND PORCELAIN, Crown, New York, 1944.
Danckert, L.	HANDBUCH DES EUROPÄISCHEN PORZELLANS, Munich, 1954.
Hannover, E.	POTTERY AND PORCELAIN, three vols., London and New York, 1925.
Hofman, F. H.	DAS PORZELLAN DER EUROPÄISCHEN MANUFAKTUREN IM 18 JAHRHUNDERT, Berlin, 1932.
Honey, W. B.	EUROPEAN CERAMIC ART: DICTIONARY OF FACTORIES, ARTISTS, etc., London, 1952. EUROPEAN CERAMIC ART, Boston Book, Boston, 2nd ed., n.d. THE ART OF THE POTTER, London, 1940; Boston Book, Boston, n.d.

Imber, D.	COLLECTING DELFT, Arco, London, and Praeger, New York (American title: COLLECTING EUROPEAN DELFT AND FAIENCE), 1968.
Leach, Bernard	POTTER'S BOOK, Faber, London, 3rd ed., 1945; Transatlantic, Levittown, New York, 1965.
Rosenthal, E.	POTTERY AND CERAMICS, Penguin Books, Harmondsworth, 1949.
Savage, George	PORCELAIN THROUGH THE AGES, Penguin Books, Harmondsworth, 1954; Pelican Books, Baltimore, Md, rev. ed., 1963. POTTERY THROUGH THE AGES, Penguin Books, Harmondsworth, 1958; Barnes & Noble, New York, 1963.
Schmidt, R.	DAS PORZELLAN ALS KUNSTWERK UND KULTURSPIEGEL, Munich, 1925. Translated by W. A. Thorpe: PORCELAIN AS AN ART AND MIRROR OF FASHION, London, 1932.

MARKS

Behse, A.	DEUTSCHE FAYENCEMARKEN BREVIER, Braunschweig, 1955.
Burton, W., and Hobson, R. L.	HANDBOOK OF MARKS ON POTTERY AND PORCELAIN, London, 1928.
Cushion, J. P., and Honey, W. B.	HANDBOOK OF POTTERY AND PORCELAIN MARKS, Faber, London, 1965.
Cushion, J. P.	POCKET BOOK OF ENGLISH CERAMIC MARKS, Faber, London, 1965; Boston Book, Boston, n.d. POCKET BOOK OF GERMAN CERAMIC MARKS, Faber, London, 1961; Boston Book, Boston, n.d. POCKET BOOK OF FRENCH AND ITALIAN CERAMIC MARKS, Faber, London, 1965; Boston Book, Boston, n.d.
Chaffers, W.	MARKS AND MONOGRAMS ON POTTERY AND PORCELAIN, various English and American editions from 1878; Reeves, London, 1968; Dover, New York, two vols., 15th ed., n.d.
Danckert, L.	HANDBUCH DES EUROPÄISCHEN PORZELLANS, Munich, 1954.
Godden, G.	ENCYCLOPAEDIA OF BRITISH POTTERY AND PORCELAIN MARKS, Jenkins, London, and Crown, New York, 2nd rev. ed., 1968. HANDBOOK OF BRITISH POTTERY AND PORCELAIN MARKS, Jenkins, London, and Praeger, New York, 1968.
Honey, W. B.	EUROPEAN CERAMIC ART: DICTIONARY OF FACTORIES, ARTISTS, etc., London, 1952.
Justice, J.	A DICTIONARY OF MARKS AND MONOGRAMS ON DELFT POTTERY, London, 1930.

AMERICAN

Cox, Warren	BOOK OF POTTERY AND PORCELAIN, Crown, New York, 1944.
Ramsey, John	AMERICAN POTTERS AND POTTERY, New York, 1939.
Watkins, L. W.	EARLY NEW ENGLAND POTTERS AND THEIR WARES, Shoe String, Hamden, Conn., 1968.

CHINESE AND JAPANESE EXPORT PORCELAIN
(see also under *Japanese Pottery*)

Beurdeley, M.	PORCELAIN OF THE EAST INDIA COMPANIES, Barrie & Rockliff, London, and Tuttle, Rutland, Vt (American title: CHINESE EXPORT PORCELAIN), 1962.
Crisp, F. A.	ARMORIAL CHINA, London, 1907.
Garner, Sir H.	ORIENTAL BLUE AND WHITE, Faber, London, 3rd ed., 1970.
Hyde, J. A. Lloyd	ORIENTAL LOWESTOFT, Newport, Mon., 1954.
Jourdain, M., and Jenyns, R. Soame	CHINESE EXPORT ART IN THE EIGHTEENTH CENTURY, London, 1950; Tudor, New York, 1968.
Mudge, J. McC.	CHINESE EXPORT PORCELAIN FOR AMERICAN TRADE, 1785–1835, New York, 1962.
Phillips, J. G.	CHINA TRADE PORCELAIN, Metropolitan Museum, New York, 1956; London, 1957.
Staehelin, Walter	THE BOOK OF PORCELAIN: The Manufacture . . . of Export Porcelain in Eighteenth Century China, translated from the German by Michael Bullock, Lund Humphries, London, and Macmillan, New York, 1966.
Tudor-Craig, Sir A.	ARMORIAL PORCELAIN OF THE EIGHTEENTH CENTURY, London, 1925.
Volker, T.	PORCELAIN AND THE DUTCH EAST INDIA COMPANY, Leiden, 1954.

DUTCH

de Jonge, C. H. J.	OUD-NEDERLANDSCHE MAJOLIKA EN DELFTSCH AARDEWERK, Amsterdam, 1947. DELFT CERAMICS, translated from the Dutch DELFTS AARDEWERK, Praeger, New York, 1970. DUTCH TILES, Praeger, New York, and Batsford, London, 1970.
Havard, H.	LA CÉRAMIQUE HOLLANDAIS, Amsterdam, 1909.
Hudig, F. W.	DELFTER FAIENCE, Berlin, 1929.
Justice, J.	DICTIONARY OF MARKS AND MONOGRAMS ON DELFT POTTERY, London, 1930.
Neurdenberg, E.	OLD DUTCH POTTERY AND TILES, translated by B. Rackham, London, 1923.
Rackham, B.	NETHERLANDS MAIOLICA, London, 1926.

ENGLISH POTTERY
(see also under *Victoriana*)

Barnard, H.	CHATS ON WEDGWOOD WARE, London, 1924; New York, 1925.
Bemrose, G.	19TH CENTURY ENGLISH POTTERY AND PORCELAIN, Faber, London, 1952.

Burton, W.	HISTORY AND DESCRIPTION OF ENGLISH EARTHENWARE AND STONEWARE, London, 1904.
Garner, F. H.	ENGLISH DELFTWARE, Faber, London, 1948; New York, 1948.
Hodgkin, J. E. and E.	EXAMPLES OF ENGLISH POTTERY NAMED, DATED AND IN- SCRIBED, London, 1891.
Honey, W. B.	ENGLISH POTTERY AND PORCELAIN, rev. R. J. Charleston, Black, London, 6th ed., 1969; Barnes & Noble, New York, 5th ed., 1964. WEDGWOOD WARE, Faber, London, 1948; New York, 1948.
Jewitt, L.	CERAMIC ART OF GREAT BRITAIN, London, 1878.
Lomax, C. J.	QUAINT OLD ENGLISH POTTERY, Manchester, 1909.
Mankowitz, W.	WEDGWOOD, Spring Books, London, 1968; New York, 1953.
Meteyard, E.	LIFE OF JOSIAH WEDGWOOD, London, 1865.
Nance, E. Morton	THE POTTERY AND PORCELAIN OF SWANSEA AND NANTGARW, London, 1942.
Pountney, W. J.	OLD BRISTOL POTTERIES, Bristol, 1920.
Price, E. Stanley	JOHN SADLER, West Kirby, 1949.
Rackham, B.	MEDIEVAL ENGLISH POTTERY, Faber, London, 1947; New York, 1949. EARLY STAFFORDSHIRE POTTERY, Faber, London, 1951; New York, 1951. CATALOGUE OF THE SCHREIBER COLLECTION IN THE VICTORIA AND ALBERT MUSEUM, vol. II, London, 1929.
Rackham, B., and Read, H.	ENGLISH POTTERY, Benn, London, 1924; New York, 1924.
Rhead, G. W.	THE EARTHENWARE COLLECTOR, London and New York, 1920.
Savage, G., and Finer, A.	SELECTED LETTERS OF JOSIAH WEDGWOOD, Cory Adams & Mackay, London, 1965.
Towner, Donald C.	HANDBOOK OF LEEDS POTTERY, Leeds, 1951.
Whiter, Leonard	SPODE: A HISTORY OF THE FAMILY, FACTORY AND WARES FROM 1733 TO 1833, Barrie & Jenkins, London, and Praeger, New York, 1970.
Williamson, F.	THE DERBY POT-MANUFACTORY KNOWN AS COCKPIT HILL, Derby, 1931.

ENGLISH PORCELAIN
(see also under *Victoriana*)

General

Bemrose, G.	19TH CENTURY ENGLISH POTTERY AND PORCELAIN, Faber, London, 1952.
Dixon, J. L.	ENGLISH PORCELAIN OF THE EIGHTEENTH CENTURY, Faber, London, 1952; New York, 1952.

Eccles, H., and Rackham, B.	ANALYSED SPECIMENS OF ENGLISH PORCELAIN, London, 1922.
English Ceramic Circle	COMMEMORATIVE CATALOGUE OF AN EXHIBITION OF ENGLISH POTTERY AND PORCELAIN AT THE VICTORIA AND ALBERT MUSEUM, London, 1949.
Fisher, S. W.	THE DECORATION OF ENGLISH PORCELAIN, Boston Book, Boston, 1954; London, 1956. ENGLISH BLUE AND WHITE PORCELAIN OF THE EIGHTEENTH CENTURY, London and New York, 1947.
Godden, G.	ENCYCLOPAEDIA OF BRITISH POTTERY AND PORCELAIN MARKS, Jenkins, London, and Crown, New York, 1964. AN ILLUSTRATED ENCYCLOPAEDIA OF BRITISH POTTERY AND PORCELAIN, Jenkins, London, and Crown, New York, 1966. HANDBOOK OF BRITISH POTTERY AND PORCELAIN MARKS, Jenkins, London, and Praeger, New York, 1968.
Hobson, R. L.	CATALOGUE OF ENGLISH PORCELAIN IN THE BRITISH MUSEUM, London, 1905.
Honey, W. B.	OLD ENGLISH PORCELAIN, London and New York, 1948.
King, W.	ENGLISH PORCELAIN FIGURES OF THE EIGHTEENTH CENTURY, London, 1925.
Rackham, B.	CATALOGUE OF THE HERBERT ALLEN COLLECTION, London, 1923. CATALOGUE OF THE SCHREIBER COLLECTION, VICTORIA AND ALBERT MUSEUM, vol. I, London, 1930.
Savage, George	18TH CENTURY ENGLISH PORCELAIN, Spring Books, London, new ed., 1964; New York, 1952.

Biographical

Cook, Cyril	THE LIFE AND WORK OF ROBERT HANCOCK, Chapman & Hall, London, 1948; New York, 1948.
McAlister, Mrs D.	WILLIAM DUESBURY'S LONDON ACCOUNT BOOK, London, 1931
Tapp, Major W. H.	JEFFRYES HAMETT O'NEALE, London, 1938.

Bow

Hurlbutt, F.	BOW PORCELAIN, London, 1926.

Bristol (see Plymouth)

Caughley

Godden, G.	CAUGHLEY AND WORCESTER PORCELAIN, 1775–1800, Jenkins, London, and Praeger, New York, 1969.

Chelsea

Blunt, R. (Ed.)	CHEYNE BOOK OF CHELSEA PORCELAIN, London, 1924.

Bryant, G. F.	CHELSEA PORCELAIN TOYS, London, 1925.
Hurlbutt, F.	CHELSEA CHINA, London, 1937.
King, W.	CHELSEA PORCELAIN, Benn, London, 1922; New York, 1923.
MacKenna, F. S.	CHELSEA PORCELAIN: TRIANGLE AND RAISED ANCHOR WARES, Lewis, Leigh-on-Sea, 1948. CHELSEA PORCELAIN: RED ANCHOR WARES, Lewis, Leigh-on-Sea, 1951. CHELSEA PORCELAIN: GOLD ANCHOR WARES, Lewis, Leigh-on-Sea, 1952.

Coalport

Godden, G.	COALPORT AND COALBROOKDALE PORCELAINS, Jenkins, London, and Praeger, New York, 1970.

Derby

Gilhespy, F. B.	DERBY PORCELAIN, Leigh-on-Sea, 1950; Tudor, New York, 1965.
Haslem, J.	THE OLD DERBY CHINA FACTORY, London, 1875.
Hurlbutt, F.	OLD DERBY PORCELAIN AND ITS ARTIST-WORKMEN, Laurie, London, 1925.

Liverpool

Boney, Dr Knowles	LIVERPOOL PORCELAIN, London, 1957.
Gatty, C. T.	THE LIVERPOOL POTTERIES, Liverpool, 1882.
Mayer, Joseph	HISTORY OF THE ART OF POTTERY IN LIVERPOOL, 1885.
Smith, Alan	THE ILLUSTRATED GUIDE TO LIVERPOOL HERCULANEUM POTTERY, 1796–1840, Barrie & Jenkins, London, and Praeger, New York, 1970.

Longton Hall

Bemrose, W.	LONGTON HALL PORCELAIN, London, 1898.
Watney, Dr B.	LONGTON HALL PORCELAIN, Faber, London, 1957; New York, 1957.

Lowestoft

Godden, G.	THE ILLUSTRATED GUIDE TO LOWESTOFT PORCELAIN, Jenkins, London, and Praeger, New York, 1969.
Murton, A. E.	LOWESTOFT CHINA, Lowestoft, 1932.
Spelman, W. W. R.	LOWESTOFT CHINA, London and Norwich, 1905.

Minton

Godden, G. MINTON POTTERY AND PORCELAIN OF THE FIRST PERIOD, Jenkins, London, and Praeger, New York, 1968.

Plymouth, Bristol and New Hall

Hurlbutt, F. BRISTOL PORCELAIN, London, 1928.

MacKenna, F. S. COOKWORTHY'S PLYMOUTH AND BRISTOL PORCELAIN, Leigh-on-Sea and New York, 1946.
CHAMPION'S BRISTOL PORCELAIN, Leigh-on-Sea and New York, 1947.

Owen, H. TWO CENTURIES OF CERAMIC ART IN BRISTOL, London, 1873.

Stringer, G. E. NEW HALL PORCELAIN, London, 1949.

Trapnell, A. E. CATALOGUE OF A COLLECTION OF PLYMOUTH AND BRISTOL PORCELAIN, London, 1912.

Rockingham

Rice, D. THE ILLUSTRATED GUIDE TO ROCKINGHAM PORCELAIN, Barrie & Jenkins, London, and Praeger, New York, 1970.

Spode

Whiter, Leonard SPODE: A HISTORY OF THE FAMILY, FACTORY AND WARES FROM 1733 TO 1833, Barrie & Jenkins, London, and Praeger, New York, 1970.

Welsh

John, W. D. NANTGARW PORCELAIN, London, 1948.

Meager, K. S. SWANSEA AND NANTGARW POTTERIES, Swansea, 1949.

Nance, Morton POTTERY AND PORCELAIN OF SWANSEA AND NANTGARW, London, 1943.

Williams, I. J. GUIDE TO THE COLLECTION OF WELSH PORCELAIN IN THE NATIONAL MUSEUM OF WALES, 1931.

Worcester

Barrett, F. A. WORCESTER PORCELAIN, Faber, London, 1953; New York, 1953.

Hobson, R. L. WORCESTER PORCELAIN, Quaritch, London, 1910.
CATALOGUE OF THE FRANK LLOYD COLLECTION OF WORCESTER PORCELAIN IN THE BRITISH MUSEUM, London, 1925.

MacKenna, F. S. WORCESTER PORCELAIN, Leigh-on-Sea, 1950.

Sandon, H. THE ILLUSTRATED GUIDE TO WORCESTER PORCELAIN, 1751–1793, Jenkins, London, and Praeger, New York, 1969.

Savage, George	THE AMERICAN BIRDS OF DOROTHY DOUGHTY, Worcester Royal Porcelain Company, Worcester, 1965.
	THE BRITISH BIRDS OF DOROTHY DOUGHTY, Worcester Royal Porcelain Company, Worcester, 1967.
	THE STORY OF WORCESTER PORCELAIN AND THE DYSON PERRINS MUSEUM, Pitkin, London, 1969.

FRENCH AND BELGIAN POTTERY

Arnaud d'Agnel, G.	LA FAÏENCE ET LA PORCELAINE DE MARSEILLE, 1912.
Brongniart, A.	TRAITÉ DES ARTS CÉRAMIQUES, OU DES POTERIES CONSIDÉRÉS DANS LEUR HISTOIRE, LEUR PRATIQUE, ET LEUR THÉORIE, Paris, 1844.
Damiron, C.	LA FAÏENCE ARTISTIQUE DE MOUSTIERS, Lyon, 1919.
	LA FAÏENCE DE LYON, Paris, 1926.
Davillier, J. C.	HISTOIRE DE FAÏENCES ET PORCELAINES DE MOUSTIERS, MARSEILLE, ET AUTRES FABRIQUES MÉRIDIONALES, Paris, 1863.
Forestie, E.	LES ANCIENNES FAÏENCERIES DE MONTAUBAN, ARDUS, NEGRE-PELISSE, AUVILLAR, BRESSOLS, BEAUMONT, etc., Montauban, 1876; new ed., 1929.
Gauthier, J.	FAÏENCES ET PORCELAINES RUSTIQUES, Paris, 1929.
Giacomotti, J.	FRENCH FAÏENCE, in English, Fribourg, 1963; Boston Book, Boston, n.d.
Hanauer, A.	LES FAÏENCIERS DE HAGUENAU, Rixheim, 1907.
Haug, H.	LES FAÏENCES ET PORCELAINES DE STRASBOURG, Strasbourg, 1922.
	LES FAÏENCES DE STRASBOURG, Strasbourg and Paris, 1950.
Lane, A.	FRENCH FAÏENCE, Faber, London, rev. ed., 1970; New York, 1948.
Meaudre de Lapouyade	ESSAI D'HISTOIRE DES FAÏENCERIES DE BORDEAUX DU XVIIIᵉ SIÈCLE À NOS JOURS, Bordeaux, 1926.
Poncetton, F., and Salles, G.	LES POTERIES FRANÇAISES, Paris, 1929.
Pottier, A.	HISTOIRE DE LA FAÏENCE DE ROUEN, Rouen, 1870.
Solon, M. L. E.	A HISTORY AND DESCRIPTION OF OLD FRENCH FAÏENCE, London, 1903.
Warmont	RECHERCHES HISTORIQUES SUR LES FAÏENCES DE SINCENY, ROUY, ET OGNES, Paris, 1864.

FRENCH PORCELAIN

Alfassa and Guérin	PORCELAINE FRANÇAISE, Paris, 1932.
Auscher, A. S. A.	HISTORY AND DESCRIPTION OF FRENCH PORCELAIN, London, 1905.
Bourgeois, E.	LE BISCUIT DE SÈVRES AU XVIIIᵉ SIÈCLE, Paris, 1909.

Chavagnac, Comte X. de, and Grollier, Marquis A. de	HISTOIRE DES MANUFACTURES FRANÇAISES DE PORCELAINE, Paris, 1906.
Haug, H.	LES FAÏENCES ET PORCELAINES DE STRASBOURG, Strasbourg, 1922.
Honey, W. B.	FRENCH PORCELAIN OF THE 18TH CENTURY, Faber, London, 1950; New York, 1951.
Soil de Moriame, E. J., and Desplace de Formanoir, L.	LES PORCELAINES DE TOURNAY, Tournai, 1937.
Savage, George	SEVENTEENTH AND EIGHTEENTH CENTURY FRENCH PORCELAIN, Spring Books, London, and Tudor, New York, 1969.
Verlet, Grandjean, and Brunet	SÈVRES, Paris, 1953.

GERMAN PORCELAIN

Bayer, A.	ANSBACHER PORZELLAN, Ansbach, 1933.
Berling, K.	FESTSCHRIFT DER KÖNIGLICHEN SÄCHSISCHEN PORZELLAN-MANUFAKTUR MEISSEN, 1710–1910, Leipzig, 1910.
Braun, E. W., and Folnesics, J.	GESCHICHTE DER K. K. WIENER PORZELLANMANUFAKTUR, Vienna, 1907.
Christ, H.	LUDWIGSBURGER PORZELLANFIGUREN, Berlin, 1921.
Graul, R., and Kurzwelly, A.	ALT-THÜRINGER PORZELLAN, Leipzig, 1900.
Hand and Rakebrand	MEISSNER PORZELLAN DES 18. JAHRHUNDERTS, 1710–1750, Dresden, 1957.
Hayward, J. F.	VIENNA PORCELAIN OF THE DU PAQUIER PERIOD, London, 1952.
Hofmann, F. H.	FRANKENTHALER PORZELLAN, Munich, 1911. GESCHICHTE DER BAYERISCHEN PORZELLANMANUFAKTUR NYMPHENBURG, Leipzig, 1921–1923.
Honey, W. B.	DRESDEN CHINA, Troy, New York, 1946; London, 1947. GERMAN PORCELAIN, London, 1947; New York, 1948.
Lenz, G.	BERLINER PORZELLAN: DIE MANUFAKTUR FRIEDRICHS DES GROSSEN, 1763–1786, Berlin, 1913.
Meyer, H.	BÖHMISCHES PORZELLAN UND STEINGUT, Leipzig, 1927.
Morley-Fletcher, H.	MEISSEN, Barrie & Jenkins, London, and Doubleday, New York, 1970.
Pazaurek, G. E.	DEUTSCHE FAYENCE UND PORZELLAN HAUSMALER, Leipzig, 1928. MEISSNER PORZELLANMALEREI DES 18. JAHRHUNDERTS, Stuttgart, 1929.
Poche, E.	BOHEMIAN PORCELAIN, London, n.d. (recent).
Röder, K., and Oppenheim, M.	DAS HÖCHSTER PORZELLAN, Mainz, 1930.

Sauerland, M.	DEUTSCHE PORZELLANFIGUREN DES 18. JAHRHUNDERTS, Cologne, 1923.
Savage, George	EIGHTEENTH CENTURY GERMAN PORCELAIN, Spring Books, London, 1968; Tudor, New York, 1968.
Scherer, C.	DAS FÜRSTENBERG PORZELLAN, Berlin, 1909.
Schnorr von Carolsfeld, L.	PORZELLAN DER EUROPÄISCHEN FABRIKEN DES 18. JAHRHUNDERTS, Berlin, 1912.
Schönberger, A.	MEISSNER PORZELLAN MIT HOROLDT-MALEREI, Darmstadt, n.d. (recent).
Zimmermann, E.	DIE ERFINDUNG UND FRÜHZEIT DES MEISSNER PORZELLANS, Berlin, 1908. MEISSNER PORZELLAN, Leipzig, 1926.

GERMAN AND AUSTRIAN POTTERY

Bayer, A.	DIE ANSBACHER FAYENCE FABRIKEN, Ansbach, 1928.
Falke, O. von	DAS RHEINISCHES STEINZEUG, Berlin, 1908.
Feulner, A.	FRANKFURTER FAYENCEN, Berlin, 1935.
Hofmann, F. H.	GESCHICHTE DER BAYREUTHER FAYENCEFABRIK, Augsburg, 1928.
Hüseler, K.	DIE HAMBURGER FAYENCEN DES 17. JAHRHUNDERTS, Flensburg, 1925.
Kolschau, K.	RHEINISCHES STEINZEUG, Munich, 1924.
Meyer, A.	BÖHMISCHES PORZELLAN UND STEINGUT, Leipzig, 1927.
Pazaurek, G.	STEINGUT: FORMGEBUNG UND GESCHICHTE, Stuttgart, 1927.
Riesebieter, O.	DIE DEUTSCHEN FAYENCEN DES 17. UND 18. JAHRHUNDERTS, Leipzig, 1921.

A brief account is given by Savage, POTTERY THROUGH THE AGES. The subject is covered in numerous entries by Honey, EUROPEAN CERAMIC ART: DICTIONARY OF FACTORIES, ARTISTS, etc., and Hannover devotes space to it. Otherwise, books on German faïence in English hardly exist. The best general work in German is that of Riesebieter.

ITALIAN PORCELAIN

Chompret, Dr J.	RÉPERTOIRE DE LA MAJOLIQUE ITALIENNE, Paris, 1949.
Eisner, Eisenhof, Baron A. de	LA PORCELLANA DI CAPO-DI-MONTE, Milan, 1925.
Lane, A.	ITALIAN PORCELAIN, London, 1954; New York, 1955.
Morazzoni, G.	LE PORCELLANE ITALIANE, Milan, 1935.
Rackham, B.	CATALOGUE OF ITALIAN MAIOLICA IN THE VICTORIA AND ALBERT MUSEUM, London, 1940. ITALIAN MAIOLICA, London and New York, 1952.

528

JAPANESE POTTERY

Morse, A.   CATALOGUE OF JAPANESE POTTERY IN THE MUSEUM OF FINE
                            ARTS, BOSTON, 1901.

Jenyns, Soame   JAPANESE POTTERY, Faber, London, and Praeger, New York, 1970.

RUSSIAN PORCELAIN

Lukomsky, G.   RUSSISCHES PORZELLAN, 1744–1923, Berlin, 1924.

Ross, M. C.   RUSSIAN PORCELAINS, University of Oklahoma Press, Oklahoma, and
                            Bailey Bros., London, 1969.

SCANDINAVIAN

Hayden, A.   ROYAL COPENHAGEN PORCELAIN, London, 1911; New York, 1912.

Hüseler, K.   GESCHICHTE DER SCHLESWIG-HOLSTEINISCHEN FAYENCEN IM
                            18. JAHRHUNDERT, Breslau, 1929.
                            DIE KIELER FAYENCE-MANUFAKTUREN, Flensberg, 1923.

Marsson, E.   DIE STRALSUNDER FAYENCEFABRIK, Berlin, 1928.

Strale, G. H.   RÖRSTRAND ET MARIEBERG, Stockholm, 1872.

SPANISH

Casal, M.   HISTORIA DE LA CERAMICA DE ALCORA, Madrid, 1919.

Frothingham, A. W.   CATALOGUE OF HISPANO–MORESQUE POTTERY IN THE COLLEC-
                            TION OF THE HISPANIC SOCIETY OF AMERICA, Hispanic Society, 1936.
                            TALAVERA POTTERY, Hispanic Society, New York, 1944.

van der Put, A.   HISPANO-MORESQUE WARE OF THE 15TH CENTURY, London, 1904.

SWISS

Ducret, S.   ZÜRCHER PORZELLAN DES 18. JAHRHUNDERTS, Zürich, 1944.
                            DIE LENZBURGER FAYENCEN UND OFEN DES 18. UND 19. JAHR-
                            HUNDERTS, Aarau, 1950.

Molin, A. de   HISTOIRE DOCUMENTAIRE DE LA MANUFACTURE DE NYON,
                            1781–1813, Lausanne, 1924.

RESTORATION AND PRESERVATION

Grotz, G.   THE FURNITURE DOCTOR, Doubleday, New York; British edition revised
                            by George Savage, Jenkins, London, 1970.

Lucas, A.   ANTIQUES: THEIR RESTORATION AND PRESERVATION, London and
                            New York, 2nd ed., rev., 1932.

Plenderleith, Dr H. J.   PRESERVATION OF ANTIQUITIES, London, 1934 and 1956; Oxford, New
                            York, 1956.
                            PRESERVATION OF LEATHER BOOKBINDINGS, London, 1946.

Scott, Dr A.	CLEANING AND RESTORATION OF MUSEUM EXHIBITS, London, 1921, 1923, and 1926.
Savage, George	THE ART AND ANTIQUE RESTORERS' HANDBOOK, Barrie & Rockliff, London, and Praeger, New York, rev. ed., 1967.

SILVER AND SHEFFIELD PLATE

Abbey, S.	THE GOLDSMITHS' AND SILVERSMITHS' HANDBOOK, London, 1952; Princeton, N.J., 1953.
Avery, Clara Louise	EARLY AMERICAN SILVER, New York, 1930.
Bradbury, F.	GUIDE TO MARKS OF ORIGIN ON BRITISH AND IRISH SILVER PLATE, various editions. HISTORY OF OLD SHEFFIELD PLATE, London and New York, 1912.
Buck, J. H.	OLD PLATE: ITS MAKERS AND MARKS, New York, 1903.
Buhler, K. C.	AMERICAN SILVER, New York, 1950.
Burton, E. M.	SOUTH CAROLINA SILVERSMITHS, 1690–1860, Tuttle, Rutland, Vt, 1960.
Castro, J. P. de	THE LAW AND PRACTICE OF HALL-MARKING, Technical Press, London, 1935.
Cellini, B.	TREATISE ON GOLDSMITHING, translated by Ashbee, London, 1898; Dover, New York, 1966.
Clarke, H. P.	JOHN CONEY, SILVERSMITH, 1655–1722, Boston, Mass., 1932.
Cripps, W.	OLD ENGLISH PLATE, London, 1878; reprinted (recent), Tudor, New York.
Currier, E. M.	MARKS OF EARLY AMERICAN SILVERSMITHS, Portland, Me, 1938.
Curtis, G. M.	EARLY SILVER OF CONNECTICUT AND ITS MAKERS, Meriden, Conn., 1913.
Cutten, G. B.	THE SILVERSMITHS OF NORTH CAROLINA, Raleigh, 1948. THE SILVERSMITHS OF VIRGINIA, Dietz, Richmond, Va, 1952.
Davis, Frank	FRENCH SILVER, Praeger, New York, and Barker, London, 1970.
Delieb, E.	INVESTING IN SILVER, Barrie & Rockliff, London, and Clarkson Potter, New York, new ed., 1970. SILVER BOXES, Jenkins, London, and Clarkson Potter, New York, 1969.
Dennis, F.	THREE CENTURIES OF FRENCH DOMESTIC SILVER, two vols., Metropolitan Museum, New York, 1960.
Dent, H. C.	WINE, SPIRIT AND SAUCER LABELS, London, 1933.
Dickinson, H. W.	MATTHEW BOULTON, Cambridge University Press, England and New York, 1937.
Evans, J.	THE GREAT GOLDSMITHS OF LONDON, London, 1936.
French, H.	JACOB HURD AND HIS SONS, SILVERSMITHS, 1702–81, Cambridge, Mass., 1939.

Graham, J.	EARLY AMERICAN SILVER MARKS, New York, 1936.
Hayward, J. F.	HUGUENOT SILVER IN ENGLAND, 1688–1727, Faber, London, 1959.
Heal, A.	LONDON GOLDSMITHS, 1200–1800, Cambridge University Press, England and New York, 1935.
Hiatt, N. W., and L. F.	THE SILVERSMITHS OF KENTUCKY, 1785–1850, Louisville, Ky, 1954.
Hill, H. D.	ANTIQUE GOLD BOXES, New York, 1953.
How, C. E. P., and J. P.	ENGLISH AND SCOTTISH SILVER SPOONS, three vols., London, 1952.
Hughes, B., and T.	THREE CENTURIES OF ENGLISH DOMESTIC SILVER, 1500–1820, Praeger, New York, and Lutterworth, London, 1968.
Hughes, G. Bernard	SMALL ANTIQUE SILVERWARE, Batsford, London, 1957.
Jackson, C. J.	ENGLISH GOLDSMITHS AND THEIR MARKS, Batsford, London, 1949; Dover, New York, 2nd ed., n.d.
Jones, E.	OLD SILVER OF EUROPE AND AMERICA, London and New York, 1928.
Maryon, H.	METALWORK AND ENAMELLING, London, 1912; New York, 1913.
Oman, Charles	ENGLISH DOMESTIC SILVER, Black, London, 1949; Barnes & Noble, New York, 6th ed., 1965.
Penzer, N. M.	PAUL STORR, Batsford, London, and Boston Book, Boston, 1954. THE BOOK OF THE WINE-LABEL, London, 1947; New York, 1948.
Phillips, P. H. S.	PAUL DE LAMERIE, Batsford, London, 1935; Saifer, Philadelphia, n.d.
Phillips, J. M.	AMERICAN SILVER, New York, 1949.
Pleasants, J. H., and Sill, H.	MARYLAND SILVERSMITHS, 1715–1830, Baltimore, Md, 1930.
Rosenbaum, J. W.	MYERS MYERS, GOLDSMITH, 1723–95, Philadelphia, 1954.
Stone, Jonathan	ENGLISH SILVER OF THE EIGHTEENTH CENTURY, Cory, Adams & Mackay, London, and October House, New York, 1965.
Taylor, Gerald	SILVER, Penguin Books, Harmondsworth, 1956; Pelican, Baltimore, Md, rev. ed., 1964. CONTINENTAL GOLD AND SILVER, Michael Joseph, London, 1967.
Wardle, Patricia	VICTORIAN SILVER AND SILVER PLATE, Jenkins, London, 1963; Universe Books, New York, 1970.

STYLES
(see also *Furniture*)

Ackerman, J. S.	PALLADIO, Penguin Books, Harmondsworth, 1967, and Baltimore, Md, 1969.
Amaya, Mario	ART NOUVEAU, London, 1966; Dutton, New York, 1966.
Battersby, Martin	THE WORLD OF ART NOUVEAU, Arlington, London, 1968.

Bazin, Germain — BAROQUE AND ROCOCO, Thames & Hudson, London, and Praeger, New York, 1964.

Blunt, A. — ARTISTIC THEORY IN ITALY, 1450–1600, Oxford University Press, Oxford and New York, 1956.

Boehn, M. von — MODES AND MANNERS, four vols., London, 1935; Blom, Bronx, New York, n.d.

Boger, Louise — THE COMPLETE GUIDE TO FURNITURE STYLES, New York, 1959.

Carritt, E. F. (Compiler) — A CALENDAR OF BRITISH TASTE FROM 1600 TO 1800, Routledge, London, 1948.

Clark, Sir Kenneth — THE GOTHIC REVIVAL, Penguin Books, Harmondsworth, and Baltimore, Md, 1964.

Colombier, Pierre du — LE STYLE HENRI IV–LOUIS XIII, Paris, 1941.

Harris, John — REGENCY FURNITURE DESIGNS FROM CONTEMPORARY SOURCE BOOKS, 1803–1826, London, 1961; Transatlantic, Levittown, N.Y., n.d.

Hawley, H. — NEO-CLASSICISM: STYLE AND MOTIF, Cleveland Museum, 1964.

Henderson, G. — GOTHIC, Penguin Books, Harmondsworth and Baltimore, Md, 1968.

Hibbard, Howard — BERNINI, Penguin Books, Harmondsworth, 1967; and Baltimore, Md, 1969.

Hitchcock, H. R. — GERMAN ROCOCO: THE ZIMMERMANN BROTHERS, Allen Lane, London, and Penguin, Baltimore, Md, 1969.

Honour, Hugh — CHINOISERIE, London, 1961; Dutton, New York, 1962.

Kimball, Fiske — CREATION OF THE ROCOCO, Norton, New York, 1964.

Kitson, Michael — THE AGE OF BAROQUE, Hamlyn, London, and McGraw, New York, 1966.

Levey, Michael — EARLY RENAISSANCE, Penguin Books, Harmondsworth, and Baltimore, Md, 1968.

Martindale, Andrew — MAN AND THE RENAISSANCE, Hamlyn, London, and McGraw, New York, 1966.

Nolhac, Pierre — VERSAILLES AND THE TRIANONS, London, 1906.
VERSAILLES ET LA COUR DE FRANCE, Paris, 1925.

Percier, C., and Fontaine, P. E. L. — RECUEIL DE DÉCORATION INTÉRIEURE, Paris, 1812.

Savage, George — CONCISE HISTORY OF INTERIOR DECORATION, Thames & Hudson, London, 1965; Grosset & Dunlap, 1966.

Schönberger, Arno — THE AGE OF ROCOCO, Thames & Hudson, London, and McGraw, New York (American title: ROCOCO AGE: ART AND CIVILISATION OF THE EIGHTEENTH CENTURY), 1960.

Shearman, John — MANNERISM, Penguin Books, Harmondsworth, and Baltimore, Md, 1967.

Sitwell, Sacheverell — BRITISH ARCHITECTS AND CRAFTSMEN, Pan Books, London, new ed., 1960; New York, 3rd ed., 1947.

Speltz, A., and Spiers, R. P.	THE STYLES OF ORNAMENT, Batsford, London, n.d.; Peter Smith, Magnolia, Mass., n.d.
Strange, T. A.	A HISTORICAL GUIDE TO FRENCH INTERIORS, London, reprint, 1950.
Summerson, John	INIGO JONES, Penguin Books, Harmondsworth, and Baltimore, Md, 1967.
Tapié, Victor	THE AGE OF GRANDEUR, London, 1960; Praeger, New York, rev. ed., 1966.
Winckelmann, J. J.	GESCHICHTE DER KUNST DES ALTERTUMS, various editions; Ungar New York (American title: HISTORY OF ANCIENT ART), two vols., n.d.

TEXTILES: CARPETS, RUGS, TAPESTRIES, ETC.

Ashton, L.	SAMPLERS, London, 1926.
Faraday, C. B.	EUROPEAN AND AMERICAN CARPETS AND RUGS, Grand Rapids, Mich., 1929.
Flemming, H.	AN ENCYCLOPAEDIA OF TEXTILES, Berlin, 1934.
Glazier, R.	HISTORIC TEXTILE FABRICS, London and New York, 1923.
Griffin, C. G.	PRACTICAL BOOK OF ORIENTAL RUGS, Philadelphia and London, 1911.
Hunton, W. G.	ENGLISH DECORATIVE TEXTILES, London, 1930.
Kent, W.	THE HOOKED RUG, New York, 1930; London, 1931.
MacIver, P.	THE CHINTZ BOOK, Stokes, New York, 1923.
Marillier, H. C.	ENGLISH TAPESTRIES OF THE 18TH CENTURY, London, 1930.
Swain, M.	HISTORICAL NEEDLEWORK: A STUDY OF INFLUENCES IN NORTHERN ENGLAND, Barrie & Jenkins, London, and Scribner's, New York, 1970.
Tattersall, C.	THE CARPETS OF PERSIA, London, 1931.
Tattersall, C. E. C., and Reed, S.	HISTORY OF BRITISH CARPETS, F. Lewis, Leigh-on-Sea, 1966; Textile Book, Metuchen, N.J., 1967.
Thomson, W. G.	A HISTORY OF TAPESTRY, London, rev. ed., 1930; New York, 1931.
Victoria and Albert Museum	NOTES ON CARPET KNOTTING AND WEAVING, Tattersall, London, 1939.
Weigert, R.-A.	FRENCH TAPESTRY, London, 1962; Branford, Newton Centre, Mass., 1963.
Wolfe	HOW TO IDENTIFY ORIENTAL RUGS, London, 1927.

TREEN

Gould, M. E.	EARLY AMERICAN WOODEN WARE, Tuttle, Rutland, Vt, 1962. EARLY AMERICAN HOUSE, 1620–1850, Tuttle, Rutland, Vt, rev. ed., 1965.
Pinto, E. H.	TREEN, OR SMALL WOODWARE, London and New York, 1949.

ULTRA-VIOLET RADIATION

Rorimer, J. J.	ULTRA-VIOLET RAYS AND THEIR USE IN THE EXAMINATION OF WORKS OF ART, New York, 1931.

VICTORIANA

Bøe, A.	FROM GOTHIC REVIVAL TO FUNCTIONAL FORM, Oslo and Oxford, 1957; New York, 1958.
Brooklyn Museum	VICTORIANA, New York, 1960.
Buck, A.	VICTORIAN COSTUME AND COSTUME ACCESSORIES, Jenkins, London, 1961; Universe Books, New York, 1970.
Floud, Peter	THE EARLY VICTORIAN PERIOD, 1830–1860, Connoisseur, London, 1957. VICTORIAN FURNITURE, Connoisseur, London, 1957.
Godden, G.	VICTORIAN PORCELAIN, Jenkins, London, 1961; Universe Books, New York, 1970. AN ILLUSTRATED GUIDE TO STEVENGRAPHS AND OTHER VICTORIAN SILK PICTURES, Barrie & Jenkins, London, 1970.
Lichten, F.	DECORATIVE ART OF VICTORIA'S ERA, New York, 1950.
Maas, J.	VICTORIAN PAINTERS, Barrie & Jenkins, London, and Putnam, New York, 1969.
Morris, B.	VICTORIAN EMBROIDERY, Jenkins, London, 1961; Universe Books, New York, 1969.
Peter, M.	COLLECTING VICTORIANA, Arco, London, 1965; Praeger, New York, 1968.
Pevsner, N.	HIGH VICTORIAN DESIGN (1851 Exhibition), London, 1951.
Pugh, P. D. Gordon	VICTORIAN STAFFORDSHIRE PORTRAIT FIGURES, Barrie & Jenkins, London, and Praeger, New York, 1970.
Shinn, C., and D.	THE ILLUSTRATED GUIDE TO PARIAN WARE, Barrie & Jenkins, London, 1970.
Symonds, R. W., and Whineray, B.	VICTORIAN FURNITURE, London, 1962.
Victoria and Albert Museum	EXHIBITION OF VICTORIAN AND EDWARDIAN DECORATIVE ART, London, 1962.
Wakefield, H.	VICTORIAN POTTERY, Jenkins, London, 1962; Universe Books, New York, 1970.
Wardle, Patricia	VICTORIAN SILVER AND SILVER PLATE, Jenkins, London, 1963; Universe Books, New York, 1970. VICTORIAN LACE, Jenkins, London, 1968; Praeger, New York, 1969.
Woodhouse, C. Platten	VICTORIANA COLLECTOR'S HANDBOOK, Bell, London, 1970.

WOOD-CARVING

Maskell, A.	WOOD SCULPTURE, London, 1911.